EDITORIAL BOARD

ENCYCLOPEDIA OF
ARCHITECTURE
DESIGN, ENGINEERING & CONSTRUCTION

JOSEPH A. WILKES, FAIA
Editor-in-Chief

ROBERT T. PACKARD, AIA
Associate Editor

VOLUME 1
Aalto, Alvar
to
Concrete—General Principles

A WILEY-INTERSCIENCE PUBLICATION
JOHN WILEY & SONS
New York • Chichester • Brisbane • Toronto • Singapore

Library of Congress Cataloging in Publication Data:

Encyclopedia of architecture.

"A Wiley-Interscience publication."
Includes bibliographies.
1. Architecture—Dictionaries. I. Wilkes,
Joseph A. II. Packard, Robert T.

NA31.E59 1988   720′.3   87–25222
ISBN 0–471–80747–8 (v.1)
ISBN 0–471–63351–8 (set)

Printed in the United States of America

10 9 8 7 6 5 4 3 2

EDITORIAL STAFF

Editor-in-chief: Joseph A. Wilkes, FAIA
Assistant Editor: Robert T. Packard, AIA
Editorial Manager: Karen M. Trost

Production Manager: Margery Carazzone
Editorial Supervisor: Joan Pokorny
Production Supervisor: Shirley Thomas
Production Assistant: Gemma Finn

CONTRIBUTORS

Robert Albrecht, *University of Washington, Seattle, Wash.,* Cold Wet Climate, Building in

Kathryn H. Anthony, PhD, *University of Illinois, Champaign, Ill.,* Behavior and Architecture

Architectural and Transportation Barriers Compliance Board, *Washington, D.C.,* Architectural and Transportation Barriers Compliance Board (ATBCB)

F. John Barbour, AIA, *Setter Leach & Lindstrom, Minneapolis, Minn.,* Ceilings

Edward L. Barnes, *Edward Larrabee Barnes Associates, P.C., New York, N.Y.,* Barnes, Edward Larrabee

P. Kenneth Barnes, AIA*, *Fort Lauderdale, Fla.,* American Society for Testing and Materials (ASTM)

Gunnar Birkerts, FAIA, *Gunner Birkerts & Associates, Architects, Birmingham, Mich.,* Birkerts, Gunnar

Lester Bloch, *Somerset Wood Products Co., Somerville, N.J.,* Architectural Woodwork

Carol J. Burns, *Harvard University, Cambridge, Mass.,* Amusement Parks

Stephanie C. Byrnes, *American Institute of Architects, Washington, D.C.,* Architectural Libraries

Trevor Carnahoff, PE, *Norr Partnership Ltd., Toronto, Ontario, Canada,* Airports

Ann Carper, *American Institute of Architects, Washington, D.C.,* American Institute of Architects (AIA)

William J. Cavanaugh, FASA, *Cavanaugh Tocci Associates, Inc., Sudbury, Mass.,* Acoustics—General Principles; Acoustical Standards

Hyman Chessin, PhD, *Brick, N.J.,* Chrome Plating

Meredith Clausen, *University of Washington, Seattle, Wash.,* Belluschi, Pietro

Edwin B. Crittenden, FAIA, *CCC Architects, Anchorage, Alaska,* Cold Dry Climate Construction

Manuel Cuadra, *Technische Hochschule Darmstadt, Darmstadt, FRG,* Behnisch, Gunter; Bohm, Gottfried

Colin H. Davidson, *Universite de Montreal, Montreal, Quebec, Canada,* Building Team

Charles M. Davis, FAIA, *Esherick Homsey Dodge & Davis, San Francisco, Calif.,* Aquariums

Donald D. Destito, *Memphis, Tenn.,* Brass and Bronze

Richard P. Dober, AICP, *Dober & Associates, Belmont, Mass.,* Campus Planning

David C. Duchscherer, PE, *Duchscherer Oberst Design, Buffalo, N.Y.,* Bus Maintenance Facilities

Benjamin P. Elliott, FAIA, *Duane, Elliott, Cahill, Mullineaux & Mullineaux, Rockville, M.D.,* Church Architecture

Bernard Feilden, CBE, FSA, FRIBA, Hon FAIA, *Norfolk, U.K.,* Cathedrals

David Fogle, *University of Maryland, College Park, M.D.,* Burnham, Daniel

Patrick J. Galvin, *Galvin Publications, East Windsor, N.J.,* Baths

Stephen C. Gatschet, AIA, *Mirick Pearson, Batcheler, Architects, Philadelphia, Pa.,* Computerization

Reinhard Goethert, PhD, *Massachusetts Institute of Technology, Cambridge, Mass.,* Cluster Development and Land Subdivision

* deceased

Marji Grant, *American Institute of Architects, Washington, D.C.,* American Institute of Architects (AIA)

Robert C. Greenstreet, PhD, *University of Wisconsin, Milwaukee, Wis.,* Arbitration in Construction

Clayford T. Grimm, PE, *Austin, Tex.,* Brick Masonry

Kingston W. Heath, PhD, *University of North Carolina, Charlotte, N.C.,* Bridges

Mark A. Hewitt, *Bergenfield, N.J.,* Chambers, William

Holly Hulse, *Bozeman, Mont.,* Bridges

Reginald R. Isaacs*, *Cambridge, Mass.,* Albers, Josef; Bauhaus; Breuer, Marcel

Paul A. Kennon, Jr., FAIA, *CRSS, Houston, Tex.,* Caudill Rowlett Scott Serrine

Benjamin B. Kine, PhD, *Rohm and Haas, Philadelphia, Pa.,* Acrylics

David L. Klepper, *Klepper Marshall King, White Plains, N.Y.,* Acoustical Design—Places of Assembly

Stephen Kliment, FAIA, *New York, N.Y.,* Careers in Architecture

James T. Lendrum, FAIA, *Phoenix, Ariz.,* Climate and Design

Evan Ling, PhD, *Aquamet, Bethesda, Calif.,* Brass and Bronze

Eliot J. Locitzer, *HRH Construction Corp., New York, N.Y.,* Concrete—Architectural

John Loss, AIA, *Architecture and Engineering Performance Information Center, University of Maryland, College Park, M.D.,* Architecture and Engineering Performance Information Center (AEPIC)

Richard E. McCommons, AIA, *ACSA News, Washington, D.C.,* Association of Collegiate Schools of Architecture (ACSA)

A. Stanley McGaughan, FAIA, *American University, Washington, D.C.,* Competitions, Architectural Design

Paul G. McHenry, Jr., AIA, *Albuquerque, N.M.,* Adobe Construction

Edward P. McNamara, PhD, *San Angelo, Tex.,* Ceramic Tile

John Macsai, FAIA, *John Macsai & Associates, Chicago, Ill.,* Apartment Buildings—High-Rise

Louis L. Marines, *American Institute of Architects, Washington, D.C.,* American Institute of Architects (AIA)

Robert L. Miller, *Robert L. Miller Associates, Washington, D.C.,* Communications in Architecture

William C. Miller, AIA, *Seaton Hall, Manhattan, Kan.,* Aalto, Alvar; Asplund, Erik Gunnar

Harry S. Nachman, *John Macsai & Associates, Chicago, Ill.,* Apartment Buildings—High-Rise

Volkmar Nickol, *Technische Hochschule Darmstadt, Darmstadt, FRC,* Bohm, Gottfried

George M. Notter, Jr., FAIA, *Notter Finegold and Alexander, Inc., Washington, D.C.,* Adaptive Use

Robert T. Packard, AIA, *Reston, Va.,* Bacon, Henry; Behrens, Peter; Bulfinch, Charles; Computer-Aided Design and Drafting (CADD)

Rein Pirn, *Bolt Beranek & Newman, Cambridge, Mass.,* Acoustical Insulation and Materials

Thomas Porter, *Cornfield, Sunningwell, UK,* Color in Architecture

Raymond Rhinehart, *American Institute of Architects, Washington, D.C.,* American Institute of Architects (AIA)

Edimir Rocumback, *Bozeman, Mont.,* Bridges

Jay L. Rogers, *Argus Division, Witco Corp., Brooklyn, N.Y.,* Antistatic Agents

Bernard B. Rothschild, FAIA, FCS, *Atlanta, Ga.,* Bonds and Sureties

John Rutherford, *Esherick Homsey Dodge & Davis, San Francisco, Calif.,* Aquariums

Linda Sanders, *North Carolina State University, Raleigh, N.C.,* Barragan, Luis; Botta, Mario

Richard G. Saxon, RIBA, *Building Design Partnership, Manchester, UK,* Atrium Buildings

Ronald E. Shaeffer, *Florida A & M University, Tallahassee, Fla.,* Concrete—General Principles

Earl Starnes, FAIA, AIP, *University of Florida, Gainesville, Fla.,* Architecture/Planning Relationship

Charles A. Szoradi, *Charlottesville, Va.,* Alberti, Leon Battista

Charles Szoradi, AIA, *Washington, D.C.,* Ammann & Whitney; Banks

Michael A. Tomlan, *Cornell University, Ithaca, N.Y.,* Architectural Press, U.S.

Ernest E. Trolio, PE, *Concrete Industry Board, Inc., New York, N.Y.,* Concrete Forming

Ivor H. Updegraff, PhD, *Stamford, Conn.,* Amino Resins

Charles B. Vick, *Forest Products Laboratory, Madison, Wis.,* Adhesives

Barbara L. Wadkins, *New School of Architecture, Chula Vista, Calif.,* Archigram; Banham, Reynar

Thomas Walton, PhD, *The Catholic University of America, Washington, D.C.,* Architectural Styles

Ralph Warburton, FAIA, *University of Miami, Coral Gables, Fla.,* Bacon, Edward N.

J. W. Weaver, PhD, *University of Delaware, Newark, Del.,* Cellulose and Cellulose Derivatives

Clive Weston, *Esherick Homsey Dodge & Davis, San Francisco, Calif.,* Aquariums

Thomas E. Will, *Rohm and Haas, Philadelphia, Pa.,* Acrylics

James E. Woods, PE, PhD, *Honeywell Inc., Golden Valley, Minn.,* Air Quality

Tony P. Wrenn, *American Institute of Architects, Washington, D.C.,* American Institute of Architects (AIA)

Ivan Zaknic, *Lehigh University, Bethlehem, Pa.,* Burgee, John

Walter G. Zelley, *New Kensington, Pa.,* Anodized Finishes

PREFACE

"Once upon a time the writing of encyclopedias was a glorious adventure and, if your work ever reached a conclusion, i.e., if you eventually got out of prison and could prevent the printers from mutilating your proofs at the last minute, you might even initiate a revolution." Excerpt from a review of THE NEW BRITANNICA by C. K. Ogden (1926).
From READING I HAVE LIKED by Clifton Fadiman, Saturday Review of Literature.

In the many contacts made during the progress of this work with people in the construction field—architects, engineers, educators, industry members and others, no one has questioned the need for a comprehensive Encyclopedia of Architecture. On the contrary, in many cases the initial contact was met with comments such as "It's about time!", "An Encyclopedia would be most useful," etc. Without these words of encouragement the task of the editors would have been infinitely more difficult. When Wiley approached the American Institute of Architects with the idea of publishing a comprehensive Encyclopedia of Architecture, the proposal was received with enthusiasm. Although other architectural encyclopedias of limited coverage have been published, none has approached the complete scope of this project. It includes all aspects of architecture and engineering from the standpoints of design, education, regulation, and other myriad aspects of the profession, as well as the construction industry as a whole, including the technologies and the laws involved as well as the many economic considerations. Surveys by the publisher indicated a broad interest in such an enterprise. In addition to educators, architects, engineers, students, consultants in acoustics, lighting, interior design and landscaping, and the construction industry from the small contractor to the manufacturers of building materials and assemblies, interest has been expressed by members of the legal profession and the real estate community. Lastly, it is expected that the Encyclopedia will serve the general public where there has developed over the last several decades a great interest in the design and development of man's built environment and the preservation of the historic legacy.

The goal was to prepare an encyclopedia which would serve this audience as a first source of information with sufficient coverage to satisfy the needs of the average reader. For those whose interest is greater, articles include references and bibliography for further reading. In addition, many entries direct the reader to other encyclopedia articles on related subjects.

Preparation of the material for this Encyclopedia required the knowledge and tireless efforts of a number of people to whom the editor is most grateful. Credit for initiating the Encyclopedia goes to Dr. Martin Grayson, former publisher of Encyclopedias for John Wiley & Sons. Robert T. Packard, AIA, who served as editor for the seventh and editor emeritus for the eighth edition of Architectural Graphics Standards, another publication of John Wiley & Sons, has served as associate editor of the Encyclopedia where his store of knowledge has proved invaluable. Bob Packard has worked on all phases of the project and has also prepared a number of articles.

Karen (Thomsen) Trost joined the Wiley staff in mid-1986 and has since performed the many and diverse duties of assistant editor. She has organized the flow of manuscripts between authors, reviewers, and editors, proofed articles, often providing valuable editorial input, and maintained contact with the many authors to ensure the scheduled delivery of their material.

After the decision was made to publish an Encyclopedia, the first item on the agenda was to determine the material to be covered. An initial "Word List" was prepared using architectural and construction dictionaries and suggestions from diverse sources in associated fields.

At this time it was decided to appoint an advisory committee to assist the editors. Letters of invitation to serve were sent by Mr. George M. Notter, Jr., FAIA, then president of the American Institute of Architects. The very positive response to these invitations was most encouraging. The committee of eight members includes the following: William Allen, CBE, LL.D, RIBA, and Hon. FAIA, a leading British architect, who has helped provide authors from the U.K. and other overseas areas to give the Encyclopedia a more international coverage; Arnold F. Butt, AIA, an architect, educator and planner, and former associate and colleague of the editor, helped in defining the coverage of the urban planning articles and, through his long association with the NCARB, reviewed the material for those entries; Sarah P. Harkness, FAIA, a prominent architect and founding member of one of the country's most prestigious firms, The Architects Collaborative. Ms. Harkness contributed to the Encyclopedia and gave the clarion call to members of her firm (including her husband, John C. Harkness) and others to do so; James T. Lendrum, FAIA, member of a nationally recognized architectural firm in Phoenix, former head of the Small Homes Council at the University of Illinois, and former head of the Architectural Department at the University of Florida. Mr.

Lendrum has also contributed articles to the Encyclopedia; Joseph P. Loring, a well-known mechanical engineer and head of his firm in N.Y. Mr. Loring's technical expertise has helped define many of the mechanical issues and recruited authors for several articles; Ieo Ming Pei, FAIA, because of several overseas commitments, was unable to take an active role on the committee in the early development but agreed to serve in an ex officio capacity; Herman D. J. Spiegel, Hon. FAIA, teaches structural design at Yale University School of Architecture, and heads a structural design firm with offices in New Haven and Washington. On many occasions Mr. Spiegel gave valued advice regarding structural design articles, and provided names of authors; Danforth W. Toan, FAIA, is a founding partner of the New York firm of Warner Burns Toan and Lunde which has produced outstanding educational and commercial projects in many areas of this country and abroad. Dan Toan has taught design, served on several national AIA committees, and prepared the article on Libraries for the Encyclopedia.

One of the first tasks of the Advisory Committee was to review the "Word List," representing the subjects to be covered by entries in the Encyclopedia. Many suggestions were made for additions, deletions, and other modifications to the list at the initial review and over the life of the project. Following the preparation of the "Word List" the task of author acquisition began, and continued for over three years. Announcements in AIA and ACSA publications brought forth many volunteers. Seeking authors for many of the approximately 600 articles was interesting, if time-consuming. It necessitated many letters and phone calls, following suggestions, leads, and referrals, but the final list represents an amazing cross-section of the construction industry. The list included practicing architects, educators from deans to librarians, consultants, engineers, material manufacturers' representatives, writers from the construction press, and freelance technical writers. For most this assignment was in addition to their regular day-to-day activities. It required many hours of research, drafts, and revisions to accommodate the comments of, in some cases, as many as five reviewers. The authors were also responsible for acquiring artwork and permission for its use. Last, but certainly not least, credit must be given to the unsung efforts of the reviewers, usually remaining anonymous but, nevertheless, representing an important check on accuracy and completeness of the entries.

If this Encyclopedia can supply a need in the industry, if the search for information and definition, history, and state-of-the art practice can be met, the great effort by all involved will be amply rewarded.

JOSEPH A. WILKES, FAIA
Annapolis, Maryland

DEDICATION

For her health in so many ways, this encyclopedia is dedicated to my wife Margaret.

CONTENTS

CONVERSION FACTORS, ABBREVIATIONS AND UNIT SYMBOLS

Selected SI Units (Adopted 1960)

Quantity	Unit	Symbol	Acceptable equivalent
BASE UNITS			
length	meter[†]	m	
mass[‡]	kilogram	kg	
time	second	s	
electric current	ampere	A	
thermodynamic temperature[§]	kelvin	K	
DERIVED UNITS AND OTHER ACCEPTABLE UNITS			
* absorbed dose	gray	Gy	J/kg
acceleration	meter per second squared	m/s^2	
* activity (of ionizing radiation source)	becquerel	Bq	l/s
area	square kilometer	km^2	
	square hectometer	hm^2	ha (hectare)
	square meter	m^2	
density, mass density	kilogram per cubic meter	kg/m^3	g/L; mg/cm^3
* electric potential, potential difference, electromotive force	volt	V	W/A
* electric resistance	ohm	Ω	V/A
* energy, work, quantity of heat	megajoule	MJ	
	kilojoule	kJ	
	joule	J	N·m
	electron volt[x]	eV^x	
	kilowatt hour[x]	$kW·h^x$	
* force	kilonewton	kN	
	newton	N	$kg·m/s^2$
* frequency	megahertz	MHz	
	hertz	Hz	l/s
heat capacity, entropy	joule per kelvin	J/K	
heat capacity (specific), specific entropy	joule per kilogram kelvin	J/(kg·K)	
heat transfer coefficient	watt per square meter kelvin	$W/(m^2·K)$	
linear density	kilogram per meter	kg/m	
magnetic field strength	ampere per meter	A/m	
moment of force, torque	newton meter	N·m	
momentum	kilogram meter per second	kg·m/s	
* power, heat flow rate, radiant flux	kilowatt	kW	
	watt	W	J/s
power density, heat flux density, irradiance	watt per square meter	W/m^2	
* pressure, stress	megapascal	MPa	
	kilopascal	kPa	
	pascal	Pa	
sound level	decibel	dB	
specific energy	joule per kilogram	J/kg	
specific volume	cubic meter per kilogram	m^3/kg	

Quantity	Unit	Symbol	*Acceptable equivalent*
surface tension	newton per meter	N/m	
thermal conductivity	watt per meter kelvin	W/(m·K)	
velocity	meter per second	m/s	
	kilometer per hour	km/h	
viscosity, dynamic	pascal second	Pa·s	
	millipascal second	mPa·s	
volume	cubic meter	m^3	
	cubic decimeter	dm^3	L (liter)
	cubic centimeter	cm^3	mL

* The asterisk denotes those units having special names and symbols.

† The spellings "metre" and "litre" are preferred by ASTM; however "er-" is used in the Encyclopedia.

‡ "Weight" is the commonly used term for "mass."

§ Wide use is made of "Celsius temperature" (t) defined by

$$t = T - T_0$$

where t is the thermodynamic temperature, expressed in kelvins, and $T_0 = 273.15$ by definition. A temperature interval may be expressed in degrees Celsius as well as in kelvins.

ˣ This non-SI unit is recognized by the CIPM as having to be retained because of practical importance or use in specialized fields.

In addition, there are 16 prefixes used to indicate order of magnitude, as follows:

Multiplication factor	*Prefix*	*Symbol*
10^{18}	exa	E
10^{15}	peta	P
10^{12}	tera	T
10^{9}	giga	G
10^{6}	mega	M
10^{3}	kilo	k
10^{2}	hecto	h[a]
10	deka	da[a]
10^{-1}	deci	d[a]
10^{-2}	centi	c[a]
10^{-3}	milli	m
10^{-6}	micro	μ
10^{-9}	nano	n
10^{-12}	pico	p
10^{-15}	femto	f
10^{-18}	atto	a

[a] Although hecto, deka, deci, and centi are SI prefixes, their use should be avoided except for SI unit-multiples for area and volume and nontechnical use of centimeter, as for body and clothing measurement.

Conversion Factors to SI Units

To convert from	*To*	*Multiply by*
acre	square meter (m²)	4.047×10^3
angstrom	meter (m)	$1.0 \times 10^{-10†}$
atmosphere	pascal (Pa)	1.013×10^5
bar	pascal (Pa)	$1.0 \times 10^{5†}$
barn	square meter (m²)	$1.0 \times 10^{-28†}$
barrel (42 U.S. liquid gallons)	cubic meter (m³)	0.1590
Btu (thermochemical)	joule (J)	1.054×10^3
bushel	cubic meter (m³)	3.524×10^{-2}
calorie (thermochemical)	joule (J)	4.184†
centipoise	pascal second (Pa·s)	$1.0 \times 10^{-3†}$
cfm (cubic foot per minute)	cubic meter per second (m³/s)	4.72×10^{-4}
cubic inch	cubic meter (m³)	1.639×10^{-5}
cubic foot	cubic meter (m³)	2.832×10^{-2}
cubic yard	cubic meter (m)	0.7646

To convert from	To	Multiply by
dram (apothecaries')	kilogram (kg)	3.888×10^{-3}
dram (avoirdupois)	kilogram (kg)	1.772×10^{-3}
dram (U.S. fluid)	cubic meter (m^3)	3.697×10^{-6}
dyne	newton (N)	$1.0 \times 10^{-5\dagger}$
dyne/cm	newton per meter (N/m)	$1.0 \times 10^{-3\dagger}$
fluid ounce (U.S.)	cubic meter (m^3)	2.957×10^{-5}
foot	meter (m)	$0.3048^\dagger$
gallon (U.S. dry)	cubic meter (m^3)	4.405×10^{-3}
gallon (U.S. liquid)	cubic meter (m^3)	3.785×10^{-3}
gallon per minute (gpm)	cubic meter per second (m^3/s)	6.308×10^{-5}
	cubic meter per hour (m^3/h)	0.2271
grain	kilogram (kg)	6.480×10^{-5}
horsepower (550 ft·lbf/s)	watt (W)	7.457×10^2
inch	meter (m)	$2.54 \times 10^{-2\dagger}$
inch of mercury (32°F)	pascal (Pa)	3.386×10^3
inch of water (39.2°F)	pascal (Pa)	2.491×10^2
kilogram-force	newton (N)	9.807
kilowatt hour	megajoule (MJ)	$3.6^\dagger$
liter (for fluids only)	cubic meter (m^3)	$1.0 \times 10^{-3\dagger}$
micron	meter (m)	$1.0 \times 10^{-6\dagger}$
mil	meter (m)	$2.54 \times 10^{-5\dagger}$
mile (statute)	meter (m)	1.609×10^3
mile per hour	meter per second (m/s)	0.4470
millimeter of mercury (0°C)	pascal (Pa)	$1.333 \times 10^{2\dagger}$
ounce (avoirdupois)	kilogram (kg)	2.835×10^{-2}
ounce (troy)	kilogram (kg)	3.110×10^{-2}
ounce (U.S. fluid)	cubic meter (m^3)	2.957×10^{-5}
ounce-force	newton (N)	0.2780
peck (U.S.)	cubic meter (m^3)	8.810×10^{-3}
pennyweight	kilogram (kg)	1.555×10^{-3}
pint (U.S. dry)	cubic meter (m^3)	5.506×10^{-4}
pint (U.S. liquid)	cubic meter (m^3)	4.732×10^{-4}
poise (absolute viscosity)	pascal second (Pa·s)	$0.10^\dagger$
pound (avoirdupois)	kilogram (kg)	0.4536
pound (troy)	kilogram (kg)	0.3732
pound-force	newton (N)	4.448
pound-force per square inch (psi)	pascal (Pa)	6.895×10^3
quart (U.S. dry)	cubic meter (m^3)	1.101×10^{-3}
quart (U.S. liquid)	cubic meter (m^3)	9.464×10^{-4}
quintal	kilogram (kg)	$1.0 \times 10^{2\dagger}$
rad	gray (Gy)	$1.0 \times 10^{-2\dagger}$
square inch	square meter (m^2)	6.452×10^{-4}
square foot	square meter (m^2)	9.290×10^{-2}
square mile	square meter (m^2)	2.590×10^6
square yard	square meter (m^2)	0.8361
ton (long, 2240 pounds)	kilogram (kg)	1.016×10^3
ton (metric)	kilogram (kg)	$1.0 \times 10^{3\dagger}$
ton (short, 2000 pounds)	kilogram (kg)	9.072×10^2
torr	pascal (Pa)	1.333×10^2
yard	meter (m)	$0.9144^\dagger$

† Exact.

Acronyms and Abbreviations

AA	Archigram Architects	ABNT	Associacao Brasileira de Normas Tecnicas
AAA	American Arbitration Association	ABPMA	Acoustical and Board Products Manufacturers Association
AAMA	American Architectural Manufacturers Association	ABS	Acrylonitrile-butadiene-styrene
AASHO	American Association of State Highway Officials	AC	Alternating current
AASHTO	American Association of State Highway and Transportation Officials	ACA	American Correction Association; Ammoniacal copper arsenate
AAT	Art and Architecture Thesaurus	ACEC	American Consulting Engineers Council
ABA	Architectural Barriers Act	ACI	American Concrete Institute

ACSA	Association of Collegiate Schools of Architecture
ADC	Air Diffusion Council
ADPI	Air Distribution Performance Index
ADR	Alternative dispute resolution
AEC	Atomic Energy Commission
AEG	Allgemeine Elektricitats-Geselschaft
AEPIC	Architecture and Engineering Performance Information Center
AFD	Air filtration devices
AFNOR	Association Francaise de Normalisation
AGC	Associated General Contractors of America
AGTS	Automated guideway transit systems
AHAM	Association of Home Appliance Manufacturers
AHU	Air handler unit
AI	Articulation Index; Artificial Intelligence
AIA	American Institute of Architects
AIA/F	American Institute of Architects Foundation
AIA/SC	American Institute of Architects Service Corporation
AICP	American Institute of Certified Planners
AID	Agency for International Development
AIKD	American Institute of Kitchen Dealers
AISC	American Institute of Steel Construction
AISI	American Iron and Steel Institute
ALS	American Lumber Standards
AMA	Acoustical Materials Association
AMCA	Air Moving and Conditioning Association
ANSI	American National Standards Institute
APA	American Planning Association; American Plywood Association
ARE	Architect Registration Examination
ARI	Air-Conditioning and Refrigeration Institute
APR	Air purifying respirators
ARCC	Architectural Research Centers Consortium
ARLIS/N	Art Libraries Society of North America
ARMA	Asphalt Roofing Manufacturers Association
ARP	Air raid precaution
ASA	Acoustical Society of America
ASCE	American Society of Civil Engineers
ASET	Available safe egress time
ASHRAE	American Society of Heating, Refrigerating, and Air Conditioning Engineers
ASHVE	American Society of Heating and Ventilating Engineers
ASID	American Society of Interior Designers
ASLA	American Society of Landscape Architects
ASM	American Society for Metals
ASTM	American Society for Testing and Materials
ATA	Air Transportation Association of America
AtBat	l'Atelier des Batisseurs
ATBCB	Architectural and Transportation Barriers Compliance Board
ATC	Air Transport Command
ATM	Automatic teller machine
ATMA	American Textile Machinery Association
A/V	Audio/video

AWG	American wire gauge
AWI	Architectural Woodwork Institute
AWPA	American Wood Preservers Association
BBC	British Broadcasting Company
BBN	Bolt Beranek and Newman
BBP	Butylbenzyl phthalate
BCMC	Board for the Coordination of the Model Codes
BDA	Bund Deutscher Architekten
BEEP	Black Executive Exchange Program
BFSM	Building Fire Simulation Model
BH	Boxed heart
BIA	Brick Institute of America
BOCA	Building Officials and Code Administrators International
BOMA	Building Owners and Managers Association International
BOSTI	Buffalo Organization for Social and Technological Innovation
BRA	Boston Redevelopment Authority
BRB	Building Research Board
BRI	Building-related illness
BSR	Board of Standards Review
BSSC	Building Seismic Safety Council
btu	British thermal unit
BUR	Built-up roofing
BV	Bolt value
CAA	Clean Air Act
CABO	Council of American Building Officials
CACE	Council of Architectural Component Executives
CAD	Computer-aided Design
CADD	Computer-aided Design and Drafting
CAGI	Compressed Air and Gas Institute
CAJ	Committee on Architecture for Justice
CARF	Committee on Accreditation of Rehabilitation Facilities
CBD	Central business district
CBR	California bearing ratio
CCA	Chromated copper arsenate
CCR	Ceiling cavity ratio
CCTV	Closed-circuit television
cd	candela
CDA	Copper Development Association
CDC	Community design center
cfm	cubic feet per minute
CFR	Airport Crash, Fire and Rescue Service
CIAM	Les Congres Internationaux d'Architecture Moderne
CIB	International Council for Building Research, Studies, and Documentation
CKD	Certified kitchen designer
CLTD	Cooling load temperature difference
CMU	Concrete masonry unit(s)
CPD	Continuing Professional Development
CPE	Chlorinated polyethylene

CPM	Critical path method
CPU	Central processing unit; Computer processing unit
CPVC	Chlorinated Poly(vinyl chloride)
cps	cycles per second
CR	Cavity ratio; Condensation resistance
CRI	Color Rendering Index
CRREL	Cold Regions Research and Engineering Laboratory
CRS	Caudill Rowlett Scott
CRSI	Concrete Reinforcing Steel Institute
CRSS	Caudill Rowlett Scott Sirrine
CRT	Cathode ray tube; Computer relay terminal
CSI	Construction Specifications Institute
CSPE	Chlorosulfonated polyethylene
CSRF	Construction Science Research Foundation
CU	Coefficient of utilization
CUA	The Catholic University of America
CVS	Certified value specialist
DAL	Federation of Danish Architects
dB	decibel
DC	Direct current
DHHS	Department of Health and Human Services
DOD	Department of Defense
DOE	Department of Energy
DOL	Department of Labor
DOP	Dioctyl phthalate
DOT	Department of Transportation
DP	Data processing; Degree of polymerization
DPLG	Diplome par le gouvernmente
DPU	Data processing unit
DWV	Drain-waste-vent
EDRA	Environmental Design Research Association
EERI	Earthquake Engineering Research Institute
EIP	Ethylene interpolymers
EJCDC	Engineers Joint Contract Documents Committee
EPA	Environmental Protection Agency
EPCOT	Experimental Prototype City of Tomorrow
EPDM	Ethylene propylene diene monomer
EPI	Emulsion polymer/isocyanate
ERM	Escape and rescue model
ESD	Electrostatic discharge
ESI	Equivalent sphere illumination
ETP	Electrolytic tough pitch
ETS	Environmental tobacco smoke
E&B	*Environment and Behavior* (journal)
FAA	Federal Aviation Administration
FAIA	Fellow of the American Institute of Architects
FAR	Floor area ratio
FBI	Federal Bureau of Investigation
fc	footcandle(s)

FCARM	Federation of Colleges of Architects of the Mexican Republic
FCR	Floor cavity ratio
FEMA	Federal Emergency Management Agency
FG	Flat grain
FHA	Federal Housing Administration
FHWA	Federal Highway Administration
FIDCR	Federal Interagency Day Care Requirements
FIDS	Flight Information Display Systems
FIRM	Flood insurance rate map
FmHA	Farmers Home Administration
FOHC	Free-of-heart center
fpm	feet per minute
FR	Flame retardant
FRP	Fiber glass-reinforced plastic
FRT	Fire retardant treated
FS	Factor of safety
FSES	Fire Safety Evaluation System
ft	foot (feet)
GAO	General Accounting Office
GATT	General Agreement on Tariffs and Trade
GDP	Gross domestic product
Glulam	Glue-laminated wood
GMAW	Gas metal arc welding
GRP	Glass-reinforced plastic
GSA	General Services Administration
GSIS	Government Service Insurance System
GTAW	Gas tungsten arc welding
h	hour(s)
HABS	Historic American Buildings Survey
HDO	High-density overlay
HEGIS	Higher Education General Information Survey
HEPA	High-efficiency particulate absolute
HHS	Department of Health & Human Services
HID	High-intensity discharge
HOK	Hellmuth Obata and Kassabaum
HPL	High-pressure laminate
HPS	High-pressure sodium
HUD	Department of Housing & Urban Development
HVAC	Heating, Ventilating, and Air Conditioning
Hz	Hertz
I	Candlepower
IACC	International Association of Conference Centers
IALD	International Association of Lighting Designers
IAPS	International Association for the Study of People and their Physical Surroundings
IATA	International Air Transport Association
IBD	Institute of Business Designers
ICAO	International Civil Aviation Organization
ICBO	International Conference of Building Officials
IDP	Intern-Architect Development Program
IDSA	Industrial Designers Society of America

IEC	International Electrotechnical Commission
IEEE	Institute of Electrical and Electronics Engineers
IES	Illuminating Engineering Society
IF	Industrialization Forum
IG	International Group
IIC	Impact insulation class
IIT	Illinois Institute of Technology
ILS	Instrument landing system
in.	inch(es)
INCRA	International Copper Research Association
IP	Image processing
ir	Infrared
IRA	initial rate of water absorption
ISO	International Organization for Standardization
IUA	Institute Universitario di Architettura; International Union of Architects
JAE	*Journal of Architectural Education*
JAPR	*Journal of Architectural and Planning Research*
JCAH	Joint Commission on Accreditation of Hospitals
JEP	*Journal of Environmental Psychology*
JSAH	*Journal of the Society of Architectural Historians*
KCPI	Knife cuts per inch
KD	Kiln-dried
kg	kilogram
kip	1000 pounds
km	kilometer
kPa	kilopascal
ksi	kips per square inch
kW	kilowatt(s)
l	liter
lb	pound
LCC	London County Council
LDR	Luminaire dirt replacement
LLF	Light loss factor
LOF	Large ordering framework
LPS	Low-pressure sodium
LRI	Lighting Research Institute
m	meter
MAI	Member of the Appraisers Institute
MARTA	Metropolitan Atlanta Rapid Transit Authority
MC	Moisture content
MDF	Medium density fiberboard
MDI	Methylene diisocyanate
MDO	Medium density overlay
MDP	Main distribution panelboard
MERA	Man and Environment Research Association
MGRAD	Minimum Guidelines and Requirements for Accessible Design
MIA	Marble Institute of America
min	minute(s)
MIT	Massachusetts Institute of Technology
MLS	Master of Library Science
mm	millimeter

MOE	Modulus of elasticity
MOR	Modulus of rupture
MPa	Megapascal
msec	millisecond(s)
MSHA	Mine Safety and Health Administration
MSR	machine stress-rated
μm	micrometer
NAAB	National Architectural Accrediting Board
NAHB	National Association of Home Builders
NAPF	National Association of Plastic Fabricators
NASA	National Aeronautics and Space Administration
NAVFAC	Naval Facilities Engineering Command
NBC	National Building Code
NBCC	National Building Code of Canada
NBFU	National Board of Fire Underwriters
NBS	National Bureau of Standards
NC	Network communications; Noise criteria
NCAR	National Council of Architectural Registration
NCARB	National Council of Architectural Registration Boards
NCIDQ	National Council of Interior Design Qualification
NCS	Natural color system
NCSBCS	National Conference of States on Building Codes and Standards
NDS	National design specifications
NEA	National Endowment for the Arts
NEC	National Electric Code
NEH	National Endowment for the Humanities
NEMA	National Electrical Manufacturers Association
NFPA	National Fire Protection Association
NGR	National grading rule
NIBS	National Institute of Building Sciences
NIC	Noise insulation class
NIOSH	National Institute for Occupational Safety and Health
NKCA	National Kitchen Cabinet Association
nm	nanometers
NMTB	National Machine Tool Builders Association
NR	Noise reduction
NRC	Noise reduction coefficient
NSF	National Science Foundation
NSSEA	National School Supply and Equipment Association
OEM	Original equipment manufacturer
ORBIT-2	Organizations, Buildings and Information Technology (study)
OSB	Oriented strand board
OSHA	Occupational Safety and Health Administration
P/A	*Progressive Architecture* (journal)
PACO	Probing Alternate Career Opportunities
PADC	Pennsylvania Avenue Development Corporation
PAPER	People and the Physical Environment Research
PAT	Proficiency analytical testing

PB	Polybutylene
PBS	Public Building Service
PC	Personal computer
PCB	Pentachlorobiphenyl
PCD	Planned community development
PCEH	President's Committee for the Employment of Handicapped
PET	Polyethylene teraphthalate
PIB	Polyisobutylene
PMR	Protected membrane roof
PMS	Pavement management system
POE	Post-occupancy evaluation
ppm	parts per million
PRF	Phenol-resorcinol-formaldehyde
PSAE	Production Systems for Architects and Engineers
psf	pounds per square foot
psi	pounds per square inch
PTO	Power take-off
PTV	passenger transfer vehicle
PUD	Planned unit development
PVA	Paralyzed Veterans of America; Poly(vinyl acrylic)
PVAc	Polyvinyl acetate
PVB	Polyvinyl butyral
PVC	Poly(vinyl chloride)
PWF	Permanent wood foundation
RAIC	Royal Architectural Institute of Canada
RBM	Reinforced brick masonry
RCR	Room cavity ratio
REI	Relative exposure index
REIT	Real estate investment trust
RF	Resorcinol-formaldehyde
RFC	Reconstruction Finance Corporation
RFP	Request for proposal
RIBA	Royal Institute of British Architects
RL, R/L	Random length
ROI	Return on investment
rpm	revolutions per minute
R/UDAT	Regional/Urban Design Assistance Team
SAC	Sound absorption coefficient
SAE	Society of Automotive Engineers, Inc.
SAR	Stichting Architecten Research
SBCC	Southern Building Codes Congress International, Inc.; Standard Building Construction Code
SBR	Styrene butadiene rubber
SBS	Sick building syndrome
SCFF	Silicone-coated fiber glass fabrics
SCS	Soil Conservation Service
SCSD	School Construction System Development
sec	second(s)
SERI	Solar Energy Research Institute
SG	slash grain
SHHA	Self-Help Housing Agency
SIC	Standard Industrial Classification
SJI	Steel Joist Institute
SLA	Special Libraries Association
SMACNA	Sheet Metal and Air Conditioning Contractors' National Association
SMPS	Society for Marketing Professional Services
SMU	Southern Methodist University
SOCOTEC	Societe de Controle Technique
SOM	Skidmore Owings and Merrill
SPP	Speech privacy potential
SPRI	Single Ply Roofing Institute
SSPB	South Side Planning Board (Chicago)
ST	Structural tubing
STC	Sound transmission class
STD	Standard
STL	Sound transmission loss
TAC	The Architects Collaborative
TAS	Technical Assistance Series
TCFF	Teflon-coated fiber glass fabrics
TDD	Telecommunication devices for deaf persons
TDI	Toluene diisocyanate
TEM	Transmission electron microscopy
TH	Technische Hochschule
TL	Transmission loss
T-PV	Temperature-pressure relief valve
TV	Television
TVA	Tennessee Valley Authority
TWA	Time-weighted average
T & G	Tongue and groove
UBC	Uniform Building Code
UCC	Uniform Commercial Code
UCI	Uniform Construction Index
UDDC	Urban Design and Development Corporation
UF	Urea-formaldehyde
UFAS	Uniform Federal Accessibility Standards
UIA	l'Union Internationale des Architects
UIDC	Urban Investment Development Company
UL	Underwriters Laboratories
ULI	Urban Land Institute
UNESCO	United Nations Educational, Scientific, and Cultural Organization
USCOLD	United States Committee on Large Dams
USDA	United States Department of Agriculture
USPS	United States Postal Service
uv	ultraviolet
VA	Veterans Administration
VAT	Vinyl asbestos tile

VCP	Visual Comfort Probability Factor		WAA	Western Association of Architects
VCT	Vinyl composition tile		WHO	World Health Organization
VDT	Video display terminal		WMMA	Woodworking Machinery Manufacturers Association
VG	Vertical grain			
VISTA	Volunteers in Service to America		WP	Word processing; Word processor
VLH	Very low heat		WPA	Work Progress Administration (Later Work Projects Administration)
VOC	Volatile organic compound			

AALTO, ALVAR

Alvar Aalto (1898–1976) is considered a modern architect, yet his work exhibits a carefully crafted balance of intricate and complex forms, spaces, and elements, and reveals a traditionalism rooted in the cultural heritage and physical environment of Finland. Over the course of his 50-year career, Aalto, unlike a number of his contemporaries, did not rely on modernism's fondness for industrialized processes as a compositional technique, but forged an architecture influenced by a broad spectrum of concerns. Aalto's is an architecture that manifests an understanding of the psychological needs of modern society, the particular qualities of the Finnish environment, and the historical, technical, and cultural traditions of Scandinavian architecture.

Hugo Alvar Henrik Aalto was born in the Ostro-Bothnian village of Kourtane in 1898. The family soon moved to Alajärvi, where his mother, Selma Hackstedt Aalto, died in 1903. By 1907 Aalto's father, J. H. Aalto, a government surveyor, had remarried and moved the family to the central Finnish city of Jyväskylä. In Jyväskylä the young Aalto attended the Normal School and the Classical Lyceum, and in the summer months during his teens often accompanied his father on surveying trips. Aalto entered the Helsinki Polytechnic in 1916, and became a protégé of Armas Lindgren (who was partner of E. Saarinen and H. Gesellius during the formative period of Finnish National Romanticism). While a student, he worked for Carolus Lindberg on the "Tivoli" area for the 1920 Finnish National Fair, and served in the militia during the civil strife following the Russian Revolution. After graduating from the Polytechnic in 1921, he sought employment in Sweden; unable to secure a position with Gunnar Asplund, he worked for A. Bjerke on the Congress Hall for the 1923 Göteborg World's Fair.

After having executed several buildings for the 1922 Industrial Exhibition in Tampere, Aalto established his practice in Jyväskylä in 1923. While securing local commissions, Aalto also followed the normal practice in Finland of participating in architectural competitions. In 1924 he married the architect Aino Marsio. Exemplary of the classicism found throughout Scandinavia during the 1920s, Aalto's early work was influenced by contemporary Nordic practitioners such as Asplund and Ragnar Östberg, as well as by the simple massing and ornamentation of the *architettura minore* of northern Italy. His work evolved from the austere quality of the Railway Workers Housing (1923), to the more Palladian inspired Workers Club (1924–1925) (both in Jyväskylä), and from there to the deftly refined and detailed Seinäjoki Civil Guards Complex (1925), Jyväskylä Civil Guards Building (1927), and the Muurame Church (1927–1929). Composed of simple, well-proportioned volumes rendered in stucco or wood, these works are characterized by their sparse decoration and selective use of classical elements.

In 1927 Aalto won the competition for the Southwestern Agricultural Cooperative Building (1927–1929), and

moved his office to Turku. Located on the southwest coast of Finland, Turku, the former Swedish capital, was a major cultural center where Aalto made numerous contacts that proved important to his development. His friendship with architect Erik Bryggman was coupled with Turku's proximity to Sweden, where associations with Asplund and Sven Markelius provided connections with the continental architectural avant-garde. Aalto not only attended the 1929 meeting of Les Congres Internationaux d'Architecture Moderne (CIAM), but traveled regularly throughout Europe, making him one of the most knowledgeable architects in Finland of the "new architecture."

During the six years spent in Turku (1927–1933), Aalto designed the series of buildings that would establish his international reputation. His architecture evolved from the stripped classicism of the Agricultural Cooperative Building toward a full acceptance of the formal and theoretical canons of International Style modernism or "functionalism" as it was termed in Finland. The *Turun Sanomat* Newspaper Building (1928–1930) was the first work in Finland to incorporate Le Corbusier's *les cinq pointes d'une architecture nouvelle*. The Standard Apartment Block in Turku (1929), the Paimio Tuberculosis Sanatorium (1929–1933), and the Turku 7th Centenary Exhibition complex (designed in collaboration with Bryggman in 1929) indicate Aalto's level of understanding of both International Style modernism and the other avant-garde movements in art and architecture that occurred in the late 1920s and early 1930s. In addition to functionalist principles, Aalto's work demonstrated an awareness of Russian Constructivism and the Dutch de Stijl movement, not to mention the work of Johannes Duiker, Andre Lurçat, and Laszlo Moholy-Nagy. During this period, Aalto was an active polemicist who advanced the cause of modernism in Finnish architecture.

Aalto moved his office to Helsinki in 1933, hoping the capital would provide greater opportunities for commissions, as well as bringing him closer to the city of Viipuri where the Municipal Library (1927–1935) was under construction. Although he would not receive a major public commission in Helsinki for another two decades, Aalto's practice expanded. This was an important period of transition in his work which, with the Viipuri Library, included his house and office in the suburb of Munkkiniemi (1934–1936), the Finnish Pavilions for the 1937 Paris and 1939 New York World's Fairs, the Villa Mairea (1937–1938), and the factory and workers' housing at Sunila (1935–1954). At this time he received the patronage of Harry and Maire Gullichsen, prominent industrialists, for whom he had designed the summer house Mairea on the Ahlström estate in Noormarkku. The Gullichsens provided Aalto with entry into Finland's industrial establishment, which resulted in a number of factory and housing commissions throughout Finland, including the complexes at Sunila, Inkeroinen, Kauttua, Vaasa, Karhula, and Varkaus for the Ahlström and Strömberg companies. In 1935, with the assistance of Maire Gullichsen and with Nils Gustav

Hahl as director, the firm of Artek was formed, which produced and marketed Aalto's furniture, fabric, and glassware designs.

During the mid-1930s Aalto's work began to embody a more tactile, romantic, and picturesque posture, becoming less machinelike in imagery. The presence of these characteristics in his work, coupled with a seemingly rekindled interest in Finnish vernacular building traditions and a concern for the alienated individual within modern mass society, signals a movement away from the functionalist tenets that formed his architecture in the early 1930s. In renouncing industrialized production as a compositional and formal ordering sensibility, Aalto moved toward a more personal style which solidified over the next decade, a direction achieving maturity in his work executed after World War II.

The characteristics of this direction are manifest in the specific architectonic concerns, issues, and elements that form a continuity of thought and formal expression throughout the remainder of Aalto's career. Centrality, as seen in the recurring presence of exterior courtyard spaces and courtlike interior atria, became an important organizational property in Aalto's work. The library at Viipuri and the 1937 Finnish pavilion in Paris incorporate an interior court, whereas the Villa Mairea is composed about an exterior courtyard. The conical skylights that illuminate the Viipuri reading room and the Paris Pavilion exhibition area provide a sense of externality to each space, and are precursors to the numerous forms Aalto developed to light his interior spaces. Within the Viipuri reading room court, Aalto includes staircases, landings, and handrails as dynamic elements celebrating human action and movement. The sinuous, undulating line and surface appear as important compositional elements in Aalto's work at this time, as witnessed in the undulating ceiling of the Viipuri Library meeting room, the three-story flowing display wall in the 1939 Finnish Pavilion in New York, and the figural geometries in the Villa Mairea's plan order. Continually exploring the tectonic possibilities of the undulating surface, Aalto demonstrates a unique sensitivity to the dynamics of the sinuous element in architecture. Aalto's material vocabulary changed at this time also, moving away from the machine aesthetics of the International Style toward a more expressive use of materials and textural effects. Wood, brick, and numerous other materials create a tactility and richness of expression that complements the formal changes in his work.

These changes exemplify the qualities and images that have become inextricably associated with perceptions of Aalto's architecture. Furthermore, they exist at a multiplicity of scales of realization in his buildings. The undulating surface is not merely a form, spatial construct, or building element, but is replicated at the detail level in his architecture and applied designs, seen in his glass vases, furniture designs, door handles, and light fixtures, not to mention in his paintings and experimental sculptures. This recurrence of form at varying scales throughout Aalto's work is representative of both the totality of the design conception found in his work and the importance of detail development in his buildings.

The problems of postwar reconstruction and rehousing following the 1939–1940 Russo-Finnish War consumed Aalto's efforts in the early 1940s. An avid supporter of planned and systematic postwar rebuilding and redevelopment, Aalto felt Finland could provide a paradigm for the entire reconstruction of Europe. Both his work and writings of this period focused on the research and procedures necessary to develop appropriate housing types and planning systems for reconstruction properly. After the war, as a result of his friendship with William Wurster, Aalto was named an adjunct professor at the Massachusetts Institute of Technology (1946–1948; he had held a similar post there in 1940). He received the commission for the Baker House Dormitory at MIT (1946–1949), a work considered to be a preview of his postwar developments. Aino, his first wife and collaborator of 25 years, died of cancer in 1949. In 1953 Aalto remarried, to the architect Elissa Makiniemi.

The time between 1945 and the early 1960s was incredibly productive for Aalto; he not only secured more commissions than any time in his career, but also produced his most important work. Often lauded as being uniquely Finnish in feeling, a quality characterized by the use of red brick, copper, and wood, the Säynätsalo Town Hall (1950–1952, Fig. 1), the Jyväskylä Teachers College (1953–1956), the Public Pensions Institute in Helsinki (1952–1956), the Rautatalo Office Building in Helsinki (1953–1955), the House of Culture in Helsinki (1955–1958), and the Technical Institute in Otaniemi (1956–1964) are exemplary of this period. The picturesque volumetric massing of these buildings, their responsiveness to landscape and site (be the context urban or rural), the juxtaposition of materials and textural effects, the rich vocabulary of forms developed to manipulate natural light, and the concern for the smallest detail (such as lighting fixtures, handrails, and door handles) demonstrate Aalto's maturity. In these works the themes that emerged in the late 1930s matured and solidified, achieving a calm, self-assured realization.

Centralization continues as a dominant theme in Aalto's buildings. From the small courts in Aalto's summer house at Muuratsalo (1953) and studio in Munkkiniemi (1955), to the plaza spaces in the Säynätsalo Town Hall and House of Culture, to the large agoralike void in the Teachers College, the exterior court orders and regulates these complexes. Similarly, the multileveled skylighted atria found in the Rautatalo Building, the Public Pensions Institute, and the main classroom building and library in the Teachers College create the feeling of being in a protected external space. The undulating surface appears with an infused vitality as large serpentine walls in the Baker House Dormitory and the House of Culture, whereas the competition entries for the Kongens Lyngby Cemetery (1951) and the Malm Funeral Chapel (1950) transform its usage into the fan-shaped plan that became the basis for a number of Aalto's library, housing, and auditorium plans over the next two decades.

The last 20 years of Aalto's practice, beginning with the Vuoksenniska Church (1956–1958), produced a more complex, expressive architecture. In contrast to the "bronze" imagery of the 1950s, Aalto returned to a material vocabulary, which created an architecture of bright, reflective, and smooth surfaces. Although there is thematic con-

A

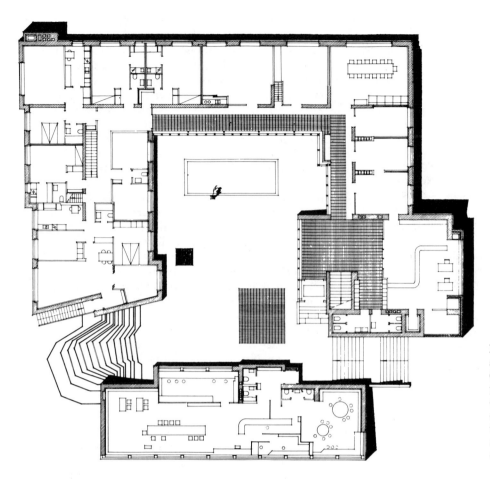

Figure 1. The village center, Säynät-salo (1950–1952): plan at the entrance (upper) level, showing the formal approach staircase leading into the courtyard, with the administrative accommodation grouped in a "U" around three sides of the court and the library arranged along its base (1). Courtesy of Schocken Books.

tinuity with his earlier work (light, sinuosity, centralization, and tactility still figure importantly in the designs), more explicit reference to classical and romantic ordering sensibilities emerge at this time. Going beyond the simple duality of pairing organic and geometric elements, Aalto's later works seem to fuse both classical restraint and romantic exuberance. The civic complex in Seinäjoki (1958–1965), the cultural center in Wolfsburg (1958–1963), Finlandia Hall (1962–1965), the Rovaniemi Library (1968), and the Riola Church in Italy (1966–1978), along with Vouksenniska, represent the best work of this period. The projects produced in the last decade of his practice indicate a slackening of creative power. The Alajärvi Town Hall (1969), the Lappia House in Rovaniemi (1975), the Aalto Museum in Jyväskylä (1973), and the Lahti Church (1978), for example, suffer from reduced design participation and a general indifference toward detailed development by the aging Aalto.

Aalto, who died in 1976, developed a rich and complex architectural language that explored the full range of expressive means available to the architect. His concerns, light, space, texture, scale, form, sinuosity, and the celebration of human action and movement, were addressed through the process of building. The uniqueness and variety of the responses he developed for these concerns result from the fact that he never forgot the role and purpose of an architect. For Alvar Aalto believed architecture to be an affirmative act, and the architect's purpose to design

and build. Thus, through responsive and responsible design, Aalto was able to create an architecture that was extremely humane, yet profoundly tangible in its presence.

BIBLIOGRAPHY

1. M. Quantrill, *Alvar Aalto, A Critical Study,* Schocken Books, New York, 1983, p. 130.

General References

K. Fleig, ed., *Alvar Aalto,* 3 Vols., Verlag für Architektur Artemis, Zurich, 1963, 1971, and 1978. The set of complete works on Aalto (Vols. 1 and 2 were reissued in 1983 and 1984, respectively).

B. Hoesli, ed., *Alvar Aalto Synopsis: Painting, Architecture, Sculpture,* Birkhauser, Basel, 1970 (2nd. ed., 1980).

F. Gutheim, *Alvar Aalto,* Braziller, New York, 1960.

W. C. Miller, *Alvar Aalto: An Annotated Bibliography,* Garland Publishers, New York, 1984.

L. Mosso, *L'Opera di Alvar Aalto,* Edizioni di Communita, Milan, 1965.

E. Neuenschwander and C. Neuenschwander, *Finnish Buildings: Atelier Alvar Aalto, 1950–1951,* Verlag für Architektur, Zurich, 1954.

J. Pallasmaa, ed., *Alvar Aalto: Furniture,* Museum of Finnish Architecture, Helsinki, 1984.

P. D. Pearson, *Alvar Aalto and the International Style,* Whitney Library of Design, New York, 1978.

D. Porphyrios, *Sources of Modern Eclecticism: Studies on Alvar Aalto,* St. Martin's Press, New York, 1982.

M. Quantrill, *Alvar Aalto: A Critical Study,* Schocken Books, New York, 1983.

A. Ruusuvuori, ed., *Alvar Aalto 1898–1976,* Museum of Finnish Architecture, Helsinki, 1978 (catalogue for the Aalto memorial exhibition).

G. Schildt, ed., *Alvar Aalto: Sketches,* M.I.T. Press, Cambridge, Mass., 1978. Contains 32 reprints of Aalto's written texts.

G. Schildt, *Alvar Aalto: The Early Years,* Rizzoli, New York, 1984. The first volume of the projected 3-volume biography.

G. Schildt, *Alvar Aalto: The Decisive Years,* Rizzoli, New York, 1986. The second volume of the projected 3-volume biography.

WILLIAM C. MILLER
Kansas State University
Manhattan, Kansas

ABS PLASTICS.   See PLASTICS, ABS

ACCREDITED PROGRAMS.   See EDUCATION, ARCHITECTURAL

ACOUSTICAL DESIGN—PLACES OF ASSEMBLY

OUTDOOR SOUND PROPAGATION

The transmission of sound in a free space environment involves the falloff of sound intensity by 6 dB, or to 25% of its intensity, for every doubling of distance. A further decrease in sound energy is evident in an outdoor facility because of the sound absorption by the audience as sound travels directly over people's heads. The well-known Greek and Roman outdoor theaters countered this problem by arranging the audience in steeply tiered fashion and by arranging them as close to the performers as possible, reducing the distance sound energy was required to travel and ensuring direct line-of-sight transmission from the performers to all members of the audience without much audience absorption. These two measures contributed to the acoustical success of these outdoor theaters; a third, and perhaps most important contributing factor, was the location of the theaters at quiet sites. Late afternoon performances required sites with the setting sun behind the audience, with strong implications for prevailing wind direction and sound refraction toward the audience. Finally, in Roman theaters in particular, a wall behind the performers added to the direct sound, with reflected energy arriving at listeners' ears with a short enough time interval (less than 30 ms) after the direct sound to reinforce both the clarity and loudness of the direct sound. These sound-reflecting walls may be thought of as the beginning of creative room acoustics, a first step in designing the ceiling and wall spaces of concert halls, opera houses, theaters, and worship spaces so that these surfaces contribute constructively to the listening conditions of the people assembled in them.

TRANSITION TO INDOOR ACOUSTICS

Figure 1 shows the transition from outdoor acoustics to indoor acoustics. Figure 1a shows an audience outdoors on a flat plane, with both inverse square law and audience attenuation reducing sound levels for listeners at the rear. Figure 1b shows the sloped seating, reducing audience absorption attenuation. Figure 1c shows the reflector behind the performers, adding reinforcement by reflected sound energy; in Figure 1d, the reflector is developed into a full stage shell with reflections both from behind and from above. Finally, in Figure 1e, shell surfaces are extended to envelop the audience, providing additional reinforcement by reflected sound energy, and the transition to an indoor theater is complete. In this example, the shaping of the walls and ceiling can assist both clarity and loudness, but possibilities also exist for sound-reflecting surfaces to reduce clarity and produce reverberation, echoes, and focusing and flutter effects (rapidly repeating echoes). All of these effects, if not properly controlled, can interfere with good hearing conditions. So, in comparing the indoor facility with the outdoor, there are positive possibilities for improving hearing conditions, but also negative possibilities or potential problems.

Reverberation

The acoustical phenomenon of reverberation is inherent in every indoor space. If the audience and seating were removed from Figure 1e, air absorption were eliminated (a physical impossibility), and all of the interior surfaces, including the floor, were made perfectly sound-reflecting (also a physical impossibility), a sound once initiated in that space would continue forever, perfectly reflected between the wall, ceiling, and floor surfaces; this lingering of sound energy when the sound source has ceased is what is meant by reverberation. Of course, in a real space, some sound energy is lost with each reflection from a wall and ceiling surface, more is lost with reflection from the audience or seating, and air absorption makes what is usually a small additional effect into one that is not so small at high frequencies and in very large spaces. The effect of all of this sound absorption is to give a finite length of time in which lingering sound energy can be heard. This is usually defined as the reverberation time, the time required for sound energy to decay 60 dB, or to one-millionth of its initial intensity. In any real indoor space, the reverberation time will vary with frequency, sometimes only slightly, but sometimes considerably; when one refers to a single number reverberation time, one usually refers to the time at 500 or 1000 Hz, or an average of the 500–1000 Hz range.

For many years, achieving the proper reverberation time was considered a prime goal in the design of concert halls, opera houses, theaters, and worship spaces, along with such important matters as freedom from echo, flutter, focusing effects, and unwanted noise. Today, there are some that dispute its importance altogether, and most consider it to be one of a number of important factors. Those who still consider it important usually assign an ideal reverberation time to a space, depending on its func-

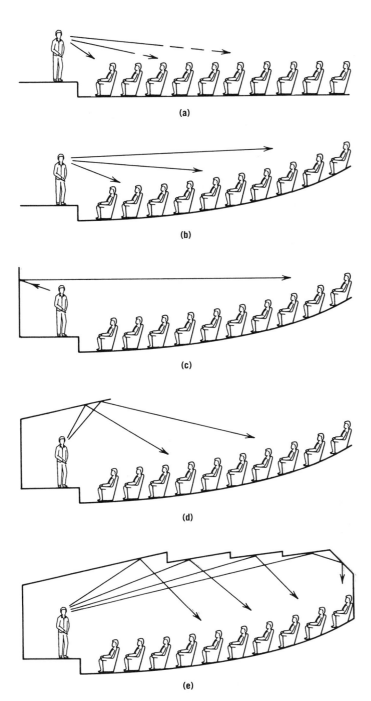

Figure 1. Stepped transition from outdoor to indoor conditions: **(a)** outdoors with no slope; **(b)** outdoors with sloped seating; **(c)** reflector behind performer added; **(d)** complete stage shell added; and **(e)** indoor auditorium.

tion. Figure 2 is an example of one such set of criteria, developed primarily by Russell Johnson. The variation in ideal reverberation times as a function of space use from 1 s or less for a drama theater, particularly one in-the-round, to over 3 s for some types of organ and choral music, particularly of the Romantic era, is striking.

Articulation

The concept that many favor as a replacement for reverberation time as the most important of several important factors is articulation, expressed as an Articulation Index

(AI), or, on the negative side, as the Articulation Loss of Consonants. These concepts were first developed to aid in the evaluation of electronic speech communication and amplification systems, where an AI of 0.75 or better, or an Articulation Loss of Consonants of 0.15 or less, is indicative of a satisfactory system from the standpoint of intelligibility. Figure 3 shows the relationships between AI, random-word intelligibility, and sentence intelligibility, and Figure 4 shows the application of the AI to criteria for spaces for music performance. Generally, a low AI or a high Articulation Loss of Consonants corresponds with spaces where the sound swims or floats, such as a large

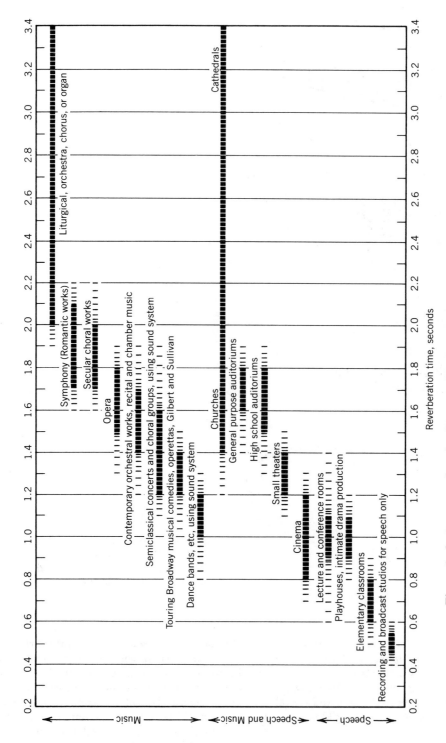

Figure 2. Optimum reverberation (500–1000 Hz) for auditoriums and similar facilities. Courtesy of Bolt Beranek and Newman, Inc.

6

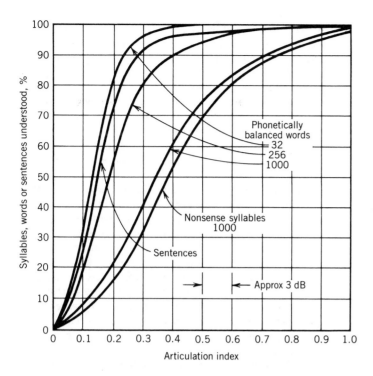

Figure 3. Approximate relationship between Articulation Index and intelligibility for skilled talkers and listeners. The numbers give the size of the test vocabulary. Courtesy of Klepper Marshall King Associates and Bolt Beranek and Newman, Inc.

cathedral suitable for organ music, while intimate spaces such as small drama theaters must, and usually do, have a high AI, or a low Articulation Loss of Consonants.

The main difficulty with the use of articulation in acoustical design is the difficulty of its assessment when the calculation must be based on architectural drawings. The calculation of reverberation time can be reduced to one of several formulas that relate the reverberation time to the room's volume, surface areas, sound-absorbing coefficients for the specific areas, and, at high frequencies, air absorption coefficients, but the calculation of the AI or the Articulation Loss of Consonants is not so simple. Computer-assisted ray tracing is one approach to overcoming difficulties in calculations. In existing rooms or in models,

the AI or Articulation Loss of Consonants can be measured with little more complication than reverberation time. For this reason in particular, some acoustical consultants insist that models be built for important projects with unusual or pioneering geometry.

In evaluating the AI or the Articulation Loss of Consonants, most acousticians consider that sound energy arriving at the listener's ear within 30 ms after the direct sound contributes to articulation; sound energy arriving between 30 and 50 ms after the direct sound may contribute to articulation, have no effect, or reduce articulation, depending on the relationship of this energy and the energy that precedes or follows it; and sound energy arriving more than 50 ms after the direct sound reduces articulation.

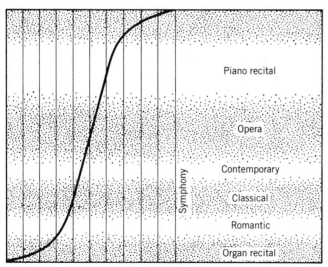

Articulation index (AI)

Figure 4. Articulation Index criteria for music performance spaces. Note that contemporary refers to serious classical contemporary music and not to rock, etc. Courtesy of Klepper Marshall King Associates and Bolt, Beranek and Newman, Inc.

Indeed, an impulse of energy arriving after 50 ms delay can be heard as a separate echo if loud enough. Usually, high articulation corresponds with short reverberation time and low articulation corresponds with long reverberation time, but this correlation can be distorted. Suspended overhead panels in a reverberant space can increase articulation, for example.

CONCERT HALLS

Concert halls represent one of the most fascinating types of interior places of assembly, and may have benefited more from acoustical research than any other building type, research that has perhaps reduced the element of change in design, but not eliminated it completely. Two important attributes of a concert hall, the reverberation time and the AI, have already been discussed. In 1962, after research based on the evaluation of 54 concert halls, Dr. Leo L. Beranek identified 18 characteristics, 17 of which could be evaluated on a rating scale, and only about half from architectural drawings (1). Today, it is not certain that even as many as 17 rating scales can truly characterize a concert hall, but there can be profit by reviewing these attributes; it is suggested that the reader refer to the section beginning on page 61, Chapter 4, of Beranek's *Music, Acoustics and Architecture* (1).

Intimacy or Presence

Beranek defined this attribute as the quality that makes a hall sound small, and related it to the length of time between the arrival at the listener's ear of the direct sound and the first reflected sound, with 20 ms or less as optimum. Beranek considered this characteristic three times as important as any of the 17 other subjective music–acoustics attributes.

In 1962, Beranek did not consider as important the relative strength of the first reflection and subsequent early reflections, with respect to the direct sound and its reflected sound arriving later. His later opinion, as well as that of others, was that failure to consider the proper strength of the early reflections led to early criticism of New York's Philharmonic Hall as being too dry, despite a measurably satisfactory reverberation time (2). Today, this author joins others in largely replacing intimacy as the major attribute by articulation, which must not be too high or the music will lack liveness; if it is too low, the music will lack sufficient clarity.

Other Attributes

Many of Beranek's other 17 attributes are considered by most acousticians as important today. Some, like freedom from echo and freedom from noise, are basic, have been considered so for a long time, and are applicable to nearly all places of assembly in addition to concert halls. (At this time, at least one acoustician believes in echo in moderation.) Some acousticians stress the importance of diffusion, a quality concerning the spatial orientation of the reverberant sound. This quality has been measured by

determining the direction from which sound arrives at the listener's location and the strength from each direction, with sound energy arriving evenly from all points around the listener considered to be the most diffusion, but not necessarily the best. Another approach is to measure the instantaneous difference between the signals at each of the listener's two ears, with greater differences indicating greater diffusion and, consequently, higher quality (assuming the same program material, of course).

Christopher Jaffe, who is probably involved in more concert hall projects than any other North American acoustician, believes he can summarize the essential attributes into five: (1) reverberation time throughout the spectrum; (2) arrival time of mid- and high-frequency reflections; (3), arrival time of low frequency reflections; (4) minimum masking of low power instruments; and (5) both minimum masking of low power instruments and arrival time of mid- and high-frequency reflections on stage. He associates a musical vocabulary and an architectural vocabulary for each of these characteristics expressed in the scientific vocabulary. However, most acousticians would agree that there are more characteristics to be considered than these five.

Lothar Cremer and Helmut A. Muller, two widely experienced German acoustical consultants, have analyzed a number of concert hall rating schemes in their book, *Principles and Applications of Room Acoustics,* including several developed by serious researchers in many countries (3). They find worth in several of the rating schemes, and find that these can lead to useful recommendations for optimal halls, but they also conclude that no existing rating scheme can yield a single-number quantity for the excellence of a hall, and that such a rating scheme is probably impossible to achieve (3).

Even solid agreement in the acoustical consulting profession on the truly critical attributes would leave the designer with a complicated problem; with disagreement on the relative importance of different attributes and with the suggestions of others, creation of a straightforward set of design principles seems quite far away. How, then, does one go about designing a concert hall with a good chance of success?

The Shoe Box Approach

The traditional or European shoe box-shaped concert hall and Western music grew up together and no doubt influenced each other. Middle Ages and Renaissance music performances often took place in spaces called oratories, which were rectangular-shaped rooms and similarly shaped ballrooms in palaces. When concerts moved out of palaces and were attended by the newly emerging middle class, the design of these oratories was copied in the design of the first concert halls (4,5). When Wallace Clement Sabine, a pioneer in architectural acoustics in the United States, assisted in the design of the now highly regarded Boston Symphony Hall, he based the design on the already existing rectangular shoe box Boston Music Hall, and on such successful European halls as Leipzig's Neus Gewandhaus, which was destroyed in World War II. One of the most successful modern concert halls is Salt Lake City's

Symphony Hall, for which Dr. Cyril H. Harris was the acoustical consultant (Fig. 5). This is a shoe box-shaped hall, but the ceiling slopes gently downward toward the front of the hall and is no more than 40 ft over the floor at the conductor's position, an improvement in the ability of musicians on stage to hear each other over certain older shoe box halls such as the aforementioned Boston Symphony Hall.

The shoe box approach to concert hall design makes an analogy to musical instrument design: eg, there is a considerable amount of information about violin acoustics, but most successful new violins have designs based on old violins; therefore, let new concert halls copy old successful ones. Dr. Harris has emphasized a continuity of practice in his approach, with each hall only slightly different from the one preceding, a careful and conservative approach that can work well when the architect does not rebel.

Note that the surfaces of these shoe boxes are not smooth and slick, either in the old halls or in the new halls. Side and rear balconies break up the smooth geometry, and detailed modulation is presented by niches and statues in the older halls and by deliberate surface modulations in both ceiling and wall areas in the new halls.

The late Robert A. Shanklin and Arthur H. Benade have shown that use of the shoe box form is no guarantee of acoustical success, particularly if insufficient diffusion is employed. Indeed, several halls, highly regarded for audience acoustics, have problems with regard to onstage communication (6). Symphony Hall has been mentioned previously, and there are examples of more modern halls with onstage communication difficulties. The shoebox may be a good beginning, but other aspects of acoustical design, such as the proper volume, echo control, and good sight lines, still need to be considered. Adequate diffusion is also important; Figure 6 is one example of adequate diffusion.

If the hall is small enough, the shoe box approach agrees with the importance that many modern acoustical consultants attach to lateral (side-to-side) reflections. Indeed, Nicholas Edwards of Artec Consultants states that a reverse-fan-shaped hall, which is wider at the front than at the rear, is an improvement on the traditional shoe box. This approach has been applied in moderation (two-degree splays) by Russell Johnson at the Pike's Peak Center in Colorado Springs and in a project completed in Calgary. The Pike's Peak Center has been judged successful for orchestral music, a real achievement for what is basically a multiuse auditorium.

In general, the modern shoe box hall seems applicable for concert halls seating up to 2000 people, or perhaps 2500 at the most. If the hall is to remain narrow, with many lateral reflections arriving before 30 ms as well as after 30 ms after the initial sound, increasing the seating capacity too much can place the rear of the hall too far from the stage for any visual intimacy, regardless of acoustical excellence. This objection to the shoe box, plus the architect's natural inclination to be creative and not to copy old forms, has led to considerable experimentation with other shapes. Certainly, the shoe box does not have a monopoly on acoustical success, and the importance of the strength of lateral reflections seems diminished when one considers such successful halls as the Jerusalem Congress Hall (Binyanae Ha-Oomah) in Jerusalem, Israel, and the Tanglewood Music Shed in Lenox, Mass., which are definitely fan-plan halls (Figs. 7 and 8).

Panel Array Halls

The use of sound-reflecting panels in concert halls is widely misunderstood. Their use was blamed for the acoustical deficiencies of Philharmonic Hall, but it is possible that it was the quantity and arrangement of the panels, and not their use per se, that was at fault, a sort of "too much pepper in the soup" phenomenon. Many acoustical consultants first used sound-reflecting panels to cure focusing effects and improve sound distribution in domed auditoriums, as in the Aula Magna in Caracas, Venezuela, MIT's Kresge Auditorium in Cambridge, Mass., and the auditorium of the Reorganized Church of Jesus Christ of the Latter-Day Saints in Independence, Mo. Randomly arranged 4 × 4-ft plaster panels were successfully used to interrupt the focusing effects of a multibarrel vault ceiling at the Spaulding Concert Hall of Hopkins Center at Dartmouth College, designed by Harrison and Abramovitz, with the clear space above the panels adding to the room's reverberant volume, while the panel array assured good sound distribution of early reflected sound. This favorable combination of early reflected sound with ample reverberation led several acoustical consultants to extend the use of sound-reflecting panels to auditoriums without focusing effects; examples include the San Diego Civic Center Auditorium, Clowes Hall at Butler University in Indianapolis, the Jacksonville (Fla.) Civic Auditorium, the Jackson (Miss.) Civic Auditorium, Branscomb Memorial Auditorium on the Florida Southern College campus, and the Salle Pelletier in Montreal. Luckily, none of these halls was disfigured by too much early sound, as was the initial Philharmonic Hall in New York.

Today, perhaps the most ardent user of sound-reflecting panels in concert halls is Dr. Theodore J. Schultz, who emphasizes the need for adjustability in the panel array, both as to height and to tilt; he insists on considerable rehearsal and concert time in the hall with the orchestra in order to determine the optimum adjustment. Dr. Schultz had the primary responsibility for the acoustics of four recent concert halls, one completed in 1980 and the others in 1982, all considerable departures from a rectangular shoe box conception: Baltimore's Meyerhoff Concert Hall, San Francisco's Louise M. Davis Hall, Toronto's Roy Thompson Hall, and Melbourne's Victorian Arts Center. All may be described as roughly horseshoe crab in plan, and all have considerable seating behind the orchestra, usable for chorus as well as audience. The sound-reflecting panels in these halls provide early reflections for the main floor seating, reflections to improve communication within the orchestra, and reflections to the audience and chorus behind the orchestra.

Concert Hall In-the-Round

The desire to bring the audience close to the stage has extended beyond wide fan-plan halls and oval-shaped halls

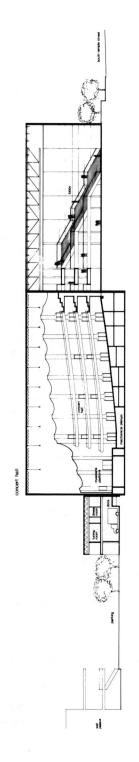

BUILDING CROSS SECTION A-A

(a)

Figure 5. **(a)** Symphony Hall in Salt Lake City, Utah, a modern example of a shoe box concert hall. Dr. Cyril Harris of Columbia University was acoustical consultant.

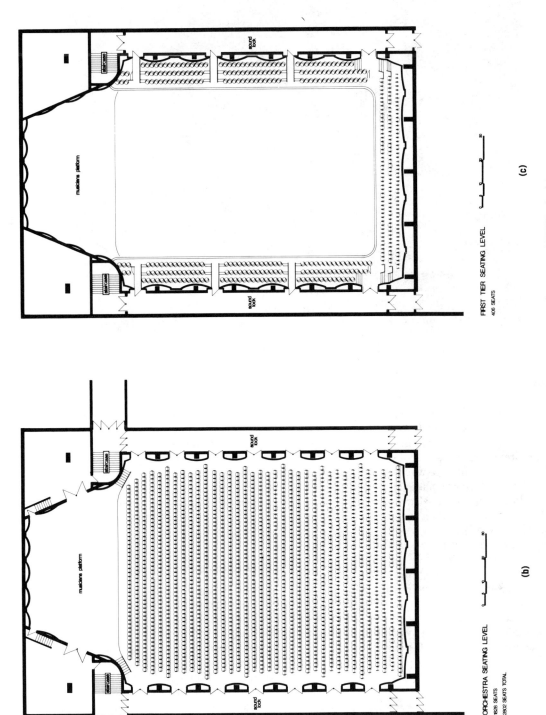

ORCHESTRA SEATING LEVEL
1628 SEATS
2802 SEATS TOTAL

(b)

FIRST TIER SEATING LEVEL
406 SEATS

(c)

Figure 5. (*continued*) **(b)** Main Floor. **(c)** First Balcony. Courtesy of FFKR, Architects.

11

Figure 6. Example of onstage wall diffusion at the Finger Lakes Performing Arts Center, Canandaigua, New York. Courtesy of Handler/Grosso, Architects.

to nearly circular halls with the concert stage near the center. The first of two important halls of this type was the Philharmonic in Berlin; H. Scharoun was the architect and Dr. Lothar Cremer was the acoustical consultant. A more recent hall of the same type was Boettcher Concert Hall in Denver, for which Christopher Jaffe was the acoustical consultant. Both halls use panel arrays to complement irregularly-shaped wall and ceiling surfaces to distribute sound energy. The experience of several acoustical consultants indicates that the concert hall in-the-round is not a wise choice for a basic design, unless sophisticated use of electronics will supplement the natural acoustics of the hall, or a relatively small proportion of the seating is behind the orchestra. Good acoustics may be achieved in the main part of the audience facing the orchestra, but achieving an equally good listening environment in a large area behind the orchestra is difficult indeed.

The Concert Hall's Other Uses

The concert halls discussed thus far were designed specifically for symphony and choral concerts. Some have adjustability to optimize the acoustics for varying sizes of performing groups and/or varying periods of music (the Romantic period requiring more reverberation and less definition, according to many, than the Classical and Modern periods). Yet even the most single-purpose concert hall will, today, be used for lectures, popular music concerts, films, and even conventions. A good electronic sound

system can go a long way toward adapting a concert hall to these uses; but such a sound system, combined with adjustable sound absorption to reduce reverberation time, can be even more effective in assuring that all uses of the room will benefit from good hearing conditions. This need for adjustability will be explored further when multipurpose auditoriums are discussed; with today's economic climate, nearly every concert hall, theater or opera house is a multiuse room.

The Electronic Concert Hall

When the Royal Festival Hall in London opened in 1951, it was criticized for lack of adequate bass response and lack of reverberation. The causes of these defects were several, including too low a room volume and the use of sound-absorbing elements. Instead of major architectural surgery, the hall has been improved by a subtle and sophisticated electronic system. The late P. H. Parkin, then of the British Building Research Station, developed a system called Assisted Resonance, using multiple amplification channels, each having a rather narrow bandwidth, and each adjusted to have a gain just under feedback (7). Together, when properly adjusted, these amplification channels provided the hall with additional reverberation time and additional bass energy without being obviously artificial. Almost simultaneously, John Ditamore was experimenting with broad-band amplification and reverberation at Purdue University, using reverberation chambers and

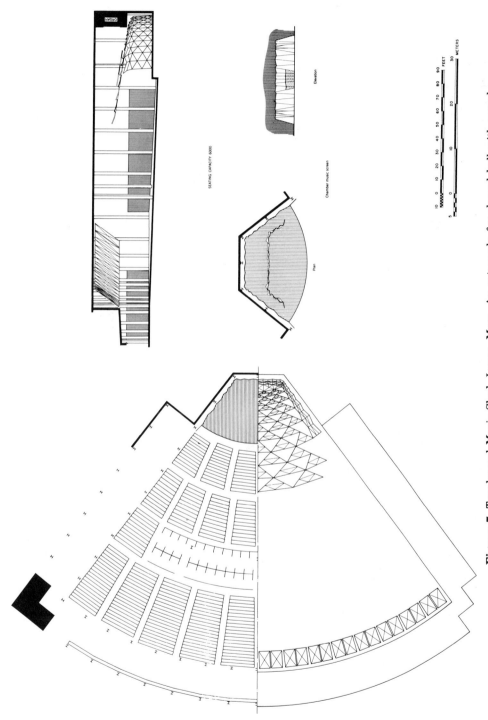

SEATING CAPACITY 6000

ORGAN

Elevation

Chamber music screen

Plan

Figure 7. Tanglewood Music Shed, Lenox, Mass. An extremely fan-shaped hall with sound-reflecting panels that is reasonably successful (8).

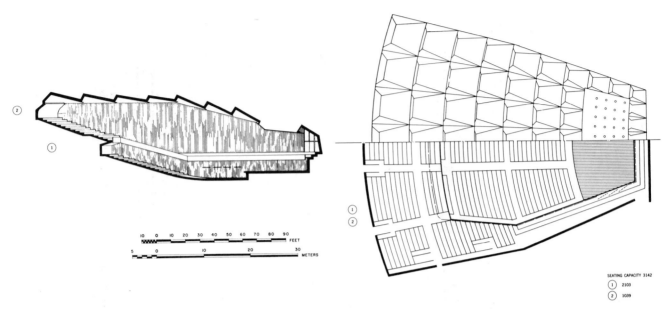

Figure 8. Jerusalem Congress Hall (Binyanae Ha-Oomah) in Jerusalem, Israel, a successful fan-shaped hall. Architects: Recheter-Zarchy-Rechter. Acoustical consultants: Bolt, Beranek and Newman, Inc. (9).

tape recorders converted into tape-loop delay devices. Today, the most vocal (and possibly the most experienced) exponent of the use of electronics in the concert hall is Christopher Jaffe, who has used both multiple narrow-band Assisted Resonance systems and wide-band systems in several of his multiuse halls and concert halls. He points out that multiuse halls must be deadened for their theatrical and popular music uses anyway, so there is no reason not to start out with theater acoustics and add liveness and warmth for orchestral music, with the use of electronics. His work at the Circle Theatre, the new home of the Indianapolis Symphony Orchestra, among others, has been praised by hard-to-please critics. John Ditamore and the author have also produced a wide-band electronic reverberation and surround system for the University of Western Michigan's Miller Hall in Kalamazoo, and a fairly simple, but effective, reverberation system for the University of Hartford's Lincoln Theatre in West Hartford, Conn.

It is relatively easy to use electronics to provide an optimum concert hall sound in a few seats in an auditorium; the trick is to provide such an environment for a wide seating area. The problems in doing so have many similarities to the problems of providing such sound by architectural means. There may well be a growth in the number of concert halls that employ some type of electronic reverberation, although many musicians will probably still prefer passive (ie, nonamplified) acoustical environments.

OPERA HOUSES

The basic difference between the typical opera house and the typical concert hall is that the opera house has a proscenium separating the stage area from the audience, and behind the proscenium, a stage tower to permit rapid changes of scenery by flying scenery in the stagehouse. Also, while the concert hall developed its traditional shoe box shape from the Renaissance oratory, the horseshoe-shaped opera house developed from the typical court theater, which arranged the audience in boxes at the rear and at both sides, with many levels from floor to ceiling. The goal was minimum distance from the audience to the stage, and a limitation was the degree of balcony cantilever possible at that time. Modern use of the horseshoe is evident in such halls as the new Metropolitan Opera House and the New York State Theater, both at New York's Lincoln Center. Dr. Cyril M. Harris and Dr. Vilhelm L. Jordan were acoustical consultants for both of these opera houses. Classic opera houses, such as the Vienna Staatsoper (reconstructed after World War II with 1658 seats) and Milan's La Scala, usually seated less than 2200 people (and would seat considerably less with up-to-date seating standards), but the new Metropolitan Opera House seats 3900 with modern seating standards and is acoustically successful. Of course, voices of international stature are essential to fill this house.

A more typical modern opera house, actually a space usable either as a concert hall or as an opera house, is the Ordway Music Theater in St. Paul, Minn., which seats approximately 1800. Home of the St. Paul Chamber Symphony, it is also the home of resident opera and theater groups. It has several adjustable acoustical features, which allow reverberation times from as low as 1.5 s for theater and some opera use, up to 2.0 s for orchestral concerts. Basically, however, it is the classic horseshoe-shaped opera house. R. Lawrence Kirkegaard was the acoustical consultant (Fig. 9).

Of course, different types of assembly spaces are used as opera houses, including arenas and coliseums seating over 10,000 people. However, the use of such spaces for opera, as for symphony orchestra, becomes more a matter of correct sound system design than room acoustics design, once adequate sound-absorbing treatment has been applied to assure control of reverberation and echo. Again, referring to Figure 2, it is seen that the reverberation time considered ideal for opera, about 1.3–1.8 s, is lower than that considered ideal for orchestral music alone, due, in part, to the demand for intelligibility from singers when they are singing languages that are understood. A second reason is the historical one that operas were originally composed to sound good in the horseshoe-shaped opera houses then in existence, which had reverberation times considerably lower than concert halls, largely because nearly all wall areas were papered with people.

Orchestra Pits

An orchestra pit is an important component of an opera house or multiuse auditorium. The traditional placement of the pit just in front of the stage has both historical and acoustical reasons. The most important is the requirement of musical coordination of the singers with the orchestra. The second is the greater ease with which the louder volume of the pit orchestra may be brought into balance with the singers' voices.

Pits are often constructed too small for their purpose in modern halls because of the architect's desire to bring the audience as close to the stage as possible. A good design figure for pits is 16 ft^2 (1.6 m^2) per musician. This is not much different from the requirement for stages for orchestras. In many cases, the larger the pit, the better the orchestral sound.

Pits where small, Mozart-sized orchestras perform should be completely open. Examples include most European opera houses and the Metropolitan Opera and New York State Theatre at Lincoln Center in New York. Pits where Wagner's operas predominate should be partially covered, to develop a more mysterious sound from the orchestra, and to allow better balance with the singers. The best example of this is the Bayreuth Festspielhaus. Some modern pits are a compromise between the two types.

Note that the partially covered pit usually involves projection of the pit under the stage to keep the singers close to the audience. A large pit may be constructed partially under the stage, and then equipped with movable panels to provide a completely open pit for Mozart-sized orchestras and a larger, partially covered pit for Wagner.

In plan, a pit should not be disproportionately long and narrow. A reasonable seating arrangement for the orchestra should be maintained.

Pits in halls where modern musical comedy is to be performed usually require some adjustable sound-absorbing treatment because musical comedy orchestration is not generally written with the same consideration for singers' voices as is Classical and Romantic opera. Certain modern operas can benefit from this treatment as well. Usually, this adjustable treatment is in the form of curtains on the upstage pit wall. Sometimes, the curtains are supplemented by carpet squares placed under the musicians with the loudest instruments, with the floor area left hard and sound-reflecting under the strings and the woodwinds.

Pit railings should be solid, even when removable, since open railings, even when draped, tend to allow too much sound energy to reach listeners in the front rows.

THEATERS

In any theater, the goal of high speech intelligibility overshadows any other acoustical design consideration. Other acoustical goals are speech naturalness, lack of distortion or harshness, and a wide dynamic range, from a whisper to a yell. Of course, these goals should apply to all seats and all likely acting positions. These goals may be achieved by proper room acoustics design in moderate-sized theaters; in large theaters, sound reinforcement is essential. Nine hundred- and 1000-seat proscenium theaters are possible without electronic amplification, but theaters-in-the-round require amplification above a 600-seat level, because of the difficulty in providing reinforcement behind the actor's back through room acoustics.

In contrast to a concert hall, a proscenium theater is probably best served by a moderate fan plan, which puts a larger number of the audience closer to the stage than does a rectangular plan; for the same reason, a one-balcony plan is better than one level of seating, except in the smallest of theaters. Thrust-stage and in-the-round theaters are complicated by the fact that, in the speech range where much intelligibility lies (the f's, s's, and t's), levels are roughly 10 dB lower behind the speaker's head than in front of it. The best thrust-stage and in-the-round theaters are, therefore, quite small, and the unidirectional theater with a mild fan plan has an acoustical advantage when compared to other theaters of the same audience size. Monumental design with high ceilings, useful in assuring adequate reverberation (through adequate volume) in concert halls, is not practical in speech theaters, where the goal of high intelligibility demands a low reverberation time and high articulation, best met by low ceilings that reflect sound quickly to the audience no more than 30 ms after the direct sound from the actor's mouth. Ensuring

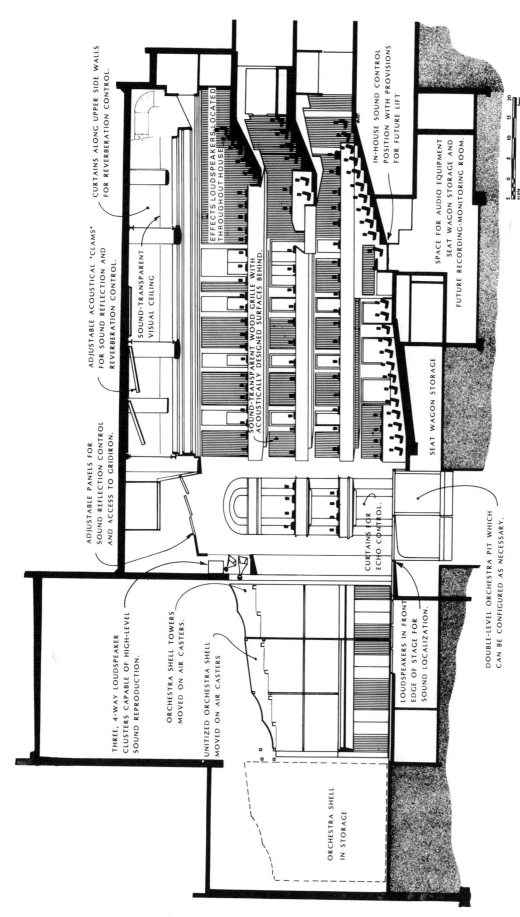

LONGITUDINAL SECTION

Figure 9. Ordway Hall, Saint Paul, Minn. A good example of a modern horseshoe-shaped hall, and one with many adjustable surfaces and devices to optimize acoustics for a variety of uses. Architect: Benjamin Thompson. Acoustical consultant: R. Lawrence Kirkegaard. Courtesy of R. Lawrence Kirkegaard.

The following labels appear within the figure:

CURTAINS ALONG UPPER SIDE WALLS FOR REVERBERATION CONTROL.

ADJUSTABLE ACOUSTICAL 'CLAMS' FOR SOUND REFLECTION AND REVERBERATION CONTROL.

SOUND-TRANSPARENT VISUAL CEILING

ADJUSTABLE PANELS FOR SOUND REFLECTION CONTROL AND ACCESS TO GRIDIRON.

EFFECTS LOUDSPEAKERS LOCATED THROUGHOUT HOUSE.

IN-HOUSE SOUND CONTROL POSITION WITH PROVISIONS FOR FUTURE LIFT

SOUND-TRANSPARENT WOOD GRILLE WITH ACOUSTICALLY DESIGNED SURFACES BEHIND.

SPACE FOR AUDIO EQUIPMENT SEAT WAGON STORAGE AND FUTURE RECORDING-MONITORING ROOM.

SEAT WAGON STORAGE

THREE, 4-WAY LOUDSPEAKER CLUSTERS CAPABLE OF HIGH-LEVEL SOUND REPRODUCTION.

ORCHESTRA SHELL TOWERS MOVED ON AIR CASTERS.

UNITIZED ORCHESTRA SHELL MOVED ON AIR CASTERS

CURTAINS FOR ECHO CONTROL.

LOUDSPEAKERS IN FRONT EDGE OF STAGE FOR SOUND LOCALIZATION.

DOUBLE-LEVEL ORCHESTRA PIT WHICH CAN BE CONFIGURED AS NECESSARY.

ORCHESTRA SHELL IN STORAGE

16

such quick reflections for all members of the audience can be difficult, because the ceiling and wall sound-reflecting surfaces must be coordinated with stage lighting covers and openings and the visual design requirements for the theater. Note that in some theaters where monumentality and its consequently high ceilings are essential, specially shaped side balconies can provide short-delayed sound reflections for the central main floor; underbalcony soffits can provide reflection for the seats under them; and the main ceiling can be shaped to reflect sound energy quickly to the balconies. All wall and ceiling surfaces that do not produce quick reflections (reflections arriving at the listener's ear within 30 ms of the direct sound) should be treated with efficient sound-absorbing material to ensure adequate control of echo and reverberation. Reverberation can be a positive contribution in music spaces but not in speech theaters. Successful theaters have been built with measured reverberation times between 0.3 and 1.7 s, all having good speech intelligibility without electronic reinforcement. Lower reverberation times are essential for thrust-stage and in-the-round theaters, because there is very little direct energy behind the actor's back to begin with; the higher reverberation times are applicable only to the larger proscenium and other unidirectional fan-plan theaters, particularly those using hard box sets that can efficiently reinforce an actor's voice. Today, the calculation of reverberation time should be a check on acoustical design of theaters, not the basis of design, but an important check.

The large theater of the Alley Theatre in Houston, Tex., is a good example of consideration for acoustics in theater design. It is a mild fan plan, with a steep rake and a relatively low ceiling shaped to reflect sound from the stage directly to the audience with minimum delay. The rear wall surfaces have an efficient sound-absorbing treatment of carpet over glass fiber. The reverberation time is 1 s, unoccupied, and slightly lower when occupied. (Upholstered seats compensate for the missing audience in the empty theater.) Ulrich Franzen was the architect (Fig. 10).

MULTIUSE AUDITORIUMS

For the purposes of this discussion, multiuse auditoriums are defined as spaces devoted to a wide variety of cultural activities: concerts, opera, theater, motion pictures, and dance. Larger spaces that are used for sports activities, such as coliseums, stadiums, and arenas, will be discussed elsewhere in this article.

As has already been seen, there are important acoustical differences between a speech theater and a concert hall, with the opera house falling somewhere between the two. A motion picture theater is similar to a speech theater in that it requires low reverberation time and complete freedom from rear wall echo or any return of energy from the rear of the theater. Acoustics are not usually particularly critical for dance presentations, although concert hall acoustics can enhance the sound of a pit orchestra. (A most important consideration in the dance theater is a resilient stage floor!)

In the 1950s and 1960s, a large number of performing arts centers were built throughout North America, and most were designed to some type of compromise acoustics, midway between the requirements for speech and music. Many turned out to be less than acceptable acoustically, and prompted several acoustical consultants to say "multiuse is no use." Today, there are acoustical consultants who will refuse to work on a multiuse facility, feeling that the results in such a facility could only damage their reputations, regardless of the degree of attention to acoustics. Those who do work on multiuse facilities usually attempt to obtain as much adjustability as the budget will allow, so that the completed auditorium will approximate the acoustics of a first-class concert hall when the auditorium is used as such, yet also be deadened, or reduced drastically in reverberation time, when used as a theater. Actually, even the older, fixed acoustics multiuse auditoriums had some adjustability, usually in the form of a stage enclosure that could be flown out of the way when the auditorium was used as a theater or opera house and be in position as a hard sending end for concerts.

A list of features of an auditorium that can be converted from one use to another might include the following:

1. Movable stage enclosure or concert shell.
2. One or more pit lifts that can provide flexibility to allow the front of the auditorium to be used as pit area, audience seating area, or a stage extension. (Note that a movable pit rail is also required, and possibly a choir lift also at the rear of the stage.)
3. Adjustable auditorium side wall and rear wall curtains or drapes stored in enclosed pockets to allow maximum reverberation for concert use, and exposed for theater use, and/or adjustable drapes above a sound-transparent or panel array ceiling, and/or banners that retract into the ceiling, are exposed for speech and are retracted for music.
4. A sound-reflecting proscenium fire curtain (wall) that can provide a sound-reflecting backdrop for musicians located on a thrust stage in front of the proscenium in addition to, or instead of, a movable stage enclosure.
5. An adjustable sound-reflecting ceiling that lowers to close off volume (and possibly balcony seating capacity) for theater use, and raises to increase volume for symphony use, thereby adjusting reverberation time without the use of adjustable sound-absorbing drapes.
6. Sound-reflecting panels or a canopy that can pivot and/or raise and lower for a different pattern of reflection for speech as opposed to concerts.
7. A well-designed, installed, and operated sound-reinforcement system that can bring out the voices in a Broadway musical comedy over the sound of the pit orchestra.
8. An electronic reverberation–surround system that can make a speech acoustics room suitable for concerts.

The longitudinal section of Ordway Hall, designed around classical opera house principles but most definitely a multiuse auditorium, illustrates a good many of these

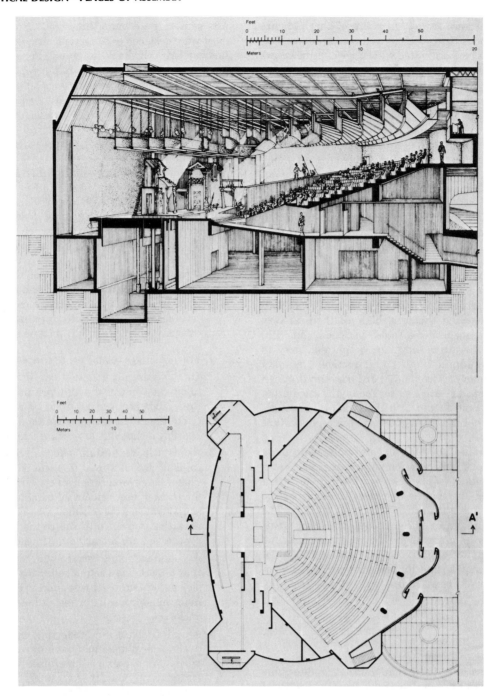

Figure 10. The Alley Theatre, Houston, Tex. Sound-reflecting surfaces provide early reflections to the listeners. Theater consultant: George Izenour. Acoustical consultants: Bolt, Beranek and Newman, Inc. and Ulrich Franzen and Associates (10). Courtesy of McGraw-Hill, Inc.

adjustable features (Fig. 9). As pointed out earlier, certain of these features may be applicable to the pure concert hall; they may also be applicable to the pure theater to provide it with some multiuse capabilities.

Movable Stage Enclosures

There are several types of movable stage enclosure, all of which have the purpose of converting the sending end of a basically theater- or opera-type stage designed for best handling of scenery into an efficient sending end for concert hall use.

Stage enclosures that are the simplest and easiest to handle are usually fairly low, have considerable area open to the backstage volume, and are relatively lightweight, possibly using thin plywood or thin glass fiber-reinforced plastic. These enclosures are lowest in efficiency in that considerable sound energy travels not out to the audience, but into the stagehouse through the enclosure material at low frequencies and through the openings. The theory is that the stagehouse acts as part of the reverberant envelope of the room and can contribute through its volume to the room reverberation, as delayed energy from the stagehouse eventually travels to the audience and is heard as reverberation. In some cases, however, this process is destroyed by the presence of sound-absorbing scenery and curtain material in the stagehouse, resulting in an anemic, dead, screechy sound, one that might be an improvement over no stage enclosure at all, but that certainly does not approximate concert hall acoustics. In many high school auditoriums, this is the only kind of stage enclosure that can be afforded. Obviously, its performance could be greatly improved by removal of all soft goods (teasers, tormentors, and other drapes and scenery) from the stagehouse for concert performances, allowing the stagehouse to contribute its reverberation to the room. This would bring about an improvement not only in liveness or reverberation, but also in bass response. Unfortunately, logistical considerations, usually lack of storage space or labor, prevent the removal of soft goods in some situations.

The second type of stage enclosure attempts, with varying degrees of success, to cut off the volume of air in which the orchestra performs from the stagehouse volume where soft goods are stored. Surface weight of the wall and ceiling panels must be at least 2 lb/ft^2 for bass energy to be reflected efficiently. Typical materials include ¾-in. plywood or well-damped 12-gauge steel, usually with a simulated wood finish. Whereas the lightweight enclosure can usually be handled on a manual rigging system, this heavier type of enclosure is best moved with electric or hydraulic winch systems, especially for the ceiling panels. Instead of leaving gaps between ceiling panels into which normal theatrical border lights are inserted, a better approach is to build the lighting directly into the ceiling panels. While 2 lb/ft^2 is definitely the lower limit for surface weight of the enclosure material, it is far from an upper limit. The heavier the material, the better the bass response of the enclosure will be. Very heavy enclosures may use some storage technique other than flying the ceiling panels, including storage of the entire enclosure in a separate upstage room, and rolling it on wheels or moving it on air casters into operating position when needed. The most frequent technique for moving side and upstage walls is to roll them as towers on wheels; however, air casters are coming into greater use for this application. In the design of such an enclosure, it is important to remember that the typical symphony orchestra occupies between 1600 and 2000 ft^2 of stage area; a large chorus can easily add 400 ft^2 or more.

The third type of stage enclosure is more complex. With it, attempts are made to develop some reverberation in the stage area, while cutting off the useful stage area from the sound-absorbing stagehouse. One good example of this type of enclosure is in use in Milwaukee's Uihlein Hall, an enclosure constructed primarily of heavy, damped steel. This construction forms a large outer enclosure some 45 ft tall, within which a series of light-transparent, sound-reflecting acoustical panels is suspended. The suspended sound-reflecting panels in their orchestra or chamber music positions contribute articulation or clarity, and provide good onstage communication for the musicians, while the space above, up to the ceiling of the enclosure, adds room volume and reverberation. With this enclosure, the stage area and the hall itself truly become one room (Fig. 11).

A different approach was used at the Virginia Center of the Performing Arts (Marcellus, Wright, Cox, and Smith, architects), a restoration of the Loew's Grace Street Theatre in Richmond, Va., as a multiuse performing arts center. Peter Frink was the theater consultant; with the author's collaboration, he designed a basic, heavy wood stage enclosure somewhat wider than necessary to accommodate the orchestra alone. Within the enclosure are partial height, sound-diffusing side walls on casters that can just fit the size of the orchestra, or be brought in to accommodate smaller chamber groups. The volume of the enclosure between the inner side and outer walls of the enclosure has hard, sound-reflecting boundary surfaces, and develops reverberation that adds to the liveness of music and even affects the measured reverberation time. The approach used in Milwaukee could not be used in Richmond because the proscenium height (approximately 32 ft) was already fixed by the restoration nature of the project, ruling out a higher stage enclosure.

The stage enclosure may be the most important item in making a multiuse auditorium into a fair approximation of a good concert hall. However, a close-to-ideal enclosure that is difficult to use is not as good as a less satisfactory enclosure that is relatively easy to use, since the enclosure that is difficult to use will often not be used when it should. This might lead to musicians playing in front of sound-absorbing drapes, with very poor acoustical results. In Richmond, hydraulic elements raise and lower the stage enclosure wall and ceiling panels; in Milwaukee, electric winches accomplish the same thing. Close collaboration between the architect, theater consultant, and acoustical consultant can ensure a good acoustical design with proper mechanization and sufficient storage space for the stage enclosure elements.

WORSHIP SPACES

Churches and synagogues resemble multiuse auditoriums in that both speech and music are expected to have good acoustics. Of course, one cannot constantly change movable acoustical panels or drapes during a typical service; speech acoustics and music acoustics must coexist at all times. Speech intelligibility is important in almost every worship space. The proper environment for worship music will depend on the type of music performed. An amplified gospel choir requires a relatively low reverberation time and a high AI, while traditional church music, and particularly choirs of men and boys performing the music of English cathedrals, requires a relatively long reverberation time, often even longer than 3 s. Size is also an important consideration. Cathedral acoustics in a small, wood church would sound unnatural, as would dry, lecture hall acoustics in a large cathedral. A description of four very different architectural styles may point out the degree of variation in the acoustical design of worship spaces.

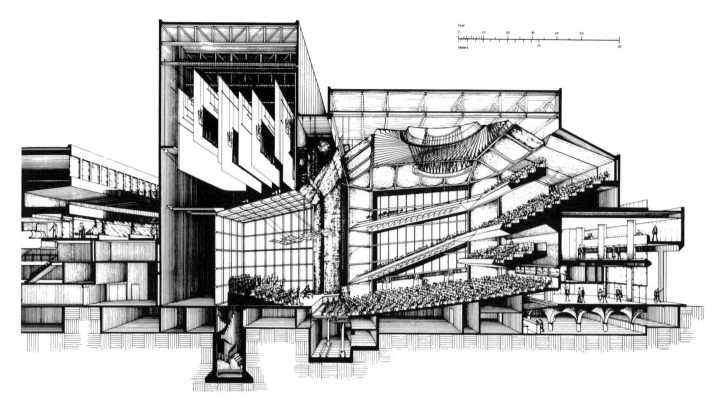

Figure 11. Uihlein Hall at the Performing Arts Center, Milwaukee, Wis. The stage enclosure is high to develop reverberation near the source, while articulated sound-reflecting panels aid definition and onstage communication. Architects: Harry Weese and Associates. Theater consultant: George Izenour. Acoustical consultants: Bolt, Beranek and Newman, Inc. with R. Lawrence Kirkegaard as job captain (11). Courtesy of McGraw-Hill, Inc.

Cathedrals

Large cathedrals or cathedral-type spaces usually house large pipe organs, and the music appropriate to such spaces was composed with large, reverberant spaces in mind. Of course, today, speech must also be intelligible, but long reverberation times are required for the musical portion of the service. The usual modern approach in reconciling these seeming opposites is to: (1) design the room with hard, sound-reflecting surfaces that do a good job of distributing music sound energy throughout the space, allow the congregation to hear themselves sing, and allow the large room volume to assure a high reverberation time; and (2) design a sophisticated speech–sound amplification system that can place the amplified speech energy into the sound-absorbing congregation seating area, without directing large amounts of amplified energy at the wall and ceiling surfaces. This concept is easy enough to state; its implementation requires close cooperation between the architect, acoustical consultant, and sound system contractor. Detailed descriptions of the sound systems necessary to assure high intelligibility in a reverberant space are not within the scope of this discussion, but there are a number of sound systems that are within the possible repertory of the acoustical designer. They are: (1) the large central cluster of directional horn loudspeakers over the usual speaking positions; (2) distributed loudspeakers pointing down and usually located 12–15 ft above the floor

in chandeliers; (3) column loudspeakers mounted on building columns, facing away from the speaking position and receiving a signal progressively delayed further away from the speaking positions, with each covering a relatively small area; and (4) pew-back loudspeakers, also using signal delay, with one small loudspeaker for every three or four people. Some variations and combinations of these basic types are possible.

Note that, in years past, attempts were made to make large cathedral spaces good for speech by massive applications of sound-absorbing treatment. Such churches became acoustically dead, very bad for music, and not much good for speech either, since they were too large for the unaided voice, and the sound-absorbing walls and ceilings did not distribute sound energy. So they then needed complex and expensive sound systems. Once the decision to use sound systems is made, there is no reason to make such spaces acoustically dead. As long as microphones can be located close to the person who is speaking, a sound system can provide high intelligibility, provided that the amplified sound energy is concentrated on the sound-absorbing congregation.

Small Churches

An opposite of the cathedral is the small, low, meeting-house style church, which may have a moderate-sized pipe organ or an electronic instrument. Music may be important, but the style of architecture precludes a long reverberation time. Speech can be intelligible without electronic amplification because of short distances, and the music program should feature music that has emotional impact in an intimate acoustical environment. Concave surfaces that may require sound-absorbing treatment should be avoided, and sound-reflecting surfaces should be used to distribute sound energy evenly and to control echo.

Medium-Sized Churches

Many churches will fall halfway between the extremes just described. Cathedral acoustics may not be possible in such spaces, but mid-sized churches can possess good concert hall acoustics, with reverberation times in the 1.8–2.0 s range. Surfaces should be hard and sound-reflecting; in certain cases, pew cushions may be applied to control the difference between full and empty acoustical conditions. A moderate- to large-sized pipe organ will usually be present or planned for. A relatively simple sound system, usually of the central cluster variety, can ensure good intelligibility, even for weak-voiced speakers. Cathedral-style music will not sound bad in such a space, and the acoustics will be appropriate to the size.

Evangelical Churches

The large evangelical church will be quite different from the three described above. An electronic organ, a piano, and an amplified choir are the main music sound sources, and the music is more similar to contemporary popular music than to traditional liturgical music. Preachers employ a wide dynamic range of voice levels. The service is often televised, and the entire church can be considered a large TV sound studio.

The acoustical design of these large evangelical churches is basically similar to that of a large speech auditorium, with reverberation times in the 1.0–1.5 s range. Rear walls should usually be sound-absorbing, and ceilings arranged so that reflections arrive at the listeners' ears within 30 ms of direct sound. The sound amplification systems often resemble the portable systems used for rock concerts.

Organ–Choir Arrangement

In any of the four varieties of worship spaces, the organ, organ console, piano, if any, and choir should be located within a 40 ft radius, if possible, to avoid delay problems. The organist–choir master must hear the organ and the choir without excessive delay. If the organist and choir director are two individuals, they must also be close to each other for proper coordination, as should the pianist, if any.

An exception to this placement rule is the antiphonal organ, which may be at the opposite end of the church, and which is intended for special effects and for keeping the congregation synchronized along the length of the church. Antiphonal choirs are also special, and require considerable skill on the part of the choir director and singers.

Choirs and organs should be located behind the altar on the upstage chancel wall facing the congregation, or in a balcony or gallery at the rear of the church. The organ and choir should face down the main axis of the church with good line of sight to the director and congregation. Divided chancels and transept placement are less satisfactory.

Both the choir and the organ should be somewhat higher than the congregation. In small churches, platforms may be used; in larger churches, some sort of balcony is preferable. Choir members should not stand under very low ceilings; ceiling heights above choir platforms should be in the 20–30 ft range. In cathedral-like spaces, nearby sidewalls can provide the reflection necessary for good communication among choir members.

Materials

Finish materials for worship spaces should usually be hard and sound-reflecting, as for concert halls. Wood paneling absorbs low frequency energy unless it is bonded to something more massive, and its use should be avoided. Brick, stone, and concrete are all appropriate materials for church interiors. Plaster is also good, but should be relatively thick. Carpet should not be used, except in evangelical churches, and should particularly be avoided near the choir and organ. When sound-absorbing treatment must be used to control reverberation or echo, it should not be placed on the ceiling, which should be hard and sound-reflecting to distribute sound energy. Pew cushions reduce the quality of congregational singing; however, they are sometimes necessary to control reverberation when only a portion of the congregation is present. Upholstered pews are normal for evangelical churches with amplified music.

SPORTS FACILITIES

This category of assembly spaces includes coliseums and indoor arenas and stadiums intended for sports activities, which are also usable for conventions and large popular music events. On occasion, these facilities may house serious cultural activities, including orchestral concerts and plays, and sometimes curtains are used to divide a portion of the seating area to form a theater seating area. These are large facilities, with seating capacities of well over 5000. The largest examples are the various domed stadiums, such as Houston's Astrodome and Seattle's King Dome, which can house entire baseball fields and their surrounding seating stands.

Sound Absorption

The basic problem with all of these facilities is that the surfaces are too far from the listeners and/or performers to provide much useful reinforcement by reflected sound energy. Instead, reflections from the boundary surfaces are heard as echoes. The basic acoustical design consists of making these surfaces sound-absorbing by means of massive applications of acoustical treatment. The acoustical materials used must have high absorption coefficients in the speech frequency range, particularly 200–4000 Hz. Concrete structures may employ thick sound-absorbing form boards, which are left in place on the underside of the concrete. Steel structures may employ perforated metal roof decks, consisting of a sandwich of perforated metal on the bottom, glass fiber in the middle, and continuous metal above. Inflatable domes should employ special sound-absorbing fabrics which can sag beneath the actual dome material. The airspace between the sound-absorbing fabric and the dome material above is necessary for efficient sound absorption.

Wall surfaces are usually also treated. Hard seats may be essential in some projects for reasons other than acoustics, but upholstered seats are better, and sometimes perforated seat bottoms (which expose sound-absorbing material within the seat) are also necessary to control the buildup of reverberation that occurs when occupancy is low.

The concept of reverberation time is somewhat meaningless in regard to such large spaces. Even with all significant areas treated efficiently, reverberation times can run to 4.0 or 5.0 s, because of the tremendous volume of these spaces. (If room surfaces are left untreated, reverberation times as high as 10 s have been recorded.) The important goal is to treat any potential echo-producing surface and not to aim for a particular reverberation time.

A final reason for the massive application of sound-absorbing treatment in these spaces is control of crowd noise. In large, untreated sports spaces, crowd noise can build up to the point where even massive, high-level sound systems cannot communicate emergency information. With treatment, crowd noise during an exciting part of a sports event can usually be held to broad-band levels of approximately 95 dB (flat), and the sound system can be designed to override such levels without causing instantaneous ear damage.

Cultural Events

The accommodation of cultural events in these large spaces should, after proper treatment of boundary surfaces, be similar to that of outdoor facilities. Stage enclosures or concert shells are useful for symphony orchestras and choruses. Beyond that point, the problem faced is basically one of proper sound system design, with the emphasis on achievement of adequate levels, proper coordination in time with sound from the live source, and uniformity of coverage. Some acoustical consultants would also include provision of electronic reverberation and surround sound.

BIBLIOGRAPHY

1. L. L. Beranek, *Music, Acoustics and Architecture,* John Wiley and Sons, Inc., New York, 1962. Reprinted by Krieger, Huntington, N.Y., 1979, pp. 61–71, Chapt. 4.
2. L. L. Beranek, F. R. Johnson, T. J. Schultz, and B. G. Watters, "Acoustics of Philharmonic Hall, New York, During its First Season," *JASA* **36**(7), 1247 (July 1964).
3. L. Cremer and H. A. Muller, *Principles and Applications of Room Acoustics* (translated from German by T. J. Schultz), Vols. 1 and 2, Elsevier Applied Science Publishers, Ltd., Barking, UK, 1982, pp. 503–591 and 592–634, Chapts. 111.2 and 111.3. Published in German by S. Hirzal Verlag, Stuttgart, FRG, 1978.
4. R. S. Shankland, "The Development of Architectural Acoustics," *Am. Sci.* **60**(2), 204.
5. R. S. Shankland, "Acoustics of Great Historical Buildings and their Relationship to Modern Design," AAAS Annual Meeting, Philadelphia, Pa., Dec. 28, 1971, unpublished.
6. A. H. Benade, "From Instrument to Ear in a Room, Direct or via Recording," *JAES,* **33**(4), 218 (Apr. 1985).
7. P. H. Parkin and K. Morgan, " 'Assisted Resonance' in the Royal Festival Hall, London, 1965–1969," *JASA,* **48**(5), Pt. 1, 1025.
8. Ref. 1, p. 142.
9. Ref. 1, p. 349.
10. G. C. Izenour, *Theatre Design,* McGraw-Hill, Inc., New York, 1977, p. 181.
11. *Ibid.,* pp. 346–347.

General References

V. O. Knudsen and C. M. Harris, *Acoustical Designing in Architecture,* John Wiley and Sons, Inc., New York, 1950. Reprinted by the American Institute of Physics for the Accoustical Society of America, New York, 1980.

R. H. Talaske, E. A. Wetherill, and W. J. Cavanaugh, eds., *Halls for Music Performance,* American Institute of Physics for the Acoustical Society of America, New York, 1982.

D. Lubman and E. A. Wetherill, eds., *Acoustics of Worship Spaces,* American Institute of Physics for the Acoustical Society of America, New York, 1985.

D. Klepper, "Speech Acoustics for Theatre," *JAES* **22**(1), 15 (Jan./Feb. 1974).

T. J. Schultz, "The Design of Concert Halls," *Forum* **14**(2 and 3), 57 (Summer/Fall 1976).

M. R. Schroeder, D. Gottlob, and K. F. Siebrasse, "Comparative Study of European Concert Halls: Correlation of Subjective Preference with Geometric and Acoustic Parameters," *JASA,* **56**(4), 1195 (Oct. 1974).

J. P. A. Lochner and J. F. Burger, "The Influence of Reflections on Auditorium Acoustics," *J. Sound Vib.* **1**(4), 426 (1964).

M. Barron, "The Subjective Effects of First Reflections in Concert Halls—The Need for Lateral Reflections," *J. Sound Vib.* **15**(4), 475, 1971.

A. H. Marshall, "A Note on the Importance of Room Cross-Section in Concert Halls," *J. Sound Vib.* **5**(1), 100 (1967).

M. Forsyth, *Buildings for Music,* The MIT Press, Cambridge, Mass., 1985.

See also ACOUSTICAL INSULATION AND MATERIALS; ACOUSTICAL STANDARDS; ACOUSTICS—GENERAL PRINCIPLES; CHURCH ARCHITECTURE; NOISE CONTROL IN BUILDINGS; OPERA HOUSES AND THEATERS; SOUND REINFORCEMENT SYSTEMS.

DAVID KLEPPER
Klepper Marshall King
Associates, Ltd
White Plains, New York

ACOUSTICAL INSULATION AND MATERIALS

Acoustical insulation is both a term that describes a process and a descriptor of certain materials. The process is that of reducing noise or vibration. The materials are those that in one way or another aid in this process. Many common building materials are not specifically known for their acoustical properties, although they profoundly affect sound. Other, generally newer, materials have been developed for specific acoustical purposes. Both are discussed in this article because both are relevant.

Insulation, as used in an acoustical context, can have one of two meanings. Literally, it means something that separates, that stops or reduces the transfer of sound. This is analogous to attenuation, as between two rooms that need to be insulated from one another. But insulation also implies materials that offer little or no attenuation, yet are used for acoustical purposes. In such cases, they provide absorption. It is essential that these two roles of insulation be clearly understood. Failing this, materials are liable to be misused, often with dire acoustical results.

SOUND ATTENUATION

The basic concept in architectural acoustics is best described as follows. Consider a pair of adjacent rooms, as illustrated in Figure 1. One, the source room, contains noise, whose transmission into the other, the receiving room, is to be reduced or prevented. The degree to which this is possible depends mainly on the attenuation offered by the wall (or floor–ceiling) between the two rooms. It also depends on so-called flanking paths that may allow sound to bypass the principal barrier; these must offer comparable attenuation.

In this concept, the reverberant sound level in the source room is compared with the resultant reverberant sound level in the receiving room. Each of these levels, and therefore the difference between them, is expressed in decibels. Thus, attenuation also is expressed in decibels.

Attenuation is described more precisely by two well-defined terms. First, the sound-level difference between two rooms that one measures or experiences is called noise reduction (NR). However, the sound-level difference due to the principal barrier (and not to other factors, as explained below) is called transmission loss (TL). TL is a specific property of the barrier under consideration. NR is not. The relationship between the two is expressed by

$$NR = TL - 10 \log S + 10 \log A_2$$

where S is the surface area of the barrier and A_2 is the amount of acoustical absorption that is present in the receiving room. (S and A_2 must be expressed in compatible units: square meters and metric sabins, or square feet and sabins.) It is apparent that if $S = A_2$, then NR = TL. In the real world of buildings, exact equality of S and A_2 is rare, but so are large differences. In general, NR due to a partition lies within a few decibels of its TL.

It should be clearly understood that for a partition or other barrier to offer the expected attenuation it must be complete in all respects. It must extend across the full height and width of the opening between the two rooms, contain no acoustically inferior elements (like doors), and absolutely no holes or cracks. The latter, if present, may seriously degrade performance.

TL, and therefore noise reduction and attenuation in general, is frequency dependent. The TL of a perfectly limp material, like lead sheet, increases 6 dB per octave. (Theoretically, TL also increases 6 dB with every doubling of mass.) However, most materials are not limp, and their TL curves are not straight. This is illustrated in Figure 2, which compares 2.5-mm (0.1-in.) lead with 100-mm (4-in.) concrete block and a comparably thick stud wall.

Analyzing and designing for sound insulation by frequency requires familiarity with the various materials' acoustical properties. It is best left to qualified acousticians. Architects, engineers, and builders should, however, be familiar with the single-number method of assessing TL. In the United States and Canada, it is the sound transmission class (STC) of a material or combination of materials (1–3). STC is determined as follows. A standard curve is fitted to the TL curve so that the sum of the deficiencies in the 16 ⅓-octave bands from 125 to 4000 Hz is no greater than 32 dB and no single deficiency exceeds 8 dB; upon such fitting, STC is given by the standard curve's position at 500 Hz. The resultant number does not represent TL at any frequency. It merely permits comparison of diverse materials, but with these qualifications.

1. As noted in Figure 2, all three curves correspond to an STC 40 rating. But they are distinctly dissimilar and, therefore, unequal at any given frequency.
2. Heavy materials like concrete and masonry perform well in the lower frequencies, are relatively ineffi-

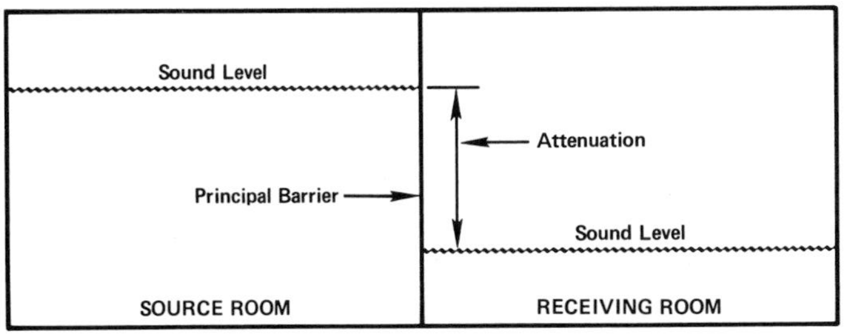

Figure 1. Schematic illustration of airborne-sound attenuation between two rooms.

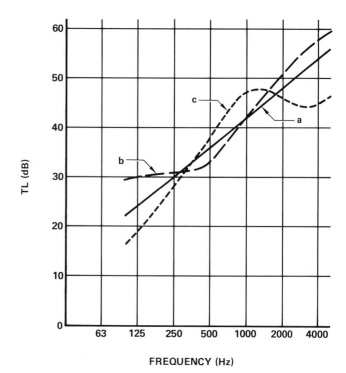

Figure 2. Some typical transmission-loss curves, all rated STC 40. **a,** lead sheet; **b,** concrete block; **c,** gypsum board on studs.

cient in the 500 Hz range, and regain their excellence in the higher frequencies.

3. Lightweight materials like gypsum board or plaster on studs (also glass) perform poorly in the low frequencies, quite well in the middle frequencies, and again less well at the highest frequencies of interest.

It follows that heavy barriers are required in order to contain low-pitched sounds, like those of mechanical equipment or of musical instruments. Considerably lighter barriers, such as stud partitions, may be employed where nothing more than speech insulation is involved. (Speech intelligibility, and hence distraction due to unwanted speech, is almost entirely governed by sounds in the 500–4000 Hz range.)

STC ratings of various materials, as well as some construction details, are further discussed later in this article.

Before leaving the subject of attenuation, some other forms of this process and some terms related to it should be mentioned. Next to airborne-sound attenuation, as illustrated in Figure 1, architects and other building professionals should also have a grasp of the following.

Shielding. This is provided by incomplete barriers, for example, the partial-height partitions often used in open office spaces. Their performance is almost always limited by their size and not by their TL. To be at all effective, they must extend well beyond the line of sight between the source and the receiver, and sound must not be allowed to reflect over or around the barrier (hence the need for very absorptive surfaces; see Sound Absorption). In practice, barrier attenuation seldom exceeds 20 dB. It is therefore unnecessary to build them of high-TL materials.

Impact Noise. This is generated by direct, physical con-

tact with a surface whose other side is exposed to an adjoining room. A typical case is that of footsteps and their transmission to the floor below. Attenuation is achieved by avoiding hard contact (ie, by covering the floor with a resilient material) and/or by resiliently separating the floor from the ceiling below. Impact noise attenuation of floor–ceilings is rated much like airborne attenuation, except that a standard tapping machine is placed and operated on the floor; its noise is measured in the room below and then normalized (4). Like airborne attenuation, impact attenuation is frequency dependent. Like STC, the single-number rating for impact sounds, the impact insulation class (IIC), is determined through curve fitting.

Vibration. This is generated by mechanical equipment. No piece of rotating, reciprocating, or vibrating equipment is perfectly balanced. The imbalance causes it as well as its supporting structure (floor, beam, etc) to vibrate. If unchecked, the vibration may be felt or heard as noise, often a considerable distance from the equipment. Attenuation is achieved through use of vibration isolators (spring and elastomeric mounts or hangers, flexible sleeves and connections) that allow the equipment to float free of the structure. There are no standards as such. To be effective, the natural frequency of vibration-isolated equipment must be substantially lower than the driving frequency. For mounts and hangers, this means ample static deflection.

Duct-borne Noise. This is from ventilation fans. Such noise propagates along ducts and enters rooms through the air supply and return grilles. (Note that sound travels almost equally with and against airflow.) Attenuation is achieved by internal lining of the ducts with an absorptive material and/or by inserting commercially available silencers. Large HVAC systems serving acoustically sensitive spaces may require 30 m (100 ft) or more of lined duct between the fan and the room.

SOUND ABSORPTION

As sound strikes a surface, it is transmitted, reflected, or absorbed. Usually, all three events occur. The percentage of energy transmitted tends to be very small, generally less than 1%, which would correspond to a transmission loss of 20 dB (the transmitted sound level, in decibels, equals 10 log of the transmitted energy fraction). All remaining energy is partially reflected and partially absorbed.

The processes that result in acoustical absorption are friction and resonance. Each is briefly discussed below.

Absorption through friction occurs when sound has access to the fine pores and interstices that one finds in porous and fibrous materials. The air molecules are restrained from continuing their cycle of compression and rarefaction. The energy thus lost is converted into heat. Most acoustical materials whose purpose is to absorb sound are based on this principle.

Absorption through resonance occurs when a stiff but not totally rigid system (eg, a plate or a confined volume of air, as in a Helmholtz resonator) is set in motion by sound. The system will absorb and dissipate the energy if its natural frequency corresponds to that of the incoming sound. Few products use this principle by design, but there are many building materials (glass, wood paneling, gypsum board, etc) that, if not well restrained, will resonate and thus absorb sound.

Acoustical absorptivity is quantified by the sound absorption coefficient α, which represents the fraction of the incident energy that is absorbed. Highly reflective materials have coefficients near zero, highly absorptive materials near one. It should be noted that virtually no material is perfectly reflective or perfectly absorptive. In general, materials with coefficients below 0.20 are rather reflective, whereas those with coefficients of 0.80 or higher are very absorptive.

Absorption, like attenuation, is frequency dependent. Porous–fibrous absorbers are most efficient in the higher frequencies, but also perform well in the middle and low frequencies if sufficiently thick or if backed by an airspace. Resonant absorbers, on the other hand, work best in the low frequencies (specifically, at their natural frequency) and are quite reflective at other frequencies. This is illustrated in Figure 3.

Absorptivity, like TL, can be described by a single number. The descriptor used in the United States and Canada is called the noise reduction coefficient (NRC). It is determined by averaging the sound absorption coefficients at 250, 500, 1000, and 2000 Hz and rounding off the result to the nearest multiple of 0.05. The NRCs of the four materials in Figure 3 would be 0.75 for both the glass fiber and the suspended tile, 0.30 for the carpet, and 0.10 for the wood paneling.

Like any simplification of a complete set of performance data, the NRC is flawed. It suggests equality of the tile and the glass fiber, yet they are not equal. If low-frequency absorption were required, suspended tile would be far better than an inch of glass fiber (in direct contact with a solid surface). If the best possible performance in the 500–4000 Hz speech intelligibility range were required, glass

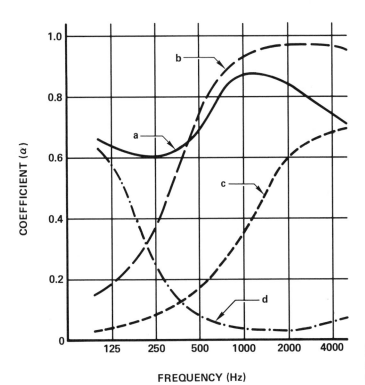

Figure 3. Some typical sound-absorption curves. **a,** suspended acoustical tile; **b,** 25-mm glass fiber board; **c,** carpet; **d,** thin wood paneling.

fiber would be better. It should be noted that despite their clearly unequal NRCs (0.75 and 0.30), tile and carpet can be almost equally absorptive near 4000 Hz.

Acoustical absorptivity of materials is determined by one of two methods: in a reverberation chamber (5) or in an impedance tube (6). The latter yields normal-incidence absorption coefficients, from which random-incidence coefficients can be estimated. The reverberation chamber method more closely simulates the conditions encountered in buildings, where sound impinges on the material from many different directions. Most of the absorption data published by manufacturers of acoustical materials are based on this method. A brief description follows.

A sample of the material, usually 244 × 274 cm (8 × 9 ft), is placed in a very reverberant, hard-surfaced room of some 250 m^3 (9000 ft^3). Reverberation time is then measured and compared with the reverberation time of the same room, but without the sample. Since reverberation time is inversely proportional to absorption, and since the room's absorption without the sample is known, that due to the sample can be calculated and then divided by the sample area. The resultant number per unit area is the absorption coefficient α. The absorption provided by a square foot of totally absorptive material (α = 1) is called a sabin; that of a square meter of such material is called a metric sabin. The significance of sabins, as opposed to α, is discussed below.

A word of caution: sometimes the reverberation chamber method yields coefficients in excess of 1, owing to diffraction effects along a sample's edges. Such numbers are unrealistic because α = 1 means total absorption. A realistic maximum for any material is 0.99.

Absorption data are often accompanied by a mounting type that describes one of several conditions, as standardized by the ASTM (7). Comparable designations by the Acoustical and Board Products Manufacturers Association, which predate the ASTM standard, may still be found in product literature. The most common conditions are

ASTM Type A or ABPMA No. 4. Sample placed directly against a reflective test surface.
ASTM Type B or ABPMA No. 1. Sample cemented to gypsum board, for example, to simulate glued-on acoustical tile.
ASTM Type E-400 or ABPMA No. 7. Sample supported 400 mm (approximately 16 in.) off the test surface— to simulate a suspended ceiling.

Every acoustical event involves a source, a path, and a receiver. As discussed earlier, attenuation usually involves two or more spaces, one of which is the source room. One speaks of attenuation between rooms. Absorption, on the other hand, affects the acoustics of one room, which contains both the source and the receiver. One speaks of absorption in a room, where it can serve any of the following purposes.

Reduction of Reverberation. The reverberation time of a room is usually given by the Sabine equation, which, in a simplified form, may be written as

$$T = 0.16 \ V/A \quad \text{(metric units)}$$

or

$$T = 0.05 \ V/A \quad \text{(English units)}$$

where T is the reverberation time in seconds, V is the room volume in cubic meters or cubic feet, and A is the combined absorption of all finishes and furnishings (plus that of air) in metric sabins or sabins. It is obvious that rooms containing little absorption can be very reverberant. Covering some principal surfaces with even moderate absorbers will greatly reduce reverberation. Further treating an already absorptive room will not result in a further, drastic reduction in reverberation.

Efficiency (as given by α or NRC) is not as important as the total number of sabins. Larger areas of less efficient materials are just as effective as smaller areas of more absorptive materials. Reverberation time is halved with every doubling of absorption.

Reduction of Noise Levels. Except in the immediate vicinity of a source, the sound level (in a room) due to that source tends to be the same regardless of distance. Such a reverberant sound level may be expressed by

$$L = P - 10 \log A$$

where L is the sound level in decibels, P is the sound power level (here treated as a constant) of the source, and A again represents the absorption in sabins. L is thus controlled by A. A room containing few or inefficient absorbers will be noisy. Adding or upgrading the absorbers will make it less noisy, but not by very much if the room is already quite absorptive.

Again, total absorption is more important than the efficiency of individual materials. Every doubling of absorption reduces the reverberant noise level by 3 dB, which, incidentally, is not nearly as drastic a change as a halving of the reverberation time.

Elimination of Discrete Reflections. A typical case is that of echoes off a distant surface, like the rear wall of an auditorium. Here, it is not the repeated interaction between sound and the material (reverberant sound will strike it many times and lose some of its energy at every contact), but a single contact that matters. In that one instant, the sound level must be appreciably reduced. The reflected level L_r, relative to the incident level L_i, both in decibels, is given by

$$L_r = L_i + 10 \log (1 - \alpha).$$

It follows that a material whose α is 0.50 will reduce the level by just 3 dB—hardly enough to eliminate an echo. Absorption coefficients of 0.80, 0.90, or higher usually are required to eliminate discrete reflections. Efficiency, and not the total number of sabins, is of the essence.

Improvement of Attenuation. Here the two roles of insulation converge again. Absorption helps attenuation in two situations: if located in a buffer space between the source and receiving rooms and if applied to the boundaries (especially ceilings) of large but low rooms containing both the source and the receiver.

In the first of these cases, sound that is in transit from the source to the receiver is reduced by very much the same mechanism as in noise-level reduction. Typical examples include absorptively treated sound locks, as between a lobby and a hall, and, on a smaller scale, insulation in the stud space of partitions. In the second case, one is more concerned with the individual reflections, as in elimination of discrete reflections. Examples include open offices and, in a somewhat analogous manner, acoustically lined ventilation ducts.

COMMON BUILDING MATERIALS

As noted in the introduction to this article, every material has certain acoustical properties. Space does not permit a review of these properties in detail, or coverage of every conceivable material, but an overview is warranted. The most commonly encountered materials, regardless of their value as acoustical insulators, are briefly described, and their properties as sound attenuators and/or absorbers are discussed.

Brick. Brick is a modular building block, made of clay. It is often used to build load-bearing walls, but is also used for non-load-bearing partitions, such as facing (brick veneer), and as paving.

Owing to its considerable mass [approximately 2.1 kg/dm^3 (130 lb/ft^3)], brick attenuates airborne sound very well. Exceptionally high orders of attenuation can be achieved with two parallel but unconnected brick walls. Joints must be fully mortared or otherwise sealed.

Absorption is negligible since there is little or no porosity. Brick is a good sound reflector at all frequencies.

Concrete. Concrete is a mixture of Portland cement, stone and sand aggregates, and water, cured into a hard mass of superior compressive strength. It is often reinforced with steel and used for structural slabs and walls.

Normal-weight concrete [approximately 2.3 kg/dm^3 (144 lb/ft^3)] is among the best attenuators of airborne sound. Lightweight concrete is less effective, unless of equal mass per unit area. Like any hard surface, concrete readily accepts and transmits impact sounds.

Concrete provides virtually no absorption. There are, however, aerated concretes that are intentionally porous. These can be fairly absorptive.

Concrete Masonry Units. These are modular building blocks made of concrete. They are usually manufactured with hollow cores. Normal-weight units can support considerable loads. Lightweight units (eg, cinder block) are generally used for non-load-bearing partitions only.

Attenuation depends on weight. Lightweight units may be adequate in noncritical cases. Normal-weight units, especially if solid or with sand-filled cores, attenuate sound very well. Two unconnected concrete masonry walls (like those of brick) can provide exceptionally good attenuation.

Since its surface is somewhat porous, concrete masonry (especially cinder block) is slightly absorptive, unless painted or otherwise sealed. If sealed, it becomes a good all-frequency reflector.

Glass. Glass is a usually light-transparent sheet made of a mixture of silicates. It is used principally to glaze windows and other openings that need to be closed, but without excluding light.

Despite its mass [approximately 2.5 kg/dm^3 (156 lb/ft^3)], glass is a marginal sound attenuator because it is thin and the mass per unit area is quite small. Superior performance is provided by well-separated double glazing and by certain types of laminated glass (see Acoustical Materials).

Almost totally reflective in the higher frequencies, glass resonates and, through this mechanism, can contribute appreciable absorption in the low frequencies.

Gypsum Board. Gypsum board is a fire-resistive sheet material made of calcined gypsum and certain additives sandwiched between sheets of special paper. It is used most typically as a finished sheathing on studs and joists.

Although not very heavy [approximately 0.8 kg/dm^3 (50 lb/ft^3)] or thick, gypsum board on studs or joists attenuates sound quite well. Performance is best in the middle frequencies. Very good results can be achieved with multiple layers, with resilient separation between the two faces of the partition, and with absorptive material in the stud space. Joints must be perfectly sealed.

Absorption is negligible, except for absorption due to resonance in the low frequencies.

Masonry. Masonry is any of a large variety of stone-like materials (eg, brick or concrete masonry units).

Metals. Metals are any of a family of alloys, but especially steel, which is commonly used to provide structural support. (See also Lead Sheet under Acoustical Materials.)

Plaster. Plaster is a pasty substance made of sand, water, and a binder such as cement or perlite. It is applied as a finish to either masonry or lath that is attached to studs or joists.

Plaster skins applied to studs or joists attenuate sound much like those made of gypsum board (see above). If applied to masonry, the improvement over the unplastered masonry is small or negligible.

Plaster provides very little absorption except in the low frequencies, if suspended or furred out from a solid surface (see Acoustical Plaster under Acoustical Materials).

Plywood. Plywood is a laminate of several layers of wood veneer. It is used in wood construction as an underlayment for floors or as finished paneling on walls.

Plywood is relatively ineffective as an attenuator because of its modest mass [approximately 0.6 kg/dm^3 (36 lb/ft^3)], specifically its mass per unit area, but often adequate in combination with other materials or where high performance is not required.

It can be a strong low-frequency absorber if thin and furred out from a solid wall. Otherwise, it is quite reflective.

Resilient Tile. Resilient tile is one of a family of floor tiles (also sheets), usually made of vinyl resins and asbestos fibers, but also of asphalt, rubber, or cork. It is used as a finish on concrete as well as other substrates.

Such tile has little effect on the attenuation provided by the substrate. However, the tile's nominal resiliency (especially if foam backed) provides some attenuation of high-frequency impact sounds.

Absorption is negligible; resilient tile is almost as reflective as concrete or any other hard floor finish.

Steel Decking. Steel decking is sheet steel, usually corrugated for greater strength, installed between structural supports (beams, purlins) as a form or base for other materials. It is also used for noise barriers along highways, for example.

Attenuation is usually governed by the combined mass of the deck and the topping. If the topping is concrete, which is typical of floors, the additional mass of the steel tends to be negligible. If used as an outdoor barrier, attenuation invariably is limited by barrier height.

Steel decking is highly reflective unless free to vibrate and hence to absorb low-frequency sound by resonance (see Acoustical Decks under Acoustical Materials).

Steel Joists and Trusses. These are structural members of many different configurations, including beams, designed to support floors and roofs. (Similar properties hold for joists and trusses made of other structural materials.)

On their own, these members do not attenuate sound, but their spacing and rigidity can affect vibration isolation. In general, rigid structures, that is, stiff, closely spaced supports, are more favorable than long-span structures that deflect more.

Such joists and trusses provide negligible absorption, but may diffuse sound if exposed to the room.

Steel Studs. Steel studs are framing members for partitions, usually fabricated in the shape of an angular C (channel studs) and covered with gypsum board.

Such studs are slightly resilient, which tends to decouple the partition's two faces and thus help attenuation (see Wood Studs). They are more effective with absorptive material in the stud space. They are most effective if two separate rows of studs are used to support the two faces of the partition.

Studs have no effect on absorption.

Stone. Stone is a natural material of considerable mass used for load-bearing walls, as a facing (stone veneer), and as paving.

Airborne sound attenuation depends on mass; stone can be very effective if thick and well sealed. However, it provides no impact insulation as a paving.

Stone does not absorb sound unless it is porous.

Wood Decking. Wood decking is one of several structural materials supported by beams or trusses to form floors and roofs. It is often exposed as a finished ceiling.

Owing to its relatively low mass (as compared to concrete), wood decking provides only nominal attenuation unless ballasted with heavier materials.

Wood decks are generally reflective, but unsealed cracks between the boards have been known to contribute a fair amount of absorption.

Wood Paneling. Wood paneling is a relatively thin wood finish made of boards or panels. It is usually attached to furring and thus kept clear of the solid wall surface behind the paneling.

Wood paneling provides negligible improvement over the attenuation provided by the basic wall.

It absorbs low-frequency sound by resonance and may lead to serious bass deficiency in music rooms unless it is thick and/or well restrained, for example, attached directly (without airspace) to the solid wall.

Wood Studs and Joists. These are framing members for partitions and floors, especially in wood-frame buildings. They are covered with gypsum board, plaster, or in the case of floors, with plywood and a variety of finishes.

Such studs and joists are quite rigid; the two sides of a partition remain well coupled (see Steel Studs). Attenuation can be improved considerably by resilient channels (see Special Devices) and by absorptive material in the stud or joist space. Staggered studs are best.

Studs and joists have no effect on absorption.

ACOUSTICAL MATERIALS

These include a great variety of materials and products whose purpose is strictly acoustical or that are commonly perceived as having acoustical value. Again, the listing may not include every product that may be so classified, but familiarity with those described should help in drawing conclusions regarding other similar materials.

Only the principal acoustical purpose of each material is discussed. Unless otherwise noted, those that attenuate sound do not absorb, and those that absorb do not offer much attenuation. This should be obvious since in order to stop sound, a material must be solid, and in order to absorb, it typically must be porous.

Acoustical Decks. An acoustical deck is a structural decking, usually made of perforated steel, backed by an absorptive material such as glass fiber (see below). The term also includes decks made entirely of fibrous materials (see Fibrous Plank).

Acoustical decks absorb sound. Their NRC ranges from about 0.50 to as high as 0.90. If exposed as a finished ceiling, they can greatly reduce noise and reverberation in spaces such as gymnasiums, factories, and workshops.

Acoustical Foams. These are any of a variety of cellular materials, usually made of polyurethane. They are manufactured either with open cells (air can be blown into and through the material) or with closed cells (each cell is sealed; material is airtight).

Open-cell foams are excellent sound absorbers, provided they are sufficiently thick. NRC ranges from approximately 0.25 for 6-mm (0.25-in.) foam to 0.90 and higher for 50-mm (2-in.) or thicker foams. Their uses include padding for upholstered theater seats to stabilize reverberation regardless of occupancy.

Closed-cell foams also absorb sound, but less efficiently and less predictably. They are more often applied to ringing surfaces, such as large metal plates, to provide damping.

Acoustical Plaster. Acoustical plaster is a plasterlike product, distinguished by its porosity after it dries. It was originally intended to create jointless surfaces (like those of ordinary plaster) that absorb sound, which ordinary plaster does not.

The performance of acoustical plaster is highly dependent on the correct mix and application technique. NRCs on the order of 0.60 have been obtained under controlled conditions, but field installations usually yield much less. Acoustical plaster is not a reliable sound absorber.

Acoustical Tile. Acoustical tile is a widely used ceiling material made of mineral or cellulose fibers or of glass fiber (see below). It is available in a variety of modular sizes from approximately 30 × 30 cm (12 × 12 in.) to 61 × 122 cm (24 × 48 in.) and larger. It is usually suspended in a metal grid, but certain varieties can be glued or otherwise attached to solid surfaces. It is prone to damage when contacted and is therefore not recommended for surfaces, especially walls, that are within human reach.

The absorptivity of acoustical tile ranges from approximately NRC 0.50 for the least efficient tiles to NRC 0.95 for the best (typically glass fiber) lay-in panels. Suspended tiles provide more low-frequency absorption than glued-on tiles. Membrane-faced tiles provide less high-frequency absorption than those whose faces are porous. In general, thicker tiles perform better than the thinner varieties.

Some acoustical tiles also attenuate sound. They are distinguished by an STC rating (in addition to the NRC rating), which quantifies attenuation through the suspended ceiling, along a standardized plenum, and through the ceiling of the adjoining room (8). This is of vital importance where the plenum is continuous, that is, where partitions stop against or just above the ceiling. Such tiles are usually made of mineral fiber and backed by a sealed coating or foil. The two-room STC ratings range from about 30 to 45.

Carpet. Carpet is any of a variety of soft floor finishes made of synthetic materials like nylon or natural materials like wool. It is either glued directly to the floor or installed over an underlayment of hairfelt or foam rubber.

The absorptivity of carpet depends primarily on the total thickness of the pile and the porous or fibrous underlayment (if present and provided the carpet does not have an airtight backing). NRCs range from 0.20 to about 0.55. Absorptivity is best in the high frequencies. Carpet is the only sound absorbing floor finish.

Carpet also attenuates impact sounds because it prevents hard contact with the floor. If sufficiently thick, it can be extremely effective. However, on wood floors, it will not eliminate low-frequency thuds.

Cellulose Fibers. Cellulose fiber is one of a variety of fibers that form the basis for materials such as acoustical tile, wood wool, fibrous spray, and so on (see Mineral Fibers). Each of these materials is designed to absorb sound, as discussed under the relevant headings in this article.

Curtains and Fabrics. These are a range of textiles that are used on their own (as curtains) or as coverings for other materials that may or may not be sound absorbing.

Curtains absorb sound if they are reasonably heavy [at least 500 g/m^2 (15 oz/yd^2)] and, more importantly, if their flow resistance is sufficiently high—to the point of severely impeding, but not stopping, airflow through the material. A light curtain may have an NRC of only 0.20; a heavy, flow-resistant fabric, draped to half area, may rate NRC 0.70 or more.

Fabrics attached directly to hard surfaces do not absorb sound. However, if stretched over materials such as glass fiber (see Fibrous Board), and provided they are not airtight, they make an acoustically excellent finish that fully preserves the substrate's absorptivity.

Duct Lining. Duct lining is one of a few materials that are literally acoustical insulation. It is usually made of glass fiber and comes in thicknesses of up to 50 mm (2 in.). The lining is mechanically fastened to the interior surfaces of sheet metal ventilation ducts. In high-velocity ducts, it may be faced with perforated metal to prevent erosion.

Duct lining absorbs sound and thus prevents noise propagation along ducts. Compared with an unlined metal duct, which may attenuate midfrequency sound by 0.15 dB/m (0.05 dB/ft), a duct with 25-mm (1-in.) lining will yield 3 dB/m (1 dB/ft). Low-frequency attenuation is not as good.

Ducts made entirely of glass fiber exhibit similar properties, but due to their very low mass they allow sound to escape into the surrounding space.

Fibrous Batts and Blankets. These are usually made of low-density glass fiber and serve two distinct acoustical purposes.

If exposed to the room, as a wall finish (behind fabric or an open grillage) or as a ceiling finish (behind perforated pans or spaced slats), they absorb sound and thus reduce noise and reverberation in the room. Performance depends on thickness and on the properties of the facing. It can be as high as NRC 0.90.

If used between the two faces of a partition (typically in the stud space, but also above suspended ceilings where the ceiling and the floor above form the partition), batts and blankets improve attenuation. They do it by absorbing sound that is in transit through the partition's cavity. If the cavity is bridged by rigid ties (eg, wood studs), there is little improvement. With steel studs, about 6 STC points are gained. Performance again depends on thickness, but the batt or blanket should never completely fill the cavity.

Fibrous Board. Fibrous board is similar to batts and blankets, but is of higher density—up to approximately 0.32 kg/dm^3 (20 lb/ft^3), but more usually near 0.1 kg/dm^3 (6 lb/ft^3).

Such rigid or semirigid boards, especially those made of glass fiber, are excellent sound absorbers. They are available with a variety of sound-transparent (usually fabric) facings, for use as wall or ceiling panels. Ratings range from approximately NRC 0.75 for 25-mm (1-in.) glass fiber board to NRC 0.90 for 50-mm (2-in.) board. Less porous or thinner boards, such as those made of mineral fiber, are somewhat less absorptive.

Fibrous Materials (Loose). These are also similar to batts and blankets and include all loose insulation that can be blown or dumped in place. They serve much the same purpose as batts within a partition; that is, they improve attenuation through the partition.

Fibrous Plank. Fibrous plank is a rigid (often structural) material, usually made of coarse fibers, such as wood fibers, embedded in a cementitious mix. The structural properties of certain planks allow them to be used as roof decking.

The fibrous surface absorbs sound. Performance depends on thickness and ranges from approximately NRC 0.40 for 25-mm (1-in.) plank to NRC 0.65 for 75-mm (3-in.) plank. If exposed to the room, fibrous plank reduces noise and reverberation in the room.

Fibrous Spray. Fibrous spray is any of a variety of sprayed-on insulating materials, often specified for fireproofing reasons. Previously made of asbestos fibers, which are now known to be a health hazard, most contemporary sprays contain cellulose or mineral fibers of various descriptions.

Fibrous spray is inherently porous and therefore absorptive. However, performance is highly dependent on thickness and application technique. A well-applied coat of 25-mm (1-in.) thickness may achieve or exceed NRC 0.60.

Glass Fiber. Glass fiber is an excellent sound absorber, available in the form of batts, blankets, and boards. The manufacturing process ensures consistent porosity at a very fine scale. Applications include a great many sound-absorbing treatments, insulation as in stud walls and ducts, and various applications in industrial noise control. Compressed blocks or sheets of glass fiber are also used to form resilient supports/hangers (see Elastomers under Special Devices) or as joint fillers where rigid ties are to be avoided.

The absorptivity of glass fiber depends on flow resistance, which, in turn, is affected by the material's thickness, its density, and the diameter of the fibers. In most applications, the thickness of the board or blanket is the most important parameter.

Laminated Glass. Laminated glass is a sandwich of two or more sheets of glass with viscoelastic interlayers that provide damping as the sandwich is flexed.

Certain types of laminated glass offer substantially better sound attenuation than an equal thickness of monolithic glass. For example, 13-mm (0.5-in.) plate glass rates approximately STC 30, whereas 13-mm laminated glass may approach STC 40.

Lead Sheet. In its purest form, lead sheet is sheet metal made of lead or a lead alloy. It is also available in combination with other materials, for example, as leaded vinyl. It is often used to close off the plenum above a room whose partitions extend only to a suspended ceiling.

Lead provides excellent attenuation per unit thickness because it is heavy [approximately 11 kg/dm^3 (700 lb/ft^3)] and limp. Furthermore, lead is easily shaped to conform to irregularities, which helps avoid holes in barriers that must be tightly sealed.

Metal Pans. Perforated metal pans, backed by fibrous batts, are an alternative to acoustical tile. Similar panels can also be used on wall surfaces. The pan itself has little acoustical value, but the size and spacing of its perforations (not just the percent openness) affect performance.

Depending on the perforation pattern and the type and thickness of the batt, the absorptivity may range from NRC 0.50 or lower to NRC 0.95. If the batts are encased in plastic, high-frequency absorptivity is impaired. Perforated pans do not attenuate sound unless equipped with a solid backing.

Mineral Fibers. Mineral fibers are a very common family of fibers used in the manufacture of acoustical tile, blankets and boards, fibrous spray, and so on (see Cellulose Fibers).

Sealants. Sealants are a family of nonhardening compounds used to seal joints and cracks in many construction types. They are especially applicable to gypsum board partitions and where services (ducts, pipes) penetrate a partition.

The acoustical value of sealants lies in their ability to render partitions airtight. Failing this, attenuation may be seriously compromised.

Slats and Grilles. Often believed to have acoustical value, slats and grilles (made of wood, metal, etc) serve only to protect the material behind them. Typically, the material behind is glass fiber, which is absorptive. Absorptivity is maintained if the slats or grille members are small and widely spaced. Increasing their size and/or reducing the space between them generally results in some high-frequency reflectivity.

SPECIAL DEVICES

The products discussed below are manufactured and used for strictly acoustical purposes. A few absorb sound. Most attenuate sound or vibration. Each is briefly discussed with reference to its properties and its typical applications.

Air Springs. Functionally comparable to steel springs and to those made of elastomers (see below), air springs are probably the most effective vibration-isolating devices available today. They are generally custom-designed for critical applications where only extremely low levels of vibration can be tolerated.

In principle, an air spring consists of a trapped volume of air encased in a flexible jacket. There are no mechanical ties between the building structure and whatever is to be isolated. Since air is compressible, it acts as a spring. The stiffness of these springs is controlled by air pressure and the jacket design. Isolation efficiencies well in excess of those practical with steel springs can be engineered.

Duct Silencers. Duct silencers, also called sound traps, are commercially made units designed to fit rectangular or round ventilation ducts of various sizes. They are available for a range of pressure-drop conditions and in several standard lengths. American-made rectangular silencers are 91 cm (3 ft), 152 cm (5 ft), or 213 cm (7 ft) long; round silencers are typically two to three times as long as their diameter.

Silencers, typically containing glass fiber-packed baffles, absorb sound and thus attenuate duct-borne noise. They perform much like duct lining (see above), but more efficiently. Performance is fair in the low frequencies, best in the midfrequencies, and quite good in the high frequencies. Long, high-pressure-drop silencers generally provide more attenuation than those that are shorter and/or less resistive.

Elastomers. Elastomers are a family of elastic, rubber-like materials (especially neoprene) used in the manufacture of resilient mounts and hangers (see below) and of other devices whose purpose is to avoid rigid contact.

The efficiency of the elastomer is related to its hardness (durometer), geometry, and loading. Durometer typically ranges from 30 (softest) to 70 (hardest). A typical recommended loading for a 40-durometer waffle pad made of neoprene is on the order of 4.2 kg/cm^2 (60 lb/in.^{2}).

Flexible Connections. These are typically flexible inserts made of canvas or leaded vinyl (see Lead Sheet under Acoustical Materials) and located between two pieces of metal duct. In a broader sense, flexible connections also include flexible conduit and various types of flexible hose.

The common purpose of all of these connectors is to create resilient breaks in ducts and pipes and thus to prevent vibration from being conducted along these otherwise rigid elements. Flexible connections are essential in all duct, pipe, and conduit runs between a piece of vibration-isolated equipment and the building structure.

Functional Absorbers. Made primarily for industrial applications in the form of free-hanging cylinders, functional absorbers combine surface absorptivity with tuned resonances that further contribute absorption. Performance of these units is usually given in sabins per unit. Like absorptive room finishes, they help reduce noise and reverberation in the room.

Gaskets. Gaskets are airtight seals made of pliable materials such as neoprene or vinyl, especially for acoustical doors and sound-rated partition systems. They are also used for other applications where airtightness cannot otherwise be achieved.

The sole purpose of acoustical gaskets (or sound seals) is to eliminate air leaks, which are also sound leaks. A perfect fit is essential if the attenuation capabilities of a door (or other) panel are to be fully realized.

Resilient Clips and Channels. These are specially designed mechanical connectors, typically made of light-gauge sheet metal, for use between studs or joists and a finished gypsum board or plaster surface. Resilient channels are very effective in combination with wood studs or joists, which are quite rigid.

Such clips and channels serve to break the rigid connection between a partition's two faces, which appreciably reduces sound transmission through the partition. Fibrous batts (see above) are usually recommended for the stud or joist space of partitions, including floor–ceilings, whose faces are resiliently attached.

Resilient Hangers. Resilient hangers are any of a variety of springlike devices designed to support suspended ceilings, suspended pieces of mechanical equipment, or ducts and pipes connected to equipment. The resilient elements may be steel springs, pieces of elastomeric material, or compressed glass fiber.

Resilient ceiling hangers perform much the same task as resilient clips or channels (see above), but more efficiently; they improve attenuation. Resilient equipment hangers, on the other hand, are primarily vibration isolators; they are a direct counterpart to the resilient mounts (see below) specified for floor-mounted equipment.

Resilient Mounts. Resilient mounts are equivalent in purpose to resilient hangers and may also incorporate steel springs or elastomer or compressed glass fiber elements (see Air Springs.)

Aside from their common role as vibration-isolating supports for mechanical equipment, there are mounts (usually 50 mm (2 in.) tall, made of solid neoprene or neoprene-covered glass fiber) designed to support so-called floating floors. Such double floors, consisting of a structural slab and a floating slab, offer exceptionally good sound attenuation.

Space Units. Space units are blocks of fibrous–porous material made of mineral fibers, foamed glass, or any other substance of comparable porosity. In appearance similar to acoustical tile, but typically about 50 mm (2 in.) thick, these units are intended for spaced application to hard wall and ceiling surfaces.

Space units absorb sound. In composition not significantly different from acoustical tile, their efficiency is helped by exposure of their sides.

Steel Springs. Generally of the coil type, steel springs form the core of most resilient mounts and hangers. They are sometimes engineered to provide static deflections of up to 130 mm (5 in.), although deflections between 25 and 50 mm (1 and 2 in.) are much more common. For comparison, static deflection of elastomer mounts/hangers seldom exceeds 13 mm (0.5 in.). Consequently, steel springs can offer considerably lower natural frequencies, and therefore greater isolation efficiencies, than any other springs except special-purpose air springs.

Steel springs (often in combination with elastomeric

Table 1. Airborne-sound Insulation of Selected Constructions and Building Elements

Constructions and Building Elements	STC[a]
Floor and roof constructions	
Wood floors without ceiling	20–30
with rigidly attached ceiling[b]	30–40
with resiliently attached ceiling[b]	45–55
Concrete slabs without ceiling	40–55
with suspended ceiling[b]	50–65
Floating slab on structural slab	55–70
plus suspended ceiling[b]	65–80
Lightweight decks (no concrete)	25–35
with concrete topping	35–45
Suspended ceilings[c]	
Unrated acoustical ceilings	10–30
Attenuation-rated acoustical ceilings	30–45
Simple solid ceilings	45–55
Thick solid ceilings topped with batts	55–65
Wall constructions	
Simple stud walls (no insulation)	30–40
Single-stud walls with insulation	40–50
Double- or staggered-stud walls	45–55
Simple masonry walls	35–55
with resiliently furred skins	50–65
Double (tieless) masonry walls	60–75
Demountable partitions	30–45
Operable (eg, folding) walls	25–50
Doors and windows	
Ordinary ungasketed doors	15–25
Fully gasketed (acoustical) doors	30–50
Tandem doors in common wall	35–55
Tandem doors with sound lock	40–70
Typical single glazing[d]	25–35
Special laminated glazing	35–45
Well-separated double glazing	40–55

[a] Sound transmission class.

[b] Solid ceilings, such as gypsum board or plaster; acoustical (tile or lay-in) ceilings attenuate sound less effectively.

[c] These ratings describe horizontal insulation between adjacent rooms that share a common ceiling plenum; for vertical insulation, see Floor and roof constructions.

[d] Includes insulating (thermal) glass, whose small airspace limits acoustical performance.

inserts, to reduce high-frequency transmission along the coil) are used primarily to isolate vibrating equipment such as fans, pumps, compressors, and so on. They are also used in ceiling hangers designed for critical applications. Steel spring mounts for floating floors are available, but their use is confined to unusual conditions.

Sway Braces. These include resilient connectors of various designs whose purpose is to provide structural, specifically lateral, support, but without creating any rigid ties. The insulating medium is typically neoprene or glass fiber attached to steel clips or angles.

Sway braces are used to brace free-standing walls in double wall constructions where rigid ties would seriously harm attenuation. Functionally similar angle braces are used to lend stability to masonry walls whose tops must, for sound insulation reasons, be kept free of slabs above.

Table 2. Acoustical Absorptivity of Selected Building Materials and Treatments

Building Materials and Treatments	NRC[a]
Floor finishes	
Concrete, marble, terrazzo, etc	0.00
Resilient tile or wood on solid	0.05
Wood on joists	0.10
Average glue-down carpet	0.25
Thick carpet without underpad	0.35
Impermeably backed carpet on pad	0.40
Permeably backed carpet on pad	0.55
Wall finishes	
Brick or plastered block	0.05
Gypsum board or plaster on studs	0.05
Heavy plate glass	0.05
Ordinary window glass	0.10
Thin wood paneling	0.10
Painted concrete block	0.10
Unpainted concrete block	0.15
Unpainted cinder block	0.25
Lightweight curtains	0.30
Medium-weight curtains	0.50
Heavy curtains	0.70
Fibrous–cementitious panels (average)	0.50
19-mm (0.75-in.) mineral fiber panels	0.60
25-mm (1-in.) glass fiber panels	0.75
50-mm (2-in.) glass fiber panels	0.90
Ceiling finishes	
Steel or sealed wood deck	0.05
Suspended gypsum board or plaster	0.05
Acoustical plaster (field test)	0.15
Mineral fiber tile (minimum)	0.50
Acoustical plaster (lab test)	0.55
25-mm (1-in.) fibrous spray	0.65
Acoustical steel deck (average)	0.70
Mineral fiber tile (maximum)	0.80
Well-perforated metal pan with batts	0.85
Glass fiber ceiling board	0.90
Audience areas	
Hard seats or pews, unoccupied	0.10
Cushioned pews, unoccupied	0.40
Well-padded seats, unoccupied	0.55
Seated audience (any seats)	0.80

[a] Noise reduction coefficient.

PERFORMANCE TABLES

Tables 1 and 2 provide a general overview of the acoustical performance that can be expected of some typical constructions and materials. Good detail is assumed in all cases. Attenuation is given in terms of the STC, and absorptivity is indicated by the NRC, both as discussed earlier in this article.

BIBLIOGRAPHY

1. *Standard Classification for Determination of Sound Transmission Class,* ASTM E413–73 (Reapproved 1980), ASTM, Philadelphia, Pa.
2. *Standard Method for Laboratory Measurement of Airborne Sound Transmission Loss of Building Partitions,* ASTM E90–81, ASTM, Philadelphia, Pa.
3. *Standard Method for Measurement of Airborne Sound Insulation in Buildings,* ASTM E336–77, ASTM, Philadelphia, Pa.
4. *Standard Method of Laboratory Measurement of Impact Sound Transmission Through Floor–Ceiling Assemblies Using the Tapping Machine,* ASTM E492–77, ASTM, Philadelphia, Pa.
5. *Standard Test Method for Sound Absorption and Sound Absorption Coefficients by the Reverberation Room Method,* ASTM C423–81a, ASTM, Philadelphia, Pa.
6. *Standard Test Method for Impedance and Absorption of Acoustical Materials by the Impedance Tube Method,* ASTM C384–77 (Reapproved 1981), ASTM, Philadelphia, Pa.
7. *Standard Practices for Mounting Test Specimens During Sound Absorption Tests,* ASTM E795–83, ASTM, Philadelphia, Pa.
8. *Standardized Mountings for Ceiling Sound Transmission Tests by the Two-room Method,* AMA-1-II, Acoustical Materials Association, New York, 1964.

General References

K. E. Kinsler and A. R. Fry, *Fundamentals of Acoustics,* John Wiley & Sons, Inc., New York, 1962.

L. F. Yerges, *Sound, Noise and Vibration Control,* Van Nostrand Reinhold Co., New York, 1969.

A. Lawrence, *Architectural Acoustics,* Applied Science Publishers Ltd., Barking, Essex, England, 1970.

L. L. Beranek, ed., *Noise and Vibration Control,* McGraw-Hill Inc., New York, 1971.

M. D. Egan, *Concepts in Architectural Acoustics,* McGraw-Hill Inc., New York, 1972.

M. Rettinger, *Acoustic Design and Noise Control,* Chemical Publishing Co., Inc., New York, 1972.

H. Kuttruff, *Room Acoustics,* John Wiley & Sons, Inc., New York, 1973.

V. O. Knudsen and C. M. Harris, *Acoustical Designing in Architecture,* American Institute of Physics, New York, 1978 (originally published 1950).

C. M. Harris, ed., *Handbook of Noise Control,* McGraw-Hill Inc., New York, 1979.

Catalog of STC and IIC Ratings for Wall and Floor/Ceiling Assemblies, Office of Noise Control, California Department of Health Services, Berkeley, Calif., 1980.

Gypsum Construction Handbook, United States Gypsum Co., Chicago, Ill., 1982.

R. S. Jones, *Noise and Vibration Control in Buildings,* McGraw-Hill Inc., New York, 1984.

Also selected papers published in the following journals:

Acustica

Applied Acoustics

The Journal of the Acoustical Society of America

See also ACOUSTICAL DESIGN—PLACES OF ASSEMBLY; ACOUSTICAL STANDARDS; ACOUSTICS—GENERAL PRINCIPLES; NOISE CONTROL IN BUILDINGS; OFFICE BUILDINGS; OPERA HOUSES AND THEATERS; RESIDENTIAL BUILDINGS; SOUND REINFORCEMENT SYSTEMS.

REIN PIRN
Bolt Beranek and Newman Inc.
Cambridge, Massachusetts

ACOUSTICAL STANDARDS

National and international standards bodies as well as scientific, technical, and trade associations provide standards that enable architects and building engineers to specify products, materials, and systems that will satisfy the desired acoustical criteria. Similarly, measurement standards and recommended practices are available both for laboratory measurement under idealized circumstances and for conformance measurements under actual use or field conditions. The U.S. Department of Commerce, National Bureau of Standards (NBS), publishes a comprehensive listing with annotated summaries of practically all international and U.S. acoustical standards currently in force as well as those in the draft and proposal stages (NBS Special Publication 386, "Standards on Noise Measurements, Rating Schemes and Definitions: A Compilation." Order SD Catalogue No. C13.10386, Superintendent of Public Documents, U.S. Government Printing Office, Washington, D.C. 20402. Price: $1.10 (U.S.)). In addition, complete copies of any particular standards may be ordered directly from the standards-producing organizations throughout the world. These organizations will have available up-to-date lists of their current standards as well as those in the preliminary draft or "working document" stage.

Listed alphabetically by country in Table 1 are the addresses for standards organizations throughout the world having acoustical standards of interest to architects and building engineers.

Table 1. Worldwide Listing of Standards Organizations That Maintain Acoustical Standards

Albania	*Komiteti i Cmimeve dhe Standarteve Prane Keshillit te Ministrave Tirana
Algeria	Institut algérien de normalisation et de propriété industrielle 5, rue Abou Hamou Moussa B.P. 1201—Centre de tri Alger
Argentina	Instituto Argentino de Racionalización de Materiales Chile 1192 C. Postal 1098 Buenos Aires

Table 1. (*continued*)

Australia	Standards House 80 Arthur Street North Sydney, NSW 2060
Austria	Österreichischer Arbeitsring für Lärmbekämpfung Regierungsgebäude 1012 Wien
	Österreichisches Normungsinstitut Leopoldsg 4 1020 Wien
Bangladesh	Bangladesh Standards Institution 3-DIT (Extension) Avenue Motijheel Commercial Area Dhaka 2
Belgium	Institut Belge de Normalisation 29 av. de la Brabanconne 1040 Bruxelles
Brazil	Associacão Brasileira de Normas Técnicas (ABNT) Av. Almirante Barroso 54 Rio de Janeiro
Bulgaria	State Committee for Science and Technical Programs 21, 6th September Str. 1000 Sofia
Canada	Standards Council of Canada 2000 Argentia Rd, Suite 2-401 Mississauga, Ontario
Chile	Instituto Nacional de Normalización Matias Cousino 64—6° piso Casilla 995—Correo 1 Santiago
China	China Association for Standardization PO Box 820 Beijing
Columbia	3 Instituto Colombiano de Normas Técnicas Carrera 37 No. 52–95 PO Box 14237 Bogota
Cuba	Comité Estatal de Normalización Egido 602 entre Gloria y Apodaca Zona postal 2 La Habana
Cyprus	Cyprus Organization for Standards and Control of Quality Ministry of Commerce and Industry Nicosia
Czechoslovakia (CSSR)	Office for Standards and Measurements Praha 1, Nové Město Václavske Namĕsti 19
Denmark	Arbejderbeskyttelsesfondet Vesterbrogade 69 1620 København V
	Dansk Standardiseringsrad Aurehøjvej 12 2900 Hellerup
	Miljøstyrelsen Kampmannsgade 1 1604 København V

Table 1. (*continued*)

Egypt	Egyptian Organization for Standardization 2 Latin America Street Garden City Cairo–Egypt
Ethiopia	Ethiopian Standards Institution PO Box 2310 Addis Ababa
Finland	Suomen Standardisoimisliitto PL 205 00121 Helsinki 12
	Lääkintöhallitus Siltasaarenk 18A 00530 Helsinki 53
France	L'Association Francaise de Normalisation (AFNOR) Tour Europe 92080 Paris, La Defense
Germany (FRG)	Beuth Vertrieb GmbH Bruggrafenstr. 4–7 1000 Berlin 30
	Beuth Vertrieb GmbH Kamestr. 2–8 5000 Köln
	Verlag Stahleisen GmbH Postf. 8229 4000 Düsseldorf
Germany (GDR)	Amt für Standardisierung der Deutschen Demokratischen Republik Mohrenstrasse 37a 108 Berlin
Ghana	Ghana Standards Board PO Box M.245 Accra
Greece	Hellenic Organization for Standardization Didotou 15 106 80 Athens
Hungary	Magyar Szabványügyi Hivatal Ullöl ut 25 Budapest PF24, 1450
India	Indian Standards Institution Manak Bhavan 9 Bahadur Shah, Zafar Marg. New Delhi 110002
Indonesia	Badan Kerjasama Standardisasi LIPI–YDNI (LIPI–YDNI Joint Standardization Committee) Jln. Teuku Chik Ditiro 43 PO Box 250 Jakarta
Iran	Institute of Standards and Industrial Research of Iran Ministry of Industries PO Box 2937 Tehran
Iraq	Central Organization for Standardization and Quality Control Planning Board PO Box 13032 Aljadiria Baghdad

Table 1. (*continued*)

Ireland	Institute for Industrial Research and Standards Ballymun Road Dublin–9
Israel	Standards Institution of Israel 42 University Street Tel Aviv 69977
Italy	Servizio Tecnico Centrale Ministero dei Lavori Pubblici Roma
Ivory Coast	Direction de la Normalisation et de la Technologie Ministere du Plan et de l'Industrie B.P. V65 Abidjan
Jamaica	Jamaica Bureau of Standards 6 Winchester Road PO Box 113 Kingston 10
Japan	Japanese Standard Association 1–24, Akasaka 4 chome, Minato-ku Tokyo
Kenya	Kenya Bureau of Standards Off Mombasa Road Behind Belle Vue Cinema PO Box 54974 Nairobi
Korea, Democratic People's Republic of	Committee for Standardization of the Democratic People's Republic of Korea Committee of the Science and Technology of the State Sosong guyok Ryonmod dong Pyongyang
Korea, Republic of	Bureau of Standards Industrial Advancement Administration Yongdeungpo-Dong Seoul
Libyan Arab Jamahiriya	Libyan Standards and Patent Section Department of Industrial Organization and Services Secretariat of Light Industries Tripoli
Malaysia	Standards and Industrial Research Institute of Malaysia Lot 10810, Phase 3, Federal Highway PO Box 35, Shah Alam Selangor
Mexico	Dirección General de Normas Calle Puente de Tecamachalco N°. 6 Lomas de Tecamachalco Sección Fuentes Naucalpan de Juárez 53 950 Mexico
Mongolia	State Committee for Prices and Standards of the Mongolian People's Republic Marshal Zhukov Avenue, 51 Ulan Bator

Table 1. (*continued*)

Morocco	Service de normalisation industrielle marocaine Direction de l'industrie Ministere du Commerce et de l'industrie 5, rue Arrich Rabat
Netherlands	Nederlands Normalisatie-Instituut Polakweg 5 Rijswijk (Z-H)
New Zealand	Standards Association of New Zealand Private Bag Wellington
Nigeria	Nigerian Standards Organisation Federal Ministry of Industries No. 4, Club Road P.M.B. 01323 Enugu
Norway	Norges Standardiseringsforbund Hàkon 7 gt 2 Oslo 1 Oslo Helseràd St. Olavs Plass 5 Oslo 1
Pakistan	Pakistan Standards Institution 39 Garden Road Saddar Karachi–3
Peru	Instituto de Investigacion Tecnologica Industrial y de Normas Tecnicas Jr. Morelli—2da. cuadra Urbanizacion San Borja—Surquillo Lima 34
Philippines	Product Standards Agency Ministry of Trade and Industry 361 Sen. Gil J Puyat Avenue Makati, Metro Manila 3117 Manila
Poland	Polski Komitet Normalizacji i Miar ul. Elektoralna 2 00–139-Warszawa
Portugal	Inspeccão Geral dos Produtos Agricolas e Industriais (Reparticão de Normalizacão) Avenida de Berna-1 Lisboa-1
Romania	Oficiul de Stat Pentru Standarde Str. Edgar Quinet 6 Bucarest 1
Saudi Arabia	Saudi Arabian Standards Organization PO Box 3437 Riyadh
Singapore	Singapore Institute of Standards and Industrial Research Maxwell Road PO Box 2611 Singapore 9046
South Africa	South African Bureau of Standards Private Bag X191 Pretoria 0001

Table 1. (*continued*)

Spain	Instituto Nacional de Racionalización y Normalización Serrano Nr. 150 Madrid 6
Sri Lanka	Bureau of Ceylon Standards 53 Dharmapala Mawatha PO Box 17 Colombo 3
Sudan	Standards and Quality Control Department Ministry of Industry PO Box 2184 Khartoum
Sweden	Liber Förlag Fack 10320 Stockholm Sveriges Menanförbund Box 5506 11485 Stockholm Sveriges Standardiseringskommission Box 3295 10366 Stockholm
Switzerland	Eidgenössische Drucksachen und Materialzentrale Bern 3
Syria	Syrian Arab Organization for Standardization and Metrology PO Box 11836 Damascus
Tanzania	Tanzania Bureau of Standards PO Box 9524 Dar es Salaam
Thailand	Thai Industrial Standards Institute Ministry of Industry Rama VI Street Bangkok 10400
Trinidad and Tobago	Trinidad and Tobago Bureau of Standards Century Drive Trincity Industrial Estate Tunapuna PO Box 467 Trinidad and Tobago
Tunisia	Institut national de la normalisation et de la propriété industrielle BP 23 1012 Tunis–Belvedere
Turkey	Türk Standardlari Enstitüsü Necatibey Cad. 112 Bakanliklar Ankara
United Kingdom	British Standards Institution 2 Park Street London, W1A 2BS Department of the Environment Department of Transport 2 Marsham Street London SW1P 3PY
United States	Acoustical and Board Products Association (ABPA) 205 West Touhy Avenue Park Ridge, Ill. 60068

Table 1. (*continued*)

Acoustical Society of America (ASA)
American Institute of Physics
335 East 45th Street
New York, N.Y. 10017

Air-Conditioning and Refrigeration Institute
(ARI)
1815 North Fort Meyer Drive
Arlington, Va. 22209

Air Diffusion Council (ADC)
435 North Michigan
Chicago, Ill. 60611

Air Moving and Conditioning Association
(AMCA)
30 West University Drive
Arlington Heights, Ill. 60004

American Gear Manufacturers Association
(AGMA)
1330 Massachusetts Avenue, N.W.
Washington, D.C. 20005

American National Standards Institute
(ANSI)
1430 Broadway
New York, N.Y. 10018

American Society of Heating, Refrigerating,
and Air Conditioning Engineers (ASHRAE)
345 East 47th Street
New York, N.Y. 10017

American Society for Testing and Materials
(ASTM)
1916 Race Street
Philadelphia, Pa. 19103

American Textile Machinery Association
(ATMA)
1730 M Street, N.W.
Washington, D.C. 20036

Association of Home Appliance Manufacturers
(AHAM)
20 North Wacker Drive
Chicago, Ill. 60606

Compressed Air and Gas Institute (CAGI)
122 East 42nd Street
New York, N.Y. 10017

Department of Housing and Urban
Development (HUD)
Washington, D.C. 20401

Federal Aviation Administration (FAA)
Washington, D.C. 20591

Federal Highway Administration (FHWA)
Washington, D.C. 20590

General Services Administration (GSA)
Public Buildings Service
Washington, D.C. 20405

Institute of Electrical and Electronics
Engineers (IEEE)
445 Hoes Lane
Piscataway, N.J. 08854

International Conference of Building Officials
(ICBO)
5360 South Workman Mill Road
Whittier, Calif. 90601

Table 1. (*continued*)

	National Machine Tool Builders Association (NMTB) 7901 Westpark Drive McLean, Va. 22101
	National School Supply and Equipment Association (NSSEA) 1500 Wilson Boulevard Arlington, Va. 22209
	Society of Automotive Engineers, Inc. (SAE) 400 Commonwealth Drive Warrendale, Pa. 15096
	Woodworking Machinery Manufacturers Association (WMMA) 1900 Arch Street Philadelphia, Pa. 19103
USSR	The State Committee of Standards 9, Leninsky Prospekt 117049, Moscow, M-49
Venezuela	Comisión Venezolana de Normas Industriales Avda. Andrés Bello-Edf. Torre Fondo Común Piso 11 Caracas 1050
Vietnam, Socialist Republic of	Direction generale de standardisation de metrologie et de controle de la qualite 70 rue Tran Hung Dao Hanoi
Yugoslavia	Savezni zavod za Standardizaciju Slobodana Penezica-Krcuna br.35 Pošt Pregr 933 11000 Beograd
Zambia	Zambia Bureau of Standards National Housing Authority Building PO Box 50259 Lusaka
International	International Organization for Standardization (ISO) 1, Rue de Varembé Geneva, Switzerland

WILLIAM J. CAVANAUGH,
FASA
Cavanaugh Tocci Associates,
Inc.
Sudbury, Massachusetts

ACOUSTICS—GENERAL PRINCIPLES

. . . we must choose a site in which the voice may fall
smoothly, and not be returned by reflections so as to convey
an indistinct meaning to the ear. For there are some places
which naturally hinder the passage of the voice, . . . those
(dissonant) places in which the voice, when first it rises up-
wards, strikes against solid bodies above, and is reflected,
interfering as it settles down with the rise of the following
utterance . . . those (circumsonant) in which the voice moves
around, is then collected in the middle where it dissolves without the case-endings being heard, and dies away in sounds

of indistinct meaning . . . those (resonant) in which the words, striking against a solid body, give rise to echoes and make the case-endings sound double . . . those (consonant) in which the voice reinforced from below rises with greater fullness, and reaches the ear with clear and eloquent accents. Thus if careful observation is exercised in the choice of sites, such skill will be rewarded by the improved effort of the actor's voices. . . . Whoever uses these rules, will be successful in building theaters . . .

Vitruvius, ca last century B.C. (1)

Acoustics as a discipline applied to the design of individual buildings and groups of buildings (as in urban design) is a relatively new technology. Although in ancient Roman times Vitruvius recorded his observations on the acoustics of theaters, very little can be found in the architectural archives until the late nineteenth and twentieth centuries, following Wallace Clement Sabine's pioneering work at Harvard University on the development of a practical theory on room reverberation and the absorption of sound by building materials and furnishings. Down through the centuries prior to Sabine's discoveries, great scientific minds such as Newton, Helmholtz, and Lord Rayleigh, to name a few, had provided understanding of the fundamentals of acoustic wave motion and sound propagation, but it was left to Sabine and his successors in the period after 1900 to observe, measure, and develop practical quantitative methods for controlling the acoustical environment in and around buildings and to provide the basis for useful criteria by which architects could design spaces to accommodate satisfactorily the wide variety of spaces and types of activities in contemporary buildings. The acoustical environment in any indoor or outdoor space intended for human activity must be one in which the character and magnitude of all of the sounds are compatible with the intended use of the space. Desired sounds such as a lecturer's voice, amplified stereo music, a live concert, or an instrumental recital must be heard with sufficient loudness, clarity, and naturalness and without distortion or masking from other undesirable sounds. Acoustics is, or should be, of concern in other than the obvious listening spaces such as churches, concert halls, broadcast studios, and so on. In practically every occupied space, undesired sounds (ie, noise) must be controlled to acceptable levels to assure a hospitable environment for such diverse activities as concentrated mental activity, relaxation, recreation, and sleep. In many work environments, the ability to communicate warning signals to fellow workers may be paramount. Recent tragic fires in hotels and high-rise office buildings have hastened the need for improved acoustical standards for the audibility of alarm systems and intelligibility of life-saving voice instructions to building occupants deprived of normal intercommunication. In short, the acoustical environment in all buildings is of concern to all associated with the design, construction, and occupancy of buildings.

The late Robert B. Newman, a professor of architectural acoustics at the MIT School of Architecture and the Harvard Graduate School of Design, often opened his lectures with the admonition, "Let there be no surprises." By the post-World War II period, when Newman began his teach-

ing activities, architectural acoustics had developed to the point where a designer no longer had to wait to see if the senior executives could hear voices between adjacent offices in a new corporate headquarters building, or whether everyone could hear well in the new recital hall, or, indeed, whether all 60,000 spectators in a new sports stadium could hear announcements as well as see an event. The relative balance in the old dictum that acoustics was "all art and little science" was shifting. This is not to say that acoustical horror stories in buildings have been eliminated, but with courses in acoustics available to architecture students and the proliferation of excellent new texts on the subject, more and more building design professionals are knowledgeable in acoustics and are applying that knowledge on a day-to-day basis. With a fundamental understanding of the basic nature of sound sources, the transmission and control of sound in building spaces, how building structures and materials interact with sound waves, how and when a sound source needs to be electronically amplified, and perhaps most importantly, what kind of acoustical criteria are appropriate for the various activities to be housed, building designers will be able to demonstrate consistently that satisfactory acoustical environments are not only possible and practical, but can be predicted in advance. Corrective acoustics after a building is completed and occupied is always difficult and costly if, indeed, a practical solution is possible at all.

Since the great post-World War II reconstructions in Europe and the massive urban and suburban expansions in many developed countries, national and international building standards and codes have incorporated meaningful acoustical performance standards. In most countries of Europe, minimum performance requirements for airborne and impact sound isolation between multifamily dwelling units are a matter of course. In the United States during the 1970s, largely as a result of the Environmental Protection Act of 1969, nearly all federal agencies were mandated to develop and implement criteria and standards toward ensuring safe and environmentally sound working and living environments. For example, the U.S. Department of Labor (DOL) has jurisdiction over the workplace environment and, through its Occupational Safety and Health Administration (OSHA) standards, provides that workers will not be exposed to damaging noise levels. Designers of industrial buildings must know the relative contributions of the building enclosure to the noise environment as well as what measures can be specified to meet OSHA standards. The U.S. Department of Transportation (DOT) has cognizance of the noise impact of air, road, and rail transportation vehicles and systems. Besides establishing noise limit standards for new highways, air terminals, and rail lines, DOT agencies support ongoing research on transportation system noise and are a rich source of design data for building designers and urban planners. For example, the designer of a building near a major highway or airport must consider the impact of these intrusive noise sources on the building's site, layout, and exterior shell construction, as well as which, if any, outdoor activities will be feasible.

The University of Massachusetts Boston Harbor Campus constructed during the 1970s was located under a major flight track to and less than 3 mi from Boston's Logan International Airport. This potentially serious noise impact was recognized in advance, and the master plan study required design architects to meet stringent acoustical criteria in the planning and design of the exterior constructions. As a result, the completed academic buildings have massive, largely masonry exterior walls with minimal glazed areas. Special double-glazed acoustical sash was installed in all classrooms, faculty offices, and critical teaching spaces. The interfering roar of jets approaching only about 300 ft overhead has been successfully excluded from the academic spaces. A concomitant result of the aircraft noise exclusion design was superior thermal insulation of the completed buildings which coincided with the energy crisis and fuel oil shortages of the mid-1970s. The project convincingly demonstrated the advantage of a coordinated approach in the overall environmental design of buildings. Fortunately, the fundamental physical principles governing such things as thermal and acoustical wave behavior are compatible, and considered together, as in the University of Massachusetts Boston Campus design, can lead to good results for both environmental disciplines.

Other federal agencies, such as the U.S. Department of Housing and Urban Development (HUD), promulgate standards that ensure all federally subsidized housing will be sited in acceptably quiet environments or that it will be designed with appropriate sound attenuation features. Likewise, demising ("party") walls and floor–ceiling constructions must meet minimum performance requirements for airborne and structure-borne sound transmission. The General Services Administration (GSA), the largest provider of building spaces for federal agencies, has adopted strict standards for acoustical performance for sound isolation from exterior and interior noise sources, for HVAC systems and equipment, for "open-plan" acoustical privacy, as well as for the acoustics of courtrooms, hearing rooms, and so on.

The acoustical performance standards activities of federal agencies eventually influence the building codes and standards of state and local governments as well. Many states, notably California, and large cities, notably New York City, have extensive acoustical performance requirements in their building codes. Building designers, developers of construction systems and details, specifiers of materials, and all who participate in the design construction process must be aware of these acoustical performance requirements if they are to produce truly acceptable buildings from an overall standpoint.

A SYSTEMS APPROACH

Every building acoustics problem can be analyzed in terms of a system of source(s) of sound and the airborne and structure-borne path(s) through which the sound will travel to the ultimate receptor(s) of the sound. As Figure 1 illustrates, the sound may be desirable sound, which the receptor should hear with adequate loudness and clarity, in which case the designer's task is to do everything possible to enhance the propagational paths. On the other hand, like the auditorium air-conditioning system equipment of Figure 1, the source may be undesirable sound (by definition, noise), and the designer must provide adequate attenuation of the sound at the source and along all propagational paths to avoid interference and masking

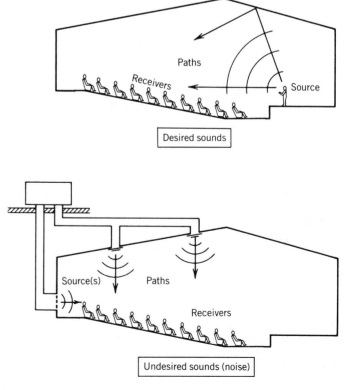

Figure 1. Every building acoustics problem, whether the enhancement of desired sounds or the control of undesired sounds (noise), can be considered in terms of a system of sound source(s), path(s), and receptor(s).

of the desired sound. Obviously, the building structures and materials influencing the propagational paths for sound transmission are those within the designer's immediate control. However, a basic understanding of sound sources, including their sound emission characteristics, directivity, and interaction with nearby or attached building elements, is also necessary. For example, one designs a performance stage in a typical multiuse auditorium for a wide variety of types and positions for sources over a relatively large performance area. Knowledge of the strength and directivity of voice and music sound sources is required to produce an acoustically adequate "sending end" of the auditorium. Likewise, to assess properly the multiple paths for typical HVAC system noise sources (fans, compressors, control valves, air supply diffusers, etc) one must have a general feel for the acoustic output of these various sources and their interaction with the architectural enclosure details, supporting structures, and so on. Furthermore, since people are the ultimate receptors of the desired or undesired sounds, the designer must have a fundamental grasp of how people are likely to react to sounds in order to properly select design criteria. The building designer must keep in mind too that people's reactions to sounds in many building acoustics environments are predominantly subjective and qualitative in nature. There are wide variations in what constitutes acoustical comfort levels, just as there are for thermal comfort levels. Perfection in acoustics is most often an elusive goal, but one that can be approached only through better quantitative understanding of people's needs and expectations. The latter is the subject of ongoing and continuing research in architectural acoustics.

A building designer's advance knowledge of the source and receptor aspects of the overall acoustic transmission system is essential for a balanced, comprehensive architectural solution. Selection of appropriate design criteria is an important first step, and this requires commonsense judgment and knowledge of the expectations of people who will be performing and listening in a new auditorium or of those who will occupy a new office building. Likewise, a firm grasp of the critical or demanding design criteria for a particular space may influence a designer to seek solutions at the source or in the early planning stage. For example, the substitution of quieter alternative equipment or the relocation of the potentially noisy mechanical equipment spaces or particularly loud activities away from critical areas may be accomplished early enough in design that an acoustic problem will never materialize.

The following discussion of general principles (how sound is generated and how its magnitude and tonal characteristics are described and quantified) is intended as a basis for understanding how the source path receiver approach may be systematically applied to solving acoustics problems in and around buildings. Likewise, this discussion should provide background for other articles on acoustics in this encyclopedia. In all of this, the building designer and others involved in decisions that will influence the acoustical environment must keep in mind that people rarely respond to just one aspect of the sensory environment. They respond to the overall environment in ways that are not always fully understood. Good acoustics alone is not enough if the temperature and humidity are not right, or if the spectator cannot see the performing stage comfortably. People are remarkably adaptive too, and thus there are few absolutes in acoustical and other largely sensory-based building criteria. Accordingly, acoustics is rarely the most important aspect of building design, but it is at least a significant consideration in most buildings. The designer's studied application of relatively few fundamental principles in controlling sound in buildings will inevitably produce better acoustical environments and better buildings.

SOUND GENERATION

Sound is generated whenever there is a disturbance of an elastic medium. Once this disturbance occurs, whether it is in air from the vibrating string of a musical instrument or in a solid floor surface from the impact of a dropped object, the sound wave will propagate away from the source at some rate depending on the elastic properties of the medium.

Sound, in its simplest form, can be generated by striking a tuning fork, as illustrated in Figure 2. The arms of the tuning fork are set into vibration, and the air molecules immediately adjacent to the vibrating surface are alternately compressed and rarefied as the surface goes through each complete to-and-from movement. This cyclical disturbance of the air molecules is passed on to the adjacent molecules and thus travels outward from the source. The outwardly progressing sound may be thought of as a "chain reaction" of vibrations. The originally disturbed air molecules do not continue to move away from the source. Instead, they move back and forth within a limited zone and simply transfer their energy to the adjacent molecules.

The pressure disturbance created by the vibrating tuning fork cannot be seen by the naked eye, but ultimately the sound wave may reach a human ear, causing the eardrum to vibrate and, through an ingeniously complex mechanism, finally producing the sensation of hearing in the brain. Although the ears are perhaps the most sophisticated sound-measuring device, some useful measuring instruments that approximate closely the sensitivity of the ear have been developed and give the numerical quantities necessary for scientific experimentation and engineering applications. With a simple sound wave generated in air by a vibrating tuning fork (as with all other more complex sound waves), there are basically two measurable quantities of interest: the frequency of the sound wave and its magnitude.

Frequency

The frequency of a sound wave is the number of complete vibrations occurring per unit of time (per second). Musicians refer to this as pitch; this basic frequency or rate of repetition of the vibration defines the character of the sound. Low-frequency sounds, like that of a deep bass voice, are classified as "boomy." High-frequency sounds, like that of a steam jet, may have a "hissing" character.

The unit of measure is termed Hertz and is abbreviated

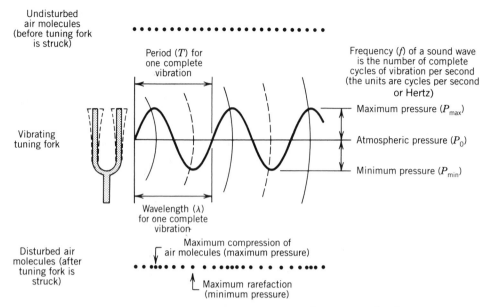

Undisturbed
air molecules
(before tuning fork
is struck)

Period (T) for
one complete
vibration

Frequency (f) of a sound wave
is the number of complete
cycles of vibration per second
(the units are cycles per second
or Hertz)

Maximum pressure (P_{max})

Vibrating
tuning fork

Atmospheric pressure (P_0)

Minimum pressure (P_{min})

Wavelength (λ)
for one complete
vibration

Maximum compression of
air molecules (maximum pressure)

Disturbed air
molecules (after
tuning fork is
struck)

Maximum rarefaction
(minimum pressure)

Figure 2. A tuning fork illustrates how a simple pure tone develops.

Hz (older acoustical textbooks and publications may use cycles per second or cps). The tuning fork described above generates sound at only a single frequency. A simple musical tone would have a fundamental tone along with one or more harmonically related tones. All other common sounds, music, speech, and noise, are more complex because they contain sound energy (ie, vibrations) over considerably wider ranges of the human audible spectrum (20–20,000 Hz). Figure 3 illustrates how these simple and more complex common sounds compare.

Figure 4 illustrates the frequency ranges for some typical sounds. For comparison, the frequency range of the piano keyboard is also shown. Thus, most sounds contain energy to some degree over rather wide ranges of the audible frequency range.

Frequency Bands. For measurement purposes, the audible frequency range may be divided into convenient subdivisions, as shown in Figure 5. Measurements may be made over the entire range or, by utilizing electronic filters in the measurement system, the frequency range may be divided into segments such as octave bands or one-half, one-third, one-tenth, etc, octave bands. Full octave bands generally yield sufficient frequency information about a sound source, but in some laboratory measurements, such as in measuring the sound transmission loss characteristics of walls and so on, one-third octave band measurements are made. The sound sources commonly encountered in buildings, as well as the acoustical performance of products and materials for sound control, are generally frequency dependent (ie, vary with frequency). It is important to keep in mind that a wide range of frequencies is involved, even if simple averages or single number values are ultimately used to describe sound levels or specify products.

Wavelength of Sound

Another fundamental property of a sound wave that is related to its frequency is its wavelength. This is the physical distance within which the complete cycle of disturbance takes place. There is a basic relationship between the velocity of sound in a medium (eg, air, concrete, etc) and its frequency and wavelength given by the expression

$$c = f\lambda$$

where

c = velocity of sound

f = frequency

λ = wavelength

For example, middle C on the piano has a frequency of 256 Hz in air, where sound travels at about 1100 ft/s. Thus, the wavelength would be 4.3 ft. If a 256-Hz sound wave were excited in water, where the speed of sound increases to 4500 ft/s, the wavelength would be 17.5 ft.

It is useful to keep in mind the range of wavelengths encountered in the audible frequency range for various building acoustics problems. For example, in the laboratory, sound transmission loss and other measurements on building components are usually made starting at the one-third octave band centered at 100 or 125 Hz up through the one-third octave band centered at 4000 Hz. The wavelengths corresponding to these frequency limits are approximately 9 and 0.25 ft, respectively. Generally speaking, it takes rather massive and generally large elements to control low-frequency sound where the wavelengths are

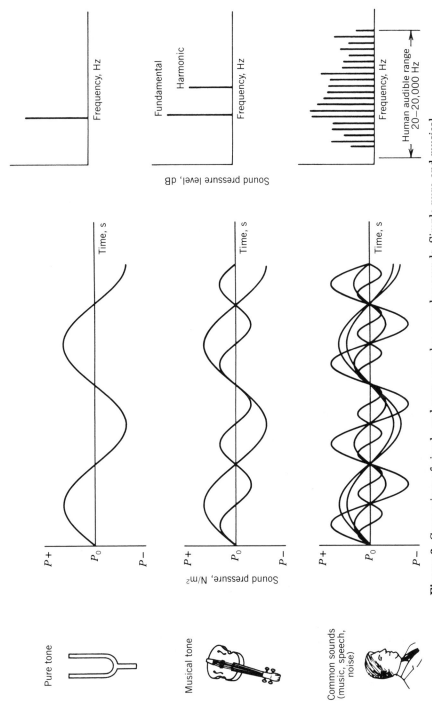

Figure 3. Comparison of simple and more complex everyday sounds. Simple pure and musical tones contain sound energy at a fundamental frequency or fundamental plus harmonically related frequencies only. Common everyday sounds contain sound energy over a wide range of the human audible spectrum.

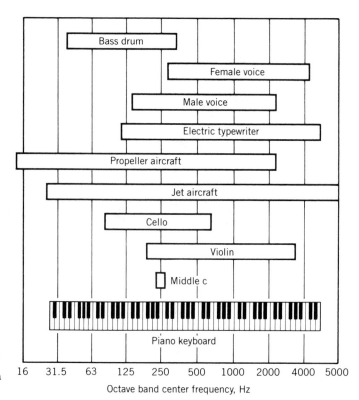

Figure 4. Comparison of the frequency ranges of some common sounds with that of a piano keyboard.

large. On the other hand, thinner, smaller building elements can provide effective sound control at high frequencies where the wavelengths are smaller.

Magnitude of Sound

In addition to the tonal character (ie, frequency) of a sound, the intensity or magnitude of acoustical energy contained in the sound wave is also of concern. Sound intensity is proportional to the amplitude of the pressure disturbance above and below the undisturbed ambient atmospheric pressure (Fig. 2). The pressure fluctuations may be minute, yet a healthy ear has the ability to detect very faint sound pressure differences down to as little as 3×10^{-9} psi. At the same time, for short periods the human ear can tolerate the painful roar of a jet engine at close range, which may

be a million times as intense, say, 3×10^{-2} psi. Although sustained exposure to such intense sounds can cause hearing damage, the range of intensities or pressures that define the magnitude of sound energy is, like the wide range of frequencies the ear can accommodate, very large. Because of the wide dynamic range, as well as the fact that the human ear responds in a roughly logarithmic way to sound intensities, a measurement unit called the decibel is used for quantifying sound levels. The decibel unit is abbreviated dB.

THE DECIBEL SCALE

The decibel scale starts at zero for some chosen reference value and compares other intensities, pressures, or sound

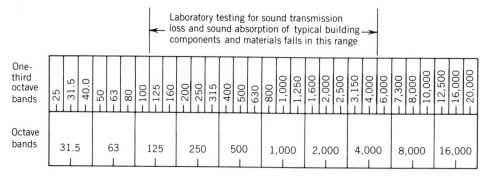

Figure 5. Standard octave and one-third octave frequency bands divide the full audible spectrum into convenient segments for measurement and analysis. Laboratory test standards for the acoustical performance of many building components extend from bands centered at 100 Hz to those at 4000 Hz.

powers to that reference value. For sound pressure level measurements, a reference value of $2 \times 10^{-5}\,\text{N/m}^2$ is chosen. This is the threshold of hearing for a typical healthy, young person. The sound pressure level in decibels for any sound for which the pressure is known is given by the following expression:

$$L_p = 20 \log \frac{p}{p_0}$$

where

L_p = sound pressure level in decibels

p = measured sound pressure of concern

p_0 = reference sound pressure, usually taken to be $2 \times 10^{-5}\,\text{N/m}^2$ [older texts and publications may show the equivalent reference values of $2 \times 10^{-4}\,\mu\text{bar}$ (dyn/cm^2)]

Fortunately, acoustical instruments give the measured decibel values directly. However, it is important to realize that since this is basically a logarithmic scale, there are a few precautions to be observed when combining decibel units, as will be discussed later.

Figure 6 compares typical sounds measured in terms of pressure with those in terms of sound pressure level. The convenience of the compressed decibel scale is obvious in dealing with the tremendous range of sound magnitudes that can be accommodated rather well by a healthy human ear.

Figure 7 indicates octave band frequency spectra for three common types of sound compared with upper and lower threshold limits. An air-conditioning fan has a great deal of low-frequency sound compared with the middle- and high-frequency sound, causing it to sound "boomy" to an observer. An air jet is generally just the reverse and contains considerable high-frequency "hissy" sound energy. Human speech covers a relatively wide range of frequencies and at the same time produces fluctuating levels in the process of continuous speech. The dynamic range covers some 30 dB, between the lowest and highest speech sound levels produced.

Fortunately, it is not always necessary to measure the full frequency range of the various sounds of concern in many building acoustics problems. When the frequency characteristics are known for a type of sound source and are generally repeatable and/or constant, simple single-number sound level values may be adequate. Figure 8 shows typical octave band spectra for various transportation noise sources along with their simple sound level equivalent values.

SIMPLE FREQUENCY-WEIGHTED SOUND LEVELS

The human ear does not simply add up all of the energy for a sound over the entire audible range and interpret this value as the loudness of sound. The ear discriminates against low-frequency sounds (ie, it weights, or ignores, some of the low-frequency sound energy). A given sound level will appear to be louder in the middle- and high-frequency range than at lower frequencies. Electronic filters, or weighting networks, can be incorporated in a sound level meter to permit the instrument to approximate this characteristic and to read out sound level values that correspond well with the way the human ear judges the relative loudness of sounds.

Figure 9 illustrates the conversion of a sound source spectrum measured over the full frequency range to single-number values. Two frequency weightings are commonly used on standard simple sound level meters: the C scale and the A scale. The C scale is a flat frequency weighting; essentially, all of the sound energy is summed and converted to an overall value. The units of this value are usually dBC to denote the frequency-weighting network used. The A scale network corresponds to the way a human ear responds to the loudness of sound at different frequencies; low-frequency sounds are filtered out, or ignored, whereas middle- and high-frequency sounds are left relatively unfiltered. After the A weight filtering in the sound level meter, all of the remaining sound energy is summed and converted to a single value that can be read directly on the meter. Such simple A scale sound levels are actually the most common and useful descriptors for many of the sounds encountered in buildings and are expressed in dBA. They are adequate for a simplified analysis of many prob-

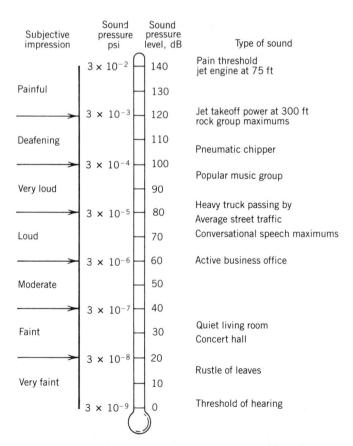

Figure 6. An acoustic thermometer compares the magnitude of sound pressures of sounds in pounds per square inch with the equivalent logarithmic quantities, decibels, used in acoustical standards.

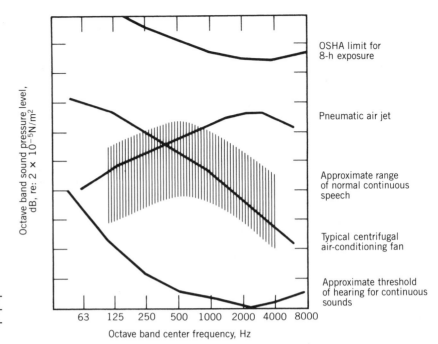

Figure 7. Typical octave band spectra of common sounds compared to the threshold of audibility for healthy, young ears and hearing damage risk criteria.

lems and for the specification of simple sound tests as long as the frequency content of the noise sources of concern is known or implied beforehand. Figure 10 shows the range of many common interior and exterior sound sources as would be measured with A frequency weighting using a standard sound level meter.

COMBINING MULTIPLE SOURCES

Sound energy levels in decibel units from independent sound sources may not be added directly. The sound pressure levels must be converted to arithmetic units, added, and then reconverted to decibel units. For example, if two sound sources each measured 50 dB when operated independently, they would measure 53 dB when operated together. Using Figure 11 to confirm this, two identical sources (the difference between the two sound levels is 0 dB) will result in an increase in sound level of 3 dB with both sources operating. Also from Figure 11, if there were a 10-dB difference between two sources, the contribution from the quieter source would be negligible.

Thus, whenever multiple sound sources are involved, the total sound output may be estimated using the procedure of Figure 11 to combine them, two sources at a time.

RELATIVE SOUND LEVELS

The subjective difference between two sound source levels or conditions is often of interest in evaluating the effectiveness of various sound control measures. Figure 12 shows that a 1-dB change in sound level is just detectable in a controlled laboratory environment. A 3-dB change (which is actually a doubling of the sound energy level) would be just perceptible in a typical room environment. On the

other hand, a 10-dB change is required to cause a subjective sensation of doubling of loudness (or halving). These rather unique characteristics of the human hearing response must be borne in mind in dealing with practical sound control problems in buildings. In other words, a 1- or 2-dB improvement alone may not represent a significant result and may not be worth the cost of the control measure.

SOUND OUTDOORS VS SOUND INDOORS

In order to appreciate fully how sound behaves inside rooms and how it is transmitted from space to space within buildings, it is helpful to consider first how sound behaves outdoors. With a simple, nondirective source, the sound intensity will fall off as the distance from the source is increased. The sound wave moving outward from the source spreads its energy over an ever-increasing spherical area. This commonly observed reduction in sound level with distance in a "free-field" acoustical environment follows the geometrical principles of spherical or cylindrical spreading (Fig. 13). For simple point sources (spherical spreading), the falloff rate is 6 dB per doubling of distance from the source. If the source is a long, narrow (cylindrical) radiator of sound (as might be the case with a steady stream of road traffic), the rate of falloff is reduced to 3 dB per distance doubling. In any case, typical sources outdoors generally fall within the 3–6 dB per doubling of distance falloff rate. In addition, some further losses (or gains) may be present in real-life situations because of atmospheric effects, wind, temperature, ground foliage, and so on. However, these effects can usually be neglected for first-order approximations of expected sound losses outdoors where distances are not very large.

Indoors, as can be seen in Figure 13, sound intensity will fall off with distance only very near the source (in

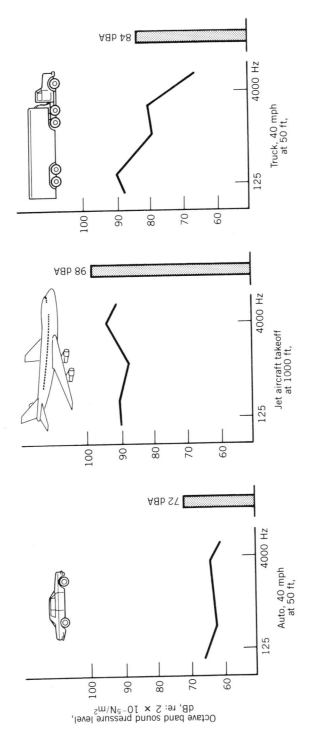

Figure 8. Examples of common exterior noise levels due to transportation sources (data from U.S. Environmental Protection Agency report).

45

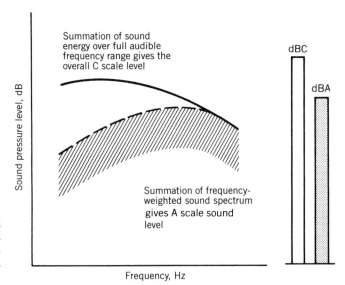

Figure 9. Frequency-weighting characteristic of standard sound level meters, which yield simple, commonly used overall sound levels (decibels with A scale weighting in dBA and decibels with C scale, or essentially unweighted flat frequency weighting, in dBC).

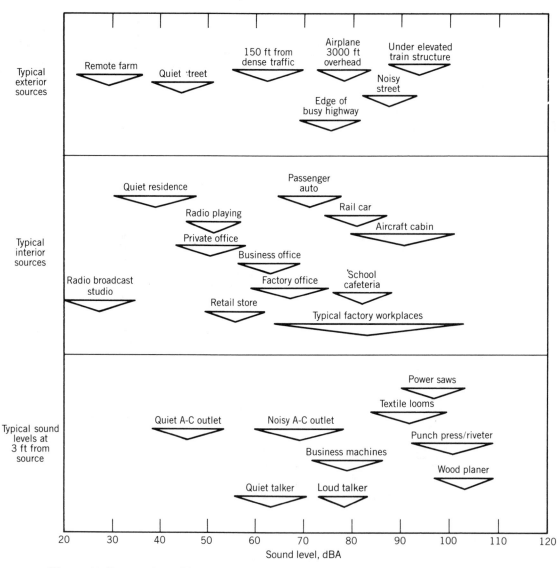

Figure 10. Ranges of sound levels in decibels with A scale frequency weighting (dBA) for typical interior and exterior sound sources.

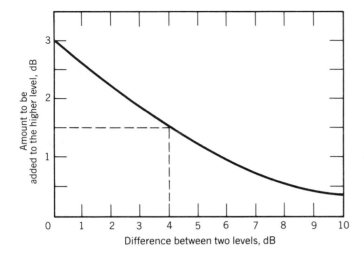

Figure 11. Nomograph for combining two sound sources in decibels. In the example shown, two sound sources produce sound levels of 50 and 54 dB, respectively. What level would be produced with both sources operating together? Difference, $54 - 50 = 4$ dB; amount to be added to the higher level, 1.5 dB; sound level with both sources operating, $54 + 1.5 = 55.5$ or 56 dB.

most building situations, within several feet). As one continues to move away from the source, the reflected sound from the floor, walls, and ceiling of the room begins to overwhelm the direct sound component that continues to be emitted from the source. Within the reflected or reverberant sound field, the sound level remains generally constant throughout the room no matter how far away from the source a listener is located. If the room surfaces are basically hard and sound reflective (plaster, concrete, glass, etc), there will be very little loss of sound at each impact of the sound wave on the room surfaces, and the built-up reflected sound level will be relatively high. If soft, porous materials (rugs, draperies, acoustical tiles,

etc) are placed on room surfaces, there will be appreciable losses each time reflected sound waves encounter room surfaces. Accordingly, the built-up reflected sound levels will be lower. This is the principal effect of placing sound-absorbing materials on the surfaces of rooms (ie, to lower the sound level in the reverberant field dominated by reflected sound). Ultimately, if completely efficient sound-absorbing materials are placed on all boundary surfaces of a room, outdoor conditions are approximated where only the direct sound remains. Note that Figure 13 shows that the application of absorbing materials to room surfaces does not affect in any way the direct sound that continues to decrease with distance near the source.

SOUND TRANSMISSION BETWEEN ROOMS

When greater reduction of sound than is possible by room sound-absorbing treatment alone is required, full enclosure of the receiver by means of separate rooms may be necessary. Figure 14 illustrates schematically the simple case of sound transmission between adjacent enclosed rooms. In essence, a sound source will develop a reverberant sound field in one room (the source room), and its sound pressure level will depend on the total absorption available from the source room boundary surfaces. In this simple case, assuming that the sound can travel to the adjacent room (the receiving room) only by the common wall, the transmitted sound level will depend on three factors: (1) the sound-isolating properties of the wall (ie, sound transmission loss), (2) the total surface area of the common wall that radiates sound into the adjacent receiving rooms, and (3) the total sound absorption present in the receiving room. The reduction of sound between rooms is given by the expression

$$L_1 - L_2 = \text{TL} + 10 \log \frac{A_2}{S}$$

where

L_1 = sound pressure level in the source room in decibels

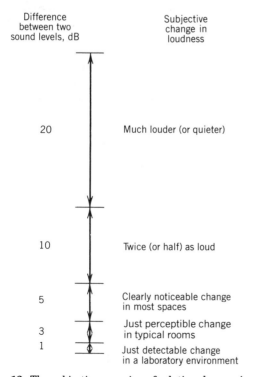

Figure 12. The subjective meaning of relative changes in sound levels measured in decibels.

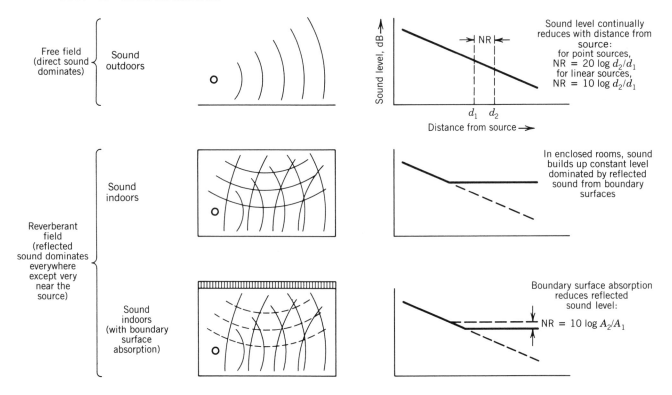

Figure 13. Diagrams showing the relative differences in sound behavior outdoors (free field) vs indoors (reverberant field).

L_2 = sound pressure level in the receiving room in decibels

TL = sound transmission loss of the common wall in decibels

A_2 = total sound absorption in the receiving room in square feet (or square meters)

S = common wall surface area in square feet (or square meters)

The transmitted sound level (L_2) in any given situation will be audible and possibly disturbing to the receiving room occupants if it exceeds the ambient or background sound level in the room. Thus, the background sound level is an extremely important part of any sound isolation problem. The background sound level may be thought of as

the residual sound level present without the offending noise present in the source room. The common wall may be thought of as a large diaphragm radiating sound into the receiving room—the larger it is, the more sound is radiated. On the other hand, absorbing material in the receiving room tends to reduce the buildup of reflected sound radiated into the receiving room. Thus, the A_2/S correction term in the room-to-room sound reduction expression accounts for the particular environment in which a wall construction is used. This correction is rarely more than ±5 dB, but under some circumstances can be significant.

In any event, the greatest loss in sound energy from room to room is generally provided by the common wall (or floor–ceiling) construction. Typical lightweight partition or floor systems may have sound transmission losses

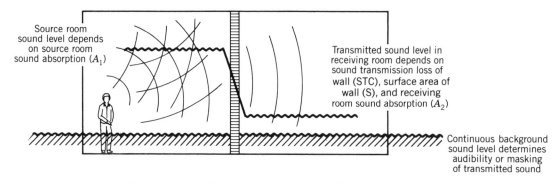

Figure 14. The essentials of the sound transmission problem between enclosed rooms.

on the order of 20 dB. Massive and/or double constructions can achieve sound transmission loss values of 40–60 dB or greater.

ACOUSTICAL DESIGN CRITERIA

Architectural and engineering applications of the basic concepts of sound control in buildings require the establishment of reasonable criteria and standards. A typical building may contain literally hundreds of kinds of spaces intended to house a variety of activities, sometimes in a single space designated for multiple purposes. The optimum acoustical environment for one activity may be impossible for another. Even some apparently unitary-use rooms, such as a music recital hall, may need an adjustable acoustical environment to handle the needs of various sizes and types of performing groups as well as variations in the acoustical environment for music of different periods (classical or romantic vs contemporary, etc).

Criteria have been or can be developed for every source path receiver situation in and around buildings. Criteria for acceptable background sound levels in various kinds of rooms and for acceptable degrees of sound isolation from exterior sources as well as from sources within a building have become part of the building technology literature. With time, many of the developing criteria have come to form the basis for standards and codes. It should be kept in mind that in most building situations, people are the ultimate receptors of the sounds in question. The somewhat variable and often confusing responses observed in various situations should not be too surprising where the end result is so often largely subjective. Criteria that have withstood the test of time, when intelligently applied, can minimize the risks in the engineering design decisions involved. The building designer's task is simpler, of course, when the criteria have found their way into hard-and-fast standard values that must be met in a particular building code. The responsibility may then be shifted to the later stage of the building project where those responsible for the field execution of a specified acoustical construction will provide the assurance that code requirements are satisfied.

CRITERIA FOR BACKGROUND SOUND LEVELS

The general background or ambient sound levels in a space are an extremely important element of its acoustical environment. They form the noise floor, so to speak, against which the occupants hear the desired sounds in the space. Continuous background sound can cover up or mask the minor intrusive sounds within a space or those transmitted from an adjacent space. Just as there is a wide variety of kinds of spaces in buildings, there is an equally wide range of acceptable background sound levels. For critical spaces, such as radio broadcasting or recording studios, very low background sound levels must be assured to be able to pick up the faintest desired musical or speech sounds. On the other hand, such low levels in a typical office environment would be "deafening" in that practically all of the normal activity sounds would become objectionable. A higher level of background sound in such spaces becomes more comfortable for the occupants. The general objective is quiet, that is, a comfortable level of background sound appropriate for the particular space involved. The objective is not silence, the virtual absence of sound, as might be desired in very critical recording studios or acoustical laboratory testing chambers.

Noise criteria (NC) curves have been used extensively for engineering design and specification of building noise control elements and are shown in Figure 15. These criteria curves specify allowable sound pressure levels in octave bands of frequency over the full audible range. The numerical value assigned (ie, the NC number) is the arithmetic average of the levels in the 1000-, 2000-, and 4000-Hz bands (the frequency range most important to the understanding of speech). Each criterion curve generally permits higher levels of low-frequency sound compared with middle and upper frequencies and follows the general pattern of human response to sound over the audible range. Low-frequency sounds are generally less annoying than high-frequency sounds within the limits expressed by the various NC curves.

Also indicated in Figure 15 is the approximate single-number A scale frequency-weighted equivalent values in dBA for the individual NC curves. For example, a background sound environment that just matched the NC 35 curve would measure 42 dBA with a simple sound level meter. For some building applications, the more detailed octave band analysis is necessary for engineering design or specification. However, the use of simple A-weighted sound levels in many types of analyses is appropriate. In addition, Figure 15 also shows the general subjective judgment a typical building occupant might express relative to the background sound environment represented by the various NC curves and their equivalent dBA values.

Table 1 lists recommended criteria ranges for typical spaces in buildings in terms of both NC curves and dBA values. Selected criteria may be used for design purposes in developing HVAC system noise control measures and in specifying system components such as air-conditioning diffusers, fluorescent light ballasts, and so on. The background sound level criteria and the extent to which they are realized in a finished building have important implications for other related acoustical design aspects in particular situations (eg, those involving acoustical privacy within and between rooms).

CRITERIA FOR COMMUNICATION IN HIGH-NOISE-LEVEL AREAS

In most industrial plants, building mechanical service areas, and other such areas, the production process or system equipment noise cannot be controlled to reasonably low levels for optimal acoustical comfort from a practical standpoint. In these spaces, it is often a matter of simply providing the best possible environment for speech communication or telephone usage. Or, if very high noise levels are likely, it may be a matter of protecting the exposed workers' hearing.

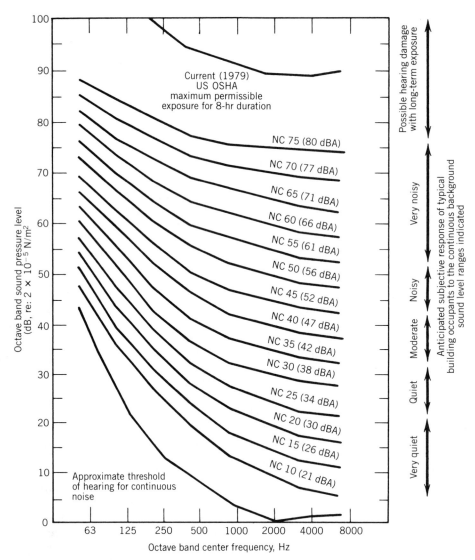

Figure 15. Background NC curves used for design and specification of acceptable acoustical environments in building spaces.

Table 2 indicates the nature of speech reception possible in various noise environments as well as a person's ability to carry on telephone communications.

Table 3 indicates the current OSHA permissible noise exposures for various durations. Note that these are upper-limit criteria for exposure and are not recommended design values. Even if an industrial noise environment falls below these limits (say, a typical worker's exposure is less than 90 dBA for an 8-h workday), there is still a potential hearing damage hazard. There is current legislative action in progress toward lowering the exposure limit to 85 dBA from 90 dBA for 8-h exposure, with corresponding reductions for shorter exposure durations. A building professional may well be involved in critical decisions concerning an industrial building design since the building or equipment enclosures can influence the plant noise levels to which personnel are exposed.

CRITERIA FOR SOUND ISOLATION BETWEEN DWELLING UNITS

The Federal Housing Administration (FHA) of HUD recommends criteria for all federally subsidized housing to ensure that both airborne and impact sound transmission between dwelling units will be controlled. Constructions that meet the criteria and are properly installed in the field will provide good sound insulation between dwelling units and should satisfy most occupants. Since the level of background sound varies in different building site environments, three grades are established.

Grade I. These environments are generally quiet suburban and peripheral suburban areas where the nighttime exterior background noise levels might be 35–40 dBA or lower. In addition, Grade I is applicable

Table 1. Recommended Criteria for Steady Background Sound in Typical Building Spaces

Type of Space or Activity	Criteria Recommended NC Curve	Sound Level, dBA
Workspaces in which continuous speech communication and telephone use are not required	60–70	65–75
Shops, garages, contract equipment rooms	45–60	52–65
Kitchens, laundries	45–60	52–65
Light maintenance shops, computer rooms	45–55	52–61
Drafting rooms, shop classrooms	40–50	47–56
General business and secretarial offices	40–50	47–56
Laboratories, clinics, patient waiting spaces	40–50	47–56
Public lobbies, corridors, circulation spaces	40–50	47–56
Retail shops, stores, restaurants, cafeterias	35–45	42–52
Large offices, secretarial, relaxation areas	35–45	42–52
Residential living, dining rooms	30–40	38–47
General classrooms, libraries	30–40	38–47
Private, semiprivate offices	30–40	38–47
Bedrooms, hotels, apartments with air conditioning	30–40	38–47
Bedrooms, private residences, hospitals	25–35	34–42
Executive offices, conference spaces	25–35	34–42
Small general-purpose auditoriums (less than about 500 seats), conference rooms, function rooms	35 (max)	42 (max)
Small churches and synagogues	25 (max)	38 (max)
Radio, TV, recording studios (close microphone pickup)	25 (max)	38 (max)
Churches, synagogues (for serious liturgical music)	25 (max)	38 (max)
Large auditoriums for unamplified music and drama	25 (max)	38 (max)
Radio, recording studios (remote microphone pickup)	20 (max)	30 (max)
Opera performance halls	20 (max)	30 (max)
Music performance and recital halls	20 (max)	30 (max)

Table 2. Nature of Speech Communication Possible in Various Background Sound Levels

Background Sound Level, dBA	Voice Effort Required and Distance	Nature of Communication Possible	Telephone Use
55	Normal voice at 10 ft	Relaxed communication	Satisfactory
65	Normal voice at 3 ft Raised voice at 6 ft Very loud voice at 12 ft	Continuous communication	Satisfactory
75	Raised voice at 2 ft Very loud voice at 12 ft Shouting at 8 ft	Intermittent communication	Marginal
85	Very loud voice at 1 ft Shouting at 2–3 ft	Minimal communication (restricted prearranged vocabulary desirable)	Impossible

to dwelling units in high-rise buildings above about the eighth-floor level and to apartment buildings desiring maximum sound insulation regardless of location.

Grade II. These environments are generally average suburban and urban residential areas where the nighttime exterior background noise levels fall in the 40–45 dBA range.

Grade III. These environments are generally noisy suburban or urban areas where the nighttime exterior background noise levels exceed 55 dBA. This category is considered to be the minimum desired sound isolation between dwelling units.

Table 4 indicates key criteria for airborne and impact sound isolation criteria in terms of minimum sound transmission class (STC) and impact insulation class (IIC) values for each of the three grades.

CRITERIA FOR ACOUSTICAL PRIVACY IN OPEN-PLAN SPACES

There are obvious architectural and cost advantages for certain kinds of activities if the individual subarea activities need not be fully enclosed with walls that extend to the ceiling. The open office landscape has become an in-

Table 3. Permissible Noise Exposures in Industrial Environments[a]

Duration per Day, h	Permissible Sound Level, Slow Meter Response, dBA
0.25 or less	115
0.5	110
1	105
1.5	102
2	100
3	97
4	95
6	92
8	90

[a] From Paragraph 1910.95, Occupational Safety and Health Act, U.S. Department of Labor.

Table 4. FHA Criteria for Sound Insulation Between Dwelling Units[a]

	Quality and Location Grade		
	Grade I	Grade II	Grade III
Party walls	STC 55	STC 52	STC 48
Party floor–ceilings	STC 55	STC 52	STC 48
	IIC 55	IIC 52	IIC 48
Mechanical equipment room to dwelling unit	STC 65[b]	STC 62[b]	STC 58[b]
Commercial space to dwelling unit	STC 60	STC 58	STC 56
	IIC 65	IIC 63	IIC 61

[a] From Ref. 2.

[b] Special vibration isolation of all mechanical equipment is required.

creasingly popular way to provide office space for large corporations and for the major federal government builder of facilities, the GSA. A significant factor in the degree of success such spaces enjoy is the acoustical environment. The open plan is really not new. Many church-basement Sunday school classrooms functioned without walls. The classical bank lobby, where loan officers discuss confidential financial information with customers, has been around for many years. Why is it, then, that some of these spaces function adequately from the acoustics standpoint and others do not? Distressed bank loan officers feel cheated when they move from the old monumental bank lobby where they enjoyed complete privacy to the new low-ceilinged, heavily acoustically treated open office landscape where they can readily hear conversations from adjacent desks.

The basic acoustical problem is really no different from the case of adjacent enclosed spaces. Adequate privacy involves sufficient attenuation of sound from source to listener locations where its relative annoyance will be a function of the degree of cover (or "masking") provided by the continuous background sound present. Figure 16 illustrates schematically the similarities and subtle differences between the two situations. Clearly, the containment and buildup of reverberant sound in enclosed rooms is

no longer present in open-plan spaces. Sound in the open space continually falls off with distance at a rate dependent on the relative sound absorptivity of the floor and ceiling surfaces. The relatively large attenuations provided by the fully enclosing partitions give way to lesser attenuation where only line-of-sight barriers, if any, exist between the source and listener.

Experience indicates that background sound levels normally produced by building air distribution systems rarely provide the spatial uniformity necessary to achieve acceptable privacy conditions in typical office spaces. In fact, practically all open landscape installations utilize carefully designed electronic masking systems to assure uniform background sound at the proper level and tonal character. Typically, such systems must be operated near the upper limits of acceptability for average building occupants (about NC 45 or 52 dBA). Criteria for the characteristic frequency spectrum shape of an electronic sound-masking system should form an important part of its performance specifications.

The Public Building Service (PBS) of the GSA has promulgated criteria and standards for the design, specification, and evaluation of systems and components used for open office spaces in federal buildings. In essence, the PBS/GSA criteria of acceptability are given in terms of a quantity known as speech privacy potential (SPP). The SPP is the sum of the background sound level and the attenuation between typical source and listener locations. The background sound level is quantified using a modified NC curve rating method. The workstation-to-workstation sound reduction is an average attenuation value taken along a source receiver path and is rated using a modified noise insulation class (NIC') method. With the PBS method of evaluation, acoustical privacy is satisfactory when the SPP is equal to or greater than 60 (ie, SPP ≥ 60). For example, an NC 40 background sound level in combination with sound attenuation from source to receiver of NIC' 20 would satisfy the PBS criterion.

CRITERIA FOR ASSEMBLY SPACES AND ROOMS FOR LISTENING

Auditoriums, music and drama performance halls, conference rooms, sports stadia, classrooms, and for that matter, all spaces where audiences listen to some desired sound source or sources must satisfy certain fundamental acoustical requirements in order to permit satisfactory listening conditions. The basic objectives are simply stated in terms of two aspects: first, the control of all undesired sounds, from exterior sources, adjacent spaces within the building, the HVAC systems serving the space, and so on, and second, the control of all desired sounds the audience has come to hear so that they are adequately loud and properly distributed without echo or distortion throughout the space.

The first requirement is rather obvious, but often there are serious oversights, such as inadequate control of HVAC system noise, which can mask significant parts of the desired speech or music program. The poor acoustics of a church or school auditorium can often be corrected by sim-

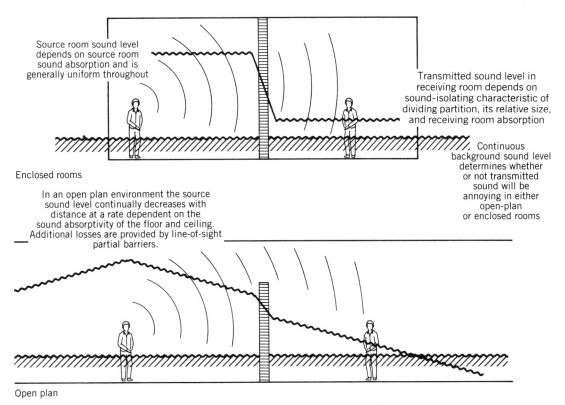

Figure 16. Schematic illustration of the relative similarities and differences between enclosed rooms and open-plan arrangements.

ply turning off the air-conditioning fans. Such situations should never occur. Properly chosen background sound levels (Table 1) and sound-attenuating constructions designed to exclude all potential intrusive sounds will satisfy this extremely important first requirement. Table 1 also suggests the range of acceptable background sound levels for various types of auditorium spaces, depending on their size and type of program material. Small conference rooms or classrooms, where speaker-to-listener distances are small, are obviously less demanding than larger performance auditoriums with a wide range of critical uses.

The control of the desired sounds is a much more complex matter since in most listening spaces the full range of sources (speech through music) must be accommodated and the audience itself is spread over a relatively large part of the room. Systematic study of typical source-to-receiver paths enables the designer to overcome even the most complex architectural acoustics configurations.

To begin with, the source must be made adequately loud at all possible listener locations. This is accomplished by taking advantage of the natural reinforcement of the principal room surfaces that can direct reflected sound in mirrorlike fashion from sources to the listener. In larger rooms, or for some sources that are weak to begin with, electronic reinforcement systems must supplement the natural loudness of the desired sounds. The coordination and integration of sound amplification system equipment with the basic room acoustics design is often the most important part of the overall acoustical design. In some

very large auditoriums, sports arenas, and so on, electronic amplification systems alone provide adequate loudness.

Another corollary requirement associated with the loudness requirement is that the desired sound be distributed uniformly throughout the listening space without long delayed discrete reflections (echoes), focused reflections, repetitive reflections (flutter echoes), or other undesirable colorations of the original source. These detailed design considerations are important, but rarely amenable to simple criteria. Simplified ray diagram analyses for the various principal source locations can reveal the general pattern of sound distribution throughout the space and the presence of possible deleterious reflection. In general, reflected signals that arrive within about 40 ms after the direct sound has arrived (ie, a path difference of 40 ft or less between the direct and reflected sound) contribute to the apparent loudness of the sound. Reflected sounds of sufficient level arriving after about 60 ms can be distinguished as discrete separate signals (or echoes). Intermediate delays between about 40 and 60 ms may simply result in fuzziness of the received sound, with no real contribution to its loudness or intelligibility.

A final requirement for good listening conditions is adequate reverberation control. Excessive reverberation can destroy speech intelligibility, yet inadequate persistence of sound can make the music sound dead. In most rooms, the selection of reverberation criteria is largely a matter of judgment and, in some cases, compromise between the ideal for either extreme, music or speech.

GLOSSARY OF TERMS

Absorbing Materials. Materials that dissipate acoustic energy within their structure as heat and/or mechanical energy of vibration. Usually building materials designed specifically for the purpose of absorbing acoustic energy on the boundary surfaces of rooms or in the cavities of structures.

Acoustical Analysis. The detailed study of all pertinent sound sources, sound transmission paths, and sound receptors in the context of a particular acoustical problem.

Acoustical Environment. The overall environment, interior or exterior, that affects the acoustic conditions of the space or structure under consideration.

Acoustical Treatment. The use of acoustical absorbing or reflecting materials or sound-isolating structures to improve or modify the acoustical environment.

Airborne Sound. Sound transmitted through air as a medium rather than through solids or the structure of a building.

Amplification. Usually the increase in intensity level of an audible signal produced by means of loudspeakers and associated electrical amplification apparatus.

Amplitude. The maximum displacement to either side of the normal or rest position of the molecules or particles of the medium transmitting a sound wave.

Architectural Acoustics. The control of sound in and around buildings.

Attenuation. Reducing the magnitude of a sound signal by separation of a sound source from a receptor, acoustical absorption, enclosure, or a combination of these or other means.

Audibility Threshold. The sound pressure at which a typical young, healthy person with normal hearing begins to respond.

Audible. Capable of producing the sensation of hearing.

Background Sound Level. The generally lowest or residual sound level present in a space above which speech, music, or other sounds may be heard.

Coupling. Any means of joining separated elements in any media so that sound energy is transmitted between them.

Cycle. The entire sequence of movement of a particle (during periodic motion) from rest to one extreme of displacement, back through the rest position to the opposite extreme of displacement, and back to the rest position. The unit for one cycle per second is Hertz (Hz).

Decibel (dB). A basic metric for describing the magnitude of sound. A division of a uniform scale based upon 10 times the logarithm to the base 10 of the relative value being compared (sound intensity, pressure squared, or power) to a specified reference value.

Diffraction. The ability of a sound wave to "flow" around an obstruction or through openings with little loss of energy.

Diffusion. Dispersion of sound within an enclosure such that there is uniform energy density throughout the space.

Direct Sound. A sound field produced and dominated by the sound waves emanating directly from a source (also referred to as the "near field").

Distortion. Any change in the transmitted sound signal such that the sound received is not a faithful replica of the original source sound.

Distribution. The pattern of sound intensity levels within a space; also, the patterns of sound dispersion as the sound travels within a space.

Echo. Any reflected sound of sufficient intensity and delay in arrival to be heard as distinct from the source.

Field Sound Transmission Class (FSTC). A rating of the field-derived airborne sound transmission loss data for a structure determined in accordance with the procedures of ASTM E 336 and E 413.

Flanking Paths. Any paths for sound transmission that bypass or circumvent the primary path through the structure under consideration.

Flutter. A rapid reflection or echo pattern between parallel sound-reflective walls with sufficient time between each reflection to cause a listener to be aware of separate discrete signals.

Focusing. Concentration of reflected acoustic energy within a limited location in a room as the result of reflections from concave surfaces.

Frequency. The number of complete cycles per second of a vibration (or other periodic motion). The unit is Hertz (Hz).

Frequency Analyzer. An instrument capable of measuring the acoustical energy present in various frequency subdivisions (1/1, 1/3, 1/10 octave bands, etc) of a complex sound.

Frequency Band. A subdivision of the frequency range of interest for measurement or analysis purposes (eg, octave band, 1/3 octave band, etc).

Frequency Spectra. The distribution of sound energy over a frequency range of interest (eg, the octave band sound pressure levels for a particular sound source plotted over the audible frequency range).

Hearing. The subjective response to sound, including the entire mechanism of the external, middle, and internal ear system and the nervous and cerebral operations that translate the physical stimuli into meaningful signals.

Intensity. The rate of sound energy transmitted in a specified direction through a unit area.

Intensity Level. A measure of the magnitude of sound intensity on a logarithmic scale; a value equal to 10 times the logarithm to the base 10 of the ratio of a sound intensity to a reference intensity. (The reference intensity is usually taken to be 10^{-16} W/cm^2.)

Isolation. The ability of materials or constructions to resist the transmission of sound or vibration through them.

Loudness. The subjective response of the human hearing mechanism to changing sound pressure.

Masking. The obscuring or covering up of one sound by another.

Noise. Unwanted sound.

Noise Insulation Class (NIC). A rating of the measured room-to-room noise reduction determined in accordance with the procedures of ASTM E 336 and E 413.

Noise Reduction. The reduction in level of unwanted sound by any of several means (eg, by distance in outdoor space, by boundary surface absorption, by isolating barriers of enclosures, etc).

Noise Reduction Coefficient (NRC). The arithmetic average of the sound absorption coefficients of a sound-absorbing material at 250, 500, 1000, and 2000 Hz rounded to the nearest 0.05.

Pain Threshold. A sound intensity level sufficiently high to produce the sensation of pain in the human ear (usually about 120 dB).

Pitch. The subjective response of the human hearing mechanism to changing frequency.

Reflected Sound. The resultant sound energy returned from a surface(s) that is not absorbed or otherwise dissipated upon contact with the surface(s).

Resilient Mounting. Any mounting or attachment system that reduces the transmission of vibrational energy from a vibrating body or structure to an adjacent structure.

Resonance. The natural, sympathetic vibration of a volume of air or a structure at a particular frequency as the result of excitation by sound energy at that particular frequency.

Reverberant Sound. A sound field produced and dominated by reflected sound from room boundary surfaces.

Reverberation. The persistence of sound within a space after the sound source has stopped.

Reverberation Time. The time in seconds required for a sound to decay, roughly speaking, to inaudibility after the source ceases. (Strictly, the time in seconds for the sound level at a specific frequency to decrease 60 dB in level after the source stops.)

Room Shape. The configuration of enclosed space, resulting from the orientation and arrangement of surfaces defining the space.

Room Volume. The cubic volume of space enclosed by the room boundary surfaces.

Sabin. The measure of sound absorption of a surface equivalent to 1 ft^2 of a perfectly absorptive material (named after Wallace Clement Sabine, a pioneer in architectural acoustics).

Sound. A vibration in a medium, usually in the frequency range capable of producing the sensation of hearing.

Sound Absorption Coefficient. The ratio of sound-absorbing effectiveness (at a specific frequency) of 1 ft^2 of acoustical absorbent to 1 ft^2 of perfectly absorptive material; usually expressed as a decimal value between 1.0 (perfect absorption) and 0 (perfect reflection).

Sound Control. The application of acoustical principles to the design of structures, equipment, and spaces to permit them to function properly and to create the desired environment for the activities intended.

Sound Leak. Any opening in a structure that permits airborne sound transmission with little or no loss compared with the basic structure.

Sound Level. A measure of sound pressure level as determined by instrumentation with standardized frequency-weighting characteristics (eg, A scale sound pressure level in dBA).

Sound Level Meter. A standard electrical instrument for determining sound pressure level.

Sound Pressure. The change in pressure at a point due to sound energy relative to the static pressure at that point without the sound wave.

Sound Pressure Level. A measure of the magnitude of sound pressure on a logarithmic scale; a value equal to 20 times the logarithm to the base 10 of the ratio of a sound pressure to a reference pressure (the reference pressure is usually taken to be 2×10^{-5} N/m^2).

Sound Transmission. The propagation of sound energy through various media.

Sound Transmission Class (STC). A rating of the laboratory-derived airborne sound transmission loss data for a structure determined in accordance with the procedures of ASTM E 90 and E 413.

Sound Velocity. The velocity at which a sound wave propagates through a medium (eg, in air, the speed of sound is approximately 1100 ft/s).

Sound Wave. A disturbance that is propagated in any medium (gas, liquid, or solid) by energy transfer between adjacent molecules.

Structure-borne Sound. Sound energy transmitted through solid elements of a building structure.

Transmission Loss (TL). A logarithmic measure of the decrease in sound power during transmission from one point to another (or through a panel, wall, etc); a value in decibels equal to 10 times the logarithm to the base 10 of the ratio of transmitted-to-incident sound power.

Vibration. A cyclical alternation in pressure or direction of movement.

Vibration Isolation. Any of several means of minimizing transmission of structure-borne sound from a vibrating body to the structure in or on which it is mounted.

Wavelength. The distance between adjacent regions of a sound wave where identical conditions of particle displacement, pressure, and so on occur.

BIBLIOGRAPHY

The material in this article has been adapted from "Acoustical Control in Buildings," in Huntington and Mikadeit, eds., *Building Construction*, 5th ed., John Wiley & Sons, Inc., New York, 1980, Chapt. 10, by the author and from material the author has found useful in courses for architectural students at the Rhode Island School of Design, the Boston Architectural Center, and Roger Williams College.

1. Vitruvius, "De Architectura," in F. V. Hunt, *Origins in Acoustics: The Science of Sound from Antiquity to the Age of Newton*, Yale Press, New Haven, Conn., 1978, Chapt. 8. This translation from the Latin indicates an extraordinary understanding of the principles of acoustical design of spaces for hearing.
2. R. D. Berendt, G. F. Winzer, and C. B. Burroughs, *A Guide to Air-borne, Impact and Structure-borne Noise Control in Multi Family Dwellings*, U.S. Department of Housing and Urban Development, Washington, D.C., Sept. 1967.

General References

H. F. Olson, *Acoustical Engineering*, D. Van Nostrand Co., 1960.

L. L. Beranek, *Music Acoustics and Architecture*, John Wiley & Sons, Inc., New York, 1962.

C. E. Crede, *Vibration and Shock Isolation*, John Wiley & Sons, Inc., New York, 1965.

L. Cremer and H. A. Müller, *Principles and Applications of Room Acoustics,* Vol. 1, Applied Science Publishers, Barking, UK, 1978 (English translation by T. J. Schultz).

L. L. Doelle, *Acoustics in Architectural Design, Bibliography 29,* National Research Council, Ottawa, Canada, 1965.

R. B. Newman and W. J. Cavanaugh, "Acoustics," in J. H. Callender, ed., *Time Saver Standards,* 4th ed., McGraw-Hill Inc., New York, 1966.

L. F. Yerges, *Sound Noise and Vibration Control,* Van Nostrand Reinhold Co., Inc., New York, 1969.

A. Lawrence, *Architectural Acoustics,* Elsevier, New York, 1970.

L. L. Beranek, ed., *Noise and Vibration Control,* McGraw-Hill Inc., New York, 1971.

L. L. Doelle, *Environmental Acoustics,* McGraw-Hill Inc., New York, 1972.

M. D. Egan, *Concepts in Architectural Acoustics,* McGraw-Hill Inc., New York, 1972.

W. C. Sabine, *Collected Papers,* Dover Press, New York, 1972.

L. Cremer, M. Heckl, and E. E. Unger, *Structure Borne Sound,* Springer-Verlag, New York, 1980.

D. Davis and C. Davis, *Sound System Engineering,* Howard W. Sams and Co., Indianapolis, Ind., 1975.

Standards on Noise Measurements, Rating Schemes, and Definitions: A Compilation, NBS Special Publication 386, National Bureau of Standards, Washington, D.C., 1976.

T. D. Northwood, ed., *Benchmark Papers in Acoustics, Architectural Acoustics,* Vol. 10, Dowen, Hutchinson, and Ross Inc., Stroudsburg, Pa., 1977, pp. 250–267.

M. Rettinger, *Acoustical Design and Noise Control,* 3rd ed., Vols. 1 and 2, Chemical Publishing Co., Inc., New York, 1977.

F. V. Hunt, *Origins in Acoustics: The Science of Sound from Antiquity to the Age of Newton,* Yale Press, New Haven, Conn., 1978.

C. M. Harris, ed., *Handbook of Noise Control,* 2nd ed., McGraw-Hill Inc., New York, 1979.

W. J. Cavanaugh, "Acoustical Control in Buildings," in Huntington and Mikadeit, eds., *Building Construction,* John Wiley & Sons, Inc., New York, 1980, Chapt. 10.

V. O. Knudsen and C. M. Harris, *Acoustical Designing in Architecture,* American Institute of Physics, New York, 1980.

R. Talaske, E. A. Wetherill, and W. J. Cavanaugh, eds., *Halls for Music Performance—Two Decades of Experience,* American Institute of Physics, New York, 1982.

D. D. Reynolds, *Engineering Principles of Acoustics,* Allyn and Bacon, Boston, Mass., 1981.

T. D. Rossing, *The Science of Sound,* Addison-Wesley Publishing Co., Inc., Reading, Mass., 1983.

R. Jones, *Noise & Vibration Control in Buildings,* McGraw-Hill Inc., New York, 1984.

D. Lubman and E. A. Wetherill, eds., *Acoustics of Worship Spaces,* American Institute of Physics, New York, 1984.

"Sound Control," in *ASHRAE Guide and Data Book,* Systems Vol., American Society of Heating, Refrigeration and Air Conditioning Engineers Inc., New York, 1984, Chapt. 32.

R. Talaske, ed., *Spaces for Drama,* American Institute of Physics, New York, 1986.

Also selected papers in the following journals:

Journal of the Acoustical Society of America
Journal of the Audio Engineering Society
Noise Control Engineering
Sound and Vibration

See also ACOUSTICAL DESIGN—PLACES OF ASSEMBLY; ACOUSTICAL INSULATION AND MATERIALS; CEILINGS; NOISE CONTROL IN BUILDINGS; SOUND REINFORCEMENT SYSTEMS.

WILLIAM J. CAVANAUGH,
FASA
Cavanaugh Tocci Associates,
Inc.
Sudbury, Massachusetts

ACRYLICS

SURVEY

The term acrylic is frequently used to describe a distinct chemically related class of polymers (plastics) that are noted for their outstanding water-clear color and the stability of their physical and chemical properties, even under extremely severe service conditions. Architects are most familiar with acrylic glazing, lighting fixture diffusers, display cases, transparent tanks, models, machine windows, roofing, siding, decorative panels, and advertising signs; acrylics, however, are also used as the building blocks for many other products frequently specified by architects, namely, paints, mastics, caulking, adhesives, floor polishes, textile materials, rug backings, and other products where outstanding wear and durability are required. Physical and chemical properties of the generic class termed acrylic polymers can be manipulated to vary from those of an extremely tacky adhesive to those of a rubber, a tough plastic, or even a hard powder. The fundamental unit from which a polymer is made is called a monomer. Many monomer units (molecules) combine to form a polymer molecule. Acrylic and methacrylic monomers are chemically related to each other by virtue of their chemical structure. Acrylic monomers add to each other such that the ratios and characteristics of the monomers in the unit and the length of the polymer chain determine the physical and chemical nature of the plastic or polymer that is formed. For a more complete and detailed discussion of the chemistry of acrylic and methacrylic ester polymers, see Ref. 1.

The acrylic plastic technology developed during World War II found many applications in the building construction boom that followed the war. Sheet glazing applications met the safety glazing requirements that were increasingly being incorporated into local and regional building codes. Acrylic sheet with a wide design selection, ranging from clear to tints and colors, was particularly adaptable to skylight glazing and sign applications (2). The skylight glazing could be thermoformed (shaped or formed by softening the plastic with heat) into aesthetically pleasing shapes that imparted rigidity for greater load-bearing capacity (3). Sign faces made of acrylic sheet could be thermoformed in limitless custom combinations of shapes, logos, and graphics. Second-surface painting accented sign features, and back lighting provided spectacular night displays. Acrylics in molding pellet form, used for injection and extrusion molding processes, found architectural applications as lighting diffusers similar to those used extensively in automotive lighting lenses (4). Many other architectural applications were developed for acrylic sheet and molding pellets that utilized their combination of unique properties and fabrication simplicity. Even today, this uniquely versatile material has not been fully exploited in the architectural field. New applications will depend on the confidence and experience of the designer and possibly on the development of alloying elements that will enhance specific applications.

The cast sheet types, as typified by Plexiglas G acrylic plastic sheet, are available in a broad range of sizes, colors, and patterns, as shown in Table 1. Clear, colorless acrylic sheet is as transparent as the finest optical glass. It transmits 92% of the light with an average haze measurement of only 1%. Gray and bronze transparent acrylic sheet colors provide a convenient way to reduce solar heat gain and glare in window glazing, skylights, transparent enclosures, and sun screens. Each of the basic colors is available in five standard tint densities to provide a range of visible light and solar energy transmittance values. They transmit light nearly uniformly across the visible spectrum so that there is little distortion of natural colors. Light transmission values are the same for any thickness in a specific tint density (5, 6).

White acrylic translucent sheet densities provide a range of light transmittance and diffusion (7). The most appropriate combination of light transmission and diffusion, with adequate lamp-hiding power, can be selected for lighting diffuser panels. A diffusing medium breaks up the light rays and scatters and redistributes them in all directions. White translucent sheet is also used in skylight glazing to transmit diffused light, thus eliminating interior bright spots. Solar heat gain through skylights can be reduced in direct relation to the white tint density. Light transmittance values for white translucent sheet vary with thickness, whereas solar transmittance over the total spectrum is relatively independent of sheet thickness.

Acrylic mirrors are colorless or have a neutral bronze tint. They are available in a standard sheet size of 48 × 96 in. (121.9 × 243.8 cm) and in 0.125 in. (0.318-cm) and 0.25-in. (0.635-cm) thicknesses.

MOLDING POWDERS AND PELLETS

Acrylic molding pellets are used by commercial extruders to produce extruded acrylic sheet, rods, and tubing and objects of complex shape. The physical properties of sheets and other shapes produced from molding powder and pellets, which are melted and extruded or cast, have been compiled (4, 7).

The various grades of molding powder and their characteristics as well as a detailed summary of properties of objects made from molding powder pellets have also been published (7).

DESIGN AND USE OF ACRYLIC OBJECTS

Careful consideration should be given to building codes and approvals before design is begun. The following will aid the architect and designer in selecting options.

Acrylic Plastic Building Codes

Acrylic Sheet and Fire. Acrylic sheet is a combustible material. In general, the same fire precautions that are observed in connection with the handling and use of any ordinary combustible material should be observed when handling, storing, or using acrylic.

Building codes define good practice in the use of acrylic sheet or light transmission and control on a design and

Table 1. Acrylic Sheet—Typical Types and Grades[a]

Type	Distinguishing Characteristics	Thickness Range, in.	Largest Sheet Size, in.	Supplied in				
				Colorless	Colors	Patterns	Form	Weatherability
Plexiglas G	Standard, all-purpose grade	0.03–4.25	120 × 144	Yes	Full range	Yes	Unshrunk	Excellent
Plexiglas II-UVA	Meets MIL-Spec P-5425	0.06–1	72 × 96	Yes	Limited	No	Shrunk	Excellent
Plexiglas II-UVT	UV-transmitting	0.06–1	72 × 96	Yes	No	No	Shrunk	Excellent
Plexiglas G-UVT	UV-transmitting	0.06–1	72 × 96	Yes	No	No	Unshrunk	Excellent
Plexiglas 55	Higher craze resistance. Use for aircraft glazing	0.08–2.75	72 × 96	Yes	No	No	Shrunk	Excellent
Plexiglas UF-3	UV-filtering	0.06–0.25	48 × 96	Yes	No	No	Unshrunk	Excellent
Plexiglas Mirror	Image-reflecting Plexiglas plastic	0.125–0.25	48 × 96	Yes	Yes	No	Unshrunk	Indoor use only
Plexiglas MC	Utility grade	0.1–0.25	72 × 96	Yes	No	No	Unshrunk	Excellent

[a] Ref. 2.

Table 2. Acrylic and Fire[a]

Fire Response Characteristics	Recommended Practice
The ignition temperature of acrylic sheet is higher than that of most woods, but it will ignite readily, and when involved in fire, will burn vigorously and generate heat rapidly.	Install acrylic sheet away from sources of intense heat or flame. Enclose edges of acrylic sheet components. Observe building code stipulations and restrictions. Do not use more acrylic sheet than required to perform the function required of it. Employ fire protective systems, eg, sprinklers, fire detectors, and automatic vents, as hazard analysis indicates.
Acrylic sheet softens when heated above 260°F (126.7°C), which is approximately 300°F (148.9°C) below its ignition temperature.	Do not use acrylic sheet as a supporting element or in any location where resistance to fire penetration is required.
Acrylic sheet, if held in position when burning, will drip burning droplets.	In overhead lighting, mount acrylic in free channel mountings to assure fallout prior to ignition. When used in interior window systems, mount the acrylic sheet in such a manner as to assure fallout prior to ignition. Extinguish burning acrylic sheet with water or fire extinguishers.
When installed as a wall or ceiling finish or when laminated to a substrate, acrylic sheet provides a surface over which flames may spread rapidly and release heat and gases, contributing to flashover.	Do not install acrylic sheet as applied wall or ceiling finish or as a substrate surfacing material for large interior surface areas in building applications unless the areas are protected by an automatic sprinkler system and approval is obtained from the controlling jurisdiction.
Large-area installations of acrylic sheet such as enclosures and continuous sections of interior window systems are provided for in building code regulations because they do not conform to area limitations and therefore require special permits based on analysis of all relevant fire-safety considerations.	Relevant considerations are the use of the structure (occupancy); location (exposure); height and area; nature of interior, not arrangements (decorations, finishes, and furnishings); availability and construction of fire exits; need for special fire-protection systems such as sprinklers, automatic heat and smoke vents, early warning devices, and deluge systems or water curtains. Unless there are extenuating circumstances, sprinkler systems should be used.
Burning acrylic sheet does not produce either excessive quantities of smoke or gases more toxic than those produced by burning wood or paper. The concentration of carbon monoxide and/or carbon dioxide released by burning acrylic sheet is a factor of the quantity of acrylic sheet involved and the conditions of burning.	The use of acrylic sheet is restricted, not because of the character of its products of decomposition, but because of its combustibility and burning characteristics.

[a] Ref. 7.

engineering basis that takes into account the combustibility and fire characteristics of the material.

The fire hazard when using acrylic sheet can be kept at an acceptable level by complying with building codes and observing established principles of fire safety. In Table 2, fire response characteristics of acrylic sheet are listed in one column, and the design, engineering, and fire protection implications of the characteristics are in the adjacent column.

Acrylic Sheet Code Approvals. Copies of the approvals of acrylic sheet under various codes can be made available on request by most manufacturers. In addition, reports on the status of acrylic sheet under federal government regulations can be provided promptly. Most manufacturers also provide assistance via code consultants and engineers in obtaining approvals for installation of acrylic objects that constitute justifiable exceptions to existing restrictions. A considerable amount of information is available to support such applications. Approvals of general interest include ICBO Research Recommendation No. 1084; BOCA Report No. 77–67 and SBCC Report No. 7246; New York City Board of Standards and Appeals Calendars 444–60–

SM, 657–64–SM; New York City Department of Water Supply, Gas & Electricity approval for use in signs and lighting fixtures; New York City MEA 107–69–M, MEA 146–80–M, MEA 139–80–M; and California Fire Marshall File No. A2560–007. Reviews of fire hazard assessment and the legal aspects and implications of the use of plastic materials in building construction may be found in Refs. 8 and 9.

General Acrylic Sheet Design Characteristics

Acrylic plastic sheet brings a uniquely favorable combination of fabrication simplicity and design characteristics to those architectural applications that primarily require optical clarity and light transmission control. Further design characteristics are as follows.

Impact Strength. Acrylic plastic sheet has better breakage resistance than most types of glass. Acrylic sheet is not prone to thermal stress cracking as is glass. A comparison with various types of glass is given in Table 3.

Weather Resistance. The excellent weatherability of acrylic plastics, in comparison with other plastics, is well documented. The weathering resistance of Plexiglas plastic

Table 3. Impact Resistance of Glass Compared with Acrylic Sheet[a]

Material	Breakage Thickness, in.[b]	Average Breakage Height of Drop, in.[b]	Average Speed of Ball At Moment of Impact, mph[c]	Average Impact Strength, lb·in.[d]
Double-strength window glass	0.125	3.7	3.3	25
Laminated glass	0.25	16.5	23.0	110
Plate glass	0.25	16.5	23.0	110
Wired glass	0.25	16.7	23.0	112
Tempered glass	0.25	87.0	51.0	582
Acrylic sheet	0.125	98.0	54.0	716
Acrylic sheet	0.1875	123.8	60.0	828
Acrylic sheet	0.25	162.5	70.0	1086

[a] Ref. 2.
[b] To convert in. to cm multiply by 2.54.
[c] To convert mph to km/h multiply by 1.609.
[d] To convert lb · in to kg · cm multiply by 1.155.

samples exposed to adverse conditions has been monitored by Rohm and Haas Co. for many years. Outdoor exposure tests on a large number of clear samples over a 10-year period in Pennsylvania showed an average of more than 91% light transmission, which is a loss of only 1% (2, 6). Inspection over a period of many years revealed no readily visible effects in nearly all test samples.

Weight. See Table 4. The weight of acrylic sheet is less than half that of glass and 43% that of aluminum, a factor that gains importance where it is desirable to keep the size of supporting structures to a minimum.

Surface Hardness. Abrasives scratch the surface of acrylic sheet. The exercise of reasonable care during installation and subsequent maintenance procedures minimizes scratching and preserves the appearance of colorless transparent glazing. Scratching is less discernible in decorative colored and patterned acrylic sheet applications.

Chemical Resistance. Most household cleaners may be used on acrylic sheet. However, the material is affected by paint thinners, turpentine, and similar solvents. Stress and temperature are influencing factors in chemical resistance. Any application subject to frequent chemical contact should be confirmed by reference to existing chemical resistance data or by appropriate field testing. The effects of various chemicals on acrylic are shown in Table 5.

Sound Abatement. Acrylic sheet provides sound reduction characteristics comparable with those of glass, but with much better breakage resistance. Additionally, acrylic sheet can be simply formed to enhance the aesthetics of sound barrier applications. The comparison of its noise reduction with that of other building materials is given in Table 6.

Thermal Expansion and Contraction. Acrylic sheet is subject to dimensional changes due to thermal expansion and contraction that are generally greater than those of other materials with which it is used in construction. Allowances must be made for these differences, particularly in exterior applications subject to wide temperature variations. The channel depth or rabbet depth should be sufficient to allow for expansion and contraction. Through-bolting or other types of inflexible fastenings that do not provide for dimensional changes lead to failure. Sealants and tapes should be sufficiently extensible to accommodate dimensional changes of the acrylic. A comparison of the coefficients of thermal expansion of the acrylic with those of other building materials is given in Table 7.

Humidity Expansion and Contraction. Some allowance is generally made for dimensional changes in exterior stan-

Table 5. Chemical Resistance of Poly(methyl methacrylate)[a]

Not Affected By	Attacked By
Animal oils	
Mineral oils	
Most inorganic solutions	High concentrations of alkalis and oxidizing agents
Low concentrations of alcohols	High concentrations of alcohols, eg, methanol, ethanol, 2-propanol
Paraffins	
Olefins	
Amines	
Alkyl monohalides	Alkyl polyhalides, eg, ethylene dichloride, methylene chloride
Aliphatic hydrocarbons; higher esters, ie, > 10 carbon atoms	Aromatic hydrocarbons, eg, benzene, toluene; xylene lower esters, eg, ethyl acetate; isopropyl acetate phenols, eg, cresol; aliphatic acids, eg, butyric acid, acetic acid

[a] Ref. 1.

Table 4. Weight of Plexiglas Acrylic Plastic[a]

Thickness in. (cm)	Weight/ft², lb (/m², kg)
0.125 (0.318)	0.75 (3.67)
0.1875 (0.476)	1.1 (5.38)
0.25 (0.653)	1.5 (7.34)

[a] Ref. 7.

Table 6. Comparison of Noise Reduction Characteristics of Acrylic Sheet with Other Materials[a]

Construction Material	Approximate dB Noise Reduction[b]
0.25-in. acrylic sheet	29
0.5-in. acrylic sheet	33
1 in. acrylic sheet	35
Double glazed acrylic sheet	38
0.125-in. glass	25
0.25-in. glass	27
1 in. plywood	26
0.125-in. steel	37
0.0625-in. sheet lead	38
Wood stud partition	38

[a] Ref. 7.
[b] Noise reduction obtained from enclosures is dependent on the completeness of the enclosure, tightness of joints, and so on. The above dB noise reductions represent complete, absolutely tight enclosures without any openings, large or small. These results are seldom achieved; however, they are rarely required to reduce noise sources to below hearing damage criteria. The main purpose of this table is to indicate the noise reduction capabilities of commonly used materials in terms of dB.

Table 7. Comparison of Coefficients of Thermal Expansion,[a] **Acrylic Sheet vs Other Materials**

	In./in./°F	Cm/cm/°C
Acrylic sheet[b]	41×10^{-6}	73.8×10^{-6}
Aluminum	12.9×10^{-6}	23.2×10^{-6}
Copper	9.1×10^{-6}	16.4×10^{-6}
Steel	6.3×10^{-6}	11.3×10^{-6}
Plate glass	5×10^{-6}	9×10^{-6}
Pine, along grain	3×10^{-6}	5.4×10^{-6}
Pine, across grain	19×10^{-6}	34.2×10^{-6}

[a] Ref. 2.
[b] In outdoor use where temperature varies widely, acrylic sheet should be installed in a channel frame engaging the edges of the material so that it is free to expand and contract without restraint.

dard applications of acrylic sheet due to changes in humidity. Dimensional changes in response to temperature occur almost instantly compared to humidity changes, which can take many days to come to equilibrium at any given humidity. Since the humidity in exterior applications is rarely stable long enough to produce equilibrium conditions, the maximum dimensional change will be relatively insignificant compared to temperature changes.

Rigidity. External factors affecting the rigidity of acrylic sheet include temperature, humidity, load, and load time. Different temperature and/or humidity conditions on the inner and outer surfaces of acrylic sheet may cause the sheet to deflect somewhat in the direction of the higher temperature and/or humidity. However, this type of deflection is temporary, and the sheet will return to its original flatness when temperature and humidity equalize on both sides of the sheet. Deflection does not affect visibility through flat transparent acrylic sheet, but may cause distorted reflections. In translucent or opaque panels where visibility through the material is not required, surface textures or formed designs will eliminate specular reflection.

Acrylic sheet is not as rigid as many other materials used in building construction applications; however, it is more rigid than any other thermoplastic sheet material. The short-term modulus of elasticity of Plexiglas G and MC sheet is 450,000 psi (3103 MPa). This value is used to determine deflections under short-term loads such as wind or snow loads associated with glazing applications. Deflection under short-term loading is temporary and mostly recoverable when the load is removed.

For calculation purposes, the modulus of elasticity should be reduced by as much as 50% for Plexiglas G to compensate for the effect of long-term loading. Long-term load occurs in glazing applications because of the weight of the acrylic sheet, and deflection is at a maximum for flat panels mounted in a horizontal plane. Similar deflections occur in interior applications of flat acrylic panels used as lighting diffusers. Dead load deflection due to the weight of the acrylic sheet will be permanent and should be considered relative to the aesthetics of the applications. Deflection can be virtually eliminated with appropriate thermoformed shapes. The typical flat sheet dead load deflections shown in Table 7 apply to Plexiglas G. The long-term modulus of elasticity of Plexiglas MC is less than that of Plexiglas G.

Service Temperature. The allowable continuous service temperatures for Plexiglas G [180–200°F (82.2–93.3°C)] and Plexiglas MC [170–190°F (76.7–87.8°C)] are sufficiently high for exterior applications and fluorescent lighting.

Light and Solar Energy Transmittance. Clear, colorless acrylic plastic sheet has excellent optical clarity (92% light transmission) and resistance to discoloration on exposure to light. The gray and bronze tints (solar control series) and the translucent whites provide additional design versatility for optimum light transmission combined with effective reduction in solar heat gain and glare in glazing applications. Transmission values for the various tint densities are given in Tables 8 and 9. Light transmittance values of white translucent materials vary with the thickness of the sheet. Radiant solar energy transmittance is independent of the material thickness (2).

Design Stresses. Maximum strength values are based on the specific parameters and procedures established by the ASTM test method (2). These are ultimate values useful for quality control, procurement, and comparison purposes. Allowable design stresses are not determined by application of an established safety factor against these values. They have instead been determined from the results of long-term testing of acrylic sheet under stress, both indoors and outdoors. Test results reflect the time and temperature dependence of the load–stress relationship and the effects of an outdoor environment. Acrylic sheet differs from grade to grade and from manufacturer to manufacturer. It is therefore sometimes critical to use the correct guide for a specific application, as illustrated below.

Allowable long-term stresses under continuous load have thus been established as 1500 psi (10.4 MPa) for Plexiglas G and 750 psi (5.2 MPa) for Plexiglas MC sheet in outdoor architectural applications. Allowable stresses under short-term load, such as wind load, may be as much as twice the allowable long-term stresses without causing

Table 8. Light and Solar Energy Transmittance of White Translucent Acrylic Sheet[a]

White Translucent Color Number	Total Solar Energy Transmittance 0.1875-in. thick, %	Light Transmittance, %		
		0.125-in. thick	0.1875-in. thick	0.25-in. thick
Colorless	90	92	92	92
W-2067	66	72	60	53
W-2159	62	64	51	43
W-2254	59	60	48	40
W-2447	52	53	42	36
W-7138	37	41	32	26
W-7328	27	32	22	17
W-7420	18	22	16	11
W-7508	8	9	6	4

Light and Heat Transmittance

[a] Ref. 6.

surface crazing. Crazing is a network of fine surface cracks attributed to the action of stress, solvents, and environmental exposure, alone or in combination. It appears on the tension surface.

Deflection under load also varies with load duration. The short-term modulus of elasticity, as a measure of stiffness, for Plexiglas G and MC is 450,000 psi (3,103 MPa). The long-term value for Plexiglas G is reduced to 225,000 psi (1,552 MPa). Similar to the reduction in long-term allowable stress as noted above for Plexiglas MC, the long-term modulus of elasticity will also be less than that for Plexiglas G. Plexiglas MC should not be used in applications such as aquarium glazing where long-term stress and deflection are more critical design factors.

Fabrication and Maintenance of Acrylic Sheet

Prior to processing acrylic sheet, the appropriate technical literature should be obtained from the manufacturer for each fabrication procedure involved. The technical literature gives detailed information for the proper handling of acrylic sheet and also provides safety and health precautions. Accessory equipment and materials suppliers should be consulted for specific health and safety information on their products (2).

Cutting. Acrylic sheet may be cut with power saws used for wood or metal or by scribing and breaking. Scribing is limited to straight cuts in materials 0.25 in. (0.635 cm) or less in thickness.

Circular saws for straight cutting and band saws for curves or straight cuts in thick material are preferred. Alloy steel tempered blades may be used where the quantity of sheet to be cut does not warrant the use of more expensive carbide-tipped blades. The saw should be adequately powered. A 10-in. diameter saw should be powered by a motor of about 2 HP, and a 14-in. diameter blade by a motor of approximately 5 HP. Cut edges should be finished free of chips and tool marks by scraping and/or sanding. Breakage resistance will be sustained at a maximum when the edges of saw cut sheets or the edges of

Table 9. Light and Solar Energy Transmittance of Solar Control Acrylic Sheet[a]

Plexiglas Sheet		Transmittance, %		Shading Coefficient, Vertical Glazing	
		Visible	Solar	Single	Double
Number	Color	Light	Energy	Glazed	Glazed[b]
2538	Neutral gray	16	27	0.52	0.36
2537	Neutral gray	33	41	0.63	0.49
2094	Neutral gray	45	55	0.74	0.61
2514	Neutral gray	59	62	0.80	0.68
2515	Neutral gray	76	74	0.89	0.78
2370	Bronze	10	20	0.46	0.30
2412	Bronze	27	35	0.58	0.43
2404	Bronze	49	56	0.75	0.62
2539	Bronze	61	62	0.80	0.68
2540	Bronze	75	75	0.90	0.79
Colorless Plexiglas sheet		92	85	—	—

[a] Ref. 6.
[b] Tinted Plexiglas sheet outside, ¼-in. air space, and colorless Plexiglas sheet inside.

drilled holes are free of notches. A carbide-tipped blade of the triple-chip style is advised. This tooth style is also called square or advanced. More complete details may be obtained in Ref. 10.

Drilling. Acrylic sheet may be drilled using high-speed twist drills commonly used for metals. However, the best results are obtained by modifying the drills. Drills should first be ground to a tip angle of 60°. The cutting edge should then be dubbed off to a 0° rake angle, and the back lip clearance angle ground to 12–15°. Moderate speeds and light pressure should be used to avoid "grabbing." Further details may be found in Ref. 11.

Machining. Acrylic sheet machining characteristics are similar to those of brass or copper. The acrylic may be turned, routed, shaped, tapped, threaded, and ground on a centerless grinder. Cutting edges of the tools should be shaped to have a scraping rather than cutting characteristic; that is, there should be no rake. Water or soluble oil and water is the preferred coolant. Chattering can be prevented by holding both the work and the tools firmly. For details, see Ref. 11.

Forming. Acrylic sheet is a thermoplastic material that softens when heated and hardens when cooled. Specific grades of acrylic sheet have specific forming temperatures. For example, Plexiglas G and K can be formed to almost any shape when heated to 290–360°F (143.3–182.2°C), and Plexiglas MC can be formed when heated to 175–350°F (135–176.7°C). The shape is retained when the material is cooled. Forming is done at relatively low pressures, and the molds can be made of low-cost wood and plaster; custom shapes in small quantities can then be made at moderate cost. Three-dimensional shapes can also be thermoformed with positive air pressure, without the use of male or female forms.

Acrylic flat sheets can be cold-formed (bent to a smooth curvature while cold) against curved mullions and then held in position with continuous retainer strips. Only simple curves can be formed in this manner. Compound curvatures must be thermoformed. Again, each grade of sheeting has its own unique characteristic. For instance, the cold-forming radius of Plexiglas G sheet should be no less than 180 times the sheet thickness. By contrast, the cold-forming radius of Plexiglas MC should be no less than 300 times the sheet thickness. For more details, see Refs. 7 and 12.

Cementing. Joints between acrylic sheets can be made using solvent cements such as methylene chloride or a polymerizing cement such as PS-30 cement, which can be obtained from plastics distributors. Solvent cements, which depend on softening of the acrylic, form a cohesive bond, whereas the polymerizing cement forms a new polymer in the joint space. Polymer joints have better strength characteristics than solvent-cemented joints. Polymer joint strength can also be improved by annealing. For more details, see Ref. 13.

Maintenance. Acrylic sheet should be washed with a mild soap or detergent and lukewarm water solution. A clean, soft cloth or sponge and liberal applications of the solution should be used. The sheet should be rinsed well and then dried by blotting with a damp cloth or chamois. Window cleaning solutions, scouring compounds, or gasoline or strong solvents such as alcohol or acetone should not be used. The surface luster of acrylic sheet can be enhanced by application of a good grade of automotive paste wax. It should be applied in a thin, even coat and polished with a dry, soft cloth such as cotton flannel. This treatment will improve the appearance of surfaces that exhibit minor scratches.

Surfaces. Surfaces that show more pronounced scratching can be improved by carefully following recommended sanding, buffing, and polishing procedures. A muslin wheel dressed with tallow and abrasive may be used, followed by buffing with a clean, soft cotton flannel wheel. A surface speed of 1800–2000 rpm and light pressure are recommended. However, these procedures may cause thickness variations that can affect optical and strength characteristics. The best practice is to avoid scratching by careful handling and by following recommended cleaning procedures.

Antistatic Coatings. Coatings that will extend resistance to the accumulation of electrostatic charges for a period of several months are available for acrylic sheet surfaces. However, in most glazing applications, occasional rain or washing removes static accumulation.

ARCHITECTURAL APPLICATIONS

The following general recommendations apply to exterior architectural applications.

1. Preferably, acrylic sheets or panels should be installed in a complete channel-type perimeter frame.
2. Sheet edges must be free to expand and contract without restraint within the depth of the channel.
3. The channel depth, also referred to as the rabbet depth in glazing applications, must be sufficient to accommodate dimensional changes due to temperature, humidity, and deflection under load, plus a safety factor to assure adequate grip along sheet edges under fully contracted conditions.
4. Acrylic panel dimensions must be trimmed to provide the proper expansion clearances within the channel frame. To reduce stress cracking, edges should be clean cut and finished free of chips or prominent tool marks.
5. Sealant compounds and accessory materials used in acrylic sheet applications must be compatible with the acrylic sheet. Sealants should provide adequate recoverable elongation to accommodate maximum differential movement between the acrylic sheet and frame.
6. Rigid fastenings cannot be used to connect acrylic sheet with other materials without risk of failure. In applications requiring through-bolted-type connections, the joints should be designed to allow lateral slip, with oversized holes to accommodate differential movement. Edge stresses and stress concentration at the holes are critical factors in this type of fastening system.

7. Acrylic sheet panels should be formed into appropriate rigidizing shapes wherever practical to virtually eliminate deflection and increase load capacity.

Glazing

Acrylic plastic sheet has long been used for primary window glazing and for exterior storm window glazing. A more recent idea is to use acrylic sheet on the interior side of the primary windows. Unlike exterior storm windows, where some venting of the cavity to the exterior is desirable to minimize condensation, acrylic sheet can and should be mounted virtually airtight on the interior side. Advantages of this include a tight perimeter seal to prevent the warm, moist interior air from contacting the colder prime window glazing and condensing, while at the same time eliminating unavoidable drafts around operable and poor-fitting prime windows. In addition, inside mounting can utilize thinner acrylic and simpler mounting and sealing systems since the panels are not subject to wind loading and exterior temperature extremes. Other advantages include a reduced level of sound transmission and a material that meets the requirements of the ANSI Z97.1 standard for safety glazing for thicknesses of 0.080 in. (0.203 cm) or greater.

The thickness of acrylic sheet prime window glazing necessary to support a specified wind load is determined by what is commonly referred to as the large deflection theory for flat plates. This theory allows the sheet to deflect enough to carry a significant portion of the load in direct tension. Deflection under wind load is temporary and recoverable. Deflection, as was arbitrarily established and set by precedent as a maximum of 5% of the short dimension of the sheet, is the limiting factor in glazing design. Stress under wind load is generally well below the allowable short-term stress for acrylic sheet. Recommendations for prime window glazing also apply to exterior storm windows, except that the use of sealants is optional in storm window glazing.

Small Light Glazing

Small light glazing, up to 24 × 24 in. (61 × 61 cm), can be installed like typical glass glazing: 0.0675-in (0.159-cm) expansion clearance should be allowed in each sash dimension. An acrylic sheet thickness of 0.125 in. (0.318 cm), available in standard clear and tinted sheet sizes, will provide a wind load capacity in excess of 40 psi (0.28 MPa) for 24 × 24 in. (61 × 61 cm) sizes.

Intermediate and Large Light Glazing Steps

1. Determine acrylic sheet thickness and rabbet dimensions vs load and panel sizes (6).

2. Determine expansion clearance required in each panel dimension (6).

3. Select sealant (6).

General Glazing Notes

1. Rabbet depth and expansion clearance (6) do not include tolerances in size and the squareness of the installed sash. Acrylic sheet glazing panels should be cut to fit each field-measured sash opening, allowing the proper expansion clearance.

2. Expansion clearance and sealant width (6) are based on cutting acrylic sheet panels to size and installing sealants in ambient temperatures near 70°F (21.1°C). Ambient temperatures that vary more than 20°F (11.1°C) from this median will require adjustment in the expansion clearance and sealant width.

3. One should hold reasonably close to the recommended expansion clearances. Excessive clearance could result in insufficient grip along sheet edges under fully contracted conditions.

4. The filler tape specified includes materials such as polyethylene and polyurethane foam tapes of medium density. Denser or firmer tapes will require a bond breaker between the tape and the sealant.

5. The sealant manufacturer's recommendations should be referred to for proper use and application of sealants. Other generic glazing compounds such as butyl types and polysulfides may be used, subject to specific approval and recommendations by the manufacturer for application on acrylic plastic glazing. Keyed-in gasket systems are limited to proven proprietary original equipment manufacturer's systems such as storm doors and skylights. Structural gaskets are generally not recommended.

Heat Transfer in Glazing Applications

The thermal conductivity of acrylic sheet is approximately one-fourth that of glass of equal thickness. This results in a better U value (lower heat loss) in single glazing. However, conducted heat loss through glazing is most effectively reduced by using multiple glazing. Winter heat loss through double glazing is roughly one-half that of single glazing. Summer heat gain also is reduced through multiple glazing.

Depending on the density of the tint, the use of solar gray or bronze tints can produce a very significant reduction in direct solar heat gain. The darker the tint is, the greater the reduction in direct solar heat gain. Tinted heat-absorbing acrylic sheet glazing is only effective in reducing direct solar heat gain when it is installed as the exterior light. The value of tinted sheet installed as the inner light is to reduce glare, but not the air-conditioning load. It acts the same as clear sheet with respect to reducing conducted heat loss and consequently the heating load.

U values for various acrylic sheet thicknesses and double glazing are given in Table 10. Shading coefficients for the range of solar gray and bronze tint densities are given in Table 8.

Skylights

Flat acrylic sheet can be used in skylight glazing following the design and installation details previously given for window glazing. In addition, permanent dead load deflection due to the weight of the sheet must be considered

Table 10. U Factor for Vertical Windows[a] **(Btu/h/ft²/°F)**[b]

Construction	Winter Heat Loss[c]					Summer Heat Gain[d]				
	Sheet Thickness, in.[e]					Sheet Thickness, in.[e]				
	0.125	0.1875	0.25	0.375	0.5	0.125	0.1875	0.25	0.375	0.5
Single glazed	1.06	1.01	0.96	0.88	0.81	0.98	0.93	0.89	0.82	0.76
Double glazed, ¼-in. air space	0.55	0.52	0.49	—	—	0.56	0.53	0.50	—	—
Double glazed, ½-in. air space	0.47	0.45	0.43	—	—	0.50	0.48	0.45	—	—

[a] Ref. 6.
[b] To convert btu/h/ft²/°F to W/m²/K multiply by 5.678.
[c] 15-mph wind velocity.
[d] 5-mph wind velocity.
[e] To convert in. to cm multiply by 2.54.

relative to aesthetics and function. Dead load deflection of approximately 0.5 in. (1.27 cm) has been shown by precedent to have little effect on aesthetics. It is not discernible from below and does not distort visibility through the glazing, although there may be some distortion in specular reflections. Flat skylight glazing panels should have a slope of at least 10° off the horizontal to assure rain runoff from dead load deflected areas. The greater potential for leakage in near-horizontal skylight installations warrants consideration of self-flashing details and/or perimeter gutters. Perimeter gutters are also used to intercept condensation.

Although used in flat sheet skylight installations, acrylic sheet has found far greater use and aesthetic appeal because of its fabrication versatility in formed skylight shapes. Formed shapes virtually eliminate deflection, increase load capacity, and simplify installation and sealant details. The most popular skylight shapes are vault arches, free-blown dome shapes, and pyramidal shapes.

Acrylic sheet barrel vault arches can be cold-formed in the field against smoothly curved mullions, as long as the radius of curvature is no less than 180 times the sheet thickness for cell cast and no less than 300 times the

sheet thickness for special-process Plexiglas MC types. Where design requires thicker sheets and/or sharper curvatures, the acrylic sheet can be shop-thermoformed. The heated sheet is draped over a simply curved arch form with the surface of the form properly prepared to minimize markoff on the formed panel. Figure 1 illustrates one of the many uses of cold-formed acrylic sheet.

Free-blown dome shapes are easily and economically formed by clamping the heated acrylic sheet over an open-end box and then applying a vacuum or positive air pressure. The sheet must be heated above the softening temperature. Since the sheet does not contact any form in the functional area, there is no mark-off to mar the appearance or optical clarity. The pyramidal shape is formed in a manner similar to that of the free-blown dome shape, with the additional insertion of a male ridge form. The sheet contacts the ridge form only along the ridge lines of the formed pyramidal shape. Mark-off is confined to these narrow bands so that there is no significant effect on the overall appearance and optical clarity of the finished unit. The use of acrylic sheet free-blown dome shapes as a roofing material is shown in Figure 2.

Figure 1. Use of cold-formed acrylic sheet. Courtesy of Rohm and Haas.

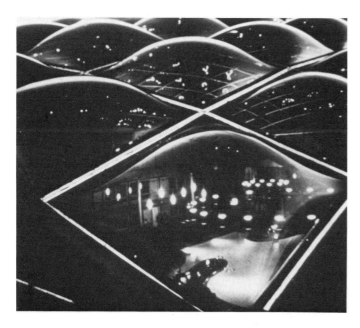

Figure 2. Transparent roof constructed from free-blown dome-shaped acrylic sheet. Courtesy of Rohm and Haas.

Skylight *U* Values and Shading Coefficients. Total winter and/or summer heat transfer through acrylic sheet skylights can be approximated by using the *U* values and shading coefficients (3). The conventional *U* values tabulated are suitable for estimating heating and cooling loads for sizing the equipment. However, determination of the overall functional economy of skylights should include solar heat gain and day lighting advantages. Essentially, solar heat gain during the heating season and day lighting during the cooling season are positive credits in the annual net energy balance through skylights.

Lighting

Acrylic sheet has outstanding optical properties and excellent resistance to prolonged exposure to both natural and electric light sources. This exposure stability, proven over many years of in-use experience, combined with good breakage resistance, strength characteristics, chemical resistance, and resistance to yellowing, makes it a preferred material for lighting lenses and diffusers, indoors and outdoors.

Acrylic sheets are easily cut to size for use as flat panels in lighting fixtures or luminous ceilings with due consideration for dead load deflection. Panels are commonly rigidized by thermoforming the sheets into the typical pan and spherical shapes used in lighting applications or by incorporating thermoformed ribs. Standard flat sheet colors and patterns provide light control by diffusion and shielding.

Acrylic molding pellets are easily processed by injection molding or extrusion for large-volume production of lighting lenses and diffusers. Injection molding provides crisp detail in optical elements, and the extrusion process produces continuous sheets or profile shapes for diffusing, refracting, and shielding applications. Both sheet and molding pellets are available in formulations specifically intended for controlling ultraviolet transmission.

Fluorescent Lighting. Many years of continuous exposure test data have proven that acrylics can withstand the effects of fluorescent lighting. Only a barely perceptible change in yellowness index occurs as measured by ASTM D-1925. The low operating temperature of fluorescent lighting allows exceptional freedom in designing the shape, size, and installation details for the part.

High-Intensity Discharge Lighting. Whether the lighting source is mercury vapor or sodium vapor, acrylics can be used effectively in lenses and diffusers, provided suitable precautions are taken to prevent excessive heat buildup. Also, mercury vapor lamps characteristically have high ultraviolet (uv) transmission; therefore, special uv-absorbing acrylic sheet should be used for maximum resistance to yellowing.

Incandescent Lighting. Incandescent lighting emits less uv radiation than fluorescent, but does generate more heat. The fixtures must then be properly designed to dissipate this heat and to allow adequate lamp-to-acrylic distance.

Installation Design. Lighting fixtures and supports for diffuser panels must allow for differential dimensional changes due to temperature and humidity fluctuations. An expansion clearance of 0.0625 in. (0.1587 cm) and a contraction allowance of 0.0625 in. (0.1587 cm) should be allowed in the fixture or frame for each foot of acrylic dimension for indoor applications. The allowances should be doubled for outdoor applications. Acrylic lenses and diffusers should not be rigidly fastened to metal lighting fixture frames or supports. Adequate ventilation and sufficient space between the lamp and the surface of the acrylic must be provided in the lighting fixture.

Signs

The availability of cast acrylic sheet after World War II revolutionized the design and construction of signs. For years a plastic sign was an acrylic sign, and acrylic plastic sheet served the sign industry well. Over the years, several additional plastic materials have become available to the sign manufacturer. These materials generally offer a specific advantageous characteristic or property such as sharper forming definition or exceptionally high impact strength. Standard acrylic sheet with its overall balance of properties will continue to find extensive application in signs, augmented by the use of, for example, extruded Plexiglas DR sheets for those applications requiring somewhat higher impact strength and sharper forming definition.

Acrylic flat sheets for sign faces are designed to resist wind loads in the same manner described above for acrylic sheet window glazing. However, since signs utilize translucent acrylic sheet color or clear acrylic sheet with the second-surface painting, a variety of reinforcing methods that blend with the sign appearance and extend the area of the sign face can be used. Flat faces can be reinforced with cemented ribs or tiebacks cemented to the back surface and spaced in accordance with design wind load requirements. Thermoformed corrugated and channel shapes can increase the load capacity of a sign face and also utilize tiebacks to further increase the overall area.

Sign lighting design utilizes lamp spacing, the lamp-to-acrylic distance, lamp characteristics, and the light transmittance of the acrylic to achieve the desired brightness of the sign background and logo.

Sign faces are generally installed in a complete perimeter frame similar to that required for glazing. The rabbet depth in sign applications will normally be greater than that required for glazing since there is no modifying effect of a warm interior temperature associated with glazing.

Specialty Applications

The specialty applications listed below may require special design analysis and/or special consideration of building codes and fire restrictions. Based on extensive field and laboratory experience, specific grades of acrylic are recommended for specific applications.

Bullet Resistance Glazing. Plexiglas SB/AR-3 is a special acrylic sheet produced with an abrasion-resistant coating for bullet resistance glazing applications. Plexiglas SB and SB/AC-3 in 1.25-in. (3.175-cm) thickness is rated by Underwriters Laboratories as resistant to bullets fired from medium-power handguns (UL-752MP5A).

Hockey Rink Glazing. Cast sheet (Plexiglas G) in 0.5-in. (1.27 cm) thickness has been used for protective glazing around hockey rinks to resist the impact of hockey pucks and the physical abuse from the players.

Sun Screens. Acrylic solar tints installed on the exterior side of windows subject to direct sunlight can control glare and solar heat gain with either partial or full window coverage.

Fascia. Thermoformed acrylic panels can supply decorative shapes and/or identifying logos, in colors, to the fascia of a building. Additionally, the acrylic sheet fascia panels can be backlighted to provide a striking night appearance.

Aquariums. Acrylic is in use in a number of large aquarium glazing applications. Even in thicknesses of several inches, it retains its optical clarity with no significant drop in light transmission. Pressure applications of acrylic plastic go back to specially designed windows in the submersible vessel "Trieste" used by August and Jacques Piccard in their deep ocean explorations. Piccard found that, unlike glass, acrylic plastic yields under compression without fracturing and thus transfers some overload beyond the elastic limit to the surrounding hull.

Chairmats. Plexiglas MC and G with patterned surfaces are used as chairmats to protect the carpeting but allow it to show through.

Solar Collectors. Acrylic sheet, with its thermoforming characteristic that allows some rigidizing shape, has been used for collector glazing applications varying from photovoltaics to low-temperature flat plate collectors.

Acrylic Mirrors. Acrylic mirrors are intended primarily for relatively small interior applications for decoration, display, and/or safety considerations that require the breakage resistance of acrylic plastic sheet.

ACRYLIC ALLOY SHEET

Acrylic alloy polymers are an alloyed mixture of poly(vinyl chloride) (PVC) and an acrylic polymer. Materials of this type have high strength and impact resistance, are resilient, and have excellent abrasion resistance, dimensional stability, and electrical and chemical resistance. Their thermoforming characteristics are excellent. They generally are recommended for interior application; however, their weathering resistance is adequate for many applications. The acrylic alloy polymer does not ignite readily; however, at temperatures in excess of 400°F (204°C), hydrochloric acid fumes may be released. In a fire, it will burn and produce thick acrid smoke. Its physical properties have been published (14). The main uses of the acrylic alloy polymer are in wall coverings and in objects made by the thermoforming of a sheet of the materials.

Wallcoverings and Thermoformed Objects

Acrylic–PVC alloy polymers are extremely durable and tough. When compared with other wall covering systems, such as vinyl wall covering, painted plaster, ceramic tile, stainless steel, or decorative laminates, the acrylic alloy polymer provides a unique combination of durable features at reasonable installed cost. The acrylic–PVC alloy of polymer has

- Excellent stain and corrosion resistance.
- High impact, scuff, dent, and gouge resistance.
- Cleanability with household and commercial cleaners.

- Easy installation.
- Low installation and maintenance costs.
- Underwriters Laboratories listing.

Instructions for the cutting and machining of acrylic–PVC alloy sheet may be found in Ref. 15; thermoforming instructions may be found in Ref. 16; installation as a wall covering may be found in Ref. 17.

Protective Coatings

Both acrylic solution and emulsion polymers are utilized as the binder or vehicle for a broad range of coatings that can be classified as paints, vertical and roof mastics, latex modified stucco, floor polishes, wood finishes, and so on. In addition, caulks, adhesives, and grouting adhesives are formulated from the acrylic. Both the solution polymer and the emulsion polymer are moderate- to high-molecular-weight polymers that form films just on the evaporation of water or solvent. For this reason, final properties are achieved relatively rapidly under actual use conditions and do not depend on a chemical reaction. A paint is defined as any pigmented liquid, liquifiable or mastic composition, designed for application to a substrate in a thin layer which is converted to an opaque solid film after application; used for protection, decoration, or identification, or to serve some functional purpose such as filling or concealing surface irregularities, the modification of light and heat radiation characteristics, etc (18). In contrast to the paint, which is a thin coating, one of the definitions of a mastic is a high-build or thick coating.

Paint or Thin-film Coatings

Acrylics are widely used in all types of paint formulations. The clarity, toughness, light resistance, chemical resistance, and property stability make the acrylic ester dispersion (emulsion or latex) polymers prime candidates as paint vehicles. They are used as the vehicle or binder for interior, exterior, flat, semigloss, gloss, primer, and top coat, trade sales, or industrial coating paint systems.

Paint is composed primarily of the vehicle or binder, pigment, fillers, and additives incorporated to achieve specific properties. The pigment, usually titanium dioxide, is used to achieve opacity or hiding of the substrate. The vehicle or binder binds the pigment to the substrate and to other pigment particles. Extenders are usually clays or calcium carbonate emulsion paint that provide bulk and lower the cost of the paint film. In water-based emulsion paint, or latex paint, spherical polymer particles in the submicron (less than 0.001 mm in diameter) range, which are prepared by emulsion polymermization, are used as the vehicle. When the paint is applied to a substrate, water evaporates, leaving behind the paint film. Removal of water allows the acrylic plastic particles to contact the pigment, extender, and each other. On contact, deformable polymer particles adhere to their surroundings. The fusion of the ingredients of the paint film to each other allows the forming of a continuous and cohesive film. Acrylic paints have had about 35 years of use history; in terms of durability, they have consistently outperformed paints based on oils, alkyds, butadiene–styrene, and vinyl acetate. Typical paint formulations and specifications are given in Ref. 18. As further background, general techniques for manufacturing acrylic latex paints are given in Refs. 1 and 19. Water-borne maintenance coatings are making significant inroads into the maintenance market because of concern for pollution by solvents, the toxicity of lead and chromates in conventional oil paints, the economy of paint, and performance on less than ideal surfaces. Acrylic latex coatings are competing in the marketplace for use in the production of structural steel (20), bridges, tanks, galvanized metal, and so on. The chemistry of water-based acrylic polymers used for industrial finishing is detailed in Ref. 15.

Solution polymers are applied to surfaces either clear or formulated with pigment. Clear acrylic solution coatings are used to protect the luster of polished zinc, copper, and brass (21, 22). The solution polymer-based paint is used where rapid drying, adhesion to greasy or other hydrophobic surfaces, extremely high gloss or extremely smooth finishes are required. The technology and formulation of high-solids-solution acrylic resins as baking enamels (factory-applied finishes that require high temperature to attain ultimate properties) are reviewed in Ref. 23.

Vertical Mastics

Exterior elastomeric masonry coatings serve both in new construction and to bridge and cover flaws and cracks in old construction. The vertical mastic is applied in thick films (usually from a water-based system), which, on the evaporation of water, form an elastic membrane that remains elastic even at low temperature (ie, −35°C), is nontacky, and resists dirt pickup at high temperature. Conventional thin paint films must be relatively hard at normal use temperature in order to achieve the toughness, abrasion resistance, and low degree of permeability that is required. As a consequence, conventional paint films tend to be brittle at low temperatures; however, they are adequate for the task for which they were designed. Vertical mastics provide for low-cost, lightweight, and easy construction or repair of building walls with high insulation value. Vertical mastic development had its origin in Europe after World War II. The need for new, rapid, and inexpensive methods to facilitate the rebuilding of Europe advanced this technology.

Vertical roof mastics, as contrasted with horizontal roof mastics, tend to be available in many more colors. The properties and formulation of vertical roof mastics are given in Ref. 24.

Details and examples of solid vertical wall construction and standard panel construction are illustrated in Figures 3–6.

Roof Mastics (Horizontal Mastics)

Acrylic latex-based roof mastics are reflective protective coatings that can be applied over existing roofing substrates such as galvanized steel, wood, conventional built-up roofs, or polyurethane foam asphalt shingles, or they

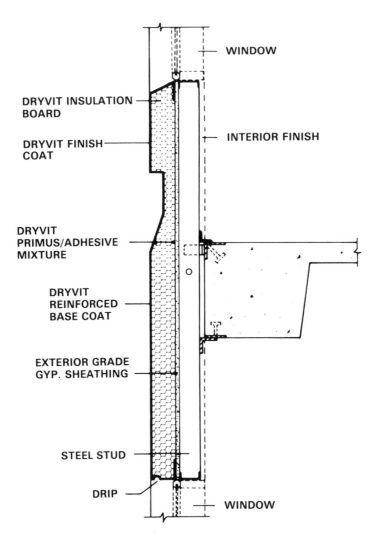

DRYVIT INSULATION
BOARD

DRYVIT FINISH
COAT

DRYVIT
PRIMUS/ADHESIVE
MIXTURE

DRYVIT
REINFORCED
BASE COAT

EXTERIOR GRADE
GYP. SHEATHING

STEEL STUD

DRIP

WINDOW

INTERIOR FINISH

WINDOW

SPANDREL PANEL

Figure 3. Spandrel panel (29). Courtesy of Dryvit System Inc.

can be applied over new elastomeric and/or roofing materials. The mastic coatings, which are usually 30–50 wet mils thick, are considerably thicker than those applied with conventional paint. Conventional paints do not have the capacity to expand and contract with the substrate as do the elastomeric mastics. Properly formulated acrylic latex roof mastics remain flexible, even at temperatures as low as 30°F (−1°C), are tack free at elevated roof temperatures, and resist dirt pickup. The acrylic roof mastic protects underlying surfaces, substances, and spaces from heat, light degradation, water, and water vapor. The acrylic roof mastic applied over polyurethane foam protects the urethane foam from uv sun radiation. Unprotected polyurethane foams, which are applied as insulating materials, crumble and split when exposed to sunlight and moisture. An unprotected polyurethane foam is destroyed on even modest exposure to sunlight if not protected by the acrylic latex-based roof mastic. Water and moisture further accelerate the degradation (27).

The protective acrylic roof mastic not only serves as a barrier to uv radiation, but also reduces the temperature

of the roof and the temperature of the interior under the roof. A comparison between black roof shingles and shingles covered with an acrylic roof mastic is given in Table 11. These data show the considerable difference between the temperature on and under the roof surface and that of the confined air space below the roof. Cooler roof conditions also result in less thermal shock to the roof and connecting members. For air-conditioned structures, lower air-conditioning costs result.

Acrylic latex-based roof mastics, which utilize the ingredients commonly found in paints, caulks, adhesives, and similar substances, are easily formulated and are easily applied by airless sprayers, squeegees, or trowels (28). These water-based finishes, compared with most of the conventional finishing materials, offer minimal hazards to workers; there are no obnoxious fumes, and the application equipment is lightweight and easy to handle. In contrast, the conventional equipment used to apply bitumen coating is bulky, heavy, and dangerous because of the high application temperatures.

Environmental pollution is minimized with acrylic mas-

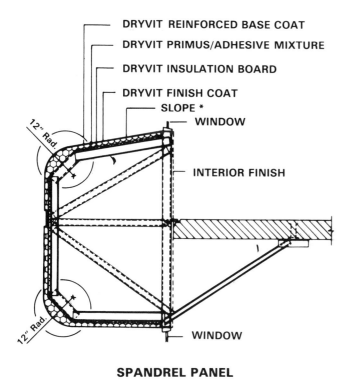

DRYVIT REINFORCED BASE COAT
DRYVIT PRIMUS/ADHESIVE MIXTURE
DRYVIT INSULATION BOARD
DRYVIT FINISH COAT
SLOPE *
WINDOW

INTERIOR FINISH

12" Rad.

12" Rad.

WINDOW

SPANDREL PANEL

* SLOPE MUST BE A MINIMUM OF 6″ OF RISE
IN 12″ OF HORIZONTAL PROJECTION

Figure 4. Spandrel panel (29). Courtesy of Dryvit System Inc.

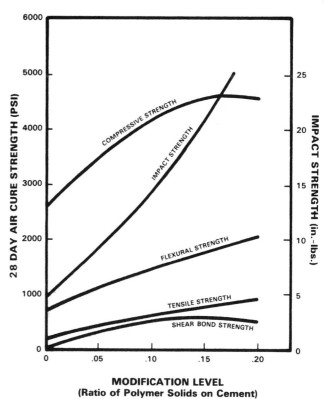

**PERFORMANCE PROPERTIES
vs.
LEVEL OF POLYMER MODIFICATION**

**MODIFICATION LEVEL
(Ratio of Polymer Solids on Cement)**

Figure 5. Performance properties vs level of polymer modification (25).

tic, and cleanup is done with water, not flammable solvents. Application and drying are rapid, thus minimizing labor costs (28).

Elastomeric Roofing Materials

Elastomeric roofing, in the past decade, has become a strong competitor for use in low-sloped industrial roofing. Bituminous built-up roofing is increasing in cost and diminishing in quality as the quality of tar decreases and labor costs increase.

Elastomeric roofing is available in preformed sheets or as a liquid mastic. Membranes formulated from acrylic polymers and applied as a liquid mastic solidify on evaporation of water or solvent to form a continuous, seamless weather barrier. Fluid-applied elastomeric membranes form much better weathertight seals than do the sheet-applied membranes. The above is especially true for roofs with extreme curvatures or surface shapes that are interrupted by vent openings, skylights, or equipment. The application equipment, like that used for the vertical mastic, is simple, and the application is rapid. Airless sprays, brushes, rollers, squeegees, and trowels are used. The thickness of the membrane is controlled by the amount applied, the workmanship of the applier, and the roughness of the surface.

Sheet-applied membranes generally cost more than fluid-applied membranes, and they are more difficult to install, especially over irregular surfaces. Sheets offer an advantage in that they can be applied over a greater temperature range than liquids; they are produced under carefully controlled factory conditions, and thus their quality is good. On the negative side, elastomeric sheet membranes require more care to prevent puncture by sharp projections in the substrate. Seams of the membranes are bonded to prevent leakage. The membrane may be bonded to the roof or held in place with a ballast of gravel or concrete pavers.

A comparison of the design and installation criteria for liquid-applied vs sheet-applied coatings is given in Table 12.

The choice of the acrylic polymer to be used for a specific application is extremely critical. The term acrylic can be applied to a large number of chemical compositions that can differ widely in properties. It is extremely important to use an acrylic vehicle that was specifically designed for the task. As an example, acrylics can vary widely in their ability to adhere to polyurethane foam. High-density foam frequently is preferred by designers because it is tougher and better able to endure pedestrian traffic or the vibrations of heavy equipment such as air-conditioning equipment. However, as the density of the foam increases, it becomes increasingly difficult for a coating to adhere to it. There are, however, acrylic dispersion polymers that are designed to adhere to polyurethane foams of varying

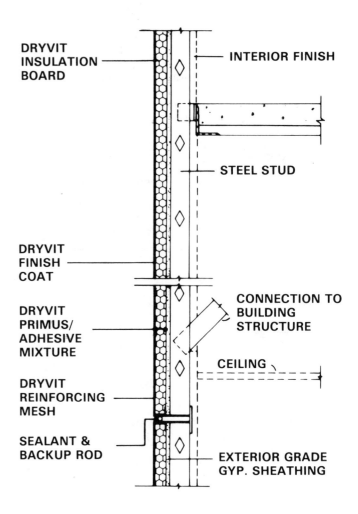

Figure 6. Panel at solid vertical wall (29). Courtesy of Dryvit System Inc.

PANEL AT SOLID VERTICAL WALL

densities and where the bond between the polyurethane foam and the coating is stronger than the cohesive force within the foam. Another example is ponding resistance, the resistance to water that lays on the surface for an extended time period. Older acrylic compositions failed by allowing water to pass through the film and also by blistering. Specifically designed and properly formulated acrylics have the required resistance. Thus, the proper choice of acrylic vehicle is vital for success. If possible,

tests should be performed to make certain that an optimum system will be employed.

Acrylic–Cement Coatings

Acrylic–cement mixture applications range from those for cement admixtures, bond coatings, surface coating binders, adhesives, mastics, and bitumen improvers (26) to those for composite structured insulation and protective coatings

Table 11. Effect of Surface Temperature on Interior Temperatures[a]

		Temperature, °F					
		Black Shingle		Reflective Mastic		Differential	
Weather Conditions	Air	Roof Surface	Interior	Roof Surface	Interior	Roof Surface	Interior
Complete shade	71	62	69	58	68	4	1
Bright sun	84	108	94	88	85	20	9
Bright sun	114	115	130	112	107	43	23
Bright sun	111	153	110	102	93	51	17
Bright sun	112	140	126	118	111	22	15

[a] Ref. 27.

Table 12. Design and Installation Criteria for Elastomeric Roof Coatings, Liquid Applied vs Sheet Applied[a]

Criteria	Liquid Applied	Preformed Sheet
Fastening/adhesion	• Continuous bond (spray, brush, roller)	• Loose laid • Mechanically fastened • Bonded (adhered)
Laps/splices	• No joints	• Heat fused • Solvent welded • Solvent and tape (clean lap is essential; overheating or excessive solvent may lead to failure)
Perimeter	• Self-sealing, allow for expansion and differential movement	• PVC-clad metal • Adhesive bond • Heat fused (all components must be well anchored)
Repair of damage	• Clean and recoat with same or compatible compound	• Use approved patching materials and cement
Prefabricated	• No prefabricated accessories	• PVC-clad flashings at curbs for use with PVC • Adhesives or heat fused at horizontal flanges; counterflash with same materials at edges
Ballast	• No ballast	• Loose-laid systems require ballast
Coatings	• Some systems are multicoat	• Some systems use uv-resistant coating on unballasted systems, eg, hypalon over neoprene
Compatibility over bitumen	• Depends on the particular compound and formulation • No compatibility problems experienced with acrylic systems	• Depends on the particular compound or formulation
Installation constraints and substrate	• Clean, dry substrate • Low-wind conditions for spray application • No foot traffic until membrane is cured • Apply second coat in a direction perpendicular to first • Some moisture permissible with acrylic latex systems	• Low-wind conditions • Clean substrate, no sharp projections • Cold temperature and excessive solvent retard weld time • Some moisture permissible with permeable materials • Clean lap joint essential, especially with EPDM
Susceptibility	• Gouging or thin coat could lead to premature failure of membrane	• Visual discoloration from overheating could be a potential failure point • Cigarette burns must be avoided (also flammable solvent)
Structural capacity of roof deck	• Materials are lightweight, therefore suitable over existing roofs	• Most systems may be used over existing roof; if ballast is used, check structural capacity of deck
Slope	• No real slope restrictions; most can be applied from horizontal to vertical	• Fully adhered and mechanically fastened systems may be used at greater slopes than loose-laid systems

[a] Ref. 28.

that can be applied on-site or can easily be prefabricated into lightweight strong panels that are inexpensively applied to new or existing structures.

Acrylic Modifiers for Cement

Acrylic polymer modification of cement produces stronger, more durable, water- and abrasion-resistant compositions that bond to a variety of substrates, including concrete, masonry, brick, glass, wood, metal, and polymeric foam. Acrylic-modified cement has superior freeze/thaw resistance, proven long-term durability on exterior exposure, good chemical resistance in general-purpose applications, and unequaled resistance to discoloration on exposure to sunlight and weather.

Acrylic latex, when properly incorporated (thoroughly mixed and unagglomerated) into a cement mix and applied under typical application conditions, tends to form a continuous matrix on hydration and drying. The acrylic polymer spheres form a continuous polymer matrix that coats the hydrated cement agglomerates and grains. The polymer matrix acts as a barrier to moisture leaving the cement, providing better hydration of the cement and also forming a polymer network, which increases the durability of the final product. The surfactant on the polymer particle surface acts as a lubricant between sand and stone parti-

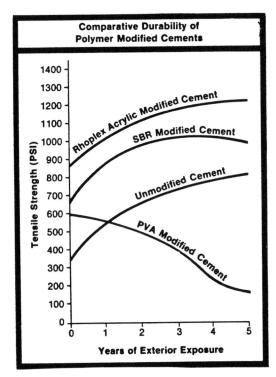

Figure 7. Comparative durability of polymer-modified cements (26). Courtesy of SCI.

cles, thereby improving the workability of the cement. In addition, the acrylic latex, by providing a lubricant, increases the density of the cement by allowing better particle packing, thereby lowering the tendency for cracking due to shrinkage of the cement on drying. The polymer film on the inner surface of the cement greatly increases adhesion of the cement to substrates, and that on the outer surface, along with the better packing or higher density, provides a water-resistant material with excellent freeze/thaw characteristics and chemical resistance.

Typical physical strength properties of modified vs unmodified cement are available (26). Marked improvement in physical properties under both wet and dry test conditions is noted.

The comparative durability of polymer-modified cements is quantitatively shown in Figure 7. The acrylic does not discolor, as does the styrene–butadiene type, or decrease in properties because of hydrolysis, as is typical of the poly(vinyl acetate) type (25,26).

Acrylics are also available as finely divided powders (> 60 μm). Acrylic powders are intended primarily for use in one-package dry mortar mixes.

Spray-applied acrylic–cement coatings are formulated from white cement, pigment, aggregates, and acrylic polymer particles plus performance additives. With the spray-applied mortar, application time is minimized, and the amount of mortar used is reduced. Since less material is needed, the layers are thin and light. Unmodified cement is singularly fragile in thin sections; properly modified acrylic–cement thin sections are strong, durable, and water-resistant. Cement-modified mortars can be used indoors or outdoors. Spray coats are particularly well suited for decorative finishing and refinishing. The thin spray

coat can be used to preserve the outline of moldings or other architectural details that might be obscured were the coating applied by troweling. Mortars of this type are also excellent penetrants and pore sealants for heavy-duty cement objects, concrete block, and masonry. Multiple-substrate surfaces of buildings can be coordinated by using a cement spray coat that adheres uniformly to the individual surfaces. Starting formulations for acrylic latex-modified mortar, acrylic powders, and white mortar spray coats modified with acrylic latex have been published (26,30). The properties of acrylic-modified cement and acrylic powders are also available.

Composite Cement Acrylic Systems

Outsulation, a system of Dryvit Systems, Inc., West Warwick, R.I., is an example of a newer trend in building construction. Outsulation consists of four major components: expanded polystyrene insulation, a cementitious acrylic-modified adhesive, a woven fiber glass-reinforced mesh, and a 100% acrylic finish coat (31). Figure 3 illustrates the construction of the composite. The acrylic-modified adhesive joins the polystyrene insulation and the fiber glass mesh or substrate to the building; the outer acrylic finish provides protection, color, and texture to the building. Outsulation can be used to retrofit existing buildings or in new construction. The systems can be fitted and applied directly to the building or prefabricated into sections and then installed on the building. The manufacturer claims that an energy savings of 30–40% is frequently experienced on the retrofit of existing buildings. Dryvit states the following advantages of Outsulation (29):

1. The panels weigh far less than brick or precast concrete, thus reducing weight and wall costs.
2. It reduces thermal shock and provides sealing thermal bridges.
3. Oversized panels of complicated shapes and incorporating windows can be raised in place easily, thus increasing speed of construction.
4. Lightweight cranes or rigging are all that is required to raise panels into place.
5. Panels are quickly welded and/or bolted to the building frame from the inside.
6. The exterior surface of the panel is fade- and stain-resistant.
7. Aesthetic details and three-dimensional shapes may be easily incorporated into a panel during fabrication.
8. The choice of surface textures and colors allows for infinite design possibilities. Detailed examples of solid vertical wall and spandrel panels are given in Figures 4–6.

BIBLIOGRAPHY

1. B. B. Kine and R. W. Novak in M. Grayson, ed., *Encyclopedia of Polymer Science and Engineering,* 2nd ed., Vol. 1, John Wiley & Sons, Inc., New York, 1984, pp 234–299.
2. *Plexiglas Design and Fabrication Data,* PL-1p, Rohm and Haas Co., Philadelphia, Pa., 1983.

3. *Structural Design Requirements for Dome Skylights Using Plexiglas Acrylic Plastic Sheet,* Pi-969b, Rohm and Haas Co., Philadelphia, Pa., 1975.

4. *Plexiglas Injection and Extrusion Molding Pellets,* PL-165f, Rohm & Haas Co., Philadelphia, Pa., 1968.

5. *Transparent Plexiglas Solar Control Series,* PL-791E, Rohm and Haas Co., Philadelphia, Pa., 1973.

6. *Plexiglas in Architecture,* PL-1047K, Rohm and Haas Co., Philadelphia, Pa., 1980.

7. *Plexiglas Molding Pellets for Lighting,* PL-926b, Rohm and Haas Co., Philadelphia, Pa., 1980.

8. F. J. Rarig, *NFPA Fire.* **67**(2), 34–38 (1973).

9. F. J. Rarig, *Progressive Architecture* (Oct. 1970).

10. *Cutting Plexiglas Acrylic Sheet,* PL-2K, Rohm and Haas Co., Philadelphia, Pa., 1983.

11. *Machining Plexiglas Brand Acrylic Sheet,* PL-3L, Rohm and Haas Co., Philadelphia, Pa., 1983.

12. *Forming Plexiglas Acrylic Sheet,* PL-4N, Rohm and Haas Co., Philadelphia, Pa., 1983.

13. *Cementing Plexiglas Brand Acrylic Sheet,* PL-7N, Rohm and Haas Co., Philadelphia, Pa., 1985.

14. *Kydex 100 Acrylic PVC,* PL-1409, Rohm and Haas Co., Philadelphia, Pa., 1982.

15. W. H. Brendley, Jr., and E. C. Carl, *Paint Varn. Prod.* **63,** 23 (1973).

16. *Kydex Sheet Thermoforming Manual,* PL-962b, Rohm and Haas Co., Philadelphia, Pa., 1980.

17. *Kydex Wallcovering Installation Manual,* PL-1006g, Rohm and Haas Co., Philadelphia, Pa., 1984.

18. *Paint/Coating Dictionary,* Federation of Societies for Coating Technology, Philadelphia, Pa., 1978.

19. *Resin Reviews,* Vol. 18, Rohm and Haas Co., Philadelphia, Pa. 1968, p. 23.

20. R. N. Washburne, *Am. Paint Coatings J.* **67,** 40 (1983); K. E. Buffington, *Maint. Eng.* (Mar. 1976); D. W. Zunker, *J. Coating Technol.* **48,** 37 (1976).

21. *Met. Finish* (Mar. 1966).

22. *Protecting the Surface of Copper and Copper Brass Alloys,* International Copper Research Association, New York.

23. R. R. Kuhn, N. Roman, and J. D. Whiteman, *Mod. Paint Coatings,* **71,** 50 (Sept. 1981).

24. *High Performance Elastomeric Wall Coatings,* 81A75, Rohm and Haas Co., Philadelphia, Pa., 1985.

25. *Cement Modifier Troubleshooting Guide,* 83D11, Rohm and Haas Co., Philadelphia, Pa., 1983.

26. R. Dennis, "Latex in Construction Industry," presented at the Meeting of the Road and Building Materials Group of the SCI, UK, Nov. 15, 1984.

27. *Mod. Paint Coatings,* 72 (Mar. 1982).

28. *Elastomeric Roof Mastics,* 83E4, Rohm and Haas Co., Philadelphia, Pa., Feb. 1982.

29. *Panelization with Dryvit Outsulation,* DS210, Dryvit System Inc., West Warwick, R.I., 1985.

30. J. A. Lavelle and P. E. Wright, *Resin Reviews* 24 (2), Rohm and Haas Co., Philadelphia, Pa., p. 3, 1974.

31. *Rohm & Haas Reporter* **39**(2), 10 (Summer 1981).

General References

J. Redtenbacher, *Liebiges Annalen Der Chemi* **47,** 125 (1843).

F. Englehorn, *Berichte* **13,** 433 (1880).

G. W. A. Kahlbaum, *Berichte* **13,** 2348 (1880).

E. H. Riddle, *Monomeric Acrylic Esters,* Reinhold Publishing Corp., New York, 1954.

M. Salkind, E. H. Riddle, and R. W. Keefer, *Ind. Eng. Chem.* **51,** 1282, 132 B (1959).

Chem. Week, 39 (Nov. 1981).

Chem. Purchasing, 13 (Jan. 1983).

Mod. Plast. **62,** 1 (Jan. 1985).

Cutting and Machining Kydex, Pl-1058b, Rohm and Haas Co., Philadelphia, Pa., 1979.

Preparation, Properties and Uses of Acrylic Polymers, CM-19ci, Rohm & Haas Co., Philadelphia, Pa., 1981.

See also Antistatic Agents; Foamed Plastics; Glass in Construction; Moisture Protection; Paints and Coatings; Plaster Systems; Plastics; Plastics, ABS; Roofing Systems; Sealants; Stucco, Synthetic.

Benjamin B. Kine, PhD
Thomas E. Will
Rohm and Haas Company
Spring House, Pennsylvania

ACSA. See Association of Collegiate Schools of Architecture (ACSA)

ADAPTIVE USE

Adaptive use is the field of architecture concerned with continuing a building or structure in service by means of creating a new use for it, or with reconfiguration of a building so its original use can continue in a new form that meets new requirements. It is sometimes called building modification or retrofitting. Adaptive use allows the recapture of the value the original building once held, using it and transforming it into new energy for the future. The success of adaptive use lies in the architect's ability to seize the potential of an existing structure and use it in its new life.

Adaptive use is preservation in that the original exterior form and even some parts of the interior are spared from destruction. It is restoration in that these elements of the building may be retained or reconstituted in their original or restored form. Adaptive use always involves the renovation or renewing of the structure, but differs from this simple term because of the reconfiguration required and the changes of use that are made.

Adaptive use concentrates on buildings that, while solid pieces of architecture, have fallen into disuse and disrepair. It tries to create spaces and environments where people feel comfortable, because they speak to an earlier age that people miss and want to see again.

The philosophy behind this type of architecture is expressed in an old New England proverb: "Use it up; wear it out; Make it do —or do without." So it is not surprising that the most intensive application of adaptive use has been in the New England area, not only because buildings with reuse potential abound there, but because community and development values are receptive to dealing with the built environment in this way.

HISTORY OF ADAPTIVE USE IN THE UNITED STATES

"There was an old woman who lived in a shoe . . . Would you?" The adaptive use illustrated by this variation on the familiar nursery rhyme would seem stranger to Americans than to most other peoples of the world. The belief that new is better has been ingrained almost since the start of the American nation. The dominant influence of the frontier in American history put a premium on new spaces and new opportunities. The United States is still the leading example of the disposable society, its economy heavily oriented to planned obsolescence. In Europe and the Orient, by contrast, the cultural value system keeps people from automatically discarding what they use. There is a respect for materials, an appreciation of nature, and a sense of renewal and growth through the continued use of possessions.

When U.S. cities undertook renewal after World War II, their first instinct was to tear down, start fresh, and build anew. New federally sponsored programs sought the elimination of neighborhood slums and blight, the construction of housing for the poor and elderly, and the building of new intracity freeways. As a consequence, entire city neighborhoods were torn down and often replaced by sterile mid- and high-rise buildings with neither beauty, joy, nor human dignity in their design. For middle income and affluent citizens, the dream environment became the suburb, with its new one-family houses and good schools. Inner city neighborhoods not gutted by urban renewal were often decimated or divided by highways intended to bring suburban workers to the city.

1958–1968: Decade of Discovery

The period 1958–1968 saw a reaction against renewal; many new projects deteriorated. Their unappetizing spaces were mistreated by their tenants. The buildings themselves were hard to maintain and keep secure against theft and vandalism. As the devastation created by urban renewal and highway building became clear to neighborhood residents, they formed community organizations designed to stop it. At the same time, a growing nostalgia was developing for the more graceful and human environments of the past.

This decade saw a gradually expanding back-to-the-city movement, with new interest in renovation and restoration of the existing downtown housing stock, and the growing power of the civic alliances formed to encourage preservation. The idea of adapting old buildings for commercial use was slower to spread. Because developers saw little profit in investing in run-down neighborhoods, financing was difficult to obtain. The very first attempts made were in Gaslight Square in St. Louis and Old Town in Chicago. Here, areas of small town houses and commercial buildings were restored and converted into restaurants and shops. Initially, they proved to be solid economic values, but some of these areas did not remain commercially viable over time. However, this very failure led to a better understanding of what was required to create an exciting physical environment that would draw the public and its spending to the area.

Pioneer Square in Seattle is perhaps the best example of how concerns about people brought forth development solutions, first for the buildings surrounding the Square and later as part of a rejuvenation of the center city. Seattle showed that it respected and valued its homeless by permitting them free and unregimented use of areas such as Pioneer Square, a wonderful and comfortable space near the waterfront and old marketplace. This caring approach brought many street people to Pioneer Place, and soon drew attention to the space itself. In the late 1950s, architects and developers who noted the attractive human scale of the square began to direct their attention to the buildings that faced onto it. By 1968, these same buildings had brought a new life into the downtown with new people, jobs, and residences joining those already there. Today, development has spread along the waterfront to a renewed Pikes Place Market, another focus for continued urban vitality.

The mid- and late 1960s saw pioneering efforts at adaptive use in San Francisco and Boston, two cities with an especially rich stock of fine old architecture. In San Francisco, an 1890s chocolate factory adjacent to Fisherman's Wharf was converted, in stages, into a multilevel specialty shopping and restaurant center known as Ghirardelli Square, with close to 200,000 ft^2 of usable space. The very special location of Ghirardelli Square, in an area that already drew enormous numbers of tourists, was an important characteristic of its reuse potential, but its success turned on the ability of the architects to reuse the existing structure in a meaningful new configuration at reasonable cost, in an area where new construction would have been prohibitively costly.

In Boston, the Prince Macaroni Building became an important prototype. Built during World War I as a warehouse for spaghetti awaiting shipment to American soldiers overseas, it had served out its first useful life by the early 1960s and was slated for demolition (Fig. 1). Its location on the edge of Boston's harbor, with spectacular views of both city and sea, made it a natural site for apartments. Again, because financing was not easily available, the imaginative use of structural resources was essential. For example, the architects wished to add 2½ floors to the top of the structure, where better views of the water could command higher rents. Code loadings for the warehouse foundations would support this addition. By designing narrow apartments that ran the length of the building from water to city, and by limiting elevator access and corridor to every third floor with access to individual apartments by interior stairs, the harbor view living areas could take advantage of the full 12-ft ceiling height (Fig. 2). When it became clear that a major expense would be incurred every time the 12-in. structural slab was penetrated, it was decided to lay piping and ducts on top of the slab and punch holes through it only for toilet piping. These systems were covered with a raised floor in the rear bedroom and kitchen–dining areas. The cost of construction was under $12/ft^2, very modest for 1967.

1968–1978: Decade of New Strategy

By the end of the 1960s, a new awareness was emerging in American cities about the value of older buildings and their potential for new uses as housing, offices, and shops.

(a)

Figure 1. Prince Macaroni Building, Boston, Mass. Architects: J. Timothy Anderson & Associates, Inc. **(a)** A derelict warehouse, the Prince Macaroni Building on Boston's waterfront awaited demolition. Courtesy of the architects. **(b)** Converted to apartments with views overlooking harbor and city, the Prince Macaroni Building became an adaptive use prototype. Courtesy of Hutchins Photography, Inc.

(b)

This set the stage for a new strategy for architecture and planning. Central to this strategy was growing public concern for the preservation of built resources reflected in the rise of the preservationist movement as a civic, cultural, and political force. Thousands of citizens became involved in the development of historic districts and the designation of historic landmarks. Their opposition to the bulldozing of older structures brought a stop to the urban renewal clearance of the 1960s.

The energy crisis of the early 1970s provided another breakthrough. Living in and commuting to the suburbs became more expensive. The cost of labor and materials

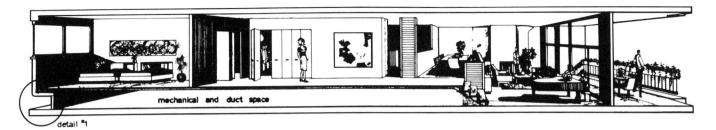

mechanical and duct space

detail #1

TYPICAL APARTMENT SECTION A-A

Figure 2. Prince Macaroni Building in Boston, Mass. Section through typical apartment showing raised floor and full-height living area. Courtesy of Notter Finegold + Alexander Inc.

for new construction rose sharply. Reuse of existing buildings could not only save fuel and transportation costs, but could itself be a major energy savings strategy, since the energy (BTU) component involved in the manufacture of new construction material was very high. For the first time, adaptive use had an economic advantage over new construction in terms of both time and money.

These pressures and changes also led to government policies that gave significant encouragement to adaptive use. Local tax easements and abatements, federal Urban Development Action grants, and various types of subsidized loans lured investors and developers into the field. By far the most powerful incentive was the investment credit in federal tax law, first enacted in 1978, which offered a dollar-for-dollar reduction in tax owed for investment in rehabilitation. Credits in the 1981 tax law ranged from 15% of cost in the case of nonresidential buildings over 30 years in age to 25% in the case of certified rehabilitation of certified historic structures.

1978–1988: Decade of Acceptance

By the end of the 1970s, adaptive use had established its niche in the urban framework and its practitioners had developed increasingly sophisticated systems and solutions. The stage was set for a virtual explosion of projects throughout the nation. Schools, libraries, public buildings, theaters, residential structures, hotels, commercial buildings, railroad stations, factories, and warehouses underwent adaptive treatment. Festival marketplaces sprang up in one community after another. Citizen involvement in preservation continued at an even higher level of interest. A literature of adaptive use grew up, allowing architects to learn from each other's experiences.

By the mid-1980s, major developers across the country had completed or undertaken major reuse projects. An estimated $11 billion had been invested in historical rehabilitation since 1977. The federal government had granted an estimated $2.2 billion in tax credits covering 16,805 projects. While a decade earlier, only 10% of the nation's architects reported adaptive use as a significant portion of their practice, by the mid-1980s, this had risen to over 80%. The convergent forces of economics, public concern, building resource and energy constraints, and tax incentives had joined with architectural ingenuity to result in a major nationwide initiative that changed the character and dynamics of U.S. cities.

ADAPTIVE USE IN EUROPE

During the same period, European countries used this architectural technique to add to their already rich heritage of preservation. The festival marketplace concept, illustrated in the U.S. by Boston's Faneuil Hall Marketplace and Baltimore's Harbor Place, was duplicated in such places as London's Covent Garden market, where the old wholesale shops that sold fruits and vegetables closed for a period of six years, were renovated, and reopened in 1980 as arcades, with boutiques, wine bars, shops, and entertainment. In Paris, the firm of Reichen and Robert made a major contribution to the urban fabric by successfully adapting many fine old industrial structures, such as a nineteenth-century factory in Tourcoing reconstituted as apartments and related commercial space, and La Villette, a former slaughterhouse grounds on the edge of Paris that was changed into a public park (Fig. 3). The Grande Halle at La Villette, a former cattle pen but one of the finest nineteenth-century cast-iron and steel industrial structures in Paris, was transformed into a flexible multipurpose public space. Completed by the architects Janvier and Jules de Merindol in 1866, the Grande Halle's special feature is simply five acres of unobstructed space. The challenge was to preserve this transparency and still provide for an ever-changing program—the ultimate multipurpose space. The exterior was carefully restored. The interior has been developed with new mezzanines along each side connected with bridges that provide a movable framework for scenery and lighting, and new underground support and service spaces have been added. All of this has been done with a minimum of intrusion, completely separate in their support and always clearly identified as new. The result is at once unique and appropriate.

ADAPTIVE USE AS A DESIGN PROBLEM

Most structures chosen for adaptive use have stood for over half a century. Some have already seen more than one use. The very fact that they still stand, while so many neighboring structures have been demolished, means they have some kind of special character. It could be their location, an outstanding design, some special spatial arrangements, superior materials, or any combination of these or other qualities.

The secret of successful adaptive use is to identify that

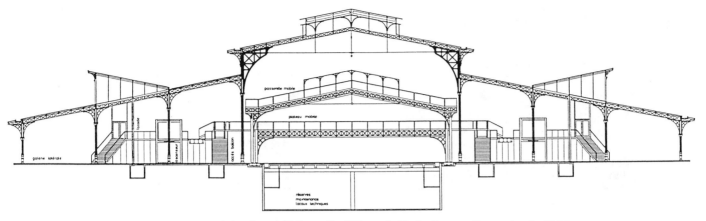

Figure 3. Section of the Grand Halle at La Villette in Paris, France. Conversion by Reichen and Robert of late nineteenth-century livestock market into five acres of unobstructed public exhibition space.

special value or character in the existing structure and fit it to the new use that is planned. All good architecture, old or new, must have that something special. In new buildings, the architect can create it; in old buildings, the architect must discover it.

Once this is done, the architect must determine whether the planned use can fit within the structure. Important questions that must be asked include:

- Will the new use work dimensionally?
- Is access possible and appropriate?
- Can the desired circulation plan be achieved?
- What kind of space will there be when it is finished?

These steps are no different from those involved in other architectural solutions. The extra dimension lies in evaluating existing systems, translating the new program into the existing structure, rearranging existing spaces and circulation, and finding new space. It is necessary to find the right fit. To discover it in an existing building is to find the soul of the building. To work with it is to achieve the delight and joy essential for design excellence in any type of architecture. By using design skill and judgment, the architect not only lets the new program work in the building, but maintains that specialness which gave the building its longevity in the first place.

Old City Hall, Boston, Mass. (Architects: Notter Finegold + Alexander Inc). This is one of the first examples of adaptive use of larger public structures during the 1968–1978 period (Fig. 4). Constructed in the 1860s over the existing foundations of a Bulfinch courthouse and designed in the French Empire style, it stood on prime property in the heart of the city. When city hall functions moved to a newer and larger building, a great deal of public discussion took place over what to do with it. Rather than allow its demolition and sale of the land for high rise development, the city of Boston leased the existing structure to a developer for 99 years in return for a percentage of the profits. The developer looked to the architect to find ways to secure another century of life for the structure.

There had been essentially no changes on the exterior since it was built. Only maintenance and a general cleaning were needed to restore it to its original appearance. Fixed glass was installed against the exterior trim and used to replace the double-hung windows to support installation of a new mechanical system. The interior was much more complex. To make the project economically viable, net rentable floor space had to exceed 80%. This required maximization of all available space, including new construction in both attic and basement, and a wholly new basic configuration of the building's plan.

The special feature that proved key to the development was the building's central space. Originally, it consisted entirely of a monumental stairway, extending through all four stories. As there was no realistic way to preserve the stairway under existing codes, the architects had to choose between treating it as open space, and making practical use of it. They chose the latter alternative, using the central space for new fire stairs, elevators, mechanical risers, an interior circulation system, and toilets. This freed the entire ring of the outer area for use as rentable space. This arrangement resulted in an unusually high net-to-gross ratio compared with new construction of the time, and allowed development of either multitenant or single-tenant floors (Fig. 5).

The existing structural masonry walls presented another challenge. Though very thick, they had been made from lime mortar instead of cement. Their structural capacity was severely limited, and by code no new loads could be added to them. A completely new structural system made of steel had to be placed in the center of the building, just within the masonry walls in the new circulation area, to support the new core elements and the new cooling towers on the roof. For the air systems to heat and cool the outer ring of rentable space, the architects chose pipes instead of the metal ducting in common use at that time. The smaller size of the pipes allowed them to penetrate the walls much more easily. (This was the first major use of water to heat air pumps in buildings of this type, a technique that has succeeded in many older installations adapted since that time.)

As often happens when the right systems are put in place, further analysis showed that during the spring and

(a)

(b)

Figure 4. Old City Hall, Boston, Mass. Architects: Notter Finegold + Alexander Inc. **(a)** The distinguished facade of Boston's Old City Hall before conversion. **(b)** Boston's Old City Hall after conversion to modern commercial office and restaurant uses. Courtesy of the architects.

fall, different exposures had different heating and cooling requirements at the same time of day. The net changes for water temperature when it returned for reheating or cooling was thus quite small, and the net energy usage for this purpose was minimal. To maximize energy savings in the colder months when more electric heat would be used, a separate exterior fin tube was placed around the entire outside perimeter and tied to an external thermostat. This supplemented the basic system by using circulating warm water to maintain a minimum of 65°F during the colder months. Individual heat–pump units located in the ceiling of the offices outside the ring of inner walls were fed by this piping system, an inexpensive way to allow individual offices to choose their own thermostat settings.

Door and window trim posed another challenge. Because the thickness of the walls varied so greatly, an inexpensive material had to be found that could be cut to any length and could also bend easily to fit the arched forms of the windows. Simple oak flooring was selected. Its use on the exterior wall also allowed the new glass, set against the existing frames, to be joined to a new wallboard, which was furred out from the existing masonry exterior wall to create a dead air space for insulation.

Old City Hall shows how adaptive use relies on the original building for its own solution. Offices mix comfort-

ably with restaurant uses and banking on the first floor and basement. Basement space expands outward onto the front lawn. Law offices are stacked vertically in the original tower. The solutions were simple, but the effect is not.

The project used new techniques because it was testing new concepts of adaptive use and because funding was limited. The initial budget was $22/ft^2$ without tenant standards, about two-thirds that of comparable space in new buildings of the time. Twenty years later, its rents have remained competitive with the newest of the high-rise offices because of the specialness of the original structure and the fit of the solution.

Butler Square, Minneapolis, Minn. (Architects: Miller Hanson Westerbeck Bell Architects Inc.). Built in 1906 to be a warehouse, this impressive, milltype structure occupied a full city block, boasted an impressive 500,000 ft^2, and was listed on the National Register of Historic Places. It was abandoned in 1964, but ten years later reopened as Butler Square, an early example of interior atrium design of office–retail space (Fig. 6).

The exterior was essentially unchanged, except for lowering the spandrels to allow floor-to-ceiling glazing. The key to the design solution for the interior was the building's unique structural system made of heavy timber. The beams, purlins, and decking of the system were exposed and became the ceiling of the new space throughout (Fig.

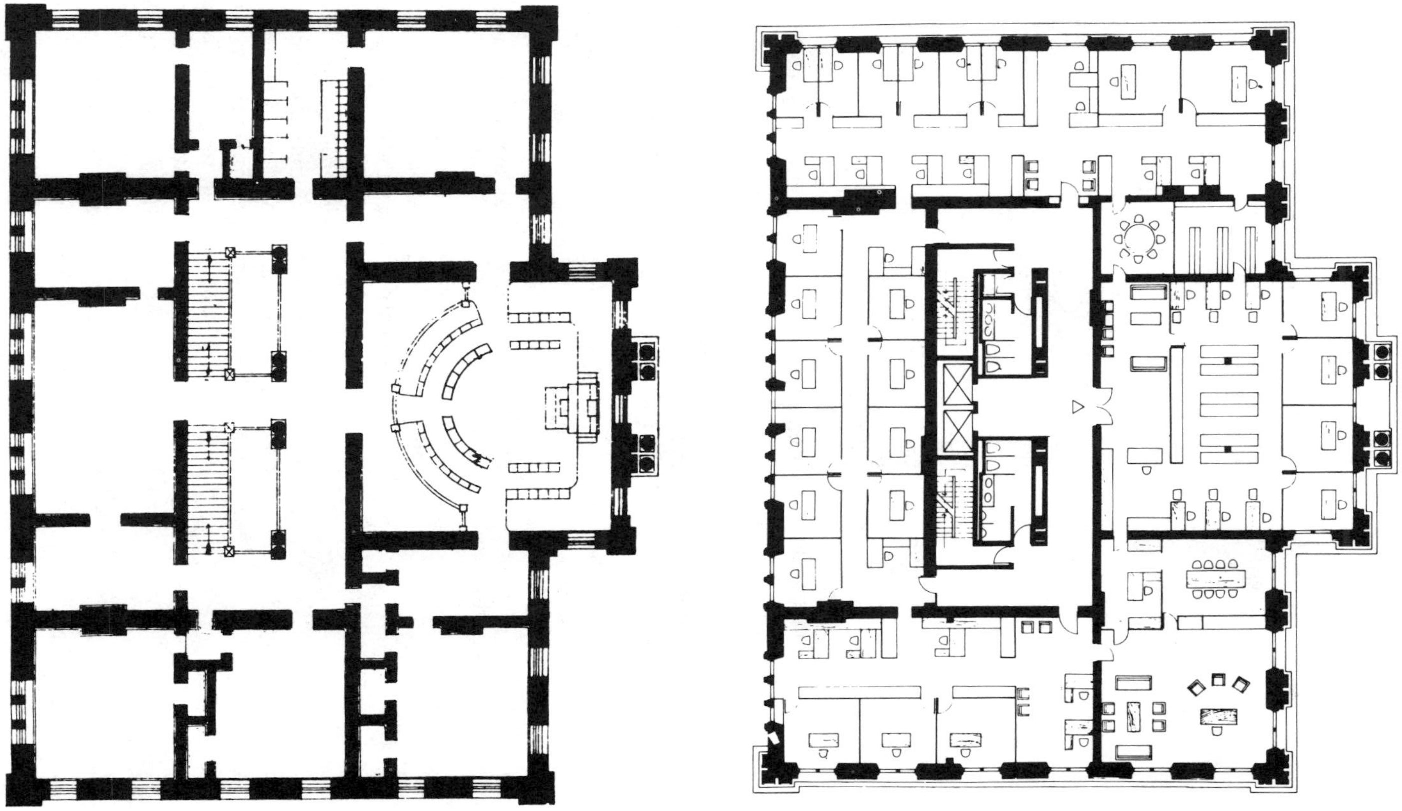

EXISTING PLAN

NEW PLAN

Figure 5. Floor plans of Old City Hall, Boston, Mass., before and after conversion. Architects: Notter Finegold + Alexander Inc. Courtesy of the architects.

Figure 6. The interior skylit atrium of Butler Square in Minneapolis, Minn., creates a dynamic office environment for workers in this converted mill structure. Architects: Miller Hanson Westerbeck Bell Architects Inc. Courtesy of the architects.

6). Mechanical space was created by raising the floors above the deck, rather than by dropping the ceiling. Individual bays were dismantled from the top down, creating an irregularly shaped skylit atrium, which brought in natural light and conserved energy (Fig. 7). The materials removed in the work were recycled in the details of other parts of the building.

The *Architectural Record* of December 1985 stated: "Butler Square is the compleat conversion—evidence that a strategically sited building, located in an area that has been declared ripe for renewal otherwise, can be turned to the service of commonly recognized commercial and business needs. But more than this, it is a reminder, in fundamental design terms, that the resources of the past and the requirements of the present day not only hinge upon each other in these belt-tight times. They can enhance each other. While it is recognized today that the profession

Figure 7. Butler Square, Minneapolis, Minn. Phase one section. Architects: Miller Hanson Westerbeck Bell Architects Inc. Courtesy of the architects.

of architecture is in a state of retrenchment, it is also in a state of reflection. At Butler Square, there are elements of both, and a good look at architecture's future—as it really was" (1).

Mechanics Hall, Worcester, Mass. (Architects: Notter Finegold + Alexander Inc). Sometimes a building can be restored to its original use simply by providing structural additions and new systems that make the use possible within the limitation of new code, access, and safety requirements. This was the case in Mechanics Hall, a wooden building constructed in 1857 with a concert hall on its third floor capable of accommodating 1700 people. The hall, which once hosted Caruso, Paderewski, Sousa, and others, had remarkable acoustics, but local interest in live musical performances waned. The hall was gradually relegated to hosting arena performances, wrestling, and finally roller skating. It was condemned as a fire hazard and closed in 1975. Its owners, the Mechanics Hall Association, had to choose between razing it, ending almost a century of its service to the community, and restoring it by providing the code requirements necessary for it to begin a new century of music and artists.

The architects' evaluation of the building's systems had to pay special attention to circulation and egress. The primary means was a wonderful monumental stair that led from the front entry up to a small, comfortable second floor hall, before branching left and right, then back and front to serve all four corners of the third floor auditorium. It was an impressive entrance, but as an exit it was a fire hazard because the entire audience had to leave the building through a single front door. The design treated the original rear wall of the building as a horizontal exit with a 2-h separation. A new back porch was built to the rear of the original building, providing a holding area of safe refuge at the third floor level of a glassed-in addition, easily accessible from the back street (Fig. 8). Additional new stairs as well as elevators were provided in this structure. The original hall was zoned into quadrants that carried vertically through the building, with separate controls and detection for smoke and fire, and the building was fully sprinklered. Throughout the process, the architects collaborated with state fire and code officials, who provided clear insight and judgment. Give and take on code issues is often essential if the special quality and character of fine old buildings is to be maintained. This process showed that code issues are essentially judgment issues based on clear thinking and common sense. They can admit some degree of flexibility without compromising safety.

The exterior of the hall, which fronted on Worcester's Main Street, was dirty. The original store fronts had been replaced by garish signs. For some obscure reason, two piers had been removed to widen the front doors. The exterior was cleaned and the piers replaced with fiber glass molded over existing cast-iron panels to replace those that were missing. New store fronts were designed, based on woodworking details from the original period (Fig. 9). Once the scaffolding and screens shielding the work were removed and a cleaned and restored front once again seen on Main Street, the other commercial establishments on the block experienced a 10% increase in sales even before the restored Mechanics Hall opened.

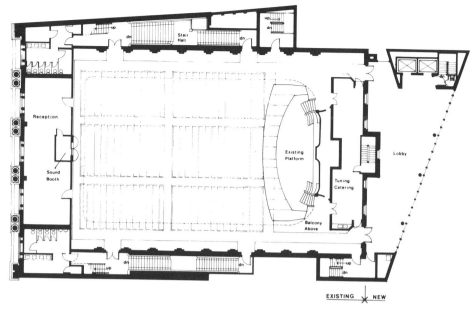

MECHANICS HALL

Figure 8. Mechanics Hall, Worcester, Mass. Floor plan with historic hall (left) and lobby addition (right). Architects: Notter Finegold + Alexander Inc. Courtesy of the architects.

Inside, common sense continued to govern. Once the egress walls and systems had been adapted to allow the hall to return to its original use, the interior finishes were restored to their original condition. New mechanical and electrical systems were put in place, and new cooling units were installed through the roof into the truss area. New steel plates were bolted into place on site to the truss connections to increase their capacity. Air was fed to a linear diffuser in one line along the bottom of the mezzanine structure. There is always the danger that, in a performance hall, too much change will affect the acoustics. This diffuser was the only addition to the original concert hall space, except for new chandeliers.

Though the original program anticipated only 25 or so performances annually, the hall was soon booked 365 days a year, often with more than one performance a day.

(a)

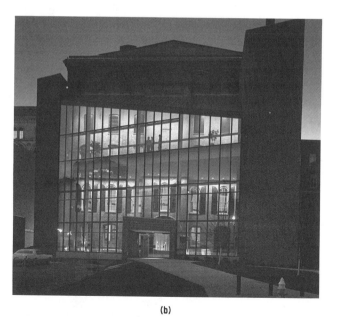

(b)

Figure 9. Mechanics Hall, Worcester, Mass. **(a)** Restored and refurbished, the fresh facade of Mechanics Hall boosted real estate values on Worcester's Main Street. **(b)** A sensitive addition to the rear of Mechanics Hall provides a unique night view of the historic building and adds safety features that meet building code requirements. Courtesy of Steve Rosenthal.

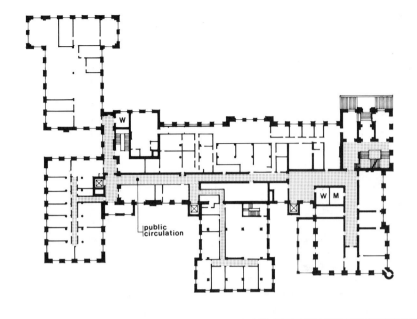

SECOND FLOOR EXISTING PLAN

AUDITORS' MAIN BUILDING
Washington, D.C.

(a)

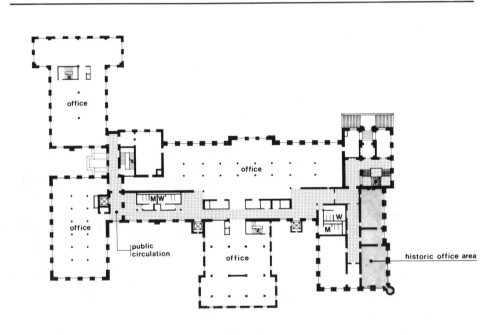

SECOND FLOOR NEW PLAN

AUDITORS' MAIN BUILDING
Washington, D.C.

(b)

Figure 10. Auditors' Main Building, Washington, D.C. Architects: Notter Finegold + Alexander/
Mariani. **(a)** Prior to renovation, the Auditors' Main Building was a warren of poorly lighted,
inefficient offices. **(b)** Open-plan offices within space restored to its original volume and accessed
through a clearly defined circulation system. Courtesy of the architects.

This impressive schedule, which also greatly enhanced the cultural reputation of the community, is a tribute not just to the vision of the Mechanics Hall Association, but to what the building always was.

Auditors' Main Building, Washington, D.C. (Architects: Notter Finegold + Alexander/Mariani). Some of the most impressive old structures in the United States are owned and operated by the federal government. Around 1976, the General Services Administration (GSA), the government's housekeeping arm, began to take a closer look at the possibility of keeping these buildings in service by adapting them to the new space requirements and systems. Its first effort was with the Auditors' Main Building in Washington, D.C., just before the Fourteenth Street Bridge. Originally the first Bureau of Printing and Engraving, it had been relegated to typical office functions of the GSA office support system. As one of the three public red brick buildings on the Mall (the other two are part of the Smithsonian Institution), it seemed highly desirable to develop some public use for the site. (Ultimately, Congress selected a portion of the site for the U.S. Holocaust Memorial Museum.)

The architect's study had to deal with many of the most important concerns of the second decade of adaptive use between 1978 and 1988. The design had to conform to the Cooperative Use Act of 1976, which required analysis of the building's response to the economics of the community, the environmental impact of the proposed uses on the community, the potential for energy conservation through reuse of existing structures, and the appropriateness of including public space in federal projects. The study, which developed over eight years, proved positive. The building is currently under construction and is scheduled for completion in 1989. While eight years is a long time, it places in perspective the magnitude of change that was occurring as one new value after another emerged and was included in the adaptive use process.

The original main building and its early additions required only cleaning, brick repair, and restoration of the original window sash. The interior plans developed logically (Fig. 10). With the elevators already fixed in their location and recently modernized, corridors were moved to relate better to the elevators. New toilets were located off the corridors. Wings of the building were treated as open-plan areas to accommodate the new space standards of the GSA. Since the open-plan layouts worked well with modular furniture and task lighting (Fig. 11), the dropped ceiling was eliminated, exposing the original vaulted ceiling whose interesting character was emphasized with indirect lighting. In some areas, where the original windows established by exterior elevation alone were above eye level, new floors were raised to accommodate them. Where attic roofs were too weak to bear office loads, new floors were suspended from roof structures which offered the extra capacity. Each space is unique and exciting, yet each was created in direct response to its own character and constraints. The new systems used will provide a modern life for this impressive old structure.

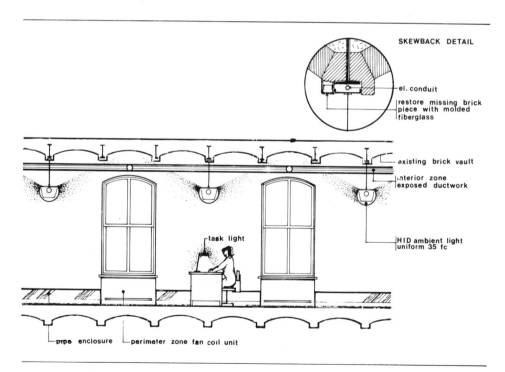

SKEWBACK DETAIL

el. conduit

restore missing brick piece with molded fiberglass

existing brick vault

interior zone exposed ductwork

HID ambient light uniform 35 fc

task light

pipe enclosure   perimeter zone fan coil unit

SECTION THROUGH OFFICE

AUDITORS' MAIN BUILDING
Washington, D.C.

Figure 11. Auditors' Main Building in Washington, D.C. Section showing indirect lighting and mechanical system within historic shell. Courtesy of the architects.

Figure 12. A modern addition echoes important nineteenth-century architectural features of the Robert Elliott House in Chevy Chase, Md. Architect: Hugh Newell Jacobsen. Courtesy of Robert C. Lautman.

Robert Elliott House, Chevy Chase, Md. (Architect: Hugh Newell Jacobsen). Older buildings do not have to be large in size or monumental in scale to be given new life. They need only exhibit a sense of their own value and comfort

Figure 13. At The Oaks, Oak Park, Ill. A bleak, narrow lightwell became a skylit atrium surrounded with single-loaded corridor galleries. Architects: Nagle, Hartray & Associates, Ltd. Courtesy of the architects.

with their own style. The Robert Elliott House presents adaptive use on a residential scale with an addition larger than the original structure (Fig. 12).

The original was built on a corner site in 1871. Its style and location gave important character to its surroundings. As the Washington, D.C. suburbs grew, its main house was torn down, and what remained experienced many changes. In 1975, the architect expanded what had been a Gothic Revival cottage into a modern dwelling with an addition that is both original and reflective. The addition echoes the details of the original and is linked by a new entry, totally contemporary in its presentation. Both structures have modern interiors. This solution allows the site to retain its influence on the neighborhood and the community, and still provide a contemporary living style for its owners.

The Oaks, Oak Park, Ill. (Architects: Nagle, Hartray & Associates, Ltd.). Here, a deteriorated residential hotel was rehabilitated to provide, as the architects state, "a better environment for the elderly than could be achieved with a new structure." The solution focused on the major problem of the existing building, an inadequate, very narrow light well in the center of the plan. This defect was transformed into an opportunity by a single reconfiguration of the plan: the old light well was skylit, landscaped as an interior garden, and surrounded on each side with single-loaded corridors which overlooked the courtyard (Fig. 13). The result is a new atrium space, much more common area, and, most important, a community atmosphere.

Institute of Contemporary Art, Boston, Mass. (Architects: Graham Gund Associates, Inc.). This is a good example of how a new use was carefully fitted into an existing building whose outstanding value was its special sense of place in the community. Boston's Institute of Contemporary Art, seeking a building with a strong sense of identity for its first permanent home, looked to a former police station, designed by Arthur H. Vinal in 1886 in the vernacular of H. H. Richardson. The building enjoys a prominent location and a strong public identity, with its great stone walls and arched entrance.

The exterior could be carefully restored, but the interior had to be analyzed carefully to determine whether it had the structural possibilities to become a gallery area with enough spatial variety to exhibit different types and sizes of art. The program also called for a restaurant and theater, all three fitting within a relatively small area of 22,000 ft^2. The solution was to create a large, 2½-story space, just inside the arched windows of the facade, which serves as the entrance for restaurant and theater. The central stair leads on to the various galleries (Fig. 14). The result affords a sense of place that is both personal and public. Through the careful sculpting of its interior space in support of the new use, the building retains its very public face and supports its neighborhood.

Center for American Art, Yale University, New Haven, Conn. (Architects: Herbert S. Newman Associates). An art gallery designed by Louis Kahn in the 1950s was no longer large enough and needed new and remodeled gallery space. In addition, a new 400-seat lecture hall was to be added to the gallery to replace a smaller one which had become obsolete. All of this had to be done without disturbing

Figure 14. The central stairs and gallery of the Institute of Contemporary Art in Boston, Mass. Architects: Graham Gund Associates, Inc. Courtesy of Steve Rosenthal.

the landmark Kahn Building or the historically significant sculpture court beside it, with its three giant elms. The solution places the new lecture hall underground, beneath the sculpture court (Fig. 15). The existing two-story lecture hall was then converted into two single floors of gallery space. The new complex is an excellent demonstration of how compact urban spaces can expand without harm to landmark buildings or spaces.

The jury which gave this design an AIA Honor Award commented that "while the conversion of its main lecture hall into exhibition space at once reflects and reinforces the two architectural sites of the museum complex, the resulting new lecture hall beneath the surface of an exist-

Figure 15. The sculpture garden at the Center for American Art at Yale University in New Haven, Conn. Architects: Herbert S. Newman Associates, A.I.A., P.C. Courtesy of Norman McGrath.

ing sculpture court is a grand example of architectural respect through sublimation."

Faneuil Hall Marketplace, Boston, Mass. (Architects: Benjamin Thompson & Associates, Inc.). Faneuil Hall Marketplace was created out of the wholesale market designed in 1826 by Alexander Parris. By the 1960s, the warehouses and stores had become dilapidated. They were condemned and abandoned in that decade, offered by the city for development in 1970, and fully completed in 1978, bringing to a close the first decade of adaptive use in Boston (Fig. 16).

This urban design solution, reflecting the excitement of the marketplace as a place for people to congregate, has become the prototype for the festival marketplace in the U.S. The restored buildings and their new interiors consist of three block-long buildings. The streets between them are edged by glass canopies that extend from the central market area, so that the entire six-acre site is public space virtually year-round. Retail shops, restaurants, and offices flow effortlessly through the existing bays of the older structures on three levels. The distinction of this project lies in its respect for the original fabric, allowing the sense of the original building to come through with dignity and power.

Turtle Bay Towers, New York, N.Y. (Architects: Rothzeid, Kaiserman, Thomson & Bee). Large buildings in urban settings are often selected for adaptive use simply because they are there. To start over and build again would be a waste of time and energy. It is a challenge at a very basic level to find the true fit for such a resource. Turtle Bay Towers emerged from a 24-story factory loft constructed in 1929 in downtown Manhattan, which had been damaged by a gas explosion in 1974. A major portion of the brick facade was blown out from top to bottom, in a V shape. Except for the passenger elevators, there was no other structural damage.

The building was adapted for residential use in 1977, under tight budget constraints. It was the first major project to make use of New York City's tax abatement program, which offered incentives for conversion of commercial structures to residential use.

One special characteristic of the building was its original wedding cake design, undertaken to conform to the then existing city zoning code. In the new design, areas lost to the original zoning were reclaimed through the use of greenhouse-type windows at the end of each loft unit, which opened onto terraces formed by the wedding cake design (Fig. 17). Twenty different setback variations were used to maximize urban and river views.

Another special feature arose from the nature of the destruction caused by the explosion. To take the place of the destroyed passenger elevators, the service elevator shafts were adapted for passenger use. Since passenger elevators are smaller, the rear portion of the shafts could be used for glass-enclosed planting areas at the rear of the cab, enhancing the ordinarily drab experience of taking an elevator in a high-rise apartment. Rather than restoring the blown-out space as part of the building, which would have been a costly effort, the passenger shafts were simply cut away, leaving a small open space which begins as a street level courtyard and goes up the entire height of

Figure 16. Exterior view of Quincy Market and Faneuil Hall, Boston, Mass., showing glassed-in arcades and sidewalk cafes. Architects: Benjamin Thompson & Associates, Inc. Courtesy of Steve Rosenthal.

the building, providing natural light to the west wall of the apartments.

The tax abatement regulations required a high ratio of bedroom apartments to studios. The old building had 12-ft high ceilings and 8-ft windows running the width of most apartments. These were used to develop unique apartment designs, narrow and up to 80 ft deep, which run from the exterior terraces to the elevator core (Fig. 18). Bedrooms are located midway, raised above eye level for privacy, yet open to light because of the absence of the outside wall.

All of these solutions come specifically out of the details and characteristics of this unique existing structure, letting the building, in its new role, be what it wants to be.

Central Grammar School, Gloucester, Mass., (Architects: Notter Finegold + Alexander Inc). Of the many types of buildings particularly suitable for adaptive use, perhaps none have been more available in the past two decades than surplus school buildings. As the school age population declined, schools were closed in almost every city and town.

Their very age—most were turn-of-the-century or early twentieth century structures—made them most appealing in form, character, and design. Their brick exteriors made them particularly workable in design terms.

Central Grammar School in downtown Gloucester, Mass., was built in 1889 and closed in 1971. It is a wonderful brick and stone structure in the center of town, across from city hall and down the street from the town library and shops, a perfect location for housing for the elderly (Fig. 19). The Massachusetts Housing Finance Agency, which used federal and state funds to help finance low income and elderly housing, had occupied space in Boston's Old City Hall and was able to see first hand the advantages of adaptive use.

The plan called for two-story units that used the attic space and unusually shaped apartments that filled leftover spaces such as stairwells. But the key to the solution was the use of the classrooms in their original configuration. Many efforts to adapt old school buildings have foundered on cost considerations because it was felt necessary to

Figure 17. Facade of Turtle Bay Towers in New York City showing stepped-back greenhouse additions. Architects: Rothzeid, Kaiserman, Thomson & Bee, P. C. Courtesy of William Rothchild.

Figure 19. The entrance to Central Grammar Apartments in Gloucester, Mass. Architects: Notter Finegold + Alexander Inc. Courtesy of Phokion Karas.

go to the expense of tearing down the classroom walls. The Central Grammar solution created its typical apartment by taking the standard 30 × 30 ft classroom as it was, inserting a kitchen and bath unit essentially freestanding within the space, and by its own placement, making a living room and bedroom out of the rest (Fig. 20). The existing woodwork and trim around the outside walls

of the classroom were left in place. By circumventing demolition costs, the solution made the project economically feasible. These additional funds were then used to turn attic spaces into unique units with loft spaces and harbor views.

Because it was the first of its kind, the plan needed to be carefully explained to skeptical local officials. Interestingly, its strongest advocates were the potential tenants who came to every public meeting to speak up for just these features: stairs for those who were still physically active; interesting spaces to relieve boredom (the attic spaces provided views to the water from balconies cut in the roof behind the parapet, not unlike the widow's walks of old); and natural wood, kept in its original position wherever possible. The wide school corridor became a public visiting space, a promenade, or even living space, as each tenant put out a piece of furniture or a picture to proclaim his or her identity.

Another elderly housing project, a high-rise, also publicly financed, was constructed at the same time just two blocks away on the site of another school that had been razed a few years earlier. The economic advantages of adaptive use can be seen by comparing the two:

	High-rise	Central Grammar
Average apartment size	600 ft^2	900 ft^2
Total development cost	$25,700/unit	$22,500/unit
Rentable floor area	61% of gross	79% of gross
Construction time	18 months	10 months

Market Square, Newburyport, Mass. (Architects: Notter Finegold + Alexander Inc). With the growing awareness

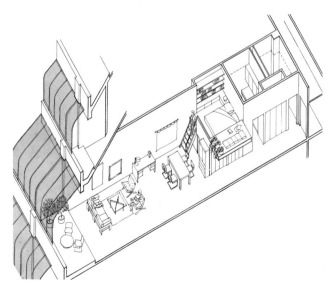

Figure 18. Cutaway isometric section illustrates the unique bedroom design for the very deep apartment in Turtle Bay Towers, New York, N.Y. Courtesy of the architects.

Second Floor

Figure 20. Typical floor plan of Central Grammar Apartments in Gloucester, Mass., showing variety of bath–kitchen core placements within individual apartments. Courtesy of the architects.

of the potential available in the untapped resources of existing building stock, architects, planners, and developers have looked beyond individual buildings to the combined value of a series of structures, working together in urban settings and neighborhood plans. Newburyport, Mass., was one of the earliest examples of this innovative process.

The town lies north of Boston near the New Hampshire line. Once a thriving seaport that challenged Boston as the major ocean port of New England, it had settled into a quiet inactivity, watching suburbs grow around it and new suburban malls begin to compete for business with its center core. Newburyport attempted urban renewal in the 1960s. Almost 90% of its downtown structures were demolished to make room for it, but new development never came.

Many other towns faced a similar dilemma and did nothing about it; Newburyport determined a new direction. In 1970, the new director of the redevelopment agency, Paul McGinley, asked the town to reevaluate its plans and consider the potential for integrating the remaining historical structures into a comprehensive plan for open spaces and waterfront development. The usual procedure at that time was for a town to restore the outside of a block of buildings, and then sell them to a single developer who would restore the interiors. Newburyport decided on a new strategy. Twenty to 30 small developers were offered individual buildings for the price of $1, provided they complete the work described by the architect's plans. The town, with the help of federal funds, promised it would contribute quality improvements, such as street and sidewalk repair, multilevel access, plantings, and underground utilities. The individual developer's work had

to be finished and approved before the city would furnish its portion of the public improvements.

To assure uniformity of the investors' work, the town found that common sense was often more effective than detailed technical descriptions. Since sand determines the basic color of mortar, the town brought a truckload of the original sand to the middle of the site for each masonry contractor to use. With the individual work in place, the town completed its part of the bargain. The spaces between the rows of buildings were filled with sidewalks, landscaping, etc, to create courtyards, which abound today with shoppers, residents, and an occasional festival. The building owners elected to operate stores and lease apartments to tenants above, or live upstairs and rent commercial space below. This mix has always supported community development and growth in cities of all sizes.

Newburyport won its competition with the suburban mall. Every available building has been restored in the same manner as Market Square (Fig. 21). Almost 20 years later, construction of new buildings is beginning again. With reclaimed space, contained traffic, and restored buildings, Newburyport has made contact with its past and taken a giant step toward its future.

Charlestown Navy Yard, Boston, Mass. (Architects: Notter Finegold + Alexander Inc). In 1974, the Charlestown Navy Yard, a 130-acre parcel with a vast complex of masonry industrial buildings, was declared surplus by the federal government. The city of Boston, through its Redevelopment Authority, acquired the property and prepared a master plan for the use of approximately half of it (Fig. 22). The first project for the site involved adaptive use of a large high bay industrial building to create 367 units of housing. Like many industrial structures with large

(a)

(b)

Figure 21. Market Square Historic District, Newburyport, Mass. Architects: Notter Finegold + Alexander Inc. **(a)** Deteriorated buildings within Newburyport's Market Square Historic District. Courtesy of the architects. **(b)** After restoration, historic Market Square experienced a major commercial and residential renaissance. Courtesy of Phokion Karas.

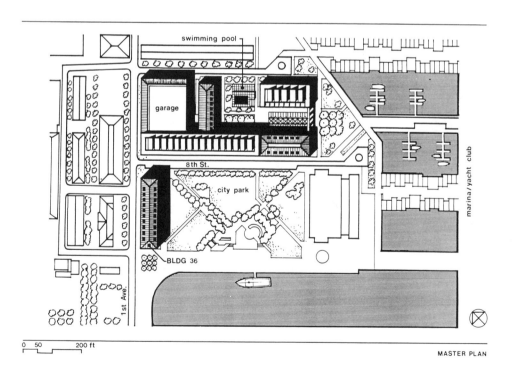

MASTER PLAN

CHARLESTOWN NAVY YARD
Charlestown, MA.

Figure 22. Site plan of Charlestown Navy Yard in Boston, Mass., shows juxtaposition of new and renovated structures with harbor, courtyards, and parks. Architects: Notter Finegold + Alexander Inc. Courtesy of the architects.

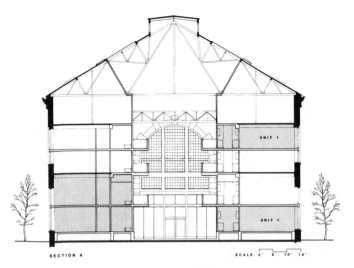

Figure 23. Charlestown Navy Yard, Boston, Mass. Section through central atrium and infill apartments within former high bay industrial structure. Courtesy of the architects.

open spaces, this building was actually a complex of structures joined together, often two and three deep. The strategy of the design solution identified the most important historic structures (the whole Yard was a National Register property) and developed a plan that carved them out from the others.

Three major buildings were identified. Some secondary structures joined to them were removed, in some cases leaving the original structures as a type of trellis and outdoor sculpture. Others were replaced with trees to form courtyards. On the side facing the water, buildings added to the front were removed and their foundations left under earth mounds, an archaeological footprint for the future. In one building, a garage was created by inserting a new steel structure within the original walls. As these adaptations were made, a new sense of place and community began to form.

The interior of the major building to be adapted for housing had no original floors, only high crane rails and intermediate mezzanines. The skylit space was retained in a new circulation atrium, and new floors were added on each side (Fig. 23). The central atrium was divided by bridges and elevators, offset to establish a rhythm within the length of the structure. The upper floors extended into the roof monitors and provided access to the roof. Windows were placed in the plane of the roof and organized by the major framing members of the original factory sash. In some of the interior courts, windows were introduced in the line of the cornice for intermediate floors. All of these modifications were carefully considered to allow the maximum configuration of units within the constraints of the existing fabric.

Because this was the first project on a very large and somewhat isolated site, interconnecting the various buildings with the central skylit atrium helped provide a unifying internal circulation that connected service and security functions with the courts and buildings, helping to give the whole the feel of a community.

Ellis Island National Monument, New York Harbor (Architects: Beyer Blinder Belle/Notter Finegold + Alexander Inc). Just as each community has buildings that symbolize its people and their history, so does a nation. Such is Ellis Island, first stopping place for tens of millions of American immigrants.

The Statue of Liberty was carefully restored in preparation for its centennial in 1986 by architects Swanke Hayden & Connell. Its copper was resecured to its original frame and its interior furnished with new platforms, elevators, and stairs to allow better movement of visitors up and down. The main building of Ellis Island, which opens in 1989 as a museum exhibiting the story of immigration to America, presented different challenges (Fig. 24). Restoration of the original features is exact. Design issues were debated with great energy and resolved in accordance with a philosophy of preservation and detail consistent with the Secretary of the Interior's Standards for Rehabilitation. The canopy at the front of the building, which evokes but does not copy the original it replaces, is detailed in a manner consistent with current technology. The new dining terrace to the east is similar to the canopy in color and form but differs in material and detail. Inside, the Great Hall, with its Guastovino vaults, has been exactingly restored. It was decided to locate the stairs where they were at the time the vaults were put in place, instead of in their original position. The stairs are rebuilt to the exact configuration of the time. Only materials and details show they are new. On each side of the Great Hall are wings that were added to provide office space for immigration officials. This area has been adapted to provide support for the hall's new use as a museum.

As in Mechanics Hall, code and safety issues were significant. Horizontal exits have been created to eliminate multiple stairs. A skylight has been added over the light court areas, and escalators connect the floors of the museum. The original exterior walls have been exposed to show where the original building stopped. Off the new atrium space new theaters and galleries have been added. The new use has found a proper home.

1988—: NEW BEGINNINGS

New beginnings have as their roots the understanding and acceptance of discovery. Adaptive use as a technique has expanded its application from the individual building to groups of buildings and has become the resource for preservationists to maintain the large context of neighborhoods, districts, and even whole towns. The postmodern era today has experienced a great deal of support from preservationists who, perhaps oversimply and maybe unknowingly, have responded to the historical image or recall of that work. The result has been a confluence of goals that share a common purpose: to evoke a sense of history and the roots of society. These goals will continue to challenge cities to retain their older structures as a means of continuing the excitement of the urban environment. These existing structures will strengthen even more their influence over the character of the new infill architecture

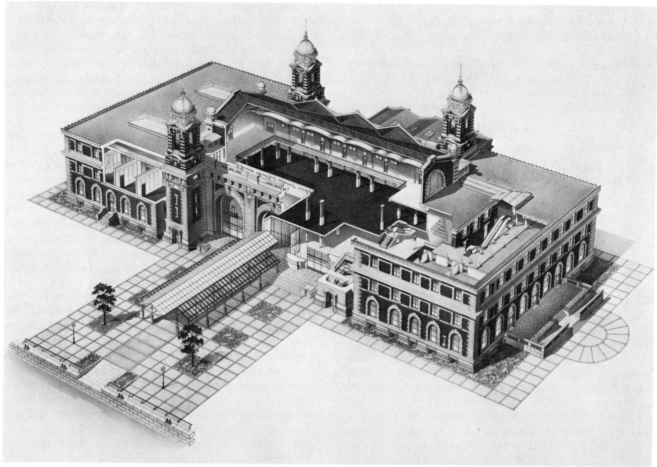

Figure 24. Ellis Island National Monument in New York Harbor, New York, N.Y. Cutaway rendering of the restored Main Immigration Building that is to be the national museum of immigration. Architects: Beyer Blinder Belle/Notter Finegold + Alexander Inc. Courtesy of Zvonimir Tesla.

as well as the spaces which remain. This new emphasis on the context of cities and the respect for older architecture will grow in the U.S. as it has in other countries and cultures, because it contributes to the comfort people feel with an earlier age as they are drawn back into the parts of cities that had been previously abandoned and now have found new uses and renewed life.

The built environment today is being changed by public needs and public tastes. This is a time of finite resources and shrinking usable spaces. As a better understanding of what the public wants and needs is developed, and as the value of existing buildings is determined, the basic decisions about how cities are going to look, and whether they are going to work, will be made by the people who will live in them. Adaptive use and new architecture will respond to those same needs and perhaps a new architecture will be born of the goals of the people who will use it out of the context of the people who have known it.

BIBLIOGRAPHY

1. *Architectural Record* (Dec. 1985).

General References

Urban Land Institute, *Adaptive Use: Development Economics,* *Process and Profiles,* Urban Land Institute, Washington, D.C., 1978.

Adaptive Use: A Survey of Construction Costs, Advisory Council on Historic Preservation, Washington, D.C., 1976.

D. Maddex, ed., *All About Old Buildings: The Whole Preservation Catalog,* Preservation Press, Washington, D.C., 1985.

B. Diamonstein, *Buildings Reborn: New Uses, Old Places,* Harper & Row, Publishers Inc., New York, 1978.

G. Bunnell, *Built to Last: A Handbook on Recycling Old Buildings,* Preservation Press, Washington, D.C., 1977.

M. Ashworth, *Glory Road: Pennsylvania Avenue Past & Present,* Link Press, McLean, Va., 1986.

A. D. Huxtable, *Goodbye History, Hello Hamburger,* Preservation Press, Washington, D.C., 1986.

J. M. Fitch, *Historic Preservation: Curatorial Management of the Built World,* Mc-Graw Hill Inc., New York, 1982.

M. F. Schmertz, *Architectural Design, New Life for Old Buildings,* Mc-Graw Hill Inc., New York, 1982.

S. Cantacuzino, *New Uses for Old Buildings,* The Whitney Library of Design, New York, 1975.

National Trust for Historic Preservation, *Preservation and Building Codes,* Preservation Press, Washington, D.C., 1975.

Boston Development Authority, *Recycled Boston,* Public Information Department, Boston, Mass., 1976.

M. T. Will, *Recycled Buildings: A Bibliography of Adaptive Use Literature Since 1970,* Vance Bibliographies, Monticello, Ill., 1979.

Notter Finegold + Alexander Inc, *Recycling Historic Railroad Stations: A Citizen's Manual,* U.S. Department of Transportation, Washington, D.C., 1978.

D. Stanforth, *Restored America,* Praeger Publishers, New York, 1975.

W. C. Shopsin, *Restoring Old Buildings for Contemporary Uses,* The Whitney Library of Design, New York, 1986.

S. Cantacuzino and S. Brandt, *Saving Old Buildings,* The Architectural Press, London, 1980.

GEORGE M. NOTTER, JR., FAIA
Notter Finegold + Alexander Inc
Washington, D.C.

ADHESIVES

The American Society for Testing and Materials (ASTM) defines an adhesive as a substance capable of holding materials together by surface attachment (1). The mechanisms by which a liquid adhesive makes intimate contact with a surface, undergoing physical and chemical changes to bond surfaces together, is highly complex and understood only in part. Nonetheless, adhesives appropriately selected for compatability with adherend and service conditions can be used to great advantage in building construction. Adhesives increase strength and stiffness of building components, uniformly transfer and distribute stresses, and combine dissimilar materials that could not be joined otherwise. Applications in building construction vary widely in structural capabilities, from huge glued-laminated beams that support roof loads to nonstructural applications where adhesives support only wall coverings and decorative trim. Within the last 45 years, age-old animal and vegetable adhesives have essentially been replaced by chemically synthesized adhesives that enable the user to bond practically all materials from microchips to jet aircraft. The construction industry is the largest user of adhesives, but by far the largest proportion is used to manufacture building materials such as plywood, particle board, gypsum board, hard board, doors, sandwich panels, glass-fiber insulation, and various factory-laminated products. The amount of adhesive used in the construction industry to assemble building materials at construction sites and in small shops is unknown, but it is this latter group of adhesives and their applications that this article addresses. Mechanisms of adhesive bonding and the natures of bonding surfaces and polymers that are common to most adhesive applications are also discussed.

MATERIALS IN ADHESIVES

Practically all adhesives used in building construction are made from organic polymers of either synthetic or natural origin. Polysaccharides and proteins are the natural polymers. Since early civilization, natural polymers derived from animal and plant materials have been used as adhesives. Animal, casein, blood, soybean, starch, dextrin, and cellulosic adhesives are still in use today, although they are being replaced by synthetic polymers. Natural rubber is the other natural polymer used in both latex and solvent systems, but here again, the natural material is being replaced by synthetically derived rubbers.

Natural rubber and synthetic rubbers are elastomers. An elastomer is a generic term meaning a macromolecular material that, at room temperature, is capable of recovering substantially in size and shape after removal of a deforming force (1). These are extremely useful materials and undoubtedly make up the largest class of adhesives used in building construction. Adhesives based on elastomers range from relatively low-strength pressure-sensitive tapes, to contact-bond and mastic adhesives, to tough structural metal-bonding adhesives made from nitrile rubber and phenolic resins.

Synthetic polymers constitute the largest group of adhesive products by far. These polymers can be chemically designed and formulated to perform an almost infinite variety of bonding functions. Synthetics can be broadly classified as thermoplastic and thermosetting polymers. Thermoplastic resins are long-chain polymers that do not undergo chemical change on heating. They soften and flow with heat and harden again on cooling. They have limited resistances to heat, solvents, and long-term loading. Common thermoplastics are polyvinyls, acrylics, polystyrenes, and polyamides. Thermosetting resins make excellent structural adhesives because they undergo chemical change on addition of heat. They form cross-linked polymers that have high-strength properties, resist deteriorations by most chemicals, and support high long-term loads without deforming. Resorcinolic, amino, and epoxy resins are examples of thermosetting adhesives.

An adhesive formulation is a mixture of several materials that are added in various ratios to a base material in order to impart the desired strength, durability, and adhesion properties. Solvents are used to disperse or dissolve base materials, to act as a vehicle for the fluid system, and to provide viscosity control. Fillers can be used to control adhesive penetration of porous surfaces, to serve as thixotropes to control flow and penetration, and just to thicken and reduce cost. Reinforcing agents improve mechanical properties such as toughness, impact resistance, and shrinkage. Extenders are fillerlike materials that usually have a small degree of adhesion capability, but are added to a system to improve certain working properties while cutting cost. Certain chemicals or base materials may be added to plasticize and tackify resins, whereas other types called fortifiers are added to improve resistance to moisture or heat. Catalysts are chemicals used to speed chemical setting of the base polymers. Acids, bases, salts, peroxides, and sulfur compounds are a few examples. Catalysts do not enter into the chemical reaction; they simply increase the rate of reaction. Other chemicals may be added, such as preservatives, acid scavengers, antioxidants, and wetting agents, all depending on the type of adhesive and the property needing improvement.

ADVANTAGES, LIMITATIONS, AND SAFETY

The function of an adhesive is to fasten members of an assembly together and to maintain the integrity of the assembly under the expected conditions of service. In building construction, adhesives fulfill this role in a great variety of applications, from structural bonds that are expected to contribute great strength and stiffness under severe service conditions for the life of the structure, to nonstructural applications where bonds only support the weight of decorative trim. Even though nails, screws, bolts, rivets, and clips are still the most common means of fastening building materials together, synthetic adhesives are making significant inroads. When adhesives are properly matched to the stresses and service environment of the application and are used in accordance with the manufacturer's instructions, they offer several distinct advantages that cannot be equaled by mechanical fasteners.

At the top of the list is the ability of adhesives to distribute stresses uniformly over the entire joint area, thereby avoiding concentration of stresses, which can lead to failures. Joint continuity allows transfer of stresses from one component to another so that all members share the load. If a rigid adhesive is used to laminate pieces of lumber into a beam or arch, the result is a structural member of greater strength and stiffness than the sum of its individual components, even when the lumber is laminated with mechanical fasteners.

The advantage of effective stress transfer can be used to design new or conventional composite building components of diverse shapes and sizes at lower costs. For example, adhesives have been used to laminate layers of plywood into structural shells for complex roof systems (Fig. 1). Conventional applications such as the widely used stressed-skin panel system enable the designer to use materials of smaller size, of lower grade, and in smaller numbers to reduce material and assembly costs, weight, and volume while increasing the strength and stiffness of the component (Fig. 2). The cost of structural beams can be lowered by more effectively locating laminates of higher quality and moduli in the outer tension and compression members, where stresses are higher, and using materials of lower quality and moduli in the core members, where stresses are lower.

Elastomeric adhesives are capable of yielding to and absorbing stresses under short-term dynamic loading. Such adhesives are used to assemble manufactured housing because they reduce excessive stress concentrations around windows, doors, and joints, where damage can occur when these units are transported over highways and lifted at construction sites.

Adhesives permit the bonding of a variety of materials that may be dissimilar in composition, thermal expansion, modulus, and thickness. Thin sheet materials may be bonded where other joining methods would cause distortion or otherwise be impossible or impractical. Examples include bonding aluminum or hardboard skins to honeycomb or foam cores in making various lightweight sandwich panels. Wall covering, floor covering, and counter tops are examples of where adhesives can be used to avoid

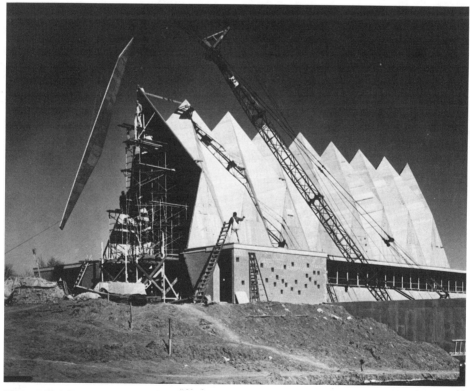

Figure 1. Adhesive bonding of roof planes allows creative solution to an architectural design problem. Courtesy of Forest Products Laboratory, USDA Forest Service.

Figure 2. Adhesive-bonded stressed-skin panels used in roof and floor systems of panelized housing. Courtesy of Forest Products Laboratory, USDA Forest Service.

marring smooth surfaces by protruding fasteners, overlaps, and irregular contours. Fewer fasteners can also reduce or eliminate the marring of surfaces by nail popping in gypsum board and resilient-tile floor coverings. Fibers, particles, and thin films could not be joined at all without adhesives. Examples are aluminum foil, paper, vinyl and fiber sheet materials, glass-wool insulation, fiber glass mat composites, sandpaper, veneered surfaces, particle board, and many others. Adhesives between dissimilar metals can reduce corrosion caused by galvanic action. If an organic adhesive is used to bond copper tubing to steel supports, galvanic corrosion can be prevented. Heat-sensitive material can be joined with adhesive that would be distorted or destroyed by brazing or welding. Adhesives can also be a good barrier to moisture and chemicals. When two metals of dissimilar coefficients of thermal expansion are joined and separated by a flexible adhesive, less stress develops with temperature changes.

Finally, there are many very important high-value building materials that have been reconstituted from low-value materials with adhesives. Examples are hardboard, particle board, flake board, plywood, composite panels and lumber, and finger-jointed lumber, not to mention a host of paper products.

The advantages of adhesive bonding can be realized, but not without knowledge of and careful attention to every aspect of the bonding process. Here lies the greatest limitation to the use of adhesives. A great variety of performance properties and working characteristics are available in an assortment of adhesive products. Realizing the desired results in a particular bonding job, however, requires that an adhesive be selected on the basis of performance requirements relevant to the expected service environment. These include the adhesive's strength and resistance to creep under static loading in the primary stress mode, its resistance to heat and moisture along with repeating stresses that accompany dimensional changes from heat and moisture, and its resistance to chemicals, microorganisms, and fire. Since the adhesive must properly wet, flow, penetrate, and solidify on a particular type of adherend, it must be chemically and physically compatible with the surface. Adhesives vary in working characteristics; these characteristics dictate how and under what conditions an adhesive must be applied and cured. Careful consideration must be given to preparing and maintaining clean surfaces; preparing and applying the adhesive; providing control over processing time, temperature, and relative humidity; and providing jigs, presses (sometimes with heat), and other processing equipment. The cost of these provisions is also an important consideration. It is extremely important to have adequate inspection and quality control procedures to ensure that bonded joints, particularly structural joints, will perform as expected in service. The unfortunate result of failure in quality control is unexpected failure in service. Even if bonded joints are found inadequate before being put into service, they usually cannot be dismantled easily and repaired, so materials, time, and labor are lost. To avoid such unsatisfactory results, it is essential to have knowledge and control of the critical aspects of the bonding process. The responsibility for material specifications and workmanship must be clearly established and placed in the hands of qualified people.

Although toxicity is not a major problem with most adhesives used in building construction, adhesives nonetheless contain chemicals that can be toxic if exposed to sufficient concentrations for prolonged periods of time. For example, resorcinol and urea resins react with formaldehyde to form thermoset adhesives that are nontoxic in the cured state. However, free formaldehyde is released from powdered hardeners during mixing, application, and cure (particularly when curing with heat). Adequate ventilation must be provided to remove gases. Formaldehyde gases may react with proteins of the body to cause irritation, if not more serious inflammations of the mucous membranes of the eyes, nose, and throat. Allergic reactions may also occur. The safe working limit for formaldehyde is 0.02 ppm in the air.

Many construction adhesives contain organic solvents that have dangerously low flash points. Generally, however, unless these materials are confined within empty containers or nonventilated rooms, they do not reach dangerous concentration levels. Unfortunately, tragic explosions have occurred simply because of cigarette smoking where solvent-based adhesives were being used. Adhesive producers have made efforts to change formulations to include less flammable solvents.

Other adhesive components may be subject to hazard-ous polymerization. For example, isocyanate in polyurethane systems can polymerize on contact with strong alkalies, strong mineral acids, and water. It can also cause irritation to the eyes and skin on contact and respiratory and gastrointestinal irritation if inhaled or ingested.

Health and safety regulations require that toxic and hazardous chemical substances be identified and visibly labeled to warn of dangers. Instructions are provided on proper handling procedures, protective clothing and gear, procedures for dealing with spills and fire, as well as first-aid procedures. These instructions also provide material safety data sheets on new products as a partial fulfillment of the OSHA hazard communication standard and worker "right-to-know" laws.

ADHESIVES USED IN BUILDING CONSTRUCTION

Resorcinol–formaldehyde (RF) and phenol–resorcinol–formaldehyde (PRF) resin adhesives have filled a great need in the building industry as wood-bonding adhesives for structural applications. Since commercialization in early World War II, when they were used to assemble wood aircraft and naval vessels, they have proven their exceptional strength and durability even under the most severe service conditions. They are capable of sustaining high long-term loading without creep. Their exceptional performance properties relative to other adhesives used to bond wood are shown in Table 1, and in the exterior exposure tests shown in Figure 3. Since resorcinolic-type adhesives can be cured at room temperature, they are well suited for shop, and in some instances on-site, laminating. For these reasons, RF and PRF resins have become the standards for structural adhesives, particularly for laminating beams and bonding stressed-skin panels (Fig. 2).

RF and PRF adhesives are marketed as two-component systems; that is, resin and hardener are separate and mixed just before use. In laminating plants, they are ap-

Table 1. Estimated Relative Performance Capabilities of Room-temperature-curing Adhesives in Douglas Fir Lumber Joints[a]

Adhesive Type[b] (Number of Components)	Shear Strength (Compression)					Delamination		
	Dry	Vacuum-pressure Soak	1 mo, ≥ 80% Relative Humidity	Boil–Dry–Boil	Dry Heat, 65°C	Three Cycles Soaking–Drying	10 Years Outdoor Weathering	One Year Dead Loading, 690 kPa
Douglas fir lumber	1[c]	1	1	1	1	1	1	1
PRF (two-part)	1	1	1	1	1	1	1	1
Epoxy, slow cure[d] (primer plus two-part)	1	2[c]	2	2	1	1	1	1
EPI (two-part)	1	2	2	3	2	1	1	1
Polyurethane (two-part)	1	2	2	3	3	1	1	3
UF (two-part)	1	2	3	3	3	3	4	1
PVAc, cross-linked (two-part)	1	3[c]	3	4	3	3	4	3
Casein (two-part)	1	4[c]	3	4	3	4	4	1
PVAc (one-part)	1	4	4	4	4	4	4	4

[a] Refs. 2–8.
[b] Adhesives represented are of the highest quality available.
[c] 1, very high; 2, high; 3, moderate; 4, low.
[d] Epoxy adhesive specially formulated for bonding to wood.

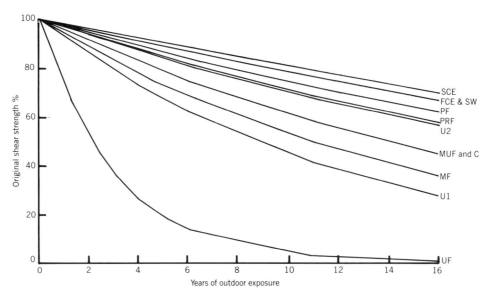

Figure 3. Durability of 10 adhesives during 16 years of outdoor exposure (3). SCE, slow-cure epoxy; FCE, fast-cure epoxy; SW, solid wood; PF, phenol–formaldehyde; U2, polyurethane 2; MUF, melamine–urea–formaldehyde; C, casein; MF, melamine–formaldehyde; U1, polyurethane 1; UF, urea–formaldehyde. Courtesy of Weyerhaeuser Co.

plied by powered roller–spreaders or extruders. In the field, a brush or hand roller is adequate. Open and closed assembly times vary according to reactivity, air and wood temperature, humidity, moisture content of wood, and spread rate. Even though lumber is planed to clean and smooth the bonding surfaces, pressures of 690–1380 kPa ensure intimate contact between adhesive and wood. The time a laminate remains under pressure may vary from 4 to 16 h.

PRF adhesives with gap-filling capability are not available except on special request, although there is a need for them in the construction industry. Conventional PRF adhesives are too thin to bridge gaps between rough, uneven plywood and lumber surfaces. Therefore, large presses, clamps, or extensive nailing must be used to apply enough pressure to bring intimate contact between adhesive and wood. Certain thickening and reinforcing agents can be incorporated into a PRF resin to make an extrudable, nonsagging adhesive that will bridge gaps of 1.5 mm or more. Instead of driving nails 10–15 cm apart, they can be spaced 30–40 cm. Nails are needed only to hold the assembly together until the adhesive sets. Even with thickening ingredients, the strength, rigidity, and durability of the adhesive in thick bondlines still exceeds the strength of plywood (2).

RF resins are prepared by reacting 1.0 mol resorcinol with formaldehyde in a low enough molar ratio, approximately 0.55:0.65, to make a formaldehyde-deficient prepolymer. When the adhesive bond is to be made, more formaldehyde is added to the prepolymer to complete the thermosetting reaction. Resorcinol is so reactive that polymerization can be completed at room temperature. A lower-cost phenol–resorcinol copolymer resin can be prepared by reacting phenol with formaldehyde to form a resole and then reacting it with resorcinol or resorcinol–formaldehyde, all depending on the type of copolymer de-

sired. Molar ratios, concentrations, catalysts, and reaction conditions can be varied to yield a great variety of adhesive products.

Isocyanates are highly reactive materials that crosslink with a variety of polyols to produce polyurethanes. These materials are highly polar and develop strong hydrogen bonds. They bond to an unusually wide variety of surfaces, such as wood, metal, plastic, glass, rubber, ceramics, and nylon. Polyurethanes have high cohesive strength and impact resistance, as well as excellent cryogenic properties. Their chemical structures can be controlled to produce a rigid film in thin bondlines or a highly flexible film in thick bondlines.

Polyurethane-type adhesives have certain properties that make them particularly suited to bonding wood assemblies: notably fast cure rates, gap-filling characteristics, and little or no pressure requirement during bonding (6). A one-part fast-curing system is capable of developing wood failure within 15 min. The bonds have high dry strength, and they are tough and flexible. A two-part system has been developed with improved heat and watersoak resistance. These were areas of weakness in polyurethane adhesives, along with their questionable ability to withstand long-term static loading at elevated temperatures. Their performance relative to several wood adhesives is shown in Table 1. Figure 3 shows the durability of two polyurethane adhesives during 16 years of exterior exposure.

The polyurethane reaction is also used to produce elastomeric construction adhesives. These are high-molecular-weight one-part systems with free isocyanate groups that react quickly on contact with the surface or moisture in the air.

One of the newest isocyanate-based adhesives is the highly versatile emulsion polymer–isocyanate (EPI) adhesive (8). It is capable of bonding to a wide variety of surfaces, and for more than 10 years it has been used in structural applications where skin materials such as plywood, aluminum, fiber glass-reinforced plastics, acrylic sheets, gypsum board, hardboard, particle board, impregnated paper, and vinyl film have been bonded to lumber framing. They have also been used in hollow-core and solid flush doors, lumber finger joints, and wood I-beams.

EPI is a two-component adhesive that requires mixing before use. The aqueous emulsion phase contains the base polymer. During mixing, the isocyanate phase is protected from reacting with the water contained in the emulsion phase, but as water evaporates and diffuses into the substrate, the protective mechanism deactivates and the two phases are brought into molecular contact for reaction.

EPI adhesive is perhaps the strongest and most durable wood adhesive that will chemically set at temperatures as low as 4°C. Once the two components are mixed, the pot life can be several hours. It can be spread with conventional hand or powered equipment. Assembly times are quite flexible, allowing 0–30 min open time and 0–60 min closed time. Press times are relatively short: 1 h at 21°C with fast-setting system. The adhesive meets all requirements for structural laminated wood products intended for exterior applications. Its relative structural performance capabilities on wood are shown in Table 1.

Epoxy resin adhesives are more widely used than any other adhesive type, primarily because of their high strength, excellent adhesion to a wide variety of surfaces, cure at ambient conditions, resistance to moisture, heat, and creep, and low shrinkage on setting. They have penetrated more fields of manufacturing, and have been used to bond more diverse materials, than any other adhesive type, including bonds to metal, glass, ceramics, plastic, wood, concrete, and others. In the United States, they have not often been used for structural applications in building construction; they are used only for repairs to structural and facial members, filling cracks and voids, and laying stone and ceramic floor tiles.

Most current applications are semistructural in the sense that the adhesive is not expected to sustain a high level of stress for long periods of time. Epoxies are capable of shear strengths of 25–35 MPa, but for such bonds as concrete-to-concrete and concrete-to-metal (10), no more than 350 kPa sustained load is ever reached. New concrete does not bond well to old, but if the epoxy resin is used to interface the old and new concretes, then bonds develop that have greater mechanical strength than the concrete. This technique is commonly used to enlarge structures or to repair existing concrete structures as in conduct walls, buttresses, pillars, and the joining of precast structural elements. Fastening steel bolts and fasteners into concrete is commonplace, as is injecting epoxy adhesive to repair cracks in concrete structures. Steel sheets or plates may be bonded to concrete beams to strengthen the composite. Steel reinforcement wires and posttensioning tendons may be bonded to concrete. In these cases, the adhesive does not support design loads, but it must be strong and durable, with enough resistance to creep at elevated temperatures to enable the adhesive-bonded metal additions to reinforce the structure.

Most epoxy adhesives considered for structural bonding of wood do not perform satisfactorily where high strength and resistance to delamination must be maintained during water saturation or outdoor exposure. However, two epoxy formulations have performed extraordinarily well over 16 years of outdoor exposure. As indicated in Figure 3, they have resisted strength deterioration as well as solid wood (3). The relative strengths and durabilities of one of these epoxies has been rated in Table 1 along with other structural adhesives. Both epoxies bonded well because the wood surfaces were primed before bonding with a 2% aqueous solution of polyethyleneamine. Apparently, these two epoxies, and others in their normal formulations, do not wet and flow effectively enough to penetrate porous wood surfaces; however, the primer overcomes this problem.

The reactive epoxy group is a three-membered ring consisting of an oxygen atom attached to two connected carbon atoms. On curing, these rings are opened by catalysts to form cross-linking networks. Epoxies owe their high chemical adhesion to epoxide, hydroxyl, amine, and other polar groups in the molecule. The most common epoxies used in adhesives are derived from bisphenol A and epichlorohydrin, and they are cured with reactive hardeners containing primary and secondary amine groups. The aliphatic amines set at room temperature, but aromatic amines require elevated temperatures. Various other hardeners such as acid anhydride, tertiary amines, mercaptans, and others may be related with epoxides to produce adhesives of varying mechanical properties, durabilities, and working characteristics. Generally, epoxies can be formulated to create a great variety of mixtures so that once a surface is properly cleaned, subsequent wetting, spreading, and penetration should not be a problem in developing a bond.

Urea–formaldehyde (UF) resin adhesives are not used often in building construction, but they are used in shops to make built-in furniture and to laminate various wood assemblies. UFs develop very strong bonds to wood, and they have structural capability as long as the joints remain free from moisture, particularly at elevated temperatures (4,5). The weakness in urea resins is that they are subject to hydrolysis, and of course, heat and moisture accelerate that process (Table 1 and Fig. 3). The adhesive is brittle and has poor gap-filling capability, so good-fitting joints are essential.

UFs are available as room-temperature-setting adhesives. In ready-mix form, the spray-dried resin powder, solid acid-forming catalyst with buffer, and fillers are mixed with water just before use. The pot life of the mix is 6–8 h, although complete chemical setting requires several days.

UF resins are products of the condensation reaction of 1.5–2.0 mol formaldehyde with 1.0 mol urea. The methylol ureas formed in the partial polymerization process are dispersed in water at high concentrations and can be converted to a powder by spray drying. When the soluble powder is mixed with the acid-forming catalyst at the time of use, the polymerization reaction is completed.

Within the last 25 years, great volumes of a variety of elastomeric adhesives have been used in the building industry to assemble materials at construction sites, in shops, and in manufactured housing plants. Even though

Figure 4. Elastomeric construction adhesive used on-site to install nail-glued plywood floor system. Courtesy of Forest Products Laboratory, USDA Forest Service.

Figure 5. Elastomeric panel adhesive used to bond paneling to wall studs. Courtesy of Forest Products Laboratory, USDA Forest Service.

elastomeric flooring and contact adhesives were in use earlier, the introduction of mastic-type construction adhesives essentially revolutionized the industry by bringing in new adhesive products and ways of assembling building materials for both semistructural and decorative purposes (Figs. 4 and 5). The variety of elastomeric-based adhesives available is extraordinarily wide, ranging from the general-purpose to those designed for highly specialized applications. The base materials are the natural and synthetic rubbers, including latex, neoprene, styrene–butadiene, polyurethane, and reclaimed rubber. Other nonelastomeric polymers such as acrylic, poly(vinyl acetate), asphalt, and copolymers of vinyl acetate with acrylic or ethylene and hydrocarbon resins may also be used. Most of these same polymers are used to make construction sealants (11).

Mastic construction adhesives have a number of unique working characteristics that make them well suited for building construction. Perhaps most important is their ability to bridge gaps between rough and poorly fitting lumber and plywood surfaces with a minimum of pressure from nails. They have viscosities ranging from 150,000 to 400,000 mPa · s (=cP) and can be extruded from a cartridge with a caulking gun (Figs. 4 and 5) to give a bead that does not slump on a vertical surface and can bridge a 7-mm gap. Construction mastics also tolerate a wide range of temperatures and moisture conditions in the air and on bonding surfaces. Adequate bonds can be developed even on very dry, wet, or frozen lumber surfaces (Table 2).

Mastic construction adhesives are not strong enough to fail solid wood in shear, but in plywood-to-lumber constructions they are capable of failing plywood. As a class, mastics do not have a high degree of water resistance, but they can support more than 700 kPa in a water-saturated condition. Since mastics are made from elastomeric materials, they have the ability to yield under stress (Table 2). This can be a distinct advantage where adhesive-bonded assemblies undergo dimensional changes with changes in moisture or where assemblies are subjected to short-term dynamic loadings. Mastics are used extensively in construction of manufactured housing to ensure the units can be transported from factory to building site without incurring significant damage to the finish or structure. See Table 2 for performance capabilities of typical construction and panel adhesives.

The semistructural capability of mastic adhesives imparts strength and stiffness to bonded assemblies beyond that possible with nailed construction. This results in economy of materials. For example, when wood floor systems are nail-glued, the added stiffness and strength resulting from the composite T-beam action permits reductions in the thickness of plywood skins, depth of floor joists, grade of floor joists, and amount of nailing. Furthermore, the floors feel firm under foot, and floor squeaks and nail popping are eliminated (Fig. 4).

Mastic construction adhesives generally meet the highest performance requirements of any adhesive in the mas-

Table 2. Strength and Durability of Typical Elastomeric Construction and Panel Adhesives[a]

Adhesive Base	Shear Strength					Strength Loss, 6-mo. Cyclic Relative Humidity, %	Shear Deflection, 2 Wk Dead Load, 345 kPa, mm
	Dry, kPa	Wet, kPa	Wet–Redried, kPa	Wet Lumber, Cured 21°C, kPa	Wet Lumber, Cured 2°C, kPa		
Neoprene	2282	800	724	972	1007	4	0.13
Neoprene	2247	896	1275	758	503	32	2.64
Styrene–butadiene	3902	1634	2392	972	1275	29	2.39
Neoprene	3468	1020	2075	2034	0	13	0.13
Polyurethane	1613	1455	1917	641	517	2	1.68
Neoprene	2392	765	1406	1213	0	4	1.12

[a] Ref. 12.

tic class. Therefore, it is necessary to compound these adhesives with higher levels of elastomer and resins than would be required for panel, wallboard, and floor-covering adhesives. A high-strength mastic might contain 30–50% neoprene or styrene–butadiene rubber and up to 45% phenolic resin or resin blend. Fillers help to control mastic consistency and reduce cost. Aliphatic, aromatic, and chlorinated solvents are commonly used to dissolve or disperse the solids into a uniform mixture of the desired viscosity. Other additions might include antioxidants, preservatives, stabilizers, cure accelerators, acid scavengers, and solvent release agents.

Mastics are also compounded as panel and wallboard adhesives. They have lower strength, and moisture and creep resistance than construction and subfloor adhesives and should be used only in nonstructural applications where moisture would not be encountered (Table 2). These adhesives are applied from a cartridge with a caulking gun or from a can or pail with a spatula, a trowel, or pressure equipment. They are used to install sheet materials such as decorative wall paneling, gypsum board, plywood, and hardboard to existing walls, studs, or furring strips (Fig. 5). These are good general-purpose adhesives that can be used to install flooring, ceiling, and wall tiles, fixtures, and decorative trim. These adhesives reduce or eliminate mechanical fasteners and the marring effects of nail popping, hammer marks, or exposed nails.

Floor-covering adhesives are available for vinyl, vinyl asbestos, rubber, and asphalt tiles, vinyl rolled goods, and carpeting. Generally, these adhesives are water-resistant enough for interior and exterior use. They can be applied to dry concrete above and below grade as well as to plywood and particle board surfaces. Flooring materials usually are installed when the adhesive is wet or tacky, and as solvents evaporate, the adhesive sets.

Mastics for rubber, vinyl, and cork tiles are rubber-based with water vehicle or resin-based with alcohol. Rigid asphalt and vinyl-asbestos tiles are bonded with asphalt emulsion, asphalt cut backs, and rubber-based systems with water vehicle. The asphaltics must be dried before placing tiles, but the rubber-based systems must be wet. Latex or other emulsion systems should not be used with wood parquet or strip flooring because the wood will absorb moisture from the adhesive and swell, causing the floor to buckle. Mastics are also specially formulated for com-

mercial and residential carpeting with impregnated, laminated foam and jute backing. Vinyl foam backing must have a special emulsion adhesive. Mastic adhesives for ceramic tile flooring are solvent and latex types, which are similar to ceramic adhesives used for walls, except the floor adhesives dry faster. The same mastic-type adhesives used for ceramics can be used with natural and simulated brick and stone. Mastics are also used to install vinyl and rubber cove base. They have enough wet grab to resist curling of the rolled cove base.

Contact-bond adhesives are so named because they develop a permanent bond as soon as two adhesive-coated surfaces are brought into contact and pressed together. Once the contact has been made, the surfaces cannot be repositioned. Generally, one or more thin coats of adhesive are applied to both surfaces, allowed to air dry to a tack-free state, and then positioned and pressed together. Roll pressure ensures intimate contact between both surfaces. Setting takes place by loss of solvent through evaporation and diffusion.

Contact-bond adhesives are used in nonstructural applications, particularly where sheet materials are laminated to rigid and flat surfaces. Typical applications in building construction are for bonding high-density laminates to countertops in kitchens and bathrooms and double-laminating gypsum board or paneling to gypsum board.

Most contact-bond adhesives are made from neoprene, although styrene–butadiene and natural rubbers are common. A typical neoprene contact is made by mill mixing neoprene with magnesium oxide, antioxidant, and zinc oxide, and then churn mixing with tertiary butyl-phenolic resin and an appropriate mixture of organic solvents to give 15–30% solids. Organic solvents in contacts are slowly being replaced by water systems because of dangers from toxic fumes and fire. Water-based contacts are slower-drying and lack the rapid bond strength development and high ultimate shear strength of the solvent-based contacts.

Poly(vinyl acetate) (PVAc) emulsion adhesives are known as white glues. They have gained wide acceptance among consumers and industrial users because they develop strong bonds quickly at room temperature, are ready to use and easy to apply, and generally require a minimum of skill to develop good bonds. In the building industry, the greatest volume of PVAc adhesive is used to construct manufactured housing. They provide temporary strength and stiffness to the structure, which helps prevent damage from racking, bending, and shearing stresses that develop while the units are transported over highways. Once the units are on permanent foundations, normal structural loads are carried by mechanical fasteners. PVAcs are used in manufactured housing to bond particle board or plywood decking to floor joists, to bond interior paneling or gypsum board to wall studs, and to assemble parts of built-in cabinets. They are used for the same purposes, but to a lesser extent, for on-site building construction.

PVAcs have a wide range of strength properties (5). Some develop very high shear strengths of 20 MPa on high-density hard maple, and on lower-density species, shear strengths are lower but failure of the wood in the shear area is very high. PVAc is thermoplastic, however, and when joints are highly stressed for prolonged periods of time, they creep. The rate of creep increases sharply at elevated temperatures. PVAcs set by loss of moisture, so when joints undergo prolonged exposure to moisture, they soften and are less capable of carrying high service loads. Many limitations in earlier formulations have been minimized through compounding or cross-linking. Water and heat resistance have been improved by adding thermosetting resins. So-called aliphatics are high-tack, high-strength PVAc formulations designed for carpentry. They are borated and contain higher molecular weight resins that give better creep and heat resistance than did older formulations. When vinyl acetate is copolymerized with certain cross-linkable comonomers, polymer chains can be cross-linked when catalysts are added at the time of setting. These cross-linked emulsions have significantly improved resistance to creep, heat, and moisture. The relative performance capabilities of PVAc and cross-linked PVAc are shown in Table 1.

PVAc emulsions are prepared by the emulsion polymerization process wherein vinyl acetate monomer, alone or in combination with other vinyl monomers, is polymerized in water under precisely controlled temperature and pressure in the presence of suitable emulsifying agents. PVAc is a brittle solid at room temperature; it must have an external plasticizer to lower its glass-transition temperature so a flexible adhesive film can form. When vinyl acetate is copolymerized with ethylene, the latter acts as an internal plasticizer to lower the glass-transition temperature (13). PVAc formulations can be compounded to yield a wide variety of working and strength properties by including varying amounts of plasticizers, emulsion stabilizers, tackifiers, fillers, solvents, wetting agents, and fungicides.

Casein adhesives (4,5,14) develop good structural bonds to certain species of wood, particularly southern pine, Sitka spruce, and Douglas fir. They do not produce high wood failure on high-density hardwoods, however. At the present time, caseins are used in wood panel-to-frame constructions and in the manufacture of hollow- and solid-core flush doors. They have been used structurally in beams, rafters, trusses, box beams, and floor systems. Caseins are suitable for interior structural applications, but they do not have the resistance to moisture to withstand water soaking or exposure to prolonged high-humidity conditions where condensation can occur. For example, rafters laminated with casein should not be used in cow barns where high-humidity conditions, poor ventilation, and frequent condensation occur. As long as the user understands the moisture limitations of caseins in structural applications and follows the manufacturer's instructions for their preparation and use, they make good structural adhesives for the job site. They can be used at lower temperatures than PVAc, UF, or PRF adhesives. The minimum temperature for casein is 2°C; however, at this temperature, the press time must be longer than at the optimum temperature of 18–24°C. Performance of casein adhesives relative to other adhesives on wood is indicated in Table 1 and Figure 3.

Casein is a proteinaceous material made by precipitation from skim milk under mildly acidic conditions. Its high molecular weight accounts for its colloidal properties and its value as an adhesive. When di- or polyvalent metal ions such as calcium hydroxide are added, the insoluble salt calcium caseinate is formed by cross-linking with the carboxylic acid groups of the different protein molecules. When the bond is formed with the monovalent sodium hydroxide, the adhesive has less water resistance (13). Formaldehyde may also be used for cross-linking amino groups to improve moisture resistance.

BONDING MECHANISMS

Adhesion is defined by the ASTM as the state in which two surfaces are held together by interfacial forces, which may consist of valence forces, interlocking action, or both (1). Valence forces are forces of attraction produced by the interactions of atoms, ions, and molecules that exist within and at the surfaces of both adhesive and adherend. These primary and secondary valence forces give rise to what is generally called specific adhesion. These forces are of the same type that produce cohesion of particles within an adhesive. Interlocking action, also called mechanical bonding, means surfaces are held together by adhesive that has penetrated a rough or porous surface structure and anchored itself during solidification. Both valence forces and interlocking action are essential to effective bonding, but the extent to which each occurs with different types of polymers and adherends is generally acknowledged to be uncertain. Bonding to porous surfaces such as wood, paper, and textiles was thought to be primarily mechanical, but now there is evidence supporting bonding by primary valence forces as well. On the other hand, bonding to hard metal surfaces was believed to involve only valence forces, but this is no longer the accepted view. Metal surfaces roughened by etching or made microscopically porous with a layer of oxide are capable of interlocking with adhesive to produce exceptionally strong bonds.

The three types of intermolecular attractive forces that are the most important in adhesive-bond formation are described here. These include dipole–dipole forces, which occur between polar molecules, London forces, which attract nonpolar molecules to each other, and the hydrogen bond, which is a special type of dipole–dipole force (13,15–

17). Such intermolecular attractive forces have been variously named, but here the generalized van der Waals forces, named after the scientist who postulated their existence in 1873, refers to both dipole–dipole and London forces (15).

Purely covalent bonds (15) are the strongest of chemical bonds. They form when atoms of nonmetals interact by sharing electrons to form a molecule. A purely covalent bond consists of a pair of electrons that are shared by two identical atoms, the simplest being the hydrogen molecule. When two atoms of different elements are joined by a covalent bond, the electron density of the bond is not symmetrically distributed around the two nuclei, which results in a difference in the ability of the two atoms to attract electrons. This causes the molecule to become polarized with a positive and a negative charge. Polarized covalent bonds in molecules give rise to intermolecular attractive forces called dipole–dipole forces (15), where positive and negative poles of molecules attract one another. In a polar molecular substance, the molecules are lined up in positive–negative–positive–negative sequence. The attractions between molecules are considered very important in interfacial adhesion, particularly where polar surfaces such as wood, paper, and glass combine with adhesives containing phenolic and aliphatic hydroxyls.

There are also intermolecular forces that attract nonpolar molecules to each other. These molecules have no permanent dipoles, or dipole–dipole forces, as do the polar molecules. Yet some molecular forces exist, and their existence was postulated by London in 1930. The so-called London forces (15) arise from the motion of electrons, and at any one instant of time, instantaneous dipoles are created by an instantaneous distortion of the electron cloud of a molecule. The instantaneous dipole of one molecule induces matching dipoles in neighboring molecules. These momentary, ever-changing, and synchronized dipoles produce the attractive forces. London forces are not very strong, but the strongest occur between large, complex molecules as in polymers that have large electron clouds that are easily distorted or polarized. Although London forces also exist among polar molecules, they are the only attractive forces existing between nonpolar molecules such as polyethylene, natural rubber, styrene–butadiene, and butyl rubbers (17).

A special type of dipole–dipole force is the hydrogen bond (15). Intermolecular attractions of certain hydrogen-containing compounds are unusually strong. They occur in compounds where hydrogen is covalently bonded to highly electronegative elements of small atomic size. The electronegative element exerts such a strong attraction on the bonding electrons that the hydrogen is left with a significant positive charge. The positively charged hydrogen and the unshared pair of electrons on the electronegative atom of another molecule attract each other to form the strong hydrogen bond. Hydrogen bonding accounts for high solubilities of some compounds containing oxygen and nitrogen in hydrogen-containing solvents such as water. Such forces of attraction between molecules are important in interfacial attraction of adhesive polymers to surfaces such as wood with its polar hydroxyl groups in cellulose.

WETTING AND SETTING

Two solid surfaces normally will not bond to each other even if they have high surface energies, are polished and flat, and are forced together under high pressure. This is because the surfaces make intimate contact at only a few points; the number of points of contact becomes insignificant relative to the overall area of the joint. Intermolecular forces of attraction are effective only at distances of less than 4 nm. In order for two solid surfaces to be held together, a liquid adhesive must make intimate contact and spread freely over both surfaces. This is called wetting. Molecules of the adhesive must diffuse over or into the surface to make contact with the molecular structure of the surface where intermolecular forces of attraction become effective. As will be discussed later, adherends are quite different in terms of their attractive energies, surface roughness and chemistry, and bulk properties. Surfaces may appear to be smooth and flat, but on microscopic examination, numerous peaks, valleys, and crevices can be seen. Therefore, the liquid adhesive must wet, flow, and penetrate the valleys and crevices while displacing or absorbing air, water, and other impurities bound to the surface. Pressure is normally used to force the liquid to flow over the surfaces while forcing out gas occlusions and other blockages to complete wetting.

Wetting of a surface occurs readily when the contact angle between the edge of a drop of adhesive and the solid surface is low. The contact angle approaches zero when the surface has high attractive energy, the adhesive has an affinity for the substrate, and the surface tension of the adhesive is low. Over 180 years ago, Young described the contact angle of a sessile drop of liquid resting on the plane of a solid surface as it was affected by three surface tensions, as shown in Figure 6. His equation is

$$\gamma_{SV} - \gamma_{SL} = \gamma_{LV} \cos \Theta$$

where γ_{LV} is the surface tension at the interface of the liquid and vapor phase, γ_{SL} is the surface tension at the interface of the solid and liquid, γ_{SV} is the surface tension at the interface of the solid and vapor, and Θ is the contact angle (18). Young's approach is still used in various thermodynamic and intermolecular considerations of adhesion to surfaces. It is to be noted that the contact angle is not considered a reliable measure of molecular attraction between solid and liquid; it is rather a relationship between

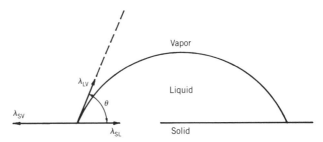

Figure 6. Contact angle of a drop of liquid on a plane solid surface as influenced by three surface tensions.

three phases of contact and gives information on relative strengths of attraction between solid and liquid, and liquid and vapor (19).

When the viscosity of a liquid film is increased, or it is solidified to the point where the film effectively resists shear and other forces tending to separate the surfaces, then the surfaces are effectively bonded. An adhesive film changes from the liquid to solid phase essentially by one of three mechanisms: (1) solvent permeation or evaporation from the film as in water-based adhesives, (2) polymerization of the liquid film as in resorcinolic resins, or (3) cooling of a hot film as in hot-melt adhesives. The mechanisms by which an adhesive joint is made strong or weak are extremely complex. In general, though, the adhesive joint must have sufficient deformability to reduce the buildup of stresses that occur during the solidification process and while the joint is in service (18).

BONDING SURFACES AND THEIR PREPARATION

The surfaces of building materials, particularly wood surfaces, are highly contaminated and replete with minute cracks and crevices. These surface conditions cause gas pockets and blockages that prevent complete wetting by an adhesive. They are also concentration points for stresses. Even though construction adhesives are capable of molecular bonding, the sources for interfacial blockage seem so numerous as to reduce seriously the opportunities for molecular bonding. One of the greatest contributions to joint strength can be made by preparing clean and smooth surfaces.

To be useful in building construction, adhesives must bond to several types of materials, including wood, metals, plastics, concrete, brick, glass, rubber, and ceramics. The surface and bulk properties of each material differ drastically, and these properties must be understood so their surfaces can be properly prepared for effective bonding.

Wood is the most complex bonding surface. It is heterogeneous and highly variable in terms of its surface chemistry and roughness as well as its bulk properties, including density, dimensional stability, porosity, and moisture content (20). These properties are sharply different not only from species to species, but from tree to tree within a species. Furthermore, when a piece of wood is cut from a tree, three surfaces distinctly different in porosity and dimensional stability are presented, depending on whether the cut was made radially, tangentially, or transversely to the grain. Each surface can have a profound influence on the effectiveness of adhesive bonds.

Chemically, wood is composed primarily of polysaccharides, lignin, and extractives (2). Cellulose, the principal polysaccharide, is a high molecular weight linear polymer that makes up about 50% of the cell walls by weight. Lignin is a large complex polymer that makes up 16–33% of the wood. Extractives are the various solvent-extractable compounds that make up 5–30% of the wood's weight. Cellulose makes wood a highly polar surface, but lignin is much less polar (20). Extractives vary in amount and chemical nature and can dramatically affect the bondability of wood. Nonpolar extractives such as terpenes and

fatty acids may inhibit bonding, whereas others may be present in such quantities that they cannot be dissolved and dispersed by the adhesive (20). The wood's surface can be chemically modified further by accumulating extractives and debris, overheating, and burnishing, all of which affect the degree to which the surface can be wetted by an adhesive.

Wood contains moisture that it gains or loses with changes in ambient moisture. The amount of moisture affects the depth of adhesive penetration and curing time, particularly with aqueous adhesives. The proper amount, depending on the type of adhesive and whether it is cured with or without heat, is critical to the development of sound bonds.

Wood shrinks and swells with changes in moisture. If such changes occur while the adhesive is setting or after, severe stresses develop, which in some instances can lead to failure. Dense woods develop higher stresses in bondlines with moisture-induced dimensional changes, so denser woods require stronger adhesive bonds.

Wood surfaces must be free of irregularities for bonding, but they are simple to prepare. Cutting the wood to shape, drying, and surfacing just before bonding ensures dry, smooth, and clean surfaces.

Plastics are relatively homogeneous in physical structure and chemical composition. Plastics have no microstructure, voids, or molecular orientation, and their physical properties are essentially the same in all directions. Thermoplastics are not as strong and stiff as cross-linking thermosets.

Surfaces of plastics, particularly plastics from nonpolar monomers, have low energy. This makes adhesives more difficult to spread. When melted, however, they readily wet and flow. Preparation of high-energy plastics such as fiber glass laminates based on epoxy or polyester resins requires only that surfaces be dry, clean, and of solid integrity. This is usually accomplished with abrading and solvent cleaning. Low-energy surfaces such as fluorocarbons and polyolefins require etching in solvent or acid solutions to increase surface energies. Some plastics may be bonded with the same plastic material dissolved in a solvent so that little or no surface preparation is required.

Metals are crystalline structures of metallic elements held together by very strong atomic forces of attraction. When different metallic elements are mixed together in various proportions, alloys that have their own distinct physical and chemical properties are formed. Metals have no microstructure. They are very dense, but alloys are usually of lower density. Normally, adhesive bonds to metals fail cohesively because the metals are so strong relative to the adhesive.

Metals have very-high-energy surfaces, but careful and thorough surface preparations are absolutely necessary for bonds to develop optimum strength, particularly when the bonds will be exposed to severe service environments. Weak surface layers, organic contaminants, oxides, absorbed gases, and moisture, which reduce surface energy or prevent intimate contact with solid metal, must be completely removed before bonding. Specific cleaning procedures are usually required for each type of metal. Generally, physical and chemical altering of the surface increases energy level. Chemical altering, not to be confused with chemical cleaning, means the chemical reacts with some component of the substrate, which results in metal loss or formation of an oxide. Surface preparations may include one or more procedures, such as solvent cleaning (liquid or vapor), alkaline cleaning, abrading, chemical treatment, washing with water, drying, and perhaps priming with dilute solutions of an adhesive to prevent further contamination.

BIBLIOGRAPHY

1. American Society for Testing and Materials, "Standard Definitions of Terms Relating to Adhesives, D 907–82," in *1984 Annual Book of ASTM Standards, vol. 15.06 Adhesives,* ASTM, Philadelphia, Pa., 1984, pp. 44–52.

2. Forest Products Laboratory, *Wood Handbook: Wood as an Engineering Material,* U.S. Government Printing Office, Washington, D.C., 1974, USDA Handbook No. 72, pp. 1-1–3-25, 9-1–9-6.

3. D. Caster, "Correlation Between Exterior Exposure and Automatic Boil Test Results," *Proceedings of the 1980 Symposium "Wood Adhesives—Research, Application, and Needs,"* Forest Products Lab., USDA Forest Service, Madison, Wis., Sept. 23–25, 1980, pp. 179–188.

4. Forest Products Laboratory, "Durability of Water-resistant Woodworking Glue," Forest Products Lab., USDA Forest Service, Madison, Wis., Report No. 1530 (revised), Sept. 1956, pp. 1–40.

5. R. H. Gillespie, "Effect of Internal Stresses on Bond Strength of Wood Joints," Forest Products Lab., USDA Forest Service, Madison, Wis., Report for Department of Housing and Urban Development, Sept. 1976, pp. 1–69.

6. E. R. Harrell, "Developments in Polyurethane-type Adhesives," *Proceedings of the 1975 Symposium—Adhesives for Products from Wood,* Forest Products Lab., USDA Forest Service, Madison, Wis., Sept. 24–26, 1975, 1976, pp. 207–221.

7. A. A. Mara, "Applications of Wood Bonding," in *Adhesive Bonding of Wood and Other Structural Materials,* Pennsylvania State University, University Park, Pa., EMMSE Project, 1983, pp. 374–377.

8. T. F. Terbilcox and E. R. Luckman, "Aqueous Emulsion Polymer/Isocyanate Adhesives," Ashland Chemical Co., Columbus, Ohio, 1984, Paper No. 18, 31 pp.

9. C. B. Vick, "Gap-filling Phenol-resorcinol Resin Adhesives for Construction," *Forest Prod. J.* **23,** 33–41 (Nov. 1973).

10. W. C. Wake, ed., *Developments In Adhesives—1,* Applied Science Pub. Ltd., London, 1977, pp. 25–72.

11. J. R. Panek and J. P. Cook, *Construction Sealants and Adhesives,* 2nd ed., John Wiley & Sons, Inc., New York, 1984, 348 pp.

12. C. B. Vick, Elastomeric Adhesives for Field-gluing Plywood Floors," *Forest Prod. J.* **21,** 34–42 (Aug. 1971).

13. R. V. Subramanian, "The Adhesive System," in *Adhesive Bonding of Wood and Other Structural Materials,* Pennsylvania State University, University Park, Pa., EMMSE Project, 1983, pp. 137–186.

14. M. L. Selbo, "Selecting Adhesives for Wood Products," *Adhesives Age,* 36–41 (Oct. 1973).

15. C. E. Mortimer, *Chemistry: A Conceptual Approach,* 3rd ed., D. Van Nostrand Co., New York, 1975, pp. 73–81, 123–126, 252–256.

16. A. N. Gent and G. R. Hamed, "Fundamentals of Adhesion," in *Adhesive Bonding of Wood and Other Structural Materials,* Pennsylvania State University, University Park, Pa., EMMSE Project, 1983, pp. 51–84.

17. I. Skeist and J. Miron, "Introduction to Adhesives," in *Handbook of Adhesives,* 2nd ed., Van Nostrand Reinhold Co., New York, 1977, pp. 3–17.

18. W. A. Zisman, "Influence of Constitution on Adhesion," in *Handbook of Adhesives,* 2nd ed., Van Nostrand Reinhold Co., New York, 1977, pp. 33–71.

19. J. J. Bikerman, *The Science of Adhesive Joints,* Academic Press, New York, 1961, pp. 33–37.

20. J. D. Wellons, "The Adherends and Their Preparation for Bonding," in *Adhesive Bonding of Wood and Other Structural Materials,* Pennsylvania State University, University Park, Pa., EMMSE Project, 1983, pp. 85–134.

General References

F. A. Keimel, "Adhesives," in R. E. Kirk and D. F. Othmer, eds., *Encyclopedia of Chemical Technology, Vol. 1,* 3rd ed., John Wiley & Sons, Inc., New York, 1978, pp. 488–510.

I. Katz, *Adhesive Materials—Their Properties and Usage,* Foster Pub. Co., Long Beach, Calif., 1964, 440 pp.

A. A. Marra, dir., *Proceedings of the Conference on Theory of Wood Adhesion,* University of Michigan, Ann Arbor, Mich., July 26–Aug. 4, 1961, 1964, 73 pp.

C. V. Cagle, *Adhesive Bonding Techniques and Applications,* McGraw-Hill Inc., New York, 1968, 351 pp.

J. Shields, *Adhesives Handbook,* Butterworth & Co., Ltd., London, 1970, 355 pp.

H. Schonhorn, "Adhesion," in R. E. Kirk and D. F. Othmer, eds., *Encyclopedia of Chemical Technology, Supplement Vol.,* 2nd ed., John Wiley & Sons, Inc., New York, 1971, pp. 16–27.

M. L. Selbo, *Adhesive Bonding of Wood,* No. 1512, U.S. Government Printing Office, Washington, D.C., 1975, USDA Technical Bulletin, 122 pp.

R. H. Gillespie, D. Countryman, and R. F. Blomquist, *Adhesives in Building Construction,* U.S. Government Printing Office, Washington, D.C., 1978, USDA Handbook No. 516, 160 pp.

W. C. Wake, *Adhesion and the Formulation of Adhesives,* 2nd ed., Applied Science Pub., New York, 1982, 332 pp.

A. Pizzi, ed., *Wood Adhesives Chemistry and Technology,* Marcel Dekker, Inc., New York, 1983, 364 pp.

See also SEALANTS

CHARLES B. VICK
Forest Products Laboratory,
USDA Forest Service
Madison, Wisconsin

ADOBE CONSTRUCTION

The word adobe is thought to be derived from an Arabic word *adob,* meaning "muck" or "sticky glob." The word adobe was carried from North Africa to Spain to Latin

America, where it is in common use today. The word can assume different meanings, including soil, bricks, or building. By definition here, the word earth may be substituted for adobe, but, in general, adobe refers to sun-dried mud brick. Several forms of earth wall construction are common on a global basis. They include earth bricks, both molded and cut from sod (*terrones*), rammed earth (*pisé*), puddled mud, and wattle and daub (*jacál*). The various systems are known by different names in different localities and are often built side by side or in combination.

The use of earth wall building systems is not limited to arid lands, as commonly believed, but is used in many climates. All of these systems use a mixture of earth and water, which is dried by the sun. Erosion from rainfall has only a small effect on vertical earth surfaces (1). The earth surface is sometimes additionally protected from moisture and erosion with plaster or other coatings. Certain other ingredients, such as Portland cement, lime, asphalt, or plant juices, can be added to an earth mixture for walls or plaster to provide additional strength or waterproof qualities to the basic material. An overhanging eave or gable roof can also offer significant erosion protection in areas of high rainfall. Horizontal surfaces, such as parapet walls, are particularly vulnerable to rainfall damage, which can be reduced by the application of stone, fired brick, or stabilized (waterproofed) adobe bricks.

HISTORY

Historically, adobe is one of the oldest forms of building materials in the world, examples of which have been found as early as 7000 B.C. at Jarmo (present day Iraq). Earth wall buildings can be found today throughout Europe, in the UK, France, Germany, and Holland; Africa; the Mediterranean countries; India; and China. Examples in Middle and Far Eastern countries date from the earliest known civilizations, where over the centuries very sophisticated masonry forms were developed, such as arches, domes, and other vaulted structures (Fig. 1). Adobe was widely used in Peru, Mexico, and many other Latin American countries in the pre-Spanish era (Fig. 2). Particularly outstanding pre-Spanish monumental examples of adobe construction can be found in the North Coastal plain of Peru at Chan-Chan dating from 1000 A.D. Examples in western China at Gaochang, Xinjiang are more than 2000 years old.

The use of adobe was widespread in the United States prior to the expansion of the railroads. It was not limited to the arid lands of the West, but included the Eastern seaboard as well. The establishment of railroad systems provided economical transportation and distribution of new types of building materials manufactured in Eastern factories, so these materials gained favor. Prior to that

Figure 1. Iranian village, 1972. Village is built entirely of unstabilized earth brick, with roof structures in various vault forms, such as arches, domes, and barrel vaults. Large building in background has been in continuous use since 400 B.C.

Figure 2. Taos Pueblo, N. Mex., 1947. This 5-story adobe and stone apartment house has been occupied for more than 1000 years.

time, buildings were constructed of locally available materials. The early West, particularly the semiarid and arid Southwest, used adobe very widely for most building projects. The idea of a modular masonry unit, while widely known elsewhere in the Western Hemisphere in pre-Hispanic times, was not known to the indigenous dwellers of the southwestern United States until its introduction by the Spanish explorers.

The use of adobe in industrialized nations gradually diminished as other more durable building materials became readily available. Its use, however, continued until the advent of World War II for many smaller and rural buildings, where transportation costs were excessive or funds were limited. In times of economic distress, adobe has been periodically rediscovered. A number of these buildings, many of considerable age, are still in use today (Fig. 3).

CURRENT USE

The current use of adobe is widespread on a global scale for indigenous, rural, and residential purposes, except in most industrialized countries. It has been estimated that more than 50% of the world's population currently lives in earth homes (2). In the southwestern United States,

the current use of adobe for new construction is principally for luxury homes (Fig. 4) emulating historical architectural examples (Fig. 5). A growing segment of the residential market is in owner-built homes, where adobe is chosen as the primary building material due to its availability, low skill requirements, and thermal characteristics, which are compatible with solar energy applications (Fig. 6). A ready supply of adobes is available in many New Mexico cities. In 1981, more than 4 million bricks were produced in the state of New Mexico (3). Adobe brick production is inhibited by rain, snow, freezing temperatures, and high humidity. In colder, more humid areas, which make production and curing of adobe bricks too difficult, other forms of earth wall construction are used, such as rammed earth.

Some modern building codes, such as the Uniform Building Code, inhibit the use of earth wall construction (unburned clay masonry) with restrictive regulations which do not recognize the properties of the material and successful historical applications. The state of New Mexico has written its own building code for adobe, recognizing local tradition and technology spanning hundreds of years. Many other state and municipal code authorities are following suit using the New Mexico adobe code as a model. Lending institutions in New Mexico, including the FHA, recognize and accept adobe as a viable and even premium building material, while lending institutions in other loca-

Figure 3. Warehouse building, Gallup, N. Mex., 1983 (ca 1915). The adobe brick walls serve well today after seventy years, even with vibration from adjacent railroad.

(a)

(b)

(c)

Figure 4. (a) P. G. McHenry home, Corrales, N. Mex., 1973. This adobe home utilizes traditional building methods with some modern technology. It was built with gravel foundations, a state-of-the-art heating–air conditioning system, and modern doors and windows. **(b)** Modern adobe home, Albuquerque, N. Mex., 1978. Traditional styling blends well with mountain setting. Note solar water heater concealed on the roof. **(c)** Modern interior of adobe home shown in **b.** Soft lines and sculptural qualities of walls provide a striking setting for artworks.

Figure 5. Stinson house, Santa Fe, N. Mex., 1975. Traditional latillas (peeled poles) in a herringbone pattern, with hand carved corbels (beam end supports) serve function, tradition, and decoration.

tions may have serious reservations or restrictions. The School of Architecture and Planning at the University of New Mexico offers undergraduate- and graduate-level courses on earth architecture, and has a special collection of bibliographic materials and photographs on earth architecture. The University of New Mexico Community College and other organizations also offer courses and workshops for nonprofessional owner-builders several times each year.

FUTURE

The increased use of earth wall construction in the future is a certainty. Rising energy costs are directly reflected in all building material prices through the energy costs for production and the energy costs for transportation to the point of use. The energy costs for production of cement, steel, aluminum, and glass are high; the energy costs for earth walls are low. The skill levels and tools required

(a)

(b)

Figure 6 (a) Modern adobe home, Albuquerque, N. Mex., 1978. Pueblo styling combined with modern passive solar design and a privacy wall utilize solar benefits with privacy in an urban setting. **(b)** Modern adobe home, Albuquerque, N. Mex., 1975. Parts of this luxurious home were a milk barn in a dairy during World War I.

for the use of modern high tech materials are high, that for earth wall construction low. While many applications require the use of modern materials, most residential and small commercial buildings do not, in which case the lower cost earth materials could be utilized. A valid example would be infill panels for concrete frame buildings. The rapidly rising need for housing, particularly in developing nations poor in energy resources and import credits, will force the utilization of lower cost local materials. In addition, labor surpluses in many of these same nations can make use of the labor-intensive nature of earth wall construction. While modern materials, such as cement and steel, are preferred by governments and owners, most of these nations recognize the fact that they have no choice and must use earth.

Seismic activity is prevalent in many parts of the world, and the destruction of adobe buildings from seismic events has resulted in human casualties. Many of these casualties have been attributed to adobe construction, giving it an undeserved reputation for seismic vulnerability. All unreinforced masonry buildings have high potential for seismic damage, whether made of brick, stone, or adobe. Studies in India, Peru, and many other countries have resulted in the development of simple design principles to improve the seismic resistance of earth wall buildings. The number of technical and reference publications on earth construction technology is increasing, both in the compilation of existing data and the giving of results of new research on materials and building systems design (4).

CHARACTERISTICS

Ideally, walls of adobe brick or compacted earth are composed of dense, fully compacted, consolidated soil that is completely dry. The presence of sand and aggregate gives strength, and the clay–silt provides a waterproofing and bonding agent. Wall thickness has a wide range, with high walls and historical buildings often thicker. Adobe bricks and earth walls are vulnerable to water in terms of erosion from running water and/or loss of compressive strength from immersion or saturation. Ambient rainfall on vertical surfaces causes minimal erosion, but rainfall on exposed horizontal surfaces, such as the tops of walls, can cause serious maintenance problems. Humidity changes and freeze–thaw cycling have little, if any, measurable effect. Water with high levels of soluble salts can damage wall bases by recrystallization, which separates the particle structure. They can be severely damaged or destroyed by immersion (flooding) or by streams of running water (concentrated erosion). The durability of the wall is mainly determined by its compressive strength and water resistance supplied by the clay. This will generally be a minimum of 300 psi for bricks (5) and 100–800 psi (6) for rammed earth, depending on its age and dryness. Clay content would be ideal at approximately 15%, but can vary widely. Some forms of puddled mud walls may be much less dense and consequently less strong. Calculated pressures for most conceivable designs will seldom exceed 10 psi, so even poorly made adobes or badly compacted walls usually exceed minimum requirements. Satis-

factory soils for the manufacture of adobe bricks, earth mortar, and earth walls are available in nearly any location on the globe. Some are satisfactory as they occur naturally, and some must be modified to some degree with other soils or additives. Ideally, the best soils are alluvial deposits with a variety of granular materials, ranging from coarse aggregate (stones) ½ in. or less and coarse sand to fine sand, silt, and clay. The proportions can vary widely and still be suitable for adobe brick or earth walls. The most reliable test to determine the suitability of soil for bricks is to manufacture test bricks from the proposed soil source. Modifications or amendments can be made at that time. The ideal proportions, which are seldom found naturally, are shown in Table 1.

Simple field tests have been devised to give information on clay–silt-sand ratios (Figs. 7, 8, and 9).

Different types of clay are found in various locations over the earth, ranging from inert types, such as kaolins, to extremely expansive types, such as montmorillonites. The expansion is caused by water entering the molecular structure of the clay. Clay type must be determined by laboratory analysis, but expansive types seem to have little effect on the qualities and stability of the finished brick or earth plaster, so identification of the clay type may be of minimum importance.

Waterproofing agents (stabilizers) are sometimes mixed with the soil and water to reduce erosion and the capability to absorb water. Common stabilizers used are manure, Portland cement, lime, asphalt emulsion, ashes (primitive fly ash), plant juices, and, infrequently, chemical compounds, such as poly(vinyl acrylic) (PVA) compounds. Proportions of stabilizers required will vary with soil properties and must be determined by field testing. The use of stabilizers in locations where they are not needed can add greatly to the cost without adding to the quality.

Adobe Brick Walls

Adobe brick walls are built in a similar manner to other masonry walls. The larger size brick affords the opportunity to build walls one brick thick, which is not always possible with smaller masonry units. Mortar is made from the same soil as the bricks and mixed with water. This earth mortar can be stabilized, or conventional mortar may be used.

Sizes and Shapes. Adobe bricks are made worldwide in a variety of sizes and shapes. Most frequently, they

Table 1. Ideal Proportions for Adobe Soil[a]

	%, Total	AASHO Std[b] Particle Size, mm
gravel	23	over 2.000
coarse sand	23	2.000–0.425
fine sand	30	0.425–0.075
silt	32	0.075–0.005
clay	15	less than 0.005

[a] Ref. 7.
[b] American Association of State Highway Officials Standard.

Figure 7. Soil jar test. A mixture of soil and water after settlement will show relative proportions of ingredients.

Figure 8. Soil rope test. A stiff mixture of soil and water rolled into a rope indicates the plasticity, or clay content, of a given soil.

Adobe Brick Manufacturing. Bricks may be made by various methods with different degrees of mechanization, depending on quantity requirement, available labor, and available capital for manufacturing machinery. This can range from one man with one mold who can make 100–200 bricks per day, to mechanized handling and molding equipment that can produce 20,000 bricks per day. Most molding processes will require a drying and curing time of one week or more (Figs. 11 and 12). Recently developed hydraulic pressing machines can be mobile, and make up to 4000 bricks per day which are usable at once without further drying.

are rectangular or square, but some are formed as cones, dentil shapes, plano convex, and wedges. Ideally for masonry design, the length of a brick should be twice the width and light enough in weight for one man to handle. Thinner, smaller adobe bricks are less subject to severe shrinkage cracking upon manufacture and will be lighter weight for easier handling.

Testing. Laboratory tests of bricks are frequently made to determine compressive strength, modulus of rupture, and, less frequently, water absorption or erosion (for stabilized units). Additional tests are sometimes conducted to determine particle size, clay type, and moisture content. Some building regulations require laboratory testing, but this is not always feasible or practical. Most reasonably well-made adobe bricks will have a minimum compressive strength of 250 psi and a modulus of rupture of 50 psi or more (8).

A simple field test has been devised to test the general toughness quality of the brick: a totally dry brick is dropped on one corner on a hard surface from a distance of 3 ft. Well-made dry bricks suffer little damage (Fig. 10).

Figure 9. Soil trowel test. High clay mixtures adhere to metal surfaces; sand mixtures slide off cleanly.

Figure 10. (a) Drop test indicates homogeneity and dryness. **(b)** Minor damage to corner indicates a satisfactory brick.

Rammed Earth Walls

Rammed earth walls have the same approximate requirements and properties as adobe brick walls. In general, they must be thicker to accommodate tamping devices, with a minimum thickness of 18–24 in. Forms to make these walls may be patented forming systems which can be either rented or job-built (Fig. 13). The moisture content of the soil material being placed in the wall is ideal at approximately 10% (9). A lesser amount will not consolidate and a greater amount is too plastic, preventing full compaction and requiring longer to dry before forms can be removed. The moisture content may be determined with the ball test. The soil mixture must be able to be squeezed into a ball by hand. If a ball will not form, moisture content is too low and moisture must be added. The ball is then thrown against a hard surface and will shatter if moisture content is 10% or less.

Filling and tamping must be done in 6–8 in. lifts to ensure uniform compaction. The compaction may be accomplished by pneumatic equipment or with hand tamps. Initial compressive strength of properly compacted walls will be 90–100 psi, strong enough to allow construction to proceed. Age and drying may increase the compressive strength to 500 psi or more.

Insulation Values

True insulation values of earth walls are generally lower than popularly believed, but provide thermal mass for a flywheel effect, which is useful in raising the comfort factor in many climates and solar applications. The flywheel effect is the thermal mass effect that dampens ambient tem-

Figure 11. Adobe production. Large quantities of adobe bricks can be molded using modern material handling equipment.

Figure 13. Forming for rammed earth walls can be conventional, as shown, or with small simple slip forms.

Figure 12. Adobe production. Small quantities of adobe bricks can be made by hand with simple molds.

perature swings with adequate mass. The indoor temperature will average the outdoor high–low temperatures. Steady state U values (laboratory conditions—a laboratory test where a constant temperature and stable conditions measure heat transmission through a particular wall assembly without the variances which occur in a field test) are affected and modified by climate zone, wall compass orientation, and wall color (10). These effective U values should be recognized and accounted for in building design.

Table 2. Insulation Properties of Earth Walls

Wall Thickness, in.	Steady State U Value	Possible Variation From Other Factors	
		Low	High
10	0.240	0.050–0.241	
14	0.189	0.040–0.193	

The thermal mass effect will tend to average out daily ambient high–low temperatures, varying only slightly in a 24-h period. In general, it is best to insulate certain walls in certain climates on the exterior to achieve maximum thermal benefits. Research indicates that optimum wall thickness for thermal values is 10–12 in. (11).

CONSTRUCTION DESIGN

Walls

Earth wall thickness is determined by several factors: wall height–thickness ratio recommended for seismic risk zone, insulation values needed, and brick sizes available. Multistory construction is feasible with earth materials, but becomes less cost-effective with added material handling costs.

Foundations

Foundations for earth walls have the same requirements as conventional construction, recognizing the high weight factors and problems with differential settlement of masonry walls.

Roof Structures

Conventional roof structure designs are compatible with earth wall buildings. Arches and vaulted masonry forms are common in many parts of the world, and can be effective if design features are incorporated to prevent moisture infiltration into the wall fabric.

Window and Door Detailing

Conventional window and door detailing is suitable, providing the water vulnerability of the wall fabric is recognized. Where such infiltration may be of minor consequence in conventional construction, it may cause major damage to earth walls. Anchorage must be provided with wood plugs, inserts, or wood adobes (12).

Seismic Design

Research projects indicate that the primary design criteria for improved seismic response by earth-walled buildings are as follows:

1. Sound earth substrata siting for building, with good drainage.
2. Square building plan with minimum rectangularization.
3. Minimum unsupported wall lengths, with minimum size openings.
4. Adequate wall aspect ratios generally not more than 1:8 or 1:10, possibly supplemented by buttressing. (The aspect ratio is the relationship of wall height to wall thickness, eg, 10 in. thick × 100 in. high = 10:1 aspect ratio.)
5. Wall reinforcement, vertical and/or horizontal.
6. The use of bond or collar beams to improve wall moment resistance.
7. Maximum 2 stories.
8. Lightweight roof structure and roofing material.

SURFACE TREATMENTS

Earth walls may be protected from erosion by the use of plaster, made either of earth materials or cement stucco. Either choice has drawbacks and advantages. Earth plasters are economical, but require more frequent maintenance. Cement stucco is more costly initially, but requires less short-term maintenance. Cement stucco, due to its waterproof quality, may also conceal other structural damage. Penetrating coatings, while apparently successful initially, have been found to accelerate the damage to earth walls and are not of great value. Most stabilizers must be mixed with the base material prior to molding or application to be effective.

BUILDING REGULATIONS

Fragmented information sources and lack of familiarity with earth construction have created a void with respect to regulations for earth wall buildings, or unrealistic building regulations that do not recognize accepted successful practice. The state of New Mexico has adopted the most knowledgeable and comprehensive regulations, which are sometimes used as a model for other building code authorities.

SUMMARY

Earth wall buildings can provide answers for high quality buildings with minimum cost and utilization of local resources of material and manpower. The techniques devel-oped over many millenniums are valid today in almost any climate.

BIBLIOGRAPHY

1. P. G. McHenry, Jr., *Adobe and Rammed Earth Buildings,* John Wiley & Sons, Inc., New York, 1984, p. 119.
2. S. Mutal, *Adobe,* Regional Project on Cultural Heritage and Development, UNDP, UNESCO, Lima, Peru, 1984, in Spanish and English, p. 29.
3. E. W. Smith, *Adobe Bricks in New Mexico,* New Mexico Bureau of Mines and Mineral Resource, New Mexico Institute of Mining and Technology, Socorro, N. Mex., 1982.
4. G. W. May, Ed., *International Workshop Earthen Buildings in Seismic Areas,* conference proceedings, Vols. I-III, University of New Mexico, Albuquerque, N.M. September 1981. J. Vargas N. Ed., *Memorias Seminario Latin Americano de Construcciones de Tierra en Areas Sismicas,* Pontifica Universidad Catolica, Lima, Peru, May 1983.
5. Ref. 3, p. 35.
6. R. L. Patty, *Puddled Earth & Rammed Earth Walls,* Agricultural Engineering Bulletin **20,** No. 8, University of South Dakota, Vermillion, S. Dak., 1939, pp. 60 and 61.
7. Ref. 1, p. 51.
8. Ref. 3, p. 38.
9. G. F. Middleton, *Build Your House of Earth,* Compendium Pty, Ltd., Melbourne, Australia, 1975.
10. D. K. Robertson, *Expanded Revision of Effective "U" Values,* New Mexico Energy Institute, Albuquerque, N. Mex., 1981.
11. F. Wessling, "Transient Thermal Response of Adobe," *Adobe News,* No. 6 (1975).
12. Ref. 1., pp. 114, 117.

PAUL G. MCHENRY, JR., AIA
Paul G. McHenry, Jr. and
Associates
Albuquerque, New Mexico

AEPIC.   See ARCHITECTURE AND ENGINEERING PERFORMANCE INFORMATION CENTER (AEPIC)

AIA.   See AMERICAN INSTITUTE OF ARCHITECTS (AIA)

AIR CONDITIONING.   See MECHANICAL SYSTEMS

AIRPORTS

THE AIRPORT ENVIRONMENT

To architects and engineers, the planning, design, and construction of an airport represents a unique challenge. No other project type requires a working knowledge of such a broad range of disciplines to be brought to bear for a successful solution. In addition to the full scope of architectural services, engineering disciplines, including heavy civil, municipal, structural, mechanical, and electrical, and electronics are required, as well as economics, environmental sciences, and specialist services of transportation planning, systems analysis, computer simulations and modeling, materials handling, etc. To make the task more challenging, it is debatable whether the ideal airport has yet been designed; each of the current examples contains elements that have achieved success, but none can be readily transposed in total from one location to another. In the airport environment, the only constant is change itself; consequently, the one attribute that is of paramount importance is flexibility, ensuring that the airport will not be overwhelmed by inevitable technological advances and economic perturbations.

This article is not intended to cover all of these aspects in any detail, but rather to present a basic understanding of the airport system together with examples and references to literature where the reader can explore the subject in greater depth.

Airports are a part of the worldwide air transportation system of airlines, airways, and airports that in 1985 carried an estimated total of 166.67 billion t-km (103.56 billion t-miles) of passenger, freight, and mail traffic on scheduled domestic and international services (1). Of this total, passengers accounted for 73.8% of the load, freight for 23.6%, and mail for 2.6%. Regional distribution of scheduled air traffic in 1985 is shown in Table 1.

Airports perform the role of providing an interface through which aircraft can land and take off safely, and be staged to facilitate the loading and unloading of passengers, freight, and mail that are either carried to the airport by surface transportation modes or transferred between aircraft.

Number of Airports

The total number of civil aerodromes in the 157 International Civil Aviation Organization (ICAO) contracting states in 1985 was 36,050, of which 14,899 were land aerodromes open to public use (1). The United States has by far the most airports open to public use, with over 37% of the world's total.

Table 1. Regional Distribution of Scheduled Air Traffic[a,b]

Region	Distribution
North America	38.5
United States	
Canada	
Europe	32.7
Asia and Pacific	17.7
Latin America and Caribbean	4.9
Middle East	3.5
Africa	2.7

[a] Ref. 1.
[b] Percentage of t-km performed by airlines registered in each region.

Standards

The ICAO, created as a special agency of the United Nations in 1947, provides the machinery for international cooperation within the air transportation industry. One of its main activities is the establishment of international standards, recommended practices, and procedures covering the technical fields of civil aviation including airports (2). As each standard is adopted by ICAO, it is put into effect by the 157 member states (countries) through their respective regulatory agencies, such as the Federal Aviation Administration (FAA) in the United States. The ICAO, FAA, and their counterpart agencies in other countries publish continually updated series of manuals and advisory publications covering the full range of airport planning, design, and construction topics, the most pertinent of which are included in the bibliography at the end of the article. Depending on their ownership, airports may also come under the jurisdiction of other federal, state, or municipal authorities, requiring the architect to check with those authorities on requirements to observe building codes and municipal bylaws.

Airport Activities

The types of activities that take place at an airport depend to a large extent on the role of the airport within the context of the regional or national aviation system. Such roles vary from the handling of predominantly general aviation, defined as all civil flying not classified as commercial air carrier, to the handling of international and domestic air carrier traffic at major gateway airports such as John F. Kennedy International Airport (JFK) in New York and Heathrow Airport in London. In the case of the two examples cited, the range of activities may include:

1. The processing of international and domestic passengers and their baggage using the airport as an origin or destination.
2. The processing of passengers and baggage connecting from one flight to another.
3. The processing of inbound, outbound, and transfer air freight and airmail.
4. The preparation and transfer of in-flight catering from flight kitchens to aircraft.
5. The provision of airport emergency services, such as fire fighting, crash, and rescue.
6. The performance of aircraft maintenance services on either a scheduled or emergency basis.
7. The provision of air traffic control services.
8. The provision of aircraft refueling services.
9. The provision of ground transportation services to and from the airport.
10. The provision of airport maintenance functions, such as snow clearing, airfield maintenance, and building janitorial services.

Airport Size

The size of an airport is usually measured more by the annual volume of traffic that is processed than it is by

Table 2. Ten Busiest Airports in the World[a,b]

Airport	Annual passengers	Land Area, acres
O'Hare, Chicago	49,954,362	7,000
Hartsfield, Atlanta	42,494,630	3,800
Los Angeles International	37,674,983	3,500
Dallas–Fort Worth	37,104,026	17,520
Heathrow, London	31,289,254	2,715
Kennedy, New York	28,945,288	5,200
Newark	28,576,586	2,300
Stapleton, Denver	28,485,927	4,600
Haneda, Tokyo	27,167,402	1,055
San Francisco International	25,018,395	5,207

[a] Refs. 3 and 4.
[b] Based on 1985 passenger statistics.

the land area within its boundaries or the floor area of its buildings. In Table 2, the 10 busiest airports in the world are listed together with 1985 traffic volumes and their approximate land areas.

The area of land required for an airport is of great significance, however, because of its size and location, by necessity, close to the population centers which it serves. The requirement for airport land area is related primarily to the airside configuration, particularly the number, length, and orientation of the runways needed to accommodate the number and range of aircraft types that use the airport. In many cases land within the airport boundaries is also used for functions that do not necessarily relate to the primary function of the airport. Such users may include the military, aerospace companies, research and development functions, and major aircraft maintenance bases (as distinct from the line maintenance functions normally carried out at airports). Noise protection, however, requires land areas much in excess of that required for the runway system. The size of airport terminal buildings bears a much closer relationship to the number of passengers processed, as will be discussed in subsequent sections of the article.

Economic Impact

The economic impact of airports, particularly those serving the larger population centers, is substantial. Economic analyses carried out by Transport Canada in 1980 indicate that Lester B. Pearson International Airport in Toronto, which handled over 14 million passengers that year, was one of the largest employers in the Toronto area, with 14,000 people directly employed at the airport. In addition, indirect employment from activities created to serve the airport and secondary employment in service-sector activities whose existence depends directly or indirectly on those employed at the airport accounted for another 42,500 jobs. This reflects an employment multiplier of 3.0 compared to a multiplier of 2.6 for New York's three major airports, where similar studies have been carried out (5).

Environmental Impact

The most significant environmental impact from airports is that caused by aircraft noise. Most noise exposure lies within the land area immediately beneath and adjacent to the aircraft approach and departure paths. A number of noise measurement techniques exist, generally involving some formulation of decibel level, duration, number of occurrences, and time of day (6). Much has been done to reduce the problem, such as the development of quieter aircraft engines, procedures for noise abatement, and the imposition of operational curfews.

HISTORICAL BACKGROUND TO AIRPORT DEVELOPMENT

The history of practical requirements for airports can be traced back to 1903, the Wright brothers, and the first powered flight by a heavier-than-air craft at Kittyhawk, N.C. Rapid development followed, with the first air transport company (airline) to operate with aircraft formed in the UK in 1916, and the first scheduled domestic air service in Germany in 1919. The first international air services operated between London and Amsterdam, and London and Paris in 1920. The early aircraft of the 1900s were lightweight and traveled at considerably slower speeds than do modern aircraft, thus making them very susceptible to crosswinds. To take off and land they had to head directly into the wind. For this reason, the best type of airfield was a large, reasonably smooth field that would provide sufficient runway length, normally no more than 800 m (2,625 ft) in any direction. Because of their light weight, the aircraft did not require strengthened strips or runways. As aircraft developed during the 1920s, becoming heavier and more numerous, they could no longer be supported by natural turf strips, and the concept of runways evolved. By 1928, there were 807 airports in the United States, 392 of which had landing strips or runways (7).

As air traffic rapidly increased, so too did the need to regulate the airport environment. In the United States, the Aeronautical Branch of the Department of Commerce assumed that responsibility by issuing airport rating regulations (8). These regulations applied to general equipment and facilities, size of effective landing area, and night-lighting equipment. An airport in the late 1920s that met the requirements was St. Louis Airport in St. Louis, Mo., illustrated in Figure 1.

Airport buildings housed some or all of the following functions, depending on the role of the airport and the type and volume of traffic: hangars, repair shops, storage sheds, manufacturing buildings, garages, administration, control tower and offices, restaurants, passenger waiting rooms, clubhouse facilities for flying clubs, pilots' building with lockers and showers, hotel or other sleeping accommodations, radio building, post office, and freight warehouse. The administration building frequently combined passenger, administrative, and flyers' functions under one roof. At the larger airports being developed in the 1930s these buildings were often grand in scale, emulating the characteristics of the great railroad terminals, and providing the new air transportation industry with a sense of solidity and permanence. The most prominent European examples of the period were Croydon Airport near London, and Tempelhof Field in Berlin.

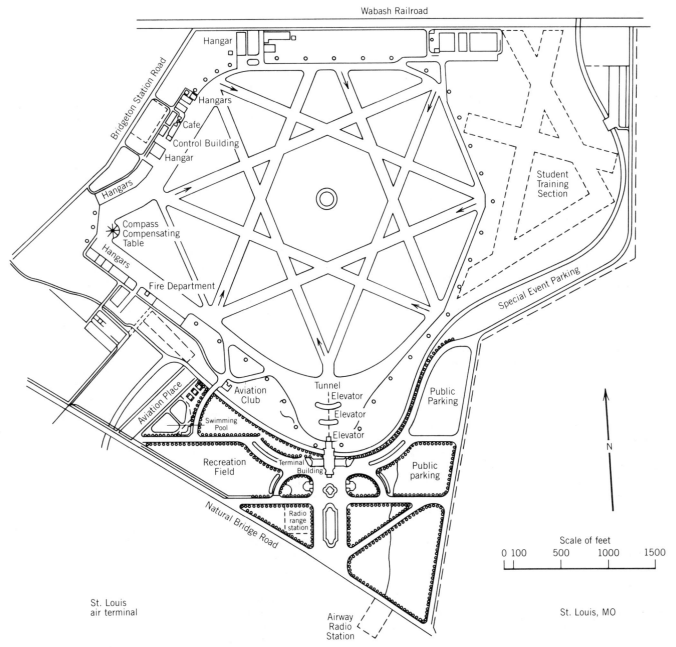

Figure 1. St. Louis Airport as it appeared in the late 1920s (7). Courtesy of Harvard University Press.

The early history of Tempelhof Field (9) typifies the difficulties faced by airport engineers and architects as they attempt to keep up with the increasing pace of change. Operations commenced at the airport in 1923, and the construction of the terminal complex commenced in 1926. The pace of construction could not keep up with the rapidly growing traffic volumes; the planning was overwhelmed by some 50 makeshift buildings that had appeared by 1930. A firm sense of planning direction was eventually taken in 1933 by the new regime, and a new concept was approved for the new Central Airport that was to be rebuilt from the ground up. Besides having to satisfy the airport function, this concept had to satisfy the needs of the Reich

Air Ministry, in fact housing all of its functions, and finally it had to be a location for huge public gatherings (for as many as 200,000 people). The air terminal building embodied many new ideas, such as the processing of passengers, baggage, freight, and visitors on separate levels in an area that was 30 times that required to handle the traffic of that time. The building was complete except for a few portions, and was used subsequently for civil air transport and military functions through 1975, at which time civil operations were transferred to new facilities at Tegel. When the building began in 1936, Berlin had established itself as the primary European airport, ahead of London, Paris, and Amsterdam. Other impressive structures combined terminal facilities with hangar accommodations at Littorio Airport in Rome and, in the United States, at Wichita Airport and Mines Field (Los Angeles).

Designers were becoming increasingly aware of the need to provide better levels of efficiency and safety, particularly at the medium to large size airports. The Lehigh Airports Competition, sponsored by the Lehigh Portland Cement Company in 1929 (10), contributed many new ideas, such as the use of taxiways to permit aircraft to travel safely from the hangars or terminal buildings to the runways, the use of parallel or double runways dedicated to either takeoffs or landings, the separation of passengers from the main operational areas of the airfield by the use of underground tunnels or walkways connecting the passenger terminal building with loading points on the apron, and the increasing provisions made for the comfort and convenience of passengers. The first prize winners in the competition were the Americans A. C. Zimmerman and William H. Harrison who presented a concept embodying many revolutionary ideas that were used successfully some 40 years later. Of particular interest was their concept of connecting the main passenger terminal with a star-shaped loading point located on the apron by means of underground walkways. This loading point was a satellite building containing telescopic steel tunnels that could be extended out on tracks to reach the doors of arriving or departing aircraft, the forerunner of the now familiar loading bridges introduced in the 1960s. The satellite concept has since been used successfully in the past 40 years at some of the world's largest airports.

From their beginnings in the 1920s, airports went through constant and rapid growth up to the present time. Worldwide air traffic volumes increased as point-to-point travel times decreased, and general levels of service including reliability and frequency of service increased.

A major contributor to the growth of civil aviation has been technological advance in aircraft performance (11). Over the period from 1945 to 1985, speed has increased from 320 to 980 km per hour (200 to 609 mph), range has increased from 4000 to 10,000 km (6210 miles), and payload has increased tenfold. Improvements have occurred in comfort and safety, and operating costs, measured on a cost-per-seat kilometer basis, have actually declined.

In addition to the requirement to cope with the rapid growth in civil aviation, there have been other major influences on airport development, such as:

1. Economic perturbations, particularly of the 1970s and 1980s, causing uncertainty in air traffic forecasts and attendant difficulties in decision making for major projects. Emphasis has swung from the development of major new facilities even at the risk of exceeding capacity, to operational optimization wherein the maximum use of existing facilities has been the overriding concern.

2. The increased use of aircraft and airports by political terrorists in the 1970s and 1980s, requiring ever-increasing tightening of security measures, including checks on passengers and their baggage, freight consignments, and airport personnel.

3. Fuel price instability of the 1970s and 1980s, particularly the spiraling rises after 1974 and the Arab oil embargo, placing increased emphasis on the requirement for airport designs that would enhance aircraft maneuvering efficiency on the runway, taxiway, and apron–gate system, thereby reducing fuel burn.

4. The saturation of major airports in the large population areas coupled with limits on available land area, leading to the development of multiple airport systems and the resulting problems of inequities in the utilization of staff, equipment, and facilities. Examples of this are Paris with Orly and Charles de Gaulle airports, Montreal with Dorval and Mirabel airports, and Washington with National and Dulles airports (12).

5. Deregulation of the air transportation industry, which began in the United States, and is proceeding in some other countries. The main impact of this phenomenon on airports has been the development of route networks in response to market forces rather than regulated demand. Out of it has emerged the hub-and-spoke concept whereby airlines are providing services that require the passenger to take connecting flights more frequently to reach a destination. William B. Hartsfield Atlanta International Airport, which serves a high proportion of connecting passengers, requires different facilities from one in which the proportion of originating and terminating passengers is predominant.

Historically, the 1930s were significant in that aircraft became larger, heavier, and faster, requiring defined and strengthened runways of increasing length. The costs of airport development were increasing as was the requirement for additional airports. Most airport locations for the major cities of the world were selected by the end of the 1930s. At this particular time, locations were selected on the basis of the closest proximity to the population centers which they served, provided that adequate space, free from obstructions, could be found.

The 1940s saw rapid advances in aircraft technology resulting from World War II, which have continued to the present time. In many cases, sufficient room for further expansion was not available. New locations had to be found for airports in cities such as London, where Heathrow Airport was developed in the late 1940s to accommodate additional growth which could not be accommodated at Croydon. LaGuardia Airport (New York), designed and constructed in the late 1930s with four runways, was opened to commercial traffic in 1940 and remains operational today, although two of its original runways are no longer usable because of insufficient length. A second airport was constructed at Idlewild (later to be renamed John F. Kennedy International Airport), to handle principally the large growth in international traffic. In the same time period, similar situations were occurring in Paris with the development of Orly International Airport to join Le Bourget, and in other cities such as Los Angeles and Baltimore.

The 1950s saw the introduction of the jet age in commercial air transportation, which was most demanding on airports in terms of additional runway length requirements. Runway lengths of 1000 m (3280 ft), which were adequate for the twin-piston-engine aircraft of the 1930s, had increased to 3000 m (9843 ft) to accommodate the new generation of four-engine jet aircraft of the late 1950s and early 1960s. In addition to the expansion of all large commercial airports, new airports were being constructed in cities such as London, where Gatwick Airport was opened in the late 1950s. Major airport developments were planned, designed, or constructed in this decade at O'Hare (Chicago), Toronto, Hong Kong, New York, Philadelphia, Orly (Paris), Greater Pittsburgh, and Zurich. New technology applied in this period included moving sidewalks at Love Field in Dallas and the planning of the transporter concept for Dulles serving Washington, D.C.

A great deal of developmental activity took place in the 1960s and early 1970s, including the acclaimed design of Dulles Airport (Washington), the massive Dallas–Fort Worth Airport, and Houston Intercontinental; major terminal expansions at JFK and Newark airports in the New York area, Kansas City, Boston, and Miami; and innovative concepts using automated guideway systems at Tampa and Seattle–Tacoma. Outside the United States, major developments were occurring at Rio de Janeiro, Copenhagen, Frankfurt, Amsterdam, and in Paris with the opening of the new Charles de Gaulle Airport at Roissy in 1974. At the peak of this activity in 1968, there appeared to be no limits to growth, with annual increases averaging 16% having been achieved in the decade. Many projects were on the drawing boards of planners who were anticipating not only a continuation of this growth, but also continued technological developments in aircraft. This period saw the introduction in 1970 of the Boeing 747 aircraft followed by other wide-bodied aircraft such as the MacDonnell–Douglas DC-10, Lockheed L1011, and Airbus Industrie A300. These aircraft, with vastly increased operating weights and quantum increases in dimensions (length, wingspan, and doorsill height), had dramatic impact on airport development, requiring larger separation between runways and taxiways, increased maneuvering and parking space on aprons, and more efficient loading and unloading methods. Inside the terminal buildings, planners had to resize virtually all facilities to accommodate single-flight loads in excess of 400 passengers, where previously maximum flight loads rarely exceeded 200 passengers.

The second half of the 1970s and the first half of the 1980s saw economic pressures applied to airport development in the Western world by the effects of the oil crisis of 1973–1974 and by recession, particularly in the 1980s. The number of large-scale developments had decreased significantly, with the exception of major developments at Mirabel (Montreal), Atlanta, Los Angeles, Heathrow's Terminal 4 (London), Stockholm, and Zurich. The focus of activity had shifted to the developing world; major new airports were being developed in the Arab world, notably at Jeddah and Riyadh in Saudi Arabia, in Kuwait, and at virtually every center in the Arab Emirates. In the Far East, growth rates remained strong, resulting in major airport construction in Tokyo, Singapore, Taipei, Jakarta,

Kuala Lumpur, and Manila. Tokyo's new second airport at Narita was virtually complete by 1972, but did not become operational until 1979 because of opposition from a coalition of farmers, other landowners, and students.

THE AIRPORT MASTER PLAN

An airport can be described as a system comprising two basic subsystems: (1) an airside system of runways, taxiways, and air traffic services; and (2) a landside system of ground transportation, parking and curbs, and sections of buildings open to the public. The passenger terminal complex is of great importance and consists of the apron, terminal building, and ground transportation facilities, providing an airside–landside interface for the purposes of processing, loading, unloading, or transferring passenger, freight, mail, and catering services. The aircraft apron must be considered an integral part of the passenger terminal complex.

Every airport, regardless of its size, should have a current master plan for future development. With the rapid growth in air traffic, there is a continuing need to expand existing facilities, and in some cases where there is no further room for the requisite expansion, to either relocate the airport to a new site or construct an additional airport. All of the airport systems interrelate closely, so that in an efficient airport there is a requirement to maintain a balance of individual subsystem capacities—the overall efficiency being related to that of its weakest link. The airport master plan sets a framework, within which individual facilities development planning decisions can be made by the appropriate authorities secure in the knowledge that such developments will not be mutually conflicting. Both ICAO and FAA have published comprehensive guidelines on the preparation of airport master plans (13,14); these publications are essential reference material to the airport architect. Layouts of four selected airports are contained in Figure 2. The following discussion relates to some of the more important aspects of airport master planning.

The Airside System

The layout of the airside system is of primary concern because of the large areas of land required to accommodate the physical characteristics of the runway–taxiway system and associated zoning restrictions. Airport land use within its boundaries is controlled by three different types of zoning criteria: horizontal separation criteria that ensure the safe maneuvering of aircraft on the ground; obstacle clearance criteria that ensure the integrity of airspace in the immediate vicinity of the airport; and zoning to maintain the integrity of electronic aids to landing and navigation. All of these zoning criteria are clearly stipulated in ICAO Annex 14 (2). The implications of some of these criteria on the siting of airport facilities, such as passenger terminal buildings, air cargo buildings, and hangars, are typically shown in Figure 3.

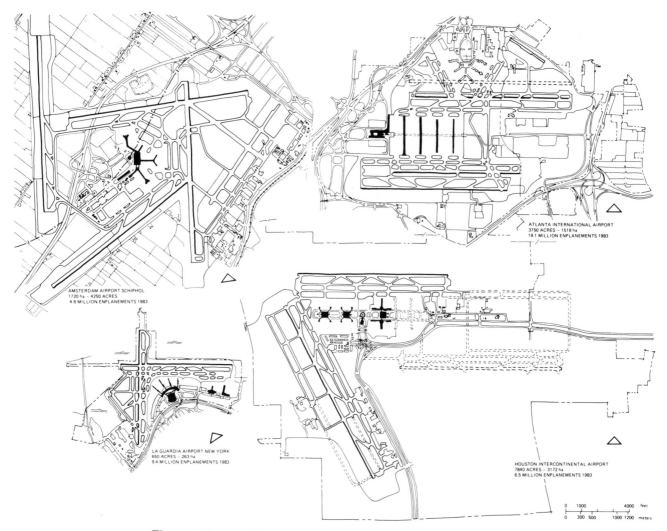

Figure 2. Layouts of four selected airports reduced to the same scale (15).

Runways and Taxiways

The length of runways is a determinant of the performance and weight characteristics of the critical aircraft that are to be accommodated, of the temperature and altitude of the airport, and of the runway slope and its surface condition. The higher the temperature, the more runway length is required; similarly, the higher the altitude, the more length required (16). Orientation of runways depends on the direction of the prevailing winds, although in broad terms they should be oriented so that aircraft are not directed over the most populated area and obstructions are avoided. Aircraft that are landing or taking off are able to use the runway as long as the wind component at right angles to the runway, referred to as crosswind, is within specified limits. For runways serving air carriers (length exceeding 2100 m (6890 ft)), ICAO specifies that the runway should be oriented so that aircraft may be landed at least 95% of the time with crosswinds of 20 knots (37 km/h) or less (2). At busy airports, an inability

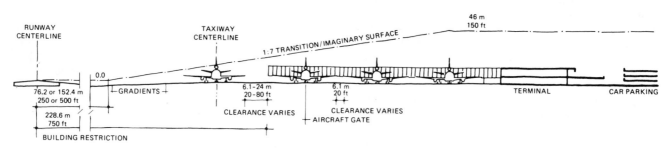

Figure 3. The effect of zoning criteria on siting of airport buildings (15).

to operate for the remaining 5% of the time may be unacceptable, and consequently, additional crosswind runways may be required, especially if there is a significant proportion of general aviation activity that is generally more susceptible to crosswinds.

The number of runways required is a function of the demand on the airport, measured in terms of the number of aircraft movements that are required to be accommodated in the peak period. The airside capacity of an airport is a function of the runway configuration, the mix of aircraft types to be accommodated in the peak period, the number and location of taxiway exits which affect runway occupancy times, and airspace constraints (17). Adequate provision of taxiways is essential to provide uninterrupted flow of aircraft between runways and aircraft gates, thereby ensuring that the maximum capacity of the runway system can be achieved.

Standards covering the physical characteristics of runways, including shoulders, strips, end safety areas, clearways and stopways, taxiways, including shoulders and strips, holding bays, and aprons, are laid down in ICAO Annex 14 and by the FAA in Ref. 18. These standards relate to lengths, widths, slopes, and pavement strengths as well as separation criteria.

The Ground Transportation System

The landside ground transportation system consists of the main access roads, internal circulation, including interterminal transportation in multiterminal airports, passenger terminal curbs, and car parking. Ground transportation to and from most airports is provided by private automobile and by public transport, including taxis and buses. At many European airports, such as Heathrow and Gatwick airports (London), Schipol (Amsterdam), Frankfurt, and Zurich, rail access has been provided, in some cases linking up to the entire regional rail network. National Airport in Washington, D.C., also provides rail access. These systems provide increased convenience to airport users, although they are expensive to implement and rely heavily on user acceptance of public transit to maintain the high levels of ridership needed to establish cost effectiveness. In North America, the private automobile is by far the dominant means of airport ground access, but many authorities such as in Atlanta, Cleveland, and Boston, have made provision for regional rail transit connections in the future.

Recognizing the advances in technology that have resulted in major decreases in point-to-point air travel times, planners of the ground transportation system at airports continuously strive to reduce delays on the ground which in some cases, during the peak periods, can equal air travel times for short-haul routes.

The Internal Road System

The internal road system is required to provide access to the passenger terminal building arrival and departure curbs; to provide access to both short-term and long-term public parking lots; to connect terminal buildings in multiterminal airport systems; to provide circulation routes for employees and their parking lots; and to provide service road connections to the passenger terminal building for delivery of supplies to the air cargo building complex and to the other airport, airline, and aviation support facilities. An airside service road with restricted access is also required to provide connections to the terminal building and apron for mail, freight, baggage, and catering supplies. Opportunities do exist to minimize delays on the public ground transportation system through effective planning of the internal transportation system. Conversely, it is in this component of the system that inordinate delays will be encountered if capacity shortfalls are not prevented. In particular, inadequate capacities of the approach roads, feeder roads to the terminal curbs, and parking structures can be the cause of serious constraints.

Some of the newer airports have introduced peoplemover technologies to enhance movement of the public and employees on the landside, although with varying degrees of success. Notable examples in the United States are Dallas–Fort Worth Airport in Texas and Seattle–Tacoma Airport in Washington State, which provide automated guideway transit connections from the parking lots to the terminals. Good examples of interterminal transportation systems using more conventional technologies that operate particularly well are the Red Bus system at Kansas City Airport, and the bus system at Logan (Boston).

Automobile Parking

Automobile parking for the public and employees is a major consideration, particularly at North American airports, and is an important source of revenues to the airport authority. There are two categories of public parking: short-term parking located close to the terminal building, and long-term parking, which can be located more remotely. Sufficient areas of land close to the terminal building are difficult to provide, particularly at busy airports with more than 5 million annual passengers. In these cases, parking structures are a convenient solution because they can be located to provide access to the terminal within reasonable walking distance.

The planning and design of the ground transportation system must take demand into account, which is related to the peak volumes of originating and terminating passengers, rather than to the enplaning and deplaning passenger volumes which include transfer passengers. These volumes can differ greatly as is the case at Hartsfield (Atlanta) where approximately 75% of all enplaning and deplaning passengers are transferring between flights and hence do not use the ground transportation system. Data for the design of each component of the system are normally provided through surveys which include: passenger-to-visitor ratios; percentage of passengers by type of vehicle; occupancy type of vehicle; percentage of use of short- and long-term parking; and intra-airport vehicle volumes (13).

The Airside–Landside Interface

To restrict access from the landside to the airside, a security fence is provided, which has a number of controlled and supervised access points through which the majority of the airport's traffic is processed. The requirement to maintain the integrity of this security system is growing with the increase in the number of terrorist-related incidents at the world's airports.

Straddling this interface are the airport facilities that process passengers, freight, in-flight catering, and supplies, and that provide aircraft maintenance functions. The terminal building is dealt with in some depth in the next section. Landside–airside interface in this facility is provided at the aircraft gates and at control points on the terminal service road which serves the terminal complex. Within the terminal, there may be some restricted areas if the terminal serves international passengers requiring processing through government inspection functions of health, immigration, customs, and agriculture.

Air Cargo

Air cargo is carried in the holds of regular passenger aircraft, by specialized all-freight aircraft, and by aircraft that operate with configurations which can vary to suit combinations of passenger and freight loads (commonly referred to in the industry as combis). It is estimated that approximately 70–80% of all air cargo, however, is carried by passenger aircraft. The air cargo facilities are owned and operated through a number of different means: a single airline handling both its own cargo and that of other airlines; a consolidated operating company, more common in Europe and the Far East than in North America; or a developer acting as a landlord with either single- or multiple-operating tenants. Prominent examples in each of these categories are: Lufthansa Air Cargo Terminal in Frankfurt, which is the largest air cargo operation in the world operated by a single airline; the Hong Kong Air Cargo Terminal at Kai Tak Airport, which handles the majority of all air cargo passing through Hong Kong; and the new Vista Cargo Centre at Pearson Airport in Toronto which will have multiple tenants, including a consolidated operating company and a combination of airlines, brokers, and forwarders. In many large airports, there is frequently more than one cargo terminal; it is possible that all three types of terminal exist at one airport.

Guidelines for the planning, design, and implementation of air cargo terminals have been published by the International Air Transport Association (IATA) in its *Airport Terminals Reference Manual* (19).

Site planning for cargo terminals should be carried out in the context of the airport master plan, allowing adequate space for future expansion, and respecting airport zoning criteria. The location of the air cargo terminal should consider the requirements for an aircraft parking apron for freighter aircraft immediately adjacent to the airside face; clear access via an airside road to the passenger terminal apron for the movement of freight to and from passenger aircraft; and ready access to the ground transportation system. The size of the aircraft apron relates directly to the forecast of the number and sizes of aircraft that will use the facility at the same time, this information being available only from the prospective operator.

There are no standards as such for the design of cargo terminals because of the variety of users and the different types of operations. For terminals handling predominantly international cargo, there is a requirement for bonded facilities, a relatively larger storage area, and customs-oriented documentation procedures. Domestic operations require relatively less warehouse space, and the emphasis is on speedy storage and retrieval systems. Another important influence on the design is the volume of cargo that would be transferred between domestic and international carriers.

The program for the cargo terminal is provided to the architect directly by the owner–operator, or is arrived at in close consultation between the two parties. The building program would consider the total volume of air cargo forecasted for the design year; the type of operation and tenants; ratios of export–import and transfer–transhipment volumes; percentages of containerized and palletized cargo; distribution of consignments by weight and volume; distribution of packages per consignment; planned dwell times; destination distribution; and arrival patterns of trucks at the landside face delivering or collecting shipments. The two most important decisions that can be made from these data are the type of materials handling systems to be employed and the number of truck docks required. The selection of the materials handling system to be employed will determine the basic building envelope, including the optimum depth, building grid, and clear heights to the underside of the superstructure. The number of truck docks required will determine building length. To ensure the maximum utilization of the cargo processing floor area, offices are usually located on a mezzanine floor above the landside areas. In these areas, floor-to-floor heights can be reduced because container storage takes place further in toward the center of the terminal.

The most commonly used building system is structural steel, because it is most adaptable to the wide spans desired. This type of system is also readily expandable and can accommodate the inevitable changes to internal layouts that are bound to occur during the life of the building. Different types of cladding systems such as metal or precast concrete have been used successfully. Special attention is required, however, to columns and walls up to a height of at least 3 m (10 ft) to protect them against damage by equipment moving around the cargo floor, especially forklifts.

The landside area also requires thoughtful planning to ensure the efficient and safe maneuvering of trucks, a large proportion of which may be articulated vehicles 20 m (66 ft) or more in length. Experience has shown that, where these areas have not been adequately planned, the resulting operation becomes most inefficient, in some cases chaotic, as the truck drivers attempt to maintain service time expectations in a congested environment. Design of the truck dock area should incorporate the latest principles and technology of truck terminals, including the use of dock levelers to accommodate truck bodies of varying heights and door seals to save energy. The area should be well lit to permit safe nighttime operation.

Comparison of the floor areas and cargo handling capacities of a number of major terminals is shown in Table 3.

Table 3. Comparison of Floor Areas and Cargo Handling Capacities

Cargo Terminal	Floor area, ft^2	Capacity, annual t
Lufthansa Cargo Terminal Frankfurt International Airport Frankfurt	624,300	530,000 (1984) 550,000 (planned)
KLM Cargo Centre Schipol International Airport Amsterdam	530,670	271,000 (1981–1982) 500,000 (planned)
Air France Cargo Terminal Charles de Gaulle International Airport Paris	430,560	250,000 (1980) 500,000 (planned)
SATS Air Freight Terminal Changi International Airport Singapore	306,780	237,000 (1985)
Hong Kong Air Cargo Terminal Kai Tak International Airport Hong Kong	865,430	383,000 (1984) 680,000 (planned)

Air Traffic Control Towers

The air traffic control tower performs the functions of approach control of aircraft as well as the control of aircraft maneuvering on the airfield. Ideally, the control tower should be located as close as possible to the operational centroid of the airfield, although other influences such as siting to provide unobstructed sight lines and to minimize sun glare will control the siting process. The controllers in the control cab are required to have an unobstructed view of the entire surface movement area of the airport (runways, taxiways, and aprons) as well as the airspace surrounding the airport, particularly the approach and departure areas.

Air traffic control towers have been built as free-standing structures or in the form of control cabs located on top of other airport structures such as terminal buildings. The height of the tower is determined by sight line criteria, considering both existing structures and future development.

In addition to the control cab itself, the control tower generally includes a number of ancillary facilities which will vary in size and number depending on the specific requirements of individual airports. These facilities include staff support areas, such as washrooms, lockers, showers, briefing area, lounge and kitchenette, telecommunications equipment areas and workshops, administration offices, and associated mechanical and electrical services areas. Normally, it is considered good practice to locate certain minimum staff support areas as close to the cab as possible, usually directly below the cab.

The size and internal layout of the cab is determined by the number of controllers required to monitor the flight movements of the airport and the corresponding size and location of the equipment consoles, which may also be dictated by the airport layout. Although there are examples of small cabs with central console layouts, the consoles are generally arranged on the perimeter of the cab facing the most active areas of the airport. This provides maximum vertical visibility for the controllers. Ceiling and windowsill heights are dictated by viewing angle requirements.

The control tower and cab must be designed to facilitate the maintenance of existing equipment and installation of new equipment. This may take the form of a raised access floor or a service level below the cab so that new cabling can be easily installed. In some cabs, such as at Schipol, a depressed access corridor between the console and the perimeter glazing permits technicians to service equipment without interfering with the controllers' area itself. Recent towers in Canada have been designed with separate internal maintenance corridors behind and below the consoles, which not only permit access to the equipment without entering the cab, but also reduce the distance from the controller to the exterior glazing, which improves visibility and minimizes the size of the cab.

Visibility is the key design consideration of the cab. Most cabs have a multisided exterior perimeter in order to reduce internal reflections and minimize the size of mullions and roof supports. Again, in Canada, recent towers are designed with 15- to 18-sided perimeters with butt-jointed glass and a tripod roof support to provide maximum unobstructed visibility. The glass is normally sloped outward from 15 to 30°F to reduce reflection and glare. Studies have indicated that double glazing produces greater visual distortion than single glazing, although in extremely cold climates double glazing may be required to reduce fogging or condensation on the windows.

Maintaining an acceptable level of comfort in the cab despite the exposure to tremendous heat gain through the broad expanse of glass is a particular challenge for the mechanical engineer. The cab mechanical system must be well integrated into the overall cab design so that it does not compromise visual and acoustical standards. In colder climates, the air supply system also serves to reduce the chances of fogging on the inside surface of the glass and freezing on the outside. Lighting type and location must be carefully considered to eliminate glare. The use of acoustically absorbent finishes such as antistatic carpet and acoustical ceilings are also important in creating an effective working environment for the controllers.

Because of its inherent prominence on the airport site, the air traffic control tower is often accorded a design significance that is equaled only by the passenger terminal building. As such, architects are challenged to interpret the basic functional requirements of this unique building type into a structure that will serve as a landmark and visual symbol of the airport or country it serves.

Aircraft Maintenance Bases

The scale of aircraft maintenance functions at an airport is not solely related to the size of the airport. More important is whether the airport is a base of operations for one or more air carriers, in which case it is most likely that major base maintenance functions will be carried out on the fleet. At other airports, it is common for the airlines to construct facilities for line maintenance functions, such facilities being considerably less complex than those required for base maintenance. An interesting exception to these general statements is that of American Airlines in the United States, currently with a fleet of more than 330 aircraft, which is based at Dallas–Fort Worth Airport in Texas. Most of the major maintenance on this fleet is carried out at Tulsa Airport in Oklahoma, even though Tulsa is not a major city on American Airlines' route network.

Aircraft maintenance hangars, particularly those for wide-bodied aircraft, are some of the most visible buildings on the airport site. To accommodate a single Boeing 747 aircraft, the hangar requires a clear height to underside of structure of approximately 24 m (79 ft), a width of approximately 69 m (225 ft), and a length of 76 m (250 ft). Siting of the hangar must respect the obstruction clearance zoning, and care should be taken to ensure that the large building faces do not produce unwanted interference or reflection to electromagnetic signals from landing aids, particularly the Instrument Landing System (ILS) localizer (20). Another siting consideration is the need to provide taxiway links to connect the maintenance base with the terminal apron, and to provide an apron adjacent to the hangar. The hangar may be oriented to provide access at either end to accommodate more than one aircraft, in which case an apron is required at both ends. The apron normally requires a designated position for engine run-ups, at which location jet blast protection must be provided by a specially designed blast fence.

A number of structural steel systems have been used successfully for large-span hangar buildings, the selection of the optimum system being dependent on the size of the facility and whether there is a requirement for an overhead traveling crane system. For a single-bay, wide-bodied aircraft hangar with no requirement for an overhead crane, the simplest building system is a welded steel portal frame structure.

There are several examples of large hangar structures that house more than one aircraft simultaneously, a relatively recent one being the Singapore International Airlines hangar at Changi Airport. This facility, commissioned in 1982, has 20,000 m² (215,280 ft²) of column-free hangar space which will accommodate three B-747 aircraft side by side or up to seven narrow-bodied aircraft. The steel roof structure with dimensions of 218 × 92 m (715 × 302 ft) weighing 2500 t is supported at 12 points by roof assembly brackets mounted on the U-shaped workshop–administration annex. Truss depth varies from 8 to 15 m (26 to 49 ft). The roof trusses were fabricated on Batam Island, 20 km (12.4 miles) away, and ferried to the site. The roof assembly was hoisted into position using hydraulic jacks leaving a clear internal height of 29 m (95 ft).

Special technological features of large aircraft hangars are the door systems used, specialized fire protection services such as underwing protection of larger aircraft using oscillating foam monitors activated by sensitive alarm systems, and the type of crane and docking systems used to permit maintenance to all sections of the aircraft.

Flight Catering Facilities

Flight catering facilities prepare meals and refreshments intended for onboard consumption. At smaller airports which do not serve major scheduled airlines, food is often prepared for aircraft in the airport restaurant kitchen or in the kitchen of a local hotel, the resulting meals being kept relatively simple, or limited to snacks. At larger airports, however, particularly those which form points of origin for major air carriers, or which are major stopover points for long-haul aircraft, there is generally a substantial demand for passenger meals; these are prepared in flight kitchens located at the airport.

Flight kitchens are generally sited in areas of the airport designated for support facilities, and not in prime passenger terminal areas. They require good road access on the landside because of major food delivery and garbage collection functions, and require direct access to the aircraft apron areas serving the passenger terminal.

Flight kitchens are designed to produce meals to satisfy a given design day demand which is based on forecasts for enplaning passengers, and can be typically categorized in three capacity classifications—up to 10,000 meals per day, up to 25,000 meals per day, and over 25,000 meals per day. All three classifications generally employ automation in meal tray assembly and wares-washing activities; however, the automation of storage areas and galley equipment handling becomes a consideration in the over 25,000 meal per day kitchen because of the volume of production and floor space requirements. Examples of flight kitchens in the low and high capacity classifications are the Marriott Chateau Flight Kitchen at Pearson in Toronto, and the SATS In-Flight Catering Centre at Changi in Singapore.

The Marriott Chateau Flight Kitchen, built in 1972, was originally designed to produce 7000 meals per day and has a gross building area of 4000 m² (43,056 ft²). Food production and storage activities are handled on one level, and administration offices are located on an upper mezzanine. The flight kitchen serves 12 airlines, resulting in a current demand of up to 9000 meals per day.

The SATS In-flight Catering Centre, completed in 1981, has a gross floor area of 50,500 m² (543,582 ft²), of which 38,000 m² relates to food production activities, and the remainder to SATS airport administration offices. It was designed to have a production capacity of 50,000 meals per day, and to serve over 30 carriers in addition to Singapore Airlines. The building operates on three levels, with receiving and storage on the lowest, food production at the center (which corresponds to the inbound and outbound docks), and administration at the top. The food storage areas are 9.4 m (30 ft) high, include a freezer-holding capacity of 5000 m^3 (176,573 ft^3), and are served by turret-type forklifts on a steel guiderail. Airline galley equipment is stacked in up to 1800 special cages designed for each aircraft type on racks up to 14.2 m (46.6 ft) high, with an automatic retrieval system. A tow motor system transports trolleys of galley equipment to a series of programmed destinations in the kitchen where they are loaded with food, and then towed to refrigerated holding areas assembled by airline flight, and ready for pickup at the adjacent outbound dock.

The plan layout of a flight kitchen should reflect the flow of food production activity that it accommodates. Figure 4 illustrates the process flows which were the basis for the design of the SATS In-flight Catering Centre previously described. Steel and reinforced concrete are both commonly used structural systems for this building type, with bay sizes typically in the 8 m (26.2 ft) to 10 m (32.8 ft) range. Depending on location, a variety of exterior materials are used, including precast concrete, metal panels, and masonry. For reasons of hygiene, special attention is required in the selection of materials and finishes for interior surfaces in order to ensure ease of maintenance.

Crash, Fire and Rescue

According to data published by the ICAO, approximately 75% of aircraft accidents occur on or in the vicinity of an airport. The principal objectives of the Airport Crash, Fire and Rescue Service (CFR), therefore, are saving lives and minimizing the result of accidents on or in the airport vicinity. The ICAO Standard for Response Time is "not more than three minutes, and preferably not more than two minutes, to any part of the movement area in optimum conditions of visibility and surface conditions" (21). Response time depends on a series of factors: the location of the fire station; access roads to the different airport areas; physical planning of the fire station building; CFR vehicle characteristics; the alarm system; and personnel training.

In addition to response time, siting of the fire station is affected by the requirement for direct line of sight along the entire length of active runways. Sufficient area on the site is required for the building, training area, and exterior parking areas for the CFR and employee vehicles.

ICAO classifies airports into categories 1–9 on the basis of the length and service frequency of the aircraft using the airport. From this classification, the volume of foam-extinguishing agents transportable to the emergency site can be determined and the required number of major vehicles to accomplish this is established. If the required response time cannot be attained by the major vehicles, a specialized rapid intervention vehicle, with a limited amount of foaming agent, is also provided.

Where climatological conditions might affect vehicle performance, the fire station must provide shelter for the CFR vehicles. Other requirements for the fire station include:

1. Extinguishant storage and filling facilities for minor maintenance and deployment of appliances and equipment.
2. Domestic and administrative facilities.

At smaller sites, CFR facilities simply consist of a vehicle bay within the general airport maintenance area. At large airports, the facility can consist of an all-purpose-designed building with several vehicle storage bays, office and operational facilities, and personnel sleeping, eating, and changing areas, the latter group often being located on an upper level.

THE PASSENGER TERMINAL COMPLEX

Architecturally, the passenger terminal complex is the most challenging component of the airport to the designer. More than a building designed to accommodate a static population, it is a subsystem within the overall airport system that should be designed dynamically to process passengers (as many as 25,000 per hour at O'Hare in Chicago) and their baggage, vehicles, and aircraft as efficiently and comfortably as possible through the requisite facilities between the terminal road and curb and aircraft parked on the apron.

The architect is normally engaged by the owner who may be a federal, state, or municipal government department, a statutory airport authority, or an individual airline. Throughout the project, he will have to interface with user groups such as the airlines individually or in groups represented by an airline consultative committee, government agencies, particularly when the airport is one designated to handle international traffic, security forces, concessionaires, ground handling agents, and other groups designated by the owner.

Planning Principles

The general size and scope of the terminal facilities is directly related to the amount and type of traffic that is expected to flow through the terminal in a selected planning period. The amount of traffic that flows through the terminal can vary widely over the hours of the day, being dependent on the schedules of the airlines using the terminal. The passenger arrival and departure peaks may occur at different times during the day, as may the maximum aircraft gate occupancy. These peaking phenomena are particularly pronounced at the smaller terminals, which may have a relatively low number of flights during the day, but with the majority of flights occurring around a peak period of an hour or so. At busier airports, the peaking phenomenon may not be as pronounced, the traffic being relatively high over a peak period lasting three hours or more, perhaps twice per day. In other cases, particularly those airports serving relatively high proportions of tourist-related traffic, there may be pronounced seasonal fluc-

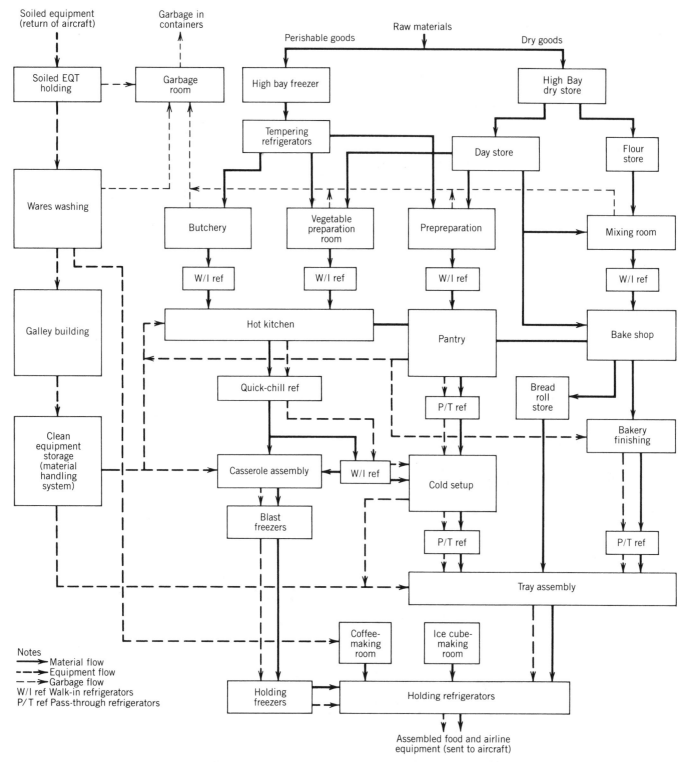

Figure 4. Process flow chart for the SATS Inflight Catering Centre at Changi International Airport, Singapore. Courtesy of NORR Airport Planning Associates.

tuations in traffic. It is not realistic for the designer to design for the absolute peak traffic expected in the design year if such volume will be achieved only once or twice during that year. Instead, standards have been adopted by the different airport authorities the world over to select representative daily and hourly traffic volumes for design

purposes. Daily volumes are variously referred to in the industry as busy day, design day, peak planning day, and standard busy rate. They all refer to the selected criterion which determines the level of traffic for which the facilities will be designed. Commonly used standards are: the average day of the peak month; the average weekday of the three consecutive busiest months; the fortieth busiest day of the year; the second busiest day of the peak week of normal airport traffic; or the 90th-percentile standard adopted in Canada, which provides that at least 90% of the total annual passengers will experience levels of congestion equal to or better than design standards.

Selection of the design year is another step in developing the building program. Over the past 50 years, with the exception of a few years in the mid 1970s and early 1980s, traffic has been in a continual state of growth. On the one hand, it is important that the terminal complex be designed for traffic levels that will eventuate some years after the commissioning of the facilities to avoid the disruption to operations caused by too-frequent expansion programs. On the other hand, the designer should be aware that characteristics of that traffic may change dramatically over the period to the extent that design decisions taken at one point in time may require considerable corrections, or may even render the design obsolete by the time that the design traffic levels mature. One approach to selection of the design year is to consider a period of ten years from the commissioning of facilities to the commissioning of the next phase. The designer would plan for the facilities to open at levels of service higher than design levels; to reach design levels at the midpoint of the planning period; and then to decline to the lowest acceptable levels at the end of the period just prior to the commissioning of the next phase. Adoption of this planning philosophy will ensure that capital is not tied up in over-provided facilities for an unreasonable length of time. It also provides the airport authority with the flexibility of monitoring the new facilities over a reasonable period to see what changes, if any, need to be made in the planning of subsequent phases, and minimizes the frequency of disruption to operations during subsequent construction phases. It also indicates that development of terminal facilities at a particular airport is a continuing process, and one that must be carried out within the framework of an overall master plan covering a period of at least 20 years.

Air Traffic Forecasts

Air traffic forecasts for annual volumes of passengers, freight, and aircraft movements are prepared by a number of different organizations within the industry. In the United States and Canada, official forecasts are prepared by the FAA and Transport Canada, respectively. FAA forecasts are used by the FAA only, for annual budget preparation, National System planning, manpower, and airport aid programs. These organizations prepare national, regional, and individual airport forecasts which are updated on a regular basis. Airline trade organizations, such as the International Air Transport Association (IATA) and the Air Transportation Association of America (ATA), provide extremely useful forecast information in a form which is readily usable for the development facilities programs. It is also not uncommon for the airport authority to commission a consultant to develop air traffic forecasts. ICAO publishes useful information on air traffic forecasts, including methods of converting annual forecasts into planning criteria such as design hour and design day volumes in

its Airport Planning Manual (13). More detailed information is contained in the ICAO document *Manual on Air Traffic Forecasting* (22).

Terminal Facilities

The facilities comprising the terminal complex, as discussed in this article, are best defined under the two major flows of people and baggage through the building:

1. The enplaning sequence, consisting of departing passengers and their baggage who have arrived at the airport with or without accompanying well-wishers via the ground transportation system, and those who are transferring between flights.
2. The deplaning sequence, consisting of arriving passengers and their baggage who will proceed through to the ground transportation system and leave the airport with or without accompanying greeters, and those who intend to transfer to the enplaning sequence.

The types of facilities required depend on the category of traffic handled at the terminal, whether domestic, international, or combinations of domestic and international. At some designated airports in Canada, Bermuda, the Virgin Islands, St. Croix, and St. Thomas, passengers bound for the United States are precleared through U.S. Federal Inspection Services constituting another category of traffic referred to as transborder traffic. The extent of international inspection facilities also varies between countries. In the United States, there are no international inspection services required on the enplaning sequence for international passengers; the same applies for Canada with the exception of transborder passengers. In virtually every other country, however, exit checks by immigration and customs officers are carried out on all enplaning international passengers. A representative list of terminal facilities is contained in Table 4, which also illustrates the scope of facilities found at different terminals in various countries. This table is not intended as a designer's checklist, but rather as an indication of the range of facilities that may be required at various locations. The designer would ascertain the full scope of required facilities in close consultation with the airport authority.

In addition to the previously mentioned facilities, there are space requirements for supporting functions such as airline, administrative, and operational offices; lounges and ramp operations; airport authority administration and operations offices; government inspection services offices; and interview and search rooms. As in other building types, the architect obtains program information for these functions through interviews and directly from the owner. As airport authorities become increasingly aggressive in pursuing commercial opportunities, concessions such as restaurants, bars, retail outlets, car rental, and hotel kiosks have increased in importance. The location of these can be critical to their revenue generating capabilities; generally, the more exposed they are to the maximum number of potential customers, the more successful they will be.

Table 4. Facilities Required at Different Types of Terminals

Enplaning facilities	Domestic	International North America	International Other	Deplaning facilities	Domestic	International North America	International Other
departure road–curb	X	X	X	aircraft at gate	X	X	X
public concourse	X	X	X	health check			at some airports
baggage security check		X	X	transit–departure lounge	X	X	X
ticketing and check-in	X	X	X	duty-free concessions			at some airports
departure tax collection			some countries	primary inspection check		X	X
immigration check			X	immigration check		X	X
customs check			X	baggage claim	X	X	X
security check	X	X	X	customs check		X	X
departure lounge	X	X	X	public concourse	X	X	X
duty-free concessions		X	X	arrivals road–curb	X	X	X
passenger waiting rooms	X	X	X				
aircraft at gate	X	X	X				

The Building Program

The essential ingredients of the building program for the passenger terminal complex are:

1. The number of aircraft gates required by sector served (international or domestic) and by aircraft size.

2. The number of processors represented by counters and servers required for functions, such as reservations and ticketing, check-in and seat assignment, security check, and government inspection services.

3. The space requirements for holding areas, such as the public concourses containing passengers and their visitors, departure lounges, passenger waiting lounges (also referred to as gate lounges or hold rooms), and baggage claim areas.

4. The area requirements and size and type of mechanical handling system for outbound and inbound baggage makeup and breakdown areas, respectively.

5. The number and exposed length of baggage claim dispenser units.

6. The full scope and area requirements for concessions, such as bars, restaurants, retail outlets, duty-free shops, car-rental booths, hotel reservations, insurance sales, and information booths.

7. A comprehensive program of requirements for airline, airport authority, and government inspection services, offices, and operational support functions.

8. The length of curb required for arrivals and departures, by vehicle type (private cars, taxis, buses, and courtesy vehicles).

9. Flow diagrams and facilities functional relationships for each type of passenger flow (arriving, departing, transfer, and transit passengers for international and domestic sectors).

The calculation of the program of requirements is a complex exercise, mainly because of the inherent dynamic nature of the traffic that the terminal complex is designed to handle. Planning documents prepared by industry asso-

ciations, such as IATA and ATA (19,23), and government organizations, such as FAA (24,25) and Transport Canada's Airports Authority Group, are essential reference material. Another useful source of information is *The Airport Passenger Terminal* by Walter Hart (15). The degree of precision used in determining the program depends to a large extent on the quantity and quality of available data. At the higher end of the scale, the best type of information on the demand side of the equation is in the form of a representative schedule of flights for the design day, referred to as a nominal schedule, including arrival and departure times, airline and aircraft type, and predicted flight loads. Armed with these schedules and with data gathered by surveys on processing times, passenger-to-visitor and passenger-to-bag ratios, and passenger flow and distribution characteristics, including arrival rate of passengers at the check-in facilities, it is possible to carry out a simulation of the terminal system for the design day. Such simulations can be carried out manually, which in a large facility may be prohibitively time consuming, or by computer-modeling techniques. The data derived from the simulation are then combined with space standards and service time standards appropriate to the jurisdiction, in calculations resulting in a logical program of requirements.

There are other rules of thumb that, although empirical in nature, have been proven over the years to provide reliable program information. These methods are enumerated in the material referenced in the preceding paragraph. Regardless of which method is used, the program is bound to come under close scrutiny because of its direct relationship to capital costs; hence, it is strongly advised that the designer undertake cross-checks on the program using a number of different methods at his or her disposal.

Another important consideration in the development of the building program is the level of service to be provided to the users. Terminal complexes do not have precise handling capacities, as for example would processing facilities for goods or products. An example of this is Terminal 1 at Pearson (Toronto), which was designed in the late 1950s to handle 3.3 million annual passengers. In 1985, the terminal, with slightly expanded facilities, handled 7.5 million passengers. There is a vast difference in the levels of service provided to users in 1964 when the terminal opened to that provided currently, measured in terms of congestion levels experienced by design day passenger volumes. Transport Canada, after extensive surveys of existing terminals, has adopted a range of standards for space allocations per occupant corresponding to designated levels of service (26). By using these standards, it is possible to design to a preselected level of service for design day traffic in the design year.

Site Planning Considerations

The terminal complex is optimally located where it affords the most expeditious (shortest and fastest) routing of arriving and departing aircraft between the terminal gates and the runway system, while at the same time providing for an unconstrained ground transportation system connecting the terminal curbs to the regional road network. The complex must respect zoning and aircraft clearance criteria, which together will define limits to the available site (2,18,27). The airports illustrated in Figure 2 are examples of the different attempts to achieve optimal siting of the terminal complex within different runway configurations. One of the better examples of airside efficiency is that of Hartsfield (Atlanta), which has the terminal gates optimally sited with respect to the runway–taxiway configuration. Arriving and departing aircraft have unconstrained routings between the runway system and terminal gates employing dual aircraft taxi flow between piers, 305 m (1000 ft) center to center, resulting in desirably low levels of aviation fuel burn by aircraft maneuvering on the ground.

Terminal–Apron Layout

In terms of site utilization, the method of parking aircraft at the terminal has a greater impact than the arrangement of internal facilities. The layout of the apron–gate area must respond to the requirement to stage aircraft in such a way as to permit efficiency of loading, unloading, and servicing, as well as to permit unconstrained maneuvering of aircraft to and from the gate, and to and from the runway–taxiway system. Two commonly used methods of parking aircraft at gate employ either self-maneuvering stands on which the aircraft maneuvers into and out of the stand under its own power; or the power-in–push-back method in which the aircraft maneuvers into the stand under its own power, and is pushed out for departure using special tractors with a tow bar attached to the aircraft nosewheel. In some cases, a power-in–power-back method is used wherein the aircraft maneuvers into and out of its gate position under its own power, thereby eliminating the need for a tractor. This method, however, is restricted to two or three engine aircraft and is employed only at some airports. The former two methods are illustrated in Figure 5.

Access to and from the gate is provided by means of defined apron taxilanes. The layout of the taxilanes is such as to provide a taxiing aircraft with the requisite clearances from other parked or maneuvering aircraft or fixed obstructions. Criteria used in the layout of aprons are stipulated in ICAO and FAA guidelines (27, 28). The dimensions and servicing requirements of the aircraft in modern airline fleets are laid out in manuals prepared by and available from aircraft manufacturers, such as the Boeing Co., McDonnell Douglas Corp., Lockheed Corp., Airbus Industrie, British Aerospace, Inc., etc (a summary of applicable aircraft data is included in Ref. 29). Where the aircraft parking configuration is such that a maneuvering aircraft is required to pass more than four to six parked aircraft, it is advisable to provide two-way taxilanes to reduce delays caused by conflicts between the push-back operation for departing aircraft and arriving aircraft maneuvering to the gate. These requirements translate into relatively large apron areas and building perimeters. A 20-gate terminal, for example, typically handling an annual volume of five million passengers with a fleet mix containing 30% wide-bodied aircraft, would require an airside building perimeter of approximately 1 km (3280 ft).

Terminal–Apron Concepts

The reference manuals (15,19,24,25,30) all agree with the categorization of terminal concepts into four types which differ in the method of linking the main terminal building with the aircraft gates, and the degree of centralization of passenger processing. The four concepts, commonly referred to as pier, satellite, linear, and transporter, are illustrated diagrammatically in Figure 6. Prominent examples representing the four concept types are listed in Table 5.

In the pier concept, enplaning and deplaning passengers are processed in the main terminal area which is connected to the gates by an elongated building element containing hold rooms and aircraft gates. There are many variations to the pier concept. In some examples, the main terminal area is centralized and is connected to the gates by single- or multiple-linear piers; one example is LaGuardia (New York), which has the main terminal in a curved form with four radial piers. In another example, Schipol (Amsterdam), the central terminal area is connected to the gates by four piers, three of which are Y-shaped. In other examples, such as O'Hare (Chicago), the central terminal area consists of three unit terminals, from which emanates a system of three Y-shaped and three linear piers. This terminal area is undergoing a major expansion under a $1.5 billion capital program. Other pier configurations commonly used are the T-shaped pier at Heathrow Terminal 3 (London), and Sky Harbor Terminal 2 (Phoenix).

In the satellite concept, the aircraft gates are grouped around satellite structures connected to the main terminal area by links which can be either above grade or underground. Passengers move through the link either by walking, using moving sidewalks, or by automated guideway transit systems (AGTS), also referred to as people movers. The most prominent example of the satellite concept is Hartsfield (Atlanta), the second busiest airport in the world. The proportion of connecting passengers is high, at around 75%, and as a result the main terminal area is relatively small compared to the satellites. There are presently four rectangular satellites located perpendicular

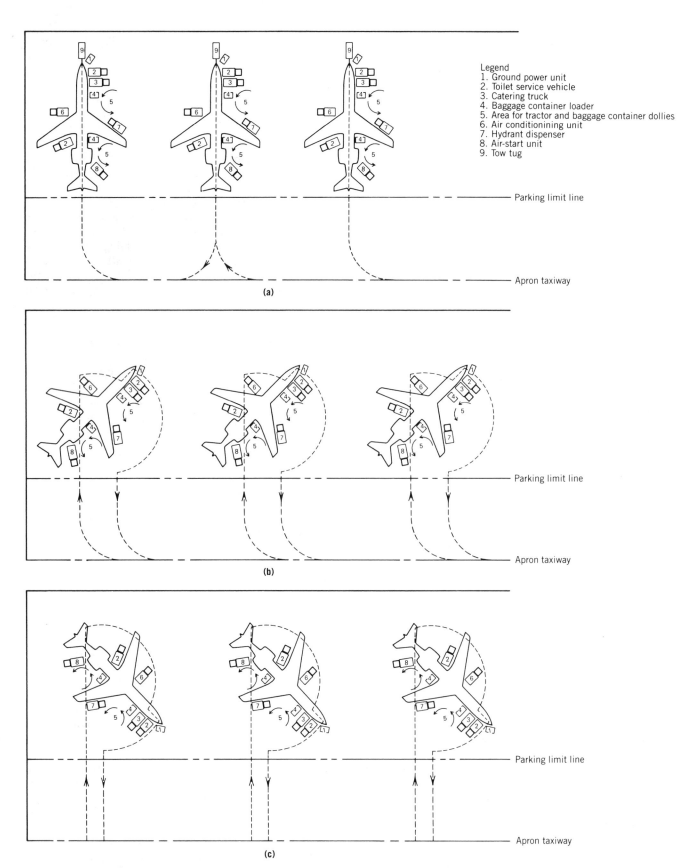

Figure 5. Aircraft parking configurations at gate: **(a)** taxi-in–push-out; **(b)** taxi-in–taxi-out; and **(c)** taxi-in–taxi-out (19). Courtesy of IATA.

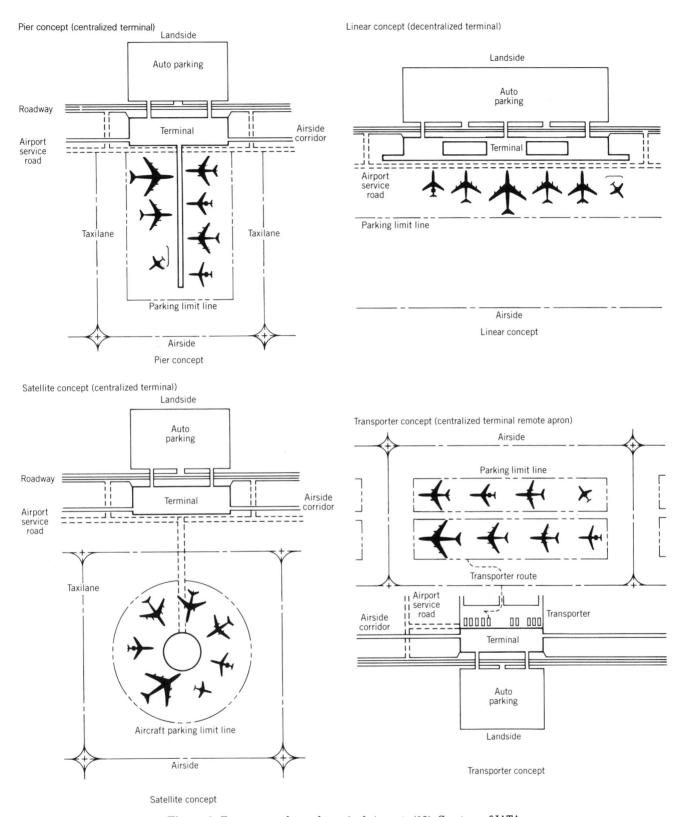

Figure 6. Four commonly used terminal concepts (19). Courtesy of IATA.

to the parallel runway system, and one pier attached to the main terminal area with a total of 140 gates. The satellites, referred to as concourses, are between 610 and 732 m (2000 and 2400 ft) long, and are connected to the main terminal area by an underground AGTS. Other examples of the satellite concept employing AGTS technology are at Tampa, Orlando, Seattle–Tacoma, and Miami in the United States and at Gatwick (London), in the UK.

Table 5. Airports Employing the Four Terminal Concepts

Pier	Satellite	Linear	Transporter
O'Hare, Chicago	Hartsfield, Atlanta	Dallas–Fort Worth	Dulles, Washington
Heathrow T3, London	Houston Intercontinental	Heathrow T4, London	Mirabel, Montreal
LaGuardia, New York	Miami International (international satellite)	Charles de Gaulle T2, Paris	Jeddah
Frankfurt	Newark	Pearson T2, Toronto	
Schipol, Amsterdam	Charles de Gaulle T1, Paris	Kansas City International	
	Tampa		
	Seattle–Tacoma		
	Narita, Tokyo		

Miami Airport is also interesting in that the main terminal area is one of the largest examples of the pier concept with more than 76 gates on seven radial piers. Eleven international gates are located on a satellite which is connected to the main terminal area by AGTS. Examples of the satellite concept, which uses a pedestrian concourse with or without assistance from moving sidewalks, are Narita (Tokyo), Charles de Gaulle Terminal 1 (Paris), Houston Intercontinental, and Newark.

The linear concept was introduced in the late 1960s. Aircraft are gated in a single line against an elongated terminal building which can have either a straight or curved linear form. The terminal building utilizes essentially decentralized processing in the basic form in which the intention is for the passenger to move through the terminal in essentially a transverse flow, minimizing walking distances. This concept is utilized at Kansas City. Where there is a high proportion of connecting pasengers, however, walking distances become undesirably long. To counteract this, various means of assisting passenger movement are employed at different airports. Such is the case of the best-known linear concept at Dallas–Fort Worth, where interconnecting passengers can use either the AGTS or bus transportation system. Other recent examples of the linear concept are Heathrow Terminal 4 (London) and Charles de Gaulle Terminal 2 (Paris).

In the transporter concept, the aircraft are parked remotely from the terminal building with passengers being transferred between terminal and gate by passenger transfer vehicles (PTV). The concept is often employed in countries that have good climates, where the apron geometry is constrained and decisions have been made not to use passenger loading bridges. Specially designed PTVs, referred to as mobile lounges, are used at some airports; their main advantage is the ability of the vehicle to elevate from ground level to the doorsill of the aircraft, or to the second level of the terminal building for passenger loading and unloading. The terminal building in this concept is not required to provide an aircraft parking perimeter, providing flexibility of design and permitting the use of centralized processing. Prominent examples of where the transporter concept is a feature of the design are Dulles (Washington) and Mirabel (Montreal). At Dulles, long-haul aircraft park remote and shorthaul aircraft, whose passengers are normally transferring to long-haul aircraft, at fixed terminal gates. The use of transporters is also employed at airports where the basic concept is pier, satellite, or linear, when additional remote gates need to be accessed either on a scheduled or ad hoc basis.

There are advantages and disadvantages to each of the concept types that have been discussed in some depth in the literature (15,19,24,25). Some of the considerations that may be used in evaluating different concepts are outlined in Ref. 30.

Terminal Building Layout

After the building program and a choice of apron–terminal concept, the two critical design decisions that affect the terminal building layout are the degree of centralization of processing to be adopted, and the choice of the number of building levels to be used.

Centralization usually means that most enplaning and deplaning passenger processing functions, related to aircraft gate positions regardless of their locations, are carried out in a centralized area which may be on one or two levels. In the centralized terminal, the only functional areas that are decentralized are the departure gate lounges, also referred to as hold rooms. The satellite, pier, and transporter concepts lend themselves to centralized processing.

Decentralization in various degrees means that passenger processing areas are provided to support a selected group of dedicated aircraft gates. Kansas City has three circular unit terminals, each employing the linear terminal concept with high degrees of decentralization; for example, each unit terminal has 14 departure lounges and four baggage claim areas.

There are advantages and disadvantages to each concept. The decentralized concept in its strictest form offers the opportunity to reduce walking distances within the terminal. Generally accepted maximum walking distances between entry to the building and the aircraft gate, or between gates for connecting passengers, is 300 m (1000 ft). Theoretically, the enplaning passenger can enter the building from the curb opposite the aircraft gate dedicated to his particular flight, and hence would have to walk through the depth of the building without significant lateral digression. Similarly, the deplaning passenger would have reduced walking distances between gate, baggage claim, and the curb if dedicated bag claim areas were supplied to a limited number of gates. There is also greater control of the passenger by the airline, because the passenger does not need to travel long and often confusing distances from check-in to the aircraft gate. Another advantage is that adequate curb lengths are easier to provide in the decentralized linear concept than in the centralized concepts for obvious geometric reasons. These advantages would be diluted significantly if the passenger were connecting from one airline to another, because he would then be required to travel laterally along a linear terminal. Experience with large decentralized terminals such as Pearson Terminal 2 (Toronto) has shown that these distances can be uncomfortably long. Passenger convenience would also be reduced if the passenger had parked his or her car in the lot closest to the originating gate, and he or she were to return at a different gate or on a different airline, again requiring possibly long walking distances back to the car. From a terminal operations viewpoint, centralization has distinct advantages in that duplication of staff is minimized, and daily utilization of centralized facilities is generally much higher than in the decentralized case.

Normally, terminal buildings have been designed to provide one level, one-and-a-half levels, or two levels of passenger processing. The one-level concept is used in smaller terminals processing up to 2 million annual passengers. A typical example of a one-level layout for a small terminal is shown in Figure 7, in which the curbs, enplaning and deplaning passenger functions, and decentralized inbound and outbound baggage areas are located on a single level. Passengers access the aircraft parked on the adjacent apron by walking across the apron and using aircraft stairs. The one-and-a-half level concept is often an expansion from what was previously a one-level concept, where to enhance passenger convenience and safety the

airside corridors or concourses have been double-decked to facilitate second-level passenger loading via loading bridges. As in the one-level concept, enplaning and deplaning passenger processing (with the exception of security which is normally carried out on the upper level), curbs, and baggage systems are located at grade.

For larger terminals handling more than 1.5–2 million annual passengers, two levels of passenger processing are most commonly provided. Typically, in the two-level concept, the departures level is on the upper floor and arrivals is at apron level, providing the most cost-efficient means of integrating inbound and outbound baggage systems. In this case, it is possible to have inbound baggage breakdown areas and outbound baggage makeup areas located at apron level, necessitating level changes for baggage conveyers for the outbound system only. One of the principal advantages of the two-level concept is that it lends itself to the adoption of the two-level roadway, thereby separating arrival and departure vehicle flows at the curb, and providing greater opportunity to provide requisite arrival and departure curb length. A third level (underground) is necessary in the satellite concept where the link from the main terminal area to the satellite is below grade, such as at Hartsfield (Atlanta), or typically in the satellite–pier concept at Los Angeles. Figure 8 shows an example of the layout of a two-level terminal using the satellite concept, which would typically be used for a one-sector terminal, such as that used for domestic operations.

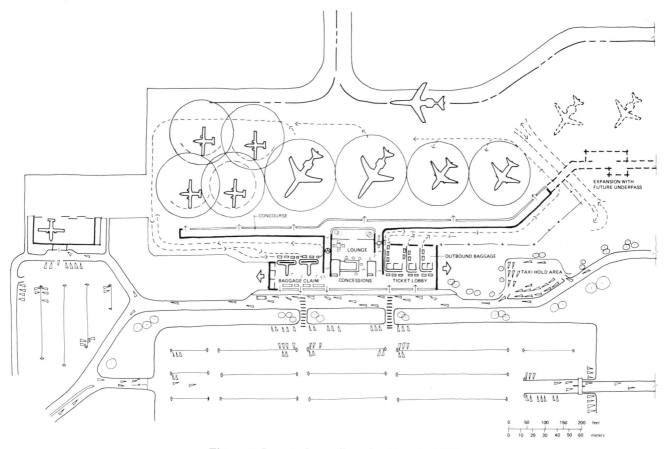

Figure 7. Layout of a small one-level terminal (15).

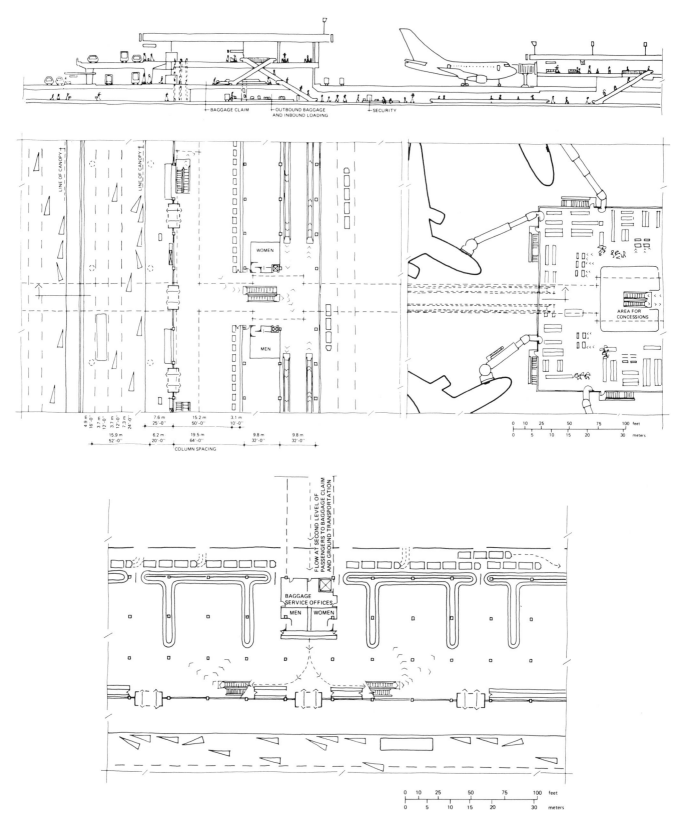

Figure 8. Layout of a two-level terminal using the satellite concept (15).

In some terminals outside the United States, there may be specific requirements to separate and secure passenger flows by sector, not only on the deplaning sequence, but also on the enplaning sequence. Examples of this require- ment are all terminals, outside of the United States and Canada, handling both international and domestic traffic, and in Canadian terminals handling a third sector of Can- ada–United States traffic, referred to as transborder wherein departing passengers are precleared through Federal Inspection Services. These requirements will greatly influence the choice of concept, including the degree of centralization to be used and the number of levels of processing to be employed.

The FAA, in its report entitled *The Apron–Terminal Complex, An Analysis of Concepts for Evaluation of Terminal Buildings* (30), has produced a chart that indicates the applicability of the various concepts previously described, relating to the number of annual enplanements to be handled and the proportion of connecting passengers. This chart, which interrelates with Figure 6, is reproduced in Table 6.

Special Systems and Equipment

The terminal complex requires the full range of mechanical and electrical building systems that would be expected for any major public building, but in addition special equipment and systems have been developed over the years to improve efficiency. Most of these special systems are unique to airport terminal buildings and therefore are of special interest.

At the airside interface, two different systems have been developed to facilitate safe and efficient passenger loading and unloading. The most familiar is the passenger loading bridge, also referred to as boarding bridge, which provides a direct articulated connection between the terminal and the aircraft. There are a number of variations to loading bridge design, although the main differences relate to the range of movement of the bridge head. Here, the two basic options available are the fixed bridge and the apron drive or swing bridge. The fixed bridge is mounted on fixed pedestals, the outer one of which is capable of moving vertically to mate with a variety of aircraft doorsill heights, with horizontal adjustment made through a telescoping bridge head. In the fixed bridge concept, all aircraft, regardless of their dimensions, are generally required to park on the same centerline. The apron drive bridge has an articulated powered undercarriage under the outer pedestal, enabling the bridge head to move universally on the apron within the limits of the telescoping bridge length. Although the apron drive bridge system concept is considerably more expensive than the fixed bridge, it has the significant advantage of being able to

Table 6. Identification of Applicable Concepts Related to Terminal Size[a]

Airport size by enplaned pax year	Concepts Applicable	Linear	Pier	Satellite	Transporter	Physical Aspects of Concepts	Single-level Curb	Multilevel Curb	Single-level Terminal	Multilevel Terminal	Single-level Connector	Multilevel Connector	Apron-level Boarding	Aircraft-level Boarding
Feeder under 25,000		X					X	X					X	
Secondary 25,000–75,000		X					X	X					X	
75,000–200,000		X					X	X			X		X	
200,000–500,000		X	X				X	X			X		X	
Primary over 75% pax OD[b] 500,000–1,000,000		X	X	X			X		X		X	X	X	X
Over 25% pax transfer 500,000–1,000,000		X	X	X			X			X	X	X	X	X
Over 75% pax OD 1,000,000–3,000,000		X	X	X			X	X			X	X	X	X
Over 25% pax transfer 1,000,000–3,000,000		X	X				X	X			X	X	X	X
Over 75% pax OD over 3,000,000		X	X	X			X	X			X	X	X	X
Over 25% pax transfer over 3,000,000		X	X				X	X			X	X		X

[a] Ref. 30.

[b] Origin–destination.

serve a greater number of aircraft parked around the same building perimeter, because there is greater flexibility in the location of aircraft parking stands.

The loading bridge is normally connected to the terminal at the upper-level gate lounge, which means that both enplaning and deplaning passengers use the second level, up to the point where deplaning passengers, in the two-level concept, descend to the lower level to claim baggage. The separation of enplaning and deplaning passengers becomes a requirement when domestic and international passengers use hold rooms and gates in the same general area of the terminal. An interesting variation on this concept is the new boarding pier at Terminal A in Zurich, in which the loading bridges are connected to the terminal pier at the upper and lower levels by a split-level fixed portion of the bridge. This permits vertical separation of enplaning and deplaning passengers. Similarly, at Kai Tak in Hong Kong, the loading bridges are designed to mate with the terminal at two levels; in this case, the fixed portion of the bridge can be raised or lowered for enplaning and deplaning and passenger loading and unloading, respectively.

Other specialized technologies developed for the transfer of passengers between terminal and aircraft are used at airports employing the transporter concept, as discussed previously. The mobile lounge is used at many airports, Dulles (Washington) being the first and perhaps best known example. The latest version of the original Plane-Mate mobile lounge has a capacity of 150 passengers. It is a specially designed vehicle with a hydraulic lift-elevating passenger compartment and a loading bridge-type coupling, allowing it to mate with terminals or aircraft with doorsill heights from 1.75 to 5.58 m (5.75 to 18.3 ft). In addition to the mobile lounge, specially designed buses and vehicles to transport handicapped passengers between the terminal and aircraft have been developed, information and specifications for which can be found in the trade catalogues or specific directories (31).

Many of the better examples of terminal design have relied on people-mover technologies to reduce the impact of walking distances, particularly in the link between the main terminal area and remotely located aircraft gates. This is particularly true in the satellite concepts and those concepts with relatively long pier or pier–satellite combinations. The two most important technologies developed for this purpose are the moving sidewalk (power walks), moving ramps (power ramps), and the automated guideway transit systems (AGTS).

Moving sidewalks have been used extensively in terminals all over the world since the 1960s, as horizontal adaptations of escalator technologies. They have application in many parts of the terminal system, including connections from car parks or rail terminals to the check-in public concourse, connections between main terminal areas and satellites, and along aircraft loading piers. They have been used in the horizontal application or in the inclined mode (power ramp) as an interlevel connector. Typically, speeds range from 0.5 to 0.7 m per second (1.64 to 2.3 ft/s) and capacities range from 6000 to 17,000 passengers per hour. Typical performance specifications of a number of different products can be found in Ref. 31.

AGTS systems have been discussed previously in this article. For airport applications, a number of types of systems have been installed, three variations of which are: the Westinghouse system, using electrically powered rubber-tired vehicles on guideways; the Wedway system of rubber-tired passive vehicles, powered by track-mounted linear induction motors; and the People Mover Group's Maglev system, using a magnetic levitation suspension system to support passive vehicles driven by track-mounted linear induction motors. These systems have been installed at the following airports: Westinghouse at Gatwick (London), Atlanta, Tampa, Orlando, Seattle–Tacoma, Miami, and Las Vegas; Maglev at Birmingham (UK); and the Wedway system at Houston Intercontinental. One of the early systems to be introduced is the LTV Airtrans system at Dallas–Fort Worth, which is a rubber-tired powered vehicle system operating on a trough-shaped concrete guideway. All of these systems have computer-controlled starting, stopping, and door operations and operate in either single- or multicar configurations.

Baggage handling systems, especially at larger airports, present a particular design challenge. Outbound systems must be efficient enough to accept and load passenger baggage at the latest possible time before departure, this baggage coming either from the check-in counters or transferred from another aircraft. Inbound systems are required to deliver baggage to the claim area as soon as possible after flight arrival, preferably coinciding with the arrival of the first passengers in the baggage claim areas. Outbound systems normally consist of linear conveyer systems carrying baggage from the check-in areas to the outbound baggage rooms, or baggage makeup areas, as they are often referred to, where baggage is sorted by destination and loaded into containers or carts staged close to the sorting area. The major technological advances contributing to efficiency in the outbound system are the automatic sorting systems installed in a number of airports. Although there are variations, generally in these systems baggage on the conveyer passes through an encoding station where tags are either manually or automatically read into a computer; the computer then tracks each piece of baggage and sends information to a sorting station where the baggage is sorted for loading. The encoding stations can have three input modes: manual encoding on a keyboard, voice encoding, or the most sophisticated method, the optical tag reader employing laser technology. The sorting methods are either horizontal diverting techniques employing pusher–puller systems such as those used at LaGuardia (New York), Dallas–Fort Worth, Denver, Atlanta, Kennedy (New York), and Houston; radial arm-belt guides, such as is used at Heathrow Terminal 3 (London); or vertical tilt devices. The tilt devices can either be discrete buckets with each containing one piece, such as the system at Seattle–Tacoma, or the tilting slat principle used at Frankfurt, Geneva, and Zurich. Information on these systems is contained in Ref. 31.

For the inbound system, the technology is in the baggage dispenser devices, which are fed from the baggage breakdown areas by linear conveyers. Baggage is either directly fed with both offloading and claiming on one continuous device, or remotely fed, offloading on a belt that feeds a remotely located circulating device. The remote feed device is usually a circulating conveyer, generally oval shaped with a tilted bed with room for two pieces of luggage simultaneously, fed from above or below by inclined belt conveyors, passenger access to the dispenser being available from all sides. The direct-feed type is usually a flat-bed circulating device and passes directly from offloading through the passenger baggage claim area. Sizing methodologies for both types of baggage dispenser are included in Refs. 15, 19, and 23–25, and representative performance outline specifications are contained in Ref. 31.

Other technologies with particular application to airport terminals are the remotely controlled and operated flight information display systems (FIDS), and x-ray technologies used in security applications. Integrated flight information display systems consist of a network of closed-circuit-television (CCTV) monitors located strategically throughout the arrival and departure areas, the whole system being operated from one or more control centers or input stations, and may include large-size display boards for large public areas. The large display boards employ a number of technologies, including the electronically controlled flap system used extensively worldwide, large area liquid-crystal displays, and other methods of producing dot matrix displays with light sources. Current systems being offered by manufacturers can be complex, incorporating not only flight information but also other control system information for airport management and security personnel. Airport security continues to increase in terms of requirements and scope. X-ray technology is used extensively, along with metal detection systems, and current developments in bombsniffing technologies aimed at detecting explosives in passenger baggage and cargo. Representative information on current systems available is contained in Ref. 31.

EXAMPLES OF AIRPORT ARCHITECTURE

Airport architecture is intensely program driven, not only in terms of spaces and functional layout, but in terms of a required response to an operational plan that increasingly strives for efficiency. Most importantly, the need for airports to achieve economic and financial balance in an era of fierce competition between airlines and resulting low yields presents the architect with a challenge that must be met without sacrificing imaginative design.

The terminal complex is the meeting point between people and planes—the human dimension in a high technology environment within the scale of the current generation of wide-bodied aircraft. Air travelers experience airport architecture from two sequential visual and psychological perspectives as they proceed through the terminal system between ground transportation and the aircraft; these experiences can differ greatly from airport to airport.

From the approach road system, the passenger may be reassured and attracted by the recognizable imagery of the terminal building, presenting a clear indication of where he or she must go; or he or she may be confronted and confused by a maze of roadway systems and parking lots surrounding the indistinguishable low rise forms of multiple terminal buildings. This is particularly relevant in the case of multi-terminal airports or large linear terminals where there are a number of decision points in the roadway system, and consequently, where directional signage information systems are most essential.

There are examples of terminals with distinct forms, immediately recognizable from the ground some distance from the airport. An excellent example is the magnificent Eero Saarinen-designed Dulles terminal building rising dramatically out of a rural landscape and providing a sense of excitement, orientation, and reassurance to the passenger even before arrival at the terminal. This is in stark contrast to National, Washington's other airport, wherein the passenger is greeted by a formidable maze of access roads and parking lots, and a low rise terminal with a clutter of piers and parked aircraft. Other successful attempts at providing exciting and recognizable forms to the approaching passenger include the soaring tentlike structure of the Haj Terminal at Jeddah designed by Skidmore, Owings & Merrill, and Norman Foster's design of the new London Stanstead Airport terminal which is intended to have an unassertive and low profile, but at the same time to manifest a strong and recognizable presence. There are airports in which the architect has used the parking structure integrated with the terminal to provide strong vertical forms, such as that achieved at Tampa, Seattle–Tacoma, Pearson Terminal 1 (Toronto), and Charles de Gaulle Terminal 1 (Paris). Interestingly, in all of the previously quoted examples except Toronto, a separation has been made between the terminal building and parked aircraft, either by the use of the transporter concept at Dulles, or by variations on the satellite concept at the others.

Once inside the terminal building, feelings of excitement and freedom of movement may be evoked by the design of open spaces and clear organizational relationships, appropriate and accessible concessions, and comfortable waiting areas, supported by the quiet technology of computerized check-in and information systems. Alternatively, the passenger may be alienated by overprocessing and regimentation in oppressive and overcrowded surroundings of noise and confusion. The degree to which the architect has succeeded in creating the former will be reflected by the commercial performance of the concessions. There is also little doubt that the passenger's experience at any airport will be most positive if he encounters on-time departures, correct information, including up-to-date information on delays, fast baggage claim, and efficient ground transportation facilities.

Much has been written on the subject of airport architecture, especially in the form of articles in periodicals. Useful bibliographies of such articles are published covering both planning and design topics for architects as indicated in Refs. 32 and 33. An especially informative periodical covering the latest developments in airports in general is listed in Ref. 9. Typically, these articles cover airport developments of special note from a variety of perspectives, including the planning considerations, and architecture and construction materials and methods.

In researching the different approaches to airport architecture that have been taken over the years, it may be interesting to view these approaches from a number of perspectives.

At the smaller airports that are required to accommodate few narrow-bodied aircraft on the apron at any one time, it may be reasonable to separate the terminal building from the aircraft. The link between terminal and aircraft can be provided by passengers walking across the apron, or by a busing operation. In these cases, the building can be considered somewhat independently. Two approaches have been taken in these cases: the common, simple, rectangular one-level form, which has little concern for architectural expresssion, but at the same time reflects the basic interior functions; or the case in which the architect has seized the opportunity to promote a particular expression appropriate to the surrounding environment. An example of the latter approach is the Ke-aloe Airport on the island of Hawaii, in which the design objective was to create a Hawaiian environment preserving the cultural and physical heritage of the islands within the context of land and air traffic of the jet era.

At the larger airports, there are many variations on the theme. There are a number of prominent examples of large airport terminal developments, such as Schipol, (Amsterdam), Frankfurt, and O'Hare (Chicago), which embody the approach of form follows function. All of these examples incorporate combinations of linear and Y-shaped piers; the main generators of the building form appear to have been passenger flows, the type of operation, and the requirement to maximize building perimeter for parked aircraft.

Examples of terminal developments that have been strongly influenced or generated by an overall airport master plan include the curved linear concept at Dallas–Fort Worth and the satellite concept at Hartsfield (Atlanta). Both of these are massive airports handling over 35 million annual passengers, and both use the area between parallel runways for phased development of terminal facilities. Dallas–Fort Worth uses the concept of semicircular unit terminals mirror imaged by a central spineroad system. Presently, there are three terminals in operation, but in the ultimate plan it was envisaged that the semicircular form would be repeated to provide 13 unit terminals with a total capacity of over 150 million annual passsengers. Atlanta uses the satellite concept wherein the space between the parallel runways is occupied by four satellite-pier concourses and parked aircraft only, the terminal and road system being located at one end of the runway system. The master plan allows for the addition of a fifth concourse for an ultimate capacity of 70–80 million passengers. An appreciation for the planning logic of both of these airports is best gained from the air; from ground level, the massive scale of the total developments is overwhelming.

There are also examples of airport architecture as sculptural or symbolic statements heavily influenced by the concept of flight. The most famous examples are both by Eero Saarinen—the previously mentioned Dulles terminal near Washington, D.C., and the birdlike form of the TWA terminal at Kennedy in New York. The concrete and glass terminal at Dulles with its dramatic catenary roof structure and sculpted concrete control tower centered behind, has been voted the most admired of recent American buildings in the *AIA Journal*'s bicentennial poll. Another example of the symbolism of flight is the terminal at Kuwait International Airport, designed by Kenzo Tange, with a form resembling the sleek Concorde ready for takeoff.

In the Middle East and Far East, there are many examples of airport architecture reflecting the cultural and historical idiom. One of the largest and most recent examples is the opulent King Khaled International Airport, near Riyadh, Saudi Arabia, designed by Helmuth Obata and Kassabaum to adhere to the Islamic tradition as well as to harmonize with the desert's natural beauty. Also in Saudia Arabia is the spectacular Haj Terminal at the King Abdulaziz International Airport in Jeddah, designed by Skidmore, Owings & Merrill. Designed specifically to accommodate up to 1 million pilgrims who arrive by air over a three-week period to visit Mecca, the terminal is a 42-hectare (104 acre) teflon-coated fabric structure. From the approach roads, it appears as a shimmering tent city, articulated with gleaming white columns.

Examples in the Far East where the architect has attempted to provide contemporary terminal facilities using the indigenous vernacular are Cenkareng International Airport in Jakarta, Chiang Kai-shek International Airport in Taipei, Kimpo International Airport in Seoul, and Kuching International Airport in Sarawak (East Malaysia).

BIBLIOGRAPHY

1. *ICAO Bull.,* **41**(6), 19 (June 1986).

2. *Aerodromes, International Standards and Recommended Practices, Annex 14 to the Convention on Civil Aviation,* 8th ed., International Civil Aviation Organization, Montreal, Canada, 1983.

3. *Worldwide Traffic Report for the Calendar Year 1985,* Airport Operators Council International, Washington, D.C.

4. Federal Aviation Administration, 1984 Airport Master Records, FAA Form 5010–1.

5. *Port of New York Authority, Jamaica Bay, and Kennedy Airport Study,* Vol. 2, Environmental Studies Board, National Studies Board, National Academy of Sciences, and National Academy of Engineering, Washington, D.C., 1971.

6. *Aircraft Noise, International Standards and Recommended Practices, Annex 16 to the Convention on Civil Aviation,* 3rd ed., International Civil Aviation Organization, Montreal, Canada, July 1978.

7. H. V. Hubbard, M. McClintock, and F. B. Williams, *Airports, Their Location, Administration and Legal Basis,* Harvard University Press, Cambridge, Mass., 1930.

8. A. Black, *Civil Airports and Airways,* Simmons-Boardman Publishing Company, New York, 1929.

9. H. Conin, "Tempelhof—Story of a Crossroads of the Air," *Airport Forum,* No. 3 (July 1975).

10. *American Airport Designs* published for the Lehigh Portland Cement Company by Taylor, Rogers & Bliss, Inc., New York, 1932.

11. Booz, Allen Applied Research, Inc., *A Historical Study of the Benefits Derived from Application of Technical Advances to Civil Aviation,* Vols. I and II, Joint DOT–NASA Civil Aviation Policy Study, Department of Transportation, Washington, D.C., Feb. 1971.

12. R. de Neufville, "Planning for Multiple Airports in a Metropolitan Region," *Built Environ.* 10 (3), (1984).

13. *Airport Planning Manual,* Master Planning Doc 9284-AN/902, International Civil Aviation Organization, Montreal, Canada, Pt. 1. 1977.

14. *Airport Master Plans,* Advisory Circular 150/5070–6A, Federal Aviation Administration, Washington, D.C., June 1985.

15. W. Hart, *The Airport Passenger Terminal,* Wiley Interscience, New York, 1985.

16. *Aerodrome Design Manual, Runways,* 2nd ed., International Civil Aviation Organization, Montreal, Canada, Pt. 1, 1984.

17. *Airport Capacity and Delay,* Advisory Circular AC 150/5060, Federal Aviation Administration, Washington, D.C., Sept. 23, 1983.

18. *Airport Design Standards—Transport Airports,* Advisory Circular AC 150/5300–12, Federal Aviation Administration, Washington, D.C., Feb. 28, 1983.

19. *Airport Terminals Reference Manual,* 6th ed., International Air Transport Association, Montreal, Canada, 1985, 7th ed. pending.

20. *Site Requirements for Terminal Navigational Facilities,* AC 150/5300–2C, Federal Aviation Administration, Washington, D.C., Sept. 1973.

21. *Airport Services Manual,* 2nd ed., International Civil Aviation Organization, Montreal, Canada, Pt. 1, 1984.

22. *Manual on Air Traffic Forecasting,* Doc 8991–AT/722, International Civil Aviation Organization, Montreal, Canada, 1972.

23. *Airline Aircraft Gates and Passenger Terminal Space Approximations,* AD/SC Report No.4, Air Transport Association of America, Washington, D.C., July 1977.

24. *The Apron and Terminal Building Planning Manual,* Report No. FAA–RD–75–191, Federal Aviation Administration, Washington, D.C., July 1975.

25. *Planning and Design Guidelines for Airport Terminal Facilities,* Advisory Circular AC150/5360–7A, Federal Aviation Administration, Washington, D.C., Sept. 1976.

26. *Interim Level-of-Service Standards CASE 1977,* Document AK 14–06–500(c), Canadian Air Transport Administration, Ottawa, Canada.

27. *Aerodrome Design Manual, Taxiways, Aprons and Holding Bays,* 2nd ed., International Civil Aviation Organization, Montreal, Canada, Pt. 2, 1983.

28. *Airport Design Standards—Transport Airports,* Advisory Circular AC150/5300–12. Chg. 1, Federal Aviation Administration, Washington, D.C., Mar. 14, 1985.

29. *Aircraft Data,* Advisory Circular AC/5325–5B, Federal Aviation Administration, Washington, D.C., July 30, 1975.

30. *The Apron–Terminal Complex, Analysis of Concepts for Evaluation of Terminal Buildings,* Report No. FAA–RD–73–82, Federal Aviation Administration, Washington, D.C., Sept. 1973.

31. D. F. Rider, *Jane's Airport Equipment 1985–86,* 4th ed., Jane's Publishing Co., Ltd, London.

32. F. Z. Louie de Irizarry, *AIRPORT ARCHITECTURE: A Bibliography of Periodic Articles,* Vance Bibliographies, Monticello, Ill., Jan. 1982.

33. *ARCHITECTURAL PLANNING FOR AIRPORTS: Site Selection, Geometric Design of the Landing Area, Terminal Design,* Vance Bibliographies, Monticello, Ill., Jan. 1980.

TREVOR CARNAHOFF
NORR Partnership, Limited
Toronto, Canada

AIR QUALITY

Within the last decade, the quality of indoor air has become a major environmental factor in the design, construction, and operation of residential, commercial, and institutional buildings. Energy conservation efforts have resulted in tighter and better insulated buildings; reduced capacities of heating, ventilating, and air conditioning (HVAC) systems; and control strategies that minimize air movement in occupied spaces. Thus contaminants traditionally considered as innocuous have been detected in concentrations that can be deleterious. Effluents from new sources, such as copy machines and synthetic building materials, have intensified the concern for acceptable indoor air quality. As methods of detection have improved, awareness of the possible effects of long-term exposures to low level concentrations of the many indoor contaminants has increased. The objectives of this article are to provide a brief historical perspective of indoor air quality control, to introduce the basic concepts, to describe some of the manifestations of indoor contaminants, and to describe the primary methods of control.

HISTORICAL PERSPECTIVE

Early Development

The conflict between energy conservation and indoor air quality is as old as human desire for shelter in permanent structures. Investigation of indigenous architecture reveals the use of vent holes in the roofs of structures to exhaust pollutants from small fires built indoors for warmth. Before the discovery of glazing materials, long-term occupancy was limited because of the minimal amount of daylighting. However, when the Romans first began to glaze windows, the uses and sizes of buildings began to vary from simple dwellings to large places of worship. Thus the use of windows in buildings for lighting and for natural ventilation has a history almost as old as buildings themselves.

Codes and Standards

During the Middle Ages, indoor air quality was often noted to be unacceptable. In 1600, King Charles I of England promulgated one of the earliest recorded regulations for ventilation control. To improve removal of smoke, odors, and heat, he specified that no house could be built with a ceiling height of less than 10 ft, and that the windows had to be higher than they were wide (1). In 1824, T. Tredgold, a Welsh mining engineer, recommended minimum requirements of 4 cubic feet per minute (cfm) (ie, 2 L/s) of outdoor air per person for carbon dioxide (CO_2) control (2). Based on his concern for tuberculosis contagion, J. S. Billings recommended in 1893 that 30 cfm (15 L/s) per person of outdoor air be considered a minimum ventilation rate for continuously occupied spaces, but that rates of 45–60 cfm (23–30 L/s) were preferable (3). These recommendations led the American Society of Heating and Ventilating Engineers (ASHVE) to adopt 30 cfm per person as a minimum ventilation rate in its first standard promulgated in 1895 (4). By 1925, the codes in 22 states of the U.S. required this minimum ventilation rate (5).

In 1923, the New York State Commission on Ventilation found, based on an eight-year study of classrooms, that control of occupancy odor should figure prominently in ventilation requirements, but that the justification for ventilation rates had to rest on grounds of comfort rather than on health. As a result of that study, the Commission recommended a minimum ventilation rate of 10–15 cfm (5–8 L/s) per student for control of odor and CO_2 concentrations, if the classroom space per student was at least 250 ft^3 (9 m^3) (6). Subsequent studies by C. P. Yaglou and his associates in the 1930s indicated that a minimum of 5 cfm (2.5 L/s) was needed to maintain CO_2 concentrations below 0.6%, even when the room volume per person was large, but that the ventilation rate per person required to maintain an odor-free environment increased logarithmically as the room volume per person decreased (7). The Yaglou studies have served as the primary reference in codes and standards for the last 50 years.

The *American Standard Building Requirements for Light and Ventilation-A 53.1* was published by the American Standards Association in 1946 (8). Although it dealt primarily with natural means of providing light and ventilation, it specified criteria, typically as cfm/ft^2, as an apparent attempt to rationalize the personal requirements of ventilation and space with building criteria of floor area and standard ceiling heights. In 1973, the American Society of Heating, Refrigerating, and Air Conditioning Engineers (ASHRAE) published a revision and update of the 1946 standard: *ASHRAE Standard 62–1973: Standards for Natural and Mechanical Ventilation* (9). In this revision, the ventilation rates were again specified as personal requirements (ie, cfm/person), but two sets of criteria were published: minimum ventilation rates to accommodate energy conservation, and recommended ventilation rates for comfort in odor-free environments. Other important considerations included the recognition of recirculation and filtration for ventilation, and the need for cleaning outdoor air when its quality was not acceptable.

In response to concerns for energy consumption in buildings, *ASHRAE Standard 90–75: Energy Conservation in New Building Design* was published in 1975 (10). By 1980, that standard and its codified counterparts, which were expected to reduce energy requirements in new buildings by 15–60% had been adopted by 45 states, and had influenced building codes in Canada and Europe (11–13). A major conflict resulted, as this standard stated that the minimum column in Standard 62–73 for each type of occupancy was to be used for design purposes. This statement had the effect of eliminating the recommended values and caused concern that the quality of the indoor air could become deleterious. To address these concerns, the ventilation standard was again revised in 1981 as *ASHRAE Standard 62–1981: Ventilation for Acceptable Indoor Air Quality* (14). Major revisions included: listing required ventilation rates for smoking and nonsmoking areas rather than minimum and recommended values; specifying a more objective method for determining required recirculation air rates as a function of air cleaner efficiencies; and introducing an alternative to the conventional ventilation

rate procedure, identified as the indoor air quality procedure. This alternative specified objective and subjective performance criteria (ie, contaminant concentrations and odor acceptability) that could be used to evaluate acceptability of occupied spaces in place of the traditional prescriptive criteria (ie, ventilation rates). To date, this indoor air quality standard is the most generally recognized in the U.S., yet it is admittedly not comprehensive.

While traditional prescriptive codes and standards provide design criteria that can be inspected and evaluated during design and construction, they provide no assurances that occupant exposure will be acceptable. Conversely, performance standards provide measurable criteria for occupied spaces, but they offer little guidance on how to design or construct building systems that will provide the required environmental control. Thus, care should be taken to ensure that prescriptive and performance criteria can be rationalized. In standards such as ASHRAE 62–1981 that contain both types of criteria as alternatives, it is not intended that compliance with both criteria be demonstrated. Rather, it is intended that compliance with one alternative imply compliance with the other (15). However, other codes and standards that specify only one method of compliance may lead to conflict with other criteria. Air quality problems can often be prevented if codes and standards are used as minimum guidelines for acceptable design and operation rather than as strict specifications for design. Actual design conditions often dictate that ventilation rates exceed minimum standards if acceptable conditions are to be provided.

BASIC CONCEPTS

General Definition

Although the air quality within occupied spaces is generally recognized as an important environmental factor to control within buildings, the concept of indoor air quality remains vague. For example, in the 1981 National Academy of Sciences publication *Indoor Pollutants,* methods of identifying, monitoring, and controlling indoor pollutants were addressed, but indoor air quality was not defined (16). In this article, the following general definition is assumed:

> Air quality is the nature of air that affects an individual's health and well-being.

In this definition, the meaning of health and well-being is also assumed to be that stated in the Constitution of the World Health Organization (WHO) (17):

> Health is a state of complete physical, mental, and social well-being and not merely the absence of disease or infirmity.

Stress–Strain–Susceptibility. When an occupant is exposed to an environmental force, pressure, or influence (stress), a physiological or psychological response (strain) results as a function of the occupant's predisposition to that stress (susceptibility). Although these relationships are usually assumed to cause adverse effects, this is not necessarily so. In most cases, a certain amount of stress is desirable to maintain a state of well-being, but excessive stresses should be avoided.

Strains depend on the concentrations of the stressors and the exposure times. Thus, for some stresses that result in cumulative doses, strains from long-term exposures to low level contaminant concentrations may have more severe effects than short-term exposures to high level concentrations. Responses to environmental stresses are also affected by organismic and adaptive factors (18). Organismic factors (ie, age, sex, genetics, rhythmicity, body type, psyche, drive, and physical condition) are intrinsic to the occupant. Adaptive factors (ie, activity, incentive, social exposure, clothing, and ingesta) provide some means for the occupant to control personal responses to environmental stressors.

Health and Comfort. Effects from exposures to environmental stressors may be described objectively and subjectively. The WHO definition of health implies that both descriptions are needed. Objective measures are expressed as quantitative values of the occupant's physiological or behavioral strains. Subjective measures are usually expressed as affective responses, such as comfort and acceptability. When the stressors result in a complete state of well-being or contentment, a comfortable (ie, healthy) strain may exist. The amount of deviation from these ideal conditions that can be accepted without discomfort or adverse health effects is dependent upon the occupant's abilities to respond to the deviations. As the ability to respond through organismic or adaptive factors diminishes, susceptibility to the adverse effects of the stresses increases. Air quality control is a necessary but not sufficient condition for occupant health and comfort; ie, if acceptable conditions are provided, individuals have an opportunity to be healthy or comfortable. However, personal limitations, eg, disease or social stress, may preclude healthy or comfortable strains even in the presence of acceptable environmental conditions. Thus a professional responsibility for those in the building industry is to provide environmental conditions within acceptable ranges of the susceptible occupants.

Ventilation

Whether a person is indoors or outdoors, air is required for respiration. Physiologically, this process is defined as ventilation or, more specifically, respiratory ventilation: the inhalation of fresh air followed by the exhalation of alveolar gas (19). The primary purpose of respiratory ventilation is to oxygenate and detoxify pulmonary blood by inspiration of oxygen (O_2) and expiration of carbon dioxide (CO_2), and other alveolar gases. However, other contaminants can also exist in the inspired air at concentrations that are likely to cause adverse health effects. Contaminants at these concentrations are commonly described as air pollutants.

For a person confined within an enclosed space, the concept of ventilation is confounded. While the life scientist thinks in terms of respiratory ventilation, engineers and architects think in terms of room ventilation (14): "The

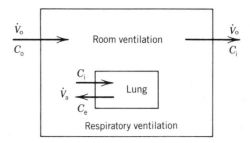

Figure 1. A two-compartment model of the coupling between room and respiratory ventilation (20).

process of supplying and removing air by natural or mechanical means to and from any space. Such air may or may not be conditioned." Although these concepts of ventilation are different, they can be related through a simple two-compartment model, which represents an occupant in an enclosed space. In Figure 1, the concentration of the inspired air is assumed to be the same as the uniformly mixed indoor air C_i; the concentration of the expired air is C_e; and the concentration of the outdoor air is C_o. The rate of emission of contaminant from the occupant is assumed equal to the net generation rate of the contaminant in the room. The respiratory and room ventilation rates are $\dot{V}_a$ and $\dot{V}_o$, respectively.

In steady state, the relationship of the room and respiratory ventilation rates may be expressed as the ventilation ratio

$$\frac{\dot{V}_o}{\dot{V}_a} = \frac{C_e - C_i}{C_i - C_o} \tag{1}$$

An example of this relationship between room and respiratory ventilation rates is shown in Figure 2 for CO_2.

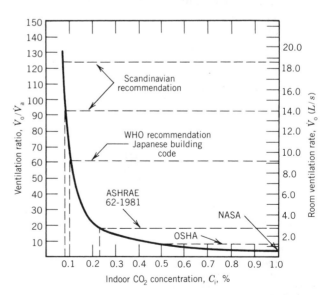

Figure 2. Relationship between the ventilation ratio $\dot{V}_o/\dot{V}_a$ and the concentration of CO_2 within a uniformly mixed occupied space C_1. The relationship between room ventilation rate $\dot{V}_o$ and CO_2 concentration for the assumed respiratory rate $\dot{V}_a$ of 0.15 L/s (0.3 cfm) is also shown (20).

While concentrations that are acceptable by NASA (21), OSHA (22), and ASHRAE standards (14) have been set for prevention of adverse health effects to the populations of concern, the Japanese standard (23) and the WHO and Scandinavian guidelines (24, 25) have probably been set to correlate with concentrations of other contaminants that also exist with the specified CO_2 levels, and that are the sources of objectionable indoor conditions, eg, odorous, stale air.

Technical Definition

To provide control of acceptable indoor air quality, it is necessary to define the technical nature of the control problem. Air is a thermodynamic mixture of dry air and water vapor at a given barometric pressure. The composition of dry air, as defined by ASHRAE for standard temperature and pressure, is shown in Table 1. The moisture content of the indoor air will normally vary from between 1 and 2% by volume. It should be noted from Table 1 that, with few notable exceptions, contaminants account for a very small fraction of the volumetric percentage of air. Yet, it is this fraction that contains the air pollutants. The following technical definition, which was first used in Iowa in 1982, is therefore assumed for the remainder of this article (26):

Air quality is an indicator of how well air satisfies three requirements for human occupancy:
1. Thermal acceptability.
2. Normal concentrations of respiratory gases (ie, O_2 and CO_2).
3. Suppression of other contaminants below levels that are deleterious or cause odor discomfort.

Thermal Acceptability. Four physical factors, ie, dry-bulb temperature, mean radiant temperature, water-vapor pressure, and air velocity, and three adaptive factors, ie, metabolic activity level, insulation value of clothing, and exposure time, most significantly influence human thermal response. Because of the sensitivity of this response, a necessary condition for acceptable indoor air quality is the provision of an acceptable thermal environment. In the U.S. and Canada, the most common standard of thermal acceptability is *ASHRAE Standard 55–1981: Thermal Environmental Conditions for Human Occupancy* (27).

Respiratory Gases. The primary gases of concern in respiratory ventilation are O_2 and CO_2. In sedentary activity, an adult occupant will inspire approximately 6 L/min of air and consume ca 0.2 L/min O_2 (21). Depending on the diet of the occupant, the corresponding emission rates of CO_2 will range from 0.16 L/min for a high carbohydrate diet to 0.20 L/min for a high protein diet. The ratio of CO_2 expired to O_2 inspired is known as the respiratory quotient (ie, RQ = 0.8–1.0). If activity increases to three times sedentary (ie, 3 Mets where 1 Met = 57 watts/m^2 of body surface area heat dissipation rate), the O_2 consumption and corresponding CO_2 emission rates will increase approximately 3–5 times. Thus activity level influences not only the amount of heat that must be dissipated from the occupant, but also the amount of room ventilation required to maintain acceptable concentrations of O_2 and CO_2.

For a sedentary occupant, the amount of room ventilation required to maintain an acceptable CO_2 concentration of 1000 ppm (ie, 0.10%) is more than five times that required to maintain an acceptable O_2 concentration of 20.5%. Thus, in most indoor environments, if room ventilation rates are provided to achieve acceptable dilution of CO_2 (eg, to ≤ 1000 ppm), the corresponding concentrations of O_2 should be more than sufficient for its oxygenating function in respiration.

Other Contaminants. Four basic classifications of airborne contaminants are gases and vapors, bioaerosols, inert particulates, and radionuclides. When concentrations of these contaminants are not controlled within acceptable levels, adverse strains can result, ranging from acute discomfort (eg, unpleasant odors, headaches, eye irritation, and nausea), to frank illness (eg, fever, infections, and carcinomas). Although thermal acceptability and respiratory sufficiency typically account for most of the complaints regarding unacceptable indoor environmental conditions, recent focus on indoor air quality has been on these other contaminants. Four basic reasons can be cited for this recent concern: changes in building control strategies for improved energy efficiency and cost effectiveness have resulted in reduced room ventilation rates; new processes (eg, photocopying), synthetic materials, and increased occupancy density have increased generation rates of contaminants; new methods of detecting the presence of contaminants at low concentrations have been developed; and the level of awareness of health implications of exposure to these contaminants has increased in the general public (16).

Table 1. Composition of Dry Air[a]

Component	Symbol	Volume, %	Concentration at Standard Conditions[b]
nitrogen	N_2	78.084	894 g/m^3
oxygen	O_2	20.948	274 g/m^3
argon	Ar	0.934	15 g/m^3
carbon dioxide	CO_2	0.0314	565 mg/m^3
neon	Ne	0.00182	15 mg/m^3
helium	He	0.000524	428 μg/m^3
methane	CH_4	0.000200	1309 μg/m^3
hydrogen	H_2	0.000050	41 μg/m^3
trace gases[c]		0.000006	123 μg/m^{3d}
Total		*100.000000*	

[a] Ref. 28, Chapter 6.
[b] Ppm$_v$ × (MW/24,500) = g/ms^3, from Appendix A, ASHRAE Standard 62–1981 (14).
[c] Trace gases include sulfur dioxide, krypton, xenon, ozone, and other natural and anthropogenic components.
[d] Concentration based on an assumed average mol wt of 50.

Basic Control Strategies

Exposure to airborne contaminants within enclosed spaces may be controlled by three basic processes: source control, which limits the emissions of the contaminants into the occupied space; removal control, which collects the contaminants from the air in the occupied space; and dilution control, which exchanges the air in the occupied space with air from outdoors or from other parts of the building. The relationship among these basic processes is shown schematically in Figure 3, and may be expressed as a simple, steady-state mass balance (29):

$$\Delta C = \frac{\dot{N} - \dot{E}}{\dot{V}_o} \qquad (2)$$

In this equation, ΔC represents the difference between concentrations in the occupied space C_i, and in the air to be used for dilution control C_o

$$\Delta C = C_i - C_o \qquad (3)$$

These concentrations are expressed in terms of contaminant mass per unit volume or per unit mass of air (eg, $\mu g/m^3$ or $\mu g/kg$).

The term $\dot{V}_o$ in equation 2 represents the rate of air exchange for dilution control, and is expressed in terms of air volume or mass per unit time (eg, m^3/h or kg/h).

The term $\dot{N}$ represents the difference between the emission and remission rates (ie, net generation rate) of contaminant within the occupied space; it is expressed in terms of contaminant mass per unit time (eg, $\mu g/h$).

The term $\dot{E}$ represents the removal rate of the contaminant from the occupied space, and is expressed in terms of contaminant mass per unit time (eg, $\mu g/h$). As seen in Figure 3, the removal rate can be estimated as

$$\dot{E} = \dot{V}_r e C_u \qquad (4)$$

In this equation, e is the removal efficiency of the air cleaner evaluated in terms of the contaminant to be removed

$$e = 1 - (C_d/C_u) \qquad (5)$$

where C_d and C_u represent the concentrations of the contaminant downstream and upstream of the air cleaner, respectively. $\dot{V}_r$ is the air circulation rate through the air cleaner, and is expressed in terms of air volume per unit time (eg, m^3/h). C_u is the concentration of the contaminant challenging the air cleaner, and, in the simple case where the air in the occupied space is uniformly mixed, its value can be estimated as that of the occupied space C_i.

The simple, steady-state mass balance of the occupied space, expressed as equations 2–5, provides important insight for air quality control strategies:

1. Source control (ie, minimizing $\dot{N}$) is the only process that can eliminate occupant exposure to the contaminant.
2. If indoor sources cannot be eliminated, exposure of occupants will exist, and removal and dilution control must be relied upon to provide acceptable conditions. Applications of removal or dilution control imply mixtures of the contaminants exist within the occupied space, and therefore assume that minimal concentrations of the contaminants are acceptable.
3. Indoor concentration cannot be controlled at values less than outdoors unless the removal rate $\dot{E}$ exceeds the net generation rate $\dot{N}$.
4. If the contaminant concentrations in the outdoor air are above acceptable values for indoor air quality, the outdoor air must be cleaned before it can be used for dilution control.
5. Priority of control should be first to minimize the net generation rate; second, to provide minimum outdoor air for normal respiration; and third, to optimize removal and dilution rates to provide acceptable conditions, energy efficiency, and cost effectiveness.

MANIFESTATIONS OF INDOOR AIR CONTAMINANTS

Types and Sources

Literally thousands of contaminants are present in most indoor environments. Because of this vast array and the limited methods of control, strategies to control each contaminant may be impractical and unnecessary. Thus, if contaminants can be identified and characterized, common control strategies may be employed to provide for the health and comfort of the occupants.

Physical factors that influence or modify human responses may be characterized as originating from four environmental zones; two within and two outside of the building (29). These factors may also be classified by dimensional continua. Mass stressors can be represented by particle size, from small molecular weight gases (eg, mean particle sizes as small as 10^{-5} μm to large airborne dust particles (eg, particles with mean diameters as large as 100 μm). To characterize mass stressors, their state (eg, solid, liquid, vapor, or gas), and their concentration (eg, mass per unit volume of air) must also be defined. In addition, biological contaminants are also characterized as living or dead matter. Energy stressors can be represented by wavelength, from short wavelengths due to high energy ionizing radiation (eg, 10^{-4} μm) to long wavelengths due to radio waves, sound, and vibration (eg, 10^5 μm). To characterize energy stressors, their potential (eg, temperature, sound pressure level, illuminance, or energy level) must also be defined.

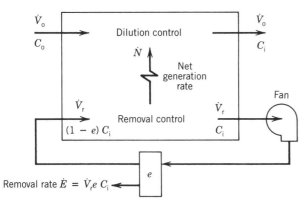

Figure 3. One-compartment, uniformly mixed, steady-state model for indoor air quality (29).

Indoor Sources. The most immediate zone with respect to the occupant, defined as the microenvironment, contains those stressors to which the occupant is intimately exposed. It includes boundaries such as the occupant's clothing and personal breathing space. Contaminants must penetrate the microenvironment for occupant exposure to occur. Contaminants emitted within the microenvironment include chemicals or microbials captured in the clothing, sidestream tobacco smoke, and endogenous bioeffluents (eg, CO_2, butyric acid, water vapor, skin flakes, and bioaerosols from sneezes and coughs).

The next most immediate source of contaminants is the minienvironment. Its boundaries include walls, ceilings, and floors, and exclude the boundaries of the microenvironment. The minienvironment is the zone where control (eg, temperature, humidity, and ventilation) is normally employed to achieve acceptable conditions within each occupant's microenvironment. Contaminant concentrations within the minienvironment are represented as C_i in equations 2 and 3. Contaminants generated in the outdoor air or in other zones in the building must penetrate the minienvironment and microenvironment for occupant exposure to occur. Many of the contaminants contained in outdoor air are also generated within the minienvironment, including products of combustion, biocides, and other volatile organic compounds (VOCs). The primary sources of contaminants generated within the minienvironment are building materials, the occupants themselves, and processes conducted indoors:

- Building materials that emit contaminants include masonry and wood products (eg, inert particulates, radon, formaldehyde, and other VOCs); thermal and acoustic insulation (eg, asbestos, glass fibers, and formaldehyde); fabrics such as carpeting, drapery, upholstery, and wallpaper (eg, fibers and VOCs); and paints and adhesives (eg, lead, mercury, and VOCs). The generation rates of contaminants from these sources, shown as $\dot{N}$ in equation 3, are functions of the mass of the material, the surface area exposed to the minienvironment, the thermal conditions of the materials and the minienvironment, and the vapor-pressure or concentration gradients of the contaminants between the materials and the minienvironment.

- Occupants are significant sources of contaminants within the minienvironment. The type and amount of contaminants are influenced by the occupants' activity levels and states of health (eg, water vapor, CO_2, butyric acid and many other VOCs, bacteria, and viruses); by their clothing (eg, fine particulates, VOCs, and microbials); by the pets and plants they own (eg, mites, dander, molds, and spores); and by insect and microbial populations associated with human occupancy.

- Processes conducted within the minienvironments may be the primary sources of contaminants to which occupants are exposed. Many of the processes commonly occur in most types of buildings (eg, residential, commercial, and institutional). These processes include:

1. Indoor combustion, such as tobacco smoking, the use of combustion appliances, and vehicle garages. More than 3800 airborne contaminants (eg, gases, vapors, and particulates) have been identified indoors as functions of environmental tobacco smoke (ETS). Of these, more than 60 are known or suspected carcinogens (30).

2. Housekeeping, such as floor, window, and wall cleaning, furniture and appliance cleaning, bedmaking, dusting, sanitizing, and deodorizing. House dust describes a complex indoor contaminant that includes molds, bacteria, mites, pollen, human and animal hair and dandruff, textiles, food particles, and decomposed materials. House dust can be aerosolized if it is not carefully removed. Moreover, products used in housekeeping can be sources of contaminants. For example, in a study of seven hospitals, 143 different chemical compounds used in 88 deodorizers, detergents, and solvents were identified. Of these, 12 were considered very toxic, 29 moderately toxic, and 23 were suspected carcinogens (31).

3. Food processing, such as preparation, serving, disposal, and dishwashing. Gases, vapors, and inert and biological particulates can be emitted by these processes.

4. Laundry procedures, such as sorting, washing, drying, folding, and storing are sources of microbials, VOCs, and water vapor.

5. Office procedures may be sources of gaseous, vaporous, and particulate contaminants, and ionizing and nonionizing radiation. Typing, photocopying, and high speed printing processes can aerosolize small diameter carbon particles, ozone, and aliphatic hydrocarbons. Carbonless paper is often the source of VOCs. Some concern also exists that x rays and nonionizing radiation can be emitted from video display tubes.

6. Environmental control systems can ironically become sources of contaminants. If the outdoor air is contaminated, indoor conditions may be aggravated unless this air is cleaned before it is used for ventilation. Also, contaminants may be transported between minienvironments within the same HVAC system if local exhaust devices (eg, fume hoods and kitchen exhaust fans) or removal devices (ie, filters and air cleaners) are not employed. If the systems are not properly maintained, inert and biological contaminants can accumulate on components and in the ductwork, and be aerosolized into the minienvironments.

Outdoor Sources. The zone immediately outside the building may be defined as the mesoenvironment. It contains those external factors that perturb control of the minienvironments. The boundaries of the mesoenvironment are less precisely defined, but include property sites and local landscaping; the mesoenvironment excludes the boundaries of the minienvironments (ie, building boundaries). The quality of the air in the mesoenvironment requires special care, as sources or factors within it may either amplify or mitigate the contaminant concentrations in the ambient (outdoor) air. Thus, factors such as location of cooling towers or stacks from stationary combustion plants in relation to makeup air intakes can highly influence the quality of the indoor air. Contaminants in the mesoenvironment may be characterized as originating from above-grade or below-grade sources:

- Above-grade sources influence the quality of the outdoor air used for ventilation of the minienvironments. The mesoenvironment is the source of ventilation or infiltration air supplied to occupied spaces (ie, C_o in equations 2 and 3). Above-grade sources include:

  1. Vehicular traffic, such as drive-up windows, loading docks, trash, and garbage pickups.
  2. Stationary combustion plants, such as central heating plants, cogeneration facilities, and incineration facilities.
  3. Heat rejection equipment, such as cooling towers and air-cooled condensers.
  4. Exhaust systems, such as toilet exhaust fans, fume hood discharges, or general building exhausts.
  5. Waste systems, such as plumbing vents, liquid and sump discharges, and solid waste facilities.
  6. Landscaping, such as dirt fill, berms, grass, plants, shrubs, trees, and waterways.

- Below-grade sources influence the quality of indoor air by diffusion of contaminants through the minienvironmental boundaries. Concentrations of below-grade contaminants may be represented as C_o in equations 2 and 3. Below-grade sources include:

  1. Soil surrounding the building substructure. Soil gases can diffuse through air channels in the soil, and other chemical and biological contaminants can be transported with the movement of soil water. Some contaminants exist naturally in the soil, eg, radon. However, many others are due to anthropogenic factors, such as fertilizers, biocides, sewage, and industrial waste.

     Radon is an odorless, colorless, radioactive gas that is a decay product of radium, a natural element in the earth's crust. A significant difference between radon and other indoor air pollutants is that radon is radioactive, an emitter of ionizing radiation. It is a suspected cause of lung cancer (32). Incidences of indoor radon exposure have been primarily manifested within residential facilities; however, no evidence exists that exposure in other types of structures is precluded.

  2. Services such as natural gas, domestic water, and sewage systems that transport contaminants into the minienvironment.

The zone outside the boundaries of the mesoenvironment may be defined as the macroenvironment. It contains both natural and anthropogenic sources of contaminants that have been the subject of outdoor air quality regulation for the last twenty years. For purposes of indoor air quality control, obvious sources in the macroenvironment should be recognized. Concentrations of contaminants from these sources and from the general macroenvironment should be considered in a manner similar to that employed in designing and controlling the indoor thermal environment; concentrations which are not expected to be exceeded by more than a given percentage of time should be considered as design values of C_o in equations 2 and 3.

Human Responses

A building and its occupants form a psychosocial environment which, together with the physical and chemical qualities of environment, determine the overall responses of the occupants. A fundamental objective of environmental control is to not only prevent the existence of deleterious or unpleasant conditions, but to provide for the comfort and well-being of the occupants. In most cases, occupant responses within nonindustrial buildings are not caused by intensive exposure to specific stressors; rather responses are caused by extensive exposure to multiple stressors. Objective and subjective responses of building occupants may be classified as those that are (33):

- Perceived and result in physiological strains.
- Not perceived, but cause physiological strains.
- Perceived, but do not cause physiological strains.

Perceived Physiological Responses. Physical stressors that stimulate the four basic types of sensory receptors (ie, thermoreceptors, olfactory receptors, auditory receptors, and visual receptors) are included in this category. These stressors are usually recognizable, and changes in their values are usually sensed by the occupants. Examples are warm or cool air, odorous gases and vapors (eg, butyric acid from occupant bioeffluents and pyridine from ETS), noise, and bright or dim lighting. Control of these stressors will elicit physiological strains (eg, vasomotor control) that are acceptable and can be pleasant or comfortable to the occupants. However, if acceptable limits are exceeded or stressors are not recognized (eg, strange odors), complaints of discomfort will usually result. Symptoms associated with unacceptable stressors in this category include headaches and fatigue from heat, glare, noise, and odors; nausea from heat, noise, and odors; eye irritation from low humidity, glare, and odorous compounds; and throat and respiratory irritations from cold drafts, low humidity, and odorous compounds.

Nonperceived Physiological Responses. Stressors that do not affect the sensory receptors or that only affect them at values above those that cause physiological strains are included in this category. Examples are odorless gases and vapors (eg, carbon monoxide and radon); carcinogenic or mutagenic compounds (eg, polychlorinated hydrocarbons and volatile amines); gases and vapors with odor recognition thresholds above irritation thresholds (eg, formaldehyde, oxides of nitrogen, and ozone); inert particulates (eg, asbestos and nicotine); and bioaerosols (eg, bacteria, fungi, and spores). Few if any beneficial physiological responses result from exposure to this category of stressors. Deleterious responses include infections, respiratory disorders, and neurological disorders. Symptoms associated with stressors in this category include headaches, fatigue, dizziness, drowsiness, nausea, irritation of eyes, throat, skin, and upper and lower respiratory tracts, fever, and loss of memory. Control of these stressors is more difficult because sensory perceptions of the occupants cannot be relied upon; detection by instrumentation is required to identify the presence and concentrations of the contaminants.

Perceived Nonphysiological Responses. Psychosocial stressors are included in this category. Examples of these stressors are labor–management climate, collegial relations, and job satisfaction. Occupant dissatisfaction with these stressors can result in a transfer of complaints to the physical environment. Thus physical stressors may be perceived by occupants to have greater strains if excessive psychosocial stressors also exist. Symptoms associated with stressors in this category are the same as those described for the other two categories. Control of responses in this category is probably the most difficult because sensory perceptions of the occupants have been influenced by the psychosocial factors. Detection by instrumentation is required to identify the presence or absence of the contaminants, and counseling of the occupants may also be required.

Problem Buildings. When the complaints of a set of symptoms, including headaches, eye irritation, sore throat, fatigue, dizziness, drowsiness, and nausea persist at frequencies significantly above 20% among occupants for periods of longer than two weeks; when the sources of complaints are not obvious; and when occupants usually obtain relief outside of the building; the building is considered to manifest sick building syndrome (SBS) (34). The symptoms associated with SBS are actually related to responses of acute discomfort rather than frank illness (eg, fever, infection, and tissue deterioration). If symptoms of frank illness are present, the condition is often classified as a building-related illness (BRI). Examples of this latter condition are occurrences of nosocomial infections in hospitals, humidifier fever, and legionellosis. An important difference between situations classified as SBS or BRI is that the etiology of the SBS may not be necessary, as complaints are often resolved by increasing system ventilation, by discussions with the occupants, and by improved system maintenance. On the other hand, the etiology of a BRI incidence must usually be determined before a solution can be implemented. When diagnosis of SBS or BRI reveals methods of control that can mitigate the problems, the building is then described as a problem building, and engineering solutions are usually employed.

METHODS OF CONTROL

Environmental control within occupied spaces relies upon three mechanisms: conduction, radiation, and convection. Conduction controls heat, noise, and vibration transmission through the structural elements of the building (ie, through the boundaries of the minienvironments). However, with the exception of control within hostile environments where special clothing and protection are required, conduction is only of minor importance to human responses from mini- or microenvironmental stressors. Radiation of energy within the visible spectrum is the fundamental mechanism for control of lighting. Long-wave radiation is the primary mechanism for control of acoustics within enclosed spaces; ir radiation is an important mechanism for control of sensible heat transfer to and from occupants. Convection is of equal importance as ir radiation for control of sensible heat transfer within occupied spaces. Moreover, convection is totally relied upon to dissipate latent heat and bioeffluents from the occupants, indoor processes, and building materials. When forced air systems are used for control of heat and mass transfer, convection also indirectly influences the acoustic environment as noise is a by-product of energy dissipated by the air transport.

Evolution of HVAC Control

Early methods of thermal and air quality control relied upon radiation and natural convection for heat transfer. Examples of systems that supplied heat by these mechanisms are fireplaces, stoves, steam radiators, and gravity furnaces. Indoor air quality was determined by the availability of infiltration air and openable windows. These systems were reasonably effective for local heating and ventilation in small buildings, but were inadequate and sometimes unsafe in large buildings. After the discovery and harnessing of electrical power, forced air systems were introduced which could provide heating more uniformly to many occupied spaces within a building. At the turn of the twentieth century, the theory of refrigeration was reduced to practical methods of cooling occupied spaces. As a result, forced air systems evolved that could provide comfort by heating, humidifying, cooling, dehumidifying, and ventilating the occupied spaces. Moreover, these methods contributed to the development of large buildings.

Until the energy shortages of the 1970s, the primary objective of HVAC control was to maximize the comfort of the occupant. Energy consumption and operating costs were important, but were not the primary factors in determining the design of the systems. During the last decade, however, they have become dominant factors in the design and operation of environmental control systems.

Today, a wide variety of systems is available to provide environmental control. In many older residences, heating is still provided by radiant or natural convection systems while infiltration is relied upon to provide ventilation. As these structures have been insulated, caulked, and sealed to reduce thermal transmission, less infiltration air has become available for ventilation, unless special efforts such as installing air-to-air heat exchangers have also been taken. In newer residences, central forced air heating and cooling systems have often been installed which also typically depend on infiltration for ventilation air. Complaints of condensation on windows and poor air quality have been associated with some of these systems, primarily because alternatives to infiltration have not been considered in their design and operation. Newer residences that have been designed to minimize energy consumption typically have disregarded the need for ventilation air, and, as a result, a controversy has arisen that energy-efficient housing is not environmentally acceptable. Larger buildings in the U.S. primarily rely on forced air systems to provide thermal and air quality control. Trends in these buildings have been toward variable air volume systems for energy conservation. As with residential design, disregard for air movement and ventilation of occupied spaces is the most typical cause for complaints manifested as SBS. Therefore, the conflict between energy efficiency and environmental acceptability is as pervasive in large buildings as in residences.

Air Movement Control

Conventional methods of convection control require mixing of the thermal and contaminant loads within the occupied spaces before dilution or removal control can be applied. For thermal acceptability, air movement is characterized by the local eddy currents or omnidirectional air velocity around the occupant (35). For acceptable air quality, air movement is usually characterized by its exchange or ventilation rates. If room air distribution patterns are not sufficient to dilute or remove contaminant or thermal loads from the microenvironments, the effectiveness of the system will be impaired as excessive air exchange rates will probably be used as compensation, with the expected effects of increased energy consumption, nonuniform mixing in the occupied spaces, and drafty or uncomfortable subjective responses. Thus air distribution patterns within occupied spaces may be as important to the effectiveness of the ventilation system as the air exchange, ventilation, or supply air flow rates.

Within Rooms. The room air distribution system must be responsive to the thermal loads in the space, the indoor air quality requirements, and the acoustic room criteria. To meet all of these criteria simultaneously requires care in the selection and placement of the supply and return air terminals. The effectiveness of distributing the supply air to the occupants is conventionally determined in terms of the Air Distribution Performance Index (ADPI) (36). This concept is based on the ability of the supply air to remove sensible cooling loads from the occupied space. Although it was originally intended as a guide in the selection and location of supply air terminal units (eg, diffusers and grilles) for cooling, the ADPI can serve as a reasonable index for evaluating the uniformity of the thermal conditions of the air throughout the room for heating or cooling. The ADPI is defined as the percentage of total points measured in an occupied space that meets the criteria

$$-3 \leq \theta \leq +2°F \tag{6}$$

and

$$0 \leq V_x \leq 70 \text{ fpm} \tag{7}$$

where

$$\theta = (t_x - t_c) - 0.07(V_x - 30) \tag{8}$$
draft effective temperature

t_c = average dry-bulb temperature in the occupied space, °F

t_x = dry-bulb temperature at the sampling point within the occupied space, °F

V_x = omnidirectional air velocity at the sampling point within the occupied space, feet per minute (fpm).

As a criterion for evaluation of air movement to provide acceptable thermal conditions within an occupied space, a minimum ADPI of 75% is suggested. Additional information on using ADPI for design or evaluation can be obtained from the *ASHRAE Handbook of Fundamentals* (28).

Although the ADPI can provide insight into expected performance for thermal control, it has several limitations as it does not consider environmental variables other than dry-bulb temperature and omnidirectional air velocity, nor does it provide for an evaluation of the amount of supply air that can bypass the occupied space because of short-circuiting of air from the supply to the return air terminal devices. The common practice of locating both supply and return air devices in the ceiling or on opposing high sidewalls has been shown to result in less than 50% of the supply air reaching the occupants before it is returned to the system (37). Thus a more general method of evaluating air movement for thermal and air quality control is being developed in terms of ventilation efficiency or ventilation effectiveness. Several definitions have been proposed, and are generally expressed as: "The fraction of room ventilation air that ventilates the personal space" (37–39).

One proposed method of evaluating ventilation efficiency is based on analysis of the system in terms of a stratified room compartment, as shown in Figure 4.

From this model, a steady-state ventilation efficiency n_v may be expressed as

$$n_v = \frac{\dot{V}_v}{\dot{V}_o} = \frac{1-s}{1-sr} \tag{9}$$

where

$\dot{V}_v$ = ventilation rate supplied to occupied space

$\dot{V}_o$ = ventilation rate supplied to room

s = stratification factor, defined as the ratio of the initial (I_o) and steady-state (I_{ss}) decay rates divided by the

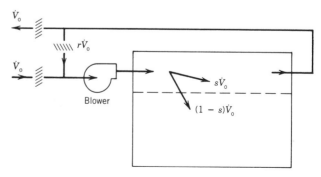

Figure 4. Two-compartment model of a room with stratification s, ventilation rate $\dot{V}_o$, and percentage of recirculation air r (37).

initial decay rate (I_o) of a tracer gas such as sulfur hexafluoride

$$s = (I_o - I_{ss})/I_o$$

r = percent of recirculated air during period of evaluation

As a criterion for evaluation of air movement to provide acceptable thermal and air quality conditions within an occupied space, a minimum ventilation efficiency, n_v, of 80% is suggested. For additional information regarding the development of standards on ventilation efficiency or ventilation effectiveness, the reader is advised to follow the development of ASHRAE Standard 129P and the revisions of ASHRAE Standard 62–1981.

Between Rooms. Transport of thermal and contaminant loads between rooms occurs because of thermal and contaminant mass gradients and interzonal air pressure differences. In facilities such as hospitals, laboratories, and cleanrooms, interzonal transport can be critical to the health of the occupants and to the processes conducted within them, yet air movement between rooms is one of the least controlled factors in HVAC systems. In most cases, direct feedback control is not employed; rather, indirect methods are relied upon such as designing a 10% excess of supply or return air for positive or negative pressurization of a room with respect to its surrounding spaces.

To assess the effectiveness of pressurization control between rooms or zones, tracer gas techniques may be employed. One such procedure has been described as the relative exposure index (REI) (39). It may be used to compare the occupant exposures to a contaminant in several rooms or areas C_i to exposure in a reference room or area, C_R

$$\mathrm{REI} = \left. \frac{\int_0^\infty C_i dt}{\int_0^\infty C_R dt} \right|_{C_j(0) = \text{local}} \tag{10}$$

In this procedure, the tracer gas is introduced as a pulse at time zero into the room in which the suspected contaminant source exists $C_j(0)$, and allowed to decay for a sufficient period to obtain reliable data. If the resultant REI is > 1.0, the data indicate that exposure may be greater in room i than in the reference room R, when the source is located in the room or area j. For cases where positive pressurization is desired in room R, the REI should be > 1.0 for several trials with tracer gas emitted at various locations j, and concentrations measured in several rooms i. Conversely, for areas where negative pressurization is desired in room R, the REI should be < 1.0 when tracer gas is emitted at various locations j, and concentrations measured in several rooms i. For additional information on the use of the REI procedure or other similar tracer gas methods, the reader is referred to Refs. 37–39.

Integrated Systems

Modern HVAC systems are capable of providing surprisingly close tolerance control of thermal and air quality criteria, as evidenced by the success of dimensional labora-

tories and class-10 to class-1 cleanrooms (40). Applications of these technologies have had slow acceptance for general control of residential and public access buildings. A basic reason for this hesitancy may be the dearth of criteria and methods available to evaluate the performance of these systems, especially the interactive effects between thermal and contaminant loads.

Methods to evaluate these systems have recently been discussed at ASHRAE and at the American Society for Testing and Materials (ASTM). One such method proposes to relate acceptability criteria to physical system characteristics (41). A schematic of the characteristic system is shown in Figure 5. In this figure, the region of primary concern within the room (ie, personal space or microenvironment) is shown as Compartment 1, and the remainder of the room (ie, minienvironment) is shown as Compartment 2. The relationship between the mini- and microenvironments is represented by a filtered room supply $\dot{m}_2 (1 - e_1)x_2$ and a room coupling coefficient a, a factor which is related to ventilation efficiency n_v.

Room Control. For either a constant or a variable air volume system, the steady-state thermal and air quality performance may be related to acceptable room exposure criteria as expressed by equation 11.

$$K_2 = \frac{x_2}{x_0} = \frac{H(1 - e_2) + M + Q_2}{H(1 - e_2) + M + e_2} \tag{11}$$

where

K_2 = room acceptability factor x_2/x_0

H = outdoor air ratio = $\dot{m}_0/\dot{m}_m$

M = passive-to-active air exchange ratio = $\dot{m}_i/z\dot{m}_m$

$\dot{N}$ = net contaminant generation rate in the minienvironment = $z\dot{N}_s + \dot{N}_2$

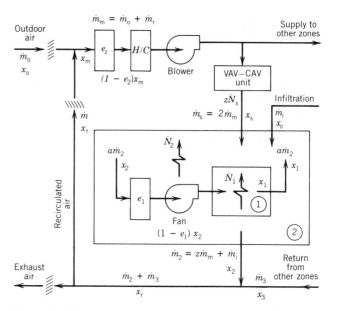

Figure 5. Characteristic system schematic for micro- and minienvironmental control for thermal and air quality acceptability (41).

Q_2 = room contamination factor = $\dot{N}/z\dot{m}_m x_o$

e_2 = minienvironmental air cleaner efficiency, evaluated in terms of contaminant removed

$\dot{m}_i$ = mass air-flow rate into minienvironment by infiltration or natural ventilation

$\dot{m}_m$ = mass air-flow rate delivered by the main air handling unit

$\dot{m}_o$ = mass air-flow rate of outdoor air provided by the main air handling unit

x_2 = contaminant concentration in the minienvironment (ie, contaminant mass per unit mass of air)

x_o = contaminant concentration in the outdoor air

z = fraction of room supply air to system supply air = $\dot{m}_s/\dot{m}_m$

Functional relationships for equation 11 are shown in Figure 6 for the assumed value of M = 0.1, which is representative of a tight envelope. These relationships indicate that, for a fixed value of e_2, the values of H and Q_2 can be manipulated to achieve the desired value of K_2 by optimizing the percentage of outdoor air and the zone supply rate (ie, $z\dot{m}_m$) for energy and operating costs. From Figure 6, it may be seen that a minimum value of K_2 is not always achieved by maximizing the percent of outdoor H into the occupied space. Rather, as in cleanroom applications where values of Q_2 are small (ie, $Q_2 < e_2$), K_2 can be minimized to values < 1.0 by minimizing the value of H.

Personal Exposure Control. The steady-state expression for room control, equation 11, assumes uniform mixing throughout the minienvironment. Because uniform mixing is not always desirable, room control alone may not be sufficient to provide the required thermal or air quality for personal exposure control. When assessment of personal exposure control is desired, a steady-state relation between the mini and microenvironments shown in Figure 5 may be expressed as follows (41):

$$K_1 = \frac{x_1}{x_2} = (1 - e_1) + Q_1 \tag{12}$$

where

K_1 = personal acceptability factor x_1/x_2

$\dot{N}_1$ = net contamination generation rate in the microenvironment

Q_1 = personal space contamination factor = $\dot{N}_1/(a(z\dot{m}_m + \dot{m}_i)x_2)$

a = room coupling coefficient = $\dot{m}_1/\dot{m}_2$

e_1 = microenvironmental air cleaner efficiency, evaluated in terms of contaminant removed

x_1 = contaminant concentration in the microenvironment (ie, contaminant mass per unit mass of air)

Functional relationships from equation 12 are shown in Figure 7. These are valid for all values of H and M. This figure indicates that the values of e_1 and Q_1 can also be manipulated to achieve the desired value of K_1. For example, if $z\dot{m}_m$ is low because the room thermal load is satisfied in a variable air volume system, the room coupling coefficient a can be increased to maintain the desired value of K_1.

CONCLUSIONS

From this article, it can be concluded that improved equipment and products together with methods of analysis and design are now available that can provide a high degree of environmental acceptability with energy efficiency and cost effectiveness. However, achieving this performance also demands a greater commitment from all parties concerned to design, operate, and maintain the buildings under a consistent set of criteria for the lifetime of the building.

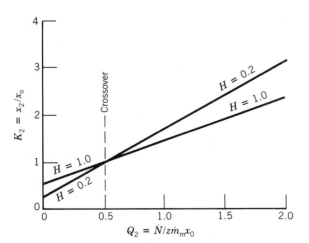

Figure 6. Relationships between the room acceptability factor K_2 and the room contamination factor Q_2, when the air cleaner efficiency e_2 is fixed at 0.5, and the passive-to-active air exchange ratio M is fixed at 0.1 (41).

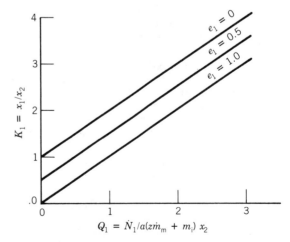

Figure 7. Relationships between the microenvironmental acceptability factor K_1 and the microenvironmental contamination factor Q_1 as a function of the air cleaner efficiency e_1 for all values of outdoor air ratio H and the passive-to-active air exchange ratio M (41).

It is also concluded from this article that continuous updating of the education, training, and skills of those responsible for the performance of the buildings and their systems will be required as the pressures for higher costs and better environmental quality persist.

Within the last decade, serious constraints on resources (eg, energy, capital, and operating expenses) have significantly influenced the designs and operations of buildings. In most cases, acceptable environmental control strategies have been utilized. Yet, in other cases, unacceptable compromises to the well-being of the occupants have resulted. While the dilemma has recurred several times throughout history, technological developments have recently occurred that can either amplify or diminish the effects.

BIBLIOGRAPHY

1. C. E. A. Winslow and L. P. Herrington, *Temperature and Human Life,* Princeton University Press, Princeton, N.J., 1949.

2. T. Tredgold, *The Principles of Warming and Ventilating—Public Buildings and Dwelling Houses,* published by J. Taylor, London, 1824.

3. J. S. Billings, *Lectures on Ventilation,* Engineering Record, New York, 1893.

4. Proceedings of the First Annual Meeting, *ASHVE Trans.* **1,** 40 (1895).

5. A. K. Klauss, R. H. Tull, L. M. Roots, and J. R. Pfafflin, "History of the Changing Concepts in Ventilation Requirements," *ASHRAE J.* **12**(6), 51 (1970).

6. New York State Commission on Ventilation, *Ventilation,* E. P. Dutton, New York, 1923.

7. C. P. Yaglou, E. C. Riley, and D. I. Coggins, "Ventilation Requirements," *ASHVE Trans.* **42,** 133 (1936).

8. *American Standard Building Requirements for Light and Ventilation-A53.1,* American Standards Association, Washington, D.C., 1946.

9. *ASHRAE Standard 62–73: Standards for Natural and Mechanical Ventilation,* American Society of Heating, Refrigerating, and Air Conditioning Engineers, New York, 1973.

10. *ASHRAE Standard 90–75: Energy Conservation in New Building Design,* American Society of Heating, Refrigerating, and Air Conditioning Engineers, New York, 1975.

11. *Codes for Energy Conservation in New Building Construction,* Washington, D.C., 1977. Prepared by the National Conference of States on Building Codes and Standards (NCSBCS), Building Officials and Code Administrators International, Inc. (BOCA), International Conference of Building Officials (ICBO), and Southern Building Code Congress International, Inc. (SBCCI).

12. *Impact Assessment of ASHRAE Standard 90–75,* U.S. Government Printing Office, Washington, D.C., 1976. Prepared for the Federal Energy Administration.

13. C. T. Zegers, "ASHRAE: Providing HVAC and R Leadership," *Consulting Eng.* **44**(1), 78 (1980).

14. *ASHRAE Standard 62–1981: Ventilation for Acceptable Indoor Air Quality,* American Society of Heating, Refrigerating, and Air Conditioning Engineers, Atlanta, Ga., 1981.

15. J. E. Woods, J. E. Janssen, and B. C. Krafthefer, "Rationalization of Equivalence between the 'Ventilation Rate' and Air Quality Procedures in ASHRAE Standard 62" in J. E. Janssen,

ed., *Managing Indoor Air for Health and Energy Conservation,* Society of Heating, Refrigerating, and Air Conditioning Engineers, Atlanta, Ga., 1986, pp. 181–191.

16. Committee on Indoor Pollutants, *Indoor Pollutants,* report by the National Research Council, National Academy Press, Washington, D.C., 1981.

17. "Constitution of the World Health Organization," *Off. Rec. W. H. O.* **2,** 100 (1946).

18. F. H. Rohles, "The Ecosystem Complex: A New Approach in Specifying the Man-Environment Relationship," *J. Environ. Syst.* **1**(4), 321 (1971).

19. J. H. Comroe, *Physiology of Respiration,* Year Book Medical Publishers, Inc., Chicago, Ill., 1969.

20. J. E. Woods, "Status—Ventilation Models for Indoor Air Quality" in H. D. Goodfellow, ed., *Ventilation '85,* Elsevier, Amsterdam, The Netherlands, 1986, pp. 33–51.

21. J. F. Parker and V. R. West, *Bioastronautics Data Handbook,* 2nd ed., Publication No. NASA SP-3006, NASA, Washington, D.C., 1973.

22. *Occupational Safety and Health Standards-Subpart Z-Toxic and Hazardous Substances, Code of Federal Regulations,* Vol. 29, U.S. Government Printing Office, Washington, D.C., 1982, Pt. 1910.

23. *Law for Maintenance of Sanitation in Buildings* (published in English in 1982), Law No. 20, Building Management Education Center, Tokyo, Japan, Apr. 14, 1970.

24. WHO Working Group, *Health Aspects Related to Indoor Air Quality,* EURO Reports and Studies 21, World Health Organization, Regional Office for Europe, Copenhagen, Denmark, 1979, pp. 1–32.

25. B. Berglund, U. Berglund, and T. Lindvall, "Characterization of Indoor Air Quality and 'Sick Buildings,' " *ASHRAE Trans.* **90**(Pt. 1B), 1045 (1984).

26. J. E. Woods and E. A. B. Maldonado, "Development of a Field Method for Assessing Indoor Air Quality in Single Family Residences" in *Final Report: Development of Energy Management Program for Buildings in Iowa-Fourth Year,* Vol. 1, Iowa State University, ISU-ERI-Ames 82469, May 1982. Sponsored by the Iowa Energy Policy Council, Des Moines, Iowa.

27. *ASHRAE Standard 55–1981: Thermal Environmental Conditions for Human Occupancy,* American Society of Heating, Refrigerating, and Air Conditioning Engineers, Atlanta, Ga., 1981.

28. *ASHRAE Handbook: 1985 Fundamentals Volume,* American Society of Heating, Refrigerating, and Air Conditioning Engineers, Atlanta, Ga., 1985.

29. J. E. Woods, "Sources of Indoor Contaminants," *ASHRAE Trans.* **89**(Pt. 1A), 462 (1983).

30. Committee on Passive Smoking, *Environmental Tobacco Smoke: Measuring Exposures and Assessing Health Effects,* report by the National Research Council, National Academy Press, Washington, D.C., 1986.

31. D. Rainer and G. S. Michaelsen, *Hospital Ventilation Standards and Energy Conservation: Chemical Contamination of Hospital Air, Final Report,* Lawrence Berkeley Laboratory, University of California, Berkeley California, Report LBL 10475, Mar. 1980.

32. *Indoor Air Quality Environmental Information Handbook: Radon,* U.S. Government Printing Office, Washington, D.C., Publication No. DOE/PE/72013–2, U.S. Department of Energy, Assistant Secretary for Environmental Safety and Health, and Office of Environmental Analysis, Jan. 1986.

33. Committee on Indoor Air Quality, *Policies and Procedures*

for Control of Indoor Air Quality in Existing Buildings, report by the National Research Council, National Academy Press, Washington, D.C., 1987.

34. L. Molhave, B. Bach, and O. F. Pedersen, "Human Reactions to Low Concentrations of Volatile Organic Compounds," *Environ. Int.* **12,** 167 (1986).

35. P. O. Fanger, *Thermal Comfort,* McGraw-Hill Inc., New York, 1973.

36. R. G. Nevins and P. L. Miller, "Analysis, Evaluation and Comparison of Room Air Distribution Performance–A Summary," *ASHRAE Trans.* **78**(2), 235 (1972).

37. J. E. Janssen, T. J. Hill, J. E. Woods, and E. A. B. Maldonado, "Ventilation for Control of Indoor Air Quality: A Case Study," *Envir. Int.* **8,** 487 (1982).

38. M. Sandberg, "What is Ventilation Efficiency?," *Build. Environ.,* **16,** 123 (1981).

39. E. A. B. Maldonado and J. E. Woods, "A Method to Select Locations for Indoor Air Quality Sampling," *Build. Environ.,* **18,** 171 (1983).

40. J. G. King, "Air Cleanliness Requirements for Cleanrooms," in R. R. Raber, ed., *Fluid Filtration: Gas,* Vol. 1, ASTM STP 975, American Society of Testing and Materials, Philadelphia, Pa., 1986, pp. 383–389.

41. J. E. Woods and B. C. Krafthefer, "Filtration as a Method for Air Quality Control in Occupied Spaces" in Ref. 40, pp. 193–213.

JAMES E. WOODS
Honeywell, Inc.
Golden Valley, Minnesota

Air-Supported Structures. *See* MEMBRANE STRUCTURES

ALBERS, JOSEF

Few artist teachers have had greater influence upon contemporary architects and designers than had Josef Albers. In part, this was a result of his pedagogic methods, as demonstrated at the Bauhaus in Weimar, Dessau, and Berlin from 1923 to 1933, at Black Mountain College in North Carolina until 1949, and at Yale University thereafter. His influence also became pervasive through his own work, which exemplifies the greatest discipline, rationality, and psychological insight in his study and artistic representation of rectilinear form, proportion, symmetry, and color harmony. His art has been compared with that of the de Stijl movement and the architecture of Mies van der Rohe.

Born in Bottrop, Westphalia, in 1888, Albers began his formal study of art in 1913 at the Royal Society of Art. After World War I, he enrolled at the Academy of Art in Munich where he studied with Franz Stuck and Max Doerner before enrolling at the Weimar Bauhaus in 1920. He became the first Bauhaus student to be promoted to Young Master and began teaching there in 1923, succeeding Johannes Itten. With László Moholy-Nagy, he reorganized the important Vorkurs at the Bauhaus. Albers's friendship with Walter Gropius continued after the latter resigned as Bauhaus Director in 1928. With the closing of the Bauhaus by the Nazis in 1933, Gropius helped Albers leave Germany, writing friends in the United States to help him get acquainted.

In 1959, Walter Gropius wrote enthusiastically about Albers, whom he considered the most outstanding art teacher alive. Writing to Albers in 1963, Gropius noted that in a recent publication the Bauhaus role of Itten had been overemphasized and that Albers's had been represented too weakly. He advised him to speak up for history's sake. However, in 1966, Albers still felt himself unappreciated by the historians of the Bauhaus and, loyally supported by his wife, Bauhaus weaver Anni, refused further communication about the school. Albers continued to teach, lecture, paint, and exhibit, receiving worldwide recognition for his pedagogic and artistic contributions in a career that had also included elementary school teaching, furniture and graphic design, typography, and photography.

BIBLIOGRAPHY

General References

J. Albers, "The Educational Value of Manual Work and Handicraft in Relation to Architecture," in P. Zucker, ed., *New Architecture and City Planning,* 1944.

J. Albers, *Poems and Drawings,* The Readymade Press, New Haven, Conn., 1958.

F. Bucher, *Josef Albers, Despite Straight Lines; An Analysis of his Graphic Constructions,* Yale University Press, New Haven, Conn., 1961.

J. Albers, *Homage to the Square,* Yale University Press, New Haven, Conn., 1962.

J. Albers, *Interaction of Color,* Yale University Press, New Haven, Conn., 1963, 1967, and 1975.

E. Gomringer, *Josef Albers,* George Wittenborn, New York, 1968.

J. Albers, *Search versus Re-search, Three Lectures,* Trinity College, Trinity College Press, Hartford, Conn., 1969.

W. Spies, *Josef Albers,* Abrams, New York, 1970.

H. Albrecht, *Josef Albers,* Farbe als Spock, Dumont Schauberg, Cologne, FRG, 1974.

S. Hunt, ed., *Josef Albers,* Princeton University Press, Princeton, N.J.

See also BAUHAUS.

REGINALD R. ISAACS
Cambridge, Massachusetts

ALBERTI, LEON BATTISTA

Leon Battista Alberti (born 1404, Genoa–died 1472, Rome) was an architectural theoretician who took the concept of building design out of the hands of craftsmen of the Middle Ages and placed it in the intellectual minds of the Renaissance men of the Quattrocento. Alberti (Fig. 1) was able to do this, in part, because he had a superior education and social position. With his seminal work, *De Re Aedificatoria* (1), Alberti advanced architecture on the

Figure 1. Leon Battista Alberti, self-portrait, bronze plaque (ca 1435). Courtesy of the National Gallery of Art, Samuel H. Kress Collection, Washington, D.C.

turned to the papal court in Rome, where he became architectural advisor to the great humanist Pope Nicholas V (1447–1455), who succeeded in ending the Papal Schism, reestablishing the authority of the Church of Rome, and bringing the Holy See back to the city. Suddenly, Rome's appearance became a top priority. During this time, the city's architecture consisted of houses built along the Tiber River and among the crumbling ancient monuments. Alberti became involved in the restoration of the city, in which he lived until his death in 1472, working as an architect and a prolific writer and thinker.

Literary and figurative arts sparked Alberti's drive to pursue architecture. He was primarily a man of letters. In fact, he believed that architecture should be approached through the study of the *artes liberales* and through the knowledge of drawing rather than through the more traditional long apprenticeship in the studio of a sculptor, painter, or senior architect. He believed that the architect must possess intelligence and persevering zeal and be able to judge well that which is fitting. For Alberti, the task of the architect was twofold, ie, to design and to execute, so to build is as necessary as to theorize (4). Regarding professional conduct, Alberti advised that future architects should not immediately run and offer their services to every man who has plans to build; he thought that one's work lost its dignity when it was being done for evil men (5).

To understand Alberti's impact, theory, and role as a universal Renaissance man fully, he must be compared with Filippo Brunelleschi. Both men traveled to Rome to measure the classical ruins carefully and to interpret how the proportions, motifs, and elements correlated to the Vitruvian principles. Both men applied what they learned to the theories that would become the crux of architecture in the early Renaissance. Their different theories relied on the integration of classical features with a structure organized according to harmonious proportions. The difference in theory is in the way each man interpreted the classical features. Brunelleschi took a feature, such as a Roman column, and reproduced it exactly, yet used it in an imaginative way, such as in designing an entire facade with columns. In contrast, Alberti had a tendency to take, for example, a Roman triumphal-arch or a temple-front motif and reproduce it with imaginative alteration of certain details, such as a change in the proportions of a column. Three of Alberti's major works, San Francesco (1447–1450) (Fig. 2), Santa Maria Novella (1456–1470) (Fig. 3), and the Palazzo Rucellai (1452?–1470?) (Fig. 4), reveal that although he was interested in maintaining the proportionality of recognizable classical motifs, he was far more excited about combining the Doric, Ionic, and Corinthian orders to form his own imaginative composite orders.

A second difference in theory between Brunelleschi and Alberti stems from their interests as young adults. Whereas Brunelleschi was apprenticed as a goldsmith, Alberti became, in his youth and throughout his life, fascinated with painting as a two-dimensional window into a three-dimensional world. The result is that Brunelleschi's buildings are more three dimensional, and his columns and entablatures have structural integrity. For Alberti, especially in his early work, the facade, like a painting,

wave of intellectual fervor that began with the early Renaissance in Florence and rolled across Italy and Western Europe. Not only did Alberti spark enthusiasm with his written work, but he left monuments to prove that his concepts were sound in stone as well as in word. He was the first and most important theoretician of the early Italian Renaissance.

Alberti was born into one of the great Florentine mercantile families that had been exiled from the city for political reasons. At the age of 11 he was sent to Padua to obtain a humanistic education in the liberal arts (Latin, Greek, music, etc). He later went to Bologna to study canon law. Denied his inheritance, Alberti first supported himself in 1432 as a secretary at the papal chancery in Rome. When at age 30 in 1434 he followed Pope Eugene IV to Florence, he was exposed to the most recent work of Massaccio, Donatello, and Brunelleschi. In this period, he wrote an early work, *Della Famiglia* (2), inspired by the writings of Cicero and Seneca. In this work, Alberti philosophized that virtue was a matter of action, not of right thinking (3). Later, this philosophy would be extended to the discipline of architecture, when he put into action the theories stated in *De Re Aedificatoria* (1452). In 1444, Alberti re-

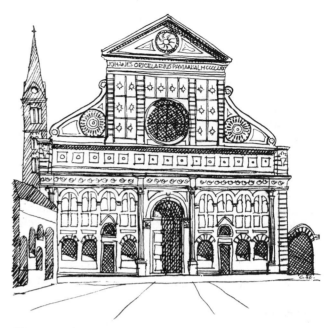

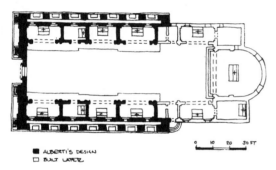

Figure 3. Santa Maria Novella, Florence (1456–1470). Drawing by Charles Szoradi (1986).

spective. By 1436, Alberti had written *Della Pittura* (8), dedicating the Italian text to Brunelleschi. In this work, Alberti says that the architect derives his architectural designs from pre-existing paintings; for example, the architect first learned about columns and entablatures from the painter (6).

Figure 2. San Francesco, Rimini (1447–1450). Drawing by F. J. Menendez (1986).

became an exercise in two-dimensional surface decoration (see Santa Maria Novella, Fig. 3, and Palazzo Rucellai, Fig. 4).

Unlike the Greek and Gothic architects, who saw ornament and structure as one, Alberti formulated in his writings the idea of ornament as an element separate from structure, similar to the classical Roman point of view. He believed that structure could be hidden in favor of appearance. For example, in some of his buildings the actual size of the stones that make up the facade revetments are larger than they appear, as in the Palazzo Rucellai. Alberti was concerned with both the image that the building creates and with the eye, which contemplates and enjoys that image (6).

Another difference between Alberti and his contemporaries, such as Michelozzo and Brunelleschi, is that he was directly involved only with the design of his projects and not with their execution. In fact, Alberti often battled with the construction architects to have his proportions respected (7).

Painting was the first art form that Alberti approached, and it was Brunelleschi who eventually introduced him to the latest methods of painting with mathematical per-

Figure 4. Palazzo Rucellai facade, Florence (1452?–1470?). Drawing by F. J. Menendez (1986).

Della Pittura is an example of how Alberti was compelled to analyze, interpret, and write about something he was interested in, but his *De Re Aedificatoria*, dedicated to Pope Nicholas V, is an example of his clarity of thought. Though completed in 1452, it was first printed in 1485. The work makes a coherent whole of the fragmented knowledge of the architecture of ancient Rome and interprets it for the Early Renaissance. In 1438, when Alberti was 34, Marchese Leonello encouraged him to become interested in architecture and to restore the classic text of Vitruvius (9). A few years later, still having had little experience in architecture, he started to work on his treatise. *De Re Aedeficatoria* provides a sense of continuity between ancient and "modern" architecture, connects history and theory to actual architectural practice, and establishes architecture as an intellectual discipline. Alberti based the ten-chapter work on the principles of the Vitruvian trilogy of *utilitas* (utility), *firmitas* (firmness), and *venutas* (delight). In defining delight or beauty, Alberti tells us that it is made up of *numero* (number), *finitio* (proportion), and *collocatio* (location). These three elements come together to produce a total greater than the sum of its parts. This total he calls *concinnitas*. For Alberti, *concinnitas* was a harmony and concord of all of the parts, so that nothing could be added or subtracted except for the worse. The union of parts or specific elements is only achieved through harmonious use of proportions. He said that the numbers that have the power to give consonance to sounds are the same that can fill the eyes and spirits with joy (4). Thus, proportionality and the resulting interest in pure geometric forms become integral to Alberti's view of architecture. His concern with understanding the whole building and how man relates to each element, as well as how he relates to the total conceptual theme, is a direct reflection of the Renaissance idea of humanism. He protested against those who believed that architectural laws are inconstant and obeyed no laws, but were merely a matter of choice (6).

San Francesco, Rimini (1447–1450) (Fig. 2). Sigismondo Malatesta gave Alberti his first commission to rebuild a church into a temple for Malatesta and his court of humanist thinkers. In Alberti's view, the structure of the building could be hidden, disguised, or invalidated in order to attain the desired appearance (10). The upper part of the front and the rotunda for the eastern end of the nave were never completed. The front facade is based on a triumphal arch built for the Roman Emperor Augustus, which is nearby. The two sides consist of huge arcaded niches meant to hold the sarcophagi of Malatesta, his mistress, and scholars and poets of his court. This arcade juxtaposes volumes with voids and lights with shadows. San Francesco is historically important because it is the first illustration of Alberti's idea of subordinating the structural meaning of the building to the meaning of the design by using the ancient Roman model of the triumphal arch.

Santa Maria Novella Facade, Florence (1456–1470) (Fig. 3). Alberti's next major project was also an exercise in facade decoration. When Alberti was hired to design the front facade of the Santa Maria Novella, it had a base constructed in the characteristic Florentine Gothic green and white marble. Interested in incorporating the existing Gothic rose window with a 2:1 overall facade ratio, Alberti introduced a pronounced attic story to make the composition successful. To maintain consistency and to satisfy his desire to use both antique and local sources for a design, he used classical temple-front motifs but included details from one of his favorite local buildings, the twelfth-century San Mineato al Monte (4). Alberti widened not only the doorway but the whole facade to satisfy the proportions. The entire portal is derived from the entry door to the Pantheon in Rome, and the ends of the facade project beyond the width of the church. An undisputed aspect of Alberti's excellence is his ability to take a classic form, reinterpret it, and apply it in an innovative way. For example, the volutes that link the upper and lower facade sections while hiding the side-aisle roofs testify to his creative genius. The facade of Santa Maria Novella became one of the most frequently used models for High Renaissance and baroque churches.

Palazzo Rucellai Facade, Florence (1452?–1470?) (Fig. 4). Giovanni Rucellai gave Alberti a chance to exercise his theories by commissioning him to design the facade of his existing Florentine city palace. For this commission, Alberti used a contemporary prototype rather than an ancient one. The Medici Palace designed by Michelozzo (begun in 1444) stood as an example of what a house for a powerful Renaissance businessman should look like. The Rucellai, like the Medici Palace, had three-story rusticated facades with heavy cornices and two-part windows contained by heavy arches. Alberti went one step further and superimposed the classic Doric, Ionic, and Corinthian pilaster system over the rustication which gives the facade an ornamented quality. It has been remarked that the architectural elements, columns, and capitals are like those borrowed from a painter (10). Every detail has an ancient prototype except the two-part window openings. The Rucellai would remain an important prototype for palaces of the next three centuries.

San Sebastiano, Mantua (1460–1472) (Fig. 5). Alberti's long-standing connections with the powerful Gonzaga family of Mantua resulted in a commission to replace a pre-Romanesque church on the southern edge of the city with the mausoleum of San Sebastiano. A free-standing building with a central plan based on the Greek cross, it actually includes two churches: a "lower" basement crypt and the "upper" main sanctuary. Alberti put into practice his thesis on how to divide a temple plan into four parts, giving two of these parts to the breadth of the chapel (5). The plan includes the subdivision of a larger square into smaller squares by the rules of geometry and the harmonies of arithmetic. The facade is based on the standard form of a Roman temple and on a specific triumphal arch, that of Orange, France (11). The concept used at San Sebastiano echoes the traditions of the Byzantine mausoleum and temple plans of Ravenna, Italy. Unfortunately, the project was never completed. What was built was neglected for centuries, and then greatly altered (7). However, its central plan contributed to the development of the Greek cross-design churches of the sixteenth century (11).

Sant' Andrea in Mantua (1470–1494) (Fig. 6). Alberti's last commission is the best example of his architectural work, even though he spent only his last two years on

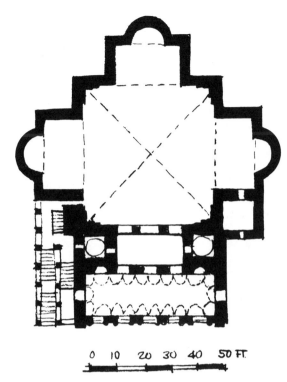

Figure 5. San Sebastiano, Mantua (1460–1472). Drawing by Charles A. Szoradi (1986).

ATTRIBUTED TO
L.B. ALBERTI   OTHERS

Figure 6. Sant' Andrea, Mantua (1470–1494). Drawing by Charles A. Szoradi (1986).

its development. Alberti's design was executed by Fancelli and completed in 1494. The transept and dome are not part of Alberti's design and were not completed until later centuries. Sant' Andrea was designed for Lodovico Gonzaga as a pilgrimage church which required a large nave with clear sightlines to allow worshipers to view the relics. To achieve this, Alberti broke away from the traditional basilican plan with aisles, which was dominant from the fourth to fourteenth centuries; instead, he designed a powerful central nave that is directly flanked by side chapels (4). The coffered barrel vault at Sant' Andrea is an architectural realization of an image in one of Masaccio's paintings completed half a century earlier.

Alberti used the exterior triumphal-arch unit in the interior to organize the dimensions of the three side chapels comprising the length of the nave. The structural system of the walls is a honeycomb of piers and vaults derived from the structure of the Pantheon (4). The portico facade is topped by a pediment and a vaulted canopy-like structure that acts as an umbrella over the large rose window that lights the nave. Alberti believed that the appearance of the building must be a result of its design and not of its structure (10). Sant' Andrea demonstrates this principle. Sant' Andrea is considered Alberti's greatest work, as well as one of the most important churches of the Quattrocento. It became the model for many other churches, such as St. Peter's and Il Gesù in Rome, which emulated, yet never surpassed, its design.

Alberti, one of the greatest architects of the fifteenth century, is as well-known for his writings on his theory of architecture as he is for his actual building designs. He changed architecture from a craft to an intellectual pursuit. The expression of his theory, *De Re Aedificatoria,* goes far beyond establishing architecture as an intellectual pursuit, because it also imbued in the minds of succeeding architects deep reverence for closely recreating the scale and grandeur of antiquity and the power of creative manipulation of forms. Because of his position in the papal court, Alberti was directly involved in the renewed interest in rebuilding the city. Many of his buildings became prototypes for later designs of the Renaissance and baroque eras.

Like his contemporaries, Alberti sought to reconcile the old with the new. He was an *Oumo Universales,* a true Renaissance man concerned with the whole and completeness, with harmony and rational order, rather than with just details. The completeness of his architectural theories is also reflected in his character. Alberti has been called the first great dilettante-architect, fitting the criteria that Baldassare Castiglione set down about a half century later in his *The Courtier* (1513) (12). Alberti was a gentleman of great ability. He was an outstanding athlete, superb horseman, and witty conversationalist. He also composed music, wrote plays, painted, and was even an expert on law. His architecture is what he is most remembered for, and in his treatise he carefully codified his solutions to the new problems of architecture, yet maintained enough flexibility so that the solutions could be adapted by others to deal with future problems. Alberti was considered an authority whose teachings extended into the Cinquecento until the Palladian generation adapted them to formulate a new repertoire of solutions to new problems and requirements.

BIBLIOGRAPHY

1. L. B. Alberti, *De Re Aedificatoria,* 1485, English translation by J. Leoni (*Alberti's Ten Books on Architecture*), Transatlantic Arts, Inc., New York, 1966.

2. L. B. Alberti, *The Albertis of Florence: Leon Battista Alberti's Della Famiglia,* 1441, English translation by G. A. Guarino, Bucknell University Press, Lewisburg, Pa., 1971.

3. J. Gadol, *Leon Battista Alberti, Universal Man of the Early Renaissance,* University of Chicago Press, Chicago, 1969.

4. E. J. Johnson in A. K. Placzek, ed., *McMillan Encyclopedia of Architects,* The Free Press, London, 1982.

5. L. Benevolo, *Storia dell'architettura del Rinascimento,* 1968, English translation (*The Architecture of the Renaissance*), Westview Press, Inc., Boulder, Colo., 1978.

6. J. Burckhardt in P. Murray, ed., *The Architecture of the Italian Renaissance,* University of Chicago Press, Chicago, Ill., 1985.

7. L. H. Heydenreich and W. Lotz, *Architecture in Italy 1400 to 1600,* English translation by M. Hottinger, Penguin Books, Baltimore, Md., 1974.

8. L. B. Alberti, *Della Pittura,* 1436, English translation by J. R. Spencer (*On Painting*), Yale University Press, New Haven, Conn., 1956.

9. Vitruvius, *De Architectura,* 1st century B.C., English translation by M. H. Morgan (*The Ten Books of Architecture*), Dover Publications, Inc., New York, 1960.

10. F. Borsi, *Leon Battista Alberti,* English translation by R. Carpamini, Phaedon Books, Oxford, UK, 1977.

11. J. R. Spencer in B. S. Myers, ed., *McGraw-Hill Dictionary of Art,* McGraw-Hill, Inc., New York, 1969.

12. N. Pevsner, *An Outline of European Architecture,* 6th ed., Penguin Books, Baltimore, Md., 1960.

General References

G. C. Argan, *The Renaissance City,* George Braziller, Inc., New York, 1969.

CHARLES A. SZORADI
Charlottesville, Virginia

ALUMINUM

HISTORY

Despite its status as the most abundant metal in the earth's crust, aluminum had to await the development of modern technology before it became a widely used metal, second only to steel in worldwide consumption.

In its natural oxide form, as alumina, aluminum has been in use for some 7000 years in pottery. However, mass 20th-century use of metallic aluminum required the invention of industrial electrolysis and the electrochemical liberation of aluminum from its ore in 1886 by Charles Martin Hall in the United States and by Paul L. T. Heroult in France.

Metallic aluminum was first exhibited in bar form eight years before Hall was born, at the Paris Exhibition of 1855. Then more precious than gold, these aluminum bars were valued at $115/lb. Although production costs dropped during Hall's childhood, it remained a semiprecious metal. Hall was obsessed during his studies at Oberlin College in Ohio with finding a better way to produce the metal. He continued his efforts after graduation, working in an old woodshed with equipment that included a skillet, a secondhand gasoline stove, and handmade crucibles.

Success came in February 1886, a few months after Hall's 22nd birthday. At about the same time, Heroult, another 22-year-old, discovered essentially the same electrolytic process in Paris. Each of the young scientists received a patent in his respective country, and the aluminum industry was born. More than a century later, the Hall–Heroult process continues to be used throughout the world to produce aluminum economically.

The first aluminum building product appeared in the era of chemical aluminum production: in 1884, a solid, 6-lb, cast-aluminum pyramidal cap was mounted at the apex of the Washington Monument, where it remains today, still in excellent condition.

During World War I, an aluminum alloy called Duralumin was developed in Germany. This technological breakthrough opened a new vista for high strength, heat-treated aluminum alloys. Two production developments, anodizing and extruding, came in the 1920s, extending the range of aluminum. During World War II, 2 million tons of aluminum went into the production of 300,000 U.S. military aircraft.

PRODUCTION

Aluminum is one of the few metals whose mining operation is much less efficient than its smelting. Bauxite is currently the common form of aluminum ore. Bauxite occurs in the tropical and subtropical belt around the globe. It is baked by the sun and leached out by rain to leave a relatively high concentration of aluminum oxide (Al_2O_3).

Aluminum production proceeds through three basic steps: mining, refining, and smelting.

Since most bauxite lies at or near the earth's surface, it is mined by open-pit methods: dug out by power shovel or dragline. Before the refining process begins, it is crushed and milled into tiny particles and dried in a rotary kiln. The refining process removes impurities to produce pure alumina ready for shipment to the smelter.

Despite many practical modern improvements, the commercial process for smelting aluminum into its elementary constituents—aluminum metal and oxygen—remains the same basic process developed by Charles Martin Hall. The alumina is first dissolved in a bath of molten cryolite in cells (known as "pots") connected in electrical series into a "potline." High amperage, low voltage direct current passes through the cryolite bath through carbon anodes suspended in each carbon-lined steel pot. Molten aluminum flows to the bottom (the cathode); oxygen combines with the carbon anode to produce oxides of carbon. Periodically, the molten aluminum is siphoned off, ready for casting or alloying.

Primary aluminum production, direct from aluminum ore, consumes large quantities of electrical energy. The industry has consequently focused intense efforts on improving production energy efficiency. Since World War II, average energy consumption has dropped from 12 to 6.5 kwh/lb. As a complementary energy-conservation strategy, the industry is also increasing its secondary production by recycling aluminum scrap. Recycling cuts energy consumption by 95% compared with primary production. Nearly 30% of the total U.S. aluminum supply is derived from recycled scrap.

ADVANTAGES

A unique combination of light weight, strength, corrosion resistance, electrical conductivity, heat reflectivity, formability, and suitability for a wide variety of durable finishes makes aluminum the most versatile metal used in building construction. It comes in castings, forgings, bars, rods, wire, tubing, electrical conductor, plate, sheet, foil, and extrusions.

Major building uses range from specialized structural framing, where light weight is paramount, to windows, doors, curtain walls, electrical conductors, heat-reflective foil insulation, and vapor barrier.

Aluminum has excellent corrosion resistance, a property exploited in its use for curtain walls, roofing, siding, doors, windows, grillework, louvers, and other exposed building components. Highly resistant to normal weathering, aluminum also resists most industrial atmospheres, salt air, and many acids. Alkalis are among the few substances that attack the protective oxide coating. Lacquers or strippable plastic tapes can protect aluminum from contact with wet concrete, mortar, or plaster.

Aluminum's corrosion resistance comes from the metal's naturally occurring oxide coating. As soon as it is exposed to air, the newly smelted metal forms this hard, tightly bonded, glasslike surface film, which protects the interior metal. If scratched, the newly exposed aluminum surface immediately re-forms a protective oxide coating. Aluminum reacts faster than most metals when exposed to oxy-gen. However, aluminum's oxidation is self-limiting, whereas with most metals oxidation is progressive.

High radiant heat reflectivity and correspondingly low emissivity make aluminum reflector foil an excellent wall insulator. In contrast to most construction materials, which absorb 90% of the radiant energy impinging on them, aluminum foil reflects about 95% of this energy and thus acts as an insulator when it faces an air space.

Good electrical conductivity, second only to copper among the world's commonly used metals, makes aluminum suitable for electrical conductor cable. The greatest economy afforded by aluminum's light weight is in large conductors. As a consequence, aluminum has long dominated the market for overhead transmission lines, service drop cables, and service entrance cables. More recently, it has been used for underground distribution and wiring of commercial buildings.

THE INDUSTRY

Aluminum produced from ore is far more difficult and costly to produce in metallic form than steel. However, once cast into a basic ingot, it is more easily worked into mill products, plate, sheet, rod, etc.

Some of the major U.S. aluminum producers are vertically integrated, marketing aluminum building products through national or regional distribution centers. But because of the relatively low capital investment required in fabrication plants, there are hundreds of independent aluminum building product manufacturers selling siding, doors, windows, louvers, and other building products throughout the United States.

Per capita use of aluminum roughly parallels a nation's technological-industrial development as well as its standard of living. U.S. consumption leads the world, at 59 lb annual per capita consumption, followed by the FRG at 52, Sweden at 43, and Canada and Switzerland at around 42.

Aluminum building products cover a tremendous range in the building and construction fields, accounting for about 20% of total domestic shipments in a typical year. Residential doors and windows constitute the largest tonnage of any aluminum building product, about one-third of the total building and construction market. Residential siding runs second. There are many other products in addition to these dominant ones. In the residential fields, storm doors and windows are popular, along with such aluminum accessories as gutters, downspouts, soffits, louvers, vents, and flashing.

In the commercial and industrial fields, windows, roofing, curtain walls, grilles, ductwork, lighting fixtures, hardware, and so-called "store fronts and entrances" are among the most popular items. High strength aluminum alloys are used in power-transmission-line towers and in remote locations where periodic maintenance and painting would be extremely costly. In powder or paste form, aluminum finds use in heat-reflective coatings over so-called "smooth-surfaced" bituminous roofs.

PROPERTIES

Aluminum is a lightweight, nonmagnetic metal with a density of roughly 0.1 lb/in.^{3} (2.7 g/cm^3), about one-third that of steel or copper. Among its most important chemical and physical properties are high strength-to-weight ratio, high heat reflectivity (and correspondingly low emissivity), high thermal and electrical conductivity, superior corrosion resistance, and adaptability to every major form of metalworking: casting, forging, drawing, machining, rolling, and extruding.

Alloying elements improve aluminum's performance across the entire spectrum of desirable properties: improved strength, corrosion resistance, ductility, workability, and weldability. Through a combination of alloying, cold working, and/or heat treatment, commercially pure aluminum can be strengthened by a factor of seven—from 13,000-psi to nearly 90,000-psi tensile strength.

Aluminum deteriorates through galvanic corrosion when in contact with iron, steel, copper, brass, and bronze. With iron and steel, the corrosion is very slow and can be readily prevented by painting the iron or steel with a good-quality exterior-grade primer and top coat or bituminous paint. Direct contact with copper, brass, or bronze should be avoided, and drainage of water off these metals onto aluminum should not be permitted. Galvanic corrosion is insignificant when aluminum is in contact with zinc (which even tends to protect aluminum), stainless steel, monel, lead, and galvanized or cadmium-plated steel. With galvanized and cadmium-plated steel, however, when the zinc or cadmium is consumed, the steel will rust, which may cause staining. In industrial environments, this can happen in a relatively short time, and the precautions advised for iron and steel should be followed.

Highly corrosive environments, such as those on the seacoast and around chemical plants, mine and mill complexes, refineries, etc, may promote corrosion even though aluminum alone has good corrosion resistance. In these environments recommendations of appropriate protective measures should be sought from specialists.

Alloy Temper System

The major alloying elements are copper, manganese, magnesium, silicon, and zinc, singly or in combination. Of most interest to architects, engineers, and other building industry experts are the 1000, 3000, 5000, and 6000 series, where the first digit in the series designation denotes the alloying elements, if any.

The 1000 "pure" (99%+) aluminum series exploits aluminum's inherent corrosion resistance and the heat reflectivity of its polished surface for insulating reflector foil. The 3000 (manganese) series adds strength to the pure aluminum for sheet used to produce roofing, siding, and other architectural products requiring good workability.

For still higher strength, plus weldability and corrosion resistance in salt air, sheet made from the 5000 (magnesium) series is used for such exposed architectural products as grilles and ornamental trim. Used principally for extruded shapes, eg, doors, windows, structural shapes, bridge railings, etc, the 6000 (magnesium/silicon) alloy series provides the required combination of good formability, weldability, and strength.

As it does for steel, cold working increases aluminum's strength and hardness. Rolling to "full-hard" condition doubles the 13,000-psi tensile strength of commercially pure aluminum. Heat treatment can further increase the strength of some alloys, and aluminum alloys are accordingly divided into heat-treatable and non-heat-treatable classes.

Heat-treatable alloys (the 2000, 6000, and 7000 series) contain alloying elements (copper, magnesium, zinc, and silicon) that singly or in combination are more soluble at elevated temperatures than at room temperature. These heat-treatable alloys can thus be subjected to a combination of heating, quenching, cold working, and aging to realign the alloyed metal's crystalline structure into stronger patterns. In contrast, the non-heat-treatable alloys (the 1000, 3000, 4000, and 5000 series) gain their strength solely through the hardening effects of the alloying elements, plus cold working.

Like the alloy system, the temper system has its own designation system. Temper, which refers to heat treatment and cold working, is designated by suffixed letters as follows:

F = *as-fabricated.* This classification applies to the products of shaping processes in which no special control over thermal conditions or strain hardening is employed. For wrought products, there are no mechanical-property limits.

O = *annealed.* The annealed classification applies to wrought products that are annealed to obtain the lowest strength temper and to cast products that are annealed to improve ductility and dimensional stability. The O may be followed by a digit other than zero, indicating a variation with special characteristics.

H = *strain hardened (wrought products only).* This designation applies to products that have their strength increased by strain hardening, with or without supplementary thermal treatments to produce some reduction in strength. The H is always followed by two or more digits. The first digit following the H indicates the specific combination of basic operations as follows:

- H1—strain hardened only—applies to products that are strain hardened to obtain the desired strength without supplementary thermal treatment. The number following this designation indicates the degree of strain hardening.

- H2—strain hardened and partially annealed—applies to products that are strain hardened more than the desired final amount and then reduced in strength to the desired level by partial annealing. For alloys that age-soften at room temperature, the H2 tempers have the same minimum ultimate tensile strength as the corresponding H3 tempers. For other alloys, the H2 tempers have the same minimum ultimate tensile strength as the corresponding H1 tempers and slightly higher elongation. The number following this designation indicates the degree of strain hardening remaining after the product has been partially annealed.

- H3—strain hardened and stabilized—applies to products that are strain hardened and whose mechanical properties are stabilized either by a low temperature thermal treatment or as a result of heat introduced during fabrication. Stabilization usually improves ductility. This designation is applicable only to those alloys that, unless stabilized, gradually age-soften at room temperature. The number following this designation indicates the degree of strain hardening remaining after the stabilization treatment.

The digit following the designation H1, H2, and H3 indicates the degree of strain hardening. The third digit, when used, indicates a variation of a two-digit temper.

W = solution heat-treated. This classification is an unstable temper applicable only to alloys that spontaneously age at room temperature after solution heat treatment. This designation is specific only when the period of natural aging is indicated, for example W1/2 h.

T = thermally treated to produce stable tempers other than F, O, or H. The "T" designation applies to products that are thermally treated, with or without supplementary strain hardening, to produce stable tempers. The T is always followed by one or more digits:

- T1—cooled from an elevated-temperature shaping process and naturally aged to a substantially stable condition—applies to products that are not cold worked after cooling from an elevated-temperature shaping process or in which the effect of cold work in flattening or straightening may not be recognized in mechanical-property limits.

- T2—cooled from an elevated-temperature shaping process, cold worked, and naturally aged to a substantially stable condition—applies to products that are cold worked to improve strength after cooling from an elevated-temperature shaping process or in which the effect of cold work in flattening or straightening is recognized in mechanical-property limits.

- T3—solution heat treated, cold worked, and naturally aged to a substantially stable condition—applies to products that are cold worked to improve strength after solution heat treatment or in which the effect of cold work in flattening or straightening is recognized in mechanical-property limits.

- T4—solution heat treated and naturally aged to a substantially stable condition—applies to products that are not cold worked after solution heat treatment or in which the effect of cold work in flattening or straightening may not be recognized in mechanical-property limits.

- T5—cooled from an elevated-temperature shaping process and artificially aged—applies to products that are not cold worked after cooling from an elevated-temperature shaping process or in which the effect of cold work in flattening or straightening may not be recognized in mechanical-property limits.

- T6—solution heat treated and artificially aged—applies to products that are not cold worked after solution heat treatment or in which the effect of cold work in flattening or straightening may not be recognized in mechanical-property limits.

- T7—solution heat treated and overaged/stabilized—applies to wrought products that are artificially aged after solution heat treatment to carry them beyond a point of maximum strength to provide control of some significant characteristic. This designation applies to cast products that are artificially aged after solution heat treatment to provide dimensional and strength stability.

- T8—solution heat treated, cold worked, and artificially aged—applies to products that are cold worked to improve strength or in which the effect of cold work in flattening or straightening is recognized in mechanical-property limits.

- T9—solution heat treated, artificially aged, and cold worked—applies to products that are cold worked to improve strength.

- T10—cooled from an elevated-temperature shaping process, cold worked, and artificially aged—applies to products that are cold worked to improve strength or in which the effect of cold work in flattening or straightening is recognized in mechanical-property limits.

As a sample of aluminum designation, alloy 6061-T6, used for sheet, gets its T6 thermally treated temper designation from a solution heat treatment at 990°F followed by a rapid quench in room-temperature water, then a precipitation or artificial aging heat treatment at 320°F for about 18 h.

ENERGY-RELATED PROPERTIES

Aluminum "thermal-break" windows and sliding doors are the latest evolutionary improvement in this important class of aluminum building products. Developed in the mid-1960s, in response to the troublesome problems of condensation forming on the inside surface of conventional metal-framed and single-glazed windows, these high quality thermal-break windows also conserve heating and cooling energy. They have permitted design of aluminum windows as energy-efficient as wood. Compared with conventional single-glazed aluminum windows, thermal-break windows offer the following improvements:

Insulating material (the "thermal break"). usually vinyl or polyurethane sandwiched within or sheathing the frame to prevent rapid heat loss or gain through the highly conductive metal.

Double or triple glazing. ie, an insulating air space sandwiched between two or three panes of glass, respectively.

These same energy-conserving features also serve to prevent condensation on interior surfaces of the window, since both energy conservation and condensation prevention depend on improved insulating quality (which raises the interior surface temperature of glass and frame, thereby making them less likely to fall below the interior dewpoint temperature, at which condensation occurs).

A product-labeling program, instituted in early 1977 by the American Architectural Manufacturers Association (AAMA), marks the first effort to provide scientific assurance to customers that such products will perform as rated. Under this product-labeling program, a manufacturer can have products tested for water infiltration, strength, and heat loss through air leakage. A condensation resistance factor (CR factor) also provides an index for assessing a given window's performance after temperatures have been recorded at 24 interior points on glass or frame surfaces during tests by an independent testing laboratory. (The higher its CR factor, the more effective the window is in preventing condensation at low outdoor temperature.)

FORMING AND CASTING

The overwhelming bulk (roughly 85%) of aluminum building and construction products is fabricated from sheet or extrusions, with each accounting for roughly half of that 85%. Window and door sections are extruded; residential and industrial siding is fabricated from aluminum sheet. Extruded pipe and tube, and foil, which merely continues the basic extruding and sheet-rolling processes noted above, account for a large portion of the remaining 15%. Castings represent only a tiny portion of the total building and construction market.

The so-called "mill products" fabricated from ingots can be loosely categorized as follows: (*1*) plate (0.25 in. thick and greater); (*2*) sheet (0.006–0.249 in. thick); (*3*) foil (less than 0.006 in. thick); (*4*) rod (⅜-in. diameter or greater); (*5*) bar (rectangular, hexagonal, octagonal cross sections, with at least one perpendicular distance between faces of ⅜ in. or greater); or (*6*) wire (less than ⅜-in. diameter). As their diminishing thicknesses indicate, plate, sheet, and foil are produced by the same basic process, continued further as thickness decreases. Preheated ingots are hotrolled down to ¼-in. thickness. Sheet is cold-rolled from plate down to 0.006-in. thickness, and foil is further cold-rolled to even thinner sections. Heat-treatable plate and sheet go into a furnace after the rolling operation, whereas non-heat-treatable plate and sheet go directly to finishing operations.

Rods, bars, and wires can be similarly produced by hot-rolling down to slightly oversized dimensions, followed by cold-rolling to final size. Continuous casting provides an alternative method for producing these mill products. In the continuous-casting process, the metal is cast in a cylindrical wheel with outside lugs that retain the molten metal. It moves between two moving belts directly onto a rolling mill.

Roll forming is a mass-production process, and other operations can be performed on the aluminum at the same time, such as seam welding, hole punching, and the automatic cutoff of parts to size. Roll-formed architectural products include moldings, gutters, downspouts, roofing, siding, and frames for window screens. Prepainted sheet can be readily roll formed.

Brake forming, which is forming aluminum on a press brake, can produce a variety of shapes with simpler tooling than in roll forming. However, length is limited by press size, and the production rate is necessarily lower. Simple bending can also be done in a folding brake.

"Blanking" and "cutting" describe the cutting of aluminum sheet to desired outline shapes. "Piercing" and "perforating" refer to making holes through the sheet. In blanking, a punch with the desired outline presses the sheet through a matching die. Automatic presses can mass-produce flat shapes with this method. Stacks of sheet can also be trimmed or cut to outline by a router or sheared in a guillotine-action shear.

Embossing, in which aluminum sheet is shaped or patterned by pressing it through mated rollers or dies, produces a raised pattern on one side and its negative indented on the other side. Aluminum sheet may also be shaped by drawing it through the gap between two mated dies in a press. Drawing produces large wall or spandrel panels with considerable depth of contour.

Aluminum owes part of its tremendous shaping versatility to the modern extrusion process. Billets are heated in a furnace to plastic state at 800°F and pushed by hydraulic ram through a die that forms the desired cross section. Aluminum cross sections have become increasingly complex over the past 10 years. Extrusions are much more adaptable to intricate cross-section shapes than rolling. Extruding produces a variety of architectural products, including structural members, tube and pipe, and such functional and decorative components as window and door frames, fascia, gravel stops, handrails, and coping.

Intricate, complex cross sections are most advantageous in window frames, which require fins, grooves, and other projections or indentations for glazing, thermal breaks, air-pressure-equalizing channels, and other features. The extrusion process has greatly increased the efficiency of aluminum structural shapes, making it possible to eliminate wasted metal in rolled cross sections, reducing their weight by an estimated 8–10% for the same strength. In addition to greater efficiency than the earlier rolled shapes, which are patterned on structural steel shapes, the number of new extruded aluminum structural shapes has been cut roughly in half. Better joining is still another advantage offered by the extruded shapes.

With aluminum extrusion, the size of the press limits the size of the die, whose diameter, in turn, determines the maximum width of an extrusion. Sometimes a final part wider than the diameter of the die can be made by extruding it in a curled shape within the die circle and then straightening it. Extruded parts can also be designed for joining by interlocking edges, welding, brazing, or fastening.

Casting of aluminum usually involves three techniques: sand casting, permanent-mold casting, and die casting. In sand casting, sand with a binder is packed around a pattern, which is then removed. Molten aluminum is poured in, reproducing the shape of the pattern. A sand casting's rough surface texture may be attractive in some applications and thus retained. Alternatively, the surface can be machined smooth or otherwise finished. Sand casting is the most economical casting method for low volume production or very large parts.

With permanent-mold castings, molten aluminum is poured by gravity or low pressure into a reusable metal mold. The process is used for relatively large volume production. In die casting, molten aluminum is forced under high pressure into permanent molds. This process is suitable for mass production of precisely formed castings.

Two relatively uncommon forming techniques are superplastic forming and powder metallurgy. In superplastic forming, a sheet of appropriately formulated aluminum alloy is heated and then stretched by pressurized air over a positive mold or into a negative mold. The process can produce complex and deep forms but is slow and appears best suited to limited production runs. With powder metallurgy, a powdered aluminum alloy is compacted in a mold, often in finished shape, and heated to a temperature at which the particles fuse into a unified solid. This technology is used to produce high strength parts.

Joining

Aluminum can be joined by most processes used to join steel, including various resistance and fusion welding processes, adhesive bonding, weldbonding, mechanical fastening and soldering, or brazing techniques. Gas tungsten arc welding (GTAW) and gas metal arc welding (GMAW) are commonly used. The GTAW process is used for joints requiring good appearance and for thin gauges of metal. The GMAW process is faster and more economical.

Adhesive bonding can help distribute loads and resultant stresses more evenly in joined parts that can be obtained with spot welding or mechanical fastening. Adhesive-bonded joints damp vibrations effectively, and metals with different expansion coefficients can be joined with adhesives of suitable flexibility. Flexible adhesives are often used to join aluminum, or other metals, to a nonmetal. Adhesives can be selected to resist particular types of stress, although it is usually best to design for shear or compression. Weldbonding, ie, combining spot welding and adhesive bonding, offers better resistance to peeling forces than adhesive bonding alone.

Mechanical fasteners may join aluminum to metallic or nonmetallic components. Preferred fasteners are aluminum or stainless steel, but coated-steel fasteners may be used in some instances. Mechanical fasteners used with adhesives provide properties similar to those of weldbonded joints.

Riveting practices for aluminum are well-defined. Speeds can approach that of spot welding with some types of riveting equipment. Mechanical clinching is also sometimes used in joining aluminum sheet panels.

FINISHES AND COATINGS

For many purposes, the natural appearance and durability of aluminum as fabricated are entirely adequate. However, aluminum can also be given mechanical, chemical, coated, laminated, or anodized finishes to meet specific practical and aesthetic requirements. Atmospheric exposure can induce surface roughening and soiling. Where appearance is a primary consideration, aluminum should be anodized or given a protective coating.

There are three basic mechanical finishing processes: buffing, directional texturing, and nondirectional texturing. Buffing with fine abrasives and polishing compounds produces smooth surfaces including "specular," produced by buffing only, and "smooth specular," produced by buffing and polishing. Specular surfaces can have strong visual impact, but on large surfaces, their mirrorlike quality will emphasize any distortion. Directional textured surfaces of various degrees of coarseness, from "brushed" to "hand rubbed" and from "coarse satin" to "fine satin," are applied by polishing with a wire brush, stainless-steel wool, or aluminum oxide grit. Forming and welding marks can be obscured by hand rubbing, and directional satin finishes are both attractive and easy to restore after welding, thus their popularity in architectural applications. Nondirectional texturing is produced by "shot" or "air blasting" with materials of various sizes and hardness. Size and type of blasting materials should be based on metal thickness to avoid distortion from the pressure of the blasting.

Chemical preparation includes cleaning, etching, and brightening. Cleaning of non-etched surfaces is done with an organic degreasing solvent or an inhibited chemical cleaner. It prepares the aluminum surface for anodizing or other finishes. Etching is done by immersing the metal in a caustic solution, producing a silver–white surface often called "frosted." This texture minimizes surface blemishes and can vary from a coarse to a fine matte finish. For large runs, chemically etched finishes are more economical than mechanical matte finishing. For small orders, mechanical finishing may be more economical. Brightening by a special dip solution produces "highly specular" or "diffuse bright" finishes. Exposed to weather, brightened aluminum may not retain its original appearance, so consultation with an aluminum finisher is recommended before specification.

Coatings such as lacquer are sometimes used as temporary protection for finishes against discoloration by contact with alkaline materials such as mortar, cement, and plaster.

ANODIZING

Anodizing is the primary technique for enhancing the durability of an aluminum finish. The name comes from aluminum's role in the process as the anode, or positively charged terminal, in the electrolytic acid bath. This electrolytic surface treatment produces a more uniform and thicker protective surface oxide coating than is natural. The anodized coating is 1000 to 2000 times as thick as the natural oxide coating, which is less than one-millionth of an inch thick.

Although anodizing originally produced only a clear protective coating, techniques were soon developed to dye the aluminum surface before it was sealed to produce a wide variety of colorful finishes.

For its first three decades, anodizing featured a sulfuric acid bath as the electrolyte. In the late 1950s, however, the industry developed new anodizing processes, performed under specific currents and voltages in complex organic–inorganic acid electrolytes. These anodizing techniques, called integral-color anodizing, produce an even more durable finish than sulfuric acid anodizing. Finishes come in colors ranging from natural silver through pale gold, bronzes of varying hue, and grays that end in dead black.

These relatively new hardcoat-anodized films range up to 1.2 mil (thousandths of an inch), nearly double the thickness of conventional anodized coating and roughly 3000 times that of natural oxide film. Depending on their quality and the atmosphere in which they perform, hardcoat-anodized finishes should last from 20 to 80 years.

In addition to improved durability, these hardcoat-anodized coatings produce integral, colorfast coatings that are highly resistant to erosion and fading from solar radiation. Architects should consult manufacturers regarding resistance to fading before specifying pigmented anodized aluminum for exterior uses.

The Aluminum Association classifies architectural anodic coatings in two categories. Architectural Class I coatings are 0.7 mil or thicker and are recommended both for interiors and exteriors subject to weathering. Architectural Class II coatings are between 0.4 and 0.7 mil thick and recommended for interior areas not subject to excessive wear or abrasion and for exterior areas that are regularly cleaned and maintained, such as store fronts and entrances.

Electrolytic color anodizing produces durable earth-tone colors by a two-step electrolytic process. The first step typically involves sulfuric acid anodizing with a second electrolytic deposition treatment in a suitable metal–salt solution. Integral-color anodizing, on the other hand, produces thick oxide films colored by the composition of the aluminum alloys employed, as affected by process temperature, voltage, current density, and time. Both processes can produce colors in Architectural Class I thicknesses with dense, hard surfaces highly resistant to abrasion.

APPLIED FINISHES

Because of its inherent corrosion resistance, aluminum provides an excellent substrate for organic coatings. Applied to a suitably pretreated aluminum surface, properly applied organic coatings do not chip, peel, or crack. Used for years on residential windows, doors, roofing, siding, and other components, improved organic coatings have entered new fields, notably high-rise commercial office towers.

Organic coatings, strictly defined, include a vast range of materials applied as liquids, powders, or films. The least costly organic coatings include bituminous coatings, paints, and shellacs applied with such simple conventional techniques as brushing, rolling, and air-spraying. For exterior finishes on aluminum curtain walls, however, only a few organic coatings provide the required durability, defined as a 20-year useful life. These high performance organic coatings fall into the following categories: fluorocarbons; siliconized acrylics; siliconized polyesters; and plastisols. These resinous polymers form the matrix protecting the pigments, which give the organic coating its color.

Fluorocarbons are the most durable of these new organic coatings. They are among the most stable resins known, with excellent resistance to erosion, solar radiation, and general weathering. Other organic coatings, however, may be superior for certain specific qualities. Siliconized acrylics and polyesters, for example, may offer slightly superior color and gloss retention in some formulations.

By general expert consensus, the proper chemical pretreatment of the aluminum substrate is of vital importance to the ultimate quality of an aluminum finish of any type, whether anodized, porcelain enamel, or organic coating.

Porcelain enamel coatings, made of inorganic vitreous materials, are the hardest and most durable of architectural metal finishes. Commercially available for some 30 years, these coatings are available in an almost limitless variety of permanent colors with excellent uniformity.

The major drawback to porcelain enamel is its high cost, the highest of any aluminum finish. It also requires greater care than organic coatings in choice of aluminum alloy.

PRODUCTS

A typical group of building products is described and illustrated below:

Flashing (Fig. 1). Aluminum flashing is used in concrete construction, brick masonry, stucco, with aluminum and vinyl siding, and for reroofing. Preformed flashings are available in a variety of widths, lengths, and styles, or custom-formed from aluminum coil stock, available in vari-

Figure 1. Flashing. Courtesy of the Aluminum Association.

ous gauges, lengths, and widths. Aluminum flashing is formed from rolls of coil stock, used at joints to make buildings watertight. Flashing should have allowance for expansion and contraction and be installed to allow inspection and repair.

Preformed Wall and Roof Panels (Fig. 2). Preformed vertical aluminum wall and roof panels are available in vented, flat, concave, and convex designs in gauges of 0.19–0.040 in. Baked-on enamel colored finishes are available in 18 colors. Panels are supplied with furring section or stringer, standoff system, and trim components. Vertical panels may span from 39 in. to 21 ft 10 in. Preformed vertical aluminum wall and roof panels have baked enamel finishes and may be bonded to foam insulation. The panels used for facades are lightweight and dimensionally stable but cannot carry loading. Panels come in a variety of styles.

Sandwich Composite Wall and Roof Panels (Fig. 3). Panels are available in clear anodized surface, or a variety of standard coil-coated, painted colors, and a wide spectrum of custom colors and finishes. Panels are fabricated to provide a 1.04 U-value, a thermal resistance (R) of 0.961, and thermal conductivity of between 260 and 230. Panels can be routed, engraved, drilled, sandblasted, formed, molded, or otherwise shaped. Panels are 0.157 in. (4mm) and 0.236 in. (6mm) thick, and 4 and 5 ft wide, in lengths

Figure 3. Sandwich composite wall and roof panels. Courtesy of the Aluminum Association.

up to 28 ft. Sandwich composite wall and roof panels are made of two thin sheets of aluminum with a thermoplastic core for interior and exterior building surfaces. Material is virtually flat in its basic form but can conform to curves or angles. The panels are lightweight, durable, nearly maintenance-free, and resist temperature changes and corrosion; they dampen sound and vibration and do not buckle or oil-can. Panels are used in beam cladding, column covers, curtain walls, and fascia uses for both low- and high-rise construction.

Skylights (Fig. 4). Skylight frames are rigid and insulated, with self-flashing perimeters and permanent weather sealing in conjunction with tempered glass or plastics. Skylights are made in standard sizes and shapes or may be custom-formed from aluminum extrusions. Aluminum skylights are available sized to suit a number of uses where overhead illumination is desired. Most popular residential installations are in kitchens, dens, hallways, and windowless bathrooms. They may be installed singly or in multiple installations. Skylights may be fixed or movable for ventilation.

Exterior Soffits (Fig. 5). Aluminum interlocking soffit panels are available in plain, center-vented, or triple-vented styles. They are designed with hidden nailing

Figure 2. Preformed wall and roof panels. Courtesy of the Aluminum Association.

Figure 4. Skylights. Courtesy of the Aluminum Association.

Figure 6. Example of a curtain-wall system. Courtesy of the Aluminum Association.

flanges and bridged perforations. Standard colors are black, brown, or white, with other colors available, warranted for long use. Trim pieces include frieze runner, quarter-round frieze molding, universal trim, and J channel. Soffit panels are made in standard widths of 4, 6, 8, and 10 in. and in lengths up to 12 ft. Aluminum soffits protect the underside of roof overhangs. Soffits are manufactured in a variety of standard widths and lengths, in systems of interlocking solid or vented panels. In another application, long lengths of aluminum coil stock are formed to fit around special contours of existing wood trim. Soffits are normally installed at right angles to the building wall, with external corners mitered. Soffits are often used in conjunction with aluminum fascia and eave trim.

Curtain Walls (*Fig. 6*). Aluminum curtain walls include extrusions, glazed areas, and optional opaque panels. Extrusions are of 6063-T5 or 6063-T6 alloy and are tempered with Architectural Class I A44 electrolytically deposited color. Industrial walls are available in stock sizes with or without fenestration. Aluminum curtain walls are non-

bearing exterior building walls of metal or a combination of metal, glass, and other surfacing materials supported by or within a metal framework. Standard systems are the stick (wall installed piece by piece); the unit (wall entirely of large framed pre-assembled units); the unit and mullion (mullion members separately installed with pre-assembled framed units placed between them); the panel (homogeneous units formed from sheet metal or as a casting); and the column cover and spandrel (column cover sections, long spandrel units spanning between column covers, and infill glazed units). Custom walls employ any of the five systems or a combination.

Sliding Doors (*Fig. 7*). Aluminum sliding doors and frames of extruded aluminum are of not less than 0.062-in. metal thickness. The quality level is established by the AAMA. Aluminum finishes include clear anodized,

Figure 5. Exterior soffits. Courtesy of the Aluminum Association.

Figure 7. A sliding door with one movable and one fixed door. Courtesy of the Aluminum Association.

Figure 8. Example of an aluminum entrance with double doors. Courtesy of the Aluminum Association.

bronze, and white, with other colors optional. Patio units include weatherstripped panel stiles, sill, and head. Sliding screen doors are available. Doors are usually installed with one fixed and one movable door. Standard doors are available up to 8 ft high, with up to 5-ft-wide panels. Aluminum-framed sliding doors are made in a wide variety of styles and sizes, including double or triple glazing and with thermal breaks in the frame to eliminate frost and condensation on the interior of the door. Pile weatherstripping on both the operating and fixed panels reduces air infiltration. Operating panels have ball-bearing, weathersealed, and adjustable rollers.

Store Fronts and Entrances (Fig. 8). Aluminum extrusions may be designed to provide doors for any size entrance. Door frames are usually of 6063 T52 alloy, with a minimum thickness of 0.125 in. Doors are bolted, welded construction, with tempered glass, weatherstripping, and aluminum thresholds. Other doors include folding grilles, and closures in a wide variety of styles and sizes, with clear or anodized bronze, gold, or black finishes and tempered glass or polycarbonate plastic glazing. Store fronts and entrances of aluminum may be of widely varying designs. Balanced doors are used where effects of wind or interior suction are a problem, such as large heavy doors, or barrier-free openings, and for air-supported structures. For shop-

ping malls and other indoor locations, folding or sliding aluminum grilles with tempered glass or polycarbonate glazing are used for security at night or for limiting public access. These sliding mall walls are practical for wide entrances. For narrow store fronts, rolling aluminum grilles are efficient.

See also ANODIZED FINISHES; CORROSION; ENVELOPES, BUILDING; FENESTRATION SYSTEMS; METALLIC COATINGS.

BIBLIOGRAPHY

General References

The following publications of the Aluminum Association, Inc., Washington, D.C., are recommended for further reading:

Aluminum Standards and Data, 1984.

Welding Aluminum, 1984.

Designation System for Aluminum Finishes, 1980.

Care of Aluminum, 1983.

Specifications for Aluminum Structures (Construction Manual Series, Sect. 1), 1982.

Illustrative Examples of Design (Construction Manual Series, Sect. 2), 1978.

Engineering Data for Aluminum Structures (Construction Manual Series, Sect. 3), 1981.

Specifications for Aluminum Sheet Metal Work in Building Construction (Construction Manual Series, Sect. 5), 1980.

Designing Solar Systems with Aluminum, 1985.

This article was done with the help of The Aluminum Association and used material from *Aluminum in Building and Construction* and *The Aluminum Book* (both Aluminum Association publications).

AMERICAN COUNCIL FOR CONSTRUCTION EDUCATION (ACCE).   See EDUCATION—CONSTRUCTION.

AMERICAN INSTITUTE OF ARCHITECTS (AIA)

PART ONE: 1857–1899

Architecture, like most professions, trades, and industries in the mid-1800s, required no formal training, was governed by no standard practices or documents, and was largely dependent on the personal tastes, background, and location of the practitioner. But in the world being created by the Industrial Revolution, factories were beginning to produce standard sizes and interchangeable parts; a machine built in Kansas City could be fixed in Pittsburgh. This movement toward common standards and minimum requirements led New York architect Richard Upjohn to gather together a dozen of his colleagues on February 23, 1857, to form a society of architects.

Upjohn introduced his idea to 12 of his colleagues, observing that the lack of professional standards had been felt by all present. They discussed the purposes an association could serve, and after much discussion, adopted a motion to found an architectural organization. A committee was appointed to draft a constitution and bylaws, and 11 additional architects were invited to attend the next meeting.

At the next meeting on March 10, the Constitution and Bylaws Committee presented a draft. The first article proposed that the name of the organization be the New York Society of Architects, but Thomas U. Walter of Philadelphia moved that the name reflect a larger, national vision. He suggested, and the others adopted, the name The American Institute of Architects (Fig. 1).

The constitution was specific about the objective of the Institute and the means for accomplishing that objective (1):

Article II. The object of this Institute is to promote the scientific and practical perfection of its members and to elevate the standing of the profession.

Article III. The means of accomplishing this end shall be regular meetings of the members for the discussion of subjects of professional importance; lectures on topics of general interest; the collection of a library, designs and models, to which the members shall have access; social intercourse among its members, and other means which the future may develop.

Discussions of religious or political subjects were prohibited.

Two classes of membership were established: professional architects and associate members. To become a member, a practicing architect had to be nominated by two members. The nomination was posted for 30 days, after which it was voted on at a regular meeting. Three or more no votes meant automatic rejection. Honorary and corresponding members were also approved.

By April 15, 1857, this constitution had been approved, embossed on sheepskin, and printed. In ceremonies that night, the embossed copy was signed in New York University Chapel, New York City. The original document is preserved in the AIA archives and contains the signatures of 49 founders. The founders recognized that if the organization were to grow in size and influence, communication was essential. Therefore, at the same April 15 meeting at which the constitution was signed, they identified a publication—*The Crayon* (2)–to carry items for and about the AIA, including minutes of AIA meetings and activities. Two years later, the Institute renewed that authorization and gave similar authorization to the *Architects and Mechanics Journal*.

In addition to a drive for standardization, the Industrial Revolution was profoundly reshaping the United States in other ways. During the latter half of the nineteenth century, society witnessed an unprecedented accumulation of wealth by U.S. corporations and entrepreneurs. Newly formed labor unions demanded that workers be given a share of the profits. That concern was a burning issue for nineteenth-century architects as well, reflected in the AIA's early concern over standard fees and fair payment for competitions. To address the first concern, the AIA adopted a standard schedule of fees in 1866. Although some architects worried about the legality of dictating fees for professional services, the overwhelming majority were more concerned about the lack of recourse for underpayment or nonpayment.

The second concern evolved from the standard practice in most design competitions of requiring architects to submit drawings of great detail and research for no payment whatsoever. The AIA set out to discourage this practice by urging members not to participate in such competitions and by urging competition sponsors to abide by certain rules that protected the architect.

The first grave challenge to confront the AIA, however, was not professional. It was the Civil War. By 1861, the architects found their fledgling association in debt, chiefly for rent of their headquarters. On November 6, 1861, the trustees reluctantly agreed to give up the lease, sell the furniture, and store the library. For the next three years, meetings were sporadic and often lacked a quorum. It was not until March 5, 1864, that the Institute was able to schedule regular meetings once more. Before the end of that month the membership received the following notice (3):

The regular meetings of the Institute having been intermitted in consequence of the War, recent measures have been taken to revive them. To this end, resolutions were adopted on the 5th and the 15th . . . to procure a room for the Institute, in the lower part of the city . . . to hold meetings in the afternoon instead of the evening . . . and that the meetings be held more especially for business purposes. . . . At the same meeting, it was resolved to cancel all unpaid dues up to the first of January last.

Figure 1. The American Institute of Architects Seal; design by H. Van Buren Magonigle. Courtesy of The American Institute of Architects Archives.

In 1864, the total membership of the AIA was 35, with 28 listed as professional members. There were also 12 Honorary Members, including seven Europeans.

A New Constitution and Leadership

In the wake of the Civil War, the AIA sensed a capability for improving society, while improving the profession and its members. To address these emerging concerns, the first annual meeting was held and a new constitution was adopted in 1867. The proceedings of that annual meeting, published by the AIA, was the first major publication by the ten-year-old organization.

AIA founder and president Richard Upjohn, in his address at that first convention, noted that (4):

> We feel that it is highly important, nay essential, to a large and tangible success, that there should be a liberal interchange of professional thoughts among us. . . . The first constitution of our association was drawn up to express the views and further the purpose of the Institute. . . . It will be observed, on examination of the different articles of this constitution, that the Institute in the outset of its career, had in view the benefits which its superior facilities might accomplish in matters connected with the planning, constructing and laying out of a city or cities. . . . Though the Institute is established for the pursuit and communication of such knowledge as is conducive to the development of architecture, it will nevertheless, it is hoped, be a source of public improvement and reform, beyond the mere scientific and artistic limits of the pursuit, and thus be, in no slight degree, a helper of civilization. . . . In this view of our American Institute of Architects, we see it to be no mean contributor of good to our fellow-citizens.

The 1867 Constitution contained the following (5):

Article II. The objects of this Institute are, to unite in fellowship the Architects of this continent, and to combine their efforts so as to promote the artistic, scientific, and practical efficiency of the profession.

Article III. The means of accomplishing this end shall be: regular meetings of the members, for the discussion of subjects of professional importance; the reading of essays; lectures upon topics of general interest; a school for the education of Architects; exhibitions of architectural drawings; a library; a collection of designs and models; and any other means calculated to promote the objects of the Institute.

Article IV. 1. The Institute shall consist of Fellows, Associates and Honorary Members.

2. The condition of membership as Fellows or Associates shall be, the honorable practice of the profession, in accordance with the Constitution and By-laws of the Institute.

3. No member shall accept direct or indirect compensation for services rendered in the practice of his profession, other than the fees received from his client. . . .

Article VI. The Institute shall hold an Annual Convention, and such other meetings as shall be ordered.

Article VII. Members in any city and its suburbs may organize and maintain a Chapter of the Institute . . .

At the Institute's tenth annual convention in 1876, held in Philadelphia to mark the nation's centennial, President Upjohn, who had served as AIA president for 18 years, was succeeded by Thomas Ustick Walter of Philadelphia. Walter held that office for 11 years. A complete list of AIA presidents is shown in Table 1.

Table 1. AIA Presidents 1857–1986

Richard Upjohn	New York	1857–1876
Thomas Ustick Walter	Philadelphia	1877–1887
Richard Morris Hunt	New York	1888–1891
Edward H. Kendall	New York	1892–1893
Daniel Hudson Burnham	Chicago	1894–1895
George Browne Post	New York	1896–1898
Henry Van Brunt	Kansas City	1899
Robert S. Peabody	Boston	1900–1901
Charles Follen McKim	New York	1902–1903
William S. Eames	St. Louis	1904–1905
Frank Miles Day	Philadelphia	1906–1907
Cass Gilbert	New York	1908–1909
Irving K. Pond	Chicago	1910–1911
Walter Cook	New York	1912–1913
R. Clipston Sturgis	Boston	1913–1915
John Lawrence Mauran	St. Louis	1915–1918
Thomas R. Kimball	Omaha	1918–1920
Henry Hubbard Kendall	Boston	1920–1922
William B. Faville	San Francisco	1922–1924
Dan Everett Waid	New York	1924–1926
Milton Bennett Medary	Philadelphia	1926–1928
Charles Herrick Hammond	Chicago	1928–1930
Robert D. Kohn	New York	1930–1932
Ernest John Russell	St. Louis	1932–1935
Stephen Francis Voorhees	New York	1935–1937
Charles Donagh Maginnis	Boston	1937–1939
Edwin Bergstrom	Los Angeles	1939–1941
Richmond Harold Shreve	New York	1941–1943
Raymond J. Ashton	Salt Lake City	1943–1945
James Richard Edmunds, Jr.	Baltimore	1945–1947
Douglas William Orr	New Haven	1947–1949
Ralph Walker	New York	1949–1951
Glenn Stanton	Portland	1951–1953
Clair William Ditchy	Detroit	1953–1955
George Bain Cummings	Binghamton	1955–1956
Leon Chatelain, Jr.	Washington, D.C.	1956–1958
John Nobles Richards	Toledo	1958–1960
Philip Will, Jr.	Chicago	1960–1962
Henry Lyman Wright	Los Angeles	1962–1963
J. Roy Carroll, Jr.	Philadelphia	1963–1964
Arthur Gould Odell	Charlotte	1964–1965
Morris Ketchum, Jr.	New York	1965–1966
Charles M. Nes, Jr.	Baltimore	1966–1967
Robert L. Durham	Seattle	1967–1968
George E. Kassabaum	St. Louis	1968–1969
Rex Whitaker Allen	San Francisco	1969–1970
Robert F. Hastings	Birmingham	1970–1971
Maximilian O. Urbahn	New York	1971–1972
S. Scott Ferebee, Jr.	Charlotte	1972–1973
Archibald Coleman Rogers	Baltimore	1973–1974
William Marshall, Jr.	Norfolk, Va.	1974–1975
Louis de Moll	Philadelphia	1975–1976

Table 1 (continued)

John M. McGinty	Houston	1976–1977
Elmer E. Botsai	Honolulu	1977–1978
Ehrman B. Mitchell, Jr.	Philadelphia	1978–1979
Charles E. Schwing	Baton Rouge	1979–1980
R. Randall Vosbeck	Alexandria, Va.	1980–1981
Robert M. Lawrence	Oklahoma City	1981–1982
Robert C. Broshar	Waterloo	1982–1983
George M. Notter, Jr.	Boston	1983–1984
R. Bruce Patty	Kansas City	1984–1985
John A. Busby, Jr.	Atlanta	1985–1986

Members and Chapters

As membership grew, the qualifications, requirements, and categories of membership expanded as well. When the 1867 membership list was printed, it recorded the names of 56 members: 47 Fellows (the highest category of membership that replaced "Professional member") and 9 Associates. There were 19 Honorary Members as well. According to the 1867 constitution, membership was conditional upon the honorable practice of the profession, in accordance with the Constitution and Bylaws of the Institute (5). Under this provision, the AIA in 1888 admitted its first woman member, Louise Bethune, a practicing architect in Buffalo, as an associate member. In 1889, she was advanced to Fellow, the first female FAIA.

A major change instituted by the constitution of 1867 was the authorization of chapters. The Institute saw the small groups of local architects around the country as a great source of potential members. However, after witnessing the catastrophic results of the Civil War, the Institute moved to create a system that allowed for participation in the national organization without subjugation of local concerns or desires. As Upjohn stated in his 1867 convention address (4),

> The sentiment of independence in local legislation [of chapters] was essential to the usefulness and dignity—and even to the self-preservation—of the various groups of practitioners in architecture at the great centers distant from New York; while, at the same time, it seemed apparent that to make a truly national organization, and to coordinate the activities of different localities for mutual benefit, and prevent counter-action, weakening to the whole body and prejudicial to its interests, it was necessary that the ties between the new organizations and the parent one should be strong and enduring.

AIA chapters sprang up across the country: New York in 1867, Chicago and Philadelphia in 1869, Boston and Cincinnati in 1870, Albany in 1873, Rhode Island in 1875, Baltimore and San Francisco in 1881, Indianapolis and St. Louis in 1884, and Washington, D.C., in 1887. A list of chapters and state associations as of 1986 is given in Table 2.

Table 2. Chapter and State Organizations—AIA Components by Region

CALIFORNIA

California Council of Architects

Cabrillo
California Central Coast
California Desert
Central Valley
East Bay
Golden Empire
Inland
Los Angeles
  San Fernando Valley Section
Monterey Bay
Orange County
Pasadena and Foothill
Redwood Empire
San Diego
  North County Section
San Francisco
San Joaquin
  Sequoia Section
San Mateo County
Santa Barbara
Santa Clara Valley
Sierra Valley
Ventura County

CENTRAL STATES

Iowa
(Statewide chapter)

Cedar Rapids Section
Des Moines Section
Eastern Iowa Section
Northwest Iowa Section

Kansas Society of Architects
(Statewide chapter)

Flint Hill Section
Lawrence Section
Topeka Section
Wichita Section

Missouri Council of Architects

Kansas City
Mid-Missouri
St. Louis
Springfield

Nebraska Society of Architects

Lincoln
Omaha
Western

Oklahoma Council of Architects

Oklahoma
  Oklahoma City Section
Tulsa

EASTERN CENTRAL STATES

Indiana Society of Architects

Central Southern Indiana
Fort Wayne
Indianapolis
Nothern Indiana

Kentucky Society of Architects

Central Kentucky
East Kentucky
Northern Kentucky
West Kentucky

FLORIDA/CARIBBEAN

Florida Association of Architects

Broward County
Daytona Beach
Florida Central
  Clearwater Section
  Polk County Section
  St. Petersburg Section
  Tampa Section
Florida Gulf Coast
Florida North
Florida North Central
Florida Northwest
Florida South
Florida Southwest
Indian River
Jacksonville
Mid-Florida
  Brevard County Section
Palm Beach
  Martin County Section
  Spanish River Section

U.S. Virgin Islands

St. Croix Section
St. Thomas/St. John Section

Table 2 (*continued*)

Puerto Rico

GULF STATES

Alabama Council of Architects
Birmingham
East Alabama
Mobile
Montgomery
North Alabama
Northeast Alabama

Arkansas
(Statewide chapter)
Fort Smith Section
Northwest Arkansas Section

Louisiana Architects Association
Baton Rouge
Central Louisiana
Louisiana Coastal
Monroe
New Orleans
Shreveport
South Louisiana
Southwest Louisiana

Mississippi
(Statewide chapter)
Gulf Coast Section

Tennessee Society of Architects
Chattanooga
East Tennessee
Memphis
Middle Tennessee
Watauga
West Tennessee

ILLINOIS

Illinois Council of Architects
Central Illinois
    Bloomington–Normal Section
    Champaign–Urbana Section
    Decatur Section
    Peoria Section
    Sangamon County Section
Chicago
Eastern Illinois
Northeast Illinois
Northern Illinois
Southern Illinois
Western Illinois

MICHIGAN

Michigan Society of Architects
Detroit
Flint Area
Grand Valley
Huron Valley
Mid-Michigan
Northern Michigan
Saginaw Valley
Upper Peninsula
Western Michigan

MIDDLE ATLANTIC STATES

Delaware Society of Architects
(Statewide chapter)

Washington
Architects in Government Section

Maryland Society of Architects
Baltimore
Chesapeake Bay
Potomac Valley

Virginia Society of Architects
Blue Ridge
James River
    Charlottesville/Albemarle Section
Northern Virginia
Tidewater

West Virginia Society of Architects
(Statewide chapter)

NEW ENGLAND

Connecticut Society of Architects
(Statewide chapter)

Maine
(Statewide chapter)

Massachusetts State Association of Architects
Boston Society of Architects
Central Massachusetts
Western Massachusetts

New Hampshire
(Statewide chapter)

Rhode Island
(Statewide chapter)

Vermont
(Statewide chapter)

NEW JERSEY

New Jersey Society of Architects
(Statewide chapter)
Architects League of Northern New Jersey Section
Central Section
Newark Suburban Section
Shore Section
South Jersey Section
West Jersey Section

NEW YORK

New York State Association of Architects
Bronx
Brooklyn
Buffalo/Western New York
Central New York
Eastern New York
Long Island

NEW YORK (*continued*)
New York City
Queens
Rochester
Southern New York
Staten Island
Westchester/Mid-Hudson

NORTH CENTRAL STATES

Minnesota Society of Architects
Minneapolis
Northeastern Minnesota
St. Paul

North Dakota
(Statewide chapter)
Fargo Section

South Dakota
(Statewide chapter)

Wisconsin Society of Architects
Northeast
Northwest
Southeast
Southwest

NORTHWEST

Alaska
(Statewide chapter)
Central Alaska Section
Northern Alaska Section
Southeast Alaska Section

Hawaii Society of Architects
Hawaii Island Section
Maui Section

Guam and Micronesia

Idaho
(Statewide chapter)
Central Idaho Section
Eastern Idaho Section
Northern Idaho Section

Montana
(Statewide chapter)
Billings Architectural Association Section
Kalispell Section

Oregon Council of Architects
Central and East Oregon
Portland
Salem
Southern Oregon
Southwest Oregon

Table 2 (continued)

Washington Council

Central Washington
Northwest Washington
Seattle
Southwest Washington
Spokane
Vancouver

OHIO

Architects Society of Ohio

Akron
Cincinnati
Cleveland
Columbus
Dayton
Eastern Ohio
Toledo

PENNSYLVANIA

Pennsylvania Society of Architects

Bucks County
Central Pennsylvania
Eastern Pennsylvania
Middle Pennsylvania
Northeastern Pennsylvania
Northwestern Pennsylvania
Philadelphia
Pittsburgh

SOUTH ATLANTIC STATES

Georgia Association

Atlanta
Augusta
Golden Isles

SOUTH ATLANTIC STATES *(continued)*

Middle Georgia
South Georgia
Southwest Georgia
West Georgia

North Carolina
(Statewide chapter)

Asheville Section
Charlotte Section
Durham Section
Eastern Section
Piedmont Section
Raleigh Section
Winston-Salem Section

South Carolina
(Statewide chapter)

Hilton Head Section

TEXAS

Texas Society of Architects

Abilene
Amarillo
Austin
Brazos
Corpus Christi
Dallas
El Paso
Fort Worth
Houston
Lower Rio Grande Valley
Lubbock
Northeast Texas
San Antonio Hill Country Section

TEXAS *(continued)*

Southeast Texas
Waco
West Texas
Wichita Falls

WESTERN MOUNTAIN REGION

Arizona Society of Architects

Central Arizona
Rio Salado Chapter
Southern Arizona

AIA Colorado

Colorado North
Colorado South
Colorado West
Denver

Nevada Society of Architects

Las Vegas
Northern Nevada

New Mexico Society of Architects

Albuquerque
Farmington
New Mexico Southern
Santa Fe

Utah Society

Central Utah
Northern Utah
Salt Lake

Wyoming
(Statewide chapter)

Merger with the Western Association of Architects

Meanwhile, a rival association was gaining strength and members in the West—the Western Association of Architects (WAA). Founded in 1884, the group was especially strong in the Midwest and the South, where AIA representation was sparse. The WAA's first president, John Wellborn Root, who was also a Fellow of the Institute, called upon his organization to consider merging with the AIA. At the AIA's and the WAA's 1889 conventions, both in Cincinnati, the consolidation was ratified by both groups. The Western Association was folded into the AIA in order to retain the AIA's 1857 charter. Upon consolidation, the "new" AIA had 465 members.

Since all members of the Western Association had gone by the title of "Fellow," and the WAA refused to give up its single class of membership, the AIA made all its active members Fellows as well. It was not until 1898 that the Bylaws were revised to reestablish the category of associate member and thereby reimbue the title of Fellow with its former higher status.

Committees and Correspondence

As the AIA grew, it became increasingly necessary to establish a system for addressing specific issues. Thus, the AIA inaugurated its committee system, a network that to this day coordinates much of the Institute's activities on pressing issues facing the profession. The first two permanent committees of the AIA, the Committee on Education and the Committee on the Library and Publications, represented the AIA's firm commitment to ensure that architects, like other professionals gaining status in the nineteenth century, received proper education, both as undergraduates and as practicing professionals. Since most formal architectural education was centered in Europe, the Institute appointed a secretary of foreign correspondence to ensure a continued flow of information from, and increasingly, to, architects abroad.

Publications

The AIA's increasing self-confidence was reflected in an official proposal to establish an AIA periodical, recorded as early as 1865. The idea surfaced on a regular basis, but it was not until 1900, with the publication of the *AIA Quarterly Bulletin* (6), that a full-fledged AIA periodical began. Prior to that, the AIA had authorized other magazines to carry its news. In 1876, the first issue of *American Architect and Building News* reported that the ninth AIA convention in Baltimore had passed a resolution making the *American Architect and Building News* the organ of publication of the Institute. It succeeded *The Crayon* and the *Architects and Mechanics Journal* and was later joined by *Inland Architect,* an official organ of the AIA.

Before the turn of the century, the Institute did publish under separate cover its constitution, committee reports, special addresses to the members and its convention proceedings. Copies of all these publications are in the AIA Archives, as are issues of the *AIA Quarterly Bulletin* and subsequent AIA publications.

Publication of Standard Documents

One of the primary goals of the Institute was to establish some uniformity in the design process, specifications, and fees, mirroring the national drive for codification and standardization. The Institute published its first document, *A Schedule of Charges* (7), in 1866 in response to mounting requests for standardization of fees. From that time forward, architects could standardize their charges, take action against other architects who undercut AIA charges, and use the documents as proof in court and elsewhere of the established fees to which architects were entitled. Soon after, the AIA published its first document on the conduct of competitions, revised many times over the years. By the end of the 1870s, the AIA had drafted at least two versions of an owner-contractor agreement, and other drafts appeared during the 1880s. In 1888, the AIA, the Western Association of Architects, and the National Association of Builders jointly published a standardized building contract, the first uniform contract (8).

During the era, prominent members of the Institute frequently wrote articles for publication. One of the most influential pieces was written by Glenn Brown, who served later as AIA secretary. Brown wrote an article for *American Architect and Building News* (9) in which he exposed the government's inept contracting of design and building services. He revealed that the government regularly paid at least one-third more for preparation of architectural drawings than private architects received for similar work. In addition, he wrote that government drawings were often inferior to private sector work, as was the actual construction. His exposé was the major catalyst for passage and active application of the Tarsney Act, a law controlling the conduct of government design competitions (discussed below) in the late nineteenth and early twentieth centuries.

Conventions

From 1867 to 1899, the annual AIA convention increasingly served as a forum for discussion of major issues facing the profession. During the nineteenth century, discussions arose out of convention addresses, reports of officers and committees, reports of host chapters, and votes on Institute policy. Prominent issues of the day included the development of fireproof buildings, the relationship between architects and engineers, legislation affecting architectural practice, and architects' responsibility within the design/construction team. Many of the issues discussed at these early conventions have reemerged in the last quarter of the twentieth century. AIA President Thomas Ustick Walter's address of 1878 could well be taken from a speech at the AIA's 1986 convention (10):

> An architect is always considered by the public as responsible for his designs, whether he is employed to see them executed or not. . . . Should they be committed to unskilled hands . . . he need not expect that public opinion will exonerate him from a certain degree of blame, however perfect his design of construction may have been.

As the influence and membership of the Institute expanded, so did the geographic diversity of sites for the annual meetings. The 1867 constitution called for annual conventions to be open to all members, and the Institute set out to make sure convention sites reflected the national image sought by the Institute. New York City and Chicago meetings were intended to recognize Northern and Midwestern centers of architectural practice. Similarly, Washington meetings recognized the seat of the federal government and the need for the profession to influence legislation beneficial to architects and to secure government work for qualified members of the Institute.

The first convention was held in New York City in 1867; the 1870 convention was held in Philadelphia; in 1871, the organization traveled north to Boston; in 1872, it went west to Cincinnati; in 1896, it went south to Nashville. A complete list of locations is given in Table 3.

To demonstrate and increase the national influence and image of the AIA further, conventions were often scheduled to coincide with major fairs and exhibitions. The 1876 convention in Philadelphia coincided with the Centennial; the 1893 convention in Chicago, with the World's Columbian Exposition, an exposition that profoundly influenced the practice of architecture for the next 50 years. The huge central exhibition was planned by eminent architects, most of them prominent members of the AIA, and was brought together by architects, artists, planners, and others in the creation of a great classical city. The exhibition embodied the European beaux-arts tradition, showing how the architect, planner, sculptor, muralist, landscape architect, and others could work together to create a harmonious whole. Its planning, neoclassical buildings, and monumentality established the look of public buildings in this country until well into the 1940s. As more and more members took part in shaping Institute policy, the convention became one of the best forums for formulating Institute policy.

National Headquarters

As the twentieth century approached, members increasingly considered the need to influence federal architecture and develop legislation affecting architects. The growing national and international importance of Washington, D.C., helped focus attention on a proposal from the Wash-

Table 3. Meeting Sites for the Convention of The American Institute of Architects

#1	1867		New York		#63	1930		Washington, D.C.
#2	1868		New York		#64	1931		San Antonio
#3	1869		New York		#65	1932		Washington, D.C.
#4	1870		Philadelphia		#66	1934		Washington, D.C.
#5	1871		Boston		#67	1935		Milwaukee
#6	1872		Cincinnati		#68	1936		Williamsburg, Va.
#7	1873		Chicago		#69	1937		Boston
#8	1874		New York		#70	1938		New Orleans
#9	1875		Baltimore		#71	1939		Washington, D.C.
#10	1876		Philadelphia		#72	1940		Louisville, Ky.
#11	1877		Boston		#73	1941		Yosemite Valley and Los Angeles
#12	1878		New York		#74	1942		Detroit
#13	1879		New York		#75	1943		Cincinnati
#14	1880		Philadelphia		#76	1944		Indianapolis
#15	1881		Washington, D.C.		#77	1945	April	Atlantic City, N.J.
#16	1882		Cincinnati		#78	1946	May	Miami Beach, Fla.
#17	1883		Providence and Newport, R.I.		#79	1947	April	Grand Rapids, Mich.
#18	1884		Albany, N.Y.		#80	1948	June	Salt Lake City
#19	1885		Nashville, Tenn.		#81	1949	March	Houston
#20	1886		New York		#82	1950	May	Washington, D.C.
#21	1887		Chicago		#83	1951	May	Chicago
#22	1888		Buffalo, N.Y.		#84	1952	June	New York
#23	1889		Cincinnati		#85	1953	June	Seattle
#24	1890		Washington, D.C.		#86	1954	June	Boston
#25	1891		Boston		#87	1955	June	Minneapolis
#26	1892		Chicago		#88	1956	May	Los Angeles
#27	1893		Chicago		#89	1957	May	Washington, D.C.
#28	1894		New York		#90	1958	June	Cleveland
#29	1895		St. Louis		#91	1959	June	New Orleans
#30	1896		Nashville, Tenn.		#92	1960	April	San Francisco
#31	1897		Detroit		#93	1961	April	Philadelphia
#32	1898		Washington, D.C.		#94	1962	May	Dallas
#33	1899		Pittsburgh		#95	1963	May	Bal Harbour, Fla.
#34	1900		Washington, D.C.		#96	1964	June	St. Louis
#35	1901		New York		#97	1965	June	Washington, D.C.
#36	1902		Washington, D.C.		#98	1966	July	Denver
#37	1903		Cleveland		#99	1967	May	New York
#38	1904		Washington, D.C.		#100	1968	June	Portland
#39	1905		Washington, D.C.		#101	1969	June	Chicago
#40	1906		Washington, D.C.		#102	1970	June	Boston
#41	1907		Chicago		#103	1971	June	Detroit
#42	1908		Washington, D.C.		#104	1972	May	Houston
#43	1909		Washington, D.C.		#105	1973	May	San Francisco
#44	1910		San Francisco		#106	1974	May	Washington, D.C.
#45	1911		Washington, D.C.		#107	1975	May	Atlanta
#46	1912		Washington, D.C.		#108	1976	May	Philadelphia
#47	1913		New Orleans		#109	1977	June	San Diego
#48	1914		Washington, D.C.		#110	1978	May	Dallas
#49	1915		Washington, D.C.		#111	1979	June	Kansas City
#50	1916		Minneapolis		#112	1980	June	Cincinnati
#51	1918		Philadelphia		#113	1981	May	Minneapolis
#52	1919		Nashville, Tenn.		#114	1982	June	Honolulu
#53	1920		Washington, D.C.		#115	1983	May	New Orleans
#54	1921		Washington, D.C.		#116	1984	May	Phoenix
#55	1922		Chicago		#117	1985	June	San Francisco
#56	1923		Washington, D.C.		#118	1986	June	San Antonio
#57	1924		Washington, D.C.		#119	1987	June	Orlando
#58	1925		New York		#120	1988	May	New York
#59	1926		Washington, D.C.		#121	1989	May	St. Louis
#60	1927		Washington, D.C.		#122	1990	May	Houston
#61	1928		St. Louis		#123	1991	May	Washington, D.C.
#62	1929		Washington, D.C., and New York					

ington, D.C., Chapter to move the Institute headquarters from New York to the nation's capital.

In 1898, the Institute leased the Octagon (Fig. 2), a Washington residence built between 1798 and 1800. Designed by William Thornton, the original architect of the U.S. Capitol, as a residence for John Tayloe III, the Octagon also served as a temporary home for James and Dolley Madison after the White House was burned during the War of 1812. (James Madison signed the Treaty of Ghent at the Octagon in 1815, ending the war.) In this historic building, the American Institute of Architects established its new headquarters. It purchased the house in 1902, and the AIA national headquarters building, completed in 1973, is to the rear of the Octagon.

Historic Preservation

The selection of the Octagon illustrates one AIA priority: historic preservation. In the late nineteenth century, the AIA embarked on its first campaign to save significant historic structures. The preservation effort was conducted at both national and local levels. National activity began officially in 1890, when R. M. Upjohn, son of the Institute's first president and one of the founders of the AIA, proposed a Committee on Conservation of Architecture. His idea was unanimously adopted by the AIA. From 1891 to 1897, the standing committee known as the Committee on Conservation of Public Buildings was primarily concerned with preservation of the New York Treasury Building and New York Customs House.

At the same time, chapters were quite active in preservation campaigns in their own communities. In 1893, the New York Chapter supported preservation of New York City Hall, and the Rhode Island Chapter held a competition for "drawings to preserve a record of the best classical work in this state prior to 1840" (11); in 1894, the Boston Chapter helped save the 1789 Massachusetts State House from demolition, and in 1898, Philadelphia proposed an extensive program to preserve and restore Independence Hall.

Figure 2. The Octagon, Washington, D.C. Courtesy of John Tennant.

Education

Education continued to be another primary concern of AIA members. When the AIA was founded, there were no architecture schools in the United States. Training came from apprenticeships with experienced architects or study abroad. Establishing schools of architecture emerged as one of the AIA's foremost goals.

The Institute created a Committee on Education, one of its first committees, to address this concern. In 1865, less than 10 years after the AIA's formation, the first architecture school in the United States was established at the Massachusetts Institute of Technology by AIA trustee William R. Ware. Ware toured architectural schools in Europe in 1867, and met his first MIT classes in September 1868. By 1879, the program had 30 students.

Meanwhile, James Bellangee began teaching architecture at the University of Illinois in 1870, establishing Illinois's first definitive curriculum in architecture. In 1871, a school of architecture was established at Cornell University by one of the AIA founders, Charles Babcock, and, in 1873, AIA member A. L. Brockway established Syracuse University's School of Architecture. The following year, the University of Pennsylvania set up a school of architecture. In 1876, the University of Michigan began instruction in architecture; Columbia University began in 1881; Columbian (now George Washington University) in 1884; and Armour (now Illinois Institute of Technology) in 1889. By 1898, these nine American architecture schools had a total of 362 students.

The influence of the European model was not limited to the formation of American architecture schools but extended to other types of training as well. Architects who had attended the Ecole des Beaux Arts in Paris opened American ateliers in which students were coached by experienced professionals. AIA member Richard Morris Hunt opened the first such American studio in New York. Ateliers continued to be a popular means of training architects until well into the twentieth century.

Concern on the part of AIA members over education after graduation from school or training prompted two future AIA presidents, Charles F. McKim and Daniel Burnham, to start the American Academy in Rome in 1894. The two men raised $800,000, leased the Villa Aurelia, and offered architects the opportunity to pursue an advanced education, of their own curriculum, in the company of their peers. In 1897, the school was enlarged to include painting, sculpture, and landscape architecture.

As one manifestation of an emerging national demand for action to protect public health and safety, a movement began in the late 1800s to require licensing, or registration, for architects, but no federal law requiring formal registration was passed. The first state registration law was passed in Illinois in 1897, but other states were slow to follow. Indeed, Vermont and Wyoming did not require registration for architects until 1951.

Compensation and Competitions

The noisy copyright fight being waged around the country during the latter half of the nineteenth century echoed a compensation-related question: Once architects' drawings are used, to whom do they ultimately belong? The AIA was nearly unanimous in its response. Members agreed, and were upheld by court decision, that "drawings are the instruments of service and therefore belong to the architect" (12). This concern over offering payment for services, including drawings, was directed toward competitions as well as client services. Architects continued to balk at competitions that were characterized by work without compensation. In the 1870s, the New York Chapter officially registered its opposition to such competitions by refusing to participate in the competition for the design of a new city post office.

Why, then, did the AIA support the Tarsney Act of 1896, which stated that the government would hold competitions for the design of public buildings? The Institute's support of the act was predicated on the Secretary of the Treasury's promise to try to have the act amended to include payment for competitors and, meanwhile, to keep the drawings simple enough to preclude using a winner's entry as a working drawing obtained without payment. The law was also intended to ensure choice of the best architects to design public buildings. Though the act may have clarified the relationship between architects and the government-as-client, opponents' claims that (1) the procedure it prescribed was still too expensive, (2) it did not ensure the best design would be built, and (3) capable government architects were available, led to the bill's repeal within 15 years.

PART TWO: 1900–1957

The American Institute of Architects entered the twentieth century with nearly 1000 members. Its purpose, as reflected in the 1900 Constitution, was "to organize and unite in fellowship the Architects of the United States of America, and to combine their efforts so as to promote the artistic, scientific, and practical efficiency of the profession" (13), almost identical to the 1867 aims.

During subsequent decades, the goals underwent further refinement, until, by the Institute's centennial in 1957, they were (14)

> To organize and unite in fellowship the architects of the United States of America; to combine their efforts so as to promote the aesthetic, scientific and practical efficiency of the profession; to advance the science and art of planning and building by advancing the standards of architectural education, training and practice; to coordinate the building industry and the profession of architecture to insure the advancement of the living standards of our people through their improved environment; and to make the profession of ever-increasing service to society.

Membership and Chapters

As the Institute continued to articulate its purpose and structure, membership categories and requirements grew, and the chapter network expanded. In an atmosphere sympathetic to broadening membership, the Institute decided in 1900 to admit architectural draftsmen if they were over 30 years old; employed by a Fellow for at least five years,

and recommended by that Fellow and two others; and had fulfilled the requirements of associate membership. In 1906, the rules were further liberalized when the five-year-employment requirement was dropped. The vague relationship between chapter membership and national membership also called for definition. In 1911, the AIA passed a Bylaw requiring all national AIA members to belong to a local chapter, or where there was no local chapter, to a "chapter-at-large." These changes provided every member an equal say in AIA policy, since most policy decisions were voted on by convention delegates, selected and sent by the chapters.

In 1916, the chapter-at-large system was abandoned. New chapters were formed so that a chapter existed for every locality. And, by 1917, the AIA ruled that chapters could no longer elect new members of their own. Members of chapters had to be either national AIA members or relegated to associate status within the chapter with the understanding that they would apply for AIA membership within three years. In addition to individual chapters, regions gained clout as they banded together to address regional issues. This trend grew stronger during the early years of the Depression. As people turned to local civic groups for support, it was the AIA's state associations that had the most influence over members. The 1932 convention helped ensure consistency among state organizations when it passed a resolution to allow state associations to pay to become Institute State Association members. The AIA further institutionalized local organizations by setting up a state association in every state that did not already have one in 1935.

By the Institute's centennial, a 1956 Bylaw amendment had set the following criteria for membership (15): U.S. citizenship, proven competency (state registration was considered proof), honorable standing in the profession and the community, and willingness to uphold the Bylaws of the AIA and its standards of conduct. Application for membership had to come through, and include approval by, the chapter.

Member Dues and Institute Finances

During the first half of the twentieth century, the dues structure underwent frequent adjustment as a fair and equitable rate was sought. To put Institute finances on a more even keel, the 1909 convention resolved to keep a balanced budget and to set aside 15% of the initiation fees and annual dues as an emergency fund. Not surprisingly, the Institute finances never kept a steady course. In 1918, the operations deficit of the Institute was $4,831. The convention reported in 1920 that the emergency fund had been tapped three times. (The convention called for and won creation of a less accessible endowment fund.) In 1922, the treasurer reported a $9,000 surplus, only to appear a year later and report that members were $25,000 in arrears.

To give some logic to dues, the Institute in 1924 adopted a procedure developed by the Washington State Chapter: to base dues on a firm's billings. A principal would pay some percentage of the firm's billings as dues; nonprincipals would pay a nominal fee. After only a few years, however, the Institute's finances were rocked along with those of the nation with the stock-market crash and the ensuing Depression. Work was hard to find, and once it was completed, compensation hard to obtain. Membership, which had reached 3000 by 1930, diminished. In 1933, meetings were canceled, the staff was winnowed down, and pay was lowered. By December 31, 1933, 1663 members owed dues totaling $77,948. The Board offered everyone a clean slate for $25 each. Still, by the end of 1934, members were $20,676 in arrears. A final warning was given in 1936 to the 1022 who collectively owed $31,659. Within 45 days, 447 had paid, 195 had set up installment plans, and 359 had let their membership lapse. At that point, membership stood at 2742. By 1935, the financial picture throughout the country began to brighten, chapters provided additional funds to help the national organization, and the books were in the black again.

More adjustments were made to the dues schedule during the years leading up to the AIA's 100th birthday. During World War II, enlisted men and women had their dues remitted. By the end of the War, the Institute had run for several years on a greatly reduced income because of the problems of the 1930s and World War II. Inflation rose as thousands of workers reentered the domestic labor force, and in 1946, dues were raised. By 1950, dues had risen again and membership had topped 9000.

Administration and Staff

Like the country itself, the Institute's growing membership, as well as the developing needs of the members, required a large administration. By 1911, there were standing committees on education, practice, finance, contracts and specifications, allied arts, government architecture, and competitions. All of these reported to the Board, one of whose officers was the secretary. The secretary was a member elected by the membership. Between 1857 and 1913, when power over the day-to-day affairs of the Institute passed from the elected secretary to a professional executive secretary, a great many prominent architects held the position. The last of the elected secretaries was Glenn Brown of Washington, D.C., who held the job from 1898 to 1913.

During that period, the AIA certainly reached its peak of power and influence. The move from New York to Washington, the purchase of the Octagon, the establishment of an AIA magazine, the first award of the AIA Gold Medal, the establishment of the McMillan Commission Plan for

Washington and of the U.S. Commission of Fine Arts, the construction of the Lincoln Memorial, and plans for the establishment of an AIA research collection of art, published works, and architectural records all occurred during Brown's term.

The Institute amended its Bylaws in 1914 to require an executive secretary, predecessor to the executive vice president. The first person to take the job was Charles Harris Whitaker. In 1915, Whitaker was succeeded by Edward Crawford Kemper, who served for 35 years. Table 4 lists the AIA's officeholders.

In 1916, the AIA named its first official Institute historian. In 1925, it established a scientific research department; in 1933, the Institute officially recognized the importance of its public image when it engaged the first AIA publicist. By 1935, the AIA had hired a full-time Washington representative to keep watch on the Capitol. By 1940, the official Institute staff consisted of Kemper, his assistant, his secretary, the treasurer, the historian, the publicist, and the Washington representative. In 1943, the Institute's first membership secretary was named to link in an official way the national organization with the local, state, and regional groups. In 1946, the first director of the department of education and research was appointed.

During World War II, as membership grew and the number of available workers dwindled, the Board took on many administrative duties. It continued to perform these services after the war until 1949, by which time Board responsibilities had expanded so widely that a committee was urged to restructure the administration of the Institute. The Institute dramatically increased the scope of the executive secretary's job and renamed the post "executive director." Edmund R. Purves was appointed the first executive director and put in charge of "all duties and work as shall be set out by the Board [including] detailed executive duties and managerial work for the administrative offices of the Institute" (16). To coordinate committee and staff activities, each committee was assigned a staff executive by the executive director to carry out liaison and planning work. Thus, the Institute staff became executor of the committee's mandates as well as those of the Board. By the AIA's 1957 centennial, the staff comprised some 50 people, including 15 department heads.

Institute Headquarters

The expansion of the duties of the Board, and later the staff, led the Institute to enlarge its headquarters. In 1902,

Table 4. Secretaries/Executive Secretaries/Executive Directors/ Executive Vice Presidents of the AIA

Secretary	Executive Director
Glenn Brown, 1898–1913	Edmund R. Purves, 1949–1966
	William H. Scheick, 1966–1969
Executive Secretary	
Charles Harris Whitaker, 1914–1915	**Executive Vice President**
Edward Crawford Kemper, 1915–1949	William L. Slayton, 1970–1977
	David O. Meeker, Jr., 1978–1983
	Louis L. Marines, 1984–

the AIA decided to buy the Octagon building it was leasing and to embark on a costly compaign of repairs and improvements. By 1912, the AIA realized that it would eventually be necessary to build additional office space to meet the needs of the growing staff, but for 28 years, the Institute debated design and requirements. Successive conventions discussed the need for an exhibition hall, an assembly hall, headquarters offices, and a library. During the years, Glenn Brown, Ernest Flagg, Henry Bacon, and McKim, Mead, and White, among others, provided designs for buildings never built. Finally, in 1940, a collaborative team of three member architects, Dan Everett Waid, Dwight James Baum, and Otto Eggers, was chosen to design the new space, built on AIA property adjacent to the Octagon site. Waid, who contributed over $300,000 to the AIA during his lifetime, paid for four-fifths of the new addition. After letting the government use the new addition for nine years during and after World War II, the AIA moved into its addition in 1950. At that time, it also built a permanent library and repaired the courtyard wall and garden.

Publications

As the real estate industry boomed in the early 1900s, building types, systems, and materials were becoming more complex, and architects were increasingly in need of contract guidance. In 1901, the AIA heeded members' requests for additional standard documents. It established the Committee on Contracts and Lien Laws. The next year, the AIA retained outside legal counsel to help the committee draw up its documents. And in 1907, the committee, by that time called the Committee on Contracts and Specifications, began developing an entire family of standard contract documents for architects.

The AIA published its first edition of standard documents in 1911 (17). It comprised general conditions of the contract for construction, a standard form of proposal, an invitation to bid, instructions to bidders, a standard form of agreement, and a standard form of bond. The effects were twofold: architects maintained a prominent position on the design/construction team and the AIA greatly increased its income by sales of standard documents to the entire construction industry.

The second edition (18), including the newly created standard form of subcontract and letter of acceptance, came out in 1915, drafted by a joint committee made up from the AIA's document committee, the National Association of Builders' Exchanges, and attorneys. In 1916, the committee issued the first standard form for an owner–architect agreement. The third edition (19) of standard documents came out in 1918, a fourth (20) in 1925, and a fifth (21) in 1937.

The Institute also published various books, reports, committee minutes, and transcripts of convention activities. The most noteworthy of these was the *Handbook of Architectural Practice* (22), published in limited edition in 1917 and first published in full in 1920. In 1900, the Institute had launched its first periodical, *The American Institute of Architects Quarterly Bulletin.* The Bulletin contained architectural bibliographies, chapter news, membership-election results, revisions of Bylaws, and illustra-

tions. The final Bulletin was published in October 1912, at which point a slick monthly magazine called the *Journal* (the *Journal of the American Institute of Architects*) began (23). For the first three years, the *Journal* was sent only to members who subscribed, but by 1920 the convention asked that all members receive the *Journal,* and that funds be taken from annual dues to cover the subscription.

The Institute also decided to set up a separate corporation to publish the magazine, and in 1920, the Press of the American Institute of Architects was formed, based in New York City. Bonds were sold to finance the enterprise. A structural services department was added to the editorial side of the magazine. Well-known artists who worked with architectural subjects were commissioned to do work for the *Journal,* including J. J. Lankes, Edwin Howland Blashfield, and Henry Winslow.

One ambitious undertaking of the Press was to have been *The Octagon Library of Early American Architecture,* conceived as a multivolume illustrated history of American architecture. Volume One, *Charleston, South Carolina,* was published in 1927 (24). The work contained maps, photographs, drawings, and text. Volume Two was to have been about New Orleans, but the Press was dissolved before the volume was printed. Two architectural monographs and two works of architectural photography, all part of the series, were published. These works are valuable historical documents not only on architecture, but on the art of photography and printing as well. They also include Louis Sullivan's two books, *The Autobiography of an Idea* (25) and *A System of Architectural Ornament According With a Philosophy of Man's Powers* (26). Both have become standard works, seldom out of print since the AIA first published them in the mid-1920s.

Despite its undoubted service to the profession, the AIA Press still ran a deficit. In 1926, the convention resolved to drastically limit the size and content of the *Journal.* Advertising was eliminated, the cost of *Journal* operation was limited to the amount allocated from dues, the *Journal* operation was moved from New York City to the Octagon, and the Press was put up for sale.

In December 1928, with the deficit problem still unresolved, the AIA discontinued publication of the *Journal* and started a more modest monthly bulletin called *The Octagon* (27). It carried formal notices of meetings, transactions, Bylaws changes, convention actions, member and officer elections, and occasional letters and articles from members. The publication was a successful vehicle of Institute news for 15 years. In the 1940s, there was renewed interest in publishing a newsstand-quality monthly magazine, and in 1944, a new *Journal of the American Institute of Architects* (28) replaced *The Octagon.* In 1948, the Board also launched the *Bulletin of the American Institute of Architects* (29) to carry official announcements of the Institute, plus reports of factual and technical information that the AIA's committees had gathered, such as had been contained in *The Octagon.* The *Memo* (30), a biweekly news organ for all members, was established in 1950 for getting fast-breaking news to the members quickly.

In 1954, the Committee on Organization proposed combining the *Journal* and the *Bulletin* to attract more ads and to incorporate into one publication news of the current works of members; results of research; excerpts of committee meetings and panel discussions; reference list guides; information on specifications, standards, codes, and zoning; and other technical material. The first issue of the newly restructured *Journal* (28) was printed in May 1957, 100 years after the AIA's founding.

Annual Conventions

The AIA has always maintained the founders' commitment to annual meetings. It is at these conventions that changes in the ruling structure, ideals, and leadership of the AIA are proposed, debated, voted on, and enacted.

The AIA's 1900 convention in Washington, D.C., was planned to celebrate the centennial of the federal capital's move to its permanent home on the Potomac in 1800 and to encourage the District to create a responsible planning group to oversee future development of the city. At that time, Washington was plagued by haphazard and disjointed development. There was no comprehensive plan for government expansion and development of parks in accordance with the original L'Enfant Plan of the eighteenth century.

The convention resolved "that a committee of five be appointed to formulate a resolution to be presented to Congress looking to the appointment of a Commission for the consideration and recommendation of a general plan for the improvement of the National Capitol" (31). The lobbying worked: Senator James McMillan (R-Mich.) met with officers of the Institute. The papers read at the convention in support of such a planning commission were reprinted as a Senate document. The convention, the papers, and a subsequent meeting led directly to the creation of the historic Senate Park or McMillan Commission, which developed a park plan for the District of Columbia that restored the openness of the Mall and established orderly development of the Federal Triangle, Ellipse, and Lafayette Square areas near the White House, and of areas along Rock Creek and the C&O Canal.

Conventions were enjoyed as much for their pageantry and display of award winners as for their policy-making role. A favorite event at conventions after 1907 was presentation of the AIA Gold Medal (Fig. 3). In 1923, a grand convention pageant at the Lincoln Memorial in Washington, D.C., honored Henry Bacon, architect of the memorial. President Warren G. Harding and Chief Justice William Howard Taft presented Bacon with his medal (Fig. 4).

Convention activities suffered a serious setback with the Depression. By 1933, there was no money for travel or for the convention itself. Regions were instructed to elect new regional directors and have the incumbents resign. National officers were asked to continue service until the following year's convention.

World War II affected the life of the Institute just as it did the nation. In 1944, there was no convention, and in 1945, the war prompted the government to limit the size of all meetings and conventions. Only 50 delegates were allowed at the 1945 AIA convention, held in Atlantic City, N.J.: the 15 members of the Board of Directors as delegates at large and 35 delegates sent by chapters and

Figure 3. The American Institute of Architects Gold Medal; design by Adolph A. Weinman. Courtesy of The American Institute of Architects Archives.

states. This number amounted to one delegate for every 160 members. By 1954, however, the convention had resumed its prewar size and importance.

Honors and Awards

Since the first days of the AIA, the title of "Fellow" has carried with it varying degrees of honor and respect. The minutes for the October 22, 1867, meeting show that H. H. Richardson was advanced to Fellowship on that day, perhaps the first official Fellow of the AIA. Although Fellowship was originally a natural progression from associate membership, at the end of the nineteenth century it became a special honor to which only a small number of members have been elevated.

As of 1898, the Board was permitted to nominate no more than 20 associates each year for Fellowship, to be voted on by convention delegates. In 1922, the president of the AIA appointed a jury to recommend candidates for Fellowship. This jury consisted of six Fellows, from across the United States, serving six staggered terms. At first, the jury merely made its recommendations to the Board, which had the final say. By 1935, however, the jury had been given sole authority for selection of candidates and election of Fellows.

By 1957, several award programs had been established by the Institute to reward, recognize, and encourage architects and architectural achievements. The highest honor was—and still is—the Gold Medal, first awarded in 1907. The initial recipient was Sir Aston Webb, a British architect best known for his design of much of Buckingham Palace. Then and now, the Gold Medal recognizes outstanding contributions to the profession and tradition of

Figure 4. 1923 Gold Medal (awarded to Henry Bacon) pageant at the Reflecting Pool, Lincoln Memorial, Washington, D.C. Courtesy of The American Institute of Architects Archives.

architecture by a single architect. The list of winners over the years includes most of the best known twentieth-century architects, including Henry Bacon, Jean Louis Pascal, Louis Henry Sullivan, Frank Lloyd Wright, and I. M. Pei. A complete list of the recipients appears in Table 5. A complete summary of the honors and awards program is given in Part Three.

Education

Throughout its history, the Institute has been as concerned with proper education and training for future peers as it has been with recognizing excellence within the profession. AIA members had been instrumental in starting the first nine schools of architecture in the country. By 1912, 36 schools offered architecture courses; by 1956, this number had nearly doubled to 66, of which 51 were accredited.

The number of students grew quickly as well. In 1911 there were 1450 students enrolled in U.S. architecture schools; by 1930, there were 4622, and by 1950 there were more than 11,500.

In addition to forming schools, the AIA also suggested curricula. Early in the twentieth century, the Committee on Education proposed a course of study steeped in the arts and humanities as well as in technical training. These proposals were to change drastically as the requirements for architects became more technologically complex. In 1915, the Association of Collegiate Schools of Architecture (ACSA) was founded to establish and monitor educational standards for architecture schools in the United States. The AIA in turn created a School Medal, to be conferred annually on an exceptional student, upon the recommendations of the deans. By 1920, the AIA began campaigning for a five-year course of study. The National Architectural

Table 5. Gold Medalists (The Gold Medal is the highest honor that the American Institute of Architects can bestow. It is awarded by the Board of Directors in recognition of most distinguished service to the architectural profession or to the AIA.)

Sir Aston Webb	1907	Louis Skidmore	1957
Charles Follen McKim	1909	John Wellborn Root II	1958
George Browne Post	1911	Walter Gropius	1959
Jean Louis Pascal	1914	Ludwig Mies van der Rohe	1960
Victor Laloux	1922	Le Corbusier	1961
Henry Bacon	1923	Eero Saarinen	1962
Sir Edwin Landseer Lutyens	1925	Alvar Aalto	1963
Bertram Grosvenor Goodhue	1925	Pier Luigi Nervi	1964
Howard Van Doren Shaw	1927	Kenzo Tange	1966
Milton Bennett Medary	1929	Wallace K. Harrison	1967
Ragnar Östberg	1933	Marcel Breuer	1968
Paul Philippe Cret	1938	William Wilson Wurster	1969
Louis Henry Sullivan	1944	Richard Buckminster Fuller	1970
Eliel Saarinen	1947	Louis I. Kahn	1971
Charles Donagh Maginnis	1948	Pietro Belluschi	1972
Frank Lloyd Wright	1949	Richard Joseph Neutra	1977
Sir Patrick Abercrombie	1950	Philip Cortelyou Johnson	1978
Bernard Ralph Maybeck	1951	I. M. Pei	1979
Auguste Perret	1952	Josep Lluis Sert	1981
William Adams Delano	1953	Romaldo Giurgola	1982
Willem Marinus Dudok	1955	Nathaniel Alexander Owings	1983
Clarence S. Stein	1956	William W. Caudill	1985
Ralph Walker		Arthur C. Erickson	1986
Centennial Medal of Honor, 1957			

Accrediting Board (NAAB) adopted that recommendation in 1950. The Board itself had been formed 10 years earlier through collaboration of the AIA, the National Council of Architectural Registration Boards (NCARB), and the ACSA. This board makes regular visits to accredited schools to make sure they continue meeting the established requirements and to schools seeking accreditation.

Early in the twentieth century, no such accreditation existed, no state laws required registration of architects, and many practicing architects had no formal education. The AIA addressed this problem first at home, by suggesting a test for prospective members to check their qualifications and evaluate their education. By 1897, a diploma from certain schools permitted AIA membership. The first state registration law was passed in Illinois in 1897, and in 1919 the AIA drafted a model state law on registration, by which time the influence of state and local AIA chapters had already led several states to adopt or consider their own drafts. Since legislation developed on a state-by-state basis, uniformity and unanimity were difficult to achieve.

As a natural evolution of the successful atelier training method in Europe, the Institute established a mentor system in 1934 whereby, upon graduation, students could be assigned to practitioners, not necessarily their own employers, who would advise the students on their progress at work and help them understand the larger implications and applications of architecture. The first trial of this system, however, lacked the support necessary to make it effective. The war precluded a swift remedy, and it was not until 1950 that the AIA established a program for architects-in-training.

At the same time, the AIA's Committee on Education and its department of education and research undertook a major comprehensive survey of the profession and the training of its members. Entitled *The Architect at Mid-Century* (32), the survey examined the function and place of the architect in the 1950s, the nature of architectural practice, the principal aptitudes and skills necessary to practice architecture, the problems of registration, and the training period between graduation and the licensing exam. The first volume of the survey ran more than 500 pages and included tables with data on school enrollment, accreditation, and value as perceived by graduates. The survey resulted in 42 major recommendations, many of which were adopted by the AIA as well as the ACSA, NCARB, and the NAAB.

The AIA shouldered an expanded commitment to educating the public when it used $10,000 bequeathed by member Albert Kahn to start the AIA Foundation. Founded in 1942, the Foundation was established as a nonprofit, charitable corporation dedicated to educating architects and the public on the subject of architecture and the related arts. Such education was, and still is, achieved through scholarships, exhibitions, lectures, preservation, publications, and research.

Historic Preservation

Historic preservation has continued to be an AIA priority, although over the years its focus of concern has shifted. In the early part of this century, the AIA's approach to preservation paralleled that of President Theodore Roosevelt, involving conservation of natural resources more than building or area preservation. In 1908, Roosevelt invited the AIA to participate in the U.S. President's Conference on Conservation of Natural Resources. The Institute's

Committee on the Conservation of Natural Resources addressed Roosevelt's agenda and researched conservation and preservation issues. The findings of the President's conference, supported by an AIA proposal originating in the committee, led to the passage of the National Parks Service Bill in 1916.

Preservation efforts during this period were largely led by local chapters. The Philadelphia Chapter's preservation committee was appointed by the city's mayor to restore Congress Hall; the New York City Chapter kept a new courthouse from overshadowing the historic City Hall; and the Louisiana Chapter saved the 1792 Cathedral of St. Louis.

In 1914, the AIA national Preservation Committee broadened its scope and became the Committee on Conservation of Natural Resources and Historic Monuments. The new chairman, William Ellicott, was involved in planning Washington, D.C.'s national park and is credited with founding the national Capital Planning Commission. After World War I, the committee's name was changed again to the Committee on Preservation of Historic Monuments and Scenic Beauties, auguring society's renewed emphasis on preserving historic architecture. Under chairman Horace W. Sellars in 1917, the committee began its call for greater documentation of historic structures to aid preservation and restoration. Over the next 10 years, Sellars pushed for a nationwide survey, which would provide detailed measurements, drawings, and photographs of significant historic buildings, as a preservation tool.

The chapters continued their work as well. Chicago began its efforts to restore the 1893 Fine Arts Building; New York attempted to save the Harlem River High Bridge; New Orleans assisted in rehabilitation of the Canal Street Plaza; Boston helped restore Faneuil Hall; Virginia appealed for and received help from AIA headquarters to restore Monticello; Pittsburgh fought for preservation of H. H. Richardson's Allegheny County Jail; Central Illinois conducted a survey of early architecture; Tennessee assisted in preserving and restoring Andrew Jackson's home; and the South Carolina Chapter joined Charleston, S.C., citizens in saving old houses.

As architecture schools gained prominence and respect, students and chapters often worked together on projects of recording and surveying. One committee member, impatient with the government's reluctance to sponsor a national survey, embarked on his own photographic survey. In 1930, Leicester B. Holland received a $5000 grant from the Carnegie Foundation to found a national Pictorial Archives of Early American Architecture.

However, the final impetus for government-backed historic surveys came from the Philadelphia Chapter, which in 1931 conducted its own survey of Colonial buildings in the city. The survey was conducted as much to give work to unemployed draftsmen as to record historic architecture. The idea caught on. Not only could such a survey document this country's rich history of early architecture but it could help relieve the massive unemployment of the Depression. (In New York City alone, there were more than 2500 unemployed architects in late 1932). In 1933, the Historic American Buildings Survey (HABS) began to photograph and catalogue significant architectural structures. The idea was so popular that the AIA signed a pact with the National Park Service and the Library of Congress pledging to make the survey permanent.

Convention resolutions adopted between 1935 and 1940 opposed any material alteration of the central portion of the U.S. Capitol, a fight the AIA waged for many years. The AIA lost on the East Front, which was extended, but eventually won on the West Front, which was restored.

Compensation and Ethics

In the twentieth century, the AIA's concern over compensation, like that of professionals across the country, led to questions about fees as well as ethics. Two practices affecting fees attracted the Institute's attention. One involved architects banding together to win contracts. At first, the Board frowned upon this procedure, then modified the censure to require simply that the Committee on Practice review the arrangement. In the mid-1920s, the controversy was largely eliminated when state governments started requiring that one individual (registered) architect sign the drawings and accept legal responsibility for them.

The AIA also began to consider the use of a code of ethics among its members to deal with allegations of professional misconduct. In 1909, the AIA established a *Circular of Advice Relative to Principles of Professional Practice and Canons of Ethics* (33). These principles stated that it is improper to (1) engage in building; (2) guarantee an estimate; (3) accept payment from anyone other than a client; (4) pay to advertise; (5) take part in a competition not approved by the AIA; (6) try to obtain work through means other than competition for a job that is being awarded by a competition; (7) attempt to influence the awarding of a competition; (8) accept an award for work for which a competition was held and for which one was an adviser or preparer of the program; (9) injure falsely or maliciously a fellow practitioners' reputation; (10) undertake work in which there is an unsettled claim; or (11) compete on the basis of charges.

In 1912, minor revisions were made. In 1918, the advertising prohibition was modified, and in 1919, the Institute approved publicizing standards, aims, and progress of the profession but not of particular architects. Architects' complaints about the ethics of competitions were largely quieted in the early 1920s, when competitions began to be held for the purpose of choosing an architect, not a specific design.

The advent of national advertising caused the AIA to examine another issue of professional conduct: advertising by architects. The use of architects' portraits in advertising materials or building services was deplored. However, in 1955, the AIA sanctioned the use of a portrait, if in the context of the advertisement the portrait could not be construed as an endorsement of a particular product and if its use was approved by the Committee on Public Relations. In 1956, the Institute again ruled out use of portraits altogether, except under special circumstances approved by the Board of Directors.

On the Eve of the Centennial

As the AIA approached its 100th birthday, it was a healthy professional organization of 11,000 members. Throughout those first 100 years, the AIA's development, activities, and structure at times followed social trends, and at other times set them. Along the way, the AIA reaffirmed its responsibility to society, a commitment evident in the AIA's strong support for historic preservation, professional conduct, ethics, proper education, standard documents, and quality design for public, as well as private, architecture.

PART THREE: 1957–1986

The AIA's 100th anniversary was marked by ambitious celebration plans, optimism for the profession, and a convention that drew 4300 people to Washington, D.C., the largest convention up to that time. In his opening address (34), President Leon Chatelain, Jr., summed up the contrast between the Institute's founding and its health 100 years later. "The mood of the founders of the Institute," he said, "was one of solemn determination to create a profession out of an ill-defined craft." In 1957, by contrast,

> The architectural profession has never been in a more secure position. You and your predecessors have achieved much: For one thing, a truly American architecture has been created; for another, the evolution of your practice has been nothing short of amazing. Today you are equipped with knowledge, skill, availability of materials and access to a vast storehouse of technology to keep not just abreast, but ahead of the needs of your clients. And you have superimposed on all of this a creativity that is the marvel of our age.

Public events focused print, radio, and television attention on the centennial and the contributions of architects to society. The Postal Service issued a 3¢ AIA Centennial Stamp, the design of which was chosen by an AIA competition committee. Fellow Henry H. Saylor, editor of the AIA Journal from 1944 to 1956, wrote a history of the AIA's first 100 years, which was published in the May 1957 issue (3). "100 Years of American Architecture," an exhibition of 75 American buildings illustrating American architecture at its best, was shown at the National Gallery of Art, and an exhibition catalogue was produced (35).

In addition to awarding the Gold Medal that year to Louis Skidmore, the Board of Directors also gave a "Centennial Medal of Honor" to honor the architect of the century, defined as an individual noted for architectural design and service to the Institute. It was given to New York City architect Ralph Walker, former Institute director and president. Walker is generally credited with devising the Manhattan art deco style through such distinguished skyscrapers as the Barclay Vesey and the Irving Trust Company buildings. Forty-eight members were advanced to Fellowship during the centennial convention, the largest group up to that time.

Governing Structure

Following the centennial, the Institute continued to respond to the issues facing its members by creating new programs and an organizational structure that allowed staff to manage them most effectively. The Institute today remains governed by Bylaws, which, depending on the nature of the Bylaw, may be amended by the Board or by the membership according to specified procedures. The Institute's 19 regions are proportionately represented on the Board by 32 elected regional directors. Each region is made up of one or more states; the number of directors from each region is determined by membership figures. The Board also includes eight officers (president, first vice president, three vice presidents, secretary, treasurer, and the executive vice president as an *ex officio* member), a public member elected by the Board, the president of the American Institute of Architecture Students (*ex officio*), and the chair of the Council of Architectural Component Executives (who serves *ex officio* and without vote) for a total as of this writing (1987) of 43 members. (See below for an explanation of CACE.)

Directors of regions are elected by a regional convocation of delegates representing the members of each chapter within the region or by vote of the members of the region. Regional directors serve for staggered three-year terms so that each year one-third of the directors retires. The public director serves for two years; the student representative and CACE chair serve for one year each. National officers are elected by delegates at the annual convention of the Institute. Each officer's term is one year except those of the treasurer and secretary, who serve for two years.

The Institute's programs and activities are carried out by commissions and committees. Established in 1963, commissions oversee the activities of the committees under their jurisdiction (the Design Commission, for example, has jurisdiction over committees on design, education, and housing), provide coordination among committees and commissions, and maintain liaisons between the Board and committees. Previous commissions on professional society, education, professional practice, architectural design, the public, communications, and government affairs have been reorganized into three commissions: design, membership services, and practice. Commissions are composed of Board members assigned by the incoming president, and each is chaired by an Institute vice president, assigned by the president.

The committees carry out specific responsibilities assigned to them by the Board, which often include holding conferences and publishing proceedings. Most committees report to the Board through the commissions. (A few committees concerned primarily with AIA internal affairs, such as the Finance Committee and the Media Advisory Committee, report directly to the Board through the Executive Committee. These are called Committees of the Board.) The Board decides which committees are open and which are limited. Generally, limited committees are charged with short-term or specific projects that require a high level of expertise, and open committees pursue more general policy issues of interest to the overall membership. Open committees are, as the name implies, open to all members who meet attendance and participation requirements.

In 1977, the Board approved the concept of "corresponding committee membership," which allows members to receive the proceedings and other mailings that are sent to open committee members. Corresponding members are encouraged to attend committee meetings but are not required to do so. Approximately 600 corresponding members joined in 1978; by 1986, their ranks had more than quadrupled to 2500.

Corporate Structure

For efficiency, tax, and endowment reasons, management was reorganized in 1981 into three corporations responsible for the programmatic, profitmaking, and educational activities of the Institute. The American Institute of Architects Corporation (AIA) continued the professional programs and activities for the membership. The profit-making AIA Service Corporation (AIA/SC) merged the existing Service Corporation (established in 1970) with the Production Systems for Architects and Engineers (established in 1969). As the nonprofit educational arm of the Institute, the AIA Foundation was formed through the merger of the existing Foundation and the AIA Research Corporation. The AIA/SC and the AIA merged in 1986 to take advantage of changes in federal tax law, so the Institute now consists of the AIA and the AIA Foundation.

Membership and Chapters

AIA membership climbed steadily from 13,878 corporate members (later changed to "members" and henceforth referred to as "regular members") and emeritus members in 1960 to 22,710 regular and emeritus members in 1970. In 1973, the national associate membership category was started for interns (architects not yet registered) and individuals employed in a professional capacity under a licensed architect. In 1980, associate members accounted for 5075 of the Institute's membership; regular and emeritus members numbered 30,666. By 1986, the Institute's membership rolls topped 50,000, with 42,186 regular and emeritus members and 8350 associate members, an increase of more than 100% in the past 25 years.

Prospective applicants apply for membership through the local chapter. The completed application form must contain the names of two sponsors who are AIA members as well as proof of registration (for regular or emeritus members). The component's membership committee reviews the applications and forwards a recommendation for admission or rejection to the AIA for final determination.

The Institute's structural system of state organizations, chapters, and sections (generally called "components") encourages an expanded, local AIA presence. It is at these levels that most members have the most extended contact with the Institute. Through the components, members can participate in and take advantage of many of the same types of programs offered at the national level, such as meetings, professional-development seminars, honors programs, exhibits, conventions, document sales, and bookstores. Since a major concern of AIA members has been a lack of public understanding and appreciation of what architects do, a component's public awareness activities are an important way of increasing the presence of architects in local communities.

The Bulletin component newsletter and other regular communications from the Institute keep its 168 unstaffed components, 125 staffed components, and their elected officers informed about the Institute's programs and services. In 1969, the Institute established the Council of Architectural Component Executives (CACE), which in 1986 was composed of the executive directors of the 125 staffed chapters, to strengthen components by encouraging the exchange of information and expertise. The annual Grassroots program, begun in 1966 as a series of forums in Washington, D.C., St. Louis, and San Francisco, provides component staff and officers with leadership and management training and opportunities for fellowship. At Grassroots, held early in the year in Washington, D.C., attendees are briefed on Institute issues and policies; participate in workshops on membership, government affairs, public relations, and other issues affecting components; lobby their Congressional representatives; and hear talks by Institute officers, legislators, and other experts. The Institute helps defray travel expenses of all component officers.

Chapters and sections are formed upon petition to the Board secretary. The Board acts on petitions after notification and consultation with the component from which the proposed chapter or section is to be formed, other affected chapters, the Membership Services Commission, and the Secretary's Advisory Committee. A component's bylaws—rules of internal organization and governance—determine a component's formal organization. Most components model their oganizational structure after the Institute's. Each component is required by the Institute to have bylaws that represent an agreement among a component's members on how the component will operate. Bylaws typically include provisions relating to organization, membership, meetings, elections, governing bodies, dues, finances, and affiliations. The Institute also requires chapters to meet certain minimum standards of service to members in the areas of architectural knowledge, communication, education, organization, and public policy.

Dues

Originally intended to be temporary, the supplemental dues that an AIA-member firm pays now play an integral role in the Institute's finances and are based on the total number of registered architects employed by the firm, including employers. Currently, supplemental dues provide for a credit for each registered architect in the firm who is an AIA member; this credit is intended to reward firms that hire AIA members or encourage employees to become members. Emeritus members and associate members are not included in the calculation of supplemental dues. Dues were reduced in response to the economic downturn of the 1970s, but since then dues at the national level have risen. Because the AIA is a three-tiered organization, members are assigned to state and local chapters and are therefore liable for state and local chapter dues, which are determined by those organizations. A member of the Chicago chapter, for instance, will pay national dues, Illinois Council dues, and Chicago Chapter dues. Members in some states (such as Connecticut, which does not have local chapters) or the District of Columbia (which does not have a state chapter) pay only one set of dues in addition to national dues. There are no regional dues.

Institute Headquarters

Construction of a new national headquarters complex was considered at the 1961 convention. In 1962, the headquarters building underwent interior remodeling and some refurnishing. In 1964, a national two-stage competition for the design of a new building was held. The following year, the Philadelphia architecture firm Mitchell/Giurgola Associates was selected to design the new building. Chosen from seven finalists in a national competition that drew 221 submissions, the winning design envisioned a five-story, red-brick structure with a semicircular glazed wall. The estimated cost for 50,000 ft^2 of usable floor space was $1,450,000, with an additional $30,000 allocated for sculpture and other fine arts.

In 1967, the Institute purchased property adjacent to its headquarters, which necessitated a restudying of the initial design and a change in the building program. The project suffered a setback in September 1967, when the U.S. Commission of Fine Arts, charged with ensuring architectural harmony in the nation's capital, failed to approve the competition-winning design presented at the 1967 convention because of objections to the building's size, mass, and relation to the historic Octagon House. The architects proceeded with a new design that was given a preliminary review by the Commission in February 1968. Later that year, Mitchell/Giurgola resigned as headquarters architects.

To keep the headquarters project alive, the Committee on Institute Headquarters developed guidelines early in 1969 for the selection of architects, and architects were invited for interviews. Later that year, Norman Fletcher and John C. Harkness of The Architects Collaborative in Cambridge, Mass., were hired as architects for the new building. In 1970, the U.S. Commission of Fine Arts approved their design. The approved design was a 130,000-ft^2 seven-story structure, with two basement levels and a parking garage extending 15 ft under the Octagon garden. Basic construction costs were estimated at $6.2 million, with supplementary costs (including professional fees, contingency funds, taxes, and interest), bringing the total to $7.9 million.

At the close of 1970, the Institute's staff moved to 1785 Massachusetts Avenue, N.W., for a two-year stay. The 1957 headquarters building and adjacent buildings were demolished and a contract was let to the Volpe Construction Company for construction. The new building was dedicated in 1973 (Fig. 5).

Octagon Restoration

Minor renovations of the Octagon had been made since the Institute purchased the building in 1902. A major structural restoration, including replacement of the second-story floor and strengthening of the staircase, took place between 1949 and 1956. In 1966, the Institute began a campaign to raise $950,000 (plus $43,500 for expenses) for the AIA/F to buy and restore the Octagon to its ca

1828 condition. In a little over a year, $1,000,428 had been pledged, and in 1968 the AIA Foundation purchased the Octagon from the AIA for $1 million.

J. Everette Fauber, Jr., was the architect for the 1968–1970 Octagon restoration, which included architectural research into some original construction documents, reconstruction of two second-floor rooms, the replacement of some of the third-floor floorboards, a more accurate reproduction of the original fanlight over the front door, and a new cypress shingle roof. In 1984, the AIA Foundation began a program to restore the Octagon's interior and exterior "finishes" (as opposed to its structure): paint, wallpaper, woodwork, interior detailing, and furniture. Restoration of the entrance hall and refurbishing of the exhibition galleries have already been completed. Designated as a National Historic Landmark in 1961, the Octagon began an exhibits program in 1970 and was accredited by the American Association of Museums in 1973.

Documents

For more than 100 years, the Institute's documents have been standards in the industry and enjoy industrywide acceptance. Because they establish the contractual duty of the architect, they play an important role in defining liability and accountability. Until the 1950s, architects were rarely involved in court cases because of legal concepts that limited their liability. However, when these concepts were modified by the courts between the late 1940s and mid-1950s, architects increasingly found themselves being sued by owners, contractors, and such parties as contractors' employees injured on construction sites.

In the landmark case of Day vs National-U.S. Radiator Corporation, tried in 1958, a Louisiana architecture firm was sued for the accidental death of a subcontractor's employee. Two lower courts found the architects negligent in supervising the job on which the employee was killed, although the Louisiana Supreme Court later overturned the ruling. In response, the AIA reworded certain passages in the 1961 and 1963 editions of its General Conditions and Owner–Contractor and Owner–Architect Agreements. The new language in these documents described the architect's role in the construction process as that of the owner's representative, responsible for observing the progress of the work. This was a significant change, for the old language had stated that the architect was responsible for supervision and inspection of the work. In addition, interpretation of the word supervision by past court decisions had broadened its meaning and implied a degree of authority beyond any definition ever intended by users of AIA contracts. The new language clarified the role that architects had customarily been practicing.

By 1986, AIA documents numbered more than 80 and covered all key industry agreements. New editions of most standard documents are published on a rotating basis.

Publications

Since its inception in 1912, the *AIA Journal* has grown from a respected house organ to a major professional magazine with a circulation of about 61,000. By the 1960s,

Figure 5. The American Institute of Architects headquarters, Washington, D.C.; architects: The Architects Collaborative. Courtesy of Gordon H. Schenck, Jr.

advertising fully supported the *AIA Journal,* and in 1964, a publisher was hired to manage its operations. In the early 1970s, the magazine was redesigned and new editorial and publishing leadership enlisted. In 1983, it was renamed *Architecture* to signal its expanding editorial role as a voice for the profession. Also that year, the Institute first published *Architectural Technology* as a quarterly (and later bimonthly) periodical for research, technical, practice, and design information. Its 1986 merger with *Architecture* now provides practice and design information in one publication.

The first edition of the *Building Products Register* was published in 1961 (36). It included 1300 product listings and helped architectural specifiers research building materials. Production Systems for Architects and Engineers, Inc. (no longer in existence) was established in 1969 to promote the development of practice aids for architects. In 1970, the first sections of its master construction specification guide, *MASTERSPEC* (37), were published. Updated quarterly, *MASTERSPEC* is available in printed and computerized form. *MASTERGUIDE* (38), first published in 1985, is a comprehensive reference source providing access to information about building product manufacturers and suppliers. It is published annually in five regional editions. The AIA also edits and updates architectural reference materials such as *Architectural Graphic Standards* (39),

and *The Architect's Handbook of Professional Practice* (40), and produces a range of publications for internal use, members, clients, and the public.

Another source of information to members and the public, the AIA information center, contains more than 20,000 books, 450 periodicals, and vertical files of ephemeral material on architects, architecture, and related subjects such as historic preservation, interior design, landscape architecture, and urban planning. Its rare book collection contains items from a number of architects' libraries and from the nineteenth-century library of the AIA. In addition, its audiovisual collection of slides and films contains a large section on contemporary buildings. Also a part of the information center, the AIA Archives is the largest existing U.S. collection of data on the profession of architecture. Among its holdings are the minutes of the AIA Board from its first meeting in 1857 to the present, the proceedings of all AIA conventions, and publications and papers of AIA officers and committees. Files on more than 100,000 individual architects and more than 100,000 photographs of architects, architectural activities, and architectural subjects are also in the archives collection.

The AIA Foundation's Prints and Drawings Collection contains the historic records of Richard Morris Hunt and includes 12,000 of his original architectural drawings and 13,000 collected European and American photographs of

Hunt and Hunt projects, most of them from the nineteenth century.

Annual Conventions

The annual AIA convention continues to serve as the Institute's primary business meeting while providing members with important opportunities for learning and fellowship. The location and scheduling of conventions are determined by the Board, and their themes, financing, and general arrangements approved by the Convention Committee with the assistance of the host chapter committee. Income is derived from registrations, exhibit space, and fees for professional-development seminars and special breakfasts and dinners. The convention's annual business meeting includes annual reports of the Board and the Treasurer, the nomination and election of officers, accreditation of delegates, Bylaw changes, and consideration of proposed resolutions. Other convention activities center on theme programs, professional-development sessions, tours, and special events such as the presentation of honors and awards. There is also a major exhibit of new products and technology featuring a cross section of products and services for the architectural profession.

Honors and Awards

Over the years, the Institute's honors and awards program has encouraged outstanding architecture and contributions to the profession by architects, clients, the public, and individuals in related disciplines. Depending on the honor or award, nominations may be made by registered architects, AIA members, chapters, committees, or Board members. Selection is made by jury or the Board, again depending on the honor or award. The following discussion summarizes the Institute's awards programs.

Fellowship. Advancement to the College of Fellows remains the highest honor the AIA can bestow on any member with the exception of the Gold Medal, which may be presented to an AIA member or architect of another nation. Fellowship is conferred on members of 10 years' good standing who have made significant contributions to the advancement of the profession. Upon election, Fellows automatically become members of the College of Fellows.

In response to Board concern in the late 1950s about the exact purpose of the College, Chancellor of the College Roy Larson and its officers explained that "its pursuits should, without apology, be on the intellectual level and its real purpose, the promotion of excellence in architecture and the creative arts." Among the activities they felt were in keeping with its purpose were encouraging informal group discussions, commissioning articles and essays by scholars on architecture, planning, and related arts, establishing close ties with foreign architects, and contributing to the field of architectural education. The College of Fellows Fund was launched in 1963 to sponsor such projects. By 1970, the Fund had reached its goal of $100,000, and College sponsorship of activities began in earnest. The first project was a grant to George McCue, one of the first architectural critics in the country, to write a history of the Octagon, which was published in 1976 (41). In 1978,

the College of Fellows awarded a grant, supplemented by government sources, to hire an architectural archivist and registrar/conservator to organize the AIA/F Prints and Drawings Collection. The College has also been active in the areas of architectural record conservation, preservation of the Institute's archives records on microfilm, and funding student internships in the AIA Archives.

In 1982, the College celebrated its thirtieth anniversary by publishing a combined history of the College and a directory of Fellows selected to date. Most recently, the College sponsored an ongoing project documenting the lives and accomplishments of Gold Medal winners through videotaped interviews of winners and spouses, biographies, and a history of the Gold Medal by architectural historian Richard Guy Wilson, which was published in 1984 (42).

Honorary Fellowship. The Institute confers Honorary Fellowship for "esteemed character and distinguished achievements" on architects who are not U.S. citizens and whose primary practice is not in the United States. The presidents of the Royal Architectural Institute of Canada (RAIC) and the Federation of Colleges of Architects of the Mexican Republic (FCARM) are named each year as *ex officio* Honorary Fellows of the Institute.

Honorary Membership. Honorary membership is awarded to nonarchitects in recognition of outstanding service to the architectural profession and to society as a whole. Recent selections include arts patron Paul Mellon, *Engineering News-Record* editor-in-chief Arthur J. Fox, Jr., and Swedish humanitarian Raoul Wallenberg.

Honor Awards. Started in 1949, the AIA's annual Honor Awards program remains the Institute's best known recognition of design excellence. Any work of architecture, such as a building, extended use project, complex of buildings, urban design, or interior, designed by any architect registered in the United States and built by a date specified in the Honor Awards program is eligible. The written and visual documentation accompanying each entry is microfilmed by the Institute archives, and slides of all entries are maintained in the Institute information center slide library.

Institute Honors. Institute Honors, started in 1917, recognize and encourage distinguished achievements by nonarchitects that benefit either the environment or the architectural profession. Individuals or organizations responsible for works that relate to or influence architecture are eligible. Recent recipients include the Cranbrook Academy of Art, architectural writer Esther McCoy, and the design team for the Games of the XXIIIrd Olympiad, Los Angeles, 1984.

Architectural Firm Award. Established in 1961, the Architectural Firm Award is the highest honor the AIA can bestow on an architecture firm for consistently (defined as "at least 10 years") producing distinguished architecture. The award was instituted to recognize the contributions that firms, rather than individual architects, make. Recent winners include Venturi, Rauch & Scott Brown of Philadelphia, and Esherick Homsey Dodge & Davis of San Francisco.

Twenty-Five Year Award. The Twenty-Five Year Award, started in 1969, annually recognizes one architectural project that has best withstood the test of time. Eligible projects must have been designed by an architect registered in the United States and completed 25–35 years prior. The General Motors Technical Center near Detroit, designed by Eero Saarinen with the firm Smith, Hinchman & Grylls, and the Solomon R. Guggenheim Museum, designed by Frank Lloyd Wright, are recent winners.

Henry Bacon Medal for Memorial Architecture. First given in 1966, the Henry Bacon Medal for Memorial Architecture is awarded every two years by the Institute on behalf of the AIA/F for excellence in memorial architecture. Maya Ying Lin's Vietnam Veterans War Memorial in Washington, D.C., is a recent winner.

Edward C. Kemper Award. The Edward C. Kemper Award, first bestowed in 1950 in honor of a former executive director of the Institute, is given each year by the Board to an AIA member who has contributed significantly to the Institute and to the profession.

Whitney M. Young Jr. Citation. Established in 1972 as a memorial to the late executive director of the National Urban League, the Whitney M. Young Jr. Citation is given to an architect or architecturally oriented organization in recognition of a significant contribution to social responsibility.

Throughout its history, the Institute has administered numerous additional awards programs, often in cooperation with other organizations. Those currently in existence (and the years they were first bestowed) are the R.S. Reynolds Memorial Award (1957), sponsored by the Reynolds Metals Company for distinguished architecture using aluminum; the Louis Sullivan Award for Architecture (1970), sponsored by the International Union of Bricklayers and Allied Craftsmen for masonry excellence in building design; the Library Buildings Award (1963), cosponsored with the American Library Association for well-designed, functional libraries; the Naval Facilities Biennial Award (1968), cosponsored with the Naval Facilities Engineering Command (NAVFAC) for outstanding architectural projects designed and constructed for the Navy or certain other government agencies; the AIA/ACSA Topaz Medallion for Architectural Education (1976), cosponsored with the Association of Collegiate Schools of Architecture for an outstanding educator; the Citation for Excellence in Community Architecture (originally the Citation for Excellence in Urban Design, 1965), administered by the Design Commission for outstanding urban design, city planning, and community development projects; and the Henry Adams Medal and Certificate Program (1914), for first- and second-ranked students at accredited architecture schools in the United States and Canada.

Architectural Education and Professional Development

The Intern-Architect Development Program (IDP) was formally launched in 1976 as a joint venture between the Institute and the National Council of Architectural Registration Boards (NCARB). Intended to close the gap between formal education and licensure, the program focused on the experience gained in design and construction documents, project administration, and office management. *SupEdGuides* (43), a series of supplementary learning units on specific office-practice topics, were developed for intern-architects and other young professionals. By 1986,

every state but Hawaii had endorsed, accepted, or adopted the IDP training standards as part of their registration requirements.

The Institute also began to develop a nationwide Continuing Education Network in 1977 to extend professional-development resources to practicing architects. The network coordinates and evaluates courses, seminars, and workshops, and the AIA maintains records and course listings. The Institute's current professional-development efforts include the Energy in Architecture program, AIA-sponsored workshops on design and practice topics; and audiocassettes and correspondence courses. The Institute's professional-development program is also expanding into new delivery formats based on video and teleconferencing technologies.

National Role

As the owner of historically significant Washington property, the AIA has been instrumental in the preservation and design of Washington, D.C. In the tradition of the McMillan Commission, it supported, during the Kennedy Administration, legislation to establish a joint House–Senate committee to study planning procedures for metropolitan Washington, and supported the establishment of an advisory council to oversee the orderly development of Pennsylvania Avenue. The resulting Pennsylvania Avenue Development Corporation, originally headed by Gold Medal winner Nathaniel A. Owings, continues the revitalization of "America's Main Street."

In 1981, the Vietnam Veterans Memorial Fund conducted the nation's largest design competition, following AIA-approved procedures, for the Vietnam Veterans War Memorial between the Washington Monument and the Lincoln Memorial. The design of a V-shaped, black-granite memorial by Maya Ying Lin, an architecture student at Yale University, was selected from entries by more than 3800 architects, sculptors, landscape architects, and artists who registered for the competition. When some veterans' organizations and others protested the abstract and symbolic nature of the memorial, the AIA waged a successful campaign to preserve its design integrity, the competition itself, and recognized standards of professional practice.

For many years, the AIA continued its opposition to a proposed expansion of the West Front of the Capitol on the grounds that its structural weaknesses could be corrected and that the last original facade should be restored. The expansion would also have destroyed portions of the nineteenth-century Olmsted-designed terraces and grounds for the Capitol. In 1983, the Institute and the National Trust for Historic Preservation lobbied extensively for restoration and sponsored a rally on the Capitol steps, which drew members of Congress and nearly 1000 participants. The Institute's view finally prevailed later that year when legislation was adopted containing provisions for a $49 million restoration plan.

Urban and Minority Issues

When racial tensions flared in cities across America, the Board of Directors adopted a resolution in 1967 calling for the Institute to find solutions to urban environment problems. Two years later, the AIA established a new, nonprofit entity—the Urban Design and Development Corporation (UDDC)—which was funded for two years at $100,000 per annum. Its charge was to educate public and private institutions to be responsive to human needs in reshaping the physical environment. In mid-1970, it merged with the Urban Design Center of Urban America, and in 1971, it was reorganized. In 1972, the UDDC became the AIA Research Corporation.

Civil rights leader Whitney M. Young, Jr., addressed the 1968 convention in Portland, Ore., and challenged the Institute to assess its minority representation; at that time, fewer than 150 black members were included. In response, President George E. Kassabaum called for the creation of a special task force reporting directly to the Executive Committee to recommend measures that the AIA could implement immediately and on a long-term basis in the areas of civil rights and equal opportunity. A seven-person task force, four of whose members were black, was appointed. The task force defined its charge as twofold: to increase the number of minorities entering the profession and to increase the profession's social commitment and involvement in practice in the ghettos. The task force also urged increased minority representation on AIA committees and studied means of identifying, guiding, and recruiting minority students.

One of the Institute's first steps was to increase the AIA Scholarship Fund by $15,000 for the disadvantaged. A more formal program of scholarships for minority and disadvantaged students began in 1970, when the AIA/F received a $500,000 matching grant from the Ford Foundation. During the first year, more than a score of disadvantaged minority students received support for tuition, room, and board for five- and six-year architecture programs. Candidates were required to show scholastic ability and demonstrate an interest in urban design problems. The AIA Foundation/Ford Foundation Minority/Disadvantaged Scholarship Program was taken over by the AIA in 1972, and in 1973 a $600,000 fund drive was begun among members, large architecture firms, allied construction firms, and foundations and corporations. The goal of the drive was to finance the program for three more years and then turn it over to components. In its first three years, 96 minority students were given scholarships to attend 36 schools of architecture and had an attrition rate lower than average. The present scholarship program supports up to 20 students per year and is funded by the AIA Foundation with member support.

The task force's report contained recommendations for greater involvement of the profession in low-income housing, the model-cities program, and other social, physical, and economic programs. Among the report's major features were guidelines for the operation of community design centers (CDCs). These centers allowed architects to volunteer their time to provide rehabilitation of houses and community facilities and assist in block improvements and tenant action. The AIA helped find sources of funding for communities unable to pay for architectural expertise. The AIA's new Community Services Department assisted more than 60 CDCs across the country, and encouraged chapter support. The AIA and VISTA (Volunteers in Service to America) helped place 70 architects in 25 CDCs for professional and advisory contributions. In 1986, the AIA's Urban Design Committee serves as a liaison with the Community Design Center Directors Association, a loose organization of CDCs.

In 1970, the AIA and the National Urban League embarked on programs to create on-the-job training placements and a Summer Fellowship Training Program for professors and instructors at black architecture schools. The Black Executive Exchange Program (BEEP) was also started. This "practitioner on campus" program of seminars at black architecture schools acquainted black students with the problems and responsibilities of black practitioners. During that same period, the Council of Black Architectural Schools (Hampton, North Carolina A&T, Prairie View, Southern University, Tennessee, and Tuskegee) was formed with AIA support to pursue accreditation of its architecture schools. Hampton, Southern University, and Tuskegee are now accredited.

Community Development

The Institute's Regional/Urban Design Assistance Teams (R/UDAT) program has continued the AIA's involvement in community design. Between 1967 and 1986, R/UDATs have advised more than 90 cities, towns, and communities on local design issues. The R/UDAT process begins when a local government, community organization, or AIA chapter recognizes a local urban design or community-planning problem and asks the AIA for help. With the advice of the AIA, the community sets up a local steering committee and submits an application to the R/UDAT Task Group. After reviewing and approving the application, the Task Group works with the community to design a R/UDAT that can meet the needs and resources of the community and utilize the capabilities of the R/UDAT program effectively. Team members are selected from a volunteer pool of architects and other design professionals, economists, sociologists, growth management and development experts, preservationists, political scientists, and lawyers. After an intensive four-day workshop is held, a report with recommendations is presented to the community. Local officials and design professionals then begin the task of weighing and implementing the recommendations, assisted by follow-up visits by the R/UDAT Task Group when necessary.

R/UDATs have addressed such issues as downtown revitalization, environmental conservation, transportation planning, and park and open-space development in communities ranging from Lynn, Mass., to Seattle, Wash. Solutions to urban design problems are also being jointly discussed by the Institute and the Royal Institute of British Architects. At his request, the Prince of Wales visited the AIA in 1985 to discuss community architecture with architects from the R/UDAT program and representatives of revitalized neighborhoods in Baltimore, Md., and Savannah, Ga.

Women in the Profession

The role of women in the Institute came under greater scrutiny in the 1970s. Delegates at the 1973 annual convention approved a resolution aimed at improving the status of women in the profession. Delegates called for a study of ways to encourage more women to become architects and to become more involved in Institute activities. The resolution also called for a program to implement the equal-opportunity section of the AIA's Personnel Practices Manual. After two years' work, the Task Force on Women in Architecture developed an affirmative-action plan, which was adopted by the Board. Goals of the plan included integrating women into the profession at salary and responsibility levels equal to those of their male counterparts, encouraging increased AIA membership for women, and ensuring at least 20% female representation on national committees by the end of 1976. Although considerable progress has been made toward these goals over the past 10 years, a 1983 study showed that women members still have not achieved parity in responsibility, salary levels, or Institute representation (almost 7% of AIA members in 1986 were women). The Women in Architecture Committee, which received full committee status in 1985, maintains a liaison network with female members in chapters across the country and continues its work to integrate women into the profession fully. The Committee has also taken the lead in sponsoring an exhibition of women in architecture. The exhibition is scheduled to open in 1988, in honor of the 100th anniversary of Louise Bethune's induction into the AIA. (Reflecting the national concern with women's rights, the Institute in 1981 changed the location of its annual convention from New Orleans to Minneapolis because Louisiana had not adopted the proposed equal rights amendment to the Constitution.)

Environmental Issues

As the environment became more of a concern in the early 1970s, the AIA instituted a national advertising campaign aimed at enlisting the public in a crusade for a better environment and against urban blight and pollution. In 1972, the Institute issued the first report of the National Policy Task Force—a call for action for the acquisition, conservation, and design of land—to widespread public acclaim. The report, "America at the Cutting Edge: A Strategy for Building a Better America" (44), advocated policies regarding the rebuilding of cities, new-town development, urban growth, and housing for middle- and low-income families. The objective of the report, to build and rebuild America to a higher level of quality by the year 2000, used as tools tax policies, government funding, and a land bank for future development. A group of task-force members appeared before the platform committees of both the Democratic and Republican Parties in 1972 and came away with platform planks that paralleled important aspects of the report. A second report was published in 1973, and a coalition of related organizations was formed to lobby for enactment of many of the reports' recommendations.

Energy Issues

Beginning in the mid-1970s, the Institute responded to the energy crisis by developing programs that taught architects how to design more-energy-efficient structures. The Institute's *Energy Handbook* (45) was introduced in 1975, and two position papers, "A Nation of Energy Efficient Buildings by 1990" (45) and "An Integrated National Energy Policy" were later published. The Institute's 1981 theme, "A Line on Design and Energy," stressed the role architects could play in freeing the nation from its dependence on fossil fuels.

Historic Preservation

In its second century, the AIA has continued its long-term efforts on behalf of historic preservation. It was instrumental in the passage of the Historic Structures Tax Act in 1976 (part of the Tax Reform Act of 1976), which removed incentives for demolishing old buildings and allowed rapid write-offs of rehabilitation costs for certain historically significant buildings. The AIA also supported the National Historic Preservation Fund Act, which increased authorized funding levels for a program of matching grants to states for their preservation efforts. The Institute endorsed provisions of the 1981 Tax Act that enabled building owners to receive tax incentives for increased building rehabilitation, and it urged Congress to maintain federal historic preservation funding.

In other preservation activities, the Institute participated in successful efforts to save New York's Grand Central Station from demolition, add Eero Saarinen's Dulles International Airport to the National Register of Historic Places, and establish a National Museum of the Building Arts in the Washington, D.C., Pension Building.

Legislative Priorities

Over the years, the Institute has been active on a wide range of issues, including a national housing policy, land-use planning, conservation of energy and the proper management of other natural resources, mass-transit financing, highway beautification, acid-rain abatement, establishment of the metric system, campaign financing, embassy security, and restrictions on surface mining. A signal federal legislative success for the profession was the enactment in 1972 of the Brooks–McClellan–Percy Bill (known as the A–E Selection or Brooks bill), the result of intense lobbying by the Institute. This law requires that design quality, not price, be the criterion for selecting architects and engineers for federal projects. The legislation is particularly important because it has become a model for the procedures of many states and local agencies that generally follow federal procurement procedures. The Institute continues to lobby against legislation that would weaken qualifications-based selection procedures.

Ethics

Like many professional organizations, the AIA has over the years maintained a code of ethics and professional conduct which governs the conduct of its members. For many years, a member who violated the AIA's standards was liable to charges of unethical conduct, and if found guilty, disciplined by the Institute. Before 1970, the *Standards of Ethical Practice* contained a statement that an architect could not enter into competitive bidding against another architect on the basis of compensation. In 1968, the Department of Justice informed the AIA that in its opinion the standard was in restraint of trade and a violation of the Sherman Antitrust Act. In 1970, a revised ethical standard was adopted which, among other provisions, allowed an architect (after being selected on the basis of professional qualifications) to reach an agreement with the client or employer about the nature and extent of services provided and the compensation.

The Justice Department maintained that the new language placed the same limitation on members and that agreeing to uphold the ethical standards amounted to an agreement in restraint of trade. In 1971, the Antitrust Division of the U.S. Department of Justice served a Civil Investigating Demand (similar to a subpoena) that required the AIA to turn over all documents on matters relating to the Institute's position on and enforcement of anticompetitive bidding. Later that year, the Justice Department informed the AIA that it intended to file for action for injunctive relief under the provisions of the Sherman Act relating to competition. (Similar action was brought against the National Society of Professional Engineers in 1972. After six years of litigation, the U.S. Supreme Court ruled that the Society's ethical ban on competitive bidding for engineering services violated the Sherman Antitrust Act.)

In January 1972, the Executive Committee retained counsel specializing in antitrust law, and two months later directed its attorneys to negotiate a consent decree for Board consideration. (A consent decree does not imply wrongdoing, but determines the future actions of its signers.) Later that year, the AIA signed a consent decree in which it agreed to remove the ethical prohibition against competitive bidding. However, the AIA remained free to influence legislation affecting competitive bidding and encourage clients to adopt its preferred method of selection. The majority of the Board of Directors accepted the decree, and it was endorsed by more than a two-thirds vote at the Houston convention. Delegates also approved a special assessment of $10 on each corporate member to defray the cost of redoubling lobbying efforts to promote the AIA method of architect and engineer selection.

In 1975, the Ethics Task Force studied the *Standards of Ethical Practice* in terms of the realities of current practice and legal constraints. The proposed changes included lifting the ban on advertising, permitting members to engage in contracting and other activities, and lifting the restriction against architecture design competitions not previously approved by the Institute. A revision of the standards was submitted at the Philadelphia convention in 1976 but was rejected by an overwhelming vote to defer. The convention referred the question back to the Board with instructions to appoint a task force.

A revised professional ethics code was adopted at the 1977 convention. The new statement of ethical principles clarified the difference between aspirational "ethical standards" and enforceable "rules of conduct," all categorized under a general "canon." The revisions retained the ban on advertising but allowed members to advertise specialty services in telephone directory listings if they were not in boldface type. These standards were later refined to allow architects to purchase "dignified" advertisements and listings. Other legal action based on the AIA's code of ethics was brought against the Institute in 1977 after member architect Aram Mardirosian was suspended for violating the "supplanting" ethic. This standard prohibited an architect from obtaining another architect's commission until the second architect had evidence that the original architect's contract has been terminated. In 1979, a U.S. District judge ruled that the "supplanting" standard in the AIA's code of ethics was in violation of the Sherman Antitrust Act.

In 1981, the Institute dropped the mandatory code of ethics and in the following year adopted a voluntary statement of ethical principles. Three years later, the Board of Directors approved a resolution directing that a model code of professional responsibility be created and that strong and effective methods of enforcement be investigated. In 1986, the membership adopted a revised code of canons, ethical standards, and rules of conduct (the last of which is mandatory). The revised code establishes guidelines of conduct relating to the public, clients, and colleagues in architecture and related professions and industries, and to the art and science of architecture. It also includes penalties that would be imposed by a newly created National Judicial Council.

125th Anniversary

The Institute celebrated its 125th anniversary in 1982. President Reagan proclaimed the week of April 18–24 "National Architecture Week," and the final block of stamps in the Postal Service's four-year American architecture series was unveiled at a first-day-of-issue ceremony in the AIA courtyard. The last set depicted buildings by Frank Lloyd Wright, Ludwig Mies van der Rohe, Walter Gropius, and Eero Saarinen. The year-long celebration of events and exhibits included a parade, concerts, dance programs, tours, and other ceremonies in Washington, D.C., and at chapters throughout the country. An Octagon exhibition, "To Unite in Fellowship," contrasted the offices of a modern-day architect with those of an architect practicing 125 years ago. Another exhibition, "For the Record . . . The First 125 Years," consisted of an archival collection of artifacts and Institute memorabilia on display at Institute headquarters. An illustrated brochure chronicling the highlights of the Institute's first 125 years was also published, and the *AIA Journal* devoted an issue and time line to the anniversary.

PART FOUR: THE CHALLENGES AHEAD

Concerned that it remain responsive to the needs of a changing profession, the Institute in the early 1980s established a framework to ensure the AIA's continued service to the profession and the public. Delegates to the 1980 convention passed a resolution directing the Board of Directors to oversee a study of the directions, principles, purposes, and roles of the Institute at all levels during the decade. This study was carried out by the Direction

'80s Task Force and two outside consulting groups, and a report was presented to delegates at the 1982 convention in Hawaii. The Task Force recommended the AIA make a major commitment to managing the body of knowledge essential to the design of the built environment; improve professional and public education; support public policy affecting the practice of architecture; improve communications for members and the public; and strengthen state and local components. These recommendations and their implementation still affect much of the Institute's planning procedures.

As the Institute moves toward the twenty-first century, it faces many of the same issues that its founders encountered in 1857. Architectural education, professional development, compensation, professional responsibility, and federal and state procurement of architectural services remain areas that demand the Institute's best efforts if the profession is to continue to prosper and provide the public with quality design. Yet other changes present new challenges to architects. The questions of accountability and liability in a litigious age may place restraints on the architects' traditional role as leaders of the building team and affect their ability to be compensated adequately. Federal tax-reform proposals pose threats to the building industry by altering laws affecting incentives for urban growth and the preservation of the nation's historic resources. In addition, computers and other new technologies offer challenges as well as unbounded opportunities for both younger and older architects.

By mobilizing its financial and human resources to respond to the issues facing the profession, the AIA will continue to ensure a dynamic and creative future for its architects and architecture.

BIBLIOGRAPHY

As indicated, many of the references below may be obtained from The American Institute of Architects, (AIA), Washington, D.C.

1. Constitution, 1857, Record Group 501, AIA Archives.
2. *The Crayon,* Stillman & Durand, New York, 1855–1861, AIA Library.
3. H. H. Saylor, *The AIA's First Hundred Years,* Octagon Press, AIA, 1957.
4. P. B. Wight, ed., *Proceedings of the Annual Convention of the American Institute of Architects,* Raymond & Caulon, New York, 1867, Record Group 504, AIA Archives.
5. Constitution, 1867, Record Group 501, AIA Archives.
6. *The American Institute of Architects Quarterly Bulletin,* AIA, 1900–1912.
7. *A Schedule of Charges,* 1866, Record Group 801, Series 8, AIA Archives.
8. *Standard Form of Agreement,* 1888, Record Group 801, Series 8, AIA Archives.
9. G. Brown, "Government Buildings Compared With Private Buildings," *American Architect and Building News* (Apr. 7, 1894), AIA Library.
10. Committee on Library and Publications, *Proceedings of the Eleventh and Twelfth Annual Conventions of the American Institute of Architects,* Alfred Mudge & Son, Boston, 1879, Record Group 504, AIA Archives.
11. Committees, Historic Resources, Record Group 801, Series 2, AIA Archives.
12. P. R. Baker, *Richard Morris Hunt,* The MIT Press, Cambridge, 1980, pp. 80–87.
13. Constitution, 1900, Record Group 501, AIA Archives.
14. Constitution, 1957, Record Group 501, AIA Archives.
15. Bylaws, 1956, Record Group 501, AIA Archives.
16. Ref. 3, p. 49.
17. *Standard Documents,* 1st ed., 1911, Record Group 801, Series 8, AIA Archives.
18. *Ibid.,* 2nd ed., 1915.
19. *Ibid.,* 3rd ed., 1918.
20. *Ibid.,* 4th ed., 1925.
21. *Ibid.,* 5th ed., 1937.
22. *Handbook of Architectural Practice,* 1920, Record Group 801, Series 8, AIA Archives.
23. *The Journal of the American Institute of Architects,* Press of the American Institute of Architects, Washington, D.C., and New York, 1913–1928.
24. A. Simons, *Charleston, South Carolina,* Press of the American Institute of Architects, New York, 1927.
25. L. H. Sullivan, *The Autobiography of an Idea,* Press of the American Institute of Architects, New York, 1924.
26. L. H. Sullivan, *A System of Architectural Ornament According With a Philosophy of Man's Powers,* Press of the American Institute of Architects, New York, 1924.
27. *The Octagon,* AIA, 1928–1943.
28. *Journal of the American Institute of Architects,* AIA, 1944–June 1983.
29. *Bulletin of the American Institute of Architects,* AIA, 1947–1957.
30. *The Memo,* AIA, 1950–1978.
31. G. Brown, ed., *Proceedings of the Thirty-Fourth Annual Convention of the American Institute of Architects,* Gibson Brothers, Washington, D.C., 1900, Record Group 504, AIA Archives.
32. T. C. Bannister, ed., *The Architect at Mid-Century,* Reinhold Publishing Corp., New York, 1954.
33. *Circular of Advice Relative to Principles of Professional Practice and the Canons of Ethics,* 1909, Record Group 801, Series 8, AIA Archives.
34. L. Chatelain, Jr., "Opening Address," *Journal of the American Institute of Architects,* **28,** 57 (June 1957).
35. F. Gutheim, *1857–1957, One Hundred Years of Architecture in America,* Reinhold Publishing Corp., New York, 1957.
36. *Building Products Register,* AIA, 1960.
37. *MASTERSPEC,* Production Systems for Architects and Engineers, Inc., Chicago (1970), Washington, D.C. (1972).
38. *MASTERGUIDE,* AIA, 1985.
39. *Architectural Graphic Standards,* 7th ed., John Wiley & Sons, Inc., New York, 1981 (1st ed., 1932).
40. *The Architect's Handbook of Professional Practice,* AIA, 1963/1972.
41. G. McCue, *The Octagon,* AIA, 1976.
42. R. G. Wilson, *The AIA Gold Medal,* McGraw-Hill, Inc., New York, 1984.
43. *SupEdGuides; An AIA Supplementary Education Program for Intern-Architects,* 1977–1981.
44. A. Holden, *The First Report of the National Policy Task Force of The American Institute of Architects, January 1972,* Holden, Yank, Raemsch & Corser, New York, 1972.

45. *Energy; AIA Energy Notebook: An Information Service on Energy and the Built Environment,* AIA, 1975–.

46. Energy Steering Committee, *A Nation of Energy Efficient Buildings by 1990,* AIA, 1975.

General References

Refs. 1, 4, 36, 38, 39, and 46 are good general references.

Many of the following references can be obtained from The American Institute of Architects, Washington, D.C.

AIA Convention Proceedings, Record Group 504, AIA Archives.

Annual Report of the Board, AIA, 1956–1984.

Bylaws, AIA, 1981.

Component Operations Manual 1986, AIA, 1986.

Direction '80s, *1982 AIA Convention Report,* AIA, 1982.

Membership Annuary/Directory, Record Group 803, Series I, AIA Archives.

Rules of the Board, AIA, 1986.

The American Institute of Architects: The Organization's Role, History, and Activities, AIA, 1985.

The First 125 Years, AIA, 1982.

G. Brown, *1860–1930 Memories,* W. F. Roberts Co., Washington, D.C., 1931.

W. C. Cokern, Jr., "Architects, Preservationists and the New Deal: The Historic American Buildings Survey, 1933–1942," Ph.D. thesis, George Washington University Microfilms, Washington, D.C.

N. R. Greer and S. Abercrombie, "One Hundred and Twenty-Five Years . . . ," *AIA Journal,* **71,** 70–77 (Apr. 1982).

T. Holleman, *A History and Directory of the College,* College of Fellows of The American Institute of Architects, Washington, D.C., 1984.

J. Hulbrink, "The Committee on Historic Preservation: The Early Years, 1890–1931," unpublished, 1985, AIA Archives.

G. McCue, *The Octagon, Being an Account of a Famous Washington Residence: Its Great Years, Decline & Restoration,* The American Institute of Architects Foundation, Washington, D.C., 1976.

M. E. Osman and co-workers, "Highlights of American Architecture, 1776–1976," *AIA Journal,* **65,** 88–158 (July 1976).

See also CONTRACT DOCUMENTS; INSPECTION, OBSERVATION AND SUPERVISION; PROFESSION IN CONTEMPORARY SOCIETY; ROLE OF THE ARCHITECT; ROYAL INSTITUTE OF BRITISH ARCHITECTS (RIBA).

LOUIS L. MARINES
ANN CARPER
MARJORY A. GRANT
RAYMOND P. RHINEHART
TONY P. WRENN
The American Institute of Architects
Washington, D.C.

AMERICAN NATIONAL STANDARDS INSTITUTE (ANSI)

The American National Standards Institute (ANSI), a private, nonprofit organization founded in 1918, is the coordinator of voluntary standards activities in the United States and is the agency that approves standards as American National Standards. It is also the coordinator and manager of U.S. participation in the work of nongovernmental international standards organizations.

As national coordinator, ANSI assists organizations involved in standardization in reaching agreement on needs for standards, establishing priorities, planning to meet identified needs, and avoiding duplication of effort. ANSI also offers standards-developing organizations a neutral forum for resolving differences and provides procedures and services to help them use their resources effectively.

It is a federation of the standards' competence existing in technical, trade, professional, labor, and consumer organizations, government agencies, commerce, and industry. These groups cooperate within ANSI to reach agreement on standards needs and priorities and to resolve differences that may arise. They also voluntarily submit standards to ANSI for approval.

APPROVING STANDARDS

ANSI approves standards as American National Standards when it is satisfied that its consensus and due process requirements have been met.

For each standard, ANSI's Board of Standards Review (BSR) evaluates evidence submitted by standards-developing groups that those directly and materially affected have reached substantial agreement—consensus—on the standard's provisions. It also assesses evidence that the standard was developed under an open process that gave the interests affected an opportunity to express their views and that all comments were carefully considered. If the BSR is satisfied, it takes action on approval.

Currently, there are some 8000 American National Standards. They provide definitions, ratings, symbols, test methods, and performance and safety requirements for a wide range of products, equipment, components, and systems in virtually every field and discipline.

Of the many ANSI standards used by designers, building owners, code writers, and enforcement officers, one frequently referenced is ANSI Standard 117.1 (latest revision 1986), "Providing Accessibility and Usability for Physically Handicapped People."

REPRESENTING U.S. INTERESTS IN INTERNATIONAL STANDARDIZATION

The Institute is the coordinator and manager of U.S. participation in the activities of the world's major nongovernmental international standards bodies—the International Organization for Standardization (ISO) and the International Electrotechnical Commission (IEC). Through ANSI, U.S. industry, business, and other interests are able to influence international standards that affect trade.

ANSI participates in almost all of the ISO's more than 2000 technical committees and subgroups and administers some 285 secretariats.

The Institute cooperates closely with federal government agencies on trade issues that involve standards and in carrying out U.S. responsibility for the Standards Code of the General Agreement on Tariffs and Trade (GATT).

PROVIDING INFORMATION AND ACCESS TO THE WORLD'S STANDARDS

ANSI is the prime source of standards in the United States. It makes available all approved American National Standards, standards and drafts of the ISO and the IEC, proposals of regional groups tied to the Common Market, and the specifications of 89 national standards organizations that are members of the ISO.

To keep members and the public informed, ANSI publishes an annual catalogue and supplements and makes available the latest catalogues issued by ISO, IEC, and more than 50 ISO members. *Standards Action,* a biweekly, solicits comments on standards being considered for approval and reports on newly published standards. The *ANSI Reporter* informs members of policy-level actions of ANSI, the ISO, and the IEC and of standards-related actions of the U.S. government.

COOPERATING WITH GOVERNMENT

ANSI has had close cooperative relationships with all levels of government for nearly 70 years. Federal agencies and state and local authorities are ANSI members. Government representatives serve on ANSI boards and councils. The Institute's advice is sought by federal agencies, congressional committees, and state and local legislative bodies.

Because of these long-term relationships, ANSI is effective in encouraging government acceptance and sound application of voluntary standards. Many federal agencies and state and local governments adopt American National Standards for procurement and to provide for safety and such services as communications and transportation.

ORGANIZATION AND FINANCING

ANSI is governed by a board of directors representing all of the interests cooperating within the voluntary standards system. Several councils, boards, and committees carry out institute programs with the support of a staff of 100 people.

Major sources of ANSI income are the dues of its members—220 standards-developing organizations and some 1000 large and small companies—and the sale of publications.

See also AMERICAN SOCIETY FOR TESTING AND MATERIALS; HANDICAPPED ACCESS LAWS AND CODES; REGULATIONS—BUILDING AND ZONING.

AMERICAN SOCIETY FOR TESTING AND MATERIALS

The American Society for Testing and Materials (ASTM) was founded in 1898 in order to develop consensus standards for materials, products, systems, and services. Prior to its founding, conditions in the marketplace were chaotic. The earliest use of standardization was in the production of firearms.

The ASTM has grown to a membership of 30,000, which is approximately 50% producers, 25% users, and 25% public. Committee membership is limited to technically knowledgeable people in the group's area of interest. The ASTM's definition of standard is the process of formulating and applying rules for an orderly approach to a specific activity for the benefit and with the cooperation of all concerned.

The ASTM has been cooperating with other standards for years, setting up associations throughout the industrialized world. Inasmuch as the ASTM is not a governmental body and is composed of volunteer members, progress is slow; however, foreign standards generally are set by governmental agencies and have slightly greater political influences. Whatever the source, standardization is an absolute necessity in any industrialized society.

The ASTM produces the following types of standards:

1. Standard definitions, which create a common language for a given area of knowledge.
2. Standard practices, which suggest accepted procedures for performing a given task.
3. Standard methods of testing, which prescribe ways of making a given measurement.
4. Standard classifications, which set up categories in which objects or concepts may be grouped.
5. Standard specifications, which define boundaries or limits on the characteristics of a material, product, system, or service.

As previously mentioned, there are three types of members in the ASTM: producers, users, and those representing the general public's interest. In general, these are defined as follows:

1. Producers are manufacturers, suppliers, and laboratories.
2. Users are architects, engineers, and governmental agencies.
3. General interest agencies are academics and others with a knowledgeable interest.

The composition of committees must be balanced so that the producers are equaled in number by users and general interest members. There are approximately 33,000 members in the ASTM, belonging to 138 main committees. Each committee is broken down into a number of subcommittees, which in turn are composed of a number of task forces. Main committees and their subgroups meet twice a year, and balloting is carried out by mail.

A new standard is originated by a group representing a specific segment of industry or by a governmental agency concerned about the need for a consensus standard for a particular discipline. The procedure is rather complex, requiring several proposals at task force conferences, followed by the final formation of a new subcommittee and/or assignment to an existing main committee. There is great care taken that at all stages each decision is made on a consensus basis.

The process of formulating a new standard is long and painstaking. At each stage, from the task force through the main committee balloting, a member of the committee may object in writing with accompanying reasons. Before issuance as a standard, the work is reviewed and edited and again reviewed. A new standard requires about five years to complete.

Each standard is reviewed periodically and, using the same process as for a new standard, updated. This action, depending on its importance, is generally shorter.

The ASTM has been particularly valuable to the construction design professions. Some of its first endeavors were in the fields of raw materials such as steel, cement, stone, and so on. With subsequent updating, these standards have been in continuous use for many years.

The most important publication for architects and engineers is a two-volume edition entitled *Compilation of A.S.T.M. Standards in Building Codes*. These volumes contain almost all of the standards and test methods for the commonly used construction materials. When using construction specifications, writers often refer to ASTM designation numbers only.

In the case of building codes, the above publication has provided the basis for the inclusion of testing and specifications as formal code requirements. There is one major concern: because of the constant upgrading required by the ASTM publication, many places will not allow the "ASTM . . . latest edition" as a legal provision, and therefore many codes are not synchronous with the latest edition. Regardless of the upgrading difficulty, these standards are referred to constantly by national model codes, as well as by state and municipal codes. ASTM standards referenced in building codes include specifications, test methods, practices, classifications, definitions, and guides. Subject areas addressed include

Acoustical materials	Iron castings
Adhesives	Lime
Aggregates	Liquid penetrant
Aluminum	Masonry products
Asbestos–cement products	Mechanical testing, metals
Bituminized fiber pipe fittings	Metallic coated iron and steel coatings
Brick	
Building construction	Natural building stone
Cement	Nickel and nickel alloy pipe and tube
Clay pipe and tile	
Concrete and concrete admixtures	Paint
	Plastics
Copper and copper alloys	Plastic pipe and fittings
Electromagnetics	Radiographs
Electrical conductors	Refractories
Fasteners	Roofing
Fences	Rubber
Fire tests	Sealants
Flammability tests	Security
Fuel, oil, solvents	Soils
Gypsum and plaster	Steel

Testing agencies	Ultrasonic techniques
Testing methods, general	Wood and wood preservatives
Thermal insulating materials	

Each year, the ASTM publishes a great variety of studies as well as proceedings of its technical committees and symposia. The 16-section *Annual Book of A.S.T.M. Standards* consists of 67 volumes. There is an annual updating service, which is issued quarterly and carries about 1500 new and revised standards each year. Of particular interest to the design professions are the sections on "Construction," "Iron and Steel Products," "Non-Ferrous Metal Products," "Paints, Related Coating and Aromatics," "Plastics," and "Electrical Insulation and Electronics."

The International Organization for Standardization (ISO) has had close ties with ASTM for many years. The ISO is the European body similar to the ASTM, but it has problems due to the varied nationalities that compose its membership. In general, European standards are government promulgated and a subject of national pride, thereby slowing adoption. Many of the ISO and ASTM standards for testing are being studied for uniformity so that common international standards can be developed.

The usefulness of ASTM cannot be overvalued. The standardization of testing, measurements, quality control, and organization have been and continue to be of inestimable value, particularly to the construction industry.

BIBLIOGRAPHY

General References

The publications referenced in this article are available from the American Society for Testing and Materials, 1916 Race St., Philadelphia, Pa. 19104.

P. K. BARNES
Ft. Lauderdale, Florida

AMINO RESINS

Amino resins are thermosetting polymers made from compounds containing the amino group NH_2. Urea is the most commonly used amino compound, accounting for over 80% of amino resins. Melamine is the next most commonly used and accounts for most of the remaining 20%. Other amino compounds are used to a very minor extent.

urea   melamine

Formaldehyde is used to link the amino compounds, forming a polymer network. The reaction takes place in two steps. First, the formaldehyde reacts with the amino group to form a methylol compound. This is known as methylolation or hydroxymethylation:

$$R—NH_2 + HCHO \longrightarrow R—NH—CH_2OH$$

The second step is a condensation reaction that involves the linking of monomer units with the liberation of water to form a dimer, a polymer chain, or a complex cross-linked polymer network. This is usually referred to as a polymerization or simply cure:

$$RNH—CH_2OH + H_2NR \longrightarrow RNH—CH_2—NHR + H_2O$$

The first reaction is most important for manufacturing the resin and the second is most important for the user of the resin who is applying it as an adhesive, a molded plastic article, or using it to modify the properties of paper or cloth.

Urea is the most important building block for amino resins for two reasons: first, because urea–formaldehyde is the largest selling amino resin; and second, because urea is used to make melamine, the amino compound used to make the next largest selling type of amino resin. Urea is also used to make a variety of other amino compounds, such as ethyleneurea, and other cyclic ureas that are used in the manufacture of amino resins. Urea is manufactured in immense quantities for use as a fertilizer and cattle-feed supplement. Only about 10% of the total urea production is used in making amino resins; hence, amino resins and plastics have a secure source of low cost raw material, so long as urea remains an important agricultural chemical.

Amino resins are manufactured throughout the industrialized world to provide a variety of useful products. Adhesives represent by far the largest market. They are used primarily in the manufacture of fibrous and granulated wood products. Special types of amino-resin adhesives are used for the assembly of wood furniture. Amino resins are also used to cross-link or cure other resins, such as alkyds and reactive acrylic polymers, for example, protective surface coatings used on appliances, automobiles, etc. Some amino resins may be used to modify the properties of other materials. Amino resins can improve the strength of paper even when it is wet. Molding compounds based on amino resins are used for parts for electrical devices. The primary outlets for amino resins based on melamine are decorative laminates used on tables and counter tops, and molded plastic dinnerware.

Amino resins and plastics have been in use for more than 50 years. Compared to other segments of the plastics industry, aminos are mature products, showing only a modest growth rate. They represent about 4% of U.S. plastics and resins production. The future for amino resins seems to be secure, since they are based on an abundant, low cost raw material, and since they can provide qualities that are not easily obtained in other ways. New developments will probably be in the areas of more highly specialized materials for treating textiles, paper, etc, and for

use with other resins in the formulation of surface coatings, where a small amount of an amino resin can significantly increase the value of a more basic material.

The first practical commercial product based on an amino resin was introduced in the mid-1920s. It was a molding compound invented in the UK by Edmond C. Rossiter (1). The new product was based on a resin made with an equimolar mixture of urea and thiourea reinforced with purified cellulose fiber. The new product could be supplied in light translucent colors, and the surface was hard and not easily stained; furthermore, it had no objectionable phenolic odor like the molding compounds based on phenol–formaldehyde resin that had been introduced about 10 years before. In short, the product was unique for its time. Although the use of thiourea gave the moldings better gloss and improved water resistance, it had the disadvantage of staining the steel molds. As amino-resin technology advanced, it was found that the amount of thiourea in the formulation could be reduced and finally eliminated altogether.

Also during this time, urea–formaldehyde resins were being developed in Europe. It was discovered that urea–formaldehyde resins might be cast into beautiful, glass-clear transparent sheets, and it was proposed that it might serve as an organic glass. Lack of water resistance, however, prevented commercialization. Melamine resins were introduced about 10 years after Rossiter's urea-molding compound came on the market. Products made with melamine were very similar to those made with urea, but with some superior qualities. The Henkel Co. in Germany was issued a patent for a melamine resin in 1936 (2). Melamine resins then moved rapidly into applications already established by urea, and soon formulations for molding, laminating, and bonding, as well as textile and paper treating, were available from a number of manufacturers. The remarkable stability of the symmetrical triazine ring made these products very resistant to chemical change once the resin had been cured to the insoluble, cross-linked state.

The simple methylol compounds and the low molecular weight polymers obtained from urea and melamine are soluble in water. They are quite suitable for the manufacture of adhesives, molding compounds, and some kinds of textile-treating resins. However, amino resins for coating applications require compatibility with film-forming alkyd resins or copolymer resins with which they must react. Furthermore, even where compatible, the free methylol compounds are often too unstable for use in coating-resin formulations that may be stored for some time before use. Reaction of the free methylol groups with an alcohol to convert them to alkoxy methyl groups overcomes both problems. This is shown in the equation below.

$$RNHCH_2OH + HOR' \rightleftharpoons RNHCH_2OR' + H_2O$$

With the replacement of the hydrogen of the methylol compound with an alkyl group, the material becomes much more soluble in organic solvents and is much more stable. This condensation reaction is also catalyzed by acids and is usually carried out in the presence of a considerable excess of the alcohol to suppress the competing self-condensation reaction. After neutralization of the acid catalyst, the excess alcohol may be stripped or left as a solvent for the amino resin.

The main advantages of amino resins are water solubility in the uncured state, allowing easy application to and with other water-soluble or water-wettable materials; the absence of color, which allows unlimited colorability with dyes and pigments; and good hardness and abrasion resistance in the cured state. Limitations of these materials include the release of formaldehyde during cure and in some cases after cure, and poor outdoor weatherability for urea moldings. Repeated cycling of wet and dry conditions can cause surface cracks. Melamine moldings, however, have relatively good outdoor weatherability. Formaldehyde is a very reactive gas that can be irritating to the mucous membranes. As more emphasis is placed on the quality of air and the control of pollution, some restrictions are being applied in the manufacture and use of urea–formaldehyde-resin-based products. For example, the use of urea–formaldehyde foams for insulating the outside walls of older houses has been banned in several states because of the slow release of formaldehyde. A high concentration of methylol groups can lead to the release of formaldehyde as follows. Two methylol groups may combine to form a dimethylene ether linkage and liberate a molecule of water:

$$2 \, RNHCH_2OH \rightleftharpoons RNHCH_2\text{—}O\text{—}CH_2NHR + H_2O$$

The dimethylene ether so formed is less stable than the diaminomethylene bridge and may rearrange to form a methylene link and liberate a molecule of formaldehyde:

$$RNHCH_2\text{—}O\text{—}CH_2NHR \rightarrow RNHCH_2NHR + HCHO$$

A recent patent describing an amino resin for wood composites of low formaldehyde emission suggests the use of a urea–formaldehyde resin having only 1.0–1.2 mol of formaldehyde for each mole of urea (3). The patent further suggests that the low ratio resin might be combined with a melamine cross-linker such as trimethoxymethylmelamine or hexamethoxymethylmelamine. Formaldehyde emission is said to be much lower than for a conventional particleboard.

Trimethoxymethylmelamine (TMMM)

Hexamethoxymethylmelamine (HMMM)

APPLICATIONS

Adhesives

Adhesives are by far the most important product based on amino resins. They may be very simple reaction products of urea or melamine with formaldehyde, or they may be complex formulated products that include plasticizers, extenders, curing agents, or hardeners. The large-volume products such as plywood and chipboard glues are often made as needed at the mill or supplied by some chemical company from a plant nearby. These are usually simple solutions of methylol compounds of high reactivity, limited storage life, and short cure time. Unlike laminating resins, the adhesive must not saturate the wood chips or veneers, but must remain in the glue line on the surface of the chips or between the plies. In general, the adhesives are made at high viscosity so that they will stay put in the glue line. Thickeners and extenders such as finely powdered pecan shells, wheat flour, etc are often used. All of the water in the adhesive formulation need not be removed before curing since it can diffuse through the wood. Laminating resins, on the other hand, must be of low viscosity so that they will quickly saturate the cloth or paper to be laminated. All of the water or other solvents must then be substantially removed before the laminate is pressed.

Furniture-assembly glues are highly developed compositions that are generally cured by adding a hardener or curing agent just prior to application. Urea–formaldehyde adhesives may be cured at room temperature by adding a catalyst such as ammonium chloride. A slow-acting basic material such as triethanolamine is often added to neutralize excess catalyst acid that otherwise might damage the wood. Amino resins may, of course, be cured with heat using less active catalysts. Very rapid cures may be achieved by applying heat in the form of microwave radiation. The moist amino-resin adhesive absorbs the high frequency radiation more than the dry wood, thereby concentrating the heat in the glue line where it is needed.

Melamine adhesives have excellent water resistance, whereas urea-based adhesives are lower cost, but somewhat more water sensitive. Often, the best all-around balance between cost and performance is struck with a blend of urea–formaldehyde and melamine–formaldehyde resins. It is not uncommon for amino-resin adhesives to contain modifiers like benzyl alcohol or furfuryl alcohol to make the resin less rigid so that it will be better able to relieve stresses imposed by shrinkage during cure and loss of water in glue lines of nonuniform thickness. These gap-filling adhesives are useful in furniture assembly. Urea–formaldehyde adhesives may also be blended with poly(vinyl acetate) (PVAc) to provide the short clamping time of the PVAc together with the heat and water resistance of the amino resin.

Laminated Plastics

Decorative laminated plastic sheet for counters and tabletops (Fig. 1) makes use of both phenolic and melamine resins. The phenolic resin is used in the backing or support

Figure 1. The use of Colorcore surfacing material in a cafe. Courtesy of the Formica Corp.

sheets, whereas the melamine resin performs both decorative and functional roles in the print sheet and in the protective overlay. Colorlessness, hardness, transparency, and stain resistance are essential for the decorative printed pattern to show through and yet provide a long-lasting working surface (Fig. 2). Good transparency is achieved because the refractive index of cured melamine–formaldehyde resin is near that of the cellulose filler fibers, so there is little scattering of light. Low cost and good all-around mechanical properties are provided by the phenolic backing layers. In this instance, phenolic and amino resins are combined to achieve an objective that neither could perform alone. To make such a laminated plastic sheet,

Figure 2. The use of Colorcore surfacing material in a fast-food restaurant. Courtesy of the Formica Corp.

the paper web is passed through a dip tank containing resin solution, adjusted for pickup on squeeze rolls, and then passed through a heated drying oven to remove most of the water or solvent. Phenolic resin is used from alcohol solution; melamine resins are best handled from water or water–alcohol mixtures. Once dried, the treated paper is fairly stable, and if stored in a cool place, may be kept for several weeks or months before pressing into laminated plastic sheets.

A melamine–formaldehyde resin for saturating the print and overlay sheets of a typical decorative laminate might contain 2 mol of formaldehyde for 1 mol of melamine. In preparing such a resin, some polymer is desirable to inhibit crystallization of methylol melamines. To effect this result, the reaction is continued until about one-fourth of the reaction product has been converted to low molecular weight polymer. Viscosity tests and cloud-point dilution tests are used to follow the buildup of polymer in the reaction mixture.

Decorative melamine laminates for countertops may be made so that they can be postformed to fit around curves. It is common to modify the melamine resin with a few percent of a toluenesulfonamide–formaldehyde resin to make it more flexible. When heated, these plasticized sheets are easily bent to curve up at the back of the counter top or down at the front. In addition, the postforming laminates may be slightly undercured compared to the regular grade. Special cigarette-resistant laminates are made by placing a thin metal sheet between the phenolic core and the printed decorative sheet. A burning cigarette left on a counter or table in a restaurant will not leave a black, burnt spot, because the metal film distributes the heat to a much larger area.

Wood Products

By far the most important application for amino resins is in the manufacture of reconstituted wood products. These are derived from materials that would otherwise be waste. For example, planer shavings can be formed into useful particleboard. Logs that are too small for conversion into lumber or plywood can be reduced to small particle form and then molded into useful boards. The board may have three layers, consisting of a core of coarse flakes with an overlay of fine flakes or wood fibers on each of the surfaces.

In the manufacture of particleboard, the aqueous solution of amino resin is sprayed on the wood chips as they tumble in a rotating drum. The amount of resin used may be from 6 to 10 parts of resin solids per 100 parts of dry wood. A wax emulsion is also applied. This will reduce the tendency of the finished board to absorb water. The wood flakes are generally made by a specially designed machine that cuts the flakes in the direction of the wood grain. A typical flake might be about 1 in. long, 0.25 in. wide, and not more than 0.10 in. thick. The cellulosic material may also be reduced to fibers. In this case the wood chips are ground in an attrition mill to form a pulp or water slurry having only about 2% by weight of wood fiber. An amino resin may be added to this slurry and then caused to precipitate onto the fibers by adding a small amount of an acid. The resulting mat may be used in the manufacture of hardboard or used for surfacing flakeboard.

A fairly recent and rapidly growing application for amino resins is in the manufacture of shingles and roofing mats. The resins are used as binders for the fiber glass mats used for these products.

The U.S. markets for amino resins are summarized in Table 1.

Many large chemical companies produce amino resins as well as the raw materials, ie, formaldehyde, urea, and melamine. Since the technology is very highly developed, sales must be supported by adequate technical service to select the best grade of resin and see that it is applied and cured under the best conditions. About 40 companies produce both urea and melamine resins, approximately 20 firms make only urea resins, and about five companies produce only melamine resins. The largest producers of amino resins are American Cyanamid Co., Borden Chemical Co., Chembond (a subsidiary of Getty Oil), Georgia-Pacific Corp., Gulf Oil Co., Monsanto Chemical Co., and Reichhold Co. Each of these companies is believed to produce over 45,000 metric tons of resin annually (100% solids basis).

TOXICITY OF AMINO RESINS

The two amino compounds used in the manufacture of amino resins are nontoxic. Urea is used as a feed supplement for ruminant animals such as cattle and sheep. The rumen microorganisms convert the urea to protein, which then can be used by the animal. Melamine has caused no ill effects in rats even when they are fed high concentrations. Fully cured amino plastics, like urea–formaldehyde molded bottle caps and molded melamine–formaldehyde plastic dinnerware, are also considered to be nontoxic.

Some amino resin-based products may release formaldehyde. These include the insulating foam mentioned earlier and the reconstituted wood products such as plywood, particleboard, and medium density fiberboard. When these products are used in the construction of homes, the released formaldehyde can pollute the indoor atmosphere. At present, there is no specific law in the United States stating the maximum concentration of formaldehyde that may be allowed in domestic indoor environments. In several countries, including the United States, various government agencies have proposed maximum safe levels for formaldehyde (5). The U.S. Department of Housing and Urban Development (HUD) (6) has issued a comprehensive study of formaldehyde release from the plywood and particle board that is commonly used in the construction of manufactured homes, also known as mobile homes.

Formaldehyde is highly reactive and combines easily with the proteins of the human body. Even at low concentrations, formaldehyde vapor can irritate the eyes, nose, and throat. This discomfort usually disappears in a short time when clean air is provided. Occasionally, however, an acute allergic reaction develops, and complete removal from formaldehyde exposure is required. Formaldehyde has also been found to cause cancer in laboratory animals.

In the manufacture of amino resins, every effort is made to recover and recycle the raw materials. However, there may be some loss of formaldehyde, methanol, or other solvent as tanks and reactors are vented. Some formaldehyde, solvents, and alcohols are also evolved in the curing of paint films, and the curing of adhesives and the resins applied to textiles and paper. The amounts of material evolved in curing amino resins is relatively small and may not justify the installation of complex recovery equipment. However, in the development of new resins for adhesives, coatings, and for treating textiles and paper, the greatest emphasis is being placed on those formulations that evolve a minimum of by-products (7).

Many amino resins used in coatings may contain solvents such as n-butyl alcohol and xylene. The acute oral (rat) LD_{50} values for n-butyl alcohol and xylene are 0.79 and 4.3 g/kg, respectively. Hexamethoxymethylmelamine, which is commonly used as a cross-linking agent for many different coating resins, has an acute oral (rat) LD_{50} value > 5 g/kg. The combusion or thermal decomposition of cured amino resins can evolve toxic gases: formaldehyde, hydrogen cyanide, and oxides of nitrogen. Amino resins, especially those based on melamine, have good heat resistance. Flammability is quite low and is classified as self-extinguishing or nonburning.

Table 1. U.S. Distribution of Applications of Amino Resins, 1983–1984[a]

Application	1983[b]	1984[b]
Bonding and adhesive resins for		
Fibrous and granulated wood	415	433
Laminating	17	20
Plywood	20	26
Molding compounds	33	35
Paper treatment and coating resins	33	46
Protective coatings	35	39
Textile-treatment and coating resins	31	36
Export	10	12
Other	7	8
Total	*601*	*655*

[a] Ref. 4.
[b] In 10^3 metric tons.

BIBLIOGRAPHY

1. Brit. Pats. 248,477 (Dec. 5, 1924), 258,950 (July 1, 1925), and 266,028 (Nov. 5, 1925), E. C. Rossiter (to British Cyanides Co., Ltd.).

2. Ger. Pat. 647,303 (July 6, 1937) and Brit. Pat. 455,008 (Oct. 12, 1936), W. Hentrich and R. Köhler (to Henkel and Co. GmbH).

3. U.S. Pat. 4,409,293 (Oct. 11, 1983), J. H. Williams (to Borden, Inc.).

4. *Mod. Plast.* **62**(1), 67 (1985).

5. M. Bowtell, *Adhesives Age* **28**(5), 42 (1985).

6. *Federal Register* **49**(155), 31996–32013 (Aug. 9, 1984).

7. L. Calve and G. Brunette, "Reducing Formaldehyde Emission from Particleboard with Urea-Salt or Sulfite Liquor," *Adhesives Age* **27**(7), 39 (1984).

General References

I. H. Updegraff in J. I. Kroschwitz, ed., *Encyclopedia of Polymer Science and Engineering,* Vol. 1, 2nd Ed., John Wiley & Sons, Inc., New York, 1985, pp. 752–789.

C. P. Vale and W. G. K. Taylor, *Amino Plastics,* Iliffe Books Ltd., London, 1964.

See also ADHESIVES; PLASTIC LAMINATES; WOOD—STRUCTURAL PANEL COMPOSITES.

IVOR H. UPDEGRAFF, PhD
Stamford, Connecticut

AMMANN & WHITNEY

Some of the most original and beguiling architecture of the twentieth century has been made possible due to the genius of the structural engineer. The firm of Ammann & Whitney (New York, N.Y.) has been in the vanguard of the architectural engineering field since 1946, when two of the most celebrated engineers of their day came together to form what now is considered one of the best structural engineering firms in the United States. Bridge designer Othmar H. Ammann and reinforced-concrete structure specialist Charles S. Whitney combined their respective talents to make seemingly "impossible-to-build" architectural designs a reality. Magnificent soaring designs such as Eero Saarinen's TWA Terminal at John F. Kennedy Airport and the Verrazano-Narrows Bridge (both New York, N.Y.) owe their realization to Ammann and Whitney.

Whereas the Ammann and Whitney firm in itself is responsible for many of the architectural wonders of the past two decades, the careers of the two founders must be examined before gaining a true appreciation for the company as it is known today. The better known of the two founders was Othmar H. Ammann (1879–1965) who was born and raised in Schaffhausen, Switzerland. In 1902, he received an engineering degree from the Swiss Federal Polytechnic Institute. Emigrating to the United States in 1904, he eventually (1912) settled in New York, N.Y., which he had always considered "the most exciting place for an engineer to work" (1).

During the years 1912–1923, he was chief assistant to the famous bridge engineer Gustav Lindenthal, helping design such noted projects as the Hell Gate Bridge (New York, N.Y.).

In 1923, he set up his own firm in New York, and in 1924 he was appointed chief engineer of bridges of the Port of New York Authority. Perhaps inspired by the work of an earlier fellow immigrant engineer, John A. Roebling, designer of the Brooklyn Bridge, Ammann designed many celebated bridges in the New York City area, beginning with the Goethals and Outerbridge Bridges in 1928. He also designed the Bayonne Bridge (1931), the Triborough Bridge (1936), the Lincoln Tunnel (1937), the Bronx-Whitestone Bridge (1939), and the Throgs Neck Bridge (1961), among others, all in New York. He capped his career with the Verrazano-Narrows Bridge completed in 1964, one year before his death.

Ammann served as chief engineer of the Port of New York Authority from 1930 to 1937 and as director of engineering from 1937 to 1939. From 1934 to 1939, he also served as chief engineer of the Triborough Bridge and Tunnel Authority, working closely with its chairman, Robert Moses.

His *chef d'oeuvre,* however, may have been the George Washington Bridge (1931) (Fig. 1) over the Hudson River, linking Ft. Lee, N.J. with Washington Heights, N.Y. Considered a perfect synthesis of art and engineering, the span inspired Le Corbusier to write (2):

> The George Washington Bridge over the Hudson is the most beautiful bridge in the world. Made of cables and steel beams, it gleams in the sky like a reversed arch. It is blessed. It is the only seat of grace in the disordered city. . . . When your car moves up the ramp the two towers rise so high that it brings you happiness; their structure is so pure, so resolute, so regular that here, finally, steel architecture seems to laugh.

Figure 1. George Washington Bridge, New York. Courtesy of Port of New York Authority.

The towers of the bridge were to have been faced with stone in the beaux-arts style. According to Le Corbusier, the designers said (3):

Stop! no stone or decoration here. The two towers and the mathematical play of the cables make a splendid unity. It is one. That is the new beauty.

and Le Corbusier continues his praise:

Drawing cannot give you the inexpressible sensation of a work thus suspended between water and sky. Neither can photography. The reader of these lines, then, will not be able to appreciate as I do, in the fervor of his heart, the miracle which happened at the right moment when a sensitive and soberminded man cried: "Stop!"

(Note: the lower traffic level was added in 1962.)

In addition, Ammann served as a consultant to Joseph B. Strauss, chief engineer, in the design and construction of the Golden Gate Bridge (San Francisco, Calif.) (1937). All said, Ammann enjoyed a brilliant career working for the New York Port Authority and the Triborough Bridge and Tunnel Authority before "retiring" in 1939 to return to private practice as a consulting engineer.

Not as well known, but equally brilliant, was Charles S. Whitney (1892–1959). Born in Bradford, Pa., he graduated from Cornell University (Ithaca, N.Y.) in 1914, before settling in Milwaukee, Wis. In 1922, he established a highly successful structural engineering practice in that city, where he became known for his innovative contributions to the advancement of the theory and practice of reinforced concrete design, including shells, domes, and arches, using ultimate strength design and plastic theory. (He wrote widely on the subject, publishing many articles and books throughout his lifetime.)

Among the most noted projects designed by Whitney before joining forces with Ammann are the Lakeside Park Bridge in Fond Du Lac, the Milwaukee County Expressway System, and the art nouveau West Sixth Street Bridge (Racine, Wis.), a reinforced concrete bridge ornamented with terra cotta. In 1941, Whitney served as chief architect, planning for the $30 million Camp McCoy in Wisconsin in partnership with the firm of Mead, Ward & Hunt.

He was a strong believer in the union of engineering and architecture. He proposed the necessity for harmony and unity as well as efficiency and truthfulness. He wrote: "The (Modern) Bridge Engineer has a thorough scientific training but he must become a serious student of architecture" (4).

He first met Ammann when they both worked on the Bronx Viaduct of the Hell Gate project in the office of Gustav Lindenthal. They kept in contact through the years and in 1946, the firm of Ammann and Whitney was founded and eventually grew to a firm of 1000 employees, with an office in Milwaukee headed by Whitney and another in New York City headed by Ammann. They immediately enjoyed success in the development and application of the latest state-of-the-art technology to attain practical and economic design solutions. Their best-known work includes the structural engineering for architect Eero Saarinen's cavernous, yet light, TWA Terminal at JFK Airport (1958–1962) (Fig. 2), with its powerful Y-shaped exterior supports and impressive light and airy cantilevering, and the same architect's Dulles International Airport Terminal outside Washington, D.C. (1962), where the structural clarity of the building shows through to make it an appropriate portal for the nation's capital. The terminal is the youngest building in the list of National Historic Landmarks. Ammann & Whitney was also charged with the master plan, design, and supervision of construction for the airport itself. Hundreds of honors and awards were bestowed upon them, including the American Institute of Architect's Allied Professional Medal in 1962, which was given jointly to Ammann and, posthumously, to Whitney.

An equally important, though not as well-known, contribution in airport design in the late 1950s was the series of unique cantilevered airplane hangars which provide

Figure 2. TWA Terminal, John F. Kennedy Airport, New York. Courtesy of Ammann & Whitney.

large unobstructed floor areas. Ammann and Whitney pioneered an innovative fire-proof, cable-suspended folded plate roof structure of reinforced concrete. This particular hangar design may now be seen in many of the world's major airports.

Ammann & Whitney is also known for its dome structures, including the Assembly Hall of the University of Illinois (Urbana, Ill.) (1963), done in conjunction with Harrison and Abramovitz, Architects. This unique design implements not one but two domes measuring 400 ft in diameter; that is, one dome serves as a roof resting on an upturned dome base, creating an interior completely free of columns. Equally as impressive, but unique in an altogether different way, is the Pittsburgh Arena (1963) (Fig. 3), designed with Mitchell and Ritchey, Architects, famous for its retractable domed roof. As befits the "City of Steel," the roof of the arena is a 415-ft diameter sheath of stainless steel. It is divided radially into eight 45° sections, six of which are movable and may glide over the two fixed sections, allowing the enclosed auditorium to become an open-air stadium in 2.5 min. The firm recently worked on a very different sort of project, performing all rehabilitation and upgrading engineering services for the herculean Arecibo radio telescope observatory in the mountains of Puerto Rico, with a 1200-ft diameter dish nestled in a natural hollow and fed by an elaborate system suspended far above. It is the largest radio telescope in the world.

One of the firm's specialties is the design and construction of bridges around the world, not the least of which is the Verrazano-Narrows Bridge across New York Harbor between Brooklyn and Staten Island, completed in November 1964 (Fig. 4). At that time the longest suspension bridge in the world, it is 6690 ft long, including a main span of 4260 ft. There are 143,000 miles of wire in its cables, enough to stretch halfway to the moon.

Its two 690-ft towers help support a double deck which carries 12 lanes of traffic. The effects of temperature are such that the center of the main span, which is approximately 230 feet above the mean high water level, may be 12 ft lower in summer than in winter.

From 1966 to 1976, Milton Brumer and Boyd Anderson, senior partners, directed the firm. In 1976, a long-time associate, Edward Cohen, became head of the firm. He

Figure 4. Verrazano-Narrows Bridge, New York. Courtesy of Ammann & Whitney.

had been with Ammann & Whitney since 1947, during which time he participated in most of the firm's major projects and formed a close working relationship with the two illustrious founders. Cohen, the recipient of many professional honors and awards, continues to carry out the tradition of excellence of Ammann & Whitney. Projects, among many, included the completion of the structural engineering work for the Lincoln Center of the Performing Arts with Harrison and Abramovitz; the Nelson D. Rockefeller Plaza New York State Government Center (Albany, N.Y.), again with Harrison and Abramovitz; the Colliding Beam Accelerator and other research facilities at Brookhaven National Laboratory and elsewhere; and the imposing Perimeter Acquisition Radar Building (Grand Forks, N.D.) in 1978, the largest in a series of blast-resistant structures that the firm designed for the U.S. military. The largest aboveground hardened structure in the world, the latter is designed to withstand the effects of a nuclear attack. They have prepared manuals for the military for protection against conventional blast and are currently providing services for improvement of security for U.S. embassies.

Of late, Ammann & Whitney is also becoming well-

Figure 3. Pittsburgh Civic Arena, Pittsburgh. Courtesy of Ammann & Whitney.

Figure 5. West facade of U.S. Capitol, Washington, D.C. Courtesy of the Architect of the Capitol.

known for its work in historical restoration, including the structural, mechanical, and electrical engineering phases of the restoration of the Statue of Liberty in New York Harbor (1986 rededication, Swanke Hayden Connell, Architects). This project required not only meeting modern building requirements and codes, but also strengthening and provision of new environmental systems while remaining faithful to the original materials and intent of the monument. Along this same line of historical restoration, Ammann & Whitney is currently involved with the restoration of the west facade of the U.S. Capitol Building (Washington, D.C.), scheduled to be completed in 1988 (Fig. 5). This project, being carried out with George M. White, Architect of the Capitol, involves the restoration of the only remaining portion of the original structure that is still visible. It requires the replacement of over 30% of the original porous sandstone with longer lasting limestone, the strengthening of the facade with stainless steel tendons, and pressure grouting the rubble stone foundations.

Their first historic restoration project was the strengthening and lightning protection of the Yorktown Victory Monument in the 1950s by making it the first posttensioned granite structure in the world.

Ammann & Whitney have combined their work in rebuilding the U.S. infrastructure with historic restoration in converting the Roebling Delaware Aqueduct Bridge (1847) to carry vehicular traffic while remaining true to the original construction (Beyer Blender Belle, Architects).

With headquarters overlooking New York Harbor (96 Morton St., New York, N.Y.) the firm continues to blaze trails in many fields of engineering.

BIBLIOGRAPHY

1. F. C. Kunz and O. H. Ammann, *Design of Steel Bridges,* McGraw-Hill Book Co., Inc., New York, 1915.
2. Le Corbusier, *When Cathedrals Were White,* McGraw-Hill Book Co., Inc., 1964.
3. P. Goldberg, *The City Observed,* Vintage Books, New York, 1979.
4. O. H. Ammann, "Bridges of New York," *J. Boston Soc. Civ. Eng.* (July 1937).

General References

O. H. Ammann, "The Hudson River Bridge," *Eng. News* (Feb. 1928).

C. S. Whitney, *Bridges: A Study in Their Art, Science & Evolution,* Ridge Publishers, New York, 1928.

O. H. Ammann, *Proceedings of the American Institute of Consulting Engineers,* Nov. 4, 1931.

O. H. Ammann, "Planning the Lincoln Tunnel Under the Hudson," *Civ. Eng.* (June 1937).

O. H. Ammann, "Verrazano-Narrows Bridge: Conception of Design and Construction Procedure," *J. Constr. Div. ASCE* (Mar. 1966).

E. Cohen, "The Engineer and His Works: A Tribute to Othmar Hermann Ammann," *Ann. N.Y. Acad. Sci.,* **136** (Sept. 1967).

Encyclopedia Britannica, Vol. 5, Helen Hemingway Benton Pub., Chicago, 1974.

E. Cohen and F. Elias, "Restoring the U.S. Capitol West Front," *Mil. Eng.* (July 1985).

See also Bridges.

Charles Szoradi, aia
Architect and Planner
Washington, D.C.

AMUSEMENT PARKS

Among the organized leisure-time entertainments that have become popular in the twentieth century is the amusement park. Evolved from a lengthy and varied tradition, the amusement park is but one example of employing entertainment to concentrate people in a centralized location in order to promote commerce. Other examples included here as influential in the development of the amusement park are world's fairs and expositions, pleasure gardens, and picnic groves.

Millions of people today enjoy amusement parks as a means of entertainment, education, or simply as a temporary escape from the everyday world. Present-day amusement parks can be divided into two broad categories: theme parks, typified by Disneyland and Disney World; and ride parks, such as Coney Island. The basic elements that define a modern amusement park are common to both types: the roller coaster, big merry-go-round, Ferris wheel, penny arcade, shooting gallery, flat rides, fun house, dark ride, midway, and picnic facilities. The amusement business is a multibillion dollar industry operating in various forms throughout the world.

HISTORICAL DEVELOPMENT

Early social antecedents of the amusement park include feast and the fair, defined thus (1):

> **Feast** n [fr. ME feast, festival; fr. L, solemn, festal; akin to holidays, temple] 1a: an elaborate meal often accompanied by ceremony or entertainment; banquet b: something that gives unusual or abundant pleasure.

Fair *n* [fr. ML, weekday or fair; fr. LL, festal day; fr. L holidays—FEAST] 1: a gathering of buyers and sellers for trade 2: a competitive exhibition.

Providing a gathered populus with both amusement and commerce originated with the founding of large marketplaces. In ancient Egypt, religious festivals were accompanied by commercial fair activity. In Greece, the crowds gathered for Olympian games were likewise supplied by fair vendors. The Roman successors to Augustus, in an age glutted with ostentatious wealth, extravagant pleasure, and search for entertainment, provided excuse and opportunity for vast building enterprises: thermae for bathing and games, amphitheaters for gladiatorial contests, theaters for drama, circuses for races, and the forum as the center of public life and commerce. Although these distinct building types have been adopted for many different uses over time, their influence on the activities and architectural forms of amusement continues to be felt. In medieval Europe, fairs were instrumental in the revival of commerce, intellectual life, trade routes, and political stability. They were supported by the church not only for their religious affiliations with saints' feast days but for the income from admission tolls and concession and pilgrimage fees.

The modern fair had its inception in the public art shows of the eighteenth century, which were intended to promote excellence through competition, advance artists' sales and reputations, improve public taste, and enhance the nations' reputations for creativity. The British established the precedent, but it was through the French that the world's fair found its form (2).

WORLD'S FAIRS AND INTERNATIONAL EXPOSITIONS

Louis XIV and the Ecole des Beaux Arts supported French public art shows as part of the Greco-Roman historical revival. In 1797, a public exhibition combining sales and entertainment was successfully undertaken to delete a surplus in the French national warehouse caused by an English blockade of shipping. In 1798, Napolean joined the prestige of the government to that of the industrial revolution by means of a three-day trade fair of French-manufactured goods at the Champ de Mars, which included temporary facades designed by Jacques Louis David. By the mid-nineteenth century, other countries held similar but smaller fairs; France, however, was the only government providing direct sponsorship.

The first international trade fair, the Great Exhibition of the Industry of All Nations, was organized by Prince Albert as president of the Royal Society of Arts, which had sponsored the UK's first public art shows as well as exhibitions of agricultural equipment. Due to political opposition, financing was arranged through private subscribers, who were to be reimbursed from entrance fees. For this fair, Joseph Paxton designed what *Punch* magazine dubbed the Crystal Palace. Built in 1851, the Crystal Palace measured as many feet and covered 18 acres of Hyde Park. Using principles developed in greenhouse design and borrowed from rail-line construction, Paxton created a building with 300,000 panes of glass (each measuring 49×10 in.) laid in an iron mullion system over 3230 prefabricated, hollow iron pillars. It was constructed in less than six months without scaffolding. The Crystal Palace had a profound impact on architecture and engineering, influencing construction technology, structural systems, building size, spatial order, and architectonic language.

In order to reestablish preeminence in world fairs, the French, at the Exposition Universelle of 1867, demonstrated the engineering prowess for which they were famed in the late nineteenth century. Displays were held in an elliptical glass and iron building derived in form from Frederic le Play's encyclopedic categorization of the world. This building was to symbolize the world, and Gustave Eiffel was employed to supervise its construction. There were displays of the first distillation of petroleum and the making of aluminum. Surrounding this were gardens and, for the first time at a French fair, an amusement park.

The 1889 Exposition Universelle included a Palais des Machines made of steel and glass with a clear span of 115 m and length measuring 420 m. More spectacularly, the engineer Eiffel erected the tallest structure in the world, the Eiffel Tower. Although construction costs were partially subsidized by the national government, Eiffel received admission fees for 20 years, after which time the tower reverted to the city of Paris. It paid for itself within weeks of the closing of the fair, and Eiffel became a national hero and a wealthy man.

In contrast to the architectural and engineering developments of the continental expositions, the fairs in the United States were remarkably uninnovative. For the 1853 New York World's Fair organized by Horace Greeley and held at Reservoir Square, now Bryant Park, there was constructed a crystal palace in a Greek-cross plan with gothic and oriental styling. Unfortunately for U.S. architecture, the superficial taste for the exotic and antique prevailed in later U.S. fairs. P. T. Barnum, the fair's president, promoted the idea that there should be more to a world's fair than displays and exhibits. He was instrumental in incorporating a large amusement area on the fairground, where he introduced General Tom Thumb and the hurdy gurdy. The New York Palace was lit by more gas lights than were found in the entire city at that time; when the building caught fire in 1853, it collapsed in 12 min.

The main building for the 1876 International Centennial Exhibition in Fairmont Park, Philadelphia, was designed by H. J. Schwarzmann, the landscape architect of the park. The building was of a beaux-arts style with Moorish interior details by Frank Furness (3). Engineering innovations on exhibition included the Westinghouse air brake, Edison's duplex telegraph, and Bell's telephone. Shown in the Women's Building Annex were a mural by Mary Cassat and the Froebel blocks that would greatly influence Frank Lloyd Wright (4).

The World's Columbian Exposition in Chicago of 1893 was the prototype and impetus for the modern amusement-theme park, but its design was said by Frank Lloyd Wright to have set back modern architecture 50 years. An architecture as impressive and transitory as a movie set, it was the expression of a "new world that dared no innovations" (5). Chaired by Daniel Burnham, the building committee included Louis Sullivan, John Wellborn Root, Stanford White, and Frederick Law Olmsted. After Root's untimely death, the eclectic Venetian gothic approach was mandated. Sullivan's transportation building, with its original ornament and freedom from historicizing style, was the only memorable structure at the fair. The whole "city" was constructed of wood frame by legions of carpenters, including Walt Disney's father. The architectural importance of the Columbian Exposition is not a stylistic one; rather, for the first time, people in the United States experienced an environment designed in a consistent scale and vocabulary with a visual order marshaled toward enjoyment. This was the first theme park in the United States (6). Moreover, the midway area of the Columbian Exposition gave birth to the amusement park and to the carnival in the United States. Whereas previous world fairs had only traces of an amusement zone, the Midway Plaissance was an amusement area complete in itself, running for a mile on what is today the campus of the University of Chicago. There, in competitive response to the Eiffel Tower, George W. Ferris operated a 200-ft diameter moving wheel with a capacity to carry over 6000 passengers hourly in streetcar-sized gondolas. Eadwaerd Muybridge presented moving pictures of birds and wrestling athletes. Just outside the gates of the fair, on the back lot of Buffalo Bill's Wild West Show, was a motley crew of unofficial amusement people who, when threatened to be shut down by fair administrators, joined together as a collective and formed the United States' first carnival (7).

The Pan-American Exposition in Buffalo of 1901 was built in the style of the Spanish Renaissance. Frederick Thompson and Elmer Dundy introduced the first of the illusion rides, "Trip to the Moon," with lunar airstrip landing in green moon grottos, amidst green midgets and green cheese, all staged in a single, large green building.

The 1904 Louisiana Purchase Exposition in St. Louis is memorable for its famous song, "Meet Me in St. Louis, Louis." Attractions included the first U.S. Olympics, Washington University as an exhibit, and the display of the wireless telegraph.

San Francisco's Panama-Pacific Exhibition of 1915 celebrated the completion of the Panama Canal. Marcel Duchamp's "Nude Descending a Staircase" was exhibited in Bernard Maybeck's classical Palace of Fine Arts, which was later rebuilt as a permanent structure.

Whereas the architecture of the U.S. fairs catered to the popularly accepted pseudo-classical styles, the European fairs reflected and affected the evolution of modern architecture. The lush art nouveau of the 1900 Paris Exposition (including Hector Guimard's Paris metro facades) gave way to an intellectual interest in geometric and cubistic solutions to formal questions. The Deutsche Werkbund Exposition in Cologne in 1914 provided the modern movement with one of its most influential works in the model factory of Walter Gropius. At the Paris Werkbund Exposition in 1925, Joseph Hoffman and Frederick Kiesler contributed innovative projects, and Le Corbusier built the Pavilion de l'Espirit Nouveau. The 1927 Werkbund Exhi-

bition in Stuttgart contributed to the development of economical and modern housing. The International Exposition in Barcelona of 1927 featured the German Pavilion by Mies van der Rohe as a reception hall for the German ambassador. It was an architectural monument of tremendous importance and formal invention; it was remembered long after the fair and was reconstructed in 1986. In this, the European fair was consistent in providing a free forum for architectural discourse.

Establishing industrial design as a profession in the U.S. during the 1930s, Norman Bel Geddes and Raymond Loewy applied stage design processes and theatrical perceptual systems in designing the 1933 Century of Progress fair in Chicago and, in 1939 with Henry Dreyfus and Walter Dorwin Teague, the New York World's Fair. The trylon and perisphere of the latter were the symbols of a streamlined optimism about the future; from a balcony in the perisphere, visitors surveyed Democracity, "a perfectly integrated metropolis" designed by Henry Dreyfus. The Futurama exhibit by Bel Geddes showed a 1960s world entirely streamlined by movement principles of free-flowing people and goods. There were pavilions designed by Gropius and Breuer, Markelius, and Aalto. The fair was in a simple, undecorated style to which Wright commented, ". . . having seen the handwriting on the wall, New York eclectics were crowding to be the first to be modern" (8). The extensive midway included vaudeville shows by Abbott and Costello and Gypsy Rose Lee.

In response to New York as the World of Tomorrow, the San Francisco Golden Gate Exhibition of 1939 turned its attention to the historical themes of the Pacific Basin; it used a stylistic blend of Mayan, Incan, Malayan, and Cambodian architecture. This fair's greatest contribution to design was the one-piece bathing suit for women (9).

The Brussels Fair in 1958 succeeded because of its architecture, with Le Corbusier's Philips exhibition a bold experiment using precast hyperbolic–paraboloid concrete shells. The Seattle Fair in 1962 introduced a modern monorail and the Space Needle (Fig. 1) as an updated version of the Eiffel Tower. The tradition of multinational corporations' sponsorship of pavilions escalated, so that the New York World's Fair of 1964 was dominated by the publicity of business; it was the great acclaim that Disney received for his displays at this fair that convinced him a market would exist for Disney World. Expo 67 in Montreal included architecture by Frei Otto and Arthur Erickson, as well as Buckminster Fuller's glass geodesic dome and Moshe Safdie's Habitat housing project. At Osaka in 1970, the Japanese constructed the instant city envisioned by Archigram; pavilions were built by Kenzo Tange, Kiyonari Kikutake, and Kisho Kurokawa.

PLEASURE GARDENS

The pleasure garden had come into existence after the Renaissance with the concentration of population in cities and an increase in leisure time. In the U.K., the pleasure garden was part of an evolutionary process orginating with country inns and taverns and resulting in the amusement park. The French pleasure garden originated with

Figure 1. Seattle skyline view with Space Needle. Courtesy of Seattle–King County Convention and Visitors Bureau.

gardens at Vaux le Vicomte and Versailles (10). Stationary amusement areas became profitable and were established near cities to attract the urban population at leisure.

Vauxhall Gardens, the first internationally famous pleasure garden, opened south of London in 1611 and operated until 1850. Although admission to the grounds of Vauxhall Gardens, including dance pavilions and band concerts, was free, individual entertainment concessions within the grounds charged admission. The Prater, established in Vienna in the 1850s, replaced Vauxhall as the world's outstanding pleasure garden. Two thousand acres in size, it was the site of the 1873 World's Fair. The Prater's Ferris wheel is one of the world's largest even today.

Among Vauxhall's preeminent successors is Tivoli Gardens in Copenhagen, which derives its name not from the Italian gardens at Villa d'Este but from a successful contemporary pleasure garden in Paris. Built in 1843 on three of the *glacis* of the outer ramparts of the city wall, the site would not accommodate the axial plan of a typical pleasure garden. Instead, a tree-lined promenade was developed on top of the berm, providing views of the attractions located below. At Tivoli in Copenhagen, structures are presented as an atmospheric backdrop rather than as a formal architectural expression. Spatial order is established by means of zones, each with a specific function and architectural definition. As such, the visual influence

of Tivoli at Copenhagen can be seen in all of the major U.S. amusement parks today. Tivoli's success is due to its limited size, beautiful setting, and ability to adapt and change to accommodate the city of Copenhagen as it grows around the park. It is simultaneously an amusement park, cultural center, and urban park. It could not have been conceived originally in its existing complexity, for it is the product of a 100-year process. Through its various areas, which appeal to diverse strata of population, Tivoli at Copenhagen is said to be an exceptionally democratic urban institution.

PICNIC GROVES

The U.S. counterpart to pleasure gardens, the picnic grove evolved from a primarily rural phenomenon and developed into the amusement park and resort. Many of the social movements of the nineteenth century instigated architectural invention; the evangelical Chatauqua, the grange movement, and Shaker communities are exemplary. These movements renewed an interest in a landscape tradition and established the recreation industry in America. Oak Bluffs, a Protestant religious settlement and bathing resort on Martha's Vineyard, is one example typical in intention and built scale. In the 1830s, it was similar to hundreds of other contemporary revival camps at which people slept in tents with straw bedding. By 1859, the Martha's Vineyard Camp Meeting was the world's largest, with 12,000 people in attendance one August Sunday. That year, a Providence family shipped over a small house with fanciful wood carving and Victorian gingerbread trim. Soon many other houses similar in style were built, frequently on the same platforms the tents had been previously. The Gothic double doors typically used were meant to recall the tent flaps. In 1879, the large circus tent was replaced by a glass tabernacle famed for its iron filigree.

TROLLEY PARKS

The trolley park originated in New England. Like the resort and picnic grove, the trolley park grew as an extension of the transportation system. Charged a flat monthly rate for electricity, the traction companies, operators of trolley lines, built electrically powered amusement parks at the end of the trolley lines. This encouraged use of trolley cars on weekends when business was otherwise slow; it also generated additional revenues from fares for rides and games. Once successful, the trolley parks were often sold by companies who saw them solely as a means to expand fares. The parks were frequently sold for fast profit to private interests that had no long-range plans and consequently were unwilling to invest or update. Most buyers were from the circus or the traveling carnival. Without maintenance, the equipment became rundown and dangerous. Larcenous games on the midway, fraudulent advertising, and short-changing became more common. Many communities undertook efforts to restore these corrupted parks. When such campaigns were unsuccessful, the parks were frequently bought outright by the city, the county government, or the chamber of commerce.

CONTEMPORARY AMUSEMENT PARKS

Early Examples

Lake Compounce (Bristol, Conn.) was built on land that had been held by the same family since 1684. In continual operation since 1846, it is the oldest U.S. amusement park (11). By 1900, the largest, most successful and best-managed amusement park was a Coney Island of the midwest, located on the banks of the Ohio River 20 miles upstream from Cincinnati. Because it was subject to periodic flooding, Coney Island of Ohio was regularly rebuilt, maintained, and updated, and so had the most up-to-date rides for years. Edward Schott, son of the original founder, created the clean amusement park image, where trash was quickly disposed. In the 1950s, he was enlisted by Walt Disney to aid in the design of Disneyland. Desiring a high class resort, tobacco tycoon Abbot Kinney built over 30 miles of Venetian Canals on the coast near Los Angeles in 1904 complete with imported gondoliers. Soon amusement park piers surrounded Venice, Calif., but the health problems associated with the stagnant canals led to the failure of the adjacent housing development. The area,

fallen into disrepair, was taken over by the city of Los Angeles and many of the canals have since been filled. Atlantic City, N.J., is second only to Coney Island as the most famous amusement park in combination with a water resort. The boardwalk of Atlantic City is unique; 60 ft wide and 4 miles long, it is built of steel and concrete and overlaid with pine planking in a herringbone pattern. The picture postcard was introduced here in 1885, as was salt-water taffy.

Coney Island

The original amusement parks were basically designed for adults rather than for children. The transition was spurred by the immensely successful diverse development of the most famous park in the history of amusement, Coney Island, N.Y.

The site was established in the mid-seventeenth century with the growing interest in ocean bathing. Construction included only smaller, lightweight buildings, beer gardens, cabarets, and bathing piers, until the construction of the first luxury hotel, Ocean Pavilion in 1874, which was financed by the owner's invention of the "red hot" hot dog. Other grand hotels followed, culminating in 1881 with Lucy, the Margate Elephant Hotel. Measuring 122 ft high, its front legs were 60 ft in diameter and housed a tobacco store and diorama. In the hind legs were the entrance and exit to guest rooms above; in the head was the vista room, which faced the ocean. This hotel made the elephant the unofficial symbol of the amusement park for the next 50 years.

Structures from various U.S. world fairs were later reconstructed on Coney Island. In 1877, the Sawyer Observatory from the Philadelphia Centennial was removed to Coney Island and renamed the Iron Tower. George Tilyou brought together the Ferris wheel from the Chicago Exposition in 1893 and Thompson and Dundy's "Trip to the Moon" from the 1901 Buffalo Exposition. These were used, in combination with his own mechanized horseracing ride, to update the attractions in Tilyou's Steeplechase Park. It was the first park to charge a flat rate (25¢), and it became the prototype for the other amusement parks at Coney Island and in the rest of the United States (12).

In 1895, Captain Billy Boyton, a professional diver and pioneer of underwater living, opened Sea Lion Park. It was the first fully enclosed amusement park with grouped rides, including the first shoot-the-chutes water ride and the first loop-the-loop roller coaster. Taken over by Thompson and Dundy in 1903, it was rebuilt as Luna Park. Dundy organized financial backing of over $1 million, only $22 of which was left on opening night for making change. However, within the first 2 hours, over 40,000 people paid the 10¢ admission. Thompson, who had left the Ecole des Beaux Arts in the midst of his architectural education, designed the park based on a lunar theme. It included a skyline of pinnacles, spires, towers, and minarets, to which more were continually added. The park was extremely successful and influenced amusement parks built all over the world prior to World War I. However, when Dundy died in 1907, Thompson's extravagance went unchecked and he died bankrupt in 1919.

In 1904, Senator William Reynolds opened Dreamland, intending it to be the park to end all parks. At a cost of $3.5 million, it boasted the biggest ballroom in the world with a capacity of 25,000 dancers. It included a small city for 300 midgets, a simulation of a submarine and an airplane ride (before the first airplane had flown), a Swiss panorama, and the canals of Venice. Two grand spectacles competed with vaudeville: a six-story hotel was set on fire every night in "Fighting Flames"; and Pompeii, reconstructed at a cost of over $2000, was engulfed daily in fiery flowing lava. The premature babies of the New York metropolitan area were rescued and displayed in the Incubator Building. Although all the buildings of Dreamland were painted flat white, the Incubator Building was disguised as "an old German farmhouse," on its roof "a stork overlooking a nest of cherubs" (13).

Fire did not come only in controlled spectacle. Built of wood and lath, the amusement parks at Coney Island were susceptible to burning; owners paid $5.50 per $100 of insurance, compared with normal fire insurance of 3¢ per $100. Steeplechase Park burned down in 1907, was rebuilt, and revived strongly. Dreamland burned to the ground in 1911. With the creation of more side shows and the extension of the subway, attendance grew from 100,000 on a Sunday in 1900 to 1,000,000 on a Sunday in 1925. Coney Island was closed briefly during the Depression of the 1930s, but revived in the 1940s with the return of servicemen from World War II. In a state of disrepair, Luna Park burned down in 1946, and the site was cleared for a parking lot.

Coney Island still has an operation called Steeplechase Park, but today it consists of only a dozen rides, all outdoors. The Wonder Wheel still dazzles visitors, and Astroland, doing capacity business with a Space Tower soaring 300 ft over Brooklyn, is still adding rides every year.

The era of amusement parks began in the 1890s and flourished in the years before World War I. It coincided with a critical period in U.S. history, when the nation came of age as an urban, industrial society. In an era of changing economic and social conditions, which created the basis for a new mass culture, amusement parks prospered as there were no other widely available inexpensive forms of entertainment. The decline of the amusement park in the 1920s and 1930s can be attributed to the ascent of the automobile as the major recreation vehicle. With a car, a family could organize its own entertainment. At the parks, family patronage was replaced by undesirables, toughs, and gangs. Both the advent of movies and the Depression aggravated this decline, and between 1921 and 1936 the number of amusement parks dwindled from 1500 to 500. An interest in amusement parks was rekindled in the 1940s, but the introduction of television made this revival brief as people in the United States stayed home to be entertained. The general decline of the traditional amusement park can be variously attributed to managerial neglect; disastrous fires; an underestimation of patron sophistication, which began to surpass the standard park's offerings; the pay-one-price policy, which frequently could not be high enough to cover investment costs; the rapid growth of cities, leading to parking problems, escalating land values, and buyouts by developers; but, most impor-

tantly, the effects of vandalism and the costs of increased security. In the 1950s, Walt Disney combined the amusement park with film to create a unique and new form of entertainment, which has largely determined the development of the current latter-day amusement park.

Disneyland: Destination Park

Walt Disney combined the vitality of Tivoli, the beauty of Dreamland, and the cleanliness and efficiency of Coney Island in Ohio with movie-making design processes in Disneyland at Anaheim, Calif. Use of scripts established a separate cinematic identity or theme for each of Disneyland's five lands. By storyboard techniques, the camera or the viewer was led through a perceptual sequence of well-controlled visual experiences cast against desired backdrops. This storyboard sequence was translated into the architecture of Disneyland, producing a visual order with controlled vistas and an intimacy of scale (14). Rather than the typical rides of other amusement parks, Disney provided cinematic continuation in the short skits of his characteristic dark rides, such as "Pirates of the Caribbean" and "Peter Pan." The success of Disneyland is due in part to its symbiotic relationship with national television; the early Disneyland television show premiered on ABC in exchange for financial backing for the park.

The construction of Disneyland was the consummate example of the multiple theme park, and it instigated the next generation of parks, the destination park. A trip to Disneyland can necessitate a stay of several days, and the proximity of Disney hotel and restaurant accommodations is effective in providing for and capitalizing on all of the necessities.

Disney World in Florida is built on a slightly larger scale than its California predecessor. Even so, the Florida park has dimensions that are inapplicable to any functioning U.S. city. Main Street, for example, is 55 ft wide, far less than the 80- to 100-ft widths of principal streets in the horse-and-buggy days. The great axial vista between Cinderella's Castle and the railroad station encompasses three plazas, two city blocks, an island, and two strips of water, yet totals just 900 ft, the distance between Fifth and Sixth Avenues in New York City (15). The adjoining buildings are correspondingly miniaturized; ground floors are only seven-eighths full height, and successive stories diminish progressively so that the third floors are about half size.

The Disney concern with scale and space, though effective in its context, does not come out of any environmental design traditions. The compression of size and manipulation of relative scale stems from Walt Disney's hobby of model railroading and from film set design, where space is at a premium and illusions are mandated by tight quarters. The effect of such tricks is to make the viewer feel comfortable and important.

The technical innovations of the Disney parks are legion. Disneyland's private utility district generates much of its own power, and uses waste heat from turbines to supply energy for air conditioning as well as steam and hot water. The size of the submarine fleet of Disney World ranks ninth in the entire world. The political jurisdiction within which Disney World operates is a government in which all voters and elected officials must be property owners within the 43-square-mile area. Five-acre parcels, sold to directors, are repurchased and resold as directorships change hands. As a result, the Disney organization has a remarkably free hand to master plan, zone, and build on its own property with few of the normal reviews and constraints of county or state government. Disney World has its own building code, which stresses performance standards, and it has thereby been able to build nonconventional structures including two hotels from prefabricated steel modules. EPCOT, the Experimental Prototype City of Tomorrow, was the title of Walt Disney's last and most compelling project (Fig. 2). However, it has been realized after his death not as a working utopia nor even as a living community; it is a merchandise mart about future prospects in energy, space, information processing, and transportation underwritten by the United States' largest corporations. Even without the real EPCOT, Disney World's role as the greatest amusement park seems secure (16). Its competitors lack the obsessive concern for quality and detail that has become a trademark of the Disney organization.

Other Types of Theme Parks

The early amusement park designed primarily for the entertainment of adults has been transformed by the Disney example into parks that are thematically developed and cater to clean entertainment for the entire family. Types of present-day parks include reconstructed towns, reenacted histories, storylands, kiddieland settings for characters from current books and cartoons, water and submarine parks, wild life habitats and exotica, and thrill-ride parks. Circulation is a critical issue in every park, and most successful parks are organized by one of two types of circulation. The linear structure of a grand axis, as for example at Taft's Kings Dominion or Kings Island in Ohio, provides a forceful organization which is dynamic

and always clear. The continuous loop, as typified in the theme park design of Randall Duell, allows for spatial diversity yet insures that a visitor sees everything. Examples include Marriott's Great America parks in California and Illinois. Rather than using architectural backdrops to establish a thematic identity, many parks are developing technologies including lasers, holography, and interactive video, and these changes may affect the formal organization of future parks.

PARK EQUIPMENT AND RIDES

The renaissance of amusement–theme parks in the 1960s shifted the emphasis to conventional rides for parks that could not hope to muster the expertise or finances to support Disney-type dark rides. As such, the amusement park rides can be likened to the furniture of the park, used to activate or define space while providing various degrees of enclosure, color, and activity. The more prominent these rides are visually, the more the park is an amusement park rather than a theme park.

Carousels

In the UK it is called the roundabout, in France the carousel, and in the United States the merry-go-round. Rich in history, the carousel is the ancestor of all of today's flat rides. From the Italian word for jousting, *carosello* (a corruption of the diminutive word for quarrelsome), came the name for the rotating frame on which jousters could ride while trying to spear a brass ring with their lance. In 1662, Louis XIV staged a jousting tournament which gave its name to the Place du Carrousel. With a triumphal arch by Percier and Fontaine to mark this spot between Tuileries and the Louvre, the Place du Carrousel is today more famous for its blue and red lit fountains commemorating the aristocratic and peasant blood shed there during the revolution.

Figure 2. Kodak's "Journey into Imagination," Epcot Center, Orlando, Fl. Reprinted courtesy of Eastman Kodak Company.

Figure 3. The "Loch Ness Monster" at the Old Country, Busch Gardens, Williamsburg, Va. Courtesy of Busch Gardens.

Through its age-old tradition and familiarity, the merry-go-round is a fixture of both ride park and theme park. The German El Dorado Carousel, installed at Coney Island in 1911, is the exemplar of the highly esteemed German carousel. Sixty feet in diameter, its 48-ft height contained three tiers of platforms revolving at different speeds. By tradition, the U.S. carousel turns counterclockwise, whereas the European model turns clockwise. Since carousel horses are deeply carved and jewelled only on the outer side, the origin can be differentiated easily. The carving of wood horses, a signature mark for various manufacturers, is an art lost today. Fiber glass or aluminum horses are lighter and cheaper to make. The market for new carousels has declined as old parks are dismantled and carousels simply change hands.

Roller Coasters

Today's roller coaster (Fig. 3) traces its beginning to seventeenth-century St. Petersburg, where ice slides were built on wood frameworks. Dangerously high speeds were achieved by shooting down a 50° iced incline more than 70 ft in length. The French adapted the mechanism to a warmer climate in 1804 by making the ramps from many rollers to accommodate sliding toboggans. Today's large slides, water flumes, and skateboarding attractions are direct descendants.

In 1884, Le Marcus Thompson, a Sunday school teacher concerned with the dearth of organized amusements for young people, introduced the Switch Back Railway at Coney Island. It was a gravity mechanism that worked between stationary towers at either end. Within one year, this roller coaster had been modified to include features standard to all future models: the power operated chain elevator and an oval tract to bring passengers back to their starting point. Boyton's Sea Lion Park at Coney Island opened with the first water flume and a 360° loop-the-loop. The loop created back pains and whiplash, but was readapted into the elliptical version featured today. At Chicago's 1893 Midway, the roller coaster ran on frozen pipes shaded by the nearby Ferris wheel. When it was moved to Coney Island into full sunlight, the ice melted and the ride ground to a halt.

More than any other amusement park ride, a roller

coaster must look as dangerous as it is safe to ride. Roller coasters run faster in the rain or on hot days when the packing grease is thinned. A lower car gives a greater feeling of speed, even though it is close to the center of gravity. Railings that flash past are effective in conveying a sense of speed and danger; conversely, the lack of railings at the crest can convey a fear of falling off. Tracks that weave over, under, or beside other tracks or construction intensify spatial effects. Actual speeds achieved on roller coasters typically vary between 25 mph on curves and 35 mph in valleys. Roller coasters are expensive capital expenditures, but are prominent identifying fixtures; through increasing park capacity, they can pay for themselves in a season or less. Frequently, they are arranged in pairs, with tamer versions for those with weaker stomachs. The tallest roller coaster in the world is the Moonsault Scrambler in Fujikyu Highland Park, Japan. It is 246 ft tall and includes drops equivalent to falling off a 15-story building.

Ferris Wheels

George Washington Gale Ferris gave his name to the Ferris wheel and provided a drawing card for the Colombian Exposition. Weighing 3 million pounds and measuring 264 ft tall, the Ferris wheel had a capacity of 2160 people and a speed of 20 min per revolution. It required special engineering for expansion and contraction due to atmospheric changes. This wheel was the largest, but not the first of its kind. Pleasure wheels and early "teeter totters" of wood had been used in Europe and the Orient for centuries. In the UK, they are called perpendicular roundabouts.

Ferris's design was based on calculations by J. W. Graydon, a marine engineer, whose own Graydon wheel included first- and second-class cars. Spectators could pay to climb through either of the 150-ft high observation towers supporting the wheel or to pass through the wheel's hollow axle from one tower to the other. The only large wheel surviving today is the Prater in Vienna; damaged by U.S. bombers in World War II, it was subsequently restored and later played an important role in Orson Welles' film "The Third Man."

Flat Rides

Over 100,000 applications for inventions of amusement park devices are on file at the U.S. Patent Office in Washington, D.C. Many have followed developments in transportation: rides simulating bicycles, automobiles, airplanes, zeppelins, and rockets have all been built as park flat rides. For instance, when bicycles were still a novelty, an 1882 amusement park ride called "Flying Velocipedes" had bikes bolted to the outside of a circular frame, and the riders provided the power. However, too many riders shirked their share of the pedaling, and the ride was pronounced a failure. The first circular, undulating flat rides were built in the UK as early as 1845 and were called "Venetian Gondolas." A modern version called "Lover's Lake" includes a rolling canopy that comes up and over the string of cars. Both boats and cars are used for dark rides, passages through dark tunnels which include mechanical frights and electrical shocks.

Circle swings are among the most venerable of all amusement devices. In the simplest form, seats are suspended from chains attached to a frame revolving horizontally on a central post. Many manually operated circle swings are still made for public playgrounds and school yards. The first modern circle swing was installed at Elitch's Gardens in Denver in 1904. Circular rides in which the radial arms are center-mounted to a sleeve that rises up the mast are increasing in popularity. They provide an added dimension of motion for the articulated arm action.

The first new type of ride to be developed recently is the "Pillow Ride" or "Moon Walk." It is in fact not really a ride; customers amuse themselves by jumping up and down. Because initial investment is low, these rides generate profit quickly. The Dodgem is another popular ride, where the driver of an electric car steers into and bumps other cars. Power is provided through a pole from each car reaching up to contact the electrically charged ceiling. This is essentially the same principle used to operate electric trolleys. Getting patrons off at the end of the ride period is simple—the attendant simply shuts off the electricity.

Sky Towers and Sky Cars

The 1933 Chicago Century of Progress sky cabin was a precursor to today's skyrides. There is no major park in the United States that does not feature a sky car or lift ride to give the visitor an overview of the park. Seattle's Space Needle brought renewed popularity to a trend most obviously marked by Eiffel's Tower in 1889. In an age of high-rise construction, these observation towers nevertheless continue to proliferate and draw crowds.

BIBLIOGRAPHY

1. *Webster's Seventh New Collegiate Dictionary,* G. & C. Merriam Co., Springfield, Mass., 1970, pp. 299 and 305.
2. L. Wasserman, *Merchandising Architecture: Architectural Implications and Applications of Amusement Theme Parks,* National Endowment for the Arts, 1978, p. 4.2.
3. J. Maas, *The Glorious Enterprise: The Centennial Exhibition of 1876 and H. J. Schwarzmann, Architect-in-Chief,* American-Life-Foundation, Watkins Glen, N.Y., 1973, p. 96.
4. Ref. 2, p. 4.5.
5. S. Giedeon, *Space, Time and Architecture,* Harvard University Press, Cambridge, Mass., 1967, p. 11.
6. Ref. 2, p. 4.7.
7. J. McKennen, *A Pictorial History of the American Carnival,* Carnival Publishers, Sarasota, Fla., 1972, p. 35.
8. Ref. 2, p. 4.11.
9. Ref. 2, p. 4.12.
10. Ref. 2, p. 5.1
11. A. Griffin, *Step Right Up, Folks,* Henry Regnery Co., Chicago, 1974, p. 7.

12. R. Koolhaas, *Delirious New York,* Oxford University Press, New York, 1978, p. 48.

13. Ref. 2, p. 5.7.

14. Ref. 2, p. 7.7.

15. J. Pastier, *The AIA Journal,* 30 (Dec. 1978).

16. Ref. 16, p. 36.

General References

Abitare **200,** 22 (Dec. 1981).

AIA Journal **67,** 26 (Dec. 1978).

Architectural Record **63,** 183 (Feb. 1928).

A. Bass, *Technology Review* **86,** 18 (Oct. 1983).

P. Blake, *Architectural Forum* **136,** 24 (June 1972).

D. Braithwaite, *Fairground Architecture: The World of Amusement Parks.* Praeger, New York, 1968.

"Building for Pleasure and Leisure," *Architects Association Journal* **80** (Sept.–Oct. 1964).

R. Cartmell, *Smithsonian* **8,** 44 (Aug. 1977).

W. Clasen, *Exhibits: Industrial and Trade Fairs,* Architectural Press, London, 1968.

F. R. Dulles, *America Learns to Play,* D. Appleton-Century Co., New York, 1940.

D. Francis, *Popular Science* **155,** 82 (July 1949).

F. Fried, *A Pictorial History of the Carousel,* A. S. Barner, New York, 1964.

B. Gill and D. Whitney, *Summer Places,* Methuen, New York, 1978.

J. S. Hamel, *Electrical West* **115,** 57 (Dec. 1955).

S. Hunter, *A Family Guide to Amusement Centers,* Walker & Co., New York, 1975.

J. F. Kasson, *Amusing the Millions: Coney Island at the Turn of the Century,* Hill and Wang, New York, 1978.

S. Koppelkamm, *Glasshouses and Wintergardens of the Nineteenth Century,* Rizzoli, New York, 1981.

G. Kyriazi, *The Great American Amusement Parks: A Pictorial History,* Citadel Press, Secaucus, N.J., 1976.

W. F. Mangels, *The Outdoor Amusement Industry, from Earliest Times to the Present,* Vantage Press, New York, 1952.

E. McCullough, *Worlds Fairs Midways,* Exposition Press, New York, 1966.

D. Meredith, *Science Digest* **86,** 58 (Aug. 1979).

N. Meredith, *Journal of Popular Culture* **15** (1), 108–115, (1981).

C. W. Moore, *Perspecta* **9–10,** 65 (1965).

T. Onosko, *Funland, U.S.A.,* Arno Press, New York, 1978.

N. Pevsner, *A History of Building Types,* Princeton University Press, Princeton, N.J., 1976, Chapt. 15.

M. Puzo, *New York* **12,** 28 (Sept. 3, 1979).

J. Ulmer, *Amusement Parks of America: A Comprehensive Guide,* Dial, New York, 1980.

G. Weedon and R. Ward, *Fairground Art: the Art Forms of Travelling Fairs, Carousels and Carnival Midways,* Abbeville Press, New York, 1981.

CAROL BURNS
Harvard University
Cambridge, Massachusetts

ANODIZED FINISHES

Aluminum has several inherent characteristics that render it especially well suited for architectural use. These include ease of fabrication, resistance to corrosion, versatility in finishing, and the combination of lightweight with high strength. Casting, sheet, and extrusion alloys have all been used in building products, with the last two having the greatest emphasis today. Alloys are selected according to their performance and aesthetic properties. Surface is an especially important characteristic, for it affects the weatherability and maintenance of a structure as well as its initial appearance. As a result, both anodizing and painting have significant roles in the use of aluminum, and it is important to identify the most effective application of each.

The applications of aluminum in architecture can be categorized as residential and nonresidential, with the nonresidential being divided into farm and industrial, general commercial, and high rise buildings. A brief discussion of these categories indicates where anodizing can be used to advantage, and likewise, where some other finishing method may be more appropriate.

In residential construction, aluminum is used for siding, soffit and fascia, gutters and downspouts, roofing shingles, and windows and doors. Siding, soffit and fascia, gutters and downspouts, and roofing shingles are sheet products which are postformed from coil-painted stock. The quality of these paint finishes is very high, with warranties offered of up to 30 and 40 years. Anodizing is not a factor in this market. Aluminum's major competitor for the pastel color siding business is extruded vinyl, based primarily on lower cost. Windows and doors, on the other hand, use large quantities of aluminum extrusions, and these are produced with both anodized and painted or vinyl-laminated finishes.

Nonresidential farm and industrial buildings employ roofing and siding in a variety of corrugated or ribbed forms. These are sheet products ranging in thickness from 0.44 to 0.53 mm for farm buildings, to 0.60 to 1.25 mm for industrial uses. A key example of this type of industrial construction is the Vehicle Assembly Building at Cape Kennedy, Fla., one of the largest structures in the world for enclosed volume space. Although agricultural–industrial applications sometimes use bare metal, the predominant finishing treatment is painting. This is most effectively done by coating coil stock and postforming. Anodizing is not usually found in this category.

The general commercial category encompasses a wide variety of products such as storefronts, windows, doors, ornamental metalwork and trim, solar shading devices, railings, copings, and gravel stops. Anodizing has proven to be especially effective on products of this type, and is used in conjunction with mechanical polishing or brushing treatments, or chemical-etching treatments to produce various decorative appearances. Usually, standard maintenance practices can be employed without difficulty, and therefore, moderate thickness anodized films are sufficient.

High rise aluminum curtain wall buildings were introduced with the Alcoa Building (Fig. 1), constructed in Pittsburgh in 1952, using anodized panels of a silicon-contain-

Figure 1. The Alcoa Building, Pittsburgh, Pa. Courtesy of Aluminum Company of America.

ing alloy. Many large buildings have followed, including the John Hancock Center, Chicago, in 1969; the World Trade Center, New York, in 1971; and the Sears Tower, Chicago, in 1974. A curtain wall does not support vertical loads and, in that sense, is not a part of a building's structural frame. Its primary function is to enclose the building and keep the weather out. Curtain wall systems can provide the effect of vertical lines, horizontal lines, a grid, or some other overall texture for a building. Usually, sheet products are employed for curtain walls, although occasionally some cast panels are used. For grid effects, both sheet and extrusions are employed. Anodizing has been the dominant finishing treatment for aluminum curtain wall buildings in clear, gray, black, gold, and various earth tone bronzes. Because of the nature of this application, heavy anodized films are desirable. In the past, some porcelain enamel was used on high-rise buildings, but it is rarely seen today. On the other hand, organic coatings have been steadily improving in quality each year, and now they are beginning to make an appearance on large buildings to participate in what was previously the sole domain of anodized finishes.

The use of aluminum in architectural applications has

been encouraged by the R. S. Reynolds Memorial Award. Established in 1957 by the Reynolds Metals Company and administered by the American Institute of Architects, this award is conferred annually on an architect or team of architects who, in the judgment of the profession, designed a permanent, significant work of architecture, in the creation of which aluminum has been an important contributing factor. In 1984, a municipal art museum in Moenchengladbach, FRG, won the award; in 1985, the recipient was the General Foods Corporation Headquarters in Rye, New York.

An extensive overall treatment of the characteristics and properties of aluminum, including architectural applications and finishing processes, can be found in the three-volume set *Aluminum,* published by the American Society for Metals (ASM) (1), and in the Kirk–Othmer *Encyclopedia of Chemical Technology* (2).

SURFACE WEATHERING AND CORROSION

In architectural applications, the effects of weathering and corrosion on surface appearance are usually of concern. A suitable surface finishing treatment can provide a desirable initial appearance, requiring a minimum of maintenance effort. Anodic coatings, for example, enhance surface appearance and also provide excellent resistance to weathering. Paint can also be used effectively for the decoration and protection of aluminum alloys.

Weathering effects vary with the environment—seacoast, urban, industrial, rural, or combinations of these. Sheltered surfaces are more vulnerable to corrosion than those that are boldly exposed and washed with rain. Likewise, vertical surfaces are much less susceptible to attack and discoloration than horizontal or inclined areas.

Galvanic corrosion, which results from contact with dissimilar metals, must always be considered when working with aluminum. For example, when aluminum is used with steel structural members, some corrosion of the aluminum may be expected if condensation and dirt collect at the faying surfaces. Such joints can be protected with caulking, sealants, or paint. Paint protection is very effective, but it is important that it be applied to the cathodic (steel) areas. When only the anodic (aluminum) area is protected, local coating failure results in a small active anodic site. Galvanic action is intensified as a small anode seeks to protect a large cathode. Deep pitting and sometimes perforation result.

Atmospheric weathering of anodized members proceeds slowly by general attack, which roughens the surface and causes dulling, and by a random pitting attack. Pitting is a function of the chance deposition of solid pollution particles on the surface and on the heterogeneities of the anodic coating itself.

As indicated before, degree and type of weathering are affected markedly by the geometry of the exposure and thus the amount of rain washing the surface receives. Film thickness plays a major role in determining the extent and severity of the penetration of the coating by pitting attack. On the other hand, lack of sealing promotes staining and blooming effects. Anodic films formed on the various aluminum alloys differ in their resistance to weathering attack. Thus it is important to first select an appropriate alloy, and then to ensure that it is processed with good finishing practices.

THE ANODIZING PROCESS

Anodizing is an electrolytic oxidation process in which the surface of a metal, when made the anode in a suitable electrolyte, is converted to a protective, decorative, or otherwise functional coating. When aluminum is made the anode in a dibasic or tribasic acid solution, the surface is converted to an aluminum oxide coating. This coating is an integral part of the metal and therefore adherent. The appearance and properties of anodic finishes are governed principally by three factors:

1. The aluminum alloy and temper.
2. The surface treatment prior to anodizing.
3. The type of electrolyte and the operating techniques used in the anodizing process.

Much commercial anodizing of aluminum is done in a room-temperature sulfuric acid solution which produces a coating with a well-defined pore structure. This allows continued growth of the coating up to a thickness of about 0.025 mm, and provides a means for impregnating the coating with various colorants or protective materials. Porous coatings form at the metal interface and progress inward; therefore, the first coating to be formed remains at the surface while the last is near the substrate-coating interface. These coatings consist of close-packed cells of oxide, predominantly hexagonal in shape, each of which contains a single pore. Cell size increases linearly with voltage, while pore size is a function of electrolyte type. Table 1 shows some typical data for a sulfuric acid anodic coating.

Various oxide-coating properties are affected by alloy composition, including appearance, continuity, abrasion resistance, weight, density, porosity, dielectric strength, and coating composition. The metallurgical structure of the alloy has significant effects on both the density and appearance of the anodic coating. Alloy constituents or impurities may impart coloration to the coating, or their presence may cause opacity as opposed to translucency, thus producing a dull rather than a metallic appearance. Fabrication processes, such as rolling or extrusion, and thermal treatments, including welding, also affect the microstructure of aluminum alloys and, as a result, their response to anodizing. Primary intermetallic precipitate particles may be broken up or deformed by rolling or extruding, and may be transformed into other intermetallic compounds during thermal treatment. Finally, the physical texture of the metal is very important to the appearance of the finish, for anodizing faithfully reproduces the surface to which it is applied.

Anodizing and surface treatment in general are extensively discussed by Wernick and Pinner (3) and in the ASM *Metals Handbook* (4). Diggle, Downie, and Goulding's article provides a thorough treatment of anodic mechanisms and structures (5).

SPECIFIC PROPERTIES OF ANODIC COATINGS

Corrosion Resistance. Properly applied, adequately sealed anodic coatings provide good protection against corrosion. For outdoor architectural applications, the minimum thickness for a low maintenance surface is 0.018 mm; 0.025 mm is preferable. The chemical resistance of anodic coatings is generally satisfactory in the pH range 4–8.5. However, care must be taken during construction because alkaline building materials (mortar, cement, and plaster) can attack and stain the coating. A clear acrylic lacquer can be applied to protect the finish during erection, and it has the added advantage of minimizing soil accumulation during service.

Hardness–Brittleness. Anodized coatings are both hard (9 on the Mohs scale) and brittle. Fine hairline cracks (crazing) can be seen on the convex side of bends. Heating the part can also produce crazing because the coefficient of expansion of the oxide is lower than that of the base metal. The temperature at which crazing occurs depends on the thickness and density of the coating; for a conventional 0.013 mm sulfuric acid coating, it is about 121°C. Because anodic coatings do have a relatively low elongation value, anodized aluminum cannot go through severe forming operations.

Reflectance–Emissivity. The total reflectance of anodically coated aluminum can be made to vary from about 4% for near-black integral colors to 53% for light colors, to about 85% for clear coatings. Emissivity is a function of both the electrolyte and the thickness of the coating employed. However, coatings thicker than 0.010 mm have about the same emissivity values in the range of 0.8–0.9. The coating color has little effect on emissivity.

Dielectric Strength. Aluminum oxide is a good dielectric. Sealed coatings of 0.013 mm can show an average voltage breakdown value as high as 500–600 V.

Dimensional Changes. In conventional sulfuric acid anodizing, the increase in thickness of the anodized part is approximately one-third the total thickness of the coating applied. For hard or integral color anodizing, the increase in dimension of the part is approximately one-half the coating thickness. Sharp edges and corners should be avoided on parts to be anodized because of the corner effect. The coating grows perpendicular to the surface from which it is formed, and a void occurs because the coating cannot fill the gap at the sharp edge. When using a 0.025 mm coating, the bend radius should not be less than 0.8 mm.

Table 1. Data for Sulfuric Acid Anodic Coatings[a]

Property	Value
Pore diameter, angstroms	Approximately 100
Number of pores, pores/cm^2	50–75 billion
Density, g/cm^3	2.96 (before sealing)
Pore volume, %	15.8

[a] Typical processing conditions: 15% sulfuric acid, 21°C, 1.29 amp/dm^2, and 12–22 V.

COLORED OXIDE COATINGS

Although clear anodic coatings have many applications, the widespread use of anodized finishes in architecture demands that some variety of colors be available. The nature of the anodizing process and the structure of the coatings formed offer several possible approaches to obtaining color. These are summarized in Table 2.

Dye impregnation in the pores of the coating has long been recognized as a versatile method for obtaining colored anodic finishes. However, dye adsorption alone has not been considered to provide the color tone–stability required for long-term outdoor exposure on buildings. Certain combination processes have been developed with the objective of overcoming such limitations (6). Inherent instability characteristics of organic dyes were addressed as early as 1940 with the development of processes to precipitate inorganic pigments in place in the pores of the coating. Although theoretically sound, this approach was hampered by the sensitivity of the chemical precipitation reactions involved, with the result that very few pigments showed the consistency of color and performance desired. The most effective performer has been gold iron oxide, which can be precipitated from a ferric ammonium oxalate solution in a process that is relatively simple to control. It has been used to a limited extent on certain high-rise buildings with an acceptable resistance to weathering; an example is the Hilton Hotel in downtown Pittsburgh.

However, it remained for the integral color and the electrodeposition processes to promote the use of colored anodized finishes in high rise buildings. The term integral color coating is used to define that type of finish which obtains its color in the anodizing process itself and not by a posttreatment. The first approach to this depended on the response of certain aluminum alloys to sulfuric acid anodizing of the conventional type. For example, aluminum–silicon alloys (4XXX) contain small particles of elemental silicon that are unaffected by the anodizing treatment and remain dispersed in the oxide coating, imparting a gray color. Also, aluminum alloys with chromium or copper in solid solution produce light-gold anodic coatings, while manganese yields a tan to brownish shade. As mentioned previously, the Alcoa Building employed an aluminum–silicon alloy to produce a gray anodized finish. This finish is still in excellent condition after over 30 years of service.

Table 2. Methods for Obtaining Colored Anodic Coatings

Method	Variations
Pore impregnation	Adsorption of dyes in pores
	Precipitation of pigments in pores
	Electrolytic deposition in pores
Integral color formation	Conventional electrolytes, Selected alloys
	Special electrolytes, Selected alloys
Combination processes	Integral color and dye adsorption
	Electrolytic deposition and dye adsorption

To expand to the fullest the use of anodized aluminum in buildings, it was necessary to obtain colors beyond the silicon alloy grays. This need was met by the introduction of mixed organic-sulfuric acid electrolytes, which operated at lower temperatures and higher voltages to produce a wide range of earth tone colors as well as grays and blacks. Kaiser's Kalcolor was the first of these processes to be commercialized, and their 1962 patent (7) describes an electrolyte containing sulfosalicylic acid and sulfuric acid. In the years following, many other patents and processes of this type appeared throughout the world. The major aluminum suppliers also directed substantial effort to developing specific alloys for optimum use of this type of integral color anodizing. As a result, the use of anodized high-rise buildings did grow markedly over the next decade, and their weathering performance to date has been very satisfactory. Integral color anodizing has been reviewed extensively in the literature (8–11).

Yet another approach to color-anodized finishes known as electrolytic coloring was developed in depth by the work of Asada (12) in the mid-1960s. Electrolytic coloring is a two-step process involving conventional anodizing followed by deposition of metallic pigments in the pores of the coating to achieve a range of stable bronzes and blacks useful in architecture. Normally, alternating current is used in the deposition step, and tin, nickel, and cobalt are the metals most often deposited. The first commercialization of this coloring approach was by Alcan as the Anolok process (13), based on the original Asada patent. As is customary with new technologies, interest in electrolytic coloring spread rapidly, and many patents have appeared throughout the world describing principally AC but also some DC deposition. Commercial use of electrolytic coloring developed more rapidly in Europe than in the United States, perhaps because of the firm entrenchment of integral color anodizing in this country. Accordingly, more extensive weathering performance data can be derived from European exposures (14). Electrolytic coloring is now prevalent in the United States as well. Sheasby has provided a thorough discussion of electrolytic coloring (15).

There are some advantages that electrolytic coloring offers over integral color anodizing, and these are primarily cost—rather than quality—oriented. First, AC electrolytic deposition processes are relatively alloy-insensitive, thus offering a broader alloy selection to the user. Second, it is a lower energy-consuming processing system. This occurs because the higher voltages of integral color anodizing are avoided, and because the refrigeration needs are appreciably less. Finally, electrolytic coloring can be installed in a conventional anodizing line with a minimum of new capital investment. It is only necessary to provide the electrodeposition tank and an AC power supply.

SEALING

It is standard practice to follow the actual anodizing operation with a step known as sealing. The purpose of sealing is to plug the pores of the coating, which increases both resistance to staining and to corrosion, and improves the durability of colors.

A traditional sealing treatment is immersion in boiling deionized water which fills the pores with hydrated aluminum oxide. Purity of the water is very important here, and small amounts of phosphates, silicates, and fluorides can severely inhibit the sealing reaction. For architectural applications, it is common to use sealing solutions with additions of a metal salt such as nickel acetate. This results in the precipitation of metal hydroxides which help plug the pores of the coating. Metal salt sealing solutions are especially effective in improving the performance of colored architectural coatings, and also render the sealing solution itself much more tolerant of impurities without adversely affecting performance. Rising energy costs have now prompted the development of low temperature (80–85°C) and ultralow temperature (30–35°C) sealing treatments.

A problem aspect of the sealing reaction is the formation of smudge, a chalky outer layer on the surface of the coating. Metal salt solutions that are the most effective sealants also produce a heavier smudge. Since this results in an unattractive appearance of the final finish, it must be handled in some way (16). Three general approaches can be used:

1. Removing the formed smudge by scrubbing or polishing.
2. Dissolving the formed smudge from the surface with an acid treatment.
3. Minimizing smudge formation by the use of surfactants or other additives in the sealing solution.

The second and third methods or a combination of the two are generally employed in commercial processing today. A further caution must be observed if the anodized finish is to receive a subsequent lacquering or painting step; an excess of surfactants or wetting agents added to the sealing solution to decrease smudge formation can markedly affect the bonding of subsequent coatings. Reviews of sealing mechanisms and processes have been provided by John and Shenoi in Ref. 17 and by Baker in Ref. 18.

SURFACE PREPARATION

Surface treatments on aluminum prior to anodizing include both mechanical and chemical processes. Mechanical finishes may be used to remove or mask scratches and pits, extrusion die lines, and other surface imperfections as well as to achieve a desired texture or appearance. Brushed (directional) and blasted (nondirectional) finishes are sometimes used on curtain walls, but they are not generally recommended. Buffed finishes are only practical on extruded members; satin directional finishes are also used on extrusions. Blasting finds its greatest application on castings. The effects of mechanical pretreatments are often subtle, and hence not readily seen at a distance of 5 m or more. Because of this and in the interest of economy, the aesthetic benefits of a mechanical finish need to be carefully assessed before such finishes are specified.

Chemical treatments are important because the aluminum surface must be clean and active for the uniform starting of the anodic coating. Materials to be removed include residual lubricants, soil, thermally formed oxide from heat-treating operations, and surface debris from rolling, extrusion-fabricating steps, or mechanical finishing. Therefore, cleaning cycles should consist of solvent degreasing or inhibited chemical cleaning for organic soil removal; an acid deoxidizing treatment if resistant thermal oxides are present; and a metal removal treatment to uniformly activate the surface and create the desired final appearance. The most widely used preanodizing metal removal process for architectural applications is sodium hydroxide etching. It is readily controlled and provides the diffuse type finish generally desired. A metal removal of 0.025 mm per surface should be adequate. Etching solutions leave a smut on the surface from the alloying constituents in the metal. This residue is removed in oxidizing acid desmutting solutions prior to anodizing.

A discussion of all aspects of surface preparation may be found in Wernick and Pinner's work (3) and in the ASM *Metals Handbook* (4). Durney concentrates on chemical cleaning and etching (19).

DESIGNATION OF FINISHES

Because of the many proprietary designations for finishes on aluminum, the Aluminum Association (AA) has developed an identification system broad enough to cover all types of finishes now in use and to meet anticipated future needs (20). The broad categories considered are as follows:

1. Mechanical finishes.
2. Chemical finishes.
3. Coatings:
   - Anodic coatings.
   - Resinous and other organic coatings.
   - Vitreous coatings.
   - Electroplated and other metallic coatings.
   - Laminated coatings.

Obviously, any system embracing all of the potential finishing combinations will of necessity be somewhat detailed and complex. It is thoroughly described in the AA manual, and anyone involved in specifying aluminum finishes should obtain a copy. Table 3 shows the nomenclature that this system employs to describe various types of architectural anodizing, but omits the additional symbols that would be used to identify accompanying mechanical and chemical pretreatments.

STANDARDS FOR ANODIZED ARCHITECTURAL ALUMINUM

Anodic coatings for architectural use are divided into two broad classifications. Class I coatings are for use on exterior surfaces which will receive little or no maintenance. (An exception are Los Angeles exposures, where special maintenance of Class I is recommended.) Class II coatings, which are thinner than Class I, are for use on maintained

Table 3. Designation of Architectural Anodic Coatings

Coatings	Class I[a]	Class II[b]
Clear coating conventional anodizing	A41	A31
Integral color anodizing	A42	A32
Impregnated color coating (dye or pigment)	A43	A33
Electrodeposited color coating	A44	A34
Other	A4X	A3X

[a] Class I architectural = 18 μm (0.018 mm) and thicker.
[b] Class II architectural = 10–18 μm (0.010–0.018 mm).

exterior surfaces (21). Table 4 shows the specifications for these coatings.

To ensure ultimate satisfaction with an architectural anodized finish, the owner, architect, contractor, and suppliers need to reach an initial agreement on the pertinent factors involved. These factors include the following:

1. Mechanical pretreatment, if any.
2. Chemical pretreatment.
3. Thickness–weight of anodic coating.
4. Color and degree of color match.
5. Adequacy of seal.
6. Gloss that is acceptable.
7. Clear protective overcoating, if any.
8. What constitutes a significant surface.

The most controversial aspects of architectural anodized material have repeatedly been appearance and color difference. Appearance of anodized work will vary with alloy composition, fabricating techniques, mechanical and chemical pretreatment variations, and control of the anodizing cycle. Therefore, some variation in appearance will always be present. As mentioned previously, designing to accept variation with all anodized finishes is most important. It is necessary for the finisher to define the range of color and gloss that he expects to hold on a given lot of metal with a given process, and for this to be acceptable to the architect and owner. This is best controlled by establishing an approved set of range samples in advance, which represent the agreed upon limits of variation. Both the architect and the fabricator should have a set of these samples available for use during the construction period (22).

TESTING ANODIC COATINGS

The first critical evaluation to be made on an anodic coating is the amount applied. If a measurement is to be made on a building panel itself, it is necessary to use a nondestructive test. Eddy current instruments meet this need very well; they are accurate, portable, and easy to use. The light-section microscope is another nondestructive technique, although the coating must be clear for its use. For referee situations, or if a test coupon is available, the more accurate although destructive cross-section microscopic method can be used. Coating weight determination, which is the most accurate method for obtaining an average value, involves weighing, dissolving the film, and reweighing; this is also a destructive test.

Seal quality is another useful evaluation; three types of testing are used for this. The first technique employed for measuring seal quality was the dye stain test. It still has some value if care is taken in its application. Later, impedance methods, which were first promoted in the automotive industry, were more broadly accepted for evaluating sealing, although these are not useful for the two-step processes. However, the most discriminating test for seal quality is the acid dissolution method, using a warm phosphoric acid–chromic acid solution, for example. Unfortunately, this is also a destructive test and its use requires a representative test coupon.

Color and gloss can be measured by approved optical instruments. These are nondestructive tests and, if desired, can often be made in place on a building. When used in conjunction with accepted color range samples, color instrument data can be very useful. Another important contribution that color measuring instrumentation can make is the change in a finish that occurs on exposure. This aids in addressing the performance characteristics of the finish.

Fortunately, organizations such as the American Society for Testing and Materials (ASTM) and the International Organization for Standardization (ISO) have prepared procedures for testing anodic coatings, and these can be specified by those responsible for evaluating surface quality (21). Table 5 shows some of the available test methods.

Table 4. Specifications for Class I and Class II Coating

Category	Minimum Thickness, μm	Minimum Weight, mg/cm^2	Minimum Applied Density, g/cm^3	Maximum Acid Dissolution,[a] mg/dm^2
Class I	18	4.2	2.32	40
Class II	10	2.4	2.32	40

[a] Weight loss test for sealing quality.

Table 5. ASTM Tests for Coating Evaluation

ASTM Method	Test	Property Tested
B110	Voltage breakdown	Dielectric strength
B117[a]	Salt spray	Corrosion resistance
B136	Stain resistance	Seal quality
B137	Coating weight	Quantity of coating
B244	Eddy current instrument	Coating thickness
B368[a]	CASS	Corrosion resistance
B457	Impedance	Seal quality
B487	Microscopic–cross-section	Coating thickness
B680	Acid dissolution	Seal quality
B681	Light-section microscope	Coating thickness
D658[a]	Air blast-abrasive	Abrasion resistance
D1044[a]	Taber abraser	Abrasion resistance

[a] Not specifically for anodic coatings.

CARE AND MAINTENANCE OF ANODIC COATINGS

The care and maintenance of anodic finishes is an important subject if the optimum in appearance and performance is to be realized. Two broad subjects need to be considered:

1. Care of finished part before and during erection of the building.
2. Care of the finish on the building in service.

It has already been mentioned that alkaline building materials (mortar, cement, and plaster) will attack and stain the anodic coating if they contact it during the construction period. First, it is necessary that this risk is recognized and that as much care as possible is exercised in handling aluminum and other materials (23). Especially, it is important to remove construction soil from curtain wall members as soon as possible. A preventive measure sometimes employed to alleviate this problem is the use of a strippable coating. This temporary coating is applied by the finisher, and remains in place until the assembly of that portion of the structure is complete, at which time it is peeled off. Although they can be effective, strippable coatings do involve some nuisance and cost.

The most effective and, of course, most expensive approach to extend the performance of an anodic coating is the application of a clear, nonyellowing lacquer top coat by the finisher. A good lacquer coating will not only provide protection during the construction period but will also facilitate dirt removal and help maintain an attractive appearance on the structure for a long period. Air-dry lacquers only have been used for this purpose because of the crazing effect of thermal cures on the oxide. A desirable lacquer film thickness is 0.010–0.015 mm, and this is best applied in two thin coats rather than in a single heavy coat. In addition to cost, another objection sometimes encountered in the use of lacquer is the relatively high gloss imparted to the surface by standard lacquer formulations. Where gloss is objectionable, it is necessary to specify a low gloss formulation. Such formulations should be carefully evaluated before use to ensure that they will not develop a deleterious appearance on weathering.

Changes that can occur on an anodized finish in outdoor exposure include: dust and soot accumulation, surface mottling, pitting and corrosion product, bloom (whitening), and color changes. Cleaning and maintenance can minimize the occurrence of these changes.

The extent of cleaning required on architectural finishes is a function of the environment and the amount of natural rain washing that the building experiences. High visibility areas, ie, ground and low level elevations in direct sight, are the most important for cleaning. Less visible areas usually need less frequent or perhaps no cleaning.

The AA offers a manual containing the latest information on various categories of commercial cleaners (24). The five principal categories that they employ are mild soaps, detergents and nonetching cleaners, solvent and emulsion cleaners, abrasive cleaners, etching cleaners, and special-duty cleaners. Lightly soiled architectural surfaces may be cleaned with mild soap, detergents, or nonetching cleaners. Application can be by swabbing or brushing, and should be followed by thorough rinsing. Solvent and emulsion cleaners are useful for oil and grease stains, but care must be taken to check the effect of solvents on any lacquer or paint coatings. Heavily soiled and weathered finishes require more aggressive treatments. Abrasives are usually employed and can be incorporated in the cleaner formulation, or provided by steel wool or abrasive pads. On large surfaces, power-driven brushes or pads can be employed. Although an anodic coating is harder and more scratch-resistant than bare aluminum, it is still a thin film on a soft substrate, and it can be damaged by an excessively harsh abrasive. Etching (chemically attacking) cleaners, which are often used on bare aluminum, are not recommended for anodized surfaces. In particular, cleaners should not contain sodium hydroxide, phosphoric acid, trisodium phosphate, hydrochloric acid, hydrofluoric acid, or fluorides.

If it becomes necessary to perform a major cleaning operation on a building, consideration should be given to extending the time before cleaning will be needed again by incorporating a protective agent into the cleaning system. This might be a wax, a silicone, or some other clear filming material. Waxes are best for handrails, doors, window frames, etc and are generally not as practical for high-rise buildings. Silicone products, on the other hand, are one class of materials suitable for application to clean, dry, anodized curtain wall panels.

SUMMARY OF DESIGN CONSIDERATIONS

For the most effective use of aluminum in buildings, especially in curtain wall construction, certain design parameters need to be considered:

1. Aluminum has a relatively high coefficient of expansion; allow for expansion and contraction caused by temperature changes.

2. Aluminum is susceptible to galvanic corrosion; avoid contact with dissimilar metals and avoid drainage of water from uncoated dissimilar metals onto aluminum.

3. Metal products are subject to poultice corrosion; avoid contact with absorptive materials that hold moisture.

4. There are a wide variety of aluminum alloys; work with the suppliers to select the proper alloy for both strength and finish.

5. Welding-filler wire alloys often produce a dark appearance after anodizing; select the proper filler wire alloy to obtain the desired anodized appearance.

6. Anodized panels of the same color often will not visually match if butted together; use projections, such as mullions, at the junctions of adjoining panels to break the surface continuity by means of shadow lines, thus deliberately minimizing the effects of color range.

7. Flop is a fascinating differential appearance effect that is a product of the viewing angle, refraction of light through the anodic film, reflection from the aluminum surface, and further refraction through the anodic film as light returns to the viewer's eye; achieve flop effects by slightly deviating the planes of adjacent pieces prepared by the same anodizing process.

8. Differential shadow depths or highlights increase the eye interest created by color; deliberately select two color tones from the same family to produce a planned pattern.

9. Unusual harmony effects can be obtained with colored oxide finishes; use two strongly contrasting panels side by side, or use contrasting colors on jointure projection or insert members.

BIBLIOGRAPHY

1. K. R. Van Horn, ed., *Aluminum,* Vols. 1–3, American Society for Metals, Metals Park, Ohio, 1967.

2. M. Grayson and D. Eckroth, eds., *Kirk–Othmer Encyclopedia of Chemical Technology,* 3rd ed., Vol. 2, John Wiley and Sons, Inc., New York, 1978, pp. 129–188.

3. S. Wernick and R. Pinner, *The Surface Finishing and Treatment of Aluminium and Its Alloys,* 4th ed., Robert Draper, Ltd., Teddington, UK, 1972.

4. W. G. Wood, ed., *Metals Handbook, Surface Cleaning, Finishing and Coating,* 9th ed., Vol. 5, American Society for Metals, Metals Park, Ohio, 1982, pp. 571–610.

5. J. W. Diggle, T. C. Downie, and C. W. Goulding, *Chem. Rev.* **69,** 365 (1969).

6. C. T. Speiser, *Aluminum Finishing Seminar Technical Papers,* Vol. 1, The Aluminum Association, Washington, D.C., 1982, pp. 121–144.

7. U.S. Pat. 3,031,387 (April 24, 1962), B. E. Deal and L. Swanson (to Kaiser Aluminum and Chemical Corp.).

8. F. L. Church, *Mod. Met.* **18,** 36 (Sept. 1962).

9. J. M. Kape, *Light Met.* **26,** 26 (Dec. 1963).

10. W. C. Cochran, *Aluminum Finishing Seminar Technical Papers,* Paper A-7, The Aluminum Association, Washington, D.C., 1973.

11. S. John and B. A. Shenoi, *Met. Finish.* **74,** 48 (Sept. 1976).

12. U.S. Pat. 3,382,160 (1968), T. Asada (to Fuji Manufacturing Corp.).

13. P. G. Sheasby and W. E. Cooke, *Trans. Inst. Met. Finish.* **52,** 103 (Summer 1974).

14. J. Patrie, *Rev. Alum.* **436,** 37 (Jan. 1975).

15. P. G. Sheasby in Ref. 6, pp. 145–160.

16. H. J. Gohausen in Ref. 6, pp. 163–175.

17. S. John and B. A. Shenoi, *Met. Finish.* **74,** 31 (July 1976).

18. B. R. Baker in Ref. 6, pp. 177–199.

19. L. J. Durney in Ref. 6, pp. 69–77.

20. *Designation System for Aluminum Finishes,* 7th ed., The Aluminum Association, Washington, D.C., 1980.

21. *Standards for Anodized Architectural Aluminum,* 5th ed., The Aluminum Association, Washington, D.C., 1978.

22. W. F. Koppes, *Aluminum Curtain Walls,* Vol. 8, Architectural Aluminum Manufacturers Association, Chicago, Ill., 1973.

23. *Care and Handling of Architectural Aluminum from Shop to Site,* Architectural Aluminum Manufacturers Association, Chicago, Ill., 1982.

24. *Care of Aluminum,* 4th ed., The Aluminum Association, Washington, D.C., 1977.

See also ALUMINUM; COLOR IN ARCHITECTURE; CORROSION.

WALTER G. ZELLEY
New Kensington, Pennsylvania

ANSI. See AMERICAN NATIONAL STANDARDS INSTITUTE (ANSI)

ANTIRUST AGENTS. See CORROSION

ANTISTATIC AGENTS

Antistatic agents are chemicals that are added to materials such as plastics in order to reduce their tendency to acquire electrostatic charge and thus prevent problems associated with electrostatic discharge (ESD).

The earliest known record of electrostatic phenomena is credited to the Greek philosopher Thales (640–546 B.C.), who noted that a piece of amber, when rubbed, attracted small, light objects. Indeed, the term electricity is derived from *elektron,* which is the ancient Greek term for amber.

Early explanations of electrostatic charges assumed that they were generated by the mechanical work dissipated in friction. In 1757, Johan Wilcke first constructed a "triboelectric series" of materials, "tribo" being derived from the Greek for friction, or rubbing. Such a list compares materials that accept progressively more negative charges. The magnitude of charge developed was supposed to be relative to the position of the material in the series. Two materials near each other would produce less static electricity when in contact than would materials at opposing ends of the series.

PRACTICAL THEORETICAL CONSIDERATIONS

Triboelectric series are based on erroneous presumptions, and analysis results in confusing and misleading conclusions. These lists, which originally included fur, glass, wood, amber, and hair, should have been discarded years ago. Unfortunately, the triboelectric series has instead been continuously updated with the inclusion of synthetic fibers, plastics, and other polymeric materials.

In reality, any material can acquire a very high positive or negative charge independent of friction or contact with a different substance. Additionally, plastics and synthetic fibers can, and often do, acquire static charges of both signs simultaneously. Different materials can dissipate static charges at vastly different rates.

The static phenomenon inherent in a multitude of common and useful materials is generally considered to be undesirable, yet its elimination or reduction is not readily accomplished. The complexities of static electricity, known and investigated for 2500 years, have yet to be fully understood.

Static electricity, or electrostatic charge, may be defined as a deficiency or excess of electrons on an insulating or ungrounded surface. Electrons are defined as being negatively charged. Thus, an excess of electrons results in a negative charge, and a deficiency results in a positive charge. There is actually only one kind of electricity. Electrons, whether motionless (static) on an insulator such as polyethylene or traveling near light speed through a conductive copper wire as an electric current, all obey the same laws and may be defined using the same dimensions.

ESD BEHAVIOR CLASSIFICATION

The entire behavioral range of electrostatic phenomena as it pertains to ESD has been classified in terms of surface resistivity according to the Department of Defense Handbook DOD HDBK-263 (1). Surface resistivity, a widely used measurement, is numerically equal to the surface resistance between two electrodes forming opposite sides of a square. Although units or dimensions are in ohms, reference is usually made in ohms per square. The usefulness of surface resistivity measurements lies in the fact that the size of the square, hence the size of the test piece and the test apparatus, is immaterial.

The four classifications of ESD behavior in which materials may be categorized are: conductive, static dissipative, antistatic, and insulative. These are defined in Table 1.

The very high electrical resistance of insulative materials is desirable for certain applications, for example, polyolefin jacketing for high-voltage cable, flexible poly(vinyl chloride) (PVC) wire jacketing for ordinary electrical wiring, and rigid PVC conduit pipe for electrical wire and cable containment. For most uses and applications, the insulative nature of polymeric plastics and fabrics causes a buildup of static charge, which is undesirable. It is these materials that are made antistatic through the use of antistatic agents. Antistatic materials and surfaces neither spark nor acquire dust and dirt from the air due to electrical attraction. They prevent a host of potential problems in hospital operating rooms, microelectronic processing locations, and ordinary computer workstations.

The static dissipative ESD range is, overall, the most desirable and the least obtainable. Commonly available construction, manufacturing, and furnishing materials are not static dissipative. They cannot be made static dissipative by simply incorporating higher levels of antistatic additives, nor are there "static dissipative additives." Neither the chemistry of ESD-reducing additives nor the electrical nature of materials seems to allow this. Static dissipative products are fabricated from composites, laminates, bonded layers of electrically dissimilar materials, foam structures, and combinations thereof. They may incorporate antistatic additives as well as conductive materials in a specific portion of their structures.

The most conductive materials are metals. They too will hold a static charge, but only when ungrounded. If grounded, they do not exhibit static phenomena. Conductive additives for polymers include flaked aluminum and conductive carbon black. These additives function by forming a continual conductive pathway of contacting particles. Loadings, therefore, are high, and initial physical properties are changed. Low levels of conductive additives do not result in static dissipative performance. When the loading drops below the level where particle contact can occur, performance drops off sharply into the high antistatic or insulative range.

Table 1. Classification of ESD Behavior

Conductive	Surface resistivity is less than or equal to 10^5 Ω/square.
Static dissipative	Surface resistivity is greater than 10^5 Ω/square, but less than or equal to 10^9 Ω/square.
Antistatic	Surface resistivity is greater than 10^9 Ω/square, but less than or equal to 10^{14} Ω/square.
Insulative	Surface resistivity is greater than 10^{14} Ω/square.

HOW AN ANTISTATIC AGENT WORKS

Some brief points on theory and observable antistatic behavior are helpful in discussing how additives are used to transform polymeric building and furnishing products that are intrinsically insulative into antistatic materials. Static electricity is primarily a surface phenomenon. Common plastics and synthetic fabrics, for example, readily acquire charges in excess of 15,000 V by friction or by contacting any other surface, including air. This charge is not distributed evenly over the surface.

Static charge dissipates or decays in two ways: through conduction within and along the surface of the material and by radiation to the air. An internal antistatic additive will cause this to happen by directly or indirectly introducing functional ionic species to the compound. Electrons will conduct from site to site along the surface and then rapidly transfer into (or out of) the compound to air and/ or ground, thus eliminating potential difference, charge, and static. Hydroxyl groups in antistatic agent molecules attract ionic species from the air and, in conjunction with being hydrophilic, form these dissipation sites. Additionally, ionic species can be incorporated directly into an antistatic molecule. Alone, however, these chemical prerequisites are insufficient.

An internal antistatic agent is added to the plastic or polymer compound mixture prior to processing. After processing, the antistat must be able to migrate through the finished material to the surface, but without appearing as either a sensible powdery coat (bloom) or greasy film (exudation). This is accomplished by selecting an antistat that has only limited solubility in the polymer. If the antistat is too compatible, it will not move out of the polymer to the surface and therefore will not afford functionality. Thus, the additive must have just the right balance of incompatibility and mobility in a particular polymer system. Consequently, the level of antistat employed can be critical, and an effective antistat in one material will not necessarily work in another.

A monomolecular layer is all that is necessary to expose, or form with ambient materials, ionic electron transfer sites. The many references to hydrophilicity, hygroscopic antistats, and the necessity of forming a thin layer of water on the surface are misleading. Moisture is necessary and high humidity is desirable, but there need be no gross physical wetting of the surface in any sense.

PRINCIPAL ANTISTATIC GROUPS

Antistatic agents are arbitrarily but conveniently grouped as being ionic, nonionic, or amines. Essentially, they are all organic compounds. Ionic species consist of a positively charged portion, or cation, and a negatively charged portion, or anion. If the cation provides the functionality, it is called a cationic antistat. Quaternary ammonium salts are the most important type of cationic antistats. If the negative portion provides the antistatic quality, it is an anionic type. Detergentlike materials, such as sulfonates, are in this category. Nonionic types include ethoxylated and propoxylated aliphatic and aromatic molecules, glyceryl monostearates, and other glycerol compounds. The amines employed are usually of the ethoxylated alkyl type. Certain waxy materials act as dry lubricants on surfaces, reduce friction, and result in less static buildup. However, they cannot contribute to charge dissipation. Only a small number of the hundreds of antistatic agents listed in the literature are commercially useful.

ANTISTAT SELECTION FOR SPECIFIC MATERIALS

There are two basic approaches to ESD control with antistats. The antistat can either be incorporated in the material itself for durable permanent protection or be applied to the surface for nondurable protection. For internal use in plastics and other synthetic polymers, the choice of antistat is critical.

The surface resistivity of polyolefins is lowered some five orders of magnitude through the use of N,N-bis(2-hydroxyethyl) alkyl amines as internal permanent agents. Polyethylene is readily made antistatic with the incorporation of only 0.1% alkyl amine. High-density polyethylene and polypropylene do not lose their insulative quality as readily and require higher levels of antistats. These additives are usually prepared as a concentrate in polyolefin prior to compounding. Solid and liquid forms are available.

Alkyl amines are relatively ineffective in PVC. Further, amines have an adverse effect on thermal stability during processing, causing discoloration or even burning. In fact, all antistats used in PVC have a negative effect on some other quality of the polymer. It is therefore necessary first to make a choice based on the properties most critical to a particular need and second to adjust the heat stabilizer system. In rigid PVC, internal antistats of the quaternary ammonium salt type afford the best functionality. The best of these additives has a tolerable effect on heat stability. In flexible PVC, certain ethoxylated nonionic types are the best overall choices. Further adjustments to the overall flexible formulation will enhance performance. The proper use level in rigid PVC is 1–2% and in flexible PVC 2–8%. These use levels are considerably higher than in polyolefin.

Polyurethane film and thermoplastic are successfully made antistatic with certain quaternary compounds added at a 2–5% level. As a rule, antistatic agents cannot be incorporated directly into either part of a urethane foam compound system, as the functional portions of the antistat molecule also happen to be reactive in urethane chemistry.

Polyacetals, cellulose acetate, and acrylics can be rendered antistatic by incorporating quaternary antistats in their formulation.

Of the commercially popular polymers, polystyrene is probably the most difficult to imbue with antistatic properties. Nevertheless, several antistats are marketed as being functional in styrene. Polycarbonate is processed at too high a temperature to tolerate most antistats and, along with polyethylene terephthalate (PET), cannot therefore be made in an antistatic form yet. Engineering resins would require at least 2 or 3% of an additive to become antistatic. However, available antistatic agents of almost any type would severely affect the processing and dimensional stability of the product, rendering its major attributes useless. Thus, the use of internal durable antistats in polymers, resins, and plastics is far from universal.

EXTERNAL TREATMENTS WITH ANTISTATIC AGENTS

Surface treatment avoids all of the inherent problems associated with internal antistats. Excellent ESD protection is provided without, as a rule, any effect on the polymer's physical properties. The drawback is that externally applied antistats are not permanent. Although they can be quite resistant to handling and dry abrasion, they are readily removed by washing. Certain ethoxylated nonionic and quaternary antistats provide the best antistatic protection. Such combinations are high wetting, clear, nonvolatile, and very adhesive. When applied from a 1 or 2% aqueous or aqueous–alcoholic solution, they provide an invisible, even, nontacky coating. Application is by spraying, wiping, or dipping. Clear materials such as styrene, acrylics, polycarbonates, and acetates can successfully be treated. Polyester (PET) fabrics, carpeting, and containers also are afforded ESD protection by surface treatment. In essence, any material can be satisfactorily surface treated. When the geometry of the structure allows, application should be to both surfaces, even if only one surface requires protection. Electrically, the uncoated insulative side has the adverse effect of raising the charge of the treated side. Applications include large acrylic cover cases for displays and acrylic office partitions.

The above discussion deals with essentially flat, integral surfaces. Complex surfaces, such as closed- and open-celled foams, carpeting, and fabrics can also be treated. The "surfaces" of these materials are actually throughout the structure, and a treatment can permeate the entire volume of the material. The geometry of foams containing an antistatic agent further enhances charge dissipation. Closed-cell foams such as expanded polystyrene paneling and parts are successfully treated prior to expansion and formation of the part. Open-cell foams such as polyurethane, fabrics, and carpeting are either dipped or sprayed.

A permanent coating would obviously be desirable for many applications. Such a coating would be a thin layer of some hard, clear polymer heavily loaded with an antistatic agent that would maintain excellent adhesion to the substrate. The thin coating actually would contain an antistat of the internal type, which must migrate to the surface in order to achieve its functionality. The antistat would, however, migrate to both surfaces, including the substrate side, and more than likely interfere with adhesion. Permanent antistatic coatings remain inherently difficult to create.

APPLICATIONS

For the most successful prevention and control of static electricity problems, antistatic agents are usually but a part of a total design concept. Deep pile or plush carpeting installations can be used as an example. Nylon carpeting will generate charges in excess of 30,000 V just by being walked on. The carpeting should be manufactured with an antistatic agent in the base. Also, an antistat can be included in shampoo solutions or just sprayed on at regular intervals. Ambient low-humidity conditions should be avoided through the use of humidifiers. Initial room design should avoid, when possible, prominent or readily contacted sources to ground. A steel outside corner member under plaster would be undesirable. A person walking across nylon carpeting and then touching the wall corner would suffer an annoying shock if 30,000 V were discharged to ground.

Conveyer belts are commonly surfaced with PVC or urethane. Antistatic grades should be specified, as moving belting readily develops static charge. PVC wall covering can be manufactured in antistatic grades, as can transparent PVC strip curtain walls. Rigid PVC pipe furniture, if constructed from an antistatic grade, will not attract dust or dirt.

A hospital environment requires ESD protection to prevent the possibility of sparking in the presence of flammable anesthetic vapors. Normally, insulative portions of curtains, interior paneling, and partitions should be manufactured from antistatic grades.

Computer room facilities also require ESD protection, as a static discharge can instantly discharge an entire day's work just by the operator touching the keyboard. Furnishings, flooring, PVC chairmats, and fixtures should be antistatic or protected by antistat surface treatments.

TEST METHODS

There appear in the older literature numerous test methods based on dust, ash, and fluorescent pigment pickup. Quantities, attraction distances, and static cling patterns have been rigorously scrutinized in carefully controlled environments. Many pages have been devoted to various methods of inducing charge on materials by friction. These tests could never truly be quantified or standardized.

Two other main groups of test methods of a more quantitative nature involve measurement of initial static charge acceptance followed by decay rate utilizing an electrometer and various resistance measurements. These groups have been narrowed down and have evolved into two reproducible test methods that are now standardized and accepted by industry. Surface resistivity, the resistance method of choice, has already been mentioned. The apparatus consists of a high-voltage source, an electrode unit, and a device, such as an electrometer, to detect current between the electrodes. The standard test procedure is according to the American Society for Testing and Materials's ASTM D-257. Complete equipment is available. For example, Keithley Instruments, Inc., Cleveland, Ohio, manufactures a functionally integrated high-voltage source, electrometer, and resistivity adapter. The other acceptable test method is the Electrostatic Decay Test as described in Federal Test Method Standard 101C, Method 4046 (2). This test is a measure of the ability of a material, when grounded, to dissipate a known charge that has been induced on its surface. The testing apparatus is commercially available. For example, Electro-Tech Systems, Inc., Glenside, Pennsylvania, manufactures a complete static decay meter.

Standards have been established for specific environments. In a hospital, for example, sparking in a potentially explosive atmosphere can be eliminated when furnishings and interiors meet the National Fire Protection Association NFPA-56A Standard for the Use of Inhalation Anesthetics (3). Section 4–6.6.3 (a) in Reference 3 requires a specimen's potential to drop to 10% of its maximum value in 0.5 s or less, according to Test Method 4046 of Standard 101C. Section 4–6.6.3 (b) requires that the surface resistivity be less than 1×10^{11} Ω/square according to ASTM D-257, utilizing 40 V of interelectrode spacing. In order to meet the standard, a material must pass either one test or the other. Many antistatic materials are manufactured to meet the requirements of the military specification MIL-B-81705B (4), which requires specimens to decay to 0% of initial charge in not more than 2.00 s according to Method 4046 of Standard 101C.

BIBLIOGRAPHY

1. *Electrostatic Discharge Control Handbook for Protection of Electrical and Electronic Parts, Assemblies and Equipment (Excluding Electrically Initiated Explosive Devices)*, Department of Defense, Washington, D.C., May 2, 1980, Military Handbook, DOD-HDBK-263, 75 pp. Available from the Naval Publications and Forms Center, Philadelphia, Pa.

2. Federal Test Method Standard 101C, Test Procedures for Packaging Materials, Method 4046 Electrostatic Properties of Materials. Available from the General Services Administration, Specifications Section, Washington, D.C.

3. NFPA-56A-1978 Standard for the Use of Inhalation Anesthetics, Sec. 4–6.6, Antistatic Accessories and Testing. Available from the National Fire Protection Association, Inc., Battery March Park, Quincy, Mass.

4. "Quality Assurance Provisions," MIL-B-81705B Military Specification, Barrier Materials, Flexible, Electrostatic-Free, Heat Sealable, Paragr. 4.8.3 and Table 1. Available from the Defense Technical Information Center, Cameron Station, Alexandria, Va.

General References

D. H. Lehmicke, "Static in Textile Processing," *American Dyestuff Reporter* **38**, 853 (1949).

F. H. Steiger, "Evaluating Antistatic Finishes," *Textile Research Journal* **28**, 721 (1958).

J. R. Huntsman and D. M. Yenni, Jr., "Test Methods for Static Control Products," Static Control Systems/3M, 3M Center, St. Paul, Minn.

J. L. Rogers, "Antistatic Tests and Agents for Plastics," *SPE Journal* **29** (Jan./Feb. 1973).

J. L. Rogers, "Controlling Static Electricity in PVC Packaging," *Journal of Vinyl Technology* **6** (June 1984).

See also FLOORING MATERIALS—CARPETING; PLASTICS.

JAY L. ROGERS
Argus Div. Witco Corp.
Brooklyn, New York

APARTMENT BUILDINGS, HIGH-RISE

HISTORY AND DEFINITION

High-rise apartment buildings first developed in the United States toward the end of the nineteenth century as a result of social, economic, and technological factors: it became fashionable to live in apartments, an affluent stratum of the population sought urban housing, downtown land was becoming scarce, and technology made it possible to build higher than three or four stories. Living in an apartment or sharing a building with others became socially acceptable first in New York in the 1870s. Prior to that time, apartment living was considered acceptable only for the poor in exploitive tenement buildings, which appeared around 1850.

Historic antecedents existed for both luxury and tenement housing. The first apartment buildings emulated a French prototype imported from the Paris of the eighteenth century and the early apartments in fact were fashionably called "French flats." The poor people's tenement, often considered to have been invented in New York, had its historic predecessor in ancient Rome. However, one of the earliest examples of multistory housing can be found on this continent in the adobe pueblos in New Mexico.

All of these early examples, the fashionable eight-story Dakota apartment building in New York, the six-story Roman tenement, or the three-story Taos Pueblo, had one thing in common: they were denser and taller than the surrounding residential fabric—they were "high-rises."

Today, a high-rise is defined as a building requiring electric elevators (seven stories and above), mid-rise is a building that can be serviced with hydraulic elevators (four to seven stories), and low-rise is a two- to four-story walk-up.

The multistory predecessor of the high-rise apartment building, like the fashionable Dakota in Manhattan (1879), was only made possible by improvements in hydraulic elevators (such as safety devices by Otis) and the stretching of masonry construction toward its limits. True high-rises were a result of further technological advances, primarily the introduction of iron and steel construction by William Le Baron Jenney in 1884 in Chicago, the invention of plunger hydraulic elevators and later electric elevators.

Technical progress can only generate building types, however, if there is an economic and social need to be satisfied. After the immense population growth of the 1880s combined with a centrifugal movement of the well-to-do to the suburbs, there was also a desire to live in the fashionable enclaves of the inner city, such as Central Park in New York, Chicago's Gold Coast, and similar areas in other large cities.

These early high-rises carried on their exterior the eclectic taste of the nineteenth century upper class. They applied any number of historic styles in a spirit of stylistic arbitrariness, although the classical language predominated with clearly defined base, top, and middle. They could also afford high quality detailing, noble materials, and frequent and rich ornamentation.

It was when high-rise living became affordable by the middle income population after the turn of the century, and growing during the postdepression years, that ornamentation became sparse if not nonexistent; face brick replaced stone or terra cotta on the exterior, flat roofs were substituted for gable windowed copper mansards. This reductive attitude comfortably accompanied the simplified aesthetics of the modern movement that had spread to the United States during the 1930s and 1940s.

By the time the post-World War II housing boom occurred, architects were ready to develop a minimalist exterior (curtain wall, exposed concrete frame, flat roof without parapet, etc) and to use cheaper details in the interior (metal stud and drywall instead of gypsum block and plaster for partitions, no moldings to cover cracks, etc) in order to satisfy the developers' need for reduced construction cost necessary to tap a growing middle income market. The engineers also responded to new challenges of cost reduction and increased density (heights). Flat-plate concrete was fireproof, labor saving, and fast; new caisson technology and wind-bracing techniques combined with improved elevator speeds allowed the high-rise to jump from 12 to 15 stories (1930s) to 24 to 30 (1950s), to 45 and much higher (1960s). Advances in environmental control systems, such as electric heat, mechanical bathroom and kitchen ventilation, noncentral air conditioning, etc, also contributed to reaching the desired heights and densities.

The simplified, unornamented exteriors on the high-rise apartment buildings of the modern movement lent themselves to some outstanding architectural solutions. The purist, cubist facades of forerunners such as Gropius's Spandau project (1929) or of the paradigmatic Highpoint apartments by Lubetkin and Tecton (London, 1933) (Fig. 1) developed into a richly varied architectural language in the United States after World War II despite cost limitations, a remarkable achievement. Metal curtain wall exteriors reached unequaled sensitivity in the work of Mies

Figure 2. Mies van der Rohe: 860–880 North Lake Shore Drive, Chicago (1967). Photo credit: Hedrich-Blessing.

van der Rohe (860 and 880 North Lake Shore Dr., Chicago) (Fig. 2) and some of his followers (Lake Point Tower by Schipporeit & Heinrich, Chicago) (Fig. 3). Exposed concrete grids, pioneered by Le Corbusier (Unite D'Habitation, Marseilles) (Fig. 4) found varied application in the work of Jose Luis Sert (Peabody Terrace, Cambridge, Mass.) and I. M. Pei (University Plaza, New York; Washington Square East, Philadelphia) (Fig. 5). Masonry-clad exteriors showed immense versatility as exhibited on projects by Davis Brody & Associates (Waterside, New York) (Fig. 6), Sert, Jackson and Associates (Roosevelt Island, New York), Paul Rudolph (Crawford Manor, New Haven, Conn.) (Fig. 7), Harry Weese & Associates (Lake Village, Chicago), and Gruzen & Partners (Arthur Schomburg Plaza, New York).

THE ECONOMIC EQUATION

All of this had to be achieved under strenuous budgetary constraints if high-rise developers were to succeed in reaching a broader market. Architecture of high-rise apartment buildings became part of a complex economic equation. The hard costs (land and construction), together with

Figure 1. Lubetkin and Tecton: Highpoint Apartments, London (1933).

Figure 4. Le Corbusier: Unité d'Habitacion, Marseilles (1952).

Figure 3. Schipporeit & Heinrich: Lake Point Tower, Chicago (1967). Photo credit: John Macsai.

Figure 5. I. M. Pei and Partners: University Plaza, New York, N.Y. (1966). Courtesy of I. M. Pei and Partners. Photo credit: George Cserna.

the soft costs (loan interest during construction, fees, marketing, etc), are usually paid for by actual investment money (equity) and borrowed money (mortgage). On one side of the economic equation is income (rents less vacancies), minus expenses (management, utilities, maintenance, taxes) and mortgage payments; on the other side of the equation is the cash flow generally expressed in terms of a percentage of the equity. In some cases, low cash flow or no cash flow is accepted because of tax savings and expected property appreciation, whereas at other times, there is no profit allowed, as in the case of some subsidized housing. In the case of condominiums, sales price replaces rent. In all cases, the equation still must work. In a time of inflation (growing taxes, rising interest rates), the user's ability to pay commensurately higher

Figure 6. Davis Brody & Associates: Waterside, New York, N.Y. (1973). Courtesy of Davis Brody & Associates. Photo credit: Robert Gray.

rents is rare or nonexistent, and there is increased pressure on the architect to keep construction costs low. All design decisions in the field of housing are affected by the economic equation; this is especially true in the field of high-rises, which, by their very heights, are the most expensive of all housing types.

Aside from normal caution in the selection of materials and detailing, there are some fundamental planning strategies related to the economics of high-rise apartment buildings. First, the taller the building the more expensive it becomes as it requires deeper and costlier foundations, costlier wind-bracing, faster and costlier elevators, longer distances, and time for both labor and material to travel

during construction. Local codes require additional costs for smokeproof stair towers, sprinklering, or compartmentation. Floor area (in relation to economical concrete pouring sequence), floor length (in relation to crane reach), and floor configuration (amount of expensive perimeter in relation to floor size) are additional cost factors. The one factor on which the architect can have the greatest impact is the design of the actual floor expressed in net to gross efficiency ratio. As a result of these conditions, the accepted net rentable area, gross floor area less exterior walls, corridors, corridor walls, elevators, stairs, and other core elements should be at least 80% of the gross floor area.

rooms) requiring daylight and natural ventilation, and an interior zone which is artificially lit or borrows light from the exterior zone and is mechanically ventilated (entry hall, kitchen, bathrooms, laundry rooms of deluxe units). The dining area can be in either zone; in ideal situations, the kitchen is in the exterior zone (Fig. 8). Dwelling units also divide into living zone (living room, dining room, kitchen) and sleeping zone (bedroom, bathroom) and should be so planned that from a defined entry it is not necessary to cross the living zone in order to enter the bedroom, that there is access to a bathroom from the entry, that the bathroom can be accessed from the bedroom in maximum privacy. In some cases, the sleeping zone is divided into two with a bedroom (and its own bath) on each side of the living–dining room. The advantage of this layout is that it allows two unrelated people to share an apartment, thus saving rent.

Dwelling units can be oriented in one direction (most common), in two adjacent directions (corner units), or in two opposite directions (row-houses, through-apartments) (Fig. 9).

The sizes of the various dwelling units, including room sizes and certain critical room dimensions (such as bedroom width), should be part of the owner's program. Sizes will vary depending on the economic level of the market to be reached. The dwelling unit, like the typical apartment floor, is most efficient when it accommodates all of the required spaces with minimum waste and circulation (15–20%). Apartments that are narrow and deep (deeper than 25 ft) seem to be the most economical to build, since they result in minimal expensive building perimeter; however,

Figure 7. Paul Rudolph: Crawford Manor, New Haven, Conn. (1965). Courtesy of Paul Rudolph. Photo credit: Robert Perron.

MARKET AND USER

As important as construction cost is, it is only one factor in the complex equation; the market is the other. The lowest cost building is not necessarily the most desirable one. Cost is only meaningful as it relates to marketability.

Knowledge of the market and understanding of the needs of the projected user are fundamentally important in planning the basic component of any apartment building, the dwelling unit. The potential user's age group, family size, lifestyle, and previous housing experience should be expressed in the owner's program in terms of room sizes, room locations, interconnections, number of closets, type of kitchen, etc. This program, together with the apartment mix (number of efficiencies, one-bedroom, two-bedroom, etc, apartments) and restrictions by local building codes as well as lending agencies (FHA, HUD, etc), will be the architect's guide in dwelling unit design.

DWELLING UNIT

Most dwelling units can be divided into an exterior zone containing the habitable spaces (living rooms and bed-

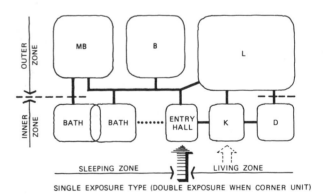

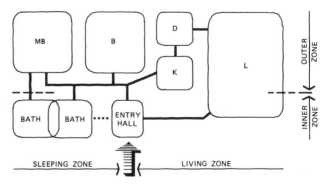

Figure 8. Diagram of outer and inner zones in two typical dwelling units (1).

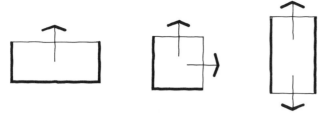

Figure 9. The three orientations of dwelling units (1).

if the apartment is too deep, the inner zone will be unpleasantly dark (Table 1).

The size of the living room, the largest single space in the apartment, can vary from HUD minimum of 160 ft^2 for a one-bedroom unit to 300 ft^2 for an average middle income apartment, or 400 ft^2 when it is a combined living–dining room. Minimum width is 12 ft, ideal width is 16 ft, although any living room dimension and configuration should be tested by furniture layouts.

Dining can be accommodated in a separate alcove (100 ft^2) which opens from the living room and is adjacent to the kitchen for proper service, or by a separate dining room (140 ft^2 or more). The dining alcove might be located in the inner zone of an apartment or in the outer zone along the exterior wall, which makes the apartment considerably longer. In all cases, direct connection between dining room and kitchen is most important.

The kitchen is most often in the inner zone and should be adjacent or close to the entrance. When it is located along the exterior wall and enjoys direct daylight, the advantages are such that crossing part of the living space in order to get to the kitchen is tolerated. Kitchens can be L-shaped, U-shaped, or galleys. The average apartment kitchen is 80–100 ft.^{2} Kitchens should be planned so that they can accommodate a breakfast table and chairs. A kitchen without any daylight is unpleasant to work in; even if it is located in the inner zone of an apartment, a kitchen should have borrowed light through a large opening, double doors, or a pass-through.

Bedroom or bedrooms constitute a separate zone of the apartment. Each bedroom requires a proper wardrobe closet. In many markets, the master bedroom is supposed to adjoin a private bathroom. Middle income averages are 180 ft^2 for a master bedroom and 150 ft^2 for a secondary bedroom. In order to locate beds and drawers, minimum length and width of the bedroom is critical. In planning bedrooms, furniture layouts are even more important than for living rooms.

Bathrooms within one apartment or bathrooms of adjacent apartments should back up each other whenever possible for the sake of plumbing economy. The minimum size is 5 × 7.5 ft.

In planning the wardrobe storage for bedrooms, walk-in closets are preferred. Walk-through dressing closets that connect the sleeping area of an efficiency apartment with the bathroom are essential to assure privacy for dressing when a guest is present. In addition to the wardrobe closets in the bedrooms, each apartment must have a guest closet at the entry, a linen closet near the bedrooms, and a utility closet for vacuum cleaners, brooms, step ladders, and other paraphernalia.

From the point of view of design, balconies are often highly desirable, but are costly and should be justified by market demand. When they are provided, the minimum width should be 5 ft. Indented or semiprojected balconies get more frequent use than fully projected ones (Fig. 10).

VERTICAL CORE ELEMENTS

The configuration of a dwelling unit will depend not only on its inner functional needs, but also on the location of the building's vertical core elements such as stairs, elevators, and refuse chutes. Prototypical apartment plans are modified when a section of the apartment floor area is "borrowed" to accommodate parts of these vertical core elements (Fig. 11). Borrowing can be compensated for by projecting part of the apartment on the exterior, resulting in a varied exterior building configuration (Fig. 12). Core elements can also be planned in such a manner that they are totally independent of the dwelling unit and do not require borrowing. In some cases, it is possible to express the core separately on the exterior, thus providing added design options, but the result also adds to the building length and, consequently, cost (Fig. 13).

The most important vertical core elements are the stairs and elevators. In high-rises, the first serve as fire exits and the second distribute users and goods, and serve the fire department in case of an emergency. All codes call for fireproof construction (Class I) for high-rise apartment buildings and require a minimum of two exits with enclosures of 2-hr fire rating. The maximum travel distance to a stair and the maximum dead end corridor beyond a stair is determined by the building code. Stairs, therefore, tend to be near the ends of apartment buildings, whereas elevators and other core elements are usually centrally located. This placement provides even distribution of ten-

Table 1. Gross Sizes of Apartments[a,b]

Unit	Low	Medium	Luxury	HUD Minimum
Efficiency (1 bath)	450	500–550	600+	380
1-Bedroom (1 bath)	650	700–800	900+	580
2-Bedroom (2 baths)	950	1100–1200	1250+	750
3-Bedroom (2 baths)	1250	1350–1450	1600+	900

[a] Ref. 1.
[b] All measurements are in ft^2.

Figure 10. Apartment prototypes (1).

225

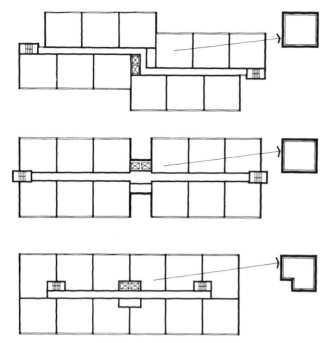

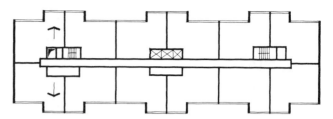

Figure 11. Typical floor as a result of vertical core arrangements and "borrowing" (1).

Figure 12. Varied exterior building configuration resulting from accomodating vertical core elements (1).

ants from the elevators and roughly equal distance, if possible, to the garbage chute. The number and speed of elevators is determined by complex calculations and requires the help of a consultant. As a minimum, two elevators are needed in case one is being serviced. In structures up to 20 or 25 floors, one of the elevators also serves as a freight elevator. Beyond this height, the number of elevators can be reduced if the normal 350 fpm speed is increased to 500 fpm or more. When a separate freight elevator is required, it need not be in the center of the building. In fact, it often has a better connection to the ground level loading area when it is located near one end. There should be an anteroom between the freight elevator and the apart-

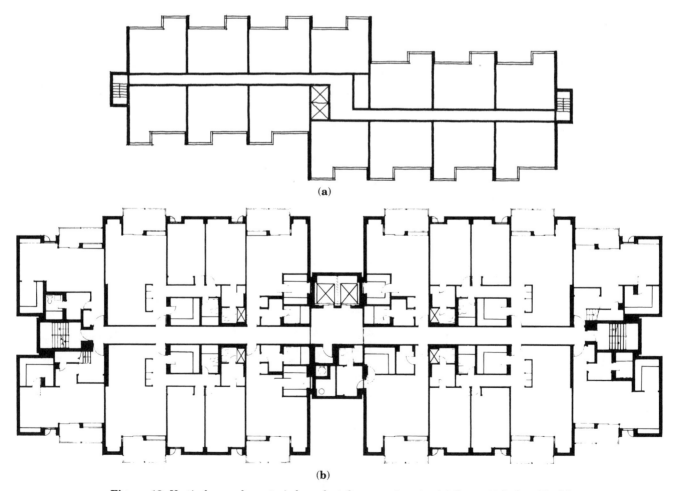

(a)

(b)

Figure 13. Vertical core elements independent from apartments: (**a**) Sequential plan (1); (**b**) Symmetrical plan (Keyes, Lethbridge & Condon: Tiber Island, Washington, D.C., 1965).

ment corridor, as well as between the corridor and the refuse chute to keep the corridor litter free.

HIGH-RISE TYPES

The type of an apartment building will be determined by the way the dwelling units are placed along the horizontal distributor (corridor) and the way they relate to the vertical core elements (stairs and elevators). Linear distribution, with elevators in the center and stairs toward the ends, is the most common and is called the corridor-type. It can be single loaded with dwelling units on one side of the corridor (infrequently used), or, most frequently, double loaded with dwelling units on both sides, called a central corridor-type. In order to eliminate long corridors,

the number of apartments a vertical core serves can be reduced, resulting in through-apartments with two opposite exposures. A series of these single cores can form a core-type apartment building. This is obviously an expensive design requiring multiple elements of stairs and elevators, the cost of which is not offset by the saving of some long corridors. When the distributing corridor is radial (tripod, cross, etc) or forms a ring, the point-block apartment building is created with all vertical core elements centrally located. There are many variants of the point-block such as square, circle, I, or pin-wheel shape. Any of these apartment building types can have regular elevator stops on every floor or can become skip-stop-type where elevators stop on every second or third floor resulting in various mixtures of apartments, one level, two story, trilevel, etc. (Figs. 14 and 15).

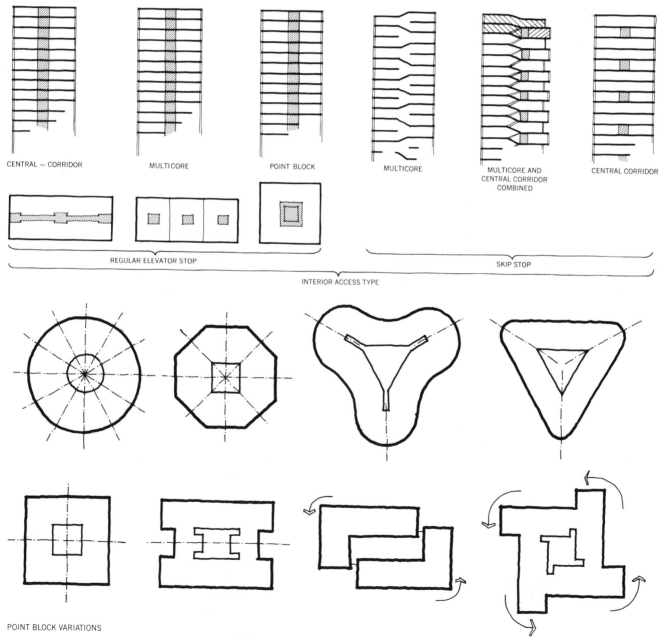

Figure 14. High-rise types (1).

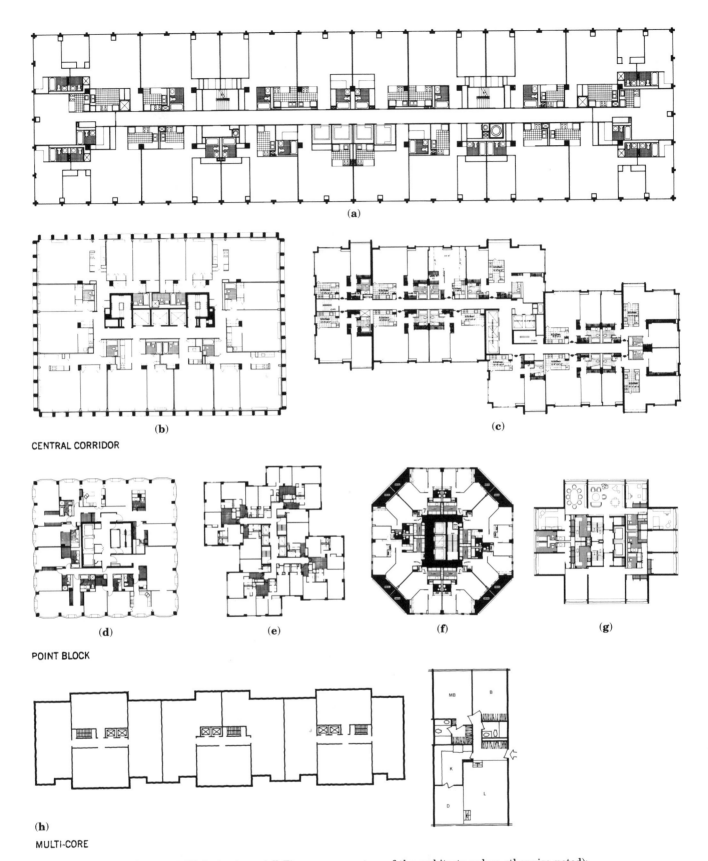

CENTRAL CORRIDOR

POINT BLOCK

MULTI-CORE

Figure 15. High-rise types (all Figures are courtesy of the architects unless otherwise noted): (**a**) Stanley Tigerman: Boardwalk, Chicago (1973); (**b**) I. M. Pei & Partners: Washington Square East, Philadelphia (1963); (**c**) Solomon, Cordwell, Buenz & Associates: Hawthorn House, Chicago (1967); (**d**) Solomon, Cordwell, Buenz & Associates: 1555 N. Astor, Chicago (1974); (**e**) Davis Brody & Associates: Waterside, New York, N.Y. (1973); (**f**) The Gruzen Partnership: Arthur Schomburg Plaza, New York, N.Y. (1972); (**g**) Skidmore, Owings & Merrill: Dorchester Apartments, Chicago (1967); (**h**) Hausner & Macsai: Harbor House, Chicago (1966) (1).

228

PARKING AND COMMON AREAS

Whereas the tower containing the dwelling units is the most important and most expensive part of an apartment building, it must relate properly to other components: the parking garage, the service linkages (loading and refuse removal), the lobby, laundry, storage, and recreation spaces known as the common areas.

The number of parking spaces to be provided is generally determined by zoning ordinance unless market conditions demand a higher number than zoning. There is rarely adequate land available to park the cars in the most economic fashion, on grade, in the open. Parking is usually provided in a two-, three-, or four-story garage structure. Ideally, much of this structure should be underground, but high watertables or other underground conditions prohibit more than a one-story deep basement on many sites. Consequently, a one-, two-, or occasionally three-story "box" that is alien to the surrounding urban fabric must be skillfully integrated with the tower. This presents one of the most difficult high-rise design problems. At times, the site is large enough to permit locating the garage separately from the tower, allowing each to have a framing system and bay sizes most conducive to its proper functioning. When site limitation forces the garage to be under the tower, either a mutually satisfactory bay size is found or the tower columns are transferred, a solution that is expensive but preferable to compromising the marketability of all of the residential floors. Tower shear walls and elevators obviously cannot be transferred and must be accommodated by the parking layout. The cost of an under-the-tower garage is high also because most codes require that the garage be sprinklered and because tower elevator and stair cores need a 4-hr fire separation when entered from the garage levels. Ramps are difficult to locate under the tower and pose a special problem. For this reason, split level parking, which requires a considerably shorter ramp, is often preferred. A critical component of an apartment building garage is the entrance. Ideally, it is designed so that tenants can be dropped off or picked up at the lobby either before entering or after leaving the garage proper.

Zoning ordinances also determine the number and size of off-street loading spots. Between these and the freight elevator there must be a corridor wide enough to accommodate carting out garbage from the compactor room under the trash chute. The receiving room, maintenance shop, building storage, mechanical room, electric gear, and telephone equipment room constitute the balance of service space in the base of the tower. Tenant locker areas, providing 15–25 ft^2 of bulk storage space for each tenant, must be located in the tower base also. Both the loading entrance and the main lobby entrance must be secured with an intercom system, which might be supplemented by the presence of a doorman in the lobby, a receiving clerk at the loading entrance, and television surveillance.

Of all of the common interior spaces of an apartment building, the lobby is the one that makes the first impression. It attests to the quality of the building as a whole; it welcomes, it orients. The main lobby with an adjacent mailroom, the first floor elevator lobby, and the connecting passage between them usually receives special interior design treatment. Less visible common areas include the central laundry (unless in certain deluxe buildings each apartment has its own washer and dryer), a community recreation room with a kitchen, and an optional swimming pool and sauna. In large projects, it is not unusual to see a health club, tennis courts, handball court, exercise room, day-care center, and shops.

VOLUME AND COST

It is obvious that each high-rise apartment project is different in multiple factors: site conditions, zoning ordinances, building codes, user needs and expectations, and amenities required. Nevertheless, there are enough constants for the architect to have some idea of the volume and, consequently, gain an indication of the final cost at an early stage of the design process.

A hypothetical program calls for 20% efficiency apartments requiring 550 ft^2, 40% one-bedroom and 40% two-bedroom apartments requiring 800 ft^2 and 1200 ft^2, respectively. Assuming that the zoning ordinance has been checked and that the site can accommodate 200 units with 10 units on a floor, a floor area neither too small nor too large can be created. This means that the net rental square footage will be

40 efficiencies	@	550 ft^2 =	22,000 ft^2
80 one-bedrooms	@	800 ft^2 =	64,000 ft^2
80 two-bedrooms	@	1200 ft^2 =	96,000 ft^2
Total net rentable space			= 182,000 ft^2

Allowing between 15 and 20% of the gross floor area of the typical floors for exterior walls, corridors, stairs, elevators, etc, the net rentable space is increased by 20% to be safe:

net rentable	= 182,000 ft^2
plus 20% nonrentable	= +36,400 ft^2
total tower	= 218,400 ft^2

There are no balconies in the program (if there were, they would be added at 50% of actual square footage). Common areas, lobby, laundry, community room, tenant lockers, and mechanical and maintenance spaces usually can be accommodated by adding 6–8% to the total tower square footage. Obviously, stores, health clubs, and other unusual amenities increase this percentage.

total residential tower	= 218,400 ft^2
plus 7% for common areas	= +15,300 ft^2
total exclusive of parking	= 233,700 ft^2

Zoning requires 60% parking and in a hypothetical urban location this is adequate. Sixty percent of 200 is 120 cars. If there were an enclosed parking garage on the ground floor and in the basement adjacent to and behind the tower, the roof of the garage could be used as a recreation deck. Allowing for driving isles, ramps, and exit stairs, each car requires approximately 350 ft^2 of garage space. If the garage were under the residential tower, depending on the configuration and the column spacing of the tower, this figure would be increased to a minimum of 450 ft^2.

building exclusive of parking	= 233,700 ft^2
parking 120 cars @ 350 ft^2/car	= +42,000 ft^2
total building	= 275,700 ft^2

Since it is practically impossible to separate the higher square-foot cost of the tower from the lower square-foot cost of the garage, the cost figures quoted for high-rise apartment buildings usually apply to a total average building square footage, including garage. Assuming $52.00/ft^2 current construction cost for high-rise apartment buildings, the total cost would be 275,700 ft^2 @ $52.00 or $14,336,400. An important planning factor is that this figure does not include cost escalation between estimating and the time of bidding.

Obviously, many factors influence the cost of a building. A decision about a door handle can be significant if it is repeated 200 times. Certain parts of the high-rise apartment building, however, represent a larger portion of the total cost than others, so that from the point of construction cost they call for special attention. Generally, construction cost breaks down as follows:

Element	% of Total Cost
Structural frame and foundations	25–32
Heating, air conditioning, ventilation, plumbing, electrical, and fire protection	24–29
Exterior "skin"	7–10
Partitions	7–9
Elevators	3–6
All other trades	20–25

The two largest components that affect cost are the structure and the mechanical systems of the building. Whereas many trades are included under mechanical systems, structure usually refers to a single major trade, concrete. The foundation, if handled by the caisson trade, is a small, separate portion. The structural system, therefore, has major significance as far as the financial success of a high-rise apartment building is concerned.

STRUCTURE

The structure of a high-rise apartment building represents a significant part of the overall construction cost. However, unlike hardware, mechanical apparatus, finishes, etc, the structure is not subject to a range of economic decisions; deluxe or modest, it must stand up. Having satisfied design requirements of strength and function, the same design can be used in low rent-subsidized or exclusive apartment construction.

The cast-in-place reinforced-concrete flat plate structure is almost exclusively used for high-rise apartment construction, except in areas where the design is governed by seismicity. The flat plate floors are either reinforced totally with mild reinforcement or a combination of mild reinforcement and prestressing steel which is site post-tensioned. The selection of reinforcement type is dependent on construction market conditions to a minor extent and on spacing of columns to a major extent.

Maximum economy in any structure results when the structural elements "work" the least to resist the applied loads. In a flat plate, closely spaced columns result in the least slab thickness. Because of minimum reinforcement requirements, this results in the least amount of reinforcing steel. As the distance between columns increases, the slab bending increases, demanding thicker slabs and increased reinforcement. Beyond certain spans, high strength reinforcement (prestressing) becomes economical.

All but the most luxurious apartment buildings can accommodate interior column spacings of approximately 15–16 ft, the maximum living room dimension. Further, within this maximum span, columns may be arranged in a rigid grid or in "scattered" layout, which eliminates architectural restraints and allows placement of columns where they fit into the architectural plan.

The rigid column layout facilitates the use of "flying forms," where entire sections of shores and forms are lifted intact from floor to floor. The rigid grid layout results in longer spans and, therefore, when spans are in the neighborhood of 20 ft, the advantages of mild reinforcement are defeated and posttensioning is advantageous.

Posttensioning in the greater than 20-ft span range allows for slab thickness less than required for mild reinforcement. Slab concrete strength must reach specified limits prior to stressing the high strength strands. This necessitates leaving shores and forms in place longer or using high strength concrete.

If parking is required under the tower, >20-ft aisles are used, thus dictating larger column spacing throughout the building height or using closer spaced columns in the tower and transferring to more widely spaced columns in the parking area. The latter approach becomes very costly. The most economical solution is to avoid the problems and place the parking garage outside the tower. Of course, this is only feasible if land is available.

Columns are usually square or rectangular. The square column is least expensive; however, the rectangular columns are more adaptable to apartment layouts. Long narrow rectangular columns (6–8-in. wide) fit well into closets and corners, often replacing partitions as well as reducing slab spans.

High-rise apartment structures require resistance to lateral loads—wind and earthquakes. This resistance is to prevent the building from turning over, sliding, and swaying. The means of providing this resistance is dependent on the building height.

Concrete columns and slabs alone can provide satisfactory resistance to lateral loads, up to about 10 stories in height. To use the frame only above this height requires increased slab thickness and a substantial increase in reinforcement. Because the frame is relatively flexible, higher buildings might sway, possibly creating problems with interacting architectural and mechanical elements (windows, partitions, pipes, etc).

Buildings between approximately 10 and 40 stories require the addition of stiffer elements to supplement the frame resistance. Shear walls generally satisfy this function. The lateral loads are distributed through the slab, which behaves as a deep, thin beam in the horizontal plane (diaphragm) and transfers the lateral loads to the shear walls and frame according to their relative stiffnesses. Vertically continuous shear walls are thought of as vertical cantilevered beams, restrained at the foundations, and resisting both axial (gravity) and lateral loads.

Exterior concrete bearing walls that form a tube provide a uniquely efficient structural system. Variations in the tube have been used economically for apartment buildings in the 40–60-story range. The extent of window openings dictates the structural behavior. Smaller openings allow a closer approximation to the pure tube behavior, with stiff columns and spandrels providing the tube effect. Increasing the size of openings diminishes the column and spandrel stiffness, and the structural response tends to approach regular frame action.

Economical lateral load resistance for apartment structures of more than 60 stories requires interaction of the exterior "bearing wall" and interior shear resisting elements generally consisting of the vertical core walls (around stairs and elevators). To provide the necessary interaction, stiff framing elements between the interior and exterior structure are required. These interconnecting elements need not occur at every floor, but only as required to distribute the lateral forces.

MECHANICAL AND ELECTRICAL DESIGN CONSIDERATIONS

Tension is a word associated with structural in engineering parlance, but it is pervasive in mechanical–electrical design of high-rise buildings. The tension comes between the operation of systems, particularly heating and cooling on the one side, and their installation costs and their compatibility with the remainder of the building elements on the other side.

The rejoinder to that statement may well be, "Of course, the first consideration must be satisfactory operation. The systems have to work." But this answer oversimplifies a very real issue. What is "satisfactory" operation? The definition might be quite different in a mountainview luxury high-rise and a low income multiple building project. What may be the significance of a 10-year equipment life expectancy compared to a 30-year predicted life at 10% higher first cost? At 30%? At 50%?

Finally, the mechanical–electrical systems must fit unobtrusively and effectively into the building. If the architect is aware of the many possible pitfalls, there has been a team effort from the earliest schematic design phase, so the architectural solution, the structure, and the mechanical–electrical systems have evolved together, as members of a single family. In the same relationship, the various trades in the mechanical–electrical disciplines grow together, but, for clarity, will be considered separately.

Heating, Ventilating and Air Conditioning (HVAC)

The first decisions on heating, ventilating and air conditioning belong to the developer or owner.

The primary concern is cooling. Except for geographic areas where hot weather virtually never occurs and for some low cost public housing, there will usually be at least convenient provisions for occupant-installed cooling in the United States. More frequently, there will be installed cooling systems.

Next is the question of heating. Again, the answer is geographic, this time with a hint of economic undertone. Some places need no heat. In others, it is an occasional luxury.

The type of fuel needs to be chosen. Cost, availability, local custom, and impact on rental or sales are factors that an experienced developer or owner can evaluate. Design engineers can contribute reasonable estimates of operating costs. Even crystal ball gazing, in an attempt to foresee future trends, may be resorted to. Coal, oil, gas, electricity, or solar power are possibilities, each with its advantages and drawbacks. If electricity is elected, will it be feasible to generate on site? There may be political implications in that question and its answer.

The choice between central systems for heating and cooling, or an independent plant for each dwelling unit must be made. For condominium ownership, there are obvious advantages in individual ownership and control, in that exact heating and cooling costs can be paid directly and need not be assessed by averaging. For rental units, local custom may determine. Are tenants accustomed to providing their own heating and cooling, or do they expect it to be included in the rent? The owner's own experience and expectations in operating the building may be important here. There are other considerations. Central systems have lower maintenance costs and, usually, lower operating costs. The widespread consequences of equipment breakdown and the difficulty of changing from heating to cooling and vice versa are unfavorable and consequently a deterrent, particularly in climates with highly changeable seasons. Finally, the choices are not mutually exclusive. Systems of central heating with individual cooling or, less frequently, central cooling with individual heating have been installed in many buildings.

Coordination with structural design is vital in system selection and in design of details. In concrete slab construction, the size and location of openings can be of crucial importance, especially with respect to heavy loading areas with their concentrations of reinforcing bars. With considerations of economy, structure, and aesthetics well in mind, the design team can finally select an HVAC system.

Central Systems. Central heating in high-rise buildings is done by circulating steam or hot water from a boiler plant. With hot water, the boiler plant can be located at any level of the building, top, bottom, or intermediate. For steam, it is impractical, although possible, to locate other than at the bottom of the building. The great advantage in hot water, however, is its temperature flexibility which allows adjustment to suit the weather. As to the boilers themselves, a high-rise building should have at least two for standby purposes in case of breakdown. Modern technology and the need for energy conservation stress multiple boiler installations, in which many small boilers are sequenced to follow the varying heating load quite closely, thus operating at high efficiency. Somewhat greater boiler room space is generally needed for this type of installation.

Central cooling in large buildings is accomplished by circulation of chilled water, usually through the same pipes that carry heating water in winter. Separate piping systems for heating and cooling water are so expensive as to be very seldom used. The common system makes for problems in changeable climates, as noted previously. In either event, the water is chilled in a mechanical refrigeration plant, usually powered by an electrically driven compressor or compressors, although in favorable circumstances fuel-powered chillers can be used for economic reasons. Heat rejection from the chiller plant is usually through recirculated water cooled by evaporation in the familiar "cooling tower," although in high-rise buildings of small floor area air-cooled condensers might be used. Either kind of equipment is very large, and some architectural effort is spent to conceal it without damaging its effectiveness.

The dwelling unit heating–cooling devices are ideally located on the exterior walls of living rooms, dining rooms, and bedrooms, where the maximum heating and cooling loads occur. They take the familiar forms of heating convectors located under windows or extending the entire length of the exterior wall, or of the familiar "fan-coil" units, which are forced heating–cooling convectors, either of the underwindow type or in the form of simulated columns, floor to ceiling, containing within themselves the common riser pipes, which serve an entire tier of such units.

Another central heating system embodies apartment "panel" heating, usually affected by warming entire ceilings of the exposed rooms, although wall or floor panels can also be used. This system has the great advantage of requiring no space in the apartment livable areas, but is somewhat slow in response to temperature changes and has lost favor on that account. Panel cooling is theoretically feasible, but requires an auxiliary air system for dehumidification, is touchy to control, and has found very little usage.

Unitary Systems. Probably the most common individual HVAC unit is the familiar room cooling unit inserted in a window or especially prepared wall opening, always on an exterior wall in order to use outdoor air for condensing purposes. When an electric heating coil is inserted into this unit, it can serve a room both for heating and cooling. Its advantages include low comparative first cost and flexibility in operation, cooling or heating being instantly available even in unseasonal weather. Its disadvantages are short equipment life (although replacements are easily installed) and a tendency to higher noise level than other systems, not to mention the difficulties the architect faces in designing elevations that are "pockmarked" with such through-wall units.

More sophisticated are apartment furnace units, including self-contained cooling systems, which distribute warmed or cooled air through the dwelling unit in season. If the refrigeration machine is air-cooled, the unit must be located on an outside wall or balcony, for access to outside air. An attractive alternative is a water-cooled heat pump unit served by a central circulating water system. This water condenses refrigerant in the cooling season and provides the source of heat in heating season. Any apartment can be on either heating or cooling service at any time. If there is a preponderance of heat removal, central boilers make up the deficit. If condensing heat is raising the circulating water temperature, a cooling tower removes the surplus. In this sense, the system combines individual and central features.

Other combinations of individual and central features may be in convector heating with through-wall room coolers, a common design. Individual apartment furnaces may be combined with a central chilled water system, or individual apartment cooling units may be fed by a central heating water or steam system.

In the selection, required space for the HVAC system and its necessary location or its flexibility in location are important considerations in the whole team effort. Common and/or attached commercial areas may be heated and cooled by conventional systems, either fed by central building systems or independently. The latter choice is another ownership decision.

Ventilation. The trend to interior bathrooms and, frequently, kitchens has been architecturally successful in providing more exterior living space, but has had energy consumption drawbacks. Such interior spaces must be ventilated to remove fumes and water vapor by exhausting air. Whatever air is exhausted from a structure must be made up by entrance of an equal volume from outdoors, and that volume must be warmed in winter and, perhaps, cooled in summer if the entire structure is to be cooled. A customary method of introducing makeup air is feeding it into the common corridors at each living level and providing means for its entrance into the apartments by grilles or by designed cracks between the apartment entrance door and its frame. This method has the additional advantage of maintaining fresh, odorless corridors.

Bathroom and, if necessary, kitchen mechanical exhaust may be individual or central. Individual small residential ceiling or wall exhaust fans are often controlled by switch with the room lights, and a method of routing a discharge duct from each fan to outdoors must be devised within the structure or via false beams. Obviously, the point of discharge must not cause a nuisance at windows or other ventilating openings.

Common exhausts usually take the form of vertical ducts into which each bath or kitchen in a tier of apartments empties via a register, which permits equalization of the amounts of air exhausted. Provisions must be made to shield sound from one room entering another. Kitchen and bathroom stacks must always be kept separate. This method of constant exhaust is very wasteful of energy. A marked improvement has been developed in the introduction of small motorized dampers behind the registers. These dampers open only when the room light is on. Capacity of the common exhaust blower is automatically reduced or increased based on the number of dampers open at any time.

Common or private laundry facilities require at least removal of clothes dryer exhaust, which is vapor-laden air. Finally, automobile fumes must be exhausted from indoor parking facilities. This is usually large volume exhaust, very wasteful of heat (if the garage is heated), and should be controlled by devices sensitive to the presence of carbon monoxide.

There is an additional unwanted though unavoidable condition in cold weather. The well-known "chimney effect," in which warmed building air tends to rise and escape out the top, replaced by cold, denser outside air coming in at the bottom of the building, can be a plague in high-rise buildings. Its only cure lies in designing and building as tight as possible. Entrance doors should be revolving type if permitted by code. Stairway doors should be tight-closing and always kept closed. Elevator doors should be closed even when elevators are waiting at ground floor level, and the doors should close as tight as possible to their frames. The upper level doors, hatches, and windows should also be tight, so the warm air cannot escape. Pipe, duct, and chimney shafts should be sealed top and bottom, and pipe sleeves through floors packed with a compressible material, so air cannot pass through the space between pipe or duct and its sleeve.

Plumbing

Reasonably quiet operation of sanitary fixtures and careful control of water pressures are major criteria in plumbing design. It is assumed that the primary task of providing enough water and adequate piping to get rid of the waste has been accomplished simply by adhering to the governing plumbing code.

Good practice and, in many cases, code requirements restrict water pressure zones to approximately 15 stories in height. For taller buildings, the height must be divided into two or more strata, none more than the 15-story limitation and each supplied with water at only enough pressure to serve itself. This may be accomplished by multiple pumps or by pressure regulating valves for the various zones. Both hot and cold domestic water must meet this requirement.

Domestic hot water systems must include full circulation to permit water to move through the piping system during periods of minimal use so that hot water is available anywhere in the building with no more than a few seconds' wait. Heating can be done by independent water heaters using whatever fuel has been found best for the building, or in combination with the space heating system. Individual apartment water heaters save the entire cost of the hot water distribution and circulating system, but their cost usually exceeds the piping cost, and maintenance of a great number of small heaters is expensive.

Drainage stacks carrying kitchen sink wastes in high-rise buildings must have a lower zone of three to five floors drained separately from the floors above. That is, the waste stack serving the upper floors runs "express," without connections, through the lower floors. The purpose of this is to avoid backup into the lowest floor sinks of foamy suds. These suds form when the wastes that carry dishwasher detergent residue hit the horizontal turn in a vertical stack. This kind of backup into lower fixtures can also occur when ordinary wastes from a great height strike the stack turn. For this reason, when a building exceeds approximately 30 stories it is well to consider running double or triple sets of stacks or, if physically feasible, to offset a single stack every 30 floors or so to interrupt the free fall of wastes from great heights.

Fire Protection

Greatly expanded concerns of fire hazards in high-rise buildings in recent years have led to new code requirements for protection. In response, designers of many such apartment buildings have included complete systems of automatic sprinklers, carefully integrated into the structural and partition layouts in order to be effective but reasonably unobtrusive. In addition, the familiar standpipe arrangement with one or more fire hoses on each floor helps the fire department fight fires at high floors. Portable, easily handled fire extinguishers are placed in stairs or halls and in storage, equipment, and other areas where small fires may occur.

Electrical Work

As in plumbing, there are not many options in placement of lights, receptacles, switches, and electrical fittings in apartments. Some code restrictions apply to location of apartment circuit breaker panels, which may or may not be in closets, may or may not be in kitchens, etc, according to local codes. Selection of lighting fixtures for living and common areas is an important architectural function.

There are choices in the methods of distribution of electrical power, however. In buildings with exceptionally high electrical loads, principally electrically heated high-rises, economies may be realized by distributing vertically at high voltages, perhaps up to 13,200 V. This makes for comparatively small electrical risers, but does, of course, necessitate installation of transformers at periodic levels of the building, to reduce the voltage to utilization levels. In order to encourage electric heating, utilities have been known to underwrite some of the cost of such high voltage distribution systems.

In planning the typical apartment floor core area, the designer must remember to allow for at least one electric distribution closet on each floor. In high-rise buildings, the electrical distribution is almost invariably efficient and comparatively economical through vertical main riser(s) with apartment feeds tapped off at one, two, or three floor intervals. Where the building has large floor areas, more than one riser and associated tapoff closet may well be least expensive. Depending on the method of distribution, such closets may be as little as 8 to as much as 35 ft^2 in floor area.

A rich field for electrical innovation is in special systems and their integration into overall control of a building. Rapidly developing electronic technology has led to great improvement in fire safety, security, intercommunication, energy management, and outside communications systems, with the ability to combine all of these functions at single control consoles.

SPECIAL USERS

Before considering issues connected to the exterior of high-rise apartment buildings, newly developed user needs should be considered. Demographic changes in the United States and economic developments resulted in such recent trends as smaller, more compact dwelling units; sharing of dwellings by two unrelated adults; loft or partially unfinished apartments for younger residents to complete on their own; and apartments more conducive to home occupations. These are differences in lifestyles and do not fundamentally alter what has already been said about the dwelling units of high-rises. Two user groups, however, require considerable changes. Interestingly, neither of these groups are entirely new; what is new is the architect's sensitivity to them.

The first group is the physically handicapped, the wheelchair-bound users who need wider parking spaces, ramps in lieu of steps, corridor rails, wider doors, and wider toilet stalls and bathrooms. They also need adaptations of facilities such as counters, grab bars, wall phones, or drinking fountains to the height of a person in a wheelchair. Whereas privately funded apartment buildings provide apartments for the handicapped only if local codes require it, public funding agencies call for a number of such dwelling units and have extensive requirements assuring accessibility for the wheelchair bound.

A larger and more diverse group whose needs are far less defined by codes is the elderly; they represent the fastest growing segment of the population and the largest housing market with unmet needs. To design for them successfully requires the understanding of the aging process (2,3). The environment designed for the elderly must be supportive of their age-related losses (lack of stamina, limited reach, arthritic joints, reduced mobility, poorer vision, etc) and must provide them with a range of options.

In terms of this article, the dwelling unit for the elderly is smaller than the average apartment (500–600 ft^2 for a one-bedroom unit) and buildings for the aged consist predominantly of one-bedroom apartments or occasional two-bedrooms where the bedrooms are split on each side of

the living room (Fig. 16). Doors are wider (all 2 ft 8 in.) to accommodate wheelchairs, and bathroom doors swing out. Although the apartment is small, the kitchen must be a decent size to permit a small breakfast table and should be totally open to the living room. Kitchen storage, counter heights, oven location, burner controls, and freezer compartments of refrigerators should all be carefully considered and located with the physical limitations of the elderly in mind.

Bedrooms should accommodate two twin beds (for emergencies, since there is usually a single occupant) and the passage from the bedroom to the bathroom should be direct and well lit. Both bedroom and bathroom should have emergency signals. Flexible shower connections, lever-type door handles, easy-to-operate window hardware, large and readable signage, and nonslip flooring are all part of the microenvironment to be considered when the user is elderly. In addition, the location of storage space is preferable in the apartment proper rather than in a remote locker room.

Well-lit, secure, public spaces with proper signage are essential. Waiting space at the elevators, daylight in the typical floor corridor, and balconies make life more pleasant for a population that is generally at home during the day.

Lobbies gain special significance when designed for the elderly. They are the "front porch," where social contacts are made and where the world is observed. The laundry room also becomes a social magnet, thus requiring daylight and, like the lobby or community room, needs to have toilet facilities nearby. The community room becomes a most important center for recreation and, if it is visible from the lobby, participation is encouraged. Craft or hobby rooms should be included. Congregate housing, as opposed to independent housing, provides central dining and kitchen facilities in addition to the housekeeping service and occasionally, if possible, amenities such as a library,

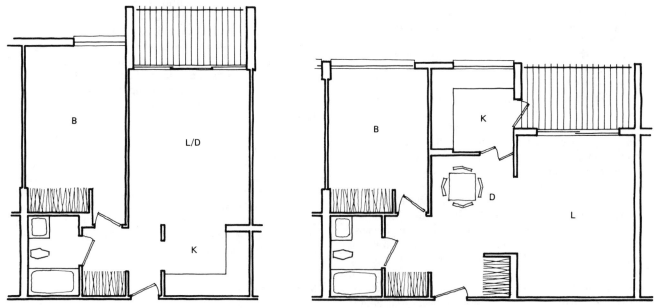

Figure 16. Typical dwelling units for the elderly (1).

gift shop, commissary, or beauty shop. Housing for the elderly requires considerably less parking than other types (30–50%).

EXTERIOR

The exterior of a high-rise apartment building, like that of any structure, does not automatically emerge, *sui generis,* from the solution of function, economy, and structure. Additional factors play significant roles: first and foremost, the architect's aesthetic theory and design intentions; and second, the influence of surrounding buildings, landscape, or unoccupied space, called the context.

The many areas of concern the designer faces can be grouped under four headings: the building volume and its articulation; the relation of the volume to the ground and its relation to the sky; the treatment of the middle of the volume, its surface, and fenestration; and the way the building relates to the environment or context within which it is being built.

The architect's opportunity to "shape" the volume of a high-rise apartment building is limited. Various housing types have inherent shapes; the corridor type is predominantly a "slab" and the point block is basically a "tower." Within these generic shapes, the designer has some options to mold the volume, to break it up and give it a more human, residential scale in contrast to unbroken large volumes that tend to be monumental. The repetitive character of high-rises and the rationality demanded by the "economic equation" in housing prevents unlimited liberty in volume articulations. For instance, to undulate the volume or to break it up and thereby decrease its efficiency ratio below 80% is rarely affordable. However, when the volume manipulation has rational motives within the limits of economic sensibility it will be a welcome design generator: projections to accommodate large vertical cores or to facilitate diagonal views from living rooms; bay windows, not only to allow angled views but to help sunlight penetrate the apartment; indentations, to give wind protection and intimacy to balconies; and breaks in the volume, to reduce visual length of corridors or to accommodate a diagonal property line are but a few of the possible design variations (Fig. 17).

Figure 17. Volume manipulations in a high-rise (1).

As important as the shape of the volume is, so is the exterior surface material and its fenestration, whether a residential or monumental scale is intended. Of the major options, the curtain wall tends to be monotonous and hardly expressive of what happens behind its undifferentiated facade; exposed concrete frame and brick cladding are more conducive to a "readable relationship" between interior and exterior, provided such correspondence is stylistically preferred. A curtain wall gains richness by the refinement of its detail and its color as well as by the total shape of the building. The major issue is the depth between concrete face and glass, the three dimensionality thus achieved in addition to proportional relations between columns and floor slab or between solid members and glazed void. Masonry cladding, the most residential in scale, has rich color and texture. Here, the major design issue besides the possible changes in color is the size and shape of windows, their relation to the amount of brick, and the character of the detail that catches light, casts shadow, and emphasizes and embellishes around the opening. Repetitive openings can be particularized by being different in shape and size for living rooms or for bedrooms,

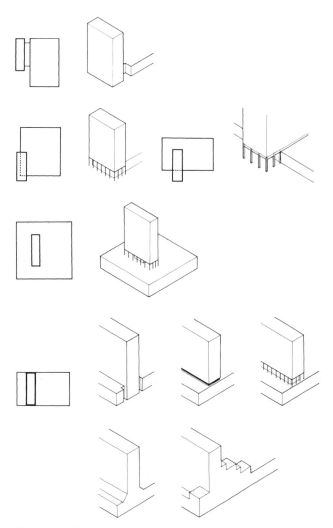

Figure 18. The relationship of the residential tower to its base (1).

and thus lend themselves to the creation of varied rhythms, which are further enriched on skip–stop schemes, and in the case of two-story apartments when living spaces are on one floor and sleeping spaces on the floor above or below.

A difficult part of any exterior, exposed frame, curtain wall, or masonry cladding is the turning of the corners. Should it be strong and sharp (90°), or softened by angle or rounding? Should it be solid, or opened by corner windows? Should it have the difficult-to-solve corner column, or should it be cantilevered?

High-rise apartment volumes, more often vertical than horizontal in proportions, "stand" on the grade and unless a proper base is provided they tend to visually "sink" into the ground due to apparent gravitational forces. In most cases, a natural base is provided by the functionally different first floor and the volume of the parking garage. The relationship of the residential tower to this base can be of three kinds: the tower stands in front of its base (the two are vertically articulated) or overlaps it; the tower stands on its base (the two are horizontally articulated); there is no clear articulation, but a purposeful ambiguity instead (Fig. 18). The major issue of the ground floor and base, besides its relation to the tower, is its proximity to the viewer. Here is the first contact the user or the visitor makes with the building, which calls for attention to scale and enrichment of detail.

Whereas the top of the building does not have the visual proximity the base has, the way it silhouettes against the sky is important. First, the soaring verticality inherent in any high-rise demands a crowning "weighing down" element. Second, vertical core elements (elevator, penthouses, stairs) and mechanical items (stacks, fan housings) need thoughtful coordination in their massing. Third, the possibilities offered by top-floor (penthouse) apartments—higher ceilings, fireplaces, roof terraces, skylights, etc—should be taken advantage of.

URBAN CONTEXT

It is the exterior of the building (volume, choice of material and color, language, ornament) that will determine if it will "fit" its environment, if it will be harmonious or out of step, if it will appear small or large compared to the surrounding scale. This relation to the neighboring fabric is referred to as contextual fit.

A high-rise by its nature is not a very contextual building type. Unless surrounded by other high-rises, it tends to stand out, to overwhelm. Even if several high-rises are planned, rarely is the development so extensive as to require a large enough number of towers that can relate to each other in height and position. The picture, compared to the dense urban fabric of the European city with buildings of equal heights filling the block from street to street, is usually an unregulated, unrelated outcropping of high-rises of various heights. This chaotic image is far less the result of Le Corbusier's vision of the city as towers in the park than it is the outcome of a *laissez-faire* attitude to development, an attitude that puts property rights above the rights of the community and avoids regulation.

Figure 19. The Hodne/Stageberg Partners Inc.: 1199 Plaza, New York, N.Y. (1975). Courtesy of Thomas Hodne Architects, Inc. Photo credit: Norman McGrath.

Even in this unregulated growth there have been laudable attempts to "relate" the high-rise apartment building to its neighbors. 1199 Plaza in New York by The Hodne/Stageberg Partners (Fig. 19), the Coney Island apartments by Hoberman & Wasserman (Fig. 20), and the Roosevelt Island apartments by Sert Jackson and Associates (Fig. 21) are all attempts to meet a low-rise neighborhood or a river edge by starting out with four–five-story buildings and "stepping-up" to high-rise heights. Stylistically, however, these are all modern buildings and in terms of style tend to disregard their neighborhoods. At the other end of the spectrum, the 320 N. Michigan Avenue apartment building by Booth/Hansen & Associates in Chicago relates to its context totally in a stylistic way by reinterpreting its basically modern facade in a revived classical language, an approach that, if well done, can result in excellent fit (Fig. 22). Another solution is Ulrich Franzen's 800 Fifth Avenue apartments in New York, which use a low "frontispiece" that matches in height, scale, and classical language the old buildings along the avenue, while the unadorned, more economical, modern tower is pushed back just far enough not to interfere with the frontispiece standing as a good neighbor.

Franzen's building is reminiscent of the stepped-back New York high-rise of the 1920s, where the lower mass could relate to and work harmoniously with the adjacent dense matrix of the city, while the tower portion as a free-standing "obelisk" could be a lone marker or part of an ensemble of towers. Stuart Cohen referred to high-rises that "function at two scales, always deferring to the space of the street. Only from a distance, as a romantic element of the city skyline, did the building assert itself as a figure" (4). Wishing the high-rise away as Leon Krier,

Figure 20. Hoberman & Wasserman: Coney Island, Site 5/6, Brooklyn, N.Y. (1972). Courtesy of Hoberman & Wasserman. Photo credit: Norman Hoberman.

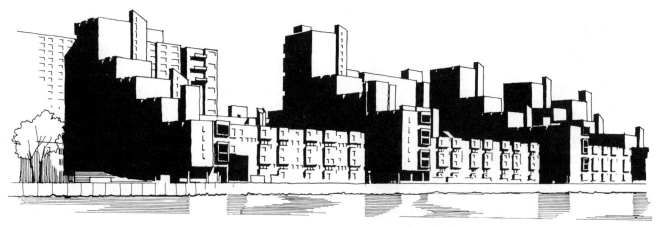

Figure 21. Sert, Jackson and Associates: Roosevelt Island, Parcel 3, New York, N.Y. (1974) (1).

critic of current cities, does, or dealing with the high-rise only as a formal element (marker, gatepost, etc) as is done in Collage City by Colin Rowe "ignores the typical clustering of skyscrapers that results as a solution to urban density and land values" (4). If high-rise apartment buildings are to succeed in an urbanistically well-designed city, they need to be perceived both as freestanding objects and as part of the urban fabric.

SOCIAL IMPLICATIONS

Lack of contextualism has been just one of the accusations leveled against high-rise apartment buildings; the other relates to social responsibility and claims that the high-rise is an asocial building type.

In responding to this criticism, the privately financed market rate housing must be separated from subsidized public housing. In the private sector where the tenant (or in the case of condominiums, the buyer) exercises free will through the pocketbook, the high-rise is not only tolerated, but for a large segment of the urban market, it seems to be the preferred housing type. This is true for young marrieds and empty nesters in the suburbs as well, where recent zoning changes have paved the way for multistory structures. Surveys indicate that even the elderly, about whom it was said for years that they want to live near the ground in low-rises, show no clear preference.

The source of the problem is high-rise public housing, which, in the minds of its critics, has become the prime cause of social ills. The accusation is twofold: on the one hand, public housing destroyed the residential fabric of the city through urban renewal; on the other hand, the high-rise as a type became the hotbed of crime and antisocial behavior.

The story is well known. The white exodus to the suburbs left a vacated housing stock that was then occupied by underprivileged blacks, millions of whom poured into the big cities from the newly mechanized South. Housing that was available for blacks was purposely neglected by the absentee owners, not to mention abused by the new occupants. Clearly, the United States faced an unprece-

dented challenge. The best minds, the most sincere efforts, and visionary dreams of the New Deal and Fair Deal were turned toward the problem of the newly created slums, and the Housing Act of 1949 was born—urban renewal.

Urban renewal based on Le Corbusier's fashionable utopian schemes was a failure. Streets were destroyed. The existing rich, though dilapidated, urban fabric was erased and replaced by towers and slabs in a parklike no-man's land. Whereas Le Corbusier's goals of space, sun, and green, so similar to the Garden City ideals, worked well with ground-related low-rise housing, it created unexpected problems with high-rises. The park that no one surveyed or claimed as his territory became unsafe and lifeless. In addition, buildings were designed by the "bottom line" philosophy; their bland brick facades, small windows, and later their exposed concrete frame bore no relation to the surrounding neighborhood. For this insensitivity, modern architecture's antihistorical bias may only be partially blamed. Minimum standards, rushing for results, and the elitist arrogance of planning agencies are equally to blame for public housing failure.

The demolitions resulting from slum clearance led to a net loss of housing inventory. In addition, the poor, especially blacks and Latinos, could not afford the rent in the units that replaced the old housing. They spilled over into the adjacent neighborhoods. The self-exacerbating result was more white exodus, creating even more slums.

If these exiled poor were provided public housing, they were not much better off. Public housing meant federal subsidies to local housing authorities who built, owned, and ran projects; they could rent only to people below certain federally established income ceilings. High land costs resulted in high-rise buildings. Regardless of the architecture, an urban renewal policy that crowded families without adequate assistance and with large numbers of children into high-rise buildings, a living mode in which they had no previous experience, was doomed to fail. These projects and the high-rise housing form became stigmatized; people came to believe that the architecture of the high-rise caused the problems of the poor rather than merely reflecting the symptoms of an ailing society.

Although modern architecture can be blamed for ignor-

Figure 22. Booth Hansen & Associates: 320 N. Michigan, Chicago (1984). Photo credit: John Macsai.

ing context, it is hardly to be blamed for the failure of U.S. public housing. First, high-rise or low-rise, apartment size, amenities, and location were not decisions in which the architect had a share. Second, public housing was doomed to fail regardless of its architectural style, because of bureaucratic ignorance and the racism of urban politics.

BIBLIOGRAPHY

1. J. Macsai, *Housing,* 2nd ed., John Wiley & Sons, Inc., New York, 1983.

2. M. P. Lawton, *Planning and Managing Housing for the Elderly,* John Wiley & Sons, Inc., New York, 1975.

3. L. A. Pastalan and D. H. Carson, eds., *Spatial Behavior of Older People,* Institute of Gerontology, University of Michigan, Ann Arbor, Mich., 1970.

4. S. Cohen, "The Tall Building Urbanistically Reconsidered," *Threshold II,* University of Illinois at Chicago, 1983.

General References

ANSI A117.1, *Making Building Accessible and Usable by the Physically Handicapped,* American National Standards Institute, New York, 1971.

R. Arnheim, *The Dynamics of Architectural Form,* University of California Press, Berkeley, Calif., 1977.

R. F. Babcock, *The Zoning Game,* University of Wisconsin Press, Madison, Wis., 1969.

J. Barnett, "In the Public Interest: Design Guidelines," *Architectural Record* (July, 1987).

L. Benevolo, *History of Modern Architecture,* M.I.T. Press, Cambridge, Mass., 1976.

B. C. Brolin, *Architecture in Context,* Van Nostrand Reinhold Co., New York, 1980.

S. Davis, ed., *The Form of Housing,* Van Nostrand Reinhold Co., New York, 1977.

J. DeChiara and J. H. Callender, eds., *Time-Saver Standards for Building Types,* McGraw-Hill, Inc., New York, latest edition.

W. von Eckardt, *A Place to Live,* Dell, New York, 1967.

H. Engel, *Structure Systems,* Praeger, New York, 1968.

K. Frampton, *Modern Architecture, a Critical History,* Oxford University Press, New York, 1980.

S. P. Harkness and J. N. Groom, *Building Without Barriers for the Disabled,* Whitney School of Design, Watson-Guptill, New York, 1976.

H.U.D. Minimum Property Standards, U.S. Department of Housing and Urban Development, Washington, D.C., latest edition.

M. A. Jones, *Accessibility Standards,* Capital Development Board, State of Illinois, Springfield, Ill., 1978.

J. C. Kirschenmann and C. Muschalek, *Residential Districts,* Watson-Guptill, New York, 1980.

T. Y. Lin and S. D. Stotesbury, *Structural Concepts and Systems for Architects and Engineers,* John Wiley & Sons, Inc., New York, 1981.

K. Lynch, *Site Planning,* M.I.T. Press, Cambridge, Mass., 1971.

M. Mayer, *The Builders,* W. W. Norton, New York, 1978.

W. J. McGuiness, B. Stein, and J. S. Reynolds, *Mechanical and Electrical Equipment for Buildings,* 6th ed., John Wiley & Sons, Inc., New York, 1980.

O. Newman, *Community of Interest,* Anchor/Doubleday, Garden City, N.Y., 1980.

O. Newman, *Defensible Space,* MacMillan, New York, 1972.

C. G. Ramsey and H. R. Sleeper, *Architectural Graphic Standards,* John Wiley & Sons, Inc., New York, latest edition.

S. E. Rasmussen, *Experiencing Architecture,* M.I.T. Press, Cambridge, Mass., 1959.

C. Rowe and F. Koetter, *Collage City,* M.I.T. Press, Cambridge, Mass., 1980.

M. G. Salvadori and M. Levy, *Structural Design in Architecture,* Prentice-Hall, Inc., Englewood Cliffs, N.J., 1967.

R. Sherwood, *Modern Housing Prototypes,* Harvard University Press, Cambridge, Mass., 1978.

F. H. Spink, *Housing for a Maturing Population,* Urban Land Institute, Washington, D.C., 1983.

JOHN MACSAI
John Macsai & Associates
Chicago, Illinois

EUGENE P. HOLLAND
Holland & Associates
Schaumburg, Illinois

HARRY S. NACHMAN
Harry S. Nachman Associates
Chicago, Illinois

APARTMENT BUILDINGS—LOW RISE.   See MULTIFAMILY HOUSING

APPLIANCES.   See KITCHEN DESIGN, COMMERICAL; KITCHENS, RESIDENTIAL

AQUARIUMS

ARCHITECTURAL DESIGN ISSUES

During the 1970s, the United States' exploration into outer space gave birth to a new kind of museum—one that attempts to simulate space and one that houses space artifacts—the National Aerospace Museum in Washington, D.C. The 1980s brought exploration into another kind of space—underwater space—and a new type of facility was created, one that not only exhibits underwater inhabitants, but also attempts to explore the depths of the sea by exhibiting its cycles, motion, and atmosphere. This kind of exploration stimulated a new kind of museum; thus the modern aquarium was developed. This new facility has many elements of a museum. Clearly, it is a new building type which must wear two hats, that of a museum and that of a highly technical plant which pumps different kinds of water to provide nourishment for the fish and mammals exhibited. In contrast to a museum, which displays essentially static items, whether they be sculptures or airplanes, an aquarium requires many more choices, both as to how it exhibits its creatures and how it communicates information about them.

Aquariums serve many functions. Like art museums, they are visual, sensational, and educational. They also promote reflection, but not into the past. Instead, they take the viewer down into the depths of the sea where one can watch sea creatures living, eating, and surviving.

This provides an opportunity for the viewer to observe evolution on the spot. Depending on its purpose, an aquarium can be designed either to entertain and evoke sensation, or to educate. Obviously, these decisions must be made at the earliest stage of the project.

Since living things are to be exhibited, many of the same issues arise that are involved in zoo design, specifically how to house living inhabitants. Another important decision is whether the aquarium's purpose will be to exhibit ocean or freshwater animals, or perhaps both. An aquarium may focus on a specific regional area, it may exhibit aspects and creatures connected by a geographic region, or it may simply display a series of interesting exhibits that talk about the ocean and its inhabitants. These decisions require many meetings among the aquarium director, the aquarist, the curators, the architect, and the exhibit designers. All of these decisions are integrated by the aquarium staff and design team, and become the program or story line of the facility. Behind the public exhibit spaces are the tanks which hold the animals, and behind them are holding tanks for animals in reserve and spaces for the curators to work and to take care of the animals. Then there are the unique and complicated support spaces involving life support systems for the exhibits, and pump and filter rooms. Threading its way through all of this space is the supply-and-return piping which carries the life-giving fluid, whether it be salt water or fresh water. Beyond these technically specialized areas are the common spaces, ie, the book shop, the restaurant, the mechanical rooms, and, of course, the public exhibit space.

There are two different exhibit sequence approaches: the prescribed path approach which directs the visitor and does not allow deviation, and the random path approach. Examples of the prescribed path method are the New England Aquarium in Boston and the National Aquarium in Baltimore, both designed by Cambridge Seven Associates. The Monterey Bay Aquarium, designed by Esherick Homsey Dodge & Davis, is an example of the second, the random path approach (Fig. 1). The advantage to this approach is that it allows the crowd to find its own path and/or to use many different paths. Both methods are valid, and both have been successful. Each method evokes a different experience and must be thoroughly considered during the design process. In addition to fish viewing through exhibit windows, there is the educational issue. This can be accomplished by graphics on or adjacent to the exhibits, by videos with which the viewer interacts to elicit a response from the creatures viewed, or via a computer programmed for interactive experience, awareness, and fun. These kinds of exhibits can be very educational and worthwhile, but are both complicated to develop and expensive to achieve.

The other major exhibit issue is an experiential one, and that is the evolution of fish display. In the last ten years, aquariums have attempted to display fish in an environment as close as possible to their natural environment. In the past, fish were displayed in a tank with minimal background. Now the intent is to present the fish as truthfully as possible. One of the ways this is accomplished is by installing rockwork inside the tank made from fiber glass or gunite painted to resemble real rocks. Sometimes this material is placed in the ocean for up to four years so that organisms will attach to it as they normally would to real rocks. These artificial rocks are then removed from the ocean and placed in the display tanks. This procedure has been so successful that organisms continue to adapt to it if their artificial environment provides the necessary nutrients. As audience participation grows and technology improves, exhibitry techniques become increasingly sophisticated and more expensive to achieve.

The exhibit tanks range in size from small, or jewel tanks of 100 gal, all the way up to major tanks that are 50,000–500,000 gal in size. Smaller tanks are used to display relatively small animals or a cross section of a particular community.

Figure 1. Monterey Bay Aquarium, Monterey, Calif. Courtesy of Jane Lidz.

The big tanks are for displaying mammals such as sea otters, sea lions, seals, or dolphins. The size of the tanks is regulated by an act administered by the Marine Mammal Agency under the Department of Agriculture. This act sets the size, depth, and number of animals by formula and is quite specific.

Other big tanks are used to display groups or communities of the larger fish, such as sharks, grouper, bass, rockfish, or kelp forests and their related fish, and anything else special to the exhibit story. These tanks may be 16–30 ft in depth, and can be in the size range of 200,000–500,000 gal.

Feeding in the small tanks is accomplished from behind the exhibit wall by curators who dump the food directly into the tank or by turkey basters aimed directly at the attached animals. Even if the aquarium has raw seawater available, augmented feeding is required to achieve a balanced nutritional diet for the creatures.

The most common procedure is to feed the mammals and sharks from the top of the tank. Although some feeding is done by divers in tanks for show, this is not recommended in general; the cross section of animals in the tanks must be carefully considered before deciding to use this method.

Raw seawater availability allows a much wider diversity of animals to be displayed, including nudibranchs and filter feeders—the so-called turf of the sea. Because it is raw water, it causes faster clogging of the seawater lines and more maintenance, but in terms of exhibit potential, the tradeoffs are beneficial.

Another important issue is that of crowd flow, especially on holidays and weekends. Aisle widths and distances between exhibits must be adequate in order to provide room for people to move in either direction. Around large exhibits, these widths should be no less than 16 ft to allow bidirectional travel. These spaces should be generous and attractive and spaced appropriately so crowds do not bunch up, causing restriction and bottlenecks (Fig. 2).

Light is another important issue for both the architect and the exhibit designers. Many aquariums are filled with backlit exhibit windows; these produce the effect of jewels glowing in black boxes (Fig. 2). Recent aquarium curators and designers have begun to question this concept. Areas where natural light penetrates into the exhibits provide relief for the viewer from the one-dimensional experience of darkness. An example of this approach is the Monterey Bay Aquarium that includes large areas of both exhibit types, and also allows the visitor to go outside for additional viewing or rest (Fig. 3). This approach mitigates museum fatigue, and allows the visitor to alternate his experience between the real and the simulative. Providing both dark space exhibits and naturally lit exhibits presents more problems for the architect and exhibit designer. Light reflection on exhibit windows makes natural lighting more complicated.

Site issues revolve around visitor access. Both tour buses, which often arrive in great numbers, and school buses must be handled expeditiously. Parking is another related problem.

Whether or not the site is located by the ocean determines whether seawater can be drawn from it or whether it will have to be made artificially. The site geology is certainly important because water loads are very heavy (500,000–750,000 gal for a specific large tank) and must be accommodated on suitable foundations. Floor loadings must be designed for exhibit tanks and should be 350 psf live-loading in order to provide reasonable flexibility.

Probably the most crucial technical issue to be confronted by the architect is that of material selection on both the outside and the inside of the building. The paramount issue here is corrosion and its drastic effects on all ferrous materials. Since all aquariums contain large concentrations of salt water, this atmosphere contains salt which deposits on all materials. Salt buildup causes severe corrosion, damage, and ultimately failure. Exterior wall materials must be carefully considered and must include reinforced, precast concrete, or glass fiber-reinforced con-

Figure 2. Viewing area in the Monterey Bay Aquarium, Monterey, Calif. Courtesy of Jane Lidz.

Figure 3. Outdoor viewing and resting area at the Monterey Bay Aquarium, Monterey, Calif. Courtesy of Jane Lidz.

crete, with adequate cover over the reinforcing. Other choices are mineral fiber paneling, such as fiber glass-reinforced plastic panels or pressure-treated wood. All exterior studding systems must be evaluated very carefully. Some inadequately galvanized metal stud systems have suffered severe damage. Wood stud wall framing must be fully pressure-treated and carefully detailed to avoid dry rot, mold, and other effects of high moisture conditions. In general, all metal paneling systems must be carefully analyzed because of lack of corrosion resistance.

Window frames must be galvanized steel with PVC coating of suitable mil coverage. All hardware, handles, cranks, and operators must be either bronze or 316 stainless steel. Installation clips, screw fastenings, and miscellaneous metal must be carefully detailed and followed through precisely because of corrosion problems. Glazing is accomplished by using conventional glazing materials. Where possible, PVC or plastic snap-on beads should be used. Aluminum windows can be used, but must be finished with fluorocarbon coating of proper mil thickness to prevent the aluminum from developing severe surface corrosion.

Door frames must be detailed out of galvanized stock 16 gauge or heavier, and painted with marine epoxy, three coats on the exterior surfaces, and coated with coal tar epoxy on the inside concealed portion. Sharp edges or returns will corrode over time if not closed. Frame bottoms must be detailed 2 in. off the floor with a closed end in order to avoid corrosion. When stainless steel (even 316) has been used, it has corroded seriously. Aluminum frames can be considered for doors and frames, but should be at least 0.125 in. thick and protected with fluorocarbon paint inside and outside. Without exception, all hardware must be of either 316 stainless steel or bronze with brass pins. Painted steel hinges with steel pins will fail soon after installation. Panic bolts are particularly problematic because their interior parts are not made with corrosive-resistant materials, and therefore corrode and become difficult to operate. All thresholds should be of bronze. Experience has proven that it is the only material that holds up in this corrosive environment. Special caution must be given to all detailing of exterior systems regardless of material.

Roof materials are very susceptible to corrosion. Built-up roofs, tile, clay or composition, mineral fiber tile, slate, or concrete shingles are all good choices provided they are installed with noncorrosive fasteners such as brass or copper. Metal roofs, especially of ferrous metals, should not be used. Coated aluminum can be considered, provided it is heavier than normal gauge, but only with careful detailing. If the site is on the ocean, all roof flashings must be of 16- or 20-oz copper to obtain the best long-lasting performance. Type 316 stainless steel or aluminum flashings have failed in salt air exposure. All clips, fastenings, screws, and hardware must be carefully selected both for salt air resistance and electrolytic compatibility. Experience has proven that either coated, extruded aluminum or copper is the best choice for all exposed mechanical louvers, fresh air intakes, and exhaust louvers.

All of the foregoing information applies equally to the interior environment, but with even more emphasis. Exteriors dry off during the day. Interiors are continuously exposed to dampness and never have the chance to dry off; therefore, corrosion problems are exacerbated. Plastics have proven useful here. The wall separating the viewer from the tanks and the back of the enclosure can be made of glass fiber-reinforced concrete, which is impervious and inert. If properly designed, it can span from floor to ceiling without intervening metal studs, which corrode. The exhibit tanks are made of fiber glass with acrylic windows. Miscellaneous items, such as stairways, railings, ladders, standing platforms, duct supports, pipe supports, etc, can be made from materials such as PVC or fiber-reinforced plastics, which are corrosion-resistant. However, these materials are not equal in strength to common aluminum or steel, and conseqently must be carefully detailed. All interior fasteners must be carefully selected for corrosion resistance.

Flooring materials are particularly difficult because throughout the normal course of operations salt water is constantly spilling on the floor. Pipes break or valves fail, and amounts of salt water often stand for long periods of time before being discovered. All floor materials that are of resilient types fastened by various kinds of cement to a substrate are not recommended. Ceramic tile and stone set in a mortar bed are very durable and resistant to salt water. Thin-set mastics or mortars should be avoided. Wood flooring should be avoided anywhere. Flooring in the support areas should favor epoxy-coated concrete systems with grit for safety purposes. Most, if not all, service areas should be bound by concrete curbs with the topping turned up at the faces. Since there is no way to tell what will eventually sit on top of these curbs, a serious problem exists because some walls need to be fire-rated and this may cause problems. Ordinary thin gauge metal studs will corrode almost immediately. Water-resistant gypsum board or Keene cement plaster can be used over the studding, but saturation of the facing materials is a permanent problem and must be carefully studied. Pressure- and fire-treated wood framing has been used with some success, but mold and dry rot are serious threats. Walls must be finished with three coats of marine epoxy systems, each coat carefully applied with adequate drying time between each, before the exhibit tanks are set and filled. All paints inside the building suffer potentially severe problems. A painting consultant is highly recommended.

Glazing the major tanks is accomplished by cast or laminated acrylic windows, or by laminated glass, with individual laminations up to ¾ in. thickness. Glass panels are restricted in size to about 10 × 13 ft, depending on the manufacturer. Acrylic windows can be cast in a single piece up to 8 × 26 ft and in thicknesses up to 10 in. Larger panels can be made of acrylic with an almost invisible bonded joint. Many combinations are possible if one works closely with the manufacturers. Presently, there are two manufacturers making acrylic windows of this type, one in Japan and one in the United States. The detailing of the rebates for the glazing must be carefully done, and the manufacturers' instructions must be followed exactly. Windows are sealed using a three-part polysulfide system in conformance with the instructions. The sealant must be tested for compatibility with the tank waterproofing system. The opening must be plumb and in plane so that windows are not subject to stress, and sealing must be the same all around the perimeter. If all of the requirements are followed through with absolute care, the installation should not leak.

Waterproofing the tank interior is a problem. One approach is to use three coats of marine-compatible epoxy coating. Because the water is so heavy and its level must be dropped periodically for maintenance or collection problems, the concrete moves almost imperceptibly and therefore creates the possibility of leaks. Epoxy coatings do not span. Another solution has been to use crystalline capillary coatings, most of which were developed in Europe for tunnel work. These coatings also produce mixed results. The quality of the concrete work in tanks must be of the finest caliber so that shrinkage and cracking are minimized. Joints should be minimized, and water stops should be avoided by carefully cleaning and preparing joint surfaces before placing them adjacent to the concrete sections. Most coatings require that the concrete surface be sandblasted and dried to a moisture content of 20% or less before application. Both the concrete surface temperature and the ambient temperature must be 60°F or greater at time of application. A problem that complicates tank integrity is that artificial gunite rockwork is often placed and sculpted over the top of the waterproof coating. This requires elaborate attention to the inserts and correct placement and material selection so that the armature underlying the gunite is held firmly in place without disturbing the waterproofing. Quality in materials and in workmanship is primary in these large tanks.

The general appearance of aquarium ceilings is the subject of much debate. While in a more conventional building it is desirable to hide the mechanical services from view, it may be more practical not to do so in an aquarium because of the complexity of the mechanical systems, and the fact that these systems require frequent servicing. The other issue is that exhibits are eventually replaced, and this may require redoing extensive seawater piping, drains, and electrical work. If these systems are buried behind ceilings, accessing them is very expensive. This is an issue of visual aesthetics vs plant flexibility; exhibitry technology will continuously evolve in order to retain visitor interest.

Flexibility for future changes of exhibits is an important issue. On the whole, an aquarium should add a major exhibit or modify existing ones every five years to maintain visitor interest and return. Flexibility of the seawater and lighting systems is very important if exhibits are changed drastically or exhibit walls are moved. Experience has shown that the exhibits are changed in minor ways constantly, and new ones are interspersed in the existing context. Therefore, capacities of seawater and electrical systems should be adequate to handle the imminent changes.

The architectural design of an aquarium requires not only the traditional skills in design, detailing, and coordination, but also a great awareness of materials, corrosion, and a constant vigilance against substitution during construction. Failure to appreciate these issues can result in death to the animals or significant damage to the facility.

AQUARIUM STRUCTURES

Aquarium structures experience the same natural forces as other structures, ie, gravity, earthquake, and wind, and must be designed to resist these forces over an appropriate design life. The engineering design principles are routine, if sometimes complex, and merit no further discussion here. Aquariums experience other less common destructive forces, such as seawater and atmospheric corrosion, and, in the case of coastal sites, such marine hazards as tidal flooding, storm waves, beach and bluff erosion, offshore currents, tsunami forces, and long-term sea-level changes. The most persistent and destructive of all of these forces is corrosion, the single most important factor in selecting materials and systems for aquarium structures. Table 1 outlines the general suitability of various structural materials for several classes of aquarium-building elements.

Structural plastics are relatively new products, and are not yet available in a full range of sizes. Beams up to 10 in. in depth are stocked in wide flange, channel, angle, and tube configurations in glass fiber-reinforced resins. Structural plastic stairs, handrails, ladders, gratings, bolts, plates, rods, and weirs are now made by several manufacturers. Large fiber glass cylindrical elements are available for tanks and filter towers. Structural plastics may eventually supplant reinforced concrete as the dominant material for aquarium use. Plastics in general are combustible and may require fire protection depending on the use.

Pressure-treated wood has a long history of successful use for marine structures of many types. It is still used for foundation pilings, piers, and small tanks, and marine plywood is often used for vessels and flooring. Some species of wood such as redwood are toxic, and may require treatment or coating when used for tanks supplying exhibits; in addition, certain wood preservatives used in pressure treatment are highly toxic to marine life.

Steel is commonly used in aquarium structures, but must be coated or corrosion-resistant when exposed to seawater or to atmospheric corrosion. Stainless steel is moderately corrosion-resistant, but is not economical for building structural systems. Type 316 L stainless steel is more corrosion-resistant than Type 304 in most applications. Special steel alloys have been developed for high corrosion resistance and are often used in pumps, filters, and valves. Monel metal has seen some use for secondary marine structures and equipment, and titanium is frequently used in seawater heat exchangers.

Concrete is used more than any other structural material in aquarium construction. When carefully specified, mixed, and placed, it is a highly corrosion-resistant material and can be used for a wide variety of aquarium structural elements. Within the last 20 years, significant advances have been made in designing and producing concrete for marine use. Marine concrete differs from ordinary concrete in formulation, reinforcing, and placing techniques. Special cements and aggregates are used, and admixtures, such as fly ash or silica fume, are incorporated to increase durability. Galvanized reinforcing has been used in the past and has proven effective, but is being supplanted by epoxy-coated reinforcing steel.

Table 1. Structural Materials for Building Aquariums

Structure Exposure	Examples	Appropriate Materials
Submerged	Intakes Foundations	Structural plastic Marine concrete Pressure-treated wood
Tidal	Foundations Seawalls Exterior exhibits	Structural plastic Marine concrete
Seawater-filled	Large exhibit and storage tanks	Marine concrete Fiber-reinforced plastic
Onshore, exposed to seawater spillage	Quarantine tank and behind-the-scenes floor areas	Marine concrete Coated, reinforced concrete
Onshore, exposed to atmospheric corrosion	Building structural elements	Exposed marine concrete Coated, reinforced concrete Coated carbon steel Pressure-treated wood
Onshore, secondary structures	Davits Pump platforms Hoists Large filters	Reinforced concrete Coated carbon steel Type 316 stainless steel Aluminum Monel metal Pressure-treated wood Structural plastic

Structural Design Considerations

Primary Seawater Processing Systems. The biochemical processes that take place in seawater are complex and poorly understood. In theory, it is possible to maintain aquatic life in a seawater vessel exposed to sunlight with no external processing of the fluid medium if the life forms within the vessel are properly selected and proportioned. In practice, this is not achievable because stored and unprocessed seawater becomes sterile, the Ph drops, ammonia accumulates, oxygen levels drop, water temperatures approach ambient temperatures, and the inhabitants die. The function of the primary seawater system is to supply seawater of sufficient quality and quantity to meet the total basic requirements of exhibit vessels. The ocean itself is a vast vessel of seawater, with physical characteristics varying significantly both seasonally and geographically, particularly in the shallow coastal areas that supply the great majority of aquarium animals and plants. Each species exhibited has unique habitat requirements and a unique capacity to adapt to change in the environment. For this reason, primary seawater systems alone are seldom adequate, and secondary seawater processing systems of differing characteristics are usually required at individual exhibits. Design of these secondary systems is the province of the professional aquarist and is only briefly discussed here. Three seawater system types—open, closed, and combined—are illustrated in Figure 4.

The ultimate open system consists of the ocean itself with human access provided by above-water or submerged structures. This is the common definition in commercial aquaculture and applies to a few aquarium exhibits. In aquarium design terminology, however, an open, or flow-through, system utilizes a continuous flow of ocean seawater passing through enclosed exhibits and discharged back to the ocean with no recirculation. Advantages of this system include a natural supply of nutrients, less need for sterilization, and savings of recirculation and secondary processing costs if the natural source is of high quality. Disadvantages include lack of quality and clarity control during seasonal changes, and the possibility of system shutdown due to ocean storms, pump breakdown, or source pollution. Open systems are seldom used for aquarium primary seawater systems, but are often used in commercial aquaculture.

Closed systems use imported natural seawater or artificial seawater. The fluid is continuously recirculated throughout the system. Losses due to evaporation, filter backwash, spills, and leakage are made up by adding artificial seawater. Advantages of closed systems include a high degree of clarity and quality control. Disadvantages include the lack of natural nutrients, the costs of procuring or manufacturing seawater, the necessity of a high level of secondary processing, including biological filtration, and higher energy costs for controlling water temperature. Closed systems are used for all inland aquariums and for some coastal aquariums lacking a seawater supply of high and consistent quality.

Combined systems pump a substantial flow of natural seawater through the aquarium supplemented by recirculation and additional filtration of a significant flow of primary fluid. This system provides a higher level of quality and clarity control than an open system, provides natural nutrients, and incorporates a high degree of operational flexibility by varying the ratio of flowthrough and recirculated primary seawater. Most coastal aquariums use combined systems.

After the site is chosen, the first step in the design of a seawater system is to gather as complete information as possible about the quality of the natural seawater

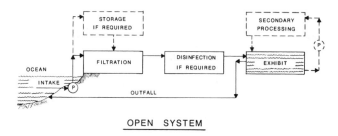

OPEN SYSTEM

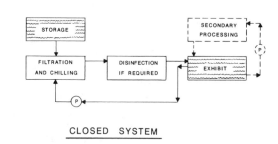

CLOSED SYSTEM

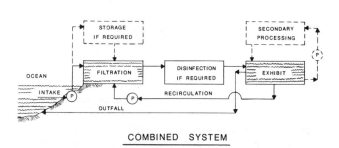

COMBINED SYSTEM

Figure 4. Seawater system types—open, closed, and combined.

source, if the site is coastal. Data should include range of salinity, Ph, temperatures, turbidity, oxygen content, and likelihood of occurrence of toxic dinoflagellate blooms, oil spills, toxic wastes, and ocean storms, which might pollute the water source. Coastal ocean water quality varies seasonally, often daily, and a record extending over a long time period is necessary for accurate evaluation. The second step is to select one of the three types of seawater processing systems described previously—open, closed, or combined.

After the type of system is chosen, the third step in design is to determine the total design flow rate and, in the case of a combined system, the design recirculation rate. The information required is a detailed list of species to be exhibited, their habitat requirements, and the dimensions of all aquarium water vessels, including exhibit tanks, backup tanks, quarantine tanks, and seawater storage tanks. Although formulas for estimating maximum biomass–water volume ratios are occasionally used in densely populated commercial aquaculture vessels, most aquarium exhibit water volumes that have low population densities are determined by viewing considerations. Aquarists often estimate required exhibit flowthrough rates on experience, expressed in a ratio of flow rate–exhibit water volume called turnover time, which may vary

from a few minutes for small jewel tanks where maximum water quality is required, to several hours for large tanks containing cetaceans. An estimate of total flow rate can be made by multiplying water volumes by turnover times and, if a combined system is used, subtracting the estimated recirculation flow rate to obtain the flow rate through seawater.

The final step in system design is to select and detail system elements. Primary seawater system processing elements in the case of combined seawater systems include at least intake, pumping and transmission, filtration, and outfall elements, with storage and sterilization elements sometimes required. Secondary processing, including secondary filtration, biological filtration, oxygenation, heating or chilling, and pressurization, is usually necessary for individual exhibits. Selection and engineering design of essential seawater system elements require assembly of design criteria, listing physical characteristics of source seawater, habitat requirements for major exhibit seawater, design ranges of flowthrough and recirculated water flows, public health requirements for water quality, federal regulations for marine mammal exhibits, state and local zoning and land use regulations, and marine and geological hazards. Ocean tidal ranges must be known in order to set intake pump elevations, and to prepare ocean current and storm wave criteria for system and structure design.

Intakes. Seawater intakes are of two general types. The first type is a sand well system, usually onshore, that collects seawater flowing through subtidal sand and pumps it to the aquarium exhibits. This type of system has the advantage of producing prefiltered seawater, which usually requires no additional primary filtration. Disadvantages include the fact that sand well seawater is relatively free of natural nutrients, may vary in salinity due to periodic freshwater intrusion, and entails high construction and pump energy costs where high flow rates are required. The second type, the offshore intake, consists of an intake screen at or above the ocean bottom and below the lowest predicted low tide level. The intake is usually screened, with the screen area sized to restrict flow velocities to 0.5 ft/s or lower in order to minimize intake of juvenile marine animals. Pumps may be submerged in seawater directly in the ocean or in an enclosed wet well, or mounted above high tide elevation in a dry well structure. Combined static and dynamic head losses cannot exceed the suction lift capacity of the pump, usually less than 15 ft, limiting the maximum elevation at which the intake pump can be mounted. Intake pipes are often constructed in pairs to permit periodic cleanout so that marine organisms that enter the pipe and rapidly grow to sufficient size to obstruct water flow may be removed.

Primary filtration systems are usually designed to remove particulate matter by mechanical means, although some types, such as sand filters, may have significant biological filtration (Table 2).

Diatomaceous earth (DE) filters consist of a septum, or mesh sleeve, coated with a precoat and a body coat of diatomaceous earth particles. A DE filter is capable of filtering out particles as small as 0.1 mm, but the cost of maintenance and filter media replacement usually limits

Table 2. Characteristics of Primary Filtration Systems

Filter Type	Filter Media	Flow Type	Common Flow Ranges, gpm/ft² of Contact Surface	Comment
DE	Diatomaceous earth	Gravity Pressure	0.001–0.003	Not economical for high flow rates
Slow rate	Granular	Gravity	0.02–0.2	Occupies large area
Rapid rate	Granular	Gravity Pressure	1–8	Frequently used
High rate	Granular	Pressure	10–20	Occupies small floor area
Screen	Stainless steel Plastic mesh	Gravity	45–5500	Velocity may be limited by regulations

use of DE filters to secondary filtration, where water prefiltered by granular media is polished to a high degree of clarity.

Slow rate filters usually employ a layer of graded sand with a small head of water, an underdrain system to collect the filtered water, and a flow-reversal system to backflush particulate matter from the sand at the end of a filter cycle. The slow rate filter can remove some types of bacteria, but requires too much floor area for use in most aquariums. This type of filter is capable of biological filtration.

Rapid rate filters are similar to slow rate filters, but vary the sand media size and layer depth, and increase the operating head to produce a greater flow rate. Pressure vessels are occasionally used, but most rapid rate filters are enclosed in open concrete compartments. This type of filter has been commonly used in older aquariums, but is being supplanted by high rate filters for primary filtration.

High rate filters usually consist of sand media placed over gravel-encased underdrain pipes in vertical or horizontal pressure-resistant steel or reinforced plastic. This type of filter occupies a minimum area and is economical to operate, but requires frequent backflushing and does not usually remove a high percentage of particulate matter below the 15-mm size. All filter pipe and fittings in contact with seawater should be plastic. Present technology limits the maximum diameter of reinforced plastic shells to about 4 ft. Larger pressure vessels must be fabricated of steel.

Type 316 stainless steel should be used, or carbon steel with a corrosion-proof coating or lining. High rate filters have little biological filtration capacity.

Gravel and packed-tower biological filters are sometimes used in primary seawater systems. Gravel biological filters are usually incorporated into exhibit tanks by placing a few inches of calcareous gravel on a suspended screen or perforated plate on the tank bottom. Bacterial cultures in the gravel convert ammonia, which is toxic to most marine life, to nitrite, and nitrite to nitrate. Filtered water is drawn from beneath the filter and elevated to the top of the tank, often by means of an airlift pump. Packed-tower filters provide a substrate of plastic surfaces rather than gravel. They are usually constructed of circular sections with an interior seawater supply riser. Biological filters are not always required for open systems and combined systems, but are usually essential for closed systems, and for many individual exhibit tanks. Other types of biological filters include granular activated charcoal and foam fractionation systems. These are usually found in secondary seawater systems.

Sterilization of aquarium seawater discharge is sometimes mandated by public health agencies or water quality control authorities. Its primary function of sterilization in aquarium systems is control of disease organisms and, in general, disinfection (destruction of organisms harmful to the seawater user is a more appropriate term). Three common methods of disinfection are listed in Table 3.

Table 3. Common Methods of Disinfection

Agent	Forms	Where Used
Chlorine	Chlorine gas Chlorine powder Electrolytic generator	Large vessels for marine mammals; must be carefully controlled
Ozone	High voltage generator of ozone gas	Suitable for high flow rates, but may leave oxidant residuals
Ultraviolet	Irradiation by means of mercury vapor lamps	Suitable for for general use, but expensive for high flow rates

In general, disinfection agents of any kind should be used with caution and are seldom required in primary seawater processing systems.

Material Selection. Materials and equipment used in aquarium seawater systems must be highly resistant to atmospheric and saltwater corrosion as was previously stated. In addition, many commonly used materials contain substances toxic to various forms of marine life. These include:

1. Chlorine, which is toxic to many forms of marine life.
2. Minute gas bubbles, which cause embolisms in some fish.
3. Ammonia, which is highly toxic to marine life.
4. Hydrogen sulfide, which is highly toxic to marine life.
5. Heavy metal ions, ie, copper, zinc, mercury, and chromium; shellfish concentrate these ions.
6. Uncured concrete. Leached calcium compounds are toxic to some species.
7. Certain wood species. Tannic acid from redwood tanks is toxic to some species.
8. Certain plastics. Catalytic agents may contain toxic substances.

Mechanical Design Considerations

Mechanical systems for public aquariums include two basic environmental control systems: exhibits and public space. Control of the aquatic system environment is required to protect the health of the aquatic stock and to provide sufficient clarity for viewing the exhibits. As tank size increases, so does the need for greater water clarity. Light diffraction inhibits viewing. During public viewing time, the water needs to be filtered.

Some exhibits require control of water temperature for cooling to offset heat gains from pump energy, and heat transmission through tank walls and pipes; to compensate for solar gain for open tanks; or to heat tropical exhibits in temperate climates. Although exhibit stock can adapt to temperatures differing from their natural environment, the adaptation is slow, and daily temperature swings of even 2°C are harmful.

Control of the public space environment is required both for human comfort and to prevent the effects of condensation. Condensation dripping onto building finishes and furnishings creates a maintenance problem; condensation on tank windows prevents exhibit viewing, the aquarium's function. Condensation problems occur to the enclosure because of the moisture caused by public perspiration and aspiration, and by evaporation from wet surfaces. Atmospheric moisture may be removed by refrigeration or desiccant dryers. Since air cooling is usually needed for comfort conditioning, refrigeration is preferred over desiccant systems. Condensation on tank windows occurs when the temperature on the surface of the tank falls below the surrounding air dew point. Some of the atmospheric moisture is contributed at the viewing location. The supply air must be distributed so that it impinges on the window, and should have a dew point several degrees below the window surface temperature.

When it is expected that exhibits will change, provision to redistribute tank supply, return water, and conditioned air supply is needed. It may be difficult to prejudge which exhibits will be most popular and will, therefore, have a particularly high population density requiring an increase in air supply. To provide for these factors, a variable volume system with small control zones is preferred. To prevent odors in the public areas, a portion of the supply air should be exhausted via the tank support area behind the exhibit wall. A provision should be made for changing the tank water supply volume and location of supply pipe to readily accommodate exhibit changes.

The environmental control systems are subject to several material selection criteria. The aquatic stock may be harmed by even trace amounts of metal ions, such as copper and chromium, and by impressed-current and sacrificial anode corrosion protection systems. To the maximum extent feasible, tanks and seawater piping should be nonmetallic, as only the most expensive and exotic metals, eg, titanium and monel metal, have adequate corrosion resistance and are not potentially harmful to the stock. Careful material selection for each system component is necessary to control costs, and yet have a reliable, low maintenance facility (Table 4). Even those systems not directly in contact with seawater may be subject to severe corrosion because of a coastal situation, or in parts of an inland facility, because of splashing or occasional contact with salt water. Corrosion protection by barrier coatings only is unlikely to be successful because of impact damage and failure to reestablish the barrier when changes are made or coatings broken for equipment maintenance.

The need to circulate large volumes of water and provide adequate lighting and air conditioning results in aquariums becoming relatively high users of electrical energy. Mitigating measures include variable speed pumps, higher than customary motor efficiencies, heat-pump use, cogeneration systems, outside air economizer cycles, two-stage evaporative cooling systems, arc discharge lighting, and building energy management systems.

Filter backwash results in high rates of waste discharge that may overload the sewer. For this situation, the size of each filter may be reduced by increasing the number of filters and backwash cycles coordinated, or by providing a holding tank with a continuous small rate pumped discharge. In addition to floor drains to aid cleaning of public spaces, equipment areas need to be sloped to floor drains in order to reduce the slipping hazard, as spills and leaks are common in support areas.

Extensive use of plastics and glass fiber-reinforced resins for piping, tanks, and other equipment can result in avoidance of corrosion at reasonable costs. The presence of large amounts of plastics in a public access facility can be a potential hazard because of the toxic gases emitted during fires. Local building authorities may severely restrict the use of plastics within the public areas. Routing of pipe to avoid public areas and exit corridors, and placing tanks so that only glazed faces are exposed to public space can increase the acceptability of high plastic loadings in public space, and may be required. Complete building

Table 4. Materials for Environmental Control Systems

Pipe Materials	Where Used
Carbon steel	Freshwater systems
Stainless steel	Seldom used
Cast iron	Freshwater systems
Ductile iron	Freshwater systems
	Intakes
Aluminum	Seldom used
Brass	Secondary systems, possibly toxic
Bronze	Secondary systems, possibly toxic
Copper	Freshwater systems, possibly toxic
Poly(vinyl choride)	Seawater piping system, up to 12 in. in diameter
Polyethylene	Intakes
Acrylic	Laboratory
	Filters
Lexan	Filter systems
ABS	Filter systems
	Seawater waste
Fiber-reinforced plastic	Seawater piping system
Plain concrete	Seawater waste, up to 8 in. in diameter
Reinforced concrete	Seawater waste, over 8 in. in diameter
	Large intakes
	Buried transmission systems
Ceramic glass	Waste piping
	Laboratory waste
	Laboratory piping
	Heat exchangers
	Sterilization units

sprinkler systems and smoke detection and engineered smoke control systems are also beneficial.

Uncoated cast-iron pipe commonly used in drainage systems should be avoided because of the potential for trapped saltwater corrosion in accessible pipe. Fusion epoxy-coated cast iron or nonmetallic piping may be substituted.

Electrical Design Considerations

Power distribution faces the same corrosion environment as the other systems; however, equipment choices are limited or expensive. Enclosing panelboards, relays, starters, etc in sealed glass fiber-reinforced plastic enclosures, in combination with sealed cable entries, can reduce problems. Large switchgear, transformer sections, and distribution buses may only be available with steel frames and enclosing panels, and these should be provided with internal heaters or placed in heated spaces to maintain a low relative humidity. Distribution conduit should be in PVC and concealed wherever possible to reduce smoke hazards. Receptacles and permanently wired equipment in tank support areas should be provided with ground fault protection.

The corrosive environment should also be considered when selecting lighting fixtures. Industrial type fixtures used in support areas can have plastic bodies and lenses. Specialty lighting for tanks and graphics illumination may require special coatings when not available in suitable materials. Brass and bronze fixtures should not be suspended over or submerged in tanks, as the copper ions may be leached. The graphics lighting needs to be flexible, preferably controlled by a dimmer equipment rack.

Lighting of large tanks presents special problems because of the effects of water absorption and light scatter. Scattering causes loss of contrast similar to the effect of car lights in a heavy fog, where increase in light-source intensity does not increase visibility. Absorption and scattering result in a rapid loss of light intensity with distance from source. To increase viewing distance, the tank water needs to be very clear, and the light source made remote from the viewer. As large tanks are often long compared with their depth, and lights normal to the viewing direction reduce the effect of scatter, overhead lighting is usually preferred. Some of the exhibits require overhead lighting for orientation. The area occupied by the viewers should have a low light intensity to reduce obscuration due to scattering, thereby increasing viewing distance. When lights are placed close to the water surface, access for relamping from above is needed. Suspended matter in the tank water also results in differential color filtering, with significant absorption at the red end in the case of high plankton content.

The aquatic stock represents a significant investment that could be lost during a prolonged loss of electrical power. To prevent this loss, much of the aquatic life support system must be provided with an emergency power source. This emergency power system may be combined with code-required emergency power for life safety systems in the public areas. A diesel generator is the usual source.

Automation

A large modern aquarium contains many complex systems with multiple operating modes. To reduce the number of people needed to operate the systems, to aid in optimizing their operation, and to monitor operational parameters, a building automation system should be considered. As many of the systems are peculiar to aquariums, a programmable, rather than a preprogrammed, system should be used. The sensors used in the seawater system should be nonintrusive and corrosion-resistant.

BIBLIOGRAPHY

General References

H. M. M. Acton, *Aquarium,* Duckworth, London, 1923.

P. D. Addison, *Observations from an Aquarium,* Tantalus Research, Ltd., Vancouver, Canada, 1972.

American Association of Zoological Parks and Aquariums, *Research in Zoos and Aquariums: A Symposium Held at the Forty-Ninth Conference of the American Association of Zoological Parks and Aquariums, Houston, Texas, October 6–11, 1973,* National Academy of Sciences, Washington, D.C., 1975.

American Association of Zoological Parks and Aquariums, *Zoological Park and Aquarium Fundamentals,* American Association of Zoological Parks and Aquariums, Wheeling, West Va., 1982.

American Association of Zoological Parks and Aquariums, *Zoological Parks and Aquariums in the Americas,* American Association of Zoological Parks and Aquariums, Wheeling, W. Va.

J. R. Clark, *Sea-Water Systems for Experimental Aquariums, a Collection of Papers,* Research Report No. 63, U.S. Bureau of Sport Fisheries and Wildlife, Washington, D.C., 1964.

A. Evans, *Aquariums,* Dover Publications, Inc., Mineola, N.Y., 1952.

H. Gersh, *The Animals next Door: a Guide to Zoos and Aquariums of the Americas,* Fleet Press Corp., New York, 1971.

P. H. Gosse, *The Aquarium: an Unveiling of the Wonders of the Deep Sea,* J. Van Voorst, London, 1854.

F. de Graafe, *Marine Aquarium Guide,* Pet Library, Harrison, N.J., 1973.

A. D. Hawkins, ed., *Aquarium Systems,* Academic Press, Inc., Orlando, Fla., 1981.

F. Lipscomb, "A Method Using Visitor Behavior to Evaluate Exhibits in an Aquarium" in *Northwest Region American Association of Zoological Parks and Aquariums Conference,* 1978.

D. W. Lupton, *Zoo and Aquarium Design,* Council of Planning Librarians, Monticello, Ill., 1978.

T. Mikkelsen, "The Aquarium at the End of Cannery Row," *Calif. Waterfront Age* 1(2), (Spring 1985).

D. Paige, *Behind the Scenes at the Aquarium,* Albert Whitman & Co., Niles, Ill., 1979.

T. J. Samuelsen, *Occasional References on Aquarium Techniques,* Bergen Aquarium, 1978.

J. A. Sanford and J. S. Taylor, *The Design of Exhibition Facilities: a Focus on Architecture Contributions to Visitor Experiences in Zoos, Aquariums, and Related Facilities,* Vance Bibliographies, Monticello, Ill., 1985.

K. Sausman, "Zoological Park and Aquarium Fundamentals" in *American Association of Zoological Parks and Aquariums Annual Proceedings,* American Association of Zoological Parks and Aquariums, Wheeling, W. Va., 1982.

M. Schumaker, ed., *Seawater Corrosion Handbook,* Noyes Data Corporation, Park Ridge, N.J., 1979.

Seattle Aquarium Design Team, *Exhibit Program: Technical Reprint No. 59,* Seattle Department of Parks and Recreation, Seattle, Wash., Dec. 1975.

B. Serrell, "Looking at Zoo and Aquarium Visitors," *Museum News,* 37 (Nov./Dec. 1980).

B. Serrell, "Signs that 'Speak': Learning More About Label Language," *Brookfield Bison,* 1 (Aug./Sept. 1980).

B. Serrell, "Survey of Visitor Attitude and Awareness at an Aquarium," *Curator* **20**(1), 48 (1977).

B. Serrell, "Visitor Observations Studies at Museums, Zoos, and Aquariums," in *American Association of Zoological Parks and Aquariums Annual Proceedings,* American Association of Zoological Parks and Aquariums, Wheeling, W. Va., 1978, pp. 229–233.

S. Spotte, *Seawater Aquariums, the Captive Environment,* John Wiley & Sons, Inc., New York, 1979.

S. Spotte, *Marine Aquarium Keeping: The Science, Animals, and Art,* John Wiley & Sons, Inc., New York, 1973.

United States Department of Agriculture, *Marine Mammals: Humane Handling, Care, Treatment, and Transportation,* National Archives, Washington, D.C., 1979.

United States Fish and Wildlife Service, *Seawater Systems for Experimental Aquariums: a Collection of Papers.*

F. W. Wheaton, *Aquaculture Engineering,* John Wiley & Sons, Inc., New York, 1977.

See also MUSEUMS; ZOOS.

CHARLES M. DAVIS, FAIA
JOHN RUTHERFORD
CLIVE WESTON
Esherick Homsey Dodge and
Davis
San Francisco, California

Edited by Elenore Souza

ARBITRATION IN CONSTRUCTION

Arbitration can be defined as the voluntary reference of a dispute between two or more parties to an impartial third party for resolution on the basis of evidence and argument presented by the parties, who agree in advance to accept the decision as final and binding. It is used extensively as an alternative to litigation in a broad spectrum of activities, perhaps most prominently in the commercial realm, which includes construction-related disputes.

Commercial arbitration can be distinguished from two other forms of arbitration, labor and international. Labor arbitration is a process which facilitates settlements between management and labor, and tends to be used as a final alternative when other forms of resolution have failed to provide a mutually acceptable solution. International arbitration is used to deal with contentious issues arising between sovereign states that have failed to resolve their differences through the more conventional channels of diplomatic negotiation. Although some procedural characteristics of the three types of arbitration are similar, the focus of the following text is primarily concerned with commercial arbitration, specifically in relation to construction-related disputes.

HISTORICAL BACKGROUND OF ARBITRATION

Arbitration as a means of dispute resolution is not a modern phenomenon and has been practiced in various forms for centuries. It is claimed that the procedures utilized by King Solomon were in many ways similar to those currently in operation, and that Greek city states in the sixth, fifth, and fourth centuries B.C. used arbitration to resolve certain disputes (1). In later times, English merchants and traders adopted the practice of arbitration long before it received parliamentary recognition in 1867 under the first Arbitration Act. The later Act of 1889 was consolidated in 1950 and 1979 and is now adopted by most countries in the British Commonwealth.

In the United States, Abraham Lincoln once acted as an arbitrator in a land boundary dispute, while George Washington included a provision in his will requiring that any conflicts arising from its contents should be settled through the expediency of arbitration. The process began to be formalized in 1787, when the Chamber of Commerce of the State of New York established a privately run tribunal for the purpose of furthering arbitration activities, although the first American legislation was not enacted until 1920, when New York State introduced the first arbitration statute. This was followed in 1925 by a Federal Arbitration Act and, during the same decade, a number of other states introduced similar acts specifically to encourage commercial arbitration.

Today in the United States, arbitration rules and procedures are codified by the Uniform Arbitration Act, which was adopted by the National Conference of the Commissioners on Uniform State Laws in 1955 and subsequently amended in 1956, and can be used by any state wishing to develop individual arbitration legislation. Forty-three states, the federal government in Washington, D.C., and Puerto Rico currently have arbitration legislation in effect.

FORMS OF DISPUTE RESOLUTION

There are a number of mechanisms available for dispute resolution which vary both procedurally and in the degree of authority exerted upon the parties. As some of these appear to be similar to arbitration, it is useful to define the various alternatives which may be used to solve a conflict:

Negotiation. Negotiation is an internal, private affair, whereby parties discuss their differences in good faith and attempt to resolve them by joint agreement without recourse to a third party.

Conciliation. If a third party is instrumental in bringing the parties together to discuss the problem, the process is known as conciliation. The third party does not participate in the discussions, but merely helps to establish communication between the parties in dispute.

Fact Finding. In this case, the third party's role is restricted to investigating the substance of the dispute by means of informal hearings and reporting on the findings to both parties. The report is intended to clarify the situation, enabling the parties to make an enlightened judgment on how to proceed with the resolution of the dispute. It is possible that the fact finder may be asked to submit recommendations in the report based on the available facts in an effort to assist the parties in reaching a mutual agreement, although such recommendations would be strictly advisory in nature. Fact finding is often used in labor disputes as a means of clarifying the issues that have caused a conflict between management and labor.

Mediation. The process of mediation involves a more active role for the third party, who tries to forge some agreement between the disputing parties by means of joint discussion and persuasion. However, the relationship between the mediator and the parties is strictly informal; neither disputing party is bound by any advice or decisions given by the mediator.

In all of the preceding forms of dispute resolution, the third party role is the same in that it provides a purely informal, nonbinding function intended solely to facilitate the discussion and potential agreement between the parties. They therefore differ from the provisions of both litigation and arbitration, where, in both cases, the judgment of the third party is final and binding.

Litigation. The conventional method of resolving a dispute entails the instigation of a lawsuit, which is processed and considered by the appropriate court within the U.S. legal system. The decision of the judge is both binding and enforceable, although appeal may be made by either party against the decision.

Arbitration. Arbitration has already been defined as the voluntary reference of a dispute to an impartial third party, whose award is binding upon the parties involved. It differs from litigation inasmuch as the process falls outside the conventional structure of the law, and can therefore be more flexible in the manner of dealing with specific disputes. This informality can provide parties with a number of potential advantages over the normal process of applying to the courts for the resolution of a conflict.

ARBITRATION VS LITIGATION

As each arbitration is a private concern between two or more parties, much of the bureaucracy inherent in the regular court structure may be avoided. Arbitrations may be arranged relatively quickly by comparison to the lengthy delays that can be expected in the courts, saving both time and money, particularly if the dispute is obstructing an otherwise ongoing relationship as, for example, in the case of a construction project. Furthermore, as attorneys are not necessary to instigate arbitration proceedings, the hearing may theoretically be an informal, inexpensive affair, involving only the two parties, the arbitrator, and any relevant witnesses. The informality of arbitration may also give some flexibility in the location of the hearing and in the procedures to be followed, which can be tailored to the nature of the case at the discretion of the arbitrator. The hearing could even be held at the location of the dispute, such as a building site, if this is deemed appropriate.

The courts are public forums, so all disputes that are litigated are open to public scrutiny. In contrast, only parties directly involved with the dispute need be admitted to an arbitration hearing, which may be desirable to parties wishing to protect their reputations from adverse publicity or wanting to shield particular trade secrets.

A major difference between arbitration and litigation lies in the nature of the third party. In the court system, disputes are determined by a judge (sometimes with a jury in session) who is conversant with issues of law, but not necessarily with the matters involved in a particular case. The arbitrator does not necessarily have to be well versed in law, but may be a specialist in the area of contention. In matters involving complex, technical data, therefore, it may be in the parties' interests to have the dispute judged by someone with sufficient knowledge and experience to understand the nature and complexity of the problem.

Finally, arbitration awards are final and binding upon the parties and subject only to limited review in the courts. This absolute settlement of a dispute may deter parties from continuing with further action and cause them to accept the decision, whereas the courts allow an avenue of appeal which an aggrieved party may pursue, thus prolonging the proceedings.

However, despite the obvious advantages, it is claimed by the critics of arbitration that, in some instances, it may be disadvantageous for parties to forego litigation in favor of arbitration. For example, although theoretically a less expensive process, arbitration has been known to become lengthy and complex, involving attorneys and expert witnesses in much the same way as a normal court trial, in which case the savings may be largely illusory, especially when the costs of the tribunal administrator, arbitrator, and hearing room (not applicable in the court system) are appended.

Despite being an expert in a particular field, the lack of detailed legal knowledge on the part of some arbitrators may make it difficult to assess accurately questions of law that are germane to the case. Furthermore, the informality which enables the arbitrator to determine the form of the hearing and the evidence to be heard also extends to the question of precedent. Cases heard in a court of law must abide by the principle of "stare decisis," meaning they are bound to decisions previously made in cases with similar circumstances. The arbitrator is not bound in this way and may decide each case on its individual merits. This may make it difficult for the parties to ascertain the strengths of their arguments prior to the arbitration.

Although there may be advantages to a final and binding award, there are limited means of overturning what may be considered by an aggrieved party to be a wrong decision. The only recourse available may be to seek relief by introducing the same case in the courts, entailing additional legal expenses for the parties involved.

Finally, as arbitration is a private agreement between contracting parties, most state laws, in accordance with the Federal Arbitration Act, do not allow for third parties (with the exception of the arbitrator) to be involved in the hearing unless by specific agreement between the parties. Thus, disputes which concern a number of parties would, in some states, have to be settled by a series of individual arbitrations, a process which could be cumbersome, time-consuming, and costly. The court system, alternatively, allows for joint action to be brought against a number of parties and can consider several suits in one combined hearing.

ARBITRATION

Legal Basis for Arbitration

Many countries have nationally applicable laws providing a legal basis for arbitration. In the United States, the majority of states has enacted arbitration statutes to provide a legal framework for the irrevocability of the agreement and the enforceability of the award. Although there are some grounds for invalidating an award, most courts in these states will stay any court action until arbitration procedures are complete.

Many of the statutes are based in whole or in part on the Uniform Arbitration Act, which was adopted by the National Conference of the Commissioners on Uniform State Laws in 1955 and amended in 1956 and approved by the House of Delegates of the American Bar Association. In addition, the United States Arbitration Act provides for the enforcement of arbitration agreements and awards in matters involving interstate commerce and maritime and international contracts.

American Arbitration Association

Although arbitration is basically a private affair between contracting parties, most countries have a nationally recognized impartial agency which provides guidance and administrative assistance in the arbitration process. In the United States, the American Arbitration Association (referred to hereafter as the AAA) was founded in 1926 as a result of a merger between the Arbitration Society of America and the Arbitration Foundation. It is a private, nonprofit organization which offers a dispute settlement service to a broad range of potential users and is the focal point of most arbitration activity in the country. Although the officers of the Association do not personally arbitrate, they administer the procedures concerned with organizing each hearing and help the parties to select the arbitrators. Their national headquarters are based in New York City, although there are twenty-six regional offices located throughout the United States. The AAA maintains research and education roles as well, providing numerous publications and training programs for its members, and has divided its operations into a series of categories, which include Commercial and Business, International Trade, Textile and Apparel, Automobile Accident Claims, Labor-Management Relations, Interpersonal Relations, and Construction. For each category, a panel of arbitrators has been assembled containing names of suitably qualified individuals who may be called upon to serve as arbitrators on appropriate disputes.

Arbitrators

There are approximately 60,000 individuals from a broad range of professional pursuits listed on the AAA's National Panel of Arbitrators in the various categories of dispute.

They are selected based on their qualifications, reputation, and experience in a particular field as well as for qualities of integrity and fairmindedness.

National Panel of Construction Arbitrators

Arbitration has become accepted in the construction industry as an expedient means of dispute resolution, and many contracts, particularly standardized forms (for example, American Institute of Architects Document A201, General Conditions of the Contract for Construction, Article 7.9.), include provisions to allow for arbitration in the event of a dispute between the contracting parties. Arbitrators are drawn from the Construction Arbitration Panel, which is composed of members of various professional bodies, including lawyers, architects, engineers, and contractors. They are expected to adhere to the rules laid down in the Construction Industry Arbitration Rules, published by the American Arbitration Association. Arbitrators on the Construction Arbitration Panel may be directly screened and approved by the AAA or appointed by the National Construction Industry Arbitration Committee, which was founded in 1966 and is composed of representatives from ten major industry organizations.

International Commercial Arbitration

Contractual agreements between parties from different countries may be complicated by such issues as language difficulties, relative currency values, and intercountry trade restrictions. In the event that disputes arise, arbitration procedures are essentially the same as in domestic disputes, although enforcement of an award in another country can sometimes present difficulties for the successful party. Uniformity in the development of international commercial arbitration has been promoted by the United Nations Commission on International Trade Law, and rules for international arbitration have been published by the United Nations Economic Commission.

Arbitration Procedures

The process of arbitration can only be originated by voluntary agreement made between the parties to a dispute. Such agreement may be made at the time of the dispute or even after it has arisen, although it is preferable to make the agreement at the outset of the contractual relationship when the chances of mutual agreement are highest. Many standard forms of contract in the United States contain an arbitration clause that binds the parties to arbitration in the event of a dispute. Similar clauses are often drafted into nonstandard contracts as well, and the AAA has prepared a model clause which they recommend be incorporated into any contract:

> Any controversy or claim arising out of or relating to this contract, or the breach thereof, shall be settled by arbitration in accordance with the Rules of the American Arbitration Association, and judgment upon the award rendered by the arbitrator(s) may be entered in any court having jurisdiction thereof.

Should either party to a contract containing an arbitration clause be reluctant to proceed with the arbitration, the courts, under relevant state law, may enforce the agreement and stay any requested court action until the arbitration proceedings have been completed.

Selecting the Arbitrator. A single arbitrator may be sufficient to resolve many disputes, but, in more complex cases, a panel of three may be appointed. Arbitrators may be selected by the parties prior to or even during the dispute. Alternatively, an application may be made to the AAA which, upon reviewing the Demand for Arbitration (or, in the absence of an arbitration clause in the original contract, a Submission Agreement, signed by both parties at the time of the dispute), will send the parties a list of arbitrators suitably qualified to resolve the dispute in question. They are given seven days to delete any names they feel to be unacceptable, and rank the remaining names in order of preference before returning the list to the AAA. In the event that there are no names acceptable to both parties, additional lists may be submitted at the request of both parties or the AAA may appoint the arbitrator(s) independently, although not from the list of names already rejected by the parties. The arbitrator will then be notified of the appointment, although the administrative officers of the AAA would have contacted potential parties beforehand to ascertain their availability and interest to serve on the arbitration.

Acceptance of the Appointment. As the arbitrator is a neutral third party in the dispute, it is important that no conflict of interest exists that could interfere with the formulation of an impartial, acceptable judgment. Such conflict may include past or present relationships with one of the parties or their counsel, or a financial or personal interest in the outcome of the dispute. If this proves to be the case, the proposed arbitrator may have to decline the appointment, or at least disclose the full nature of the relationship to the AAA at the beginning of the proceedings, who will inform the parties and determine whether the appointment is acceptable.

If no reason exists to prevent the appointment, the arbitrator notifies the AAA, returning the "Oath of the Arbitrator" form completed and notarized. The administrative officers then proceed with the arrangement of meetings and basic procedural details. All such matters are handled by the AAA to eliminate the contact between the parties and the arbitrator prior to the hearing and also to relieve the latter of the bureaucratic burdens involved.

Prehearing Conference. A prehearing conference may sometimes be arranged at the parties' request or if the AAA believes it would be useful prior to the appointment of the arbitrator. The parties may then meet with an AAA tribunal administrator to discuss procedural matters which may help to minimize delays in the arbitration and overcome any procedural difficulties. Matters for consideration may include the composition of the panel of arbitrators, lists of witnesses, discovery of documents, on-site inspection, interpretation, specification of uncontested facts, stenographic records, use of counsel, and determination of the locale of the hearing, which may be selected by agreement of the parties or by the AAA.

Preliminary Hearing. In large, complex cases, a preliminary hearing may be scheduled by the AAA in consultation with the parties and the arbitrator to establish procedures and time frames for disclosure, identification of witnesses, and further meetings. In some cases, it may be necessary for the arbitrator to issue subpoenas for the attendance of witnesses or the disclosure of documents. This may be undertaken at a party's request or on the arbitrator's initiative, although authority will depend on state law.

Hearing. A hearing is not always necessary to resolve a dispute, and the parties may agree to allow the arbitrator to settle the matter solely on the written submissions of each side in the relationship. If a hearing is preferred, however, it can proceed when all required documentation has been exchanged and at a time and place established by the arbitrator. The hearing may be less formal in nature than a conventional court, and strict rules of evidence do not automatically apply. However, arbitrators may decide to follow a similar pattern to the courts to ensure that all relevant facts and arguments are presented.

Following the taking of an oath by the arbitrator (which may or may not be required by either the parties or state law), the arbitrator may ask for a brief statement by each party to clarify the issues involved. Although legal representation is not necessary, the parties may use attorneys to present their cases for them. After such statements have been made, the complainant will usually present the claim, supported by proof in the form of testimony, exhibits, witnesses, and perhaps expert witnesses. The latter are not specifically involved in the dispute, but are employed to give an expert opinion on the matter. All witnesses are usually examined, cross-examined by the respondent or their counsel, and reexamined by the claimant. They may be required by state law or by the arbitrator to give their testimony under oath. If a witness is unable to attend the hearing, the arbitrator may accept a signed affidavit, giving it such weight as considered appropriate. When the claimant's arguments are completed, the respondent follows the same procedure in delivering the defense and any counterclaim. The procedure may be varied to accommodate special circumstances, but the arbitrator must give full and equal opportunity to both sides to present all proof they feel is relevant to the issue. In some cases, a site visit may be instructive for the arbitrator, in which case both parties must be notified in advance to give them both an opportunity to attend.

At the close of the hearing, the arbitrator determines whether each side has any further proof they wish to present before discussion is terminated. If both parties are satisfied that they have fully presented their cases, the arbitrator closes the proceedings, from which point a fixed period of time in which the award will be made will be stated (usually thirty days). During this time period, communication between the parties and the arbitrator can only take place through the offices of the AAA. The hearing may be reopened either at the arbitrator's determination or upon the application of one of the parties, but only in the time period before the award is made. The hearing will not be reopened if this action will delay the delivery of the award past the specified deadline unless an extension is agreed upon by both parties in writing.

In the event that one of the parties attempts to slow down or obstruct the proceedings, the arbitrator may continue with the hearing in that party's absence, unless state law provides to the contrary. However, the recalcitrant party must be notified in writing of the right to attend the hearing, and the final award must be made on the evidence that is presented and not on the basis of the absent party's failure to attend.

Award. The award is made in writing, executed in accordance with relevant state law, and signed by the arbitrator. If there is a panel of arbitrators involved in the case, the majority must sign to validate the award, which is then sent to the AAA which informs the parties of its contents. The arbitrator, having signed and delivered the award, becomes "functus officio" and has no further power or duties in the matter.

The award must be made within the terms of the original agreement to ensure its validity, and does not have to be accompanied by any statements giving reasons for the decision. It is usually made in the form of a brief direction to the parties, although some arbitrators prefer to provide a brief rationale for their award in a separate document to clarify the issues to the parties. This action may be considered unwise, however, as the argument provided may give an aggrieved party more leverage if they try to have the award vacated by the courts.

Although the majority of awards will be made for finite dollar amounts, it is possible, where circumstances warrant, for the arbitrator to award specific performance of the contract by one of the parties, or to grant injunctive relief, requiring the losing party to desist from a contractual violation. Again, the arbitrator must be careful to make the award within the terms and powers extended in the original agreement to arbitrate to ensure the validity of the award.

Expedited Procedures. In circumstances where time is of the essence, parties may decide to follow the expedited procedures established by the American Institute of Arbitrators. These involve the communication of all notices to the parties by telephone, the contents of which are subsequently confirmed in writing. In addition, the expedited procedures facilitate the appointment of the arbitrator and the establishment of the hearing, which does not normally exceed one day in length. The award, unless otherwise agreed to by the parties, will then be rendered within five business days by the arbitrator.

Fees and Expenses. In the award, the arbitrator assesses the arbitration fees and expenses, including those of the AAA, equally between the parties, or in favor of the winning side if this was specifically required in the original agreement. The AAA is a nonprofit organization and so therefore only charges an administrative fee to offset its expenses. The fee is prescribed on a schedule which links the amount on a sliding scale to the combined sums of the claim and counterclaim, if any, and is payable at the time of filing for arbitration. Unless otherwise determined by the parties at the outset of the arbitration, arbitrators who are members of the National Panel of Construction Arbitrators serve the first day of each case free of charge. If the arbitration extends beyond this time, compensation is determined through the AAA, which may discuss the details of payment with the parties prior to the hearing. Other expenses, including travel and related costs of the arbitrator and the AAA personnel, are usually split between the parties unless they agree otherwise, or unless the arbitrator awards them against one of the parties.

Unless otherwise determined in the arbitration agreement or by written request of both parties, both sides are usually expected to pay their own expenses incurred in hiring legal counsel and calling expert witnesses. The cost of a stenographic record or an interpreter, if required, is usually borne by the party requesting the service.

Arbitration and the Courts

Although the arbitrator's decision is binding upon the parties and has no avenue of appeal, there are certain connections to the regular court system. Most courts in states with arbitration statutes will, eg, enforce arbitration agreements if they are validly made. Similarly, if one of the parties refuses to accept the decision given by the arbitrator and will not abide by its provisions, the arbitrator may make application to the courts to enforce it. The reneging party will thenceforth be in contempt of court if it continues to ignore the findings of the award and will face a fine or imprisonment for continued violation.

Despite the absence of a line of appeal, the courts may, in certain limited circumstances, intervene. If either party feels that the arbitrator has exceeded his or her authority or has refused to hear evidence relevant to the dispute, or if there are indications to suggest corruption, fraud, or partiality on the part of the arbitrator or that the original arbitration agreement was improper in some way (eg, if the dispute was outside the scope of the agreement and the issues are not arbitrable), they may also make application to the courts. Upon review, the award may be vacated under state law. However, the courts will not review the arbitrator's decision on the merits of the case but solely on the legitimacy and conduct of the proceedings.

BIBLIOGRAPHY

1. C. K. Wehringer, *Arbitration Precepts and Principles,* Oceana Publications, Inc., Dobbs Ferry, N.Y., 1969.

General References

J. Acret, *Construction Arbitration Handbook,* McGraw-Hill, Inc., New York, 1985.

R. Coulson, *Business Arbitration—What You Need to Know,* American Arbitration Association, New York, 1980.

M. Domke, *The Law and Practice of Commercial Arbitration* (1985 cumulative supplement), Callaghan and Company, Chicago, Ill., 1968.

S. J. Faber and S. R. Lovett, *Arbitration Handbook with Forms,* Charing Cross Publishing Co., Los Angeles, Calif., 1979.

W. H. Gill, *The Law of Arbitration,* Sweet and Maxwell, London, 1975.

G. Goldberg, *A Lawyer's Guide to Commercial Arbitration,* 2nd ed., American Law Institute/American Bar Association Committee on Continuing Professional Education, Philadelphia, Pa., 1983.

P. E. O'Keefe, *Arbitration in International Trade,* Prosper Law Publications, Sydney, Australia, 1975.

J. Parris, *Arbitrations: Principles and Practice,* Granada Publishing, London, 1983.

I. Richter and B. Kozek, *Construction Briefings,* Construction Arbitration Proceedings No. 75–8, Federal Publications, Inc., Washington, D.C., Oct. 1978.

R. M. Rodman, *Commercial Arbitration with Forms,* West Publishing Co., St. Paul, Minn., 1984.

C. M. Schmitthoff, Compiler and Editor, *International Commercial Arbitration,* Vol. I, Oceana Publications, Inc., Dobbs Ferry, N.Y., 1976.

J. Sweet, *Legal Aspects of Architecture, Engineering and the Construction Process,* 3rd ed. West Publishing Co., St. Paul, Minn., 1985.

A. Walton, *Russell on the Law of Arbitration,* 18th ed., Stevens and Sons, London, 1970.

J. G. Wetter, *The International Arbitral Process: Public and Private,* Vols. 1–5, Oceana Publications, Inc., Dobbs Ferry, N.Y., 1979.

A. T. Widiss, ed., *Arbitration: Commercial Disputes, Insurance and Tort Claims,* Practicing Law Institute, New York, 1979.

The American Arbitration Association publishes a wide range of books, pamphlets, and reprinted papers of an explanatory nature. They provide information and insight into the practices and procedures of arbitration, which have been used in the preparation of this article. In addition, the Association makes available to its members a quarterly news bulletin, an arbitration journal, and a quarterly newsletter.

See also CONSTRUCTION LAW; CONTRACT ADMINISTRATION; LIABILITY INSURANCE; MEDIATION IN ARCHITECTURAL AND CONSTRUCTION DISPUTES.

ROBERT GREENSTREET, PhD
University of Wisconsin—
Milwaukee
Milwaukee, Wisconsin

ARCHIGRAM

Archigram was a loosely knit group of young architects that emerged as a major polemic force in architectural thinking in the early 1960s in London. Led by original members Peter Cook, David Greene, and Michael Webb, and later joined by Warren Chalk, Ron Herron, and Dennis Crompton, the organization disseminated its vividly controversial ideas through *Archigram,* a series of broadsheet manifestoes published yearly from 1960 to 1970. Designed to disturb the self-satisfaction in the London architectural scene, Archigram's message was at once angry, defiant, humorous, and socially aware. With the fourth *Archigram* in 1964, the "Zoom" edition, came rapid international attention and the support of architectural critics Peter Blake and Reynar Banham.

With Ron Herron as the group's leading image maker, the publication became known worldwide for its playfully irreverent attitude toward traditional architectural design and graphics. Superman and other elements of pop iconography of the city were juxtaposed with the rocket support structures of Cape Kennedy and other images of the U.S. space program—all in a manner and with a meaning that was new to architecture.

Central to the projects and exhibitions published in *Archigram* was a belief that sophisticated technology, working in harmony with humanity, was the hope of the future. With the technology of the space age already at hand, it was felt that architects should no longer be building only from bricks and mortar. With hopes that traditional architecture could be expanded by acquiring elements from outside itself, members strove to invent new artifacts and to eliminate traditional notions of house and city from shelter design and urban planning. At the core of Archigram's thinking was a conviction that change, adaptability, and metamorphosis, already attainable through available technology, were essential to the survival of modern cities.

As would be expected from a group that accepted flexibility, ephemerality, and change as the only constants, Archigram's typical products were drawings and exhibitions. Members sought new directions, embracing technology wholeheartedly in underwater cities, living capsules, mobile villages, and the rest. Included in hundreds of projects were some of the seminal architectural statements of the 1960s, such as Living City sponsored by the Gulbenkian Foundation Grant (1963); Capsule Homes, Warren Chalk (1964); Plug-In City, Peter Cook (1964–1966); Walking City, Ron Herron (1964); Living Pod, David Greene (1965); and Instant City, sponsored by the Graham Foundation, Chicago (1968).

The Living City Exhibition, published by the *Living Arts Magazine No. 2* and displayed at the Institute of Contemporary Arts in London in June 1963, was the first group project realized by Archigram. Rather than creating a blueprint for a new city, members sought to express energy and movement. The role of architecture in the project is relatively insignificant in relation to the total environment of the city (1):

We must perpetuate this vitality or the city will die at the hands of the hard planners and architect-aesthetes. The re-creation of the environment is too often a jaded process, having to do only with densities, allocations of space, fulfillment of regulations . . .

The result of dogged adherence to the all-importance of architecture is (2)

a vast suburb without any cities, and in it the odd pocket of architects building their own houses—no longer involved.

The Walking City was a spin-off from Cape Kennedy, where several structures, some the height of 40-story office buildings, moved "serenely across the flat landscape" (3).

In Ron Herron's version, steel tanks moved mechanically, resolving urban difficulties such as transportation. Although solutions provided by visionary architecture were still considered impractical by most designers and builders, the manipulation of existing technology from NASA and Cape Kennedy seemed to provide a new avenue for solutions to urban ills.

The Plug-In City, which incorporated plug-in kits and throw-away units into traditional architecture, was the culmination of a series of ideas developed by Archigram between 1962 and 1964. The dialectic in *Archigram 2* and *Archigram 3* led to experiments with expendable buildings, and ultimately to an urban environment designed to accommodate constant change. The core of the Plug-In City is a concrete megastructure to which removable house elements planned for obsolescence are continually added and subtracted. A large-scale network of access ways and essential services is applied to the megastructure. All units are serviced and maneuvered by means of cranes operating from a railway at the apex of the structure.

The series of Capsule Homes, Gasket Homes, and Living Pods developed by members between 1964 and 1966 explored the notion of prefabricated dwellings that could stack into tower structures or be applied to megastructures. The highly sophisticated units, essentially products of an industrial design approach, departed radically from the traditional folk art of housing.

Until 1966, Archigram's projects made "direct conversation" with the traditional type of solutions of architecture: the Plug-In City, after all, was still a city, the Capsule houses still houses. By the seventh issue, "Beyond Architecture," *Archigram* was on a new track. From 1966 onward, all enclosures were gone; there was a gradual dissolve from alternatives for earlier models of useful building to strange beasts such as "suits that are homes" and other hybrid projects that were at once architecture, machine, animal-like growth, and electrical circuitry. Archigram had abandoned all traditional categories of architecture, form, and building in the name of adaptability, software, and servicing.

Archigram's chance to put theory into practice came in 1970 after it won a major international competition for the design and construction of an entertainment center in Monte Carlo. The Archigram office, established for the competition, was responsible for numerous projects and exhibitions, such as the "Malaysia" exhibition at the Commonwealth Institute in London, 1973. Archigram Architects (AA) dissolved in 1974, shortly after the Monte Carlo project was abandoned by its financial backers.

By the mid-1970s, Archigram had lost its urgency, but its impact had already been made; the dialogue had started. It has been said that (4)

The great contribution of the British avant-garde has been to open up and develop new attitudes towards living in an advanced industrial civilization where only stereotyped rejection had existed before, to dramatizing consumer choice and communicating the pleasure inherent in manipulating sophisticated technology.

If Archigram's approach did not solve the serious social and political problems in modern cities, at least it initiated alternative paths for analyzing consumer society and urbanism.

Although the images and the ideas of Archigram remained for the most part on paper, they had an enormous effect on practice around the world. From the Brutalist idea of *une architecture autre* had arisen the un-house of Banham, the noncity of Webber, and the nonarchitecture of Archigram; these paved the way for the nonbuilding later realized by Piano and Rogers in the Pompidou Center in Paris and by Cedric Price in his Inter-Action Center in London. The ideas involved with the Instant City were further developed by Arata Isozaki in his section of the Osaka World's Fair, 1970. According to Isozaki, Archigram's consistently countercultural work was totally divorced from the patterned logic that architecture had created within itself (5):

> When all values have been turned topsy-turvy, Archigram has established a new structure of values, a new syntax, and demonstrated the possibility of an independent subculture.

Members of Archigram have played a prominent role in British architecture, both as a group and as individuals. The work of former students of Peter Cook, a tenured instructor at AA in London, has been a driving force in many prominent architectural firms and major international competitions, including the Paris Park Competition, the Hong Kong Club Competition, and the Osaka World's Fair, 1970. Ron Herron has also been a major force in the AA and has acted as a visiting Professor in Urban Design at The University of California at Los Angeles (1968–1969) and served as director of Urban Design, William Pereira and Partners, Los Angeles (1969–1970).

BIBLIOGRAPHY

1. P. Cook, *Archigram*, Praeger Publishers, Inc., New York, 1973, p. 20.
2. *Ibid.*, p. 23.
3. *Ibid.*, p. 28.
4. C. Jenks, *Modern Movements in Architecture*, Anchor Press, New York, 1973, p. 298.
5. Ref. 1, p. 2.

BARBARA L. WADKINS
New School of Architecture
Chula Vista, California

ARCHITECTS COMPENSATION.   See FEES, ARCHITECTURAL

ARCHITECTS RESEARCH CENTER CONSORTIUM (ARCC).   See RESEARCH, ARCHITECTURAL

ARCHITECTURAL AND TRANSPORTATION BARRIERS COMPLIANCE BOARD (ATBCB)

The Architectural and Transportation Barriers Compliance Board (ATBCB) was created by Congress in 1973 to enforce the Architectural Barriers Act (ABA) of 1968 (1). The ATBCB was authorized under Section 502 of the Rehabilitation Act of 1973 (2).

The ATBCB is an independent federal agency with 23 board members. The President appoints 12 public members (six must be disabled) to three-year terms, and the other 11 are the heads (or their designees) of the departments of Defense, Education, Health and Human Services, Housing and Urban Development, Interior, Justice, Labor, and Transportation; the General Services Administration; the Veterans Administration; and the United States Postal Service. An executive director heads the ATBCB staff.

The ATBCB reports annually to the President and Congress on investigations, actions, and the extent of compliance with the Architectural Barriers Act (the Act).

LEGAL REQUIREMENTS

The Act requires that buildings and facilities designed, constructed, altered, or leased with certain federal funds after September 1969—when architectural accessibility specifications were first established—must be accessible to and usable by handicapped persons. Facilities covered by this law include those receiving grants or loans if standards for design, construction, or alteration are issued under authority of the legislation authorizing the grant or loan. The law does not cover every type of federal funding nor does it include privately funded construction.

The 1968 Act and later amendments gave four federal agencies—the General Services Administration (GSA), the Department of Defense (DOD), the Department of Housing and Urban Development (HUD), and the U.S. Postal Service (USPS)—authority to set accessibility standards (specifications). GSA's standards apply to federally funded construction other than that covered by HUD, DOD, and USPS standards. HUD prescribes standards for residential facilities subject to the Act, whereas DOD and USPS issue standards for facilities under their respective jurisdictions. Standards first prescribed in September 1969 have been modified over the years. The Uniform Federal Accessibility Standards (UFAS) are the standards now in effect for all four standard-setting agencies. The four agencies are required to conduct continuing surveys and investigations to ensure compliance with such standards. The GSA administrator reports annually to Congress on GSA's activities and those of other departments, agencies, and instrumentalities that implement standards under the Act.

FUNCTIONS

The ATBCB's primary legislative mandate is to ensure compliance with standards prescribed under the Act. Other main functions are to:

- Propose alternative solutions to barriers facing handicapped persons in housing, transportation, communications, education, recreation, and attitudes.
- Determine what federal, state, and local governments and other public or private agencies and groups are doing to eliminate barriers.

- Recommend to the President and Congress legislation and regulations to eliminate barriers.
- Establish minimum guidelines and requirements for standards issued under the Act and conduct research to determine the most appropriate requirements.
- Prepare plans for adequate transportation and housing for handicapped persons, including proposals to cooperate with other agencies, organizations, and individuals working toward such goals.
- Develop standards and provide technical assistance to any entity affected by regulations issued under Title V of the Rehabilitation Act of 1973.
- Provide technical assistance on removing barriers and answer questions on architectural, transportation, communication, and attitudinal barriers affecting physically handicapped persons.
- Ensure that public conveyances, including rolling stock, are usable by handicapped persons.

The ATBCB may conduct investigations, hold public hearings, and issue orders to comply with the Act. An order is final and binding on any federal department, agency, or instrumentality of the United States. A complainant or participant in the proceeding may have orders reviewed in federal court. Complete details on the complaint process are available from the ATBCB.

STANDARDS

Federal buildings or federally funded facilities covered by the Act must meet federal accessibility standards in effect when the facility was designed, constructed, altered, or leased. For example, the standards generally require at least one primary entrance to be level or ramped and restrooms to be accessible to wheelchair users. Congress required the ATBCB in 1978 to develop minimum guidelines and requirements as a basis for the standards issued by DOD, HUD, GSA, and USPS. The guidelines were published on Aug. 4, 1982 (3). The four standard-setting agencies issued UFAS on Aug. 7, 1984 (4). They must exceed the ATBCB's minimum guidelines and apply from the effective date forward to buildings and facilities subject to the Act.

TECHNICAL ASSISTANCE

Since 1978, the Board has been authorized by Congress to provide technical assistance on accessibility. Congress required that these activities be separate and distinct from the Board's compliance and enforcement responsibilities.

Technical assistance is based on information drawn from various resources. These include staff expertise and a comprehensive technical assistance file of about 2500 documents, with selected bibliographies and abstracts on a variety of accessibility-related topics. Also available are an extensive file on accessibility products and a codes and standards file on federal, state, and model code access requirements.

Technical assistance may be provided through consultation, either in person or by telephone, or referral to other agencies, organizations, or individuals.

The Board has made a particular effort to provide technical assistance to other federal agencies. Most technical assistance requests, however, are from individuals and organizations affected by federal, state, or local laws requiring accommodations for handicapped persons.

Requests for technical assistance are not considered complaints. Complaints about inaccessible federally funded facilities are filed with the Board's office of compliance and enforcement.

Board-sponsored projects often result in research reports or technical papers addressing various aspects of accessibility, summarizing research and field experience, recommending future studies, developing bibliographies, and listing references. Technical papers, final reports, or bibliographies may be requested on a variety of subjects, including such topics as alarms, orientation and wayfinding, ground and floor surface treatments, multiple disabilities through the lifespan, windows, hand anthropometrics, and TDDs (telecommunication devices for deaf persons).

Through a cooperative project with the four standard-setting agencies, the Board has published an indexed edition of UFAS. The Board also publishes a newsletter. Both UFAS and the newsletter are available upon request in print and on cassette. Technical assistance may be obtained by writing or calling the Architectural and Transportation Barriers Compliance Board in Washington, D.C.

The following list outlines the significant events in the Board's history:

1973   Section 502 of the Rehabilitation Act establishes Board to enforce 1968 Act; it is composed of heads (or their designees) of eight federal agencies.

1974   Section 502 amendments expand federal-agency membership and establish a consumer advisory panel.

1975   Board adopts "Access America" national campaign to increase public awareness about need to eliminate barriers.

1976   Architectural Barriers Act is amended to include postal facilities and all leased buildings, and to expand federal-agency membership.

1977   Board issues first citation for noncompliance with ABA.

1978   Section 502 is amended to add 11 public members; to expand Board's responsibilities to include transportation and communication barriers; and to give authority to set minimum guidelines and requirements for standards and to provide technical assistance to entities affected by Rehabilitation Act regulations.

1982   Board publishes final revised Minimum Guidelines and Requirements for Accessible Design.

1984   Four standard-setting agencies publish Uniform Federal Accessibility Standards.

1986   Indexed edition of Uniform Federal Accessibility Standards is published as a cooperative project by the Board and the four standard-setting agencies; Section 502 is amended to increase public members to 12, disabled members to six, and to provide for a public member to "hold over" until successor is appointed.

BIBLIOGRAPHY

1. Public Law 90–480, 42 U.S.C. 4151–4157.
2. Public Law 90–480, 29 U.S.C. 792.
3. Minimum Guidelines and Requirements for Accessible Design, 47 Federal Regulation 33862.
4. Uniform Federal Accessibility Standards, 49 Federal Regulation 31528.

See also HANDICAPPED, DESIGN FOR; HANDICAPPED ACCESS LAWS AND CODES.

ARCHITECTURAL AND
TRANSPORTATION BARRIERS
COMPLIANCE BOARD
Washington, D.C.

ARCHITECTURAL DESIGN COMPETITIONS.
See COMPETITIONS, ARCHITECTURAL DESIGN

ARCHITECTURAL FEES.   See FEES, ARCHITECTURAL

ARCHITECTURAL LIBRARIES

A library is an organized collection of material used for reference, education, or pleasure reading. Format of the material is irrelevant. It may be print, such as books and periodicals, audiovisuals (slides, tapes, and films), drawings and maps, or material samples. Physical location of the material within an organization may also be unimportant, as long as there is a central record of each location.

Architecture is a service profession of problem solving. In the traditional scenario, the architect takes the client's needs, adds information on the project type, as well as legal, regulatory, and financial considerations, and develops a solution that resolves design issues to satisfy the client's program. The reference library, therefore, has always played a vital role in the architectural office, although the library itself may range from a shelf or two to a full-fledged resource center staffed by a professional librarian. Testimony to the importance of the library to the profession is given by both the Royal Institute of British Architects (RIBA) and the American Institute of Architects (AIA). Each established a library soon after founding, the RIBA in 1834 and the AIA in 1857.

The purpose of the office library is to provide control over the firm's information resources, most often those which are external in nature, ie, generated outside the firm. These include reference texts and manuals, codes and standards, manufacturers' literature and trade catalogues, periodicals, and clipping files. Internal information is developed by the firm and includes its business and administrative records, operational information (person-

nel procedures, for example), project proposals and records, feasibility studies, drawings, standard details, and specifications. Control over the firm's information resources, both internal and external, minimizes duplication in dollars spent on purchases, and in staff and storage costs. Control is based on an efficient and effective retrieval system or mechanism that reduces overall research time, yet provides the architect with the widest and most thorough access to the firm's store of information.

However, since the library serves the firm and the individual members of the firm, it is important to consider their information needs and their information-seeking behavior before deciding on the organization, scope, and staffing of the library itself.

The studio approach to education used in most schools of architecture determines the practitioner's information-seeking behavior. It emphasizes creativity and in-depth analysis of design problems, supplemented by the beaux-arts tradition of learning by doing and by journal-based research. In contrast to other disciplines and professions, however, architects share information on or publish only products rather than methods or processes, so that even journal research throws the practitioner back on his or her creative resources. Each new project is approached by both student and practicing architect as the proverbial wheel, to be invented anew. This lack of information sharing is exacerbated by a weak tradition in the profession of applied research.

The role of the practicing architect is a varied one, because the architect's problem solving abilities open the way for a host of other services which may be offered to the client. The American Institute of Architects, in its 1977 document "Scope of Designated Services," describes eight phases of project-related services, from predesign through postconstruction. A ninth section lists 26 categories of so-called supplemental services that the architect may be qualified to provide, from special studies and life-cycle cost analysis to development of leasing brochures, to expert witness testimony. The private practitioner is also a business person concerned with financial and personnel management, job development, and design services marketing. The architect may also assume the role of community activist, speaking before civic groups and classrooms on the profession or the built environment. The intern architect has special information needs in preparation for the registration examination. Finally, mandatory continuing education and recertification are ongoing issues in many states, and place still other information demands on the practitioner.

It is clear, then, that the information needs of the architect extend far beyond product literature and the basic design data of *Architectural Graphic Standards* and that it is to the benefit of the firm to identify, organize, and catalogue its information resources in a way that best serves those needs.

THE FIRM LIBRARIAN

Once the decision is made to create a functioning library in the firm, one person must assume responsibility for its maintenance, at the very least. In the simplest situation, a secretary may be assigned to shelve and file material and to monitor the currency of the trade catalogues. At the other end of the spectrum, the firm commits itself to a full-time, professional librarian who systematically acquires and catalogues books, periodicals, and other types of reference material, institutes procedures for the most effective use of the material by members of the firm, and does outside research when the firm's resources are insufficient. It is also possible for a professional staff member, often a specification writer, to assume the role of librarian and take on organization and maintenance of the collection.

Of critical importance to the success of the firm library in meeting the staff members' information needs is the librarian's role in the firm hierarchy and that person's relationship to other staff. He or she should have the confidence and trust of the other employees, who understand how the librarian can help on a project and thus will use the librarian's skills to best advantage. The librarian cultivates with the other employees an ongoing, two-way communication about sources, types of material, and means of acquisition. Some ability may be required to assess the value of architectural information; that should actually be the responsibility of the technical staff using it, but the librarian must understand the workings and needs of the firm well enough to know when to acquire, when to refer, and when to do how much research. He or she must stay abreast of current projects in the firm. The good working relationship with the staff helps the librarian gain the necessary level of control over the firm's information resources to solve the firm's information needs.

The Association of Architectural Librarians (AAL), an informal network of design firm and architecture school librarians, maintains a mailing list of several hundred names. Approximately one-third comes from the academic world, but the others are in the private sector. It is a small group when compared to the 15,000 AIA-member-owned firms in the United States, but important nevertheless. It represents recognition in several hundred firms of the importance of an organized library.

The strongest argument in favor of hiring a professional librarian with a Master's degree in library science (MLS) is that person's research skills. Information, its resources, and its management are the business of library science, and a good librarian knows where and how to most efficiently look for answers. He or she knows sources and how to use them, and often has an extensive network of colleagues to consult on a particular challenge. He or she will also have extensive knowledge of local public, academic, and special library resources. It is rare to find a librarian with both an MLS and a professional degree in architecture, but this is not necessarily a drawback. Librarians, like architects, are trained as generalists, and the organized approach to research and information management is far more valuable to the firm than familiarity with the architectural profession. This can be picked up on the job. An undergraduate degree in art or architectural history is not uncommon, however, and the number of information specialists who have design firm or architecture school library experience is growing.

The firm has several options to consider when making hiring decisions. If it can put the reference and research skills of the professional librarian to good use, perhaps only part-time employment is warranted. Should this be beyond the firm's means or needs, it may be worthwhile to hire a consultant to set up the library, organize and catalogue the material, establish procedures, and train permanent staff to take over the day-to-day responsibility. The AIA Information Center has a resource packet on setting up an architectural office library. In many firms, the librarian has responsibilities beyond research and collection management, including promotional writing, proposal preparation, and coordination of educational seminars.

Salary data specifically for architectural librarians does not exist. However, the Special Libraries Association (SLA) conducts a salary survey of its membership every three years, which is tabulated by region and job type.

THE FIRM LIBRARY

Space and Budget Requirements. There are no hard and fast guidelines for space or budget requirements in the firm library. Indeed, both are a function of the type of practice a firm maintains and how much material is deemed necessary for retention. Obviously, material samples take up more space than books or slides, and a firm that specializes in planning and feasibility studies probably relies heavily on a large collection of research reports, demographic studies, and the like. The practitioner will probably be surprised at the total volume of library-type material to be found scattered at individual work stations, and clearing a discrete area large enough to accommodate it all may present a problem. Standard library shelving comes in three-foot sections, with a base and six shelves reaching 90 in. in height. A rule of thumb is to allow 9–12 in. of empty space per shelf for growth. The library should be centrally located and easily accessible to encourage frequent use by staff members. Study desks and seating are necessary, in addition to a work station for the librarian and any clerical support. A card catalog and a book truck or two will also be required. Library procedures and information retrieval are ideally suited to computerization, so provision should be made for terminals, if not at the time the library is organized, then in the near future. Positioning a photocopier in or near the library is also a consideration.

Establishing a budget requires some understanding of the firm's information needs. The library will probably use some special supplies such as catalog cards in addition to the usual office supplies, but the cost of books and periodicals may be difficult to estimate for the first year. Business resources and other materials used for job development, for example, tend to be quite expensive, but by the same token, a well-managed newspaper and journal routing system maintained by the library can eliminate redundant subscriptions. Here, an analysis of the existing collections by an experienced architectural librarian may be helpful, or the firm may choose to go without a budget for the first year in order to monitor actual expenses. In succeeding years, budget development and preparation should be the responsibility of the librarian.

Procedures. The purpose of instituting procedures in the firm library is to exert control over the material and information it contains, from ordering and purchasing through dissemination to and use by other members of the firm. Generally speaking, standard library technical functions are the identification, cataloguing, and circulation of material relevant to the parent organization's purposes.

There are many sources for identifying architectural material for possible inclusion in the firm library. Sonja Nielsen, in her article "Information Resources: An Expert's List of Books You May Need" (1), describes an all-purpose core collection. Association journals, in both the design and library fields, review new publications and carry ads for new titles. References and citations in books and journal articles, which should be scanned regularly by the librarian, are helpful guides to material which may not show up elsewhere. Most publishers concentrate on specific fields or areas of reader interest, and their catalogues and promotional mailings alert the librarian to current and forthcoming titles. Architectural bookstores, often affiliated with or run by local AIA chapters, are becoming more common; many also issue catalogues or booklists. The AIA Information Center and many architecture school libraries regularly publish accessions lists that note titles recently added to their collections. Other members of the firm should be encouraged to submit suggestions based on their own reading and research as well as current project needs. Bibliographies may suggest material that is not necessarily new, but still useful in expanding a collection in specific areas.

Periodicals may be located through two reference sources. *Ulrich's International Periodicals Directory* (2) is an annual publication found on any public or university library reference shelf. Entries, which include editorial and subscription information, are grouped in broad subject categories, cross-indexed alphabetically by title. Of particular interest to the design firm are the headings "Architecture," "Building and Construction," "Business," and "Interior Decoration." Frances C. Gretes has compiled the *Directory of International Periodicals and Newsletters on the Built Environment* (3) that groups titles into 14 categories more closely aligned to architectural practice. Three indexes cross-reference titles alphabetically, geographically, and by subject.

The librarian should be the control point for all publications purchased with firm funds, even if the material is to be a personal desk copy. This policy minimizes unnecessary or unwitting duplication, but still allows for individual needs. It is particularly useful in the case of periodicals, for each title must be recorded and each issue checked in as it arrives. Missing issues can thus be claimed promptly, an unlikely occurrence if the magazine is sent directly to the firm member. Centralizing subscriptions makes possible an annual, across-the-board evaluation of titles at renewal time. Even free publications should be checked in and scrutinized once a year for their value to the firm, for they use firm resources in the form of staff time and shelf or storage space.

Periodicals play a critical role in the design professional's current awareness, and the firm librarian is responsible for routing titles to the appropriate staff. This process has built into it several problems without easy solution. The first is the hierarchy of the list itself, whose name goes where. Compounding the problem of office politics is the time lag factor and staff members who hold on to an issue too long. The librarian can retaliate by putting these people at the bottom of the list, but again, office politics may intervene. A colleague may borrow the issue just for a moment and forget about it or lose it. In some cases, routing only a table of contents is a possibility, but puts the onus of keeping up on the staff member. Finally, currency of routing lists can be a major headache, although the advent of inexpensive database management systems for microcomputers promises relief to the librarian.

Circulation of books and other materials presents its own set of problems. Again, the issue is control, the ability to identify the current location of a book, catalogue, or sample. The most common method is a check-out card in a pocket attached to the item, a time-consuming processing task, but still the most effective. Again, automation heralds an improvement in the form of bar coding for the firm willing to invest in the hardware and software. Loan periods are generally unnecessary in the firm setting, because theoretically an item checked out needed by others is easily retrieved. An exception is reference material, such as association directories, telephone books, etc, that should be allowed to leave the library only for a few hours or overnight.

A good vehicle for communicating library acquisitions, policies, etc, to other staff is a regularly issued newsletter or accessions list. Physical display of book jackets and periodicals may also be an effective way to alert staff to new material, particularly if the library has a bulletin board or other display mechanism in a heavily trafficked area.

Classification Systems

Organizing and retrieving systems for information are two different, although often confused, systems. An organizing framework or structure provides a method for the physical arrangement of material on a shelf or in a drawer. Generally, like items are placed next or close to one another, to make browsing easy. A retrieval system, however, operates independently of the physical organization or location of information. Instead, it provides more points of access, generally based on vocabulary or a controlled list of terms. In the library setting, these two systems are represented, for example, by the Library of Congress classification system and its subject heading list. The librarian catalogues material by describing its unique characteristics (author, title, etc), places it in the proper spot in the classification system by assigning a call number, which is also the signpost to the item's place on the shelf, and finally adds further access points in the form of subject headings. The latter take the user from the card catalog to the shelf.

The problem for the firm librarian is that commonly used classification systems such as Dewey decimal or Library of Congress are designed to organize man's body of knowledge in general and are at the same time too complex for the nonlibrarian to administer, as well as not detailed enough to be useful to the architect. There are, in fact, no comprehensive classification or retrieval systems that completely meet the information needs of the practicing design professional and thus have instant applicability. At present, the most widely used classification system is the 16-division format of the old *Uniform Construction Index,* which was developed for the organization of project-related information for use by specification writers. This format, which mimics the chronological sequence of the construction process, works well for the filing and retrieval of project- and product-related data, but again, it does not suffice for all of a firm's information needs. The latest, most ambitious attempt to develop a controlled vocabulary is the *Art and Architecture Thesaurus,* a program of the Getty Trust. The novel aspect of the *AAT* is that it is a hierarchical, ie, relational, structure rather than a strictly alphabetical one. The project has been endorsed by many groups, and is currently being tested by several institutions, but the drawback for the practitioner and the firm library is its strong scholarly and academic orientation.

The solution for many firms is to use several systems, matching material with the appropriate classification scheme. Thus product literature is arranged by the 16 divisions; books, if the firm has a librarian, more often follow the Library of Congress system; if not, they are arranged loosely by subject. Reference and vertical files of clippings, articles, and other ephemera can be organized alphabetically by building type and technological issue.

Slides, photographs, and material samples are three other collections that the librarian often manages, and the nature of each requires special consideration in cataloguing and storage. Slides and photographs are used most commonly in marketing and promotion, and working copies are generally arranged accordingly. Each slide must be labeled for identification and filing purposes, and should be marked (with a red dot, for example) for easy insertion in a carousel or other projection device. Original images of the firm's work should be treated as archival record material, screened for quality before addition to the collection, and remounted from cardboard frames to plastic. These slides are filed in an order conforming to the project archives, while working copies may be arranged alphabetically by project name under building or project type. It is possible to maintain project number sequence as the organizing format if the librarian devises a card catalog or other retrieval mechanism to permit subject access. Boiler plate presentation slides should be stored together, and frequently used presentations can be shelved in boxed carousels. If the firm's slides are heavily used, the inconvenience caused by inevitable loss, damage, or change in image quality can be minimized by making multiple copies of each. These should be reviewed periodically for usefulness and color degradation. The actual storage medium depends on the firm's needs and financial resources. Acetate sleeves in three-ring binders or files may be sufficient for a small collection, protecting the slides from handling while allowing easy browsing. Special steel slide cabinets

are available, some which store the slide like a 3 × 5 in. card, so that the user must pull out each to examine it. Others store the slides on light-table-like trays, which pull in and out of the cabinet. Wooden cabinets should be avoided, as the acidity in the wood can damage the slides.

Photographs, because of their expense, exist in much smaller numbers in the firm library. Negatives and one print should be treated as the archival copies, and the others filed like the slides. Acid-free folders are useful for storage.

Critical to the successful operation of a design firm, samples present, as a category of information resources, the greatest challenge to the librarian or resource specialist. Samples of architectural products are an extension of product literature and, as such, can at least be catalogued, if not assigned additional access terms, according to the 16-division format. This is not quite adequate for interiors and furnishings samples, and for this, the librarian is left to his or her own devices. Physically similar samples should be stored together, alphabetically by manufacturer, for economy of space as well as for browsing purposes. An indexing system is mandatory, to provide cross-references to particular qualities or uses. As with product literature, currency of the material is of great importance, as is a good working relationship with the manufacturers' representatives. The firm might consider hiring an experienced consultant to set up the samples library and indexing system, which could then be maintained by others.

Records Management and the Firm Archives

The architectural firm keeps project records to document its work for promotional, reference, historical, and legal reasons. The sheer bulk of a project's contract documents, to say nothing of the supporting material, presents a daunting problem: how to store masses of information captured on diverse, often unstable, materials and in diverse formats. Expediency plays an unfortunate role in the documentation of the built environment. All too often, the firm does not take the time to analyze its records, set up an efficient retention schedule, and establish a process for transferring documents of permanent value to its archives. This level of organization does, however, pay off immediately in researching past work for a new project or a new promotional angle, in defending a lawsuit, or in designing an addition to an old project.

A records management and retention program provides the firm with a process for automatically clearing files of nonessential material, creating an index to files and past projects, and preparing material for organized storage. Retention schedules establish time periods for keeping file material and other documents on hand before they are either destroyed or placed in permanent archival storage. Here, important considerations are statutes of limitation and any applicable court decisions on liability. Conversion of some types of records to microfilm or microfiche is also a possibility, contingent on both legal requirements and the kind of use the material is expected to receive. Appropriate legal and financial counsel should be consulted before any procedure is adopted that involves the destruction of material.

Time takes its toll on all material, no matter how carefully preserved or stored, and some of the processes used to create architectural records and project files are literally self-destructive. Colors fade, inks transfer, paper brittles, and rolls of drawings are easily damaged because of their bulk. Temperature, light, and humidity controls are necessary for the permanent retention of material, as are properly constructed, acid-free folders, tubes, and boxes. Models are probably best treated by careful documentation through photography and presentation to the client. Computerized specifications and computer-aided design and drafting have added a new dimension in which changes or decisions are not documented because of the technology's instant update capabilities.

While it is clear that old records are invaluable in restoration, preservation, and renovation work, the contemporary firm may balk at the expense of and time commitment for permanently preserving the records of their own work, and modesty may prevent them from understanding fully the importance of their records to history. It may be useful to discuss the firm's situation with the local historical society or a regional architectural records repository.

Research

Directories. Two standard reference sources all too often unknown but very useful to the practitioner are the *Encyclopedia of Associations* (4) and *National Trade and Professional Associations* (5). These annual compilations list thousands of associations alphabetically and by subject, with a descriptive paragraph on the organization's purpose, membership, scope of activities (standing committees, for example), and publications. They are excellent guides to sources of statistics, standards, programming and design data, consultants and experts, and general information about a particular field or activity.

Indexes. These tools provide access to periodical articles in every imaginable field. Most can be found in large public, university, or architecture school libraries. There are many document delivery services that will provide a copy of articles not found in any local institution. The following are particularly appropriate for the practitioner (sources are listed in Table 1):

1. *Applied Science & Technology Index.* A subject index to approximately 340 English-language periodicals, this covers construction in addition to aeronautics, automation, chemistry, electricity, engineering, geology, metallurgy, industrial and mechanical arts, machinery, physics, and transportation.

2. *Architectural Index.* This annual index covers 11 periodicals in the fields of architecture, urban planning, landscape architecture, and interior design. Subject headings consist primarily of building types and geographic locations. Works by specific architects or firms can be found under the heading "Architect or designer."

3. *Architectural Periodicals Index.* Published by the British Architectural Library, this quarterly index

covers 450 periodicals from 45 countries on current practice, historical aspects of architecture and the allied arts, construction technology, design and environmental studies, and planning. Citations are arranged by subject and indexed by name; a geographic index is included in the annual cumulation.

4. *Art Index.* Issued quarterly, with annual cumulations, this index covers approximately 230 American and foreign periodicals in the fields of architecture, industrial design, urban planning, landscape architecture and interior design, in addition to archaeology, art and art history, photography and films, and related subjects. Arrangement is by author and subject in one alphabet.

5. *Avery Index to Architectural Periodicals.* This index, which covers nearly 550 American and foreign periodicals, some of them back to the nineteenth century, is extremely useful for historical research. It indexes articles on architecture, archaeology, the decorative arts, interior design, furniture, landscape architecture, housing, and urban planning. A multivolume basic set is supplemented periodically.

6. *Business Periodicals Index.* This is a subject index to approximately 300 periodicals in the fields of accounting, advertising, banking and finance, general business, insurance, labor and management, public administration, taxation, and specific industries, businesses, and trades. It is issued monthly, except August, with quarterly and annual cumulations.

7. *Engineering Index.* This international index is an alphabetical subject listing, often with abstracts, of engineering professional and trade journals, society publications, scientific and technical associations, universities, laboratories, research institutions, government agencies, and industrial organizations. Conferences, symposia, nonserial publications, and selected books are also covered. Monthly issues are cumulated annually.

8. *Reader's Guide to Periodical Literature.* This author–subject index covers approximately 180 U.S. periodicals of general interest, as well as a selection of nontechnical titles representing important scientific and subject areas. It is often useful for finding articles on more common building types and for finding articles on architectural topics in the popular press. It is issued monthly, with periodic and annual cumulations.

9. *Social Sciences Index.* Covering over 300 periodicals in the fields of anthropology, area studies, economics, environmental science, psychology, public administration, sociology, and other related subjects, this index is published quarterly, with an annual cumulation.

Data bases. Computers have taken the periodical index and the card catalog one step further in scope, currency, and ease of retrieval by making possible the creation of huge on-line data bases. Over two thousand data bases now exist worldwide which provide access to information in newspapers, journals, reports, conference proceedings,

Table 1. Indexes Available to Practitioners

Index	Source
Applied Science & Technology Index *Art Index* *Business Periodicals Index* *Reader's Guide to Periodical Literature* *Social Sciences Index*	H. W. Wilson Company 950 University Avenue Bronx, N.Y. 10452
Architectural Index	P.O. Box 1168 Boulder, Colo. 80306
Architectural Periodicals Index	RIBA Publications, Ltd. Finsbury Mission Moreland Street London EC1V 8VB UK
Avery Index to Architectural Periodicals	G. K. Hall & Co. 70 Lincoln Street Boston, Mass. 02111
Engineering Index	United Engineering Center 1345 East 47th Street New York, N.Y. 10017

symposia, and books, as well as statistical and financial data, company profiles, patent research, and medical and scientific data. The results of a database search range from a list of bibliographic references to periodical articles, reports, and abstracts, to names, addresses, statistics, and annual company reports. They may be used to locate design and technical information, to find client background and industry research, to identify competitors and consultants, and to track demographic trends (sources are listed in Table 2).

Other Libraries. The public library is a sadly underused local resource by firms without the expertise of a professional librarian. While they vary widely in terms of size and sophistication and are least likely to carry specifically design-related information, the public libraries can provide valuable general and business reference and information to the practitioner. Business reference librarians in the public arena have pioneered fee-for-service reference–research relationships with corporate clients, which have great potential for the architectural firm.

The firm also has much to gain by using the skills of the academic architectural librarian and the resources of the academic architectural library. Again, size and sophistication of the institution are variables, and, because the academic librarian's primary responsibility is to the students and faculty, the firm may not be able to get all of the help it needs. A working relationship with the general reference and business librarians is also valuable to

Table 2. Database Suppliers and Vendors

Bibliographic Retrieval Services 1200 Route 7 Latham, N.Y. 12110	Pergamon Infoline, Inc. 1340 Old Chain Bridge Road Suite 300 McLean, Va. 22101
DIALOG Information Retrieval Service 3460 Hillview Avenue Palo Alto, Calif. 94304	Systems Development Corporation ORBIT Search Service 2525 Colorado Avenue Santa Monica, Calif. 90406
Cooperative Library Agency for Systems and Services 1415 Koll Circle Suite 101 San Jose, Calif. 95112-4698	H. W. Wilson Company 950 University Avenue Bronx, N.Y. 10452
Dow Jones & Co., Inc. Information Services Division P.O. Box 300 Princeton, N.J. 08540	Newsnet 945 Haverford Road Bryn Mawr, Pa. 19010
Mead Data Central P.O. Box 1830 Dayton, Ohio 45401	

Table 3. Related Associations Accessible to the Practitioner

American Institute of Architects Information Center 1735 New York Avenue, N.W. Washington, D.C. 20006 (202) 626-7493	Association of Architecture School Librarians % Association of Collegiate Schools of Architecture 1735 New York Avenue, N.W. Washington, D.C. 20006 (202) 785-2324
American Library Association 50 East Huron Street Chicago, Ill. 60611 (312) 944-6780	Association of Records Managers and Administrators 4200 Somerset Suite 215 Prairie Village, Kans. 66208 (913) 341-3808
Art Libraries Society of North America (ARLIS/NA) 3900 East Timrod Street Tucson, Ariz. 85711 (602) 881-8479	Council of Planning Librarians 1313 East 60th Street Chicago, Ill. 60637 (312) 947-2007
Associated Information Managers 1776 East Jefferson Street Rockville, Md. 20852 (301) 231-7447	Special Libraries Association 1700 18th Street, N.W. Washington, D.C. 20009 (202) 234-4700
Association of Architectural Librarians % AIA Information Center 1735 New York Avenue, N.W. Washington, D.C. 20006 (202) 626-7493	Visual Resources Association % Department of the History of Art Tappan Hall The University of Michigan Ann Arbor, Mich. 48109

the practitioner, and again the institution may establish a fee-for-service arrangement.

AIA members and their employees may avail themselves of the services of the AIA Information Center, which was established to assist the profession in meeting its information needs. It is a fully functioning library offering traditional research and reference services, book loans, rental or sale of audiovisual materials, and access to the Institute's archives or historical records. The collections focus on practice management issues, especially those unique to the design firm, as well as building type design data. Also covered are contemporary architecture, architectural history, and the related disciplines. Table 3 lists related associations available to the practitioner.

BIBLIOGRAPHY

1. Sonja Nielsen, "Information Resources: An Expert's List of Books You May Need," *Archit. Rec., 172,* 39 (Aug. 1984).

2. *Ulrich's International Periodicals Directory,* R. R. Bowker Co., New York, published annually.

3. F. C. Gretes, *Directory of International Periodicals and Newsletters on the Built Environment,* Van Nostrand Reinhold Co., Inc., New York, 1986.

4. *Encyclopedia of Associations,* Gale Research Company, Detroit, Mich., published annually.

5. *National Trade and Professional Associations,* Columbia Books, Washington, D.C., published annually.

General References

American Institute of Architects Foundation, *Architectural Records Management,* Washington, D.C., 1985.

D. K. Ballast, *The Architect's Handbook,* Prentice-Hall, Inc., Prentice-Hall Press, Englewood Cliffs, N.J.

J. Boucher, "Does Your Firm Need a Technical Library?" *Consult. Eng., 44,* 70 (Dec. 1974).

J. Boucher, "How to Fit a Library into Your Office," *Consult. Eng., 50,* 68 (Feb. 1978).

J. Boucher, " 'Launching' Your Own Library," *Consult. Eng., 45,* 56 (Aug. 1975).

V. J. Bradford, ed., *Information Sources in Architecture,* Butterworth & Co. (Publishers) Ltd., Kent, UK, 1983.

C. H. Burnette, *The Architect's Access to Information: Constraints on the Architect's Capacity to Seek, Obtain, Translate and Apply Information,* Center for Building Technology, National Bureau of Standards, Washington, D.C., 1979.

C. H. Burnette, *Making Information Useful to Architects: an Analysis and Compendium of Practical Forms for the Delivery of Information,* Center for Building Technology, National Bureau of Standards, Washington, D.C., 1979.

P. Calderhead, ed., *Libraries for Professional Practice,* Architectural Press, London, 1972.

H. C. Dandekar, ed., *Planner's Use of Information: Techniques for Collection, Organization, and Communication,* Hutchinson Ross, Stroudsburg, Pa., 1982.

W. van Erp, *The Architecture–Interior–Design–Engineering Library: a Report on Current Practices,* Professional Services Management Journal, Newington, Conn., 1981.

F. C. Gretes, "Computers: Need Information? You Can Get a Lot with On-line Retrieval Services," *Archit. Rec., 170,* 43 (Mar. 1982).

K. L. Kalt, "Color Coding the Firm's Library for Fast, Simple Retrieval," *Archit. Rec., 167,* 66 (Jan. 1980).

K. L. Kalt, *Organizing and Managing Information in Architectural, Engineering and Consulting Firms: Analysis of a 1978 Survey,* Professional Services Management Journal, Newington, Conn., 1979.

Managing the Library: A Collection of Past Articles from Professional Services Management Journal, Professional Services Management Journal, Newington, Conn., 1981.

Massachusetts Committee for the Preservation of Architectural Records, *Records in Architectural Offices: Suggestions for the Proper Organization, Storage, and Conservation of Architectural Office Archives.* Cambridge, Mass., 1980.

M. Slavin, "Interiors Business: the Resourceful Backup," *Interiors,* **141,** 182 (May 1982).

STEPHANIE CORMIER BYRNES
American Institute of Architects
Washington, D.C.

ARCHITECTURAL PRESS, U.S.

THE ARCHITECTURAL PRESS IN THE FIELD OF PUBLISHING

A review of the first 100 years of journalism devoted to the various aspects of architecture in the U.S. provides a record and a sense of the sources for the design of buildings. To define more closely the scope of this survey, it is useful to consider the range of audiences that periodicals devoted to architectural interests may address. First, a serial can attempt to educate the public in order to broaden its appreciation of architecture and make the role of the design professional and the development of technical advances more widely understood. Such a journal may be of little or no interest to the professional, for the level of the discussion assumes the reader has limited familiarity with the issues at hand. In the following essay, most of the journals devoted to popular interests have been omitted. For a more detailed discussion of the role of popular architectural literature see Ref. 1. Second, a periodical may be cast so as to serve a community of interests including architecture. The readership of this type of journal may encompass carpenters, builders, contractors, material suppliers, or allied tradespersons, as well as architects, landscape architects, and planners in order to make it a viable economic venture. For the professional, the question is often how much a publication contains that cannot easily be obtained elsewhere. In the discussion that follows, some of these journals are included, to the degree that they are concerned with architectural matters. Third, there is the serial that is cast as a specialized, technical journal; that is, it has been published largely in the interest of those who have been trained in or practice architecture. The purpose of such a publication is largely to record the trends and developments of the leaders in the profession, which is in some instances conceived to include allied design fields. The professional journal may be of limited interest to a layperson because it presupposes a familiarity with the history, theory, and language of the profession. The subject at hand, then, is the professional architectural journals that were published during the latter half of the nineteenth century and the first half of the twentieth century. Taken together, they illustrate the roles of publishers, editors, journalists, critics, theorists, designers, renderers, draftspersons, specification writers, advertisers, and real estate agents—in fact, the role of every occupation involved with design.

This article is primarily a chronological review, highlighting events and personalities while considering and comparing the publications for both their visual and verbal content. The divisions between sections are roughly related to the major interruptions in building activity and corresponding breaks in the development of architectural journalism. As will be shown, the early, sporadic journalism in New York, Philadelphia, and Boston grew into a strong group of professional voices by the early 1880s. By the second half of that decade, there was a plethora of architectural publishing, supported by local and regional interests in architecture and building. After the collapse of many of these journals in the early 1890s, comparatively few periodicals rose at the turn of the century, and some specialization occurred. More complex relationships between publishers and advertisers grew in the 1920s, especially with the backing of trade organizations and building industries. Periodicals devoted to draftsmen, designers, and practicing architects were developed and then absorbed into more diverse publications. A major shift in aesthetic concerns—the modern movement—began to occur during the late 1920s, but during the lean years of the Depression, there was little opportunity for the realization of these ideas. After World War II, the surge of building activity gave rise to an emphasis on practice, rather than theory, and issues of social responsibility became frequent topics in professional journalism in the third quarter of the century.

EARLY ATTEMPTS AT ARCHITECTURAL JOURNALISM

The roots of nineteenth-century professional journalism in the United States lie in the United Kingdom. Just as their builders' guides and serialized architectural portfolios provided U.S. professionals with a model, so too the first periodicals in the UK were longingly looked at by architects in this country. As early as 1770, *Builder's Magazine* had appeared in London, although it was devoted to a much broader range of activity than construction. The first architectural magazine to gain widespread respect in the profession was *The Architectural Magazine and Journal of Improvement in Architecture, Building and Furnishing and in the Various Arts and Trades Connected Therewith . . . ,* conducted by John Claudius Loudon from March 1834 through January 1839. With Loudon's *Magazine* as the model, other journals were soon begun. The monthly *Civil Engineer and Architect's Journal* was begun in 1837, *Surveyor, Engineer and Architect* commenced in 1840, and *Builder, An Illustrated Weekly Magazine for the Drawing-room, the Studio, the Office, the Workshop and the Cottage,* first dated December 31, 1842, firmly established the place of the technical architectural periodical in the UK (2).

Although the need to address the profession existed in the United States during the early nineteenth century, there were few attempts to launch a serial completely devoted to architecture. The audience was too limited, and the investment was too great for subscribers to bear alone. Building materials suppliers were not numerous enough and were only beginning to establish a regional distribution network that would necessitate large-scale advertising.

The Philadelphia architect John Haviland put out a prospectus for a U.S. architectural magazine as early as 1830 or 1831, but no indication has been found that the attempt ever came to fruition. In the 1840s, architectural concerns were included in the agricultural, horticultural, and religious press and, to a lesser degree, in a few journals directed toward mechanics and investors. These, however, were not professionally oriented.

The first journal devoted to architectural professionals was *The Architects' and Mechanics' Journal. A Weekly Illustrated Record of the Progress of Architecture, Building, Engineering, Mechanics, Science, The Fine Arts, etc.,* begun in October 1859 by the owners, printers, publishers, and editors Alexander Harthill, Stephen Smith, and J. Dimon Smith of New York. A period of booming construction activity, the absence of any U.S. journal devoted to the interests of those connected with building enterprise, and an awareness of the success of professional journals in the UK convinced these booksellers that the time was right to launch such a venture. It was an impressive effort. Although few illustrations were included, virtually every aspect of construction was addressed. Aesthetic and critical essays, notes on materials and finishes, structural and mechanical systems, new appliances and inventions, comments on architectural education, gardening, horticulture, bridge construction, and tenements were all included, along with news of the building progress in various cities gleaned from newspapers or submitted by correspondents from across the country. The *Architects' and Mechanics' Journal* also published papers presented before the American Institute of Architects (AIA). Although it was an excellent journal, the nearly complete paralysis of building operations that occurred during the Civil War apparently affected the advertising income enough that Harthill and Company found it impossible to continue beyond 1861.

The Reconstruction era can be considered the "dark ages" of architectural journalism. Aside from the pattern books produced by the architectural bookseller Amos Jackson Bicknell, little was published of interest to the professional. Journals that broadened their appeal to address builders, carpenters, and mechanics in the building trades were the first to achieve success. The first of these was the *American Builder and Journal of Art,* a pragmatic monthly begun in Chicago in 1868 by the carpenter, architect, publisher, and editor Charles Lakey. Wider in scope than either the defunct *Architects' and Mechanics' Journal* or the contemporary *Manufacturer and Builder,* Lakey's monthly attempted to address a number of aspects of the building process. Reports of construction in New York and Chicago, as well as in Boston, Newport, and Philadelphia, kept the readers informed of the latest developments. The designs of Chicago architects, including William L. B. Jenney, Gourdon Randall, and James Cochrane, were succeeded by those of Edward Kendall and Lawrence B. Valk when Lakey's *Journal* moved to New York City in January 1873. Perhaps the most attractive feature of the $3/year *Journal* was the "Supplement Sheets," large tissue paper

foldouts with lithographed scale drawings, chiefly details. Lakey's *Journal* was the first, but by no means the last, periodical to cater to those in the construction trades. *Carpentry and Building,* begun in January 1879 by the New York publisher David Williams, became the largest and best-known journal in this field, although it never included the designs of a major architect. *Carpentry and Building* boasted a record-setting circulation of 20,000 copies in 1890, whereas the *Architects' and Builders' Edition* of the *Scientific American* had a circulation of 12,000, and the successor to Lakey's serial, the *Builder and Woodworker,* claimed a circulation of 8000. These figures reflected the difficulty of maintaining a number of journals devoted specifically to the interests of architects, who were much smaller in number than other members of the building trades.

Philadelphia lagged behind in the production of architectural periodicals in the nineteenth century, never developing a coterie of architects who would support one. The few journals that were published there were of brief duration. The most notable example was the *Architectural Review and American Builder's Journal,* began in July 1868 under the guidance of the architect Samuel Sloan, apparently with the assistance of Charles Lukens and Charles P. Dwyer. Sloan mistakenly believed that his was the first periodical on architecture and construction to be issued in the United States and set forth an ambitious program to make up for this deficiency. His journal included, among other things, discussions of public and private buildings, monumental and sepulchral architecture, naval construction, ornament and furniture, the strengths of materials, management of lumber yards, ornamental trees and landscape gardening, and instruction in drawing and perspective. A considerable number of fine cuts were included in each issue, displaying the designs that were proposed or being built in such cities as Boston, New York, Baltimore, Washington, and Pittsburgh, in addition to those for which Sloan was responsible in and around Philadelphia. Although the *Review* was never adopted as the official organ of the AIA, it carried regular news of the events sponsored by that organization, its committee reports, and publication notices (3).

Although the *Review* was widely distributed, this was not enough to make up for the lack of local support. It ceased publication with the November 1870 issue, although not before inspiring some competition. The *American Architect and Builder's Monthly* was even more short-lived, lasting only from March 1870 through January 1871. Its editor, the architect-lithographer Benjamin Linfoot, is known to have delineated at least one plate for Sloan's *Review,* so he knew the challenge that lay before him. Correspondents in New York, Boston, Philadelphia, Buffalo, Chicago, Montreal, Baltimore, New Orleans, Louisville, and San Francisco made this periodical truly nationwide in scope. The *American Architect and Builder's Monthly* was an extra quarto size publication, and with four full-page plates, a double plate, and 16 pages of letterpress, was considerably more elegant than the *Review.* Unfortunately, like Sloan, Linfoot did not garner enough financial support to ensure the continuation of his journal.

When a periodical directed toward architectural interests finally did take root in Philadelphia, it had none of the high goals and far-flung professional connections of either of its predecessors. The *Builder and Real Estate Advocate,* begun in September 1883, was a periodical devoted principally to local interests and supported by many of the building materials suppliers in the metropolitan area. Edited by Frank T. Woods and Frank Woods, the *Builder and Real Estate Advocate* was a vociferous proponent of a builders' exchange in Philadelphia. It regularly recorded the projects on the drawing boards of the major practitioners in the area, including Addison Hutton, George W. Hewitt & Brothers, Walter Cope, and John and Emlyn Stewardson. However, a considerable amount of the text and commentary was derived from architectural and building journals published elsewhere in the country, chiefly in New York City. The Woods's journal failed by 1891, and remarkably enough, Philadelphia never developed a strong architectural voice of its own.

Compared with New York and Philadelphia, Boston's efforts at the publication of an architectural journal came a little later and were addressed to the professional architect, not the carpenter. In keeping with the larger literary tradition of the Northeast, the first periodicals in this area emphasized architecture as a fine art and on the whole avoided the practicality and commercial overtones that were so prevalent in New York.

The publishing firm initially responsible for establishing and maintaining this high tone of aesthetic and artistic merit was that of James R. Osgood and Company, recognized successors to James T. Fields and Company, a publishing house that had a distinguished line of 250 authors and four periodicals to its credit. Osgood's interest in architectural serials seems to have arisen from his interest in reproducing accurate illustrations using the heliotype process. Almost immediately upon installing the new process, it was put to use with the publication of the *Architectural Sketch-Book,* a monthly collection of drawings of the Portfolio Club, a group of talented draftsmen and architects, most of whom practiced in the Boston area. Published from July 1873 through September 1876, it was noted for its clarity of tonal reproduction. H. H. Richardson must have been impressed, for he agreed to act as Editor when Osgood published the *New York Sketch-Book of Architecture,* begun in January 1874 and continued for the next two years.

Thus, by the time of the U.S. centennial, the desirability of a professional journal was clear from the numerous prior attempts and because the techniques necessary to provide clear and faithful illustrations had been perfected.

PROFESSIONAL VOICES RISE (1876–1891)

The first professional journal to have a significant long-term impact was the *American Architect and Building News,* begun in January 1876, published in Boston by James R. Osgood and Company. It was unusual in that it was a weekly, undoubtedly following the lead established by the *Builder* in the UK, which had proven so influential. Apparently, the *American Architect and Building News* was begun at the behest of William Robert Ware, Professor

of Architecture at the Massachusetts Institute of Technology (MIT), who convinced Osgood of the necessity of such a venture. It may have been Ware, too, who suggested the journal's first editor, William Pitt Preble Longfellow, an architect, educator, and author. It was owing to Longfellow, a Harvard graduate, that the first years of the new publication took on a higher tone and a more consciously intellectual character than others of the time. Aided by an able assistant editor, William Rotch Ware (nephew of William Robert Ware), another Harvard graduate, who had attended classes in architecture at MIT and the Ecole des Beaux Arts in Paris, the *American Architect and Building News* was extraordinary for having such well-educated guidance. Its attitudes would not greatly change; when Longfellow stepped down from his editorial chair in 1881, Ware succeeded him in the task, one that would occupy him for nearly three decades.

From the outset, it was intended that this journal cover ground similar to that of the well-known publications in the UK, and that it be nationwide in scope. Even before Osgood published the first issue, the *American Architect and Building News* was accepted as the organ of the AIA. Believing the journal to be at the cutting edge of the profession, its editors assumed an air of self-righteousness when commenting upon any building publications that did not have similar lofty ideals. Considering the number of architects in the country, the journal was widely read, although it never approached the influence of the more broadly based building journals. From a circulation of about 500 copies in the late 1870s, rising to just above 2000 copies around 1880, the *American Architect and Building News* was not well known outside the profession. With the introduction of other, specialized editions during the 1880s, it grew to about 7500 copies by the early 1890s, topping the subscription figures of all of the other architectural journals in the country. As will be shown, its importance is in the fact that it set the tone for a number of regional journals, particularly those in the Midwest.

The first major contribution to architectural journalism in New York was *Building. An Architectural Monthly, Treating on All Matters of Interest to the Building Trades,* begun in October 1882 by the editor and publisher William T. Comstock, who had previously been best known for his role as a partner with Amos Jackson Bicknell in the pattern book business. *Building* contained "articles on different subjects. . . . written by men thoroughly acquainted with the theoretical and practical questions pertaining to their own departments"(4). Comstock attempted to address the growing profession of architecture in an active, commercially oriented city. The initial issues included, for example, articles on heating and ventilation, notes on the Tudor period, the first of a series on perspective drawing, specifications for a city residence, a hillside cottage design, and notes on industrial products, building materials, and construction from points as diverse as Denver and Philadelphia. Book reviews of many of the texts that Comstock was publishing and the obituaries of noted architects around the country made this more than simply a New York City-based journal.

With the opening of its second year, *Building* added a new feature in keeping with the catholicity of Comstock's approach. This was the "Special Illustrated Edition," which contained a number of full-page lithographic illustrations selected from leading foreign publications, in addition to the regular plates. In the first issue of this edition, for example, there were 19 selections from six foreign architectural, decorative arts, and furniture journals. Considering that there were then about two dozen foreign journals dealing with architecture, carpentry, and building in France, with perhaps another three dozen periodicals being produced in the UK and Germany, the eclecticism of *Building* must be appreciated as having provided a service of considerable merit.

Throughout the 1880s and into the early 1890s, *Building* was the principal architectural journal produced in New York City, achieving a circulation of about 5000 copies. In January 1886, it followed the lead of the *American Architect and Building News* by becoming a weekly, and then reverted to a monthly in December 1886. In January 1890, it was renamed *Architecture and Building* to reflect more accurately its concerns and its audience.

When the first architectural journal to be published in Chicago appeared in February 1883, it followed the format of previous serials. *The Inland Architect and Builder. A Monthly Journal Devoted to Architecture, Construction, Decoration and Furnishing in the West* was produced by the Inland Publishing Company. A careful canvass had convinced its projectors that a regional journal would be welcomed, and an experienced editor, Robert Craik McLean, was chosen to direct it. The first issue was dated February 1883. In general, the format was that established by the *American Architect and Building News,* but there was little opinion and no specific theoretical position of the editorial staff. The two major contributions of this journal were very obvious. First, it would prove to be an effective organizing tool for many midwestern architectural groups, including the Western Association of Architects (which adopted the *Inland Architect* as its official organ) and the Chicago Architectural Club. Second, the journal provided an unbiased forum for architects working in the surrounding states to display their work. The designs of William L. B. Jenney, Dankmar Adler, Louis Sullivan, Daniel H. Burnham, John W. Root, and many others were carried, providing a look at the latest buildings under construction in many smaller and more remote midwestern cities, towns, and villages (5).

At least one other Chicago-based publication should be mentioned, namely, the *Building Budget. A Journal of Architecture and Kindred Arts.* Begun in March 1885, this monthly was conducted by Henry Lord Gay, a New England-trained architect who had traveled in Europe and worked in Chicago under William W. Boyington before establishing his own office. This periodical was more broadly cast and larger in circulation, reaching 5000 copies by 1890, when it was absorbed by the *Northwestern Architect.* Gay was an outspoken proponent of the Permanent Exhibition of Building Materials and actively advocated it in the *Budget.* The Exhibition, perhaps modeled on the similar efforts of Bicknell in New York City, was a collection of materials and appliances from all branches of the building arts under one roof; it was a state-of-the-arts display. Although Gay defended the *Budget* as an architec-

tural and building educator, it came under attack for being too much of an advertising sheet. Perhaps more disappointing were the limited number of plates and indiscriminate choice of designs, which were often unimaginative. It did, however, carry reports and notices of various state and regional associations of architects, contractors, and builders, news of building activity from the metropolitan area, and readers' contributions from the surrounding states.

In San Francisco, the first professional journal was the *Quarterly Architectural Review,* begun in January 1879 by James E. Wolfe and Franklin P. Burnham, both architects. It included a broad range of architectural information in an effort to attract as much support as possible from the building community. Renamed the *California Architect and Building News* in January 1880, it also underwent changes in format, frequency, and publisher. Wolfe continued to set a similar tone, however, by reprinting articles from Lakey's *American Builder and Journal of Arts,* Williams' *Carpentry and Building,* and the *Manufacturer and Builder,* alongside excerpts from the *American Architect and Building News.* Wolfe seemed to prefer anything that arrived in the mail from the East over what the local designer had to offer. The character of this journal did not change until the mid-1880s, when it was influenced by a number of members of the newly formed San Francisco Chapter of the AIA. At its peak, near the end of the decade, it had reached a circulation of about 3800 copies. Another journal, the *Architectural News,* was begun in San Francisco in November 1890. Its emphasis was on architecture as an art, and the editor-architect Willis Polk intended to deal with only the best in design. However, it was discontinued after only three issues were published.

On the whole, the increase in the total number of professional journals after the Civil War was very impressive. Whereas in 1870 there were only three or four periodicals that dealt with architecture and building, in 1875 there were six, and in 1880 there were 10. The most significant growth occurred in the next decade. By the end of 1885, 22 journals were active, and five years later 46 were in circulation. It was during the 1880s that professionals in such cities as San Francisco, Denver, Washington, Atlanta, Indianapolis, Minneapolis, St. Paul, Kansas City, St. Louis, Syracuse, Cincinnati, Scranton, Galveston, and Richmond found that one or more local architectural publications existed to serve their interests. Thereafter, a precipitous decline occurred. More than a dozen journals failed between 1890 and 1895, and although attempts at beginning new ones were made, only 30 dealing with architecture and building were in operation at the turn of the century. This overall pattern of expansion and contraction follows the curve of construction activity over the same period. The relationship was not, however, simply a reflection of the amount of building news to be reported. Rather, it was based on a fact that had been noted by the AIA Committee on Architectural Periodicals in 1885: because such journals circulated "among a class who materially influence contracts for building materials," they attracted advertising, which greatly supplemented the limited income derived from subscriptions (6). Thus, when the generally poor economic health of the nation in the early 1890s caused building material suppliers to suffer for lack of sales, their advertising budgets dropped accordingly. This hurt many of the newly established journals, particularly those serving more rural regions of the country.

A LEANER AND STRONGER FIELD (1891–1917)

In an article published in July 1916, architect-educator A. D. F. Hamlin reviewed the progress in the previous quarter decade of U.S. architecture and commented on the development of specialized journalism. He wrote that there were two major professional journals that had long deserved the architect's attention. These were the *American Architect and Building News,* produced in Boston, and *Architecture and Building,* originating in New York City. Another New York City publication, the *Architectural Record,* was worthy of mention because it had a much-needed seriousness of artistic and literary purpose. In Boston, the *Architectural Review* was seen as "filling in the field" between the *Record* and the others previously mentioned, while in Chicago, the *Inland Architect* had been serving the interests of the Midwest. The *Western Architect,* first published in Minneapolis, was more recently established, and *Architecture,* another comparatively young serial, was making a specialty of photographic illustrations. Last, Hamlin mentioned the *Journal of the American Institute of Architects,* devoted to "scholarly and literary work" by virtue of its position as an official organ (7). As suggested by these observations, between the early 1890s and the temporary suspension of building activities after the United States entered World War I, there were considerably fewer professional journals than in the previous period. Further, those that were established took care to define their purposes more narrowly.

The *American Architect and Building News* suffered some comparatively lean years during the mid-1890s, but managed to survive despite the competition. There was surprisingly little change in the newsprint format, which had been established in 1876. A summary of recent news collected from a wide variety of sources began each issue. This was followed by four or five articles, often lectures, reprinted from other publications, or perhaps a review of a recent exhibition and the catalogue of the Architectural League or similar professional association. The letterpress was followed in the regular edition by approximately six plate illustrations, largely of U.S. work. In the imperial and international editions, six or eight additional plates featured buildings in Austria, the UK, France, and Germany. The typical issue then closed with minor headings: books and papers, societies, communications from readers, notes and clippings, and trade surveys.

The Editor, William Rotch Ware, had little assistance in assembling this weekly. Further, at the turn of the century, he complained that the *American Architect* was finding it difficult to obtain suitable plates for publication. Whereas leading architects once rushed their projects into print, now many of these individuals had large firms that undertook their own advertising. Some architects even thought they were doing the magazines a favor by allowing them to publish a photograph. Many firms had changed

in stature, new ones had come to the fore, and the leading personalities had changed. It was becoming increasingly clear that personal solicitation was necessary to gain the needed material.

The magazine moved to New York City in 1905, aware of the fact that the potential interaction with a greater number of professionals and advertisers could only help its position. With its circulation hovering at about 3000 copies, however, financial problems became more apparent. In May 1907, the *American Architect and Building News* was purchased by the Swetland Publishing Company, and on January 1, 1909, that firm also acquired the *Inland Architect.* The latter was merged with the former to create the *American Architect,* the shortened name being adopted as the "Building News" section discontinued (8). The new Editor, E. J. Rosencrans, and the Associate Editor, William H. Crocker, immediately attempted to get the journal on a firmer footing. They employed a more upbeat magazine format and increased the number of illustrations. A typical issue might have included an article featuring recent work, a report of the activities of the AIA or the Beaux Arts Society of Architects, a review of federal legislation, and editorial comment. Henry H. Saylor briefly joined the staff as Associate Editor in 1909, adding information on topics that would be useful in the office, such as model making, drafting, and the education of an architect.

A number of departments were begun in 1909, which seemed to help stabilize the magazine by delegating responsibility for it to more than the Editor and his assistant. The first was the monthly review of the "Current Architectural Press," an idea borrowed from a contemporary publication, the *Architectural Review.* The editorial staff of the *American Architect* clearly had its eye on trying to recapture the number one position in professional journalism that the magazine had once enjoyed.

In October 1910, the *American Architect* announced that Professor Charles F. Osborne of the School of Architecture at the University of Pennsylvania had assumed editorial direction. Osborne was to commute between New York and Philadelphia, devoting himself to editorial duties during the week and lecturing on Saturdays. The former Editor, Rosencrans, and the advertising manager, G. E. Sly, purchased the journal from Swetland and established a new publishing firm, The American Architect, Inc. Under the new management, advertising increased considerably. Subscribers were urged to study the advertisements as well as the articles and plates, for the value of the architect's services lay in his ability to provide quality buildings, and this began with a familiarity with the most recent building products.

A series of articles entitled "Notes From Europe," by Francis Swales, a series on the need for consistency in decorative treatment, and another on U.S. city planning carried the journal into the second decade of the twentieth century. Departments were added to deal with legal decisions and current commentary. "Building News" was reintroduced by 1916, giving architects throughout the country the chance to see their names and projects in print, and a photograph of a "Northern Italian Detail" was included in every issue.

While the *American Architect* struggled to maintain its position, Comstock's *Architecture and Building* began to gain in stature and support. Comstock recast his journal in the widest manner, but avoided his earlier tendency to borrow material from other publications. The journal, "devoted to art, architecture, archaeology, engineering, and decoration," was published weekly in direct competition with the Boston-based serial, which it soon overtook in number of subscribers, size, and content. Articles covered a wide range of topics and often appeared in serial form. Five or six large photolithographed plates, including foldouts on coated paper, captured the work of many architects and represented a wide variety of building types. With considerable help from a staff of professionals, regular departments were established to deal with architectural engineering, art notes, book reviews, current notes, industrial progress, personnel notes, and architectural societies and associations. Although the editorial commentary was largely devoted to activities in the New York metropolitan area, the advertising section contained not only the prices for building materials in New York and Chicago, but also notices from product manufacturers, architects, and craftsmen, notices for bids and proposals, and announcements of projects and applications for building permits from cities as far away as Milwaukee and New Orleans. Beginning with the December 5, 1891 issue, *Architecture and Building* was dated at both New York and Chicago, for Comstock knew from previous experience the importance of addressing the needs of his growing subscription list in the West and Northwest (9).

Building construction was seriously hampered by the Spanish–American War, as lenders anticipated the government's needs and temporarily withheld their money from the mortgage market (10). This caused advertising revenue to fall and led Comstock to combine the weekly *Architecture and Building* with the weekly *Builder's Magazine,* which he had established in January 1899. The first issue of the new, smaller-format monthly *Architects' and Builders' Magazine* appeared in September 1899. The move consolidated Comstock's resources, and readers were told that the new format was more convenient, permitted the staff more time to prepare its work, and allowed a highly finished paper to be used to everyone's benefit.

"Devoted to the interests of architects, engineers, builders, woodworkers, and persons contemplating building," the new magazine carried several series of practical articles on topics such as sanitary fixtures, cost estimation, power sources, and bricklaying by contributors William P. Gerhard, Frederick T. Hodgson, Alton D. Adams, and Owen B. Maginnis. Most of these authors, who had worked with the Editor in the earlier building magazine, were gradually replaced by architects, who contributed material of a more thoughtful and design-oriented nature. Russell Sturgis began a series on contemporary architecture in Europe, Barr Ferree undertook a department filled with commentary that was called "In Streets and Papers," and in November 1902, Joy Wheeler Dow began his lengthy series on the "American Renaissance." As the decade wore on, the attention paid to art notes surpassed that given to industrial progress, and most of the concerns of the builder were left behind. A wide range of function types,

from apartment houses to theaters, was included, most built in the region surrounding New York City. A series of articles on building contracts emphasized the architect's right to compensation. By March 1911, when the architect-educator Thomas Nolan was appointed Editor, the transition might have been thought complete, for *Architecture and Building* became "a magazine devoted to contemporary architectural construction." Nolan's tenure at the journal was brief, however, and the Publisher's son, William P. Comstock, was appointed Managing Editor by the end of the next year. After more than 30 years in architectural publishing, William T. Comstock retired in 1913, and his son became the president of the firm.

In a move to gain editorial assistance, architect Theodore Starrett was added to the staff as a contributing editor in February, 1913. He set the tone of each issue for more than four years by providing introductory editorials with eye-catching titles such as "Unions and Porterhouse Steaks," "Too Many Middlemen," and "A Pound of Flesh," and was always ready with incisive observations and a quick turn of a phrase. Under Starrett's guidance, *Architecture and Building* enlarged its format in 1916 and promised even more improvements in the future. Unfortunately, however, he died in October 1917, and Comstock alone carried on both the publishing and editorial duties.

Hamlin's observation that the *Architectural Record* provided a much-needed seriousness of purpose on the artistic and literary side of architectural journalism was an accurate one. Established in July 1891, the *Record* was published quarterly by The Record & Guide Company in New York City. Its first editor was not an architect, but a man of letters. Harvard-educated Henry W. Desmond began this publication with the idea of entering the field on a higher level than the other journals of the period. He wanted to go beyond merely recording contemporary work and "build up 'a pile of better thoughts'" about architecture by providing examples of good work and critical commentary. As Desmond wrote, "the difficulty is that people generally are so ignorant of even the A.B.C. of Architecture" (11).

The *Record* was produced in a magazine format, approximately 6 × 9 in., reminiscent of popular literary monthlies such as the *Century*. The magazine's best-known writer, Montgomery Schuyler, was already well established in those circles and became a regular contributor from the first issue. Other early authors were Ferree, William Goodyear, John Beverly Robinson, and Banister Fletcher, who added a foreign perspective. The *Record* also enjoyed the support of Sturgis, who was responsible for submitting most of the book reviews. Practical matters were few. The "Technical Department" was an infrequent specialty item, discreetly reflecting the interests of the advertisers.

The high-minded intellectual orientation was one of the most important characteristics of this magazine. It was, however, the departments entitled "Cross Currents," "Architectural Aberrations," and "Wasted Opportunities" that gave the *Record* its memorable place in architectural journalism. The first created a chatty dialogue, by which various observations and opinions could be presented on common or related topics. The second took to task recent buildings for "bad composition" or other artistic ills, and the third criticized plans in order to "illustrate fundamental principles." A parody, the prospectus for the "Classical Design and Detail Co."(12), and another series, "Critiques of Current Buildings," underscore the insistence with which the *Record* maintained its role.

When Herbert Croly assumed the editorial chair in 1900, certain changes began to take place. The *Record* extended its interests to include the allied arts, and the number of contributors increased to include leading French and Italian writers and professionals. With the April 1902 issue, the magazine ceased to be a quarterly and became a monthly. Fine arts design was added, reportedly because of a constant demand from the subscribers and a desire to the publishers to broaden the scope and purpose of the magazine. In keeping with this change, it was deemed necessary to redesign the page layout, although readers were reassured that the *Record* would still be devoted to architects, those with professional and commercial interests in architecture, and educated laymen who kept informed on these matters.

One of the more striking developments of the new monthly was how quickly it became enamored of and subsequently disenchanted with art nouveau. Its preference for things French was evident in articles on architecture, civic art, sculpture, and decorative arts. After January 1903, however, the *Record* was devoted to "architecture and the allied arts and crafts." By 1904, behind an entirely new cover, the magazine returned to its original U.S. focus. The works of prominent architects such as Trumbauer, Platt, and Day were supplemented with the writings of Cram and Bragdon. The most obvious characteristic of Croly's editorial reign was the attention lavished upon costly domestic projects for the rich and famous.

In 1905, following the pattern established by *Architecture and Building*, the *Record* opened a Chicago office. The writing of Elmer Grey and the work of Myron Hunt, A. C. Eschweiler, Louis Sullivan, and Robert E. Schmidt, all largely residential and on a more modest scale, were added to the buildings designed by New York firms. In the same year, however, the magazine began to be transformed physically as a result of another enterprise of the parent publishing firm. This was *Sweet's Indexed Catalogue of Building Construction*, launched with the claim that it would be *the* book of catalogues for the professional, all of the same size, cross-indexed, and compiled in a logical scheme. It was the idea of company President Clinton W. Sweet to call on building material firms to inform the architectural profession with a standard-sized catalogue, to be used as a working tool, while the advertisements in the *Record* were to act as an updating mechanism. The result of this effort was almost immediately obvious, with dozens of pages of advertisements being added to each issue. The *Record* soon boasted of three times the circulation of any other contemporary architectural publication, reaching over 11,000 copies before World War I. This journal was the first to enjoy such enormous financial support.

Croly served as Editor until May 1911, at which time Desmond once again assumed the position. For more on Croly's career, see Ref. 13. This time, however, Russell F. Whitehead was the Associate Editor, and in reality,

he managed all aspects of the magazine. In 1912, Sweet sold all of his publications to Frederick Warren Dodge, who was already operating over a dozen different publishing corporations. Dodge reaffirmed the belief that *Record* should maintain the high road in architectural journalism, but with the death of some of the principal contributors and the onset of the war, the journal would never be quite the same. In 1913, Desmond died. In July 1914, the foremost contributor, Schuyler, died, and shortly thereafter, Croly became the first Editor of the *New Republic*. These three events effectively curtailed many of the strong literary ties the *Record* had enjoyed for over two decades. Thus, a new phase of the *Record* began in the spring of 1914, when Michael A. Mikkelsen, an Associate Editor of the *Real Estate Record and Builders' Guide*, assumed the post of Editor (14).

The *Architectural Review* was similar to the *Record* in attempting to take a more intellectual approach and do more than simply report the latest architectural developments. The *Review*, the second major journal to be generated in Boston, had begun in November 1887 as the *Technology Architectural Review*, a student publication of the Architectural Society of M.I.T. Its purpose was to provide U.S. draftsmen an academic model at a price within the reach of everyone. With the liberal support of its advertising patrons, Editors Bates, Kimball, and Guild were able to offer a small magazine containing student coursework.

Publication was suspended from late 1889 until November 1891, when the editors issued their new periodical, entitled the *Architectural Review*. Its purpose was the criticism of architecture. The format was simple and straightforward. It included an article by a contributor, a few plates of current work, and a review of current periodical literature. It was the last feature that distinguished the *Review*. The editors regularly passed judgment on the contents of both U.S. and UK architectural journals, and occasionally considered French, German, and Canadian periodicals as well. Although many of the early reviews were unsigned, by the late 1890s H. Langford Warren had taken on much of this task. Frequent contributors included C. Howard Walker, Russell Sturgis, R. Clipston Sturgis, John Galen Howard, and Clarence H. Blackall.

Bates and Guild, the Editors of this relatively slim, semiquarterly journal, disdained most of what was published in other architectural publications and dealt at length with only what was deemed the best. They were proud of the fact that the *Review* had no great number of correspondents, and they stood above issuing any cheap editions with dozens of plates. They were proud, too, of their extremely fine heliographic illustrations, most of which were drawings, not photographs. On the other hand, this journal was not an outstanding commercial success, for its circulation was never much above 1000 copies.

Beginning with the January 1899 issue, the *Review* appeared monthly. In general, however, the journal maintained its formula. The only noticeable change occurred in the plates, which often included photographs of newly completed buildings. "The Work of Frank Lloyd Wright" by Robert C. Spencer, for example, was a condensed monograph of the architect's work, illustrated primarily by drawings, but supplemented by halftones (15). Noteworthy also was the attention paid to the UK architect-writer

Charles R. Ashbee as he toured the U.S. promoting the aims of the National Trust for Places of Historic Interest or Natural Beauty.

During the first decade of the twentieth century, the *Review* produced several special issues, each devoted to a building type, such as churches, banks, and hotels. Three or four articles dealt with the special aspects of each type, and these were followed by as many as four or five dozen examples treated at length photographically. The examples chosen were primarily in East Coast cities.

From April 1910 until January 1912, publication was once again suspended, without explanation. The material that had been scheduled for the May 1910 issue, the drawings submitted for the Hudson Fulton Competition, appeared in the next issue, and the format was unchanged. The emphasis remained on critiques of work appearing in recent architectural periodicals, with the best possible reproductions of architectural drawings in the plate section. Title pages and indexes were not published after 1912 because the editors had found that most subscribers preferred to take out the plates and file then. The editors determined that it was wiser to put their money into the paper, something all of the subscribers could appreciate.

The longest and most notable series was entitled "Extracts from 'The Log of the Dorian,' " which began in July 1912. This was a story taken from the personal journals and notes of Francis R. Bacon who, with Joseph T. Clarke, had purchased a single-masted cutter in England in the summer of 1878 and sailed it into the Mediterranean with the idea of living cheaply and studying firsthand the Doric architecture of the Aegean. The boat, originally dubbed "The Cobweb," was renamed the "Dorian" in keeping with the purpose of the mission.

The story of the *Inland Architect and News Record* was one of little change through the 1890s. McLean continued to serve as Managing Editor, with Charles Illsley of St. Louis as Associate Editor from 1885. Special contributors included John W. Root, William P. Gerhard, William L. B. Jenney, Benezette Williams, Louis Sullivan, Daniel H. Burnham, Irving K. Pond, Allen B. Pond, Peter B. Wight, and Henry Van Brunt. Wight deserves particular notice because his role with the *Inland Architect* parallels that of Schuyler with the *Record*. Wight's articles, often cast as a series, dealt with such topics as fireproofing, Chicago in the 1850s, and the programs of the Chicago Art Institute schools.

The typical issue would include one or two installments of a series such as the translation of a theoretical or historical European work, the proceedings of a statewide architectural association or the National Association of Builders' convention, six to eight illustrations, an equal number of plates issued to subscribers who paid for the photogravure edition, a review of new publications, a synopsis of building news, and notices from Buffalo and Toronto to San Francisco, Seattle, and Tacoma. Last, there were about 30 pages devoted to advertising.

By the late 1890s, however, the journal had developed a different air. Although it carried the names of many of the same contributors, their input was limited, and each issue was only 8–12 pages long. The emphasis on recording current architectural developments continued, but an increase in the number of articles devoted to licensing, building laws, fire and safety regulations, and legal decisions indicated the magazine was serving different interests. In 1905, McLean left his post, and the Inland Publishing Company sold the *Inland Architect* to Porter, Taylor and Company of Chicago. The publication became a "monthly journal of architecture, constructive, decorative and landscape" and was printed on coated paper, similarly to many other periodicals of the period. The contributors were no longer regional practitioners, but figures from throughout the nation. They included Glenn Brown and James Knox Taylor of Washington, D.C.; T. M. Clark, Ralph Adams Cram, and the Olmsted Brothers of Boston; Albert Kelsey of Philadelphia; and Edward L. Tilton of New York. Four pages of letterpress were followed by eight plates, chiefly halftones, often laid out vertically across the foldout pages for the convenience of those who filed them in the office. This move, however, seems to have been only the prelude to the announcement that, on January 1, 1909, the *Inland Architect and News Record* would be subsumed under the *American Architect* (16).

If one were looking for a journal concerned with high-style, fashionable architecture at the turn of the century, it would be *Architecture. A Monthly Journal Edited by A. Holland Forbes*. Begun in 1899 by the Forbes Company and edited in its Fifth Avenue offices, it rivaled the *Record* for featuring the most current trends among the well-to-do. The opinions of the magazine were not those of Forbes. Rather, the contents were either prepared or revised by five specialists, referred to as the Consulting Board of Architecture, who reviewed all of the manuscripts and photographs to assure the merit in each issue.

The formula of the early issues of the periodical had two parts. First, there were photographs of country residences and formal gardens in suburban New York, Long Island, New Jersey, and Connecticut, to which were occasionally added libraries, courthouses, masonic temples, and European villas. Forbes's photogravure publication, *Architectural Gardens of Italy,* parts of which were featured and advertised in *Architecture,* was typical of the visual content of the magazine. The work was always presented at the behest of wealthy clients, and the architects were generally well established. In fact, every issue included the portrait of the prosperous architect whose work was highlighted. Second, there were reports from the Architectural League of New York City and small articles of interest to professionals in the immediate area. The need for a League organ may have been a *raison d'etre* for the journal, for the articles were short, unillustrated, and often completely unrelated to the photogravure plates.

In all, *Architecture* was an elegant magazine, suitable for display in the very best parlors and boasting a circulation of over 7000 subscribers during most of the first decade of the twentieth century. Even the "Building Trades Number," July 1902, wherein the reading pages were devoted to the advertisers' interests, was considerably more polished than the pages of many other architectural journals of the period. The December 1902 issue featured typical New York residential hotels and apartment houses, and one of the principal advertisers, New York Telephone, called attention to the convenience of private branch telephone systems in these buildings.

It was also obvious from its content, layout, and design

that *Architecture* was unusual in that it was tightly controlled by its parent company. The formula that was introduced did not develop in any noticeable fashion in the succeeding decade. There were a few additional short articles, some reprinted from sources in the UK such as the London *Building News* or *Architectural Review,* occasionally accompanied by illustrations from the same sources. In all, by about 1915, *Architecture* was considered eclectic, and its content and circulation were slipping.

The *Western Architect,* published in Minneapolis and later in Chicago, was begun in 1901. It announced itself as "a national journal of architecture and allied arts," and from its inception strove to overcome whatever provincial tendencies it might have favored. Each issue consisted of a few brief editorial paragraphs; one or two lectures from recent conventions, conferences, or committee meetings; about a dozen plates; a few notes on the events of an architectural club; and perhaps an obituary notice or two. Although special attention was given to developments in Chicago and to the architects who worked in the "Prairie spirit," the *Western Architect* maintained connections with professionals throughout the country, from Ralph Adams Cram in Boston to Charles Sumner Green in Pasadena. The former Editor of the *Inland Architect,* McLean, edited the *Western Architect* from 1905 until 1929. Not unexpectedly, the formula he developed in the Minneapolis-based journal was not noticeably different from that in the *Inland Architect*.

McLean believed that a person of refinement needed to have a critical knowledge of architecture in order to distinguish between its good and bad examples. He wrote that the illustrations in the *Western Architect* held the strongest educational value for the public because they were chosen from the best architecture and were executed by the greatest architectural artists of the day. The "pseudoarchitectural journals that print pretty pictures; the 'House, Field and Garden' kind of journal cannot be depended upon for correct technical censorship"(17). McLean provided overt guidance by occasionally contributing entire issues that were devoted to a single city, highlighting its architecture, commercial development, art, and manufacturing. For example, in 1908, Winnipeg, "The Ultimate Metropolis of Canada," and Spokane were featured. The *Western Architect* was still maturing. It would become more professional after World War I.

As the oldest architectural association in the country, the AIA had from time to time designated various periodicals as its "official organ." In addition, the Institute had for decades produced a limited number of copies of the proceedings of its annual conventions. In neither case, however, was there much room for the AIA to make editorial comments or to address the profession as a whole. American professionals needed only to look at the example provided by the Royal Institute of British Architects to feel inadequate.

Accordingly, the *American Institute of Architects Quarterly Bulletin* was begun in April 1900, and the Secretary of the AIA, Glenn Brown, was appointed Editor. The *Bulletin* carried news about the Institute and its annual conventions, chapters, members, competitions, and commissions. In addition, Brown included the titles of articles and publication information from the 43 foreign and 40 U.S. societies

and institutions and 59 other periodicals on architecture and allied subjects that the Institute regularly received. The Editor made no critical comment on the contents of these serials, but he created one of the earliest and most comprehensive periodical indexes to architectural literature then known in the United States.

By all accounts, the *Bulletin* was successful in meeting its objectives. As part of a larger reorganization of the Institute at the annual meeting in late 1912, however, Brown's responsibilities were severely altered (18). The secretary was made more or less a figurehead as the initiative was taken from the officers in the Washington office and delegated to independent committees throughout the country. He seems to have been the target of specific corrective action, for the new regime put the *Bulletin* in the hands of the Publications Committee. In January 1913, the quarterly was recast as the new monthly *Journal of the American Institute of Architects* and turned over to Charles Harris Whitaker. The directors of the Institute felt that "problems of vital interest . . . could be treated with greater hope of proper and successful solutions . . ." if they could be dealt with in a more immediate fashion and that the chapters and other members of the profession would welcome a more frequent exchange of news items (19).

At this point, the journal became more like contemporary periodicals. It was printed on coated stock and contained articles of broader interest to the profession. The facts that fewer than 500 copies would be sold each year, that only $5 was set aside to pay for the journal from a member's dues, and that no one looked to the need for adequate advertising support only meant that the publication was headed for financial trouble in the decade ahead.

In addition to the journals that Hamlin mentioned, at least one other, the *Brickbuilder,* published in Boston, is noteworthy. Begun in 1892 with Arthur D. Rogers as Editor, it was conceived as a means to improve communication between the brick and clay tile industry and architects and builders, who typically preferred wood and stone. Industry representatives felt they needed more direct access to those who made the design decisions that inevitably affected what materials were used in construction.

This was a modest undertaking at the start. The opening issues each contained a frontispiece; eight pages of letterpress, often containing essays and articles of a historical nature; eight plates of measured drawings or sketches of old work; and a photographic supplement of foreign architecture that demonstrated the long history of the use of earthen materials, particularly for ornamentation. Advertising was restricted to the cover pages (20).

Beginning with the March 1893 issue a new format with a new cover was featured. The supplements were discontinued (21). Soon contemporary work, competition designs, and contributions from industry specialists rounded out the publication, addressing practical as well as aesthetic matters. By the end of the second volume, the details of Italian architecture and such tour-de-force designs in brick as Richardson's Sever Hall at Harvard were being supplemented by departments that dealt with roofing tiles, glazing products, limes, cements, fireproofing, masons, contractors and manufacturers.

By the mid-1890s, the contents included not only all

of the regular departments, but also original contributions from C. Howard Walker, Allan Marquand, R. Clipston Sturgis, Ralph A. Cram, Bertram G. Goodhue, Charles H. Alden, and H. Langford Warren, the last of whom often took on the editorial responsibilities. By the turn of the century, the *Brickbuilder* was featuring serial articles on church architecture written by both clerics and architects and on village commercial blocks contributed by business figures. The frontispiece frequently focused on a detail of a Spanish or Portuguese church, and recent residential construction along Commonwealth Avenue and Bay State Road in Boston was often highlighted in the plates.

Rogers's journal grew slowly but steadily. By 1910, the plates illustrated the work of dozens of small firms from throughout the country. A series on architectural acoustics by Hugh Tallant, one on current brick architecture in the UK, and another on the role of burnt clay products in the rebuilding of San Francisco all helped push its circulation from 2500 copies at the turn of the century to almost twice that by the opening of World War I. Although Rogers directed the *Brickbuilder* and remained president of his publishing corporation for a number of years, by August 1912, Whitehead was appointed Managing Editor, and shortly thereafter, Ralph W. Reinhold was made Business Manager and Vice President. Almost simultaneously, a series on early American architectural details was begun, including measured drawings, alongside another series entitled "As He Is Known," consisting of biographical sketches of architects. By 1915, C. Matlack Price began a series on the use of native woods for interior finish, signaling the drift away from the exclusive focus on clay materials that had characterized the *Brickbuilder* for over two decades.

When the U.S. entered World War I, architectural journalism had been well established, with an older generation of periodicals continuing to report the latest developments alongside a newer generation that was more devoted to criticism and analysis. The *American Architect* and *Architecture and Building* survived the competitive threats of the *Architectural Record* and *Architectural Review*. The capability, and even eagerness, of the latter group to examine both architectural thought and new buildings provided a certain amount of strength and direction in U.S. architectural journalism as a whole. The most direct manifestation of this was the development of other journals specializing in one aspect of architecture, such as the *Brickbuilder*, which promoted the use of clay products, the *Architect*, which catered to a higher economic class, and the *American Institute of Architects' Quarterly Bulletin*, devoted to the particular needs of that organization. The tendency to specialize would grow in the near future, and the importance of securing substantial financial support would not be lost on those who wished to command the field.

SPECIALIZATION AND REFORMULATION (1917–1933)

As the U.S. returned to a peacetime economy, the construction industry hesitated for a few years, but then began to surge forward, setting new records. Architectural journalism soon felt this strength in its advertising revenue and reflected the activity in its text and illustrations. The

Architectural Record still laid claim to having the largest circulation of any journal in its class, about 10,000 copies, well ahead of both *Architecture and Building* and the *American Architect*. The *Brickbuilder*, which became the *Architectural Forum*, and the *White Pine Series* had the backing of particular product manufacturers and suppliers. The journal that proved most impressive, however, was dedicated to the interests of those who worked in the drafting room. It was *Pencil Points* that provided the greatest surprise in architectural journalism during the 1920s, while the rise of other periodicals, such as *The Architect*, proved to be merely a momentary burst of publishing energy, which was followed by their demise during the Depression.

The Editor of the *Architectural Record*, Mikkelsen, not only conducted the architectural journal with the largest circulation, he also enjoyed contributions from some of the best educated men in the field. Croly, who continued as a contributing editor, was joined in writing about U.S. country houses and gardens by Harold D. Eberlein and John Taylor Boyd. An air of scholarship was added by Richard F. Bach, curator of the School of Architecture at Columbia University, whose column entitled "The Architect's Library" reviewed dozens of books on colonial architecture. Architect Wesley Sherwood Bessell wrote a series on colonial architecture in Connecticut. Measured drawings were inserted as foldouts, and various buildings under restoration, such as the Paul Revere House in Boston and the Old City Hall in New York, were described. The architectural losses in Europe during World War I were of interest to professionals on this side of the Atlantic and gave yet another reason for the *Record* to follow developments abroad. Toward 1920, an installment of the long series on architectural decoration in the UK by Albert E. Bullock appeared in every issue and the cover illustrations of historic sites in Paris, Venice, and Rome, drawn by Otto Eggers, signaled to all that peace had been restored.

During the early 1920s, a change of policy was instituted, calling for more recognition of and reliance upon contributing editors. Croly was joined by George Burnap, Whitehead, A. N. Rebori, and Leon V. Solon. Solon was especially well known for his extensive series on the principles of architectural polychromy as exemplified by Grecian temples, and the accompanying color plates considerably enlivened the pages of the *Record*.

Dodge began publishing the magazine in August 1923, with little apparent change. Lithographs of New York City buildings by Birch Burdette Long were used on the covers in the mid-1920s and the photography of Sigurd Fischer and John Wallace Gillies was featured inside. Parish churches in the UK and their details dominated the pages of the 1925 issues, accentuated by an occasional article on the International Exposition of Modern Industrial and Decorative Arts in Paris.

In early 1927, the *Record* not only carried Frank Lloyd Wright's series "In the Cause of Architecture," but also began to include his designs alongside illustrations taken from books and periodicals published in northern Europe (22). However, the linkage among the various aspects of the modern movement on both sides of the Atlantic was only suggested. Developments in the Netherlands, Germany, Italy, France, and the UK were taken as news to be reported, not as examples of what U.S. buildings should be in the future. One indication of Mikkelsen's stand on aesthetic issues was the appointment, in August 1927, of A. Lawrence Kocher to the post of associate editor. Kocher's first contribution to the magazine had been a series of 15 articles on "The Early Architecture of Pennsylvania," published from 1920 to 1922. He joined the magazine as a traditionalist (23). For example, the November 1927 issue, which was almost completely devoted to "The Country House," was largely Kocher's effort.

The format remained the same until January 1928, when the page size was changed—"plainly a concession to the universal demand for standardization," according to Mikkelsen. The larger *Record* would have "a greater variety of illustrations" and would allow a "new chapter" to be opened. It was, with the very next issue.

In February 1928, Henry-Russell Hitchcock began his short association with the *Record,* as a contributing editor, by reviewing Le Corbusier's *Towards a New Architecture* (24). In April, he initiated a series of articles on "Modern Architecture," an early attempt to push aside the influence of architects who "consider themselves, broadly speaking, Traditionalists" (25). Hitchcock's reviews of foreign periodicals, begun in May 1928, must have opened many American eyes to the European modernists, for almost every month during the next two years he discussed buildings whose images were quite unlike most of what was being built in the United States, as demonstrated by the balance of the *Record* itself. With the onset of the Depression, however, domestic economic developments became more important than European design experimentation.

Whereas most of the other major architectural journals were recast at least once in the years after World War I, *Architecture and Building* remained wedded to its old format. After Starrett's death, William P. Comstock took on the duties of managing editor and publisher, and concentrated on producing a publication that catered to large architectural firms in the New York City area. Devoted to the interests of those interested in the business side of the profession, the journal suffered from a dearth of editorial material and undistinguished articles. A short series on the Hotel Commodore and the Hotel Pennsylvania by Charles Warren Hastings in 1919 and Comstock's own series on the soda fountain shop in 1920 were the extent of any serious commitment to the content of the letterpress. The illustrations were devoted to the latest apartment houses, banks, churches, hotels, and theaters. Few residences were included, although the "Dwelling House Series" gave some attention to the need for guidance in subdivision dwellings. By 1924, the "Department of Construction Materials and Appliances" was the largest section in every issue. The number of articles on nontechnical topics was curtailed, and the plates not only indicated the names of the clients and the architect, but also listed the general contractor; the subcontractors for plastering, plumbing, heating, lighting, bronze work, and painting; the stone work company; the terra cotta manufacturer; and even the manufacturer of the mail chute equipment.

At the end of the decade, *Architecture and Building* continued to record commercial construction activity, but

shortly thereafter the circulation of the journal began to fail, and the William T. Comstock Company began to consider a new format and approach. The January 1931 issue was the last "devoted to contemporary architectural construction," for henceforth it was to be known as "a journal of investment and construction." The move away from architecture and toward real estate and development interests may also have been influenced by various members of the Thompson-Starrett Company, with whom Comstock had remained in contact over the years. Unfortunately, the effort to redefine the audience of the journal was begun too late. The financially troubled monthly was able to produce only two issues in the second half of the year, and it came to an end with the March 1932 issue.

The *American Architect* continued its efforts to become a leading journal by broadening its range of attention. In 1918, for example, the formula consisted of a feature article, editorial comment, and departments dealing with commercial and financial news, criticism and comment, industrial information, and architectural engineering. The results of the competitions of the Beaux Arts Institute of Design were commonly included, adding several illustrations to the text beyond the usual number of plates.

The postwar issues showed much more building in progress, with many photographs of construction processes and techniques. As projects began, the amount of current news increased, and the new Editor, Crocker, was busy traveling around the country gathering it. The *American Architect* aggressively attempted to scoop the other journals, hoping by virtue of its weekly issuance to gain the edge in circulation. This was seen in July and August 1921, for example, when H. Van Buren Magonigle wrote to the Editor expressing his resentment at the unauthorized publication of his competition drawings, causing him to abandon a monograph project and personal embarrassment for having refused other journals the publication rights.

One of the features that had been suspended during the war was the review of the current architectural press. This omission was soon remedied, for with the August 31, 1921 issue, the *American Architect* merged with the *Architectural Review* and became known as the *American Architect and Architectural Review.* It was the intent of the Publisher to continue those features that rendered each journal distinctive, but the move clearly reduced the former's competition.

About the same time that the *American Architect* was absorbing one journal, it gave rise to another. For many years, the Beaux Arts Institute of Design had been seeking to establish its own organ in which to publish illustrations of student work, the announcements of programs, and the results of the competitions. This material had been carried by the *American Architect;* however, in the early 1920s it switched from weekly to fortnightly production, so that the Institute needed a more timely and extensive descriptive medium. Hence, the monthly *Bulletin of the Beaux Arts Institute of Design* was begun in October 1924.

By the time that the *American Architect* published its "Golden Anniversary Number" in January 1926, it could look with pride at the fact that it had contributed to the progress of the last 50 years and was expected to do so in the future. The editorial staff pointed to the fact that it had been the first to gain authorization to publish John Russell Pope's design for the Theodore Roosevelt Memorial, and it was the first to feature an article that dealt with the design of airports. When Arthur T. North began writing as a correspondent for the *Western Architect,* the occasion was taken to point out that at one time he had been the engineering editor of the *American Architect.* Departments of engineering and construction, interior architecture, law, and minor community architecture neatly structured the journal. Beginning in March 1927, a part II, entitled "Topical Architecture," was incorporated in the journal and provided not fewer than four pages on a single theme or detail, printed on art paper (26). Collections of church cupolas, chimney stacks, and eaves treatments were dealt with in dozens of photographs. The feature articles that opened such issue were devoted to topics such as landscape architecture, apartment houses, or churches or focused on a particular building designed by a well-known firm. Modern U.S. design was displayed alongside more traditional modes without apparent prejudice. The *American Architect* enjoyed the backing of a wide range of building material and appliance producers. There was no appreciable change in either content or advertising when the journal was purchased by William R. Hearst's International Publications Corporation in 1929.

The idea that a journal could be sponsored by manufacturers interested in promoting the use of one material has already been noted in the development of the *Brickbuilder.* In January 1917, the title of the *Brickbuilder* was changed to *Architectural Forum.* The ownership and management remained the same, but the former name did not seem to cover recent developments in the magazine or the work the staff wished to undertake. A broader scope was desired, recording architectural progress to aid discussion and understanding (27).

The formula changed little. The two parts, the letterpress and the plates, maintained the same appearance and feeling they had had for over a decade. As the economy of the nation began to recover from the effects of World War I, the *Forum* responded in the same manner as its contemporaries, by paying increased attention to the economics of building. In fact, it became the "illustrated architectural monthly devoted to the art, science, and business of building." An article on "The Promotion and Financing of Building Operations" appeared in the February 1919 issue, introducing readers to Charles A. Whittlemore, who within a few months became the associate editor of the "Engineering and Construction Department." C. Stanley Taylor was appointed Associate Editor for the "Architecture and Building Economics Department" in June 1919, and an "Interior Decoration Department" was added shortly thereafter. The journal seems to have been partitioned into departments even before Editor Rogers died in early 1919, having served his subscribers for 27 years (28). The *Forum* staff, undoubtedly caught off balance, hesitated only briefly before choosing Albert J. MacDonald to assume the editorial chair. The departments were maintained. Perhaps at the instigation of S. Howard Myers, who had been hired as an advertising salesman in 1919, the journal added a "Service Section" by the middle of

1921, wherein subscribers were provided with specific information regarding the design, equipment, and construction of buildings. A special feature was the Consultative Committee, made up of professionals nationally known in their respective fields, who provided extensive information on retail material price quotations and examined "Trends in Construction Activity" through figures by Dodge. The Committee played a key role in guiding the development of "Reference Numbers," begun in 1922. Special issues dealing with industrial buildings, hotels, public libraries, churches, hospitals, retail stores, and movie houses helped boost the utility of the journal and its circulation.

As building construction boomed in the early 1920s the *Forum* carried articles that displayed the most recent buildings along with others on the Greek Revival and the development of architecture in Charleston. In fact, the editorial preference was decidedly conservative. MacDonald went so far as to state that nothing could have a more beneficial effect on the future development of American architecture and decoration than the perpetuation of the best examples of colonial design (29).

In 1924, the *Forum* moved from Boston to New York City, and the following year, Rogers and Manson Company was reorganized. Former advertising salesman Howard Myers became part owner and the president of the firm, although he would relinquish the position in a few years. Meanwhile, the Editor, MacDonald, accompanied by photographer Paul J. Weber, undertook a five-month tour of Europe to examine recent architectural developments (30). Upon their return, MacDonald was replaced by Parker Morse Hooper as Editor.

A number of improvements followed almost immediately. Weber's photographs were seen in "Studies of European Precedent," infrequently added to the other plates in the journal beginning in April 1925, running through 1927. In January 1927, "The Architect's Forum" was begun, with Contributing Editors Aymar Embury II, Harvey Wiley Corbett, Taylor, Charles Loring, Alexander Trowbridge, and Rexford Newcomb further adding to the content of each issue. The most startling change, however, occurred in January 1928, when for the first time subscribers received not one, but two separately bound parts of the *Forum* every month. Part I was devoted solely to architectural design, and Part II contained engineering and business material. Each pair contained over 150 pages of editorial matter, a considerable accomplishment at that time.

As might be expected, it was in Part I, with all of its plate illustrations, that the first mention of modern European architecture occurred. Ralph T. Walker noted that, "although extremely economical, it is far from pleasing in appearance," and he found it a mistake to believe, as Le Corbusier did, that anything resolved into absolute efficiency would necessarily be to the same degree beautiful (31). The editorial staff sensed, however, that these new developments were worthy of further investigation. "Some call it 'futurist,' some 'cubist,' and some 'ultramodern,'" Hooper wrote of the Rue Mallet-Stevens in Paris, although he chose the term modernist for the housing he observed (32). Five years after the MacDonald–Weber trip, Hooper sent Sigurd Fisher to Europe to photograph the modern architecture of The Netherlands, Denmark, Germany, and Sweden, and these plates began to be regularly inserted as special sections.

Meanwhile, Part II, largely under the direction of Taylor, dealt with such topics as insulation, the use of structural steel in residences, architectural law, promotion and finance, and the business viewpoint, forecasting the time when the architect would become much more important in the economic scheme of the country.

In August 1930, the editors announced that criticism would become more integral in its review of architectural works (33). Two months later, Kenneth Kingsley Stowell, who had joined the staff in 1927 and served as the managing editor, was promoted to Editor. Roger W. Sherman, Arthur T. North, and John Cushman Fistere were hired as assistant editors. In October 1931, Myers became president of Rogers and Manson once again, to direct the journal through the depths of the Depression. Until July 1932, the staff of the *Forum* continued to produce a two-part publication; thereafter a single issue included the same items. The focus was largely on housing as a social, technical, and economic problem. The work of Clarence Stein, Henry Wright, John Nolen, and others was prominently featured; however, the inclusion of the International Housing Exhibition in Vienna in the October 1932 issue suggested that the biases of the staff would become more evident in the future.

Whereas the *Brickbuilder* and its successor, the *Forum*, were backed by the brick and clay products industry, the *White Pine Series of Architectural Monographs* was begun in July 1915 as "a bimonthly publication suggesting the architectural uses of white pine and its availability today as a structural material" (34). This 16-page, staple-bound 8 × 11 in. serial was sponsored by the White Pine Bureau of St. Paul, Minnesota. The content of the *Series* was somewhat different from other professional journals in its strong historical bias. Each issue was centered around an article featuring a seventeenth- eighteenth- or early nineteenth-century historic site.

The idea of publishing a series of monographs on early U.S. architecture as a means of advertising was largely due to the interest of the chairman of the Bureau, George Lindsey. The makeup of each issue was provided by the editor, Whitehead, who had previously served for about six months as managing editor of the *Record* and then became Editor and part owner of the *Brickbuilder* (35). Whether Lindsey, having seen Whitehead's earlier work, convinced him to take the lead role in the *Series* is not known, but the relationship between the two men was a strong one.

Through this journal, several competitions were held to encourage young architects and draftspersons to use pine, especially for suburban construction. The most important contribution the *Series* made, however, was a documentary one. As Whitehead sought good examples of early work in pine, he repeatedly turned to western Massachusetts, Vermont, New Hampshire, and Maine. He enlisted the help of the best scholars of the day, such as Joseph Everett Chandler, Frank Chouteau Brown, Aymar Embury II, and Frank E. Wallis. These authors were aided

by Julian Buckly and Kenneth Clark, two architects-turned-photographers. The illustrations include several measured drawings and historical data, which made the collection a useful reference for architects, historians, connoisseurs, and students.

In 1924, the White Pine Bureau decided to cease supporting the *Series* because some of its members wanted to advertise on their own. The Bureau gave Whitehead its approval to carry on the series using its name, but as a private enterprise. Thereafter, the Weyerhaeuser Forest Products Company provided some support, but the Editor and Publisher instituted a modest $2/yr subscription rate for what had formerly arrived free in the mailboxes of nearly 10,000 readers. Whitehead's dream, retitled the *White Pine Monograph Series* and released from the obligatory focus on a single material, was to expand beyond colonial New England to consider other materials and their use in public and religious buildings. In fact, he proposed "to cover, little by little, the whole field of Colonial and Early American architecture." The dream was only partially realized, for the *Series* would subsequently become absorbed in *Pencil Points*.

In July 1918, the *Architectural Review* adopted a smaller format. A long-time contributor, Frank Chouteau Brown, had become the Editor, and the president of the Architectural Review Company, Ralph F. Warner, was providing a series on manufacturers' housing projects. Although a number of fine plates were regularly included, the review of current architectural periodicals that had previously characterized the journal was temporarily discontinued.

In October 1918, the Architectural Review Company moved its editorial and publishing offices from Boston to New York City, and a number of changes in the form and substance of the journal soon followed. In January 1919, a leaflet devoted to the interests of draftspersons, entitled "Pencil Points," appeared in the *Review*. A year later, Brown was replaced by Eugene Clute, and three new contributing editors were appointed. C. Howard Walker reintroduced the review of current architectural periodicals, J. H. Phillips was put in charge of the interiors department, and J. F. Musselman was given the responsibility for the equipment department.

It was probably Reinhold, the president of the company as of March 1920, who wished to enlarge the scope of the leaflet, so that *Pencil Points. A Journal for the Drafting Room* was launched in June 1920. The same men were involved with both magazines (36). In August 1921, Pencil Points Press, a separate corporation, was begun in anticipation of the sale of the *Architectural Review*. At the end of the month, the *American Architect* absorbed the *Review* and became known as the *American Architect and Architectural Review*.

It was clear from the outset that *Pencil Points* was a "journal for the drafting room." On the cover, a T-square and triangle were shown interlocked. In many ways, it was directed specifically to the draftsmen who aspired to have their own offices. Among the early advertisers were several drafting room equipment and supply companies, in addition to a few book publishers and materials suppliers. Major advertisers borrowed from the parent magazine included all of the major terra cotta manufacturers on the East Coast.

Clute was the first Editor. Among the earliest contributors were Paul Valenti, whose lessons on perspective ran for several months; Arthur Guptill, who wrote on pencil rendering and sketching techniques, following his classes at the Pratt Institute; John Vredenburgh Van Pelt, former Professor in charge of the College of Architecture at Cornell University, who wrote on architectural details; and John F. Harbeson, who added a series on the study of architectural design with reference to the problems of the Beaux Arts Institute of Design. In addition, the contents included queries from draftspersons who sought good examples to learn from, whether bungalows, hotels, theaters, courthouses, or bridges. The specifications department and personnel notes announcing office moves were particularly chatty, giving the journal a personal air.

By the opening of the third volume in 1922, *Pencil Points* presented skilled draftsmen and renderers who could be looked upon as role models. The lives and work of Jules Guerin, Charles Platt, Otto Eggers, Raymond Hood, Hugh Ferriss, Harvey Corbett, Charles Maginnes, and Wilson Eyre, among others, were featured, and their accomplishments lauded. Perhaps the most heroic figure was Birch Burdette Long, who undoubtedly ranked as one of the most talented illustrators of the period. Long, who first gained notice in Chicago, attempted to memorialize himself by establishing the Birch Burdette Long Sketch Competition, the prizes for which were donated by the artist. Entries in the 1922 competition were reviewed by Long, Cass Gilbert, Trowbridge, Hood, and Clute and were then featured in the journal (37). Long's promising career came to a sudden end (38).

Because the staff had so carefully launched the journal and identified its subscribers, *Pencil Points* was a success from the start. The circulation began with 3221 copies and steadily rose to about 7800 by the end of the first year (39). Clute knew there was room for improvement, however, and solicited suggestions from the subscribers. As a result of their responses, more information of practical value was promised: references on the design of motion picture theaters, data on concrete and steel details, and methods of modeling. The January 1923 issue was devoted solely to the problem of writing good specifications.

In January 1924, Publisher Reinhold began a department labeled "Here and There, This and That." This was truly a readers' department, the contributions ranging from the funny to the serious, about architecture or anything else of interest to those in the drafting room, in any medium, from prose and poetry to verse and sketch. A $10 prize was offered for the best entry each month. Reports of office festivities were published, noting the costumes that were worn and the creative antics that highlighted these events. In addition, cartoons and poems that lampooned office routines were commonplace. Reinhold's social consciousness was evident, too, as even photographs and descriptions of orphaned children were included, with the hope that they would be adopted.

In March 1924, *Pencil Points* advertised the need for additional editorial help to carry out plans for developing the magazine and initiating a book publishing program.

Elizabeth L. Cleaver was appointed an associate editor, but this was only part of the change of command (40). In November 1925, Whitehead became the Editor, with the full backing of Publisher Reinhold. For anyone who knew these men, this was no surprise, for they had previously worked together on the *Architectural Record* and *Architectural Forum*. It was Whitehead's idea to broaden the journal to include design, planning, rendering, field sketches, measured drawings, the use of color, and "other new features." As did his predecessor, Whitehead promised to edit the magazine with readers, not for them, and he reaffirmed that *Pencil Points* was devoted to those in the drafting room (41). Reinhold and Whitehead filled out the editorial staff with the appointment of Kenneth Reid as a second associate editor in April 1926.

In addition to bringing a great amount of experience to *Pencil Points,* Whitehead also brought the ailing *White Pine Series*. In many ways, the two periodicals were similar. Both were pedantic in nature and were largely devoted to instilling values and knowledge of traditional skills in the novice. At the time, the marriage of the two seemed a compatible one.

With a full editorial staff, *Pencil Points* began to consider the publication of books. Harbeson's *Study of Architectural Design,* Eberlein and French's *Lesser French Palaces,* and York and Sawyer's *Specifications for a Small Hospital* were promised, all as drafting room aids (42). An important series of articles discussed the relationship between the draftsperson and the architect. This featured interviews with prominent architects around the country, who indicated their impressions of the role of the draftsperson. At the insistence of some readers, this was extended so that draftspersons would have a chance to comment from their point of view (43).

"Draw! Draw! Draw!" was the command, with pen and ink, charcoal, and pastel. All of this suggested to advertising representatives that *Pencil Points* was a "schoolboy paper" without significant purchasing power, which was a sore spot with the publisher and staff. Their answer was that "the students of today are the draftsmen of tomorrow . . ." (44) and that everyone, old or young, in the office might be considered a student.

From its modest start in 1920, when each issue contained only about 16 pages, to the close of the decade, *Pencil Points* had developed to the stage where it consisted of 64 pages of editorial matter and at least two color reproductions. The boom in construction activity had boosted the advertising section to where it was anticipated that eight more pages of material could be added in 1928. "The Specifications Desk" was the newest department to be added, and a series on perspective projection was begun, without the slightest hint of the changes that would take place in the drafting room with the arrival of European modernism.

In the Midwest, the story of the *Western Architect* was one of brief resurgence and decline, its last issue being published in March 1931. In 1917, the *Western Architect* was recast in a slightly smaller format, a measure of the wartime economy, to reduce the expense of publication (45). In line with Editor McLean's belief in the importance of the illustrations, there was no appreciable reduction in their size, giving the journal a more photojournalistic air. The regular contributors to the letterpress were few; McLean supplied most of the editorial commentary and several of the articles in each issue. With the demise of the *Inland Architect,* Peter B. Wight took up writing for the *Western Architect* and was often responsible for alerting readers to developments on the West Coast, working from his home in Pasadena until his death in 1925 (46,47). The most important contributor to the journal, Professor Rexford Newcomb of the University of Illinois, began with a series of articles on the Spanish Renaissance architecture of Texas and California in 1919. The architectural offices represented were extraordinarily widespread throughout the country, with well over 50 firms included during the course of a year. George C. Nimmons and Albert Kahn received repeated attention, but there were no favored firms. In October 1922, Newcomb was appointed Architectural Editor (48). He believed that the West merited a strong architectural journal and was instrumental in setting up a Board of Architectural Advisors, composed of leading professionals from Illinois, Indiana, Montana, Alabama, Kansas, Ohio, California, Michigan, Texas, Washington, Iowa, Minnesota, and Wisconsin. Although McLean continued to contribute articles and comments regularly, Newcomb presided over the selection of the plates and took a commanding lead in choosing the contents of the monthly. As construction activity surged to ever higher levels, the *Western Architect* gained strength as well. At least 18 plates in each issue featured buildings by architects working in most of the major cities of the United States, and occasionally in France, Germany, and Denmark. Newcomb's historical series on "Color in Architecture" and the addition of North as Associate Editor in charge of a current events department named "The Passing Show" ensured an interesting and informative issue every month.

In January 1930, Newcomb assumed the editorial chair, an action that was as much an acknowledgment of his past effort as an indication of his future responsibilities. Special issues on memorials, the architecture of airports, the National Parks of the West, and floodlighting suggest that the Editor had a lively interest in many emerging issues. Unfortunately, however, the *Western Architect* would not survive the economic difficulties of the period; it ceased 15 months later.

When Forbes sold *Architecture* in 1917, he had agreed not to return to the publishing business for five years. In Fall 1922, a number of architects requested that he publish a monthly that would reflect the best work being produced in the U.S. Accordingly, Forbes began the *Architect,* its first issue appearing in October 1923 (49). George S. Chappell and Kenneth Murchison were the first associate editors; Donn Barber joined them the following January. The manner of operation Forbes instituted, however, was the same one that he had made use of earlier. Whereas a Consulting Board of Architecture had reviewed the illustrations and content in *Architecture,* a Board of Architects was instituted for the *Architect,* to save "the profession valuable time in weeding out worthless material" (50).

At the outset, every issue contained from 24 to 30 plates, several pages of perspectives or line drawings, and a dou-

ble-page detail by architect-illustrator Walter McQuade. The outside cover was a Piranesi drawing, changed monthly. A journal of pretension, the staff held that "our ideal is to have publication in the *Architect* become an honor" (51). It was reputedly the only periodical of the time to print on only one side of the page; the other side was left blank.

The opening issue began with a letter from architect Barber, calling for American architects to make simple and direct use of fewer motifs and a logical choice of fewer materials. The missive itself is important for indicating that Barber was in contact with the Editor, Forbes, from the start, because the *Architect* was in many ways the logical successor to the *New York Architect,* which the architect had begun a number of years earlier.

In the first issues, Forbes's role in this periodical was paramount, for there were few contributors. The primary justification for the *Architect* seemed to be the publication of work by a litany of the best-connected architects in New York City: Platt, Magonigle, Embury II, Francke H. Bosworth, A. Stewart Walker, Leon N. Gillette, Richard Henry Dana, and John Russell Pope, among others. Many of these professionals worked in the Architects' Building, from which the journal was issued. The formula gained an element of humor in December 1923, when Chappell began a delightful serial in which Sir Christopher Wren came back to Earth and was shown New York City. This was followed by other entertaining series: "An Architect on Olympus," "An Architect's Letters to His Son," and "A Student's Note-Book, Being the History of a Strange Architectural Discovery on the Top of a Fifth Avenue Bus." (In the last story, an architectural student's bag, which contains some rather special instruments, such as a volute compass, an egg and dart layer, and a little book "Architectural Composition and Decomposition," and a notebook that describes the classes he was attending are left behind for the young narrator of the story.) By October 1924, Murchison was producing a regular column, "Mr Murchison Says," with short, cute headings ("God Bless Our Flat," "Trim Should Shrink," etc) for his observations, occasionally including a crossword puzzle to round out the department. By early 1925, the *Architect* had found its stride, and to judge from published readers' comments, it was successful. The idea of completely segregating the architecture from the advertising allowed the subscriber to page through the illustrations as one would "stroll through a gallery"—uninterrupted. The practical matters were dealt with in the advertising sections.

One of the most extensive contributors was Newcomb, who, beginning October 1927, dealt with a number of early U.S. architects. Included in this series were studies of McIntire, Latrobe, Bulfinch, Jefferson, Mills, Thornton, Strickland, and Hamilton, to name a few. Several articles on legal topics written by the attorney Leo J. Parker were also incorporated, and the photographic coverage was extended to new buildings throughout the U.S. and, occasionally, Europe.

McQuade, whom Forbes had relied upon from the beginning of the journal, became Editor in March 1928. Readers were assured that he was thoroughly imbued with an appreciation of the high standards of the journal, which he would respect in every detail. Modern ideas became evident in the medium for which the *Architect* was most celebrated—photography. The April 1928 issue included a frontispiece by Amemya entitled "Downtown," a composite photograph of buildings from various angles in the manner of "some of our more revolutionary artists who aim to give us 'impressions,' combined mental experiences rather than isolated examples." McQuade did not back away from the issues raised by modern architecture, believing that contemporary designers were wrong in imitating Greek and Roman vocabularies. He pointed to the towering buildings that were being built, however, and found them to be the most worthy monuments of the new movement in architecture; he found a power and dynamic quality that left behind petty applied detail, whatever the artistic language employed.

Another contributor, Chappell, became the Editor in January 1929. His views on the quality of the journal were similar, except that he wished to enlarge the scope of the publication by including the best available work of the allied arts of decoration, sculpture, and mural painting. These were introduced in subsequent issues, but they did not avert the demise of the *Architect,* the last issue of which was published in June 1931. The editors announced the journal was "going on the air" and would shortly be heard over the radio on Tuesdays and Thursdays. "Mr. Corbett" was to be the broadcaster (52).

The *Pacific Coast Architect,* launched in 1911, did not receive much attention for the work it featured, nor was its circulation very large. Another West Coast journal, *California Southland,* was established in 1918; the title was adopted in order to appeal to readers in the southern portion of the state, without offending those elsewhere. This journal absorbed *California Home Owner,* established in 1922. In January 1929, *Pacific Coast Architect* was combined with *California Southland,* to form *California Arts & Architecture.* The marriage of these two monthlies, published by the Western States Publishing Company, made Harris Allen the Editor, and M. Urmy Seares the managing editor. Their editorial staffs and advisory boards, and perhaps also their subscription lists, were merged to create a new journal that appealed to both professional architects and the cultured public. A magazine format that combined text and illustrations was adopted. "We propose to present, through picture and work, the atmosphere of life in California in its cultural and social aspects" (53). The major emphasis was on California homes and gardens. Particular attention was paid to the Spanish–American history of the region, and architects such as Roland Coate of Los Angeles provided many examples of modern houses designed along those lines. The work of other architects, including that of Myron Hunt, H. C. Chambers, H. Roy Kelley, Bernard Maybeck, the Newsom Brothers, and Gordon B. Kaufmann, was also found, although the journal celebrated the lifestyle of the client as often as the accomplishments of the designer. All of this was combined with book reviews, sketches, short stories, travel notes, and monthly bulletins and notices of the various architectural clubs and chapters of the AIA.

By the end of the 1920s it was apparent that U.S. architectural journalism had enjoyed a significant period of growth. The general prosperity of the field enabled editors and publishers to pay significantly greater attention to a number of topics vital to the profession. These matters included criticism, drafting techniques, historical documentation, and building materials. As a result, some journals, such as *Pencil Points* and the *White Pine Series,* were more specialized, and others, the *Architectural Forum* and *Western Architect,* for example, developed broader profiles. Neither approach was more successful than the other, but these topics offered clearly defined options in the era of consolidation that followed.

LITTLE BUILDING, BUT MUCH THOUGHT (1933–1945)

The field of U.S. architectural journalism contracted during the Depression. Whereas in 1928 there were six major periodicals, a decade later the number was reduced to only three, and most of those that survived were owned by large publishing corporations. The day of the small, independent, influential professional monthly had passed.

During the early 1930s, *Pencil Points* retained the position of having the largest circulation in the field. Each month, more than 18,000 copies were printed, equaling the sum of any two of its competitors. By 1937, however, the *Architectural Forum* had surged forward to surpass this number and went on to reach a circulation of over 38,000 copies by the opening of World War II. This was, in part, due to the fact that the *Forum* enjoyed access to the resources of a major publication network, Time, Inc., which was a tremendous asset. On the other hand, the oldest journal of the group, *American Architect and Architecture,* would not survive, despite the backing of the Hearst publishing group. This serial would be absorbed by the *Architectural Record,* one of the periodicals of the F. W. Dodge Corporation.

The rise of the *Forum* was the most important development in architectural journalism during the late 1930s and early 1940s. Compared with those of its contemporaries, both the contents and the format were distinctively promodern. In December 1932, the "International Section," a series that appeared in alternate months and was completely devoted to European modern architecture, was initiated. The first issue featured recent buildings in Austria; successive ones reviewed modern designs in Germany, France, Italy, the Netherlands, and Czechoslovakia. All were notable not only for their contents, but also for their special paper and strikingly different layout. The editorial preference for modern structures was more evident in the selection of new foreign buildings than in that of recent structures erected in the U.S. The published images of buildings in the U.S. were much more diverse in style and type. The colonial and Tudor were especially obvious in articles dealing with modernizing and remodeling and in departments such as "Master Details Series" and "Historic American Buildings Survey."

A format that alternated articles with plate illustrations was employed until April 1933, when the two were integrated and a new section was added. Entitled "Building Money," it dealt with earnings, corporate notes, loans, mortgages, and securities and followed the evolution of government financial aid programs. Money was the one topic of interest to everyone; no one could afford to ignore the latest developments in Washington. "Building Money," edited by Washington Dodge II, and then by John Cushman Fistere, was very nearly a journal within a journal.

The July 1933 issue of the *Forum* was devoted to the Century of Progress Exposition in Chicago, an event that gave the Beaux Arts-trained architects who took part in it a moment in the spotlight. For the most part, however, it was the latest architectural developments of a much smaller, more select group of modernists that found the greatest editorial support. To the subscriber who believed the favored style did not meet the needs of the average practitioner, or who held that the average person could not be educated to understand cubist or modernist designs, the editors answered only that the circulation had doubled from 6580 in 1934 to 12,500 the following year.

In May 1935, when Stowell left for the *American Architect,* Howard Myers became Editor as well as Publisher. With his interest in the latest movements in the art world, Myers became an evangelist for contemporary architectural design and trumpeted the "Coming of Le Corbusier," a "prophetic French architect . . . known throughout the world as the founder of the International Style . . ." (54). Modern European developments were included in the *Forum* with increased frequency. Ironically, in the November issue, which celebrated the visit of Le Corbusier, a letter to the Editor noted that modernism was being reversed in Germany because official Nazi policy returned to the traditional forms and methods of the nineteenth century.

It was also in November 1935 that Rogers and Manson sold the *Forum* to Time, Inc. This should not be surprising for, undoubtedly at Myers's instigation, the *Forum* had been advertising the value of the architect's services in *Time* and *Fortune* magazines.

Throughout the 1930s and into the 1940s, the *Forum* continued to examine small houses. The case histories, which appeared at least six times per year, contained interior–exterior photographs, floor plans, cost data, construction outlines, and critical comment. Notes on events, competitions, and developments in schools such as the WPA laboratory of designer Gilbert Rohde, the establishment of the New Bauhaus by Laszlo Moholy-Nagy, and the appointment of Walter Gropius to Harvard's School of Architecture, were also included.

In October 1938, Henry H. Saylor was appointed to the staff, and *The Architect's World,* a collection of abstracts and book reviews he had been publishing independently, became a regular department of the journal alongside "The Diary." Readers who had subscribed to *Architecture* would remember that Saylor contributed the "Editor's Diary," a similar chatty, semiautobiographical gossip column. Another feature, 16 pages long, entitled "Plus, Orientations of Contemporary Architecture," was introduced in December. This separately paginated section was edited by Wallace K. Harrison, William Lescaze, William Muschenheim, Stamo Papadaki, and James Johnson Sweeney and a host of collaborators, including Max Abramovitz, Josef Albers, Leopold Arnaud, Beatty and Strang, Marcel Breuer, Albert Frey, R. Buckminster Fuller, Bertrand Goldberg, Harwell Hamilton Harris, Alfred Kastner, George Fred Keck, Albert Kahn, Moholy-Nagy, Richard Neutra, Antonin Raymond, R. M. Schindler, Edward Durell Stone, and Le Corbusier, with typography and layout by Herbert Matter. The *Forum* sought to "add opinion, exploration, and new controversy . . . because out of the 'wildest' theories often come the most vital ideas" (55). In addition to all of the special sections, short articles by Naum Gabo, Sigfried Giedion, Fernand Leger, Amédee Ozenfant, and Moholy-Nagy stirred the imagination of subscribers, if the letters to the Editor were any indication. Both cheers and jeers were heard, the latter caused by what was termed Matter's "typographical nightmare" and "postwar German layout." Readers' reactions apparently led to its discontinuation in late 1939, after only three installments.

As the U.S. formally entered World War II, Time, Inc. reorganized, and Myers resumed his role as Publisher of the *Forum.* In January 1942, Ruth Goodhue was listed as the managing editor with associates George Nelson and Henry Wright, who were given an increased share of responsibility.

Along with most of the journalism at the time, the *Forum* became fully occupied with wartime considerations. The "Building Money" section was dropped, for financing of nondefense construction ground to a halt under L-41, the federal "stop building order." Remodeling continued to be a prevalent theme, whether the building under consideration was a residence, bank, or school. More in keeping with the general editorial direction was the continual emphasis on prefabrication, often included as a minor department of the journal. "Demountables" were reportedly springing up everywhere alongside public war housing, whether for naval yards or bomber production plants, such as that at Willow Run, near Detroit.

With the July 1943 issue, the *Forum* appeared in reduced format, in conformance with the orders of the War Production Board curtailing the amount of paper available for printing. The journal was not seriously handicapped by this measure, however, and continued to hold fast to its architectural ideals. Because many schemes would remain on paper, however, the editors turned their attention to gaining more popular acceptance for new design. In August, the journal began an experimental series entitled "Planning with You," a popular treatise on city planning intended to enlist public support for rebuilding U.S. cities. The series continued into 1945 and was made available to readers in pamphlet form. The *Forum* was also interested in tenant reactions to functional housing designs and reviewed the biases of consumer magazines such as *McCall's* and *Ladies' Home Journal* to examine the degree to which modern architecture was finding acceptance among the general public. The editorial staff noted that enlightened advertisers had been using images of buildings that demonstrated the practical value of the modern idiom and were attracting the consumer, whereas others failed to grasp the implications of contemporary design and planning and were merely using them to disguise out-of-date approaches.

The story of the *Architectural Record* during this period is one of considerable advance, truncated by a difficult adjustment to the war situation. In January 1933, Mikkelsen was still Editor and Kocher was Managing Editor.

C. Theodore Larson, Hooper, W. Pope Barney, Theodore Crane, Howard T. Fisher, Fiske Kimball, William Stanley Parker, and Henry Wright were all listed as contributors. The format consisted of one or two short feature articles, a portfolio of current architecture, a department of technical news and research, another smaller section on building trends and economic outlook, and various smaller items such as book reviews, correspondence, and manufacturers' announcements.

Throughout the mid-1930s, the *Record* carried features that indicated architects in foreign countries were practicing in the modern mode, whereas the majority of buildings in the U.S. were erected in the traditional colonial or Tudor fashion. Progress in housing activity was recorded, with inventories of many cities being conducted to determine the extent of blighted areas that would be replaced under one or more of the new federal programs. Public works legislation for the construction of highways, bridges, airports, power stations, museums, and health institutions supported some firms, and others were dormant.

With money for large-scale projects scarce, architects turned their attention to what was variously called remodeling or modernizing. The *Record* noted that branch banks and warehouses were altered with the application of stucco veneers. Schools were updated by removing gables, replacing sashes, and adding Moderne parapet walls. Main Street retail structures were modernized with structural glass fronts and tubular lighting.

Housing prefabrication was one of Kocher's interests, as evidenced by the houses he executed with architect Albert Frey. This received more attention in the mid-1930s, in conjunction with an emphasis on materials. For example, in November 1935, John Ely Burchard of Bemis Industries, which had been conducting a number of research experiments in housing, was quoted as believing that the profession was on the verge of a revolution in American housing design. To Burchard, it was evident that houses of the future would have walls with simpler finishes and that allowed more light and closer contact with the out-of-doors. The flat roof was deemed inevitable.

On the other hand, the *Record* continued to record developments of interest to those practicing in the traditional modes. The December 1935 issue was devoted entirely to the restoration of Colonial Williamsburg; the issue became so popular that it was republished as a book. In fact, the editors, interested in discovering how many professionals had been subscribing to the journal from its beginning, offered a bound copy of *The Restoration of Colonial Williamsburg* (56) as a prize for the oldest subscriber who would identify himself or, "if he takes his modern straight," a copy of *The New Architecture in Mexico* (57).

In February 1936, two associate editors were added to the staff: James Marston Fitch and Gene Hawley. Within a few months, their efforts became obvious in one of the most intellectually stimulating periods this journal would experience. Contributors in early 1937 included Catherine Bauer and Clarence Perry, with features on Bauhaus associate Lyonel Feininger and De Stijl architect Frederick J. Kiesler. Beginning with the January issue, every *Record* was devoted in part to the study of a building type, a

feature that would distinguish the journal from its contemporaries for a number of years to come. Retail stores were followed by industrial buildings, housing, and schools. Special issues, such as that of March 1937, which was produced by the editors of the *Architectural Review* in London, were also published. The plan was to have the editors of the *Record* and the *Review* switch places for a month. "The English *Review* is rated as the most brilliantly edited magazine in England," crowed the *Record* (58), and articles by Nikolaus Pevsner and Herbert Read underlined the point.

When, in June 1937, Kocher replaced Mikkelsen as Editor, the *Record* refined its format so as to produce "three magazines within a magazine." To the "Building Types" part, another section was added, entitled "Building News," edited by Fitch, along with a third, "Design Trends." A change in layout was put in the hands of Hawley, who was named Art Director (59). The purpose of this format was threefold: to note events without any attempt at editorial analysis, to indicate trends that developed from recurring events, and to help define standards in design as they applied to various building types.

The tempo of the *Record* in the late 1930s was near fever pitch. The typical issue opened with the "Building News" section. Fitch might highlight the mountain home of the elderly potter and once-famous socialist Bouck White at the same time he noted the movements of Gropius and Wright and the claims made by Clarence Saunders of Piggly Wiggly fame for his infamous "Keedoozle" supermarkets. Science and technology were to bring new materials, new methods, and new systems to building design. "Design Trends" came next. It included articles proposing that consumer acceptance of modern design was inevitable, as suggested by the fact that houses executed in this new style were receiving mortgage loans. The "Building Types" section, edited by R. Stanley Sweeley, was third. It urged designers faced with factory layout problems to look to flow diagrams for effective solutions. The development of time-saver standards for each of these types put the latest ready-reference material at the fingertips of subscribers.

The pace was interrupted, however, when Dodge announced the consolidation of the two oldest architectural journals in the U.S. in March 1938. With that issue, *American Architect and Architecture* was combined with the *Record*. The former journal had been created in June 1936 when the *American Architect* was combined with *Architecture*, with Stowell as Editor and Saylor as Associate Editor. However, even after that merger, the new Hearst publication seemed doomed to failure. When Dodge consolidated the two journals, the editorial staffs were united, but clearly the *Record*, devoted to technological advance, changed little.

For a few months longer, the *Record* enjoyed a large, experienced staff. In response to the claim that the reduced competition in the field would likely produce a magazine with only "one mind," the Editor responded that never again would anyone working alone be able to bring together all of the facts necessary to be able to control the policies and editorial matter of an architectural journal. The *Record* enjoyed a field staff of over 700 reporters and correspondents for Dodge Reports, who provided a wealth of information for each issue. *Sweet's Catalog Services,* for decades a principal source of information, and the *Dodge Statistical Service* were other parts of the network (60).

The year 1941 marked the fiftieth anniversary of the *Record,* and in January and February special sections were included that juxtaposed design solutions of a half-century earlier with those of the present. The emphasis was on displaying the contributions that science and technology had made to building design, a position made clear in a symposium held by the *Record* at the time. This predilection seems to have been due in part to Thomas S. Holden, who served as Editorial Director throughout the late 1930s and early 1940s and who was elected President of the Dodge Corporation in March 1941.

After the United States entered World War II, the *Record* lost many of the contributors and staff who had worked to make it so distinctive. A number of personnel changes took place. For example, in August 1941, Fitch left the *Record* for the Army, and engineer Emerson Goble, former Editor of the *National Real Estate Journal,* joined the staff, soon to become Managing Editor. At about the same time, Saylor became a regular contributor, and in March 1942, Stowell became Editor-in-Chief, having spent seven years with *American Architect* and *House Beautiful.* Douglas Haskell was made Associate Editor in September 1943.

As the war dragged on, the number of recently completed projects declined. Housing developments designed in traditional modes by Royal Barry Wills appeared alongside dormitories in modern fashion by Saarinen and Swansen. The most important critic the *Record* featured was Dean Joseph Hudnut of Harvard. His articles on such topics as "Housing and the Democratic Process" and "The Political Art of Planning" underscored the need for a harder look beyond the ideas and techniques for postwar planning to the institutions and laws that would make them real.

The most notable contribution the *Record* made to architectural journalism as a whole during the war years was the series of building types studies, wherein each month the journal collaborated with a leading magazine that served a specific building manager group. As a result, the *Record* published a study on hotels with *Hotel Management,* on gas stations with the *National Petroleum News,* and on educational buildings with the *Nation's Schools.* These studies were aimed at demonstrating the value of architect-engineer services to the client and were backed by the news-gathering and market-gauging facilities of the Dodge Corporation.

As wartime construction increased, the attention of the journal changed to reemphasize the opportunities offered professionals by prefabricated housing and remodeling, although with little of the polemics associated with the topic in the *Architectural Forum.* A building types study devoted to factory design, for example, discussed the merit of easy-to-erect modern design and underlined the importance of economy and factory air-raid protection. The emphasis on materials changed as well. Although it was anticipated that there would be no general shortage of materials, metals in particular became scarce. Plywood became ever more prominent, especially in modern designs. The postwar house would have open planning, with several rooms combined into one space to save money, division of the building into several zones, and an enlarged conception of space, with more glass.

Pencil Points underwent a slow transformation during the depths of the Depression, leaving behind its original image for a broader, more design-oriented one. Although Whitehead remained Editor, Kenneth Reid was made Managing Editor beginning with the February 1933 issue, and the publishing responsibilities were taken over by the Reinhold Publishing Corporation in September 1934. At this point, although its cover claimed it to be "an illustrated journal for the drafting room," the table of contents began to claim that the magazine had "something for everyone in the architectural profession." One of the elements that *Pencil Points* lacked was criticism. Some of the staff believed that "the profession would benefit by sincere criticism," which would be forceful and pertinent (61). However, they had repeatedly encountered reluctance and opposition when trying to get one architect to comment on another's work. In June 1934, Magonigle, who was already well known to subscribers by virtue of his autobiographical series, began a new department entitled "'The Upper Ground,' Being Essays in Criticism." His approach was to examine architecture that had appeared in several recent periodicals and to characterize the "drift—rather than the direction"—it was taking. Magonigle did not have a preconceived point of view. He acknowledged that there were too many directions to follow, that architectural design was often a regional affair, and that if the new buildings seen in the journals were taken as representative of what was being built throughout the nation, it would be found inchoate (62). In the months that followed, Magonigle reviewed the *Forum, Architecture,* the *Record,* and the *Architectural Review* (London), but he focused his criticism chiefly on the American architects for their "sleepiness," an apparent inability to rally against the restrictions being imposed by an increasingly bureaucratic government.

In the late 1930s and early 1940s a single word—design—was printed across the top of the cover. Reid assumed the editorial chair, and Whitehead was reassigned as Editor of the monograph series, clearly relegating the latter to a secondary position. The journal was no longer concerned with drafting room techniques. Even more obvious was the switch from a journal that was edited with its readers to one prepared for them. This transformation was complete by June 1940, when Editor Reid wrote (63)

. . . . we have shifted our position somewhat in the direction of stressing design rather than draftsmanship. With changes taking place in the manner of choosing and assembling materials in building, we have felt there was a need to set before our readers illustrations showing how leading designers have reacted. . . . and technical data about materials and construction methods.

The formula consisted of 6–8 short articles, 6–12 sets of plate illustrations, letters from subscribers (dubbed "The Threshing Floor"), a few selected details, data sheets provided by Don Graf, and "Here, There, This and That," which was reduced to editorial commentary. Perhaps the best known contributor to the journal was Professor Talbot F. Hamlin of Columbia University, whose essays were both the subject of commendation and the object of scorn.

The turmoil that followed the entrance of the United States into World War II was clearly reflected in *Pencil Points*. It quickly became obvious that architects needed to cooperate with engineers, planners, and housing experts if they wanted to share in government work. Victory design contracts for housing and industrial plants complete superseded country house designs and church schemes. Air-raid precaution (ARP) literature and articles on camouflage suddenly found their way to the forefront of professional journalism. In addition, Reid provided some of the most pointed, emotional editorials ever to appear in print about the architect's role during wartime. Exhortations that "the Nation's unused architectural skill should be mobilized for Post War Planning NOW!" appeared as early as February 1942 (64). *Pencil Points* had looked ahead and warned its readers that an economic Pearl Harbor was possible after the war, if proper measures were not taken immediately to plan for the return of peace.

Reid's energy was also evident in the transformation of the journal into *The New Pencil Points,* which occurred in May 1942. It would be "as fresh, exciting and vigorous as we know how to make it," he wrote, with its keynote: "Look forward—not back" (65). Reid had become an ardent advocate of the avant garde. In July, the birth of the Telesis group in California was featured. An outgrowth of the Congres Internationaux d'Architecture Moderne (CIAM) and national organizations like the Modern Architectural Research Group in the UK, the philosophy of Telesis was "the essence of Henry Wright, Geddes, Gropius, Mumford, Corbusier, [and] Unwin. For the majority of the younger planners and architects, there are among these men superficial differences, but no fundamental disagreement" (66). The message was made clear repeatedly: architects must broaden their professional knowledge to include all aspects of community design and planning. A series of articles on changing aspects of architectural practice by Arthur C. Holden; insistent headings such as "Little Plans Won't Do!" and "Farm Buildings Are Architecture," introducing the contributions of Hamlin; and satirical essays such as "The Frenzied Functionalist" and "Wilbur, Master Builder" by Thomas H. Creighton all served to reinforce the polemical position of the journal.

In June 1944, *Pencil Points* rededicated itself to "progressive architecture," which Reid defined as having the three Vitruvian principles of fitness, strength, and beauty, but to which he added another—social purpose. The architect was not only to consider the needs of the client, but also to provide for others who would see, use, or be affected by the design. The object was to create a better world.

Meanwhile, *California Arts & Architecture* was spiraling closer to many of the same issues. Allen was succeeded by architect Mark Daniels as Editor in 1933, and he served to guide the magazine in architectural matters. Ellen Leech and several other contributors provided reviews of radio programs, movies, art exhibitions, theater notes, antique auctions, and garden parties. The Western States Publishing Company, with George Oyer as President, continued to publish the magazine. Oyer urged his readers to employ architects and was interested in domestic architecture himself, frequently writing on the problems of the small house in the West. In this, the journal maintained a certain pride. It was common, the Editor noted, for a California architect to win the Better Homes in America contest, as Reginald Johnson and Winchton Risley had done, with traditional schemes evoking Spanish images. The supremacy of the contemporary California design was proven when Richard Neutra won the award.

The January 1935 issue of *California Arts & Architecture* was devoted entirely to the modern movement in architecture as it had appeared in the West. The staff believed that "no region of the United States has a greater number of outstanding and internationally known architects building 'modern' houses" (67). Among the designers featured were Neutra, Frank Lloyd Wright, R. M. Schindler, Irving Morrow, Harwell Harris, Jock Peters, Harbin Hunter, and J. R. Davidson. Pauline Schindler was Associate Editor for this issue. Modern issues appeared infrequently thereafter; however, the traditional, Spanish-inspired ranch house remained a favorite.

Oyer had sold The Western States Publishing Company to Jere B. Johnson by January 1939. Daniels also left, and for a time, although there were several architects who continued to contribute, such as Harris, Ralph D. Cornell, and Gordon B. Kaufmann, no one assumed an editorial capacity or wrote regularly for the magazine.

A major reorganization of the contents occurred in early 1940, when John Entenza was named Editor. A three-part format was established, with short, impressionistic feature articles, followed by the architecture section and, lastly, the general features. All three were generously illustrated, artistically and fashionably laid out on the page, and highlighted with bold lettering. Entenza's interests in abstract art and modern architecture were soon made clear. Articles on such artists as Matter, Jackson Pollock, Hans Hofmann, Harry Bertoia, Piet Mondrian, and Peter Krasnow and on musicians such as Lou Harrison and Charles Ives put *California Arts & Architecture* at the leading edge of the artistic world. Attitudes on architectural matters were likewise advanced. Editorial associates included Patterson Greene and Charles Eames, and the editorial advisory board included Ray Eames, William W. Wurster, Neutra, Harris, Paul T. Frankl, Harold W. Grieve, and John Byers as well as the older generation of Kaufman, William Schuchhardt, and H. Roy Kelley.

In August 1943, *California Arts & Architecture* inaugurated an annual competition entitled "Designs for Postwar Living," a search for the "kind of house that can really be built for living in a world of peace." The successful designs were to suggest a way of life for the U.S. worker, who was likely to have an enormous respect for the machine and who would insist on simple, direct, and honest efficiency. The results were judged by Neutra, Sumner Spaulding, Gregory Ain, Charles Eames, and John Rex. In August, first prize was awarded to Eero Saarinen and Oliver Lundquist.

To reinforce his point of view, in January 1945 Entenza launched "the case study house program . . . to begin immediately the study, planning, actual design, and construction of eight houses, each to fulfill the specifications of a special living problem in the Southern California area." Eight nationally known architects were chosen: Davidson, Spaulding, Neutra, Saarinen, Wurster, Charles Eames, Ralph Rapson, and Whitney Smith. Their designs were featured over the course of the next few years and others followed, as models to emulate. To demonstrate his point, the Editor personally financed the construction of 23 of these contemporary designs (68).

Entenza became both Editor and Publisher of *California Arts & Architecture* in December 1943, and by March of the following year, all explicit references to California were dropped. Henceforth, the journal became *Arts and Architecture,* and it attempted to compete on a nationwide basis with the most progressive serials in the East.

In January 1946, Creighton summarized the changes that he observed in *Pencil Points,* the *Architectural Forum,* and the *Architectural Record* (69). He found that whereas before the war there were modernized Gothic schools, modern hospitals, Georgian public buildings, modernistic recreation buildings, rambling Cape Cod houses, and modern homes, when peace returned, "not a single building was illustrated which was not designed in a contemporary, nontraditional manner." Over these four years, there had been a more careful use of materials, a more rigid analysis of plans and more honest projection of plans into the buildings as wholes. Why the change? A shortage of materials produced the unexpected result, for ostentation had to be dropped and barrenness had become a virtue. Creighton's appraisal of the progress indicated that credit went to the *Forum* for early scouting and touting and to *Pencil Points* for critical analysis, especially of community issues, and the early contributions of the rival *Record* were largely forgotten in the face of its change to an architectural engineering orientation. Aside from the "big three" eastern journals, it can be seen that *California Arts & Architecture* also contributed to the change, largely from an artistic point of view.

EDITORIAL STABILITY (1945–1964)

In 1945, the *Architectural Forum,* with slightly over 38,000 subscribers, was twice as large as either of its competitors. In fact, its lead became even greater by 1951, when it reached over 70,000 (70). It was different from its competitors in that it aimed to please not only architects, but also clients, contractors, real estate agents, and financiers. *Pencil Points,* emerging as *Progressive Architecture* after the war, also showed a healthy increase, but stood a distant second in circulation. In many ways, *Progressive Architecture* was the most concerned with professional practice and could justifiably lay claim to having "the largest architectural circulation in the world." Placing third was the *Architectural Record,* which did little to improve its position, preferring to cling to a staid format, emphasizing technological developments and business matters. Meanwhile, the *Journal of the American Institute of Architects,* launched in 1944, slowly began to develop as an influential voice, emerging as a commercial journal in the late 1950s.

All of these journals benefited by the economic recovery following World War II and the prolonged period of prosperity that came on the heels of the Korean conflict. The steady increase in construction activity from 1946 through the next decade marked the most prosperous period of growth the U.S. had ever experienced. This swelling began to hesitate in 1958 and cooled only in the early 1960s.

At the time the armistice in Europe was being signed, the *Architectural Forum* employed more women on its staff than any professional journal ever had. Eleven women, and only four men, were listed as either associate or assistant editors under Managing Editor Henry Wright. This, and the fact that Publisher Howard Myers was not a practicing architect, occasionally led disgruntled subscribers to remark that the journal had become preoccupied with a specious brand of architecture and strayed far afield from the concerns of the professional. The staff of the journal believed it was correct in its position, however, and pointed to the circulation figures to suggest there were thousands who were satisfied. The last important issue to be published under Wright's command, in November 1948, may be taken as typical. It was entitled "Measure." In brief, it promoted an understanding of the degree to which humans control and condition their environment by considering developments in the regulation of heat, atmosphere, light, sound, enclosure, aesthetics, and space. As the Editor acknowledged, this approach to the artificial environment and building design owed much to Fitch, who had studied under Wright and whose book *American Building* had recently been published (71).

Much to the consternation of many modernists, one needed only to observe the booming subdivisions to determine that the most popular house design of the mid-twentieth century was the Cape Cod cottage. It seemed that neither the builder, the realtor, the banker, nor the customer was to blame; rather, it was a lingering popular notion that had been fostered by architects who had for years used historical prototypes before World War II.

This building boom was seen as an opportunity by those who controlled the *Forum.* In March 1949, the management of Time, Inc. appointed Perry Prentice as both Editor and Publisher of the journal. He had become convinced that the *Forum* was trying to serve two different industries: the first was heavy construction, working in concrete and steel, and the second, devoted to the postwar housing boom, was working in wood. In April, for example, a reference issue devoted to the "Builder's House, 1949" addressed the merchant builder, who accounted for about 80% of the houses constructed each year. (The emergence of the large-scale builder was largely a recent development, the result of the Defense Housing Program, the war, and the introduction of mortgage insurance by the Federal Housing Authority.)

Prentice first sought to deal with this dichotomy by subordinating the magazine's title to cover both fields, changing it to the "Magazine of Building." In September 1951, he proposed that the magazine be published in two separate editions, one for "big builders" and the other for houses (72). The October issue was a "dress rehearsal" for the new magazine about houses, and for the next two months two magazines were carried in one cover. In January 1952, the "Magazine of Building" appeared in two editions: *Architectural Forum* and *House & Home.* By September 1952, the former continued with a circulation of 46,000, and the latter boasted a circulation of 100,000.

Prentice, although Editor of both periodicals, devoted most of his time to *House & Home,* which became the friend of the small contractor grown large. Unfortunately, both magazines continued to operate at a loss. *House & Home* continued to be published for another 10 years under Prentice, but he was relieved of command of the *Forum.* It was given to Del Paine, who was publisher of *Fortune* as well (73).

With a sharper focus and expanded coverage of engineering developments, the *Forum* was not to be cast as a journal that would merely reflect what was being built. Rather, it would lead discussion of what should be built. The new architectural editor, Haskell, who had worked as senior associate editor of the *Architectural Record,* received hearty congratulations from the staff at the Museum of Modern Art, for the *Forum* was perceived to have recovered its former promodern editorial stand. In addition, the journal assembled an impressive cast of associates, including Peter Blake, Jane Jacobs, McQuade, Richard Sanders, and Ogden Tanner. It was clear, however, that there was no longer one answer. "Modern architecture used to be all one thing and modern architects were comrades in arms," Haskell wrote (74), and the public understood the difference between what was traditional and contemporary because the latter was more functional. By May 1953, the cry was for a more human architecture.

Where did the *Forum* stand? It continued to act as a forum and attempted to reflect all developments. In an article that appeared in July 1953, Eero Saarinen wrote that there were six broad currents in modern architecture, each represented by one or more major practitioners: Wright and organic unity; Wurster and Belluschi and handicraft architecture; Aalto and the European individualists; Le Corbusier, devoted to function and plastic form; Gropius and the architecture for the machine age; Mies van der Rohe, the form-giver; and Nervi and Fuller, who represented the engineer-scientists (75). The options were clearly open.

Largely due to Haskell's influence, the *Forum* became the first magazine to become heavily concerned with redevelopment, a theme prominent in several articles during the mid-1950s. Questions such as what could be done for cities economically and socially were put alongside journalistic plans of action, such as those to keep cities downtown and to make urban renewal succeed by making use of private enterprise. Alarmed at the office building boom that was destroying the street life of Manhattan, Senior Editor Jane Jacobs analyzed the problem and offered her prescriptions.

In September 1955, a series entitled "Architecture in America," which examined the changes in the profession that affected the nature of buildings, was begun. The architect as organizer, the manufacturer's role in construction, the demands of corporate clients, the contractor's part, the engineer's place, and the changes in the labor force were all seen as influential. The seventh installment, entitled "Fantastic Architecture," included a portfolio of photographs by Clarence John Laughlin, which explored the unusual, personal expressions found in a firehouse or a boatman's house and called for a reevaluation of the merits of the commonplace commercial architecture of the nineteenth and early twentieth centuries.

"Can Roadtown Be Damned?" asked Haskell, questioning the tendency of thinkers in 1955 to curse at the architecture of strip highway development in the same way that others in the 1920s had condemned Main Streets. Taking its cue from articles that had appeared in the *Architectural Review,* the *Forum* began to ask the more important question: How can "Roadtown" be improved? Soon the discussion of innovative or unusual shopping centers, parking garages, and drive-in banks rivaled that of the latest designs by Mies van der Rohe, Skidmore, Owings and Merrill, and Saarinen.

In 1956, Publisher Paine embarked on a new program to widen the appeal of the journal, of which the management approved wholeheartedly. Editor-in-Chief Henry R. Luce led off in this direction with a statement on the place of "Art in American Life." Many creative manifestations were soon evident. Dealing with Washington, D.C., for example, the beauty of its civic art led to a discussion of the history of its grand plan and its present-day problems; this, in turn, led to questions associated with urban design of monumental architecture. The preservation of historic buildings and neighborhoods was set before the readers for the first time, and the misguided remodeling of the Capitol received special editorial attention.

The January 1957 issue, entitled "Technology—1977," for which the editors were indebted to Lawrence Lessing, formerly a member of *Fortune*'s Board of Editors, took a higher, literary level. Recalling the tone of the November 1948 issue, the journal restated its belief that industry was continually developing a new technology for tomorrow's architecture, that "landshaping" was being added to the art of architecture, that matter would be remodeled into new building components, that the fabrication of sandwich wall panels would offer total environmental control, and that structure was now freed by the use of thin shells, pleated slabs, space frames, and balloon structures. Humans controlled the machine. As Editor Haskell wrote the following month, the U.S. was in a position to enter a golden age of architecture.

In the late 1950s, *Forum* criticism was at its peak. There were three sections, on the art of architecture, the business of building, and technology; all examined difficult issues in a clear light. The various schemes for building over Grand Central Station, the drastic reduction in rental housing construction, the clubbiness of electricians and carpenters, and the need to "arrest the highwaymen" were a few of the campaigns the journal carried on. In 1962 and 1963, special issues on cities such as Chicago, Boston, and Washington were rooted in historical understanding and supplemented with numerous and extensive on-site interviews and investigation. The May 1962 issue of the *Forum* even listed the 100 largest architectural firms and, two months later, ranked the 100 largest clients. What about architectural design? Commenting on the apparent confusion in architectural thinking, Sigfried Giedion wrote that there appeared to be a rash of "Playboy Architecture . . . an architecture treated as playboys treat life, jumping from one sensation to another and quickly bored with everything . . ." (76).

Where in September 1945 *Pencil Points* listed "Progressive Architecture" as a subtitle, in October the journal became *Progressive Architecture. P/A,* as it came to be known, prided itself on the fact that its editors were trained as architects and that it remained the closest to the interests of the practicing professional.

In May 1946, Creighton replaced Reid as Editor. Charles Magruder was soon named Managing Editor, and George A. Sanderson was designated Feature Editor. Creighton made few immediate changes in permanent staff or the overall complexion of the journal. Instead, he gradually introduced several new features and relied upon a number of well-known columnists to make several important adjustments in the structure of *Progressive Architecture*.

In May 1946, the annual *Progressive Architecture* awards were instituted. There were two awards, the first for the best nonresidential building and the second for the best private residence, both to exemplify the contemporary design standards of fitness, strength, beauty, and purpose. The jury consisted of George Howe, Wurster, Eliel Saarinen, C. E. A. Winslow, Fred N. Severud, Reid, and Editor Creighton. The winning buildings were chiefly contemporary residential architecture from the West Coast and small institutional structures.

A year later, Creighton introduced the idea of having each of the various building types that were featured in the journal accompanied by a critique. This commentary from fellow professionals was intended to sharpen several skills. "Architects can take it," wrote the Editor, referring to the examination given retail stores, multifamily housing, single-family homes, and health care facilities that would be reviewed in the upcoming months. "The Architect and His Community" series attempted to educate the professional to his responsibilities in a broader sense by featuring the work of progressive architectural firms from throughout the country that were making contributions to the cities and towns of their regions. Firms from such points as Atlanta; Charlotte; Portland, Oregon; Burlington, Vermont; and Klamath Falls, Oregon were highlighted for having improved their municipalities.

Creighton also initiated two new columns by well-qualified writers. "It's the Law" by Bernard Tomson was begun in November 1948 and dealt with the legal aspects of architecture, engineering, and building construction. A second column, entitled "Out of School," was written by Carl Feiss, then Director of the School of Architecture at the University of Denver. It began in September 1949 (77) and continued until 1955, dealing with architectural and planning education and its relationship to practice. Feiss repeatedly expressed his belief that the professional designer should be trained for more than practice, and he demonstrated this with examples of his own work as a public official and consultant and from the history of planning and housing.

Progressive Architecture had only briefly believed that modern architecture represented the wave of the future and carried some of the earliest criticism of it (78). Creighton took to task much of the current discussion about the direction of the profession, dubbing as false any belief in current styles, the overemphasis on so-called technical problems, and the idea that the architecture of the time was a failure because there was no monumental expression of the culture (79). Creighton believed criticism was

healthy, but on the whole, he insisted, "Let's stop talking nonsense and get down to work" (80).

In January 1950, a special feature entitled "The Grand Detour" detailed the course of architecture from 1900 to 1950. A Board of Consultants, including Henry S. Churchill, Fitch, Hamlin, Carroll L. V. Meeks, and Severud guided this investigation into the question of why it took so long for design to catch up to the technological developments of the age. The answer was that society was not ready to support rapid advances in design. Despite the development of precast concrete components, corrugated steel panels, stainless steel, synthetic lumber, plastics, and so on, there was a widening of responsibilities. Architect-planners and architect-engineers were concerned with many more issues, or so it was felt. This was the one of the most thorough reviews of the construction methods, materials and equipment, architectural designs, and office practice ever to appear in print.

Houses, power and industrial buildings, hotels and motels, and the new building type, shopping centers, were featured in the early 1950s. Efforts to improve not only the content of *Progressive Architecture,* but also its format never seem to have ended. "Interior Design Data," a department from the architect's point of view, was introduced in January 1952. Page Beauchamp served as the first consulting editor for this feature. In addition to the columns by Creighton, Tomson, and Feiss, others were begun. In 1953, consultant Benjamin John Small launched "Spec Small Talk" on specifications, often gracing his writing with cartoons. Frederick Gutheim began a column on the "Washington Perspective" later in the same year.

In keeping with the general feeling of sustained optimism in the construction industry, *P/A*'s first Design Awards program was begun in 1954. This was devoted to buildings in the design stage and superseded the earlier awards program. In the first year, over 600 entries were submitted, and the competition was keen, bringing many well-known firms in comparison with the best new talent. The winners were the team of Belluschi, Walter F. Bogner, Carl Koch & Associates, Hugh Stubbins, Jr., and The Architects Collaborative, for a proposed Back Bay Center development in Boston. It was to be a shining new core for the old metropolis, within two blocks of Richardson's Trinity Church. Members of the jury were the Editor's friends and associates Howe, Eero Saarinen, Severud, and Victor Gruen.

The first issues in 1954 also showed the shift toward the use of themes to organize each issue. Ideas concerning changing family living habits, more leisure time, more general education, new structural concepts, and better health care were seen as having an impact on architecture. The use of themes allowed the staff greater flexibility in defining the material of greatest interest, unlike in the *Record,* which concentrated on a single, narrowly defined function type. When *P/A* dealt with the question of greater mobility, for example, highways, parking decks, service stations, motels, and airports were all dealt with in one issue.

With the February 1954 issue, Creighton moved its various features on office practices into one section. The first article, "Overhead," was the beginning of a series on architectural office and drafting room management, written by Siegmund Speigel. Another new series dealt with architectural public relations, documenting a number of case histories of successful exhibits, TV shows, and community education. Architectural guidebooks were noted because they helped public relations.

In a remarkably prescient column, Feiss had noted as early as November 1952 that there was a growing tendency of architectural journals to discuss art, using such authors as Sibyl Moholy-Nagy, Gropius, and Mitzi Solomon. This seemed to be leading to some relaxation of aesthetic tensions. By the mid-1950s, the phenomenon Feiss had observed was more evident. The jury of the Design Awards program for 1956, for example, remarked that architects were breaking away from the safe rectangle, using fewer pilotis, occasional dashes of color, and turning to a pitched roof as often as a flat one. There appeared to be a relaxed use of contemporary forms, which often took very plastic shapes. In fact, the jury for the awards in 1957 questioned whether architects had the sculptural understanding necessary to use such forms (81). Creighton noted that there seemed to be a continuing school of austerity in design, but at the same time, there was a growing desire for sensuous shapes and emotion-producing forms. Thin-shell concrete roofs, in the form of hyperbolic paraboloids, barrel vaults, and folded plates were much more common as the 1950s wore on. The New Brutalism and Grand Design were seen as the predominant schools of design (82).

In February 1957, a new, short series was introduced by Consulting Editor Ada Louise Huxtable, entitled "Progressive Architecture in America." The Harper Brothers Building of 1854, the Larkin Company Administration Building, the Eads Bridge, Home Insurance Building, and the E. V. Haughtwout & Company Building were a few of the structures highlighted, with the assistance of some of the best-known architects and historians of the day.

In January 1959, James T. Burns, Jr., was made News Editor, and the "News Report" was greatly enlarged, made easier to read, and generously illustrated. Burns was also given the assignment of reviewing prominent firms around the country in a series that once again featured the architect in the context of serving his community. The first editorials that dealt with historic preservation soon followed the increased news coverage. They concerned Simon Rodia's Towers and George Wyman's Bradbury Building in California, and College Hill in Providence, Rhode Island (83,84).

The word most often used to describe the jury's comments about the entries for the *Progressive Architecture* Design Awards was chaos. Stimulated by this reaction, the journal conducted a seminar by correspondence, asking some 50 architects to answer questions about contemporary theory, practice, and technology. In March 1961, the first part of the "*P/A* Symposium on the State of Architecture" indicated that although almost everyone agreed there was a considerable amount of confusion in architecture, few could agree on the reasons for it. This was illustrated in the November 1962 issue, when Craig Ellwood's house in Hillsborough, California, appeared back to back with Herb Greene's residences near Snyder, Oklahoma. In February 1964, two newly completed Yale buildings were featured: the Beinecke Rare Book Library by Skidmore, Owings and Merrill, and the Art & Architecture Building by Paul Rudolph.

Creighton served until 1963, when he went into private practice (85). Perhaps his most important contribution was the introduction of the Design Awards program, which allowed readers to get a glimpse of the immediate future. By the time he stepped down, however, a vision of what lay ahead was often as disconcerting as the present.

The *Architectural Record* emerged from World War II as the most reserved of the "big three" journals. Stowell's editorials were among the most liberal of his contemporaries', calling for a new freedom in contemporary design (86); he did not, however, enjoy the support of any group of architects or theorists, and the publisher remained most interested in the business of architecture. The most characteristic feature of the *Record* remained the building types studies, which brought forward relatively obscure practitioners from throughout the United States. Stowell was proud to acknowledge those who were responsible for bringing contemporary design to their communities. On the other hand, the work of a number of well-known architects, such as Belluschi; Neutra; Page, Southerland and Page; SOM; and Wurster, was also included. Further, having conducted the first survey of its kind, the *Record* found there were "A Thousand Women in Architecture." Of the 22% of the women who replied, it was determined that 11% were practicing. In May 1949, Stowell delivered the journal's credo, "We Believe," and among the last tenets was "We believe in publishing constructively, objectively, for the greatest number of architects, young and old, in every section of the country, without prejudice or favor . . ." (87).

The format of each issue, which changed only rarely in the next decade, began with "The Record Reports," which included recent building news from throughout the United States, a cartoon by Alan Dunn, a column written by Ernest Mickel on developments in Washington, news from Canada by John Caufield Smith, construction cost indexes, and short book reviews. Three or four illustrated feature articles made up the next section, followed by a building types study and architectural engineering notes related to the function type discussed earlier. Multistory hospitals and one-story schools received attention at least once or twice a year, often under the guidance of Associate Editor Frank G. Lopez.

Stowell continued to serve as Editor-in-Chief of the *Record* until 1949, when he left for private practice (88). In September, Harold D. Hauf, a professor of architectural engineering and chairman of the Department of Architecture at Yale, was announced as his successor (89), although he remained only until he was recalled by the Navy in June 1951. Under Hauf, there were no letters to the editor, no editorial comment, and little discussion of design issues. Perhaps because the backgrounds of Hauf and Managing Editor Goble were technical, the *Record* displayed an architectural engineering orientation, reflecting activities in other areas of the profession, but not stimulating it to explore new ideas. The publication sought to be, and attempted to profit from being, an authoritative information service (90).

After Hauf left, the journal extemporized, and Joseph B. Mason was appointed Executive Editor, serving along with Goble. To provide some thoughtful discussion, a series was commissioned that involved a number of well-known critics and professionals charged with addressing the current developments in the direction of an architecture for people, wherein architects would not be the slaves of, but rather the masters of, technology. The contributors included Churchill, Giedion, Henry Hill, Osbert Lancaster, Hudnut, Belluschi, Burchard, Hitchcock, Frank Lloyd Wright, and Lewis Mumford. Wright's article, "Organic Architecture Looks at Modern Architecture," was particularly provocative (91), and Mumford's contribution, "Function and Expression in Architecture" (92), won him the Howard Myers Award for outstanding architectural journalism in 1954.

John Knox Shear became Editor of the *Record* in November 1954. As both a teacher and a professional, Shear had already had a brilliant career, and he was only 37 years old at the time he assumed the chair. Shear, with Goble continuing as Managing Editor, sharpened the focus on current projects by Eero Saarinen, Keck & Keck, Harrison & Abramovitz, Vincent Kling, and Marcel Breuer, always a *Record* favorite.

The series, entitled "One Hundred Years of Significant Building," was begun in June 1956, consisting of buildings nominated by a panel of 50 architects and scholars. Divided into function types, the 12 groups were included in the journal through the following year to celebrate the accomplishments of the profession and honor the one-hundredth anniversary of the AIA. At the conclusion of the series, Edgar Kaufmann called for recognition of other important U.S. structures, reminding readers of the loss of the Marshall Field Wholesale Store, Larkin Building, and Hearst Hall at Berkeley. "If the original buildings that have given form to our world are not to vanish, all of them, into legend—as many too many have already—the architectural profession will need to alert the rest of the community and many of its own members to the values of these structures" (93). This was the first time that the *Record* published the cry for preservation.

Another column, "Reviewing the Record," glanced back at the contents of the magazine in 1906. "Views of Current Periodicals," reviewing some of the major architectural journals of the UK, Italy, France, and Germany, kept readers aware of developments elsewhere around the globe.

In December 1956, Dodge extended its professional magazine horizon by acquiring the *Modern Hospital,* the *Nation's Schools,* and *College and University Business,* permanently allying the heretofore frequent but sporadic collaboration between them and the *Record.* Houses were not forgotten, either, as in mid-May, apart from the regular monthly issue, the *Record* houses for the year made their appearance in a special issue devoted to the topic. In 1957, for example, the houses were designed "for a full life," with two or three "zones," emphasizing "the big room concept," with a screened-in Florida room or a patio, suggesting luxury and convenience. Among the architects whose work was featured were Evans Woolen III, Eliot Noyes, Edward L. Barnes, A. Quincy Jones, Robert A. Little, Philip Johnson, and The Architects Collaborative.

Upon the death of Shear in January 1958 (94), Goble was elevated from Managing Editor to Editor. Burchard, former Dean of Humanities and Social Studies at MIT, was appointed Consulting Editor and became very influential in directing the journal and contributing articles after having traveled abroad. The building types studies continued, with special attention given to schools in anticipation of massive federal aid for educational facilities to relieve the split sessions that the "baby boom" had caused.

In May 1959, a series of articles entitled "The Image of the Architect" was begun, with the belief that the professional should be the complete man of design, involved not only as an artist, city planner, industrial designer, landscape architect, decorator, draftsman, and graphic designer, but also as a sociologist, politician, teacher, economist, and office administrator. The search for fundamentals that the profession was carrying on was obvious in the *Record,* but the answers were not. Instead, Goble was swept up in the early 1960s with the need for a new city image, better urban redevelopment, and the death of the street. Mumford's five-part series on "The Future of the City" began to address some of the design goals for urban renewal, which were explored further in later issues. In addition, a larger, more difficult problem loomed, that of nuclear attack and industrial survival.

The reentry of the AIA into the field of architectural journalism was a slow process, which came about after World War II largely because of the devotion of a small editorial staff. The house organ at that time was the *Octagon. A Journal of the American Institute of Architects,* begun in January 1929. The *Octagon* was not considered a significant professional journal because it was concerned only with the business of the Institute, that is, the formal notices of meetings, transactions, convention actions, chapter information, prizes, competitions, and membership announcements. Furthermore, the *Octagon* was also largely unillustrated. Many members of the Institute continued to feel that it would be desirable to publish a magazine addressing all of the architects in the country, not merely AIA members. The Secretary, faced with material that was clearly related to, but outside the scope of, the Institute's affairs, found it difficult to determine what should or should not be published. In general, the *Octagon* was not expected to take on the character of a professional magazine, enter into controversy, or attempt to guide professional opinion (95). This was primarily because articles on underlying social and economic issues, for example, would sometimes stray into criticism. By the early 1930s, however, articles of technical interest, as on fungus and termite damage in buildings, were regularly being added to the official and internal documents being published.

At the recommendation of two committees constituted for the purpose of investigating the matter, the *Journal of the American Institute of Architects* was reformulated in January 1944 with Saylor at the editorial helm. Saylor already had a considerable amount of experience, having worked as a staff member of the *Architectural Review, Architecture, Country Life, American Architect, House and Garden, Architect's World,* and the *Architectural Forum.* He was mindful of the financial disasters that had befallen previous journals and strove to make the advertising cover the costs of distribution to a growing membership (96). His purpose was clear. "What the *Journal* does earnestly hope to do is pick up, as with a microphone, the Voice of the profession, and amplify it to audibility . . ." (97).

Although restricted at the outset to only 12 pages per issue and denied any embellishments that could have come from advertising revenue, Saylor valiantly carried on. He openly wondered whether "the practice of architecture has undergone a change greater than the adaptability of the individual practitioner." Often, in a soul-searching manner, he would present to the profession questions that would stimulate discussion. For many senior members of the AIA, however, the Institute and its *Journal* seemed to represent the last line of defense against the modern movement. As Gropius wrote to Joseph D. Leland, regional director of the AIA, "several men with respectable records" did not feel welcome within the Institute "as they do not see that the modern architect is given an opportunity to make his opinion known among his older colleagues" (98). Compared with the commercial magazines, the *Journal* was "stuffy" and "uninspiring," and Saylor's editorial comments were branded "forever sarcastic towards anything creative. . . . your personal idiosyncrasies" (99). The Editor's answer was remarkably even-handed: he reiterated that the publication was merely a sounding board, reflecting that which was directed against it. Soon thereafter, however, the occasional plates of early American architecture were suspended, and in August 1948, the *Journal* created a valve through which the pressure might be released in the "Guest Editorial." "The opinions expressed will be, naturally, the uninhibited ones of the Guest who occupies a particular month's driving seat. If you want to argue with him, do so in the *Journal;* if you feel that you must sue him for libel, mayhem, or whatnot, sue him, not the *Journal*" (100). In the months that followed, Burchard, Ernst Joseph Kump, Harold S. Buttenheim, Jerrold Loebl, Churchill, Elizabeth Gordon, Norman J. Schlossman, Feiss, and several others were given their turn to comment on the current state of architectural affairs. The series was curtailed in August 1950 because of the Korean War proceedings of the Committee on National Defense of the AIA.

As the 1950s wore on, the ideas reflected in the *Journal* were much more akin to those seen in the other professional periodicals. Articles on slum clearance, housing, and transportation appeared alongside architectural commentary and the speeches made at regional and annual meetings of the Institute. There were few regular columns, only "The Editor's Asides," "Life in the Martini Glass" by Alfred Bendiner, book reviews, and the necrology. Short serialized articles were occasionally furnished by Edwin Bateman Morris. Saylor's *Journal* was always hampered, however, by a combination of its pocketbook format and a lack of illustrations. After January 1957, when editorial control passed to Joseph Watterson, a number of changes were made that transformed the content and form of the publication. In May 1957, the first issue of the new *Journal,* with an enlarged format, was published and was somewhat reminiscent of the *Record* and the *Forum,* although it was a few months before the potential of the larger pages was fully realized. Watterson next addressed the contents of

the *Journal* by establishing a group of contributing editors, including David C. Baer, John Stewart Detlie, Carroll L. V. Meeks, Neutra, Charles M. Stotz, Ralph Walker, Philip Will, Jr., Edgar I. Williams, and Wurster. These professionals, as well as a number of other well-known authors, added more substance to the editorial matter. Watterson then began to secure advertising to increase the financial base. Last, dissatisfied with the layout, the Editor asked Wolf Von Eckardt to redesign the *Journal* in early 1959. Von Eckardt's subsequent columns, attempting to educate the profession to broader issues surrounding architecture, gained him a following and led to his departure for the *Washington Post* two years later. In general, readers were pleased with the changes in the *Journal,* but asked for more pictures and more articles on office practice, research, and aesthetics. The staff attempted to fulfill this request, while reminding the audience that the *Journal* was basically a magazine for architects who read, and that three other publications were already doing an excellent job of covering professional news with illustrations.

In many ways, the post-World War II era was one of the most stable editorial periods that the American professional architectural press ever enjoyed. This was largely due to the commitment displayed by Haskell, Creighton, Goble, and Saylor, although it must be added that they were assisted by many others. Perhaps due in part to this period of comparative calm, each of the journals assumed a distinct and separate role, addressing various aspects of the profession.

Many other short-lived journals have been omitted in this survey, but deserve brief mention. Among those journals that were begun before World War II were *Task* (1941–1944), *Shelter* (1930–1939), and the *Federal Architect* (1930–1945). For the educator-practitioner, one of the most obvious groups was the periodicals that were published by architectural schools. A list of the foremost "little magazines" would include the student journal *Program,* produced at Columbia University from 1961 through 1964, *Connections,* created at Harvard University from 1963 through 1969, *Perspecta, the Yale Architectural Journal,* begun in 1952, and *Oppositions,* an organ of the Institute for Architecture and Urban Studies in New York City, begun in 1973.

The general prosperity that followed World War II also gave rise to architectural journals that emphasized both broader and narrower, more regional topics. Two examples are *Trans/formation* and *Design Plus.* The former was published three times per year, from June 1950 through 1952, and dealt with arts, communication, and the environment. The editors were Harry Holtzman and James Martin, with an editorial board of Le Corbusier, Giedion, Fuller, and Marcel Duchamp. *Design Plus,* begun in 1950, was a regional magazine with an editorial staff that included Henry Wright, Lee Childress, Ezra Stoller, and 11 outstanding Florida architects.

This introduces the topic of state- and local-level professional publications. A number of these journals were started as the organs of AIA districts or chapters. These included the *Iowa Architect* (begun in 1949), *Texas Architect* (1950), *Missouri Architect* (1951), *Great Lakes Archi-*

tecture & Engineering (1954), North Carolina Architect (1954), Indiana Architect (1957), Alabama Architect (1958), and New England Architect & Builder Illustrated (1958). All of these have played a significant role in recording regional developments.

RECENT DEVELOPMENTS

A number of editorial changes in the early 1960s led subscribers of the major architectural journals into a new period, the recent past, which can only be sketched out in the broadest terms.

In 1962, Entenza left Arts and Architecture for the Graham Foundation and was succeeded by Managing Editor David Travers until the journal was suspended in late 1967.

In 1963, Creighton was succeeded by Jan Rowan who guided Progressive Architecture until 1969, when Forrest Wilson took the reins. Wilson returned to teaching two years later and Burton Holmes served in 1971 until John Morris Dixon assumed the role in February 1972.

The Architectural Record was owned by Dodge until 1962, when it was sold to McGraw-Hill. Goble, who had been valiantly fighting cancer for several years, retired in 1967 (90), and was succeeded by Walter F. Wagner, who carried on until September 1985, when Mildred F. Schmertz, on the staff of the journal since 1957, became the tenth Editor of the Record.

The Journal of the American Institute of Architects was led by Robert E. Koehler, who was named Editor in July 1965. Koehler was formerly Editor of Architecture/West, and joined the Journal as an Associate Editor in 1962, rising to Managing Editor before reaching the post at the top. Donald J. Canty succeeded him in March 1974 and still heads the publication, which was renamed Architecture in July 1983.

Perhaps most striking, in September 1964, Time, Inc. ceased its publication of the Forum. This was part of a general restructuring, for Time also sold House & Home to McGraw-Hill Publishing Company. The publishing rights were given as a gift to the American Planning and Civic Association, which was reformulated as Urban America, Inc., a nonprofit educational organization. With limited circulation, the Forum had little going for it but the editorial commitment of Peter Blake, Canty, and Paul Grotz, while James Bailey from the national AIA, and Dixon were added to the staff (101). The commitment to the problems of urban areas remained uppermost (102). Government transportation and housing programs were followed closely, monitoring Congressional activity and the unrest and riots in the ghettos. The March 1968 issue carried the first installment of Venturi and Scott Brown's book, Learning from Las Vegas, a few years before it would be published by MIT Press. Preservation activity was often included, looking at how the monuments of modernism were faring as often as recording the destruction of nineteenth-century railroad stations and post offices. In 1971, the Forum was taken over by Whitney publications, although its editorial staff remained essentially unchanged. The July–August, 1972 issue of the Forum was the last

Blake edited (103). He went on to become Editor of Architecture Plus, published from 1973 to 1975. At the Forum, William Marlin was appointed the new Editor-in-Chief, having proven himself by having been Guest Editor of the journal's eightieth anniversary issue. With continued financial difficulties, the journal came to an end in March 1974.

CONCLUSION

The architectural press has some of the same characteristics as the publishing industry as a whole, but differs in other aspects. Like most of the industry, the architectural press exists to earn money for its publishers and investors. Their principal source of income is advertising, for subscriptions have always proved problematic and at best supplement the advertising revenues. Architectural publications have suffered whenever this rule has been forgotten. The implications of this fact serve as a departing point, however, for in many other sections of the U.S. press the editorial department is secondary to advertising in importance. In architectural periodicals, particularly in the mid-twentieth century, the choice and treatment of material has generally been well ahead of public and even professional taste. The rural or remote practitioner has had every opportunity to compare his work with some of the "best" in the country and to become equipped with a wealth of new information (104). On the other hand, it is clear that an architectural publication that attempts to define its audience too broadly, to include other aspects of the building public, inherently runs the risk of failing to meet enough of the needs of the profession. Thus, the U.S. architectural press has some inherent economic and social restrictions that must be heeded as it valiantly attempts to mirror and motivate nationwide building activity.

BIBLIOGRAPHY

1. M. A. Tomlan, "Popular and Professional American Architectural Literature in the Late Nineteenth Century," Ph.D. dissertation, Cornell University, Ithaca, N.Y., 1983.
2. F. Jenkins, "Nineteenth Century Periodicals," in J. Summerson, ed. Concerning Architecture: Essays on Architectural Writers and Writing Presented to Nikolaus Pevsner, Allen Lane, The Penguin Press, London, 1968, pp. 152–165.
3. H. N. Cooledge, Jr., Samuel Sloan (1815–1884), Architect, University Microfilms, Ann Arbor, Mich. 1963, pp. 182, 183.
4. Building I(1), 1 (Oct. 1882).
5. "Retrospective Glance at the Inland Architect," Inland Architect and News Record XXI(2), 19 (Mar. 1893).
6. O. P. Hatfield and H. M. Congdon, "Report of a Committee of the American Institute of Architects on Architectural Journals," in Proceedings of the Nineteenth Annual Convention of the American Institute of Architects, Nashville, October 21 & 22, 1885, Davis & Pitman, Newport, R.I., 1880, pp. 25–28.
7. A. D. F. Hamlin, "Twenty-five Years of American Architecture," Architectural Record XL(1), 12 (July 1916).

8. "Announcement," *American Architect* **XCV**(1724), 8 (Jan. 6, 1907).

9. "Announcement," *Architecture and Building* **XV**(23), 283 (Dec. 5, 1891).

10. "Retrospective," *Architecture and Building* **XXIX**(27), 209 (Dec. 31, 1898).

11. H. W. Desmond, "By Way of Introduction," *Architectural Record* **I**(1), 6 (July–Sept. 1891).

12. "Architecture Made Easy," *Architectural Record* **VII**(2), 215–218 (Oct.–Dec. 1897).

13. D. Seideman, *The New Republic. A Voice of Modern Liberalism,* Praeger Publishers, New York, 1986.

14. "Michael A. Mikkelson, 1866–1941, In Memoriam," *Architectural Record* **LXXXIX**(3), 47 (Mar. 1941).

15. R. C. Spencer, Jr., "The Work of Frank Lloyd Wright," *Architectural Review* **VII**(6), 61–72 (June 1900).

16. "Announcement," *Inland Architect and News Record* **LII**(6), 67 (Dec. 1908).

17. [Editorial,] *Western Architect* **XI**(6),73 (June 1908).

18. G. Brown, *Memories, 1860–1930,* privately printed by the author, Washington, D.C., 1931, p. 222.

19. "Introductory," *Journal of the American Institute of Architects* **I**(1), 5 (Jan. 1913).

20. *Brickbuilder* **II**(1), 10 (Jan. 1893).

21. *Brickbuilder* **III**(12), 25 (Dec. 1894).

22. E. J. Kahn, "Nieuw Nederlandsche Bouwkunst," *Architectural Record* **LXII**(1), 77, 78 (July 1927).

23. "Professor Kocher Joins the Architectural Record Staff," *Architectural Record* **LXII**(2), 167 (Aug. 1927).

24. "The Architect's Library," *Architectural Record* **LXIII**(1), 90, 91 (Jan. 1928).

25. H. R. Hitchcock, Jr., "Modern Architecture," *Architectural Record* **LXVIII**(4), 337 (Apr. 1928).

26. "Announcing a New and Valuable Department," *American Architect* **CXXXI**(2517), publisher's page (Mar. 20, 1927).

27. "Editorial Comment and Notes for the Month," *Architectural Forum* **XXVI**(1), 26 (Jan. 1917).

28. E. J. Russell, "Arthur Durand Rogers. An Appreciation of the Man and His Work," *Architectural Forum* **XXX**(3), 91 (Mar. 1919).

29. "Editorial Comment," *Architectural Forum* **XL**(3), 132 (Mar. 1924).

30. D. J. Baum, "The Forum Studies of Architectural Precedents," *Architectural Forum* **XLVI**(5), 437 (May 1927).

31. R. T. Walker, "A New Architecture," *Architectural Forum Part I,* **XLVIII**(1), 1 (Jan. 1928).

32. P. M. Hooper, "The Rue Mallet-Stevens, Paris," *Architectural Forum* **XLVIII**(4), 505 (Apr. 1928).

33. The Editors, "Architectural Criticism," *Architectural Forum* **LIII**(4), 1 (Aug. 1930).

34. R. F. Whitehead, "A Review and a Forecast," *The White Pine Series of Architectural Monographs* **X**(6), 3–16 (1924).

35. "R. F. Whitehead, Architect, Dead," *New York Times,* 10 (Dec. 5, 1954).

36. "The Same Men," *Pencil Points* **II**(8), 5 (Aug. 1921).

37. "The Birch Burdette Long Sketch Competition for 1922," *Pencil Points* **III**(12), 11 (Dec. 1922).

38. "B. B. Long, Artist is Dead at 49 years," *New York Times,* 25 (Mar. 2, 1927).

39. "We Celebrate," *Pencil Points* **I**(5), 7 (May 1921).

40. "Here & There & This & That," *Pencil Points* **XIV**(7), 321 (July 1933).

41. "In Which We Ask Some Questions," *Pencil Points* **VII**(2), 71 (Feb. 1926).

42. "The Sixth Milestone," *Pencil Points* **VII**(5), 265 (May 1926).

43. "Pencil Points in 1927," *Pencil Points* **VII**(1), 1 (Jan. 1927).

44. *Pencil Points* **VIII**(8), 459 (Aug. 1927).

45. "Announcement," *Western Architect* **XXVI**(1) 1 (July 1917).

46. P. B. Wight, "California Bungalows," *Western Architect* **XXVII**(10), 92 (Oct. 1918).

47. R. C. McLean, "Peter Bonnett Wight, F.A.I.A.," *Western Architect* **XXXIV**(10), 100–103 (Oct. 1925).

48. "Announcing a New Editorial Policy," *Western Architect* **XXXI**(10), 110, 111 (Oct. 1922).

49. *Architect* **I**(1), 15 (Oct. 1923).

50. *Ibid.,* headpiece.

51. "Our Public," *Architect* **I**(3), 181 (Dec. 1923).

52. "On the Air," *Architect* **XV**(6), 271 (Jan. 1931).

53. "Editor's Note Book," *California Arts and Architecture* **I**(1), 15 (Jan. 1929).

54. "Coming of Le Corbusier," *Architectural Forum* **LXIII**(4), 34 (Oct. 1935).

55. "Plus," *Architectural Forum* **LXIX**(6), 432 (Dec. 1938).

56. *The Restoration of Colonial Williamsburgh in Virginia,* F. W. Dodge Corp., New York, 1935.

57. Esther Born and Ernest Born, *The New Architecture in Mexico,* The Architectural Record, W. Morrow & Co., New York, 1937.

58. "March . . . English Number," *Architectural Record* **LXXXI**(2), 1 (Feb. 1937).

59. "Behind the Record," *Record* **LXXXVI**(6), 5 (June 1937).

60. "Behind the Record," *Architectural Record* **LXXXV**(5), 7 (May 1938).

61. "An Essay in Critical Appraisal," *Pencil Points* **XV**(3), 112 (Mar. 1934).

62. "Upper Ground, 2," *Pencil Points* **XV**(7), 341 (July 1934).

63. "To the Readers of Pencil Points," *Pencil Points* **XXI**(6), 35 (June 1940).

64. "Architects Are Americans, Too," *New Pencil Points* **XXIII**(1), 16 (July 1942).

65. K. Reid, "New Beginning," *Pencil Points* **XXIII**(5), 243 (May 1942).

66. K. Reid, "The Birth of a Group," *New Pencil Points* **XXIII**(1), 45 (July 1942).

67. "Announcement," *California Arts and Architecture* **XXXXVI**(3), inside front cover (Dec. 1934).

68. "John Entenza," *Progressive Architecture* **LXV**(12), 26 (Dec. 1984).

69. T. H. Creighton, "Pearl Harbor to Nagasaki, A Review of Architectural Progress During the War Years," *Pencil Points* **XXVIII**(1), 42 (Jan. 1946).

70. D. Haskell, "75 Years of Change—Mostly Unpredicted," *Architectural Forum* **CXXI**(2), 79 (Aug.–Sept. 1964).

71. J. M. Fitch, *American Building; The Forces that Shape It,* Houghton Mifflin, Boston, 1948.

72. P. I. Prentice, "Two Magazines for Building," *Architectural Forum* **CXCV**(4), 153 (Sept. 1951).

73. R. T. Elson, *The World of Time Inc. The Intimate History of a Publishing Enterprise,* Vol. II, Athenaeum, New York, 1973, pp. 322–325.

74. D. Haskell, "Criticism vs. Statesmanship in Architecture," *Architectural Forum* **LXXXXVIII**(5), 97 (May 1953).

75. E. Saarinen, "The Six Broad Currents of Modern Architecture," *Architectural Forum* **LXXXXIX**(1), 110–115 (July, 1953).

76. S. Giedion, "Playboy Architecture," *Architectural Forum* **CXVII**(1), 116–117 (July 1962).

77. T. H. Creighton, "P.S.," *Progressive Architecture* **XXX**(8), 140 (Aug. 1949).

78. M. F. Kirchman, "Logic? . . . Or Esthetics? A Study of the Irrationalism in Some Modern Work," *Progressive Architecture* **XXVIII**(8), 41–43 (Aug. 1947).

79. The Editors, "Many Translations," *Progressive Architecture* **XXVIII**(8), 1 (Aug. 1947).

80. T. H. Creighton, "Architecture—Not Style," *Progressive Architecture* **XXIX**(12), 138 (Dec. 1948).

81. H. Creighton, "P.S.," *Progressive Architecture* **XXXVIII**(1), 216 (Jan. 1957).

82. T. H. Creighton, "P.S.: The Intellectual Fringes," *Progressive Architecture* **XXXVIII**(6), 366 (June 1957).

83. I. Reese, "Are We Going To Be Sorry Later On?" *Progressive Architecture* **XL**(9), 312 (Sept. 1959).

84. T. H. Creighton, "Historic Renewal," *Progressive Architecture* **XL**(10), 272 (Oct. 1959).

85. J. M. Dixon, "Thomas H. Creighton," *Progressive Architecture* **LXV**(12), 26–28 (Dec. 1984).

86. K. K. Stowell, "On the State of the Nation," *Architectural Record* **CIII**(2), 65 (Feb. 1948).

87. K. K. Stowell, "We Believe," *Architectural Record* **CV**(5), 85 (May 1949).

88. "Deaths," *Architectural Forum* **CXXX**(2), 89 (Mar. 1969).

89. "Harold D. Hauf, A.I.A., A.S.C.E., Becomes Editor-in-Chief," *Architectural Record* **CIV**(3), 87 (Sept. 1949).

90. J. Davern, "Emerson Goble: 1901–1969," *Architectural Record* **CXXXXVI**(6), 9 (Dec. 1969).

91. F. L. Wright, "Organic Architecture Looks at Modern Architecture," *Architectural Record* **CXI**(5), 149–152 (May 1952).

92. L. Mumford, "Function and Expression in Architecture," *Architectural Record,* **CX**(5), 106–112 (Nov. 1951).

93. E. Kaufmann, "In Summary," *Architectural Record* **CXXI**(5), 203 (May 1957).

94. "John Knox Shear, 1917–1958," *Architectural Record* **CXXIII**(2), 9 (Feb. 1958).

95. "The Octagon—Character of Articles," *Octagon* **III**(5), 27 (May 1931).

96. H. H. Saylor, *The A.I.A.'s First Hundred Years,* The Octagon, Washington, D.C., 1957. p. 95.

97. H. H. Saylor, "Gentlemen, Your Journal," *Journal of the American Institute of Architects* **I**(1), 3 (Jan. 1944).

98. "A Frank Letter and Its Answer," *Journal of the American Institute of Architects* **VII**(4), 198, 199 (Apr. 1947).

99. A. Raymond, "On the Editor's Chin," *Journal of the American Institute of Architects* **VII**(12), 277 (Dec. 1947).

100. H. H. Saylor, "Guest Editorial," *Journal of the American Institute of Architects* **X**(2), 51 (Aug. 1948).

101. A. Heiskell, "Publisher's Note," *Architectural Forum* **CXXVI**(1), 1 (Jan.–Feb. 1967).

102. L. W. Mester, "Publisher's Note," *Architectural Forum* **CXXV**(1), 1 (July–Aug. (1966).

103. P. Blake, "Forum," *Architectural Forum* **CXXXVII**(1), 39 (July–Aug. 1972).

104. E. Raskin, "Architecture in Print," *Progressive Architecture* **XXXI**(1), 11, 12 (Jan. 1950).

See also COMMUNICATIONS IN ARCHITECTURE; CRITICISM, ARCHITECTURAL; LITERATURE OF ARCHITECTURE; MEDIA CRITICISM; PATTERN-BOOK ARCHITECTURE.

MICHAEL A. TOMLAN
Cornell University
Ithaca, New York

ARCHITECTURAL RESEARCH.   See RESEARCH, ARCHITECTURAL.

ARCHITECTURAL REVIEW BOARDS.   See REVIEW BOARDS, ARCHITECTURAL.

ARCHITECTURAL STYLES

Architectural styles are a method of classifying buildings into historical or cultural periods. Based on the study of aesthetic attitudes, the use of detail, and structural techniques, scholars highlight the features a group of buildings have in common and define this shared approach as a style. In its narrowest sense, style is associated with the work of an individual architect, eg, the style of Frank Lloyd Wright or the style of Mies van der Rohe. In broader terms, style identifies the architecture of a particular region or era such as Italian Gothic or American Colonial. At an even larger scale, style is the framework for discussing the buildings of an entire culture or an extended period of time. The Egyptian or Romanesque styles are illustrative of this point. To review the significant aspects of architectural history concisely and clearly, this essay uses the term style with this last and most general meaning. The first section summarizes 12 periods that comprise the Western architectural tradition, beginning in Greece and ending with the most recent Postmodern trends. The second section is divided into five parts and briefly describes important non-Western styles.

THE WESTERN TRADITION

Greek Architecture

The history of Western architectural styles began in Ancient Greece about 800 B.C. This civilization was centered in the Peloponnesian peninsula and surrounding islands, although settlements could be found in Italy, Sicily, and in other areas along the Mediterranean coast. In these locations, numerous independent city-states developed an approach to building and decoration that, even today, continues to influence architectural design. As a theme, the Greeks stressed individuality. In a diverse landscape that included mountains, coastline, and broad plains, important public buildings such as temples, theaters, and stoas were designed as autonomous sculptural masses, each blending siting and detail in a way that uniquely responded to function.

The temple building best illustrates this process. Using stone post-and-beam construction, its form may have been derived from the megaron or rectangular hall used as an organizing element in Mycenaean palaces during the fifteenth to thirteenth centuries B.C. Similar to the megaron, the main space of the temple was a large room (*naos*), in this case housing the statue of a god. Often this area was preceded by a porch entry (*pronaos*) at one end and an additional treasury or sanctuary at the other. The perimeter of the oblong volume was gracefully denoted by freestanding columns. The entire building was usually raised on a platform of three large steps, and the roofline was marked by a triangular pediment at each end. Independent of other structures, and seen in relation to the sky and the earth, the overall impression was, indeed, that of a great sculpture. There was a careful balance of horizontal and vertical elements, and the strong Greek sunlight emphasized the details of the design, cast rhythmic shadows on the walls, and brought life to the statues in the pediment. As the details and statues were originally painted in bright colors, the impact was quite dramatic.

While most temples shared these general qualities, the real talent of the Greek architects and sculptors was their ability to translate this common form into buildings that expressed the individual characters of the gods to whom they were dedicated. The creation of orders was the most important device that made this possible. Orders are a system for detailing a classical structure. They define the elements of the column and entablature, a range of proportional sizes for these elements, and an appropriate spacing between columns. Doric, Ionic, and Corinthian were the three orders developed in Greece (Fig. 1). The Doric, in common use by the seventh century B.C., may have been derived from wooden construction, as it had a solid and

massive appearance. The fluted column had no base and the height of its shaft was four to six times the diameter. The capital was composed of two parts: a circular pad that expanded upward and a square slab that acted as a transition between the column and entablature. The entablature itself was two horizontal bands of stone: a plain frieze and an architrave of alternating triglyphs and metopes. The Ionic order, developed in Asia Minor simultaneously with the Doric, was more slender. The column had a molded base and was about nine times as tall as its width. The capital was characterized by volutes, and the entablature was most often divided into a three-part frieze and sculpted architrave. The Corinthian order, which was not a traditional feature of temples until the fourth century B.C., differed from the Ionic in having a column almost ten times as tall as its width, and a capital elaborately decorated with scrolls and double rows of acanthus leaves.

The Roman architect Vitruvius noted that the orders represented various human qualities. The Doric suggested male strength and beauty; the Ionic, feminine slenderness and grace; the Corinthian, the slight figure of a maiden and ornamentation. Thus, adapting the orders and their attributes to a particular site, the ancient Greeks were able to design temples uniquely related to their gods. Two temples in Paestum, Italy, are good examples. Both are dedicated to the earth goddess Hera, and "celebrate the city's unity with the earth and its goddess" (1). Mirroring this theme, they are located in a low, open field and employ the earth-hugging Doric order. In their detailing, however, each suggests a different relationship between humanity and the goddess. The First Temple to Hera, also known as the Basilica, was constructed about 550 B.C. with a row of columns in the center of the *naos,* nine across the front, and 18 down the sides. It spreads over the site and, under the weight of the entablature, the shafts bulge and the capitals appear squashed. The concept depicted here is the struggle between human reason and nature. The Second Temple to Hera, also known as the Temple of Poseidon, was built one hundred years later; it is compact and lean. Inside, two rows of columns open up the central space of the *naos* while six columns mark the entry facade and 14 columns line each side. Their profiles are vertical, and their capitals display a strength and sureness not seen in the earlier temple. In this case, the theme depicted is the victory of will and the harmony between humanity and nature.

A similar analysis can be used to interpret other temples, such as those at Delphi and Olympia on mainland Greece, those on the islands of Delos and Corfu, and those at Agrigentum in Sicily. Because it is so well known, the Acropolis in Athens deserves special mention. Developed during the Golden Age of Pericles in the fifth century B.C. after the Athenian victory over the Persians, this impressive complex is situated on a rocky platform that dominates the city. Although it contains numerous other structures, four buildings are particularly significant. The Propylaea (437 B.C.) is the entrance to the sacred compound; its U-shaped form welcomes visitors. The exterior Doric order suggests strength, while the interior Ionic columns imply the warmth and grace of this greeting. The

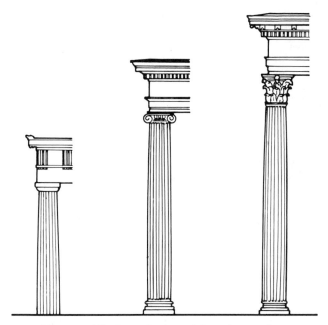

Figure 1. The Doric, Ionic, and Corinthian orders.

small Ionic Temple of Athena Nike (427 B.C.), to the side of the Propylaea, displays the cunning and feminine charm of the goddess who led Athens to victory. To the north, the Erechteion (ca 421 B.C.) is a complex design built on several levels and dedicated to the three founding personalities of Athens. Two Ionic porches represent Athena and Poseidon. A third, supported by six carved female figures known as caryatids (Fig. 2), marks the burial place of the mythical king of Athens, Erectius. Finally, the Parthenon (447 B.C.) (Fig. 3) stands above all the other buildings, literally and figuratively. Originally, a colossal statute of Athena stood inside the temple, but even without this symbol, the beautifully proportioned Doric order describes the strength of the goddess and the greatness of her city. Many refinements also enhance the perfection of this design: as horizontal lines visually appear to sag, the stepped platform curves gently upward toward the middle of each side to compensate for the optical illusion; the corner columns are thicker and closer to their neighbors, yet seem evenly spaced to the eye; and the silhouette of the shafts is slightly convex (called entasis), so that from a distance they do not look pinched in the middle.

The Greeks were equally subtle about the design of other public buildings. Architecturally, theaters and stoas deserve special comment. Theaters, such as the one at Epidauros (ca 300 B.C.), had a semicircle of terraced benches built into the side of a hill. Patrons looked down at a circular stage and a low scale set. They could also see the distant landscape, thus linking the action of the play to the site and the reality of life. The stoa was an open, extended colonnade and was used to define the boundaries of major public spaces. Sometimes shops and storage units were located along the back wall, and its form could be rectangular (the Stoa of Attalos, Athens, ca 150 B.C.), L-shaped (the stoa at Delos, ca 250 B.C.), or U-shaped (the Stoa of Zeus, Athens, ca 420 B.C.). Detailed with long rows of Doric or Ionic columns, and just one or two stories high, it was a relaxed and elegant background to the agora and temples beyond. And while the structure sheltered people, it did not isolate them from the activity and vitality of their city.

Figure 3. The Parthenon. Courtesy of the Architecture Department, The Catholic University of America.

The Greeks also developed other building types, including courtyard homes, council chambers known as *bouleuterions,* gymnasia, and town halls known as *prytaneions.* More than these particular designs, however, it is the layout of their cities as a whole that is most significant. Here, a dual strategy is evident. For residential areas, an orthogonal street grid was adapted to the contours of the site. Miletus, Turkey, and Rhodes, on the island by that same name, clearly display this pattern, a scheme attributed to the fifth-century B.C. planner Hippodamus. For sacred precincts and the market, a less rigid approach was employed. At Miletus, for instance, a large rectangular space is opened up in the center of the grid for these uses. In the Agora and the Acropolis in Athens, and at the Sanctuary of Apollo at Delphi, the plan appears somewhat random. In these cases, it is an important vista or sequence of sculptural spaces that governs the design. At the Acropolis, for example, the buildings were organized to facilitate the annual Panathenaic procession which moved past the Temple of Athena Nike, through the Propylaea, to the Parthenon, and then to the Erechteion. Like its architecture, Greek planning embodied the concept of individuality with different layouts responding to different functions.

A final era of design in Greece was the Hellenistic period (ca 330–30 B.C.), occurring after the conquest of Alexander the Great. During this time, the restrained, pristine qualities of earlier centuries were replaced by a flamboyant, almost theatrical style. Building forms were more complex; the Ionic and Corinthian orders, rather than the subdued Doric, became the norm; the once simple house grew larger and was elaborately decorated with frescoes and mosaics; and urban design stressed ceremony and drama rather than the interaction of citizens. The Sanctuary of Athena in Lindos on the island of Rhodes suggests how this transition affected architecture. The original temple was constructed in the sixth century B.C. and stood alone on an escarpment overlooking the sea. During the fourth and third centuries B.C., two large colonnades and grand staircases were built on separate terraces as an entrance to the sanctuary. What had been a meandering path to the temple was now a formal axial ascent. In terms of planning,

Figure 2. The Erechteion, porch of the caryatids. Courtesy of the Architecture Department, The Catholic University of America.

the Hellenistic approach is illustrated by the city of Pergamon. Historian Spiro Kostof describes it as "a calculated work. . . . All public buildings were framed by porticoes and set on platforms. . . . The theatre in the upper part of town was the only urban element to accept the precipitous land just as it was. The rest was all contrived" (2). Ultimately, what emerged during these last centuries of Ancient Greek design were concepts and attitudes toward building that became common features of Roman architecture.

Roman Architecture

Order and grandeur are the key elements of the Roman style, themes that are mirrored in the history of this civilization. Around 800 B.C., the Etruscans, a tribe of merchant traders, landed near the Tiber River and established a kingdom in central Italy. After less than three centuries, they controlled the northern peninsula, and had instituted a centralized and hierarchical government. The domination of this group ended when the king was overthrown in 509 B.C., but the desire for growth continued. By the end of the third century B.C., the Roman republic included Spain and all of Italy. By the end of the second century B.C., its territory included North Africa and portions of Greece. By the first century B.C., France and Germany were conquered. Geographically, this empire was at its height about 117 A.D., by which time southern England, most of Germany, and the entire Mediterranean basin was under Roman rule. Cities flourished and the population of Rome itself grew to an estimated one million people.

Not unexpectedly, this civilization left an impressive architectural legacy. The Romans borrowed many design elements and details from the Greeks, but with the Hellenistic influence and their own desire for order and grandeur, these were transformed into a new monumental and highly controlled style. The development of the temple is illustrative. For the Greeks, this building type was a beautiful sculpture. Its exterior was meant to be observed from all four sides, and was generally sited with relation to important vistas and the surrounding horizon. For the Romans, the temple was an interior space. The Maison Carrée (Nîmes, France, 16 B.C.) (Fig. 4) is typical. At first glance, its rectangular form appears Greek, but there are many significant differences. To begin with, this structure is frontal. It is raised high above the ground and is approached from only one side, up a long flight of stairs and through a colonnaded porch. The remaining sides of the building are detailed with engaged (ie, attached to the wall) half columns. Beyond this decoration, there is nothing to attract the viewer around the temple. Indeed, what is important is not a symbolic connection to the landscape, but rather an axial procession from the city to the interior sanctuary.

Axes, ceremony, and enclosed space are pervasive ideas in Roman architecture. Influenced by Hellenistic examples, the Temple of Fortuna Primigenia (Palestrina, Italy, ca 80 B.C.), displays this sense of control. In this case, worshipers ascend a series of ramps, stairs, and porticoed terraces to a theater and a small round temple at the top of the site. Both movement and space are carefully defined. Conceptually, other public buildings are quite sim-

Figure 4. Maison Carrée. Courtesy of the Clarence Ward Collection, Photographic Archives, National Gallery of Art.

ilar. The plan of the Baths of Caracalla (Rome, 212 A.D.) shows one axis moving from the entrance through the tepid, cold, and hot baths, and another crossing an expansive exercise field between two giant apses. To define its interior focus, massive walls surround the facility, which included a complex of rooms and outdoor areas that were used not only for bathing and recreation, but also for meetings and social gatherings. The Colosseum (Rome, ca 80 A.D.), like arenas in other cities, was an oval—a shape that by definition creates a long and a short axis—in this instance, behind a dramatic four-story curved facade. Theaters, too, share this characteristic. In Orange, France (Theatre, ca 50 A.D.), seats rise some 10 m around a semicircular stage and in front of an even taller architectural set. The set itself forms one axis; the visual line between the center of the stage and the back of the seating forms another. The basilica form in general, and the Basilica Ulpia (Rome, ca 110 A.D.) specifically, are additional examples of these ideas. This building type served as a place of business and a court of law. Architecturally, it was an enclosed rectangular hall with an immense central space illuminated by clerestory windows and lower aisles off to the sides. An entrance on the long wall marked one axis, while apses at both ends defined a second.

Roman planning demonstrates this same order and control. Except for older urban centers such as Rome, cities were modeled on the design of a military camp. Ideally, flat sites were selected and two main roads—the *cardo*, running north-south, and the *decumanus*, running east-west—were laid out. A grid of secondary streets filled in the plan, and near the intersection of the *cardo* and *decumanus*, a forum or civic center was developed. This could include a temple, a basilica, baths, an arena, and a theater. Residential areas might have multistory apartments as well as more spacious single-family homes with atria and gardens. Illustrating his point with a plan of Timgad (North Africa, ca 100 A.D.), author Christian Norberg-Schultz has pointed out that this rational scheme can be interpreted both literally and symbolically. On the one hand, it represents the wealth and organization of the community. On the other, it is a microcosm of the empire, with Rome as the *caput mundi* (head of the world), its power and influence spreading throughout the cardinal directions of the compass (3).

The construction of cities and buildings on such a large scale was possible because of certain engineering innovations. Sewers and abundant running water were features of every town. But from a stylistic viewpoint, the structural system was the most important Roman contribution to architecture. Rather than the monolithic carved stones and post-and-beam technique used by the Greeks, Roman designers employed bricks and mortar in various arch forms as the basis for much of their building. The simplest expression of this technology is the Pont du Gard (late first century B.C.) in Nîmes, France. This aqueduct is at once utilitarian and elegant as it carries water across the river atop three graceful tiers of arches.

The real advantage of this approach, however, was its versatility. Barrel vaults, groin vaults, domes, and apses are all derivatives of the simple arch; they may be combined in various sizes to suit the needs of almost any structure. Thus, seating at the Colosseum is supported on a network of barrel vaults, and at the Baths of Caracalla, groin vaults, barrel vaults, domes, and half domes are used to roof different parts of the building. In addition, relieving arches could be incorporated within walls to transfer weight over openings to foundations at ground level. Interestingly, while modern architects are impressed with the raw beauty of Roman ruins and their dynamic arch forms, the Romans themselves decided to conceal this structure with classical detail and marble decoration. Often used in layers because of the grand size of their buildings, this system is particularly evident on the facade of the Colosseum. A different order is applied to each of its four levels: the first uses a Tuscan order (similar to the Doric but with a molded base); the second, an Ionic; the third, a Corinthian; and the fourth, Corinthian pilasters.

To complete this discussion, three buildings deserve special mention. The first is the Pantheon (Rome, ca 120 A.D.) (Fig. 5), a unique temple erected by the emperor Hadrian to all Roman gods. A circle in plan with a monumental porch attached as an entrance, its interior can only be described as awe inspiring. It is large enough to contain a sphere over 43 m in diameter, and is dramatically lit by an oculus, or circular opening, in its dome. During the day, sunlight sweeps across the walls and floor in a wide arc. The axes of the building move in three directions. One leads from the portico to the main altar. Another crosses this at a right angle between two semicircular side altars. A third, through the oculus, connects the center of the space to the heavens above, and suggests that the temple can be interpreted as a representation of the Roman cosmos.

A second structure, also built by Hadrian, was the Villa at Tivoli, outside Rome (ca 118 A.D.). Essentially a small city, this palace is organized along two major axes that spread in a relaxed manner from a great courtyard across the hilly site. One contains the public buildings, including a stadium, an academy, temples, two baths, and headquarters for Hadrian's guard. The other is the focus of the palace itself with a hospice, libraries, and several elegant

Figure 5. The Pantheon, interior. Courtesy of the Architecture Department, The Catholic University of America.

private rooms and gardens. This complex can be compared with the Palace of Diocletian (Split, Yugoslavia, 300 A.D.). Constructed in the form of a fortified camp, it is planned around two interior streets that cross at 90° and lead to towered gateways. The front of the building, originally located on the shore of the Mediterranean, was reserved for the emperor and his court. Behind this area, courtyards were the setting for a mausoleum on one side and a temple to Jupiter on the other. Conceptually, while the scheme is quite large, it is also rigid and introspective, lacking the confidence and boldness of earlier designs. The decline of the empire had begun, and a new style of architecture emerged to replace the grand edifices of Rome.

Early Christian Architecture

Although the Early Christians spurned the materialism of Roman society, when the empire began its slow decline, it was the Church as an institution that helped maintain both spiritual and earthly order. With the Edict of Milan in 313 A.D., the emperor Constantine officially recognized the Christian faith and soon thereafter, an architectural style developed to serve increasing numbers of converts and worshipers. In the West, this combined the qualities of spaces previously used for Christian celebration—private homes and catacombs (underground galleries of tombs)—with the grand scale and form of the Roman basilica. The basilica, rather than a temple, was chosen as the model because it was free of pagan religious connotations.

Blending these precedents, the theme of Early Christian churches became "pathway," an architectural expression of spiritual growth. The typical building was composed of five elements: an atrium or courtyard; a narthex or covered porch; an interior nave and side aisles; a transept or crossing (not always present, especially in smaller churches); and an apse. These spaces were arranged on a long axis suggesting the road toward salvation. The atrium, adapted from the design of Roman houses, was the area where those interested in Christian teachings received instruction. The narthex was the entrance to the church and the place where converts were baptized. The interior resembled a basilica except that the entrance was on the short rather than the long side. This created a processional with a tall nave and two or more lower aisles off to the sides. The transept ended this symbolic walkway, and was used as the sanctuary and location for the altar. Behind this, an apse concluded the sequence and was reserved for the clergy.

The detail of these churches also emphasized spirituality. Unlike Roman buildings, exteriors were left unadorned and, at the roof level, light wooden trusses were substituted for massive brick vaulting. Inside, marble patterns and decorations were replaced by mosaics that depicted Christ, the apostles, and the saints on a shimmering gold background. The whole effect was to inspire other-worldly virtues at a time when the earthbound, imperial traditions were collapsing.

Most Early Christian churches were built between the fourth and seventh centuries, and although they can be found outside the Italian peninsula, the finest examples were those in Rome and Ravenna. In Rome, for instance, with the patronage of Constantine, a structure was built over the tomb of Saint Peter. Known as Old St. Peter's (ca 330) because it was later replaced by the Baroque church that exists today, this original edifice was enormous. Its atrium measured over 50 m and its nave over 80 m in length. The interior was marked by wide entablatures and arches supported by 100 stone columns. The pathway of the nave was echoed in four side aisles, two

on either side, and the whole procession ended at the transept—a space that contained the altar as well as the tomb of the saint, and was almost the same height as the nave. Sant' Apollinare in Classe (ca 533) (Fig. 6), erected just outside of Ravenna, is another important Early Christian basilica. It is not as large as Old St. Peter's. It does not have a transept, and therefore the altar is located in the apse at the top of a flight of stairs. In addition, it is missing the atrium that formerly graced its entrance. Still, it is an extraordinary building, particularly known for its mosaics. Along the nave arcade, various saints and bishops are shown. Over the altar, St. Apollinaris is depicted as the Good Shepherd surrounded by 12 sheep representing the faithful. Above this scene on a background reminiscent of the Garden of Eden are images of the prophets, Moses and Elijah; and symbols for Christ, God the Father, the transfiguration, and the four Evangelists. Even after 13 centuries, the colors still seem to glow in the warm clerestory lighting, and the message of this spiritual architecture remains clear and compelling.

Byzantine Architecture

At the same time Early Christian churches were being developed in the West, another religious style, known as Byzantine, was emerging in areas under the control of Constantinople. (Today named Istanbul, this eastern capital of the Roman Empire remained independent until its conquest by the Turks in 1453.) Because important ceremonies in these buildings occurred in the middle rather than at the end of the space, this architecture was based on a central plan. Thematically, emphasis was on salvation as an event, and not, as was the case with basilican plans, on growth toward Christ. In terms of form, the Byzantine style borrowed from the mausoleums built for saints and other important Christian personalities. The Church of Santa Costanza (ca 345) in Rome and the Tomb of Galla Placidia (ca 425) in Ravenna are typical of these early central plan structures. In Santa Costanza, a tall circular area is vaulted with a dome and surrounded by a lower ambulatory or walkway. To accent the altar in the middle (built over the tomb of Constantine's daughter Constantina), light enters through clerestory windows just below the dome. This places visual focus on the religious ceremony while the faithful observe from the darker and more intimate ambulatory beyond. In Ravenna, the plan of Galla Placidia's mausoleum is cruciform. Four barrel-vaulted arms are extensions off a central domed square. Although not used as a church, this layout and the elaborate mosaic decoration that covers the ceilings and walls of this building are features that became common as the Byzantine style matured.

These precedents, along with the vaulting techniques employed by the Romans, most notably in the Pantheon, offered Byzantine architects a vocabulary they exploited for nearly 10 centuries. The design of these central plan churches varied. Some were circular; some were octagonal. Others were square, cruciform, or slightly oblong. In every case, however, the dome was the dominant spatial determinant, transformed into a shimmering vision of the heavens by a hierarchy of carefully executed mosaics or frescoes.

Figure 6. Sant' Apollinare in Classe. Courtesy of the Gramstorff Collection, Photographic Archives, National Gallery of Art.

Eventually, this style spread throughout the Balkans and Asia Minor, and into Italy, Egypt, and Russia. In Greece and Yugoslavia, the many small monasteries built between the tenth and fifteenth centuries were characterized by decorative brickwork on their exteriors and a roofline of multiple small domes. The complex on Mount Athos (Greece, begun in the tenth century) and the Monastery of Gračanica (Yugoslavia, fourteenth century) are just two examples. Russian churches, such as the Cathedral of the Annunciation (1482) in Moscow, were known for their intriguing adaptation of onion-shaped domes to the central plan.

While these buildings are typical and suggest the breadth and diversity of Byzantine architecture, there are three structures that stand out as major monuments in the style: San Vitale, Hagia Sophia, and St. Mark's. San Vitale (526) in Ravenna was an imperial church and celebrated the surrender of the Goths to Justinian. The interior is adorned with remarkable mosaics: two illustrate the emperor and his wife Theodora bringing gifts to the altar; other panels depict the Old Testament sacrifices of Moses, Abraham, Melchizedek, and Abel; and above the altar, Christ's second coming is the central image. Column capitals were also elaborately incised with intricate floral patterns. All of these details enhanced the structure's subtle spacial qualities. Although the narthex entrance is unexpectedly off-center, the plan is otherwise a simple composition of concentric octagons. A central one rises three floors to a band of clerestory windows and a dome. An outer one is two stories tall and is used as an ambulatory and gallery for women with one bay reserved for the sanctuary. At ground level along the shared sides of the octagons, curved arcades gracefully link the two forms. This gesture, combined with the artwork and warm light in the church, give San Vitale an inviting human scale without sacrificing any of its spiritual impact.

It is interesting to compare San Vitale to another church commissioned by Justinian in Constantinople. Hagia Sophia (532) (Fig. 7) was designed by two mathematicians,

Anthemius of Tralles and Isodorus of Miletus, and was conceived to inspire rather than welcome worshipers. Its exterior is dominated by four massive buttresses. Inside, a dome with a diameter of about 30 m is lifted high above the central space on dramatic pendentives (curved triangular supports that serve as a transition between a square base and a domed roof). Sunlight pours in from clerestory windows at the base of the dome, and a series of progressively smaller half domes and apses mark the east-west axis. To the north and to the south, a screen of arches creates an ambulatory. When Hagia Sophia was consecrated in 537, the court poet Paul the Silentiary perceptively commented on its overwhelming grandeur (4):

> "The golden stream of glittery rays pours down and strikes the eyes of men, so they can scarcely bear to look. . . . Thus through the spaces of the great church come rays of light, expelling clouds of care, filling the mind with promise, showing the way to the living God."

More that 500 years later, the Byzantine style was still influential and was selected for the design of St. Mark's (1063) (Fig. 8) in Venice. In this case, the plan is cruciform with four equal arms, each of which, in addition to the central crossing, is covered with a hemispherical dome. The sequence of spaces is impressive as it moves from dome to dome, particularly since the floors, walls, and ceilings are richly decorated with colored marbles and gold mosaics. As the later addition of a medieval entrance facade suggests, however, just as St. Mark's was being completed, other builders were experimenting with new styles that soon replaced the Byzantine tradition in the West.

Romanesque Architecture

Experimentation is the theme of Romanesque architecture. This era—at its height between 1000 and 1200—is noted for its many regional styles. Within this diversity, there were two common threads: first, because of the increasing power and influence of Christianity, churches

Figure 7. Hagia Sophia, interior with details from its later renovation as a mosque. Courtesy of Art Resource, N.Y.

Figure 8. St. Mark's. Courtesy of the Architecture Department, The Catholic University of America.

were the most important building type; and second, following the example of Roman construction, the round arch was the basis of form, structure, and detail.

The emphasis on regionalism and local tradition has its roots in a tumultuous history. This begins in the fourth to sixth centuries, when a series of Barbarian invasions and the eventual collapse of the Roman Empire led to the depopulation of cities. Some urban areas, such as Rome and Ravenna, continued a modest existence, but most were transformed into small, fortified settlements. The stability of Europe was further upset in the seventh and eighth centuries as the Moslems conquered territories in North Africa, the Middle East, and most of present-day Spain and Portugal. In the ninth century, the Norsemen led their flotillas into France, Germany, and Russia.

Architecturally, this unstable period from 650 to 1000 is known as Pre-Romanesque, and is characterized by buildings that suggest the struggle to rebuild. San Juan de Baños (Cerrato, Spain, seventh century), San Pedro de la Nave (El Campilo, Spain, ca 700), and Worth (Sussex, England, ninth century) are typical. Referred to as cell churches, other examples of which can be found in France and Ireland, the interiors of these buildings are treated as groups of connected rooms, often in the form of a cross. And while it is possible to move among these cellular spaces, each volume is independent rather than part of a larger, more continuous form. In addition, construction is relatively crude, classical ornament is abandoned or abstracted into geometric patterns, and beyond the main entrances, openings are treated as narrow arches or thin slits.

Two notable exceptions to this trend foretell the emergence of a new and richer style. The first was commissioned by Charlemagne, founder of the Holy Roman Empire, as part of his palace complex in Aachen, Germany. Known as the Palatine Chapel (ca 792), it has a central plan and may have been modeled after St. Vitale in Ravenna. In the Byzantine style, a three-story arcade defines an octagonal form that is roofed by a mosaic-filled dome. Unlike the earlier structure, a more independent, sixteen-sided ambulatory surrounds the main space; an imperial throne is incorporated on the second floor gallery opposite the altar; and the interior details are not as refined. Regardless of inspiration, the building displays a clarity and boldness that are common features of later Romanesque designs. Similar attributes are evident in the ideal plan for a monastery in St. Gall, Switzerland (ca 820). In this case, a towered basilican church (ie, with a long nave and transept) serves as the focus for the scheme. To one side stand the cloister and refectory. Beyond this, organized on a grid, are the school, guesthouse, infirmary, barns, pens, and pavilions for other services. Although the monastery was never built, its components and sense of order became the norm. In addition, while there were many variations on the theme, the towers and basilican layout of the church were the basic elements used by almost all Romanesque builders.

After the year 1000, the invasions of Europe subsided and there was a balance between forces that enhanced stability and forces that made life more dynamic. On the one hand, feudalism and monasticism created enduring secular and religious communities. Behind the walls of castles and within the tranquil confines of monasteries, safety and order existed. On the other hand, certain events added energy to this social system. The crusades, begun in 1095 to retake the Holy Land from the Moslems, never succeeded, but perhaps more importantly, they encouraged trade and the exchange of ideas. As acts of penance and piety, pilgrimages were increasingly popular during this period. Travelers journeyed to sanctuaries in Jerusalem, Rome, France, and Spain to attain forgiveness and grace; in the process they established vital sea and land routes and left behind offerings used to build new churches and towns. Conquests also intensified the vitality of this era. When lords and kings expanded their territory, they also expanded their influence over people, institutions, wealth, and building techniques. Thus, when William the Conqueror took control of England in 1066, he brought with him the Norman customs, laws, and architectural style.

Regionalism in the Romanesque style, then, is an outgrowth of creative tension. Like the stable social forces, the round Roman arch and the basilican church plan were constants. Beyond this, however, function, local talent and materials, and a willingness to experiment were the qualities that shaped design. Several examples suggest the diversity that was possible. Some of the earliest buildings are found in Germany. Like other churches in the region, St. Michael in Hildesheim (ca 1000) has several exterior towers, and an apse and a transept at both its east and west ends. The interior elevation is two stories tall, composed of a nave arcade and a simple clerestory, and the roof is supported by a wooden truss that is peaked on the outside and flat on the inside. To help fireproof and unify the design, later churches employ stone vaulting. In this respect, those in Normandy, France, such as St. Etienne in Caen (ca 1068), are the most sophisticated. Here, six ribs and stone infilling (sexpartite vaulting) cover the square bays that make up the nave. Each rib gracefully connects to a column that, in turn, helps carry the weight of the roof down to the foundation. Along the interior elevation, which includes a clerestory, gallery, and ground level arcade, columns are detailed so that they create an alternate, A-B-A-B rhythm. This reflects the two-to-one proportions of the nave to the side aisles and unifies the entire scheme. The basilica of La Madeleine (1104) in Vézelay (Fig. 9) illustrates another style of French Romanesque architecture. In this instance, the interior is defined by a barrel vault, a clerestory, and a nave arcade. The truly special feature of this design and others in Burgundy, however, is the beautiful sculpture that decorates the capitals of columns and arched panels, or tympana, above doorways. These depict Christ, the apostles, the saints, and scenes such as the Nativity and the Last Judgment. The Church of St. Front in Périgueux (ca 1100) exemplifies yet a third approach in France. In this case, the influence is Byzantine. Great domes dominate the interior, but instead of being covered by mosaics, they are left unadorned—massive stone vaults recalling the Roman technology that is the basis of this style.

In southern France and northern Spain, the barrel vaults and two-story interior elevation (a nave arcade and gallery) that characterize pilgrimage churches are not par-

Figure 9. La Madeleine, Vezelay, interior. Courtesy of the Trachtenberg Collection, Photographic Archives, National Gallery of Art.

ticularly innovative. What is important in buildings like the Cathedral of Santiago de Compostela (1075) is the flowing plan and dramatic lighting around the altar. These emphasize the concept of procession—a path that leads down the side aisles, along the transept, behind the apse past radiating chapels, back to the front of the church, and then up the nave to the main altar, a culminating space bathed in light from clerestory windows. A last illustration of the diversity of this style is the decorative quality of Italian Romanesque. In the Cathedral at Pisa (1063) (Fig. 10), the baptistry and tower are separate elements

Figure 10. Cathedral at Pisa. Courtesy of the Architecture Department, The Catholic University of America.

of a church complex that stands in the middle of an open square. The drama of this approach is heightened by the lacy arcades and marble patterns that cover the facades of these structures. The elaborate detail ties the pieces together and makes the design appear to be a series of delicate layers.

Gothic Architecture

Filling a space with heavenly light is the fundamental concept of Gothic architecture. The idea first appeared in 1144 at the Abbey Church of St. Denis, just outside of Paris. The head of this abbey, a prominent monk named Suger, was able, with the patronage of the French king, to renovate the choir of his Romanesque building. Using pointed arches and rib vaults, the abbot brought the weight of the roof down to a skeleton of slender columns and piers. This, in turn, allowed him to replace what formerly had been solid, load-bearing walls with great panels of stained glass. The design's elegance and glowing light was an immediate success, and in Abbot Suger's words, lifted "the mind from the material to the spiritual" (5). Others soon began to emulate the style, and with a half century of almost frantic building, certain typical features emerged. Examples of these can be seen in Reims Cathedral (1211), used for the coronation of kings. Like most French Gothic churches, the structure dominates the center of the town. The west (front) facade has an imposing three-part entry reflecting the nave and two side aisles within. Towers flank a central rose window, and are tied together by a horizontal gallery of statues. The interior elevation soars 42 m and is divided into three layers: a slender nave arcade of pointed arches, a shallow triforium (a windowless arcade at the roof level over the side aisle), and an expansive clerestory. Between each oblong bay, piers of clustered columns rise through all three layers to the ribs of the vaulting, emphasizing the cathedral's height and skeletal construction. This last image is reinforced through the introduction of flying buttresses, lean exterior arches that support the weight of the roof along the nave and around the apse. The plan is compact and flowing, especially the transept that projects only slightly beyond the nave and side aisles and is well integrated with the choir and radiating chapels.

Interestingly, the origins of many of these elements can be found in Romanesque architecture. The pointed arch was used extensively in Cistercian monasteries. Rib vaulting and a three-story interior elevation were common in the churches of Normandy. The notion of a sculptural program may have been influenced by the carving in the basilicas of Burgundy, and the plans of pilgrimage churches were already sophisticated approaches to spatial integration. The essential achievement of the Gothic master masons was to synthesize Romanesque experiments with the principles of structure and lighting initiated at St. Denis. While Reims is typical, there were, inevitably, variations on the theme. The Cathedral of Laon (1160) uses a four-story interior elevation. The plan of Notre Dame in Paris (1163) (Fig. 11) is based on a square rather than an oblong bay. Bourges (1192) and later Beauvais (1247) have four, instead of the more traditional two, side

Figure 12. Salisbury Cathedral. Courtesy of James O'Hear III.

Figure 11. Notre Dame Cathedral. Courtesy of the Architecture Department, The Catholic University of America.

aisles. The Cathedral of Albi (1282) in southern France is a unique fortified design made of brick; Sainte Chapelle (1243), which adjoined the royal palace in Paris, distills the ideals of this style to the point where the church becomes a beautiful room enclosed in stained glass.

There is no doubt that Gothic architecture is a French invention. But social and economic trends during this era made it possible for this innovative building technique to be employed throughout Europe. Towns freed themselves of feudal domination and developed trading specialties; improved mapmaking and navigation enhanced the transportation system; universities such as Oxford, Cambridge, and Bologna broadened educational opportunities; and a code of chivalry was established to guide behavior. From the viewpoint of building, the notebook prepared for his students by an architect named Villard de Honnecourt—full of sketches showing plans, elevations, details, and proportions—suggested the exchange of ideas that was taking place with regard to design.

In this dynamic environment, then, the English were the next to embrace the Gothic style, and they exploited it for more than 350 years. A first phase in this history is referred to as Early English Gothic and is illustrated by Salisbury Cathedral (1220) (Fig. 12). Like the French churches, it employs the pointed arch, ribbed vaulting, oblong bay, three-story interior elevation, and flying buttresses. But there are some significant differences. Rather than in the center of town, Salisbury is located along the edge in a parklike setting. The west facade is treated as a screen, hiding the rest of the building and giving little

indication of the nave and two side aisles. The flying buttresses are modest in size and hint that, on the interior, length—not height—is emphasized. In this regard, the nave arcade and triforium appear as long horizontal bands and the columns for each of these levels are independent instead of continuous as they are in the cathedrals of France. Finally, the tradition of a semicircular choir is replaced by a rectangular chapel dedicated to the Virgin.

As time progressed, Gothic architecture in England grew more elaborate. A second, Decorated phase occurred during the fourteenth century and is characterized by more complex vaulting and tracery (the stone mullions in stained glass windows). The star pattern in the tower at Ely Cathedral (1322) and the intricate ribbing over the east end of Gloucester Cathedral (ca 1330) are examples. The last era of English Gothic is called Perpendicular. Most of these churches were constructed during the fifteenth century, and took the form of large single rooms or halls surrounded by walls of stained glass and graceful fan vaults in the ceiling. King's College Chapel (Cambridge, 1446) and Bath Abbey (1501) are typical. What is important in these cases is that a decorative motif has been substituted for the skeletal ribs and columns, formerly the essence of this style. The buildings are beautiful, but quite different from their original French sources.

Other countries also adopted Gothic design. In Spain, it was popular from the thirteenth to the sixteenth centuries. As the Cathedral of Seville (1402) and the New Cathedral in Salamanca (1509) demonstrate, the major attributes in this area include side aisles that are almost as tall as the nave, small clerestories, curvilinear ribs, and, in later buildings, a highly decorative form of detail known as Plateresque, a word that refers to the delicate craftsmanship of silversmiths. The few exceptions to this approach are in Barcelona. There, several local churches, notably Santa Maria del Mar (1328) and Santa Maria del Pino (1453), are designed as simple columned halls, free of decoration and with little or no clerestory. Many German churches have a similar hall-like quality, with varying degrees of painted and carved decoration. The truly distinguishing feature of this northern style, however, is the presence of a central tower to mark the entry on the west facade. This can be seen both at the Frauenkirche in Nuremberg (1354) and at Ulm Cathedral (1377). In all of Europe, Italy was the least receptive to the concepts of this French architecture. As the marble patterns on the facade of Siena Cathedral (ca 1226) make clear, the pointed arch was used as a visual rather than structural element. Walls were load bearing. Flying buttresses were seldom employed, often because the roof was supported by a wooden truss, as in Santa Croce (Florence, 1294), instead of on stone vaulting. And even in those instances such as the Cathedral of Florence (1296), where cross ribs are part of the design, the space under these vaults seems more like Roman domes than the oblong bays of most Gothic churches. Indeed, it is this classical heritage that ultimately emerged as the major architectural influence in Italy.

Renaissance Architecture

In the early fifteenth century, the citizens of Florence, Italy, faced a unique architectural dilemma. As the European center for banking as well as the wool and silk trades, proud civic leaders had, for over 100 years, supported the construction of a new cathedral. It was a grand undertaking. The building was more than 120 m long with the transept and the east end of the church designed as large apses with space for 15 altars and chapels. The crossing was to be covered by an enormous dome, a symbol of the city's power and wealth. The problem was that no one could figure out how to build a dome that would span the required 42 m. In addition, the situation became more complex in 1410, when a thin-wall drum was erected as a base for the dome. Fortunately, ten years later a solution was developed. A lightweight, double-shell dome was built on a skeleton of vertical ribs. These were tied horizontally by rings of sandstone, oak beams, and brick panels, and the entire job was completed without unsightly exterior scaffolding. This ingenious scheme had been devised by a designer, inventor, and goldsmith named Filippo Brunelleschi, and his creative and rational approach marks the beginning of the Renaissance style. It was a major shift from the verticality of Gothic building. The architecture of this period emphasizes four qualities: (1) it uses classical Roman and Greek details and design concepts; (2) it is human in scale rather than imperial or divine; (3) it is usually based on a proportional system; and (4) it shows a renewed interest in the central plan and a focus on the individual, including recognition of the patron and designer of a project.

Three buildings by Brunelleschi, the Florentine who initiated the Renaissance, are examples of these principles. The Foundling Hospital (1421), like most designs of this era, is an urban structure. Used as an orphanage, it faces a square and responds to this public space with a graceful arcade. In terms of detail, the scheme recalled Italy's heritage as the center of ancient Rome. The arcade used the Corinthian order. Over the delicate capitals, arches were outlined in gray stone molding, an architrave created a strong and unifying horizontal line in the facade, and triangular pediments highlighted the second story windows.

In terms of scale, the composition was elegant but not overwhelming. It was a classical approach that served people and, at the same time, satisfied Florence's self-image of its important role in history. It is clear, then, why there were other commissions in this same style. The church of Santo Spirito (1445) is interesting because it combines Brunelleschi's architectural vocabulary with the use of a proportional system. In this case, an arcade similar to that of the Foundling Hospital was reinterpreted for the nave elevation. Above the side aisle, however, arches rather than pediments defined the clerestory windows. This helped to tie together the two layers of the interior facade. But more subtle relationships among various parts of the design were also developed. Based on a square module, the width of the nave was twice the width of the side aisle. In addition, the height of the nave was twice the height of the side aisle. Thus, here, aesthetics and proportion worked together to unify the elements of the building. The Pazzi Chapel (1429) (Fig. 13) demonstrates Brunelleschi's sophistication in dealing with the central plan. The small church is almost square, with two axes carefully delineated by different kinds of vaulting. From the entrance to the altar, a person moves up a few steps and passes under a series of three domes, the largest of which marks the center of the structure. At right angles to this sequence, barrel vaults create a transept. But even with this articulation, the design is experienced as a single space, a feeling that is enhanced by the triumphal arch motif used for both the exterior and interior elevations.

By the second half of the fifteenth century, other cities and other individuals were exploring this architectural

Figure 13. Pazzi Chapel. Courtesy of the Architecture Department, The Catholic University of America.

language. Leon Battista Alberti, one of the most influential, was both a theorist and designer. In his *Ten Books on Architecture* (ca 1450), he commented on town planning and the practice of architecture, and codified the details, proportions, and appropriate uses of classicism. He also gave a clear definition of beauty (6): "A harmony of all the parts, in whatsoever subject it appears, fitted together with such proportion and connection, that nothing could be added, diminished or altered, but for the worse." Sant' Andrea (1472) (Fig. 14), a church he designed in Mantua, Italy, reflects this studied approach and demonstrates his fascination with mathematics. The facade is a triumphal arch, but instead of the slender Corinthian columns of Brunelleschi's Pazzi Chapel, Alberti used giant Corinthian pilasters, a feature common in antique architecture. The effect is bold and solid, particularly in combination with the full entablature and pediment above the central opening. The interior is equally weighty. The roof is a coffered barrel vault, and the image of a triumphal arch is repeated along the nave with a proportional system that intensifies the movement toward the main altar. On the outside, pilasters are spaced in a 1:3 relationship. Down the nave, this ratio is 1:2. In the transept, it is 2:3, and in the apse behind the altar, it becomes 1:1—the ideal—as a person reaches the visual and spiritual goal of the building.

Donato Bramante was another architect who mastered the Renaissance style. The Tempietto (1502) in Rome illustrates how he carefully studied ancient buildings. This compact structure, in the middle of a courtyard, supposedly marks the spot where St. Peter was martyred, and is modeled on a circular pagan temple. The dome is plain and the Tuscan columns are unfluted, creating a severe appearance. But this impression is balanced by elegant details: a pleasing human scale; proportions based on a system

of related rectangles; and a rhythmic pattern of shadows around the colonnade, niches, and windows.

During this period, for the first time since the collapse of the Roman Empire, designers also devoted their talents to the development of a secular architecture. Palazzos or palaces for wealthy merchants and political and religious leaders were the major building type. Generally, these grand homes were three stories tall with a central courtyard. The first floor was used for business and storage. The second, or *piano nobile,* contained public spaces, and the third was traditionally reserved as private quarters. Aesthetically, the exteriors of these edifices varied according to the location and time in which they were constructed. In Florence, the earliest palazzos—examples include the Riccardi (1444 by Michelozzo) and the Strozzi (1489 by Majano and Cronaca)—had a fortified character, with large cornices, arched windows, and heavy rustication. Occasionally, a design like the Palazzo Rucellai (1446 by Alberti) would have a more elaborate elevation, in this case with Tuscan, Ionic, and Corinthian pilasters defining the three levels, but this was the exception until the early sixteenth century. The Palazzo Farnese (1515 by Sangallo and Michelangelo) (Fig. 15) in Rome is typical of this later, more hierarchical, High Renaissance style. The entrance is pulled forward and marked by a large arch at the ground level, and by a balcony and cartouche on the *piano nobile.* Rustication, instead of a general facade treatment, is used to accent the entry and corners of the building, and windows are adorned with a variety of pediments to suggest the importance of interior spaces. These pediments are flat on the ground floor, all triangular on the top story, and alternate between triangular and arched shapes on the *piano nobile.*

Beyond the borders of Italy, the classical language of architecture was not really exploited until the second half of the sixteenth century. In France, England, Germany, and northern Europe, the most common approach until about 1550 was to apply Renaissance details to an otherwise Gothic structure. At the Chateau de Chambord (1519), designed by the Italian architect Domenico da Cortona, the pilasters, pediments, coffering, and moldings have precedents in antique buildings, but the form and composition of the palace is medieval. Similar assessments may be

Figure 14. Sant' Andrea. Courtesy of the Architecture Department, The Catholic University of America.

Figure 15. The Palazzo Farnese. Courtesy of the Architecture Department, The Catholic University of America.

made of Germany's Heidelberg Castle (1531), and Elizabethan mansions in England such as two planned by architect Robert Smithson, Longleat (Wilts, 1567) and Hardwick Hall (Derbyshire, 1590). The Palace of Charles V (1527) in Granada, Spain, is one of the few digressions from this approach. In his travels, architect Pedro Machuca may have been inspired by Bramante, for the scheme has a purity and boldness that, for its time, is unusual outside Italy. The square layout is about 61 m on a side with an expansive circular courtyard in the middle. The two-story facade is Tuscan on the lower level and Ionic above, and this chaste attitude is only interrupted at the main entrance where pairs of columns surround the doors and alternating triangular and curved pediments mark the windows. This last feature is a more personal rather than literal interpretation of classicism and hints that another stylistic phase had begun.

Mannerist Architecture

During the 1400s and early 1500s, individuals like Alberti and Bramante established the Renaissance style. But the architects that followed, throughout the sixteenth century in Italy and up to the end of the seventeenth in other parts of Europe, made some significant changes. While they based their work on a traditional classical vocabulary, these later designers interpreted concepts and details in unexpected ways and demonstrated a growing enthusiasm for landscape and urban design issues. Their approach was personal and experimental; thus the era is referred to as Mannerist. On a small scale, these architects used several techniques, many of them quite playful and whimsical. They exaggerated detail, for instance, by decorating columns and walls with oversized rustication. They layered facades, developing complex patterns of overlapping detail. They intentionally employed the correct detail incorrectly, and created designs that were ambiguous. In the garden court of the Palazzo del Tè (1525, Mantua, by Giulio Romano) (Fig. 16), for example, the triglyphs of the Doric order appear to be slipping from the entablature, and attic windows above the major openings make it unclear whether the elevation is one or two stories. On a larger scale, unlike a Renaissance building that was conceived of as a single, well-proportioned mass, a Mannerist commission was often treated as multiple volumes. U-shaped plans, entry porches, and palaces with arcades off to the sides were common. These forms, in turn, allowed architects to improve the relationships between a structure and its site. In the city, this meant enhancing a piazza or civic square. The busy and sheltering colonnade of the Uffizi Gallery (1560, by Giorgio Vasari) in Florence is illustrative. In the country, since villas were increasingly popular, this meant linking these suburban palaces with the landscape. The Villa Lante (1566, Bagnaia, Italy, by Giacomo da Vignola), for example, is designed as two pavilions in an elegant terraced garden.

In addition to the names already mentioned, Baldassare Peruzzi, Domenico Fontana, and Raphael Santi were prominent Italian architects during this period, but perhaps the most well-known and influential were Michelangelo and Andrea Palladio. The vestibule to the Lauren-

Figure 16. Palazzo del Tè, detail. Courtesy of the Architecture Department, The Catholic University of America.

tian Library (Florence, 1524) displays Michelangelo's talent and Mannerist style. The room is small yet detailed as if it were a grander and more important space. There are no exterior openings, but blind (in-filled) windows enrich the facades. These have alternating curved and triangular pediments, and are flanked by pairs of Tuscan columns. Instead of supporting the roof, however, these columns are recessed into the wall and sit atop decorative scrolls. It is the reversal of the expected; decoration supports structure instead of being supported by it. Another Mannerist tendency is evident in the scheme's sweeping staircase that would be more appropriate on the outside of a building than in this tiny entrance. As a second example, Michelangelo's plan for the Capitoline Hill (ca 1544) (Fig. 17) in Rome suggests his ability to address urban concerns as well as his Mannerist preference for visually active forms and exaggeration. In this case, a flight of

Figure 17. Capitoline Hill, view from balcony. Courtesy of the Architecture Department, The Catholic University of America.

gently sloping stairs leads to a trapezoidal piazza. On the left and right, two buildings (the Capitoline Museum and the Palazzo dei Conservatori), each two stories tall, splay outward to frame the centerpiece of the composition, the three-story Palazzo dei Senatori. A double staircase rises to the entrance of this last structure and, from a balcony at this upper level, there is a dramatic vista over an elaborate paving pattern and past a statue of Marcus Aurelius to the rooftops of the city. Finally, in an effort to give visual unity to the space, giant Corinthian pilasters are used as a motif on all of the major elevations.

Andrea Palladio was also a master of this style. His Church of Il Redentore (Venice, 1577) is a sophisticated design of overlapping detail. Inspired by Roman temples, three pedimented facades are layered in a single elevation to designate different parts of the building. One marks the entrance; another the nave; and a third, the side aisles. At the Villa Rotunda (Vicenza, 1552), the architect uses a solid square plan, but artfully subdivides this into several volumes with a dominant central rotunda and a porch and stairs coming off each of the four sides. These last elements also tie the building with the gardens beyond, another aspect of Mannerism. In the Palazzo Chiericati (Vicenza, 1550) (Fig. 18), Palladio established a U-shaped plan with a series of proportionally related rooms, marked the first floor with a colonnade along the street, and designed the second story as three volumes with two open bays around an enclosed central space.

Such freedom made it easier to exploit architecture as an expression of individuality and prestige. This fact, combined with the availability of several treatises on design (including Palladio's *Four Books of Architecture*), made the Mannerist approach to building increasingly popular in Europe, especially among monarchs and the nobility. Developments in Britain and France were particularly significant. In England, Inigo Jones's Queen's House in Greenwich (1616) and the Banqueting House in Whitehall Palace, London (1619), were inspired by Palladian villas. Later, Sir Christopher Wren translated classical details into an unusual vocabulary of towers and steeples to grace

Figure 18. Palazzo Chiericati. Courtesy of the Architecture Department, The Catholic University of America.

his community churches in London, such as St. Bride (1671) and St. Mary-le-Bow (1670). In France, the palace of the kings in Paris, the Louvre (begun in 1546), received the attention of many architects. The courtyard facade and the Pavillon de l'Horloge (1624, by Jacques Lemercier) were designed in a Mannerist fashion as several multistory volumes along a spine. The east facade (1667, by Claude Perrault) is more chaste but with a Mannerist rhythm of paired columns as its special hallmark. The Château de Maisons (near Paris, 1642) by François Mansart demonstrates this period's concern for linking building and landscape, and exemplifies the steep pitched roof typical in France during this era. A last illustration, the Place de Voges (1605, Paris, possibly by Claude Castillon), is notable as a Mannerist square with arcades and elegant private homes surrounding an attractive urban park.

Baroque Architecture

Architecturally, the baroque style manifests itself in three major areas. On the largest scale, city planning becomes a reality. Conceptually, this process involved identifying important urban buildings, squares, and spaces, and then visually and physically linking these with axial boulevards and monumental sculpture. The creation of grandiose palaces is a second baroque development. Sheer size distinguished these royal and papal homes from earlier Renaissance and Mannerist designs. In addition, however, these complexes often had elaborate gardens and *allées* that, beyond unifying landscape and architecture, symbolized the ability to control nature. Changes in the layout and details of churches were a third expression of the style. During this era, these structures were characterized by central plans, curvilinear facades, and ornate classical and sculptural decoration. Chronologically, the period begins in Italy in the late sixteenth and early seventeenth centuries and extends to the rest of Europe by the eighteenth century.

Examples of baroque planning include Christopher Wren's proposal of circular and diagonal avenues for the reconstruction of London after the Great Fire of 1666; Tsar Peter the Great's development of St. Petersburg (now Leningrad) based on French models in the first half of the eighteenth century, and the combined radial and grid layout of Karlsruhe begun in 1715. The objective in each of these was to organize the city as a sequence of plazas, vistas, and significant structures, an idea that first emerged in the plan for Rome conceived by Pope Sixtus V in 1585. The hope was to give the center of Christendom a new image, one that would replace the haphazard medieval order with a new town of classical monuments and churches. This harmony was possible because the scheme established major routes that opened up the city and visually unified the shrines frequented by pilgrims. Obelisks were used as markers to guide visitors from point to point, and piazzas were planned as settings for important buildings. Although the Pope died long before the proposal was complete, his concept and initial work were so clear that they guided design for centuries to come. Today, broad avenues such as the Via Quirinale and the Via Agostino Depretis and beautiful spaces such as the Piazza del Popolo and the Spanish Steps are a direct result of this sixteenth-century project. The plan for another part of Rome started with the construction of a single building and, after about 150 years and contributions from many architects, emerged as a dynamic component of the city's urban design. The first plan for St. Peter's was prepared by Bramante in 1505 and was subsequently enlarged by Michelangelo in 1546 and by Carlo Maderno in 1606. In a last phase of development, Pietro Bernini designed the over 250 m-long processional colonnade and piazza (ca 1667) (Fig. 19) that make this an outstanding illustration of both architecture and planning. Finally, as an interesting footnote to this process, in the late 1930s Mussolini razed the buildings from the colonnade to the Tiber River, creating the Via della Conciliazione and further expanding the impact of this scheme.

Perhaps because of its vastness, Versailles must be considered the quintessential baroque palace. Built between 1661 and 1756, this work was initiated as a collaborative effort among the architect Louis LeVau, the landscape designer Andre Le Notre, and the interior designer Charles Lebrun and, as a symbol of the nation-state and political strength, it became a model emulated by other powerful leaders. Features typical of this and other palaces are: the courtyard entrance, used to create a visual and ceremonial focus; the almost overwhelming scale, suggested in this complex by the fact that it could house up to 100,000 people; control over the surrounding landscape, illustrated at Versailles by formal gardens, fountains, canals, and forests that extended several kilometers beyond the palace itself; the emphasis on stairs as an architectural event, in this case in an impressive interior foyer and on the garden terraces; and the use of exuberant detail and decoration, a quality particularly evident, in this French example, in the Royal Chapel and the Hall of Mirrors. Some rulers, such as Peter the Great in his summer Ekaterininski Palace (1749, outside St. Petersburg, by Bartolomeo Rastrelli), tried to copy the grandeur of Versailles. Others developed their own interpretations of this style. Castle Howard (Yorkshire, 1699) and Blenheim Palace (Oxfordshire, 1704), both designed by Sir John Vanbrugh, are illustrations of English baroque where many wings spread out from a central and dominant architectural block. The Belvedere (ca 1693, by Lucus von Hildebrandt) in Vienna is notable because it is composed of an upper and a lower palace with the gardens in between. Additional examples would include the low scaled Drottningholm Castle (1660, by Nicodemus Tessin the Elder) outside Stockholm, the decorative Zwinger palace (1711, by M. D. Poppelmann) in Dresden, and the massive La Granja de San Ildefonso, the Spanish Versailles (1735, by Filippo Juvarra), near Segovia.

Five church designs, all derived from curvilinear forms, suggest the variety of baroque alternatives for this building type. The exterior facade of Sant'Ivo della Sapienza (1642, Rome, by Francesco Borromini) (Fig. 20) has concave shapes for its first two stories, convex shapes at the base of its dome, and a corkscrew motif for the roof of its cupola. This rhythmic combination hints at the interior that is made up of alternating concave and convex bays that lead to the main altar and define a complex central plan. Pulling this lively movement into a single space, the six ribs of the dome come together in a compact circle just below the brightly lit cupola. San Andrea del Quirinale (1658, Rome, by Giovanni Bernini) presents a second alternative. In this case, concave walls and a projecting semicircular porch serve as the entrance. The main altar is opposite the doorway on the short axis of an oval plan and, in a subtle shift, the longer but less important cross axis is played down by marking it with pilasters rather than side altars. Inside, the building materials are especially lavish.

Figure 19. St. Peter's Piazza. Courtesy of the Architecture Department, The Catholic University of America.

Figure 20. Sant' Ivo della Sapienza. Courtesy of the Architecture Department, The Catholic University of America.

The dome is coffered and classical details are carved in richly textured white and reddish marbles. A third design, Guarino Guarini's San Lorenzo (1668) in Turin, is baroque not only because its plan is composed of multiple and overlapping ovals and circles, but also because its tiered dome is created from a unique web of intersecting ribs and arches.

In England, St. Paul's Cathedral (1675, London, by Christopher Wren) (Fig. 21) is a fourth example of this style. The facade and details are more reserved than those in Italy, but the paired columns, the two-story base for the dome, the curved entablature in the spires, and the dramatic sequence of interior circular spaces are characteristic of this era. A fifth illustration is the Pilgrimage Church (1743, by Balthasar Neumann) in Vierzehnheiligen, Germany. In this instance, the exterior is a blend of gentle convex and concave shapes between two large towers. This simplicity contrasts with the gilding and elaborate paintings, sculpture, and stucco decoration that adorn the interior, elements typical of baroque in northern Europe. Beyond these features, however, the plan is an ingenious mix of curvilinear shapes that joyfully guides the faithful past the shrine of the Fourteen Saints to side altars and finally to the high altar in the apse of the building.

Although there is great diversity in scale and detail during this period, it is worthwhile noting that, regardless of type, these projects have three themes in common. Unlike Renaissance and Mannerist buildings that can be analyzed in two dimensions, baroque designs are concerned with the full, three dimensions of space—with urban squares, with relationships between a palace and its garden, and with complex interiors derived from curved shapes and the theatrical use of false perspective and optical illusion. These designs also stress the concept of movement: movement along the broad avenues of cities; movement up to the entrance and through a palace and into its gardens; and movement around the dynamic volumes of churches. Finally, these designs are synthetic—the grand and visually stimulating blend of architecture, painting, sculpture, and in the cases of palaces and cities, the surrounding landscape. Because it is a synthesis, baroque then can be interpreted as the culmination of the rebirth of classicism begun three centuries earlier in Florence, "the last of the great universal styles of European art"(7).

Eclectic Architecture

With the advent of the Industrial Revolution, the period from the last half of the eighteenth century to the first decades of the twentieth century was characterized by the growth of cities and major technological, economic, and social change. It was an era of dynamic tension—of rural vs urban images, of those who supported the agrarian tradition vs those who looked forward to the machine age, of an absolute monarchy vs an increasingly powerful middle class. Buildings reflected this situation. Rather than a single theme, many styles emerged, each with its own character. Still, within this diversity it is possible to identify several major trends. Some structures, including those classified as Greek revival, neoclassical, Palladian, and beaux-arts, derived their details from antique, Renaissance, Mannerist, and baroque precedents. Some were inspired by medieval architecture and were categorized as Romanesque or Gothic revival. Others go even further back in history to mimic Egyptian and Byzantine designs. Finally, certain edifices were styled after nature and technology.

Perhaps the most enduring and widespread tradition was the continuation of classicism. Even within this category, however, the approach was pluralistic. Some structures, such as the Church of the Madeleine (1806, by Pierre-Alexandre Vignon) in Paris, the State Capitol (1789, by Thomas Jefferson) in Richmond, Va., and the Second Bank of the United States (1817, by William Strickland) in Philadelphia, Pa., clearly adapted antique models. While scale and function have changed, the classical precedents are evident: Roman temples in the first two examples, and the Parthenon in the third.

In other cases, the design is Mannerist, interpreting rather than copying architecture from the past. The British Museum (1823, London, by Sir Robert Smirke), for instance, translates the Greek temple form and the Ionic order into a series of grand exhibition pavilions. In a more personal technique, Claude Nicolas Ledoux, in his toll house, the Barrière de la Villette (Paris, 1785), abstracted a classical vocabulary into stark geometric shapes—squares, rectangles, circles, semicircles, and triangles—and then used these to make allusions to a Doric temple, a Palladian arcade, and a central plan church such as

Figure 21. St. Paul's Cathedral. Courtesy of the Architecture Department, The Catholic University of America.

the Tempietto. During the second half of the nineteenth century, a baroque influence was apparent. The Paris Opéra (1862, by Charles Garnier) is illustrative. It has a ground-level arcade, a double-columned main facade, a domed theater, elaborate sculpture, paintings, and carved decoration, and a magnificent lobby and interior staircase, elements later used by other designers. In the United States, those structures emulating this French Second Empire style included the Old Executive Office Building (1871, Washington, D.C., by Alfred B. Mullet), the Philadelphia City Hall (1874, by John McArthur), and the Library of Congress (1886, Washington, D.C., by John Smithmeyer and Paul Pelz).

A last phase of classicism began in America around the turn of the twentieth century when a genre known as beaux-arts grew increasingly popular. The Boston Public Library (1887, by McKim, Mead & White) (Fig. 22) and the Union Railroad Station (1908, Washington, D.C., by Daniel Burnham) are two examples. The library was based on a similar Renaissance-inspired design in France, the Bibliothèque S. Geneviève (1845, Paris, by Henri Labrouste), and the station was modeled after the Roman Baths of Caracalla. Ultimately, however, the beaux-arts style was concerned more with planning than with individual structures. The 1893 World's Columbian Exposition in Chicago had demonstrated that architecture, landscape design, and sculpture could be combined to help create the ideal city. And with this success, architects and landscape architects went on to develop large-scale classical plans for cities such as Washington, D.C. (1902), San Francisco (1905), and Chicago (1909).

Other periods were also part of this emphasis on revivals. This is especially true with regard to building facades and decoration. The Houses of Parliament (1836, London, by Charles Barry) was a Gothic design that used precise Tudor details across a picturesque elevation of towers and spires, including the famous Big Ben. Another illustration of this secular style was Strawberry Hill (1747, Twickenham, by Horace Walpole), a lavish country home with a fortified appearance and irregular plan that recalled the image of a medieval castle. In addition, and not unexpectedly, as Trinity Church (1839, by Richard Upjohn) in New York and the Cathedral (1903, by Giles Gilbert Scott) in Liverpool suggest, religious structures often employed Gothic motifs. Occasionally, the allusions to history were more exotic. The Royal Pavilion (1815, Brighton, by John Nash) blended minarets, onion-shaped domes, and fanciful arcades in references to Islamic, Indian, and Gothic architecture. Westminster Cathedral (1895, by J. F. Bentley) in London and Sacré-Coeur (1875, by Paul Abadie) in Paris look back to Romanesque and Byzantine design. And a New York City jail, the Halls of Justice (1835, by John Haviland), was decorated as an Egyptian temple.

Two additional aspects of this eclectic era deserve mention. One is art nouveau, an organic style inspired by nature rather than history. This movement, which began in the 1890s and flourished for about 20 years, went beyond the design of buildings to include graphics, furnishings, jewelry, glass, and metalwork, and was noted for its fine craftsmanship. Architecturally, the Hotel Tassel (1893, Brussels, by Victor Horta) was one of the first structures to explore this expressionistic idiom. On the exterior, the flowing lines of balcony railings and stone columns that appeared to have taken root in the window sill, and on the interior, the elegant staircase with its flowerlike metal columns and beams, were typical details. In Paris, the Metro stations (ca 1900) designed by Hector Guimard displayed similar features, but in this case, because the sensuous curves of the metal framework were filled in with glass, there was an interesting balance between nature and light. Antonio Gaudi can also be considered an art nouveau architect. Although he was influenced by structural concepts and historical and religious themes, his designs exhibited the organic qualities essential to the style, and, as the free-form balconies, turrets, colorful facade, and skeletonlike details of the Casa Batlló (Barcelona, 1905) (Fig. 23) indicate, he had a unique imagination.

Outside this work and the historical revivals described earlier, another source of eclecticism was technology. Inspired by the potential of cast-iron and steel as building materials and the development of new techniques for the construction of bridges, a machine aesthetic emerged as an important trend during the second half of the nineteenth century. While cast-iron commercial structures (ca 1850s) in New York and the stack area of the National Library (1862, by Henri Labrouste) in Paris were significant examples of this theme, the approach was boldest in exhibition halls, markets, shopping arcades, and train sheds. An early illustration was the Crystal Palace (1851, London, by Joseph Paxton) whose open frame and glass panels rose to a height of over 20 m and covered a space more than 560 m long. Equally impressive was the fact that the entire pavilion was constructed in less than nine months. The 300-m Eiffel Tower (1887, Paris, by Gustave Eiffel) (Fig. 24) was another exhibition monument that demonstrated the versatility and dramatic potential of a style based on technology. In more practical applications, the Galleria Vittorio Emanuele (1865, by G. Mengoni) in Milan and the Gare du Nord (1862, by J. I. Hittorff) in Paris blended baroque and neoclassical details on the facades with elaborate iron vaulting to span large public areas, a combination that clearly expressed the diversity of this eclectic period.

Figure 22. Boston Public Library. Courtesy of the Architecture Department, The Catholic University of America.

Figure 23. Casa Batlló. Courtesy of the author.

Figure 24. Eiffel Tower. Courtesy of James O'Hear III.

Modern Architecture

In 1908, Viennese architect Adolf Loos prepared a manifesto that advocated a new aesthetic: "Since ornament is no longer organically linked with our culture, it is also no longer the expression of our culture. The ornament that is manufactured today has no connexion (sic) with us, has absolutely no human connexions (sic), no connexion (sic) with the world order" (8). Even among his contemporaries, Loos was a radical and, although few designers supported his extreme position, the modern, decoration-free style he espoused was already in evidence by the beginning of the twentieth century. Perhaps the best example was the skyline of Chicago that, during this time, was hallmarked by growing numbers of tall office and commercial buildings. Structures such as the Second Leiter Building (1889, by William Le Barron Jenney), the Reliance Building (1890, by Daniel Burnham and John Root), and the Gage Building (1898, by Louis Sullivan) had facades with large planes of windows, and a grid of columns and beams that indicated their skeletal, steel-frame construction and their emphasis on efficiency rather than allusions to history. In terms of smaller scale, domestic architecture, the designs of Frank Lloyd Wright were important. His prairie homes—the Robie House (Chicago, 1908) is especially well known—had ground-hugging horizontal silhouettes and combined beautiful details and references to nature with innovations that included open interior plans, window walls, built-in furniture, integrated mechanical systems, and carports, all features that would be commonplace decades later.

With this trend established and discussed in a growing body of theoretical literature, and with support from the Werkbund and the Bauhaus, two early twentieth-century German design institutions, architects began to exploit this modern idiom based on structure and technology. Philosophically, this group hoped that the new style would alleviate the clutter and confusion in cities, and offer rich and poor alike comfortable housing, open space, and sunlight. Architecturally, they expressed these objectives in buildings that, in their purest form, were dubbed the international style. Such structures subscribed to three principles: (1) the notion that architecture was volume rather than mass; (2) the belief that the chief means of ordering design was regularity rather than symmetry; and (3) the general proscription of applied decoration (9). Mies van der Rohe's Tugendhat House (Brno, Czechoslovakia, 1930) and Le Corbusier's and Pierre Jeanneret's Villa Savoye (Poissy-sur-Seine, France, 1928) (Fig. 25) illustrate these themes. Although the latter was lifted off the ground and was more sculptural, both employed open interior plans. Both used columns as structure and walls to divide space, thus distinguishing between elements that hold a building up and those that create architectural volume. Both used expansive glass windows to demonstrate that the facade was independent of structure and free to respond to interior function. Additionally, both used light, geometric form, and the nature of materials as decoration. In the United States, after the immigration of European architects such as Walter Gropius and Mies van der Rohe, and with pioneering designs such as the McGraw-Hill Building (1929,

Figure 25. Villa Savoye. Courtesy of Dhiru Thadani.

Figure 27. Dulles International Airport. Courtesy of the students, The Catholic University of America.

New York City, by Raymond Hood) and the Philadelphia Saving Fund Society skyscraper (1932, by George Howe and William Lescaze), this approach became increasingly popular. Particularly after the end of World War II, most offices and apartments reflected this lean aesthetic and often had elevations that at least superficially were variations of the international style.

In contrast to this stark manipulation of structure and technology, a number of modern designers demonstrated that the same architectural vocabulary could be handled in a more relaxed manner without creating unnecessary ornament or stylistic references. The Finn, Alvar Aalto, was a leader in this group. His projects blended brick, wood, reinforced concrete, stone, tile, color, asymmetrical plans, an ingenious use of windows and skylights, and a sensitivity to the surrounding environment in a way that was both casual and contemporary. Even a monumental commission like the Finlandia Hall concert complex (Helsinki, 1962) (Fig. 26) balanced an appropriate civic scale with an inviting entrance and a variety of textures and intimate interior spaces. In another technique, some architects used structure itself to achieve organic effects. Pier Luigi Nervi's Palazzetto dello Sport (Rome, 1956) has an

elegantly thin concrete-shell dome supported on a woven framework of concrete piers that seem to have been grown in the earth. And Eero Saarinen employed shell construction to fabricate the swooping forms of his TWA terminal (John F. Kennedy International Airport, New York City 1962), which appears to be a great bird in flight. Interestingly, at Dulles International Airport (Chantilly, Va., 1962) (Fig. 27), the same designer used a tension structure to suggest the grace and dynamic movement of air travel.

In some cases such sculptural qualities were imposed by the design, rather than having structural origins. In these cases, sophisticated technology was essential to the result, but was a means rather than an end. The spiraling gallery of Frank Lloyd Wright's Guggenheim Museum (New York City) completed in 1959 is one example. The sail-like facades of Jorn Utzon's Sydney Opera House (completed in 1973) is another. Additional illustrations of this technique are evident in the work of Louis Kahn, who juxtaposed beautifully proportioned solid and open volumes as a way to visually distinguish between major spaces and service areas in his buildings. As the Richards Medical Research Center (Philadelphia, 1957) (Fig. 28) demonstrates, however, the impact could be both functional and sculptural—in this case a structure in the image of an Italian hill town. Le Corbusier also explored this approach. The Pilgrimage Chapel of Notre Dame du Haut (Ronchamps, France, 1955), the Supreme Court (Chandigarh, India, 1951), and the Carpenter Center for the Visual Arts (Cambridge, Mass., 1961) indicate how he combined light and form into exciting architecture. A final example, the Georges Pompidou Center (1972, Paris, by Richard Rogers and Renzo Piano), is worthwhile noting because it shows that the modern sculptural vocabulary could even be extended to include the playful use of trusses, pipes, vents, and other mechanical equipment. Yet, while this style was creative in an abstract sense, it also posed problems. Many of the buildings were without scale and had little or no relationship to the people that occupied them. Others were individually attractive, but ignored their context and surroundings. Recently, as a response to these issues, a new aesthetic has begun to emerge.

Figure 26. Finlandia Hall. Courtesy of the Architecture Department, The Catholic University of America.

Figure 28. Richards Medical Research Center. Courtesy of the students, The Catholic University of America.

Figure 29. The Red Wall. Courtesy of the Architecture Department, The Catholic University of America.

Postmodern Architecture

In 1961, Jane Jacobs published a condemnation of post–World War II city planning and urban revitalization techniques. The thesis of *The Death and Life of Great American Cities* was that modern concepts such as superblocks, the separation of land uses, and the destruction of entire neighborhoods in the name of urban renewal were destroying the vitality of American cities. She urged decision makers, including designers and planners, to develop processes that were more sensitive to the existing city fabric and more accepting of diverse functions and building styles (10). Five years later, Philadelphia architect Robert Venturi made another break with the tenets of modernism, advocating a new design method, ie, "a complex and contradictory architecture based on the richness and ambiguity of modern experience." The vocabulary and rules of this alternative style were revealed in a thoughtful analysis of architectural history and emphasized visual and spatial images rather than function and technology (11). Thus during the 1960s, while most clients and designers were content with modern architecture, the philosophical groundwork had been laid for a postmodern era. Numerous examples of this approach only began to emerge during the 1970s; thus it is difficult to make definitive assessments.

It is possible, however, to outline the principles that appear to guide these projects and give illustrations. The first and dominant theme is that, unlike modern architecture that rejected the past, these structures consistently make allusions to history. Some buildings, such as Philip Johnson's Mannerist AT&T headquarters (New York City, 1978) and Venturi's Victorian Faculty Dining Room (Penn State University, University Park, Pa., 1974), make references to specific periods. Others look to vernacular architecture or historical urban design and planning models for their inspiration. The facade of the Best Products Company showroom in Richmond, Va. (1971, SITE) is a peeling brick wall that both spoofs and celebrates the warehouse building type. Kresge College (1974, Charles Moore and

MTLW) at the University of California at Santa Cruz was developed as a medieval hill town. Dormitories are terraced along the sloping site and piazzas are the focus for administrative, classroom, library, and dining facilities.

A second concept important to this style is the desire to adapt images from history in ways that are new, fresh, and sometimes shocking. It is almost always apparent that these buildings have been constructed in the twentieth century. Postmodernism is not revival architecture. The Red Wall (Calpe, Spain 1972, Ricardo Bofill and the Taller de Architectura) (Fig. 29), for instance, recalls the castles and turrets of darker ages, but its many windows and colored walls make it clear that this sun-filled resort apartment building was constructed during a brighter era. The precedents for the Piazza d'Italia (1978, New Orleans, Charles Moore with the Urban Innovations Group) (Fig. 30) with its fountains, baroque spacial qualities, and classical details are European, but the Corinthian capitals are chrome plated and, in the evening, entablatures are edged

Figure 30. Piazza d'Italia. Courtesy of the Architecture Department, The Catholic University of America.

in neon light rather than deep shadow. Even skyscrapers that emulate more recent styles, such as the art deco Transco Tower (1980, Johnson/Burgee) in Houston, use materials with a boldness and simplicity that usually distinguishes them from earlier designs.

A third element of postmodernism is a concern for context, detail, and human scale. As the Regional Library for San Juan Capistrano, Calif., (1981, Michael Graves) demonstrates, architects attempt to devise buildings that complement the surroundings as well as meet functional needs. They make frequent use of colors and textures, including woods, tiles, and marbles. And, when possible, they incorporate inviting amenities, eg, an arcade, a public square, an atrium, or in the case of the library, a reading room with a fireplace and an exterior courtyard with a fountain. While it is too soon for final evaluations regarding postmodern architecture and, indeed, many talented designers continue to develop sophisticated and sensitive modern buildings, the fact is that this style reverses certain sterile architectural trends evident after World War II. Yet there may be problems. Some structures are merely facades, and others use construction techniques that are not particularly durable. Ultimately, time will be the test that determines whether postmodernism is ephemeral or a truly lasting approach to design.

NONWESTERN TRADITIONS

The Architecture of the Fertile Crescent and Ancient Egypt

Although many ancient Near Eastern civilizations were located between the Mediterranean Sea and the fertile valleys of the Tigris and Euphrates rivers, three of the most significant were the Sumerians, the Assyrians, and the Babylonians. The Sumerians were important because researchers have identified them as the first city builders in history. From about 3000 to 2000 B.C., these people established more than one dozen large settlements between the Tigris and the Euphrates. The wealth of cities such as Kish, Nippur, Erech, and Ur was based on farming and trade, and manifested itself in fortified complexes of narrow, winding streets, and dense clusters of courtyard homes with thick walls and no exterior windows. A public square, a few broad avenues, a bazaar, and ziggurat temples were the elements that added diversity to an otherwise severe style. The Ziggurat of Urnammu (ca 2125 B.C.) at Ur was typical of these religious structures. The temple rose 21 m in three terraces to a small sanctuary at the summit, and the base was a monumental platform measuring 62 × 43 m. A procession of staircases between the levels and wall surfaces broken up by a regular pattern of indentations were other characteristics of this striking edifice, which was located in a court and surrounded by three less dramatic temples. The later Assyrian and Babylonian cultures, which emerged between the nineteenth and sixth centuries B.C., used this same form, but rather than an isolated building type, they incorporated it within large palaces. The Assyrian Palace of Sargon (eighth century B.C.) suggests the grandeur of these royal homes. Arranged around a series of courts, it covered over eight hectares and included a religious enclave with six temples and a seven-tiered ziggurat, an administrative center and service quarters, and an area for the affairs of state and the king's apartment. In terms of detail, the throne room was an expansive hall, approximately 49 × 10 m, and had colorful friezes running the length of its plaster-covered walls. Other significant spaces were decorated with equal care. The main gate and entry arch, for instance, was flanked by sculptures of man-headed, winged bulls and was surfaced with bright polychrome brick. This splendor was also evident in the city of Babylon (sixth century B.C.). Although the Babylonians had briefly risen to power during the eighteenth century B.C., it was over a millenium later, under Nebuchadnezzar II, that they made their most lasting contributions to architecture. Their fabled capital was marked by massive fortifications that on one side formed a channel for the Euphrates River by a 90-m high ziggurat—the mythical Tower of Babel—and on the other, by an elaborate palace and garden complex that impressed the entire ancient world until the city was sacked by the Persians in 539 B.C.

Simultaneous with these developments in the Near East, the Egyptians established a civilization in northern Africa along the Nile River. This endured as an independent culture from about 3000 to 500 B.C., and was known architecturally for two major building types: tombs in the north and temples in the south. In general, both emphasized the transition from life on earth to life hereafter and employed similar features: a processional entry, an exterior court or terrace, an interior ceremonial space, and a burial chamber or sanctuary. Tombs were the first structures and, although there were many variations such as stepped and bent pyramids, the most famous examples were the three Pyramids at Giza (twenty-eighth–twenty-sixth centuries B.C.). These were each highlighted by an axis that moved from the Nile via a colonnaded causeway to a courtyard and mortuary temple, and culminated at the tomb itself deep inside the crystalline-shaped mass. The sheer size of these buildings remains impressive. The largest was dedicated to the pharaoh Cheops and originally had a base 230 m square and rose over 145 m to its apex. As centuries passed, however, and the power of the priesthood grew, temples emerged as the predominant form. The Temple of Hatshepsut (ca 1500 B.C.) (Fig. 31) at Dier el-Bahari illustrates this transition. Constructed at the base of cliffs along the Nile, it substituted a sanctuary inside the mountain for the solidity of the pyramid, and defined the processional with long ramps leading to a series of terraces and ceremonial colonnades. Eventually, this kind of structure was designed as a freestanding complex. Some of these were quite elaborate and were built over several centuries, but most contain the elements used at the Temple of Khons (ca 1200 B.C.) at Karnak. There, the procession to the entrance pylons and obelisks was surrounded by two parallel rows of sphinxes. The sequence continued through an enclosed courtyard to the hypostyle hall, a covered, column-filled room with a tall central area and lower side aisles, and ended at the sanctuary, an intimate and dimly lit sacred space. Finally, although there is archaeological evidence of Egyptian cities, these were not nearly as durable as the tombs and temples, and ulti-

Figure 31. Temple of Hatshepsut. Courtesy of the Cultural and Educational Office, Embassy of Egypt.

mately, unlike the civilizations of the Fertile Crescent, the theme of this architecture must be interpreted as uniquely related to the concept of eternal order.

Native American Architecture

Archaeologists and anthropologists trace the origins of civilization in the Americas back several millenia before Christ. The evidence for these earliest settlements are skeletal remains, tools, and the ashes of long-extinguished fires, and are of little interest architecturally. At the same time, from these humble beginnings sophisticated cultures emerged that did establish significant building traditions on these continents well in advance of their colonization by European nations. In North America, in the southwest United States, the Pueblo Indians created a style that is still influential. Since 700 A.D., these people have lived in communities defined as clusters of rectangular rooms, often stacked around a courtyard or plaza in receding layers up to five or six stories tall and oriented to maximize shade during the summer and exposure to the sun during the winter. The walls of these structures were built of adobe or sandstone, and roofs were supported on logs (called vigas), the ends of which remained visible on the exterior. Until the arrival of the Spaniards, when ground-level doors were introduced, the typical entrance to these pueblos was up a ladder and then into the spaces from openings in the roof. Examples of these complexes include the Taos Pueblo (begun ca thirteenth century) in New Mexico, and the dramatic cliff dwellings (eleventh–thirteenth centuries) in Mesa Verde National Park, Colo.

In another region, the architectural legacy of ancient Mexico and Central America is particularly diverse. The most impressive buildings were pyramidal temples, a form that may have first appeared around 300 B.C. when, outside present-day Mexico City, a group known as the Olmec constructed a ceremonial earthen mound faced with stone and terraced in four stages to a height of over 20 m. This type of structure was refined by later societies; tribes not only built temples, but also established thriving cities as the centers of large empires. From about 200 to 700 A.D.,

for instance, central Mexico was ruled from Teotihuacán. This city was home for 100,000 people and spread across 20 km². Its grid of streets contained shrines, palaces, and courtyard homes, many of which were decorated with colorful frescoes. Its main boulevard, the Avenue of the Dead, was 5 km long. The Pyramid of the Moon (ca third century A.D.), rising 40 m in five levels, was at one end, and the walled Temple of Quetzalcóatl (ca third century A.D.), adorned with carved stone serpent heads, was at the other. In between, the Pyramid of the Sun (ca third century A.D.) (Fig. 32) filled a space over 213 m on a side, and had five terraces supporting a typically small, rectangular temple atop its 60-m summit. Simultaneous with this activity, the Mayans were creating a federation of towns that would eventually extend from southern Mexico through parts of Nicaragua and Costa Rica. Beginning around 300 A.D., the civilization would endure for more than 800 years, and be noted for its many urban and religious centers, such as Tikal in Guatemala, Copán in Honduras, and Uxmal and Chichén Itzá on the Yucatan peninsula. Stylistically, the early pyramid–temples in this area—the Temple of the Giant Jaguar (Tikal, ca 500) is illustrative—were steep and embellished with lavish figural and geometric motifs, especially on the facades of the temple rooms themselves. Later designs maintained this approach to decoration, but were more spread out. In addition, the Mayans developed other building types, including ceremonial ball courts and expansive stone palaces. The Palace of the Governors (Uxmal, ca 900) is typical with its monumental terraced base and one-story elevation measuring over 95 m. The last native empire in this part of the world was the Aztecs, a group of warriors that dominated much of central Mexico during the fifteenth and sixteenth centuries. Although the form and details of their architecture were similar to those of the Mayans, their talent for organization was unique. This was evident in their vast capital Tenochtitlán, a city of 300,000 inhabitants built on man-made islands in the middle of Lake Texcoco. Dikes were constructed to control the water, canals built for transportation, and causeways linked the

Figure 32. Pyramid of the Sun. Courtesy of the Embassy of Mexico.

settlement to the mainland. The town was so large that, beyond the two central markets, each of its four subdivisions had a local market. Homes and palaces were painted with colored stucco, and a grand temple precinct marked the center of the city. This contained a ball court, a school, four major pyramid/temples, and several smaller ones. It was a vibrant society that only ended with the Spanish conquest.

In South America, the Chavín, the Mochica, and the Tiahuanaco were the first tribes to build temples, fortresses, and homes, but it was the Incas, from the thirteenth to the sixteenth centuries, who were to ultimately establish the most important empire on that continent. From their capital in Cuzco (now in Peru), these people used their well-developed engineering skills to create a system of paved highways and suspension bridges that tied some 30 cities, from modern Ecuador to Chile and Argentina, into a single civilization. These same talents were also applied to individual buildings. The Citadel of Sacsahuamán (ca 1475), constructed to protect Cuzco, used three tiers of zig-zag walls to trap enemies in cross fire. The fortress, and other structures in the capital, including a huge rectangular hall dedicated to the Sun God (ca fifteenth century), display careful masonry work. Although courses were irregular, stones weighing up to 100 tons were perfectly aligned with their neighbors. High in the Andes, at the mountaintop town of Machu Picchu, this attention to detail is evident not only in the architecture, but also in the aqueducts and terraces for farming. Thus, as this brief summary suggests, there were important architectural styles in the Americas centuries before the Europeans reached the New World.

Islamic Architecture

After the death of Mohammed in 632 A.D., Islam spread quickly. By the end of the seventh century, it was a dominant influence throughout the Middle East, Asia Minor, and northern Africa. By the eleventh century, Moslems controlled territories in Russia, Afghanistan, Pakistan, and northern India. By the fourteenth century, followers could be found as far away as the Philippines and Indonesia. Although architecture was not initially an important component of this faith and power, by the eighth century a significant building tradition had emerged that enhanced the religious and political presence of Moslem leadership. Inevitably, across such a vast territory, there were variations in construction, detailing, and design. But there were also formal and conceptual elements that transcended regional differences and characterized an Islamic style. On a general level, the two most common features were courtyards and a rich decorative vocabulary. The arcaded interior courtyard was used in mosques, schools, palaces, and homes, and with the hot climate and density of Arab cities, these spaces were oases from the heat and crowded bazaars. Splendid geometric decoration was the other aspect shared by these structures. Inside and out, elaborate abstract patterns, scripts, and plant motifs covered walls and ceilings. These were done in beautiful colors and were crafted from a variety of materials, including tiles, brick, marble, carved plaster, wood, or stone.

In terms of specific building types, the mosque was the most important. Derived from the design of Mohammed's house in Medina (Saudi Arabia), it was a rectangular structure with an arched portico leading to a central open space. This court contained a well for ritual cleansing and was surrounded by a covered gallery. On the side of the edifice oriented toward Mecca, Islam's holy city, the depth of the gallery was widened as a hall for worshipers. An Imam led the service from a *mihrab,* or decorated ceremonial niche, and on Fridays delivered a sermon from an elevated pulpit known as a *minbar.* Outside, minarets (towers) were built from which a Muezzin called the faithful to prayer. As an example, the Mosque of Ibn Tulun (Cairo, 876) is noted for its spacious courtyard, its domed fountain–well, its square minaret, and its delicately carved stucco grills in the clerestory windows. In Cordoba, Spain, the Mosque (begun in 785) is remarkable for its seemingly endless rows of multistory arches, the intricate horseshoe shapes and interlocking patterns of these arches, and the beautiful mosaics that adorn the *mihrab.* A third illustration, the Mosque of Shah Abbas (Isfahan, Iran, 1612) has a great dome over the prayer hall, four minarets, elegant blue faience tilework over most of the building's surfaces, and four *iwans,* or vaulted rooms, opening onto the central court.

This last feature, the *iwan,* was also frequently seen in the *madrassahs,* or Moslem religious schools. Facing a courtyard, these large spaces were used for study and discussion while other smaller cells nearby were occupied as dormitories. The Madrassah Madir-i-Shah (Isfahan, Iran, 1706) and the Madrassah of Sultan Qaytbay (Cairo, 1472) are typical, and, with their mosques, suggest the close relationship among learning, life, and religion in the Islamic tradition. Palaces were another major building type in this culture, lavish complexes that served as cool desert retreats. As exemplified by the Alhambra (Granada, Spain, fourteenth century) (Fig. 33), these included a throne room, reception room, living quarters, and baths arranged around a relaxed series of colonnaded courts and gardens. In terms of detail, geometric patterns were evident throughout in a dramatic and colorful blend of tiles, woodwork, grills, and carved plaster stalactites hanging from the ceiling. Similar care was put into the design of tombs for religious and political leaders. Most were decorated domed pavilions, situated in the courtyard of a mosque or as a modest freestanding monument, but those in India, for instance, the Taj Mahal (described in the summary of Indian Architecture), were especially elaborate. As this review suggests, then, Moslems have an important architectural tradition, particularly in the areas of decoration, courtyard, and garden forms.

Indian Architecture

The history of India is a complex tapestry of influences; indigenous tribes, the Persians, the Greeks, the Buddhists, the Hindus, the Moslems, and other groups have played a part in its development. While not trying to sort out this complex story, it is important to describe a few monuments that suggest the general characteristics and diverse architectural heritage of this area. The Harappan civiliza-

Figure 33. The Alhambra. Courtesy of Dhiru Thadani.

Figure 34. Great Stupa at Sanchi. Courtesy of the Embassy of India, Washington, D.C.

tion, located along the rivers of the Indus Valley in north-western India, was the first urban society in this region. Based on trade and farming, it flourished from about 2500 to 1500 B.C. Although invasions appear to have brought this culture to an abrupt end, and none of its buildings have survived intact, excavations have revealed its sophisticated approach to planning and construction. The port of Lothal had a brick shipping dock over 200 m long. The citadels at the major cities of Mohenjo Daro and Harappa were up to five stories tall and contained granaries, assembly halls, and baths. In addition, both towns were organized on a grid pattern and had elaborate systems for sewerage and supplying courtyard homes with running water.

Other important buildings in India are related to Buddhism. Buddha was born in the sixth century B.C., and most of the architecture reflecting the spiritual tradition he established dates from the fourth century B.C. to the ninth century A.D. One type of structure was the stupa, a solid domed mound of earth or brick built in memory of Buddha or a Buddhist saint. Important stupas, such as the Great Stupa at Sanchi (ca late first century B.C.) (Fig. 34), were surrounded by a stone railing, had ceremonial gateways at the cardinal points of the compass, and were faced with intricately carved panels of religious figures. Another structure was the *chaityas* or assembly hall. Those carved out of living rock at Ajanta (30 were excavated between the third century B.C. and third century A.D.) are among the most famous, and use motifs that

indicate that the first of these buildings was probably constructed in wood. The typical plan is a long hall ending in an apse that contains a stupa shrine. Closely spaced columns line the walls and support a beam and stone ribs that decorate the barrel-vaulted ceiling. Light enters through a horseshoe-shaped opening in the carved entrance, and would have illuminated the procession of monks as they celebrated Buddha's wisdom and chanted scripture around the stupa.

Hindu architecture is another Indian style and is characterized by elaborate decoration and sculpture covering almost the entire surface of the building. Temple designs, most of which were developed between the seventh and fourteenth centuries A.D., vary significantly in their layout and profile, but generally have two elements in common: a rectangular shrine with a tall beehive-shaped roof and one or more lower halls off to the side. The simplest approach is exemplified by the Parasuramesvara Temple (750, Bhuvaneshvar) which is composed of two masses, the vertical sanctuary and the horizontal porch. The Lingaraja Temple (1000, Bhuvaneshvar) uses the same theme, but with a progression of four spaces, each capped by a pyramidal roof, that become taller as they near the main shrine. The Kandarya Mahadev Temple (Khajuraho, 1000) displays yet another variation. In this case, the mountainous silhouette of pavilions is given added drama because it is lifted off the ground on a stone platform. The Hindu temples of southern India were the exception to the norm. As the Arunacalesvara Temple (ca fourteenth century, Madras region) illustrates, these were citylike complexes rather than single buildings. In this area, walls and gigantic tiered gateways (some rising over 30 m) surrounded communities of religious structures that included shrines, pools for ritual ablutions, dormitories for pilgrims, and bazaars for merchants.

Interestingly, one of the most elegant examples of Indian architecture, although influenced by Hindu details, was a Moslem design. Indicative of the breadth of styles in this country, the Taj Mahal (Agra, 1630) was built by

Shah Jahan as a mausoleum for his wife. The use of white marble, stone grillework, and delicate inlays of semiprecious stones are techniques borrowed from the Hindus. But the minarets, the pointed arches, the reflecting pool, and the floral, arabesque, and chevron patterns are Moslem. Inside, a softly lit octagonal room contains the cenotaphs, and on the floor below, the tombs of both Shah Jahan and his wife. Beyond the spacial qualities of the building, however, it is the meticulous craftsmanship, especially in the multicolored inlays, that makes this one of the most extraordinary structures not only in India but in all the world.

Architecture in Burma, Cambodia, China, and Japan

While in a brief essay it is not possible to offer a complete review of oriental architecture and its stylistic diversity, the discussion of a few critical monuments is appropriate and necessary. Two edifices in Southeast Asia must be mentioned. One is the Ananda Temple (ca late eleventh century A.D.) in Pagan, Burma, and the other is the Angkor Wat (twelfth century A.D.) complex in Angkor, Cambodia. The first was a Buddhist structure intended to reproduce the spatial qualities of the Nandamula cave, the place where Indian monks had once lived after their reception by the Burmese court. The plan was a cross with four equal arms, the center of which was a massive block, constructed of white bricks, that rose in a series of tiered roofs to a gilded spire. Elaborately decorated arched porticoes formed the axial entrances to the temple, and within, two narrow concentric ambulatories allowed worshipers to process past 9-m tall statues of Buddha placed in four niches around the building's masonry core. The second example, Angkor Wat, can be characterized as a temple-mountain, and was built by and in honor of the god-king Suryavarman II. In this instance, a paved causeway led over a moat to a main gate surrounded by colonnaded walls, a sequence made especially dramatic by the reflection of the facade on the water. Beyond the entry, the complex was a stepped pyramid composed of three rectangular platforms, the base of which was almost 250 m on a side. As the climax of these spaces, the sanctuary was on the highest and smallest of these terraces, and was defined by four corner towers connected by galleries to one another and to a larger and richly sculpted tower in the center. What is remarkable is that, while in both countries the stone and brick construction techniques were simple, the concepts of order, symmetry, and procession were used with great sophistication.

Although the style of architecture was quite different, similar qualities could also be found in Chinese design. As the city of Ch'ang-an illustrates, this was certainly true with regard to urban issues. The city was modeled after a religiously inspired ideal plan and had a grid of streets oriented to the cardinal points of the compass that covered an area of about 78 km². The main north-south avenues were almost 150 m wide, and within this network, there were parks, markets, monasteries, temples, and lavish private homes. At the end of the major ceremonial boulevard, known as the Street of the Vermilion Sparrow, there was an immense government and palace complex located along the north wall. An indication of the impor-

tance of this capital is that, at its height during the eighth century A.D., the population was estimated at 2 million people.

On a smaller scale, pagodas, pai-lous (memorial gateways to the dead), temples, and palaces were important Chinese building types, and historian Paola Caffarelli has carefully documented the evolution of these structures (12). Each changed subtly during the centuries. At the same time, each also had certain general characteristics that can be noted here. Whether erected as part of a temple complex or as a secular monument to victory or good fortune, pagodas were tall pavilions of three to 15 stories. Their plans were rectangular or polygonal, and traditionally each higher floor was smaller than the last with a roof, often distinguished by a concave eave, marking the division between levels. While the first pagodas were built of wood, most of those existing today, such as the Twin Pagodas (ca tenth century A.D.) at Suchow and the decorative Pa Li Chuan Pagoda (thirteenth century A.D.) near Peking, were constructed of brick.

Another ceremonial structure was the pai-lou, a gateway of one or three openings, either dedicated to a revered individual who had died, or used as the entrance to a sacred or beautiful place. Erected with official permission, these were made of stone (the marble pai-lous at the Altar of Heaven Temple (Peking, ca eighteenth century) or wood (the pai-lou over the stairs to the Pai-t'a Temple (Peking, ca seventeenth century), and were designed with posts or piers to support an inscribed horizontal rail, which was frequently protected by projecting roofs covered with brightly colored tiles.

An additional building type, the temple, varied significantly in plan and organization. The round Altar of Heaven (Peking, begun ca 1400) (Fig. 35) with its many terraces, and the rectangular Temple of Five Pagodas (Peking, ca fifteenth century) with its large supporting platform were indicative of this diversity. Buddhist temples, such as the Temple of Honan (Canton), were usually developed as walled complexes that included a gateway, several halls, a sanctuary, and offices, kitchens, and sleeping cells for the priests. Other religious structures were domestic in scale, one room covered by a slightly concave tiled roof.

Interestingly, the feature most characteristic of these designs did not concern shape or size but construction. The Chinese developed a special approach for building with wood. First, rectangular trusses were fabricated for the roof. Once these were completed, the location of columns was determined. Next, after the vertical supports were in place, they were tied to the truss and roof with a complex system of brackets. Using this technique, walls then were merely infill, and unlike much of European architecture, it was the roof rather than the facade that became the dominant stylistic element. This focus was particularly evident in palaces and large private homes. At the Imperial Palace (developed from the mid-sixteenth century on) in Peking, for instance, it was the silhouette and roofs of the many pavilions and temples situated in the gardens that made this capital one of the most impressive in the world.

While the Japanese were influenced by and borrowed from Chinese architecture, three design features are typical of the island country and differentiate its buildings

Figure 35. Altar of Heaven. Courtesy of John J. Kennedy.

complexes of buildings. This was illustrated by the Horyu-ji Temple (Horyu-ji, Japan, seventh century A.D.) that was surrounded by a low wall, and included a gate (referred to as the chumon), a pagoda, and a two-story main hall called a kondo. Overall, the heterogeneity of oriental architecture makes it difficult to summarize briefly, but if these many styles did share one trait, it was a unique concern for the design and development of roof forms.

BIBLIOGRAPHY

1. V. Scully, *The Earth, the Temple, and the Gods,* Praeger Publishers, New York, 1962, p. 170.
2. S. Kostof, *A History of Architecture: Settings and Rituals,* Oxford University Press, Inc., New York, 1985, p. 185.
3. C. Norberg-Schulz, *Meaning in Western Architecture,* Praeger Publishers, New York, 1975, pp. 111–112.
4. Ref. 3, p. 140.
5. *Gothic Architecture* (translated by L. Grodecki and I. Paris), Harry N. Abrams, Inc., New York, 1976, p. 43.
6. L. Alberti, *Ten Books of Architecture* (translated by G. Leoni), Tiranti, London, 1955, p. 113.
7. C. Norberg-Schulz, *Baroque Architecture,* Harry N. Abrams, Inc., New York, 1971, p. 357.
8. A. Loos, "Ornament and Crime" in C. Ulrich, ed., *Programs and Manifestoes on 20th-century Architecture* (translated by M. Bullock), The MIT Press, Cambridge, Mass., 1970, p. 22.
9. H. R. Hitchcock and P. Johnson, *The International Style,* W. W. Norton & Co., Inc., New York, 1966, p. 20.
10. J. Jacobs, *The Death and Life of Great American Cities,* Vintage Books, New York, 1961.
11. R. Venturi, *Complexity and Contradiction in Architecture,* The Museum of Modern Art, New York, 1966.
12. P. Caffarelli, "China" in M. Bussagli, ed., *Oriental Architecture* (translated by J. Shepley), Harry N. Abrams, Inc., New York, 1973, pp. 293–360.

General References

Ref. 3 is a good general reference.

B. Fletcher, *A History of Architecture,* Charles Scribner's Sons, division of the Scribner Book Companies, Inc., New York, 1987.

L. Gardner in H. de la Croix and R. Tansey, eds., *Art Through the Ages,* 7th ed., Harcourt, Brace Jovanovich, Orlando, Fla., 1980.

S. Kostof, *A History of Architecture: Settings and Rituals,* Oxford University Press, Inc., New York, 1985.

M. Trachtenberg and I. Hyman, *Architecture from Prehistory to Post-Modernism,* Prentice-Hall Inc., Prentice Hall Press, Englewood Cliffs, N.J. and Harry N. Abrams, Inc., New York, 1986.

See also ART NOUVEAU; CATHEDRALS; CHICAGO SCHOOL; CHURCH ARCHITECTURE; ECOLE DES BEAUX ARTS; ISLAMIC ARCHITECTURE; LATIN AMERICAN ARCHITECTURE; RELIGIOUS ARCHITECTURE—ORIENTAL; WEST AFRICAN VERNACULAR ARCHITECTURE.

THOMAS WALTON, PhD
The Catholic University
of America
Washington, D.C.

from those of the continent. First, because of abundant forests, wood construction has remained important in Japan. Whereas in China brick and stone grew increasingly popular, with the exception of fortified structures and modern edifices from the late nineteenth century on, the Japanese have continued to use wood. Indeed, testifying to the longevity of this tradition, a few wooden temples are over 1000 years old. Second, the Japanese aesthetic was more dependent on straight lines. In general, roofs and eaves were not designed with the dramatic curves evident in many Chinese temples and pagodas. In addition, the details of buildings evolved from beautifully crafted construction rather than applied sculpture and decoration. The third trait concerned color. Unlike China, where the architecture was often painted in bright hues, natural shades were emphasized in Japan, eg, the warm tans and browns of wood, the relaxed whites and beiges of shoji screens, and the pale greens of tatami mats.

These qualities are exemplified in two major building types, the Shinto shrine and the Buddhist temple. The first was dedicated to worship of important families and ancestors. Entrance to the shrine was through a symbolic gate, or torii, that was often a simple composition of two columns topped by two parallel beams. The shrine itself was a small room raised on a platform and approached via steps under a covered porch. As the shrines at Ise (rebuilt every 20 years since the seventh century A.D.) suggest, the roofs of these structures were steeply sloped, projected well beyond the walls and were decorated with wooden crossbeams along their ridges. With the influence of Buddhist designers, later Shinto shrines were more lavish and ornamental. This hinted at the approach used in Buddhist temples. As in China, these were actually

ARCHITECTURAL WOODWORK

Architectural woodwork is the term generally used to describe all items of wood (and wood-related products) which are used to finish the interior or exterior of a building. They are usually not structural in nature but on exterior woodwork may be used to create the aesthetics that will determine the architectural style of the structure, ie, a particular exterior pediment head front entrance with certain style wood columns and a heavy cornice, dentil, and frieze might identify the exterior of a building as Georgian Colonial; a flush wall of paneling with recessed base and reveals at the top and between panels might be termed contemporary in style. An example of interior contemporary architectural woodwork is found in Figure 1, which illustrates a laminated plastic reception desk. Interior traditional architectural woodwork is shown in Figure 2.

Architectural woodwork includes standing and running trim, casework, panelwork, closet and storage shelving, miscellaneous ornamental items, stairwork and handrails, exterior and interior frames, exterior sash, screens, blinds and shutters, flush doors, stile and rail doors, factory finishing, monumental woodwork, and fire-retardant woodwork.

Some of the items may be available as stock-catalogue or lumberyard items. This is true only where the demand for certain items is sufficient to warrant it being readily available to the public. In most cases, the item has been reduced in size or quality in order to meet the demands

of mass marketing and may be greatly revised from the original architectural woodwork item. This can be illustrated by considering moulding, for example. A true architectural pattern of casing might be ¾ × 2 ⅝ in., with deep, sharp lines to its pattern. The corresponding item in a lumber yard might be 9/16 × 2 ⅛ in., with a less delineated pattern. In order to differentiate between stock and custom architectural woodwork, the Architectural Woodwork Institute of America (AWI) was established in October 1953. At that time, it represented 109 architectural woodwork firms from the United States and Canada as well as representatives of related suppliers and associations. The stated objective of the institute in 1953 was the promotion of the use of architectural woodwork accomplished through a threefold program of architect relations, publicity and public relations, and membership services. The latest (1984) description of purpose by the AWI indicates it is a not-for-profit organization representing the architectural woodwork manufacturers of the United States and Canada, devoted to the elevation of industry standards, continuing research into new and better materials and methods, and the publication of technical data helpful to architects and specification writers in the design and use of architectural woodwork.

It is important to recognize that new materials and methods are being introduced into the woodworking industry at an ever-increasing pace. Therefore, a type of material or construction which may be described in the various sections that follow may not be the only acceptable method

Figure 1. Contemporary architectural woodwork. Courtesy of Lehrer/McGovern.

Figure 2. Traditional architectural woodwork. Courtesy of Driwood Moulding.

or material. It is suggested that the latest edition of the *Architectural Quality Standards, Guide Specifications and Quality Certification Program* (*QSI*), available from AWI, be consulted for the latest information (1).

HISTORY

The development of the cabinet shop and architectural woodworking can be closely related to the construction carpenter in pre-industrial revolution times and his evolution into the cabinetmaker. During the growth of the United States, a carpenter was expected to produce the doors and windows and frames on the site, while the building was being constructed. Since everything was done with hand tools, the place where the work was performed was unimportant. The only machine tool in use was the large power saw which cut logs into slabs of wood for other uses. From that point on, all cutting and jointing was done by hand. In most cases, the carpenter or home owner built his furniture in the same way. The pre-industrial cabinetmaker produced mouldings by using a series of different knives in wooden planes.

Until the 1800s, before the advent of the power saw, most lumber was sawed from logs by using a pit saw.

This was simply a two-man saw, where one man stood on top of the log being sawed while the other stood in the "pit" underneath the log, hence the name.

During the 1700s, mechanization was growing because of developments in water, wind, and steam power at the end of the century and the breakthrough in the production of iron. This set the stage for all types of new machinery to be built, especially for the woodworking and machine-tool industries. This was true in Europe, but even more so in the United States, where the population was growing geometrically. Guilds were not a factor in the New World, and the demand for furniture, lumber, wagons, ships, and other wood products seemed insatiable. Given these circumstances, there were great opportunities for new machinery development.

By 1840, 31,000 sawmills were operating in the United States and wood processing was the second largest industry. In 1836, William Woodworth patented the first surface planer. This brought mechanization to an area that had previously only used hand planing. The first cylinder planer was built by Baxter D. Whitney in 1846. A famous planer company still bears his name. The next step was the development of a planer-matcher, whereby edges were milled to fit together as well as surface planing. The product produced was similar to flooring in use today (2). Also, during the 1850s, H. B. Smith designed one of the first successful lightweight moulders.

The period from the nineteenth century through the twentieth century has witnessed giant progress in the woodworking industry. Most of the progressive machinery has come from Europe since the early 1960s.

The invention of all of this machinery also produced areas of specialization within carpentry. The house builder continued to work at the site with mostly hand tools and a few power tools. The cabinetmaker, on the other hand, began working in a factory environment due to the size and power requirements of the machinery. These millmen set up wood shops in local communities to produce windows, doors, and cabinets.

This was the beginning of architectural woodwork as it is known today. Architectural woodwork is really the combination of custom furniture, fixture, and millwork plants.

LUMBER

The lumber in architectural woodwork is either hardwood or softwood, depending on the aesthetic requirements of the specifier. Basically, hardwoods are obtained from broad-leaf (deciduous) trees, whereas softwoods are obtained from needle-leaf (coniferous) trees. The term hard or soft does not necessarily relate to the actual hardness of the woods. There are some "soft" hardwoods (ie, basswood, phillipine mahogany) and some "hard" softwoods (ie, fir, cypress). The principal characteristics that should determine the selection of a species for a particular use include strength, hardness, stability, adaptability, and, under certain conditions, fire rating (although, with reference to fire rating, the woodworker should not be responsible for determining the applicability of any codes). For detailed information on factors which should be considered in selecting a particular species, consult Ref. 3.

Aesthetic Characteristics

From an architect's point of view, the most important reasons for using wood is its natural appearance and the warmth it imparts to the final product. Some of the special variable qualities found only in wood are listed below:

1. *Color.* The basic line of the species (ie, red vs white oak) which may be enhanced during the finishing process. Even the particular area of the tree yields different colors. The sapwood (the outer layers of the tree which continue to transport sap) is normally lighter in color than the heartwood (the inner portion of the tree which have cells filled with natural deposits). This may lead to some confusion when specifying a particular species. For example, select white birch comes from the sapwood portion of the yellow birch tree and select red birch comes from the heartwood portion of the same yellow birch tree.

2. *Grain.* This is the appearance produced by the arrangement of wood fibers and pores of the species.

3. *Figure.* This is the pattern produced, across the grain, by natural deviations from the normal grain.

4. *Method of sawing.* The manner in which a log is sawn will influence the appearance of the grain and figure. Plain sawing (Fig. 3) yields the widest boards with the least waste. Quarter sawing (Fig. 4) is available in limited amounts in certain species, and yields straight grain, narrow boards, with some flake appearance. Because there is a greater amount of waste (less yield), the cost is higher than plain sawn. Rift sawing (Fig. 5) is available only in limited quantities in some species. The appearance is similar to quarter sawn with less flake and more vertical grain. Its cost is higher than plain sawn or quarter sawn be-

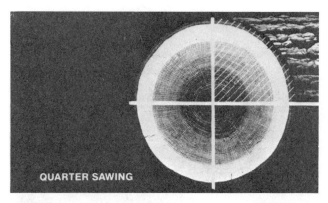

Figure 4. Quarter sawing. Reproduced by permission of the Architectural Woodwork Institute.

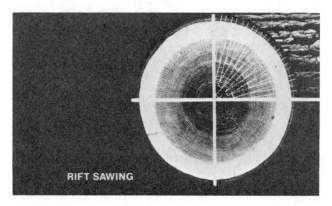

Figure 5. Rift sawing. Reproduced by permission of the Architectural Woodwork Institute.

cause of waste (less yield) and availability. It is not readily found in all species or in all thicknesses.

The supply of various species of lumber may vary based on worldwide demand as well as export regulations of the country of origin. It would be wise to consult the local AWI office before specifying an uncommon species or even large quantities of a special width or length.

Quality

The tables and rules established by the various lumber associations for grading the particular kind of lumber they represent are much less stringent than the standards established by AWI. The association grading rules are based on the percentage of board that can be realized by cutting out the defects.

For architectural woodwork, it is the final appearance of the piece in the end product that is important, not whether it was cut from a larger board that contained defects which could be eliminated. The AWI Quality Standards contain tables describing AWI lumber grades I, II, and III. They also describe the defects, variations, and amount of each permitted in each grade.

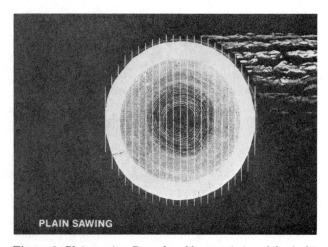

Figure 3. Plain sawing. Reproduced by permission of the Architectural Woodwork Institute.

Thickness and Width

It is important to mention the standard finished thickness which can be obtained after surfacing and sanding a rough sawn board. The architect must pay strict attention to this when detailing various wood members. It is important to adhere to the standards listed or designate nominal dimensions (ie, a 2 × 4 in. nominal piece of hardwood would actually be produced to a size of 1 ½ × 3 ½ in.) The lists below give the current industry standards.

Thickness:

Nominal Thickness Inches	Quarters	Finish Thickness (Hardwoods), in.	Finish Thickness (Softwoods), in.
1	4/4	3/4	3/4
1¼	5/4	1 1/16	1 1/16
1½	6/4	1 5/16	1 3/8
2	8/4	1½	1½
2½	10/4	2	2¼
3	12/4	2½	2½

Width:

Nominal Width, in.	Finish Width, in.
2	1½
4	3½
6	5½
8	7¼
10	9¼
12	11¼

Moisture Content

The amount of water contained in a piece of wood is termed moisture content; typically, lumber used in architectural woodwork should be dried to between 6 and 12% moisture content. This will vary according to the different geographical and climatic locations in the North American continent. For additional information, see AWI Quality Standards Section 100-S-3 and *Wood Handbook No. 72* (4).

PANEL PRODUCTS

This term refers to manufactured panels used in the production of architectural woodwork. A greater emphasis is placed on what is actually available and used by the industry in today's market. The different types of panels (by ingredients and method of manufacture) are discussed below.

Particle Board

Particle board is manufactured from natural wood reduced to particles, fibers, or chips mixed with binders and formed by the use of heat and pressure into panels.

It is commercially classified according to density. Low density describes panels of less than 37 lb/ft³. These find limited use in architectural woodwork except as cores for 1⅜, 1¾, and 2¼-in. flush doors. Medium density describes panels of 37–50 lb/ft³. The 42–47-lb density is the most popular and has the broadest application in architectural woodwork. High density describes panels over 50 lb; these are not used to a great extent because of weight, hardness, and additional cost and thus are not readily available.

Fiberboard

Fiberboard is manufactured from wood reduced to fine fibers mixed with binders and formed by use of heat and pressure into panels. Density is measured and described in the same manner as particle board. The main advantages of fiberboard (often referred to as MDF, medium density fiberboard) are a smooth surface, due to the smaller fibers used in manufacture of the board, and an edge that machines well. The smooth surface allows a better opaque finish than could be produced from standard particle board. The machinability of the edge allows the edge of the panel to assume varied contours. In this fashion, with modern finishing methods, this product is used in the furniture industry, where grains are applied and real wood is simulated.

Plywood

Plywood is manufactured from plies of wood material. Two of the most popular types are particle-core plywood and veneer-core plywood. The former (Fig. 6) is constructed of medium density particle-board core with face and back veneers or overlays, ie, plastic laminate, adhered thereto. Referred to as three-ply construction, it is readily available. Veneer-core plywood (Fig. 7) is constructed using an odd number of veneer plies with decorative face and/or back veneers or overlays.

Hardboard

Hardboard is manufactured from interfelted fibers consolidated and formed under heat and pressure into panels. The first kind, standard hardboard, is also called untempered hardboard. The second type, tempered hardboard,

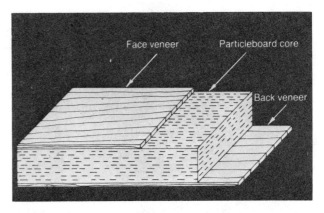

Figure 6. Panel construction with particle-board core. Reproduced by permission of the Architectural Woodwork Institute.

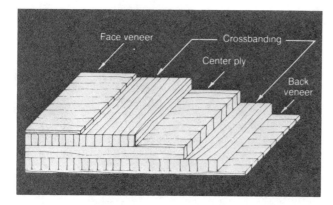

Figure 7. Panel construction with veneer-core plywood. Reproduced by permission of the Architectural Woodwork Institute.

is a standard hardboard subjected to an oil and curing treatment, which increases its stiffness, hardness, and weight. Table 1 indicates the characteristics of each type of panel relative to application in architectural woodwork.

FACING MATERIALS

Wood Veneers

Wood veneers can be classified into hardwood veneers and softwood veneers. The former is available in many domestic and foreign species. It is normally cut as plain sliced except for birch and some red oak, which are rotary cut. Rift sliced or quarter sliced is available in certain species (mostly red and white oak). All others must be custom cut. The most common species of softwood veneer are Douglas Fir and Southern Yellow Pine; other softwood veneers are in limited supply. Most softwoods are rotary cut. Plain slicing or rift cut are of limited availability on special order only.

Wood-Veneer Cuts

The following terms were mentioned previously, but an understanding of what is produced by each type of cut is essential when specifying wood veneers for aesthetic purposes.

The relationship of the cut to the annular rings of the log determines the appearance of the veneer. The principal methods of cutting veneers and the general visual characteristics of the grain are listed below:

Rotary Cut. The log is center-mounted in a lathe and turned against a razor sharp blade; the action is analogous to the peeling of an orange or the unwinding of a roll of paper (Fig. 8). Since this cut follows the annular growth rings of the log, a bold grain figure is produced. Rotary veneer is exceptionally wide, and matching at veneer joints is extremely difficult. Almost all softwood is cut this way. Lengths in all hardwoods are limited to 10 ft.

Plain Slicing or Flat Slicing. The half log is mounted with the heart side against the guide plate of the slicer; the slicing is done parallel to a line through the center of the log, cutting from the outside to the center (Fig. 9). This produces a figure similar to that of plain sawn lumber.

Quarter Slicing. The quarter log is mounted on the guide so that the growth rings of the log strike the knife at approximately right angles, producing a series of stripes which are straight in some woods, varied in others (Fig. 10). In some woods, principally oak, "flake" results from cutting through the radial "rays."

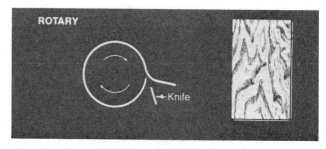

Figure 8. Rotary cut. Reproduced by permission of the Architectural Woodwork Institute.

Table 1. Panel Characteristics

Panel Type	Flatness	Dimensional Stability	Visual Edge Quality	Availability
Particle board (medium density)	Excellent	Excellent	Poor to good	Wide
Fiberboard (medium density)	Excellent	Excellent	Excellent	Wide
Particleboard, core plywood	Excellent	Excellent	Poor to good	Wide
Veneer-core plywood	Fair	Good	Poor to good	Limited
Standard hardboard	Excellent	Good	Good	Wide
Tempered hardboard	Excellent	Excellent	Good	Limited

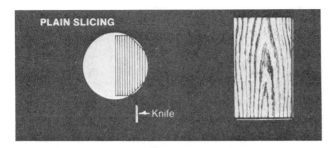

Figure 9. Plain slicing. Reproduced by permission of the Architectural Woodwork Institute.

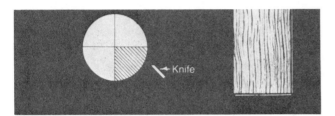

Figure 10. Quarter slicing. Reproduced by permission of the Architectural Woodwork Institute.

Half-round Slicing. This is a method of cutting in which log segments are mounted off-center in the lathe (Fig. 11). This results in a cut slightly across the annular growth rings and visually shows modified characteristics of both rotary-cut and plain-sliced veneers. This cutting method is often used on red and white oak.

Rift-Cut. Rift-cut veneer (Fig. 12) is produced in the various species of oak. Oak has medullary ray cells which radiate from the center of the log like the spokes of a wheel. The rift is obtained by slicing slightly across these medullary rays. This accentuates the vertical grain and minimizes the "flake." Combed grain is a selection from rift-cut material that is distinguished by the tightness and straightness of its grain.

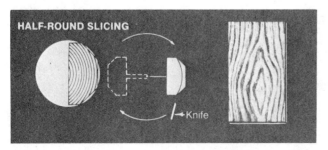

Figure 11. Half-round slicing. Reproduced by permission of the Architectural Woodwork Institute.

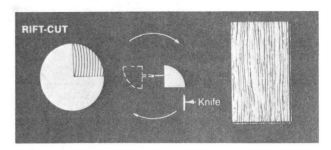

Figure 12. Rift cut. Reproduced by permission of the Architectural Woodwork Institute.

For more information concerning matching of veneers and factors affecting selection, refer to AWI Quality Standards Section 200.

Overlays

This type of facing material is available in the following varieties: high pressure laminates, low pressure laminates, medium density overlays, and cured wet films.

High pressure laminates come in varying thicknesses to suit different applications:

1. *General purpose.* 0.05 in. thick for horizontal and high usage exposure.
2. *General purpose.* 0.028 in. thick for vertical and medium usage exposure.
3. *Cabinet liner.* 0.020 in. thick for lining cabinet interiors (limited color selections).
4. *Post-forming.* 0.042 in. thick for forming radius edges (limited color selections).
5. *Backer.* 0.020 in. thick used on back of substrate to create a balanced panel.
6. *Solid metallics.* ±0.05 in. thick, usually solid aluminum with anodized finishes simulating polished and satin-finished chrome, brass, and copper.

Low pressure laminates are available in a wide range of surfacing materials for decorative and wear-resistant applications, ie, cabinet exteriors and interiors. The materials include melamine, polyesters, and vinyl. Manufacturers' data should be consulted to determine if the panel offered has the proper characteristics to meet job requirements. Medium density overlays usually consist of a crezon-impregnated paper overlay and are applied to an exterior fir panel to improve paintability. Cured wet films are comprised of materials which are sprayed or rolled onto the panels and then cured by a variety of techniques (heat, ultraviolet) to produce a relatively hard, smooth decorative surface. Manufacturers' data should be consulted for characteristics.

STANDING AND RUNNING TRIM AND RAILS

These items can be generally described as wood members manufactured to a profile for application to surfaces of wood or other material for functional or decorative purposes.

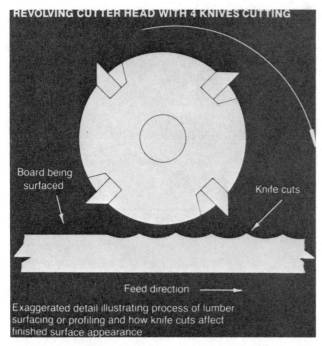

Figure 13. Exaggerated detail illustrating process of lumber surfacing or profiling and how knife cuts affect finished surface appearance. Reproduced by permission of the Architectural Woodwork Institute.

Standing trim includes items of fixed length, such as door and window casings, stops, stools or sills, aprons, etc. Each member can usually be accomplished by a single length of wood. Running trim includes items of continuing length, such as cornices, fascias, soffits, chair rails, base, shoe mouldings, etc. Rails are used on corridors in hospitals and other institutions, as well as for protection at glass openings and at stairs.

Methods for achieving surfaces and profiles on lumber are outlined below:

Sawing. Sawing produces rough surfaces that must be further processed unless a rough sawn finish is desired.

Planing. Sawn lumber is passed through a planer which has a series of knives which remove a thin layer of wood to produce a relatively smooth surface.

Abrasive Planing. Sawn lumber is passed through a powerful beltsander with tough, coarse belts which remove the rough top surface.

Molding. Sawn lumber is passed through moulders or shapers which have knives ground to a pattern which produces the profile desired. The smoothness of surfaces machined by shapers or molders (also planers) is determined by the number of knife cuts per inch (referred to as KCPI). The more cuts the closer the ridges, and therefore the smoother the result (Fig. 13).

Joints of standing trim should be plant-assembled in the following manner:

Premium grade. with lemon splines or dowels (Fig. 14).
Custom grade. with clamp nails (Fig. 15).
Economy grade. plant assembly not required.

Various grade compliance requirements and other information should be confirmed by referring to Section 300 of the AWI Quality Standards.

ARCHITECTURAL CABINETS

The term architectural cabinets should differentiate between the quality obtained when specifying a standard kitchen or other stock cabinet, as opposed to an AWI grade cabinet. Using the AWI Quality Standards (Section 400), the architect has an almost unlimited choice of design and cost considerations. The three basic types of cabinet construction are:

1. *Flush Overlay.* This is the most popular and versatile design. Door and drawer faces partially cover the body members of the cabinet with minimum spaces between face surfaces sufficient for operating clearance. There is no face frame required.

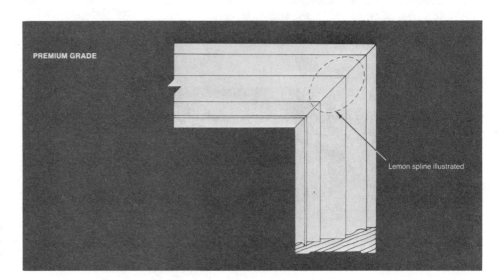

Figure 14. Standing trim with miter joint, premium grade. Reproduced by permission of the Architectural Woodwork Institute.

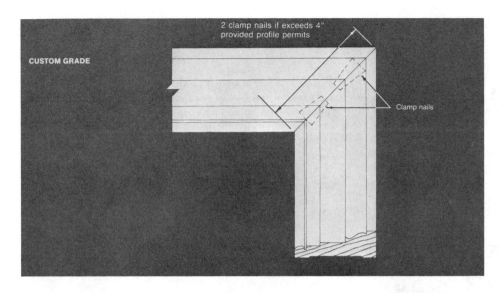

Figure 15. Standing trim with miter joint, custom grade. Reproduced by permission of the Architectural Woodwork Institute.

2. *Reveal Overlay.* Door and faces cover the body members or face frames of the cabinet, creating reveals.

3. *Exposed Face Frame.* Door and drawer faces are set within and flush with face frames or face members of the cabinets.

There are three designations that define the various cabinet parts by visibility (Fig. 16):

1. *Exposed Surfaces.* Surfaces are visible when:
Doors and drawers are closed.
Behind clear glass doors.
Bottoms of cabinets are 42 in. or more above finish floor.
Tops of cabinets are below 78 in. above finish floor.

2. *Semiexposed Surfaces.* Surfaces become visible when:
Opaque doors or drawers are opened.

Bottoms of cabinets are more than 30 in. and less than 42 in. above finish floor.

3. *Concealed Surfaces.* Surfaces are considered concealed when:
Surfaces are not visible after installation is complete.
Bottoms of cabinets are less than 30 in. above finish floor.
Tops of cabinets are over 78 in. above finish floor and not visible from an upper level.
Stretchers, blocking, and components are concealed by drawers.

There has been a reluctance on the part of some in the architectural community to accept the use of particle board as a substrate for veneers and overlays. The AWI Quality Standards, specifically, does not permit the use of veneer-core material as a substrate (core) for cabinet doors. In addition to the many ways described in Section 400, there are, due to constantly changing technology, many new materials, joint details, items of hardware, etc,

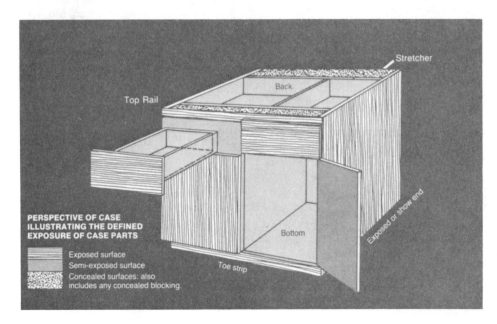

Figure 16. Perspective of case illustrating the defined exposure of case parts. Reproduced by permission of the Architectural Woodwork Institute.

which become available and may not be included in AWI Quality Standards. The architectural woodworker who is a member of the AWI may choose to introduce these to the architect on shop drawings. The architect can feel confident that if the woodworker is willing to certify that the work meets the specified AWI grade, then all of the components of the work also meet the specified grade.

Drawer Construction and Assembly

The woodworker may elect to fabricate a drawer shell and apply an exposed front fastened with screws from inside of drawer, or utilize molded plastic drawer parts, provided approval is obtained.

Extension slides are available for both full and partial extension of the drawer. Full extension slides are furnished only when specified except that full extension slides are always furnished for file drawers.

Bottoms should be set into members in grooves ¼ in. deep with a minimum ⅜-in. standing shoulder; they then should be spot glued and reinforced with glue blocks in premium and custom grades except that, at backs, the bottom may be glued and nailed to bottom edge of the back.

All joints should be glued and nailed except dovetail joints, which are only to be glued (Fig. 17).

Materials to be used are classified by grades in Table 2.

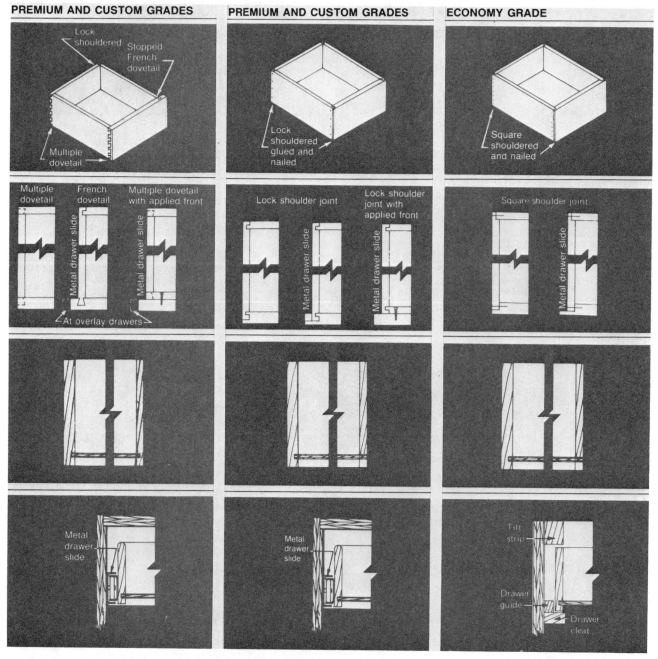

Figure 17. Drawer construction and assembly methods by AWI grade. Reproduced by permission of the Architectural Woodwork Institute.

Table 2. Classification of Drawer Materials by Grade

Item	Premium	Custom	Economy
Drawer sides, backs and semiexposed fronts	Hardwood lumber or 7-ply (min) all-hardwood ply (no voids)	Hardwood or softwood lumber of high density particle board or fiberboard	Panel product or lumber
Exposed fronts	Matches exposed body components	Matches exposes body components	Compatible with exposed body members
Bottoms	Hardwood panel product or hardboard	Panel products or hardboard	Panel products or hardboard

Laminate-clad Cabinets

Laminate thickness for all grades of cabinets should be 0.028 in. (for additional information, consult Section 400B of AWI Quality Standards). The recent development of solid integral color plastic laminate has seen many architects and designers specifying these products without regard for the ramifications. First, the solid integral color laminates cost four to five times more than regular laminate. It must be decided whether eliminating the thin black line is worth the extra expense. One option would be to use the solid integral color material on the edges only. There is a slight color differential between the two, which may not be acceptable. Another method of eliminating the thin black line might be to use solid PVC made in matching color to the face HPL (high pressure laminate). The PVC can be made to match when the quantity required (10,000–12,000 lineal feet (lf) minimum) is sufficient. There are also some stock PVC colors available in smaller quantities. One of the least desirable ways to eliminate this line is to specify that the two HPL sheets be mitered, since this usually results in a poor-quality joint. Most plastics manufacturers do not recommend mitering their product.

Although it is clearly indicated in Section 400B that particle board is a superior substrate for plastics (as well as wood veneer), it is worth mentioning again. Many times architects have specified veneer-core plywood as a substrate for plastic. The AWI Quality Standards do not permit the use of veneer-core plywood for door cores. There are several problems that can occur with veneer-core plywood: veneer-core plywood tends to warp and twist; when fir is the face veneer on the substrate, the heavy grain characteristics tend to photograph through the HPL, especially when using a color rather than a woodgrain material; and the cores of plywood have voids (the cores are made of veneers with defects) which may show as a concavity under HPL. In general, if a 42–47-lb density particle board is used, it will have almost the same strength and meet the same test requirements as plywood.

Fire-retardant Requirements for Cabinetry

The AWI brochure *Building Code Flame Spread Classifications ASTM E 84 for Interior Architectural Woodwork* (5) can be consulted to determine if cabinets are required to be fire retardant. Most national codes classify cabinets as furniture and therefore not subject to code classification. If requirements indicate the need for fire retardancy, the core specified should be fire-retardant particle board. The framing and blocking for the cabinet should be fire-retardant. There is also fire-retardant HPL available by special order if required (6).

Counter Tops

Most of the information listed under "Laminate-clad Cabinets" also applies to counter tops. The underside of tops, which are unsupported for 4 ft^2 (premium grade) or 6 ft^2 (custom grade), should have an 0.02-in. balancing sheet. When a field joint is required, it should be splined and held together with some form of mechanical fastener. Postforming has become a popular method of creating a radius edge at the front of a top and a cove at the meeting point between the counter and splash. It must be remembered that not all colors and/or sizes are available in special forming grade. Almost any radius can be bent, but because of the technology involved in the bending process, it is almost impossible to make a completely flush joint when the surface is longer than the 12-ft material available.

The area of post-forming, as well as the latest development, "softforming," offers almost unlimited possibilities in bending and wrapping plastics, metallics, and wood veneers around shaped substrates.

PANELING

Paneling is perhaps the item of woodwork most generally associated with architectural woodwork. For purposes of discussion and clarity, the subject can be divided into three types: flush wood paneling, flush plastic laminate paneling, and stile and rail paneling.

Flush Wood Paneling

The architect or designer must first indicate:

- Veneer species and type of cut.
- In the case of selecting flitches (flitch is a set of veneer slices from one particular log; the term is synonymous with "log" when referring to veneer), the source, flitch number, gross footage in flitch or flitches, yield of particular flitch species (it may take 3 or 4 ft^2 of veneer to yield 1 ft^2 of face veneer after splicing), and veneer cost per square foot.
- Method of matching within the panel face, ie, center matched, balance matched, or special matched. If the method is not specified, the woodworker may use his own discretion.

Figure 18. Wall paneling, typical articulated joint. Reproduced by permission of the Architectural Woodwork Institute.

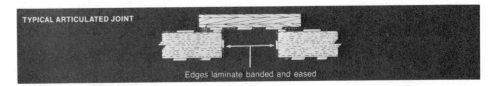

- Method of matching between panels and within each area, otherwise the woodworker will supply the sequence match.
- The grain direction of panels and articulated joints. In the absence of such indication, the grain direction of the panels is assumed to be vertical.

In terms of construction, the panels should be a minimum of ¾ in. thick for premium grade and a minimum of ⁷⁄₁₆ in. thick for custom grade. The core for both grades can be either particle board or veneer. A better job will result with the former: the panel will be flat, stable, and have virtually no "telegraphing of grain" through the face veneer.

There are two types of joints between panels (Fig. 18): butting joints, where panels meet each other only with a spline or other joint to line up faces of adjacent panels; and articulated joints, which have some form of space or reveal between panels and which can be of similar material to the panel or contrasting plastic or metal.

Flush Plastic Laminate Wall Paneling

The architect or designer must specify:

- The substrate. In this case, only 42–47-lb density particle board should be used.
- The face laminate. This is usually done by listing several acceptable manufacturers. It is helpful to the woodworker if the colors can be determined when the specifications are written.

- The thicknesses of laminate and balancing sheet, which should be the same. Section 500B of the AWI Quality Standards indicates which thickness meets which grade.
- The edging. This can be thinner than the face laminate. Solid-color (all the way through) laminate can be used as edging to eliminate the black-edge appearance.

The types of joints between panels (Figs. 18 and 19) and joint details are basically the same as described for flush wood paneling.

Wood Stile and Rail Paneling

The architect or designer should indicate:

- Veneer species and type cut.
- In the case of selecting flitches, the source, flitch number, gross footage in flitch or flitches, yield of particular flitch species (it may take 3 or 4 ft² of veneer to yield 1 ft² of face veneer after splicing), and cost per square foot.
- Method of matching within the panel face, ie, center matched, balance matched, or special matched. If unspecified, the woodworker may use his judgment.
- Method of matching between panels. If left unspecified, the woodworker will supply the sequence match.
- The grain direction of the panels. In the absence of other indication, this is assumed to be vertical. The

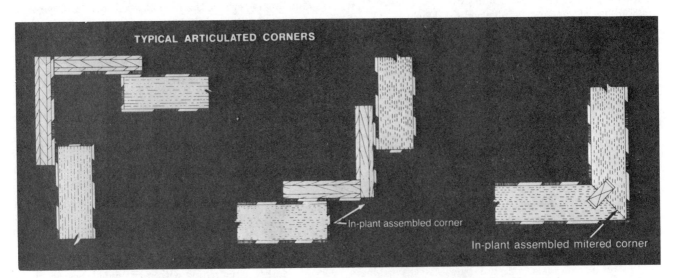

Figure 19. Wall paneling, typical articulated interior and exterior corners. Reproduced by permission of the Architectural Woodwork Institute.

Premium Grade   **Custom Grade**

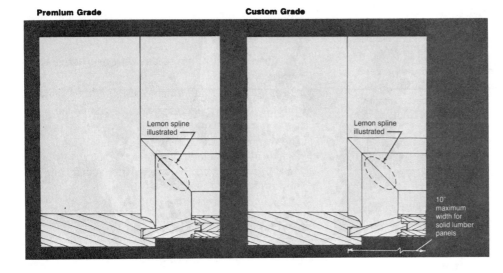

Figure 20. Typical sections of stile and rail paneling. Reproduced by permission of the Architectural Woodwork Institute.

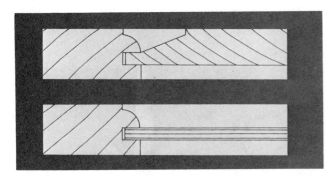

Figure 21. Panel retention with solid sticking. Reproduced by permission of the Architectural Woodwork Institute.

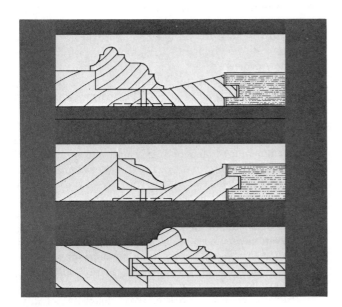

Figure 22. Panel retention with moulding. Reproduced by permission of the Architectural Woodwork Institute.

grain direction of all members other than panels should be the long dimension of that member.

Panel construction for wood stile and rail paneling is shown in Figure 20.

There are different methods of panel retention (Figs. 21, 22, 23). Regardless of which one is used, the panel should not fill the full depth of groove, so that it may expand and contract.

DOORS

Architectural Flush Doors

The constant development of architectural flush doors by companies specializing in their manufacture has made it possible to combine function, performance, and aesthetics in producing a specific wood door for a particular opening in a designed building. Function and performance are primarily controlled by the door construction.

Flush doors are manufactured with a variety of core construction and face combinations. These are described below so the specifier may select that type of door which will satisfy his function and performance criteria. AWI

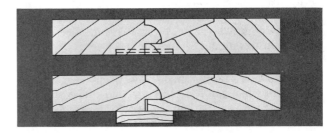

Figure 23. Panel retention, solid sticking with rear-mounted fastening. Reproduced by permission of the Architectural Woodwork Institute.

spec symbol designations are assigned to facilitate specifying.

1. *Particle Core P.C.-5.* Vertical stiles 1 ⅜ in., top and bottom rails 1 ⅛ in., glued to core. Crossbands except under plastic laminate. Maximum stability, minimum core telegraphing, excellent sound insulation. Eleven percent heavier and less costly than stave core. In stock in local warehouse.

2. *Framed (Non-Glued) Particle Core P.C.-7.* Drop-in core, premanufactured faces or hardboard. Economical and suitable for residential use. Usually has softwood edges.

3. *Staved Lumber Core S.L.C.-5.* Glued block core stiles ⅝ in., top and bottom rails 1 ¼ in., glued to core. Usually crossbanded and possesses good strength along length of door. Telegraphing is a problem which can be minimized with low sheen finishes. Long lead time, higher relative cost.

4. *Framed Non-Glued Block Core F.L.C.-7.* Similar to S.L.C., but blocks are not glued. Limited manufacturers.

In terms of face finish, if wood veneer is to be used, the architect should select the lowest grade required to meet both the aesthetic and budgetary requirements of the particular project. All too often, costly veneer faces are specified and the finish is so dark and/or opaque that less costly veneers could have been used. Various veneer cuts should not be cross-specified with different species. The standard veneers with the cuts available in each species are *birch:* rotary cut; *red oak:* plain sliced, rotary cut, half-round, quartered, rift; *white oak:* plain sliced, rift cut; and *walnut:* plain sliced. The imported exotics (teak, rosewood, etc) are mostly available in plain sliced. In many cases where plain sliced birch is called for (cross-specifying birch in place of red-oak face), a door with narrow strips of veneer is produced at a cost almost equal to that of oak. The reason birch is rotary cut is because it grows as a narrow tree; cutting the veneer in a rotary manner produces wide leaves of veneer rather than the narrow leaves that would result from slicing the log. Matching of veneers can be accomplished with all cuts, but least accurately with rotary cut.

If paint finish is to be used, a medium density overlay should be specified. This will result in a grain-free finished face.

Plastic laminate faces in 1/16 or ⅛-in. thicknesses can be applied over all solid-core faces. Crossbands are not required if ⅛-in. faces are used. If plastic laminate vertical edges are required, it must be kept in mind that further job-site fitting will not be feasible.

Exterior Use. There is a reduced warranty by most manufacturers when the doors are used on the exterior. In order to protect and extend the life of exterior doors, the following measures should be taken:

- Doors must be manufactured with a Type-I adhesive.
- A medium density overlay face must be used in place of a wood veneer.

- An aluminum cap and lite flashing and bottom flashing should be specified, especially if door is out-swinging.
- The door should be protected with overhangs or recesses in the building.
- Adequate primer and finish coats should be specified.
- If there is any glazing, the glass should be set in silicone glazing compound.
- The owner should be required to maintain the door periodically to prolong the life of the door by inserting this requirement in the specifications as a condition for maintaining the warranty.

Fire-rated Wood Doors

The wood fire door is probably the most improperly specified type of door. For accurate information that should help eliminate confusion, local code requirements should be consulted. These will give general requirements, but it is up to the architect to specify the actual type of door. Helpful interpretation of all codes can be found in the AWI publications entitled *Building Code Flame Spread Classifications ASTM E 84 for Interior Architectural Woodwork* (5) and *Fire Doors Where and When* (7).

It is wasteful for doors to be overspecified for a project, eg, most hospital patient rooms, in a sprinklered building, need only have a 20-min label door to the corridor, although many architects specify a 45-min "C" label "just to be safe." The National Fire Protection Association (NFPA) Life Safety Code 10-1331 states that "doors with a 20 minute fire protection shall be used on openings other than those serving exits or hazardous areas" (8). Since the cost per door is often multiplied by the hundreds of doors in a large structure, there are thousands of dollars to be saved, without providing substandard material, by accurately specifying the type of door to be used (ie, not overspecifying). It is incumbent upon the architect to investigate carefully the particular requirements of the project. In too many cases, the specifications are reprinted from job to job (because of the use of a word processor) and sometimes do not relate to the particular requirements of the new project.

A frequently asked question is why wood fire doors should be used instead of metal. The answers are simple. First, a wood veneer may be more desirable aesthetically than a painted surface. Second, wood is a poorer conductor of heat than metal. For instance, in the winter time an aluminum window sash may transmit the temperature to a greater degree than a wood sash under similar conditions. The same behavior is true with doors. If there were a fire in a corridor the temperature on the room side of a metal door would almost be the same as that in the corridor. This means it would be too hot to touch and might even cause combustion to occur within the room. It has been proven by testing that the opposite side of a wood door can be safely touched during a fire. Additionally, metal doors twist and warp during a fire, making them impossible to open after a fire. Wood doors do not have these problems after fires. If the fire were minor, it might also be possible to salvage wood fire doors, whereas metal doors would have to be discarded after being in a fire.

There are restrictions on what can be done to a fire door with regard to light and louver cutouts and hardware. As a result of regulations promulgated under NFPA80 (which have been adopted by many state and local authorities), all wood fire doors must be machined at the manufacturer's plant or at a licensed fabricator that has the ability to apply its own identifying label after machining or altering a door. This is to maintain the integrity of the label and prevent the unauthorized cutting or mortising of a door.

The following are some of the restrictions that affect design when using wood fire doors:

1. The maximum size for a single door is 4 × 10 ft; for pairs, it is 4 × 8 ft for each leaf.

2. If a louver is required in the door, it must be a fusible link louver with a maximum size of 24 × 24 in.

3. Metal vision panels are allowed in most fire-rated doors, but their size is restricted based on label: 90-minute and 60-minute labels, 100 sq in. maximum; and 45-minute labels, 1296 sq in. maximum in single doors and 100 sq in. maximum in each leaf of a pair.

4. Metal astragal is required with all paired label doors.

5. Transoms must have a metal transom bar; the size of the transom and total height of the opening are limited.

6. All hardware should be of a type tested and listed by Underwriters Laboratories and thru-bolted whenever possible.

7. Any variation from label requirements will result in loss of label and use of certification tag.

(These restrictions may change as additional test approvals are obtained.)

There are also special function solid-core doors available: sound-retardant or acoustical doors with decibel ratings from 35 to 51; lead-lined doors (the thickness of lead required must be specified); and electrostatic shield doors. Ref. 6 can be consulted for further information.

"3P" Doors

"3P" is defined as prefit, premachined, and prefinished. This work can be performed by any manufacturer and/or fabricator if requested by the architect. Including this work as part of the woodwork package on a project guarantees neat proper cutouts for hardware and a finish on the door that is equivalent to a furniture finish. To estimate the cost of this work accurately, the woodworker requires certain information:

Specification of clearances

The hardware schedule, which should be available at bid time

Specification of prefinishing in manufacturer's standard finishes, ie, 3-coat natural finish, 4-coat stained finish

Type of packaging to be used (polyethylene bags are adequate for protection of all finishes; cardboard cartons are more costly and may not afford better or longer protection).

Stile and Rail Doors

Stile and rail doors can be custom-manufactured for functional application in a particular project, for interior or exterior use. They must be veneered except if a softwood or mahogany is used. Stiles and rails are joined by mortise and tenon joints for premium-grade construction and dowel construction for custom grade. Panels exceeding 10 in. in width should be laminated. See AWI Quality Standards Section 1400 for additional information. There are many manufacturers of stock stile and rail doors. These specifications do not apply to stock doors.

Warranties

Manufacturers provide limited warranties for wood door products.

FACTORY FINISHING

In the early days of mill/cabinetwork, most woodwork was sent to the job unfinished; in fact, in the first half of the twentieth century, most cabinetwork was sent to the job without the hardware installed and in an unfinished state. In order to maintain standards of high quality, it has become necessary to install hardware and prefinish in the shop. The AWI Quality Standards lists nine types of finishes and their related wear and appearance characteristics. AWI Quality Standards Section 1500 goes into detail about methods and materials. It is recommended that a sample of the actual wood being used be finished in the color and method specified prior to approval of the entire project.

FIRE-RETARDANT WOODWORK

The various model codes, which include Building Operators and Code Aministrators International (BOCA), NEPA101, Uniform Building Code (UBC), and Standard Building Construction Code (SBCC), define "interior finish" similarly. In its most general terms, interior finish encompasses wall coverings, paneling, grille work, ceiling and acoustical wall, or ceiling finishes applied to the wall and ceiling surfaces of buildings. Interior finish does *not* include doors, windows, cabinets, and floor and wall coverings $\frac{1}{28}$th of an inch or less in thickness. The specific definition of interior finish for each Model Code is included in the flame-spread classification charts in the AWI publication *Building Code Flame Spread Classifications ASTM E 84 for Interior Architectural Woodwork* (5). Trim refers to such items as mouldings, baseboards, railings, and door and window trim. Under the BOCA, Life Safety, and National Building Codes, trim includes interior finishes that cover wall and/or ceiling areas which are 10% or less of the total wall and ceiling areas in a given room. This 10% rule can be used for any room by using this formula:

$$A = \frac{2H(L + W) + L \times W}{10}$$

where A=area of interior finish to be applied to the room (walls and ceiling); H=ceiling height of room; L=length of room; and W=width of room.

An interior finish material, including trim, is considered the surface or facing materials that compose the exposed portion or interior face of a wall or ceiling, whether it be an architectural or acoustical treatment or the structure itself. It includes the construction of the wall if there is no finish material applied to the basic wall construction.

Most untreated wood species commonly used as interior finish materials have flame-spread classifications less than 200 (the highest flame-spread classification permitted by the Model Codes is 200). Therefore, these untreated wood species are acceptable for many uses as interior finish or trim, depending on the use of the building and the area in which the finish is installed as indicated by the appropriate code. For more detailed information and examples of various situations, refer to the previously mentioned AWI publication. For detailed information on wood fire doors and how to specify them correctly, refer to AWI publication *Fire Doors Where and When* (7). Another AWI publication, *Building Code Applications for Miscellaneous Exterior and Interior Uses* (9), covers items such as siding, balconies, and stairs.

Treated Lumber

Certain species of hard- and softwoods are treated with chemicals to reduce flammability and retard the spread of flame over the surface. This usually involves impregnating the wood under pressure with salts and other chemicals. The vehicle for this treatment is a liquid. Therefore, treated wood must be redried before use. Check with local sources for the available species and flame spread.

Treated Panel Products

The use of fire-retardant panel products has become prevalent in situations that require decorative wood treatment and yet must meet the code requirements. Wall paneling in lobbies or public-assembly areas is a good example. The substrate can have a flame spread of 25 or less, and a wood veneer of $\frac{1}{28}$ in. or a $\frac{1}{32}$-in. plastic laminate decorative face can be applied. The panel assembly would then meet the code requirements.

Veneer-core plywoods (usually available with fir or Southern Yellow Pine faces and cores) meet the label requirements but are poor substrates for panel- or cabinetwork. There is Luan fire-treated plywood, which is somewhat better as a substrate, but the best, most stable substrate is fire-retardant treated particle board. At this time, there is only one manufacturer of this product, Willamette Industries, Inc., Albany, Oreg.; their product is called Duraflake FR.

The basic difference between the plywood and particleboard products is the manner in which they are treated to obtain their respective ratings. Plywood is immersed in treatment solution (water-borne) under pressure and then dried after treatment. This causes grain raising, warping, and a generally unstable sheet of material. Particle board, on the other hand, is manufactured with treated particles so that the treatment is "built-in" the product. The panels are flat, stable, and have the same characteristics as high quality medium density particle board. The use of this material will produce a much higher quality product than one made with a veneer-core substrate.

Where it is impractical to use fire-retardant panel or lumber products and a Class I rating is required, the use of a clear intumescent finish over the wood will provide the required rating. The coating, when exposed to temperatures of 350°F or more, develops a rigid foam ("intumescent mat") many times its dry thickness. This foam contains noncombustible, nontoxic gases, which provide a highly effective fire and heat barrier. There are several manufacturers of this product. One product which results in an acceptable finish is Albert-DS-Clear Class A Fire Retardant Coating, manufactured by American Vamag Co. Inc., Ridgefield, N.J. This coating has received both Underwriters Laboratories and BOCA approval for flame spread 5, smoke developed 0, and fuel contributed 0.

MONUMENTAL WOODWORK

This term refers to architectural woodwork of difficulty and quality which exceeds "premium" grade as defined in AWI Quality Standards. It refers to a project for which the requirements are extremely stringent and the additional costs which may be incurred are not a consideration. This might be a board room with a fancy veneered conference table or a chief executive's office with an exotic veneered credenza. It also might involve some special finish, ie, high gloss polyester. There have been some technical articles on various solutions to problem details in monumental woodwork in the 1985 editions of *Design Solutions* (10).

RECENT DEVELOPMENTS

Machinery

Most of the new innovations in machinery have come from Europe. Many machines developed for high production in Europe are being used by small and medium volume shops in the United States. Automatic edge-banding machines apply plastic laminate, PVC, and wood veneer edges to panels, as well as solid lumber (up to 1 ¼-in. thickness) edges. These machines, through the use of hot-melt adhesives, instantly glue the edges onto the panel and, on continuously moving belts, trim, end-cut, bevel, shape, sand, and/or polish the edges. These machines are costly, but by performing all of these functions at a rate of 60–100 lineal ft/min, most shops cannot afford to be without them. Large computerized panel saws which cut stacks of panels 3–4 in. thick and cut square and accurate to within 4/1000 of an inch are commonplace in today's architectural woodwork shop.

Fabrication Systems

A recent import from Europe is the "32MM System," which has been used there with success for many years. The system is used primarily for the assembly of casework and cabinetry. It operates on the basis of a series of holes, on 32-mm centers bored into the surface of cabinet sides and into the edge of horizontal cabinet members. Dowels and glue are inserted into the holes and the cabinets held under pressure in a clamping device until the glue sets. This gives the manufacturers the ability to assemble prelaminated parts without concern for the glued surfaces. The actual contact surface being glued is greater with the dowels than it would be in a conventional dado or rabbetted construction. When this system is used, the "Europeanstyle" concealed hinge is also used. This hinge is by far the most important improvement in cabinet hardware in the past 25 years. The hinges are available in all types of opening angles, ie, 90–185°. The particular hinge manufacturer should not be as critical to the architect as the function. Because each shop purchases special equipment, which may only be used with one particular hinge manufacturer, for installing the hinges, it is incumbent upon the designer/architect to specify a manufacturer or equal together with the function of the hinge. Most of these hinge manufacturers offer a complete line of hinges.

Industry Trends

The most important change affecting the architectural woodworking industry has been the enlargement of the woodworker's scope on particular projects. In addition to the traditional wood items (ie, doors, trim, cabinets), the woodworker is now asked to furnish all items that relate to finish (ie, glass, architectural metal, fabric panels, toilet partitions and accessories, hollow metal frames, and architectural hardware) because contractors and owners want to place the responsibility for coordination with one supplier. Since the woodworker normally becomes involved with the coordination of all of these related trades, it is an almost natural evolution that the woodworker enlarge the scope of his work to include these items.

BIBLIOGRAPHY

Many of the publications below can be obtained from the Architectural Woodwork Institute (AWI), Arlington, Va.

1. *Architectural Quality Standards, Guide Specifications and Quality Certification Program (QSI),* 4th ed., AWI, 1985.
2. Jones, *Planers, Matchers and Molders in America 1800–1985,* Chandler Jones, Seattle, Wash.
3. *Guide to Wood Species,* AWI, 1977.
4. *Wood Handbook No. 72,* Forest Products Laboratory, Forest Service, U.S. Department of Agriculture, U.S. Government Printing Office, Washington D.C.
5. *Building Code Flame Spread Classifications ASTM E 84 for Interior Architectural Woodwork,* AWI.
6. *Fire Code Summary,* AWI, 1986.
7. *Fire Doors Where and When,* AWI.
8. National Fire Protection Association Life Safety Code 10–1331, *Life Safety Code Handbook,* National Fire Protection Association (NFPA), Quincy, Mass., 1986.
9. *Building Code Applications for Miscellaneous Exterior and Interior Uses,* AWI.
10. *Design Solutions,* AWI, 1985, published quarterly.

General References

Additional publications from the AWI relating to architectural woodwork are available:

Artistry in Wood Series
Architectural Casework—General Detail and Specifications Guide
Five Contemporary Wood Window Concepts
High Pressure Laminates
Wall and Ceiling Treatments
Wood Mouldings—A Guide for Interior Architectural Design

See also ADHESIVES; PLASTIC LAMINATES; WOOD IN CONSTRUCTION; WOOD—STRUCTURAL PANEL COMPOSITES.

LESTER BLOCH
Somerset Wood Products Co.
Somerville, New Jersey

ARCHITECTURE AND ENGINEERING PERFORMANCE INFORMATION CENTER (AEPIC)

History will record the decades of the 1970s and 1980s as the "decades of the disasters" in response to all of the building, bridge, and other failures which shocked the world. Although it will be recognized that many failures of constructed facilities occurred during previous years, it was the dramatic collapse of large public structures during this period that caused the professions involved, the public, and the Congress of the United States to become alarmed. Specifically, it was the collapse in 1981 of the skywalks in the Hyatt Hotel in Kansas City, Mo., resulting in the deaths of 114 persons, that caused the increase in attention to safety.

During this period, the airplane crash and the train wreck were becoming more frequent and closer to home. Buildings in cities and towns began to collapse. Yet this was to be only the tip of the iceberg. The insurance industry informed the world that, indeed, everything was going badly for them. Roofs, skylights, and walls were leaking, walls were falling off buildings, elevators were not working, air-conditioning systems were malfunctioning, indoor air was polluted and poisoned, and parking structures were cracking and falling on automobiles; everyone was suing everyone to find a little justice. The building industry and the design professions were indeed in serious trouble. The media of the 1980s has been replete with stories of rising insurance premiums, unavailability of insurance, the liability crisis, and need for tort (legal) reforms.

CASES AND ISSUES

A review of recent and historical cases will illustrate some of the issues in detail.

Hartford Civic Center Coliseum, Hartford, Conn., 1978. In January 1978, after a major snowstorm, the 300 × 300 ft space frame roof of the Hartford Coliseum collapsed. The roof had been in service for over five years and had been designed for live loads of 30 lb/ft². The snow across the street was measured by investigators the day following the collapse at 23 lb/ft².

The report from investigators indicated that the roof had displayed excessive deflection prior to the day of the storm. Also, there were basic design errors as well as an underestimation of the roof dead loads: some top chord members were found to be overloaded by as much as 852%. Further investigation reports cited a lack of adequate bracing of the top chord compression members.

Later, a second opinion was offered that the failure was a result of torsional buckling of compression members in some way related to the geometry of connections. A third opinion blamed the collapse on the failure of a weld connecting the scoreboard to the roof. By the time all reports were in, it was concluded that the construction manager, the space-frame contractor, the inspecting engineers, and the city of Hartford may all have contributed to the failure.

Rosemont Horizon Stadium, Rosemont (Suburban Chicago), Ill., 1979. In August 1979, during the construction of the wood arch roof over the Rosemont Horizon Stadium, the roof collapsed, killing five construction workers and injuring 19 others. The $3 million arena was 90% complete at the time of collapse. The construction consisted of 16 wood arches spanning 288 ft which supported a purlin and girder system, the girders connected to the arches with steel angles and bolts.

According to an investigation by the Occupational Safety and Health Administration (OSHA), missing bolts, inadequate bracing, and improper construction practices led to the collapse. OSHA called for citations against five companies involved and asked for monetary penalties against the roof-erection subcontractor. In addition, the firm investigating the collapse was cited for unnecessarily exposing its employees to fall hazards.

Kemper Arena, Kansas City, Mo., 1979. In June 1979, during a wind and rain storm, a major portion of the roof of the Kemper Arena collapsed. The major space trusses that spanned 324 ft over the great space did not collapse, but the roof construction that hung from the trusses failed. The structure was built in 1974.

The investigation report indicated that the high strength bolts used to hang the roof trusses from the longspan space trusses had failed due to fatigue stress. The bolts connected the roof trusses to a steel base plate joined to the space truss by a pipe hanger. The movement of the assembly under wind load exerted a "prying" force which caused a fatigue failure in the bolts. It was also noted that the A490 high strength bolts are specified by the American Institute of Steel Construction only for static loading conditions (Fig. 1).

Congress Hall, West Berlin, 1980. In May 1980, after 23 years of use, approximately one-third of the 37,000 ft² concrete shell roof over the auditorium level of the Congress Hall collapsed, killing one person and injuring four others. When the roof failed, one of the twin edge

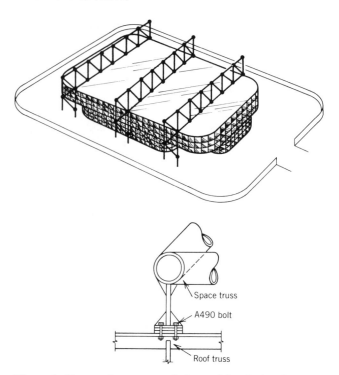

Figure 1. Kemper Arena: general view and detail of roof suspension.

arches fell and pulled a portion of shell between it and the tension ring.

The preliminary reports of the investigation teams indicated that dynamic stress and corrosion in prestressing tendons were the primary causes of failure. Highly fluctuating stresses in the tensioning steel were caused by vertical movement in the arches due to concrete creep, temperature stresses, snow, wind, settlements, and other factors. Also, humidity and carbon dioxide were able to penetrate to the tensioning elements in some areas and cause extensive corrosion, bringing about a gradual break in a sizable number of the highly stressed tensioning wires.

Further opinion stated that the collapse of the Congress Hall was due to design as well as construction shortcomings. The twin arches had experienced unavoidable up-and-down movement due to temperature change, wind, snow, vibrations, and concrete creep. The tension tendons used to resist this movement were protected by thin slabs which cracked with the constant movement; the cracks permitted corrosion. The tendons became embrittled by corrosion and hydrogen induction and finally broke (Fig. 2).

MGM Grand Hotel, Las Vegas, Nev., 1980. In November 1980, the fire at the MGM Grand Hotel taught many lessons about the lack of fire safety but at a very high cost: 85 dead and 500 injured. The fire started with an electrical short circuit in improperly installed wiring in the kitchen area; it spread unseen due in part to poor construction and also due to breaches in firewalls created to accommodate changes in ductwork and wiring.

The fire reached disaster level because of the lack of sprinklers in the casino area, the failure of manual alarms, and smoke that was permitted to flood stairwells and eleva-

Figure 2. Congress Hall, West Berlin.

tor shafts and enter the air-handling system. Serious fire damage was limited to the casino, office, and entrance area. The smoke, however, spread throughout the building.

Hyatt Hotel Walkway, Kansas City, Mo., 1981. In July 1981, during a special celebration at the Hyatt Hotel, the suspended walkways in the lobby atrium collapsed, killing 113 persons and injuring 180 others. The cause of the collapse was quickly determined: the detail for connection of walkway to hanger rod was improperly designed. It was later determined that a change in design that had doubled the force on the connection had been executed. Although the cause was known, the responsibility for error was not, and numerous investigation teams brought in at high cost tried to determine liability. The death of so many in one accident sent reverberations through professional, legal, and congressional circles for some time.

The design engineer of record was eventually held responsible for the approval of the change in detail, and the appeal processes are continuing in the courts. The court and out-of-court settlements have exceeded $60 million, and suits in excess of that are pending (Fig. 3).

Tacoma Narrows Suspension Bridge, Tacoma, Wash., 1940. In November 1940, after but a few months of use, the 2800-ft main span of the Tacoma Narrows failed during 42-mph winds.

Known as "Galloping Gertie" because of the way in which winds caused the severe waving and twisting of the roadbed, the bridge's weakness was identified as its great flexibility, vertically and in torsion. The bridge was too narrow, too light, and too thin to be stable in normal wind loads.

Damping devices were installed as the problem became obvious but were not able to reduce the vertical oscillations.

In addition, extensive model analysis was conducted to find a solution to the problem. Fortunately, no lives were lost in this failure. Although an expensive learning experience, it is an excellent example of learning from failure.

Silver Bridge, Gallipolis, Ohio, to Point Pleasant, W. Va., 1967. In December 1967, the eyebar suspension bridge collapsed with its deck loaded by a Friday traffic jam; 46 people died and nine were injured in the worst bridge failure in U.S. history. Forty years earlier the bridge had been celebrated for its unique design.

The early reports of multiple investigations indicated many possible causes, which ranged from overload and outdated design practices to inadequate inspection programs. Final investigation reports verified that the last complete inspection was in 1951 and that the collapse started with the failure of one of the 50-ft long eyebars. The eyebar fractured due to development of a critical size flaw resulting from the combined action of stress corrosion and corrosion fatigue.

It should be noted that in 1967 only 17 states had bridge-inspection programs acceptable by federal government standards. In 1968, all states had inspection programs considered acceptable.

I-95 Mianus River Bridge, Greenwich, Conn., 1983. In June 1983, after nearly 25 years of service, a 100-ft span of this three-lane bridge fell into the river below. Three deaths and three injuries resulted from the collapse, in which several vehicles fell with the failed structure. Early speculation as to the cause related to the inspection of the "pin and hanger" detail at the end of each of the two main girders. Investigators also speculated that the bridge's "pin and hanger" design may have been responsible, indicating a problem associated with "zero redundancy" with the tension connectors. It has also been noted that corrosion of the steel in the connection caused a mode of performance not anticipated (Fig. 4).

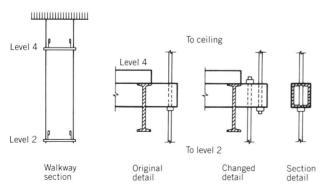

Figure 3. Hyatt Regency Walkway.

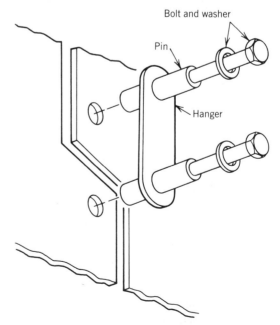

Figure 4. I-95 Mianus River Bridge: detail of connection.

Willow Island Cooling Tower (Formwork), St. Mary's, W. Va., 1978. In April 1978, the "jack-up" formwork in construction of a cooling tower collapsed, causing 51 workers to fall 170 ft to their deaths. The initial investigation report by OSHA charged that failure to follow proper procedures in use of the formwork caused the collapse. The formwork was not adequately secured to the wall; some bolts were missing and the quality of concrete was uncertain.

The State of West Virginia criticized both OSHA for failure to enforce its own regulations and those in the private sector for failing to observe OSHA regulations. The final conclusions appear to have been that human error (error of judgment) was the cause of failure.

Apartment Towers, Bailey's Crossroads, Va., 1973. In March 1973, as concrete was being placed on the 24th floor of the new Towers and the reshoring of concrete was under way at the 22nd level, the mass of concrete at those levels plus the crane on the 24th floor dropped all the way through the structure. The progressive collapse of 24 floors of what was to be a 26-story building was attributed to irregularities in shoring removal and reshoring. The accident resulted in 14 deaths and more than 30 injuries.

The contractor, concrete subcontractor, and job superintendent were indicted by a county grand jury; the concrete subcontractor was also charged by OSHA with willful violations of the Occupational Safety and Health Act. Yet, in the end, the architect and engineers were sued in federal court and found negligent of not visiting the job, not inspecting the work, and not warning the contractors regarding the curing times for concrete.

The accident also caused the industry and related professions to reconsider the issues of "progressive collapse" and study several cases recorded in recent years.

Beauvais Cathedral, Beauvais, France, 1284. In 1284, after 59 years of design and construction under the direction of three different (unknown) masters, the 158-ft-high choir vaults at Beauvais collapsed. Repairs were completed 53 years later; all of the original quadripartite vaults were replaced by sexpartite vaults, and extra unbuttressed piers were added. Work was then delayed for a few years to fight The Hundred Years War. About 1500, work began to complete the transept. During the 1560s, a 490-ft-high tower was erected over the transept crossing, though the nave work was not far advanced. In 1573, the stone tower collapsed. Damage was repaired within five years, but the tower was not replaced. Work was then stopped and the cathedral left unfinished.

The dispute over the cause has never been completely resolved. However, it is generally agreed that the towers failed because the two western piers at the crossing failed from progressive movement in a westerly direction due to insufficient lateral support from the incomplete nave.

There is no agreement as to cause of failure of the choir vaults. Speculation has ranged from (*1*) an earthquake, (*2*) inadequate foundations, (*3*) initial shrinkage of lime mortar, (*4*) creep in the mortar, (*5*) wind loads causing potential tension stress in masonry, (*6*) error in design (excessive spans between piers that were too slender), (*7*) error in detailing (collonnettes too slender), (*8*) a theory that planned construction had reached the "limits of construction" in stone (per Viollet-le-Duc), and (*9*) another theory that the failure was not of the architect as artist but of the architect as engineer (per Paul Frankl).

Observations have been made that for well over 700 years, even over thousands of years, builders and architects have experienced failures and have had the opportunity to learn from failure. Obviously, the problems are not new.

DEVELOPMENT OF CONCERN

Numerous additional accounts of similar current and historical events and their alleged causes have been written (1–6). Some materials, systems, and techniques are new. Some perceptions of the problem, their causes, and the means of relief or retribution are changing. Yet, before the collapse of the civic centers and arenas in 1978 and 1979 and the Hyatt Walkway in 1981, there appeared to be little concern expressed by professional societies, federal agencies, Congress, or other groups.

The professional societies in architecture and engineering responded to the growing awareness of performance issues in a number of ways. The American Institute of Architects (AIA) appointed the AIA Long-Span Building Panel in 1979 to review the causes for the failure of long-span buildings, especially the large civic centers, arenas, and sports complexes that collapsed in 1978 and 1979 (7). The American Society of Civil Engineers created the Committee on Forensic Engineering in 1982 (8).

The United States Committee on large Dams (USCOLD) published *Lessons from Dam Incidents, USA* in 1975 (8). In 1976, the Teton Dam, a large earth-fill dam in Idaho, failed. USCOLD published a second volume, *Lessons from Dam Incidents,* in 1979 (8).

The Congressional Committee on Science and Technology began in 1982 to hold hearings through the Subcommittee on Investigation and Oversight on Causes of Structural Failures in Public Facilities. Representative Albert Gore, Jr., of Tennessee (now Senator Gore), Chair of the House Panel, stated his interest in creating a national investigative agency and a federal repository of information on failures (9).

Several other committees of professional societies and other groups have some interest and involvement in the performance of buildings and civil structures, although it is natural that their activity is most related to the specific interests of the group (8).

Through many years of human activity in construction and design and the related performance problems, there has been no real concern or activity related to the development of a comprehensive reference of accessible data about building performance. All of the groups, agencies, and organizations associated with the construction process have some form of records or files relating to problems of the particular groups, but not one has a systematic collection of performance data that is accessible. Thus, there has been no systematic way to learn from past experiences except those that are personal and within the generation. Building and design professions have not recognized the great opportunities to learn from experience that were realized in the development of data bases in medicine, law, and chemistry. It is readily apparent that the rapid expansion of new techniques and technology in design and construction, coupled with the economic, political, and social changes of the twentieth century, both contributed to produce a rash of serious failures.

The evidence indicates that these problems will grow progressively worse in the near future. Bold measures are necessary to address problems of such magnitude. Action is necessary at all levels and in all areas: education, law, government, ethics, attitudes, values, and finance, to name just a few.

THE ROLE OF THE AEPIC

One idea that grew out of this complex set of problems and concerns was AEPIC (the Architecture and Engineering Performance Information Center). By sharing in the activities of the AEPIC at the University of Maryland, all professionals engaged in the design, construction, and use of buildings, civil structures, and other constructed facilities can more easily fulfill their obligation to remain well-informed and assist others in remaining well-informed about standards and performance failures related to their work. AEPIC provides the means for access to a data base, the first giant step toward reducing performance failures in building and civil structures (10).

The Founding of AEPIC

AEPIC was founded at the University of Maryland in July 1982. The center, a joint endeavor of the School of Architecture and the College of Engineering at the University of Maryland, was given its initial support by a National Science Foundation grant of $150,000. That grant, with considerable additional support from the University of Maryland, the College of Engineering, the School of Architecture, the Department of Civil Engineering, Victor O. Schinnerer & Co., Sperry/Univac Corp., several professional societies, and others with enthusiasm for AEPIC, has made it possible for the center to develop the systems, programs, software, and storage networks for the systematic collection, collation, analysis, and dissemination of information about the performance of buildings, civil structures, and other constructed facilities.

Architects, engineers, contractors, developers, manufacturers, lawyers, building owners and users, federal and state agencies, insurance underwriters, university and private research organizations, and others interested in the objectives of AEPIC can use this computer-based collection of performance informations for (1) planning new projects, (2) reviewing existing structures for rehabilitation or restoration, (3) teaching (case studies), (4) modifying codes and regulations, (5) planning research, (6) preparing professional texts, (7) investigating for dispute resolution, (8) developing new products for the industry, (9) implementing effective quality-control measures, (10) improving professional and industry practice, and (11) creating an in-house resource base with lessons learned from project performance.

Performance Data

AEPIC uses a broad definition of performance: "fulfillment of a claim, promise, request, need, or expectation." Obviously, a performance failure or dysfunction is the lack of fulfillment or nonfulfillment of such claims, promises, requests, needs, or expectations. The contract and breach of contract issues are fairly clear, although not always easy to resolve if the contract or promise is vague and expectations are laced with self-serving rhetoric. Moreover, the expectations of building owners and government officials for quality materials and professional service have been increased by the constant exposure to exaggerated promises and claims of excellence fed through the advertising media on behalf of product manufacturers and professional societies. Indeed, the entire society is constantly informed of the "new, super-deluxe, better-than-ever" products now available.

AEPIC's data base covers performance information about buildings and civil structures and includes all aspects of problems arising from the building envelope, structural, mechanical, and electrical systems; moisture barriers; economic and environmental concerns; and thermal, accoustical, visual, and behavioral dysfunctions. The center's performance data relate to materials, elements, systems, processes, and procedures. Information about some cases currently under litigation is included in the files. All data can be coded and classified without sensitive or personal information, to protect the privacy of involved individuals and firms. The data is stored in either computerized data files or libraries, and includes:

1. *Computerized Performance Incident or Case Files.* Professional and "informed reporter" reports on actual performance problems or malfunctions, such as water damage, masonry disintegration, structural collapse or distress, indoor air quality, etc. Victor O. Schinnerer & Co. has donated 48,000 claim reports to this file.

2. *Computerized Citation Files.* References to published information about performance problems that have appeared in journals, trade press magazines, newspapers, agency investigation reports, etc. This file currently includes *Engineering News Record* articles for the last 20 years, as well as other references.

3. *Dossier Library.* Documentation of performance data about the incidents and related information in the case files.

4. *Visual Materials Library.* Photographs, slides, and other visual materials related to the case files.

5. *Reference Library.* Current and historical codes, standards, and other technical references.

Data Sources

AEPIC uses the Performance Report and Document Citation forms, which are described and summarized in the section entitled "Format for Data Input at AEPIC." All reporters are urged to use that format to contribute data. Of course, full information and complete sets of the forms, as well as the coding and classification systems, are available. Over 150 professional advisors assisted AEPIC in developing the data forms in order to assure a broad base of applicability.

All readers are encouraged to contribute case and citation reports and to contribute to the dossier visual materials and reference libraries.

Several hundred persons and firms are members of and/or correspondents to the AEPIC. This broad range of professional and user interests includes architects, engineers, contractors, building inspectors, lawyers, federal, state, and private agencies, insurance underwriters, research organizations, building owners, managers, and their agents, and many others. Many are contributors to AEPIC resources. As may be expected, the insurance industry has been a major source of information.

Accessing Data

The computerized data base is accessed by written or telephone inquiry through the use of key words. Care and precision in the choice of words are very important in framing a query to access the data. Users and reporters choose words that are familiar to them but sufficiently standardized to permit computer cross-referencing for effective storage and search routines. AEPIC uses existing reference bases for classification and coding, and all of the users and contributors identify the reference base for their word usage, eg, CSI (the Construction Specifications Institute), ASTM (the American Society for Testing and Materials), NFPA (National Fire Protection Agency), AIA Standard Documents, etc.

Custom Services

Businesses, agencies, and institutions may contract with AEPIC to monitor and analyze performance data for a particular building or group of buildings. The data is collected and stored with appropriate coding to permit analysis. Personal identification information may be deleted from these files so that the basic information can become part of the general data base and be of assistance to all users.

Another special program is the Building and Materials Register. Owners may register buildings or products to be monitored over time and to record their performance history as it accrues.

Research organizations may use AEPIC as the primary data source and the repository for collection and analysis of research data, again in a coded format to facilitate exclusive access by the research organization that is subcontracting.

Data Analysis

AEPIC has developed computer programs for the analysis of trends over time. The insurance-claims data range over a claim period from 1958 to 1985. Trend analysis of much of the previously mentioned data has been conducted over this time. The trend analysis (Lorentz curves) shows the rate of incidence, ie, the percentage of claims related to one type of data, by year, compared with the total of all

claims of that type over all years. The base for the Lorentz curves is expanded to a normalized 1000 cases per year to remove variations in the number of claims in any one year. The rate of incidence for the architect has been unchanged over a 25-year period. This is interesting in comparison with the data that shows that the number of claims per 100 insured firms has increased dramatically over the same period of time: below 30% before 1963 and 43–47% in 1983 and 1985. (Note: Architects are involved in approximately 45% of all claims in the Victor Schinnerer data.) Similar studies show a comparable lack of change for the engineering professions, except for the structural engineer and the architectural engineer, who show a decreased rate of incidence since 1972. In contrast, the retired professional shows a drastic increase in the rate of incidence since 1976. Through such AEPIC data, it is possible to discover the trend, but additional research is needed to explain it.

Other interesting studies are derived from a comparison of AEPIC/Schinnerer data with the reports of C. Roy Vince, as (former) Vice President of Architecture and Engineering Claims Division of Shand-Morahan & Co. (11). The AEPIC Lorentz trend analysis of the building type "Factory and Industrial" indicates that rate of incidence of claims against this type has declined over the past 20 years. Yet the observations of Vince indicate an increase in the severity curve for this building type over the same period. This would seem to indicate that the percentage of claims has diminished as the severity of claims has increased. Change in methods of design and construction is the reported reason for this change.

Vince also points out that over a period of 20 years a major change has occurred in the ranking of building types on the severity curve. In 1963, assembly buildings were high on the severity curve and in 1983 they were low on the severity curve. In 1963, industrial facilities, tunnels, bridges, dams, and public buildings were low on the severity curve and in 1983 those same structures were high on the severity curve. It is observed that changes in the construction management process and the imposition of speeded-up methods of construction have led to a lack of quality control in adapting those processes.

Vince indicates that there is a growing tendency in the primarily industrialized and specialized construction areas to move away from negotiation as the primary method of resolving claims. Presumably, the trend is toward litigation. He also notes that government bodies are learning to press claims. "Design–build" firms and "complete service" firms have a frequency of claims of 250%–300% above the norm. Further studies by Shand-Morahan indicate that building failures were the highest ranked on severity of losses in the past, but current trends show that economic or financial loss claims lead the list.

In addition to the insurance-industry data, a number of other studies of performance in Europe and the U.S. have been analyzed at AEPIC. Studies of "phase of service to problem area" comparisons and variations in "phase of service" have also been conducted. From 1978 to 1983, the incidence of claims related to design in the Schinnerer data was over 60% in comparison to construction at over 26% (Fig. 5). Data from the Bureau Securitas (a French

Problem area \ Phase of service	Design	Construction	Additional services	Study and report phase	Bidding	Unspecified	Total claims in problem area
Site development construction	625 43.2%	425 29.4%	44 3.0%	89 6.2%	15 1.0%	250 17.2%	1448
Architecture	873 70.7%	307 24.9%	17 1.4%	30 2.4%	5 0.4%	3 0.2%	1235
Structural	326 61.8%	167 31.6%	4 0.8%	17 3.2%	6 1.1%	8 1.5%	528
Mechanical, electrical, environment	777 70.2%	250 22.6%	22 2.0%	31 2.8%	16 1.4%	11 1.0%	1107
Economic	31 47%	9 13.6%	3 4.5%	13 19.7%	0 0.0%	10 15.2%	66
Overall average	2632 60.0%	1158 26.4%	90 2.1%	180 4.1%	42 1.0%	282 6.4%	4384 100%

Figure 5. AEPIC data: 1978–1982.

agency), provided by a U.S. subsidiary of Société de Controle Technique (SOCOTEC), shows in a study of 10,000 failures from 1968 to 1978 that 37% of the number of failures were in design and 51% in construction. Data from the bureau also indicate that 78% of design deficiencies are related to poor or inadequate details, and that the predominant number of failures occur within the construction period or during the first year of use.

AEPIC also monitors other studies to test for correlations of data. Another study of interest to architects and engineers is a 1983 survey of 448 major building owners throughout the United States (12). Over half the owners indicated having problems with leaky roofs and heating and cooling systems. Over one-quarter indicated problems with elevators and poured concrete. In addition, of those owners with heating, ventilating, and air-conditioning (HVAC) problems, 56% felt the problem was related to design; of those with concrete problems, 60% felt the problem was related to quality of workmanship; of those with leaky roofs, 42% felt the problem was related to quality of workmanship.

Some interesting statistics emerged from the survey; 63% of the owners indicated that projects were seldom completed behind schedule, but 46% felt the contractor was usually responsible for the delay. Also, 50% indicated that projects experience cost overruns, but 52% thought that the architect (architect/designer) is usually responsible for the overrun and 41% felt the contractor is responsible for the overrun. Also, 87% of the owners thought that design changes during construction contribute to the cost overruns. It is interesting to note that more owners agree than disagree that the architect tends to sacrifice function for the sake of aesthetics.

The one good note in the survey revealed that 63% of the owners had not had any of their projects involved in litigation or formal arbitration because of building design or construction problems, including cost overruns or scheduling problems. This means, however, that over 36% had

been involved with litigation or arbitration, and herein lies part of the problem.

Extensions/Information Dissemination

The conference and workshop have been the primary modes of information transfer, next to personal verbal and written communication. The AEPIC International Conference and Workshop in 1982 and 1984 were vital means of communication in the development of AEPIC. In 1985, a successful conference, "Excavation Failures," was held, and the summation of that conference was reported in AEPIC's *Architecture and Engineering Performance Notes* (13).

Architecture and Engineering Performance Notes was begun in 1985. Volume 1 featured excavation failures and Volume 2 roofing, the number-one construction problem. Volume 3 dealt with structural failures as well as the current activities of AEPIC research.

Another major means of AEPIC extension has been the lecture circuit. The directors and board of AEPIC have presented the AEPIC agenda on numerous occasions in every region of the United States and in many other countries. Repositories are currently in development in the UK, and discussions and processes are under way in Canada and Australia.

Current Projects

In February 1986, the National Bureau of Standards (NBS) entered into an agreement with the University of Maryland's Department of Civil Engineering on behalf of AEPIC to collect documentations of 500 structural failures. This grant resulted from the earlier testimony and agreements in the Subcommittee on Investigation and Oversight on Causes of Structural Failure in Public Facilities. AEPIC had been identified in the 1984 hearings as the only data base on failures in the country and the logical resource to be used by any special projects proposed by the subcommittee.

In June 1986, the National Science Foundation (NSF) funded a grant to the University of Maryland's School of Architecture on behalf of AEPIC. The goal of this project is the improved performance of the nation's existing and future building stock and infrastructure and therefore the increased quality, longevity, and safety of the built environment through the identification of the specific failures currently being experienced. The basic objectives of the project are to (1) identify general failure priority areas based on percentage of occurrences over the past 10 years; (2) gather detailed information and data on a statistically valid sample of actual individual failures in these priority areas; (3) analyze individual cases in order to identify high correlations of recurring failures in buildings, civil structures, and other constructed facilities; and (4) identify priority areas of specific failures, their problems, potential solutions, and future research needs.

Of course, the NBS and NSF projects will add significantly to the data base of AEPIC and prove to be a great resource to its users.

Numerous other studies and projects are in process

at AEPIC. A study of the influence of mandatory low bid contracts on performance was begun at the request of the Wyoming Chapter of the American Institute of Architects (AIA). Their members, who have become sponsor members of AEPIC, have expressed hope that other chapters will join them in their efforts to improve the process of design and construction.

Additionally, a study was conducted for the Florida Board of Professional Engineers to examine the trends in claims against structural engineers within the state of Florida in comparison with other states and regions.

Other subjects being studied include (1) trends in bridge performance, (2) a historical survey of the "Sarabond" story, (3) trends in roofing performance, (4) trends in HVAC performance, (5) a historical survey of the brick veneer and steel-stud back-up performance problems, (6) trends in glass and glazing performance, and (7) trends in surveying errors. There are also plans for a number of similar studies to begin in the near future.

Curriculum and course development is an important aspect of AEPIC activity. A university course, "Performance Analysis of Buildings and Civil Structures," developed as a joint offering of the School of Architecture and the Department of Civil Engineering at the University of Maryland, was first offered as a cross-listed course in 1984. The response was overwhelming. The course has been offered each year since and is consistently oversubscribed.

Organization

The University of Maryland serves as the international center and the national repository of AEPIC (Fig. 6). A number of international repositories are proposed for development in other countries. The most advanced development is presently in the UK. The international repositories will significantly broaden the base of AEPIC users and contributors.

An advisory board of distinguished persons provides advice and guidance on AEPIC policies, programs, and technical operations. The members of the advisory board were selected for their expertise in architecture, engineering, engineering testing, geotechnical analysis, insurance, law, contracting, research, and education.

Furthermore, an advisory council and nine advisory committees have been formed to serve as liaisons between AEPIC and membership organizations, technical and trade associations, councils and institutes, and major agency media, research, educational, legal, and technical user networks. Approximately 150 members of the council and committees are assisting in the dissemination of information about AEPIC, encouraging their constituencies to contribute data, and reviewing AEPIC functions in terms of their interests as users and contributors. All persons, individually or as representatives of an organization, interested in the objectives of the AEPIC are invited to participate as a member of one of the advisory committees.

Several hundred professional firms, agencies, organizations, institutions, and individuals are correspondents to AEPIC. They have no council or committee affiliations but share information on a mutual-interest basis. Several selected individuals are appointed as correspondent reporters, who assist AEPIC from particular regions of the country by sharing news of interest, assisting in distribution of AEPIC material, and clarifying AEPIC objectives.

Future Years

The 1982 announcement of the founding of AEPIC was heralded by the local, national, and international press as great news. The staff at the National Science Foundation indicated that the AEPIC project had received more press coverage than any other project in their memory. The founding trio of the AEPIC was cited by the publisher and editors of *Engineering News Record* in their 1984 awards program for ". . . those who served the best interests of the construction industry in 1983" (14). Thus, AEPIC began to grow, experiencing some of the joys of goals achieved, as well as some of the pitfalls.

The participants of the AEPIC International Conference and Workshop in 1982 and 1984 had observed that the AEPIC data base could develop to the point that a professional designer would be expected to review the data as a matter of course in a modification of the "standard of care" issue. Although there was some dissatisfaction expressed, it was generally agreed that such a trend in the concept of standard of care would be positive.

A 1985 article in the *Villanova Law Review* details a proposal for a new standard: the informed engineer (15):

Although dicta of some courts indicate a willingness to adopt an "informed engineer" standard, all courts should expressly

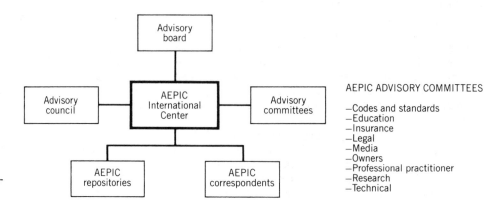

Figure 6. AEPIC organization diagram.

AEPIC ADVISORY COMMITTEES

—Codes and standards
—Education
—Insurance
—Legal
—Media
—Owners
—Professional practitioner
—Research
—Technical

recognize and apply this higher standard of care to structural engineers. The engineer should be expected to incorporate into his designs applicable advances in the profession that have reached the "professionally accepted" horizon of knowledge.

Under this standard the engineer is not held responsible for cutting-edge research or technology that is not widely disseminated to practitioners, but only for accepted techniques published in professional journals and accepted by the profession after a period of time. This national standard of the informed engineer avoids the pitfalls of strict liability, but at the same time prevents wholesale engineering practice at the "undergraduate" horizon of minimum acceptable professional conduct. The "informed standard" provides a demonstrable level of conduct provable by objective facts.

The advent of the Architecture and Engineering Performance Information Center (AEPIC) at the University of Maryland and the best dissemination of structural research support the notion of changing the standard. AEPIC opened in 1982 to collect, analyze, and disseminate information on the performance of structures in an effort to prevent perpetuation of past design and construction errors. The goal of AEPIC is to provide practicing engineers access to a computer data base of case files on successful and unsuccessful structures, photographic files, and hard-bound dossiers before they commence a similar design.

Of course, the proposal for the "informed engineer" standard can be extended to include all other design professionals, such as architects, landscape architects, land surveyors, etc. In the normal course of events, several years can be expected to pass before such ideas may become reality. In the meantime, some defensive measures are suggested (15):

A review of alternative defensive measures for the practitioner is appropriate, lest engineers and their counsel reject the "informed" standard out of hand as patently unreasonable. Six "office practice" suggestions and one possible legal solution are proposed as available alternatives to limit the impact of the "informed" standard of care.

Office Practice

1. A cardinal rule, an engineer must know the limits of his or her capabilities and never undertake more than he or she can professionally—not merely competently—complete.
2. At least one member of the firm should continually review the professional journals and periodicaly attend seminars to acquire knowledge of advances prior to their inclusion in design manuals.
3. Each design should incorporate a review of all available information on the performance of similar structures based on data obtained through AEPIC or other sources.
4. The structural engineer should retain an independent proof engineer to analyze all major designs, not just to check mathematical computations.
5. The engineer might request scale-model strength tests of innovative designs, components, or member-critical systems like the space frame. Even full-scale testing might be done in some cases.
6. The owner and engineer should consider full-time engineering supervision during the erection of critical elements of systems to ensure proper construction sequencing and procedures.

Contractual Alternatives: Indemnity Clauses

A crucial but unspoken issue underlying the structural engineer's liability is which of the parties should bear responsibility for developmental risks? In economic terms, the engineer can either increase precautions against failure by providing design redundancy, thus increasing construction costs, or, if his bargaining position is strong enough, seek indemnification from the owner for any resulting liability. Either alternative has the effect of allocating the risk of liability and/or the costs of avoiding liability to the project owner. Owners' agreements to indemnify engineers for negligent performance of design responsibilities are strictly construed but generally upheld unless prohibited by statute or against public policy. If the owner clearly and unequivocally agrees to indemnify the engineer, the engineer's liability exposure to the owner is significantly reduced. Alternatively, the parties can agree that the owner will purchase insurance to cover an anticipated risk, which has the effect of indemnifying the engineer against his own negligence.

Thus, at least some members of the bar recognize a vital role for AEPIC in the resolution of performance problems. Other defensive measures and contractual alternatives, such as peer review and project insurance, have been proposed. In peer review, selected professional peers may review the office practices of a firm with regard to quality control and quality assurance in design, construction documents, specifications, contract administration, and record keeping. It is also possible that a group of peers could review a specific project for appropriate conceptual development and accuracy. Some concern has been raised as to the possible liability exposure of the members of the peer review team if they review specific projects. Project insurance, on the other hand, would have all parties involved in a project, ie, owner, architect, engineer, contractor, etc, insured under one policy by one underwriter. Theoretically, this could remove the adversarial role of one insurance underwriter trying to recover from another: a problem could be identified and resolution could proceed. Caution has been raised for this proposal in that the rights of some parties may be abridged. It is, in one sense, a very special kind of "no-fault" insurance.

The contractual alternatives, such as those discussed in Refs. 15 and 16 and elsewhere, are more concerned with the sharing and/or shifting of liability among the designers, constructors, and owners. AEPIC has little direct involvement in proposals relating to contractual issues except insofar as a data base on performance is recognized as a tool for loss prevention and quality control within the insurance industry, the design professions, and the construction industry.

Long before the founding of AEPIC, the professional societies, associations, and institutes had a running battle with their own ambivalence related to issues such as liability, peer review, and standards of care. It is understandable that an individual would be reluctant to announce publicly his or her role in a failure of a particular building or structure, but it is difficult to understand some of the collective paranoia displayed within some groups toward the concept of a data base of performance for buildings and civil structures. There has been a tendency to blame the presence of too many lawyers in society as a prime cause of the problem rather than face the possibility that greater care may be required on the part of all. Unfortunately, some groups will then attempt to redefine their liability exposure to get out from under the liability crisis rather than recognize that an improvement in professional practice will benefit all persons—designers, constructors, and users—as well as assist in the resolution of the liability problems that face every segment of society.

Fortunately, some groups and individuals have been very positive about the presence of a performance data base. Numerous groups, firms, committees, and individuals have provided significant support and untiring service to the AEPIC.

With the expectation of this continuing support, the future of AEPIC is bright indeed.

SUMMARY AND CONCLUSIONS

Learning from mistakes or learning from failure have become common phrases in advice to professionals in the design and construction of building and civil structures. Indeed, with the recent rash of dramatic and tragic collapse failures of buildings, bridges, and other major structures, the need for that advice has become urgent. Yet it would appear that all too many experience a serious loss of memory and/or myopia when it comes to learning from their own mistakes and a rather crass indifference when it comes to learning from the mistakes or failures of others. The concept of AEPIC has been developed to assist in the struggle to learn from failures. This concept is predicated on the belief that a systematic collection, collation, analysis, and dissemination of information about the performance (failure) of buildings, civil structures, and other constructed facilities will, in fact and in deed, assist in learning from failures. Professional practice can be improved and poor practices that contribute to failure can be prevented. AEPIC has devloped a substantial computerized data base and has created the techniques to analyze trends and disseminate the lessons about technical and procedural errors and oversights. Currently, new research support grants will move AEPIC into a new level of service for all who support its concept.

Prior to the development of AEPIC, reports of performance failures were filed in isolated storage throughout the world. No centralized source of data on performance was available. AEPIC now has the resources for storage and retrieval of vital information to support a wide range of professional activities.

In the future, it is reasonable to expect that the normal procedures in the process of design analysis will include a summary of AEPIC data for the building, structure, and material type contemplated. For a little effort, it may be possible to avoid repeating many of the mistakes of the past. This should lead, ultimately, to a diminishing rate of performance failures, fewer confrontations in the courts, an improved codes and standards development process, and a reduction in insurance premiums.

Support from engineers, architects, and design professionals in private practice, education, research, government, and business, as well as constructors, building owners, lawyers, and all others who wish to improve the performance of the built environment is necessary in order to make AEPIC a helpful resource for all.

Format for Data Input at AEPIC

The major activity of the AEPIC Conference and Workshop in 1982 and 1984 was the creation of a format for data that would be useful for a wide range of users, since the needs of the researcher, the practicing professional, the educator, and the building official are quite different. Several hundred persons representing a wide range of interests have shared their concerns to produce as close to a consensus as possible for the data-reporting forms. In 1984, the Performance Report Form (long form) and the Document Citation Form were created. In 1986, the Quick Code Performance Report was created in conjunction with a Quick Code Dictionary. The Quick Code permits the recording of all of the critical data of the Performance Report long form in numerical codes for more efficient computer retrieval.

Performance Report Form

PART A: REPORTER, ACCESSIONS DATA

A110/115   describes the alpha-numeric used as a format for data, whether used on one's word processor or computer or if one uses the actual form.

A120   requests that all reports, documents, photos, etc, used in the report will be identified, labeled, and enclosed, if possible.

A130   queries the reporter as to services performed in connection with the reported event, and asks if reporter can be contacted by AEPIC or by others in regard to the event.

A140/150   asks for business card and/or name, address, occupation, professional affiliation, registration or licensure, and present position and organization of reporter.

It should be noted again that all reports in the data base are depersonalized and *no* names of persons, trade names, specific addresses, and other information of an identification type are included.

PART B: PROJECT IDENTIFICATION AND DESCRIPTION

B 200   Terminology: (Technical or professional reference for use of terms, eg, CSI, AIA, ASTM, etc)

B 210   Project Name, Function: (Building type, bridge, dam, etc)

B 220   Location: (Nearest place, milestone, state in the United States, etc)

B 230   Overall Project Systems, Materials: (Structural system, construction type, structural and cladding materials)

B 240   Overall Project Dimensions: (Length, width, number of stories, span, square feet of area, etc)

B 250   Project Dates, Cost: (Design, construction, occupancy, etc)

B 255   Alterations During or Since Construction: (Dates, costs, etc)

B 260   Component(s), Element(s) Involved, Materials:

B 270   Component, Element Dimensions:

B 280   Conditions, Agents, Catalysts: (Loads, pressures, forces, temperature, weather, accumulations, impact, vibrations, etc)

B 285   Contracts, Codes, Laws: (Applicable, allegedly violated, for design, construction; violation established, etc)

B 290   Equipment, Products, Tools: (For transport, lifting, erection, assembly, etc, related to problem)

B 295   Special Factors: (Unspecified data, nonstandard use, unusual conditions, etc)

PART C: PERFORMANCE EVENTS, ANALYSIS, CONCLUSIONS AND RECOMMENDATIONS

C 300   Description of Events: (Dates, timespans, seasons, stages, signs, conditions, observed events, persons and roles, discovery, diagnosis, initial remedial measure, results, injuries, deaths, economic losses, replacements, repair, reconstruction, progress of investigation, dispute resolution, legal proceedings, outcomes, settlements, payments, damages, etc)

C 310   Analysis: (Analysis, investigations performed, by whom—reporter, investigator, government official, etc)

C 320   Conclusions: (Apparent or established major cause or last agent, factor or error; contributing agents, etc; specific acts or omissions, missing information, unknown facts, miscommunication, noncommunication)

C 330   Recommendations: (Overall recommendations; proposed act or conduct which would avoid problem or lessen severity. Proposed changes in practice or procedure to incorporate lessons in quality assurance industry-wide)

PART D: SKETCHES, KEYWORDS, COMMENTS

D 410   Caption: [Title of sketch(s)]

D 420   Scale: [Scale of sketch(s)]
        Draw or include sketch/diagram

D 420   Keywords: (List from six to nine of the most descriptive words related to and descriptive of the event)

D 440   Comments, Postscripts

Document Citation Form

P 100   Published _____   Unpublished _____
P 110   Title:
P 200   Author(s):
P 300   Source, Publisher:
P 400   Publisher City, State:
P 500   Periodicals:
P 510   Date
P 520   Volume
P 530   Number
P 540   Pages _____ to _____
P 600   Books, Pamphlets, Serials:
P 610   Date
P 700   Series Title
P 800   Event, Date, or Timespan
P 820   Abstract:
P 850   Keywords:
P 900   Reporter Information

A brief "Quick Code" is also included with the Document Citation as a cross-reference to Performance Reports.

BIBLIOGRAPHY

1. R. DiPasquale, "Building Failures Forum," *Newsletters,* R. DiPasquale, Ithaca, N.Y., 1980–1981.

2. J. Feld, *Construction Failure,* John Wiley & Sons, Inc., New York, 1968.

3. N. FitzSimons, "An Historical Perspective of Failures of Civil Engineering Works," *Forensic Engineering: Learning from Failures,* American Society of Civil Engineers (ASCE), New York, 1986.

4. B. B. LePatner and S. M. Johnson, *Structural and Foundation Failures: A Casebook for Architects, Engineers, and Lawyers,* McGraw-Hill, Inc., New York, 1982.

5. T. H. McKaig, *Building Failures: Case Studies in Construction and Design,* McGraw-Hill, Inc., New York, 1962.

6. S. S. Ross, *Construction Disasters: Design Failures, Causes and Prevention,* McGraw-Hill, Inc., New York, 1984.

7. Long-Span Building Panel, *Toward Safer Long-Span Buildings,* American Institute of Architects (AIA), Washington, D.C., 1981.

8. Committee on Forensic Engineering, *Report of the Working Group on Information Dissemination, Committee on Forensic Engineering,* American Society of Civil Engineers (ASCE), New York, Mar. 1984.

9. United States House of Representatives, Committee on Science and Technology, Subcommittee on Investigation and Oversight on Causes of Structural Failure in Public Facilities, *Structural Failures,* Hearing before the Subcommittee, Apr. 25, 1984, U.S. Government Printing Office, Washington, D.C., 1984.

10. J. Loss, "Finally—A Data Base on Building Performance Dysfunctions," *Architectural Technology,* American Institute of Architects (AIA), Washington, D.C., Fall 1984.

11. C. R. Vince, "Construction Claims Facing Radical Shifts," *National Underwriter* (Aug. 5, 1983).

12. *Opinions of Building Owners on the Construction Industry: A Report to Wagner-Hohns-Ingilis, Inc.,* Opinion Research Div., Fleishman-Hillard, Inc., St. Louis, Mo., Sept. 1983.

13. AEPIC, *Architecture and Engineering Performance Notes,* **1** (1) (June 1985).

14. Engineering News Record Editor, "Man of the Year Awards," *Engineering News Record* (Jan, 1984).

15. J. C. Peck and W. A. Hoch, "Liability of Engineers for Structural Design Errors: State of the Art Considerations in Defining the Standard of Care," *Villanova Law Review,* **30** (2), 403–439 (1985).

16. C. R. Vince, "Construction Insurance: An Alternative Unified Risk Insurance," *Forensic Engineering: Learning from Failures,* American Society of Civil Engineers (ASCE), New York, 1986.

See also ARBITRATION IN CONSTRUCTION; CONSTRUCTION LAW; CONTRACT ADMINISTRATION; LIABILITY INSURANCE; MEDIATION IN ARCHITECTURAL AND CONSTRUCTION DISPUTES.

JOHN LOSS, AIA
Architecture and Engineering
   Performance Information
   Center
University of Maryland
College Park, Maryland

ARCHITECTURE/PLANNING RELATIONSHIP

The practices of architecture and planning are associated traditionally, institutionally, methodologically, and symbolically with the design of cities and have been enduring handmaidens in the processes of city building. Architecture, it may be said, is the art and science of organizing space and building elements in a coherent structure. Planning is, similarly, the art and science of forethought in the arrangement of land uses, city elements, pathways, open space, and service systems. Both practices deal with the intentional direction of "human activities and natural forces with reference to the future" (1) and the fusion, in harmonious actions, of technology, labor, materials, and urban service systems to some purposeful objective. The discussion of the relationship of these practices is limited to the urban setting and city building. Both architecture and planning practice may be much larger in scope. Often regional, state, or national levels of planning and design occur, but this article focuses on the city because these uniquely human activities are more specifically evident in the places, buildings, artifacts, and cultural characteristics of cities and urban places.

TRADITIONAL RELATIONSHIP

Architecture and planning include related yet differing applications of scientific method as well as historical, intellectual, and artistic traditions. These traditions have developed over many hundreds of years. Development has been influenced by cultural change, architectural styles, emerging economic and political systems, and diffusion of ideas as people moved in place and time.

As built environments evolved from agrarian villages of antiquity to more specialized human settlements, the personal power of the village chief grew into urban kingships. In the earliest efforts to build cities, people with special knowledge of building became advisers to kings and religious leaders.

The power of these leaders, believed to be divinely bestowed, permitted them to marshal craftsmen and artisans to serve civic and other purposes. Architecture and planning were one, as the management of craft, trade, and materials brought about the need for organization and building skills. The purpose of building was to aggrandize the agora, the temple, and the palace. This citadel thus became the core of the protected city and the symbol of all power. It has been argued that (2)

> . . . the key development here had already been presaged, at a much earlier stage, by the apparent evolution of the hunter into the tribute-gathering chief: a figure repeatedly attested in similar developments in many later cycles of civilization. Suddenly this figure assumed superhuman proportions: all his powers and prerogatives became immensely magnified, while those of his subjects, who no longer had a will of their own or could claim any life apart from that of the ruler, were correspondingly diminished.

The citadel thus radiated established power and the protection of the leader, whether considered god, king, or both.

The planner of the city emerged as the manager of craft and trade, the master of design and logistics, and gradually the master builder. The master builder, servant of the king or religious leader, became a specialist in these early societies. He in turn allocated prerogative and status to yet others with special skills. The master builder to the Romans became the architect. For example, the great Roman architect Vitruvius laid down standards for both building design and for city planning, including such notions as orienting streets to protect inhabitants from cold winds. Social and public health objectives appeared as collateral purposes in city building, but architecture continued to be the activity most frequently associated with the design of cities.

Towns and cities were often laid out in firm geometric patterns and fixed in place by the construction of street facades that (3)

> . . . could be regarded as static for an indefinite period of time. To lay out a square, a district or a whole town was to give it a definitive and permanent architectural form, though sufficient margin was allowed to absorb, without basic alteration, any foreseeable growth . . .

An excellent example of this is the Place de Vendôme in Paris, illustrated in Figure 1. Here Mansart, between 1685 and 1699, in honor of Louis XIV, designed and managed the building of facades to define the square. When parcels of land behind the facades were offered for sale, the buyers were required to preserve the facades. The new owners and developers could develop the property behind the facade for their own purposes. This approach to town and city planning by kings and their architects reveals the political and economic reality of seventeenth-century Europe. Planning and architecture were integrated in practice.

This relationship was slow to change, but earlier concerns for population health allowed new specialists to enter the process of city building. By the fourteenth century, official municipal physicians had made their appearance (4), thus foretelling opportunities for specialists in city planning. Yielding to the growth of institutions such as religion, mercantilism, and democracy in governance, cit-

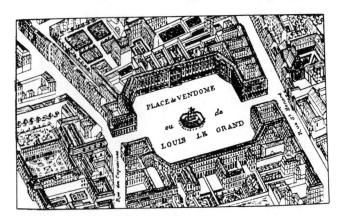

Figure 1. Place de Vendôme in Paris (from Turgot's plan, 1734). This square was designed by Mansart in the 17th century (3). Courtesy of Routledge & Kegan Paul Plc.

ies of the Middle Ages appeared to become more organic while less deterministic in planning philosophy. It has been postulated that (5)

> . . . organic planning does not begin with a preconceived goal: it moves from need to need, from opportunity to opportunity, in a series of adaptations that themselves become increasingly coherent and purposeful, so that they generate a complex, final design, hardly less unified than a pre-formed geometric pattern.

In these early cities, the architect, with legal sanction, did not practice *a priori* planning to guide an incremental growth process. This should not suggest that planning was not practiced. It often resulted from negotiation between the craftsmen and municipal officials guided by ordinance or statute which predicated conformity in style, street pattern, and any other regulation affecting the physical growth of the city (6):

> We need not doubt Descartes . . . when he observes that "there have been at all times certain officers whose duty it is to see that private buildings contributed to public ornament."

A specific example of early regulation is found in the Ordinance of 1563, The Laws of the Indies. As a part of this ordinance, Phillip II of Spain instructed colonizers and city builders of the Caribbean and the Americas with the following language (7):

> The plan of the place, with its squares, streets and building lots is to be outlined by means of measuring by cord and ruler, beginning with the main square from which streets are to run to the gates and principal roads and leaving sufficient open space so that even if the town grows it can always spread in a symmetrical manner.

As western civilization expanded to the North American continent, the responsibility for building cities shifted to the growing private sector. Concentration of civic power diffused and was shared by strong economic and industrial entrepreneurs. This trend was favored and abetted by decentralization of governmental power as young democracies emerged. The architect faced a diminishing role in the planning process. City political leaders, medical doctors or health officers, and civil engineers emerged in roles specialized to cope with new needs in city building. These needs included the building of factories and centers of commerce and the provision for water, sewer, and transportation systems. This unfolding of new roles continued as the variety, number, and character of institutions and technological advances were affected by urbanization.

In the U.S. experience, a clear recognition of private property rights contributed to the need for plotting early towns and cities. The purpose was to define boundaries of real property, but it also served to facilitate speculation in the marketplace for those with interest in land. In addition, it was necessary to define public rights-of-way to assure public access and street systems. Later, these rights-of-way accommodated water, sewer, transit, and electrical distribution systems. Thus, land surveying was added to the growing list of specialized activities involved in planning.

U.S. city planning in the nineteenth century resulted in part from a disjointed and incremental system of muddled public policies, private land interests, private and public initiatives for industrial development, and the addition of new economies. Free enterprise and weak local governments fostered an environment of freewheeling profiteering (8):

> Cities were laid out as often by real estate developers, engineers, surveyors, and even amateurs as government officials. The plan was most often a simple plotting of streets in a gridiron pattern and the subdivision of blocks into lots for sale.

In this heyday of nonplanning and laissez-faire economics, design was seldom done by architects or planners. The inevitable consequences cast the seeds of reforms and movements which grew in the late nineteenth and early twentieth centuries. These included sanitary reforms, the City Beautiful and City Efficient movements, and strivings for social equity.

ARCHITECTURE/PLANNING GROWING APART

It is the residue of these movements that has influenced the practice of architecture and planning in the United States. Sanitary reform in cities was politically fashionable and necessary. Sanitary reformers based their programs on "empirically grounded explanations of infectious disease, often dubbed the filth theory by medical historians" (9). These findings and the discovery in England during the 1840s that relatively small pipes could be used for wastewater provided the incentives and technique for the design and building of sanitary sewer systems. In addition to the existing road and street systems, this new development provided linkages between the lots and building sites of the city.

Until the last decade of the nineteenth century, the practice of architecture concerned itself with buildings on a site-by-site basis; the practice of planning was not yet a coherent set of activities. Planning remained ill-defined among scattered and discrete functions of civic bureaucracies which were primarily concerned with public health and public works.

During the last three decades of the nineteenth century (10),

> . . . architecture, on the down grade since the twenties, had by 1860 touched the bottom. Before every new manifestation of industrial society in cities and buildings, the word "ugly" became inescapable. Within thirty years the situation had changed: the foundation of a new architecture was reunited to the city development in the boulevards and parks designed in New York, Balitmore, Boston, Chicago, Kansas City, and many other communities . . .

This new idea for the design of boulevards and parks brought a new national approach to city design into focus.

The City Beautiful movement branched from these roots, as did municipal and outdoor art and civic improvements (11):

Each played a vital, if now forgotten, role in launching the movement; each had distinct historical roots predating the Chicago World's Fair; and each began with different constituencies.

As the depression of the 1890s lifted, "architects in New York and elsewhere . . . had dreamed of large-scale civic embellishments, though not comprehensive city planning" (12). These large-scale civic plans and projects resulted in many architectural design competitions in cities all over the country. Some architects advanced their own concepts for civic design. One such example, Daniel Burnham's personal scheme for the Chicago lakefront, is illustrated in Figure 2.

These activities relating to civic embellishment did not yet mean comprehensive city planning, but (13)

Certain architects by 1898–1899 favored large plans, and their thinking pointed toward the scheme for Washington in 1901 (The Senate Park Commission Plan, also known as, The McMillan Plan) and other grand designs celebrated as part of the City Beautiful.

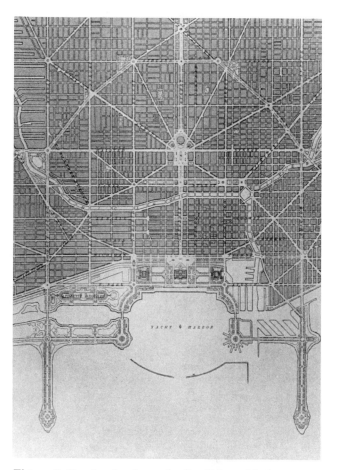

Figure 2. Burnham's scheme for the Chicago lakefront, 1909 (7).

Others, artists and architects alike, felt that the City Beautiful was an incremental process and that every bit and piece could contribute to the quality of the whole.

As for the architecture of the movement, Louis Sullivan wrote that (14):

The virus of the World's Fair, after a period of incubation in the architectural profession and in the population at large, especially the influential, began to show unmistakable signs of the nature of the contagion. There came a violent outbreak of the Classic and the Renaissance in the East, which slowly spread westward, contaminating all that it touched . . . Thus architecture died in the land of the free and the home of the brave . . . in land declaring its fervid democracy, its inventiveness, its resourcefulness, its unique daring, enterprise and progress. Thus did the virus of a culture, snobbishness and alien to the land, perform its work of disintegration; and thus ever works the pallid academic mind . . . The damage wrought by the World's Fair will last for half a century from its date, if not longer.

Sullivan's stern observations were prophetic and only a handful of architects, among them his apprentice, Frank Lloyd Wright, influenced architecture and city planning independent of the neoclassic nostalgia in U.S. cities. However, the grand planning of the City Beautiful movement seemed to give rise to new concepts in city planning. The sanitary condition and housing surveys of the late nineteenth century revealed the poor and often desperate sanitary and housing conditions in older and industrialized cities.

The concept of large-scale planning combined with the idea of Garden Cities created by Englishman Ebenezer Howard gave impetus to the development of the Greenbelt Towns of the late teens and early 1920s and the start of construction of Radburn, N.J., in 1928. These were not redevelopment projects but freestanding new towns set in regions becoming urbanized. Architects such as Clarence Stein and associates in the Regional Planning Association of America, founded in 1923, provided a fresh application of principles of design and modern city building (8,15,16). In planning for Radburn, N.J., principles of design were spurred by beliefs in social equity, the future of the automobile, pedestrian safety, and the convenience of shoppers and school children. In addition, open space and greenways were integrated into the design concepts. For a discussion of this era of U.S. architecture and planning, see Ref. 8. Particularly interesting discussions of the development of new towns and the emerging interest in social equity in city planning can be found in Refs. 15 and 16.

The most significant outgrowth of the development of Radburn and the Greenbelt Towns was the work of the Regional Planning Association of America, which brought together like-minded architects, engineers, economists, and sociologists (8,15,16). Here, the principles of design, economics, and the social sciences coalesced in planning teams which foretold the direction of architectural and planning practice. The planning of cities for the aesthetic demands of the City Beautiful movement had joined with the demands and realities of urban life.

In 1927, John D. Rockefeller, Jr., became interested

in leasing three blocks of midtown Manhattan. Rockefeller Center became a forerunner of large-scale commercial redevelopment projects following World War II. It was the only large private permanent construction project planned and executed between the Depression and the end of the War (17). The influence of this project on the practice of architecture and planning led to redevelopment projects such as La Defense Zone in Paris, as well as those in many U.S. cities. It inspired the urban-renewal programs of President Eisenhower and subsequent administrations. Architects and planners were employed in teams for these large-scale projects. These new programs, which utilized governmental powers in concert with private entrepreneurships, prepared architects and planning leaders to organize new institutions for city planning.

INSTITUTIONAL RELATIONSHIPS

From the above traditions, architects and planners saw planning as a set of activities much broader than the discrete design of buildings on separate parcels of land. Economic and social pathologies of the city were not adequately apprehended in independent designs of structure, nor were these problems moving toward any resolution. Perceived urban problems in U.S. cities brought architects, city engineers, landscape architects, and civic leaders, such as Alfred Bettman of Cincinnati, together. In 1909, the first national conference on city planning was held in the United States. The diversity of participants at this conference can be shown by its sponsors: the Committee on Congestion of Population in New York, the American Institute of Architects, the American Society of Landscape Architects, the League of American Municipalities, the American Civic Association, and the National Conference of Charities and Corrections. The first chairman of the conference was Frederick L. Ford, city engineer of Hartford, Conn.

At this first conference, many cities reported on their planning activities. These included plans and programs to improve housing and health conditions, street design, aesthetics, architectural quality of buildings for both civic and private purposes, and establishment of parks and "green spaces." Other reports recommended proposals for state legislation governing city planning and construction of buildings. It was argued that city planning should not be the responsibility of the private sector, as had been fashionable, but of city government. The scope and wide variety of issues and the diversity of professional participation growing out of this conference spurred the development of the American City Planning Institute and other organizations concerned with city planning. By the time the 27th conference on city planning was held, in Cincinnati in 1935, there were four sponsoring organizations: the American City Planning Institute, the American Civic Association, the American Society of Planning Officials, and the National Conference on City Planning.

During these years of growth and change, city planning emerged as a set of activities fashioned by the demand for social, economic, and urban systems (eg, traffic) analysis, all embedded in municipal political processes. The

traditional architectural concerns for physical planning were no longer the reasons for being in city planning. However, the general land-use plan survived the influx of urban sociologists, economists, and public administrators into the city planning realm.

Architectural schools had long been the hosts and stewards of architectural and planning education. The curricula were considered to be so similar as to preclude specialized training. During the second decade of the twentieth century, schools in the United States began to offer specialized graduate degrees in city planning. Students at first were drawn from architecture and landscape architecture, but much later, the pool of undergraduates became broader. A study in the 1960s of the San Francisco Bay area found a strong shift from undergraduate education in architecture and landscape architecture to other areas of study, such as political science, economics, law, and sociology (18):

> . . . This means that the planner is a full-time professional in a field marked by technical standards of achievement for the evaluation of performance; operates in the absence of conventional profit motives, with the presumption that he will be sparring in the intrusion of his own values and will venerate "objectivity"; and is first and foremost a community servant who will put the common good above self interest.

City planning thus shifted from the City Beautiful movement of the nineteenth and the early twentieth century to a profession dedicated to analysis of urban problems and the offering of reasoned alternatives for public policy. At its core was a holistic, systematic view of the city with all of its complex parts, in contrast to the strictly physical and architectural view, which is often piecemeal and incremental in scope.

Architects and city planners were represented by separate professional societies by the mid-1930s. The American Institute of Architects (AIA), the American City Planning Institute (later to become the American Institute of Planners, and, since 1978, the American Planning Association (APA) and the American Institute of Certified Planners (AICP), grew to be well-established national organizations with considerable influence in national politics. This same organizational influence also affected the quality and direction of the educational institutions responsible for research and training of the two professions. In addition to these associations, there are an American Society of Consulting Planners and an Association of Registered Architects.

During the 1940s and 1950s, pervasive and responsible political action, organized by architects and planners, encouraged national policies designed to improve city planning and housing. During the debates, the concept of the city master plan was given considerable currency and was supported by many national organizations, including those of architects and planners. As a result of these debates and national research, planning was supported through federal legislation which provided for city, urban, county, and state assistance programs. Thus, cities during the 1950s and 1960s received federal and state government assistance for master plans. Sanctions were applied to cities if certain planning efforts were not made by local jurisdictions. Among the purposes of these programs were provisions for housing development, open space, and transportation planning. In addition, urban-renewal programs for older cities followed World War II. Urban renewal was the subject of another national debate which brought both the architectural and planning professions into the fray.

When the debate subsided and a national policy for urban renewal was enacted, architects and planners discovered a new working relationship in planning and designing for very large and significant redevelopment projects. Many of these, including South West Washington, D.C., illustrated in Figure 3, stand as exciting evidence of cooperation and collaboration between architects and planners. Social, economic, and functional systems and architectural quality were blended in successful city building.

Transportation planners working toward the implementation of the 1954 Interstate Highway Program caused massive intrusions into developed urban areas as they located limited-access and multilane highways. These highway and redevelopment programs caused significant social and economic dislocations in many cities which resulted in part in a review of these policies by architects, planners, public agencies, and social scientists. Because of these reviews, coupled with an emerging concern for overall urban and natural environments, national policies of planning continued to add requirements for social, economic, and environmental impacts when large renewal and highway projects were proposed.

Education

Planning educators added new analytical imperatives to study programs, and architectural educators expanded into areas of urban and environmental design. However, architecture continued to serve the individual, corporate, or public client with an emphasis on its contractual re-

sponsibilities. Planners served a variety of public clients with an emphasis on civic and social responsibilities as consultants or public employees. These relationships often generated advocacy roles for planning and architecture in the milieu of municipal politics and the formulation of public policy in urban design. Architects often viewed these encounters as hopeless "in the process of social reconstruction because industrial society cannot generate the political and cultural conditions that will enable good design to flourish" (19). One author described how planning and architecture were drawing apart (20):

It seems to me that the "urban design" approach growing out of architecture is much more active at present than the "physical planning" perspective, in part because so many city planning professionals and city planning schools and departments have oriented their teaching programs to an exclusive concern with issues of social and economic policy and research.

The urban-design approach referred to is the practice of planning and architecture which focuses the two professions onto large-scale urban development and redevelopment projects. Taught in some architectural schools as a specialty in architecture and planning, it is not yet generally recognized as an independent field. However, increasing interest in urban design is found both among academics and practitioners in architecture and planning. The Institute for Urban Design is organized to educate and promulgate information on this subject.

In the late 1960s, the American Institute of Architects, in its report to the Committee for the Future of the Profession, found that (21):

The institutions for education and research are not strong when compared to other professional or academic fields. They have an unproductive record of scholarship, research, and development, particularly when compared to engineering. Most schools lag behind the practicing profession both in quality

Figure 3. Southwest Washington, D.C., urban renewal project, 1963.

of personnel, development of new theory and method, and as a training ground for professional practice.

These studied thoughts have led to reevaluations of both planning and architectural education during the 1970s and 1980s. Planning schools are tending toward a more cogent concern for physical design and public policy, and architectural schools are seeking faculty with advanced degrees and relevant research.

Educators in the universities have begun to meet this challenge by establishing six new doctoral programs in architecture; more are in the planning stage. Many federal, state, and local agencies now recognize the importance of architectural research, and regularly fund projects dealing with architectural planning disciplines. In both this country and abroad, there is a growing awareness of the need for and value of architectural research. Members of the architectural profession, faculty at the nation's schools, and leaders of the American Institute of Architects have all worked to bring about these changes. Planning schools and educators continue in widely based research efforts which have become an integrated part of training for many years.

It has been suggested by at least one author that architecture and planning education should impart three central skills to the architect or planner in order to advance city design (22):

A sharp and sympathetic eye for the interaction between people, places, place events, and the institutions that manage them. A thorough grounding in the theory, technique, and values of city design. . . . Finally, I think that a city designer must be skilled in communication, and have a passion to express and learn.

Architectural and planning educations are bound by separate institutional arrangements, but there is an intermingling of theory and research. Often this mingling occurs in faculty and student studio settings. These studios are found in planning and architectural programs housed in schools of architecture where a growing emphasis is on teaching the skills referred to above.

METHODOLOGICAL RELATIONSHIP

Architecture and planning are clearly related in their intellectual traditions. Both deal with the possibility of intervening in city building in such a way as to alter the quality, conditions, and appearance of the built environment. This is accomplished by means of the process of planning and design. One author (23) offers some insight into differentiating the process of planning by arguing that determinants and constraints provide the measure of blueprint versus process planning. Architecture is stated to be predominantly blueprint planning, whereas planning as practiced today is predominantly process. The diagram in Figure 4, taken from the same source (23), partially illustrates this differentiation.

Determinants are images and control. Images result when the designer or planner is dealing with a problem

Blueprint Planning		Process Planning
Determinants		
Firm	Image	Uncertain
Complete	Control over environment	Incomplete
Constraints		
Short	Internal time-lag	Long
Short	External time-lag	Long

Figure 4. Determinants and constraints of blueprint versus process planning (23).

or set of problems. They may be firm or uncertain. For example, an architect approaching a project on a given site often finds the environment of the proposed project is limited to the nature of site conditions and the functions and activities to be provided in the project. These functions are most often predetermined by the interest and requirements of users. Furthermore, any public policies, such as zoning and building codes, establish additional project requirements. Thus, the designer begins with a level of certainty not afforded in process planning.

Process planning is usually found in a public arena with uncertain boundaries. The planner must be more concerned with the framework within which individuals operate than with controlling their actual conduct (24). This tends to define a working space with often unclear institutional boundaries. This sometimes leads to more general plans and proposals than seen in the designs of architects. Solutions to the problem are frequently offered as alternatives; therefore, decisions are made by choosing from the set of alternatives. Examples of this are seen in alternative land-use patterns in development areas of cities. Uncertainty tends to rule process planning whereas blueprint planning is relatively certain.

Another determinant discussed in Ref. 23 is environmental and decision control. If an entrepreneur sets out to build a freestanding new community backed by a well-financed organization, he or she establishes design and planning parameters and follows the blueprint-planning process closely. There is a very controlled environment in which to pursue projected objectives. On the other hand (25),

incomplete control means that (public) planning agencies must anticipate what other agents will do, striking bargains with them and responding to opportunities as they arise.

In this bargaining model, planning activity is much more heuristic in the sense that fitness is not controlled but results from constant adjustment of strategies and objectives in the light of negotiation.

Constraints in the model discussed above (and in Ref.

25) deal with time lag. Internal time lag results from the necessary steps in the design or planning process. Very large public-works projects, such as the Interstate Highway System in the United States, are affected by the changes in technology and public attitudes during the many years that such projects require in planning and development. In blueprint planning, most often related to specific projects, the time lag is short. Time lag in comprehensive planning processes is usually long and the opportunity for plan review infrequent. This results in much public frustration with the comprehensive planning process and accordingly attenuates public support.

External time lag is evident in massive public-works projects and in process planning. In comprehensive city and community planning, with some exceptions in rapidly growing urban areas, feedback, or information regarding the impact of the plan, is slow to reach the planning agency. Similar conditions exist for public-works projects of large scope. One such example is the Interstate Highway System, which was designed for 70-mph speeds before the energy crises of the mid-1970s had a major impact on these criteria. Similar problems may affect the community planner and developer as markets and public policies affecting development change.

If the blueprint and process-planning approaches are understood, the action spaces of architecture and planning can be partly explained. Of particular interest is the determinant: image. Architecture begins with a much more focused program for design, whereas planning begins with a framework for action. It is not reasonable to relate the practice of architecture to a completely deterministic view of its scope any more than it is to attribute to planning omnipotence in the development of cities (26):

> Since time immemorial planners and architects have tried to systematize their methods of designing and carrying out the forms of buildings and towns—to be philosophers—designers competent to formulate, without error, schemas for any predetermined purpose. . . . Architecture has traditionally been produced by the interaction of a designer's experience, intellect, aesthetic sensitivity, and common sense. . . . A city, when it was consciously planned or designed at all, drew largely upon the same creative sources, with correspondingly larger but more poorly defined sets of objectives and constraints.

This argues for architecture and planning in a realm of overlapping action spaces in city building. The relationships have been historically elastic and in today's industrial and complex cities the boundaries are indeed ill-defined. Architecture is influenced by the same social, economic, and cultural forces that impact upon planning. The city is a complex of physical, institutional, and social systems that draws on the intellect of architects and planners in somewhat differing ways, but both serve the evolution of the character of urban places. It is the decision-making context that is different. Architecture reveals itself in its physical and sometimes poetic form in the controlled marketplace of the client and the client's specific purposes, whereas planning is most often found in the realm of city politics and the public forces that constrain choice for law, regulation, and public policy.

The methods thus employed by architecture and planning, although related in many ways, operate in differing decision milieus. The diagram in Figure 5 attempts to describe the activities in both the design process and the planning process. These are not neat, linear steps. The

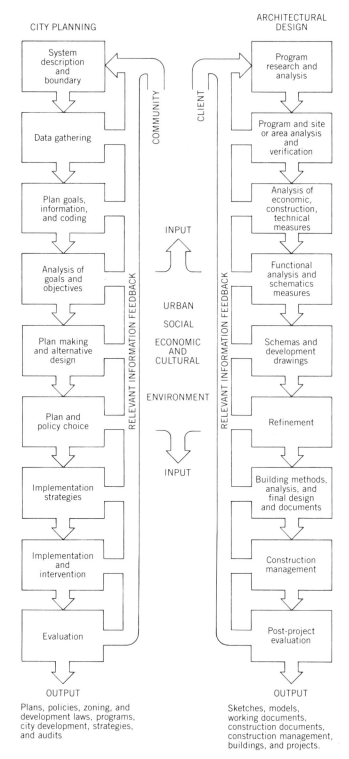

Figure 5. A flow chart diagramming architectural design and city planning processes and identifying major sets of activities and an iterative relationship.

order of the suggested activities is more for descriptive purpose than it is a reflection of absolute reality. The processes are iterative at best, even under ideal conditions.

Both architectural design and city planning are rooted in the scientific method. Theorizing and categorizing lead to data gathering and hypothesis testing. In architecture, this is not a rigorous statistical procedure as might be found in planning methods, but it flows from the imaginative, intuitive, cognitive, and intellectual strength and skills of the designer. Findings, conclusions, and intervention follow. Depending on time lag, evaluation may provide feedback to the design and planning procedures.

In this diagram, there are nine iterative and even elliptical related steps. In architectural design, these include program research and analysis, program verification, analysis of economic and environmental resources, schematic design and conceptualization, development drawings, refinement of final design concepts, construction documents, construction management, and, finally, post-project evaluation. In this diagram or discussion, no attempt is being made to describe design/build approaches in the United States. Some architects and builders engage in design/build operations today in order to reduce some of the time lag that exists in conventional approaches to design and then build.

The sequence of steps in the planning process are as follows: definition of the system and its boundaries; data gathering; recording of information and goals; analysis of goals and resources; plan making and alternative generating; plan choice; selecting strategies for implementation; implementation; and evaluation.

Architectural Design

The architectural design process usually begins with a stated building program, or it may begin with research to determine need in a particular building type. At this point, it is necessary to clarify the requirements and understand any public or private constraints that will impact upon the project. Clear understanding between the client and designer is important to the success of subsequent steps. The program is verified by the architect in order to develop a clear image of the program. In addition to verification, an analysis of the costs that will be involved and all of the urban and environmental factors which will affect the design must be understood. In these procedures, the architect finds an opportunity to view the project in its urban and environmental context. Many techniques, modern systems, and materials are available to the contemporary designer to increase the potential fitness of a final project design.

Those skills and sensitivities discussed previously as necessary to the designer are truly manifested in the conceptualization and schematic phases of the design process. It is here that architecture can fulfill a broader role in city building. It requires a conscious and articulated approach to the problem-solving process. Social, economic, and cultural values enrich the opportunity for city design. The schema is developed and choices are made by the designer and the client. The steps that follow require refinement of detail and architectural quality. They are rich in design and application of technology and building methods. Post-project analysis and evaluation are infrequently employed but can be of great benefit to the knowledge of the art and science of architecture.

The Planning Process

The planning process is first revealed in the context of its setting. It may be concerned with a limited set of systems or problems or with an entire set of urban systems and the entire city. Thus, the first step is a determination of the scope of planning. It is necessary to identify the relevant institutions, the participant groups or actors in the process, and the temporal and physical boundaries of the study area. Moreover, the characteristics of urban and environmental systems must be determined along with behavioral patterns and trends. It is also useful to identify any existing national, state, or local policies or plans that may be in effect. Data is then gathered to portray the nature and quality of the study area. Population and economic base studies, among many others, are included in this step. Information is coded and systematically organized to form a basis for analysis. Goals of the plan must be drawn from the community to be served by the plan, and carefully designed techniques for public involvement can be employed to assist in the articulation of community goals.

Plan making utilizes the skills, experience, intellect, sensitivity, and common sense of the designer and planner. Plan choice is usually a public process because the institutions of governance are vested with this responsibility. Strategies and implementation should be consistent with the resources and jurisdictional powers that are available. Evaluation is designed to retrieve relevant information with regard to the effects of the chosen plan.

The diagram of these processes advanced here is offered only to identify the major sets of activities involved in architectural design and planning. The methodological relationship is similar. There has been no attempt to identify all of the technologies used in these practices. Data gathering and research offered by architectural and planning schools and the social, natural, and engineering sciences feed the knowledge that supports these activities. Public agencies, universities, private research organizations, and professional societies provide for technological transfer using publication, continuing education programs, and seminars.

SYMBOLIC RELATIONSHIP

Architecture and planning are drawn together in literature and in the reality of the public marketplace. It has been said that (27) writing on

> . . . architecture and city planning involves more than a mere discussion of specific artistic problems. The plan of a house, the form of an office building, and the layout of a town represent nothing else than the crystallization of a living cultural situation.

It has also been suggested that (27)

> Planners think of the city not as an end in itself, but in terms of happier, more adequate human beings.

The symbolic underpinnings of architecture and planning are most difficult to differentiate. Some see this as more than a symbolic relationship in a set of activities called urban design. Urban design can be viewed as a deliberate and intentional process of (28)

> . . . giving perceptible shape to a community in creating its physical environment in response to stated social, economic, and aesthetic objectives, ultimately, to every last detail.

The old divisions of labor between architecture and planning tend to evaporate in the context of urban reality. That reality includes growing and more definitive regulatory measures to protect the health, welfare, safety, and aesthetic well-being of citizens. Architecture and planning are associated with this phenomenon in the minds of the public. It is an inescapable association; although the currents of education in recent decades have tended to flow in separate channels, the flood of reality forces confluence. This confluence is primarily the result of the overlapping action spaces of the two professional practices. A common concern for the built environment will continue to be the symbol, if not the reality, of architecture and planning.

The traditions, the institutions, the methods, and the symbolic relationships seem well-documented in the literature and practice of these professions. Architecture will continue to offer the hope of visual quality to the city; planning will continue to cope with its complex framework of public policy and the allocation of land uses. Planning will hone its social consciousness, and architecture will sharpen its focus on the anticipatory but fleeting nature of beauty. They may struggle apart, but the prospects of building cities independently is not easily supported.

BIBLIOGRAPHY

1. M. C. Branch, *Comprehensive Planning: General Theory and Principles,* Palisades Publishers, Pacific Palisades, Calif., 1983, p. 2. A thorough treatment of the comprehensive planning process as practiced in the United States today, it is a valuable source for additional reading.

2. L. Mumford, *The City in History,* Harcourt Brace Jovanovich, Inc., Orlando, Fla., 1961, Martin Secker & Warburg, Ltd., London, 1961, p. 35. A classic, this book provides essential and authoritative information on the evolution of cities for the student of architecture and city planning.

3. L. Benevolo, *The Origins of Modern Town Planning,* The MIT Press, Cambridge, Mass., 1967, p. 12.

4. Ref. 2, p. 296.

5. Ref. 2, p. 302.

6. Ref. 2, p. 311.

7. J. W. Reps, *The Making of Urban America,* Princeton University Press, Princeton, N.J., 1965, p. 29. An exceptionally rich source for the study of cities in the United States which carefully ties this development to its European heritage, it con-

tains a marvelous collection of city plan maps and early oblique views.

8. D. A. Krueckeberg, "The Culture of Planning, "in D. A. Krueckeberg, ed., *Introduction to Planning History in the United States,* The Center for Urban Policy Research, New Brunswick, N.J., 1983, p. 3. An excellent reference work on the history of planning and city building with contributions from outstanding authors.

9. Ref. 8, p. 14.

10. Ref. 2, pp. 112–113.

11. J. A. Peterson, "The City Beautiful Movement: Forgotten Origins and Lost Meanings," in Ref. 8, p. 41.

12. J. A. Peterson in Ref. 8, p. 42.

13. J. A. Peterson in Ref. 8, p. 45.

14. L. Sullivan, *The Autobiography of An Idea,* Dover Publications, Inc., New York, 1924, pp. 324–325. In this excellent book especially for students of architecture and planning, the author develops his philosophy of architecture as part of his larger view of democracy and the emerging culture of America.

15. E. L. Birch, "Radburn and the American Planning Movement," in Ref. 8, Pt. 7.

16. W. H. Wilson, "Moles and Skylarks," in Ref. 8, Pt. 6.

17. C. H. Krinsky, *Rockefeller Center,* Oxford University Press, Inc., New York, 1978, p. 5. A thorough account of the planning, development, and building of Rockefeller Center, it is well-illustrated with plans and photographs.

18. J. Dyckman, "What Makes Planners Plan," in A. Faludi, ed., *A Reader in Planning Theory,* Pergamon Press, Inc., Elmsford, N.Y., 1973, p. 244.

19. R. Gutman, "The Role of Architectural Theory in Urban Design Education," in A. Ferebee, ed., *Education for Urban Design,* The Institute for Urban Design, Purchase, N.Y., 1982, p. 21.

20. Ref. 19, p. 26.

21. G. M. McCue and W. R. Ewald, Jr., *Creating the Human Environment,* University of Illinois Press, Urbana, Ill., 1970, p. 308. The work of McCue and Ewald is considered to be pivotal in the self-evaluation of architectural education and practice in the 1960s.

22. K. Lynch, "City Design: What It Is and How It Might Be Taught," in Ref. 19, p. 108.

23. A. Faludi, *Planning Theory,* Pergamon Press, Inc., Elmsford, N.Y., 1973, p. 138. An important, comprehensive study of planning theory which carefully compares current theories in circulation and use, although a bit tedious in style.

24. Ref. 23, p. 139.

25. Ref. 23, p. 140.

26. F. Ferguson, *Architecture, Cities, and the Systems Approach,* George Braziller, Inc., New York, 1975, p. 1. Advances many approaches to the application of systems methods to planning and design.

27. P. Zucker, *New Architecture and City Planning,* Philosophical Library, New York, 1944, pp. 4 and 625.

28. M. Hoppenfield, "Planners as Architects of the Built Environment—or Vice Versa, in R. W. Burchell and G. Sternlieb, eds., *Planning Theory in the 1980s,* The Center for Urban Policy Research, New Brunswick, N.J., 1978, p. 20.

General References

All of the sources above, in their entirety, serve as good general references.

K. Lynch, *The Image of the City,* The MIT Press, Cambridge, Mass., 1960.

EARL M. STARNES, FAIA, AIP
University of Florida
Gainesville, Florida

ART GALLERIES.   See MUSEUMS

ART IN ARCHITECTURE.   See ORNAMENT IN ARCHITECTURE

ART NOUVEAU

The term Art Nouveau refers to an international art movement during the years 1895–1912. The term was derived from an art gallery in Paris called Maison de l'Art Nouveau which displayed the work of progressive artists and designers. Although the new art was called by other names in other countries, art nouveau has become the term applied to progressive art of the period.

Its style was derived from the work of William Morris in book and fabric design and other designers of the Arts and Crafts movement in England. Art nouveau is characterized by the use of waves, flames, flower stalks, or flowing hair in naturalistic or abstracted forms. The concepts of a new art not connected with the past and an integrated approach to all of the arts were identified with the style.

For many architects, artists, and designers, the art nouveau style was a passing interest; their work was identified only later with the international movement. Some architects who have been identified with the Art Nouveau include:

Great Britain (Arts and Crafts Movement)
Charles Rennie Mackintosh (1868–1928) (Glasgow School)
Charles Francis Annesley Voysey (1857–1941)

Spain (Modernismo)
Antoni Gaudi I Cornet (1852–1926)

Belgium (Art Nouveau)
Victor Horta (1861–1947)
Henry-Clement Van de Velde (1863–1957)

France (Art Nouveau)
Hector-Germain Guimard (1867–1942)

Holland (Art Nouveau)
Hendrik Petrus Berlage (1856–1924)

Switzerland (Art Nouveau)
Charles-Edouard Jeanneret (Le Corbusier) (1887–1965)

Germany (Jugenstil)
Peter Behrens (1868–1940)

Italy (Liberty)
Antonio Sant'Elia (1888–1916)

Austria (Secession)
Otto Koloman Wagner (1841–1918)
Joseph Maria Olbrich (1867–1908)
Josef Hoffmann (1870–1956)

United States (Chicago School, Prairie, Bungalow)
Louis Henri Sullivan (1856–1924)
Frank Lloyd Wright (1867–1959)
Charles Sumner Greene (1868–1957)
Henry Mather Greene (1870–1954)

See also ARCHITECTURAL STYLES; BEHRENS, PETER; BERLAGE, H.P.; GAUDI, ANTONIO; GREENE & GREENE; HOFFMANN, JOSEF; HORTA, VICTOR; LE CORBUSIER (CHARLES-EDOUARD JEANNERET); OLBRICH, JOSEPH MARIA; SANT'ELIA, ANTONIO; SULLIVAN, LOUIS; VAN DE VELDE, HENRY-CLEMENT; WAGNER, OTTO KOLOMAN; WRIGHT, FRANK LLOYD.

ROBERT T. PACKARD, AIA
Reston, Virginia

ARUP, OVE

Ove Arup, the British structural engineer, was born in 1895. He received his engineering degree in Denmark in 1922. His long career involved contracting, structural engineering, consulting (Ove Arup and Partners), and an architectural practice (Arup Associates). His large body of work includes a number of pioneering structures for well-known contemporary buildings. His awards and worldwide recognition reflect his importance as an engineer. A list of his buildings ranges from small projects to major buildings such as The Barbican, City of London (Chamberlain, Howell and Bon, architects).

During the 1930s, he served as the structural engineer for a contracting firm. An early structure of interest was the Penguin Pool in St. Regent's Park in London (1939). After the war, his engineering firm provided structural engineering services for the following projects in addition to many others: 1956–1980, The Barbican, City of London; 1972–1977, Paris, the Pompidou Centre (Piano and Rogers, architects); and 1973, Sydney Opera House (Jorn Utson, architect).

In 1964, the architectural practice was separated from the consulting engineering practice and given the name Arup Associates. They are best known for their university and factory designs.

Sir Ove Arup was the author of several books and many technical articles. In addition, many of his projects have been covered in the architectural press. The care given to even small projects was typical of Ove Arup's concern for all construction, and even as the office became very large, he continued to design.

BIBLIOGRAPHY

General References

M. Emanuel, ed., *Contemporary Architects,* St. Martin's Press, Inc., New York, 1980. Copyright the Macmillan Press, Ltd., New York, 1980.

"Arup's First Ten Years," *Architecture Plus* (Nov./Dec. 1974). *Architecture & Urbanism* (A&U) Tokyo (Dec. 1977).

ROBERT T. PACKARD, AIA
Reston, Virginia

ASBESTOS REMOVAL.   See HAZARDOUS MATERIALS—ASBESTOS

ASPHALT.   See PAVING SYSTEMS, ASPHALT

ASPLUND, ERIK GUNNAR

Erik Gunnar Asplund (1885–1940) was one of the most important Scandinavian architects of the first half of the twentieth century. His early work evolved from National Romanticism through the spare Nordic classicism of the pre- and post-World War I periods, and by 1930 embraced canonical modernism. By the late 1930s, his work had assumed a personal direction, influenced more by traditional architecture and a desire for symbolic content than by the tenets of the International Style. Asplund had a unique ability to create a sense of place in his architecture, to manifest directly the context in which his buildings were situated by manipulating landscape elements as forcefully as architectural ones. His death at age 55 from a heart attack occurred at the height of his creative powers and productivity.

Born in Stockholm in 1885, Asplund studied architecture at the Royal Institute of Technology from 1905 to 1909. After traveling to Germany on an Institute Scholarship, he returned to Stockholm and helped establish—with fellow students O. Almqvist, E. Karlstrand, S. Lewerentz, J. Östlin, and M. Wernstedt—an independent academy of design, the Klara School. Supplanting the more normative neoclassic training of the period, the Klara School, under the invited tutelage of C. Bergsten, R. Östberg, I. Tengbom, and C. Westman, assumed a romantic sensibility acknowledging the influence of Scandinavian vernacular design and handicrafts. The incorporation of vernacular and traditional sources of expression had influenced Nordic architecture since the turn of the century, creating a style known as National Romanticism. The National Romantic influences of Carl Westman and Ragnar Östberg, and in particular Östberg's ability to combine symmetrical facade composition with informal plan organization, informed Asplund's early work: the villa project for I. Asplund (1911), the Karlshamn School competition entry (1912), and the Villa Ruth (1914). These works are characterized by a vernacular imagery created through the use of traditional board and batten siding, tile-covered gable-roof forms, and carefully placed and proportioned window openings.

While continuing to use vernacular imagery, classical motifs began to emerge in Asplund's work. The first-place competition entry for the Woodland Cemetery (1915), done in collaboration with Sigurd Lewerentz, is a strongly romantic composition maximizing the naturalistic features of the site. Asplund's Woodland Chapel (1918–1919) blends romanticism and classicism; the simple steeply pitched roof recalls Swedish vernacular buildings, whereas the austere Doric portico, domed interior space, and white-rendered stucco walls reference classicism. The Villa Snellman (1917–1918), located in the Stockholm suburb of Djursholm, combines these two qualities while demonstrating Asplund's mastery of the compositional techniques found in Östberg's villa designs. In the Lister County Courthouse (1917–1921), the classic–romantic dialogue continues, but the detail qualities become somewhat idiosyncratic, even mannered, in execution. Three competition entries for urban projects entered during the period between 1917 and 1922, the Göta Square (1917) and Gustaf Adolf Square (1918), both in Göteborg, and the Royal Chancellery (1922) in Stockholm, indicate that Asplund's sensitivity in designing buildings within the historical context of the city is equal to that within the natural landscape.

Paralleling the development of classicism in Scandinavia during the 1920s, the classical–romantic duality of Asplund's earlier work gave way to a more explicit expression of classical principles. The work of this period represents a serious attempt at innovation within the context of classicism, rather than a nascent eclecticism. Two buildings in Stockholm, the Skandia Cinema (1922–1923) and the Public Library (1920–1928), demonstrate his leadership position in this Nordic movement. Whereas the Skandia Cinema projects a certain playful and idiosyncratic use of classical elements, motifs, and images, the Public Library (Fig. 1) has a simplicity and austerity reminiscent of the neoclassic architecture of the French Enlightenment. Although the initial design for the library was explicitly classical, with coffered dome, columnar entry porticos, and palazzolike facade treatment, the built work, while maintaining the same organizational *parti,* was abstracted into two simple volumetric elements: cube and cylinder. Preceded by a large reflecting pool, the building sits slightly rotated in its parklike setting, adding further monumentality to the austere volumes. The cylinder houses a great rotunda, which contains the tiered, open-stack lending hall, a monumental clerestoried space which recalls the work of E. L. Boullée. Exterior and interior surfaces are rendered in stucco, with finely proportioned openings and excellently crafted and integrated sculptural detail that provide the building with a subtle power.

The Stockholm Public Library marks the end of Nordic classicism, for "functionalism," as modernism was termed in Scandinavia, began to appear in Sweden. The 1930 Stockholm Exhibition, which celebrated the emergence of functionalism in Sweden, represented a fundamental change in sensibility for Asplund. The design for the Exhibition complex underwent three phases, the last occurring after Asplund traveled to the continent to visit extant examples of the new, "modern" architecture. The Stockholm Exhibition not only epitomized the mechanistic aesthetics of modernism but served as a propaganda instrument for illustrating its social programs. But unlike many modernist compositions, which were isolated objects sitting in green, parklike settings, Asplund's complex assumed a more dense, urban form. The light, machinelike pavilions were tied together by such traditional urban

Figure 1. Public Library, Stockholm 1920–1928. Courtesy of Tomas Mjö-berg, Swedish Museum of Architecture.

elements as squares, concourses, cul-de-sacs, and garden courtyards. The tall constructivist-inspired advertising mast was combined with light steel structures holding signs and flags that provided a festive quality to the Exhibition.

Although Asplund designed the Bredenberg Department Store (1933–1935) in a functionalist vocabulary, the State Bacteriological Laboratories (1933–1937) signaled a move away from the canons of modernism. In his last two major commissions, the Göteborg Law Courts Annex

(originally won in competition in 1913, redesigned in 1925, and finalized and built between 1935 and 1936) and the Woodland Crematorium (1935–1940, Fig. 2), Asplund's reaction to functionalism solidified. The design for the addition to the Law Courts, which were designed by N. Tessin in 1672, was initially conceived of as a direct extension of the original facade. In the final design, Asplund attempted the difficult proposition of developing a facade that would create a contrasting and harmonizing tension between the old and the new. The result not only extends

Figure 2. Woodland Crematorium, Stockholm, 1935–1940. Courtesy of Per Bonde, Swedish Museum of Architecture.

the rhythm of the original, but does so in a modern, yet traditional manner. The central interior atrium, composed of a delicate concrete framework and staircases with superbly detailed wood paneling, has a timeless quality that transcends stylistic preferences.

Asplund's final major work, the Woodland Crematorium, is a composition dominated by the manipulation of the naturalistic qualities of the landscape, making the buildings seem secondary upon approach. Yet the positioning of the primary architectural elements of loggia, wall, and cross actively gathers the surrounding landscape into a dynamic, emotional experience. The complex contains references to traditional, classical, and modern architecture; the planar quality of the buildings stems from modernism and the loggia and impluvium from classical sources, whereas the material usage and landscape design root the building to its Nordic context. The integration Asplund achieved in the complex, through the synthesis of modern with classical and vernacular precedents, makes the Woodland Crematorium, in the final analysis, one of the truly compelling buildings of the twentieth century.

BIBLIOGRAPHY

General References

Asplund: 1885–1940, Swedish Museum of Architecture and Arkitektur Forlag, Stockholm, 1985. Exhibition catalogue with essays by H. O. Andersson and K. Winter.

E. G. Asplund, W. Gahn, S. Markelius, G. Paulsson, E. Sundahl, and U. Ahren, *Acceptera,* Bokforlagsaktiebolaget Tiden, Stockholm, 1931.

C. Caldenby and O. Hultin, eds., *Asplund,* Arkitektur Forlag, Stockholm, 1985. Includes essays by K. Frampton, S. Wrede, E. Cornell, and C. A. Acking.

E. De Mare, *Gunnar Asplund: A Great Modern Architect,* Art & Technics, London, 1955.

A. Hasegawa, ed., *Erik Gunnar Asplund,* Space Design, Tokyo, 1982.

G. Holmdahl, S. I. Lind, and K. Odeen, eds., *Gunnar Asplund, Architect,* Byggmastarens Forlag, Stockholm, 1950 (Swedish ed., 1943; 2nd ed., 1981). Includes an important essay by H. Ahlberg.

E. Nagy, *Erik Gunnar Asplund,* Budapest, 1974.

S. Wrede, *The Architecture of Erik Gunnar Asplund,* The MIT Press, Cambridge, Mass., 1980.

B. Zevi, *Erik Gunnar Asplund,* Il Balcone, Milan, 1948.

WILLIAM C. MILLER, AIA
Kansas State Universtiy
Manhattan, Kansas

ASSOCIATION OF COLLEGIATE SCHOOLS OF ARCHITECTURE (ACSA)

The Association of Collegiate Schools of Architecture is a nonprofit educational organization, founded in 1912 to advance the quality of architectural education. The original organization started with 10 U.S. schools of architecture as charter members. Over the years, participation has grown to such an extent that for the sake of clarity there are now four categories of membership. Voting members are in a category designated as Full Member Schools. Members in this group are schools offering accredited professional architecture programs in the United States or government-approved professional architecture programs in Canada. This category includes virtually all of the 101 recognized schools in both the United States and Canada. All 2700 faculty at these schools automatically receive the full benefits of the Association. Each school has one vote. A category designated as Affiliates includes over 30 members and is open to schools offering nonprofessional programs or architecture courses, and foreign schools offering professional degree programs. A category designated for Individual Members is comprised of over 1000 individuals, architectural firms, architectural product associations, and individual architectural product manufacturers with an interest in architectural education. Candidacy Status is the fourth and most recent category of membership, and is open to schools offering professional architecture degree programs that do not yet have accreditation in the U.S. or government recognition in Canada, but who are working toward that goal. In 1986, there were nine such schools.

The Association is organized to offer programs and representation on three levels. Each school has a faculty councilor who serves as liaison and who conducts ACSA business at the individual school level. The schools in turn are organized into six geographic regions, which traverse both the United States and Canada. Each region elects a director who organizes activities at the regional level. A major activity is the yearly regional meeting at which refereed papers are presented and ACSA regional business is conducted. The regions also produce a variety of other special topic workshops as well as publish occasional magazines and papers. At the national level, the Association is composed of a board of directors of 13 individuals: six regional directors, five nationally elected officers, a student director, and the executive director, ex-officio. The Board of Directors maintains a variety of activities that influence, communicate, and record important architectural issues.

ACSA does not attempt unilaterally to set policy for the schools, which have long enjoyed the individual freedoms traditionally associated with and protected by the canons of higher education. Rather, it is one of the major roles of the Association to celebrate the diversity of architectural opportunity, discourse, and exploration offered by the schools. One of the desired results of these activities is to maintain the strong sense of pluralism, choice, and astonishing richness in architectural education.

The programs of ACSA at the national level are intended to provide major forums for ideas on the leading edge of architectural thought, as well as represent the varied interest of the schools with the collateral professional organizations and the public. National programs fall into six major categories; scholarly meetings, continuing education workshops, publications, public education and liaison, student competitions, and research. The scholarly meetings program is designed to give faculty the opportunity to present refereed papers on a variety of architectural topics. Each year, ACSA conducts a series of meetings for this purpose. There are six regional meetings in the fall followed by the technology conference in the winter, and the annual meeting each spring, which attracts over 350 faculty from all over the world. The continuing education program consists of a series of annual workshops, usually lasting 2–4 days, designed to improve the teaching skills and knowledge of the faculty. These programs are conducted by faculty, researchers, and practitioners recognized for their particular specialties or skills. The workshops include The Administrators Conference, where administrators of the various architectural programs meet to discuss the challenges and special nature of architectural administration; The Teacher's Seminar, jointly sponsored since 1956 by ACSA and AIA to develop the teaching skills of both young and seasoned faculty; The Architectural Issues Forum, where the work and theories of internationally recognized practitioners are presented to faculty, practitioners, and the public; The Summer Institute on Energy and Design, which focuses on the integration of energy into the design curriculum; and The Construction Materials and Technology Institute, which brings the latest developments in construction processes and teaching to the faculty.

The publications of the Association include a scholarly quarterly magazine, a newsletter published seven times annually, several annual directories outlining special opportunities, annual meeting proceedings, and special topic publications on a variety of subjects and activities. *The Journal of Architectural Education* (*JAE*), since its first issue in 1947, has brought research findings and thoughtful discussions about the state of architecture and architectural education into the academic forefront. The Journal is received by over 4000 faculty, practitioners, students, and libraries. It is listed in major referral indexes in the United States and abroad, including the RIBA Index, Review of Architectural Periodicals, the *Architecture Index,* and the *Art Index.* Widely regarded as a leading publication on new directions in architecture and architectural education, *JAE* contributors are a diverse, distinguished, and occasionally controversial group of architects and educators who have included Hugh Stubbins, Walter Netsch, Minoru Yamasaki, Paul Rudolph, Lawrence Anderson, Albert Bush-Brown, Charles Moore, James Marston Fitch, Walter Gropius, Ludwig Mies van der Rohe, José Luís Sert, Sigfried Giedion, Louis I. Kahn, William Caudill, Donlyn Lyndon, Herb Greene, Gerhard Kallman, Albert Speer, and Stanley Tigerman. *THE ACSA NEWS,* published seven times annually, presents interscholastic news in an informal style providing timely information on faculty activities, program changes, exhibits, meetings, and faculty position opportunities. This latter section offers an average of five pages in each issue of positions available throughout the world. *The Proceedings of the Annual Meeting* provides a contemporary record of faculty papers accepted for presentation at the annual meeting on topics related to architectural theory, education, and research. *Architecture Schools in North America* is the only guide to all professional degree-granting institutions in the United States and Canada. The book is intended as a reference for students, high school counselors, and anyone interested in seeing objective descriptions of all U.S. and Canadian schools. A standardized format is used to describe the program opportunities at each school and lists statistics on size, costs, student composition, libraries, faculty, etc.

Other annual publications include a *Directory of Member Schools* and a directory of *Off-Campus Study Programs: U.S. and Abroad.* Occasional publications detailing the results of student competitions, special grant projects such as design charrettes, and surveys are also available.

Public education and liaison programs take many forms, but generally activities fall into several categories: speaker programs aimed at a public as well as professional audience, community design charrettes, special projects aimed at increasing community awareness, and committee liaison activities with such groups as the American Institute of Architects, American Institute of Architecture Students, National Architectural Accrediting Board, The National Council of Architectural Registration Boards, National Institute of Architectural Education, and the Society of Architectural Historians. Special speaker programs have included an annual public forum on theoretical architectural issues in San Francisco and Chicago, sponsored in part by the Skidmore, Owings and Merrill Foundation, and such occasional conferences as the *International Conference on Barrier Free Design* at the United Nations in New York, which ACSA cosponsored and organized. ACSA has undertaken a series of programs at the local level to include local citizens in a specific local design issue. These have taken the form of design charrettes, in which a team of architects, architecture students, and faculty have undertaken projects of local interest. Design charrettes have recently been held in Philadelphia, Phoenix, and Knoxville. Each of these charrettes drew large community participation and resulted in a publication outlining various design alternatives for the communities. Obviously, these programs also provide a wonderful opportunity for students to get firsthand experience working with nationally prominent practitioners as well as contact with the public. ACSA also has received grants to document research efforts at the schools, to track recent architecture graduates, and to provide videos on local environmental concerns for showing on local public television stations.

The student programs also cross into various other categories. Special admission fees are available for all ACSA public programs, as are special membership rates to currently enrolled students.

In addition, ACSA runs a competition program aimed at both students and faculty. Each of the four competitions offered annually addresses itself to an issue that either emerges as a major concern or that ACSA believes needs attention. Such issues have included energy conscious design, building new facilities in old historic neighborhoods, looking at new building types that need attention such as the highway office park, and urban housing. Each of these competitions has a major sponsor who provides the prize money to winning students, as well as the winning school. Each year, ACSA provides over $55,000 in cash awards to students throughout the United States and Canada. ACSA's competition program draws the largest annual participation in the United States, with over 4500 students and 80 schools participating annually.

ACSA derives its financial support from three major sources: membership dues from the schools, groups, and individuals; program income; and grants and contracts from a variety of funding groups both public and private. Recent major contributors for various programs have included the American Institute of Architects, Royal Architectural Institute of Canada, the U.S. Department of Energy, the National Endowment of the Arts, the Graham Foundation, the Henry L. Kamphoefner Foundation, the Skidmore, Owings and Merrill Foundation, the American Wood Council, the Brick Institute of America, the Masonry Foundation, the Indiana Limestone Institute, the Foundation of Wall and Ceiling Industries, and General Motors.

The most recent addition to ACSA activities is in the area of research. ACSA has joined with The American Institute of Architects to form the AIA/ACSA Council on Architectural Research. The council works to establish a national agenda for architectural research, encourages research activity through funded projects, and disseminates research findings to practitioners and faculty.

For a list of ACSA Full Member and Candidate Member schools, see Table 1.

Table 1. ACSA Full Member and Candidate Member Schools (1986)

U.S. Full Members

1. Arizona State University
2. Arizona, University of
3. Arkansas, University of
4. Auburn University
5. Ball State University
6. Boston Architectural Center
7. California Polytechnic State University, San Luis Obispo
8. California State Polytechnic University, Pomona
9. California, Berkeley, University of
10. California, Los Angeles, University of
11. Carnegie-Mellon University
12. Catholic University
13. Cincinnati, University of
14. City College of City University of New York
15. Clemson University
16. Colorado, Denver, University of
17. Columbia University
18. Cooper Union, The
19. Cornell University
20. Detroit, University of
21. Drexel University
22. Florida A&M University
23. Florida, University of
24. Georgia Institute of Technology
25. Hampton University
26. Harvard University
27. Hawaii at Manoa, University of
28. Houston, University of
29. Howard University
30. Idaho, University of
31. Illinois Institute of Technology
32. Illinois at Chicago, University of
33. Illinois, Urbana-Champaign, University of
34. Iowa State University
35. Kansas State University
36. Kansas, University of
37. Kent State University
38. Kentucky, University of
39. Lawrence Institute of Technology
40. Louisiana State University
41. Louisiana Tech University
42. Maryland, University of
43. Massachusetts Institute of Technology
44. Miami University
45. Miami, University of
46. Michigan, University of
47. Minnesota, University of
48. Mississippi State University
49. Montana State University
50. Nebraska-Lincoln, University of
51. New Jersey Institute of Technology
52. New York Institute of Technology
53. New Mexico, University of
54. North Carolina State University
55. North Carolina, Charlotte, University of
56. North Dakota State University
57. Notre Dame University
58. Ohio State University
59. Oklahoma State University
60. Oklahoma, University of
61. Oregon, University of
62. Pennsylvania State University
63. Pennsylvania, University of
64. Pratt Institute
65. Princeton University
66. Puerto Rico, University of
67. Rensselaer Polytechnic Institute
68. Rhode Island School of Design
69. Rice University
70. Roger Williams College
71. Southern California Institute of Architecture
72. Southern California, University of
73. Southern University
74. Southwestern Louisiana, University of
75. State University of New York at Buffalo
76. Syracuse University
77. Temple University
78. Tennessee, University of
79. Texas A&M University
80. Texas Tech University
81. Texas at Arlington, University of
82. Texas at Austin, University of
83. Tulane University
84. Tuskegee University
85. Utah, University of
86. Virginia Poly. Institute & State University
87. Virginia, University of
88. Washington State University
89. Washington University
90. Washington, University of
91. Wisconsin-Milwaukee, University of
92. Yale University

Canada Full Members

93. British Columbia, University of
94. Carleton University
95. Laval University
96. Manitoba, University of
97. McGill University
98. Montreal, Universite de
99. Technical University of Nova Scotia
100. Toronto, University of
101. Waterloo, University of

U.S. Candidate Members

A. Andrews University
B. Drury College
C. Morgan State University
D. New School of Architecture
E. Oregon School of Design
F. Spring Garden College
G. Wentworth Institute of Technology
H. Woodbury University
I. Frank Lloyd Wright School of Architecture

BIBLIOGRAPHY

General References

All publications mentioned in this article are available through the Association of Collegiate Schools of Architecture, 1735 New York Ave., N.W., Washington, D.C., 20006.

See also EDUCATION, ARCHITECTURAL; NATIONAL ARCHITECTURAL ACCREDITING BOARD (NAAB); NATIONAL COUNCIL OF ARCHITECTURAL REGISTRATION BOARDS (NCARB); REGISTRATION EXAMINATION PROCESS, ARCHITECTS; RESEARCH, ARCHITECTURAL.

RICHARD E. MCCOMMONS, AIA
ACSA News,
Washington, D.C.

ASTM.   See AMERICAN SOCIETY FOR TESTING AND MATERIALS (ASTM)

ATRIUM BUILDINGS

The terms atrium and atrium building have come into common usage since the late 1960s. An atrium is currently understood to be a covered courtyard space within a building or between buildings. It usually passes through several levels and acts as the arrival and circulation focus of the building. An atrium building is one formed around one or more atria (the plural form atriums is also used).

There are many generic forms of atrium building, each with unique variants (see the section Worldwide Expressions). There are also closely related concepts, often called galleria, arcades, or wintergardens. The useful distinction between an atrium building and these others is that an atrium is a space with an essentially vertical emphasis. Galleria and arcades are synonymous, and indicate a covered street, a space with a horizontal emphasis, and a circulation role. A wintergarden is a glazed conservatory, either free-standing or attached to a building. Only when the building and covered space interlock and interact can the term atrium be sensibly used. However, each of the related concepts shares design ideas and construction requirements with the atrium building, and much of this article can be read as equally relevant to them.

The word atrium is Latin and had two meanings during the Roman era. First, it meant the part-roofed court which formed the focus of the public part of a house. The street entrance usually led to it via a short passage. The term was also used in the early Christian period to denote the open-air courtyard before the narthex or porch of a church. The new use of the word is a deliberate coinage by the marketing people of the Hyatt Hotel Corp., whose Regency Hyatt Hotel in Atlanta, Ga. (Fig. 1), was the first to have its covered court described as an atrium. They sought a term conveying grandeur and the resonances appropriate to a deluxe hotel, and succeeded admirably. The name stuck immediately and has been subsequently applied retrospectively to all earlier examples of the covered court. The new usage now essentially excludes unroofed courtyards.

Figure 1. The covered court at the Hyatt Regency Hotel (Atlanta, Ga.) by John Portman Associates, 1967, was the first to be called an atrium. Courtesy of John C. Portman Associates.

HISTORY OF THE MODERN ATRIUM

The term modern atrium is used to distinguish the concept of the fully covered court from its Roman predecessors. The wish to glaze over street and courtyard space and the ability to do so coincided in the UK and France at the turn of the nineteenth century. The wish to do so may have arisen from Napoleon's conquest of Egypt in 1798. Writers and artists followed closely on the army's heels and brought back many new ideas in fashion, furniture, and building. The covered bazaars of Cairo and its inward-looking courtyard houses appealed greatly to northern Europeans, whose open spaces were uncomfortable due to rain and cold. The first skylit-covered street could well be the Passage des Panoramas, Paris, 1800. It used current glasshouse technology, with wooden framing and small glass sheets, which leaked copiously.

Real progress was made in 1805 when the Shropshire ironmaster Noel Hill asked John Nash to roof over a court at Attingham Park. As a fellow freemason, Nash shared the secrets of iron framing and constructed a watertight picture gallery in the form of a Roman house atrium. Nash's protégé, Richard Porden, followed this with the much larger iron-domed stable yard at Brighton Pavilion in 1806. The Oriental style of the whole complex portrays its inspiration.

Other important early examples include Francois Belanger's roofing of the courtyard in the Halle au Ble, Paris 1813; Samuel Ware's Burlington Arcade, London, 1819; Warren and Bucklin's three-level Arcade, Providence, R.I., 1829 (Fig. 2); and Sir Charles Barry's noble Reform Club, London, 1839. This latter is a fully resolved and technically mature atrium building.

The period from 1840 to 1914 saw an ever-increasing scale of iron and glass construction around the developed world. The great exhibition and railroad buildings stretched the technology, although it was applied far less ambitiously in galleria and atria. Mengoni's Galleria in Milan, 1867, is the definitive grand covered street. Eiffel and Boileau's Bon Marché store in Paris is the most accom-

plished atrium building (1876). The prime remaining nineteenth-century atrium examples are the Barton Arcade, Manchester (1871) (Fig. 3); the Utopian Familistere housing at Guise, France (1883); the Grand Arcade, Cleveland (1888); the Rookery building (1885) and Railway Exchange (1903) in Chicago; the Brown Palace Hotel, Denver (1893) (Fig. 4); and the Bradbury building, Los Angeles (1893) (Fig. 5). The Brown Palace has, at eight stories, the tallest extant nineteenth-century atrium. The Bradbury has hydraulic elevators and iron stairs standing in the atrium, powerfully foretelling the ideas of 75 years later.

Between 1914 and 1965, the arcade virtually disappeared; the atrium is found only in the backwaters of modern architecture. Architecture in Europe and the United States moved toward solid, set-back buildings, which had more space around than inside. Courtyard planning fell completely from favor. The examples that do appear are by designers outside mainstream modernism. Frank Lloyd Wright spans the whole period. He remodeled the Rookery in 1903, when he also built the seminal Larkin

Figure 2. Modeled on the Arabian souk, the Arcade in Providence, R.I., is the earliest surviving multilevel galleria. It was built in 1828 to the design of Warren and Bucklin. Courtesy of the Rhode Island Department of Economic Development.

Figure 3. Patented glasshouse construction was added to a conventional building to produce Barton Arcade (Manchester, UK), 1871, by Corbett, Raby and Sawyer. Courtesy of R. G. Saxon.

Figure 4. The eight-story atrium of the Brown Palace Hotel (Denver, 1893, by Frank Edbrooke), considered to be the greatest surviving Western-style hotel. Courtesy of Brown Palace Hotel.

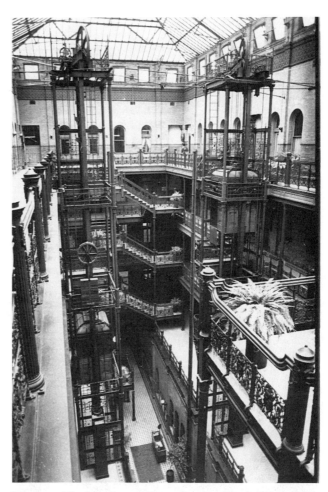

Figure 5. The first elevators in an atrium, in the futuristic Bradbury building, 1893, Los Angeles, George Wyman. Courtesy of R. G. Saxon.

Building in Buffalo, N.Y. His Johnson Wax headquarters, Racine, Wis. (1936), continues the top-lit atrium theme, and the 1959 Guggenheim Museum in New York (Fig. 6) was very influential on John Portman, FAIA, the architect most responsible later for popularizing the atrium.

In Europe, Berlage's Amsterdam Stock Exchange (1903) spawned imitators in Scandinavia, and the atrium concept continued almost unbroken in the work of Lars Sonk and Gunnar Asplund. Asplund's Law Courts annex at Gothenburg (1937) is clearly inspired by the Bradbury Building. The Italian rationalist Giuseppe Terragni was one of several Italians using glass-roofed courtyards as the centerpieces of post offices, banks, and political party buildings. The most notable example is the Casa de Fascio, Como (1936).

Department stores continued to favor the great central well concept, with the most unusual example being Liberty's store in London, by Edwin T. and Stanley Hall. This 1928 Tudor-style emporium uses several small, timber-framed atria in its intricate interiors.

The return of the atrium to center stage began in the 1950s with the reappearance of the arcade, now as an air-conditioned mall in shopping centers. Victor Gruen's Southdale Center, Minneapolis (1952), set in motion a revolution in shopping design, which eventually spilled over into all types of urban development. Two Finns developed the atrium idea alongside Frank Lloyd Wright. Alvar Aalto's Rautatalo building in Helsinki (1953) leads a series of three by Finnish-American Eero Saarinen: his U.S. Chancellery in Oslo (1959); the University of Pennsylvania women's dormitory, Philadelphia (1960); and Bell Telephone Laboratories at Holmdel, N.J. (1963). Australian architect John Andrews put forward a striking atrium-based design for the Toronto City Hall competition of 1958.

By the mid-1960s, reaction to the solid set-back building was developing in many architects' minds. John Andrews completed Scarboro College, Ontario, which is based on dramatically cut-away interiors, both linear- and court-yard-form. Colin St. John Wilson proposed a seven-story atrium at the heart of the Liverpool Civic Centre. Saarinen's successors, Kevin Roche and John Dinkeloo, created the Ford Foundation building in New York in 1967 (Fig. 7), whose great garden is embraced by a modest L-shaped office block. James Stirling designed the University of

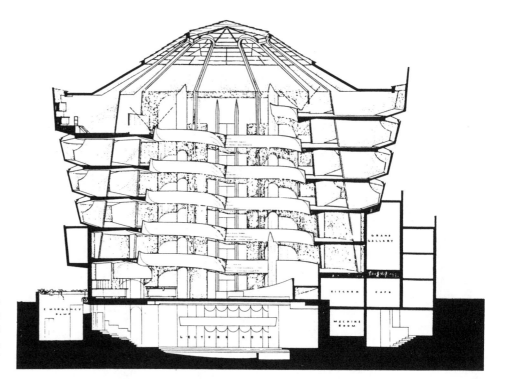

Figure 6. The Guggenheim Museum (New York), 1959, marks the high point of Frank Lloyd Wright's 60-year interest in atria. Copyright, The Frank Lloyd Wright Foundation, 1960.

Figure 7. Two-sided atrium at the pioneering Ford Foundation, New York. The original, native planting scheme had to be replaced with tropical species, revealing the climate for atrium landscapes. Courtesy of Kevin Roche John Dinkeloo and Associates.

Cambridge History Library at the same time, leaning a glass tent in the angle of an L-shaped multistory block. It was not completed until 1968.

It is in Atlanta, Ga. that the atrium can most justly claim to have been reborn, for it was here that the name was first applied to a covered court. John C. Portman, FAIA, pioneered two advances in architectural practice; he made the case for architects to be commercial developers ethically and he did it with atrium buildings. Portman's first atrium was, however, in a public housing development, the Antoine Graves houses (Fig. 8), designed in 1963 and completed in 1965. The grandeur of the result led to the concept for a hotel on the same principle, accommodation arranged like motel units with gallery access, but around a tall, roofed court. The hotel was to be 22 stories high, with visible, "wall climber" elevators, developed by Otis for the observation tower at the San Antonio Hemisfair, arranged on a tower in the courtyard.

Portman built the hotel as a speculation and tried to sell it several times during construction. The Pritzker family, which was trying to develop the Hyatt motel chain into a deluxe hotel business, took a gamble in buying it and has never looked back. A startling commercial success, a new leading chain of hotels was built within a decade, changing the concept of the luxury hotel in the process, and reintroducing the word atrium to the language.

Since 1967, atrium buildings have appeared in all of the most rapidly developing cities of the world. Hundreds are to be found in Canada and the United States, and dozens in the UK and Scandinavia. The oil-boom cities of the Middle East, Hong Kong, Singapore, and Japan

Figure 8. John Portman's Antoine Graves houses (Atlanta, 1965) were his first atria and built within the low-budget target. Courtesy of John C. Portman Associates.

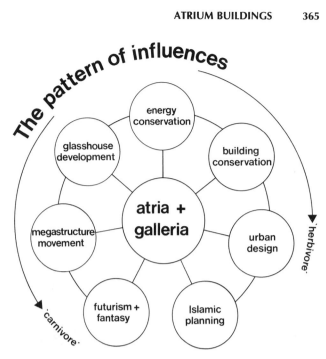

Figure 9. The pattern of influences on the atrium concept. Courtesy of R. G. Saxon.

are other major concentrations. A series of consistent themes has emerged, and several major technical challenges are being faced. The examples in the rest of this article cover the last 20 years of development.

INFLUENCES ON DESIGN

The atrium building has spread with speed and zest because it fulfills a wide range of quite disparate purposes. It is also the result of a pattern of influences running to both ends of the ethical and conceptual spectrum of architectural thought. This makes the atrium concept a robust one, with great staying power and potential for variety.

The influences (Fig. 9) range from the hard, high technology, progress-minded futurism, sometimes called carnivorous, to the soft, ecologically aware, conservationist philosophy, contrastingly called herbivorous. At the hard end are ideas from utopianism and science fiction—the dream of enclosed cities, of sublime, megalomaniac scale. The great interior as an end in itself is a theme running from the eighteenth-century Sublime period in European architecture. It is associated with fear of a future that was felt to be both terrible and magnificent (Fig. 10). The internal world is portrayed as a safe haven from chaos and danger outside, and often as a utopian community. The sanitized, crime-free world of a U.S. mixed-use atrium

development is a realization of the H. G. Wells' fantasy *The Sleeper Wakes* (1901).

Indeed, the megastructure movement of the 1950s and 1960s, most of whose fantastic schemes remain on paper, is the upwelling of these deep hopes and fears about the urban future. Realized complexes like Atlanta's Omni center and Detroit's Renaissance Center, both with checkered economic careers, project the image of beleaguered fortresses. Buildings like the Walt Disney World Contemporary Resort Hotel (Fig. 11) and the Hong Kong and Shanghai Bank Headquarters (Fig. 12) show the "Brave New World" optimism also inherent in these ideas.

On the turning point between carnivorous and herbivorous philosophies is the glasshouse phenomenon. The greenhouse is simultaneously an image of ecologically sound, energy-conserving culture and of the first industrialized buildings, capable of enclosing vast areas. Bringing the outside world indoors, under glass, softens the hard edge of modernism, promotes relaxation, and provides an imagined escape into the natural world (Fig. 13).

Enveloping a weather-free garden within a building or wrapping a building within such gardens combines utility of accommodation with this antifunctional amenity, producing a postindustrial image with which there is strong popular identification. Roche Dinkeloo's Ford Foundation (Fig. 7) and Deere West buildings are among the finest examples.

Fully into herbivorous territory are the twin conservation movements for energy and existing buildings. Energy conservation has shifted the perspective on what constitutes responsible built form. Attenuated, overexposed forms have been replaced by compact, sheltered ones. Cubic-built forms with deep daylight penetration via atria are the new norm. Buffer zones of semicontrolled environment help to reduce climatic impact in both hot and cold

Figure 10. Sir John Soane's Museum, London, 1813. Gandy's drawing of the top-lit space captures the Sublime movement's awe of the great but terrible future which they sensed. Courtesy of the Trustees of Sir John Soane's Museum.

Figure 11. The linear atrium at the Contemporary Resort, Walt Disney World, 1970, by Welton Becket. Note the through-running monorail. Courtesy of David Barnes/BDP.

extremes, and produce more comfort for less energy. Princeton University's Enerplex provides a classic example.

The forms thus favored are, of course, the familiar forms of premodern building. The return of respect for premodern building has greatly aided the atrium's progress. Historic atria have been rediscovered and restored; the U.S. National Building Museum is now based in Montgomery Miegs' Pension Building in Washington, D.C. Many new atria have also been created during refurbishments and extensions.

The revived interest in urban design is in some ways the strongest impetus for continuation of the atrium concept. As the modern movement rejected streets and courts as determinants of form, generating building shape from the internal needs of the building, so the current reaction has revived appreciation of the subtle interplay between a building and its context. Except on very small sites, it is now recognized that set-back tall blocks deliver no more space than courtyard blocks that fill the site. Outdoor plazas at the feet of towers are also clearly seen as less useful and comfortable than indoor courts.

The final notable and recurring influence is Islamic. As the historical outline showed, the covered street and arcade probably entered Western architecture as a result of contact with the Near East. It is an interesting coincidence that strong Western contact with the oil-producing Arab States in the 1960s and 1970s should have paralleled the revival of introspective building forms (Fig. 14). Many Arab clients commissioned Western architects to build in the Islamic tradition, who then explored that tradition and absorbed it into their whole approach. Henning Larsen's Saudi Foreign Ministry Building in Riyadh is one of the finest atrium buildings of the decade and is a fasci-

Figure 12. Hong Kong and Shanghai Bank Corp. headquarters, Foster Associates, 1985 (model). Futurism continues to see the enclosed vertical space as prophetic. This example is modeled on the Vertical Assembly Building at Cape Canaveral. Courtesy of Foster Associates.

Figure 13. The psychological value of garden space is proved in the extreme conditions of Alaska's Prudhoe Bay oil field. This garden atrium is artificially lit during the arctic night. WFEM, 1972. Courtesy of British Petroleum PLC.

Figure 14. Sheraton Hotel (Dubai, UAE), 1978. Rader Mileto has created a modern Islamic court, indoors, shady and cooled by running water. Courtesy of R. G. Saxon.

nating counterpoint to the same architect's Trondheim University of 1979 in Norway (Fig. 15). This campus on the Arctic Circle has a covered street matrix, and the life of the university is focused on these educational "souks." The building complex is energy-oriented and uses glasshouse technology to achieve both this and a futuristic image. Thus are the influences on atrium building design interwoven.

The following sections enlarge on the most powerful present influences: conservationism and urban design.

Conservationism

Doubts arising in the late 1960s and early 1970s about the sustainability and ecological morality of the Western approach to industrialization became a substantial influence on all aspects of thought. For architects, the issues raised centered on the use of nonrenewable energy and materials, and on the retention of existing buildings. By the mid 1980s, what were seen as issues of overriding

Figure 15. Trondheim University, Norway, Henning Larsen, 1979 onwards, brings together many influences with its glazed streets between buildings. Courtesy of The Architectural Press Ltd.

Figure 16. An energy-conserving atrium at the Gregory Bateson State Office building (Sacramento, Calif.) by the State Architect, 1981. State-of-the-art passive systems are used for winter warmth and summer cooling. Courtesy of R. G. Saxon.

urgency have settled into a balanced perspective. Energy prices will probably continue to rise in the long term, and energy conservation technology is now a central design criterion. The retention and recycling of historic and familiar structures is commonplace as economics and consumer preference for cultural continuity push in the same direction. New is no longer seen as necessarily better.

Atria are but one of many energy conserving ideas for buildings. Their impact is often quite marginal. However, they are favored as a highly visible sign of good intent, compared to the invisibility of insulation or more sophisticated systems and controls (Fig. 16). The most positive advantages to be gained are increased daylight penetration and the buffering of occupied spaces from direct contact with adverse climate. Until atria reappeared, low heating and cooling loads were mainly sought by deeper planforms, with reduced external wall area. These actually led to high lighting costs, resultant cooling loads, and oppressive interiors. Atria allow shallower occupied spaces to be used. The extensive perimeter, popular with occupants, does not need to suffer the heat gain or loss it would have experienced on an external wall. A comparatively low cost, low performance wall between occupied space and atrium can deliver superior comfort, vision, and general amenity to an external wall. Multiple atria allow the large, compact floor areas increasingly favored by tenants, with the added advantage of considerable high status perimeter.

Passive solar-heat collection is a bonus in certain building types and climates. More often, the atrium acts as a cooling device, shading occupied spaces more economically than external shade structures.

The building conservation movement has not only led to the rediscovery and restoration of historic atria, but to the creation of many more in the process of remodeling redundant buildings. Old buildings used daylighting and, therefore, shallow plan-forms. Light wells and reentrant courts are now frequently enclosed as atria, turning what was often a low amenity outlook into a high amenity one. Sullivan's Wainwright Building in St. Louis is one notable example.

With the recycling of deep-planned warehouse or industrial buildings has come the idea of cutting atria out of the oversized section. By discarding one-quarter of the floorspace, the value of the remainder has been greatly multiplied. Butler Square, Minneapolis, is one of the best-known examples (Fig. 17). Atria have allowed the extending of old buildings without losing sight of their historic facades. Glazed-over spaces act as links, with the old outdoors moved indoors, notably at the Metropolitan Museum, New York (Fig. 18). Market buildings, now often redundant for their original use, have been recycled with their covered trading areas turned into atria serving surrounding activities and acting as public resorts in themselves. London's Covent Garden Market is the best-known example.

Figure 17. Butler Square, Minneapolis, 1974–1981, Miller Hanson, Westerbeck, Bell. The 200-ft wide, nine-level timber warehouse was successfully relaunched as offices and speciality retailing by cutting out a quarter of its floorspace to make an atrium. Courtesy of R. G. Saxon.

Figure 18. Metropolitan Museum, New York, 1980. Roche and Dinkeloo connected the American Wing back to the main museum by adding this garden court. The link preserves the facade of an old house now embedded in the museum. Courtesy of Kevin Roche John Dinkeloo and Associates.

Urban Design

The new interest in urban design is also largely a conservative movement, favoring continuity of traditional forms rather than introducing radical new ones. Respectability has returned to the low-rise courtyard plan, now that it has been mathematically demonstrated (1) that it delivers floorspace as efficiently as a set-back tower or slab. The rigid, orthogonal shapes of buildings derived solely from their internal plan logic, not alien to most U.S. streetscapes, wrought havoc with European ones. The pragmatic ability of courtyard buildings to bend to the site has solved odd-site problems, however, even in the United States and allows a valued return to the street frontage line. There is also once again a strong desire to mold civic outdoor spaces by shaping buildings to frame them.

The resultant atria are developing as an urban culture of their own. In rapidly developing city centers, the connection of atria and galleria into pedestrian-movement systems creates strong pressure for all redevelopments to relate similarly. In some cities, this system is a planned

one, above (Minneapolis, Calgary) or below (Houston) street level. At-grade separation is perfectly feasible, however. A recent study (2) of the morphology of the shopping mall suggests that a network of pedestrian malls at 200–250-m intervals, with parallel motor streets at similar intervals between them, is consistent with successful historic and modern examples.

The areas around and including Toronto's Eaton Center, Philadelphia's Market Street East, and midtown Manhattan between 5th Avenue and Madison (each side of 56th St.) show the potential.

There is, however, a negative side to the urban impact of atria that should not be overlooked. The introversion of much of such development, turning away from the surrounding streets, is impoverishing those streets, and rendering them less safe and less attractive. The urban crime problem of the last two decades has created a tacit wish to control access to apparently public spaces, and the atrium/galleria/mall environment can provide this "sanitized" world. As a self-fulfilling prophecy, however, the environment on the streets now abandoned can become suitable only for locked, moving vehicles, as trade flees to the inner sancta. As Jane Jacobs observed, good urban design produces safe, self-policing streets.

CONSTRUCTION REQUIREMENTS OF ATRIUM BUILDINGS

It has become clear over 20 years of modern atrium building that the form makes several distinctive demands on design skills. These demands are in six areas:

1. Environmental design.
2. Fire-safety design.

3. Structures and skins for atrium enclosures.
4. Passenger-transport systems.
5. Indoor large-scale planting.
6. Cost planning.

Technical illustrations under each of these headings are available (3).

Environmental Design

If atrium principles are to yield significant energy savings, the basic form of the building must be influenced by environmental studies. Two aspects are central: the amount of daylighting sought and the thermal strategy of the building. Seeking to provide a given proportion of floorspace with ambient lighting levels by daylight will result in limited plan depth for any given floor-to-ceiling height. (Lighting performance can be enhanced over the conventional by optical and reflecting devices.) Space of the selected daylightable depth can then be arranged around the perimeter of the site, using atrium space to take up any difference between externally preferred shape and internally generated plan-form. East- and west-facing window facades are hardest to control for solar impact, so the preferred orientation of occupied and atrium spaces tends to be north–south.

Daylight-collecting atrium roof-forms, excluding sun when solar warming is not desirable, are the start of a light-delivering system. An atrium behaves as a daylight duct, bouncing light down to its base and into surrounding openings. More light reaches lower levels when the upper walls are highly reflective and with modest openings. Poor onward transmission results from low reflectivity surfaces and oversized windows at high levels. Reflection can be diffuse, from pale surfaces, or specular, from mirrors. Specular solar-reflecting techniques are applicable in sunny climates, whereas diffuse reflection performs better under cloudy skies. Model studies under an artificial sky are the best way to optimize design for daylight transmission. Thermal strategies are varied and depend on two decisions: does the building need its atrium to help it to keep warm, to stay cool, or to do both at different seasons; and what comfort level is desirable in the atrium? The thermal and comfort decisions interact and also affect the choice of daylight delivery system.

In extreme climates, the thermal choice will be obvious. In temperate zones, it can be variable. Residential and industrial buildings usually require heating, but commercial and office buildings rarely do, given the heat available from lighting and electronic systems. Choice of a warming atrium will lead the design in one direction; a cooling atrium will go the opposite way. A "convertible" atrium, changing its characteristics between seasons, is a third and more complex type. Each of these will be differently achieved depending on the comfort level sought in the atrium itself. Four levels are identifiable:

Canopy atrium	Roofed but not fully enclosed, providing a rain and/or sun shield only.
Buffer atrium	Unserviced enclosure, with wide seasonal and daily fluctuation in temperature. The most energy efficient in most climates.
Tempered-buffer atrium	Some moderation of extreme cold by energy input, to allow plant survival (see below) and year-round use of the space.
Full-comfort atrium	Serviced space to the same standard as surrounding space, for use as an office, bank, restaurant, etc.

Canopy atria can protect overlooking spaces against extreme cold, damp, and solar impact, but can only be involved in natural ventilation. Full-comfort atria are likely to have their own separate ventilation system, at least for the occupied floor level. Buffer and tempered-buffer atria can be involved in the ventilation system of the surrounding spaces.

Atria work like chimneys for a combination of the greenhouse and stack effects. Solar warming raises air temperature, and the buoyancy of warm air lifts it to the top, inducing negative pressure at the base of the atrium and positive at the top. This powerful effect can be harnessed economically, but if it is not required, it can be expensive or even impossible to control, hence the need to consider the thermal strategy as part of the basic conceptual design of an atrium building.

Warming buffer atria in Scandinavia frequently draw fresh air into the occupied space from a solar-warmed atrium, or discharge clean used air into it to raise atrium temperatures. In other cases, the atrium is used as a return air plenum, switching to natural extraction in summer. Extraction rates can be enhanced by a "solar chimney." A permanent or seasonal shade drawn behind sun-facing glass will induce powerful heating of the space between glass and shade. Venting the top of this space will draw air rapidly from the atrium and connected spaces even in still conditions. If the atrium is not connected to the building ventilation system, it can become temperature-stratified very easily in winter. Low velocity fans to move air downwards are then desirable, putting warmed air where occupants and plants can benefit from it.

Convertible atria are found in sunny continental climates, where sun is welcome in winter but not in summer. Motorized external shade louvers are commonly used to admit winter sun, exclude summer sun while admitting daylight, insulate the glass on winter nights, and expose it on summer nights.

Cooling atria seek to exclude direct sun at all times, although often admitting a small amount to provide sparkle accents. The aim is to retain a tank of cooled air in the heart of the complex, a modern version of the traditional function of courts in hot climates. Side-wall glazing will be preferred to roof glass, and the wall glass will usually face the pole and/or be fully shaded externally. Cooling atria are often serviced as supply plenums to the surrounding spaces.

It will be seen that the location of insulation and shading will vary considerably between thermal and comfort types. Insulation will move to the outer atrium walls as higher comfort standards are sought, as will shading for summer conditions. In canopy or buffer atria, both will be best placed on the walls of the occupied space. For warming atria in cool temperate climates, summer shading of the occupied space may still be needed, but can be economically done inside the atrium and outside the windows of the occupied space. Only in full-comfort atria is it possible to consider the complete removal of walls between occupied space and the atrium. Openable windows are possible with buffer and canopy atria, although for fire-safety reasons, windows will often be fixed in all comfort types.

One particular feature has proved valuable for daylighting and servicing performance: a projecting lantern at the top of an atrium, above all surrounding occupied space. For lighting, such a lantern will capture winter sunlighting better than a low profile roof, with potential to reflect it down to the atrium floor. In summer, the lantern will hold the bubble of hot air that inevitably forms just below an atrium roof. Accommodation alongside this hot air bubble can be uninhabitable or excessively costly to service. Finally, the lantern acts as a smoke reservoir in emergencies.

Fire-safety Design

The selected strategy for fire safety will interact strongly with the environmental design of any atrium building. The degree of separation between atrium and surrounding accommodation and the degree of involvement of the atrium in ventilating the accommodation depend as much on fire aspects as on environmental considerations.

Fire safety is a major issue for atrium design because the opening up of a building's cross section creates potential hazards not found in fully compartmentalized buildings. These hazards can be contained—there is no evidence that atrium buildings are inherently less safe than their conventional counterparts—but safety will depend more on active defense systems than on passive ones.

There are codes in some countries, states, and cities to lay down the approved form of atrium design. These regulations are by no means definitive or even logical in some cases. This section will, therefore, discuss the fire-safety issues from first principles. It is recommended that designs be developed from first principles and that the regulatory authorities be involved with the designs as much as possible to ensure mutual comprehension.

Smoke control is the key design issue, impinging immediately as it does on life safety throughout a building. Compared to conventional multistory buildings, the smoke hazard in atrium buildings is inherently increased. Smoke entering an atrium from a floor on fire can, unless satisfactory countermeasures are employed, invade other occupied levels rapidly. This compares to a conventional building, where smoke pouring from a window is unlikely to reenter another floor in hazardous quantities.

Smoke expands rapidly as it rises, until it cools to ambient air temperature, usually about 15–20 m above the fire. An atrium, therefore, allows smoke volume to multiply far more than it could inside conventional floor heights, thereby aggravating the problem of safe smoke removal.

If a full-comfort occupied atrium is desired, with space around it substantially open to the atrium, then smoke control issues are at their most acute. Fire could arise on the atrium floor or on any overlooking level. Smoke will almost certainly be channeled to the atrium for re-

moval, and its quantity will need severe limitation, probably by sprinklers. Only with controlled-fire size can an engineered smoke-removal system perform. A smoke cloud in the atrium can be lifted up to and through the roof without entering open accommodation around it if:

- Roof extract ventilation, powered or natural, operates at the rate of maximum smoke production.
- Replacement air is fed to the atrium from substantially below the fire floor in equal volume to the smoke removed, or in lesser volume in order to lower atrium air pressure.
- A general negative pressure is maintained in the atrium compared to that in overlooking accommodation.
- Floor plate edges are detailed to repel rather than capture rising smoke.
- The reservoir volume at the top of the atrium is sufficient to prevent the cloud base from descending into occupied levels. (It may prove impractical in practice to have the topmost floors open to the atrium.)

Sprinkling the atrium from its roof is counterproductive, cooling and pushing down the smoke cloud. Atrium floors with a fire load should be sprinklered from low levels, from floor edges or features like pergolas or catenaries. Where the atrium floor is designed to have a very low fire load or risk, it is possible to reverse this strategy, extracting smoke from a fire floor away from the atrium. Smoke drainage via ceiling reservoirs can prevent any spill into the atrium which, together with all uninvolved floors, is maintained at positive pressure compared to the fire floor. Lack of visible smoke makes this a good strategy for avoiding full evacuation of the building, which may be psychologically inevitable when smoke is seen in an atrium.

The smoke-extraction strategy should be parallel to the normal ventilation system, so that the normally used and maintained system is used in emergencies and excessive cost is avoided.

Where surrounding accommodation is screened from the atrium, in all comfort levels, the basic risk of smoke spread is considerably reduced. However, where operable windows are installed, the safety situation is similar to that in a fully open atrium. Only motorized windows, closing on fire detection, can make operable windows behave like fixed ones.

Where occupied space is screened from the atrium, it is not strictly necessary to control the quantity of smoke generated, as it cannot readily escape into the atrium or from there enter another floor. Sprinkling of all space is desirable in any building, however, to increase life safety and minimize property loss. The performance of the screen wall in containing radiation, smoke, and flames is important, especially if gallery escape routes are provided. Glazed screens are needed to last throughout the escape period and to minimize heat radiation to the galleries. Intumescent laminated glass offers ideal performance and is preferable to unreliable sprinklered glass. Borosilicate glass is a strong contender also. Continuous innovation in this sector can be expected. Where glass screens simply overlook the atrium directly, it is still wise to defend against breakage and falling glass and to prevent smoke damage within the atrium by toughening or wiring the glass in heat-resistant ways.

Fire on the occupied floor of a screened atrium must be dealt with as in an open-sided situation, although the cloud base can probably be allowed to descend opposite occupied floors. Linked ventilation of atrium and overlooking space again needs to be considered in light of the fire strategy. Plenum extraction from screened overlooking space via the atrium is consistent with safety; the pressure across extract grilles defends them from smoke invasion. Supply from a plenum atrium must, however, be cut off if smoke enters such a space, and must not be resumed until the atrium is flushed clean.

Means of escape from atrium buildings are not straightforward. One of the advantages for users of many atrium buildings is the easy visibility of the circulation system, with glass elevators and open stairs in the atrium facilitating orientation. These features are disadvantages in fire escape, as occupants will be familiar only with the atrium circulation routes, the ones they should not be encouraged to use if there is any risk of smoke in the atrium. Enclosed, probably pressurized stairs need to be accessible without traveling more than a minimal distance across space at risk of smoke-logging. These stairs should discharge directly to outside air at ground level, or into a place of comparable safety. It is worthwhile to position such stairs where they will intercept people making their way to the familiar atrium routes, rather than expect people to move in an unfamiliar way in emergencies. Stairs can discharge onto atrium floors if these floors are at very low risk of smoke-logging.

Those atrium buildings where all circulation is enclosed inside occupied spaces are conventional in their escape needs. A major factor in escape costs, however, will be the proportion of the building needed to be evacuated simultaneously in the event of an alarm. The limited evacuation possible in multistory buildings may not be acceptable because of visible smoke in the atrium. People may wish to leave floors not actually threatened.

Access for fire fighting needs additional consideration. Atrium buildings often fill their sites, and space for appliances to arrive must be left in a way that does not conflict with marshaling areas for evacuees. A separate service core for fire fighting may well be necessary. Glass passenger elevators cannot be used by firefighters, and a stair and elevator within a pressurized core will be needed. Service risers and controls on this stair will enable it to act as a safe bridgehead to the fire floor. Where horizontally extensive atria or malls are proposed, it may be necessary to allow fire-fighting vehicles into the atrium, or to provide special tenders to aid mobility within the extensive area.

Structures and Skins for Atrium Enclosures

Atria enlarge the familiar problems of window and skylight design to the point where new issues arise. In return, they can often reduce complication and cost in the surrounding building frame by allowing it to be lower, wider, and more economically braced than a conventional equivalent building. Atrium envelopes are often, however, the focus of ambitious design. Slopes, curves, complex shapes, and great spans are often sought, leading to construction and maintenance difficulties. Whereas many of the best-known atrium buildings have custom-designed envelopes, there is an established industry in pre-engineered atrium roofs and walls. Advice from suppliers can be very useful whether or not a pre-engineered solution is eventually specified. Major issues to check are

Movement	An atrium envelope usually moves thermally to a far greater degree than does a main building envelope. The joints between them will need to perform well.
Air-tightness	The stack pressures within atria can be severe, needing very good general sealing and high performance from any operable ventilation at top and bottom. Doors into an atrium will similarly need to resist stack pressures, while still allowing ease of access and escape. Revolving and powered sliding doors perform best.
Cleaning	Cleaning and maintenance both inside and outside atrium envelopes seem to be a problem considered too often as an afterthought. The access ways or special rigs needed can be very expensive and unsightly if not considered from the start. The cleaning solution can often be a discipline that simplifies the envelope design, generally to advantage.

A wide range of design solutions has emerged for the three basic elements of atrium envelopes: window walls, sloped or curved roofs, and flat roofs.

For vertical side walls, there have been two generic approaches: continuation of the main building frame across the void, and change to a separate, lighter structure. The continued frame allows a free-form atrium, even a flexibly defined one, and minimizes thermal discontinuity problems. High shading and insulation factors can be built in, although with corresponding loss of vistas through the wall.

The curtain-wall approach can use metal framing or suspended glass assemblies. Metal framing is economical if substantial depth of framing can be allowed, with trussed mullions or spandrels. Space trusses are particularly effective. The actual glazing can be direct into these superscale frames, or a conventional curtain wall can be supported by them. Glass can now be stuck or bolted to internal framing, giving a frameless appearance externally.

Hybrid external walls include the stepped, sunbreaking form used at the Children's Hospital of Philadelphia, spanning the side blocks, and the use of windbracing between the side blocks to carry the curtain wall, as at the Hennepin County Courthouse, Minneapolis.

Sloping surfaces can use the same techniques as vertical ones, but can also capitalize on the water-shedding nature of a slope to use lapped "patent glazing" systems. These 130-year-old, economical, industrial techniques are flexible and effective, with modern versions providing high thermal performance. Such surfaces, and those of sealed, inclined, curtain-wall variants, can be supported on rolled steel frames at major intervals, or on space trusses or frames. One gives major rhythm to the space, the other an even, shimmering effect without perceptible bays.

Curved roof-forms can introduce a degree of self-support by light glazing frames, using the stiffening effect of the curve. Many of the pre-engineered vault and dome roofs use very little material to cover major spans.

"Flat" glazed roofing is now possible, using silicone-sealed planar "armorplate" surfaces with no projecting frames. The great majority of horizontal glazed roofs consists, however, of arrays of pitched, vaulted, or pyramidal rooflights. All of these require drainage between each module, above the membrane, or by piping through into the interior. The "ridge-and-furrow" frames introduced in Victorian greenhouses are still very effective. Generous structural depth compared to span produces economy and also gives opportunities for maintenance access from the lower chord of the structure. Laylights, where a diffusing glass or louver surface hangs from the lower chord, are occasionally used, concealing all structure and shading from excessive solar impact.

Glazing materials are in constant evolution, with a very wide range of transparent, translucent, reflective, insulating, and structural performances to consider. For two decades, glass has been favored for side walls where vision is paramount, but the lighter plastics have usually been preferred for roofs. The convenient molded forms of plastic domes, pyramids, or barrel vaults, combined with light weight, have favored PVC, acrylic, polycarbonate, or glass-reinforced plastic (GRP). Multiwall sheets have good thermal performance. Some reaction is now discernible, as the aging of plastics, coupled with their fire performance, undercuts their cost advantage. Toughened or laminated glass can now often do the job better and pressed forms are becoming available.

Composite glazing materials, glass with plastic interlayers, or GRP cells with glass-fiber fill, have a special niche in delivering very high thermal performance. Where high atrium comfort is required in cold climates, these materials are ideal for roofs, although they cannot deliver side-wall view.

In hot, sunny climates, the case for fabric roofs is increasingly being made. Teflon-coated and silicone-coated fiber glass fabrics (TCFF and SCFF) are the highest performing fabrics, although also the highest cost. They will last at least as long as plastic rooflighting and deliver both structure and skin in one economical form. Unusual spans and shapes are possible in pneumatic or tensile structures. High solar incidence is necessary for effective use, as the light transmission is a low 10–15% (higher for SCFF). The reciprocal reflectivity gives excellent solar shading and good nighttime artificial light performance.

Circulation Systems

The atrium is a circulation concept. It replaces the solid block, with its often labyrinthine interior circulation routes, with an open, easily comprehensible arrangement.

Good atrium design capitalizes on this, placing arrival points in the atrium, locating vertical circulation in or looking into the atrium, and giving direct or indirect views into the space from upper level circulation. The apparent generosity with volume that the atrium approach brings is offset by two factors:

- Atrium buildings usually have fewer and larger floors than conventional buildings of the same area. This makes substantial savings possible on vertical circulation systems and, incidentally, on plumbing installations.
- Circulation equipment can often be located in the atrium void, leaving more usable area undisturbed.

Lower buildings with higher populations per floor make escalators more interesting as part of the vertical circulation system. Reliance on escalators is possible for heavily populated buildings up to four or five stories. A mix of elevators and escalators in taller buildings can provide for lower floors and for peak arrival and departure flows by escalator. The new Lloyds of London headquarters (Fig. 19) exhibits this pattern. The Hong Kong and Shanghai Banking Corp.'s new headquarters in Hong Kong (Fig. 12) teams elevators and escalators in an original manner. Escalators lift people from a plaza beneath the building into its atrium entry floor. Elevator shuttles then move them to sky lobbies, with escalators replacing local elevators to deliver staff to each stack of floors. In all-elevator buildings, the sky-lobby concept is often teamed with elevator staging; shuttles deliver people to a series of atrium spaces from which local elevators rise. A multistage tower can feel like a stack of smaller buildings, each with a "front door" atrium overlooked by its occupied space.

There are several strategies for locating elevators in atrium buildings: only a minority use glass observation elevators within the space. Those buildings that do use them choose either a separate tower or towers of elevators, or a row of attached wall-climbers along gallery circulation. Many buildings mix wall-climbers with conventional elevators to cater to the proportion of people who dislike wall-climbers and to reduce the costs of an all-custom-designed installation. Few office buildings use wall-climbers, as they are associated with hotels and leisure environments. Office elevator clusters are located with views from the lobby into the atrium, from the end of a double-banked lobby, or along the face of a single-banked set of elevators. In podium-atrium buildings, a variation on the theme is the wall-climber on the outside of the tower, which rises from within the podium space.

As mentioned above, a separate, conventional elevator will probably be needed for firefighting if main elevators or their lobbies are unprotected. Wall-climbers and escalators in atria need no fire enclosure for normal use, but they are also, therefore, useless in emergencies.

Atrium buildings have increased the demand for hydraulic elevators. This type of drive is smooth-riding, reliable, and uncluttered by counterweights or motor-rooms at shaft-top. It is slightly more expensive, however, and limited to a maximum of six stories. As lower buildings

Figure 19. A four-sided atrium, opening into three-sided form towards the top, is Lloyds of London headquarters by Richard Rogers and Partners, 1986. The lowest four levels around the atrium act as single insurance trading room. Courtesy of Lloyds of London; Richard Rogers Partnership.

spread and elevator costs are thereby reduced, its advantages can outweigh its disadvantages.

Guideway design for wall-climber elevators can follow manufacturers' recommendations, although these assume that concealment of mechanisms is desired. Exposed support and guiderail designs are also possible and can be quite minimal. Safety is the overriding factor. The public must not be able to approach the moving car or the guides and door mechanisms. Side screens of glass are sometimes used, but can be more cluttered than enclosing the guideway would have been. Glass screens or wide safety zones must be allowed where cars pass through atrium floors.

One particular circulation issue has been created by the atrium: how to relate public circulation to semiprivate circulation where both use the atrium. Office, hotel, shopping, leisure, parking, and transit users all move through many atria and galleria, with the mixed use encouraged for its good trading effect. Security and compatibility problems have arisen, however, with the crowds drawn by leisure and transit uses, for example, proving incompatible with specialty shopping. Access to private space off the atrium can also be difficult to control in a fully open arrangement. Effective designs segregate users unobtrusively. Twenty-four-hour public access is usually on a level below the entry to limited-hours spaces, with controlled access between levels. The Royal Bank (Toronto) and the San Antonio Hyatt provide very good examples, with open views between controlled-access levels. Similarly, it is sensible not to run elevators to offices, apartments, or hotel rooms past lobby level to public levels, parking, or transit. A separate elevator service from lobby to public levels is essential if security is to be maintained.

Atrium development is playing an increasing role in creating focal urban spaces, on skywalk or subway systems, at railroad and rapid transit stations. The potential for successful urban space is tremendous, if the necessary circulation precautions are observed.

Planting in Atria

The association between atria and planting is close. The greenhouse is one source of the concept, and one of the atrium's main roles is to act as a metaphor of the outdoors. There are as a result very few atria with no planting at all, and some with so elaborate an installation that the illusion of outdoors is very strong. Landscape design concepts for atria are as diverse as those for outdoor areas, although within the technical limits of indoor planting. It is those technical limitations with which this section will deal.

Plant selection for atrium use is limited compared to that available for outdoors. Low light levels and relatively high average annual temperatures, the environment of most atria, allow successful use only of tropical species used to shade conditions. Temperate plants do not get the winter rest they need. The most effective large trees have proved to be fig (*Ficus*) varieties, although palms and the umbrella tree (*Schefflera actinophylla*) are increasingly used. Giant bamboo forms a striking forest at the IBM headquarters in New York. Usable smaller-scale plants are drawn from the much wider range developed for indoor use. Ferns, ivies, and the ubiquitous philodendron are most common, with more unusual specimens used as contrasts. Permanent flowering plants are only possible in very high light levels, but are often seen as temporary potted displays.

Keeping plants alive indoors, or perhaps more realistically slowing their death rate, demands an understanding of plant physiology, and suitably designed environment and growing media. Plants live on a balance of light, heat, gases, water, and nutrients. Light provides the basic energy supply, but also information that determines the plant's shape, direction of growth, and seasonal pattern of activity. Hormones in the leaves and stems note length of day, direction, level, and color of light. Photosynthesis in the leaves derives carbohydrate fuel for the plant's metabolic process from carbon dioxide and water interacting in light. Metabolic energy is created by respiration, oxidizing part of the fuel. The rate of respiration is temperature-sensitive, doubling for every 10°C rise. A compensation point exists for any plant at which temperature and light levels balance to meet respiration fuel needs. Only above that point can growth occur, using fuel surplus for respiration needs. Continuous light is not desirable, however, as the actual construction of carbohydrates and their transport to growth points only occurs in the dark. Underground, the root system takes up water and nutrients, and pulls down carbohydrates for growth, all driven by the energy created above ground. The balance between the spread of the plant above- and underground will tend to be unnatural in indoor planting, with too little root structure for unaided stability.

Environmental conditions for plants are more demanding than those needed for a successful climatic-buffer atrium. A range of 21–24°C in daytime, falling to 15–16°C at night, suits the most widely used species. Very low temperatures, below 10–13°C, can kill tropical species, whereas the very high temperatures, found near roofs in particular, can overstress them quickly. A tempered-buffer atrium is required, if not a full-comfort one, to allow successful planting. Weekend and holiday conditions must also be maintained, even if the rest of the building is shut down. Local conditions are important too. Cold radiation through glass can kill, whereas heat burns can be caused by minor glass flaws and artificial lights placed too close. Drafts from doors and air inputs, even as low as 1.5 m/sec, will cause die-back. Humidity levels are not a problem, however.

Light is the hardest commodity to supply. A diet of 700–1000 lux for 12 h is ideal, with 500 lux for a similar period as minimal for survival. This implies 14–20% daylight factor through clear glass under an overcast sky, which is unlikely to be available year-round. Supplementary sources are most likely to be needed, running principally in daylight only, to preserve the dark period for carbohydrate formation. Supplementary sources will also be needed to correct any shape distortion caused by unequal daylight supplies around the plant. Good color-rendition lamps are needed, not just for appearance but to avoid stunted or etiolated growth resulting from overly blue or red sources. Nighttime-effect lighting can be quite separate from the main lighting provided. Its low level will not cause problems, but even so it should be turned off for 4–6 h at least.

Planting can be grown in lightweight compost or in water (hydroculture). Most large-scale installations use compost media, as it allows easy anchorage of plants. Hydroculture is gaining ground for small plants, as it is the way most are grown in the nursery and enables low maintenance costs after installation. Continuous movement of nutrient-bearing water through an inert rooting medium like clay granules can be almost completely automatic. Automatic watering systems for compost installations do exist, however, activated by sensors detecting water levels or by indicators for occasional manual top-up of reservoirs.

Whereas naturalistic appearance of plants in their setting is usually required, it is by no means universal that plants are actually "planted" in the building. Most small plants remain in their production containers, disguised by bark chippings. These potted plants can be readily exchanged. Large trees can be in a pervious or biodegradable production container, set into compost in a permanent planter. These heavy structures need integration with the building frame design, and with waterproofing and drainage systems. Water features will need similar early consideration.

Care and maintenance of planting installations is crucial. If the building owner is not a wholehearted supporter of the scheme proposed, it is better to omit it or resort to the use of artificial plants. Care can be very labor-intensive, and the skills required are not always available. Mechanical, electrical, and gardening skills will be needed if any automation is built in. Planting should go into the atrium last, after general cleaning down is done, to avoid the immediate need to dust each leaf. Plants will have been acclimatized for a period before moving, and there may be seasonal influences on when plants can best be moved.

An allowance for continuous and prompt replacement of the 10–20% losses among smaller plants is needed. Access routes and water and power supply around the installation will be very valuable in minimizing labor cost and disruption of public amenity.

It is necessary to remember that planting and some composts can represent a fire load within an atrium; some highly flammable plant materials must be avoided. Another negative factor is that, as plants live on light, they do not reflect much of it. If daylight for working illumination is at a premium, it is necessary to locate planting where it will not unduly reduce reflected light levels within the atrium.

COST PLANNING

The budget for an atrium building is somewhat differently distributed than that for a conventional building. In capital terms, there are extra cost elements as well as savings; in revenue terms, there can be significant savings; in investment terms, there can be a significant increase in value.

For capital cost, the useful comparison is between an atrium building and a tower or slab form of the same rentable floorspace. The tower is likely to stand back from plot boundaries and have external landscaping. The atrium is likely to cover the full plot, with internal landscaped space. Compared to the tower, the atrium form will have fewer floors, lighter structure, and a lesser gross area for the same rentable space. Elevators will be fewer, as will restroom areas and escape stair flights. Construction time will be reduced, lowering interest costs and bringing forward return on capital. Extra costs, on the other hand, will come from the atrium envelope and from fire-engineering requirements. Landscape costs will be similar.

Published studies suggest that where a similar floorspace depth (window to core) is taken, atrium forms are about 15% less costly per rentable unit of area. Deeper plan space is more economical to construct than shallow plan, however, and atrium office and hotel buildings are frequently shallower in plan than their conventional equivalents. Atrium costs can be slightly above conventional costs if plan depths are very different.

Operating costs favor the daylit building with effective solar shading. Where a similar capital cost is invested in climate-control systems, ie, insulation and shading, indications are that daylit atrium buildings can consume from one-half to two-thirds the energy of a deeper, conventional building. Where similar building energy performance standards are sought, the capital cost of achieving them is higher in conventional design. Landscape care costs will, however, generally be higher for interior schemes.

The most significant economic effect of atrium design has, however, been on investment value. All other things being equal, commercial atrium developments outperform conventional ones. The initial novelty value can be discounted in cities where the atrium form is already familiar, but it is still a strong effect when it applies. Lasting effects are due to the enhanced perceived value of rentable space in atrium buildings. In retail development, there can be double frontage, inside and outside; there is enhanced ability to trade on several levels; and there is increased marketability of the center as an entity, with themed identity and promotion. In office development, there is the ability to provide more window offices and corner offices in a shallower, more modeled floorplan; individual floors can be larger, meeting market demand for horizontal working relationships; and open sides to atria, with frequent stairs, can further reduce the divisive effects of multilevel space. In hotel development, the atrium provides a "resort" facility and ambience, which becomes a strong factor in the attraction of the hotel.

What is clear from experience to date is that there is no direct link between enclosed volume and capital or operating costs. Cost factors and value factors can be planned with greater sophistication in atrium design to provide generally higher added value.

WORLDWIDE EXPRESSIONS

In the period between 1967 and 1985, at least 400 significant atrium buildings have been completed. Conservatively assessed, these represent an investment of over $4 billion. The great majority are commercially developed and funded, reflected in the building types and styles of this body of work. Hotels, office buildings, shopping centers, and mixed-use complexes are the dominant expression of the modern atrium building. There are, however, interesting examples of public buildings. Two-thirds of all modern atrium buildings are to be found in North America; Canada and the United States have exploited the concept vigorously now for 20 years. London, with over 35 examples and a rapid rate of further development, is, however, probably the single most concentrated location. It has half of the UK's atria. Scandinavia is the other main European focus. In the rest of the world, it is the centers of rapid development during the 1970s and 1980s that feature atrium buildings: the OPEC members, Singapore, Hong Kong, and Japan.

This survey of examples is not, however, based on loca-

tion or building type, but on the generic form of the building: the way the atrium concept is used in relation to the surrounding accommodation. Nine generic types of atria are identifiable: five simple ones based on the degree of enclosure of the atrium by surrounding space and four complex ones involving multiple buildings or atria in a variety of ways.

Single-sided Atria. A small number of atrium buildings have a glazed court attached to one side of the building, without wrapping accommodation around this conservatory-like space (Fig. 20). The most notable is the Vancouver Law Courts by Arthur Erickson (Fig. 21). Terraced levels step back below a sloping space-frame glass roof with a wide view of the city's setting. Three fine small examples are at Truman's Brewery, Brick Lane, London; at the Irwin Bank, Columbus, Ind.; and at the Museum of Modern Art extension, New York. The Enerplex North building at Princeton University, by SOM, uses a south-side sunspace which deepens into an atrium to collect light and warmth for the whole complex.

Two-sided Atria. Here, the atrium is half-surrounded by accommodation and half-exposed (Fig. 22). The most famous example is the Ford Foundation headquarters in Manhattan by Roche and Dinkeloo (Fig. 7). Two floors at the top of the section surround the atrium, leaving a skylight at the center over a fine garden. Derived from Ford are the expansive Fourth Financial Center, (Wichita, Kans.) and the compact Spectrum Building (Denver), both fine examples at different scales. Cambridge University History Library has its reading room in the form of a glass-roofed space leaning into the arms of an L-shaped classroom block, whose galleries overlook the room. The Galaxy Theaters (San Francisco) by Kaplan, McLaughlin, Diaz exhibit an exuberant street corner glasshouse resting in the angle of a multicinema group.

Three-sided Atria. This classification covers those cases where the atrium is largely embedded within surrounding

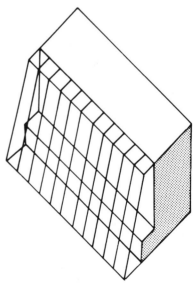

Figure 20. Single-sided atrium type (3). Courtesy of The Architectural Press Ltd.

Figure 21. Single-sided conservatory atrium at the Vancouver Law Courts. Courtesy of Architectural Press.

accommodation, but has a single side open to view (Fig. 23). Sometimes this open side is a grand entrance, as at the State of Illionis building (Chicago) by Murphy/Jahn (Fig. 24), where a segment of the great central rotunda is open to view. This is also the case at Richard Meier's

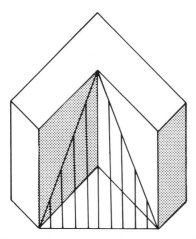

Figure 22. Two-sided atrium type (3). Courtesy of The Architectural Press Ltd.

High Museum (Atlanta) and HOK's Levi's Plaza (San Francisco). In other cases, the great glass side is a solar collector or a vista window. The Hyatt hotels at Dallas and San Antonio frame views. The Children's Hospital of Philadelphia warms the building via its south-facing atrium, shading it from overheating by wide play-decks. London has notable three-sided atria at Lloyds Chambers, Billingsgate, and Stockley House, Victoria.

Four-sided Atria. The most common atrium form is the most economical, the top-lit court completely surrounded by accommodation (Fig. 25). London has a fine collection: the 1837 Reform Club sets the tone. Richard Rogers's Lloyds headquarters uses a 12-story volume for the world's premier insurance market (Fig. 19). Arup Associates have designed two fine examples: one in Finsbury Avenue, London, an octagon of complex section; and Gateway House, Basingstoke (Fig. 26). Coutts's Bank on the Strand and the Sheraton Skyline Hotel, Heathrow, are fine landscaped spaces. Drummond Gate offices have exposed ducting and a free-standing elevator and stair tower to animate the space.

Many of John Portman's atrium hotels are top-lit spaces. They vary from the rectilinear Atlanta (Fig. 1) and O'Hare Hyatts to the baroque Atlanta Marriott Mar-

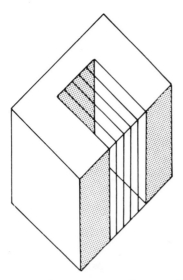

Figure 23. Three-sided atrium type (3). Courtesy of The Architectural Press Ltd.

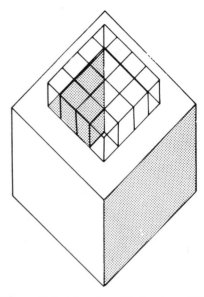

Figure 25. Four-sided atrium type (3). Courtesy of The Architectural Press Ltd.

quis, which is like the inside of a whale. His Marina Centre, Singapore, has three triangular top-lit atrium hotels.

Linear. A linear atrium (Figs. 11 and 27) is not a synonym for a galleria; that term is best used for covered streets, through-routeways usually associated with shopping. Many office buildings arrange their spaces in parallel linear wings and light them from linear courts that have open glazed ends. A good low-rise example is the Decker building at the Corning Glass headquarters (Corning, N.Y.) by Davis, Brody. Murphy/Jahn's Rustoleum headquarters, near Chicago, has entry from one end and from parking below, with stairs and ducts marching along the central cleft. Hennepin County Courthouse, Minneapolis, has twin 22-story towers with a glazed canyon between

Figure 24. Three-sided atrium in the State of Illinois building, 1985 (model). One side of the rotunda opens to the street. Courtesy of Murphy/Jahn.

Figure 26. A tempered-buffer atrium by Arup Associates, at Gateway Two (Basingstoke, UK). Naturally ventilated offices surround this multiuse space, which has underfloor heating to moderate extreme cold. Courtesy of Peter Cook/*Architects' Journal.*

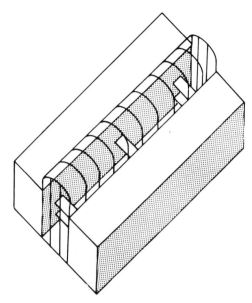

Figure 27. Linear atrium type (3). Courtesy of The Architectural Press Ltd.

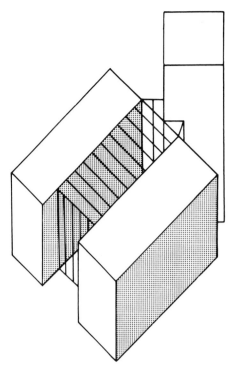

Figure 28. Bridging atrium type (3). Courtesy of The Architectural Press Ltd.

them, similar to the Irving Trust Operations Center, New York. The Mercantile Warehouse conversion (Boston) cuts a 25-ft wide, 400-ft long atrium between walls of apartments above shops. The fine small civic center at Chester-Le-Street, UK, divides its office space into four squares with two intersecting linear atria. One acts as entry lobby and the other as garden and conference space.

Bridging. The term is used to describe atria surrounded by separate building elements (Fig. 28). The atrium "spans" between different buildings or distinct elements of the same complex, and there are views out between the elements. Many of the multiuse complexes of North America are in this category: The Omni Center, Atlanta; the Plaza of the Americas, Dallas; the Eaton Center, Toronto; the First Bank Center, South Bend, Ind.; and Copley Place, Boston. A split single building works similarly, as at the Bell headquarters and the Royal Bank headquarters in Toronto, or the Triton Court and British Telecom buildings in London. Separate elevator towers or shared ones on bridges between blocks give a highly articulated space. At the Ealing Broadway office center, London (Fig. 29), a palmhouse-like atrium bridges between low-rise office elements, bringing people from the street and parking level up an escalator flight reminiscent of Chicago's Water Tower Place.

Podium. In very high density development, where floor area ratios exceed 15:1 and even 20:1, the courtyard plan can work only on the largest sites. Seeking to combine the appeal of atria with the density of solid towers, U.S. architects have created a hybrid. A conventional tower provides most of the floorspace, but with an attached atrium around the base, forming a podium (Fig. 30). There are some very fine and varied examples. For Minneapolis, Johnson Burgee designed the IDS center, a full city block with a ring of buildings around the marvelous Crystal Court. Two of the buildings rise above the roof of the court, one to be the city's tallest. Pennzoil Place, Houston,

shows the same architect enclosing space at the foot of prismatic twin towers by draping glass skirts out from the towers. Three Westin hotels by John Portman use the device: the Bonaventure, Los Angeles; the Peachtree Plaza, Atlanta; and the Detroit Plaza all feature circular guestroom towers rising through the roof of atria, which are enclosed by public rooms and retail space.

New York City has the most varied collection of podium atria. Citicorp has a seven-story shopping and office court

Figure 29. A glasshouse-style bridging atrium links two wings of the Ealing Broadway Office Centre, London, 1985, by Building Design Partnership. Escalators rise from street and parking below. Courtesy of Building Design Partnership/Martin Charles.

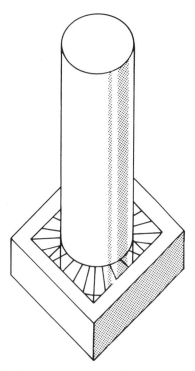

Figure 30. Podium atrium type (3). Courtesy of The Architectural Press Ltd.

around one foot of its tower (Fig. 31). Trump Tower has a similar but upmarket shopping center at the foot of an apartment tower. The IBM headquarters, alongside Trump Tower, has a glazed garden on a triangle of land at the base of a conventional office tower. Chemcourt is a retrofit podium atrium; a glasshouse has been added, covering the small plaza around the base of Chemical Bank's Park Avenue tower. The result is a marvelous urban park.

Multiple Lateral. Where any atrium form is used twice or more on one building, the phenomenon of windowed space with no external wall at all can occur (Fig. 32). This allows development of very deep building footprints, combined with the use of essentially shallow-plan space. Examples are rare, but more can be expected. The Intelsat headquarters (Washington, D.C.) by John Andrews arranges square office stacks corner to corner, roofing a chain of courts that can extend in all directions. The Central Beheer headquarters (Apeldoorn, The Netherlands) by Hertzberger sets dozens of connected 9-m square stacks of office levels under a shared roof, producing a matrix of miniature atria (Fig. 33). Simpler concepts are seen at the Royal Garden hotel (Trondheim, Norway), where a multiwing plan has each court enclosed with a linear atrium; there are conservatory atria at each end of the array. At Victoria Plaza, London, a deep plan is subdivided into three skylit courtyards.

Connected atrium buildings produce similar environments: the Finsbury Avenue complex in London will add further atria as connected phases continue, and the Milton Keynes Central Business Exchange has a ring of four connected atrium buildings, and can add more.

Multiple Vertical. A rare but significant alternative to the podium atrium in high density development is the multiple vertical or stacked atrium building (Fig. 34). Skidmore Owings and Merrill have pioneered the concept with their 33 West Monroe tower in Chicago (Fig. 35) and the Pan American Life headquarters in New Orleans. Using a three-sided atrium plan form, these tower buildings have subdivided what would otherwise have been a Portmanesque spectacular atrium into a quieter series of spaces. Each atrium is a sky lobby, coincident with the start of a local elevator bank, and can act as the front door of a

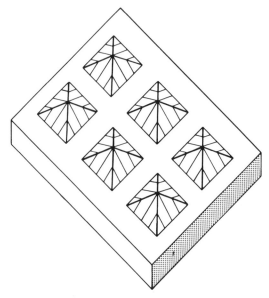

Figure 31. One of New York's many podium atria, at Citicorp headquarters, 1978, by Hugh Stubbins. One of the tower's four giant columns is on the right. Courtesy of Norman McGrath.

Figure 32. Multiple lateral atrium type (3). Courtesy of The Architectural Press Ltd.

Figure 33. Multiple lateral atria. The Centraal Beheer headquarters, (Apeldoorn, The Netherlands) consists of dozens of linked stacks of space, lit by small, cruciform atria. Courtesy of W. Jansen/Centraal Beheer.

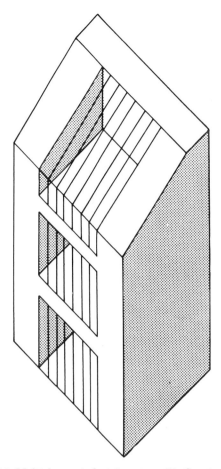

Figure 34. Multiple vertical atrium type (3). Courtesy of The Architectural Press Ltd.

major tenancy. This principle can be radically extended to produce towers taller and thicker than any planned to date, without increasing the acceptable depth of occupied space.

Other examples are worthy of study. Norman Foster's Hong Kong and Shanghai Banking Corp. headquarters (Fig. 12) has one major atrium in its lowest 10 stories and other minor ones in its upper levels to handle escalator stacks dispersing people from shuttle elevators. Helmut Jahn's 100 Wacker tower in Chicago gives small atria to each sky-lobby level, which coincide with setbacks. Jahn's extension to the Chicago Board of Trade sits an atrium office building on top of eight levels of the trading floor complex, with elevator access by shuttle to the atrium floor, then transferring to a tower of local elevators across the court. John Portman's Marriot Marquis hotel in New York starts its 42-story atrium at the eighth floor, above a series of linked foyer levels served by the same elevator tower.

Climatic Types. The way atria work climatically in relation to the surrounding space cuts across their formal classifications. In the section on environmental design above, distinctions were made between canopy, buffer, tempered-buffer, and full-comfort atria, and between warming, convertible, and cooling atria. Examples of canopy atria, those not fully enclosed and completely unserviced, include the historic Covent Garden market and Burlington Arcade (London), and the Galleria in Milan and Naples. Modern examples are the Antoine Graves houses, Atlanta (Fig. 8); Brunel Plaza, Swindon, UK (Fig. 36); and several of Charles Correa's complexes in India, sheltered by giant pergolas.

Buffer atria, enclosed but serviced only by passive means, include the University of Trondheim, Norway; Swansea Quadrant center, Wales; the Gregory Bateson Building, Sacramento, Calif. (Fig. 16); and two major historic examples—Barton Arcade (Manchester, UK) (Fig. 3) and the National Building Museum in the Old Pensions Building (Washington, D.C.).

Tempered-buffer atria, those with energy input only to control excessive temperature range, include the Sohio Operation Center at Prudhoe Bay, Alaska (Fig. 13), where atria provide a sunny, quasi-outdoors during the arctic night, and three naturally ventilated atrium office buildings in the UK: Gateway II in Basingstoke (Fig. 26), Cavern Walks in Liverpool, and the Midsummer 4 building at

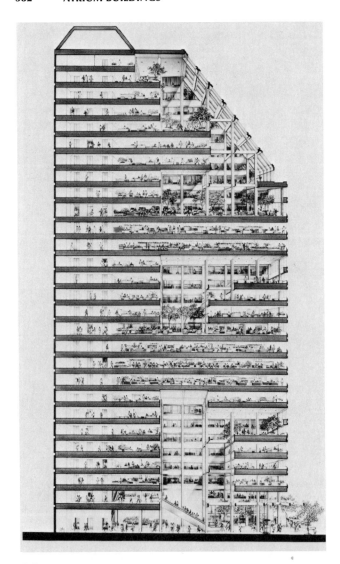

33 WEST MONROE   SECTION PERSPECTIVE

Figure 35. 33 West Monroe (Chicago, Ill.) was the first of many stacked atrium designs from Skidmore, Owings and Merrill. The section shows three atria. A development of Draper and Kramer, Inc. (Chicago, Ill.).

Milton Keynes. Full-comfort atria are very common, encompassing all hotels and most of the other U.S. office developments mentioned.

Warming atria, designed for winter solar collection, include most Scandinavian examples, where a conscious effort has been made to collect energy. Low-rise housing schemes are most notable, in particular, the Tarnan site in Landskrona, Sweden. The JCC-huset building at Kista, Stockholm, is one of the best warming atria in an office building. Multiuse projects, using office waste heat to buffer housing, are in progress. In the UK, the schools of Hampshire are following an energy related program of building. Crestwood, Yateley, Locksheath, and Netley schools are of interest, using sunspaces as atria.

Cooling atria, designed to shield occupied space from solar impact and to be a reservoir of cool air, are most

Figure 36. A canopy atrium at the Brunel Centre (Swindon, UK) shelters a shopping plaza without complete enclosure. Douglas Stephen and Partners, 1978. Courtesy of Douglas Steven and Partners/Martin Charles.

highly developed in extreme climates. A series of Arabian hotels are notable: the Sheratons at Dubai (Fig. 14) and Basra have traditional, Islamic courtyard architecture in modern form, with dim, indirect daylight. Other good examples are the Holiday Inn, Kuwait, and the Messarrah Intercontinental at Taif, Saudi Arabia. The Saudi Foreign Ministry building (Riyadh) by Henning Larsen must be the ultimate in the sophisticated modern use of traditional climate and culture-related architecture.

Convertible atria, adjusting between sunny, cold winters and hot summers, are found only in continental climates. The Gregory Bateson building (Sacramento) (Fig. 16) has the features needed, but in a very benign climate. The Solarium by WZMH (Denver, Col.) has a well-developed approach, with steerable external louvers, to admit or exclude sun and to retain winter warmth.

Worldwide expressions of the atrium concept thus range through most of the cultures and climates of the planet: in high technology or in intermediate forms, in futuristic forms or in historic recyclings, in huge and in modest scale. There is much to be learned from the first 20 years of modern atrium building to develop the truly successful applications and to avoid the pitfalls.

BIBLIOGRAPHY

1. L. Martin and L. March, *Land Use and Built Form*, Cambridge University Press, 1966.
2. B. Maitland, *Shopping Malls, Planning and Design*, Nichols Publishing Co., New York, and Construction Press (Longmans), London, 1985.

3. R. Saxon, *Atrium Buildings, Development and Design,* Architectural Press, London, and Van Nostrand Reinhold, New York, 1983 (2nd ed. 1986). The main source for this article. Technical illustrations can be found here and a full bibliography.

GENERAL REFERENCES

Carlson, Almstedt, Thor, and Wozniak, *Overglasade Rum* (in Swedish), Svensk Byggtjanst, Sweden, 1985.

Atrium buildings are also continuously covered by case-study articles in each of the major U.S. and UK architectural journals.

RICHARD G. SAXON
Building Design Partnership
London, United Kingdom

AVIARIES.   See ZOOS.

B

BACON, EDMUND N.

Born in Philadelphia on May 10, 1910, Edmund Norwood Bacon received a Bachelor of Architecture degree from Cornell University in 1932 and was elected to membership in Tau Beta Pi, the national engineering honor society. After work as an architectural designer with Henry Killam Murphy in Shanghai, People's Republic of China, and with W. Pope Barney, Philadelphia architect, he undertook graduate study in 1935 at Cranbrook Academy of Art (Bloomfield Hills, Mich.) under Eliel Saarinen. Bacon was Supervisor of City Planning at the Institute for Research and Planning in Flint, Mich. from 1937 to 1939, and was appointed Managing Director of the Philadelphia Housing Association in 1940. He served the U.S. Navy in the South Pacific from 1943 to 1946. In 1946, he became Senior Land Planner (and codesigner with Oscar Stonorov of the Better Philadelphia Exhibition) with the Philadelphia City Planning Commission.

There, he made a singularly important contribution to that city and to urban design and planning over the next several decades, building on the initial plan of Thomas

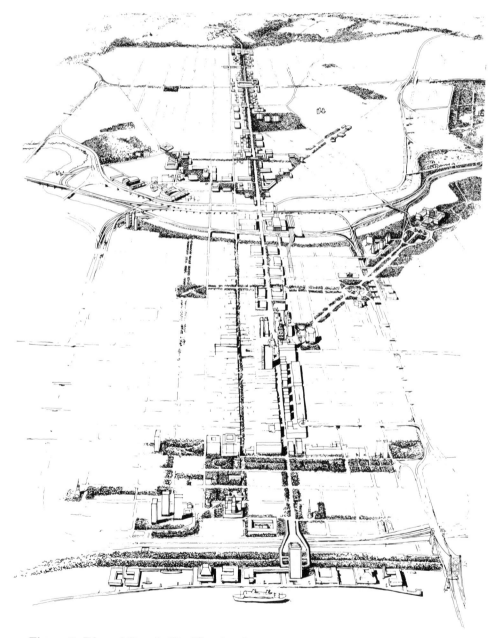

Figure 1. Edmund Bacon's City Planning Commission illustration of Philadelphia (1963) (4). Drawing by Irving Wasserman.

Holme for William Penn in 1683. This occurred particularly during his service as Executive Director from 1949 to 1970; he acquired the additional title of Development Coordinator in 1968.

During this period, he began his service as an adjunct professor at the University of Pennsylvania (1950–), and received a Ford Foundation travel and study award in 1959 and a Medal of Achievement from the Art Alliance of Philadelphia in 1961. In 1962, he was given the Man of the Year Award from the City Business Club and the Brown Medal from the Franklin Institute, both Philadelphia organizations. Bacon also received an award from the Rockefeller Foundation in 1963. *Time* featured him on its cover and in the accompanying story on "The City" in 1964, emphasizing his role in the planning of Center City Philadelphia and the Market Street East downtown development (1,2).

In 1965, Bacon participated in the White House Conference on Natural Beauty, and stated (3):

> In Philadelphia over the last several years we have developed the concept that we will move into the most depressed areas of the city; that we will establish in the center of these areas oases of beauty—parks and squares next to beloved landmarks which will serve as rallying points for neighborhood pride and identification and, in the process, identification with the city as a whole.

In the capacity of Chairman of the Conference Townscape Panel he reported (3):

> The technological capacity of American industry must be harnessed with our design knowledge if we are ever to create a higher order of urban environmental design. To achieve this objective, the panel recommends that the professional societies concerned create, with Federal aid, a National Urban Design Center. Such a center would coordinate the work of architects, planners, landscape architects, industrial and interior designers, manufacturers, and research corporations—with all who contribute to total townscape design. . . . Every city should develop a comprehensive design plan embracing elements of the environment, as part of its comprehensive planning program. . . . comprehensive design planning must be an integral part of the decisionmaking function of local or regional governments.

Bacon was appointed by President Johnson to serve on the Citizen's Advisory Committee on Recreation and Natural Beauty from 1966 to 1969, and served as a Trustee of the American Academy in Rome from 1965 to 1976. He served on the Secretary of the Interior's Potomac River Basin Task Force, 1965–1967, and on the Secretary of Transportation's Urban Transportation Advisory Council, 1969–1971.

In 1967, he wrote the major urban design text, *Design of Cities* (revised in 1974), in which he stated (4):

> I contend that human will can be exercised effectively on our cities now, so that the form that they take will be a true expression of the highest aspirations of our civilization.

As background for this, the accompanying 1963 City Planning Commission illustration (Fig. 1) presents ". . . a broad impression of the evolving structure underlying the growth and development of Philadelphia" (4).

He received the Distinguished Service Award of the American Institute of Planners in 1971 and the Gold Medal of the Royal Institute of Chartered Surveyors in 1974. A Fellow of the American Institute of Architects, he received its Medal and the R. S. Reynolds Memorial Award for Community Architecture in 1976, when he was also awarded the Fairmont Park Art Association Medal of Honor. He received the Philadelphia Award in 1983 and the Penn Club Award in 1984.

Bacon served as Professional Adviser for the FDR Memorial Design Competition in 1959, and was on the juries for the University of Miami International Campus Plan Competition and the national AIA Institute Honors in 1986. He produced the "Understanding Cities" film series in 1983. Since 1972, he has served as Vice-President, Design/Development, Mondev International, Ltd.

BIBLIOGRAPHY

1. G. Breckenfeld and co-reporters, "The City," *Time,* **84**(19) (Nov. 6, 1964).
2. R. D. Childs in R. Warburton, ed., *J. Franklin Inst.* **286**(5), 451 (Nov. 1968).
3. *Beauty for America,* U.S. Government Printing Office, Washington, D.C., 1965, pp. 77 and 635.
4. E. N. Bacon, *Design of Cities,* Viking Press, New York, 1967, revised edition 1974; Viking Penguin, 1974, pp. 13, 300, 301.

GENERAL REFERENCES

E. N. Bacon, "Time, Turf, Architects and Planners," *Archit. Rec.* **159**(3), 97 (Mar. 1976).

J. Gane, ed., *American Architects Directory,* R. R. Bowker Co., New York, 1970, p. 35.

A. Hast, ed., *Who's Who in America,* 43rd ed., Marquis Who's Who Inc., Chicago, 1984–1985, p. 132.

J. Oberlander in A. K. Placzek, ed., *Macmillan Encyclopedia of Architects,* Vol. 1, The Free Press, New York, 1982, p. 123.

S. Stephens, *Prog. Archit.* **57**(4), 46 (Apr. 1976).

Bibliographic Research Library, *Urban Planning and the Work of Edmund Bacon: A Selected Bibliography,* Vance Bibliographies, Monticello, Ill., 1984.

RALPH WARBURTON, FAIA
University of Miami
Coral Gables, Florida

BACON, HENRY

Henry Bacon, U.S. architect, was born in Watseka, Ill. in 1866. After a year at the University of Illinois, Bacon worked for many years at McKim Mead and White in New York. From 1889 to 1891, Bacon traveled abroad as the winner of the Rotch Travelling scholarship. He returned to McKim, Mead & White and became Charles McKim's personal assistant.

In 1897, he left to open a partnership and, in 1903, his own office. Bacon is best known for his collaboration with artists. He designed a number of settings and bases for sculpture, particularly with Augustus Saint-Gaudens and his long-term friend, Daniel Chester French.

Among the many large houses and other commissions he designed, his most famous is the Lincoln Memorial on the Mall in Washington, D.C. The McMillan Commission had recommended extending the Mall, with a monument to Lincoln situated at the end, as early as 1901–1902. The site was confirmed by the Fine Arts Commission in 1911. The Lincoln Memorial Commission asked Henry Bacon to prepare a design for this site and John Russell Pope to design proposals for two alternate sites.

Bacon made several drawings for the site, and John Russell Pope was asked to modify his earlier designs for the approved site. The Lincoln Memorial Commission gave final approval to the site in 1912.

Bacon's design was approved by the Fine Arts Commission and he was asked to prepare the first set of specifications for the building. With their acceptance, President William Howard Taft signed a Congressional resolution naming Bacon the architect of the Lincoln Memorial. All of Bacon's designs included a statue of Lincoln; his choice of sculptor was Daniel Chester French. There was a proposal to use a replica of St. Gauden's standing figure of Lincoln in Chicago for the memorial, but the Commission accepted Bacon's recommendation to proceed with a new sculpture by French. The cornerstone of the building was laid in 1914, and the sculpture started.

The memorial was dedicated in 1922 and has been recognized as one of the most successful monuments in Washington, D.C. The monument is shown on the obverse of the U.S. penny. In 1923, Henry Bacon was awarded the Gold Medal of the American Institute of Architects, presented by President Warren G. Harding in a night ceremony on the steps of the Memorial. Henry Bacon's award represented the high point of the influence of the Ecole des Beaux Arts and classicism in U.S. architectural design.

BIBLIOGRAPHY

General References

E. Conklin, *The Lincoln Memorial,* U.S. Government Printing Office, Washington, D.C., 1927.

R. A. Cram, *Archit. Rec.* **53,** 497 (June 1923).

R. G. Wilson, *The AIA Gold Medal,* McGraw-Hill, Inc., New York, 1984.

M. Richman, *Daniel Chester French, An American Sculptor,* National Trust for Historic Preservation, Washington, D.C., 1976.

ROBERT T. PACKARD, AIA
Reston, Virginia

BANHAM, REYNAR

Reynar Banham, one of this century's foremost architectural historians and critics, has become known for his far-reaching insights and refreshingly witty, often irrever-

ent analyses of modern architecture, including the pop movement and the development of high tech. Banham's professional writing career began in 1952 with a position on the prestigious English periodical *Architectural Review.* Since that time, his insights have appeared in numerous books and hundreds of articles. In addition, Banham has lectured and taught at institutions around the world, including the University of California at Los Angeles and the University College in London.

Banham became an integral part of the International Group (IG), a quorum of artists and writers, including the Smithsons, who invented pop art at the Institute of Contemporary Arts in London in the 1950s. Rather than rejecting mass-produced commercial culture, as did most intellectual groups of the time, the IG enthusiastically consumed movies, advertisements, and other products. Members viewed the aesthetic of pop art as no less serious than traditional values of the fine arts. During the winter sessions of 1954–1955, they explored the topic of popular culture, particularly in the products of Hollywood, Detroit, and Madison Avenue, which members regarded as prime examples of the new art forms. Other themes included expendability and the throwaway aesthetic of art forms that are consumed and discarded as quickly as they are produced. Banham identified this replaceable quality, which digs at the sensitive roots of traditional culture and design philosophy, as the real point of contention with absolutist and idealist art theorists. Banham analyzed the deepest implications of the new mass culture in a continuing series of essays for various publications including *Industrial Design* and *Architectural Review.*

The *Guide To Modern Architecture,* published in 1962, was conceived as the "hoi polloi's" guide to "know when to applaud" architectural theories that have been warped and misinterpreted. In the regaling introduction, Banham writes, "We architecture fans get a poor look-in when modern architecture is being discussed." All too often, the discussion becomes a battle between architects and the public. "Architects make high level utterances meant only to be understood by other architects. The latter write one another resentful newspaper articles about the horrors of modern architecture"(1). In 1964, he received a research scholarship from the Graham Foundation in Chicago, and soon after that he began editing the papers for the prestigious International Design Conference in Aspen. These were later compiled for the 1974 publication of *Aspen Papers: Twenty Years of Design Theory* (2), with editorial and commentary provided by Banham. Also in 1965, Banham was invited to participate in a design symposium held at the University of California at Los Angeles. His fascination with the city resulted in yearly visits until 1976 when he took up residence in Los Angeles.

In 1965, Banham also collaborated with Francois Dallegret and Richard Hamilton on the design of the Unhouse in support of dialectical creation, and the pursuit of more profound personal freedom through the construction of environments sensitive to instantaneous wish fulfillment. Banham explains, "What we want, clearly, is a miniaturized, mobile, cooking, refrigerating, televiewing, trunk-dialing, drying, martini-dispensing services robot with fitted ashtrays and book rest that will follow us around the house riding on a cushion of air like an interplanetary Hoover" (3). In effect, they used available technology to create the modern day Aladdin's lamp, a robotic maid designed for immediate gratification and growing out of the great American tradition exemplified in the luxurious executive suite and Buckminster Fuller's standard-of-living package. In his essay "The Unhouse," Banham depicts the ideal freedom of the savage returned to nature and unrestricted by his enclosure. Once all the technology and great gizmos are in place, Banham says, ". . . when your house contains such a complex of piping, flues, ducts, wires, lights, inlets, outlets, ovens, sinks, refuse disposals, . . . when it contains so many services that the hardware could stand up by itself without any assistance from the house, why have a house to hold it up?"(4).

The publication of a series of important books came in rapid succession, beginning with *The New Brutalism,* published in 1966. Banham describes this as an extraordinarily exciting period in the evolution of British ideas. As Banham had been personally acquainted with most of the British Brutalists from 1952 on, the book is hardly a dispassionate review conducted from the heights of an ivory tower. Although, according to Banham, the most significant fact about the backward-looking reformist trend was its demise, Banham explains that he was seduced by the ethical stand of Brutalism, "an idea that the relationships of the parts and materials of a building are a working morality. This, for me, is the continuing validity of the New Brutalism"(5).

In 1967 came the publication of *The First Machine Age,* in which Banham explores the significance of the industrial age in which a single housewife frequently uses more horsepower in a single day than an industrial worker did at the beginning of the century. Banham believes that the men who wrought the new machine age aesthetic were not completely equipped to handle their new environment. "While we yet lack a body of theory proper to our own Machine Age, we are still free-wheeling along with the ideas and aesthetics left over from the first"(6).

Fame and a U.S. audience came with the publication of *Los Angeles, the Architecture of Four Ecologies* (7), written in 1971 in conjunction with the production of a television program for the BBC, "Reynar Banham Loves Los Angeles." Roughly divided into two sections, ecology and architecture, the book evaluates the rich architectural diversity and underlying patterns of the city. Banham isolates four distinct environments within Los Angeles: surburbia, the foothills, the heartland, and the freeways. In 1973 came *The Age of The Masters.* Referring to Gropius, Le Corbusier, and other perpetrators of the modern movement, Banham opens with his typically rousing approach: "Now that they are all dead, it is difficult not to feel liberation as well as loss. While they lived, they tyrannized the Modern Movement"(8). He explains that the coherent body of principles of the modern great architects gave solidarity and cohesion to the profession, but attacks the traditional elitist role of the architect as form giver, creator, and controller of human environments. He argues the importance of public participation in determining their own environment. *Megastructures* (9), published in 1976, is an analysis of an architectural movement of megastructures. These vast monumental frameworks, generally of modern technology, typically were designed to maximize freedom for individuals and groups by enabling them to contrive their own environments. He examines the work of groups including Archigram in London and the metabolists in Japan.

Banham became a professor and coordinator of the art history program at The University of California at Santa Cruz.

BIBLIOGRAPHY

1. R. Banham, *Guide to Modern Architecture,* Van Nostrand Reinhold Co., Inc., New York, 1962, p. 9.
2. R. Banham, *Twenty Years of Design Theory,* International Design Conference, Praeger Publishers, New York, 1974.
3. *The Architects' Journal,* 415 (1960).
4. R. Banham, "The Unhouse," *Art in America* (Apr. 1965).
5. R. Banham, *The New Brutalism,* Reinhold, New York, 1966, p. 3.
6. R. Banham, *The Machine Age,* Harper & Row, Publishers Inc., New York, 1975, p. 12.
7. R. Banham, *Los Angeles: The Architecture of Four Ecologies,* Harper & Row, Publishers Inc., 1971.
8. R. Banham, *Age of the Masters,* Harper & Row, Publishers Inc., 1975, p. 3.
9. R. Banham, *Megastructures,* Thames and Hudson, London, 1976.

BARBARA WADKINS
New School of Architecture
Chula Vista, California

BANKS

The concept of banking has always been closely identified with the building in which it is performed. Whether a bank is seen as a place to store communal and individual wealth or as a central point for financial dealings, its importance within the community has always been great.

As economic systems have changed, forcing changes to currencies and how they are handled, the design of those financial institutions has also changed. Whether the imposing, fortified treasuries for metal coinage or today's electronically protected lines of credit stored by means of magnetic disks, the variation in the building form has been dramatic.

If the banks of the past have needed to be places of strong physical presence and image, and today's banks project a sense of openness and ease where electronic transactions are initiated and handled, tomorrow's banks might be nothing more than a projected image onto a direct linkup with the home or office. The only archaic function left for the bank of today, and perhaps of the future, is that of the safety deposit box, which has become only a minor part of its range of services.

What has not changed is the concept of the bank as a depository of trust. If the bank of the eighteenth century communicated that image by means of iron gratings and stately columns, the bank of the twentieth century does so by skillful advertising and promotion. The need to gain the public's trust remains the same.

HISTORY

The earliest known evidence of banking activities dates to the Sumerians of 2000 B.C., where cuneiform tablets record widespread trade and financial activity. Sumerian temples were used to store valuables since they were believed to be under protection of the gods.

The pre-Hellenic Mycenaeans also used these holy places as treasuries and banking centers. An extant example is the tomb of Atreus, dating to 1325 B.C. (Fig. 1).

The Greeks used already existing physical strong points within the city for the safe storage of wealth. The temple, with its religious (and often physical) impregnability, quickly filled that need, the most famous example being the Acropolis of Athens. This differed from the "hall of bankers" or market exchanges which had the opposite requirements, needing to be open and accessible to all and usually housed in a type of building derived from the religious Telesterion or meeting hall.

The Romans continued with the basic concept of retaining financial functions near the temple/civic centers. They placed them in the Tabernae, which first housed merchants but eventually developed into exclusively banking centers in the Forum. In fact, Vitruvius makes a direct reference to placing the "banker's office" in the Forum in the manner of the Greeks (1).

The collapse of the Roman Empire brought a marked reduction in long-distance commerce and banking. Catholic teaching against usury eventually left the handling of money to outsiders. Their houses became strongholds to protect them against robbery and frequent riots (2).

Slowly, during the thirteenth and fourteenth centuries, the town halls in Italian city-states, owing to their relative prosperity and commerce, began to house money-changing and money-lending activities. These buildings served a variety of functions, with civic rooms on the upper floors and market halls on the open ground floor, with financial activities performed in adjacent loggias or booths.

During the Renaissance, from the beginning of the four-

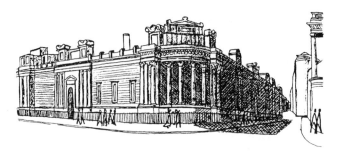

Figure 2. The Bank of England, London, Sir John Soane (1788–1833).

teenth century, banking began to emerge as a positive force, often with religious involvement. Commercial families (the Bardi, Peruzzi, Medici, Fuggers) began to issue "letters of credit" from branches in one city to another. Those branches, housed in the family palazzi, became a new model for bank buildings. A strong, secular image was imposed (3).

Later, public or exchange banks were formed (eg, in 1401 in Barcelona). These continued to use the urban palazzi as their models since their size still served the needs of the organization. When banking became a larger public concern, new prototypes were needed. These new exchanges returned once again to the Greek temple and basilican models, but these too were eventually outgrown. Larger and more complex structures were needed. The Bank of England, Sir John Soane, 1788 (Fig. 2), is a good example, its plan recalling those of imperial villas or palaces. The scale of buildings became larger and more imposing to represent the new power of the institution they housed. The use of the temple symbol and language reappeared as marks of respect and prestige.

In North America, banking began with the informal loans made by individuals or by state governments to each other. The first bank structure in the United States was designed by Samuel Blodgett in 1792 for the First Bank of the United States in Philadelphia (Fig. 3). It became the dominant prototype for bank designs over the next century.

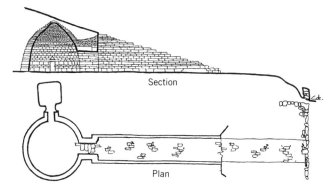

Figure 1. Treasury of Atreus, Mycenae, 1325 BC.

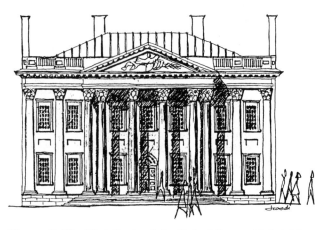

Figure 3. The First Bank of the United States, Philadelphia, Samuel Blodgett (1792).

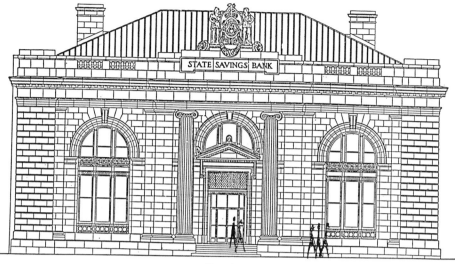

Elevation

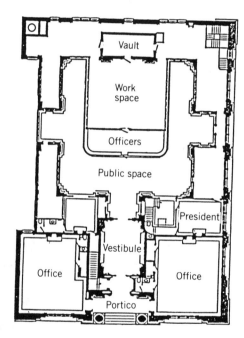

First floor plan

Figure 4. State Savings Bank, Detroit, Mich., McKim, Mead & White (1898).

The extent of the classical, beaux-arts influence can be seen in examples such as the State Savings Bank in Detroit, designed in 1898 by McKim, Mead & White (Fig. 4), with its strong cornice lines and roof ballustrades; and the Riggs National Bank of Washington, D.C., designed in 1897 by York and Savage (Fig. 5), with its strongly secured entrance, great ionic columns capped with a pediment, imposing central hall, and generous use of gilt and bronze in the interior.

When the National Farmer's Bank of Owatonna, Minn., asked Louis Sullivan to design a building for them in 1907 (Fig. 6), the result was not so programmatically different than previous bank architecture. Even while stating that "the Roman temple . . . had died a Roman death,"

Sullivan provided a proportionally large and equally impressive central banking hall with adjacent office space, a formula used well into the twentieth century.

It is only after the financial crisis of the 1930s that a physical change in the type of structure used to house the banking institution is seen. Banking facilities were expanded by the establishment of branch offices, often smaller in size and requiring less space. Such an example is the Shawmut Branch Bank in Boston by Imre and An-

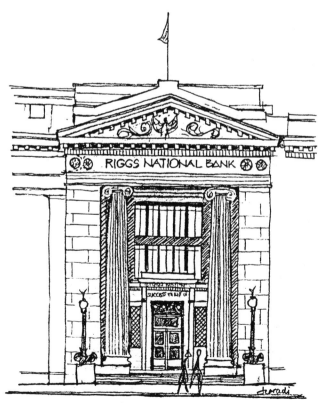

Figure 5. The Riggs National Bank, Washington, D.C., York and Savage (1897).

Figure 6. National Farmer's Bank, Owatonna, Minn., L. H. Sullivan (1907).

thony Halasz, built in 1963 (Fig. 7). The bank's plan, with its unique snail-like coiling, carries forth the idea of security and containment found in the traditional, much larger bank buildings of the past. Its jewel-like quality serves the bank's image well.

At present, the bank building is rapidly changing. Examples of large impressive corporate symbols can still be found, such as the Citicorp building in New York City by Hugh Stubbins and Associates, 1977 (Fig. 8), which, aside from fulfilling the basic institutional and functional needs of the activity of banking, also makes certain implications about the role of a bank in today's society. Attention to public needs and respect for existing institutions has become as important a message as corporate dependability and financial longevity.

DESIGN CONCEPT

Image

The financial power concentrated in a banking organization has always brought with it a social and cultural power of corresponding importance. Banks have always searched for the visual projection of that power by building and by the acquisition of symbols of power. The use of formal symbols derived from religion and from imperial models was a natural development of that search.

Since banks, especially those with public depositories, have needed to convince potential clients of their dependability and stability, a conservative image has been emphasized. In the past, the barred window, the large colonnade, and the heavy bronze doors were as much a visual means of reassuring the customer of the bank's impregnability as an actual security device. The use of heavy arches implied a certain permanence and immutability. Sullivan's National Farmer's Bank in Owatonna (Fig. 6) is a good example of this. Specific symbols became trademarks to certain organizations. For example, the high tower with a pyramid-shaped roof became associated with the Bankers Trust Building in New York City by Trowbridge and Livingstone, 1912 (Fig. 9).

Height, an element still in use today, can be a tool used to reinforce the importance of the institution within the community, the Citicorp Building in New York being an excellent example (Fig. 8).

The smaller, often suburban, branch banks must also deal with the problem of proliferation. The presence of

Figure 7. National Shawmut Branch Bank, Boston, Imre and Anthony Halasz (1963).

these banks on the corners of business streets has increased the competition for the customer's attention. The bank, competing in an already crowded visual field, needs to project an identity to the passerby quickly, and this has led to changes in how banks are designed.

Openness has become important. Technological advances, such as vandal-proof glass, camera surveillance, more sensitive alarms, high intensity illumination, etc, have allowed a greater degree of physical openness without a reduction of the required security. This can be seen in banks such as the Capital City State Bank of Des Moines,

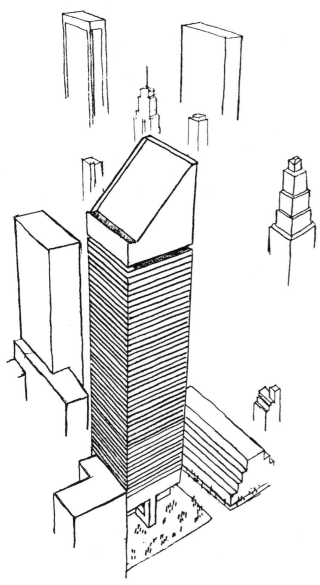

Figure 8. Citicorp Center, New York City, Hugh Stubbins and Associates (1977).

Figure 9. Bankers Trust Building, New York City, Trowbridge and Livingstone (1912).

Recent trends in architectural style have permitted the usage of the traditional symbols of banks (pediments, columns, etc) in new, interesting ways. In their awareness of the need for a image, bankers have traditionally been conscious of the fact that not all building is architecture. As has been said, "Building is about serving function, architecture is about serving art"(4).

Figure 10. Capital City State Bank, Des Moines, Iowa, Charles Herbert and Associates (1977).

Iowa, by Charles Herbert and Associates, 1977 (Fig. 10). It is a structure in which the banking activity is in full view of the passerby, showing that the bank has nothing to hide from the community to which it belongs.

Another aspect of the bank's image that is now being emphasized is the transition in material used, from the heavier, more traditional stone and brick to the lighter, pre-manufactured cladding such as steel, aluminum, and glass, which allow more daring concepts and presentations. These have become new symbols of status since they represent technological advancement, and, by implication, power. This use of the latest building technology seems to parallel the increasingly important role of communications and data-processing technologies now being used by the banks internally and in their dealings with the public. The presence of the latest electronic technology is yet another facet of the modern bank's image.

Function

At present, banks could be placed into a number of functional categories which directly affect the required building. The international organizations of banks, such as the World Bank or InterAmerican Development Bank, are large lending institutions with mainly office-space requirements. The central or national banks found in other nations can also be placed into this grouping, since they function as monetary agents for central governments and have vast office space needs. The functions and space requirements of these banks are similar to the space and building requirements of commercial banks in this post-deregulation period.

Traditional Banking Halls. For the greatest part of their history, commercial banks have used a central high ceilinged, cathedral-like hall in which rows of teller stations face the customer. These grand rooms, as can be seen in the Riggs National Bank (Fig. 11), create an atmosphere of luxury and permanence. Typically, there is a limited amount of office area adjacent to these rooms which is closed to the general public.

Yesterday's Banks. Until the recent past, private and commercial banks in cities and suburbs, although retaining the main features of the traditional banks, made certain changes to conform to new practices. An increase in the amount of space given over to officials who handled the enlarged trust, loan, and mortgage, as well as money fund, CD, and certificate departments, became necessary. An example of this is the Albany Savings Bank, Schenectady, N.Y., by Feibes & Schmitt, 1974 (Fig. 12).

With the variation in commerical hours, it is necessary for businesses to be able to make late-hour deposits. A well-lit, safely placed location needs to be provided by bank design.

One traditional service provided by these banks is the use of safety deposit boxes. Often located next to the vault or in an equally secure area, they require a number of private booths in which the customer can examine the contents of his or her deposit box with comfort. Space

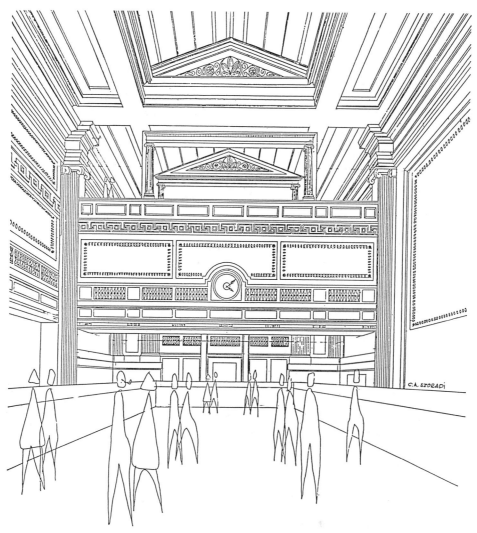

Figure 11. Main office banking hall, the Riggs National Bank, Washington, D.C., York and Savage (1907).

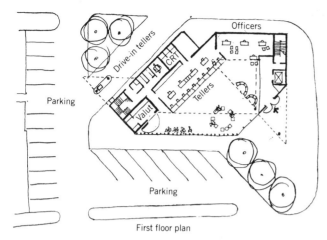

Figure 12. Albany Savings Bank, Schenectady, N.Y., Feibes & Schmitt (1974).

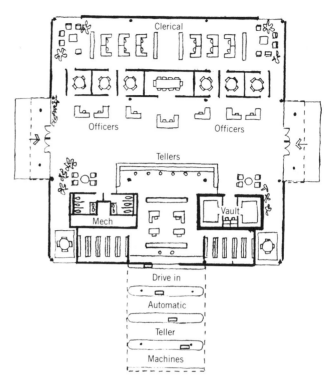

Figure 13. First National Bank of Ripon, Wisc., Hammond, Beeby & Babka (1978).

also needs to be provided for the number of officials in charge of the service, preferably close to the examination and storage areas.

Contemporary Banks. Just as the drastic change from the Renaissance mercantile organization to the individual banking institution required important changes, today's deregulation is also creating different demands in the design of the traditional bank.

Nowadays, banks are experiencing a decrease in personal-teller usage and an increase in electronic banking by businesses and individual customers. In addition, the role of highly specialized services has grown in proportion to their overall activity. A greater amount of office space is being given to banking officials, many of whom are present to deal with the public directly by providing the varied new services found in banks. The deregulation of the banking industry has allowed banks to provide a number of specialized services, from the handling of stock purchases, bullion, money funds, and securities, to the more traditional loan, mortgage, and trust roles of the past.

The shift in services has required a different type of space design. A more intimate atmosphere must be projected for personal transactions where the customer's needs are handled by a specific official and not by one of a number of tellers. Display areas are needed for advertising new or ongoing services, rate changes, or coin or bullion exhibits. Occasionally, assembly rooms in which meetings with special groups of customers can be held are also included in the designs. An example of this is the First National Bank of Ripon, Wis., by Hammond, Beeby & Babka, 1978 (Fig. 13).

The relocation of banks to the suburbs and the increased usage of the automobile demanded the provision of drive-in facilities as well as an accommodation to the scale and setting of suburban sites. Ease of automotive accessibility to drive-in tellers is critical, including provision for necessary movement and waiting areas. A good example of this is again the First National Bank of Ripon, Wis. (Fig. 13). Recently, the drive-in tellers manned by persons have been replaced by the automatic teller machine (ATM). Since the 1980s, this service has often been placed close to the

traditional night deposit boxes to provide the same requirements for lighting and safety. These ATMs are an expanding innovation in banking that has altered design requirements considerably. When the ATMs directly face a public space, a certain amount of protection from the elements needs to be provided for both the machine and its user. Along with lighting and safety, this then becomes a primary consideration, since the use of the ATM and the banking services it represents must remain a pleasant experience to the customer.

Modern office data-processing equipment has also changed the shape of the modern bank. Not only is space required for personal terminals at many of the bank officer's desks, but also at the traditional teller's stations, eg, for computer access for credit checks, wire transfers, etc. Rear counter space for a variety of new electronic office equipment must be provided. Often, the main computer equipment is placed in the headquarter's office, which becomes a centralized information center for branch offices.

The bank lobby, the most common location for ATMs, is now not just part of the entry sequence to the main banking room. It is often the only room of the bank that the customer uses; therefore, some of the design requirements formerly belonging to the banking room have shifted to the lobby. Comfortable lighting, available writing surfaces, bank-slip form containers, and surveillance/safety devices are part of these lobbies. The images, symbols, or logos of the bank as well as any material relating to an ongoing promotional campaign are prominently displayed near the machines. These electronic banking practices and changes in functions have led to shifts in emphasis from the dominant, formal presence often found in designs in the past to the more communal, personal office environment of contemporary designs.

Future

Revolutionary changes are taking place in banking and its buildings owing to technological innovations and industry deregulation. The evolution of more efficient ways of dealing with currency, from "archaic" coins and paper money to the use of signed checks and notes and then to the acceptance of plastic cards with receipts without signature requirements, will give way to electronic signals that require neither signature nor receipt. These trends are beginning to change bank design (5).

In terms of technological changes, smaller new branches with perhaps two or three people and a number of ATMs are starting to spread. Dramatic use of interior design and lighting concepts is becoming increasingly important in order to compensate for the smaller spaces used. The creation of ATM stations, unmanned and with 24-hour card-controlled access, or perhaps placed in even smaller urban or suburban structures, is also a growing trend (6). The enclosure for the ATM by Walton, Madden and Cooper in Beltsville, Md. (Fig. 14), is a good example of the latter. Eventually drive-in tellers will be replaced by the quicker, more efficient drive-in ATM; this process has already begun, especially in the suburbs.

The deregulation of the industry is allowing banks to provide more personal banking services. These new offices will acquire a clublike atmosphere in which privacy and personal contact with the financial advisers will be emphasized (7).

In the future, there will be a greater amount of direct electronic linkups with personal computers at the home and office with no signature, paper receipt, or plastic card to slow down the process. This will make banking as easy and accessible as any other household chore.

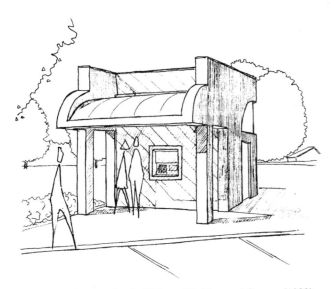

Figure 14. ATM kiosk, Walton, Madden and Cooper (1982).

SECURITY AND EQUIPMENT REQUIREMENTS

Guidelines

The Comptroller of the Currency, in the *Manual For National Banks, Minimum Security Requirements and Procedures,* describes a set of standards for the necessary security. Its purpose is to discourage robberies and help in the apprehension of criminals.

Security System

Surveillance systems need to cover all areas of the bank. The camera must allow reproduction and enlargement of an image to a 1-in. head size, operate silently, take at least one picture every 2 s, and be capable of operating for not less than 3 min.

Robbery alarms are also a requirement. They must be operable from each teller's station and capable of reaching the police, either directly or through a third party, within five minutes. The system must have a visible and audible signal to indicate a malfunction, as well as an independent power source lasting a minimum of 24 hours.

Burglary systems have similar requirements; in addition, all points of entry and equipment such as vaults, safes, ATMs, and night deposit boxes need to be connected to the system. Lighting is also required for the areas surrounding the vault if during the hours of darkness the vault is visible from outside the banking office.

Bank Equipment

Given the fast transformation of the banking format currently under way coupled with the rapid change in elec-

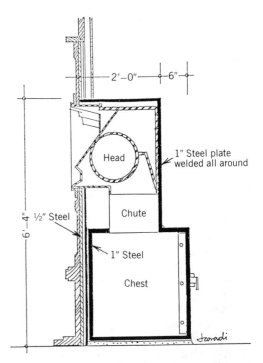

Figure 15. Night depository, cross section.

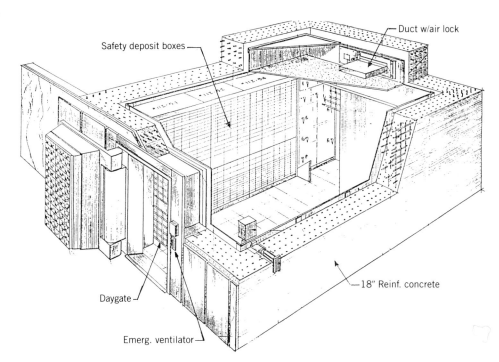

Figure 16. Vault with safety deposit boxes.

tronic equipment, its size, and applications, the equipment used in today's banks changes frequently also. Some, like the ATM and CRT consoles, have arrived within the last decade. Others, such as the night deposit box (Fig. 15) and the vault (Fig. 16), are traditional pieces of equipment which electronic improvements have modernized.

WORLDWIDE EXPRESSION

For the banking industry, the importance of image projection is a worldwide concern. Throughout the capitalist world, the bank needs to present an image of security and trust to the potential client. With the development

Figure 17. Postal Savings Bank, Vienna, Otto Wagner (1904).

of a global communications network, the larger international banks require a recognizable identity with which to operate.

Since the banking industry developed and grew within a European context, it was only natural that, in the past, it used classical symbols to project its required image, as in the Bank of England (Fig. 2). These symbols continued to be used even when banks began to spread beyond Europe.

At the turn of the century, the old beaux-arts style gave way to a number of stylistic experiments in Europe. The Secession-styled Postal Savings Bank of 1904 in Vienna by Otto Wagner (Fig. 17) exemplifies this transition.

The emergence of the Bauhaus during the 1920s began to influence U.S. design. It in turn was adopted and reshaped in the United States and coincided with the growth in this country's worldwide influence.

Today, banks throughout the world are adopting the latest stylistic innovations and banking practices to project the requisite expression of public trust. An example of this can be seen in the Banca Popolare di Verona, Italy, by Carlo Scarpa and Arrigo Rudi, 1974–1981 (Fig. 18).

BIBLIOGRAPHY

1. L. Severini, *The Architecture of Finance; Early Wall Street,* UMI Research Press, Ann Arbor, Mich., 1983, p. 6.

2. "Banks and Banking; Sect. 3: Origins of Banking," *Encyclopedia Americana,* Grolier Educational Corp., Danbury, Conn., p. 172.

3. Ref. 1, p. 9.

4. P. Eisenman, *Number 6 in a series of 12 quotations on architecture gathered for the 1985 AIA National Convention,* June 9–12, 1985, San Francisco, American Institute of Architects (AIA), Washington, D.C.

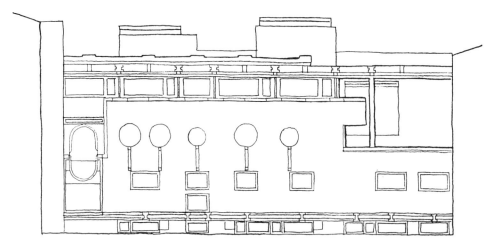

Figure 18. Banca Popolare di Verona, Italy, Carlo Scarpa and Arrigo Rudi (1974–1981).

5. T. W. Thompson, L. L. Berry, and P. H. Davidson, *Banking Tomorrow, Managing Markets Through Planning,* Van Nostrand Reinhold Co., New York, 1978, p. 2.

6. *Ibid.,* p. 10.

7. Ref. 5, p. 11.

General References

Refs. 1, 2, and 5 are good general references.

Vitruvius, *The Ten Books on Architecture,* 1st century B.C., translated by M. H. Morgan, Harvard University Press, Cambridge, Mass., 1914, reprinted by Dover Publications, Inc., New York, 1960.

The Bankers Magazine, Warren, Gorham & Lamont, Inc., New York, 1846.

"Banks," *Architecture Magazine* (May 1912).

Representative Examples of the Work of A. Moorman and Company in the Design, Construction, Reconstruction and Equipment of Bank Buildings, A. Moorman and Co., St. Paul, Minn., 1920.

A. Hopkins, *The Fundamentals of Good Bank Buildings,* The Banker's Publishing Co., New York, 1929.

A Monograph of the Work of McKim, Mead & White, 1879–1915, Arno Press, Inc., New York, 1977.

"Banks," *The Architectural Index.* Includes magazine articles from *Architecture, Architectural Record, Interiors, Forum, Architecture Plus,* 1950–1984. Erwin J. Bell, AIA, Publisher, Boulder, Colorado.

B. Fletcher, *A History of Architecture on the Comparative Method,* Charles Scribner's Sons, New York, 1975.

M. Swimmer, "New Services Alter Design of Bank Projects," *Contract Magazine* (Oct. 1984).

Comptroller of the Currency, *Manual for National Banks, Minimum Security Requirements and Procedures,* U.S. Government Printing Office, Washington, D.C.

R. C. Benore, *Diebold Catalog,* Diebold Co., Canton, Ohio, and Washington, D.C., 1984.

T. West, *Bank Studies,* Informative Design Group, Inc., Washington, D.C., 1984.

N. Pevsner, *A History of Building Types,* Princeton University Press, Princeton, N.J., 1976.

Charles Szoradi, AIA
Architect and Planner
Washington, D.C.

BARNES, EDWARD LARRABEE

Edward Larrabee Barnes graduated *cum laude* from Harvard College in 1938 and, after a year of teaching English and Fine Arts at Milton Academy, Milton, Mass., he returned to Harvard to study architecture at the Graduate School of Design. There, he studied and worked with Walter Gropius and Marcel Breuer, and was awarded the Sheldon Traveling Fellowship before graduating in 1942. As a lieutenant in the U.S. Navy he served as naval architect from 1942 to 1947. Edward Barnes established his architectural practice in New York City in 1949. He remained the sole principal of the firm until 1981 when he formed a partnership with three of his associates: John M. Y. Lee, Percy K. Keck, and Alistair MacFarlane Bevington.

Edward Barnes's architectural style started with a logical Harvard base that is structurally and functionally straightforward, and has developed over the years into a simple volumetric vocabulary often expressed with few materials, and with a strong sympathy for urban context and natural surroundings.

The early work of the office consisted of small commissions—private houses, camps, and academic projects. During the 1960s, campus planning and urban renewal projects predominated. The 1970s saw the design of the firm's first office building, the New England Merchants National Bank in Boston (1971), and its first museum, the Walker Art Center in Minneapolis (1971). The work of the office has always been diverse and continues so today. The firm's work in the 1970s and 1980s includes museums, office buildings and corporate headquarters, academic buildings, and private residences. Major works of the office include the Haystack Mountain School of Arts and Crafts in Deer

Figure 1. Dallas Museum of Art, designed by Edward Larrabee Barnes Associates P.C. Photograph by Masahiro Horiuchi.

Isle, Maine (1962); a library, music and art complex at Emma Willard School in Troy, New York (1967); dormitories at St. Paul's School in Concord, New Hampshire (1961); master planning and academic buildings at the State University of New York (SUNY) at Potsdam (1963–1973) and SUNY Purchase (1968–1979); the Chicago Botanic Garden (1976); IBM World Trade Headquarters in Mt. Pleasant, New York (1974) and IBM's corporate headquarters at 590 Madison Avenue in New York City (1983); the aforementioned Walker Art Center in Minneapolis; the Sarah Scaife Gallery at Carnegie Institute in Pittsburgh (1974); and the Dallas Museum of Art (1983) (Fig. 1).

The work of the office has been published in the leading domestic and foreign architectural magazines, and chapters devoted to its work can be found in *Architects on Architecture* by Paul Heyer (1); *The Ideal Theatre: Eight Concepts,* published by the only publisher American Federation of Arts (2); *Macmillan Encyclopedia of Architects* (3); *Contemporary Architects* published by St. Martin's Press (4); and *American Architecture Now* by Barbaralee Diamonstein (5). The master plan for SUNY Purchase was exhibited at the Museum of Modern of Art in 1971, and a retrospective of the work of Edward Larrabee Barnes from 1950 to 1974 was sponsored by the Carnegie Institute

in Pittsburgh for the opening of its Sarah Scaife Gallery. The office has won numerous awards, among them American Institute of Architects (AIA) honor awards and the 1980 AIA Firm Award.

BIBLIOGRAPHY

1. P. Heyer, *Architects on Architecture: New Directions in America,* Walker & Co., New York, 1966.

2. *The Ideal Theatre: Eight Concepts,* American Federation of Arts, New York, 1962.

3. A. K. Placzek, ed., *Macmillan Encyclopedia of Architects,* Macmillan Publishing Company, New York, 1982.

4. M. Emanuel, ed., *Contemporary Architects,* St. Martin's Press, Inc., New York, 1980.

5. B. Diamonstein, *American Architecture Now,* Rizzoli International Publications, Inc., New York, 1980.

EDWARD LARRABEE BARNES
Edward Larrabee Barnes
Associates P.C.
New York, New York

BARRAGÁN, LUÍS

Luís Barragán, prominent twentieth-century Mexican architect and landscape architect, was born in 1902 in the state of Jalisco, Mexico. Barragán grew up near the village of Mazamitla in the northwestern section of Mexico near Guadalajara on a ranch that his family owned. This landscape with its heavy red clay earth, rolling hills, intense sunsets, and frequent heavy rainfall was to have a lasting impression upon his later work. The courtyard houses, each with a fountain and large overhanging eaves, and the churches and marketplaces of Mazamitla left an indelible mark on his memory. The ranches, horses, and haciendas (Barragán was an accomplished horseman) became part of his creative genius in expressing architectural form in the landscape. An understanding of cultural traditions, of the positive–negative relationship between the public street and private introverted house, and of the use of a simple and very limited palette of materials are always recognizable in his work. Although he is a self-taught architect and landscape architect, Barragán was educated initially as an engineer. During his school days in Guadalajara, a friend introduced him to French (the only foreign langauge he speaks) literature (Proust, Verlaine, etc). Thus he had his first contact, which highly impressed him, with the writings of the French landscape architect Ferdinand Bac, who wrote (1): "The soul of gardens contains the greatest amount of serenity in all of man's work." During his first trip to Europe in his early twenties, Barragán met Bac; their mutual interests led to a friendship and together they visited Bac's gardens. This was a revelation to Barragán and aroused in him the desire to develop landscape architecture.

In 1924, another momentous event occurred when Barragán visited the Alhambra in Granada, Spain. This Islamic palace, built in the thirteenth and fourteenth centuries, is perceived from the exterior as a fortress with earth-colored stuccoed, burnt brick walls. Yet inside, it is a well-designed, organized, and complex program of rooms, intimate courtyards, and lush vegetation in informal, compartmentalized gardens, laid out asymmetrically with a free unrestrained composition. The effect of the use of water in tinkling, sparkling fountains, and tranquil reflection pools coupled with the heavy stuccoed walls, caused a profound influence on both Barragán's architecture and landscape architecture. This Moorish architecture was carried over to Latin America during the Spanish Conquest, and Guadalajara has multiple examples of this architecture in houses and public, religious, and military buildings that Barragán knew very well, the roots of which he discovered in Spain. In several early Barragán houses, the Moorish influence is clear. Barragán has said (2):

> I believe in an emotional architecture. It is very important for humankind that architecture should move by its beauty; if there are many equally valid technical solutions to a problem the one which offers the user a message of beauty and emotion, that one is architecture. . . . The construction and enjoyment of a garden accustoms people to beauty, to its instinctive use, even to its pursuit. . . . I believe that architects should design gardens to be used, as much as the houses they build, to develop a sense of beauty and the taste and inclination towards the fine arts and other spiritual values.

Barragán's best known works include the garden at El Pedregal (1945–1950), his own home in Mexico City (1947) (Fig. 1), the Chapel for the Capuchinas Sacramentarias del Purísimo Corazón de María (1952–1955), the Towers of Satellite City (1957), Las Arboledas (1958–1961) and Los Clubes (1963–1964) residential subdivisions, the stable, pools, and house for the Egerstrom family of San Cristóbal (1967–1968), and Casa Valdés (1985) (Fig. 2), a project for which Luís Barragán and Raúl Ferrera did both the exterior and interior designs, the construction, and the landscape design. Perhaps the most important of Barragán's architectural projects was the Lomas Verdes development; even though it was never built, Lomas Verdes is a completely new city concept, with very important urban development contributions and the plastic image of a contemporary city. It takes into consideration modern technology without the buildings resembling a cluster.

Another important project was the development of 13 million m^2 (865 acres) of land near Mexico City formed some 6000 years ago by volcanic action. Ruins of several early towns were buried under layers of lava rock. The project is El Pedregal (stony place) de San Angel. During

Figure 1. The terrace of Barragán's home in Tacubaya, Mexico. Courtesy of Luís Barragán and Raul Ferrera.

Figure 2. The central garden of the Casa Valdés in Monterrey, Mexico. Courtesy of Luís Barragán and Raul Ferrera.

his first visits to the Pedregal, he began to envision the potential for integrating the massive lava forms—some rising precipitously behind the tree-covered foreground into gardens and habitable environments. He started by buying a small piece of property on the edge of the Pedregal, El Cabrío (the goat's pen), where he built an intimate garden that would increase the property's value. Barragán was first and foremost a real estate broker, and at that time, the area had very little commercial value in spite of its wild beauty. Thus El Cabrío was a trial lot before buying, in association with another developer, the 4.5 million m^2 of the Pedregal de San Angel. The very distinctive native flora was complemented by Barragán with grass plateaus, fountains, and man-made walls and gates, turning it into gardens and a habitable environment. The winding streets were designed according to the urban concepts of the times, the English winding street concept that was used by architects such as Richard Neutra. Steps, garden paths, and water pools were carved into rock outcroppings and crevices. Here native flora grew easily on a layer of topsoil and created sharp, sensual contrast that heightened the beauty of the many-hued rock; transitions through areas of exotic contrast introduced an air of magic and mystery to the gardens.

In 1980, Luís Barragán received the International Pritzker Prize. This prestigious award, established only one year earlier, is awarded to the living architect or architectural group whose work demonstrates those qualities of talent, vision, and commitment that have produced significant contributions to humanity and the environment through architecture. In presenting the award to Barragán, Emilio Ambasz wrote (3):

We are honoring Luís Barragán for his commitment to architecture as a sublime act of poetic imagination. He has created gardens, plazas, and fountains of haunting beauty—metaphysical landscapes. A stoical acceptance of solitude as man's fate permeates his work.

A few of Barragán's important words from his acceptance speech follow (4):

It is alarming that publications devoted to architecture have banished from their pages the words Beauty, Inspiration, Magic, Spellbound, Enchantment as well as the concepts of Serenity, Silence, Intimacy and Amazement. All of these have nestled in my soul, and though I am fully aware that I have not done them complete justice in my work, they have never ceased to be my guiding light.

Beauty. The invincible difficulty that the philosophers have in defining the meaning of this word is unequivocal proof of its ineffable mystery. Beauty speaks like an oracle, and ever since man has heeded its message in an infinite number of ways. . . . Human life deprived of beauty is not worthy of being called so.

Silence. In the gardens and homes designed by me I have always endeavored to allow for the interior placid murmur of silence, and in my fountains, silence sings.

Solitude. Only in intimate communication with solitude can man find himself.

Serenity. Serenity is the great and true antidote against anguish and fear, and today, more than ever, it is the architect's duty to make of it a permanent guest in the home, no matter how sumptuous or how humble. Throughout my work, I have always strived to achieve serenity, but one must be on guard not to destroy it by the use of an indiscriminate palette.

. . . a garden must combine the poetic and the mysterious with a feeling of serenity and joy.

Barragán designed and constructed his own home to satisfy personal needs. In the process, he set new standards for the relationship between traditional and contemporary materials. His home in Tacubaya, Mexico, D.F., exemplifies special form characteristics drawn from memories of the convents, haciendas, and popular architecture of his childhood. It consists of a reinforced concrete structure and pine beams (5). The outer walls have few openings and are plain and high. All important rooms face inward to a garden. Inner walls are also tall and thick and white. Some interior walls rise only 7 ft, acting as partial separators of the tall spaces, and creating a dynamic quality of space flowing from one area to another. Lighting is diffused and gentle; the ambience is mystical. The colors and forms of Barragán's roof terrace have been changed many times since 1947 when the house was originally built. One of Barragán's central principles is that as man grows and changes, his spaces may change as well. Originally, a view of the garden below could be seen from the roof terrace, and a large rustic, plaster-covered, brick cross was engaged in one wall. In later alterations, this cross was removed and the wall made flush. The final form of the roof terrace encloses the inhabitant from all but the ever-changing sky.

While Barragán's terrace reflects a poetic and dreamlike atmosphere, his devout Catholic belief is reflected in the convent of Tlalpan, currently recognized as one of the few worthwhile examples of contemporary religious architecture. The convent, located in a suburb outside Mexico City (Tlalpan, D.F.), belongs to one of the most cloistered orders of the Catholic Church where sisters rarely leave the convent (Capuchinas Sacramentarias del Purísimo Corazón de María). The convent was constructed over a period of two years. Barragán, with his own funds, remodeled the cloister and gardens, designed the chapel, and supervised the construction to his complete satisfaction (1954). The walls become dynamic sculptures as light moves through the spaces. The rough plaster walls contrast with a few finely detailed wood elements. The sense of layering and meaning in this extraordinarily simple and serene convent make it a place of incredibly austere beauty totally in harmony with the rules of this order.

Although Luís Barragán calls his life's work totally autobiographical, it must also be considered as an enormous contribution to the modernists' search. While Barragán cannot be considered a modernist except in the broadest terms, he in fact has carried the cause of contemporary architecture to new heights. The quality of his architecture cannot be grasped by studying plans alone, but must be appreciated as three-dimensional, dynamic, surrealistic compositions ever-changing with the sun and moonlight. He has been a pioneer in the use of color in modern architecture.

He has been influenced by a number of artists through his life. Perhaps the most important ones have been the painters Jesús Reyes Ferreira and Gerardo Murillo ("Dr. Atl"); the poet, Carlos Pellicer; the historian, Edmundo O'Gorman; the art critic, Justino Fernández; and Barragán's only partner, Raúl Ferrera (since 1975). Barragán credits Reyes Ferreira with teaching him to see beyond the level of purely rational thinking. Dr. Atl, famed for his landscape paintings of mountains, volcanoes, and valleys, camped out at the Pedregal before it was developed, sketching tirelessly. Barragán was inspired by these drawings which helped him to clarify his vision of man in the landscape. Barragán was also influenced by Le Corbusier, whom he imitated in several of the rental apartments and houses carried out during the 1930s and early 1940s. However, although Barragán greatly appreciates Le Corbusier's talent, concepts, and architectural theories, Barragán abandoned his style because they differed in taste and composition.

Louis Kahn wrote of Barragán (6):

I asked Barragán to come to La Jolla and help me in the choice of the planting for the garden to the Studies of the Salk Laboratory. When he entered the space he went to the concrete walls and touched them and expressed his love for them, and then said as he looked across the space and towards the sea, 'I would not put a tree or blade of grass in this space. This should be a plaza of stone, not a garden.' I looked at Dr. Salk and he at me and we both felt this was deeply right. Feeling our approval, he added joyously, 'If you make this a plaza, you will gain a facade—a facade to the sky.'

When sculptor Mathias Goeritz came to Mexico as a Nazi refugee during World War II, he was probably influenced by Barragán's work, who in turn, appreciated his talent. Barragán asked Goeritz to collaborate with him in designing a sculpture for the Pedregal de San Angel, and in the design of two windows for the convent in Tlalpan. In collaboration, they followed Barragán's ideas and concepts inspired by the 12th-century towers of San Gimignano and Bologna in Italy, and designed the Towers of Satellite City. Paraphrasing his friend O'Gorman, Luís Barragan has said (5):

Before the machine age, even in the middle of the cities, nature was everybody's trusted companion, partner of the baker, the butcher, the blacksmith, the carpenter. Nowadays the situation is reversed. Man does not meet with nature, even when he leaves the city to commune with her. Enclosed in his shiny automobile his spirit stamped with the mark of the world whence the automobile emerged, he is, within nature, a foreign body. A water tank is sufficient to stifle the voice of beauty. Nature becomes a scrap of nature, and man a scrap of man. The intended dialogue between man and nature becomes an hysterical, monotonous, human monologue.

Barragán's challenge to succeeding generations of architects and landscape architects is to find the fit between the natural environment and the man-made one—to respond to the spiritual and aesthetic needs of humans by working in harmony with nature.

BIBLIOGRAPHY

1. M. Schjetnan, *L.A.* **72**(1), 71 (Jan. 1982).
2. E. Ambasz, *The Architecture of Luís Barragán,* The Museum of Modern Art, New York, 1976, pp. 2 and 11.
3. D. Bayon, *L.A.* **66**(4), 533 (Nov. 1976).
4. Acceptance speech for the 1980 Pritzker Architecture Prize, sponsored by the Hyatt Foundation, Los Angeles, Calif.
5. C. B. Smith, *Builders in the Sun,* Architectural Book Publishing Co., Inc., Stamford, Conn., 1967, pp. 74 and 78.
6. L. Barragán, "The Construction and Enjoyment of a Garden Accustoms People to Beauty, to its Instinctive Use, even to its Accomplishment," *Via 1, Ecol. Des.,* 73 (1968).

General References

L. Barragán, "Gardens for Environment—Jardines del Pedregal," *J. Am. Inst. of Archit.* **57**(4), 167–171 (Apr. 1952).

H. Fleisher, "The Gardens of the Pedregal–Contemporary Design in a Land Subdivision in Mexico," *Landscape Archit.* **68**(2), 48 (Jan. 1953).

M. Goeritz, "Sobre Luís Barragán," *Arquitectos de Mexico* **21**(1), 19 (1964).

E. McCoy, "Designing for a Dry Climate," *Prog. Archit.* **52**(8), 50 (Aug. 1971).

"Recent Work of a Mexican Architect–Luís Barragán," *Archit. Rec.* **77**(1), 33 (Jan. 1935).

"Parque de La Revolución, Guadalajara, Jalisco, México," *Archit. Rec.* **78**(3), 165 (Sept. 1935).

L. Barragán, "Dos Jardines en México, D. F.," *Arquitectura* **18,** 148 (July 1945).

"Jardines del Pedregal, Mexico City," *Arts Archit.,* 20 (Aug. 1951).

"House by Luís Barragán, Architect," *Arts Archit.,* 24 (Aug. 1951).

Y. Futagawa, ed., "House & Atelier for Luís Barragán," *G.A.* 48, A.D.A. Edita, Tokyo Co., Ltd., 1979.

LINDA SANDERS
North Carolina State University
Raleigh, North Carolina

BATHS

The modern bathroom in the United States has come full circle, to about what it was 4000 years ago in Greece. In the United States, it is developing more and more into an elegant, roomy space for relaxation and physical fitness with exercise equipment, saunas, steam, and jetted tubs for two or more, in addition to its more established functions of cleansing and grooming the body and elimination and disposal of bodily wastes.

The changes of the late 1980s resulted from three decades of new materials and changing concepts. New materials include cultured marble and onyx for walls, counters, and integral lavatories, jetted tubs for whirlpool baths, acrylics and various petrochemical concoctions for faucets and accessories, and sumptuous fiber glass fixtures that include intercoms and computerized controls that draw a bath at a preset time and temperature, and fill the room with music of choice. New concepts include more emphasis on luxury and space, and use of the bathroom for multiple purposes such as health maintenance and physical fitness. The bathroom now might be more properly called a bathing suite.

HISTORY

The history of the bathroom has been an in-and-out, up-and-down series of cycles. In prehistoric days, if there was any thought of personal cleanliness, the bathroom would have been any convenient stream or river. If there was any thought of modesty for elimination of bodily wastes, any nearby bush would do. It could have been only in a much later cultural context that the two concepts of elimination and cleanliness would come together.

But come together they did, as far back as the Minoans in the third millenium B.C. and through the centuries to the better-known and fabled baths of the Roman Empire. In about 2000 B.C., the ancient Minoan civilization's palace in the capital city of Cnossos, on what is now the island of Crete, had water-flushed sewerage systems, piped hot and cold running water, marble tubs, steam rooms, and other appurtenances of the modern bathing suite. In neither Cnossos nor Rome, however, were modesty and privacy considered factors for closing off these activities in rooms. Both bathing and elimination were public, or at least communal, as they are today in many societies.

In all societies, ancient or modern, the growth of cities has played a major part in the development of bathing and elimination facilities, although these two activities would seem to be bound together only by their mutual need for sewerage. When many people come together, there arises the need for disposal of human wastes and for water supply and distribution, which in turn inspires engineering solutions.

While human waste elimination always has been a necessity, disposal of that waste has not. Nomadic tribes simply moved away from it. Medieval castles often chuted it into the moats, but literature of that period has many references to excrement left in hallways, rooms, or stairways. Leonardo da Vinci, in proposals for building new towns, suggested spiral stairways to prevent sanitary misuse of landings. While disposal always becomes necessary in cities, and cities usually are sited because of the presence of water, it does not follow necessarily that there will be water-borne sewerage. Visitors to Calcutta in the 1940s remember well the honey dippers who roamed the streets with huge shoulder-borne buckets, gathering the waste and toting it off to wagons or trucks that carried it to collection sites.

Nor has cleanliness or personal hygiene always been either concomitant or a necessity. After the splendor of the Roman Baths, there was for several centuries a sense of rebellion against such indulgence. Early Christians tended to equate dirt with humility. King John of England is reported to have bathed only three times a year, before major church festivals. Europeans brought their bathing habits with them to North America when they immigrated and, with new freedom in the new democracy, even passed laws against bathing in several states.

As the United States developed, the outhouse and the chamber pot were common in residences. They still are in some rural areas where there is no compelling reason for change other than winter discomfort. In fact, they make sense where human and animal waste can be used for fertilizing fields. However, the course of bathroom history in the United States moved slowly toward private bathrooms, combining elimination and hygiene, into the twentieth century.

Bathing became a weekly habit. In the nineteenth century, it consisted mostly of a wooden tub hauled to the area of the home near the stove, into which hot water was poured for all in the family to use. In 1855, a wooden tub was installed in the White House. Cast-iron tubs and toilets came into production by American Standard, Inc. in the 1860s. In the 1880s, John Michael Kohler added enamel and four legs to a horse trough to refine the bathtub. Meanwhile in the UK in 1870, Thomas Crapper, an employee of Twyford's (which made teapots and similar products), invented a flush mechanism that his firm incorporated in the first mechanically flushed toilet. In 1907, Eljer introduced the vitreous china toilet. Throughout history, back to the days of the Roman Baths, private bathrooms have been the province of the wealthy. In the United States, it was around 1900 that the wealthy started incorporating tub and toilet, in some cases even a bidet, in a separate private room, although few knew (and few know to this day) the purpose of a bidet.

In his book *The Bathroom,* Professor Alexander Kira

of Cornell University attributes the U.S. standard three-fixture 5 × 7-ft. (1.5 × 2.1-m) bathroom to the building boom of the early 1920s, when each new dwelling unit was required by law to have at least one private bathroom. The three fixtures were tub, toilet, and lavatory (1). These minimal specifications, along with one bare light bulb, became standard because there was no consumer demand for more, and so there was no incentive for builders to be more creative.

Little was done to expand on the minimums in the postwar housing boom of the 1950s until late in the decade when builders, still producing tract housing on a speculative basis, started promoting multiple (but still minimal) bathrooms in their houses.

The trend toward multiple bathrooms continued through the 1970s, often taking the form of one or two complete bathrooms and one or two half-baths or powder rooms, which consisted of only a toilet and lavatory. The half-bath was largely a product of increasing affluence as family incomes increased, and social activities grew accordingly. When parties were held, half-baths provided fixture sufficiency.

Many other influences converged in the 1970s and 1980s to exalt the status of the bathroom, or at least of the master bath, not the least of which was the consumer press, as newspaper and magazine editors competed to present the newest and most far-out ideas for the home. The whirlpool or jetted bath was introduced by Jacuzzi,

Inc., and manufacturers glamorized it with exotic materials such as ceramic tile and genuine or cultured marble, often with elegant steps for easier access. Physical fitness and health maintenance became national obsessions, and the bathroom seemed a logical place for such activities. The standard 5 × 7-ft bathroom was too small, so designers looked for adjacent closet or extra-room space to borrow for enlarging or relocating the bathroom. Extra rooms often were available as children grew and moved out to start their own households.

Another influence was the growing impact of television advertising, dominated by cosmetic and grooming products, and television series that glamorized the rich. The poor are seldom without television, so even in the homes of the less well-to-do there was total exposure to fantastic bathrooms, and to the need for dramatic lighting for best use of the many cosmetics and grooming products.

So, while the standard bathroom still is undersized, there are now many more exceptions that incline toward the sumptuous.

Mimimal baths are often upgraded. Figure 1 shows a small 6 × 8-ft (1.8 × 2.1-m) upgrading suggestion by Eljer Plumbingware. The three basic fixtures are augmented by a skylight, on the upper right, and a full-wall mirror over the lavatory. The medicine cabinet recessed in the far wall is hidden by indexed wall covering.

An example of the sumptuous bath by the Kohler Co. is shown in Figure 2. It features a raised 6-ft (1.8-m)

Figure 1. Small baths can be upgraded in many ways. This is only 6 × 8 ft. (1.8 × 2.1 m), upgraded by extra-size vanity cabinet, skylight, and dropped soffit light. Recessed medicine cabinet is covered by indexed wall covering, far wall. Courtesy of Eljer Plumbingware.

Figure 2. Sumptuous bath, more common in remodeling, has raised, sunken, jetted tub of teak with matching teak lavatory, toilet seat, and tiled floor. Courtesy of the Kohler Co.

sunken jetted tub of teak, with matching teak lavatory and toilet seat, and a tiled floor.

BATHROOM FIXTURES

The three fixtures that became standard in the 1920s bathroom—tub, toilet, and lavatory—still are standard, but they have changed vastly in form, function, and the materials of which they are made.

Bathtubs

Until the 1940s, most U.S. bathtubs were freestanding cast iron on short legs, surfaced with porcelain enamel. In the housing boom of the 1950s, most were built-in, porcelain-enameled steel or cast iron without legs, nestled in against three walls with an apron to the floor on the exposed side. The 1960s saw the advent of molded fiber glass and molded cultured marble, followed by acrylics in the 1970s. The cultured marbles were basically polyester surfaced with a gelcoat. One exception was an acrylic monomer by DuPont, unique because it was a homogeneous material and therefore could be drilled, cut, or routed with woodworking tools. The DuPont material continued to be unique until the late 1980s, when materials with similar characteristics were developed by others.

Most tubs were 5 ft (1.52 m) long to fit the smaller dimension of the standard 5 × 7-ft. (1.5 × 2.1-m) bathroom. However, increasing consumer awareness of and dissatisfaction with that standard from the 1960s on led slowly to increases in bathroom size, and bathtubs changed. Now

in fiber glass or the other molded materials, they might be square, oval, round, or rectangular, even heart shaped. Widths vary as do lengths, the latter usually in 6-in. (15.2-cm) increments from as little as 54 in. (137 cm) to as much as 84 in. (213.36 cm), with 72 in. (182.88 cm) a popular size.

Another advantage of new molded tubs has been the capability of molding in seats, ledges, and shelves so a bather can sit down and find soaps and cosmetics close at hand. The molded tubs might have integral wall surrounds for new housing, or the surrounds might come in two or three pieces for moving into existing housing on remodeling jobs. In the United States, most tubs also come as dual installations with showers, as showers are more popular than tub baths. Showers have not been that popular in Europe, probably because of slow development of central heating, as noted by Professor Kira. In cold, raw environments, the warming effects of tub baths are appreciated more. Perhaps that is why the hand-held showers of European bathrooms appear to Americans as somewhat of a design afterthought. Another notable difference is the central drain in the floor of European bathrooms, that never appears in U.S. bathrooms.

In the ultimate of exotica, U.S. manufacturers also have resurrected the wood tub; however, it is, of course, different. Now it is teak with a protective acrylic urethane coating, with matching lavatories and toilet seat covers. Ceramic tile, set piece by piece, is also fairly common in western and southwestern states.

The newest development in bathtubs is the indoor spa, epitomized by the Kohler Environment, the Waterjet Bath-Womb, and the American Standard Sensorium. These are

Figure 3. The Habitat moves bath off the floor; includes steam, sauna, and shower. Courtesy of the Kohler Co.

the dénouement of bathing and health maintenance, with various combinations of steam, sauna, bathing and music, intercom, television, outer door locking control, etc.

The Environment, or the similar but smaller Habitat (Fig. 3) moves the installation off the floor and into a wall, where it needs 7–9 ft (2.1–2.7 m) of width, 66–93 in. (168–234 cm) of height, and about 4 ft (1.2 m) in depth, along with 36 in. (92 cm) of working space behind the relay box, as required by the National Electric Code. This is about the size of a closet turned on its side and recessed into the wall.

The BathWomb (Fig. 4) is 72 in. (182. 8 cm) long and fully jetted, with computerized controls for facial misting (shielded by what looks like a windshield), intercom, music, and massage, and with a tilt-out tray table on which a bather can read or enjoy lunch.

American Standard's Sensorium (Fig. 5) has computer controls on the 6-ft. tub to control all functions, including even locking or unlocking the outer door of the house. A matching box on a wall is used for presetting bathtub functions up to 24 h ahead.

But there are many lesser versions. Ordinary tubs are now available with whirlpool jets to replace standard tubs of any size. Such upgrades are common in bathroom remodeling and custom-built houses, but seldom are included in speculative housing. The Soft Bathtub, for example, is a whirlpool spa in a fiber glass shell lined with inch-thick plastic foam, in large sizes or in a size to fit the space of a standard tub.

Freestanding tubs are still produced, many of them replicas of the old claw-foot tubs of the early part of the century. Skirted tubs already described are most prevalent. Sunken tubs, with no sides finished, are considered the epitome of luxury. However, most sunken tubs in the United States are not really sunken. One reason is that it would be too dangerous to persons walking around at night. Another is that a tub can seldom be recessed into the floor in a remodeling project. It would protrude at least 20 in. (50.8 cm) below floor joists, which would push the fittings and drain line still lower. Therefore, the practice has grown to build up to the tub so that, while it rests on the floor or is supported by flanges along the rim, it has a sunken appearance. For access steps, design-

Figure 4. Bathwomb jetted tub has computerized controls for facial misting, intercom, music, and massage as well as tilt-out tray table. Courtesy of Waterjet.

Figure 5. Sensorium, in Walter Platner design, has computer control on tub, and another on wall for advance setting. Along with all intercom functions, this also controls outer doors. Courtesy of American Standard, Inc.

ers usually plan a 10-in. (25.4-cm) tread and 7-in. (17.78-cm) risers.

Newer oversized tubs for two or more can pose a weight problem. Most U.S. houses of the last 50 years have been built to specifications of the Federal Housing Authority (FHA), which has specified a floor joist load of 40 lb (18.4 kg) per ft^2, but only 30 psi (13.6 kg) in sleeping areas. The weight of an oversized tub, along with water and bathers, can double that easily. In such cases, it is necessary to spread the weight over a wider area with framework or to double the joists.

Shower baths are preferred over tub baths by most men in the United States, and probably by most women except for weekend bathing. This means showers are necessary in all tub installations. An exception would be sunken tubs, to which showers are not easily adaptable. In these cases, there would be separate shower stalls. Showers are mounted on the wall over the tub with a diverter valve directing water to either tub or shower. Separate shower stalls are usually prefabricated and have their own central floor drain.

Toilets

The British term water closet is a widely used euphemism for the word toilet in the United States, although in the UK it referred to the bathroom. By whatever term, it has been flush-operated since 1870 and made of vitreous china since 1907. Yet, there have been dramatic changes in configuration and appearance.

In the early decades of this century, especially in rural areas, the toilet tank was placed high above the toilet bowl to take advantage of pressure from gravity. Flushing was actuated by pulling a chain connected to the tank, from which water was piped down to the bowl. The two-piece toilet still is most prevalent, but the tank now is placed directly behind and only slightly above the bowl where gravity still is a factor. Old-style wood, high tank fixtures are now produced as fashionable nostalgic mementos.

Classified by configuration, there are two types of toilets: one-piece and two-piece. Classified by flushing action, there are three types: washdown, reverse trap, and siphonic.

The washdown (Fig. 6a) is still widely used all over the world, but is no longer produced in the United States.

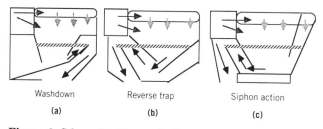

Washdown   Reverse trap   Siphon action

(a)   (b)   (c)

Figure 6. Schematic of types of toilets. **(a)** Washdown toilet has the smaller water surface, the narrowest trap passage, and is the lowest priced. **(b)** Reverse trap toilet has the larger water surface and some siphonic action. **(c)** Siphon action toilet has the largest water surface and the most efficient flushing action.

It is the lowest in price and has a narrow trap passage of less than 2 in. (5 cm). This makes it noisy and susceptible to clogging. Water surface area is about 83 in.^{2} (535.5 cm^2), leaving a lot of exposed surface subject to contamination and staining. The reverse trap actually has siphonic action, but has a 2-in. trapway that is less subject to clogging.

Water surface in the reverse trap type is slightly more than 102 in.^{2} (658 cm^2), and more of the flushing water enters from the rim holes, making flushing more efficient (Fig. 6b). In this type, as with other siphonic models, the bowl discharges at the back where a low baffle and the rush of water creates the siphoning action.

The third type, usually called siphon jet (Fig. 6c), has a larger water surface, 126 in.^{2} (813 cm^2), that covers the bottom of the bowl to totally eliminate any staining or fouling. The trapway is 2¼ in. (5.7 cm), which virtually eliminates the possiblity of clogging, and the volume of flushing water starts siphoning almost instantly. In the upgraded models, rim holes are slanted so incoming flush water creates a vortex action for maximum quiet. This system is used in one-piece toilets in which the bowl is cast as an integral part with the water tank, and these have a still larger water surface; ie, 138 in.^{2} (890 cm^2).

Some of the upgraded toilets are self-venting to whisk away odors. This is done by adding a small water channel through which the flow of water creates a vacuum that draws odors out through the rim holes. In other cases, an electrical fan is used.

A growing awareness of the need for conservation in the United States had led to recent introductions of water-saver toilets. These use high water levels and siphon action, and flush with as little as 3.5 gal (13.2 L) per flush, some as little as ½ gal (1.89 L). Flushing efficiency of such models depends on excellent engineering, so most designers tend to avoid the lower priced models.

For roughing-in, the one-piece toilet takes a ½-in. (1.27-cm) water supply line. The others take a ⅜-in. (0.95-cm) supply. Drain rough-in, depending on the model, will be 10 in., 12 in., or 14 in. (25.4 cm, 30.48 cm, or 35.56 cm).

Lavatories

There are four types of widely used lavatories: free-standing (or pedestal), wall-hung, drop-in (recessed in a cutout in the counter), and integral (molded as part of the counter). Completely aside from design considerations, the integral and drop-in models are better from a homeowner's viewpoint because they ensure some countertop space, however minimal it might be. Countertop space for toiletries and grooming is one of the prime deficiencies in U.S. bathrooms.

Pedestal lavatories add a touch of nostalgia to fashion bathrooms. The pedestal is hollow for supply and drain lines to be installed from the floor, although some are designed for plumbing in the back. Usually, they are vitreous china, although some are of marble or other exotic materials.

Wall-hung lavatories are fastened to the wall with a metal bracket with the fixture cantilevered from the wall.

Some are designed for installation in a corner. A disadvantage of wall-hung models is that all plumbing is exposed to view. An exception and recent innovation in this category is the Lift by Villeroy & Boch (Fig. 7), with a base mounted low on the wall and a bowl that can be raised or lowered to serve adult or child.

Drop-ins are lavatories designed to be installed in a cutout in a decorative laminate countertop. These were extremely popular in the building booms of the 1950s and 1960s, and continue to be popular, but have been challenged in the last two decades by the growth of cultured marble with its integral lavatories.

Integral lavatories gained immediate acceptance among homeowners and builders because they are molded in one piece with the countertop. This means a lavatory does not have to be bought and installed separately. Many such lavatory tops are made only to span a vanity cabinet, 20–36-in. wide (50.8–91.44 cm), with little counter surface. But many extend from wall to wall, providing needed counter space in the bathroom.

Figure 7. Innovation in lavatory design is Lift model by Villeroy & Boch. Lever (front) frees it for raising or lowering, for use by adult or child. Courtesy of Villeroy & Boch.

CABINETRY

Recognition of the need for storage space in bathrooms started in the 1950s, but there was little space available for it or for cabinetry made specifically for the bathroom. Some manufacturers started to make vanity cabinets primarily to hide the lavatory plumbing, but drawers and extra width came quickly and some vanity cabinets became quite elaborate. Now a wide range of cabinets is available on a stock basis, mostly from kitchen cabinet manufacturers who were easily able to alter heights and depths for use in smaller rooms.

Kitchen wall cabinets are 12 in. (30.58 cm) deep; base cabinets are 24 in. (60.96 cm) deep. For bathrooms, cabinet depths normally are 12 in., 18 in., 21 in., or 24 in. deep (30.48 cm, 45.72 cm, 53.34 cm, or 60.96 cm). Heights for the bathroom generally are 29–35 in. (73.66–88.9 cm). However, many shelves and smaller bathroom wall cabinets are 6–9 in. deep (15.24–22.86 cm). Deeper cabinets are mounted on the floor. Shallower cabinets are mounted on walls or, in many cases, recessed in the wall between wall studs, which usually are 16 in. (40.64 cm) on center. Some wall cabinets are designed to fit on the wall over the toilet tank (Fig. 8), and many base units have tilt-out or swing-out clothes hampers. Because so many bathrooms are so small, some cabinets are designed to fit in the bulkhead over the tub.

SURFACES AND MATERIALS

Several surfacing materials are available for the high moisture bathroom environment, but consideration must start with substrates, particularly in the tub area. When a bathroom is being remodeled and a tub replaced, it is necessary to strip the wall to the studs after removal of the old tub to be sure there has been no rotting. This is true especially in older homes where there might be an exterior wall that is not insulated. In colder climates, it is not

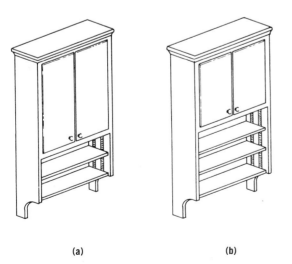

(a)   (b)

Figure 8. Some storage space is gained in bathroom with cabinets designed to fit over water closet. **(a)** Two-shelf model; **(b)** Three-shelf model. Courtesy of Wood-Mode Carpentry.

unusual to find a wall filled with ice behind the tub. To prevent this, it is necessary to install a 6-ml polyethylene vapor barrier, along with insulation if it is an exterior wall.

Backing materials commonly used to cover the wall studs include water-resistant gypsum wallboard, exterior grade plywood, and concrete-reinforced fiber glass. The gypsum wallboard has a water-resistant core, and the face and back paper are treated to resist water. It comes in 4 × 8-ft. (1.2 × 2.4-m) panels that can be screwed or nailed to the studs. Exposed joints are taped and covered with a joint compound, then finished with two or more coats of joint compound. Exterior grade plywood is made with phenolic or resorcinol resins that are not soluble in water. Grade A-C is recommended. It comes in 4 × 8-ft sheets, and its advantage is that it provides backing for mounting of accessories anywhere on the wall. If a grab bar is to be installed, ¾-in (1.9-cm) thickness is recommended. Concrete-reinforced fiber glass, developed as a base for ceramic tile, is relatively new. Bathroom moisture helps cure the Portland cement in the panels. It is installed with rustproof screws or nails.

Ceramic tile is widely used as bathroom surfacing, particularly on floors and tub surrounds, but many bathrooms are tiled everywhere except the ceiling (Fig. 9). Small mosaics are used on floors, and standard wall and countertop tiles are 4¼ or 6 in. square (10.8 cm or 15.2 cm). Tile is rated by water absorption with the following definitions: impervious, 0.5% water absorption or less; vitreous, 0.5% to 3%; semivitreous, 3–7%; and nonvitreous, 7% or more.

High pressure decorative laminate, such as Formica, Wilsonart, etc, is the most common counter surface. High pressure laminate is defined by the National Electrical Manufacturers Association (NEMA) as laminate made under 500 psi (226.8 kg) of pressure or more. It consists of several sheets of resin-impregnated kraft paper in a sandwich of melamine, topped with a decorative sheet that might have woodgrain or any other pattern reproduced photographically, and with multicolor printing. NEMA is the standard-setting agency because the melamine was originally an electrical insulating material.

These laminates are glued to a substrate, usually ¾-in. (1.9-cm) industrial-grade particle board, using contact or urea adhesives. These laminates, waterproof and available in hundreds of colors and patterns, are also excellent for bathroom walls and ceilings, where they can be installed with panel adhesives. However, they are rigid and must be cut to fit outside the bathroom, so they are difficult to move in and install. For countertops, a less expensive alternative is low pressure melamine board that is laminated on both sides by the board manufacturer. Its surface is somewhat less durable than high pressure material, but is usually considered suitable for bathroom use.

Many special tiles are used to finish off a tile bathroom installation. Pieces in Figure 9 are keyed to their applications.

Rivaling high pressure laminate popular for bathroom counters is cultured marble, favored by builders because of its cast integral lavatory. The material is opaque, but marble manufacturers also make a cultured onyx that is

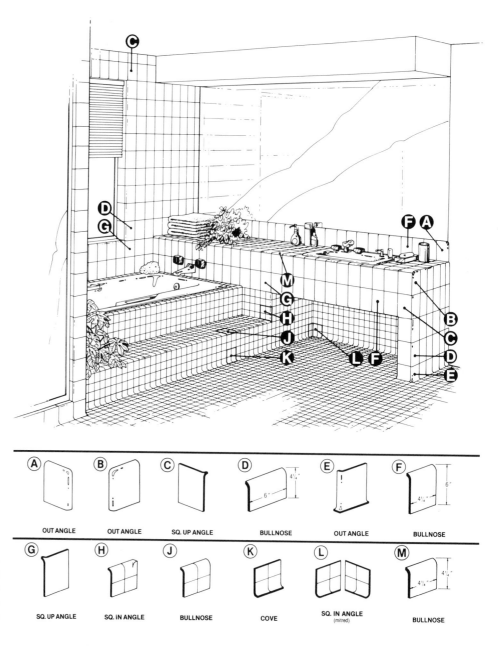

Figure 9. Inside and outside corners, coves, and other applications take special tiles. Pieces shown here are keyed to their applications. Courtesy of American Olean Tile.

translucent, and some designers gain dramatic effects with lighting behind cultured onyx panels. Cultured marble and onyx are not as durable as high pressure laminates and are difficult to repair, except for acrylic materials (see Bathtubs). Cultured marble is available in ¼-in. (0.63-cm) sheets for wall applications, and is often used for tub and shower surrounds.

Paint is often used, especially on bathroom ceilings. Either latex or alkyd is suitable, with alkyd being more durable.

LIGHTING

Bathroom lighting should be planned with two factors in mind: the size of the room, for general light level, and the placement of light to facilitate specific bathroom tasks,

such as shaving, applying makeup, pleasure reading, and, often overlooked, reading of labels for various tubes and bottles used while in the bathtub or shower.

For general lighting, small bathrooms of up to 75 ft² (7 m²) need one to three sockets totaling 60 W if fluorescent, 150 W if incandescent. Bathrooms up to 120 ft² (11 m²) need four sockets with 60–80 W of fluorescence, or 150–200 W of incandescence. Super baths over 120 ft² should have ¾-W fluorescence of 2-W incandescence for each square foot (0.1 m²).

Placement is based on location of the mirror, which is usually over the lavatory. To be effective, light should be on each side of and above the head, and reflected from a light vanity top or lavatory for shaving or applying cosmetics under the chin. Many mirrored medicine cabinets come with lighting such as this.

If lighting must be installed, there should be a ceiling

fixture over the front edge of the lavatory and side lights centered 30 in. (76 cm) apart and 60 in. (152 cm) above the floor for a small mirror. If these lights are fluorescent, the ceiling fixture should have two 24-in. (60.9-cm) 20-W tubes, and each side fixture should have one tube of this size and wattage. If incandescent, the ceiling fixture should be at least 12 in. (30 cm) in diameter with at least 100 W, and two side brackets should be mounted with one 75-W or two 40-W soft white bulbs in each.

In larger bathrooms with a larger mirror, 36 in. (91.4 cm) or more, a diffusing fixture overhead is recommended with two 36-in. (91.4 cm) 30-w tubes or two 48-in. (121.9-cm) 40-W tubes on the wall over the mirror, or in a dropped soffit with shielding. If incandescent light is used, use three or four 60-W soft white bulbs in separate diffusers at least 22 in. (55.8 cm) wide across the top of the mirror. The width and power of this overhead lighting eliminates the need for side lights. If theatrical lighting is desired (bare bulbs running up one side of the mirror, across the top, and down the other side), mount strips with four to six G-bulbs (globe type) across the top and along each side of the mirror. The bulbs should be only 15–25 W; more would be too bright for good vision.

Track lights may also be used, but they should never be aimed at the mirror itself. They should be aimed at the place where the face would be so they do not create glare.

The bathtub or shower, when in use, often is screened off from the light by a curtain, making it very difficult to read the tiny labels on the many hair conditioners, rinses, shampoos, and other concoctions used there. An added light there should be in a water-tight fixture, either by structure or by caulking. If local building codes allow, it is best to use a recessed vaporproof ceiling fixture with a 60- or 75-W bulb, and with the switch out of reach. If it is a recessed box with a closed bottom, a 100-W bulb should be used. In a half-bath or powder room where extensive grooming is usually not practiced, one wall fixture usually is sufficient. Use two 75-W or four 40-W bulbs, or two 24-in. (60.9-cm) 20-W fluorescent tubes. However, if any of these rooms have dark walls, it might double the lighting requirements.

In considering housing for older people, it should be noted that lighting requirements increase with age. A person 60 years old needs twice as much light for good vision and general well-being as a person of 40.

PLUMBING

Bathrooms are primarily water-powered rooms. This calls for supply piping that brings water into the room under pressure at from 30 to 80 psi, distributes it to the various fixtures, then carries it away under gravity power in drain–waste–vent (DWV) piping. Because it is under pressure, supply pipes can be smaller. Water usually enters the house in either 1¼-in. (3.175-cm) iron, 1-in. (2.54-cm) copper, or 1¼-in. (3.18-cm) plastic pipe. In the house, distribution piping ranges from 1 in. in diameter down to ¼ in. (6.35 mm). The common size is ⅜ in. (9.535 mm). But DWV lines must be larger because the only pressure is

gravity. These lines will be 1¼–2 in. (5.08 cm), except for lines serving toilets that are usually 3 in. (7.62 cm), sometimes 4 in. (10.16 cm).

Pipes might be of galvanized steel, cast iron, copper, brass, or several plastics, including poly(vinyl chloride) (PVC), chlorinated PVC, polybutylene (PB), and acrylonitrile butadiene styrene (ABS). The plastics have many advantages because they are very light in weight and easy to work with; joining is usually accomplished with solvents that result in a chemical weld. Copper is most common in newer homes, especially for supply lines. Galvanized steel and cast iron will be found in most older homes, and the latter is still common in DWV lines. ABS and PVC are used for DWV and cold water, CPVC for hot water lines.

When plastic pipe is used for hot water lines, the temperature-pressure relief valve (T-PV) on the water heater should be set for no more than 180°F (82.2°C), the maximum safe operating temperature for plastic pipe. Also, it cannot be worked in temperatures below 40°F (4.44°C), as cold weather slows the solvent adhesive's action, preventing it from bonding properly. Figure 10 shows bathroom supply piping in white, DWV piping in black. The

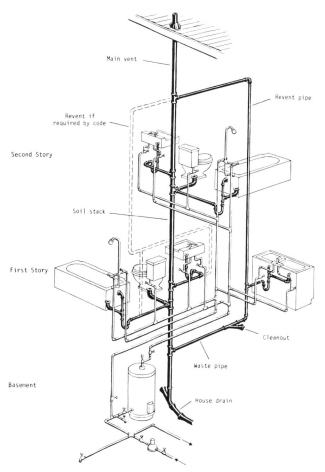

Figure 10. Typical plumbing system has supply piping in white, DWV in black. Revent pipe use varies with local building codes. This shows how upstairs and downstairs bathrooms and laundry room join same plumbing tree. Courtesy of Time-Life Books.

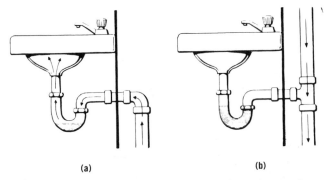

Figure 11. Drawings illustrate need for venting, showing how sewer gases can enter home without proper trap **(a)** Lower level permits gas entry; **(b)** Water in trap seals off gases. Courtesy of Popular Science Books.

T-PV sits atop the water heater. Every fixture has a trap, providing a water seal against the possibility of sewer gases seeping into the home.

Trap action is illustrated in Figure 11; this also shows the need for venting each fixture. Without venting, trap water might be siphoned off because of draining action, and sewer gases could come in as illustrated by black arrows in Figure 11a. Black arrows in Figure 11b show vent action caused by flush in a lower fixture, leaving the water seal here intact.

Some vent pipes must be added for branch fixtures, bringing vent air down the main stack from the roof. This is called reventing (Fig. 12). These must connect with a stack above all other waste lines, but it need not be the same stack as the fixture served. If distance to the stack is short, the drain pipe can also serve as the vent pipe, but this distance is governed by the pipe size. This is known as wet venting (Fig. 13). For a 1¼-in. (3.17-cm) drain pipe, the maximum distance for wet venting is 30 in. (76 cm). For a 1½-in. (3.8-cm) drain pipe the distance is 42 in. (106.6 cm).

Figure 14 shows a representative plumbing setup for a bathroom. All DWV pipes slope downward, usually ¼

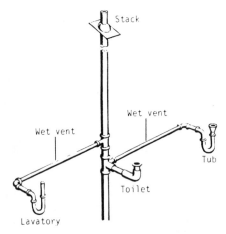

Figure 13. If distance is short to branch fixtures they can be wet vented, meaning vent and waste share the same pipe. This procedure depends on distance and pipe size. Courtesy of Popular Science Books.

in. (0.63 cm) per ft (30.48 cm). This tub trap is 42 in. (106.68 cm) from the vent stack and has a 1½-in. (3.8-cm) drain pipe, so it is wet vented to the vent stack. The multiple-outlet fitting where both tub and toilet, or water closet, are joined to the stack is called a TY fitting. If the tub trap were farther than 42 in., it would not be above the level of the TY fitting, so there would be no downward pitch.

A bathroom also needs special framing in the walls to accommodate the fixtures and medicine cabinet, as shown in Figure 15. Medicine cabinets that are recessed between

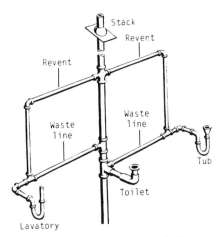

Figure 12. When branch fixtures are installed, revent pipe must be used, joining stack above all other branch fixtures. Courtesy of Popular Science Books.

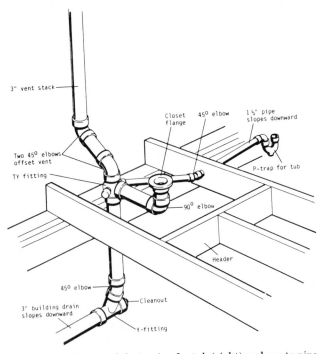

Figure 14. Horizontal drain pipe for tub (right) and waste pipe from toilet (center) must slope downward to stack due to gravity flow. Building drain, leaving house, must also slope downward. Courtesy of Popular Science Books.

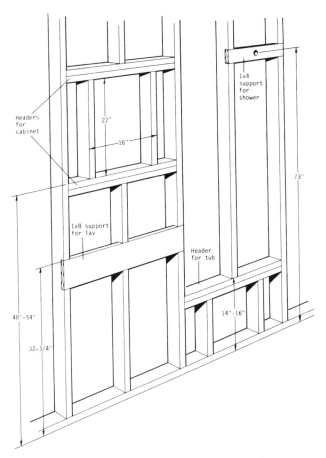

Figure 15. When studs are cut so recessed medicine cabinet can be centered over lavatory, cutout must be reinforced with headers and short stud pieces to reinforce wall. Headers are also needed for shower, tub and lavatory. Courtesy of Popular Science Books.

the studs will fit into a 16 × 22-in. opening (40.6 × 55.8 cm), although the outside will be much larger. Placement of the cabinet will be over the lavatory, which must be placed according to interior measurements, and not accord-

ing to stud placement. Therefore, it will often be necessary to cut out a section of stud at cabinet height, to install double headers to maintain structural integrity of the wall, and then to fill in short sections of stud to frame a cabinet. Extra-large medicine cabinets that can be surface mounted so this extra carpentry will not be needed are also available. For lavatory support, the studs will have to be notched for flush mounting of a 1 × 8-in. board (2.5 × 20.3 cm) to support the lavatory. Double headers will also have to be installed at the head end of the tub and, up above, a 1 × 4-in. board (2.5 × 10 cm) will have to be notched in to support the shower, which will be just above the tub surround. Heights of these framing members are shown in Figure 15.

DESIGN

Bathroom design will vary widely according to the room size, equipment, and activities desired, and the location of plumbing. However, most plumbing is relatively easy to move except for the toilet location and, to a lesser extent, the bathtub drain line. It is best to plan the bathroom in the early design stage.

The first consideration, especially in smaller bathrooms, is clearance needed for body operation at the basic fixtures. Figure 16 shows these clearances. Starting at the left, the shower is piped in at 74 in. (187.9 cm) above the floor, high enough to clear the tub surround that might be difficult to cut. The shower curtain rod goes anywhere above that point. Usual tub height is 14 in. (35.5 cm). An upper soap dish should be installed even with the upper end of a grab bar, 50 in. (127 cm) above the floor. The lower end of the grab bar should be 24 in. (60.9 cm) above the floor, even with a lower soap dish. Height of the counter will be about 32 in. (81.3 cm) above the floor. Countertops usually have a 4-in. (10.2-cm) backsplash, and the bottom of the medicine cabinet will usually be about 8 in. (20.3 cm) above that. To allow comfort at the toilet, its center line should allow at least 18 in. (45.7 cm) to the user's right and 12 in. (30.48 cm) to the user's left. The toilet

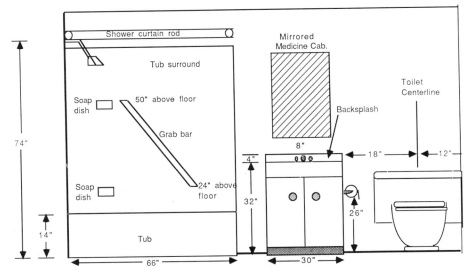

Figure 16. Clearance space must be provided in bathroom for elbows, knees, and movement. Drawing shows minimum clearances and representative dimensions, although 25% more clearance would be desirable.

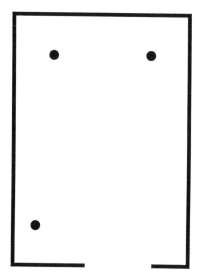

Figure 17. Standard 5 × 7-ft bathroom shows locations of water supply and DWV lines. Any of these can be moved in building stage, but in remodeling the toilet is relatively fixed because it is much more difficult to move.

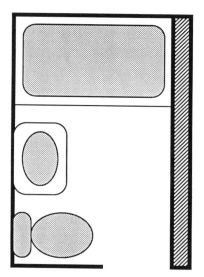

Figure 19. Another standard builder layout places 5-ft (1.5-m) tub across end. This permits use of 6-in.-deep wall shelving (15.2 cm) for minimal storage. It can fit over tub, or a shorter 54-in. (137-cm) tub can be used. In some cases, this might be extended to 9 in. deep (22.6 cm), extended over the end of tub.

paper fixture is best at 26 in. (66 cm) above the floor, and to the right front of a right-handed person. If more space is available in such an arrangement, it is best used in increasing the vanity size from a normal 30 in. (76.2 cm) to at least 36 in. (91.4 cm) by adding a bank of drawers, which would also increase the countertop space.

The next important consideration in bathroom planning is to provide, somewhere, even in the tiny standard 5 × 7-ft (1.5 × 2.1-m) bathroom, added counter or shelf and storage space. It should be noted here that 5 × 7 ft is a catch-all term for spaces that normally vary in inches anywhere under 6 × 8 ft (1.8 × 2.4 m). In the accompanying drawings, the 5 × 7 measurements are used. Figure 17

shows such a bathroom with the black dots marking locations of the drains.

Figure 18 shows how a builder might typically place the fixtures, with a standard 5-ft (1.5-m) bathtub placed along the long axis. Lavatory location at the far end makes added shelving or storage unworkable on the long wall, as it would restrict access to the lavatory.

Figure 19 shows one solution to that, placing a 4½-ft (1.37-m) tub across the short axis with a full-wall wall system (shelves and cabinets). Depth is only 6 in. (15.2 cm), but in some areas, such as open shelves at the height

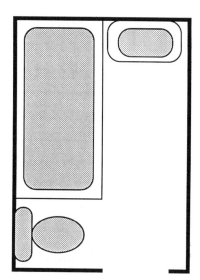

Figure 18. One standard bathroom floor plan by builders arranges bathtub on long axis. This inhibits any use of wall for storage.

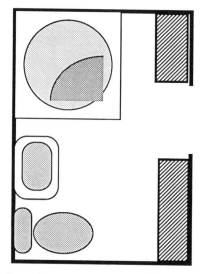

Figure 20. A much more useful improvement in the standard space would be use of a 40-in. (101.6-cm) steeping tub that has a molded seat and can also take a shower. This permits use of cabinets and shelves of standard 12-in. depth (30.5 cm) on either side of relocated door.

of the lavatory, these could be recessed between studs for a better depth of 9 in. (22.8 cm). The tub drain and supply plumbing are not altered by this change in tub direction.

Figure 20 relocates the door and uses a fiber glass soaking tub 40 in. (101.6 cm) square with molded seat, and permits any combination of shelves and cabinets a full 12 in. (30.5 cm) deep on either side of the door. Figure 21 shows one suggestion on how such a storage wall might look, with the shaded areas representing open shelving. The shaded area on the lower right might even have a pullout desktop shelf for added work area, with a mirror recessed at the wall.

SPECIAL USES

As noted, the trend is toward bathrooms expanded for various special uses and purposes, some minor and some major. For example, bathing a small child is a minor special use, and it requires open space beside the tub of 30 × 42 in. (76 × 106.7 cm), which also allows for dressing the child. However, providing for exercise and health maintenance is a major special use that might demand more space.

Equipment varies widely; a typical treadmill jogging machine might be about 51 in. long and 31 in. wide (129.5 × 78.7 cm), but space must be added for bodily movement. A floormat-type jogging machine will be about 26 × 20 in. (66 × 50.8 cm). A rowing exerciser will be about 54 in. long and 42–49 in. wide (137 × 106–124 cm). A cycle exerciser will be about 32 × 19 in. (81 × 48 cm) for a simple one, to 44 × 18 in. (112 × 46 cm) for a more elaborate one. Packaged sauna units come as small as 11 ft² (1.02 m²) for solo use, and as large as 96 ft² (8.9 m²). However, a sauna does not necessarily have to be in the bathroom. A nearby closet or the basement can be used, but the bathroom is preferred.

While home laundries are usually located in basements or utility rooms, the upstairs bathroom is an excellent place for them. Hot and cold water is available, and it can eliminate a lot of carrying. Home washers and dryers usually are about 27 in. (66 cm) wide and 25 in. (64 cm) deep. However, washers need an added 4 in. (10 cm) behind for plumbing, and dryers need the same added space for venting. A washer needs 12–18 in. (30.5–45.7 cm) above for the door, and a dryer needs 21–28 in. (53–71 cm) in front for the door swing.

However, there are now many over-under models available, some compact and some full-size. One full-size unit needs space only 28 in. (71 cm) wide, 32 in. (81 cm) deep, which allows for plumbing and venting behind, and 74 in. (188 cm) high.

Bathrooms occasionally must be designed for usage by the handicapped. To allow for a wheelchair, a bathroom should have a door at least 32 in. wide (81 cm), with, a full 5-ft. (1.5-m) circle of maneuvering space immediately inside. There should be two grab bars in the tub, 4 ft. (1.2 m) long, one vertical starting at the top of the tub, and one horizontal 3 ft (0.9 m) above the tub floor. There should be two grab bars at the toilet, one in front and one behind, each 30 in. (76 cm) long and each extending from the center line of the toilet, 30 in. above the floor. Mirrors should be not more than 40 in. (102 cm) from the floor to the bottom of the mirror, and there should be 30 in. (76 cm) clearance from the floor to the bottom of the lavatory with all pipes recessed and insulated to prevent burns.

BIBLIOGRAPHY

1. A. Kira, *The Bathroom*, Bantam Books, Inc., New York, p. 9.

General References

E. Cheever, *The Basics of Bathroom Design—and Beyond*, National Kitchen & Bath Association, Hackettstown, N.J., 1985.

N. Christensen, *The Light Book*, General Electric Lighting Institute, Cleveland, Ohio, 1983.

Consumer Products Safety Commission, *A Guide to Reduce the Incidence of Severe Bathtub Injuries*, U.S. Government Printing Office, Washington, D.C., 1985.

R. Cox, *The Custom Bathroom Remodelers Training Manual*, Bob Cox Training Schools, Baltimore, Md., 1976.

P. J. Galvin, *Remodeling Your Bathroom*, Harper & Row Publishers, Inc., New York, 1980.

M. Gilliatt, *Bathrooms*, Viking Penguin, Inc., New York, 1971.

M. Litchfield, *Renovation, a Complete Guide*, John Wiley & Sons, Inc., New York, 1982.

R. Platek, *Bathroom Specialist Training Manual*, National Kitchen & Bath Association, Hackettstown N.J., 1986.

W. Reyburn, *Flushed with Pride*, Macdonald & Co., London, 1969.

Rutt Custom Kitchens, *Planning Guide for Architects & Designers*, Goodville, Pa., 1985.

J. Chasin, *Wheelchair Bathroom*, Paralyzed Veterans of America, Washington, D.C., 1977.

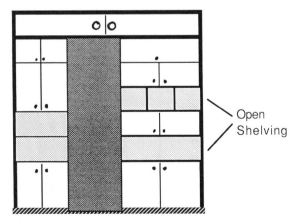

Figure 21. Elevation drawing shows how wall system (Fig. 20) might look, with combination of cabinets and open shelves. Shaded area at lower right might even have a pull-out desktop shelf for added work area, with mirror recessed in wall.

PAT GALVIN
Galvin Publications
East Windsor, New Jersey

BAUHAUS

Changes in methods of education in design were already well underway by early 1915 when architect Walter Gropius, now Hussars' Lieutenant, began to organize his own comprehensive ideas. Initially, these thoughts were at least colored by his negative experiences barely a decade earlier at the Technische Hochschülen of Munich and Berlin-Charlottenburg. In the intervening years, Gropius had accepted the idea that improvement in architectural education would result from the activities of organizations such as the Deutsche Werkbund, although he was already familiar with schools such as those directed by Bernhard Pankok in Stuttgart, and by Hermann Obrist and Wilhelm von Debschitz in Munich. Their programs differed radically from the set curricula of the prominent Kunstschülen and Technische Hochschülen that Gropius had experienced. Few of the innovative schools, however, provided as comprehensive and interrelated programs as Gropius contemplated—programs which emphasized social betterment through design and industrial production, collaborative methods and practice, and which gave encouragement to the students' own ideas rather than to education by rote and emulation of the teachers. An approach such as he envisioned would result in the fully prepared architect who would be recognized as the coordinator of planning, architecture, building, and art for a new society yet to arise. In 1915, the circumstances of the war created an opportunity that would permit him to carry out his ideas for education in design and production.

THE WEIMAR PROSPECT

Henri van de Velde, despite his contributions to architecture and education in Germany as an architect and director of the Grand Ducal Saxon School of Arts and Crafts in Weimar (Fig. 1), was a Belgian national and no longer welcome in 1915. Ordered to resign by April 1, he recommended three possible prospects as his replacement, although he favored Gropius. Responding to the opportunity, Gropius proposed that architecture, as a principal program and applied art, be included in the school's curriculum, and that the students' individual approaches should be encouraged. Although there was further correspondence with van de Velde and others in Weimar, it was not until January 1916 that Gropius was called from the war front for an interview with the Grand Duke of Saxe-Weimar. Gropius, encouraged, refined his ideas for the school, preparing a memorandum on objectives and curriculum within which he described the gifted faculty and experienced students he would attract. He emphasized the need for mechanical processes rather than handwork, following the collaboration of artists and craftsmen. Gropius suggested that industry's factories could be used as school workshops. All of this he framed carefully within the conservative policies of the Grand Duke. Although two other invitations to teach spurred his thoughts about a new kind of school, its final concept would not be formed until after the war.

The victory of the Allies and the chaotic conditions in Germany that Gropius found on his demobilization on November 18, 1918 energized him to try to restore tranquility in a complex personal life, to begin rebuilding his practice, and to participate actively in the new and old professional groups. Among the latter, organized in the ferment of the first postwar months, was the Arbeitsrat für Kunst, the objectives of which most attracted Gropius and contributed to his ideas for education, and to his belief in the need for collaborative effort and social reform through art and architecture.

THE STAATLICHES BAUHAUS WEIMAR

Upon his return to civilian life, Gropius sought to reestablish communication regarding the Grand Ducal Saxon Academy of Fine Arts. He already had support among the old faculty and the Duke's Oberhofmarschall, who fortunately had been present at the January 1916 interview and who was in charge of the Academy. Now the times were very different; Gropius expanded his proposal to include the dormant Grand Ducal Saxon School of Arts and Crafts by amalgamation with the academy. In mid-March 1919, the Oberhofmarschall agreed to the plan, and Gropius promptly proposed that the combined schools be named Staatliches Bauhaus in Weimar; the Thuringian state government approved.

The genesis of the name Bauhaus may have come from Gropius's admiration of the medieval bauhutte, a kind of building lodge or association whose members, master builders, journeymen, and apprentices, from many construction, arts, and crafts fields, lived and worked together on the sites of the great cathedrals, castles, monasteries, and other structures, motivated by the spiritual purposefulness of their endeavors.

By April 1, 1919, Gropius's contract was approved; his announcement of the opening of the Bauhaus called for a simple but revolutionary ideal: the unity of all creative art under the primacy of architecture, and the amalgamation of the roles of artists and craftsmen. This was the basis of the pedagogy of the Bauhaus. With fervor, he wrote (1):

Figure 1. The Weimer Bauhaus. Architect: Henri van de Velde.

The ultimate aim of all visual arts is the complete building!. . .
Together let us conceive and create the new building of the
future, which will embrace architecture and sculpture and
painting in one unity and which will one day rise toward
heaven from the hands of a million workers like the crystal
symbol of a new faith. . . .

The Faculty

Gropius immediately began to integrate old faculty and
to introduce the new. Among the faculty who returned
were Walther Klemm, Richard Engelmann, Max Thedy,
and Otto Frohlich. The newcomers in 1919 included Lyonel
Feininger, Gerhard Marcks, Johannes Itten, and Adolf
Meyer.

In 1920, they would be joined by Paul Klee and Oskar
Schlemmer, and in 1921, by Gertrude Grunow, Georg
Muche, and Lothar Schreyer. Wassily Kandinsky would
come in 1922. In 1923, Josef Albers was the first student
to be promoted to the rank of young master; constructivist
Lászlò Moholy-Nagy would be the last to be appointed,
completing the roster of Weimar Bauhaus design masters.
These were joined by skilled crafts masters among whom
were Josef Hartwig for the sculpture workshop, Max Kre-
han for the pottery workshop, and Christian Dell for the
metal workshop. The collaboration of the design and crafts
masters was basic to the training of students; competence
in both design and crafts was necessary in order to prepare
production models for large-scale manufacture by industry. When students completed the diploma requirements
of the Bauhaus and had become young masters, the combination of a design master and a crafts master in each
workshop was no longer necessary.

The Students

The idealistic manifesto of the school had immediately
attracted students, and classes and workshops were
quickly formed; the Bauhaus was underway. The first students, numbering almost 150, were as young as 17 and
with little or no funds to support themselves, let alone
pay tuition. Many were but a few months out of military
service. One quarter were women who would excel in their
studies. The reaction of the Weimar burghers to the students, to their appearance, and to their youthful behavior
was a negative one, and added to the suspicions of crafts
organizations not trustful of the workshops' purposes, and
to the antagonism of the Volkische Partei, concerned with
what it believed to be the school's political stance. Gropius
had anticipated such reaction; he immediately prohibited
any political activities in the school and arranged meetings
among faculty, students, and the Weimar citizens.

The Studies

The experimental and theoretical studies were directed
toward the technical and practical. The product designs
utilized new materials and new methods of industry. The
products were not only functional and attractive, but of

high quality and, produced in quantity as they were by
machine processes, were available to lower income families.

Gropius called for teamwork, yet he insisted on the
development of individual creativity, allowing the students' work to grow out of themselves without interference.
The Bauhaus philosophy provided only a general direction
that would be tested day by day. Changes in the attitudes
and work of the students were to come with increasing
insight and understanding, not by dictate.

A most unique requirement for the students was the
Vorkurs. In this studio, the students experimented with
all kinds of materials, testing and taxing them to the utmost through innovative designs and constructions in order to discover the possibilities and limits of their use as
well as to stimulate their own creativity. The success of
the Vorkurs was made most evident by the products of
the other workshops. In the fall of 1919, Johannes Itten
took charge, making it very much his own. Itten, a disciple
of Mazdaism, required his students to follow a course of
exercises, diet, costume, and thought that he believed
would better their accomplishment in the Vorkurs. Although Gropius then and later admired Itten's skill as a
teacher, he was concerned with the divisive cultist atmosphere created by Itten and a nucleus of students, mainly
painters, who had followed him from Vienna. Gropius was
well aware of the reaction of the Weimar burghers, who
were hardly acclimated to the ordinarily unusual appearance of the Bauhaus students, and were now confronted
by this exotic and highly visible new group in their midst.
In the case of Itten, whose influence and responsibilities
were extensive, Gropius actively looked for his replacement, finding it in the persons of Josef Albers and Lászlò
Moholy-Nagy; each of them would take charge of a semes-
ter of the Vorkurs. In 1923, Itten resigned, encouraged
to do so by Gropius, then under pressure from the city
and state.

Outside the school, it was a newcomer to Weimar, Theo
van Doesburg, a member and cofounder with Piet Mondrian of the de Stijl movement, who attracted the attention
of the students and faculty away from the not yet firmly
established direction of the Bauhaus. Offered a simpler
approach, almost a formula, for art and architecture, students found it more understandable and easier to practice
than Gropius's comprehensive interrelated view or Itten's
regimen of mysticism and attendant activities. Without
question, van Doesburg as well as Itten contributed to
the thinking of Gropius, faculty, and students. However,
unlike Itten, he was not accepted in the school for reason
of the rigidity of his approach and rejection of teamwork.

There would be a full complement of workshops; in
addition to the sculpture, metal, and pottery shops, there
were studios for stone and plasterwork, woodwork, joinery
and carpentry, gold- and silversmithing, ceramics, wall
painting, house painting and color decoration, stained
glass, weaving, theater, and graphic arts. There was not
at this time an architecture department although, from
the beginning, students had expected one. Although Gropius always had the intention of establishing a building
department for design, experimentation, and engineering
sciences, it would only follow the completion of the basic

Bauhaus program by a sufficient number of students who were interested. His original authorization and budget were for not more than the design of products for the crafts unions. Beginning in 1922, the prohibition would be circumvented by means of informal architecture workshops such as the one first begun by Herbert Bayer, followed the next year by Marcel Breuer with the aid of Georg Muche and others. Gropius continued, nevertheless, to react against an overemphasis on architecture at the early stages of education, believing that the fundamentals should be mastered first. He insisted that architecture be the ultimate goal of design development. Standardized housing, prefabrication, and housing development became themes of discussion long before the Bauhaus was prepared to offer formal courses and workshops in these subjects. Gropius and Meyer designed six different-sized and -shaped units that would be assembled in a diversity of arrangements and appearance. The units were compared to children's building blocks (Baukasten im Grossen). The first practical application of housing studies and related subjects was in Gropius's private office that was soon established in the school. The majority of the dozen employees were Bauhaus apprentices selected from a great number of applicants. An even more hands-on experience for the students was in the design and execution of the Adolf Sommerfeld house in Berlin under the direction of Gropius, then responsible for the carpentry workshop, and of Joost Schmidt for designing and carrying out the interiors. Another experience for students was that provided by the model house Am Horn, a showpiece of the Bauhaus 1923 Exhibition. It was designed by Georg Muche with the assistance of Adolf Meyer and Gropius's office; the interiors were completed and furnished by the students and masters of the workshops.

The Attack Against the Bauhaus

Despite every precaution taken by Gropius, by the end of 1919, the first year, antagonism against the school had become overt. It was based in part on the lack of understanding of the school's goals and its programs. Among the crafts organizations were those that wanted to receive nothing more from the school than designs for handcrafting, which were not to be adapted for large-scale production which they feared would overrun their markets. Then, too, the conservative Weimar citizen believed that the very search for new design, new materials, and new methods was tantamount to a leftist political direction. Although Gropius was still able to counter many of the complaints by appearing at public meetings and replying rationally to the charges, he knew that any respite won would only be temporary. Realizing the need for communication with Weimar society, he had announced a program of musical occasions, lectures, exhibits, and other events to which the public was invited; these became very popular. Supporting his defense of the school were the Deutsche Werkbund, the Arbeitsrat für Kunst, and the Novembergruppe, among other organizations that viewed the Bauhaus program as supporting their own purposes. In blunting the attacks at least temporarily, the school was able to advance

rapidly; the faculty was achieving integration, and the students were developing a school spirit.

Early in 1921, however, the two schools united by Gropius were separated by the government to ameliorate the growing complaints against the Bauhaus, many of which were fostered by the old faculty of the Academy of Fine Arts. It was not altogether regarded as a setback by Gropius; in actuality, the division afforded him the opportunity to replace unsympathetic teachers with new appointees who would be in accord with the program, goals, and methods of the Bauhaus. With the addition of the new masters, the faculty was complete but this, along with the growth of the student body, made the load of administrative tasks even more onerous. The need to augment the school's income to offset the then inflationary trend, and the need to continually counter the political activity of the very vocal opponents forced Gropius to engage a business manager. Gropius himself would be responsible for negotiations with the government and for obtaining financial support. He traveled widely, lecturing to raise funds and to obtain contracts for the workshop product designs.

Gropius, while often distracted by his personal problems, politics, administration and finance, private practice, the professional organizations, and the personalities of the masters and students, maintained firm control over the school's direction. The councils of faculty and student representatives quickly found that they were advisory only; Gropius offered policies and actions for discussion, received comments, and then retired to consider these and to make his decisions.

The Bauhaus Exhibition: August–September 1923

Recognizing that much of the now open opposition to the school was based on inadequate communication and a lack of knowledge of its program, purposes, and accomplishments, the Weimar and Thuringian governments insisted that an exhibition be made of the work and contributions of the Bauhaus. Planning began in late 1922 for a 1923 summer demonstration; it was to be a comprehensive display of the school's work. Although faculty and students would cooperate, the anticipated costs of the showing and its attendant activities were beyond the already strained budget of the Bauhaus. Gropius again took to the lecture circuit and sought aid from family, friends, and industry. A Bauhaus Week opened the exhibition on August 15; its slogan was "Art and Technique—A New Unity." There were classroom and workshop displays and demonstrations, lectures, music, and modern ballet and dance. The works of international architects (including Le Corbusier), painters, and sculptors were featured. Several thousand visitors came to Weimar during the opening week; among these were distinguished musicians and composers, lecturers, artists, and architects who participated in the events. The Haus am Horn was a focal point of the exhibition, receiving both praise and criticism. Despite any adverse comment, the exhibition accomplished its purpose, making known to the world the value and purposefulness of the reforms offered in education. Locally, however, the triumph of the Bauhaus exhibition only spurred the opponents to greater effort to overcome the advantage gained by the school.

Renewed Antagonism

Weimar, though the seat of the republic, was now undergoing political change, and not for the better insofar as the Bauhaus was concerned. Disparate groups, united by their antagonism to the school, pressed the government to limit if not to close it. By November 1923, Thuringia was under martial law, the better to seek out Socialists and Communists: thus it was easy to point out the school as a center of subversion. Although no incriminating evidence was found when the Bauhaus was searched, the school remained suspect. With the failure of the Socialist government to win the election, the school had little political support to meet new charges.

Although as early as 1922 a few staff members were dismissed for reasons of disloyalty and dishonesty, by early 1924 their falsehoods were again presented, this time in the infamous Yellow Pamphlet. The charges were disproven and private citizens, artists, and professionals, formerly indifferent to the School, now rallied to its aid. The earlier organized Bauhaus Circle of Friends was now strengthened and influential at least for a brief period.

By mid-1924, Gropius realized that the effectiveness of the Bauhaus was being worn away in Weimar, and he began to consider its removal to another location. By autumn, the state had examined the school's finances, and reported errors as the result of inadequate, but not dishonest, administration. Although the errors could be explained, Thuringia, under the pressure of the now ruling Völkische Partei, called for the closing of the Bauhaus by the following spring of 1925.

Gropius, despite little defense against the coalition of opponents, continued his efforts to gain time and find alternatives. There were offers from private industry to use the school for production only, dropping the education component. The combined strengths of the National Socialists and the Right could not be overcome, and to offset the order to close, Gropius and the faculty made public their decision to leave Weimar by April, 1925.

There was no dearth of invitations from cities that were attracted by the well-publicized successes of the Bauhaus. Among these offers for a new beginning, the most promising was that of Dessau, urged by Mayor Fritz Hesse.

BAUHAUS DESSAU

The mayor was convinced that the school would prove most advantageous to the city and that Dessau would encourage the Bauhaus to develop further its educational concepts. The official welcome was not shared by the Deutsche Volkspartei, the Employers' Union, crafts organizations, and suddenly organized citizen groups. The Yellow Pamphlet, as well as newspaper stories, had preceded the Bauhaus to Dessau. Nevertheless, Mayor Hesse had the support of the Social Democrats and a contract was approved on March 24, 1925. Gropius became responsible

administratively for Dessau's School of Arts and Crafts and the city's trade school, although these would not be amalgamated with the Bauhaus.

It proved to be fortunate that there were not adequate facilities for the Bauhaus; Gropius was engaged to design an appropriate building (Fig. 2). He immediately reopened his private office in Dessau, this time without the aid of Adolf Meyer, staffing it with young masters and students.

By midsummer 1925, the plans for the building were complete; construction began in September. Within a year, the shops and classrooms were occupied. There were studies, a dormitory, dining hall, and auditorium. The completion of the interior was in the hands of the masters and students of the workshops. Gropius was also engaged to design homes for the masters on a nearby wooded site (Fig. 3). These included a detached house for himself and three double houses for senior faculty members: Wassily Kandinsky, Paul Klee, László Moholy-Nagy, Oskar Schlemmer, Joost Schmidt, and Lyonel Feininger.

Although in Weimar Gropius and his faculty favored the designations of master, young master, journeyman, and apprentice, in Dessau they believed the title of professor to be appropriate, particularly since the Bauhaus was given university status. Gropius augmented the faculty with young masters, in addition to Josef Albers. These were former students in of the Weimar Bauhaus who had completed all the requirements and were considered highly competent to lead a workshop in both design and craft production: Marcel Breuer, Herbert Bayer, Hinnerk Scheper, and Guta Stölzl. The faculty and students made a greater effort than in Weimar to involve the community through festive occasions, music, and theatricals.

For students desiring to study architecture and building, the design and construction of a 60-dwelling unit project by Gropius for low income families in nearby Toerten (Fig. 4) in mid-1926 served as a research laboratory, as did the planning and building of the new school on which many of the young masters and students had found employment.

The dedication of the new building in December was a major event, well attended by interested notables from every field and thousands of the merely curious, and profusely reported across Germany. It appeared to be a most propitious new beginning for the school.

Yet every gain appeared shadowed by problems to be solved: contracts with industries for product design, increasing budgets and salaries, and differences among temperamental faculty. There was a concomitant growth of reactionary influences fostered not only by dissident teachers from other schools, but also by political leaders, officials, unions, and citizen organizations; the newspapers had a heyday. The Bauhaus was blamed for the new architecture and for every other problem, real or imagined. Gropius now felt that his remaining as director endangered the future of the Bauhaus. Then, too, he wanted to return to full-time architectural practice. Perhaps with prescience, Gropius anticipated this moment. In early 1927, Gropius had engaged architect Hannes Meyer to head the architecture department; Meyer's views on context and the interrelationships of architecture, planning, and society appeared similar to his own comprehensive approach

Figure 2. The Dessau Bauhaus. Architect: Walter Gropius.

and other principles of education and practice. On New Year's Day 1928, in a letter to Mayor Hesse, Gropius offered several reasons why he should resign, and thus permit a new director to have an uninhibited opportunity to guide the Bauhaus. Later that month, Gropius requested the mayor and municipal council to release him from his Bauhaus contract in order that he might devote all of his attention to his architectural practice. It was in this letter

that he recommended Hannes Meyer as his successor. A third letter on February 4 sent to Hesse and a statement directed to the public confirmed Gropius's resignation, although this was not to be effective until April 1.

Hannes Meyer—Director

Gropius's choice of Meyer as his successor was accepted only tacitly by the faculty and students, but was affirmed by the city government. Meyer almost immediately met with the faculty and thereafter with the students. Although he was then most diplomatic in explaining his plans, Moholy-Nagy, Bayer, and Breuer also submitted their resignations. Gropius moved his office to Berlin, and at the end of March, departed Germany for an inspection trip to the United States.

During the two months that Gropius was away from Germany, Meyer instituted many changes, not all of which

Figure 3. Masters' houses, Dessau. Architect: Walter Gropius.

Figure 4. Toerten Housing Project, Dessau. Architect: Walter Gropius.

were appreciated by members of the faculty and student body. There was a new emphasis on architecture and planning, and to accomplish this courses in art, unless contributing directly to architecture, were minimized as were several others Gropius had considered essential to a comprehensive approach to the study of architecture. Architects and planners were engaged, among them Mart Stam, Ludwig Hilberseimer, Meyer's associate Hans Wittwer, Walter Peterhans, Edward Heiberg, and Anton Brenner. (In 1929, Wittwer and Oskar Schlemmer would resign, and Hinnerk Scheper would take leave for two years.) Although the expansion of curriculum, the new faculty, and the improvement in the school's financial progress appeared most propitious, another element introduced by Meyer would prove otherwise. This was the study of Marxism and Leninism for which perhaps 10% of the students were ready and most receptive.

Despite earlier constant external pressures that could stimulate reaction by members of the school community, Gropius had been quite successful, with few exceptions, in enforcing his order to keep political activities out of the Bauhaus. Now in Meyer's time, such an order as Gropius had promulgated would have been most difficult, if not impossible, to enforce. Germany's economic and government distress had intensified and had exacerbated the already sensitive school–city relationship. Meyer had voiced no objection to the students organizing to resist those external forces. The students' tendency toward communism and action rather than to Platonic intellectualism and the discussions in the canteen was a natural development among idealistic youth.

The opposition to the school was heightened by its then current success and by public knowledge of Meyer's encouragement of the study of Marxism and support of the striking miners in Mansfield. In early 1930, Mayor Hesse asked Meyer to resign, charging him with fostering political unrest in the school by means of his espousal of Marxist ideology and methods. Nevertheless, Meyer had contributed to the growth of the school through his development of the program to include architecture and planning emphases. He had stressed its social purpose, had interrelated the independent workshops, had put the fine arts into a more appropriate balance, and had achieved good relationships with the labor unions. Despite these justifiable claims, his politics and actions were held against him, and he was persuaded to accept a financial settlement in early November 1930. Unlike Gropius, who departed Germany on the occasion of his resignation for the capitalistic U.S., Meyer now departed Germany for the communistic USSR.

Ludwig Mies van der Rohe—Director

Hesse attempted to persuade Gropius to return to the Bauhaus, but, failing to do so, accepted his recommendation of Ludwig Mies van der Rohe to succeed Meyer. Mies obtained a most favorable contract that provided, along with the perquisites of a house, consultation on city planning, patents, licenses, contracts, a six-month cancellation clause option, and the rights to the name Bauhaus, that

his work week in Dessau would be no more than three days to permit him to continue his Berlin office.

Mies's educational method appeared to be one of master and disciple and learning by rote. The social emphasis of the Gropius and Meyer curricula was reduced, as was that of the school community. Architecture, housing, and city planning were given new emphasis. Historian Ludwig Grote compared the teaching methods of Gropius, Meyer, and Mies, stating (2):

> Meyer gave some credit to Gropius for his social ideas; under Meyer, these became Socialist and active. Mies did not continue Meyer's program, but went back to Gropius's ideas and combined them with his own.

As seen by their student, Selman Selmanagic, the teaching philosophies of Meyer and Mies were quite different; Selmanagic stated (3):

> With Hannes Meyer and through his Marxism and Leninism, the main point was not only how one built, but also what and for whom. . . . But, according to Mies van der Rohe who succeeded him, it was not what one built, but how. . . .

Through all of this upheaval, the faculty remained almost intact; only Johannes Riedel, Edvard Heiberg, and Anton Brenner, all appointed by Meyer and Gunta Stölzl, who protested the manner in which Meyer was ousted, departed the Bauhaus.

Mies's changes in the school and his regulations set a sober tone in order not to draw attention from government or citizen groups. Dissident students were expelled; others resigned. The building was renovated and its reopening celebrated. There would be a brief respite, almost a truce, with the governmental officials, trade unions, citizen groups, and other critics. Political change, however, was rapid and by January 1932, National Socialists on the city council called for an end to the Bauhaus. Hesse and Mies were briefly successful in delaying this and other efforts to close the school until late August. A final action by a large majority of the city council on October 1, 1932 did close the Bauhaus, at least insofar as Dessau was concerned.

BAUHAUS BERLIN

Mies was persistent and reestablished the school, still with the name Bauhaus, in an old factory building in Berlin-Steglitz. The faculty now included Albers, Engemann, Hilberseimer, Kandinsky, Scheper, Peterhans, Lilly Reich, and Alcar Rudelt, a faculty which Mies considered minimal for the courses fundamental to architecture studies. Some students had followed Mies to Berlin, and the populous city provided others. Despite the political confusion in Germany and especially in Berlin, the Bauhaus gained momentary stability in its program, and its festivals and exhibits attracted hundreds. Unfortunately, the politics of Dessau followed the school to Berlin as had those of Weimar to Dessau. On April 1, the school was suddenly searched by the police for incriminating evidence against

Mayor Hesse on request by the Dessau city attorney general. Although none was found, on the next day the school was ordered closed. Although efforts were made to continue, the harrassment by the Gestapo was more than could be overcome, and the Bauhaus administration and faculty voted to dissolve the school on July 20, 1932. There was a summer term of sorts, but it was the end of the Berlin Bauhaus as it was the end of the Weimar government.

THE SPREAD OF THE BAUHAUS IDEA

However, it was not the end of the Bauhaus idea. With the completion of their studies, or as the result of the forced dispersions from Weimar, Dessau, and Berlin, most of the faculty and students departed the Bauhaus imbued with its legacy to teach or to practice their professions and crafts. The concepts and principles were reestablished by them, and expanded and strengthened by local cultural or physical requirements. The influence of the Bauhaüsler became almost immediately evident on five continents, although almost not at all in Germany until after World War II. Elsewhere in Europe, although delayed by the war, were schools such as Wchutemas in Moscow, the Bauhaus of Budapest, and the Skola Umeleckych Remesiel in Bratislava. In the Far East, Bauhaüslers returning to Tokyo opened the School of Architecture and Fine Arts in the Ginza; it was closed by the military government in 1936.

Within a few months of the closing of the Bauhaus in 1933, Josef Albers and his wife, Bauhaus weaver Anni Fleischmann Albers, departed Germany to teach at the recently organized Black Mountain College in North Carolina; they were followed by Bauhaüsler Xanti Schawinsky and other avant-garde teachers. It was the first school in the United States to pattern its programs on those of the Bauhaus. In March 1937, Gropius arrived at Harvard University's Graduate School of Design where changes were already being made by dean Joseph Hudnut. Harvard offered curricula in landscape architecture, town and regional planning, and architecture, and would not replicate the more comprehensive Bauhaus program. The school did, however, offer summer Vorkurs and a two-year experimental Vorkurs with Albers, Naum Gabo, and other instructors. Perhaps the Carpenter Center, ensconced in the only Le Corbusier building in the United States, provides the last Bauhaus trace at Harvard. The advent of Hudnut's successors marked the diminution of the unique qualities of the Graduate School of Design.

In October 1937, with advice from Gropius, Moholy-Nagy created the New Bauhaus on Chicago's South Side; Bauhaüsler Hin Bredendieck and other contemporary artists joined him there. In barely a year, the school disbanded and Moholy established the Institute of Design on Chicago's North Side. Following his premature death in October 1946, the institute struggled along with inadequate financial resources until 1949 when it became part of the Illinois Institute of Technology, where Mies van der Rohe had already served for a decade as director of its architecture and planning department. Although Mies had engaged

Bauhaüslers Ludwig Hilberseimer, Walter Peterhans, and Johannes Molzahn, the program would be typically Miesian rather than Bauhaus. Other schools came to reflect portions of the Bauhaus program and Gropius's philosophy and pedagogical methods; among these were Yale, Virginia Polytechnic Institute, Kansas City Art Institute School, Bennington College, the University of Illinois, and many others; three-quarters of Gropius's Harvard alumni became part- or full-time teachers, even exceeding the 50% of the Bauhaüslers who did so.

Following World War II, European schools quickly adapted to the new art and architectural directions; among these are Hochschule für bildende Kunst in Hamburg, which Gustav Hassenpflug had directed and to which Bauhaüslers Wolfgang Tümpel and others came to teach; Hochschule für bildende und Angewandte Kunst in East Berlin; and schools in Darmstadt, Wiesbaden, Giessen, Düsseldorf, and Munich. All could claim Bauhaus lineage, as could Instituut voor Kunstnijverheidsonderwijs in the Netherlands to which Bauhaüsler Johan Niegemann returned in 1937 to teach under the direction of Mart Stam.

Particularly important was the Hochschule für Gestaltung of Ulm for which Gropius had great hope. Funded by the Geschwister—Scholl Foundation with a contribution from the United States and subsidies from the city of Ulm, the state of Baden-Wurttembergand, and the German federal government, it was directed by Bauhaüsler Max Bill; the program began in 1953 with its buildings completed two years later. Unfortunately, the Hochschule, which was frequently called Bauhaus Ulm and did show the influence of the earlier Bauhaus, survived only 14 years, so difficult were the internecine and external problems of administration and finance.

Industrial production of ceramics, metalware, furniture, textiles, and automobiles reflect Bauhaus design directions. In Germany, Rosenthal ceramics, Rasch wallpapers, and Feder furniture, among other products, became internationally known. In the United States, the Container Corporation of America engaged Gropius as consultant and Herbert Bayer as director of its design work. Bauhaus work became prototypical for typography, graphic design, photography, and art everywhere. Thus the objective of Gropius and the Bauhaus of making well-designed and well-made products from quality materials was achieved, but these were so much in demand that they were not always available at prices affordable to lower income families. Also yet to be accomplished is the goal of Gropius and the Bauhaus of making industrialized production of good-quality housing of diverse designs in well-planned communities available to all. Nevertheless, what was considered by skeptics to be a near-Utopian vision of the environment and society by the Bauhaus is obviously advancing steadily toward its realization.

BIBLIOGRAPHY

1. W. Gropius, *Bauhaus Manifesto,* Weimar, FRG,. Apr. 1919.
2. L. Grote, interview, Munich, FRG, June 1965.
3. S. Selmanagic, interview, East Berlin, GFR, Jan. 1965.

General References

G. C. Argan, *Walter Gropius e la Bauhaus,* Francesco Toso, Torino, Italy.

H. Bayer, W. Gropius, and I. Gropius, *Bauhaus—1919–1928,* The Museum of Modern Art, New York, 1938, Verlag Gerd Hatje, Stuttgart, FRG, 1955.

M. Franciscono, *Walter Gropius and the Creation of the Bauhaus,* University of Illinois Press, Champaign, Ill. 1971.

W. Gropius, *Staatliches Bauhaus in Weimar, 1919–1923,* Bauhaus Verlag, Weimar GFR, 1923.

W. Gropius, *Bauhausbauten Dessau,* Albert Langen, Munich, FRG, 1930.

W. Gropius, *The New Architecture and the Bauhaus,* Faber and Faber, Ltd., London, 1935; Museum of Modern Art, New York, 1936; Florian Kupferberg, Mainz, FRG, 1964.

F. Hesse, "Von der Residenz zur Bauhausstadt" in *Erinnerungen au Dessau,* Band I; "Aus den Jahren 1925 bis 1950," Band II, Schmorl u.v. Seefeld, Buchhandlung, Hanover, 1964.

K.-H. Hüter, *Das Bauhaus in Weimar,* Akademie-Verlag, Berlin, 1976.

R. R. Isaacs, *Walter Gropius—Der Mensch und sein Werk,* Vols. I and II, Gerbrüder Mann Verlag, Berlin, 1983 and 1984.

B. M. Lane, *Architecture and Politics in Germany, 1918–1945,* Harvard University Press, Cambridge, Mass., 1968.

W. Scheidig, *Crafts of the Weimar Bauhaus,* Reinhold Publishing Corp., New York, 1967; *Bauhaus Weimar/Werkstattarbeiten,* Edition Leipzig, 1966.

H. M. Wingler, *Das Bauhaus 1919–1933: Weimar, Dessau, Berlin,* Rasch (DuMont) & Co., Bramsche, FRG, 1962; *The Bauhaus,* The MIT Press, Cambridge, Mass., 1968.

R. Isaacs, "Walter Gropius—Harvard Teacher," Centennial Address, Harvard University, Cambridge, Mass., May 18, 1983.

R. Isaacs, "Walter Gropius" in *Macmillan Encyclopedia of Architects,* Macmillan Publishing Company, Inc., New York, 1982.

R. Isaacs, "The Bauhausler" in H. M. Wingler, *Bauhaus—50 Years* exhibition catalogue organized by the Institute für Auslandsbeziehungen, Stuttgart, FRG, Pasadena Art Museum, 1970.

See also ALBERS, JOSEF; GROPIUS, WALTER; MIES VAN DER ROHE, LUDWIG.

REGINALD ISAACS
Cambridge, Massachusetts

BEAUX ARTS.   See ECOLE DES BEAUX ARTS

BEHAVIOR AND ARCHITECTURE

The relationship between architecture and human behavior has recently emerged through a field commonly known as environment and behavior. This discipline is also termed environmental psychology, people–environment studies, design–behavior, people–environment relations, and environment–behavior studies. Its roots lie in the links between the environmental design professions (architecture, interior design, landscape architecture, and city planning) and the social sciences (psychology, sociology, anthropology, and geography). This field has both a theoretical side, attempting to explain and predict phenomena related to environment and behavior, and an applied side, seeking to implement findings from various research endeavors to specific design projects.

One of the most comprehensive accounts of both the history and theory of environment and behavior can be found in Gary Moore's chapter in the *Handbook of Environmental Psychology* (1). Much of the first two sections of this article are based on Moore's work. For a more complete review of these two topics, consult the original work. It is a valuable resource to anyone seriously intrigued by field.

BRIEF HISTORY OF THE FIELD

Environment and behavior first became a recognized discipline in the 1960s with the establishment of the Environmental Design Research Association in 1968 and the inaugural issue of the journal *Environment and Behavior* in 1969. Widespread systematic research in the United States began in earnest in the late 1960s and early 1970s. However, the origins of many concepts central to environment and behavior were stated much earlier. For instance, the notion of environmental symbolism, a concept that only recently attracted the attention of researchers, was foreshadowed by the writings of the influential nineteenth-century landscape architect Andrew Jackson Downing in his book *The Architecture of Country Houses.* In it, he wrote, ". . . much of the character of every man may be read in his house"(2). In 1938, social critic Emily Post, in a book entitled *The Personality of a House,* elaborated on this idea when she wrote, "A front door of lovely design and perfect scale is like a beautiful hand held out in welcome. A hideously untidy door is like a dirty hand that is repellent to touch"(3). The symbolism accorded Japanese gardens has been described for centuries. The publication of Kevin Lynch's landmark book *The Image of the City* in 1960 helped launch the beginning of environment–behavior research in the environmental design professions (4). Lynch, an urban planner and professor at the Massachusetts Institute of Technology (MIT), was the first U.S. designer to challenge traditional modes of planning and design by carefully examining the everyday person's reaction to cities and their buildings. His basic premise in this work and others that followed was that the opinion of the "person on the street" was just as, if not more, important than that of the design professional, be it the planner, the architect, the landscape architect, or other environmental decision maker. *The Image of the City* is still one of the most widely read books in the field. Lynch's impact on the environmental design professions and on environment and behavior has been profound and long-lasting (5–8). The work of Lynch's protégé, Donald Appleyard, has had a similar influence on the field (9–12). *With Man in Mind,* a convincing plea for the use of behavioral research in environmental design written by city planner Constance Perin, also helped set this new field in motion (13).

Sim Van der Ryn and Murray Silverstein's pioneering report on *Dorms at Berkeley,* published in 1967, took a similar stance toward the architectural profession (14).

Through systematic interviewing and observations of dormitory residents, these architectural researchers discovered that the ways in which the building's occupants and the architectural community evaluated these dormitories were remarkably different. Constructed in the late 1950s as part of a major program to house thousands of University of California, Berkeley, students, the buildings had received accolades and professional awards. To a great extent, however, students who participated in this study found their dormitories unsatisfactory, largely because of their inflexible architectural designs and because some of the assumptions made by the architects about student behavior in dormitories (eg, that most students studied in their bedrooms) proved to be incorrect.

Environment and behavior's origins can also be traced back to early studies in its parent disciplines of psychology, sociology, geography, and anthropology. Berkeley psychologist Edward C. Tolman conducted early studies in the 1940s on cognitive maps of both animals and humans, setting the stage for further research in this area. A classic 1950s social psychology study discovered that the arrangement of the physical environment had a distinct influence on human behavior. Through systematic investigation, Festinger, Schachter, and Back discovered that friendship patterns of married students at MIT were closely linked to the relative location of their apartment units (15). Roger Barker and his colleagues were among the first psychologists to examine child development in its natural environment, as opposed to a psychological laboratory. Ecological psychology, a precursor of environment and behavior, was born out of this research in the early 1950s (16,17).

Research psychiatrist Humphrey Osmond's work, in conjunction with that of architect Kiyo Izumi, on the effect of psychiatric ward design on patient behavior, conducted in Canada in the 1950s, discovered the commonly used concepts of sociopetal space, which encourages group interaction, and sociofugal space, which discourages group interaction (18). Osmond's work spawned the work of Robert Sommer, a social psychologist, who described early environment–behavior research in mental hospitals, dormitories, and bars in another landmark book published in 1969 entitled *Personal Space: The Behavioral Basis of Design* (19). Along with Lynch's *Image of the City, Personal Space* is another of the most widely read and often cited works in environment and behavior. Sommer's other books have continued to have a major impact on sensitizing design professionals to users' needs (20–22).

Walter Firey's 1945 article on urban symbolism, followed in 1961 by Anselm Strauss's book *Images of the American City* and later by William Michelson's book *Man and His Urban Environment*, were among the earliest sociological accounts of environment–behavior issues (23–25). In 1947, geographer J. K. Wright was the first in his field to create the terms geosophy or terrae incognitae and to study them to analyze people's conceptions of their geographical environment (26). Two well-known books that addressed environment–behavior issues from yet another viewpoint were *The Silent Language* and *The Hidden Dimension*, written by Edward Hall, an anthropologist (27,28). These two books were mavericks in their field, among the first to try to understand proxemics, how inter-cultural communication is affected by the use of the physical environment.

AN OVERVIEW OF ENVIRONMENT—BEHAVIOR THEORIES

A number of theorists have attempted to explain the complex relationship between environment and behavior. A variety of philosophical approaches, frameworks, conceptual models, and explanatory theories have been proposed over the years, reflecting the diverse, multidisciplinary nature of the field (1). As could be expected, no one theory has gained universal or even widespread acceptance. The development of theory is an evolutionary process, with constant revision and refinement. Theory is an interpretive endeavor, so that although some theoreticians may view an idea one way, others see it differently.

Philosophical Approaches

In a recent chapter for the *Handbook of Environmental Psychology*, theoretician Irwin Altman and his colleagues proposed that three philosophical approaches underlie research and theory in environment and behavior: interactional, organismic, and transactional. This typology is based on the philosophical frameworks of John Dewey, Arthur Bentley, and Stephen Pepper. The interactional approach considers environmental factors, personal or group qualities, psychological processes, and temporal variables each as independent entities. Interactional research and theory describes the dimensions of these variables, examines their interactions, and attempts to understand causal relationships among them. To a certain extent, some environment–behavior research on crowding, environmental perception, environmental cognition, and post-occupancy evaluations (POEs) of housing projects, workplaces, and other settings adopts an interactional approach by examining how personal and group factors interact with physical design characteristics to affect attitudes, satisfaction, performance, or other outcomes.

The organismic approach examines dynamic and holistic psychological systems in which personal and environmental components exhibit complex, reciprocal relationships and influences. This viewpoint emphasizes the overall complex pattern of relationships between system components rather than the characteristics of each element in isolation or in specific relationships with other elements. Some environment–behavior research incorporating this general framework includes work on hospitals, schools, dormitories, and elsewhere that views a number of subsystems (environmental, organizational, and personal) embedded in a larger system (29).

The transactional approach stresses that people, psychological processes, places, and temporal flow form intrinsic aspects of a whole and do not exist as separate elements (30). Aristotle was a major influence on this approach with his view of causation. Some phenomenological approaches to environment and behavior, particularly in the context of homes, are transactional in many respects (31,32). The phenomenological perspective especially addresses subjective and experiential aspects of people—environment relationships, centering around meanings, feelings of attachment, and affective orientations of people to places. Related to this is a recent study of residential autobiographies and residential histories (33).

Overarching Theories

The major theories put forth in environment and behavior parallel these philosophical approaches. Based on the work of sociologist Robert Merton, theorist Gary Moore has drawn a distinction between "big T" and "little t" theories. Big T theories are those overarching theories that relate to the field as a whole, whereas little t theories pertain to only a subdiscipline within the field (1).

Concerning big T theories, one of those most widely discussed during the early development of the field was environmental determinism, a viewpoint suggesting that environment determines behavior. However, determinism was soon viewed as being overly simplistic. Basically a causal model, it did not allow for any of the more subtle nuances that might better articulate this relationship.

Another major big T theory put forward soon after was interactionism. This theory was based on the model first proposed by psychologist Kurt Lewin, stating that

$$B = f(P,E)$$

that is, that behavior is a function of the person and the environment. However, this has also been viewed as a relatively simplistic and often unidirectional model.

At present, one big T theory that has gained some support is the transactional theory (34). In contrast to the previous two, this theory emphasizes the reciprocal effects between the environment and psychological, behavioral, cultural, social, political, and economic processes. It views these variables as parts of an integrated system. Each variable can function as an independent, mediating, or dependent variable, depending on the particular situation. The transactional theory is helping to transform the nature of environment–behavior research from a focus on people's short-term reactions to isolated environmental conditions (such as lighting, density, or noise) to more complex composites of activities, places, and time. Both the spatial and temporal dimensions of research have broadened. In addition, a more Gestalt approach to research has evolved. Rather than focusing strictly on cognition, stress, or behavior, for example, the current trend is toward analyzing the linkages among these diverse processes (1,34).

Theories Within Specific Areas of Environment and Behavior

A variety of little t theories have been proposed to help explain several subdisciplines within environment and behavior. For example, the Gestalt theory has been linked to the study of environmental perception, suggesting that people perceive the environment as a whole, greater than the sum of its parts, rather than as a group of discrete entities. Developmental theories have been offered to help explain how children acquire mental images of spaces and places over time. The arousal theory has been used to address the study of performance in learning and work environments. Proponents of this theory believe that an optimal level of arousal, caused by noise for example, can help make individuals more alert and attentive, often benefiting performance on simple tasks. However, when noise is intense, it can lead to a state of overarousal, which adversely affects task performance. The theory of information overload has been used to help explain how people respond to crowded conditions in cities.

The evolution of theoretical perspectives in environment and behavior is significant because it has helped shape and direct the nature of research in the field. Much more can be said about theory than space permits here. For a more comprehensive review, consult Refs. 1, 29, and 34. In sum, these theorists suggest that the field is simply maturing from a stage of descriptive research to one of causal research and to the notion of multiple complex causalities with respect to time.

AN OVERVIEW OF ENVIRONMENT–BEHAVIOR RESEARCH METHODS

One of the chief features of environment and behavior that distinguishes it as a separate discipline, related to but distinctly different from architectural criticism, is its reliance on specific research methods. Architectural critics typically base their impressions of buildings on their own opinions of good architecture. Environment–behavior specialists base their views of architecture primarily on research about the buildings' occupants. Understanding users' assessments of architectural work is often achieved through the use of POEs. See Table 1 for a comparison of architectural criticism and POE.

Once a research problem has been clearly defined, environment–behavior researchers work out a research design that attempts to answer the problem. Research design is the arrangement of conditions to collect and analyze data in a way that is relevant to the purpose of the research. The purpose of a research endeavor generally falls into a number of broad groupings: formulative or exploratory studies to gain familiarity with or to achieve new insights into a phenomenon; descriptive studies to portray characteristics of a particular individual, situation, group, or place (with or without an initial hypothesis) or to determine the frequency with which something occurs or of its association with something else; and studies that test a causal hypothesis of a relationship between variables. For more information on research design, data collection, and analysis consult Refs. 36–39.

Once a research design has been established, a set of research methods is selected to collect the desired information. A sample is chosen from which to collect information, a standardized procedure is developed for collecting and checking the data, and the results are analyzed and reported.

Research methods used in environment and behavior are derived from parent disciplines in the social sciences, primarily psychology and sociology. The most widely used data-gathering techniques are divided into two categories: unobtrusive and obtrusive. When using unobtrusive techniques, the researcher typically does not talk with users,

Table 1. Comparison of Architectural Criticism and POE[a]

	Architectural Criticism	POE
Purpose	Communicate views to professional peers and often to the public	Give immediate feedback for a given project. Develop information for future designs—offer feedback to designers, managers, and users.
General orientation	Subjective, seen from the individual critic's viewpoint.	Objective, using systematic methods of investigation to gain the users' viewpoints.
Focus	Primarily on aesthetics—quality of design and its place in the history of artistic ideas and concepts.	Examines aesthetics, but simply as one of many design elements affecting users.
Typical process	Visit site, examine photographs or other buildings by the same designer—methods depend on the critic.	Uses relatively standard and tested procedures of investigation so that information is not biased.
Timing	Typically occurs after final drawings are produced, but before building is completed or occupied. Sometimes occurs soon after building completion.	Occurs after occupants move into building—Can be relatively soon after occupancy and can be checked periodically.
Origins	Criticism in the arts—music, drama, the literary world, etc.	Social sciences.
Similarities	Examine historical context of a building. Examine circumstances leading to the design of a building. Examine issues such as circulation, image, and fit into local context.	

[a] Ref. 35.

nor are users even aware that they are being studied; since people are less likely to react to being the subject of investigation, this is often referred to as nonreactive research. The use of obtrusive techniques, however, implies that the users are contacted and that they are aware of the study; since, in this instance, people are more likely to react to being studied, such techniques are often termed reactive measures.

Data-gathering techniques can also be viewed along a spectrum from quantitative to qualitative. Quantitative research employs standardized measurements and uniform or numerical data (37–39), whereas qualitative generally does not. Furthermore, all data-gathering techniques need to be assessed for their reliability, that is, the extent to which a research instrument is likely to produce similar results when replicated, and their validity, the extent to which the instrument in fact measures what is intended. Much of the following section is based on Ref. 40.

Depending on the information desired, observations of the behavior of building occupants and passers-by on the street may span sizable periods of time, such as a week or a month, and take into account different times of day, days of the week, and if an outdoor space is observed, weather or time of year. Researchers systematically seek to answer the following types of questions: Who is doing what with whom? In what relationship, in what context, and where? Among the types of behavior observed are the simple presence or absence of people; if they are sitting, standing, walking at a leisurely pace, or rushing by; if they are alone or in groups; if they are silent or talking with others; if they are eating, reading, or simply people-watching; how long they stay; and specifically where they are located in a particular setting. The particular kinds of behavior observed will depend on the concerns of each study.

Behavior observations are often recorded through behavioral mapping techniques, which plot out specific behaviors and their frequency on a floor plan, site plan, map, or precoded checklist and often use photography (time-lapse photography is especially useful), film, or videotape.

Physical traces involve examining the physical surroundings to learn clues about previous behavior. For example, by-products of use include places where steps are worn down and empty apartment balconies. Office partitions erected long after building completion are types of adaptations for use. Photographs hung on a wall or numbers displayed in front of a home are displays of self. Commercial signs and graffiti writings are examples of public messages (40). Another distinction can be drawn between accretion (what people have added to the environment) and erosion (what they have taken away).

Archives are used in environment–behavior research to examine data gathered for one purpose and transform it into useful information for another (40). These usually take one of three forms: words, numbers, or graphic representations. Examples of archival data that researchers might use include a speech delivered at the opening ceremonies of a new building, written architectural criticism of a building in professional architectural journals, and absenteeism or turnover rates in an office. Diagrams, photographs, plans, sketches, drawings, and models are especially useful archives for architects.

Interviews are commonly used to gain firsthand responses from either users or nonusers of a particular building or space. They differ from questionnaires and surveys in that they involve either a face-to-face or telephone conversation and in that responses are oral. A structured interview uses a predetermined set of questions, whereas an unstructured one involves a much looser free-flow of information. Questions can be either open-ended, as in an essay exam, where respondents are encouraged to elaborate on their answers, or closed, where respondents choose from several predetermined categories, as in a multiple-choice test. The purpose of interviews in environment–behavior is generally to learn how strongly a respondent feels about a particular situation or environment. Understanding this kind of information can help designers establish priorities and decide on tradeoffs for design decisions, such as privacy vs safety.

Questionnaires are similar in purpose to interviews, as is the type of questions asked. They differ from interviews, however, in that they are generally administered to a large group of people simultaneously and are often sent by mail. Any confounding effects of the interviewer–interviewee interaction are removed through the use of questionnaires. Responses are written, and little or no verbal contact is made with each respondent. Compared to interviews, questionnaires are a less costly and less time-consuming way of gathering information, and they have been used increasingly in recent environment–behavior research.

Cognitive maps are used to help understand people's images of buildings, open spaces, neighborhoods, and cities. They are among the commonly used techniques for studying environmental cognition, or people's mental representations of their physical environment. Much as in a geography class, people are asked to draw maps of an area or to identify places or parts of a building on a pre-drawn map or plan. Researchers then note such features as the order, content, strength, and accuracy of a map. Cognitive mapping is a useful way to record orientation and how people find their way around environments, and it has design implications, primarily in the area of circulation.

Time-budget studies are sometimes used in environment–behavior research to record what a person has done during a specific period of time and where that set of activities occurred. The format of these studies is either precoded or open-ended and is often similar to that of a diary.

Environmental simulation is a way of showing representations of the environment to groups of individuals. The intention is to replicate closely an existing or proposed environment and to measure people's reactions to it. Environmental simulation involves going beyond drawings, plans, and models typically used by architects. A movie camera is sometimes used to document the effect of traveling through a model. In recent years, computers have begun to be used for the same purpose, and it is expected that they will be widely used in the future.

Gaming uses simulated representations of buildings and rooms in workshops for designers and users. Gaming examines real-life situations and helps people deal with changing, complex environmental problems. A variety of design games have been developed by researcher Henry Sanoff (41). The practical application of games is to enable the public to participate in environmental decisions. For example, gaming was recently used in a design research project in a low-income public housing project in Aurora, Ill.

Participant observation is a technique borrowed from both sociology and anthropology that involves the researcher as a participant and as an observer simultaneously. For instance, in studying a housing project for the elderly, a researcher might move into the facility for a week or so, dine regularly with residents, discuss their surroundings with them informally, and attempt to gain some experience of the setting as they see it.

Rather than relying exclusively on any one data-gathering technique, most research employs a combination of methods, usually a balance between unobtrusive and obtrusive measures and qualitative and quantitative techniques (Fig. 1). Each technique has its strengths and shortcomings and is not relied upon solely. The validity and reliability of specific data-gathering techniques must be taken into account in designing any environment–behavior research project.

ENVIRONMENT–BEHAVIOR RESEARCH AND ITS DESIGN APPLICATIONS

Small-scale Settings: Interior Design and Furniture Arrangement

One research issue often studied in small-scale settings is personal space; its implications concern interior design, furniture arrangement, and space planning. Edward Hall was the first to propose the four interpersonal distance zones typically used in social interactions. The study of proxemics, "the interrelated observations and theories of human use of space as a specialized elaboration of culture," has led to distinctions among three different types of spaces (28). Fixed-feature space is that usually considered in architectural design: walls, ceilings, and floors. Semifixed features include chairs, tables, and other furniture that can be moved around in fixed-feature space. Informal space includes the distances maintained in encounters with others. Cultural variations exist. The design implications here often address seating arrangements in various settings.

Robert Sommer's *Personal Space* examines the invisible "space bubble" that surrounds human beings and the way in which people use space to reflect their behavior. He has argued that the physical arrangements of many interior spaces are inappropriate for the behavior that occurs there. His work has led to the redesign of airports and office buildings, among other places (19,22). Personal space patterns seem to differ according to cultural background, age, stage of development, personality, and sex. Researchers have also discovered that in smaller, more enclosed, and corner-like rooms with lower ceilings greater personal space is desired (43). Other research issues studied in connection with small-scale settings include territoriality, privacy, and crowding. These have also been central research issues in the study of institutional buildings and housing projects (44).

A useful perspective in examining human behavior in small-scale settings is sociologist Erving Goffman's theatrical analogy. Goffman argues that furniture, decor, physical layout, and other background items supply the scenery and stage props for performances. Places where performances are given are termed front-stage regions; these are easily accessible and open to the public. In a house, for instance, a living room, dining room, or kitchen would

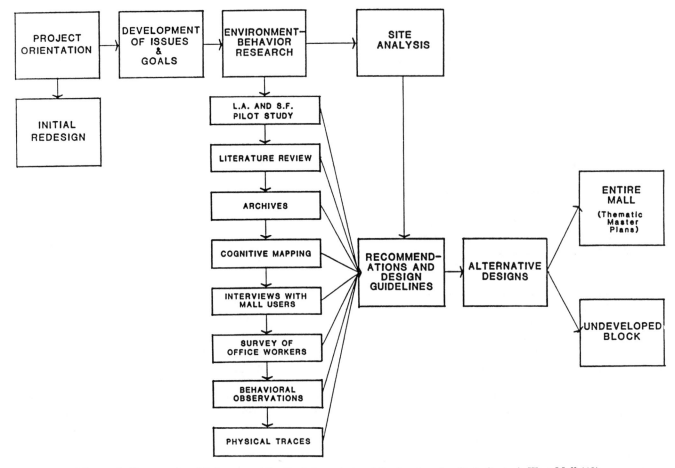

Figure 1. The use of multiple research methods in a study of the Los Angeles Civic Center's West Mall (42).

qualify. Back-stage regions are more private, hidden, and less accessible. Bedroom closets, bathroom cabinets, and dresser drawers constitute such back-stage places (45).

Some design interventions have been found to help promote a positive sense of personal space. The size and shape of rooms, degree of openness, access to the outside, complexity and displacement, brightness, and extent of partitioning are among these interventions (46).

Housing

Housing is among the most highly developed areas in environment and behavior. Although some researchers have addressed the concept of "home" and how it differs from "housing" or "house," others have examined special problems encountered in the design of housing for special user groups. This section addresses both the concept of home and user-needs research: housing for children, students, and low-income, disabled, and elderly people.

The Concept of Home. Through interviews, questionnaires, and card-sorting tasks, one large study conducted by psychologist D. Geoffrey Hayward identified nine clusters of the meaning of home. Most important was home as a relationship with others, followed (in order) by home as a social network, self-identity, a place of privacy and

refuge, continuity, a personalized place, a base of activity, a childhood home, and a physical structure (47).

Along these lines, another study examined the experience of moving and individuals' memories of favorite homes. Open-ended interviews with 97 southern California residents revealed that most people had a negative reaction to moving and a strong psychological attachment to their previous home.

In terms of Hayward's typology, the strongest concepts of home were home as physical structure and home as a place of privacy and refuge. Remembrances of landscapes surrounding the home figured prominently in most people's descriptions (48). These findings confirm previous studies that have used residential autobiographies as a way of understanding designers' attitudes toward housing (49).

Clare Cooper Marcus was among the first in the environment–behavior field to address the notion of residential symbolism, or how the homes people occupy often reflect their character and psyche. She relied on psychologist Carl Jung and his notion of archetypes as a way to help understand this relationship (50). The experience of burglary has been the topic of some fascinating recent research in France. Findings indicate that burglary victims experience a trauma similar to that of being raped. After being burglarized, they take great pains to redefine their home as a private and safe place (51).

Others have examined the meanings of different symbols within the home across a wide geographic area. The symbolism of the landscaping in front of single-family houses has also been examined. The area of residential symbolism has only recently prompted serious exploration; further research is needed. For a comprehensive overview of current research on home environments, consult Ref. 52.

Housing for Children. Although children are frequent residents of housing projects, the environments provided for them are often inadequate. A number of studies have shown that by far the greatest users of public outdoor areas in multifamily housing are children. However, such spaces are often planned more appropriately for adults. Children are often relegated to neatly labeled play areas, which are able to captivate their interest for only short periods of time. A set of guidelines for designers has been developed based on findings from a wide body of social science research to help improve the design of housing for children. A few of the findings and recommendations are summarized below.

1. Children tend to play anywhere and everywhere, not just in designated play spaces. The entire site should be designed with this in mind.

2. To increase a sense of internal security, access to the site by outsiders should be discouraged.

3. Families with small children should be located on ground-level units with enclosed yards or patios and be able to overlook an enclosed common space for preschool play from a slightly elevated position.

4. Small children tend to play close to the most frequently used entrance to a dwelling or building.

5. Boundaries between private and communal outdoor spaces need to be strictly defined.

6. Many observation studies indicate that when given a choice, children tend to play more frequently on hard surfaces than on grass. A variety of hard surface areas, away from the circulation system, should be provided for hopscotch, small ball games, jumping rope, tricycle riding, and other activities. Nonetheless, for aesthetic reasons, hard surfaces should not predominate.

7. Trees that can be used by children for climbing should be selected—ideally, they should have sturdy, low branches.

8. Play equipment should be chosen with children's preferences in mind. Children prefer equipment that moves such as swings, on which they can move such as jungle gyms, and places where they can sit, watch activity, and play quietly, such as benches and tables (Fig. 2).

9. Teenagers prefer informal gathering places where they can "check out" the action (54).

A study of over 300 children living in apartments furnished by the New York City Public Housing Authority examined the relationship between residential density (in three- vs 14-story buildings) and children's well-being. Results indi-

Figure 2. A tot lot design based on environment–behavior research (53).

cate that higher-density homes have some deleterious effects on children's health and well-being (55).

Sample Applications. Another aspect of housing for children involves the design of day care centers. As the number of dual-career and single-parent families has risen sharply, this building type has become increasingly important. Gary Moore, Uriel Cohen, Tim McGinty, and their colleagues at the University of Wisconsin-Milwaukee, conducted a series of studies detailing design needs for child care facilities and outdoor play environments. The Department of Defense, the largest purveyor of child care in the world, has adopted their results in the form of recommendations for all new Armed Forces child care centers (56,57). Both governmental and private centers have been constructed around the country based on these recommendations.

Housing for Students. A large body of environment–behavior literature, too great to cite here, is available on housing for students. Most such studies have addressed particular issues that occur in dormitory settings, such as personalization, density, and friendship formation. A sophisticated instrument for evaluating social and psychological characteristics of dormitories, the University Residence Environment Scale, was developed and administered at a renovated dormitory at the University of Rhode Island (58,59). A few researchers have taken more of a Gestalt approach, studying the dormitory environment as a whole rather than focusing on a single issue. Studies of university dorms, the International House at Berkeley, and six college dormitories in New York State are three such examples (14,60,61).

Sample Applications. Four generations of dormitories have been built at Indiana State University based on user-needs research through the cooperative efforts of a behavioral scientist and an architect (56). The student center at California State University, Los Angeles, was designed by the firm of Deasy and Bolling using behavioral research conducted by social scientist Thomas Lasswell. Management and program planning at the University of California's International House have also been influenced by environment–behavior research (61).

Housing for Low-Income People. Low-income housing has captured the attention of environment–behavior specialists, perhaps because it is here that the satisfaction (or lack thereof) of user needs is most critical. One of the most extensive studies on low-income housing was conducted by a team of researchers at the Housing Research and Development Program at the University of Illinois at Urbana-Champaign. This seminal work won the Applied Research Award from *Progressive Architecture* magazine in 1980. It examined residents' satisfaction in 37 publicly assisted housing projects located in 10 states from New York to California, in both central city and rural locations. Among the goals of this research were to identify and measure specific physical, managerial, social, and psychological factors that influenced the degree of residents' satisfaction. Over 1900 residents responded to the questionnaire, and over 18,000 behavioral observations were recorded. Results from the research indicate that most residents (66%) were satisfied with Department of Housing and Urban Development- (HUD-) assisted housing and that "the overwhelming negative image of assisted

housing frequently encountered in impressionistic and journalistic accounts is not deserved." Three major factors explained a high proportion (74%) of the total variance in overall satisfaction: satisfaction with other residents, pleasant appearance, and economic value (62). Both physical and nonphysical qualities of the housing development influenced residents' satisfaction (Fig. 3).

One of the more well-known pieces of work concerning housing for low-income residents is *Defensible Space: Crime Prevention Through Urban Design* by Oscar Newman (63). This controversial book attempts to demonstrate that the way in which housing structures are arranged on a site and the manner in which each building is designed can reduce the amount of crime occurring in a housing project. Newman's key argument is that providing residents with a clear sense of territoriality can actually help reduce crime. This could be accomplished by designing limited entrances to the building for a small number of families, by subdividing massive, anonymous, public, open spaces in the middle of housing projects into smaller, more identifiable, private or semiprivate pieces of land, and by allowing a strong sense of surveillance from each apartment unit to the open space outside. Other recommendations for designing low-income multifamily housing to increase resident satisfaction are described by Clare Cooper (64).

The study of housing for low-income people has only

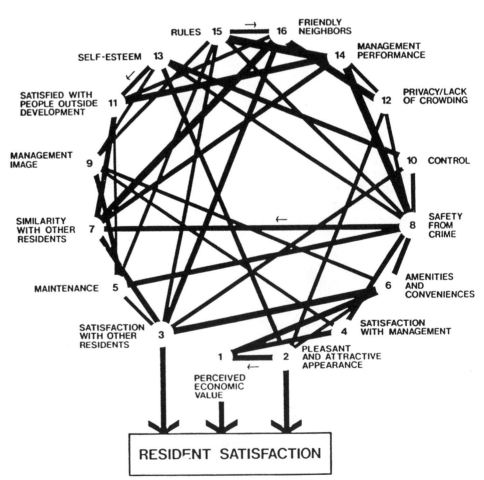

Figure 3. Model of residential satisfaction (62). Courtesy of the U.S. Department of Housing and Urban Development.

recently begun to examine the special needs of single-parent families. Needs for privacy within the dwelling unit, opportunities for social interaction within the housing project, and on-site day-care facilities are among the issues being addressed (65). One housing project exclusively devoted to providing housing for single-parent, female-headed households is Warren Village in Denver, Colo.

Sample Applications. The Housing Research and Development Program at the University of Illinois at Urbana-Champaign, has conducted post-occupancy evaluations and programming studies for several low-income housing projects in Illinois. The program's research includes design recommendations, many of which have since been implemented (53). Similarly, housing authorities in Albuquerque, N. Mex., changed design sites based on post-occupancy research, and two federally subsidized housing projects designed by Lou Sauer and Associates also made use of behavioral research in the programming process (56).

One housing project that exemplifies the behavioral design concept of defensible space is St. Francis Square, a cooperative low-rise apartment complex for low-income residents located near Japantown in San Francisco's Western Addition. A study involving interviews with almost 300 St. Francis Square residents found that residents viewed the project very favorably (66). Among the chief reasons for high resident satisfaction was the strong emphasis on exterior landscaping in three courtyards forming the core of the project, on providing each apartment unit with its own private outdoor space, and on breaking the project into smaller, discrete units.

Housing for Disabled People. The study of housing for the disabled from a user-needs perspective has been burgeoning in recent years. A number of researchers have specialized in this area and produced documents to assist designers with specific housing concerns, above and beyond the specifications of building codes (67–69).

One of the most pressing problems encountered in studying housing for the disabled is architects' frequent assumption that the disabled population is a monolithic group. Often, all units are designed for residents who are wheelchair bound, when many people suffer from different kinds of disabilities. In fact, those individuals confined to wheelchairs constitute a relatively small segment of the total disabled population. At last count, approximately 10% of the U.S. population suffered from some form of physical handicap: limited vision (5.5 million), hearing (8 million), or movement (22 million). Of these, 400,000 are permanently and totally confined to a wheelchair; the rest can walk, but have difficulty moving their hands, or need canes, braces, crutches, or other aids. Each of these disabilities requires a different kind of housing environment to help support rather than interfere with the user's behavior. The width of doorways, stair gradients, height of window controls, location of electrical outlets and light switches, and type of operative fixtures on stoves, ovens, refrigerators, sinks, and other appliances are all affected by the nature of the occupant's disability. Even industrial design is important in designing for the disabled, as often standard store-bought appliances are inappropriate for certain types of disabilities.

Standard drawings found in architects' codebooks, of wheelchair-bound people with muscular arms outstretched from the body, imply a robust, healthy person who is simply movement impaired. This picture is inaccurate, as most problems are more severe and involve weakness, muscular difficulty, and lack of coordination. To that end, a number of authors have advocated careful examination of disabled people's behavior as it occurs in their housing environments. One suggestion is the use of the performance interview or scenario, where the researcher observes disabled people carrying out a specific task, such as serving a midafternoon snack to a friend, and then holds a discussion about how easy or difficult it was to perform that task and what specific environmental features either helped them or got in their way (69).

Others have pointed out the psychosocial effects of inaccessibility (68). These include the notion that the environment sends out a negative message to disabled people, that people's mental maps of a place or a building may well be dramatically different and less accurate than those of able-bodied people, that environmental barriers serve as "no trespassing" signs to disabled users, and that disabled people often possess a high level of competence to master their environment, but that an inaccessible building fails to allow them to exercise it. All of these factors may result in strong negative consequences for their self-esteem and personal identity.

Housing for the Elderly. In recent years, as the percentage of elderly in the overall population has risen, housing for the elderly has become an increasingly important force on the national housing scene. It has also become a major focus for environment–behavior research. The location of housing sites, the scope of the program, and architectural and site design issues have been addressed by recent user-needs research. Congregate housing that provides transportation, meal service, programmed activities, outpatient medical clinics, and the like; fully independent housing projects; and alternative housing types have been studied.

Many elderly people have particular needs that require special housing environments. Failing vision and hearing, a variety of physical disabilities, as well as the psychological change of identity accompanying retirement, loss of a spouse, and relocation are among the factors that influence the design of housing for the elderly.

Several books address user needs in elderly housing and provide behavioral criteria for planning and design over and above HUD's Minimum Property Standards for Housing for the Elderly (70,71). Unfortunately, in many housing projects the minimum standards quickly become the norm. The purpose of environment–behavior research in this area has been to sensitize designers to both large-scale site planning issues (such as designing a series of buildings that face an inner courtyard, for example, thus encouraging social interaction) and small-scale interior design issues (such as designing door handles, grab bars, and kitchen cabinetry). Additional research has investigated the concept of intergenerational housing, which integrates the elderly with younger residents, as well as other alternative housing types for the elderly.

Sample Applications. One housing for the elderly project whose design was specifically influenced by POE research is San Rafael Commons in San Rafael, California. The project, designed by architects Kaplan/McLaughlin/Diaz, was influenced by the results of a POE from Martinelli House, a nearby elderly housing complex designed by the same firm (72). Among the POE's recommendations were relocating the mail area to serve as an activity hub and using outdoor courtyard furniture to encourage social interaction. A second POE was conducted on San Rafael Commons, and results indicate that resident satisfaction was extremely high (71). Another such example is the Rosa Park Towers, where environment–behavior research was used to transform an abandoned San Francisco high-rise (formerly known as the Pink Palace) into award-winning housing for the elderly.

User-needs research was also incorporated in the design of the Captain Clarence Eldridge House in Hyannis, Mass. Architect Barry Korobkin, research sociologist John Zeisel, and associated architects Donham and Sweeney collaborated on the planning and design of this congregate housing complex. The project consisted of an 8500-ft^2 addition to a nineteenth-century sea captain's house. In response to interviews with prospective tenants, residents of other elderly housing facilities, and elderly home-care personnel, the designers opted to offer each tenant a private room with its own private front porch overlooking an atrium, its own sink and toilet, showers and tubs shared by four, and shared living spaces: front and back parlors (originals of the old house), a sitting room, a large dining room, and a long front porch with rocking chairs and tables. Many residents came from nursing homes to Eldridge House and "without exception, all said it has revolutionized their lives. Some, who have been in nursing homes for a long time, say they feel they are now living for the first time in years"(73).

Institutions

Erving Goffman has drawn a distinction between total and partial institutions (74). A total institution is much more restrictive, and one of its major purposes is to protect people who cannot fend for themselves or are deemed threats to the community. These people are removed from the outside world and thus separated from society. Correctional facilities, hospitals, mental health care facilities, and nursing homes are examples of total institutions. By contrast, partial institutions require individuals to be at specific spots for prescribed periods of time (for work, learning, etc), but are far less restrictive. Time, activity, and use of the environment are somewhat regimented. Examples include schools, day-care centers, workplaces, camps, and communes.

Correctional Facilities. The study of jails and prisons, otherwise known as correctional facilities, has attracted the interest of environment–behavior researchers. In past decades, the United States has been plagued by severe prison riots; the reasons for rioting can often be traced in part to overcrowded conditions and obsolete physical environments. The social and psychological reasons for imprisonment remain controversial, and the efficiency of today's prison and criminal justice system remains in doubt. Nonetheless, some studies have implemented user-needs research in the design of prisons and jails.

Sample Applications. The San Francisco architecture firm Kaplan/McLaughlin/Diaz has done some work in this area, applying environment–behavior research to the design of correctional facilities at the Contra Costa County Detention Facility in Martinez, Calif., and elsewhere.

Another California-based firm, Patrick Sullivan and Associates (PSA), headquartered in San Luis Obispo and Palo Alto, has also employed a behavioral consultant in its design work at Kings County Juvenile Center in California. Their research findings have indicated that the severity of the crime committed should be reflected in the design of each individual cell. A prisoner who has committed a severe crime ought to be housed in a high-security cell with restricted activities and no carpeting, but with cameras, towers, and so on. In contrast, one who has committed a moderate crime would best be served in a low-security cell with high ceilings, wood doors, and private toilet facilities. More violent criminals require more stringent codes and more costly construction techniques. A common error made in prison design is to design all units uniformly. In fact, tremendous savings can be had if a variety of units are provided, so that costly security measures are only built for those who really need them. In this regard, PSA was able to save its client a considerable amount of money because of findings from user-needs research; one building was constructed at $90/ft^2 instead of $125/ft^2. The same design firm was able to save another client $34,000–39,000 per bed based on user-needs research findings indicating that rehabilitation of existing structures, rather than a new building, would better help solve the client's space problem (75).

A POE of three metropolitan correction centers in Chicago, New York, and San Diego influenced the design of the Contra Costa County Detention Center in California. In addition, researchers have developed an evaluation system supported by the National Institute of Corrections resulting in an improved generation of correctional facility designs (56).

Hospitals. As a complex and large building type, hospitals house an exceptionally wide variety of users, including nurses, doctors, paramedics, managers, administrators, executive officers, boards of directors, trustees, and most importantly, patients and their visitors. Because the user is not the paying client, architects often design hospitals that fail to take user needs into account. The spatial requirements of equipment often supersede those of human beings.

One of the major issues examined in hospitals has been environmental cognition, or how people find their way around the building. Time is of utmost importance in emergencies, so designing hospital facilities that are clearly marked is critical. The relationship of spaces, signs and graphics, color coding, lines on the floor or walls, and redundant cuing have been shown to help make hospitals more easily understood.

By examining work-sampling and staff questionnaires over an 82-day period, an extensive study compared patient and personnel preferences for different floor plans. Results indicated that in most cases, radial (round) design is superior to double-corridor (racetrack), which in turn is better than single-corridor design. Furthermore, based on average salaries at the time, it was calculated that compared with those in radial units the extra travel costs in the single- and double-corridor units amounted to about $77 per bed per year (76). Other studies have found that triangular-shaped nursing units offer the greatest flexibility and efficiency and link easily with future expansions (77).

One POE of hospitals has produced recommendations for the design of waiting rooms, and urges designers to consider the length of time people are waiting, the population mix, the type of activities that occur in the waiting room, and the range of anxiety level. Where people are most anxious, separate comfortable furniture groupings, televisions with private earphones, soft light, reading lamps, and opportunities for privacy are recommended (78).

Yet another issue addressed in the hospital POEs has been the comparison between single and double rooms as far as administering medication is concerned. Instances where nurses actually confused prescriptions for two patients sharing the same room have been documented (79). Researchers have examined the role of nature in hospital patients' recovery. Results indicate that patients recover more rapidly when treated in a room with plants or with a view of nature (80,81). A field called horticultural therapy has developed around this premise.

Sample Applications. Environment–behavior research has produced a variety of design recommendations for hospital design. In fact, the Veterans' Administration has begun to use POEs to learn more about the designs of its hospitals. The New York State Veterans' Home, designed by The Architects Collaborative, and the rehabilitation facility at Rhode Island Medical Center in Cranston, R.I., were based on user-needs research (56). POEs have also been used to assess the impact of design on institutionalized elderly patients suffering from chronic brain syndrome, an illness that leaves patients confused and immobile. User-needs research conducted at the Philadelphia Geriatric Center served as background information for the design of a new institution, and another POE was conducted in which the new design was very highly rated (56). Another project called "Plane Tree" involved the use of research to convert a San Francisco hospital into a facility for more humane care for the sick and dying.

Regarding the issue of way finding, some detailed design guidelines based on award-winning user-needs research have been developed by a research team at the University of Michigan Medical Center (82,83). Its Patient and Visitor Participation (PVP) Project gathered data from over 2500 patients and visitors and over 1200 staff in 32 different studies. Results have already been applied to the redesign of existing facilities and will also be incorporated into the design of a new $285 million University of Michigan Hospital complex.

Mental Health Care Facilities. Environment–behavior research in mental health care facilities was pioneered by Kiyo Izumi, Robert Sommer, and Humphrey Osmond. While working at a mental hospital in Canada and experimenting with a variety of seating arrangements in the day room of a mental hospital, Sommer and Osmond discovered a change in patients' behavior. When rows and columns of chairs were transformed into small-scale groupings of chairs around tables and magazines, patients who had otherwise remained quiet and withdrawn began talking with each other (18,19). Two admissions wards at one psychiatric hospital were studied as part of another experiment. One ward was remodeled based on user-needs research; the other was not. Those patients in the remodeled ward socialized more and had a more positive attitude toward their environment (84).

A number of researchers have shown that typical psychiatric facility designs serve the purposes of the administration and staff rather than the needs of the patients. Others have shown that such features as long corridors with windows at only one end exaggerate the already distorted vision of many patients (85).

Some sensitive guidelines for designers have been produced by interior designer Victoria Jane Willis based on her observations, interviews, and questionnaries at six different mental health care facilities in Indiana. Among her recommendations are that the scale, color, and shape of the building should all be given proper consideration since they help form the first impression of the building. The admissions office should be extremely private to protect the confidentiality of patients. Waiting areas need a variety of seating arrangements; accommodations for one or two people are best. Day rooms should reflect a hierarchy of spaces for different levels of social interaction, and they should include windows, clocks, and calendars to maintain time-space relationships. In the therapist's office, the doctor's chair should not block the entrance, as it could cause the patient to feel trapped.

Willis also concluded that cafeterias should avoid lines and rectangular tables; round tables are best since no one has to sit at the head. The cafeterias ought to be made to appear more like restaurants than institutions by featuring walls, ceilings, and floors of different colors and materials. Throughout the facility, mirrors, glass, and highly polished floors should be avoided, as the reflections they create tend to cause visual distortions for patients. Similarly, wood, natural materials, and live (as opposed to artificial) plants should be used to avoid confusing patients. Within each patient's room, personal storage areas and individually controlled lighting units (table or pole lamps) are desirable, as they offer a greater sense of control over the environment (86).

Sample Applications. The new Mental Rehabilitation Center at San Diego's Grossmont District Hospital, designed by Kaplan/McLaughlin/Diaz, was strongly influenced by POEs of other facilities. It features an especially strong relationship to outdoor spaces, with three different levels of security as well as a "no corridors" design (56). An addition to Herrick Memorial Hospital in Berkeley, Calif., designed by the same firm, was also influenced by POE research.

Schools. A great deal of attention has been paid to social and psychological aspects of school design. One of the most often cited studies compared big and small schools, finding that smaller schools, or "undermanned settings," elicited greater participation in student activities, greater sense of responsibility, and greater satisfaction (87). The school environment as a source of stress has been the subject of extensive research (88). Much of the research has focused on classrooms, particularly on their seating arrangements, design, density, and noise. In addition, researchers have examined the controversial debates between traditional vs open classrooms and windowed vs windowless classrooms. In these last two areas, research findings have been somewhat inconclusive and contradictory. Other research has addressed the influence of the design of special education settings on developmentally disabled students (89).

Sample Applications. A few researchers have conducted systematic POE studies of high schools in, for example, Albuquerque, N. Mex., and Rosemead, Calif. (90,91). The latter study involved a multimethod approach, including a literature review; observations of behavior and physical traces; a review of over 30 years' worth of school archives; interviews with students, faculty and staff, and the school architect; student cognitive maps; and questionnaires of approximately 230 students and faculty and staff. It developed some guidelines and recommendations, which have since been implemented by the School Board. Rosemead High School has been repainted, and the lighting in its corridors has been significantly altered as a result of the POE. At another location, the College of Osteopathic Medicine of the Pacific, Pomona, Calif., significant design changes to the campus—particularly in the campus graphics, signs, and outdoor entranceways to the campus—also resulted from a POE and a behavior-based program (92).

Office Buildings. Environment–behavior research on office environments is perhaps most comparable to that on housing environments because it has become extremely well developed and sophisticated and has produced specific design recommendations. Researchers have examined how the physical environment influences the ability of workers to perform work-related tasks. They have discovered that characteristics of the ambient environment such as heating, ventilation, and air conditioning, as well as the concentration of irritants such as tobacco smoke, asbestos fibers, and so on, may result in worker headaches, fatigue, or interference with concentration. They may even significantly impact physical and mental health. Office furnishings, layout, and the size of the workspace have been shown to influence worker satisfaction and performance. Ergonomic studies indicate that improper seating heights, reach lengths, arm angles, viewing angles, and distances affect personal comfort and efficiency. Additionally, researchers have found that natural lighting and a view

contribute to worker satisfaction. When artificial lighting is required, adjustable lighting is preferred, hence the current trend toward task lighting. Some evidence indicates that fluorescent lights can be harmful, as they decrease the ability of the body to absorb calcium (93).

Other studies have addressed privacy and social interaction in offices, discovering that both visual and auditory privacy are key ingredients to worker satisfaction. Phones and other people talking are cited as the most bothersome types of noise. Other research has examined symbolic identification or status indicators and perceptions of status. Such indicators include the size or square footage of office space; the amount of enclosure provided by walls, partitions, and doors; the location of an office (at the corner of a building, adjacent to the window wall, or close to management); and the amount and quality of furnishings. Status incongruence, or environmental symbols that are in conflict with perceived or achieved status, may impact worker satisfaction and performance as well as mental and physical health (93).

A few major studies are particularly applicable to design and have also helped to shape the direction of subsequent research. Steelcase Inc., a major producer of office furniture, conducted a comprehensive national study of office environments based on a survey of 1047 office workers from 178 federal, state, and local government agencies. Its findings revealed that about one-third (30%) of the employees work in office landscapes (the physical grouping of people working together through the use of component furniture and movable half-height partitions) or open-plan offices (usually with fixed or no partitions) and that over half (54%) use or operate data processing, word processing, or other electronic equipment. Almost half (43%) are unhappy with the way their present offices look, and three-quarters (74%) said that given better working conditions, they could probably do more work (94). A four-year study by the Buffalo Organization for Social and Technological Innovation (BOSTI), a basic research and consulting group, examined 18 environmental variables in offices, such as the amount of floor area per employee, layout, enclosure, temperature/air quality, lighting, windows, status, and privacy, through a 500-item questionnaire of about 5000–6000 workers at over 70 office sites. Respondents were questioned two to four months before a facility change to new and upgraded offices and then about eight months to a year later. Several variables were shown to affect job satisfaction, environmental satisfaction, and ease of communication on the job. These are shown in Figure 4. Job performance and satisfaction fluctuate depending on the nature of specific environmental changes. The study places a dollar value on these variables, concluding that through improved office design, companies can increase annual productivity by up to 17% of the average annual salary for clerical workers and about 15% of the annual average salary for professional/technical employees and for managers (95).

A team of researchers at the University of Michigan conducted a POE of the new State Office Building in Ann Arbor, designed by Tarapata, MacMahan, and Paulsen of Bloomfield Hills, Mich. This detailed evaluation helped set a model for future research (96). Another major study,

FACETS	BOTTOM-LINE MEASURES			
	ENV. SAT.	EASE COMM.	JOB SAT.	JOB PERF.
ENCLOSURE	■	■		■
LAYOUT	■	■		■
FURNITURE	■	■	■	
NOISE	■	■	■	
FLEXIBILITY	■	■	■	
PARTICIPATION	■		■	
COMFORT	■		■	
COMMUNICATION	■	(IS THE SAME)	■	
LIGHTING	■		■	PROBABLY
TEMP./AIR QUAL.	■		■	
FLOOR AREA		■	■	
PRIVACY	■	■		
STATUS	■	■		
PATHFINDING	■	■		
DISPLAY	■			
APPEARANCE	■			
OCCUPANCY		■		POSSIBLY
WINDOWS	POSSIBLY		POSSIBLY	

Figure 4. Environmental facets relating to environmental satisfaction, ease of communication, job satisfaction, and job performance in office environments (95). Courtesy of Workplace Design and Productivity, Inc.

"Organizations, Buildings, and Information Technology" (ORBIT-2), based on user-needs research and sponsored by 18 different organizations, has developed strategies to help businesses cope with change, the introduction of new technology, and facility management (97).

Among the newly emerging issues in office research are the impact of office automation, open-office planning, and degree of environmental control. Recent studies have discovered that video display terminals have generated a variety of physical and psychological problems, including a high level of anxiety, depression, fatigue, eyestrain, and muscle strain. Problems have been associated with keyboard height, gaze angle, lighting, and glare.

Open-office problems with privacy have resulted in worker dissatisfaction and reduced work performance. To date, no research has indicated that the greater communication promoted by open offices leads to a greater amount of work accomplished. Researchers have discovered the importance of employees being able to control heating, ventilation, air conditioning, windows or shades, and furniture (93).

Sample Applications. Environment–behavior research has influenced the design of several office facilities, including those of the Federal Aviation Agency in Seattle, an AT&T branch office, and the U.S. Senate office complex (98). Recent POEs have been conducted for Amoco, Arco, Citibank, Nestles, Proctor and Gamble, and TRW (98). One of the world's largest building clients, the U.S. General Services Administration, routinely uses POEs to evaluate its facilities; user-needs research has also been used to help design new office spaces for the engineering and research building of the Research Triangle Institute in North

Carolina. The New Zealand Ministry of Works and Development recently sponsored research to enable its client regional departments to evaluate their own government buildings; orientation and way finding have been major focuses to date (98).

Large-scale Architecture and Urban Design

A variety of work has investigated large-scale architecture and urban design, including the human use of open space. Some studies have examined how people remember buildings in cities. Results indicate the importance of the following factors: movement, contour, size, shape, use, singularity, significance, and quality (9,99). A large body of work has addressed the social and psychological impacts of highrise buildings (100).

A number of POEs of major downtown buildings and open spaces have been conducted in various cities across the country (100). A recent study of users' relations to enclosed and semienclosed public spaces found that indoor pedestrian spaces (arcades, atriums, and gallerias) perform many of the same functions as outdoor pedestrian spaces (parks and plazas) and actually perform some of them better. The study also demonstrated that agoras possess desirable qualities in their own right (101). A comparative analysis of several urban open spaces across the United States, spanning almost a decade, was conducted by William Whyte and his Street Life Project and is summarized in his well-known book *The Social Life of Small Urban Spaces* and a television film, part of the *Nova* television science series (102). Through an extraordinarily detailed set of behavior observations recorded through time-lapse photography, Whyte and his research team were able to distill the key ingredients of successful (ie, heavily used) urban plazas. These are a large amount of sitting space (one linear foot for every 30 ft^2 of plaza) and a choice of seating areas, preferably with movable chairs; adequate sun; provision of trees; protection from wind; access to water; presence of food through cafes, kiosks, and street vendors; triangulation, or the provision of an external stimulus (like a piece of sculpture, a fountain, or entertainment); and a very close relationship to and high visibility from the street.

A large body of research has linked behavioral issues to the study of the large-scale landscape. The subdiscipline of landscape assessment has become particularly well developed (103); researchers have even addressed such far-reaching topics as perceptions of the sky (104). Others have examined perceptions of and responses to a variety of environmental changes in urban settings (examining such issues as growth, urban renewal, historic preservation, gentrification, neighborhood conservation, mobility, and relocation) and rural settings (natural and recreational environments, agriculture, rural development, and energy production and development) (105).

Sample Applications. Whyte's research resulted in significant amendments to New York City's 1975 zoning codes, and his follow-up assessments have further modified zoning rules. His research has had a tremendous impact in altering the streetscape of downtown Manhattan. For example, food kiosks and open air cafes previously classified as obstructions are now viewed as amenities. Additional changes called for specific guidelines for seating, planting and trees, lighting, circulation and access from the street, access for physically disabled people, and maintenance (102). Other cities are beginning to follow suit.

Since 1975, Project for Public Spaces, Inc. (PPS), a not-for-profit organization and an outgrowth of Whyte's Street Life Project, has conducted a vast number of public space evaluations in cities and towns across the United States. Its work has helped solve problems in plazas, central business districts, urban parks, neighborhoods, cultural facilities, recreational areas, and public transportation facilities. Many of these studies have produced or will produce design and management changes based on user-needs research. These include New York City's Exxon Minipark; Dallas' LTV Center; Kansas City's Crown Center Square, designed by Edward Larrabee Barnes; New Haven's Shubert Square Entertainment District; downtown Madison, N. J.; and Detroit's Renaissance Center, designed by John Portman. Among other places studied by PPS have been Flushing Meadows–Corona Park, Museum Mile, and Rockefeller Center, designed by Harrison and Abramovitz in New York City; Larimer Square in Denver; an office–retail building on Boston's Boylston Street; and downtown Hartford, Conn.

Recently, PPS has worked for private developers helping to design and retrofit public spaces in and around mixed-use and office building projects. The organization analyzes existing circulation patterns to determine optimal locations for entrances and to predict how people will circulate and orient themselves throughout the project. It recommends potential locations for all uses for the site, especially retail spaces, and shows how these uses can reinforce lively, active public spaces. It also suggests locations for major focal points of activity, such as plazas, atria, parks, and so on and designs them to be well-used amenities. PPS usually works directly for the developer and collaboratively with the building architects. The organization has earned the nickname "the space doctors."

San Francisco's famous urban design plan of 1971, along with its most recently adopted version, have taken into account user needs in large part through the work of Berkeley researchers Donald Appleyard and Peter Bosselman. The latest set of urban design guidelines has incorporated studies of the impact of skyscrapers' shadows on pedestrian use and of pedestrian reaction to open space (106). Today, developers of proposed new structures in downtown San Francisco are required by the city's architectural review board to place a scale model of their proposal in the University of California, Berkeley, Environmental Simulation lab model and photograph it for their design review hearing. The simulator was also used to project the appearance of New York City's Times Square if the same midtown controls in effect throughout Manhattan were used there. The results were frightening: when compared to those now existing, the potential new buildings were immense. The researchers concluded that a new set of controls was needed for the theater district, ironically like those first legislated in 1916 to protect sunlight on the city streets and sidewalks (106). Had the simulator not been in use, such conclusions would have been much harder to reach.

Lynch's studies of city imageability and Appleyard's research on residents' views of their city also influenced the design of the Ciudad Guayana, Venezuela, and the Village of Woodbridge (planned by the Irvine Company with landscape design by Sasaki Walker Associates), Irvine, Calif. (4,9). Lynch's concepts of landmarks, nodes, edges, paths, and districts can be clearly seen in Woodbridge, located in Southern California's Orange County.

ENVIRONMENT–BEHAVIOR RESEARCH

Colleges and Universities

A number of colleges and universities in the United States and abroad offer courses and programs in environment and behavior. At present, U.S. doctoral programs in architecture with an emphasis on environment and behavior exist in only a handful of institutions; however, several universities offer this specialty in other departments. In 1987, about 24 universities had doctoral programs focusing on environment and behavior (Table 2).

Private Firms and Other Organizations

A small number of design firms specialize in environment–behavior research as an integral part of their practice. According to a recent informal survey of members of the Professional Practice Committee of the Environmental De-

Table 2. North American Doctoral Programs in Environment and Behavior

Architecture
Georgia Institute of Technology
University of California, Berkeley
University of California, Los Angeles
University of Michigan
University of Montreal
University of Wisconsin-Milwaukee
Psychology
Arizona State University
City University of New York
Claremont Graduate School
Colorado State University
Rutgers University
University of Arizona
University of British Columbia
University of Utah
Sociology
Michigan State University
Rutgers University
University of Kansas
Washington State University
Geography
University of California, Santa Barbara
University of Nebraska
University of Toronto
Natural Resources
University of Arizona
University of Michigan
Interdisciplinary
University of California, Irvine (Social Ecology)

sign Research Association, very few clients of these firms are architects (under 20%). Instead, most clients are government agencies, nonprofit institutions, and profit-making entities, who in turn hire architects (98).

Professional Organizations

The oldest and largest professional organization devoted to environment–behavior concerns is the Environmental Design Research Association (EDRA). Beginning in 1969, EDRA has held a series of conferences bringing together architects, landscape architects, interior designers, urban designers, planners, psychologists, sociologists, human/social ecologists, geographers, and anthropologists to discuss common research issues through papers, symposia, workshops, poster sessions, and field trips. These conferences are held annually on various university campuses across North America, and papers are published in a set of annual conference proceedings. EDRA's headquarters are located in Washington, D.C., and its membership is approximately 900. Although 27 countries are represented, about three-quarters of the members are from the United States (1).

Another organization, more international in scope, is the International Association for the Study of People and Their Physical Surroundings (IAPS). IAPS is headquartered in the United Kingdom and its members meet biannually throughout Europe. Environment–behavior research organizations have recently been established in New Zealand and Australia [People and the Physical Environment Research (PAPER), formalized in 1983] and in Japan [Man and Environment Research Association (MERA)]. These organizations are devoted primarily to the discussion and dissemination of environment–behavior research. Other organizations whose members include researchers with environment–behavior specialties are the Association of Collegiate Schools of Architecture, the American Psychological Association, whose Division 34 is devoted to population and environmental psychology, the Association of American Geographers, the International Association of Applied Psychology, and the American Sociological Association.

Major Journals and Publications

In recent years, the field has expanded to include three major journals: *Environment and Behavior* (*E&B*), the *Journal of Architectural and Planning Research* (*JAPR*), and the *Journal of Environmental Psychology* (*JEP*). A number of other publications carry occasional articles on environment–behavior research, and newsletters such as *Design Research News,* published by EDRA, the *Population and Environmental Psychology Newsletter,* published by the American Psychological Association's Division 34, and the *Architectural Psychology Newsletter,* published by IAPS, also provide updates on current scholarly activities in the field.

CURRENT TRENDS AND FUTURE DIRECTIONS

Current trends in the field include examining issues such as the behavior of salad bar patrons (which often violates the canons of hygiene); consumer behavior in supermarkets, farmers' markets, and cooperatives; commuters' responses to traffic jams; human responses to environmental pollution; residents' perceptions of nuclear power plants; and habitability in space stations (107–109). Studies are now underway by NASA/Ames Research Center's Space Habitability Research Group to try to troubleshoot the design of space station systems while they are still under conceptual development. The research team is especially interested in helping maximize work performance of astronauts and providing comfortable spaces for privacy, territoriality, and stress reduction (110).

Some other research has involved the use of behavioral studies in the design of a combined tactile/electronic guidance system for visually impaired persons. The system has been installed in two buildings and about 2000 ft (600 m) of outdoor track connecting major buildings at the University of New Mexico campus. This system allows the blind and sight impaired to travel more easily and safely, both indoors and outdoors (111,112).

Another area of research conducted through the U.S. Department of Energy addresses occupants' responses to passive solar commercial buildings (113). Other researchers have also begun to explore some of the same user groups, but in different locations: for example, the perception and use of performing arts centers by the elderly (114). Although the field has generally encompassed place research, user-group research, responses to social and technological change, basic research, and process research, the current effort is to try to better expand and more effectively integrate these different approaches.

A recent EDRA task force under a grant commissioned by the National Endowment for the Arts Design Arts Program developed a set of future priorities for the field. Gary Moore, D. Paul Tuttle, and Sandra Howell encapsulated their views in a recent book entitled *Environmental Design Research Directions.* Among the priorities identified were to more effectively communicate examples to the general public and the professions and to improve education in environmental design research (115). In this regard, some revisions to the National Architectural Accreditation Board (NAAB) guidelines, which stipulate the criteria necessary for professional accreditation of schools of architecture across the United States, will have an impact on the environment–behavior field and architectural education. The recently adopted guidelines specify that schools of architecture must include courses on social and behavioral factors that also apply that information to design. Hence, in the next few years, virtually all accredited schools of architecture will offer coursework in environment and behavior; this change alone is likely to have a profound influence on a new generation of architects.

The implementation of environment–behavior research in architectural practice is not without its difficulties. A number of scholars have pointed out the many impediments to translating research into design. Nonetheless, a solid body of environment–behavior user-needs research with applicability to particular building types, such as those listed in this article, is now developing. More and more studies that present research findings and design recommendations through both well-documented text and careful illustrations are being published, thus increasing their value to both academic and professional audiences. The expansion of this type of data base and its increased visibility will help make the field of environment and behavior even more useful to practicing architects.

BIBLIOGRAPHY

1. G. T. Moore, "Environment and Behavior Research in North America: History, Developments, and Unresolved Issues," in D. Stokols and I. Altman, eds., *Handbook of Environmental Psychology,* John Wiley & Sons, Inc., New York, 1987.

2. A. J. Downing, *The Architecture of Country Houses,* Dover Publications, New York, p. 25; originally published by D. Appleton and Company, 1850.

3. E. Post, *The Personality of a House, The Blue Book of Home Design and Decoration,* Funk and Wagnalls Co., New York, 1938, p. 7.

4. K. Lynch, *The Image of the City,* MIT Press, Cambridge, Mass., 1960.

5. K. Lynch, *Site Planning,* 2nd ed., MIT Press, Cambridge, Mass., 1981.

6. K. Lynch, *What Time is This Place?,* MIT Press, Cambridge, Mass., 1972.

7. K. Lynch, *Managing the Sense of a Region,* MIT Press, Cambridge, Mass., 1976.

8. K. Lynch, *A Theory of Good City Form,* MIT Press, Cambridge, Mass., 1981.

9. D. Appleyard, *Planning a Pluralist City: Conflicting Realities in Ciudad Guayana,* MIT Press, Cambridge, Mass., 1976.

10. D. Appleyard, "The Major Published Works of Kevin Lynch," *Town Planning Review* **49**(4), 551–557 (Oct. 1978).

11. D. Appleyard with M. S. Gerson and M. Lintell, *Livable Streets,* University of California Press, Berkeley, Calif., 1981.

12. K. H. Anthony, "Major Themes in the Work of Donald Appleyard," *Environment and Behavior* **15**(4), 411–418 (July 1983).

13. C. Perin, *With Man in Mind: An Interdisciplinary Prospectus for Environmental Design,* MIT Press, Cambridge, Mass., 1970.

14. S. Van der Ryn and M. Silverstein, *Dorms at Berkeley: An Environmental Analysis,* Center for Planning and Development Research, Berkeley, Calif., 1967.

15. L. Festinger, S. Schachter, and K.W. Back, *Social Pressures in Informal Groups,* Stanford University Press, Stanford, Calif., 1950.

16. R. G. Barker, *Ecological Psychology: Concepts and Methods for Studying the Environment of Human Behavior,* Stanford University Press, Stanford, Calif., 1968.

17. A. W. Wicker, *An Introduction to Ecological Psychology,* Brooks/Cole, Monterey, Calif., 1979.

18. H. Osmond, "Function as a Basis of Psychiatric Ward Design," *Mental Hospital* **8**, 23–29 (1957).

19. R. Sommer, *Personal Space: The Behavioral Basis of Design,* Prentice-Hall, Inc., Englewood Cliffs, N.J., 1969.

20. R. Sommer, *Design Awareness,* Rinehart Press, Corte Madera, Calif., 1972.

21. R. Sommer, *Tight Spaces: Hard Architecture and How to Humanize It,* Prentice-Hall, Inc., Englewood Cliffs, N.J., 1974.

22. R. Sommer, *Social Design: Creating Buildings with People in Mind,* Prentice-Hall, Inc., Englewood Cliffs, N.J., 1983.

23. W. Firey, "Sentiment and Symbolism as Ecological Variables," *American Sociological Review* **10**, 140–148 (1945).

24. A. L. Strauss, *Images of the American City,* Free Press, New York, 1961.

25. W. Michelson, *Man and His Urban Environment: A Sociological Approach,* Addison-Wesley Publishing Co., Inc., Reading, Mass., 1970.

26. J. K. Wright, "Terrae Incognitae: The Place of Imagination in Geography," *Annals of the Association of American Geographers* **37**, 1–15 (1947).

27. E. T. Hall, *The Silent Language,* Anchor/Doubleday, Garden City, N.Y., 1959.

28. E. T. Hall, *The Hidden Dimension,* Anchor/Doubleday, Garden City, N.Y., 1966.

29. I. Altman and B. Rogoff, "World Views in Environmental Psychology: Trait, Interactional, Organismic, and Transactional Perspectives," in D. Stokols and I. Altman, eds., *Handbook of Environmental Psychology,* John Wiley & Sons, Inc., New York, 1987.

30. S. Wapner, "Transactions of Persons in Environments: Some Critical Transitions," *Journal of Environmental Psychology* **1**, 223–239 (1981).

31. D. Seamon, *A Geography of the Lifeworld,* Croom/Helm, London, 1980.

32. A. Buttimer and D. Seamon, eds., *The Human Experience of Space and Place,* Croom/Helm, London, 1980.

33. C. Cooper Marcus, "Remembrances of Landscapes Past," *Landscape* **22**, 35–43 (1978).

34. D. Stokols, ed., "Theories of Environment and Behavior: New Directions," *Environment and Behavior,* Special Issue, **15**(3) (May 1983).

35. C. Zimring and J. E. Reizenstein, "A Primer on Post-occupancy Evaluation," *AIA Journal* **70**, 52–58 (Nov. 1981).

36. C. Selltiz, L. S. Wrightsman, and S. W. Cook, *Research Methods in Social Relations,* 4th ed., Holt, Rinehart & Winston, New York, 1981.

37. L. Kidder and C. M. Judd with E. Smith, *Research Methods in Social Relations,* 5th ed., Holt, Rinehart & Winston, New York, 1986.

38. R. W. Marans and S. Ahrentzen, "Developments in Research Design, Data Collection, and Analysis: Quantitative Methods," in E. Zube and G. Moore, eds., *Advances in Environment, Behavior, and Design: Theory, Research, Methods, and Practice,* Plenum Press, in cooperation with the Environmental Design Research Association, New York, in press.

39. S. M. Low, "Developments in Research Design, Data Collection and Analysis: Qualitative Methods," in E. Zube and G. Moore, eds., *Advances in Environment, Behavior, and Design: Theory, Research, Methods, and Practice,* Plenum Press, in cooperation with the Environmental Design Research Association, New York, in press.

40. J. Zeisel, *Inquiry by Design: Tools for Environment–Behavior Research,* Brooks/Cole, Monterey, Calif., 1981.

41. H. Sanoff, *Design Games: Playing for Keeps with Personal and Environmental Design,* William Kaufman, Los Altos, Calif., 1979.

42. K. H. Anthony, *West Mall, Los Angeles Civic Center: Environment–Behavior Research and Design Study,* Department of Landscape Architecture, California State Polytechnic University, Pomona, Calif., 1984, p. 4.

43. C. J. Holahan, *Environmental Psychology,* Random House, New York, 1982.

44. A. Churchman and R. Sebba, "Women's Territoriality in the Home," in M. Safu, M. Mednick, D. Israeli, and J. Bernard, eds., *Women's Worlds,* Praeger, New York, 1985.

45. E. Goffman, *The Presentation of Self in Everyday Life,* Doubleday, New York, 1959.

46. G. W. Evans, "Design Implications of Spatial Research," in J. Aiello and A. Baum, eds., *Residential Crowding and Design,* Plenum Press, New York, 1979.

47. D. G. Hayward, "Psychological Concepts of Home Among Urban Middle-class Families with Young Children," Ph.D. dissertation, Environmental Psychology Program, City University of New York, New York, 1977.

48. K. H. Anthony, "Moving Experiences: Memories of Favorite Homes," in D. Duerk and D. Campbell, eds., *The Challenge of Diversity, Proceedings of the Environmental Design Research Association (EDRA) Conference,* Washington, D.C., 1984, pp. 141–149.

49. C. Cooper Marcus, "Awakening the Human Man and Woman: Techniques for Raising the Consciousness of Design Students Regarding Personal Environmental Values and Biases," abstract, in D. Amedeo, J. B. Griffin, and J. J. Potter, eds., *EDRA 1983: Proceedings of the Environmental Design Research Association (EDRA) Conference,* Washington, D.C., 1983, p. 167.

50. C. Cooper Marcus, "The House as Symbol of Self," in J. Lang and co-workers, eds., *Designing for Human Behavior,* Dowden, Hutchinson and Ross, Stroudsburg, Pa., 1974, pp. 130–146.

51. P. Korosec-Serfaty and D. Bolitt, "Dwelling and the Experience of Burglary," *Journal of Environmental Psychology* **6**(4), 329–344 (Dec. 1986).

52. I. Altman and C. M. Werner, eds., *Home Environments; Human Behavior and Environment: Advances in Theory and Research,* Vol. 8, Plenum Press, New York, 1985.

53. S. Weidemann, J. Anderson, P. O'Donnell, and D. Butterfield, *Resident Safety: Research and Recommendations for Longview Place Anti-crime Program,* Housing Research and Development Program, University of Illinois, Urbana, Ill., 1981.

54. C. Cooper Marcus and W. Sarkissian with S. Wilson and D. Perlgut, *Housing as if People Mattered: Site Design Guidelines for Medium-density Family Housing,* University of California Press, Berkeley, Calif., 1986.

55. S. Saegert, "Environment and Children's Mental Health: Residential Density and Low Income Children," in A. Baum and J. Singer, eds., *Handbook of Psychology and Health,* Vol. 2, Erlbaum Associates, Hillside, N.J., 1981.

56. R. Wener, "Environment Behavior Research Success Stories," *Journal of Architectural and Planning Research,* to appear.

57. G. T. Moore, U. Cohen, and T. McGinty, *Planning and Design Guidelines: Child Care Centers and Outdoor Play Environments,* Center for Architecture and Urban Planning Research, University of Wisconsin-Milwaukee, Milwaukee, Wis., 1979 ad seriatum, 7 vols.

58. M. S. Gerst and R. H. Moos, "The Social Ecology of University Residences," *Journal of Educational Psychology* **63**(6), 513–525 (1972).

59. *Butterfield Hall Evaluation,* Research and Design Institute, Providence, R.I., 1974.

60. F. D. Becker with S. Ashworth, D. Beaver, and D. Poe, *User Participation, Personalization, and Environmental Meaning: Three Field Studies,* Program in Urban and Regional Studies, Cornell University, Ithaca, N.Y., 1977.

61. K. H. Anthony, *International House: Home Away from Home?,* Ph.D. dissertation, Department of Architecture, University of California, Berkeley, 1981.

62. G. Francescato, S. Weidemann, J. Anderson, and R. Chenoweth, *Residents' Satisfaction in HUD-assisted Housing: Design and Management Factors,* U.S. Department of Housing and Urban Development, Washington, D.C., 1979.

63. O. Newman, *Defensible Space: Crime Prevention Through Urban Design,* MacMillan Co., New York, 1972.

64. C. Cooper, "Resident Dissatisfaction in Multi-family Housing," in W. M. Smith, ed., *Behavior, Design and Policy Aspects of Human Habitats,* University of Wisconsin-Green Bay Press, Green Bay, Wis., 1972.

65. J. Leavitt and T. West, "Changing Family Structure: An Architectural Response to the Housing Needs of Single Parents," paper presented at the Association of Collegiate Schools of Architecture (ACSA) Conference, Vancouver, B.C., Canada, 1985.

66. C. Cooper, "St. Francis Square: Attitudes of Its Residents," *AIA Journal* **56,** 22–27 (Dec. 1971).

67. S. Goldsmith, *Designing for the Disabled,* 3rd ed., Royal Institute of British Architects (RIBA) Publications, London, 1976.

68. M. Bednar, ed., *Barrier-free Environments,* Dowden, Hutchinson and Ross, Stroudsburg, Pa., 1977.

69. R. Lifchez and B. Winslow, *Design for Independent Living: The Environment and Physically Disabled People,* Whitney Library of Design, New York, 1979.

70. M. P. Lawton, *Planning and Managing Housing for the Elderly,* John Wiley & Sons, Inc., New York, 1975.

71. D. Y. Carstens, *Site Planning and Design for the Elderly: Issues, Guidelines, and Alternatives,* Van Nostrand Reinhold Co., Inc., New York, 1985.

72. J. Bernstein, "Post-occupancy Evaluation Study Leads to Insights on Elderly Housing," *Architectural Record* **166,** 69–76 (Sept. 1979).

73. "Congregate Living. Captain Clarence Eldridge House, Hyannis, Massachusetts," *Progressive Architecture* **62,** 64–68 (Aug. 1981).

74. E. Goffman, *Asylums: Essays on the Social Situation of Mental Patients and Other Inmates,* Anchor/Doubleday, New York, 1961.

75. K. H. Anthony, "Clients Benefit From Behavior-based Programming: A Case Study of Patrick Sullivan Associates," paper presented at the International Association for the Study of People and Their Physical Surroundings (IAPS) Conference, West Berlin, Germany, 1984.

76. D. K. Trites, F. D. Galbraith, Jr., M. Sturdavant, and J. F. Leckwart, "Influence of Nursing-unit Design on the Activities and Subjective Feelings of Nursing Personnel," *Environment and Behavior* **2**(3), 303–334 (Dec. 1970).

77. H. McLaughlin, "Systems Study Supports Triangular Shapes," *Modern Hospital* **112,** 105–109 (May 1969).

78. H. McLaughlin, "Post-occupancy Evaluation of Hospitals: What One Such Evaluation Produced," *AIA Journal* **63,** 30–34 (Jan. 1975).

79. "One Patient, One Room: Theory and Practice," *Modern Healthcare* **3,** 65–68 (Mar. 1975).

80. C. A. Lewis, " 'Comment' Healing in the Urban Environment,

A Person/Plant Viewpoint," *Journal of the American Planning Association* **45,** 330–338 (July 1979).

81. R. Ulrich, "View Through a Window May Influence Recovery from Surgery," *Science* **224,** 420–421 (May 1984).

82. J. R. Carpman, M. A. Grant, and D. A. Simmons, *No More Mazes: Research About Design for Wayfinding in Hospitals,* University of Michigan Office of the Replacement Hospital Program, Ann Arbor, Mich., 1984.

83. J. R. Carpman, M. A. Grant, and D. A. Simmons, *Design That Cares: Planning Health Care Facilities for Patients and Visitors,* American Hospital Publishing, Inc., Chicago, Ill., 1986.

84. C. Holahan and S. Saegert, "Behavioral and Attitudinal Effects of Large Scale Variations in the Physical Environment of Psychiatric Wards," *Journal of Abnormal Psychology* **82**(3), 454–462 (1973).

85. K. Izumi, "Psychosocial Phenomena and Building Design," *Building Research* **2** (4), 9–11 (July–Aug. 1965).

86. V. J. Willis, "Design Considerations for Mental Health Facilities," *Hospital and Community Psychiatry* **31**(7), 483–490 (July 1980).

87. R. G. Barker and P. V. Gump, *Big School, Small School,* Stanford University Press, Stanford, Calif., 1964.

88. S. Ahrentzen, G. M. Jue, M. A. Skorpanich, and G. W. Evans, "School Environments and Stress," in G. W. Evans, ed., *Environmental Stress,* Cambridge University Press, New York, 1982.

89. W. F. E. Preiser and A. Taylor, "The Habitability Framework: Linking Human Behavior and Physical Environment in Special Education," *Exceptional Education Quarterly* **4**(2), 1–15 (Summer 1983).

90. W. F. E. Preiser, ed., *Albuquerque High School: A Post-occupancy Evaluation,* Institute of Environmental Education, University of New Mexico, Albuquerque, N.M., June 1981.

91. K. H. Anthony, *Rosemead High School: A Post-occupancy Evaluation and Behavior-based Program,* report, California State Polytechnic University, Pomona, Calif., 1982.

92. K. H. Anthony, *College of Osteopathic Medicine of the Pacific: A Post-occupancy Evaluation and Behavior-based Program,* report, California State Polytechnic University, Pomona, Calif., 1983.

93. J. Wineman, ed., *Behavioral Issues in Office Design,* Van Nostrand Reinhold Co., Inc., New York, 1986.

94. L. Harris and co-workers, *The Steelcase National Study of Office Environments: Do They Work?,* Steelcase, Inc., Grand Rapids, Mich., 1978.

95. M. Brill with S. T. Margulis, E. Konar, and BOSTI in association with Westinghouse Furniture Systems, *Using Office Design to Increase Productivity,* Vols. 1 and 2, Workplace Design and Productivity, Inc., Buffalo, N.Y., 1984.

96. R. W. Marans and K. F. Spreckelmeyer, *Evaluating Built Environments: A Behavioral Approach,* Institute for Social Research and Architectural Research Laboratory, University of Michigan, Ann Arbor, Mich., 1981.

97. G. Davis, F. Becker, F. Duffy, and W. Sims, *Orbit-2. Overview Report,* Harbinger Group, Inc., Norwalk, Conn., 1985.

98. M. Kantrowitz and A. Seidel, eds., *Environment and Behavior,* Special Issue: Applications of E & B Research, **17**(1) (Jan. 1985).

99. G. Evans, C. Smith and K. Pezdek, "Cognitive Maps and Urban Form," *Journal of the American Planning Association* **48**(2), 232–244 (Spring 1982).

100. D. Conway, ed., *Human Responses to Tall Buildings,* Dowden, Hutchinson and Ross, Stroudsburg, Pa., 1977.

101. Kaplan, McLaughlin, and Diaz, "Celebrating Urban Gathering Places," *Urban Land,* 10–14 (May 1985).

102. W. Whyte, *The Social Life of Small Urban Spaces,* The Conservation Foundation, Washington, D.C., 1980.

103. E. H. Zube, D. G. Pitt, and G. W. Evans, "A Lifespan Developmental Study of Landscape Assessment," *Journal of Environmental Psychology* **3,** 115–128 (1983).

104. E. H. Zube and C. Law, "Perceptions of the Sky in Five Metropolitan Areas," *Urban Ecology* **8,** 199–208 (1984).

105. J. L. Sell and E. H. Zube, "Perception of and Response to Environmental Change," *Journal of Architectural and Planning Research* **3**(1), 33–54, (1986).

106. C. Myer, "Cities in 3-D," *Planning* **52**(5) (May 1986).

107. S. C. Carstens and R. Sommer, "Stopping Sanitation Problems in Salad Bars," *Partners Quarterly* (Nov. 1985).

108. S. L. Johnson, R. Sommer, and V. Martino, "Consumer Behavior at Bulk Food Bins," *The Journal of Consumer Research, Inc.* **12** (June 1985).

109. R. Sommer, J. Herrick, and T. R. Sommer, "The Behavioral Ecology of Supermarkets and Farmers Markets," *Journal of Environmental Psychology* **1,** 13–19 (1981).

110. Y. Clearwater, "A Human Place in Outer Space," *Psychology Today* **19,** 34–43 (July 1985).

111. W. F. E. Preiser, "A Combined Tactile/Electronic Guidance System for Visually Impaired Persons in Indoor and Outdoor Spaces," in *Proceedings of the National Symposium on Access to Cultural Programs,* Bloomington, Ind., July 1983.

112. *Progressive Architecture* **1,** 148–149 (1984).

113. M. Kantrowitz, "People, Energy, and Passive Solar Commercial Buildings: Results of Occupancy Analysis in 15 Buildings," in *General Proceedings Research and Design 85: Architectural Applications of Design and Technology Research,* AIA Foundation, Washington, D.C., Mar. 1985.

114. K. H. Anthony and S. McDonald, *The Perception and Use of Performing Arts Centers by the Elderly: An Exploratory Study,* report, Housing Research and Development Program, University of Illinois, Urbana-Champaign, Urbana, Ill., 1985.

115. G. T. Moore, D. P. Tuttle, and S. C. Howell, *Environmental Design Research Directions,* Praeger, New York, 1985.

See also ASSOCIATION OF COLLEGIATE SCHOOLS OF ARCHITECTURE (ACSA); DAY CARE CENTERS; EDUCATION, ARCHITECTURAL; ELEMENTARY EDUCATION; HEALTH CARE; JUSTICE BUILDINGS—COURTS AND CORRECTIONAL INSTITUTIONS; MULTIFAMILY HOUSING; NATIONAL COUNCIL OF ARCHITECTURAL REGISTRATION BOARDS (NCARB); OFFICE-INTERIOR PLANNING; RESIDENTIAL BUILDINGS; SECONDARY SCHOOLS; SINGLE PARENT HOUSING.

KATHRYN H. ANTHONY, PHD
University of Illinois
Champaign, Illinois

BEHNISCH, GÜNTER

Günter Behnisch, German architect, was born in 1922 in Lockwitz, a village near Dresden, in what today is the German Democratic Republic. He was the second of three children. He served in the German navy from 1939 to 1945 and was a prisoner of war in England from 1945 to 1947. He finally settled in Stuttgart, Federal Republic of Germany, and studied architecture there at the Technische Hochschule from 1947 to 1951. He married in 1952 and has three children, two of whom are architects.

Behnisch worked for Rolf Gutbrod in Stuttgart from 1951 to 1952 and from then on as an independent architect, first associated with Bruno Lambart from 1952 to 1957. Since 1966, he has been the head of Behnisch & Partner with Fritz Auer (until 1981), Winfried Büxel, Manfred Sabatke, Erhard Tränkner, and Karlheinz Weber (until 1981).

He has been a Professor of Design and Construction (*Entwerfen, Baukonstruktion, und Baugestaltung*) at the Technische Hochschule Darmstadt since 1967, a member of the Akademie der Künste, Berlin, since 1982, and Dr. hc. of the Technische Universität, Stuttgart, since 1985.

Behnisch studied architecture and began his career as an architect during the postwar reconstruction period in the Federal Republic of Germany. Far away from his home town, his personal beginnings were comparable in many respects to his country's own emergence after the war. With no financial resources and without a defined social or political position, his process of self-definition was indeed parallel and comparable in content to that of the Federal Republic of Germany as a whole.

As an independent architect dedicated to succeeding in public competitions and largely dedicated, from the very beginning, to social buildings (first educational ones and also sporting installations since the late 1960s), his career had much to do with his ability to recognize and express social needs and expectations in architecture as well as the current state of technological development. Behnisch's approaches to these challenges were determined by his tools, which were much more those of an engineer than an artist. His attitude as an architect was in this sense that of a member of the technical intelligentsia and the intellectual sector of the modern middle class and was no longer that of an elitist, individualist artist. As such, Behnisch shared the ambition of this intelligentsia to develop the country in accordance with its own cultural, social, and political ideals. He saw himself as an organ of public interest in architecture. All of this made it necessary for him to develop his own goals in architecture and a personal architectural language in accordance with these goals. The results were an original architectural theory and an architecture akin to the democratic, social, and liberal ideals of modern FRG society.

By the late 1960s he had achieved these results; this made him the leader of the modern mainstream within the German architectural scene. The solidity of his theory and practical work resulted from the social and political dimensions of his argumentation and from their clear, concrete references to technological and architectonic situations, not to mention their affinity with his personal ideals, reflected in the organization and work methods at his office.

He executed the most representative and spectacular projects of the newly open, libertarian, and egalitarian German postwar society, namely, the buildings and sites for the 1972 Olympic Games in Munich and the Parliament/State Administration Buildings in Bonn, the second of which were planned in 1972 but have not yet been realized. Because of their unprecedented scale, these projects constitute the exception in Behnisch's work, which is otherwise characterized by a large number of smaller and less prepossessing buildings. Indeed, given his country's postwar development, it was precisely his background as an architect of medium-sized buildings in the social field that made him arguably the ideal architect for executing its most representative projects.

From the very outset in the early 1950s, Behnisch's architecture had two components: his naturalism, which was more akin to the use of natural materials, simple structural systems, and traditional craftmanship; and his rationalism, which was rather attuned to standardization by means of industrial building materials and modern building processes as well as more sophisticated structural systems. Whereas the latter component may be seen as universal in content and sharp in language, the former was correspondingly regional and soft, in close relation to the landscape that accompanied it.

One of the first consistent realizations of Behnisch's naturalism was the Vogelsang School, in which he tried to emphasize the low, meandering hills of Stuttgart, using building forms adapted to the situation and employing masonry, much wood, and handcrafted materials. The realization of this project, however, showed the technical limits of such building methods in an industrialized economy suffering from a decreasing number of craftsmen.

The first culmination of the rationalist component of Behnisch's architectural philosophy was the Staatliche Fachhochschule für Technik, a technical college in Ulm. It was the country's first completely prefabricated large public building, and its design required much developmental work in this field. In accordance with the principles of efficiency, this complex consisted of large, uniform precast concrete blocks with standard steel and sheet-metal detail solutions repeated throughout the building. As time passed and this kind of architecture became widespread, it eventually showed its limitations, which lay in the negative architectonic consequences of a schematic thinking reduced to formulas. It produced standardized buildings of stereotyped architecture, especially when planned by state agencies.

As a result of these two initial developments, his search went on for a synthesis, for a more individual architecture based on both prefabricated and handmade elements as well as on more complex structural systems, forms, and spaces. This process began in the mid-1960s; the buildings and sites for the Olympic Games in Munich demonstrate its first results. The idea of the organizers was to celebrate bright and open games "in the green," and not in the dreary deserts of concrete usually planned for such events. The architect's answer was the Olympic Park, a landscape with hills, a lake, paths and mounds, where some of the arenas were placed (the landscape architect was Günter Grzimek). Behnisch's goals were to realize an open, situational, versatile architecture, in an attempt to correspond programmatically to the explicit expectations. The light roofs were just the necessary complement to this project;

the field of interest went far beyond this roof (whose engineers were Frei Otto, Leonhardt, and Andrä) (Fig. 1).

The process itself is best reflected by comparing the schools In den Berglen, Oppelsbohm, Progymnasium Auf dem Schäfersfeld, and Hauptschule Auf dem Schäfersfeld, both in Lorch. The first abandoned the usual blocks of the prefabricated schools and took, in the floor plans, the form of a regular star with pentagonal classrooms and a roofed inner courtyard. The step from this to the Progymnasium brought even more irregular and complex floor plans, with only a few regular geometric parts, complex facades, and construction methods distinguishing not only the supporting parts from the enclosing, but emphasizing as many different functional elements as possible (Fig. 2). The Hauptschule presupposed a very high degree of constructive differentiation, an almost completely separate treatment of all aspects of design, and their reintegration

into architecture through the addition of all partial solutions. This kind of design came very close to the idea of collage architecture (Fig. 3).

The development of Behnisch's architectural reasoning in the 1950s was based, at least during his naturalist period, on the identification of ethical values with building methods. He saw natural materials as part of creation, like humanity itself; they were not initially meant to be used for building. They were only adapted by humans as building materials, therefore they had natural weaknesses that had to be considered and respected; these determined architectural form and space. The main criteria for his design were *Materialgerechtigkeit* and *Werkgerechtigkeit*, which roughly mean harmony with the nature of materials and their corresponding craftmanship methods. In his opinion, past speculation remained bound to the natural limits of humans—their size and strength. In this sense,

Figure 1. Olympic Park, Munich, Federal Republic of Germany (1972). Courtesy of Behnisch & Partner. Photo Credit: Christian Kandzia.

Figure 2. Progymnasium, Auf dem Schäfersfeld Lorch, Federal Republic of Germany (1973).

in his early rationalist phase, natural materials were replaced by industrial products and handicraft by industrial processes, but the old logic of the correct use and representation of materials and of the resulting architectural language on a large scale and in details remained.

Only in the 1960s, while searching for new ways, did it become clear that the logic of nature and the application of moral values to building did not apply when using materials created by human intellect and employing the superhuman force of the machine. Under these circumstances, there were no longer any guarantees of moral correctness given by nature. The whole responsibility lay on humanity; everything had to be revised, everything could be manipulated, and both materials and construction systems failed to corresond directly to architectural language.

This signified the liberation of form, made place for more formal experimentation, and obliged a revision of the basis of form. Behnisch reached this step in the late 1960s, the time when he began to teach at the Technische Hochschule Darmstadt and of the worldwide student upheavals. By then he had become conscious of the possibility of determining the basis of form, choosing the factors of design to be aestheticized, and deciding on the content of architecture and the resulting form. He began to see architecture as a metaphor for society. Classical architecture was a metaphor for a hierarchical organized society, and his architecture was a metaphor for the contemporary democratic, social, open FRG society to be built up and strengthened. Such an architecture had to emphasize society's complexity, its pluralism, its various levels, its vari-

Figure 3. Hauptschule, Auf dem Schäfersfeld Lorch, Federal Republic of Germany (1982).

ability, the different forces acting in it, and the necessity to support its weaker forces and limit the superhuman ones. The results were buildings consisting of an enormous multiplicity of simultaneously realized global and detailed solutions.

The next step, already announced in the Lorch Hauptschule, brings a new dimension of formal speculation. It applies the collage genre to architecture; it not only wants to show constructive and other contradictions because of ethical necessity and social sincerity (ie, it not only accepts contradictions such as trusses going through window panes), but makes the superimposition of such contradictory statements the formal theme of architecture itself, giving to the whole an aesthetic dimension in correspondence to the society itself.

Behnisch's main awards include the Hugo Häring Prize 1972, 1974, 1977, 1978, 1981, 1984; Großer Preis Bund Deutscher Architekten 1972; ICP Award of Honour; International Award of the UIA: Auguste Perret Prize 1981; Paul Bonatz Prize 1967, 1979, 1983; Sixth International Award for Architecture 1980; Mies van der Rohe Prize 1984, Award 1986.

BIBLIOGRAPHY

General References

G. Behnisch & Partner, "Die Verwirklichung einer Idee," *Bauen + Wohnen*, 7, (1972).

G. Behnisch & Partner, *Behnisch & Partner, Bauten und Projekte 1952–1974*, Hatje, Stuttgart, FRG, 1975.

G. Behnisch & Partner, "Vom Werden architektonischer Gestalten," *Bauen + Wohnen* **11**, 408–420 (1977).

H. Klotz, "Gespräch mit Günter Behnisch," in *Architektur in der Bundesrepublik, Gespräche mit sechs Architekten*, Ullstein, Berlin, FRG, 1977, pp. 13–63.

G. Behnisch & Partner, "Offenheit und Vielfalt," *Deutsche Bauzeitung* **3**, 12–42 (1982).

G. Behnisch & Partner, "Nicht nur Büros," *Deutsche Bauzeitung* **5**, 10–17 (1984).

G. Behnisch & Partner, "Acht Sporthallen, Entwicklung und Vergleich," *Stahl und Form* (1984).

R. Reid and D. Hauser, "Towards a Democratic Architecture," *Architectural Review* **1060**, 46–55 (1985).

E. Janofske, "Renunciation of Form in the Interest of Life," *Architectural Review* **1060**, 56–57 (1985).

P. B. Jones, "Modern Schools of Thought," *Architects Journal*, AJ-39, 60–74 (1986).

G. Behnisch & Partner, *Architekten Behnisch & Partner, Arbeiten aus den Jahren 1952–1987*, Cantz, Stuttgart, FRG, 1987.

MANUEL CUADRA
Technische Hochschule
Darmstadt
Darmstadt, Federal Republic of
Germany

BEHRENS, PETER

Peter Behrens, German architect, was born on April 14, 1868 in St. Georg, Hamburg. Orphaned at the age of 14, he inherited considerable wealth. He studied art in Karlsruhe, Dusseldorf, and Munich, and joined the Munich Secession of 1892, in reaction to the German Academy. His woodcut "Der Kuss" of 1898 is often used to illustrate the art nouveau style. Later, under the influence of the arts and crafts movement, he designed glass and pottery for such manufacturers as Villeroy and Boch, as well as silver and furniture.

He was chosen as one of a group of artists making up the Kunstlerkolonie at Darmstadt, and he designed his house there in 1901. Other early work in architecture included a proposal for a festival theater at Darmstadt.

Behrens became noted for his type and graphic designs. In addition to book type, in 1909 he designed, with Anna Simons, the inscription for the Reichstag. This inscription was restored after the bombing of Berlin, and now stands over the renovated portico of the Reichstag.

Behrens's long-term connection with the Allgemeine Elektricitäts-Geselschaft (AEG) was consistent with its use of the best architects and designers. Behrens designed lamps, electric kettles, advertising, and many architectural projects, including festival exhibition halls and, perhaps his most famous building, the Turbine Hall in Berlin in 1909, with engineer Karl Bernhard. This piece of industrial architecture has often been used as an example of a prototype modern design. Other buildings for the company followed. He designed apartment housing, a number of large private homes, and the German Embassy at St. Petersburg (1911–1912).

Behrens is well known for the fact that three of the most famous architects of the twentieth century worked as young assistants in his office. They were Walter Gropius, Ludwig Mies van der Rohe, and Charles-Edouard Jeanneret (Le Corbusier), each of whom is the subject of a separate article. The office of Behrens was recognized as the most important in Germany before World War I.

In Gropius's book *The New Architecture and the Bauhaus*, he had this to say about his experiences in Behrens's office (1):

In 1908, when I finished my preliminary training and embarked on my career as an architect with Peter Behrens, the prevalent conceptions of architecture and architectural education were still entirely dominated by the academic stylisticism of the classical "Orders." It was Behrens who first introduced me to logical and systematical coordination in the handling of architectural problems. In the course of my active association with the important schemes on which he was then engaged, and frequent discussions with him and other prominent members of Deutscher Werkbund, my own ideas began to crystallize as to what the essential nature of building ought to be. I became obsessed by the conviction that modern constructional technique could not be denied expression in architecture, and that that expression demanded the use of unprecedented forms. Dynamic as was the stimulus of Behrens's masterly teaching, I could not contain my growing impatience to start on my own account. In 1910 I set up in independent practice.

Le Corbusier worked in Behrens's office for five months in 1910. The influence of German design at that time was described by Le Corbusier in 1912 in his book *Etude sur le mouvement d'art decoratif en Allemagne* (2):

As French, I suffered in Germany; I was overwhelmed in Paris where they complained of a German invasion. The marvelous Industrial Art of Germany demands to be known. . . . Germany is a book of actualities. If Paris is the place of Art, Germany remains the great place of production. Experiences are happening there, the battles are crucial; buildings are raised and the rooms with their historic walls recount the triumph of order and tenacity.

Mies van der Rohe worked in Behrens's office from 1908 to 1911. The importance that Mies van der Rohe placed on detail reflects the training that Behrens gave in those early years. Mies was supervisor of construction for the German Embassy at St. Petersburg. Some scholars feel that Mies van der Rohe was the most sympathetic of the three to Behrens's orderly approach to design.

Behrens's building activity continued until World War I, when construction was limited to factories and aircraft hangars. After the war, he resumed his practice and through the 1920s designed a number of exhibition buildings, such as the all-glass Viennese Pavilion Conservatory at Paris in 1925 and a house, New Ways, Northampton, England (1923–1925), an early international style building.

During the Nazi period, Behrens was unfortunately identified with the anti-Semitic Austrian Werkbund and worked on the design of the proposed AEG Headquarters building as a part of Albert Speer's master plan for Berlin. The Nazi regime's rejection of the modernist movement included violent attacks on Behrens, although he was successfully defended by Speer. Behrens died in 1940 at the age of 72.

BIBLIOGRAPHY

1. W. Gropius, *The New Architecture and the Bauhaus,* MIT Press, Cambridge, Mass., 1965, p. 47, originally published by Faber and Faber, London, 1935.
2. C. Jencks, *Le Corbusier and the Tragic View of Architecture,* Harvard University Press, Cambridge, Mass., 1973. Contains his English translation of the quoted passage from C. E. Jeanneret, *Etude sur le mouvement d'art decoratif en Allemagne,* La Chaux de Fonds, 1912.

General References

A. Windsor, *Peter Behrens: Architect and Designer,* Whitney Library of Design, Watson-Guptill Publications, New York, 1981. First published by the Architectural Press Ltd., London, 1981.
T. Buddensieg with H. Rogge, *Industriekultur: Peter Behrens and the AEG, 1907–1914,* MIT Press, Cambridge, Mass., 1984. Translated by I. B. Whyte. Originally published under the title *Industriekultur: Peter Behrens und die AEG, 1907–1914,* Gerb. Mann Verlag, Berlin, 1979.

ROBERT T. PACKARD, AIA
Reston, Virginia

BELLUSCHI, PIETRO

Pietro Belluschi is a leading figure in the American modern movement: his refined, eloquent buildings have exerted a profound impact on American life. Discreet yet distinctive, Belluschi's buildings represent the soundest of the modern tradition; technologically progressive but never ostentatious, avoiding the whims of fashion or superficial style, his forms derive not from preconceived aesthetic theories but from the givens of the job itself. He seeks those simple qualities that he considers the essence of all enduring architecture. His approach is straightforward, starting with the practical givens: the needs of the client, character of the locale, and function of the building itself; from these he derives the architectural form. His philosophy is to prune away the nonessentials, paring down to the barest minimum to arrive at a simple, elegant form, never dull or merely ordinary. Molded, dramatic space, soft but compelling light, finely sculpted or crafted architectural forms—these are the elements he works with to create his buildings, of wood, brick, concrete, or metal, on any scale. He begins by studying carefully all aspects of the problem: site, client, type of building, and materials. He then proceeds methodically, designing and perfecting until finally he arrives at the most rational, aesthetically satisfying solution. It results from a deep understanding of the intricacies of the task, listening to his client, and then explaining and suggesting his own point of view. Belluschi's architecture is humanistic, with the ways of life, the tastes, and the traditions of the people he builds for uppermost in his mind. A man of considerable insight, Belluschi knows there are no perfect answers and that the art of architecture, unlike the fine arts, demands compromise between the desires of the client and those of the architect, the practical and the aesthetic, the structural and the poetic. His principal aim is to create buildings that are sources of pride and delight, that bring serenity to the soul, and that go beyond the means, the technical, structural, and practical, to achieve a more noble end, the creation of a visually or aesthetically satisfying setting for gracious living. More than shelter, Belluschi sees architecture as an art, a civilizing force to be enjoyed by all.

Belluschi was born in 1899 in Italy, in the small city of Ancona, northeast of Rome. A teenager during World War I, he served as an officer in the army and in 1920 went to the University of Rome, where he obtained a degree in civil engineering in 1922. Stifled by the weight of the past in tradition-bound Italy and infused with a spirit of adventure, he seized the opportunity to go abroad, and in 1923 came to the United States for a year of graduate work at Cornell. After receiving a second degree from Cornell and with little money at his disposal, he remained in the United States rather than returning to Italy. After considerable searching, Belluschi found a job that took him west to work in a mine in Kellog, Idaho. He stayed only nine months, doing menial work, and then pushed on to Portland, Oregon, where he secured a job with A. E. Doyle, one of the largest architectural firms in the region. Within the next several years, the principal designer in the firm left and Doyle died, leaving Belluschi, who had had no formal training in architecture, in charge.

In 1929, he received his first major commission, the Portland Art Museum, which was the building that first brought him national acclaim. Finished by 1932, on the eve of the MOMA International Style show, it was remarkably modern in its clean, crisp, unornamented forms, as well as technologically innovative in its skillful use of a monitor lighting system. It constituted an abrupt departure from the conventional historicizing architecture then practiced throughout the United States. It was a landmark in emerging modernism in this country, establishing Belluschi as one of the leading figures in the still fledgling modern tradition.

During the Depression, Belluschi turned to domestic work as a means of keeping the firm afloat. In these relatively small private residences, he united his commitment to modern forms with a love of the native land. He was inspired by the philosophy, and to a lesser degree the forms, of the waning Frank Lloyd Wright and wanted to eschew traditional forms and design with a fresh eye. Inspired too by the simple, natural vernacular buildings, the weathered timber barns and sheds of the Oregon countryside, he and several others began designing in a regionalized modernism in the mid-1930s. All traces of the Colonial or Georgian architecture then in vogue were eliminated in favor of simple, unpretentious, unpainted structures, typically horizontal in massing, with low, sweeping, gently pitched roofs and porches or terraces supported on slender posts, integrated with and yielding to their natural sites (Fig. 1). Recognized by 1941 as a distinct trend, combining modern spatial concepts and clean, unornamented forms with local materials and building customs, Pacific Northwest Regionalism was nationally heralded, with Belluschi as a leading figure.

The war years, difficult for virtually all architects, taxed his ingenuity. Building supplies and materials were severely limited, but the demand was great for rapidly built, low-cost housing, neighborhood shopping centers, and planned communities for war-related industrial workers. Accepting the challenge of new work and determined not to let the firm founder, Belluschi broadened his field of endeavor. From this point on, incorporating or drawing on whatever he could of the advanced technologies, structural innovations, and new materials developed during the war, he went on to design an astonishing array of buildings and building complexes: shopping centers, multistoried office buildings, banks, churches, community centers, college campuses, and urban designs.

Among the most significant of his buildings in this early period was the Equitable Building in Portland (1945–1948), which received immediate national attention as the first major tall office building to be built in the United States in the postwar era (Fig. 2). Widely acclaimed at the time for its innovative use of aluminum cladding, the 12-story, narrow slab, which was 3×14 bays to make maximum use of the 100×200 ft lot, was actually adumbrated in 1943 in a project commissioned by the *Architectural Forum,* which had devoted an issue to exploring new ways of using new structural techniques and resources. Belluschi's proposal, drawing on the anticipated surplus of aluminum being produced for the airplane industry, used prefabricated aluminum panels riveted to a conventional concrete-framed structure. The smooth, flush, reflective glazed and metal surfaces of the clean, unadorned Equitable Building give the impression of a thin, taut membrane enclosing a volume of space and suggest the influence of Mies van der Rohe's glass tower projects in the 1920s; they also anticipated the series of glazed rectangular slabs that were to dominate the U.S. city in the 1950s and 1960s. The Equitable, with its frankly revealed concrete structure filled solely with glass, was recognized as an early landmark in curtain wall development; it was also noted as one of the first completely sealed,

Figure 1. Sutor House, Portland, Oregon (1938). Courtesy of the Oregon Historical Society.

utilizing a faceted surface with sharp, angular, projecting bay windows and stepping back the upper reaches of the building. Its granite-clad surface, deep carnelian in hue but highly polished to catch and reflect light, gives it a clean, crisp, crystalline quality, recalling the Seagram in its dark color, meticulous craftsmanship, and precise detailing, but also his own Equitable Building in its flush, highly reflective surfaces and clarity of form. The Bank of America Building, whose configuration constantly shifts depending on the angle of vision, was immediately recognized as a major architectural monument in San Francisco; it both blended with the forms of the city and made a strong architectural statement on the San Francisco skyline with its unique, visually arresting sculptural form.

Long known for his simple, eloquent wood churches in the regional tradition, Belluschi was asked to design a second major building in San Francisco, St. Mary's Cathedral (1962–1971) (Figs. 3 and 4). Demurring at first for lack of experience in such a momentous project on such a vast scale, he ultimately accepted, relishing the challenge not only of harmonizing the form of a large prominent building with those of the city, but of reconciling the conflicting demands of the traditional church with his own commitment to modern forms: the new cathedral had to evoke the Catholic church, preserving enough of traditional symbolism to satisfy the longing of the congregation, yet speak in terms of the modern age. Seeking a form that both drew upon those of the past and acknowledged current structural techniques and modern materials, Belluschi arrived at a solution at once simple and ingenious: four thin concrete hyperbolic paraboloid shells rising from a broad base to where the warped surfaces meet at the summit, forming a cross of stained glass over the centralized nave. The simple, continuous, rising surface gave the exterior the height and verticality of the traditional spired church, and in the interior it created the lofty, uplifting spiritual space, the "holy emptiness" bathed in soft light, that Belluschi sought. The centralized plan, marking a departure from the traditional longitudinal nave, established another first: a modern cathedral designed to accommodate the recent changes in the Catholic liturgy, dispensing with the hierarchical distinction between nave and choir and uniting priest and congregation around the main altar in a single, unified space. Pier Luigi Nervi, whom Belluschi had brought in as a consultant on the structural engineering, put it well: the first cathedral truly modern, it could not have been of any other age (1).

Creating serene spaces for quiet repose was important to Belluschi, but so too was accommodating the activity of crowds and solving the problems of a modern, highly technological society on a broad, urbanistic scale. While Dean at MIT, he and his colleagues developed a program of urban studies, one of the first in the nation. After he stepped down from the deanship in 1965, Belluschi continued to practice, collaborating with established firms as principal designer and consultant. In this capacity, requiring the utmost diplomacy and tact in dealing with others, Belluschi accomplished some of the major achievements of his career. Among these was the Juilliard School (1957–1969), a conservatory for the performing arts, which he executed with associate architects Catalano and Wester-

Figure 2. Equitable Building, Portland, Oregon (1948). Courtesy of the Oregon Historical Society.

fully air-conditioned buildings. It has double-glazed windows, an advanced heating system, and an innovative traveling crane suspended from the roof for window-washing as well as a clear, elegant, refined form and sensitive proportions. It marked Belluschi's first large urban work under his own name, a major accomplishment both structurally and aesthetically. It received the AIA 25-year award in 1982.

Belluschi left his practice three years after construction of the Equitable to become Dean of Architecture and Planning at the Massachusetts Institute of Technology (MIT), a post he held from 1951 to 1965. Twenty years after the Equitable was completed, he was to do a second major multistoried office building, representing one of the great challenges of his career. This was the 52-story Bank of America building in San Francisco (1959–1970), designed in collaboration with Wurster, Bernardi & Emmons, and later SOM. The client wanted a large, visually compelling building expressive of the might of one of the largest banks in the world; the challenge lay in integrating the immense form into the relatively small-scaled forms of the San Francisco cityscape of the time. The solution, inspired by the great basaltic outcroppings of the Sierra Mountains, was to minimize the effect of bulk by fragmenting the forms,

Figure 3. St. Mary's Cathedral, San Francisco (exterior). Courtesy of Morley Baer.

Figure 4. St. Mary's Cathedral, San Francisco (interior). Courtesy of Morley Baer.

Figure 5. Juilliard School for Performing Arts, New York. Courtesy of Ezra Stoller.

A. Juilliard Theater
B. Drama Workshop
C. Lila Acheson Wallace Library
D. Orchestra rehearsal and recording studio
E. Paul Recital Hall
F. Alice Tully Hall

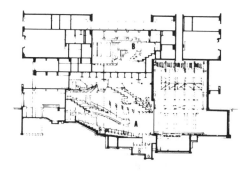

Figure 6. Juilliard School for Performing Arts, New York (cross section). Courtesy of Pietro Belluschi.

mann, in Lincoln Center, New York (Figs. 5 and 6). An astonishingly compact building given the multiplicity of spaces and enormously complicated functions it comprises (Alice Tully Hall; three theaters; several large rehearsal rooms; 15 dance, opera, and drama studios; three organ studios; 84 practice rooms; 24 classrooms; a workshop, library, and snack bar; and administrative offices) the Juilliard School has proved to be one of the most successful in the Lincoln Center complex. It is acoustically sound, economically built, simple, and unpretentious, yet elegant in design.

It summarizes well Belluschi's long-standing conviction that every architectural problem represents a challenge to create the structure most suitable to its purpose, a structure that satisfies emotional as well as physical demands. A key apologist for the modern movement, awarded the AIA gold medal in 1972, Belluschi acknowledges the importance of structure and function not as ends in themselves, but always as the means to a higher aesthetic order. "Architecture," he said in 1953, "is more than function and structure; it transcends, transforms, and redeems engineering in terms of human values for the purpose of giving pleasure to the senses as well as to the mind of man" (2).

BIBLIOGRAPHY

1. E. K. Thompson, "St. Mary's Cathedral, San Francisco," *Architectural Record* **169,** 114 (Sept. 1981).

2. P. Belluschi, "An Appraisal of Our Contemporary Architecture," *Bulletin of the American Academy of Arts and Sciences,* 5 (Dec. 1953).

General References

Ref. 2 is a good general reference.

H. R. Hitchcock, "An Eastern Critic Looks at Western Architecture," *Arts & Architecture* **57,** 21–23, 40, 41 (Dec. 1940).

J. Stubblebine, ed., *The Northwest Architecture of Pietro Belluschi,* F. W. Dodge, New York, 1953.

M. D. Ross, "The Museum Building as a Work of Art," *Notes on the Collection* (7), Portland Art Museum, Portland, Oregon, 1967.

W. L. Creese, "The Equitable Revisited," *Architectural Forum* **128**(5), 40–45 (June 1968).

M. F. Schmertz, "The Juilliard School: A Conservatory for the Performing Arts," *Architectural Record* **147**(1), 121–130 (Jan. 1970).

E. K. Thompson, "Pietro Belluschi, The 1972 Gold Medalist," *Architectural Record* **151**, 119–126 (Apr. 1972).

M. D. Ross, "The 'Attainment and Restraint' of Pietro Belluschi," *American Institute of Architects Journal* **58**(1), 17–25 (July 1972).

C. Gubitosi and A. Izzo, *Pietro Belluschi, Edifici e Progetti. 1932–1973,* Officina Edizioni, Rome, 1973.

J. Pastier, "Evaluation: Brooding, Outsize Tower (Bank of America)," *American Institute of Architects Journal* **69**(9), 49–55 (Aug. 1980).

J. Cook, "Postwar Prototype in Downtown Portland: Belluschi's Equitable Savings & Loan Building," *American Institute of Architects Journal,* **71**(8), 84–89 (July 1982).

J. P. Gaffey, "The Anatomy of Transition: Cathedral-building in San Francisco," *Catholic Historical Review* **LXX**(1), 45–73 (Jan. 1984).

MEREDITH L. CLAUSEN
University of Washington
Seattle, Washington

was an enthusiastic admirer of Wright and introduced his work to the Dutch. After his return from the United States, Berlage published an article and two books in 1912 and 1913 on what he had seen, especially in the Midwest.

Berlage was much admired for his doctrine of direct structural expression, as well as for his own work. This break from the past and the search for new design laid the groundwork for younger men and the twentieth century. In later years, Berlage's work became more refined, and shows the influence of younger architects such as Dudok. Among Berlage's other famous buildings were De Nederlanden van 1848 Insurance Company Building, The Hague (1895); Villa Henny, The Hague (1898); Diamond Workers' Union, Amsterdam (1898–1900); housing and master planning for The Hague and Amsterdam (1908–1909); Holland House, Bury Street, London (1914–1916); and The Gemeentemuseum, The Hague (1919–1935).

BIBLIOGRAPHY

General References

S. Giedeon, *Space, Time and Architecture,* Harvard University Press, Cambridge, Mass., 1949.

H. R. Hitchcock, *Architecture: Nineteenth and Twentieth Centuries,* 4th ed., Penguin Books, Harmondsworth, UK, 1977.

Richard Padovan in F. Russell, ed., *Art Nouveau Architecture,* Rizzoli International Publications, New York, 1979.

ROBERT T. PACKARD, AIA
Reston, Virginia

BERLAGE, HENDRIK P.

Hendrik Petrus Berlage was born in Amsterdam in 1856. He studied in Zurich at the Polytechnihum from 1875 to 1878 and then visited Italy, Austria, and Germany in 1880–1881. Returning to Amsterdam, he was a partner with the engineer Thomas Sanders until 1889, after which he formed his own firm. His early work was of a general Renaissance character. Later, he adopted a more round-arched style.

The building that brought him fame was the Amsterdam Exchange of 1897–1903. The vigorous heavy brick detailing and exposed metal roof framing was a real break from the general historicism of the time and prepared the way for the younger generation of the Amsterdam School. It was Berlage's total approach to design, using sculpture, paintings, ceramics, and stained glass as well as the furniture and fittings, that identifies this building as consistent with the art nouveau concept of the unity of the arts.

Berlage visited the United States in 1911 and was impressed with the work of H. H. Richardson, Louis Sullivan, and in particular, Frank Lloyd Wright. The famous "Wasmuth Portfolio" of Wright's early work had been published in Germany in 1909, and interest in U.S. work was strengthened as art nouveau's influence faded. Berlage

BIRKERTS, GUNNAR

Gunnar Birkerts was born on January 17, 1925 in Riga, Latvia. His father, Peter Birkerts (1881–1956) was a writer, philosopher, and folklorist; his mother, Merija Shop Birkerte was a philologist, folklorist, and teacher.

While still a student at the first (English) gymnasium in Riga in 1943, Birkerts's strong literary, liberal exposure helped him make an early decision to pursue art in architecture. War circumstances caused his departure from Latvia. After a temporary stay in Noerdlingen, Bavaria, he enrolled in the Department of Architecture, Technische Hochschule Stuttgart, in December 1945. The Technische Hochschule Stuttgart was strongly influenced by Paul Bonatz. The influence of Heinrich Tessenow was also present, particularly through the teachings of Paul Schmitthenner. The Dean, Richard Doecker, along with Adolph Schneck and painter Willie Baumeister, was part of the Bauhaus group, reemerging after years of nonacceptance. The Department of Architecture was situated next to the Weissenhof Siedlung, which had architectural examples by most of the members of the international set of modern architecture.

At the Technische Hochschule Stuttgart, Birkerts derived great benefit from the attention paid to *werklehre,* the exploration of building materials and building technology from the primitive to the most sophisticated. During his student years, he was much influenced by Rolf Gutbrod, who headed several design studios as well as the final diploma council. But eventually, the dominant claims of national and regional architectural rhetoric were overshadowed by his interest in the great Scandinavians and in wartime architectural developments in the United States. Birkerts was especially attracted to the work of Eliel and Eero Saarinen; there he found the fusion of U.S. and Scandinavian strains. His formal education was completed in December 1949, when he was awarded the degree of Diplomingeneur Architekt.

On December 17, 1949, Birkerts arrived in New York. He began his search for an architectural association immediately, traveling to Bloomfield Hills, Michigan, to interview with Eliel Saarinen. His projected position was postponed, and Birkerts moved to Chicago to work at the offices of Perkins & Will. After he had worked for the firm for one year, in Chicago and Rockford, Ill., the invitation to work with Eero Saarinen came.

In December 1950, Birkerts married Sylvia Zvirbulis in Princeton, N. J. They have three children: Sven Peter, Andra Sylvia, and Erik Gunnar.

Birkerts joined the office of Eero Saarinen in Bloomfield Hills in August 1951. During what he calls "the Saarinen years," the period of Saarinen's active search for an architectural identity, he was exposed to a striking array of design personalities, many of them visitors to the office. No less important was Birkerts's collaboration with his office peers, who included Kevin Roche, John Dinkeloo, Cesar Pelli, Charles Bassett, Robert Venturi, and many others. Most of the Saarinen years were spent working on the design of the General Motors Technical Center, the Milwaukee War Memorial, Concordia Senior College, and other projects. Apart from his work in the office, Birkerts became interested in furniture design. In 1954, he was named Young Designer of the Year by the Akron Institute of Art, and in 1955, he won first prize in the International Furniture Competition in Cantu, Italy (which was judged by Alvar Aalto, Gio Ponti, and Sven Markelius).

In 1956, Minoru Yamasaki invited Birkerts to join his office in Royal Oak, Michigan. Birkerts was intrigued by Yamasaki's vitality, as well as by his desire to depart from prevailing doctrine while searching for a humane architecture. Birkerts joined the office and was soon putting the experience gained with Saarinen to use in further technological explorations; the Reynolds Aluminum Building in Detroit dates from this period.

In 1957, Birkerts became Principal and Head of the Design Department at Yamasaki's office. Subsequent work with the firm involved investigations into the application of precast concrete to structural and facade designs; these projects included the Dharan Airport in Saudi Arabia, educational buildings at Wayne State University in Detroit, and others.

In 1959, Birkerts joined with Frank Straub to establish Birkerts & Straub in Birmingham, Mich. Their first commission was Lafayette 1300, a major apartment building in Detroit. During this period (1961), Birkerts was appointed Assistant Professor of Architecture at the University of Michigan. In 1963, he was appointed Associate Professor, and in 1969, he became a full Professor.

When Straub left the firm in 1962, Birkerts established Gunnar Birkerts and Associates. Numerous awards and publications helped to establish the presence of the new office. In 1962, *Art in America* included Birkerts in its "New Talent USA," as selected by Ada Louise Huxtable (1). Italy's *Zodiac* cited him in its 1963 feature "Young Architects in the U.S." (2). In 1964, John Dixon of *Progressive Architecture* devoted a major part of an issue to Birkerts's work, calling it "A Search for Architectural Principles" (3). The next year (1965), the Architectural League of New York invited Birkerts to participate in an exhibition entitled "Forty Under Forty."

Birkerts's first phase of independent practice (1960–1970) represented a certain reaction to the intricate building technology espoused by Saarinen and Yamasaki. Bold forms (the Schwartz house), space before structure (Lafayette 1300), minimal detailing (University Reformed Church and Marathon Oil), stratified walls (University Reformed Church and Lillibridge School), and most importantly, daylight in interior space (University Reformed Church and the Freeman House) were some of the dammed-up reactions that Birkerts expressed in his new commissions. Influences of Alvar Aalto and Carlo Scarpa can also be detected in his work of this period. There were also larger-scale master plan proposals for Tougaloo College in Mississippi (1966), Glen Oaks College in Michigan (1966), and the Vocational Technical Institute in Carbondale, Ill. (1967). The Lincoln Elementary School in Columbus, Ind. (1965), can be considered one of the more important buildings belonging to this phase.

The continuation, what might be called his second phase (1970–1980), represents a widening and strengthening of Birkerts's design philosophy. The need to work with building technologies of metal and glass resulted in a number of solutions expressing sculptural, minimal forms with strong graphic overtones. These include The Contemporary Arts Museum in Houston, Tex. (1970); the IBM Computer Center in Sterling Forest, N. Y. (1970); the Federal Reserve Bank in Minneapolis, Minn. (1970) (Fig. 1); the Municipal Fire Station in Corning, N. Y. (1973); the Duluth Public Library in Duluth, Minn. (1976); and the Museum of Glass in Corning, N. Y. (1976).

The IBM Office Building in Southfield, Mich. (1974), was designed as a highly efficient energy-conserving metal building with minimal apertures through the walls. The use of light reflectors and exterior wall surfaces to express graphically and metaphorically the building's solar orientation exemplifies Birkerts's architectural response to the pressing energy issues of the time.

In 1970, Birkerts was elected a Fellow of the American Institute of Architects (FAIA); in 1971, he received a Gold Medal in Architecture from Tau Sigma Delta and was elected a Fellow of the Graham Foundation and an Honorary Fellow of the Latvian Architects Association. Other honors followed: a Gold Medal in 1975 from the American Institute of Architects, Detroit Chapter, and an appointment as Architect in Residence at the American Academy in Rome in 1976.

Birkerts's stay in Rome can be considered the beginning

Figure 1. Federal Reserve Bank, Minneapolis, Minnesota (1970). Courtesy of Balthazar Korab.

of his next phase, one marked by an ongoing search for meaningful form and appropriate expression, as well as a renewed investigation of materials and uses conducive to the presentation of a building's personality. Several buildings were conceived during Birkerts's Rome stay, including the Corning Museum of Glass.

Further examples of how expressive outer forms are generated by the organic functioning of building interiors include the Iowa College of Law Building (1979) and the Ferguson Residence (Villa Ginny) in Kalamazoo, Mich. (1980). Similarly, the University of Michigan Law School Addition in Ann Arbor (1974) and the Uris Library at Cornell University (1980) are underground design solutions with great emphasis on interior space, use of daylight, and physical and emotional comfort.

In 1982, Japan's Yukio Futagawa published *Gunnar Birkerts and Associates,* an extensive monograph on Birkerts's work (with critical commentary by William Marlin) (4). Birkerts continued to garner honors and awards: in 1980, the Michigan Society of Architects presented him with its Gold Medal, and in 1981, he received the Arnold W. Brunner Architectural Prize in Architecture from the American Academy of Arts and Letters. In the later part of 1982, Birkerts was the Lawrence J. Plym Distinguished Professor of Architecture at the University of Illinois in Champaign. Birkerts became the first recipient of the Thomas S. Monaghan Architect in Residence Professorship in Architecture at the University of Michigan in 1984. In connection with that appointment, the university published a monograph entitled *Buildings, Projects, and Thoughts, 1960–1985.* In its introduction, Birkerts expresses his views on the future direction of architecture (5):

The Next Architecture is compassionate toward the human race. It seeks to accommodate, please, and inspire. It recognizes the past achievements in our civilization which are applicable and can be accommodated. The Next Architecture synthesizes the past and the present, it works with the philosophical, economic, and aesthetic principles of today, and it also projects into the future. It will be only evaluated in increments of decades. The Next Architecture is a continuation of the Modern Movement; it is the next step. It is free from inflexible design theories and stylistic and philosophical dogmas. It is not subjected to media eagerness to pronounce styles and directions. It approaches each case individually.

The main force in the Next Architecture is the appropriate inventiveness. Solutions are formulated appropriate to each problem. Appropriate inventiveness is equally effective in working with past, present, and future. It prevents creation of subjective design theories and stylistic idiosyncrasies. Careful synthesis and developed design methodology are the other forces in the Next Architecture.

This thesis, like a formula, is able to accept combinations of endless magnitudes thus providing solutions, equally endless. It would not have to be abandoned or retracted with progression of time. It says current by being appropriately innovative, preempting the need to be avant-garde for the sake of bringing on change.

BIBLIOGRAPHY

1. A. L. Huxtable, "New Talent USA," *Art in America* **50** (1), 52 (1962).

2. E. McCoy, "Young Architects in the United States," *Zodiac* **13,** 164–197 (1964).

3. "A Search for Architectural Principles—Some Thoughts and Works of Gunnar Birkerts," *Progressive Architecture* **XLV** (9), 172–191 (Sept. 1964).

4. W. Marlin, *GA Architect 2—Gunnar Birkerts and Associates,* A.D.A. EDITA Tokyo Co., Ltd., Japan, 1982.

5. G. Birkerts, *Buildings, Projects and Thoughts—1960–1985,* College of Architecture and Urban Planning, University of Michigan, Ann Arbor, Mich., 1985.

GUNNAR BIRKERTS, FAIA
Gunnar Birkerts and Associates
Birmingham, Michigan

BLAKE, PETER

Peter Blake, U.S. architect, was born in Berlin, Germany, in 1920. He emigrated to the United States in 1940 and became a naturalized citizen in 1944. He was educated in England and the United States, receiving his architectural degree from the Pratt Institute in New York in 1949.

After early office experience with Serge Chermayeff in London and George Howe, Oskar Stonorov, and Louis Kahn in Philadelphia, he was named Curator of the Department of Architecture and Industrial Design at the Museum of Modern Art in New York (1948–1950). In 1950, he was named Associate Editor, later Editor-in-Chief, of *Architectural Forum* and Editor-in-Chief (1972–1975) of *Architecture Plus,* the successor to *Architectural Forum.*

In addition to practicing architecture in New York, Blake has been chairman of the School of Architecture at the Boston Architectural Center and chairman of the Department of Architecture and Planning at the Catholic University of America in Washington, D.C., to 1986.

Blake is well known as the author of several books, including *The Master Builders—Le Corbusier, Mies van der Rohe, Frank Lloyd Wright; God's Own Junkyard;* and *Form Follows Fiasco—Why Modern Architecture Hasn't Worked.* Through education, writing, and exhibitions, Blake has made a major impact on architectural theory and public understanding in the United States.

BIBLIOGRAPHY

General References

P. Blake, *God's Own Junkyard,* Holt, Rinehart & Winston, New York, 1964.

P. Blake, *The Master Builders—Le Corbusier, Mies van der Rohe, Frank Lloyd Wright,* W. W. Norton & Co., New York, 1976.

P. Blake, *Form Follows Fiasco—Why Modern Architecture Hasn't Worked,* Little, Brown and Co., Boston, Mass., 1977.

See also ARCHITECTURAL PRESS.

ROBERT T. PACKARD, AIA
Reston, Virginia

BLIND, SIGHT-IMPAIRED: DESIGN FOR. See
HANDICAPPED, LAWS AND CODES.

BÖHM, GOTTFRIED

Gottfried Böhm, German architect, was born in 1920 in Offenbach/Main, near Frankfurt/Main, in what today is the Federal Republic of Germany. He was the third and last son of Dominikus Böhm (1880–1955), one of the most prominent Catholic church builders of his time in Germany, known for his typological and constructive innovations as well as his expressive architecture. Gottfried Böhm received his Abitur in Cologne at the Aposteln Gymnasium in 1939, served in the German army from 1938 to 1942, and studied architecture at the Technische Hochschule in Munich from 1942 to 1946 and sculpture at the Akademie der bildenden Künste in 1947. He married in 1948 and has four children, three of whom are architects.

Böhm worked in Cologne at his father's office from 1947 to 1950. In 1950, he began working for Rudolf Schwarz (1897–1961), another prominent German church architect, and in 1951 for Cajetan Baumann in New York City. Returning to Cologne, he went into a partnership with his father from 1952 to 1955, and took over the office after Dominikus Böhm's death.

Gottfried Böhm was a Professor of Urban Planning (*Stadtteilplanung und Werklehre*) in Aachen (Aix la Chapelle) at the Rheinisch Westphälische Technische Hochschule from 1963 to 1985. He has been a member of the Akademie der Künste, Berlin, since 1968, of the Deutsche Akademie für Städtebau und Landesplanung, Berlin, since 1976, of the Academie d'Architecture, Paris, since 1983, and of the Academia Pontificia ad Pantheon, Rome, since 1986. He has been a Profesor Honorario of the Universidad Nacional Federico Villarreal, Lima, since 1977, Honorary Fellow of the American Institute of Architects since 1982, and Dr.hc. of the Technische Universität in Munich since 1985.

Böhm began his professional career in the Federal Republic of Germany's postwar reconstruction period. His architecture was in many respects a continuation of his father's work. His family and social extraction made him a cultivated, urbane Roman Catholic artist with a sense for the past and for the prewar developments of the arts, especially for the more conservative, romantic, and expressive modern tendencies at that time. His connections with intellectual circles and the Catholic Church, then one of the architect's foremost patrons, permitted him to work at high professional and artistic levels from the very beginning.

His professional approach is characterized by clear concepts and correct, very conscious realizations of building types, building materials, and structural systems as the natural bases for architectural language. His artistic approach emphasizes the sculptural aspects of architecture, both on a large scale and in details. His buildings are always extremely personal, transcendent, original, and thereby singular solutions. Böhm is thus more an introverted individual artist than the expansive leader of a mainstream architectural tendency in the German architectural scene.

At the beginning of his professional work, in the late 1940s and early 1950s, Böhm went through an experimental phase influenced by the formalist U.S. versions of the

452   BÖHM, GOTTFRIED

modern movement. His contribution to the construction of wide-span church roofs was the realization of suspended reinforced-concrete shells. This development is explained by the limited financial and material resources of those years and the urgent need for quick solutions. Examples are the churches St. Columba, which is a reconstruction, and St. Paulus, both in Cologne. These solutions were soon abandoned, however, probably because of the reduced durability of tensioned concrete constructions.

A second phase, in the late 1950s, was dominated by clear and simple lines (skeleton framing, panes, and walls) of almost Miesian character, as well as Corbusian stereometrical elements (cones, cubes, and pyramids) attached to different functions. Pencil-like towers, ornamental colored windows, and other decorations were added to the clear forms. The Herz Jesu Church is an example of Böhm's work in this period. Separated from the street by a high wall, there is an entrance courtyard, followed by a kind of cloister and finally the sanctuary. The last is strictly rectangular and is defined by several rows of supports. The zone of the altar is arched over by a dome. The cloister is closed by ornamental glass panes. All special uses (church bell, baptismal font, confessional) are in freestanding round towers meant to be seen from afar (Fig. 1).

Böhm's architecture passed through a third phase, possibly the first high point in his work, through a correspondence between his individual artistic expression and the individual constructive solutions still possible at that time. In this sense, from the beginning of the 1960s his architecture was characterized by plastic volumes and spaces and by dynamic, crystalline forms. The best examples are the Pilgrimage Church in Neviges, the Bensberg town hall, and the residence for the elderly in Garath. The Pilgrimage Church in Neviges is located in a hilly countryside in the middle of the old town bearing its name. Beside the church, there are several subsidiary rooms for pilgrims, which accompany the path leading to the church. Böhm describes the project as a series of squares, which lead to the large covered square inside the church. The inner space of the latter gives the impression of a superelevated crystalline form, and the central area with the altar is surrounded by lateral chapels and a multistory gallery. Big, vividly colored glass windows in the lateral chapels and small openings in the upper zone provide light and create an almost magic, sensual atmosphere (Fig. 2).

The simple and regular structures of the 1950s had become highly complex: as in his father's work, the use of folded systems and shells predominated; however, they were no longer geometrically simple and repetitive, but highly irregular and individual. Such constructions were made by hand and exploited the possibilities of *in situ* reinforced-concrete and brick construction to the maximum.

In the 1960s, the Federal Republic of Germany had developed into a rich and highly industrialized country, with cheap industrial products and a decreasing number of craftsmen. In contrast to preceding periods, the 1970s and 1980s have been characterized by the use of modern materials and methods of production (ie, steel, sheet metals, and precast concrete instead of brick and *in situ* con-

Figure 1. Herz Jesu Church, Schildgen, Bergisch-Gladbach, Federal Republic of Germany (1958).

crete) and by rationalized structures, such as skeletons, and repetitive versions of other systems instead of the individual and irregular ones of the past decades.

In accordance with this, in his fourth phase, beginning around 1970, Böhm designed several large buildings, in which the new materials and technologies played an important part. The plastically shaped skyscraper of the Landesamt für Datenverarbeitung und Statistik in Düsseldorf, the Town Hall and Cultural Center in Bocholt, a combination of a sculptured concrete basis and steel–glass construction, and the Civic Center Bergischer Löwe in Bergisch Gladbach, a sheet-metal-covered skeleton construction, are examples from that period. The changing material conditions change the forms; they demand other forms and details.

A project of the 1980s also shows the continuing development of technology and the way Böhm uses it for creation; the Züblin Building is a standard precast concrete skeleton construction with a facade of red-colored concrete prefabs also designed by the architect. A glass hall connects the two seven-story wings of offices. The main circulation facilities, two escalators, a staircase, steps, trees, fountains, and the possibility of putting the tables and chairs of the

Figure 2. Pilgrimage Church, Neviges, Federal Republic of Germany (1964).

Figure 3. Züblin Office Building, Möhringen, Stuttgart, Federal Republic of Germany (1984).

ground floor restaurant inside the hall make it the center of the building for all people working in it (Fig. 3).

All of these attempts to individualize the usual standard building types, the stressing of the color and surface of the concrete prefabs or of the massive, plastic effect of the thin, light sheet-metal facades, serve the purpose of formal dramatization and individualization. To this day, these attempts seem to be contributions to a new architectural language that is still waiting for culmination. Böhm's demand for an integration of art and architecture, of human desires and needs and construction, seeks to create the conditions to enhance life and the possibilities of communication in an open society.

Awards for his work include Großer Preis Bund Deutscher Architekten 1975; Medaille d'Or de l'Academie d'Architecture, Paris, 1982; Fritz Schumacher Prize, Hamburg, 1985; Pritzker Architecture Prize 1986.

BIBLIOGRAPHY

General References

F. Otto, "Rheinische Kirchenbauten und hängendes Dach," *Bauwelt* **51,** 1047–1050 (1955).

G. Böhm with N. Rosiny, "Zur Wiederherstellung der Hohen Domkirche zu Trier," *Bauwelt* **22,** 810–815 (1974).

E. Schirmbeck, "Gottfried Böhm, Anmerkungen zum architektonischen Werk," *Bauen + Wohnen* **11,** 421–424 (1977).

H. Klumpp and E. Schirmbeck, "Interview mit Gottfried Böhm," *Bauen + Wohnen* **11,** 425–427 (1977).

S. Raev, "Architecture of Synthesis," *Architecture and Urbanism,* **3,** 5–7 (1978).

P. Bode, "Expressive Kraft und schöpferische Humanität: Der Architekt Gottfried Böhm," Architecture and Urbanism **3,** 37–48 (1978).

"Chronological List (of Works) 1946–1977," *Architecture and Urbanism* **3,** 55–60 (1978).

H. Klumpp, "Der Architekt Gottfried Böhm," *Werk Bauen + Wohnen* **9,** 9–12 (1980).

S. Raev, ed., *Gottfried Böhm, Bauten und Projekte 1950–1980,* König, Cologne, FRG, 1982.

Der Architekt Gottfried Böhm, exhibition catalogue, Kunsthalle Bielefeld, Bielefeld, FRG, 1984–1985.

G. Böhm, "Acceptance Address," in *The Pritzker Architecture Prize 1986 Gottfried Böhm,* The Hyatt Foundation, 1986.

Manuel Cuadra

Volkmar Nickol
Technische Hochschule
Darmstadt
Darmstadt, Federal Republic of
Germany

BOLTING.   See Steel in Construction

BONDS AND SURETIES

A surety is one who guarantees satisfactory fulfillment of an obligation that a second party has agreed to undertake for the benefit of a third party. The concept of such a guarantee of performance goes far back into history. There is reference, for example, to fidelity insurance in the Code of Hammurabi and there are Biblical warnings against suretyship. While there is evidence of written surety contracts in early history, the most usual form of suretyship was unwritten between individuals, with predictable erratic performance on the part of sureties. By the mid-eighteenth century, written and corporate contracts of suretyship began to replace oral agreements between individuals. In the United States prior to the 1870s, the construction industry relied on personal sureties; by the turn of the century, with the growth of business enterprises willing to stand behind contracts, sureties assumed corporate form.

The usual written, construction-related form of surety became and remains the surety bond, sometimes referred to as the contract or construction bond. In this, the bonding company (surety) stands behind the contractor (principal) and guarantees to the owner (obligee) satisfactory performance of contract terms by the contractor, the surety agreeing to complete the project should the contractor be unable to do so.

The performance bond and labor and material payment bond (also referred to as the payment bond) as well as the bid bond are the principal forms of surety bonds used today in the construction industry. There are several other types of bonds used with varying frequency: statutory bond, dual-obligee bond, completion bond, release of lien bond, subcontract bond, license or permit bond, and variations of many of these. Except for the bid bond, these all relate to contractual obligations in connection with construction agreements.

OVERVIEW OF CONTRACT BONDS

The earlier form of contract bond was a single document first known as the standard form of bond published by The American Institute of Architects (AIA); this was subsequently replaced by the owner's protective bond, published jointly by the Surety Association of America (SAA) and the AIA. This form was a single performance and payment bond that guaranteed the contractor's satisfactory performance of the contract. It was also intended to provide financial protection for those supplying labor and materials in the event of nonpayment by the contractor, while at the same time covering the contractor's default. However, the named obligee, the owner, had prior right of action under the bond over unnamed third parties; this had the potential of leaving labor or materials claimants unpaid because of the owner's priority in using bond funds for completion of the project. On private work, those unpaid for supplying labor or materials have a statutory right to place a lien on the owner's property, a right that is not available in connection with government construction contracts. The federal government had first addressed this situation by passage of the Heard Act in 1894, and more recently by enactment of the Miller Act in 1935 [40 U.S.C., Section 270(a)–(e)]. This latter statute required furnishing a separate bond specifically related to claims of persons entitled to payment for labor or material on government projects; the federal statute was followed by the individual states adopting similar laws, often referred to as Little Miller Acts. In the early 1940s, in the interest of conforming to such statutes as well as making it simpler to administer these claims, the single bond was augmented by a standard dual-bond form: the performance bond and labor and material payment bond (combined in AIA Document A311, hereinafter referred to as A311) still in current use. The owner's protective bond was dropped in the mid-1950s. An expanded version of the dual bond, performance bond and payment bond (combined in AIA Document A312, hereinafter referred to as A312), was published in 1984 but the A311 bonds remain available since they appear to relate more closely to the Miller Act requirements. In each case, the dual bonds are furnished as a single package, although it is possible to purchase either one separately. There is no additional cost for the two bonds furnished together; there is no premium reduction if the performance bond is furnished alone but there is an adjustment for the payment bond if issued singly.

Bonds are most often written with the penal sum of each equal to the contract price. On occasion, usually in conformance with statutory requirements, one or the other, or even both, may be written for less than the contract sum, although there is no premium advantage for such reduction. It is also possible to establish the value of the performance bond in a greater amount than the contract sum, but there is little advantage in doing so since the total cost of finishing a partially completed, defaulted project rarely exceeds the original contract sum.

Surety bond premiums, at rates established by a rating bureau, are based on the dollar amount of the contract as well as project classification, and may vary to some extent with the financial background of the contractor being bonded. The fee will vary from 0.5–1.5% of the total construction cost, and will be included in the contract sum when a stipulated cost contract is entered into. Although bond fees are related to total cost and project type, they are essentially based on empirical data related to administrative costs rather than on calculated statistical experience as is the case with insurance premiums; default by the contractor-principal is not an anticipated event. The contractor's reputation, financial situation, character and quality of staff, adequacy of plant and equipment, and performance on previous projects have an effect on the bond's cost. These same criteria will also affect the total amount of work for which a contractor may be bonded at any one time. Contractors with many projects underway may be precluded from taking on new work if they have reached their maximum bonding capacity. Since bonds are optional on private work, because of possible bonding limits it is essential that an owner make the bonding requirement known to contractors during the bidding period and, if not then, very definitely prior to entering into a construction contract.

A surety company will monitor the contractor's economic activity and work load very carefully to be certain the business is operating effectively and to its best financial advantage. Because of this close scrutiny, sureties are sometimes viewed as partners in the contractor's business operations; the cash flow from the owner to the contractor is carefully monitored or even approved by the surety as though the money were its own. For example, the AIA publishes forms that provide for the surety's consent to final payment (AIA Document G707), and consent to reduction of funds retained by the owner (AIA Document G707A). These releases, while required by terms of the construction contract (General Conditions of the Contract for Construction, AIA Document A201), reflect the surety's concern for its own interests. Because of this close relationship, choice of surety is almost exclusively left to the contractor rather than stipulated by the owner, although the owner reserves the right to approve the surety since the company's financial stability can be an important factor in the event of a contractor default.

Surety bonding is often thought of as insurance, which it definitely is not. Basically, insurance is a method of using resources provided by many to reimburse the losses of a few and is a contract between two parties, an insurer and a beneficiary. The insured risk is generally calculable and premiums are based on actuarial tables related to the risk of loss, among other things; when a loss occurs, the insurer accepts full responsibility for payment. The surety bond, on the other hand, is a three-party contract involving the contractor, surety, and owner and is based on performance capability, a factor that cannot be specifically measured; the bond is essentially a conditional promissory note. When the bond is called on, costs are paid by the surety, which, in turn, endeavors to recover the amount expended from the forfeiting principal. Despite this very basic difference in concept, when government regulation of surety companies became desirable and necessary, statutory control over sureties fell to the insurance commissioners of the states, where it still remains. While in earlier times sureties were independent companies, many insurance companies, either by absorbing these independent sureties or entering the surety market on their own, left the impression that contract bonds were an insurance industry product and thereby appeared to justify regulation by the states' insurance commissioners. Further compounding this misconception is the fact that bonds are normally prepared by the contractor's insurance agent, not the surety company directly; the bond is accompanied by a sealed power of attorney from the surety company authorizing the agent to write the bond, sometimes with specific dollar limitations.

BID SECURITY

As related to the contract for construction, the surety process starts with the bid security. This is an assurance to the owner from a bidder that, if the bidder submits the lowest acceptable proposal, it will enter into a contract within a stipulated period of time to perform the bid-on services at the proposed price and furnish any required contract bonds. The bid security may be in the form of a certified or cashier's check, actual cash deposit, irrevocable letter of credit, or bid bond. Since any form of cash security or letter of credit would impinge on the bidder's working capital or bank credit, the bid bond (AIA Document A310, hereinafter referred to as A310) is the preferred and most frequently used form of bid security. The amount set for the bid security on private work is generally 5–10%; on government projects, the amount of the bid bond is usually greater than these percentages. The cost of this bond is nominal and, for the low bidder, may be covered in the fee for the contract bonds furnished; for the unsuccessful bidders, it is absorbed as a general overhead cost. In the event the low bidder refuses, without justifiable reason, to sign the proffered agreement or if the low bidder is unable to furnish required performance and payment bonds, the bid bond would be called on to reimburse the owner for damages sustained on account of such failure to enter into a contract. The measure of damages is either the actual difference between the contract sum finally agreed on and the defaulting bidder's proposal, or the penal sum of the bond, whichever is lower. If the surety is required to make payment, it would seek to recover the paid damages from the forfeiting bidder. As suggested above, there are reasons justifying a bid withdrawal. Although not a general rule, with each situation relying on its own merits, courts have most frequently held that basic errors in material facts (eg, substantial mistakes in addition or in extending unit costs) can be considered acceptable reasons for a bid withdrawal without calling on the bond, assuming timely notification of the discovered error. On the other hand, a judgmental error (eg, estimating insufficient labor or calculating too little concrete) would not be sufficient reason for bid withdrawal.

PERFORMANCE BOND

It is an unfortunate fact that the construction industry is subject to a certain amount of economic instability. Slow payment, excessive retainage, bad weather, strikes, or price escalation can rapidly change a contractor's financial situation from one of comfortable solvency to one of financial crisis. Because of this, most private owners and all government agencies require contractors to furnish surety bonds to assure satisfactory completion of a project regardless of fluctuating financial circumstances. The performance bond covering total satisfactory compliance with contract terms is the first part of the dual bond furnished to satisfy these requirements, both public and private.

Initial conditions of the performance bond provide that, if the contractor faithfully completes the contract, the bond becomes null and void. If for any reason the contractor is unable to complete the contract or comply with contract terms, or has been declared by the owner to be in default, the surety will take one of several actions, providing the owner has faithfully fulfilled its obligations under the bond and the contract. Under the terms of the A311 bond, the surety may: (1) remedy the default; or (2) obtain bids and arrange for a contract between the owner and another contractor to complete the work. The terms of A312 are more detailed and require meetings of the owner, contractor, and surety prior to taking any specific action. The action options available to the surety in that bond are: (1) with the consent of the owner, arrange for the contractor to complete its work; (2) undertake to complete the construction contract itself; or (3) obtain bids from or negotiate proposals with contractors and arrange a contract between another contractor and the owner to complete the work. A312 also stipulates two additional options for the surety: (4) waive its rights to complete the work and offer the owner a cash settlement; or (5) deny liability in whole or in part. Payment by the surety under the performance bond when the surety is involved in completion of the work, including payment to the owner for any specific damages on account of the contractor's failure to complete, is limited to the actual cost of completion and damages, not to exceed the penal sum of the bond. The owner, in turn, must make available any remaining balance of the funds still due on the original contract.

As indicated in the additional options in the A312 bond, it is possible that the surety could seek release from its obligations under the bond. This might be occasioned by circumstances such as significant changes in the contract that materially alter the scope of contract performance, or failure of the owner to comply with specific contract terms where such failure is detrimental to the contractor's interests (eg, failure to make prompt payments). Such action on the part of the surety usually results in litigation to resolve the issues. The time limit for the owner to file suit under the performance bond is two years from a specified date.

LABOR AND MATERIAL PAYMENT BOND (PAYMENT BOND)

The second part of the dual bond furnished to satisfy bonding requirements on construction projects is the labor and material payment bond (A311), also called payment bond (A312), an abbreviated title frequently used for convenience when referring to the A311 form. As with the performance bond, the initial condition of this bond is that, if the contractor makes prompt payment for labor and materials needed in the performance of the work and no mechanics liens have been placed on the property, the bond becomes null and void. In the event of the contractor's failure to make such payments or satisfy any liens, the bond provides for payments to two categories of claimants: (1) those with direct contracts with or who have been employed by the principal; and (2) those with no such direct contract. Under the conditions of A311, claimants having direct contracts are permitted to sue on the bond without prior notice whereas a notification sequence is described in A312. Both A311 and A312 stipulate a notification sequence for claimants not having direct contracts. All claimants have the right under this bond to sue for satisfaction of their claims in courts of competent jurisdiction. The penal sum is the maximum obligation under both A311 and A312 except that, under the terms of the A312 payment bond, the outstanding contract balance may also be made available subject to the owner's priority to use such funds for completion of the work. Since filing of a claim under the payment bond is a more direct and expeditious process than the involved procedures called for by the performance bond, this is the bond form that satisfies the Miller Act requirements. Because the terms of the A312 payment bond are more detailed while the terms of the A311 labor and material payment bond are simpler and closely follow the Miller Act requirements, the A311 form continues to be available for statutory use. There is a stipulation, however, in both of the A312 bonds that, when terms of the bond are in conflict with statutory or legal requirements at the place of construction, such statutory or legal requirements supersede the bonds' terms. There is also a stipulation in both of the A312 bonds that specifically excludes third-party claims unrelated to the construction contract. The time limit for a claimant to file suit under the labor and material payment bond is one year from a specified date. If the performance bond and labor and material payment bond are called on to complete the contract, the surety, after fulfilling its financial obligations to the owner, would seek to recover its losses from the defaulting contractor-principal.

STATUTORY BOND

Statutory bonds are furnished in compliance with laws and regulations at the location of a construction project. The term statutory bond describes a bond required by statute that carries the liability imposed by that statute on principal and surety; it is not the title of any specific bond form. These statutes usually refer to public work, but do, in a few jurisdictions, apply to private projects as well. As previously described, the A311 or A312 bonds could be used to meet statutory requirements, but there is the possibility of the provisions in them being inconsistent with relevant statutes, causing their use to be questioned.

Typical examples of statutory bonds are found in those prepared by the U.S. General Services Administration:

bid bond (Standard Form 24), performance bond (Standard Form 25), and payment bond (Standard Form 25-A). Bonding requirements for federal government projects are set out in the Federal Acquisition Regulation FAR28. These requirements vary from the customary, but not mandatory, private terms in many instances, a few of which are cited here. The bid bond is required to be not less than 20% of the bid price, although a maximum dollar limit may be set for larger projects. There are specific time limits stated for acceptance of the bid and execution of the contract. Except for the time limits, the terms are less detailed than in A310. Performance bonds are required to be 100% of the contract price while payment bonds would have a maximum penal sum of 50% of the contract price for smaller work, with the percentage decreasing as the contract price increases. The specific terms of these bonds are more general than those of the A311 or A312; the performance bond, however, does specifically refer to payment to the federal government of the taxes on wages collected or withheld by the principal. To be acceptable, corporate sureties must appear in the Department of the Treasury Circular No. 570, *Surety Companies Acceptable on Federal Bonds,* a document that may also be used to evaluate qualifications of sureties in connection with private work. In lieu of a surety bond, a contractor may deposit another type of security such as certain U.S. government notes and bonds, currency, cashier's or certified checks, or bank drafts, each in an amount equal to the penal sum required for the bond.

OTHER BOND FORMS

There are variations of the usual performance bond, which, although available, are not often required. There are also additional bonds, some of which are described further, that guarantee other aspects of the construction contract. Except for the major contract bonds, titles and format as well as terms and conditions for many of these variations and additional bonds will vary from company to company.

The dual-obligee bond is similar to the standard performance bond except that the entity providing the financing is named as an additional obligee along with the owner. There are also specific terms regarding payments to the principal in accordance with contract requirements: the surety is relieved of its obligations under the bond by failure of the owner or lender to make payments to the principal strictly in accordance with the contract requirements. The dual-obligee bond is not too frequently called for so there is no standard form available.

The completion bond is a special form of performance bond wherein the owner is the principal and the lender the obligee. It warrants to the lender that the owner will apply the borrowed funds to secure proper completion of the project free of any liens or encumbrances, and assures that the mortgage is the first lien on the completed project. The surety, in effect, warrants satisfactory performance on the part of both the owner and contractor. The completion bond, too, is rarely used and is not available as a standard form.

The release of lien bond, often referred to as the lien bond, protects the owner of the property against loss if liens are filed. Contractors may furnish such a bond at the time final payment is requested in lieu of any required

releases or waivers of lien should there be any disputed claims. There is also a no-lien bond that is furnished in those jurisdictions where, by statute, construction contractors must waive lien rights. This bond substitutes for the right to file a lien in connection with such contracts, and permits a direct right of action against the surety by persons who might otherwise have had such lien rights.

The subcontract bond is one required by a contractor to be furnished by a subcontractor, and is most often the standard performance bond and payment bond, with the subcontractor as the principal and the contractor named as obligee; the terms and conditions are usually the same as those in the bond furnished to the owner by the contractor.

License or permit bonds are occasionally required from the contractor by local government entities before granting certain licenses or permits related to construction. The bond is an assurance of the contractor's knowledge and understanding of and intent to comply with applicable laws and ordinances, and provides for satisfaction of any claims or damages rising out of the contractor's actions in violation of such local requirements.

The maintenance bond warrants that the contractor will correct defective work or work not in conformance with the contract documents within a period of one year from substantial completion, or such other period of time as may be set out in the contract documents. This is not usually needed if the warranty period is for one year and if a performance bond has been furnished. If there is a warranty period longer than one year for the entire work or portions thereof, the maintenance bond would be required.

For many years, roofing bonds were furnished in response to specifications for bonded roof installation. These bonds had the manufacturer as principal, supported by a surety company, and indemnified the owner as obligee against failure of the roofing installation. They had specific dollar and time limits and covered materials only. In recent years, these bonds have been replaced by warranties given to the owner by the roofing products manufacturer without involving a surety. The warranties have a time limitation and most frequently limit the penal sum to the original cost of installation; they cover labor as well as materials and generally relate to failure of the manufacturer's products or improper installation.

Fidelity bonds, although not a requirement of the construction contract, are often used by both owners and contractors in the administration of their operations. This bond, purchased by the obligee rather than the principal, as is the case with surety bonds, covers any loss to the obligee caused by dishonest acts of an employee, who is the principal. The large dollar volume in the construction industry often suggests that the bonding of persons responsible for the disbursement of great sums of money is a prudent practice.

BIBLIOGRAPHY

General References

J. D. Lambert and L. White, *Handbook of Modern Construction Law,* 1st ed., Prentice-Hall Inc., Prentice Hall Press, Englewood Cliffs, N.J., 1982, p. 131.

Georgia Chapter, Society of Chartered Property and Casualty Underwriters, *Risk Management in Building Construction,* National Underwriter Co., Cincinnati, Ohio, 1976, p. 89.

A. Remmen, *The Contract Bond Book,* National Underwriter Co., Cincinnati, Ohio, 1978.

J. Sweet, *Legal Aspects of Architecture, Engineering and the Construction Process,* 2nd ed., West Publishing Co., St. Paul, Minn. 1977, p. 295.

C. H. Cowgill and B. J. Small, *Architectural Practice,* Reinhold Publishing Corp., New York, 1947, p. 250.

B. Rothschild, *Construction Bonds and Insurance Guide,* American Institute of Architects, Washington, D.C., 1979, p. 9.

K. Cushman, *Guidelines for Improving Practice, Insurance-12, Vol. XV, No. 5,* Victor O. Schinnerer and Co., Office for Professional Liability Research, Washington, D.C., 1987.

National Institute of Construction Law, Inc., *Construction and Design Law,* Michie Company, Charlottesville, Va., 1986, Chapt. 31.

Federal Acquisition Regulations, Part 28-Bonds and Insurance and *General Services Acquisition Regulations, Subpart 528.1-Bonds,* U.S. Government Printing Office, Washington, D.C., 1985.

J. Sweet, Ed., *Yearbook of Construction Articles, Anthology Edition,* Vol. 1, Federal Publications, Inc., Washington, D.C., 1983, pp. 89, 171, and 383.

See also CONSTRUCTION DOCUMENTS.

BERNARD B. ROTHSCHILD,
FAIA, FCSI
Atlanta, Georgia

BOTTA, MARIO

Mario Botta, contemporary architect, lives in Ticino, a small canton in southern Switzerland, in an extraordinarily beautiful landscape separated by the Alps from the rest of Switzerland. Most of his projects have been built within a few miles of Lugano where he works. This area reflects Switzerland's peculiar situation: politically it is Swiss, yet culturally it is Italian. This setting has somehow produced an unusual empathy between the architects practicing here, and has inspired what Botta describes as "a love for one's own habitat, in a constructive tradition which is extremely rigorous and closely fitted to the minimal conditions and primary demands of living" (1).

Botta was born in Mendrisio on April 1, 1943. He attended primary school at Genestrerio and secondary school at Mendrisio. By his own admission, he never liked going to school; as long as he could remember, he went against his will. At age 15, he quit school and became a draftsman in the architectural studio of Carloni and Camenish in Lugano, Switzerland. In that capacity, Botta soon realized that his natural talent for drawing could lead to his final career choice in architecture. After three years as a draftsman, he became an apprentice and was given his first major design project. Botta was put in charge of the design for a new complex to replace the parish house of Genestrerio that was to be demolished when a village road was widened. The excitement and enthusiasm with which he

developed and completed this first major design responsibility has never left him.

In 1961, Botta left the Carloni and Camenish office to attend art college in Milan, Italy. He describes himself as an external student who did not attend classes but prepared his lessons alone, then sat for the final examinations at the school. After graduation, he journeyed to Venice to enroll at the "most sophisticated and least technical of the Italian architectural schools," the Instituto Universitario di Architettura (IUA) (1). Botta remained in Venice from 1964 to 1969; during those years, through a combination of good luck and perseverance, Botta was able to make contact with three giants of the architectural world, Le Corbusier (1965), Louis Kahn (1969) and Carlo Scarpa, who was one of his teachers and his thesis professor. Botta credits his association with these three for the fact that he is "condemned" to do well: "I cannot allow myself not to do well . . ." (2). Le Corbusier has been characterized by Botta as being, for him, "the history of architecture." Corbusier represents, in Botta's early training, most of his impressions of modern architecture as well as the notion that the profession of architecture can assist society. Botta worked in the master's studio with Jullian de la Fuente and Jose Oubrerie on a new hospital project for Venice. Botta was there six months, but the master died at the beginning of his tenure. His influence, however, has been long lasting. The hospital project was exhibited in 1967 when Botta designed his first single-family house at Stabio in Ticino, Switzerland, for a friend. He was in his first year of architectural school and had just completed the work in Le Corbusier's studio. The house was meant to express the contrast between man and nature. Botta describes his design time as a preoccupation with "the quality of the 'artificial', that which is designed by man and as such in dialectic contrast to nature" (3). This project exemplifies the teachings of Le Corbusier in the use of light, in the spatial organization, and in the expression of the exposed concrete frame.

It was not until 1969 that Botta had the opportunity to meet Louis Kahn who was in Venice to install the exhibition of his project for the new Congress Building (Palais de Congrès) in the Palazzo Ducale. Botta felt it was very important to meet Kahn, and managed to help him with the exhibit and to assist Kahn in completing plans for that building. Of the time in Venice, Botta has suggested that he and Kahn did not understand each other very well. Kahn spoke no Italian, Botta no English, so all conversations occurred through an interpreter. Yet, Kahn's brilliance, his ability to distill any architectural issue to its essence, and his ability to clearly define the purpose and the depth of a problem etched a permanent impression on Mario Botta. Not only was it possible to ask Kahn's famous question "What does the building want to be?", but in his contact with Kahn, Botta found the answer: "It is not what you want, it is what you sense in the order of things which tells you what to design" (4). Carlo Scarpa, who acted in the capacity of teacher and final examiner at the completion of Botta's studies in Venice, showed Botta the "innovations of modern architecture as they were interpreted by the neo-Rationalist movement" (1). Scarpa also imparted to his apt pupil his intense love for materials, for the composition and order of those materials, and for the differences between their expressions. Scarpa's sensitivity toward the understanding of their structure and his concern for detailing materials intelligently gave Botta a philosophical direction and an appreciation for even the most common materials that has since characterized all of his built work.

After graduating from the IUA in Venice, Botta returned to Switzerland to work as a professional architect with a studio in Lugano. Botta's first built work after graduation was a single-family house at Cadenazzo in Ticino, in progress from 1970 to 1971. Having only a few months before completing his work with Louis Kahn in Venice, Kahn's lessons provided a fresh vision for Botta (3):

> . . . the light, the silence and the memory entered as structural and essential elements of architecture . . . Architecture, beyond the fantastic images and as a messianic vocation, reproposes itself every day as a system of life, as a profession, a labor, a craft. Now in this perspective architecture is essentially to me, it is a system for living, for seeing and evaluating what is around me. With this attachment every theme, every occasion of work becomes a new and enthralling adventure, a fantastic encounter and confrontation in the struggle for the transformation of reality.

Mario Botta's career has spanned more than two busy decades; in addition to his practice, he has served as a visiting professor at the Ecole Polytechnic Fédérale in Lausanne, Switzerland, for the past ten years. In 1982, he was made a member of the Commission Federale Svizzera delle Belle Arti, and in 1983, became an honorary fellow of the Bund Deutscher Architeckten (BDA). The American Institute of Architects (AIA) conferred honorary fellowship upon Botta in 1984. Today, he continues his active lecturing in Europe, North America, and Latin America.

Many of Botta's projects have been single-family houses. For him, the single-family house includes the problems and the objectives of the entire discipline of architecture. Carrying on the ideas of Kahn, Botta believes in the organization of the relationship between man and nature and the distinctive characterization of man in relationship to his own environment (5). Botta is keenly interested in history and in the study of man's habitat through time. Because the home has been the one constant through the evolution of history, Botta feels this architectural type deserves both study and elaboration. It is not only individual needs, but the collective requirements of societies that fascinate him. Another theme pervading his single-family houses is the search for the roots of a design and man's identity in a particular place. Cultural traditions are important throughout Botta's projects, and his forms are derived from—but not copied from—"the environment as a testimony of history and memory" (5).

Botta's house projects are numerous. A few of the more notable ones are the single-family houses in Switzerland at Stabio (1965–1967); Riva San Vitale (1972–1973); Ligornetto (1975–1976) with Martin Boesch; Pregassona (1979) with Rudy Hunziker; Massagno (1979–1981); Stabio (1980–1981); Viganello (1981–1982); Origlio (1982); and Morbio Superiore (1982–1983) (Fig. 1).

Figure 1. House at Morbio Superiore, Switzerland (1982–1983). Photograph by Robert McCarter.

From his houses of the early 1970s when projects were conceived as an agrarian metaphor with a linear, asymmetrical structure, Botta's designs have evolved to more formal partis where a central axis usually carries a stair to the north, a framed view to the south, and a carefully composed and structured skylight as a crown (6). His house forms are simple, elementary volumes where the exterior is independent from the interior. Internal planning is developed with a grid and suggests a layering of planes that introduce the carefully framed views and long vistas into the interior, reminiscent of the times before the Ticino landscape was consumed by a building boom.

Other projects in Switzerland include many with fellow Ticino architects: the secondary school at Morbio Inferiore with Emilio Bernegger, Rudy Hunziker, and Luca Tami (1972–1977) (Fig. 2); the library for the Capuchin monastery at Lugano (1976–1979); the craft center at Balerna (1977–1979) with Remo Leuzinger; and the Fribourg State Bank at Fribourg (1982) (Fig. 3).

Botta is fond of competitions. He has submitted numerous entries, some as individual efforts, others as collaborative gestures. Notable among them are the schemes for an urban renewal project at Lugano (1970); the master plan of the new Lausanne Polytechnic at Lausanne (1970) with Tita Carloni, Aurelio Galfetti, Flora Ruchat, and Luigi Snozzi; the school at Locarno (1970); the new administrative center at Perugia, Italy (1971) with L. Snozzi; the enlargement of the Zurich railway station (1978) with L. Snozzi; and the urban renewal project at Basel (1979).

Albert Sartoris, historian and architect, who spends

Figure 2. School at Morbio Inferiore, Switzerland (1972–1977). Photograph by Robert McCarter.

Figure 3. Fribourg State Bank, Fribourg, Switzerland (1982). Photograph by Robert McCarter.

portions of each year in Ticino, has written of Botta: "Before being logical, his original mediation is philosophical and social" (7). Botta infuses his themes with a sometimes hermetic sense of discovery. He reflects before building. With Botta, intuition precedes reason. Botta says further (8):

> More difficult to express, this aspect is essential to me for it is the poetic fact, the intuitive dimension inside the rational process. Through the experiences I had with Scarpa, Kahn, and Le Corbusier—and the names are to be understood in this sequence—I am hoping to recover the rational as well as the irrational side involved in the process of making architecture.

BIBLIOGRAPHY

1. P. Arnell, "Mario Botta: Trans-Alpine Rationalist," *A. R.* (June 1982).
2. Y. Futagawa, ed., *G. A. Document 6,* A.D.A. EDITA, Tokyo, 1983, p. 7.
3. Y. Futagawa, ed., *G. A. Houses 3,* A.D.A. EDITA, Tokyo, Japan, 1977, p. 76.
4. C. Norbert-Schultz, "Kahn Heidegger and the Language of Architecture," *Oppositions 18,* The MIT Press, Cambridge, Mass., 1979, pp. 29–47.
5. M. Zardini, *The Architecture of Mario Botta,* Rizzoli, International Publications, Inc., New York, 1984, p. 13.
6. K. Frampton, "Botta's Paradigm," *P.A.* **65** (12), 82 (Dec. 1984).
7. R. Trevisiol, ed., *Mario Botta: La Casa Rotonda,* L'Erba Voglio, Italy (Westbury NY; distribution rights for N.A. by Bellmark Book Co.), 1982, p. 85.
8. L. Dimitriv, "Transfigurer of Geometry," *P.A.* **65** (7), 54 (July 1982).

General References

K. Frampton, "Place Production and Architecture: Towards a Critical Theory of Building," in *Modern Architecture: a Critical History,* London, 1980, pp. 291 and 292.

LINDA SANDERS
North Carolina State University
Raleigh, North Carolina

BRASS AND BRONZE

Copper and its alloys, brass and bronze, show a remarkable color range—from red, through golds and various yellows, to warm silver. This wide range of attractive natural colors, along with their corrosion resistance and other outstanding properties give copper, brass, and bronze a variety of applications in the architectural field.

Metals most commonly alloyed with copper are zinc, tin, aluminum, silicon, and nickel. Of the various alloys, the brasses (copper and zinc in varying percentages) are the best known. The brasses commonly used range from 95% copper and 5% zinc, to about 55% copper and 45% zinc.

These brasses exhibit a range of colors from the redgold of 95% copper and 5% zinc through the gold of 90% copper and 10% zinc, and 85% copper and 15% zinc, to the bright yellow shown at 70% copper and 30% zinc.

These brasses, as well as those with a copper content above approximately 64%, are known as alpha brasses. They are best known for their ability to withstand a great deal of cold working (drawing, rolling, etc) without annealing. They show a somewhat higher strength than copper, increasing with the decrease in copper content. Their ductility is good; the combination of ductility and strength is even better than copper.

Those brasses that contain 64% copper and less are called beta brasses, and are especially noted for their ease of working in the hot condition. These brasses exhibit comparatively high tensile strength and high hardness. Their color is a surprising feature. As the copper content decreases under 62% (the beta content increases), they become more and more red so that at 58% copper the color is a close match for commercial bronze, which is 90% copper and 10% zinc. This is useful in that complicated architectural shapes may be made by hot extrusion, and used to match rolled panel sheets of commercial bronze.

Bronze, historically and technically, is defined as an alloy having tin as the only or principal alloying element. In modern usage, bronze is seldom used alone and the terms phosphor bronze or tin bronze are used for copper–tin alloys. In fact, the term bronze with a suitable modifying adjective has in recent years been extended to other copper alloys, such as aluminum bronze and silicon bronze. The addition of these elements to copper to produce bronzes increases strength or corrosion resistance, or both.

However, in architectural parlance, the principal architectural copper alloys are referred to as bronze, even though they are technically brasses, or nickel silvers. Because all of these alloys are beautiful, require a minimum of maintenance and improve with age, it is understandable that architects and builders refer to them as bronzes.

The principal architectural brass and bronze alloys and their properties are shown in Table 1.

Major architectural end-use applications for brasses and bronzes are readily identified from the divisions and sections of CSI's Masterformat; these have been adopted by the Construction Specifications Institute (CSI), the American Institute of Architects (AIA), the American Consulting Engineers Council (ACEC), and the Associated General Contractors of America (AGC). Illustrations of some end-use applications are located in Figures 1–7. A cross-reference for principal applications and specific brass and bronze alloys is shown in Table 2.

FABRICATION

Metal fabrication usually can be divided into two categories: primary and secondary fabrication. The primary-fabrication process involves melting, casting, and roll–extrusion. Secondary fabrications, which produce finished products for the users, usually involve cutting–machining, forming, joining, and surface finishing.

Primary Fabrication

Melting is the first step in primary fabrication; it primarily involves heating the prepared metal to above the melting point. Raw materials from which the melt is prepared

Table 1. Properties of Various Architectural Brasses and Bronzes[a]

Alloy Number[b]	C22000	C23000	C26000	C28000	C38500	C65500	C74500	C79600
Alloy Name	Commercial Bronze	Red Brass	Cartridge Brass	Muntz Metal	Architectural Bronze	Silicon Bronze	Nickel Silver	Leaded Nickel Silver
Color	Red Gold	Reddish Yellow	Yellow	Reddish Yellow	Reddish Yellow	Reddish Old Gold	Warm Silver	Warm Silver
Nominal composition, %								
Copper	90	85	70	60	57	97	65	45
Zinc	10	15	30	40	40		25	42
Silicon						3		
Nickel							10	10
Phosphorus								
Lead					3			1
Manganese								2
Density, lb/in.^{3}	0.318	0.316	0.308	0.303	0.306	0.308	0.314	
Modulus of elasticity, 10^6 psi	17	17	16	15	14	15	17.5	16
Coefficient of thermal expansion, 10^{-5} per °F	1.02	1.04	1.11	1.16	1.16	1.00	0.91	1.10
Thermal conductivity, Btu/ft^2/ft/hr/°F	109	92	70	71	71	21	26	
Electrical conductivity, %, IACS	44	37	28	28	28	7	9	
Tensile strength, ksi	40	42	50	54	66	60	56	
Elongation, %	44	44	55	45	30	60	40	
0.05% yield strength, ksi	15	16	18	21	20	25	24	

[a] Ref. 1.
[b] These alloy designations are part of the unified numbering system for metals and alloys, which is managed jointly by the ASTM and SAE, and administered by the Copper Development Association, Inc.

Figure 1. Bronze sculpture by Fritz Koenig in the plaza of New York's World Trade Center. The sculpture is 25 ft high. Courtesy of Copper Development Association, Inc.

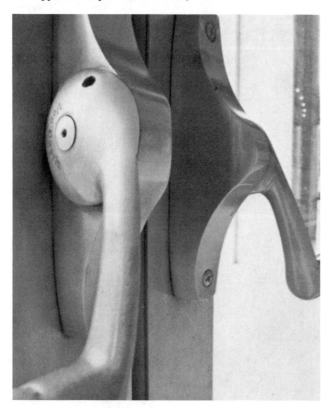

Figure 2. Bronze hardware in the lobby of New York's Metropolitan Opera House. The lever arms are forged and the panic bar is drawn tube; the housings are castings. Courtesy of Copper Development Association, Inc.

Figure 3. Mullions in the main facade of the Metropolitan Opera House in New York City are composed of extruded architectural bronze and brake-formed Muntz metal. Architects: Harrison and Abramovitz. Courtesy of Copper Development Association, Inc.

consist of virgin copper, usually electrolytic cathode, selected clean scrap, and specific alloy elements, such as zinc, tin, nickel, aluminum, or lead. The melt is protected from atmospheric oxidation by a cover of graphite, charcoal, or flux. When the composition and temperature have been determined to meet the requirements of the alloy being melted, the molten metal is then poured for casting.

Casting may be carried out in three ways: static, semicontinuous, and continuous (3). In static casting, the melt is poured into a water-cooled mold of the desired shape. In semicontinuous and continuous techniques, molten

Figure 4. Extruded architectural bronze for structure mullions in the Seagram Building, New York City. Architect: Mies van der Rohe. Courtesy of Copper Development Association, Inc.

Figure 5. Stamped bronze fascia on the Hayden Building, El Monte, Calif. Architects: Ainsworth and McClellan. Courtesy of Copper Development Association, Inc.

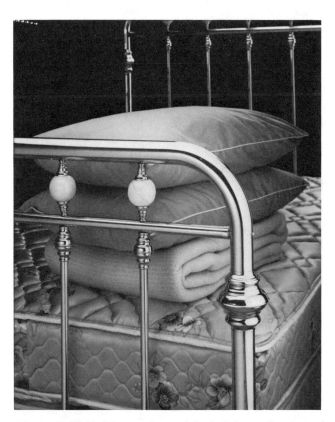

Figure 7. Welded brass tube used for bed frame. Courtesy of Revere Copper Products, Inc.

Figure 6. Solid extrusion of architectural bronze used in the spiral staircase of European American Bank, New York City. Architect: Carl J. Petrilli. Courtesy of Copper Development Association, Inc.

metal is poured into an open-end mold, and solidification is carried out mainly through direct chilling by water spray (4). The direct-chilling technique used in semicontinuous and continuous casting produces a cast material with superior microstructural integrity. Static casting, because of its slower solidification rate, exhibits more compositional inhomogeneity or segregation, and sometimes center cavities.

The direct-chill semicontinuous cast method is designed to produce large slabs from which heavyweight finished strip coils can be produced. The thick cast slabs must first be hot-rolled and then cold-rolled with a few intermediate annealings. Surface cleaning is needed if annealing is not conducted in an inert atmosphere containing hydrogen. Surface cleaning is usually accomplished by chemical means; however, mechanical means, such as grinding, minimize ecological–environmental problems.

Continuous casting produces rod and strip products without the need for hot working. The small cross-section rods and thin slabs can be directly cold-rolled to finish gauges. This method is especially beneficial for processing alloys that are susceptible to hot-short problems, such as phosphor bronze. Hot shortness is brittleness in hot metal, commonly related to impurity segregation at the grain boundary.

Rod, tube, shape, and bar products are usually produced by extrusion from billet, which may be cast by static, semi-continuous, or continuous methods. The process starts with

Table 2. Specific Applications of Architectural Brass and Bronze[a]

Application	C22000	C23000	C26000	C28000	C38500	C65500	C74500	C79600
Artwork	X	X	X	X	X	X	X	X
Bank equipment	X	X		X	X		X	X
Builders hardware	X	X	X		X		X	X
Curtain walls, store fronts	X	X		X	X		X	X
Ecclesiastical equipment	X	X	X	X				
Educational equipment	X	X	X	X	X		X	X
Elevators, escalators	X	X		X	X		X	X
Entrance doors and frames	X	X		X	X	X	X	X
Fire fighting devices	X	X		X				
Flag poles	X	X						
Floor tiles	X	X						
Food service equipment		X		X		X		
Furniture	X	X	X	X		X	X	
Grilles, screens	X	X	X		X		X	X
Identifying devices	X	X	X	X	X			
Lighting fixtures	X	X			X			
Louvers	X	X			X			
Mansards	X	X		X				
Plumbing fixtures	X	X	X					
Postal specialties	X	X	X	X				
Railings	X	X	X	X	X		X	X
Skylights					X			
Sun-control devices	X	X			X		X	X
Thresholds					X			X
Toilet and bath accessories	X	X	X		X			X
Wall coverings	X	X	X					
Wall panels	X	X		X				
Wall tiles	X	X	X					
Weather strippings	X	X						
Windows	X	X		X	X	X	X	X

[a] Ref. 2.

hot extrusion and follows with cold-drawing to the desired dimension. Intermediate annealings may be applied between cold-drawings.

For shape products, the ease with which a section can be extruded depends largely on its shape. A balanced section in which the flow of metal through the die is uniform throughout its area will extrude more easily, without uneven shrinkage or twisting, than one in which the flow tends to be too generous at one area and starved at the other. It is possible to produce almost any shape of cross-section by extrusion, but for cost effectiveness, one should avoid sudden changes in thickness, long thin fins, fine tapered edges, and deep slots. Figure 8 shows examples of various shapes.

Temper Designation

Temper is used by the copper industry to describe the metallurgical condition of a fabricated product resulting from its thermal and mechanical processing history. Temper designations are generally confined to basic metallurgical conditions involving grain size, amount of cold work, and degree of annealing.

The three basic temper categories for single-phase copper and copper-alloy plate, sheet, and strip are hot-worked, cold-worked, or annealed. Hot-worked temper is normally only applicable to plate, and is essentially the same as an annealed temper material having a similar grain structure.

The annealed tempers are determined by the grain size. Mechanical strength, work-hardening rate, ductility, and formability vary in a consistent manner with grain size. Grain size is usually determined by a metallograph or metallurgical microscope using direct-measurement method, line-intersection method, or by relative comparison with standard samples. The common nominal grain sizes in millimeters for annealed tempers are 0.010, 0.015, 0.025, 0.035, 0.045, 0.065, 0.090, 0.120, 0.150, and 0.200.

The cold-worked temper is defined by cold reduction in cold rolling and cold-drawing. The cold reduction is the percentage change in cross-section area of the work piece by cold-working. Tensile strength increases and ductility decreases with increasing cold-worked reduction. The relationship between cold reduction and temper designation is shown in Table 3.

Secondary Fabrication

Secondary fabrication is defined as the fabrication process applied to the mill stock to produce the product. Architectural brass and bronze lend themselves to a variety of fabricating techniques, including machining, forming, deep drawing, forging, stamping, laminating, and joining.

Various fabrication techniques have been well docu-

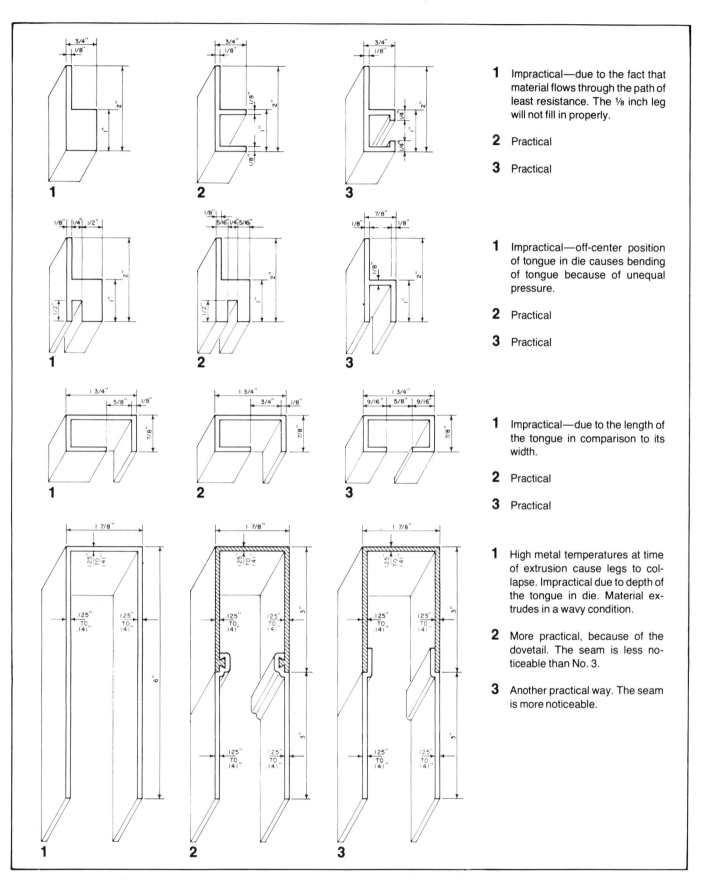

1 Impractical—due to the fact that material flows through the path of least resistance. The ⅛ inch leg will not fill in properly.

2 Practical

3 Practical

1 Impractical—off-center position of tongue in die causes bending of tongue because of unequal pressure.

2 Practical

3 Practical

1 Impractical—due to the length of the tongue in comparison to its width.

2 Practical

3 Practical

1 High metal temperatures at time of extrusion cause legs to collapse. Impractical due to depth of the tongue in die. Material extrudes in a wavy condition.

2 More practical, because of the dovetail. The seam is less noticeable than No. 3.

3 Another practical way. The seam is more noticeable.

Figure 8. Basic design criteria for extrusions. Courtesy of Copper Development Association, Inc.

Table 3. Temper Designation of Brass and Bronze

Nominal Temper	Cold-Rolled Temper		Cold-Drawn Temper	Tensile Strength of C26000	
	Reduction of Thickness by Rolling, %	B&S Numbers Hard[a]	Reduction of Area by Drawing, %	10^3 lb/in.^{2}	MPa
Eighth hard	6.0		11		
Quarter hard	10.95	1	21	49–59	338–407
Half hard	20.7	2	37	57–67	393–462
Three-quarter hard	29.4	3	49	64–74	441–510
Hard	37.1	4	60	71–81	490–555
Extra hard, full hard	50.15	5	75	83–92	572–634
Spring	60.5	8	84	91–100	627–689
Extra spring	68.65	10	90	95–104	655–717
Special spring	75.0		94		
Rivet			5–21		
Screw			15		

[a] B&S gauge numbers are a numerical scale established many years ago by the Brown and Sharpe Manufacturing Company (North Kingston, R.I.) to express the degree of reduction by rolling or drawing.

mented by the American Society for Metals in a series of handbooks (6). Metalworking in copper and its alloys, specifically for architectural applications, has also been documented by the British Copper Development Association (7).

This discussion is limited to the characteristics of architectural brass and bronze that influence their fabricating behavior, and some of the defects and difficulties that cause problems. There are four features that have the most effect on the fabricating behavior: (1) alloy chemistry; (2) microstructure and temper; (3) gauge or thickness; and (4) surface condition.

Workability and Formability. The basic crystal structure of copper and its alloys is face-centered cubic. This structure is very desirable because it allows considerable plastic deformation without fracture. Thus copper alloys are noted for their excellent press-working characteristics. The combination of strength, ductility, and work-hardening rates of coppers, brasses, and bronzes make these alloys among the most workable metals from which parts can be fabricated in presses. Table 4 summarizes the formability, workability, and machinability of various architectural brasses and bronzes.

The high zinc brasses, such as C24000 and C26000, have strengths comparable to the low carbon, mild steels. Their strength is coupled with high ductility and a relatively low work-hardening rate. They are outstanding materials for deep drawing and other press forming, including stretch forming, brake forming, and roll forming. With appropriate tool design and fabricating-process design, the most intricately shaped drawn parts can be fabricated economically from these alloys. The higher zinc C28000 brass is a two-phase alloy. It exhibits an excellent formability, but only at an elevated temperature, approximately in the range of 1100–1450°F (593–788°C).

The nickel silvers, C74500, and high silicon bronzes, C65100 and C65500, also have excellent deep-drawing characteristics like the high zinc brasses. However, they have somewhat higher work-hardening rates and require more interstage annealing than high zinc brasses.

The architectural bronze, C38500, and leaded nickel silver, C79600, are designed for high machinability. These alloys are not suitable for any forming process; however, a certain degree of forming and bending can be accomplished at an elevated temperature. The most common fabrication processes for these alloys are hot forging and pressing, and machining.

Table 4. Formability, Workability, and Machinability of Architectural Brass and Bronze[a]

Alloy Designation	C22000	C23000	C26000	C28000	C38500	C65100	C65500	C74500	C79600
Cold workability	Excellent	Excellent	Excellent	Fair	Poor	Excellent	Excellent	Excellent	Good
Annealing temperature, °C	425–800	425–725	425–750	425–600	425–600	475–675	475–700	600–750	500–620
Hot formability	Good	Good	Fair	Excellent	Excellent	Excellent	Excellent	Poor	Poor
Hot-working temperature, °C	750–875	800–900	725–850	625–800	625–725	700–875	700–875		
Machinability rating[b]	20	30	30	40	90	30	30	20	60

[a] Ref. 8.
[b] Free-cutting brass = 100.

Joining. *Mechanical Joining.* The most common joining methods for architectural components are by mechanical means, such as screws, bolts, and rivets. In some applications where a complete seal is required, soldering or adhesive joining may be applied in addition to mechanical joining. In the use of fasteners, strength, color matching, and corrosion are the main concerns. If strength permits, the use of a similar alloy for both substrate and fastener will eliminate problems relative to color matching and galvanic corrosion. Table 5 shows the most commonly used fastener alloys and their characteristics.

Metallurgical Joining. Metallurgical joining involves a metallurgical diffusion of the two metals being joined. The most common metallurgical joinings are brazing, soldering, and welding (9,10,11).

Brazing uses a nonferrous filler metal with a melting point above 800°F, but lower than that of the base metals. The molten filler metal is drawn between the closely fitted surfaces of the joint by capillary action.

Brazing produces good metallurgical bonding with good joint strength; loss of desirable properties and distortion can be minimized through proper alignment and the use of suitable jigs and fixtures. All exposed joints should be ground off to remove excess brazing alloy, thus minimizing color differences. Most common brazing alloys for copper alloys contain copper, silver, and zinc.

Soldering is a relatively low temperature joining process using lead-base or tin-base alloy, solder filler metals that melt below 500°F; it is widely used for sealing joints, especially in gutter and flashing work. In order to assure adequate strength, soldered joints are normally reinforced mechanically using clinch locks, rivets, or screws. Soldering should be confined to concealed joints since tin–lead

solders do not match the color of any of the copper alloys.

Welding is a high temperature joining process involving melting or fusion of the base metals with or without the addition of filler metal. Welding is seldom used for exposed joints because sound, color-matched welds are difficult to achieve, and joint distortion is a significant problem, except for silicon bronzes (C65500), which are readily welded.

The suitability of various metallurgical joining techniques for various architectural brasses and bronzes is shown in Table 6. Figure 9 shows a few examples of mechanical joints as well as a combination of mechanical and metallurgical joints for extruded products.

Laminations. Brass and bronze can be successfully laminated to steel, plywood, cement, asbestos board, and similar substrates to achieve economical architectural components. By utilizing the lamination technique, thinner gauges of architectural copper alloys can be employed, since strength and rigidity are imparted to the composite by the substrate.

Although metallurgical bonding can be achieved between two different metals, the more economical technique of adhesive bonding is commonly used for architectural applications. Satisfactory bonding is dependent upon: (1) surface preparation; (2) proper adhesive; and (3) bonding procedure. For exterior applications, a thermosetting or high quality thermoplastic adhesive is recommended (12,13). Edge support and edge design are critical to prevent peeling and moisture entry.

Shapes Drawn from Strip or Tube. A large amount of architectural metalwork is made of strip or tube into shaped sections by drawing, rolling, or extrusion. The cross-section could be hollow or have wood cores.

Table 5. Common Fastener Alloys of Brass and Bronze[a]

Fasteners	Characteristics
Alloys C26000, cartridge brass	Used for full range of medium strength, cold-headed, and roll-threaded screws, bolts, and nuts. Color matches only to alloy C26000 sheet, tube, and rod.
Alloy C28000, Muntz brass	Used for low strength screws, nuts, and bolts where color match is critical. Excellent color matches with alloy C38500.
Alloy C36000, free-cutting brass	Used for full range of medium-to-low strength machine screws, bolts, and nuts. Good color match with alloy C26000.
Alloys C46400–C46700, naval brass	Used for full range of medium strength screws, bolts, and nuts. Fair-to-good color match; slightly more yellow than alloy C38500.
Alloy C48500, naval brass, high leaded	Used for machine screws, bolts, and nuts of medium-to-low strength. Color match with alloys C28000 and C38500 is fair-to-good. Color is yellow.
Alloy C65100, low-silicon bronze	Used for full range of medium-to-high strength nails, screws, bolts, and nuts, where color match is not critical. Color is slightly redder than that of alloy C38500.
Alloy C65500, high-silicon bronze	Used for special hot-headed bolts, or bolts of large diameter or long lengths, where color match is not critical. Color is slightly redder than that of alloy C38500.
Alloy C74500, nickel silver 65–10	Used for full range of medium-to-high strength, cold-headed, roll-threaded (coarse-threaded) screws, alloy C74500 sheet, tube, and rod as well as alloy C79600.

[a] Ref. 2.

Table 6. Welding, Soldering, and Brazing of Architectural Brass and Bronze[a]

Joining techniques	Rating[b]								
	C22000	C23000	C26000	C28000	C38500	C65100	C65500	C74500	C79600
Oxyacetylene welding	G	G	G	G	N	G	G	G	N
Gas-shielded arc welding	G	G	F	F	N	E	E	F	N
Coated-metal arc welding	N	N	N	N	N	F	F	N	N
Resistance welding									
Spot	N	F	G	G	N	E	E	G	N
Seam	N	N	N	N	N	G	E	F	N
Butt	G	G	G	G	F	E	E	G	F
Soldering	E	E	E	E	E	E	G	E	E
Brazing	E	E	E	E	G	E	E	E	G

[a] Ref. 1.
[b] E = excellent; G = good; F = fair; and N = not recommended.

With wood cores, the principal requirement is for the metal to fit tightly over the wood without any tendency to lift. This is normally accomplished by forming a dovetailed groove or rebate in the wood, into which the edges of the metal are pressed (7). This wood-cored shape is manufactured by drawing wood and metal strip together through a special design die. It is essential that wood cores are of straight-grained, stable timber. A hardwood, such as mahogany, is usually preferred.

Casting. In certain architectural applications, direct castings of the finished form are desirable. In that case, sand mold or metal mold with the desirable shape is needed so that molten brass or bronze can be poured in.

The composition of alloys used for casting is normally different from that of wrought alloys because of different requirement criteria. Articles formed by casting usually do not require deformation; therefore, ductility of the alloy is not a critical requirement. Fluidity, which is the ability of a molten alloy to flow into thin sections, is the major requirement for cast alloy. Dross and gas formation and shrinkage are other considerations for the cast alloys. In general, higher impurity levels can be tolerated for cast alloys than for wrought alloys.

The Copper Development Association's standard handbook, *Alloy Data: Cast Products* (14) lists all of the cast alloys. For color matching with a wrought product, the user can select the alloy from the handbook that has a similar major component.

DESIGN CRITERIA

Gauge Consideration

Oil canning or buckling, which adversely affects appearance, is a common problem in the use of sheet and strip; as the metal gauge decreases, distortion becomes more pronounced. Since bright, flat metal surfaces reflect light, minor deviations in flatness become quite apparent. The problem can be eliminated or alleviated by the use of a metal with sufficient thickness, or in a more economical way, by using lamination with a backing that assures sufficient rigidity and stiffness, and minimizes distortion.

For example, a gauge of 0.100 in. or thicker may be required for an unsupported 3 × 3-ft flat sheet to avoid waves and buckles. If the sheet is deformed or corrugated with a pattern that breaks up the flat surface, or if it is made rigid by lamination, the gauge may be reduced to as low as 0.032 in. On monumental work, however, 0.080-in. gauge may be preferred; as in most instances, there is less labor involved in forming either 0.064 or 0.080-in. gauge metal than the lighter gauge.

Thermal Expansion

Thermal expansion as related to the change in temperature is an important consideration in using metals for architectural applications. A proper design allowing changes in dimension without adversely affecting the integrity of the architectural components is essential. Thermal expansion coefficients of various architectural brasses and bronzes are listed in Table 1. An example of total change in length in 100 ft for a 100°F temperature change for a few alloys, as calculated from their thermal expansion coefficients, is shown in Table 7.

Galvanic Corrosion

Galvanic action resulting in accelerated corrosion may occur when two different metals are in contact, especially in the presence of moisture. The problem can be eliminated by using insulation at the contact, such as zinc chromate or red-lead primer, bituminous or asphaltic compounds, or an appropriate sealant or tape.

Galvanic action poses more serious problems when the two metals possess a significant difference in nobility, such as that between aluminum alloy and copper alloy, or that between carbon steel and copper alloy. The less noble metals, ie, aluminum and carbon steel, will produce pitting corrosion when coupled with copper alloys. It should be noted that coupling of two different copper alloys should

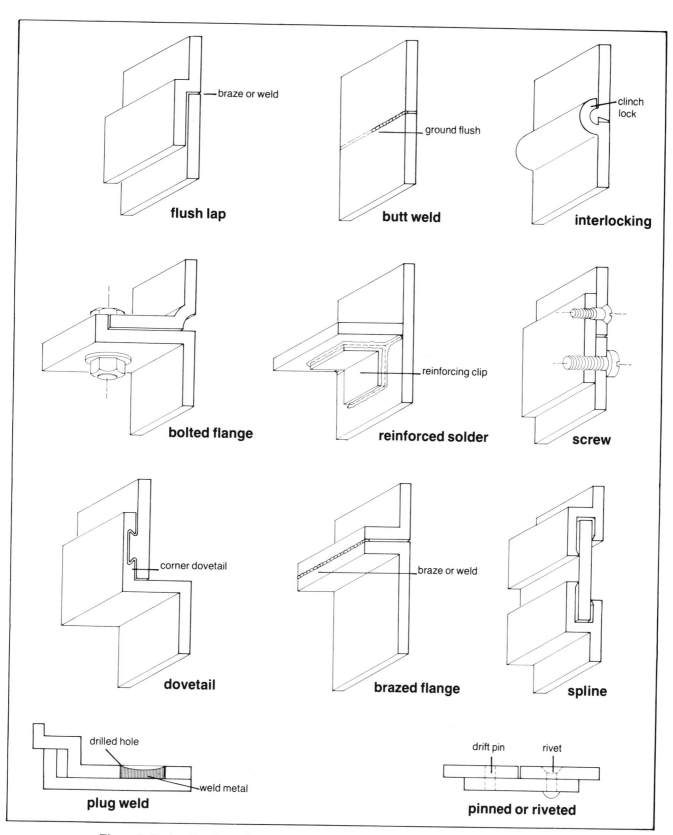

Figure 9. Design of mechanical and metallurgical joints. Courtesy of Copper Development Association, Inc.

Table 7. Change in Length Owing to Thermal Expansion[a]

Alloy	Length Change in 100 Ft Per 100°F, In.
C22000	0.122
C26000	0.133
C38500	0.139
C65500	0.120
C74500	0.109

[a] Ref. 1.

not cause galvanic corrosion. Also, direct contact of a copper alloy with stainless steel should not pose serious problems unless water is allowed to accumulate at the joint line.

Stress-corrosion Cracking

Stress-corrosion cracking can occur in most brasses and bronzes. It occurs only in certain environments and only when the material is under stress, or has residual stress from deformation applied during fabrication. The three common environments that can cause stress corrosion in brasses and bronzes are ammonia vapors and solutions, amines, and water or water vapor. The relative stress-corrosion rate of various architectural brasses and bronzes is shown in Table 8.

Stress-corrosion cracking can be prevented by a stress-relief annealing that removes or reduces the residual stresses without affecting the temper and mechanical properties of the material. This can be accomplished by a low temperature annealing. It is advisable to review design details with the fabricator to determine the need for a stress-relief annealing.

FINISHING

Because of their attractive natural appearance after weathering, brasses and bronzes are sometimes left untreated. However, there are instances where finishes are desired initially. There are four common techniques for

Table 8. Relative Stress-corrosion Cracking of Architectural Brass and Bronzes in Moist Ammoniacal Atmosphere[a]

Alloys	Time to 50% Relaxation, Hr[b]
C28000	0.35
C26000	0.51
C23000	1.53
C22000	13.1
C74500	28.3
C65500	354.0
ETP copper[c]	2000.0

[a] Ref. 15.
[b] This is the time required for a 50% stress relaxation as a result of stress-corrosion cracking. The shorter the time, the more severe the stress-corrosion cracking.
[c] ETP copper is electrolytic, tough pitch copper, which is 99.90% (minimum) copper with 0.04% nominal oxygen.

surface finishing: (1) mechanical finishing; (2) chemical finishing; (3) applied finishing; and (4) chemical coloring.

Mechanical Finishing

Mechanical finishes are produced by mechanical means to achieve the desired surface appearance. The untreated, as fabricated surface can be called a mill finish. The surfaces of mill finishes usually exhibit visible parallel lines from rolling, extrusion, or drawing.

Mechanical finishing applied on mill products can produce various desired surface appearances, such as bright polished finishes, directional textured finishes, nondirectional textured finishes, and pattern finishes.

Bright polished finishes are produced by successive processes of grinding, polishing, and buffing. Because of the cost and their high reflectivity, these finishes are not used on wide flat surfaces, but are limited primarily to small accent areas.

Directional textured finishes are among the most common and popular finishes used by the architect. These finishes appear smooth and have a soft satin texture as a result of fine parallel scratches. They are produced by wheel or belt polishing with fine abrasives, by hand polishing with steel wool, or by brushing with abrasive wheels.

Nondirectional textured finishes are matte finishes produced by sand or metal-shot spraying. The roughness of the matte surface can be varied by the use of different particle sizes of sand and metal shot. These finishes are commonly applied on the castings.

Pattern finishes are produced by a rolling process employing patterned or embossed rolls. This could be from matched-design rolls or only one roll with a pattern (16).

More details on mechanical finishing of brasses and bronzes can be found in references 6 and 17.

Chemical Finishing

Chemical finishing involves the use of a chemical to react with the metal surface. Pickling, bright dipping, and matte dipping are three major chemical finishings used by the industry (18).

Pickling is the removal of surface oxides by an acid treatment. It leaves the surface free of oxides, but not with a bright color or luster. Bright dipping gives a clean, bright lustrous surface. Prior to bright dipping, a pickling is necessary to prepare the surface for the bright dip.

The following dips are typical:

Pickling	% By Vol
Concentrated nitric acid (HNO_3, specific gravity (sp gr) 1.40)	40
Concentrated sulfuric acid (H_2SO_4, sp gr 1.83)	30
Concentrated hydrochloric acid (HCl, sp gr 1.16)	0.5
Water	29.5

Bright Dip	% By Vol
Concentrated nitric acid (HNO_3, sp gr 1.40)	25
Concentrated sulfuric acid (H_2SO_4, sp gr 1.83)	60
Concentrated hydrochloric acid (HCl, sp gr 1.16)	0.2
Water	14.8

The dips are used at room temperature; the metal is rinsed in running cold water after each dip, and immersed in sodium cyanide solution (2–4 oz/gal) with a final water rinse.

Matte Dip. To produce a light matte finish on brasses and bronzes, the metal is placed in the following solution after bright dip.

Matte Dip	% By Vol
Concentrated nitric acid (HNO_3, sp gr 1.40)	65
Concentrated sulfuric acid (H_2SO_4, sp gr 1.83)	35
Zinc sulfate ($ZnSO_4$, commercial)	1 lb/gal solution

This dip is used at 180°F; the metal is rinsed and dried in the usual manner.

Other chemical finishings can be accomplished by electrolytic polishing, etching, or electroplating.

Preservation and Coating

The natural color, warmth, and metallic tones inherent in brass and bronze can be preserved by applying transparent protective coatings. The most commonly used preservation coatings are as follows:

1. *Alkyd coatings.* The service life of this coating can be significantly improved by mixing with melamine resins, making it applicable for exterior use.
2. *Acrylic coatings.* These coatings provide good color retention and resistance to chemicals, impact, and abrasion. Two compositions are available for air drying and thermosetting. An improved acrylic developed by International Copper Research Association (INCRA) called Incralac is an air-drying lacquer which can be used in both indoor and outdoor applications (19).
3. *Cellulose acetate butyrate.* These coatings are used for interior application. They are air-drying types with moderate cost and fair-to-good performance properties.
4. *Epoxy coatings.* Epoxy coatings have excellent resistance to impact, abrasion, and chemicals. They are only available in thermosetting form. They are good for severe indoor applications.
5. *Nitrocellulose coatings.* These are the least expensive and most common air-drying coatings for interior service. When used outdoors, they must be stripped and replaced at intervals of less than one year.
6. *Silicone coatings.* Silicones provide the best potential coating at elevated temperatures or under other severe exposure conditions. For exterior exposure, ultraviolet-absorbing compounds are added to prevent darkening.
7. *Urethane coatings.* These coatings are available in both air-drying and thermosetting forms. Resistance to chemicals and abrasion are excellent. The resins are relatively expensive.
8. *Oils and waxes.* The natural color of brass and bronze can be enhanced by the frequent application of oils and waxes. These coatings are, however, primarily used for maintenance purposes on site.
9. *Opaque coatings.* Painting, vitreous enamel, and various metallic coatings and plating can be applied to brass and bronze.

Chemical Coloring

Chemical coloring of brasses and bronzes has appealed to the human artistic instinct. Coloring supplements the inherent usefulness of the metals. This added feature has been of particular value in architectural applications. Chemical coloring techniques depend on time, temperature, surface preparation, humidity, and other variables. These coloring techniques can result in greens, reds, blues, yellows, browns, black, and shades of gray. The techniques are described in plating and finishing handbooks (20,21).

Some examples of these formulae and techniques are given below (18).

Brown on Yellow Brass

Surface:	Buffed.
Preparation:	Hot alkaline cleaner, cold water rinse; cyanide dip, cold water rinse.
Solution used:	Sodium dichromate, 20 oz Nitric acid (sp gr 1.42), 2½ fluid oz Hydrochloric acid (sp gr 1.20), ¾ fluid oz Wetting agent, 1/10 oz Water, 1 gal
Procedure:	One-minute immersion at room temperature (70°F), agitating the work at 15-s intervals. Rinse in cold and hot water; dry by air blast. Coat with a clear nitrocellulose lacquer.
Remarks:	The film is easily removed when wet; after drying, it is very adherent if properly applied.

Gold on Yellow Brass

Surface:	Buffed.
Preparation:	Hot alkaline cleaner, cold water rinse; cyanide dip, cold water rinse.

Solution used:
Sodium dichromate, 20 oz
Nitric acid (sp gr 1.42), 2½ fluid oz
Hydrochloric acid (sp gr 1.20), ¾ fluid oz
Sulfuric acid (sp gr 1.84), ⅜ fluid oz
Wetting agent, 1/10 oz
Water, 1 gal

Procedure:
One-minute immersion at room temperature (70°F), agitating the work at 15-s intervals. Rinse in cold and hot water; dry by air blast. Coat with a clear nitrocellulose lacquer.

Remarks:
The film is easily removed when wet; after drying, it is very adherent if properly applied.

Blue Black on Yellow Brass

Surface:
Buffed (glossy finish), bright dipped, or matte finished.

Preparation:
Hot alkaline cleaner, cold water rinse; cyanide dip, cold water rinse.

Solution used:
Copper carbonate, 16 oz
Ammonium hydroxide (sp gr 0.90), ¼ gal
Water, ¾ gal
(An excess of copper carbonate is required.)

Procedure:
Approximately ten-second immersion at 180–200°F. Cold water rinse, alkaline rinse; cold water rinse, alcohol rinse (avoid excess accumulation of water); dry in clean sawdust. Coat with a clear nitrocellulose lacquer.

Light Green on Yellow Brass

Surface:
Bright dipped.

Preparation:
Hot alkaline cleaner, cold water rinse; cyanide dip (4 oz NaCN/gal), cold water rinse.

Solution used:
Sodium dichromate, 20 oz
Phosphoric acid (sp gr 1.71), 1¼ fluid oz
Wetting agent, 1/10 oz
Water, 1 gal

Procedure:
Immersion for 40–60 min in cold solution without agitation of the work. (It is important, of course, to use a wetting agent that is not changed in the solution.) Rinse in hot and cold water; dry by air blast. Coat with a clear nitrocellulose lacquer.

Remarks:
The film is easily removed when wet; after drying, it is very adherent if applied slowly.

The immersion time may be reduced to three minutes by the addition of 1/10 fluid oz of hydrochloric acid and slow but constant agitation. With the use of hydrochloric acid, however, the film, while formed more rapidly, has a tendency to become friable when dry. In this instance, therefore, the parts should be cleaned and covered immediately with clear lacquer.

Steel Gray on Yellow Brass

Surface:
Bright dipped.

Preparation:
Hot alkaline cleaner, cold water rinse; cyanide dip, cold water rinse.

Solution used:
Arsenic trioxide (AS_2O_3), 4 oz
Hydrochloric acid (sp gr 1.20), 8½ fluid oz
Sulfuric acid (sp gr 1.84), 2 fluid oz
Water, 1 gal

Procedure:
Immerse 5–10 s at room temperature (70°F). Rinse with cold and hot water; dry by air blast. Coat with a clear nitrocellulose lacquer.

Statuary Bronze on Yellow Brass

Surface:
Bright dipped.

Preparation:
Hot alkaline cleaner, cold water rinse; cyanide dip, cold water rinse.

Solution used:
Copper carbonate, 16 oz
Ammonium hydroxide (sp gr 0.90), ¼ gal
Water, ¾ gal

Procedure:
Immerse for approximately 10 s at 180–200°F. Rinse with cold water. Develop a brown color by immersion for a few seconds in a dilute sulfuric acid solution (2 fluid oz/gal of water). Rinse thoroughly in cold water; dry by air blast. Remove smut with a clean soft rag or sawdust. Coat with a clear nitrocellulose lacquer.

Black on Yellow Brass

Surface:
Bright dipped.

Preparation:
Hot alkaline cleaner, cold water rinse; cyanide dip, cold water rinse.

Solution used and procedure:
Suspend the work in a hot, caustic soda solution (8 oz sodium hydroxide/gal of water) for a few minutes; then transfer to another caustic soda solution of the same strength to which 1 oz of potassium persulfate/gal is added and heat to incipient boiling. Immerse the work for 10 min. Rinse thoroughly in cold and hot water; dry by air blast. Smooth the black-velvet-like film by rubbing with a clean soft cloth. Coat with a clear nitrocellulose lacquer.

Black on Copper

Surface:
Buffed.

Preparation:
Hot alkaline cleaner, cold water rinse; cyanide dip, cold water rinse.

Solution used:
Potassium sulfide, 2 oz
Water, 1 gal

Procedure: Immerse for 5–10 s at 100°F. Rinse in cold and hot water; dry by air blast. Coat with a clear nitrocellulose lacquer.

Royal Copper on Copper

Surface: Bright dipped and buffed.
Preparation: Hot alkaline cleaner, cold water rinse; cyanide dip, cold water rinse. Dry by air blast.
Solution used: Molten potassium nitrate (1200–1300°F, dark red) in an iron container.
Procedure: Immerse for 20 s. Quench in hot water; dry and buff. Coat with a clear nitrocellulose lacquer.

MAINTENANCE AND PROTECTION

Maintenance of metal surfaces covers periodic cleaning and protection of surfaces, including restoration of the original finish and color.

It is imperative that a regular maintenance schedule be established and followed with regular inspections. There should be a different maintenance schedule for interior and exterior surfaces, and those exposed to scuffing and abrasion.

On a regular maintenance schedule, most surfaces can be maintained by oiling or waxing. Some surfaces may require lacquering and, a few, polishing. Oiling can be accomplished by the use of lemon oil, lemon brass oil, or a high grade paraffin oil. Quality commercial paste waxes can be used satisfactorily. Initially, new surfaces should be oiled or waxed frequently to build up a protective film.

Restoration or renovation of surfaces that have become encrusted with dirt or corrosion products may require more drastic treatment than soap and water. These surfaces may be cleaned with a mixture of 5% oxalic acid in water and pumice powder.

To prevent damage to finished surfaces during transportation, handling, and storage, the use of protective wrappings or strippable coatings may be required. Care in the selection of protective wrappings should be exercised to avoid wrappings that contain sulfides which react with brasses and bronzes.

Strippable coatings employed may be any number of spray-on vinyl plastics or pressure-sensitive paper and/or plastic film (22,23).

TECHNICAL LITERATURE AND MATERIAL SOURCES

There are four major sources of technical literature regarding brasses and bronzes: (1) the Copper Development Association, Inc. located in Greenwich, Conn.; (2) the International Copper Research Association located in New York City; (3) the British Copper Development Association located in London; and (4) the Japan Copper and Brass Research Association located in Tokyo.

The following standards handbooks, available at the CDA office, cover material terminology, specification, toler-

ance, and sources of semifinished mill products in the United States:

1. *Standards Handbook No. 1: Wrought Mill Products—Tolerances.*
2. *Standards Handbook No. 2: Wrought Mill Products—Alloy Data.*
3. *Standards Handbook No. 3: Wrought Mill Products—Terminology.*
4. *Standards Handbook No. 4: Wrought Mill Products—Engineering.*
5. *Standards Handbook No. 5: Wrought and Cast Products—Materials Sources.*
6. *Standards Handbook No. 6: Wrought and Cast Products—Specification Index.*
7. *British CDA No. TN26: The Brasses—Technical Data.*

Also published by CDA are several important publications documenting technical aspects and materials sources specifically related to architectural applications: (1) *Contemporary Copper in Architecture;* (2) *Copper, Brass, and Bronze in Architecture;* (3) *Copper, Brass, and Bronze Design Handbook—Architectural Applications;* (4) *Copper, Brass, and Bronze for Building Products—Source Book for Doors, Windows, Curtain Walls, Store Fronts, and Hardware;* (5) *Copper, Brass, and Bronze for Building Products—Source Book for Elevators, Escalators, and Other Conveying Systems;* and (6) *Architectural Metalwork in Copper and its Alloys* (British CDA).

The following CDA technical publications are also important references in the use of brasses and bronzes for architecture: (1) *Clear Organic Finishes for Copper and Copper Alloys;* (2) *Copper, Brass, and Bronze: Maintenance, Finishes, and Coloring;* (3) *Welding, Soldering, Brazing, and Surfacing of Copper and Copper Alloys;* and (4) *How to Apply Surface Colors.*

BIBLIOGRAPHY

1. *CDA Standards Handbook—Wrought Mill Products,* Copper Development Association, Inc., Greenwich, Conn.
2. *CDA Design Handbook—Architectural Application,* Copper Development Association, Inc., Greenwich, Conn., 1977.
3. *Metals Handbook,* Vol. 5, American Society for Metals, Metals Park, Ohio, 1982.
4. M. Sugiyama, "Melting Techniques for Copper Alloy Castings," *Casting Forging* **22**(9), 1(1969).
5. *Understanding Copper Alloys,* Olin Corp., East Alton, Ill., 1977.
6. *Metals Handbook,* Vols. 2–6, American Society for Metals, Metals Park, Ohio, 1979, 1980, 1981, 1982, 1983.
7. A. L. McMullen, *Architectural Metalwork in Copper and its Alloys,* Publication No. 63, Copper Development Association of United Kingdom, London, 1963.
8. *CDA Standards Handbook—Wrought Mill Products,* Copper Development Association, Inc., Greenwich, Conn.
9. *The Brazing Book,* Handy and Harman, New York, 1972.

10. I. Kawakatsu, "Soldering and Brazing of Copper and Copper Alloy," *J. Jpn. Copper Brass Res. Assoc.* **11**, Pl-9 (1972).

11. K. Wold, "Welding Copper and Copper Alloys," *Met. Prog.* **108**, 43 (1975).

12. E. M. Huffaker and M. F. Adams, *Washington State University Programs Report No. 5* and *Final Report,* sponsored by Copper Development Association, Inc., Greenwich, Conn., 1968.

13. R. M. Kell and C. W. Cooper, *Adhesive Bonding Copper and Copper Alloys to Other Building Materials,* CDA Technical Report No. 406/6, Copper Development Association, Inc., Greenwich, Conn., 1966.

14. *CDA Standards Handbook, Alloy Data: Cast Products,* Vol. 7, Copper Development Association, Inc., Greenwich, Conn., 1978.

15. D. H. Thompson, *Materials Records and Standards,* 1961, pp. 108–111.

16. *Metal Finishes Manual,* 3rd ed., National Association of Architectural Metal Manufacturers, Oak Park, Ill., 1975.

17. "Cleaning and Finishing of Copper and Copper Alloys," *ASM Source Book,* American Society for Metals, Metals Park, Ohio.

18. *Maintenance, Cleaning, Finishing, and Coloring of Copper Brass and Bronze,* CDA Report, Copper Development Association, Inc., Greenwich, Conn., 1959.

19. *Development of an Improved Incralac,* Report No. 83, International Copper Research Association, New York, 1967.

20. *Plating and Finishing Guidebook,* Metal Industry Publishing Co., New York.

21. W. H. Safranek, *Colored Finishes for Copper and Copper Alloys,* Technical Report, Copper Development Association, Inc., Greenwich, Conn., 1968.

22. A. D. Little, *Protective Coatings for Copper Metals,* Report No. C67965, International Copper Research Association, New York, 1969.

23. *Evaluation of Clear for Protection of Copper Base Alloys,* Report No. 16, International Copper Research Association, New York, 1966.

See also AMINO RESINS; CELLULOSE AND CELLULOSE DERIVATIVES; COPPER; CORROSION; EPOXY RESINS; SILICONES; URETHANES.

EVAN LING, PhD
Diamond Bar, California

DONALD DESTITO
Memphis, Tennessee

BREUER, MARCEL

Marcel Breuer (1902–1981) was attracted to the year-old Weimar Bauhaus by its idealistic program that promised new approaches to art and architecture away from the iconoclastic methods of the past. The 18-year-old from Pecs, Hungary, demonstrated an extraordinary talent and energy in the Vorkurs and workshops. His objective, however, was architecture, and though it was not yet a part of the formal curriculum, in the spring of 1924, Breuer, with the advice of Georg Muche, began a collaborative work group to study housing and particularly high-rise structures. Breuer produced a design for a seven-story apartment block that would become a prototype. One of the first to complete his diploma requirements, he became a young master when the school moved to Dessau in 1925. It was during those years that Breuer created his famed Wassily steel and leather sling chair and other innovative furniture designs; he was then in charge of the furniture workshop.

A few months following Gropius's resignation in April 1928 from the Bauhaus, Breuer followed suit and attempted unsuccessfully for three difficult years to establish his practice in Berlin. This was followed by almost four years of wandering in Europe and North Africa. Two projects were realized during this period: the house for Harnischmacher in Wiesbaden, and the Doldertal apartment building for Sigfried Giedion in Zurich. In 1935, Gropius, who was in London, obtained employment for Breuer; there he designed his famous chaise lounge for Isokon, and with F. R. S. Yorke, he designed a noteworthy exhibition pavilion for Bristol. Two years later at Harvard, Gropius invited Breuer to assist him in the masters class in architecture as research associate (in 1938, as associate professor) and to join him in practice. Their team teaching was highly successful judging by the accomplishments of alumni. The most significant projects of the partnership were their own homes in Lincoln, Mass., and the housing project for defense industry workers at New Kensington, Pa., which established a new high standard of design for the federal government. There were other houses in New England, a mansion in Pittsburgh, and an interior for the Pennsylvania Pavilion at the 1939 New York World's Fair. Breuer resigned from the partnership in 1941 to begin his own practice and from the university in 1946. In New York, he was joined at intervals beginning in 1953 by Herbert Beckhard, Robert Gatje, Hamilton Smith, and Tician Papachristou. The first internationally important building project was the UNESCO building in Paris with Bernard Zehrfuss and Pier Luigi Nervi. Among other

Figure 1. Department of Housing and Urban Development, Washington, DC. Courtesy of the Department of Housing and Urban Development.

Figure 2. Department of Health and Human Services, Washington, DC. Courtesy of the Department of Health and Human Services.

projects of note are the St. John's Abbey Church in Collegeville, Minn., and the Whitney Museum of American Art in New York, both with Smith as associate; the building for the Department of Housing and Urban Development (Fig. 1) and that for the Department of Health and Human Services (Fig. 2), both in Washington with Beckhard as associate; and the IBM-France building with Gatje as associate in La Gaude, France.

Recognition and honors grew rapidly, particularly beginning in the 1950s. Among his awards are the Gold Medal of the American Institute of Architects, and honorary degrees from Harvard and the Technical University of Budapest. He is the subject of numerous articles and books, although too modest and too busy to have been the author of more than a few.

BIBLIOGRAPHY

General References

P. Blake, *Marcel Breuer, Architect and Designer,* New York, The Museum of Modern Art, New York, 1949.

M. Breuer, *Sun and Shadow, The Philosophy of an Architect,* Dodd, Mead, & Co., New York, 1956.

M. Breuer, "Les buts de l'architecture," *Architecture; formes et fonctions,* (9) 6–29 (1962–1963).

M. Breuer, "Genesis of Design," in G. Kepes, ed., *The Manmade Object,* G. Braziller, New York 1966, pp. 120–125.

K. Ichinowatari, ed., *MBA: The Legacy of Marcel Breuer,* Process Architecture, Tokyo, Japan, 1982.

A. Izzo and C. Gubitosi, *Marcel Breuer: Architettura 1921–1980,* Florence, Italy, 1981.

T. Papachristou, *Marcel Breuer, New Building and Projects,* Praeger Publishers, New York, 1970.

C. Wilk, *Marcel Breuer, Furniture and Interiors,* The Museum of Modern Art, New York, 1981.

See also BAUHAUS; FURNITURE; GROPIUS, WALTER; MUSEUMS.

REGINALD ISAACS
Cambridge, Massachusetts

BRICK MASONRY

HISTORY

Architecture has been the faithful chronicler of civilization. Man's cultural development is vividly recorded in buildings. Written history requires much imagination to picture how it must have been, but in architecture, each of the great ages of man can be glimpsed, the atmosphere felt, and the spatial environment sensed. This heritage is recorded in the durability of manufactured building materials, and one of the most enduring of these is brick. Technology had its origin in art. Most industrial materials, metals and ceramics alike, had their beginning in the decorative arts. Baked clay figurines preceded the useful pot. Pottery came before brick.

The introduction of ceramics into prehistoric culture was a significant intellectual development. Stoneworkers and wood craftsmen, however skilled, only rework available material. Clay workers transform unrelated materials into something entirely new. The raw materials must be correctly proportioned, shaped functionally, and burned within close temperature tolerance.

Man used clay as a building material well before he is said to have been civilized. He has used clay as a masonry unit perhaps longer than he has been civilized, about 11,000 years. He will undoubtedly continue to do so for a very long time. The architectural ages outlined in Table 1 are preserved in a universe of brick building of which a very few examples are illustrations of historical brick architecture.

BRICK TYPES

Brick belongs to the clay construction product group, which includes drain tile, sewer pipe, terra cotta, structural clay tile, and adobe. The American Society for Testing and Materials (ASTM) has standard specifications for eleven kinds of brick, ie, manhole and sewer brick (C32), clay building brick (C62), facing brick (C216), chemical-resistant brick (279), floor brick (C410), hollow brick (C652), paving brick (C902), chimney brick (C980), concrete brick (C55), glazed brick (C126), and sand–lime brick (C73). This article is concerned only with floor and paving brick, and clay building and facing brick. Building and facing brick have the same durability requirements, but only facing brick has aesthetic requirements. Sheppard (1) discusses chemical-resistant masonry; McHenry (2) discusses adobe.

BRICK MANUFACTURE

The manufacturing process consists of excavating; grinding; tempering with water; shaping; drying; and firing (3). Clay is perhaps the world's most abundant raw material for building products. It is a compound of silica and alumina with various metallic oxides, which provide characteristic colors when brick is fired. Clays occurring on

Table 1. A Summary of Brick in the History of Architecture

| Styles | Ages | Great Brick Building | | |
		Name	Location	Date
Asiatic				
Babylonian	4000–1275 B.C.	City of Ur	Chaldees, Iraq	3500 B.C.
Assyrian	1275–538 B.C.	Istar Gate	Babylon, Iraq	575 B.C.
Persian	538–333 B.C.	Xerxes Palace	Persepolis, Iran	ca 485 B.C.
Egyptian				
Ancient	4400–2466 B.C.	Pyramid	Sakkara, Egypt	ca. 3733 B.C.
Middle	2466–1600 B.C.	Pyramid of Amenemhet III	Dahshur, Egypt	ca 1820 B.C.
New	1600–332 B.C.	First Temple of Rameses III	Luxor, Egypt	ca 1180 B.C.
Ptolemaic	332–30 B.C.	Great Temple	Tanis, Egypt	ca 300 B.C.
Greek	3000–700 B.C.	House of Tiles	Lerna, Greece	ca 2000 B.C.
	700–146 B.C.	Cyrene	Tripoli, Greece	ca 600 B.C.
Roman	509 B.C.–369 A.D.	Pantheon	Rome, Italy	Rebuilt ca 118 A.D.
Early Christian	313–800	Baptistry	Ravenna, Italy	449
Byzantine	324–1453	Hagia Sophia	Istanbul, Turkey	Rebuilt 537
Islamic	622–present	Madrasa Mader-i-Shah	Isfahan, Iran	1706
Romanesque	800–1200	Cathedral	St. Albans, England	1077
Gothic	1200–1500	Cathedral	Albi, France	1282
Renaissance	1400–1850	Dome of St. Peter's Basilica	Rome, Italy	1506
Early American	1607–1850	Bruton Church	Williamsburg, Va.	1715
Contemporary	1850–present	Robie House	Chicago, Ill.	1908

the earth's surface are sedimentary. When subjected naturally to high pressure, clays become nearly as hard as slate and are termed shales. Fire clays occur well below the earth's surface and contain less oxide. Perhaps 75% of the U.S. brick production is made of surface clay and/or shale. Draglines, earth scrapers, power shovels, and shale planers are used to win the clay. The raw materials are crushed, ground, and pulverized. As much as half of the clay is ground to a particle size smaller than 0.0021 in. (0.053 mm). Water is mixed with clay to yield a plasticity suitable to the manufacturing process. Water contents of 12–15% by weight are used in the stiff-mud process, in which clay is extruded through a die. Clays having naturally high water contents are mixed with water to produce moisture contents of more than 20%, in which case the soft-mud process is used to form brick in wooden molds. To prevent the clay from sticking to the mold, sand or water is used to produce sand-struck or water-struck soft-mud brick. Excessive sand on the bed and the end of brick significantly reduces bond strength of brick to mortar, reducing the flexural strength of walls and increasing water permeance. Clays with very low plasticity are dry-pressed at pressures up to 1500 psi (10.3 MPa). Texture is achieved in the stiff-mud process by deforming the clay column as it is extruded from the die.

The formed units are dried in a kiln (the n is silent as in kil) for a day or two at temperatures up to 300°F (149°C). The dried units are then fired at gradually increasing temperatures from 1600°F (871°C) up to 2400°F (1316°C). Clays are fired to a maturing temperature, the point of incipient fusion, which varies greatly with clay materials. In the drying and firing process, a shrinkage of 5–15% occurs. High strength, low water absorption, and low moisture expansion are associated with higher firing temperatures (4,5,6) (see also ASTM C43).

PHYSICAL PROPERTIES

Brick sizes should always be listed in the following order: thickness (width), height, and length. Three types of dimensions are used, ie, nominal, specified, and actual. A nominal dimension is equal to the actual dimension plus the thickness of one mortar joint. The specified dimension is equal to the nominal dimension less the specified mortar joint thickness. The actual dimension should be equal to the specified dimension plus or minus the permissible dimensional tolerance. For example, the nominal size of a standard modular brick is $4 \times 2\frac{2}{3} \times 8$ in. ($100 \times 67 \times 200$ mm). For $\frac{3}{8}$-in. (10-mm) mortar joints, the specified brick dimension would be $3\frac{5}{8} \times 2\frac{1}{4} \times 7\frac{5}{8}$ in. ($90 \times 57 \times 190$ mm). Under ASTM C216, type FBS, the actual thickness might vary $\pm \frac{3}{32}$ in. (2.4 mm), and the length might vary $\pm \frac{1}{4}$ in. (6.4 mm) from the specified dimensions.

There are many, perhaps too many, available brick sizes. Modular sizes range from the standard size given above to $8 \times 4 \times 12$ in. ($200 \times 100 \times 300$ mm). Modular coordination (7) reduces the cost of masonry at least 5% (8). For the range of available dimensions and other physical properties, refer to Table 2. At a reasonable distance, a face dimension of 4×12 in. (100×300 mm) is aesthetically indistinguishable from face dimensions of $2\frac{2}{3} \times 8$ in. (67×200 mm), because the proportions are identical. The use of larger size brick increases mason productivity significantly and results in walls having higher compressive strength. Facing and building brick may not be cored more than 25%, but hollow brick may be cored up to 40%. Coring affects weight, strength, fire resistance, and transmission of heat and sound. Grimm (9) discusses the physics, identification, description, psychology, specification, and tolerances of brick color. There are no standard tex-

Table 2. Physical Properties of Brick, Mortar, and Brick Masonry

Item No.	Property	Units	Low[a]	Most Likely[b]	High[c]
1.0	*Brick*				
1.1.0	Size				
1.1.1	Width, nominal	in.	3	4	8
		mm	75	100	200
1.1.2	Height, nominal	in.	2	2.67	8
		mm	50	68	133
1.1.3	Length, nominal	in.	8	8	16
		mm	200	200	300
1.2.0	Compressive strength	lb/in.^{2}	1500	11,000	20,000
		kPa	10.3	75.8	126
1.3.0	Water absorption				
1.3.1	5 hr, boiling	% by weight	3	9	23
1.3.2	24 hr, cold	% by weight	2	7	17
1.3.3	Initial rate (suction)	gr/(min · 30 in.^{2})	3	5[h]	75
		gr/(min · m^2)	4650	7750	116,250
1.4.0	Weight, solid brick	lb/ft^3	100	123	145
		kg/m^3	1602	1970	2323
1.5	Expansion				
1.5.1	Coefficient of thermal expansion	10^{-4}% per °F	1.87	3.22	4.57
		10^{-4}% per °C	3.36	5.76	8.23
1.5.2	Freezing expansion	10^{-4}%	30	59	440
1.5.3	Moisture expansion, unrestrained brick at 60 yr.	10^{-4}%	40	200	540
1.6	Thermal conductivity[e]	Btu/(hr · ft^2 · °F · in.)	4	8	18
		W/(m^2 · K)	0.58	1.2	2.6
1.7	Specific heat	Btu/(lb · °F)	0.20	0.24	0.26
		J/(kg · K)	837	1004	1088
1.8	Heat storage capacity	Btu/ft^3	20	d	35
		J/m^3 ×10^6	1.3	d	2.3
1.9	Thermal diffusivity	ft^2/hr	0.016	d	0.03
		mm^2/s	0.25	d	0.46
1.10.0	Emissivity				
1.10.1	unglazed		0.85	d	0.96
	grey glazed		d	0.75	d
1.11.0	Solar radiation absorptivity				
1.11.1	red		0.65	d	0.8
1.11.2	dark brown		0.79	d	0.85
1.11.3	yellow or buff		0.5	d	0.7
1.11.4	white or cream		0.3	d	0.5
1.11.5	dark blue		0.85	d	0.95
1.12	Sound absorption[f]	%	d	0.036	d
1.13	Electrical conductivity[g]	10^{-6} g	0.5	d	0.11
1.14	Brinell hardness	No.	9	d	100
2.0	*Mortar*				
2.1	Compressive strength 2-in. cubes	psi	350	2400	4500
		MPa	2.4	16.6	30
2.2.0	Shrinkage				
2.2.1	at 28 days	10^{-3}%	27	65	103
2.2.2	ultimate	10^{-3}%	150	200	250
2.3	Coefficient of thermal expansion	10^{-4}%/°F	4.5	4.7	4.9
		10^{-4}%/°C	2.3	2.6	2.9
2.4	Thermal conductivity	Btu/(hr · ft^2 · °F · in.)	d	5	d
		W/(m^2 · K)	d	28.4	d
2.5	Weight	lb/ft^3	d	116	d
		kg/m^3	d	1858	d
2.6	Specific heat	Btu/(lb · °F)	d	0.2	d
		J/(kg · K)	d	837	d
2.7	Emissivity		0.85	0.9	0.95
2.8	Solar absorptivity, nonpigmented mortar		0.65	0.75	0.85
3.0	*Brick masonry*				
3.1	Compressive strength[j]	lb/in.^{2}	350	2000	6500
		MPa	2.4	13.6	44.8

Table 2 (*continued*)

Item No.	Property	Units	Low[a]	Most Likely[b]	High[c]
3.2	Modulus of elasticity	10^6 psi	0.2	1.2	3.9
		10^6 kPa	1.4	8.3	26.9
3.3	Modulus of rigidity	10^6 psi	0.1	0.5	1.6
		10^6 kPa	0.6	3.3	10.8
3.4	Compressive creep, brick masonry walls	10^{-4}%/psi	0.25	0.49	2.83
		10^{-4}%/Pa	0.036	0.071	0.41
3.5	Flexural strength[i,j]	lb/in.^{2}	91	137	183
		kPa	627	945	1262
3.6	Coefficient of friction on:				
	Sand		[d]	0.4	[d]
	Gravel		[d]	0.6	[d]
	Wood		[d]	0.3	[d]
	Masonry		0.65	0.7	0.75
	Metal		0.3	0.5	0.7
	Concrete		0.65	0.7	0.75
	Undisturbed dry clay		[d]	0.5	[d]
	Undisturbed wet soil		[d]	0.3	[d]

[a] Low values are estimated to have a 95% probability of being exceeded.
[b] Most likely values are the estimated modal value.
[c] High values are estimated to have a 95% probability of not being exceeded.
[d] No data available.
[e] Varies with density and moisture content.
[f] Noise reduction coefficient.
[g] At 25.1 kv.
[h] Median = 14; mean = 24.
[i] Type-S mortar, 1 PC-1/2L-4 1/2S, no air entrainment, inspected workmanship, and ASTM E72 walls.
[j] Stress normal to bed joint. Standard modular brick with ⅜-in. (10-mm) mortar joints.

tures for brick. They vary greatly with local and temporal custom.

The durability of brick is not solely a property of the material per se (10), but is also related to the severity of exposure to weather. The physical properties most closely related to durability are strength and pore size distribution. Severity of exposure is related to the climatic factors of water precipitation and freezing frequency, as well as position in the structure, ie, probability of being frozen when saturated. Thus, ASTM requirements for strength and water absorption are related to intended use, ie, position of brick within a structure (eg, pavement or wall above grade) and to local climatological data.

There are large ranges in climatic factors affecting brick durability. The weathering index (product of annual cycles of freezing and thawing in air and the annual winter rainfall in inches) is zero in San Diego, Calif., and 1820 in Huntington, W. Va. The number of annual freeze–thaw cycles occurring in ambient air may exceed 135 in some parts of the United States. Because of the effect of solar radiation, the number of freeze–thaw cycles on the south facade may be 30 cycles greater than on the north facade of the same building. Prevailing winds may produce a rather consistent suction force on one side of a building and pressure on another. Exfiltration may bring interior moisture through the wall, prompting interstitial condensation. The amount of rain absorbed by brick on one wall may be five times greater than that absorbed on another wall on the same building. East walls have been observed to produce more severe weathering than west walls in some cases.

Resistance to weathering is related to compressive strength and to the ratio of cold-to-boiling water absorption (C/B ratio), which should not exceed an average of 0.78 for brick having a severe exposure. The median compressive strength of brick produced in the United States is about 11,000 psi (75.8 MPa) and values as high as 38,000 psi (241 MPa) have been reported (Table 2). The coefficient of variation in the compressive strength of individual brick samples is about 11% but may be as high as 40%. Because durability is not precisely related to strength and water absorption, freeze–thaw testing (ASTM C67) is the best available means for predicting durability, but the test is expensive and requires ten weeks to complete (10,11). The durability of brick and the bond strength of brick to mortar are related to the initial rate of water absorption (IRA) (ASTM C67), which should not exceed 30 g/min·in.^{2} (0.0194 g/min·m^2) when bricks are laid. Other physical properties of brick are given in Table 2.

BONDS, PATTERNS, AND JOINTS

The word bond, when used in reference to masonry, may have three meanings:

1. *Structural bond.* The method by which individual masonry units are interlocked or tied together to

cause the entire assembly to act as a single structural unit.

2. *Pattern bond.* The pattern formed by the masonry units and the mortar joints on the face of a wall. The pattern may result from the type of structural bond used or may be purely a decorative one in no way related to the structural bonding.

3. *Mortar bond.* The adhesion of the mortar joint to the masonry units or to reinforcing steel.

The terms applied to various brick positions are illustrated in Figure 1.

MORTAR AND GROUT

Mortar in brick masonry functions as an adhesive to bond the brick together, as a gasket to avoid compressive stress concentration, and as a sealant in the joint between bricks. Conventional mortar for bricklaying consists of sand particles bound together by cementitious materials, ie, cement and lime. Mortars have two kinds of performance characteristics, ie, those applicable before solidification occurs and those thereafter.

It is important that mortar be workable in the plastic state, ie, have the capacity to spread easily under the mason's trowel. Workable mortars combine plasticity, consistency, cohesion, and adhesion in a manner that is ill-defined but readily recognizable to a craftsman. Water retentivity of plastic mortar is very important in establishing compatibility with brick. The properties of mortar should be matched to the properties of the masonry unit. Poor bond is created by certain combinations of brick and mortar, simply because the two materials are not suited to each other, and not necessarily because of any defect

in either. Mortar having high water retentivity should be used with brick having high IRA and during hot, dry weather. Lower water retentivity is better suited to brick having low IRA. Bond will be reduced if so much water is removed from the mortar as to prevent proper cement hydration, or if insufficient mortar paste is sucked into the pores of the brick to form a proper mechanical bond. Poor bond between brick and mortar results in reduced masonry strength and increased permeance to wind-driven rain. The time required for mortar to reach its initial set (solidification) is also an important property of plastic mortar.

The strength, durability, and extent of bond also depend on mortar air content, time lapse between spreading mortar and laying brick, brick texture on the mortared surface, and curing temperature, humidity, and wind. Important characteristics of hardened mortar include compressive strength, extensibility, shrinkage, and durability. These properties are determined by the type and proportions of the mortar ingredients.

The cement used in masonry mortar is typically Portland cement (ASTM C150) or masonry cement (ASTM 91). Non-air-entrained Portland cements are mixed with non-air-entrained lime (ASTM C207, type S) and sand (ASTM C144) in mortars for structural brick masonry. Masonry cements contain plasticizing agents and do not require the addition of lime. The ASTM specification for masonry cement does not require identification of the cementitious materials, plasticizing agents, and inert ground limestone that form the proprietary ingredients. Masonry cements are usually high in air content, which reduces bond and compressive strength of masonry. Masonry cements may be used in nonstructural applications but, in the absence of complete structural tests data on full scale walls, only non-air-entrained Portland cement–lime mortars should be used in engineered brick masonry.

In Portland cement–lime mortars, the cement content by volume ranges from approximately 11 to 44%. Lime contents range from 30% with low cement contents, to 8% with high cement contents. High cement content increases strength and durability. High lime content increases workability, water retentivity, and elasticity. To optimize these qualities, mortar should be no stronger than is necessary. Low strength mortars provide more flexible masonry, capable of absorbing larger movements without cracking. For most purposes, high cement content is not desirable. High strength mortars are necessary in reinforced brick masonry (RBM) and for durability in pavements and foundation walls.

Sand volumetric content should range from 2¼ to 3 times the sum of the Portland cement and lime. High sand contents increase setting time and reduce strength. Proper sand gradation improves workability. Excessive fines reduce strength; deficiency of fines reduces workability.

Mortar should contain the maximum amount of potable water that the mason finds suitable for workability. Bond strength increases with water content; conversely, compressive strength is reduced. Since bond strength is usually more important than compressive strength, mortar should be retempered to replace water lost by evaporation. Mortar

BRICK JOINTS

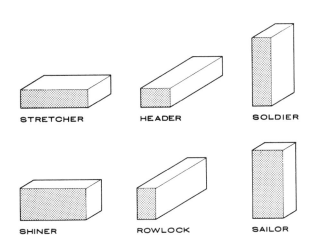

Figure 1. Terms applied to varied brick positions (12). Courtesy of the Brick Institute of America.

is not concrete. Additional water reduces the compressive strength of concrete, but typically increases the bond strength of mortar to brick.

Mortar compressive strength depends on water–cement ratio, curing, air content, age, and specimen size and shape. Field-mixed mortars have greater water contents than laboratory-mixed mortars, and therefore lower apparent compressive strength; however, field-mixed mortars are placed in absorbent brick molds and laboratory mortars in nonabsorbent molds. Strength tests on laboratory and field mortars are not comparable. Tensile strength of mortar is usually unimportant, since it is usually greater than bond strength. Other physical properties of mortar are given in Table 2.

Grout is used in reinforced brick masonry (RBM) to imbed reinforcing steel. Fine grout (ASTM C476) should be proportioned by volume: one part Portland cement, 2¼–3 parts sand (ASTM C404). For coarse grout 1–2 parts coarse aggregate [maximum size ½ in. (12 mm)] may be added. As much as one-tenth part hydrated lime may be added to either fine or coarse grout.

AUXILIARY MATERIALS

The performance of brick masonry is highly dependent on such auxiliary materials as connectors (13), shelf angles and lintels (14), reinforcing (15), flashing (16), sealants, coatings (17), and insulation. Design and construction considerations for these materials in masonry are discussed in the quality control section at the end of this article.

BRICK MASONRY STRENGTH AND ELASTICITY

The compressive strength of brick masonry prisms (ASTM 447) is a function of cement and air content of mortar;

ratio of brick height to mortar joint thickness; compressive strength of brick; mortar joint solidity, age and curing condition of test specimen; and direction of stress with regard to bed joints (18). The compressive strength of brick masonry at first crack varies greatly but is typically about 50% of ultimate strength. Quality control in compressive strength of masonry is measured by the coefficient of variation in the compressive strength test data. The average coefficient of variation in compressive strength of conventional brick masonry prisms is about 9%, with a range from 5 to 24%.

The uniaxial compressive strength and modulus of elasticity of mortars are usually considerably lower than the corresponding values for brick, while Poisson's ratio is higher. Accordingly, under axial compression, the unrestrained lateral strain of mortar would exceed that of brick. However, shear and friction between brick and mortar restrain the mortar, placing it in triaxial compression, while the brick is in axial compression and lateral tension. Thus the typical uniaxial compressive strength of brick masonry exceeds the uniaxial compressive strength of mortar. Because the tensile strength of brick is low, the typical mode of failure of brick masonry prisms in compression is by vertical longitudinal splitting.

Arrangement of properly installed headers in various patterns affects appearance (Fig. 2) but has no significant effect on wall strength. There is no significant difference between the compressive strengths of well-built metal tied and masonry bonded walls; single-wythe prisms built in stack bond or running bond; and single-wythe prisms ranging from 8 to 24 in. (200 to 610 mm) in length. Maximum allowable compressive stress may not exceed 20% of the prism compressive strength for walls and 16% for columns. The degree of restraint at the ends of compression members, magnitude and direction of eccentricity at each end,

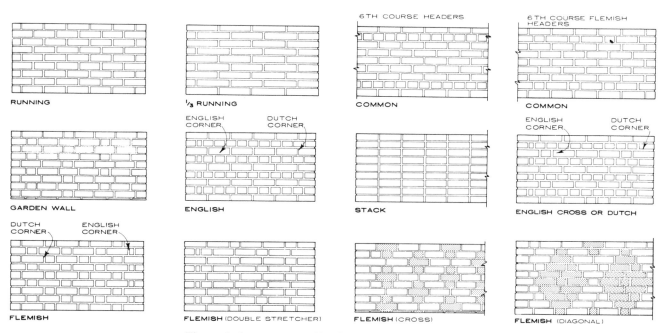

Figure 2. Arrangements of headers in various patterns (12).

and slenderness of the specimen all significantly affect compressive strength.

The modulus of elasticity of brick masonry is highly variable, but may be approximated at 600 times the compressive strength. Poisson's ratio is about 0.2. About 60% of the creep (increased strain without increased stress) at one year occurs during the first 30 days. Creep in flexure at 300 days is about 50% greater than that in compression (19,20).

The flexural tensile strength of brick masonry is a function of cement content of mortar; mortar joint solidity; direction of stress with regard to bed joint; mortar joint thickness; air content of mortar; time interval from spreading mortar to laying brick; size of test specimen; brick IRA; and cleanness of brick surface. For type-S, Portland cement–lime–sand mortar without air entrainment but with inspected workmanship in ⅜-in. (10-mm) thick joints in ASTM E72 wall panels, and with brick having an IRA between 0.17 and $1 g/(min \cdot in.^2)$ [108 to 645×10^{-6} g/ $(min \cdot m^2)$], the range in strength is shown in Table 2. With type-M mortar, the strength is about 10% greater, with type-N 23% less, and with type-O 32% less. With high IRA brick {more than 1 $g/(min \cdot in.^2)$ [645×10^{-6} g/ $(min \cdot m^2)$]} the strength is reduced about 27%. This strength reduction is avoided by wetting such bricks prior to laying them. Thinner mortar joints increase flexural tensile strength. The strength is about 2.6 times greater when stress is parallel to the bed joints. The flexural strength of mortar–brick joints tested individually is much greater than the strength of wall panels. (A chain breaks at its weakest link.) Twenty percent air entrainment, which is not unusual in masonry cement mortars, reduces brick–mortar bond strength by about 50%. Dirt or sand on the mortar bond surface of bricks reduces flexural strength.

The average shear strength of brick masonry (ASTM E519) without precompression ranges from approximately 50 to 600 psi (345 kPa to 4.1 MPa). Shear strength is related to compressive strength and compressive stress. Maximum allowable shear stress in unreinforced brick masonry is half the square root of the compressive strength plus 20% of the compressive stress, not to exceed 28–80 psi (193–551 kPa), depending on workmanship, quality control assurance, and mortar type (21). Other physical properties of conventional brick masonry are given in Table 2.

Polymer-impregnated brick masonry was first tested at the University of Texas at Austin in 1969 (22). Those tests generated the highest compressive strength of brick masonry ever reported, 17,429 psi (120 MPa). Flexural strengths were 476 psi (3.3 MPa).

CRACK CONTROL

Cracks in masonry admit water, are aesthetically objectionable, and may be indicative of structural distress. Wind-driven rain enters cracks having a width in excess of 0.1 mm. Normal visual acuity is about one minute of arc. Thus cracks can be seen at distances about 3400 times their width, depending on exposure time, contrast, and illumination. Structural cracks may be the result of restrained movement or the imposition of excessively high loads.

Three types of cracks are differentiated as facial separation cracks, cracked brick or mortar, and structural cracks. Facial separation cracks are separations between brick and mortar, typically caused by inadequate tooling of mortar joints. Well-built brick walls may have 15% of the contact length between brick and mortar cracked in excess of 0.1 mm. Cracks in face brick that are observable at distances of more than 20 ft (6.1 m) result from manufacturing defects, excessive stress, or excessive weathering. Cracks in mortar may be the result of high shrinkage and low thermal expansion of mortar combined with high thermal expansion of brick.

Structural cracks in brick masonry may result from unaccommodated movements in the supporting structure, in the masonry, or both. Soil movement due to moisture content changes in plastic soils, uneven foundation displacement, and soil subsidence can cause masonry cracks, but foundation settlement is often erroneously blamed for masonry cracks. All structural frames are subject to elastic deformation, thermal displacement, sidesway, and beam deflection. Concrete frames creep and shrink; steel shelf angles and lintels elongate, rotate, deflect, and corrode. Wood changes volume and warps with varying moisture content. Brick masonry increases in volume because of moisture, heat, and freezing while mortar shrinks. Story high, 4-in.-(100-mm-) thick brick walls crack at deflections about equal to height divided by 1800. Brick masonry veneer walls flexed to deflections of L/360 or L/600 will surely crack.

Cracked brick masonry is avoided in design by providing flexible anchorage to structural supports, ie, anchors resist tension and compression but not shear; providing properly sized and clean expansion joints at appropriate locations; and specifying proper materials.

Tie spacing should not exceed 24 in. (600 mm) vertically or 36 in. (900 mm) horizontally. Proper tie spacing depends on tie size and the widths of cavities, but not less than one tie should be provided for each 4½ ft² (0.42 m²) of wall area. Adjustable ties should not be used without adequate structural test data (ASTM E488), proving sufficient strength and stiffness. Rigid anchorage of walls to frames will not prevent differential movement; the forces generated are too great. There is one chance in 20 that the vertical differential movement between brick masonry and a concrete frame is more than 0.155%. If that movement is restrained in brick masonry having a modulus of elasticity of 1.5 million psi (10,342 MPa), the stress in the masonry is 2325 psi (16 MPa), ie, quite sufficient to crack the masonry, deflect shelf angles, shear anchor bolts, tear sealant joints, and lift the shelf angle in its insert to make the masonry self-supporting to the foundation.

To avoid these problems, horizontal expansion joints should be placed under shelf angles (14), and vertical expansion joints in brick masonry walls: within 18 ft (5.5 m) or so of corners; at changes in wall height or thickness; at pilasters, recesses, and chases; at one side of wall openings; and at horizontal intervals of about 18 ft (5.5 m). The distance between expansion joints should not exceed that which could be expected to produce enough movement to disrupt an expansion joint. If an expansion joint ⅜ in. (10 mm) wide has a sealant with a 50% compressibility, the allowable closure is 3/16 in. or 0.1875 in. (4.8 mm). There is one chance in 20 that the horizontal strain in the masonry is greater than 0.0865%. The allowable spacing of vertical expansion joints is, therefore, 0.1875/0.000865 or 217 in., or 18 ft (5.5 m). If the compressibility of the sealant were only 30%, as is often the case, there would be a 5% probability that the sealant would be overstressed if expansion joint spacing were to exceed 10.8 ft (3.3 m). Horizontal surfaces in coping and pavements are subject to much greater thermal movements than occur in walls. Accordingly, expansion joints in horizontal brick masonry should be spaced at closer intervals and over shrinkage joints in concrete base slabs.

Construction operations that affect cracked masonry include:

1. Culling excessively cracked brick.
2. Providing proper weather protection.
3. Providing anchors and ties of the specified type and size at the indicated location.
4. Properly filling and tooling mortar joints.
5. Properly proportioning and mixing mortar.
6. Placing brick in plastic (unset) mortar.
7. Providing clean and well-built expansion joints at the specified locations.

WATER PERMEANCE

One of the primary causes of building problems is water; it can cause dimensional change, corrosion, decay, efflorescence, freeze–thaw spalling and splitting, increased heat transmission, condensation, deterioration of interior finishes and building contents, tenant inconvenience, and litigation. Water permeance of brick masonry (16) is a function of: the severity of exposure to wind-driven rain, architectural design, construction quality, and maintenance continuity.

Severity of exposure to wind-driven rain is related to the driving rain index (Fig. 3) (23), the proximity of the building to a large body of water, the proximity of the wall to a corner or top edge of the building, and the degree of wall protection, eg, roof overhang. All exterior walls on buildings located within 5 mi (8 km) of a sea, large lake, or estuary, have a severe exposure as do all unprotected walls in buildings in all locations in the United States, except that walls not near the corner or top of

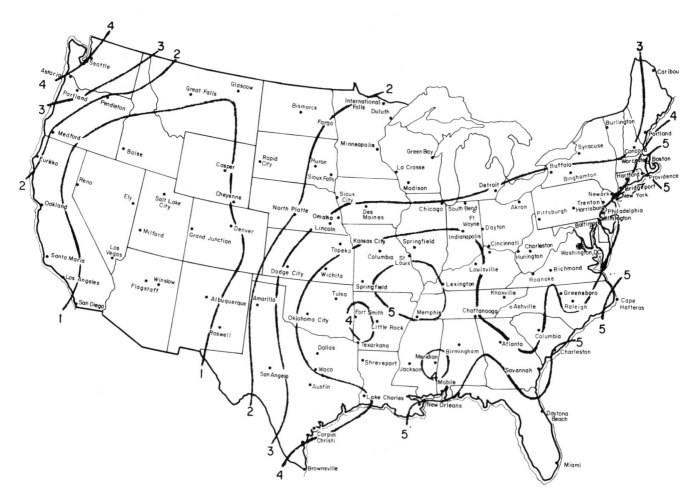

Figure 3. Driving rain index (23). Courtesy of the American Society for Testing and Materials.

buildings where the driving rain index is less than 3.0 have a moderate exposure (23).

For maximum resistance to water permeance:

1. The mortar bond surface of brick must be clean when bricks are laid.

2. The face of exterior mortar joints must be well tooled and concave or V shaped (Fig. 4).

3. All cavities having a minimum width of 2 in. (50 mm) must be clean of mortar and foreign material.

4. Mortar joints must be solidly filled.

5. All imbedded metal must be solidly imbedded in mortar or grout.

6. All control, expansion, and construction joints must be properly sealed.

7. Flashing and weep holes must be properly installed.

8. The backup of the exterior masonry wythe must be sufficiently stiff to prevent the exterior wythe from cracking under lateral loading.

These conditions notwithstanding, 4 in. (100 mm) of brick masonry no matter how built, by whom, or of what, never stopped a wind-driven rain. For that reason, two wall types are appropriate for use in severe exposure: a cavity or veneer wall in which the net air space width is at least 2 in. (50 mm); a solidly grouted single-wythe wall of hollow masonry units; or a multiwythe wall with a grout core at least 2 in. (50 mm) thick.

Water that enters masonry walls in objectionable quantities does not go through uncracked brick and does not go through uncracked mortar. It goes through cracks in brick and in mortar, between brick and mortar, or through cracked sealant joints. The water permeance integrity of an entire facade is often left to sealant joints, which have a typical life expectancy of seven years. Durable sealants can last more than 20 years. If the sealant cracks, water cascading down the wall is forced by high wind pressure into the building. A backup, double-sealant joint vented to the exterior would provide much better protection. Periodic inspection to identify deteriorated sealant and cracked masonry is necessary to ensure resistance to water permeance.

EFFLORESCENCE

Water that enters masonry may contain salts, and water may dissolve salts within the masonry. When the water evaporates, a salt crystalline residue remains. Salt deposited on the surface of masonry is a stain called efflorescence (10), which is usually white but may also be green. If evaporation occurs inside the face of the masonry, the salt crystalline residue is called cryptoflorescence. Efflorescence may be an aesthetic problem, but it does not affect durability. It may, however, be indicative of cryptoflorescence, which can be destructive. Crystallization of salt can exert pressures of nearly 10,000 psi (69 MPa). At low temperatures and high humidity levels, hydration of plaster of Paris to gypsum could exert a pressure of more than 30,000 psi (207 MPa).

The two conditions necessary for efflorescence are the presence of soluble salts in the masonry and water permeance of the masonry. Brick may be tested for efflorescence (ASTM C62). ASTM Committee C12 has a test method under development for determining the tendency for mortar to effloresce. To control efflorescence, salt content in materials and water permeance of masonry should be minimized.

HEAT TRANSFER

Dynamic heat transfer through building enclosures is a function of the thermal properties of the wall materials, climatic conditions, solar angles, and architectural design. Thermal properties include thermal conductivities and thicknesses of the materials, specific heat, density, radiant emissivity, and water retentivity. Climatological factors include interior and exterior air temperatures, wind velocity, atmospheric clarity, and duration of temperature difference across the wall (eg, degree days). Architectural design features include tilt angle and azimuth of the facade. Solar angles are peculiar to longitude, latitude, date, and hour.

In winter, the design rate of heat loss through a unit area of wall is the product of the steady state thermal transmittance (U value), temperature difference across the wall, and an M factor, which includes the effect of wall weight and local winter degree days (24). U values for masonry walls range from 0.05 to 0.4 Btu/(hr·ft²·°F) [0.28 to 2.27 W/(m²·K)], depending on the amount of resistance insulation provided. A typical U value is 0.13 Btu/(hr·ft²·°F) [0.74 W/(m²·K)]. The heat conductance of a brick surface [Btu/(hr·ft²·°F)] can be estimated empirically as 35% of the wind velocity (mph) plus 2. [1 Btu/(hr·ft²·°F) = 5.68 W/(m²·K).] The thermal inertia effect as measured by the M factor ranges from 0.62 to 1.0, depending on wall weight and the number of winter degree days. A typical M value is 0.89, ie, the heat loss rate is 11% less than measured by U value. A typical unit heat loss rate for a typical masonry wall is about 9 Btu/(hr·ft²·°F) [49 W/(m²·K)], which is about 10% of that through single-glazed windows.

In summer, the design rate of heat gain through a unit area of wall is the product of the U value and the cooling load temperature difference (CLTD), which is a function of wall type and weight, exterior and interior design temperatures, diurnal temperature range, wall color, latitude, wall orientation, time of day, and date. Maximum values

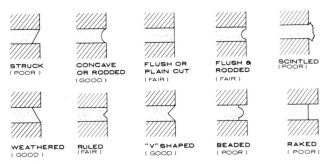

Figure 4. Types of joints (weatherability) (12).

of CLTD for brick-faced walls range from 14 to 41°F (8 to 23 K). A typical value for a south facing wall is 23°F (13 K). Typical heat gain is, therefore, 3 Btu/(hr·ft²·°F) (17 W/m²·K), a small fraction of that through windows.

The time required for heat to permeate a brick wall (time lag) is about 0.8 hr/in. (0.0315 hr/mm) of thickness plus or minus about 10%. The thermal storage capacity of brick masonry is used in passive solar heating systems to reduce fuel consumption. The proper design and construction of such systems for brick masonry buildings can result in total annual energy savings of as much as 60% (25). The ratio of total masonry volume in walls and floors to total building floor area with passive solar design may range from 0.15 to 1.15 ft³/ft² (0.046 to 0.35 m³/m²).

ACOUSTICS

Sound, like heat, needs to be walled in and out. Noise is unwanted sound. The sounds people dislike most are loud, high pitched, intermittent, irregular, impulsive, and continuing. The best place to stop noise is at its source by mounting noise generators on vibration isolators. Once propagated, noise may be airborne, transmitted through structures, or both. (See ASTM C634, *Standard Definition of Terms Relating to Environmental Acoustics.*)

Noise level is measured in decibels (dB). One dB is about the minimum sound pressure level audible to the normal human ear, and 120 dB is the threshold of feeling. Sound pressure level in a room can be reduced only to a very limited extent by increasing sound absorption within a room. Doubling sound absorption reduces noise level 3 dB, and a tenfold increase reduces noise level 10 dB.

It is necessary to control sound transmission through walls and to ensure that walls are not acoustically flanked. Where partitions go only to a suspended ceiling, sound is transmitted through the plenum. Joints between walls and other structural elements should be sealed. Cracks should be sealed around pipes and other objects that penetrate walls. Medicine cabinets and electrical outlets should not be placed back to back. Walls can be flanked by sound entering an air register and traveling through a duct to an adjoining room, through nearby windows, or through sound-porous doors on a common corridor.

Sound transmission loss (STL) is the attenuation (decrease) in airborne sound energy expressed in decibels as it passes through a building wall. In general, STL increases with sound frequency. A single-figure rating, sound transmission class (STC) in dB, provides an estimate of the airborne sound insulating performance of building walls. The STC for brick walls is approximately equal to 2.2 times the sum of the wall thickness in inches plus 16, ie, 44 dB for a 4-in. (100-mm) wall. The addition of plaster finish adds about 3 dB to the STL. The suggested minimum average STC for walls is 50 dB in hospitals, 42 dB in schools, and 48–55 dB in apartments.

FIRE RESISTANCE

Approximately one person per hour dies in the United States in a building fire, and ten others are injured. Com-

bustible wall finish is responsible for the spread of smoke and fire resulting in loss of life in 25% of all building fires having fatalities.

The term fireproof is a misnomer, which was first rejected as inaccurate in the UK in 1903, and because it is misleading, it is not used by the National Fire Protection Association (NFPA) in the United States (See ASTM E176 for definitions of terms relating to fire standards.) Brick masonry is noncombustible and has zero flame spread, zero smoke accumulation, zero toxicity, and zero fuel contribution.

Fire containment is the most important aspect of design for fire control in buildings. The fire resistance ratings for walls is measured in hours by ASTM E119 and ranges from 1 to 4 depending on combustibility of framed-in members, plaster coatings, wall thickness, and brick solidity (26).

AIR AND VAPOR PERMEANCE

Air filtration through brick masonry ranges from 3 to 22 ft³/hr·ft²·in. (0.67–4.33 L/m²·min·mm) (27). The American Society of Heating, Refrigerating, and Air Conditioning Engineers (ASHRAE) gives higher values based on older data (28).

Vapor may migrate through walls from the warm, humid side to the cold, dry side. As air moves through the wall, its temperature drops and its relative humidity increases. If temperature drop reaches the dew point, condensation occurs within the wall, ie, interstitial condensation. Condensate can cause the same problems associated with rainwater in walls. To prevent this, a vapor retarder may be placed on the warm side of any insulation in the wall. However, for buildings of normal human occupancy, the quantity of condensate is very small, and vapor barriers are not required in insulated cavity walls, unless the exterior wythe is built of glazed brick. ASTM E241 contains a good review of vapor transmission problems.

STRUCTURES

Brick masonry structural elements may be classified as arches and shells; lintels, beams, and girders; piers, columns, pilasters, and buttresses; walls; and floors and pavements.

The working (allowable) stress method of structural design for masonry is currently employed in the United States, although Europeans have long since progressed to limit state design, which consists of probability-based loading and resistance design criteria to provide explicit reliability. For most masonry, the working stress method provides inappropriately high and highly variable factors of safety. There is good evidence that the ultimate strength theory adequately predicts the strength of reinforced and unreinforced masonry walls in compression and flexure; however, additional research may be necessary to develop limit state models and resistance criteria in shear (29). It can be anticipated that within a few years the design methods for masonry in the United States will catch up with that now used for masonry in other countries and for other materials in the United States.

The structural engineering design methodology used for masonry bearing walls is currently (1987) being altered in the United States by a joint committee of the American Society of Civil Engineers (ASCE) and the American Concrete Institute (ACI). The new recommended building code requirements include provisions for concrete masonry and clay brick masonry as well, which are now covered by separate standards. Most industrialized nations of the world have rational structural engineering techniques for the design of masonry bearing wall buildings, but there are significant differences among them. The International Council for Building Research, Studies, and Documentation (CIB) has developed an international consensus. More fundamentally, there was in 1987 no coordination between those committees of the ASTM that write standard test methods and specifications for masonry materials, and their counterparts in other countries.

Figure 5. Brick shell, Piacenza, Italy.

Arches and Shells

Brick arches have been in use for six millennia and longer in all architectural epochs, wherever and whenever brick was used. They have taken many shapes, eg, segments of circles, ellipses, parabolas, catenaries, straight lines, and various combinations of these. Their shapes have frequently been named after historical architectural styles, eg, Gothic, Tudor, and Moorish. The economy of arch construction lies in its ability to span horizontally with minimum tensile stress. Tellett (30) records the historical development of structural engineering applied to arches, and Heyman (31) considers in detail the structural design of the masonry arch.

Brick masonry shells range from single- and double-curvature vaults to domes and hyperbolic paraboloids. Domes antedate the pyramids. Since the prehistoric bee-hive huts of the British Isles and the 7000-year-old mud brick domes of Arpachizah, few architectural epochs have failed to recognize the inherent economic potential of shells to enclose the most space with the least material. The first rational structural engineering analysis of a building was made on the concentric brick masonry domes of St. Peter's Basilica in Rome in 1742 (32). Clay masonry shells are being used in a variety of modern structures with impressive spans in many countries of the world, eg, Italy, Denmark, and Mexico (33) (Fig. 5). There is no valid economic reason why brick masonry shells should not be used in the United States.

Lintels, Beams, and Girders

The tensile strength of brick masonry is typically less than 5% of its compressive strength. To compensate, steel reinforcing is introduced to create reinforced brick masonry (RBM) (15). The technique antedates reinforced concrete, the early promoters of which (ca 1850) pointed to extant RBM to prove that the new idea would work. Sir Marc Isambard Brunel proposed the use of RBM in 1813, but first used it extensively in 1825 in the 50-ft

(15.24-m) diameter and 70-ft (21.3-m) deep shafts for the Thames River Tunnel in London.

An RBM lintel 4 in. (100 mm) wide and 8 in. (200 mm) high with two ¼-in. (6-mm) rods can safely support the triangular load of a 4-in. (100-mm) masonry wythe on a 7-ft 4-in. (2.2-m) span. The 65-ft (19.8-m) span of the RBM girders in St. Hedwig's Church in St. Louis, Mo., sustained test loads of 67,500 lb (302.5 kN) at each span third point in addition to dead loads with half of the allowable deflection at 24 h and with 94% recovery. The RBM girders are 1 ft 5 in. (452 mm) wide and 10 ft 2¼ in. (3.1 m) deep with six No. 10 (32-mm diameter) and six No. 8 (25-mm diameter) bars in tension, and two No. 7 (22-mm diameter) and two No. 8 (25-mm diameter) bars in compression. The RBM girders were less costly than exposed steel or reinforced concrete as determined by competitive bids.

More than 43 engineering papers have been published on prestressed and posttensioned brick masonry, which now enjoys broad use in the UK (34).

Piers, Columns, Pilasters, and Buttresses

A pier is a column laterally unsupported at the top. A column is a vertical structural member laterally supported on top and bottom, whose horizontal dimension measured at right angles to the thickness does not exceed three times its thickness. A pilaster is a column and/or vertical beam of uniform cross-section, integrally bonded in a wall from which it may project. A buttress is a pilaster having a cross section increasing from top to base.

A plain (nonreinforced) brick masonry column of moderate strength materials, nominally 8 × 16 in. (200 × 400 mm) in cross-section, and 10 ft (3.05 m) in height, can safely sustain a concentric load of 36 kips (160.4 kN), ie, about the weight of 200 men (35). If the column were 18.75 ft (5.7 m) high, it would support 103 men. If the nonreinforced column were 9.37 ft (2.8 m) high and not supported at its top, ie, if it were a pier, it could still safely support 103 men (18.6 kips or 82.7 kN).

A RBM column of moderate strength masonry materials, nominally 16 in.^{2} (400 mm), with four No. 6 (19-mm diameter) bars, 10 ft (3.05 m) in height, and concentrically loaded, can safely sustain the load of 948 men (171 kips or 761 kN).

Walls

A wall is a vertical structural member whose horizontal dimension measured at right angles to the thickness exceeds three times the thickness. A bearing wall supports a superimposed vertical load. A shear wall resists a longitudinal, horizontal load. A shear wall may or may not be a bearing wall and may or may not be laterally loaded. A panel wall is an exterior, nonbearing wall supported at each story that resists lateral loads. A curtain wall is an exterior, nonbearing wall that resists lateral loads, and is supported laterally but not vertically at each story.

Walls are classified as solid, hollow, or perforated. Solid walls may be of single or multiple wythes. Multiple wythes may be tied together by masonry units or preferably by metal ties. Hollow walls have a net air space of at least 2 in. (50 mm) but not more than 4½ in. (113 mm) between wythes. Cavity walls are hollow walls, having a continuous airspace bridged only by metal ties. Masonry-bonded hollow walls have the separated wythes tied (bonded) together by masonry units at discrete intervals vertically and horizontally. Rib walls are hollow walls tied together by transverse wythes spaced longitudinally at discrete intervals. Diaphragm walls are rib walls in which the cavity width exceeds 4½ in. (113 mm).

Walls resist horizontal loads due to wind, earth, water, granular material, seismic forces, and blast, which may act laterally or longitudinally, ie, in the plane of the wall. RBM has been widely and successfully used to resist all of those forces. The state of the art in seismic-resistant RBM has been well defined in national and international conferences (36,37). In India, one-brick-thick bearing walls have been used in seismic areas. The seismic resistance of reinforced concrete frames is greatly increased by infilling the frame with RBM walls. The structural interaction between walls and their supporting beams has been studied by many investigators. Several blast resistance test programs have established the ability of properly designed and built masonry to resist explosions of several types, including nuclear (38), fallout from which is also well resisted by brick masonry.

Perforated walls provide a screen without blocking ventilation, or they may serve as shading devices. They are used aesthetically for their peek-a-boo effect in establishing architectural sequence. They are weak in compression but usually have more than adequate lateral strength because of reduced wind loading (Fig. 6).

Bearing Walls. Prior to about the turn of the twentieth century, masonry bearing walls were the only structural system for use in high-rise buildings, which by 1891 had reached a wall thickness of 6 ft (1.83 m) in the 16-story Monadnock Building in Chicago, Ill. During the first half of this century, frames of steel and later concrete replaced

Figure 6. Perforated brick wall.

masonry bearing walls for all but two- or three-story structures.

However, recovery from World War II forced Europeans to consider more economical construction. In 1946, the Swiss Federal Materials Testing and Research Institute built a 19-ft 8-in (6-m), 1.1 × 10^6 lb (5 × 10^5 kg) press in which Professor P. Haller tested more than 1600 brick masonry walls. As a direct result of that work, three 13-story apartment buildings were built between 1951 and 1953 in Basel, Switzerland, with brick masonry bearing walls ranging in thickness from 6 to 15 in. (150 to 381 mm). The idea slowly spread through Europe and to the United States. In 1952, Davidson and Monk (39) published a feasibility study of a ten-story building with 6-in. (150-mm) brick masonry bearing walls. In 1964, a team of American architects and engineers documented the European bearing wall experience and brought the technology to the United States. In 1969, the predecessor of the BIA published *Building Code Requirements for Engineered Brick Masonry,* which provided the first rational, structural engineering design method available in the United States for masonry. This standard was soon adopted by the national model building codes. From there, the idea spread throughout the United States as brick masonry bearing walls became thinner to support higher buildings. To date, the height record is held by 20-story buildings in Denver, Colorado, where 10-in. (250-mm) RBM walls were used in this seismic region. In 1970, no universities in the United States offered engineering courses in structural masonry. By 1983, 44 universities offered such courses.

There are a number of reasons for the use of masonry bearing wall structures. With one material installed by a single trade, bearing walls define space; support the structure; provide variety in color, texture, pattern, and scale; and exclude weather, heat, noise, and fire. However, the facade of masonry bearing wall buildings may be of glass, metal, concrete, or any material when the bearing walls are perpendicular to the facade, as is often the case (Fig. 7).

The primary reason for the acceptance of the bearing wall structural system is its economy. A 1974 study by the American Appraisal Co. compared the initial cost of a nine-story apartment building in 205 cities in the United States and Canada with three different structural systems, ie, brick masonry bearing walls, brick masonry panel walls in a concrete frame, and brick masonry panel walls in a steel frame. In every city studied, the bearing wall system was least costly. The average for all cities studied showed that the steel frame building was 22% more expensive than the comparable bearing wall building, and the concrete frame structure was 14% more costly (40).

Deep-Beam Bearing Walls. Brick masonry bearing walls are most often supported on continuous concrete foundations, but it is not essential to do so. A significant savings can be achieved by reinforcing the wall and designing it as a deep beam to span about 24 ft (7 m) between spot foundations. The cost savings may be 12–26% (30).

Shear Walls. Horizontal forces acting in the wall plane generate flexural and shear stresses. Since the flexural stress must be suppressed by vertically acting dead load, such walls are called shear walls. Bearing wall buildings depend on shear walls for their lateral stability. In such buildings, vertically spanning, exterior panel walls transfer wind loads to the edge of the floor system that acts as a diaphragm, ie, a horizontal deep beam, spanning between shear walls that are parallel to the wind direction.

Thus, the wind load is transferred from the exterior walls to transverse shear walls that act as deep, vertical, cantilevers to transfer the load through the foundation to the ground. In seismic regions, the lateral forces of earthquakes are similarly distributed. Shear walls have any of several plan shapes, eg, Is, Ts, Cs, and Zs. If shear walls are symmetrically located, torsional stress and wall costs are reduced.

Panel Walls. Panel walls supported on frames of steel or concrete are the largest single use of masonry structural elements and the most neglected by building design professionals. Considering all construction materials, there is reason to believe that a building facade failure occurs approximately every working day in the United States. Notwithstanding the existence of rational, analytical methods in structural engineering (34,41,42), masonry panel walls are usually designed by antiquated rules of thumb, establishing some arbitrary ratio of wall height to thickness. As a direct result of these irrational, empirical design methods, there are many brick masonry panel wall failures each year, ie, cracks, spalls, and leaks. Indeed, many brick masonry, veneer–steel stud panel walls are designed to crack, ie, their deflection is arbitrarily limited to their height divided by 360 or 600, disregarding the fact that brick masonry wall panels are known to crack at about one-third that deflection. Shelf angles, which usually support the exterior masonry wythe of panel walls, are rarely designed for their torsional stress and deflection (14). Standards of practice for the corrosion resistance of masonry wall ties and anchors ensure coating life expectancies that are much less than the useful life of masonry buildings

Figure 7. Siedlung Alpenblich Cham (1965–1966). Architect: Josef Stockli Zug. Courtesy of Peter Guggenbuhl.

(43). Brick veneer is anchored to steel studs by the thin arris of one thread of an abraded steel screw, which is periodically bathed in a salt solution, due to copious water permeance through cracked brick masonry. At present, the prevalent architectural design of nonbearing masonry panel walls in the United States needs considerable improvement.

Three types of brick masonry panel walls are in common use, ie, brick masonry veneer over steel studs, masonry cavity walls, and composite solid walls. Veneer walls employ an exterior wythe of brick masonry 3 or 3⅝ in. (75 or 92 mm) thick; anchors across an air space of about 1 in. (25 mm); sheathing; steel studs with insulation in between; and interior dry wall. Problems with the system include interalia: insufficient stiffness of the anchors and studs, resulting in flexural cracking of the masonry; high water permeance of the cracked masonry; and rapid corrosion of anchors.

Cavity walls with brick masonry exterior wythe and brick or concrete masonry interior wythe solve the stiffness, flexural cracking, and water permeance problems. The cavity may be nominally 2–4 in. (50–100 mm) in width and may be insulated. If board insulation is used, a minimum net cavity width of 2 in. (50 mm) should be maintained on the outer side of the insulation. When glazed brick is used, a vapor barrier should be placed on the warm side of the cavity. Only the most durable brick should be used in the exterior wythe of insulated cavity walls. When properly designed, built, and maintained, cavity walls are thermally efficient, impermeable to wind-driven rain, and highly resistant to fire and sound transmission. Cavity walls are, however, weaker in flexure than solid composite walls of the same materials.

The absence of a cavity in composite solid walls results in higher water permeance, less thermal efficiency, and lower resistance to fire and sound transmission. Composite walls are better suited to those industrial facilities where environmental control is less important. For industrial plants, where walls are higher and column spacing is greater, diaphragm walls and pilastered cavity walls have been successfully used in the UK (44). There is no reason why such walls should not have broad application in the United States.

Because of the shear-resistant connection between longitudinal wythes, masonry-bonded hollow walls and rib walls have greater lateral strength than cavity walls. However, these shear connectors also increase water permeance and heat transmission, and reduce resistance to fire and sound transmission. In general, masonry-bonded hollow walls and rib walls have better performance characteristics than composite solid walls, but are not as good as cavity walls. Masonry-bonded hollow walls, rib walls, and cavity walls may be used as bearing, shear, panel, or curtain walls. Veneer walls may only be used as nonbearing walls unless the backup carries all of the load, as in brick masonry veneer over reinforced concrete. In summary, exterior brick masonry is best placed in a cavity wall.

Floors and Pavements

The Roman forum was paved with brick, as were many forums throughout the empire. In the Georgetown area of Washington, D.C., pedestrians walk today on original colonial brick sidewalks. Where properly designed and built, brick pavements are indeed durable.

Three types of bases are used: a flexible base of compacted earth covered by sand, gravel, sand on gravel, or sand–cement mixture, all of which are for flexible brick pavements; a semirigid base of asphaltic or bituminous concrete for flexible brick pavements; or a rigid base of reinforced concrete for rigid or flexible brick pavements. A cushion of 1 or 2 in. (25 or 50 mm) of sand or a cushion of asphalt-saturated felt paper is placed over the base. A setting bed of mortar, ½–1 in. (12–25 mm) thick, is placed over semirigid and rigid bases. Brick should conform to ASTM C7 for highways, C410 for industrial floors, and C902 for pedestrian and light traffic pavements in moderate or mild climates. ASTM is now developing a specification for patio brick.

Mortared or grouted joints are used for brick pavements over rigid bases. Mortar may be applied conventionally with a trowel on a mortar bed. Brick may be set on a mortar bed but with void vertical joints that are subsequently grouted; alternatively, a cement–sand mix may be swept into the joints and sprayed with a fine mist of water, in which case care must be taken to keep the brick clean. Mortar should conform to ASTM C270, type M. Brick set without mortar or grout is placed over flexible bases. Mortarless brick pavements may be swept with dry sand or a cement–sand mixture. Flexible brick pavements may be used for walks, patios, terraces, and residential driveways. Mortared or grouted brick pavements should be used for all other applications.

Pavements should be sloped ⅛–¼ in./ft (10–20 mm/m). To prevent horizontal movement, a curb or edging must be provided for mortarless pavements. Expansion joints should be placed at edges, turns, interruptions, and at horizontal intervals of not more than 12 ft (4.6 m) in each direction. Popular surface bond patterns include many variations of basket weave, herringbone, and circular, running, and stack bond.

DESIGN QUALITY CONTROL

Masonry quality control begins with good design, ie, properly prepared specifications and good detailing. The most common masonry wall failures are cracking, leaking, and spalling in that order, all of which can be eliminated by adherence to the following wall design check list:

1. *General.*
   - Comply with the building code requirements for masonry and for related subjects, such as fire resistance and sound transmission control.
   - Rigorously enforce construction contract requirements when they are correct. Correct errors as soon as possible.
2. *Clay brick.*
   - Specify ASTM C216 for solid face brick or ASTM C652 for hollow face brick where color, texture, finish, uniformity, and control of efflorescence, cracks, and warpage are required. Otherwise, specific ASTM C62 building brick.

- Specify ASTM C216 face brick or ASTM C62 building brick for greater fire resistance and lower sound transmission. Specify ASTM C652 hollow brick for lower heat transmission and lower cost.

- Specify grade-SW brick in insulated cavity walls and for all exterior use in the United States, except in coastal southern California, southwestern New Mexico, south Texas, and south Florida, in which areas grade MW may be used in walls above grade. Grade NW may be used on interiors.

- In ASTM C216, specify type-FBX face brick where a high degree of mechanical perfection and a narrow color range are required. Otherwise, specify type FBS. Do not specify type FBA without a thorough understanding of availability. Type FBS may be furnished if no type is specified.

- If minimum average compressive strength greater than 3000 psi (20.7 MPa) is required for brick, specify the required strength.

- Specify ASTM C126 for ceramic glazed brick. For exterior use, require submission of recent ASTM C67 freeze–thaw test data prior to construction and notify brick manufacturer of intended exterior use of glazed brick.

- Specify the largest modular size brick available and aesthetically acceptable.

- Do not specify brick masonry for copings or low slope sills.

- Specify low IRA brick to be protected from rain when stored. Specify cover for all walls when not being worked on prior to completion.

- Do not specify sand-finished bricks in exterior, except where the driving rain index is less than 1.5 (23) or for any use where flexural strength is important (Fig. 3).

3. *Mortar and grout.*
   - Specify ASTM C270 masonry mortar. Specify mortar type recommended in appendix to ASTM C270 except as indicated further on. Require non-air-entrained Portland cement–lime mortars for all structural uses of masonry, unless complete structural test data are provided on walls (not prisms) in compression, flexure, and shear, which justify the use of masonry cement mortar. Use cement–lime or masonry cement mortars elsewhere, eg, in veneers on low-rise buildings and for interior, nonbearing partitions.

   - Specify mortars having relatively high lime content where structurally adequate for use with brick having high IRA and for use in summer. Specify mortars having relatively high cement content for use with brick having low IRA and for use in winter.

   - Specify the weakest mortar that has adequate durability and strength. Do not specify type-O mortar for structural use or where the masonry is likely to be frozen while nominally saturated.

   - Specify type-III (high early strength) Portland cement for winter construction. Specify ASTM C207, type-S, hydrated lime. Do not permit the use of air-entrained Portland cement or air-entrained lime for structural masonry.

   - Do not permit the use of any admixture in mortar except mineral oxide pigments. Limit maximum pigment content to quantities that are known not to adversely affect the physical properties of the mortar.

   - Specify that job-mixed mortars be accurately proportioned by measuring cement, lime, and sand in cubic foot boxes. Do not permit the use of shovel measurements. Specify that three quarters of the required water, one-half of the sand, all of the cementitious materials, and all pigments, if any, be briefly mixed together in a mechanical mixer. Specify that the remaining water and sand then be charged, and mixed continuously for 3–5 min.

   - Specify ASTM C476 masonry grout. Require coarse grout when least dimension of grout space exceeds 2 in. (50 mm), otherwise specify fine grout.

   - Do not specify pargeting in cavity walls.

4. *Metals in masonry.*
   - Specify stainless steel, copper-coated steel, or hot-dip galvanized coating for all steel having less than 4 in. of masonry cover, ie, all ties, anchors, fasteners, joint reinforcements, structural reinforcing bars, lintels, and shelf angles, including their shims, washers, bolts, and inserts. Structural reinforcing steel, having less than 4 in. (100 mm) of masonry cover, should be galvanized in accordance with ASTM A123. Other hardware and miscellaneous steel should be galvanized in accordance with ASTM A153, copper coated in accordance with ASTM B227, grade-30 HS, or stainless steel, ASTM A666, types 304 or 316, grade C. Do not juxtapose dissimilar metals. Require that cavity wall ties and veneer ties have adequate stiffness to fully transfer lateral loads. Require that all metal in mortar or grout be solidly embedded.

   - Require that the materials, design, and installation of all metal anchors, ties, and attachments conform to the requirements of *Connectors for Masonry* (13), Canadian Standard CAN 3-A370-M 84.

   - Ensure that shelf angles are properly designed for torsion and shimmed to avoid rotation. Extend shelf angles longitudinally beyond column faces at corners to avoid vertical continuity of masonry. Extend horizontal leg of shelf angle under at least two-thirds of exterior masonry wythe.

   - Carefully check compatibility of construction tolerances for structural frames and for masonry walls supported on frames to ensure that compliance with the construction contract documents is not impossible.

   - Do not extend bed joint reinforcing through control or expansion joints.

5. *Flashing and coping.*

- Provide flashing under copings and sills, at the head of wall openings, at spandrels, shelf angles, and lintels, and at the base of walls. Specify the sealing of all flashing joints, and provide dams at the end of horizontal runs, ie, turned up 6–9 in. (150–225 mm) and sealed. Extend wall flashing outward beyond face of wall at least ¼ in. (6 mm) and turn down at 45° to form drip. Provide sealant in dihedral angle at wall face. Extend wall base flashing from face of wall inward through one wythe, turn up 6–9 in. (150–225 mm), and turn into a reglet or interior wythe, or extend up behind sheathing. Extend flashing upward above roofs at least 8 in. (200 mm). Do not extend flashing longitudinally through control or expansion joints.
- Extend all stone or concrete cornices, copings, sills, and wall caps 2 in. (50 mm) from the face of the wall and provide a drip at least ⅝ in. (16 mm) wide by ⅜ in. (10 mm) deep.

6. *Exterior coatings.*

- Avoid the use of all exterior coatings on brick masonry, but where necessary specify latex paint, water–cement paint, or stucco. Do not specify colorless coatings, except on walls built of highly porous masonry units, having a facial IRA greater than 1.8 g/(min·m²).

7. *Insulation.*

- If rigid board insulation is used in a masonry cavity wall, provide a total cavity width equal to the thickness of the insulation plus 2 in. (50 mm). Ensure that the board insulation is well anchored flush with the cavity face of the interior wythe.

8. *Vapor retarder.*

- Provide a vapor retarder in all walls having an exterior wythe of glazed brick. Provide vents similar to weep holes in the top of cavity walls having glazed-brick exterior wythes.

9. *Design to resist water permeance.*

- Specify only concave or V-tooled mortar joints for exterior use except where the driving rain index is less than 1.5 (23) (Fig. 4).
- Locate weep holes in the exterior face of the wall at 20–32 in. (500–810 mm) oc located immediately above the horizontal leg of all internal flashing.
- Specify that all head, bed, and collar mortar joints be solidly filled.
- Require all cavities (but not cores) to be kept clean of mortar and debris. Do not expect an air space less than 2 in. (50 mm) in width to be kept clean.
- Specify a minimum thickness of 2 in. (50 mm) for all cavities.
- Specify that the mason contractor examine all masonry units for color, cracks, chips, and warpage and that unacceptable units be culled before the units are placed in use.
- Specify that all clay brick, having an IRA of more than 0.83 g/(min·m²) [1.3 kg/(min·m²)], be wetted to a nominally saturated, surface dry condition before being laid. Do not wet brick having an IRA of less than 0.17 g/(min·in.²) [0.26 kg/(min·m²)].
- Specify that masonry units be laid within one minute of spreading mortar.
- Except for some compelling reason, design all exterior walls as veneer wall types or cavity walls, or require solidly grouted cells or cavities in all other wall types where the driving rain index is greater than 1.5 (23) (Fig. 3).

10. *Crack control.*

- In panel or curtain walls having an exterior wythe of clay brick masonry, locate horizontal expansion joints immediately below shelf angles. Design expansion joint width for a movement of 0.0015 times vertical spacing between horizontal expansion joints.
- Provide expansion joints between top of wall and underside of beam or slab above to ensure that flexural deflection does not inadvertently load a nonbearing panel wall or partition.
- Locate ⅜-in. (10-mm) wide continuous vertical expansion joints in walls at horizontal intervals of about 18 ft (5.5 m).
- Locate vertical expansion joints at pilasters, recesses, returns, chases, changes in wall thickness or height, and at one side of wall openings.
- Specify flexible anchorage for walls to frames, permitting horizontal and vertical movements in a plane parallel to the wall but rigidly resisting lateral movement. Where necessary, enclose, but do not encase, beams and columns with masonry.
- Break bond between masonry and foundations and between masonry and roofs.
- Limit deflection of horizontal flexural members supporting masonry to 1/600th of the span but not more than 0.3 in. (8 mm).
- Ensure that the anchorage and backup for brick masonry veneer are sufficiently rigid to prevent flexural cracking of the veneer.
- Ensure that the maximum differential vertical movement between adjacent columns supporting masonry does not exceed 1/500th of the distance between columns or 0.6 in. (15 mm), whichever is less.
- Ensure that the maximum differential horizontal movement between the top and bottom of a single-story segment of a column supporting masonry does not exceed 1/500th of the story height or 0.6 in. (15 mm), whichever is less.
- Specify that all expansion, construction, and control joints be free of mortar, reinforcing, flashing, or debris that would inhibit proper functioning of the joint. Ensure that movement joints are sealed with properly designed and built, durable, elastic sealant and backer rod.
- Ensure that all cracks around pipes, conduits, and other wall perforations are acoustically sealed and fire resistant.

CONSTRUCTION

The value of masonry construction in the United States in 1982 was $4.3 billion, or approximately 2.6% of all building construction dollar volume. In that year, about 20,000 masonry contractors employed approximately 109,000 construction workers whose productivity had been investigated by more than 200 researchers in 18 nations, resulting in more than 250 reports on the subject. Design decisions have a more significant effect on bricklayer productivity than do labor motivation, union work rules, or contractor efficiency (Table 3).

Brick masonry costs are reduced by the use of large, straight, solid, unbroken, single-wythe wall areas. These wall areas are faced one side and built of local, red, common, conventionally shaped, textured, packaged, large brick units laid from adjustable scaffolding on low buildings with minimum supervision, during favorable weather, with the aid of corner poles, to modular dimensions, in common bond with thin, flush cut mortar joints; the contents of the latter are high in air and lime, low in cement, and free of admixtures. It is interesting to note that masons have no control over any of those variables that in total affect their productivity to a degree that makes their own motivation relatively insignificant. Those concerned with mason productivity should investigate the unnecessary limitations placed on that productivity by designers and the contractors.

Bricklayers' unions have often been erroneously accused of conspiracy to limit by quota the number of bricks a union mason may lay during a day's work. There is no documented evidence to support that allegation. Bricklayers generally have been most receptive to innovations in tools, materials, and prefabrication, although there are some local exceptions, ie, refusal to accept corner poles on commercial work by some union locals.

Mason productivity has increased 40% in the United States in the last 60 years, principally because of improved materials-handling techniques. In 1906, normal mason productivity was 400–500 face bricks laid per 8-hr day.

Today, 570–700 is normal for the same quality of work. Depending on typical design variables, mason productivity might reasonably range from 200–1200 bricks per day. It may be indicative of the work effort of bricklayers that 21% of their work injuries result from overexertion.

MAINTENANCE AND RESTORATION

Water permeance of masonry walls may be reduced by tuck pointing, surface grouting, or coating of the masonry and the replacement of sealant joints in or adjacent to the masonry. Cleaning of masonry may involve high pressure steam, hand washing, high pressure water, chemicals, and wet or dry aggregate cleaning (17).

Tuck pointing may be necessary if mortar joints have disintegrated, after perhaps 15–50 years, depending on the environment and the quality of materials, design, and construction. Tuck pointing is accomplished by cutting away defective mortar at the wall face and replacing it with new mortar. Mortar is removed to a depth of at least ½ in. with hand or power tools. Mortar for tuck pointing should be of the same composition as the original mortar. In the absence of such information or testing to establish the original mortar mix, mortar should be proportioned by volume of one part Portland cement, one part hydrated lime, and six parts sand.

Surface grouting requires about one-seventh of the labor needed for tuck pointing. After the wall has been water soaked, a slurry of fine grout is scrubbed into the cracks in the wall face, and the grout is then cleaned from the face of the units. Proprietary or job-mixed grouts may be used.

Grimm (17) discusses 15 types of coatings for masonry, including paint, plaster, stucco, membranes, and colorless coatings. Colorless coatings do not generally bridge cracks wider than 0.5 mm. Such coatings may somewhat reduce water permeance of masonry, but they do not prevent it. They do, however, retard the normal drying-out process and, therefore, may promote damaging cryptoflorescence

Table 3. Economic Effect of Some Wall Design and Construction Changes[a]

Item Number	Design Change	Relative Wall Cost
1	None, prototypical cavity wall	1.00
2	Use economy Norman unglazed face brick [4 × 4 × 12 in. (100 × 100 × 300 mm)]	0.92
3	Lay brick in herringbone bond pattern	1.65
4	Use colored mortar in exterior wythe	1.02
5	Use modular design	0.95
6	Use close inspection	1.07
7	Use curved-wall radius of 20 ft	1.09
8	Use half as many wall openings with same area of openings	0.97
9	Increase cost of brick 25%	1.04
10	Increase cost of labor 25%	1.13
11	Use corner poles	0.85
12	Items 2 and 5 combined	0.89
13	Items 2, 5, 8, and 11 combined	0.72

[a] Ref. 8.

and contribute to freeze–thaw damage. Water–cement or latex paints are suitable coatings.

Considering the variety of stains that may occur on masonry, careful examination is necessary to identify the stain and the type of masonry material. Stains may be caused by acid, metals, asphalt, tar, carbon, soot, chalk, soil, crayons, mortar, grout, pencils, paint, rust, and florescent salts. Every cleaning operation should be tried first on a small, inconspicuous wall area. After removal of spot stains, general removal of atmospheric dirt is usually best accomplished by chemical cleaning. Very lightly applied wet- or dry-sand cleaning may be necessary for stains that are otherwise very difficult to remove. However, sand blasting is not recommended. Because of the many variables in cleaning masonry, experienced management and well-trained craftspersons are essential.

Structural damage to masonry walls may be caused by: ground movement; thermal or moisture movement; shrinkage; fire; frame, roof, or floor movement; sulfate attack; corrosion of embedded metal; frost; salts; and unsound materials. Strength and stability may be impaired by wall bulges exceeding $\frac{3}{8}$ in. (10 mm) or out of plumb by 1 in. (25.4 mm) in one story for typical brick walls 12 in. (305 mm) or more in thickness. Smaller tolerances are appropriate for cavity walls and those built with high lime or masonry cement mortars. Repair methods include use of tie-rods, buttresses, epoxy grouting, and partial demolition. Demolition methods include manual, mechanical, and explosive wrecking. Structural crack repair of masonry may be accomplished by pressure grouting with epoxy resins to prevent water entry, to restore structural integrity, or to improve appearance.

In seismic regions, many older buildings have unreinforced masonry walls that become life threatening during earthquakes. Techniques for strengthening such walls include sprayed concrete, steel frame shoring, and coring to reinforce existing brick masonry (25).

BIBLIOGRAPHY

1. W. L. Sheppard, *Chemical-Resistant Masonry,* Marcel Dekker, Inc., New York, 1982.

2. P. G. McHenry, *Adobe and Rammed Earth Buildings,* John Wiley & Sons, Inc., New York, 1984.

3. G. D. Paepe and E. H. Lapeyseu, *Bricks, Brickmaking, and Brickworks—A Selected Bibliography 1962–1970,* PB 197–066, National Technical Information Service, Springfield, Va., 1970.

4. W. E. Brownell, *Structural Clay Products,* Springer-Verlag, New York, 1976.

5. F. H. Clews, *Heavy Clay Technology,* Academic Press, Inc., Orlando, Fla., 1969.

6. "Passive Solar Heating with Brick Masonry" in *Technical Notes on Brick Construction,* Series No. 43, Brick Institute of America, Reston, Va., May–June 1981.

7. M. Vance, *Modular Coordination (Architecture): A Bibliography,* Vance Bibliographies, No. A 945, Monticello, Ill., 1983.

8. C. T. Grimm, "Estimating Masonry Wall and Column Cost," *J. Constr. Div.,* 627 (Dec. 1977).

9. C. T. Grimm, "The Color of Structures," *J. Struct. Div.,* 1871 (Sept. 1975).

10. C. T. Grimm, "Durability of Brick Masonry: A Review of the Literature," in *Masonry: Research, Application, and Problems,* STP 871, American Society for Testing and Materials, Philadelphia, Pa., 1985.

11. H. C. Plummer, *Brick and Tile Engineering,* Brick Institute of America, Reston, Va., 1962.

12. R. T. Packard, ed., *Ramsey–Sleeper Architectural Graphic Standards,* 7th ed., John Wiley & Sons, Inc., New York, 1981.

13. *Connectors for Masonry,* CAN 3-A370-M84, Canadian Standards Association, Rexdale, Canada, 1984.

14. C. T. Grimm and J. A. Yura, "Shelf Angles for Masonry Veneer," *J. Struct. Div.,* in press.

15. "Reinforced Brick Masonry" in *Technical Notes on Brick Construction,* Series No. 17, Brick Institute of America, Reston, Va., 1962.

16. C. T. Grimm, "Water Permeance of Masonry Walls: A Review of the Literature" in Ref. 23, pp. 178–199.

17. C. T. Grimm, "Masonry Maintenance and Restoration—A Guide to the Literature," *Structural Renovation and Restoration,* Boston Society of Civil Engineers, Boston, Mass., 1979, p. 71.

18. C. T. Grimm, "Strength and Related Properties of Brick Masonry," *J. Struct. Div.,* 217 (Jan. 1979).

19. D. Lenczner, "Design of Brick Masonry for Elastic and Creep Movements" in *Second Canadian Masonry Symposium,* Carleton University, Ottawa, Canada, June 9, 1980, pp. 303–316.

20. K. J. Wyatt and J. W. Morgan, "The Role of Creep in Brick Work," *Archit. Sci. Rev.* **17**(2), 22 (June 1974).

21. J. G. Gross, R. D. Dikkers, and J. C. Grogan, *Recommended Practice for Engineered Brick Masonry,* Brick Institute of America, Reston, Va., 1969.

22. D. W. Fowler and T. J. Fraley, "Investigation of Polymer-Impregnated Brick Masonry," *J. Struct. Div.* **100**(ST1), 1 (Jan. 1974).

23. C. T. Grimm, "A Driving Rain Index for Masonry Walls" in *Masonry: Materials, Properties, and Performances,* ASTM STP 778, American Society for Testing and Materials, Philadelphia, Pa., 1982, pp. 171–177.

24. "Thermal Transmission Corrections for Dynamic Conditions—M Factor" in *Technical Notes on Brick Construction,* No. 4B, Brick Institute of America, Reston, Va., Mar.–Apr. 1977.

25. J. M. Plecnic, J. J. Howard, J. H. Fogarty, and V. S. Parra, "Strengthening of Unreinforced Masonry Buildings" in *Proceedings of the Seventh International Brick Masonry Conference,* University of Melbourne, Melbourne, Australia, Feb. 1985.

26. "Fire Resistance," in *Technical Notes on Brick Construction,* Series No. 16, Brick Institute of America, Reston, Va., Oct. 1974.

27. A. J. Newman, and D. Whiteside, "Water and Air Penetration through Masonry Walls—a Device for the Measurement of Air Leakage In-Situ," *Br. Ceram. Trans. J.* **83**, 190 (1984).

28. *ASHRAE Handbook of Fundamentals,* American Society of Heating, Refrigerating, and Air Conditioning Engineers, Inc., New York, 1985.

29. B. Ellingwood and A. Tallin, "Limit States Criteria for Masonry Construction," *J. Struct. Div.* **3**(1), 108 (Jan. 1950).

30. J. Tellett, *A Review of the Literature on Brickwork Arches,* Technical Note No. 338, British Ceramic Research Association, Stoke-on-Trent, UK, Aug. 1982.

31. J. Heyman, *The Masonry Arch,* Ellis Horwood, Ltd., Chichester, UK, 1982.

32. H. Straub, *A History of Civil Engineering,* The MIT Press, Cambridge, Mass., 1952, p. 111.

33. C. T. Grimm, "Brick Masonry Shells," *J. Struct. Div.,* 79 (Jan. 1975).

34. *Code of Practice for Structural Use of Masonry,* BS 5628, British Standards Institution, London, 1978, Pts. I and II.

35. "The Contemporary Bearing Wall: Design Tables for Columns and Walls" in *Technical Notes on Brick Construction,* No. 24E, Brick Institute of America, Reston, Va., Nov. 1970.

36. R. A. Crist, and L. E. Cattaneo in L. E. Cattaneo, ed., *Earthquake-Resistant Masonry Construction: National Workshop,* National Bureau of Standards Building Science Series 106, U.S. Government Printing Office, Washington, D.C., 1977.

37. *Proceedings of the International Research Conference on Earthquake Engineering,* Institute of Earthquake Engineering and Engineering Seismology, Skopje, Yugoslavia, June 30, 1980, p. 361.

38. C. B. Monk, *Resistance of Structural Clay Masonry to Dynamic Forces—A Design Manual for Blast Resistance,* Research Report No. 7, Brick Institute of America, Reston, Va., 1958.

39. R. L. Davison and C. B. Monk, "Thin Brick Walls Are the Only Support in a Design for Multi-Story Buildings," *Archit. Rec.,* 208 (June 1952).

40. J. E. Walton, *American Appraisal Company's Comparison of Apartment Building Costs in 205 Major Markets,* Brick Institute of America, Reston, Va., 1974.

41. L. R. Baker, "Structural Action of Brickwork Panel Walls Subject to Wind Loads," *J. Aust. Ceram. Soc.* **9**(1), 1 (May 1973).

42. C. T. Grimm, "Design of Nonreinforced Masonry Panel Walls" in *Proceedings of the Second North American Masonry Conference,* University of Maryland, College Park, Md., Aug. 1982, pp. 1–11.

43. C. T. Grimm, "Corrosion of Steel in Brick Masonry" in *Masonry: Research, Application, and Problems,* ASTM STP 871, American Society for Testing and Materials, Philadelphia, Pa., 1985.

44. W. G. Curtin and K. Al-Hashimi, *Design of Brickwork in Industrial Buildings,* The Brick Development Association, Windsor, UK, 1978.

See also ADOBE CONSTRUCTION; CONCRETE MASONRY; STONE, NATURAL BUILDING.

CLAYFORD T. GRIMM, PE
Austin, Texas

BRIDGES

BRIDGE DESIGN THROUGH THE BEGINNING OF THE TWENTIETH CENTURY

The function of a bridge is to provide a passageway for people, vehicles, or materials where normal surface construction is not practical. It is this singleness of purpose that distinguishes a bridge from other forms of structures. Structure is the dominant factor, and a bridge's form should reflect this. The essence of an elegant bridge is simplicity of line, in which the structural form is expressed to full extent.

As early as 3200 B.C., the Sumerians understood arch construction, and there exists evidence of a Nile bridge from 2650 B.C. The oldest extant datable bridge (ca 850 B.C.) is a slab stone, single-arch bridge over the river Meles in Smyrna (present Izmir), Turkey. There are examples from antiquity of remarkable engineering coupled with beauty, including the stone arch bridge, the Ponte de' Quattro Capi, built in 62 B.C. to connect the city of Rome with an island in the Tiber (Fig. 1), the Hellenic bridge of the fourth century B.C. near Assos in Greece (Fig. 2), which used stone stringers, and Trajan's famous pontoon and trestle bridge, built across the Danube during his conquest of Dacia, by Appollodorus of Damascus in 106 A.D. (Fig. 3). However, the majority of large-scale spanning solutions from antiquity were based on the germ of the stone arch bridge. Sometimes builders employed imaginative embellishments above the roadbed for cover, as in the stone arch bridge over the Grand Canal, Venice, built by Antonia

Figure 1. The Ponte de' Quattro Capi, Rome, 62 B.C. Courtesy of the American Society of Civil Engineers.

Figure 2. Stone stringer bridge, near Assos, Greece, fourth century B.C. Courtesy of the American Society of Civil Engineers.

Figure 3. Trajan's pontoon and trestle bridge over the Danube by Apollodorus, 106 A.D. Line drawing by Rowland Mainstone; Courtesy of Harper Bros.

Da Ponte (1591) (Fig. 4), or multiplied the arches until the loads were absorbed by the bank abutments, as in Roman aqueducts such as the Pont du Gard used to carry water from Uzès to Nemausus (modern Nîmes) in France in the first century B.C. (Fig. 5). As early as the fourth century B.C., Rome began building aqueducts. The triple-tiered aqueduct at Nîmes is 160 ft high, the highest in the ancient world. Large uncemented blocks weighing up to two tons each formed large arch spans (some 82 ft) below, and smaller arches grouped in threes above carried the channels for water. To place the large voussoir stones in the arch, large blocks of stone projected from the middle tier to support wooden scaffolding and falsework. The water was transported a distance of 30 mi and provided each citizen of the Roman province of Nemausus with approximately 100 gal daily. The finished aqueduct stands as a testament to not only surveying and engineering skills but to a concern for mixing aesthetics with function. Yet, it was not until the nineteenth century that new experiments in the use of spanning materials and engineering principles brought the bridge as a building type into its own. For example, whereas the earliest bridge trusses date back to antiquity in wood construction, Theodore Burr of Pennsylvania (1803–1804) reinterpreted the traditional use of the king post truss by combining it with a wooden arch (Fig. 6) and is credited with the initial use of an

Figure 4. Covered stone arch bridge, Grand Canal, Venice, by Antonia Da Ponte, 1591. Courtesy of Random House.

Figure 5. Pont du Gard aqueduct, Nîmes, France, first century B.C. Courtesy of Random House.

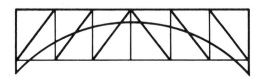

Figure 6. Burr's arch truss bridge, 1804 to late nineteenth century.

arch to strengthen a truss. Other contributors to the development of the arch truss bridge were Palmer's "permanent" bridge of 1805 (194-ft span) and Wernwag's Upper Ferry Bridge of 1812 (340-ft span), both built over the Schuylkill River. Burr's arch truss bridge was used from 1804 through the late nineteenth century; its length ranged from 50 to 175 ft (15–50 m). The type combined a wooden arch with a multiple king post and also later combined the arch with wooden trusses.

The early nineteenth century exploited the use of the truss as a structural system. Ithiel Town used closely spaced diagonal timbers (forming a lattice) to distribute the loads evenly, and his patent of 1820 (Fig. 7) anticipates the structural principle of the balloon frame (1832) in house construction. His bridge type, which consisted of a system of cross-hatched wooden diagonals with no verticals, was popular from 1820 to the late nineteenth century. The lengths of the bridges varied from 50 to 220 ft (15–66 m). William Howe followed with a truss patent in 1840, which employed both wood and wrought iron; the iron provided the essential feature of metal verticals used as tension members, and the wooden diagonals (as in Town's scheme) were utilized as compression members. The Howe Truss was used into the twentieth century; lengths were between 30 and 150 ft (9–45 m). Whereas the Howe Truss (Fig. 8) was a vast improvement over the all-wood bridge

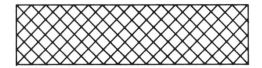

Figure 7. Town lattice truss, 1820 to late nineteenth century.

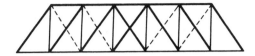

Figure 8. The Howe Truss, 1840 to early twentieth century.

Figure 9. Proposal for a 600-ft bridge across the Thames, London, 1801, Thomas Telford (detail). Courtesy of the Science Museum, London.

(especially for railroad bridges), the unprecedented loads and spans required to meet the demands of an industrialized era mandated not only iron but steel as the nineteenth century wore on, and fostered entirely new systems of support as well. For more on the history of truss bridges, consult Refs. 1–6.

As the accomplishments of the Industrial Revolution became realized in such structures as the iron and glass Crystal Palace in 1851, the predominantly steel Brooklyn Bridge in 1883, and the Eiffel Tower (1887–1889), it appeared as if the engineer, not the architect, would shape the cities of the future. It also became clear to the engineers, who had the task of producing the large-scale construction demanded, that steel could carry loads far beyond the capacity of iron or masonry.

The first steps toward the industrial manufacture of iron products took place at Abraham Darby's foundry in Coalbrookdale in Great Britain. In 1747, coke replaced charcoal for smelting iron ore and by 1750, malleable pig-iron bars were being produced. Until this point, the use of iron for construction had been little explored and was limited primarily to structural members (tie rods, chains, and supports for arches and vaults) and wrought-iron fixtures. The new technique in iron production brought about other building support materials, such as cast iron girders, beams, and columns, first put to use in St. Anne's Church, Liverpool (1770–1772) (7).

The versatile qualities of iron encouraged experimentation. The construction trades found that by means of casting, iron could be molded to lend support to complex areas; it was fire resistant, easy to use, and could span large areas with slender supports at distant centers (8,9). Designers soon began using iron for bridges; from 1775 to 1779, a 100-ft cast-iron bridge was built over the Severn at Coalbrookdale; its "five ribs were subdivided into two series of half-arches, each cast in a single piece by the Darby Foundry" (9). A structure built up from ribs consisting of openwork cast-iron voussoirs and wrought-iron straps was proposed by Thomas Telford in 1801 for a 600-ft bridge to replace the Old London Bridge across the Thames; however, because of difficulties in acquiring land and the City sponsors' feeling that the bridge design was too daring, the project was abandoned. A sketch of the design (Fig. 9) lends to the modern lines of the bridge the appearance of a futuristic intruder, as it spans the classically oriented London banks, while a three-masted wooden vessel of the day passes beneath its skeletal metal form. The advantages and new techniques of iron would soon make themselves known to the major cities of Europe and the United States.

Experimentation continued, bridges spanned longer distances, and other countries became aware of the durability and building facility of this metal. In Paris (1801–1803), for example, de Cessart and Dillon employed a cast-

iron multiple-arch structure (the first French bridge of iron) for the Pont des Arts Bridge, which continues to be used today (10).

Thomas Telford's Menai Bridge in Wales (1819–1826) represents the first monumental appearance of a metal suspension bridge (Fig. 10). This prototype of the Brooklyn Bridge was a road bridge with the roadbed hung from wrought-iron chains and for several years remained the longest bridge of this type in Britain (11). The iron chains were replaced in 1939 with four chains of high tensile steel. Other suspension bridges (Conway Castle Bridge, by Telford, 1822–1826; Rhone Bridge, by Marc Sequin, 1824) replaced chains with cables, rope spun from wire.

Besides designing the 700-ft Clifton Suspension Bridge over the river Avon, which is described as one of the masterpieces of 19th-century engineering, I. K. Brunel, a naval architect, initiated the technique of self-supporting riveted shell structures applied to building his ships (9). By the early 1830s, the new railways were increasing the demand for bridges. Robert Stephenson and Francis Thompson adopted Brunel's technique of riveting for their tubular Britannia Bridge (Fig. 11) over the Menai Straits (1845–1850): "trains were carried inside a rectangular tube of rolled iron [wrought iron, not cast] that constituted a continuous box girder" (11) which extended from between massive masonry towers. In the 1840s, rolled iron eliminated the seams needed in cast-iron beams and thus avoided the dangerous and unpredictable shearing factor.

Figure 10. Menai Bridge in Wales, 1819–1826, Thomas Telford. Courtesy of the Mansell Collection.

Figure 11. Brittania Bridge, over the Menai Straits, 1850, Robert Stephenson and Francis Thompson. Courtesy of the Science Museum, London.

The highly original tubular iron bridge consisted of four 460-ft-long wrought-iron tubes constructed on the shore. Its 1511-ft overall length made it the world's longest railway bridge until Roebling's 1855 Niagara Falls Bridge. Suspension chains to be hung from the tall towers to lend support to the iron tubes were later deemed unnecessary.

While Stephenson was laboring over his weighty beamed structure, a German immigrant, John A. Roebling, was developing in the United States the principle of Marc Sequin's lightweight, cable suspension bridge. By 1848, Roebling had already completed a 535-ft-long suspension bridge in Lackawaxen, Penn. to span the Delaware River; Roebling supposedly used this bridge as the prototype for the Brooklyn Bridge (12). A cable-spinner by trade, Roebling's first noted success at designing came in 1855 with his Niagara Falls Bridge (Fig. 12). Aided by its favorable site, and even more by its surprising ability to carry railroad trains (the first suspension bridge to do so safely), it soon gained distinction; it had been previously suspected that the vibration from the cars would break the links in chain-supported bridges. Following the failure of the bridge in Wheeling, West Va. (which then, at 1010 feet, had the longest span in the world), because of oscillations due to wind loads, Roebling secured the bridge's deck with

diagonal cable stays, something he would repeat in the Cincinnati and Brooklyn Bridges. On the Niagara Bridge, Roebling relied on numerous iron wire and rope stays tied between the bridge's deck and the floor of the valley to prevent oscillations from wind and to counter train vibrations. The original truss work was timber. The 821-ft Niagara Falls Bridge carried a single-track railroad above and carriage traffic below. The bridge was removed in 1897.

Some preconceived notions about suspension bridges are discussed in Refs. 13 and 14. Suspension-bridge designers found, for example, that the major problem would not be load but stability. A prime example of this can be seen in the failure of the Tacoma Narrows Bridge, which collapsed due to aerodynamic instability just four months after completion in July 1940. Today, all major bridges must have their aerodynamic properties tested by a wind tunnel (13) (See Twentieth-Century Bridge Design for more on the Tacoma Narrows Bridge). Ref. 13 also compares the stress difference of the Forth Railroad Bridge (1881–1890), which is over 1½ mi long and has three cantilevers, each rising to a height of 361 ft above sea level, to the Forth Road Bridge (1964). Standing alongside its counterpart (near Edinburgh), the Forth Road Bridge has a central span of 3300 ft of cable drawn between its two main towers (15) (Fig. 13). A parallel is also drawn in Ref. 13 between the stability of these two bridges to that of a cart wheel whose ruggedness and durability must withstand the cornering forces as bending stress, and vertical load as compressive and bending ones, "requiring a substantial cross-section" (Fig. 14). A bicycle wheel, on the other hand, "absorbs all cornering and loading forces as pure tension in its spokes" (13). Linked with the knowledge "that steel in tension can be made of hard drawn wire, thereby increasing its strength several times for a given weight" (13), materials and mathematics are seen working congruently. Thus, the heavy metal tubing of the Rail Bridge, which boasted the two longest clear spans in the world at 1710 ft each, stands in contrast to the

Figure 12. The Niagara Falls Bridge, 1855, John Roebling.

Figure 13. Forth Railway Bridge, 1890. Courtesy of BBC Hulton Picture Library.

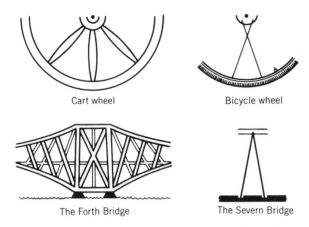

Cart wheel   Bicycle wheel

The Forth Bridge   The Severn Bridge

Figure 14. A comparison of various structural principles in bridge design.

"wire-suspended economy" of the Road Bridge (13). It must be said about the Forth Rail Bridge that because of the unique use of hollow tubing and carefully riveted construction, its bridge strutting was both strong and light for its day (16). The Forth Bridge and Brooklyn Bridge are acknowledged as "the two outstanding achievements in bridge building of the Nineteenth Century" (17).

As John Roebling finished construction on his Niagara Falls Bridge (1855) and apparently, in the winter of that year, hit upon the idea of the Brooklyn Bridge while stranded on a ferryboat attempting to cross the ice-clogged East River (18), technological improvements in iron, glass, and steel were taking place in Europe. Puddle iron was in its industrial stages in 1840; Bessemer converters were producing steel in 1856. The glass industry had also made strides from the mid-eighteenth century onward, and the marriage of iron and glass seemed to culminate in the building of Joseph Paxton's Crystal Palace in London (1851). There were critics, however, such as John Ruskin, who insisted that "the Crystal Palace was a greenhouse like others, only larger" (19). The vast greenhouse at Kew by Decimus Burton and Richard Turner (1845–1847) (in many ways more innovative in its use of materials than the Crystal Palace) possibly gave inspiration for this remark. The design of the greenhouse, however, was conceived to fit its only function of housing plants, whereas the implications of Paxton's design (for human habitation) were more far-reaching and stated an entirely different approach to the same materials. Certain features of the Crystal Palace had to be acknowledged. This huge building, 1851 ft in length to match its exhibition year, was erected in nine months thanks to prefabricated cast-iron units. Its blend of metal and glass, producing a boundless interior suggesting transparency and weightlessness, also presented new aesthetic conceptions to the architect of the future, though essentially it was a post and lintel system with metal for arches. Apparently, the greatest achievement was "the merging of interior and exterior . . . by a seemingly insubstantial and unreal tracery of walls" (19).

Three decades later (1887–1889), Gustave Eiffel (1832–1923) would use three-dimensional steel openwork to create this airy and weightless effect in his famous tower, in its day the tallest edifice ever raised by man. Eiffel

had previously built some of the world's first high towers in iron, such as the Rouzat Viaduct over the Sioule River near Gannat, France (1869). The towers flared at the base to resist wind loads and anticipated the form of his famous tower built 20 years later. The two wrought-iron towers carried a single-track rail line. The towers reached a height of 59 m and supported three trellis girders that spanned 60 m each. The viaduct at Rouzat was one of four constructed by Eiffel between 1867 and 1869 (20). Eiffel's Bon Marché department store in Paris (1876, the same year he constructed the new crescent arch format in the Duoro Bridge in Portugal) drew upon the metal and glass principles established in greenhouses and greenhouse building designs such as the Crystal Palace. Although the metal supports are exposed on the interior only, the integration of the side wall of the gallery and the glass roof brings his style very close to a pure metal aesthetic, which would be witnessed in the late 1890s when architectural detailing no longer relied on historic sources.

The Crystal Palace was a work of pure engineering principles (after such men as I. K. Brunel) which would be praised by the functionalist architects of the 1930s. Those developments in architecture, ushered in by the new technology, serve to demonstrate that Roebling's conception of the Brooklyn Bridge (as well as achievements by Eiffel, Brunel, and others) did not occur in an architectural and engineering vacuum; the idea of a suspension bridge and metal framing (as discussed) all happened years before in Europe, but the exploitation of these ideas proceeded rapidly in America with the energy and intelligence of men such as John Roebling and his son, Washington. John Augustus Roebling (1806–1869) was one of the few structural engineers of the nineteenth century who could rival the structural daring, economy, efficiency, and art of Gustave Eiffel. As has been pointed out, however, the two men took iron in opposite directions when approaching viaduct and bridge design (20). Eiffel often used rigid arches to frame his structures, as can be seen in the 1884 crescent arch Garabit Viaduct over the Truyere River near St. Flour, France; the wrought-iron two-hinged crescent arch stretches 165 m and was the world's longest arch span upon completion. It not only anticipated similar structural applications in steel, but solved many problems related to the effects of wind on high structures (Fig. 15). Roebling, on the other hand, hung structures in flexible suspension to achieve unprecedented spans.

As early as 1811, Thomas Pope, an American architect, proposed a "flying pendant level bridge" to span the 12-mi-long East River separating Manhattan (with a population of 2 million) from Brooklyn (with 1 million inhabitants) (21). His plan, although sound, was not approved and, until a bridge could be built, steam ferries (as the Fulton and Union lines) would carry an estimated 22,000,000 foot passengers and 1,100,000 vehicles a year (21).

In 1856, Roebling's original plan for the Brooklyn Bridge included "an immense multi-span bridge to arch over Blackwell Island in the East River" (18). A year later, the location was changed to the area near the city halls of Manhattan and Brooklyn. Proposals for his bridge were written to *The New York Press* in 1857 and 1860, but received little excitement because of the current economic

Figure 15. Garabit Viaduct, near St. Flour, France, Gustave Eiffel, 1884. Courtesy of Pepperfoto.

Figure 16. Cincinnati–Covington Bridge over the Ohio River, John and Washington Roebling, 1866.

crisis. *The New York Times* of May 24, 1883, made mention of two Roebling plans (22). One was for the erection of a light bridge "exclusively for foot passengers" which would rise about 185 ft above the water and cost $3 million—it received no financial backing. The second was for rapid transit between Manhattan and Long Island built as a quay system, ie, a series of quays connected with draw bridges. Others entertained ideas of tunneling under the East River, but the hazards and cost of laboring through the especially rocky river bed discouraged the idea. By the time the Brooklyn Bridge was completed, however, some questioned whether the tunneling scheme actually would have been as risky and expensive. Finally, in 1864, Roebling's plans won approval. The New York Bridge Co. was formed in 1865 and incorporated by Senator Murphy on January 25, 1867 with John Roebling as chief engineer; the company was given the authority to "construct and maintain a permanent bridge over the East River" (22). Roebling, having given the bridge its design and reality, would never live to see its completion. In the summer of 1869, while he was observing the work on the bridge, a ferryboat returning from the opposite shore landed heavily into the dock upon which Roebling was standing; his foot was caught and crushed between the piling timbers and 16 days later he died of lockjaw (23). The responsibility of completing the bridge fell to his son, Washington Augustus Roebling.

Washington Roebling graduated from Rensselaer Polytechnic Institute in 1857 as a civil engineer; after being discharged from the service in 1865 as a colonel, he took charge of the Cincinnati–Covington Bridge over the Ohio River while his father devoted his full energies to the Brooklyn Bridge. Completed in 1866, the Cincinnati Bridge (a 1057-ft suspension span, Fig. 16) served as a prototype for the Brooklyn Bridge (Fig. 17); for example, the diagonal iron-wire stays in both structures (developed in the earlier Niagara Falls Bridge) served to stiffen the flexible bridge deck and prevented dangerous oscillations in the wind. In 1899, steel cables and trusses replaced the original scheme of iron stays tied between the bridge's deck and the floor of the valley, markedly altering the appearance of the Cincinnati Bridge. The Cincinnati Bridge and the

Brooklyn Bridge were the longest-spanning bridges in the world upon completion.

One of the biggest difficulties facing the engineers of the Brooklyn Bridge was how to install underwater foundations to secure the massive stone towers, which were to rise 272 ft above the river and support four major suspension cables (21). In 1867, John Roebling sent his son to England, France, and Germany to discover the recent developments in pneumatic foundations, "a procedure of pumping air into underwater caissons" (24). This novel idea in bridge building would be used again in 1881 by the designers of the Forth Railroad Bridge. The young Roebling's findings were sent to his father and utilized in the planning of the bridge. In the year he returned from Europe, 1869, his father suffered the dock accident and Washington was appointed chief engineer.

The caissons devised by Washington Roebling for the bridge were huge wooden boxes caulked on the inside with oakum and pitched to make them airtight (the New York caisson used boiler iron for better fire protection); the exterior was covered with tin to protect against seepage and sea worms, and the over-sheathing was a layer of 3-in.

Figure 17. Brooklyn Bridge, John and Washington Roebling, 1869–1883.

planks saturated with creosote (22). In May 1870, the Brooklyn caisson (168 ft long, 102 ft wide, 22 ft deep, and capable of displacing 3000 tons) was towed to position and sunk to the river bottom where the workmen would build the foundations for the towers. The unusually rocky river base at the Brooklyn pier site made the caissons unstable; as a result, work was slow and several accidents occurred (25). Work began inside the Brooklyn tower on May 21, 1870, and by the following year (March 11, 1971), the foundations for that pier were ready; the depth of the Brooklyn foundations (below high water level) was 44.5 ft, as opposed to 78.5 on the New York side (26).

Novelty has its shortcomings, and Washington Roebling was continually faced with new and untried problems. He proved to be a resourceful and skilled engineer, however, as he met the challenge of many technical obstacles. For example, he devised a method of removing sediment through the caissons by means of "water shafts"; provided safe lighting for the caissons by taking advantage of the illumination of whitewashed sheet iron (27); developed machinery for raising stone for the towers; and discovered a unique method for spinning the steel wire into cables (24) (discussed later).

One of Washington Roebling's engineering problems came about with the building of the New York tower when the caisson hit a bed of boiling quicksand before reaching solid bedrock. If he took the foundation any lower, he stood the risk of personal injury and wasted time and money; instead, he added a cushion of sand to distribute the pressure of the foundation and the tower. This might have been more costly than his alternative decision, for the tower could have shifted into the river before the cables were fixed. Apparently, his decision was fostered more by public concern for the duration of this costly and "chancy" project, which, by its completion, would result in the loss of 20 lives. Nevertheless, the New York tower, completed in July 1876, rests on sand and settled without fault.

Washington Roebling had the perspicacity to alter his plans for the roadway. He anticipated that elevated trains would replace the cable trains because of their ability to handle greater numbers; thus, he decided to widen and strengthen the roadway, improvements that he felt considerably changed the bridge to an "almost different structure from the one originally designed" (28). To allow for this widened central span and provide headway for tall-masted ships, the two opposing towers had to be of monumental size: 350 ft from base to summit and 85,000 yd^3 of solid masonry. The bridge's central span boasted the unprecedented width of 1595 ft and the headway was 135 ft. In addition, each shore span to the tower was 930 ft long, bringing the overall length of the Brooklyn Bridge (main span and shore span) to 1 mi, 709 ft, "six times larger than any bridge of its kind built up to that time" (29).

In his 1883 essay on "The Brooklyn Bridge as Monument" (which he later believed marked the first attempt in the United States at an aesthetic analysis of a work of engineering) (30), Montgomery Schuyler criticized the Roeblings for not making the towers more sculpturally expressive of their function. He felt that the four vertical piers sustaining the weight of the cables should have pro-

jected noticeably beyond the pointed arches instead of emphasizing an abbreviated horizontal plane of masonry. Curiously, Roebling's previous Niagara Falls Bridge (1855), whose simplified tapering piers strongly stress their function, is not mentioned (Fig. 12). Schuyler also criticized what he thought was the Roeblings' failure to make form follow function; he felt that the curved metal saddle inside the pier (over which the cables were slung) should have been indicated visually instead of having the cables disappear, in an inexpressive manner, into the beetling cornice block (Fig. 18). He also thought that the masonry anchorages failed to express the resistance of the cables sufficiently. Schuyler felt that these parts (the towers' metal saddle seating and anchorages) reflected the "defects of being rudimentary, of not being completely developed" (31). Perhaps the extreme length of the bridge (for its day) and the newness of the design to the general public inspired the Roeblings to stress visually the substantial strength of the piers to a greater extent than had been done on the Niagara Falls Bridge. Certainly, there were those who felt that suspension bridges were risky and unable to shoulder the great numbers of people who would travel over them. On December 29–30, 1879, for example, *The New York Times* inundated citizens with mistrust of shoddy metal construction and poor engineering when it announced the collapse of the new Tay Railroad Bridge in Scotland (killing 90). Built by Britain's leading engineer, Sir Thomas Bouch, it had failed as a result of miscalculating wind loads (it had been built mostly of wrought iron, not steel). Also, on December 30, 1879, J. Lloyd Haigh's bankruptcy was announced (Haigh Brooklyn Works was the wire manufacturer for the Brooklyn Bridge). On January 11, 1880, *The New York Herald* ran the headline, "Will the Tay Disaster Be Repeated Between New York and Brooklyn?" Further, a noted engineer announced that the East River Bridge could not hold a fifth of the weight that was likely to be put upon it (32). The interior of the arches (33 ft 9 in. wide) (26), of a smooth texture, further suggested the penetration of mass in the tower blocks. Thus, as the editors of Schuyler's writings (William Jordy and Ralph Coe) point out in defense of the towers (33):

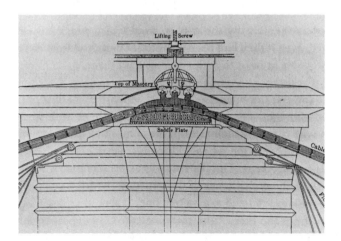

Figure 18. Saddle plates and iron rollers in the towers of the Brooklyn Bridge (Schuyler, 1883).

If the ungainly masonry piers are somewhat too blunt fully to record the organic ideal, their exaggerated massiveness provides an expressive foil for the swift swoop of the cables, [and provide] . . . the magnificent opposition of the compressive bulk of the towers against the tensile web of the cables.

Later bridges would reduce the bulk of their supporting piers by making the spanning members sturdier, thus further allowing the supporting cables to be lighter and less essential.

On August 14, 1876, the first wire was strung from both towers like a spider's steel filament. As Oliver Larkin put it, Roebling "promised to carry eighteen thousand tons on four bundles of steel wires slung from two stone towers and anchored on the earth at both ends" (34). Each of these "bundles" contained 5296 steel wires which stretched from their seating on each shore (a distance of 3578 ft 6 in.) and anchored at each end to 23-ton plates embedded in solid masonry foundations each weighing 44,000 tons. A total of 14,000 mi of anchored wire, then, comprising four cables (each with a diameter of 15½ in. and a breaking strain of nearly 12,000 tons) would carry the stress of the Brooklyn Bridge (29,35). It should be noted that the cables had more wires than the original design required, because in July 1878, Roebling's men had discovered fraud by the contractor of the Haigh Brooklyn Works, who was supplying the steel for the cables; extra wires were added to make up the deficiency in strength of the "rejected" wire already spun (36).

After the traveler ropes were stretched between the anchorages, a heavier wire rope known as the "carrier" followed. In this way, small cables for supporting the cradles (in which the building of the main cables was to take place) were secured in the tops of the towers. The spinning of the cables began on June 11, 1877, and the roadway was laid on six parallel trusses supported by four cables. The 85-ft-wide roadway provided for "two carriage tracks, two tracks for street railways, and one footway" (35).

Aside from the use of caissons, the unique achievement of the bridge was the "spinning-in-air" technique invented by the Roeblings (although in March 1868, the newspaper writer Charles B. Bender contended that the invention of air-spinning was the work of L. J. Vicat) (37); instead of twisting the wires "like the strands of a rope," which would subject them to varying degrees of strain, the wires were arranged in a parallel fashion (19 strands forming one cable) and fastened at 1-ft intervals by soft annealed wire to allow an equal share of weight (35). Washington Roebling used galvanized steel wires (the first ever) coated with linseed oil to prevent rusting; these had almost double the strength of iron wires previously used (22). The cable strands were laid in "saddles" (Fig. 18), one saddle to each cable, at the top of the towers after having first passed over iron rollers; the rollers take up the strain on the cables, and the cables are permitted to move in the saddle plate and relieve tension on the masonry towers. Nineteen and a half tons of wire could be swung in a day, and at the end of 21 months of "spinning," the longest suspension bridge in its day was finished; its cables, finally painted with white lead and oil, glistened in the sun. A new era of bridge design had dawned.

The Brooklyn Bridge essentially celebrated the merits of the suspension bridge as a safe, striking, and structurally economical solution to spanning unprecedented distances. In the century to come, the engineering principles inherent in the design of a suspension bridge would be refined and fully explored to render landmark achievements in bridge building.

Although Gustave Eiffel and John Roebling stood out as giants in their age in the structural exploration and utilization of iron and steel, Robert Maillart (1872–1940) led the way in the application of reinforced concrete in bridge design as the nineteenth century came to an end. In his work, engineering daring and monumental simplicity led to structural art. Whereas Eiffel used a sweeping wrought-iron, two-hinged crescent arch in the Garabit Viaduct near St. Flour, France, Maillart broke with the lithic and metal past in his 1901 bridge at Zuoz, Switzerland. There, Maillart's structural solution produced a low-slung concrete arch supporting a flat roadway connected by longitudinal walls. The structural solution at Zuoz has been referred to as a hollow-box girder similar to his design (and form) for the Stauffacher Bridge designed two years earlier in Zurich but without the structural honesty (38). In the Zurich bridge, the curved arch was hidden behind a stone-faced wall and the roadway deck load was transferred to the arch by concrete cross walls (38). Maillart's achievement at Zuoz in terms of structural art was to fuse expressed form with structural function through concrete. As has been noted, however, in both bridges by Maillart previously mentioned, his teacher, Wilhelm Ritter (1847–1906), was the consultant for the client and played a central role. Without any mathematical theory available to prove by calculation that the concrete hollow box for Zuoz would work, Ritter had to design a full-scale load test, giving his understanding of physical reality precedence over the accuracy of mathematical approximations (39).

Maillart was to refine the structural economy of Zuoz even more in 1904 in a design for a bridge over the Vorder Rhine River at Tavanasa, Switzerland. Because cracks had appeared near the abutments in the longitudinal walls of Zuoz, Maillart simply eliminated that section of the wall in this bridge to produce one of the most daring forms of his early career.

By 1930, in his Salginatobel Bridge near Schiers, Switzerland, even the use of stone for abutments was eliminated, creating a streamlined form with no material intrusions beyond concrete. This bridge, the longest of Maillart's career, was one of his most recognized achievements. It was a three-hinged arch of the hollow-box design. Such daring designs were likely accepted less on the basis of progressive aesthetic attitudes on the part of the clients than the fact that Maillart had a reputation for delivering successful results at an affordable price; his bid for the Salginatobel Bridge, for example, was the lowest of 18 designs (40).

Maillart's best-known work was constructed in 1933 over the Schwandbach near Hinterfultigen, Switzerland. It was a deck-stiffened arch bridge spanning 37.4 m that received stiffening support in the manner of long-span wooden railroad trestle bridges by horizontally curving

Figure 19. Concrete arch bridge built over the Schwandbach near Hinterfultigen, Switzerland, 1933, Robert Maillart. Courtesy of Losinger Co.

the roadway. Here, the economy of the arch support could hardly be taken further. Stabilizing support was achieved by integrating the arch and the roadbed with trapezoidal cross walls (Fig. 19). Maillart's bridges illustrate that minimum use of materials and money can produce maximum aesthetic appeal. In this regard, he has few equals (40). For further information on Maillart's work, see Ref. 41.

BIBLIOGRAPHY

1. T. A. Comp and D. Jackson, *Bridge Truss Types: A Guide to Dating and Identifying, Technical Leaflet,* American Association of State and Local History, Nashville, Tenn., 1977.

2. M. Hayden, *The Book of Bridges,* Galahad Books, New York, 1976.

3. N. McWhirter, "Bridges," *1986 Guinness Book of World Records,* Sterling Publishing Co., Inc., New York, 1986, pp. 183–185.

4. *The Civil Engineer: His Origins,* American Society of Civil Engineers (ASCE), New York, 1970, pp. 64–66.

5. H. S. Smith, *The World's Great Bridges,* Harper and Brothers, New York, 1953, pp. 13, 54.

6. D. B. Steinman, *Famous Bridges of the World,* Random House, New York, 1953, p. 61.

7. G. Hatje, ed., *Encyclopaedia of Modern Architecture,* Thames and Hudson, London, 1963, pp. 226–227.

8. *Ibid.,* p. 266.

9. Ref. 7, p. 267.

10. H. R. Hitchcock, *Architecture: Nineteenth and Twentieth Centuries,* Penguin Books, Baltimore, 1968, p. 119.

11. H. R. Hitchcock, "American Influence Abroad," in E. Kaufman, ed., *The Rise of an American Architecture,* Praeger Publishers, New York, 1970, p. 19.

12. "Brooklyn Bridge," *Preservation News,* 6 (Dec. 1973).

13. G. L. Glegg, *The Design of Design,* The University Press, Cambridge, UK, 1969, pp. 57–58.

14. H. J. Hopkins, *A Span of Bridges,* Praeger Publishers, New York, 1970, pp. 231–232.

15. L. Rhind, *Edinburgh: The City and Its Citizens,* Edinburgh Corp., Edinburgh, Scotland, 1971, p. 75.

16. Ref. 14, p. 160.

17. A. Tractenberg, *Brooklyn Bridge: Fact and Symbol,* Oxford University Press, Inc., New York, 1965, p. 171.

18. *Ibid.,* p. 67.

19. Ref. 7, p. 5.

20. D. Billington, "Bridges and the New Art of Structural Engineering," *American Scientist,* **72,** 23 (Jan.–Feb. 1984).

21. R. S. Holland, *Big Bridge,* MacRae-Smith Co., Philadelphia, 1934, p. 172.

22. "Building of the Brooklyn Bridge," *The New York Times,* May 24, 1883, p. 2-1.

23. Ref. 17, p. 95.

24. Ref. 17, p. 98.

25. Ref. 21, p. 173.

26. D. McCullough, *The Great Bridge,* Simon & Schuster, New York, 1972, p. 564.

27. Ref. 14, p. 223.

28. Ref. 17, p. 99.

29. Ref. 21, p. 175.

30. M. Schuyler, "The Brooklyn Bridge as Monument," in W. Jordy and R. Coe, eds., *American Architecture and Other Writings,* Atheneum Publishers, New York, 1963, p. 29.

31. *Ibid.,* p. 172.

32. Ref. 26, pp. 470, 595.

33. Ref. 30, p. 31.

34. O. W. Larkin, *Art and Life in America,* Holt, Rinehart & Winston, New York, 1960, p. 283.

35. Ref. 21, p. 176.

36. Ref. 14, pp. 224–225.

37. C. B. Bender, *The New York Times,* March 1868.

38. Ref. 20, p. 26.

39. Ref. 20, p. 27.

40. Ref. 20, p. 28.

41. D. P. Billington, *Robert Maillart's Bridges: The Art of Engineering,* Princeton University Press, Princeton, N.J., 1979.

GENERAL REFERENCES

Refs. 1, 7, 12, 22, and 41 are good general references.

The Civil Engineer: His Origins, American Society of Civil Engineers (ASCE), New York, 1970.

W. Andrews, *Architecture, Ambition, and Americans,* The Free Press, New York, 1964.

D. Billington, "Bridges and the New Art of Structural Engineering," *American Scientist* **72,** 22–31 (Jan.–Feb. 1984).

D. P. Billington, *The Tower and the Bridge: The New Art of Structural Engineering,* Basic Books Inc., Publishers, New York, 1983.

W. C. Conant, "The Brooklyn Bridge," *Harper's New Monthly Magazine* (May 1883).

"Dead on the New Bridge," *The New York Times,* May 31, 1883, p. 1-6.

G. L. Glegg, *The Design of Design,* The University Press, Cambridge, UK, 1969.

H. Russell Hitchcock, "American Influence Abroad," in E. Kaufman, ed., *The Rise of an American Architecture,* Praeger Publishers, New York, 1970.

H. R. Hitchcock, *Architecture: Nineteenth and Twentieth Centuries,* Penguin Books, Baltimore, 1968.

R. S. Holland, *Big Bridge,* MacRae-Smith Co., Philadelphia, 1934.

H. J. Hopkins, *A Span of Bridges,* Praeger Publishers, New York, 1970.

R. F. Jordan, *A Concise History of Western Architecture,* Thames and Hudson, London, 1969.

O. W. Larkin, *Art and Life in America,* Holt, Rinehart & Winston, New York, 1960.

G. McCue, *The Building Art in St. Louis,* St. Louis Chapter, American Institute of Architects, 1964.

D. McCullough, *The Great Bridge,* Simon & Schuster, New York, 1972.

E. B. Mock, *The Architecture of Bridges,* The Museum of Modern Art, New York, 1949.

The New York Times, June 12, 1883, p. 8-3.

Opening Ceremonies of the New York and Brooklyn Bridge, The Brooklyn Eagle Job Printing Dept., Brooklyn, New York, 1883.

D. Plowden, *Bridges: The Spans of North America,* The Viking Press, New York, 1974.

L. Rhind, *Edinburgh: The City and Its Citizens,* Edinburgh Corp., Edinburgh, Scotland, 1971.

M. Schuyler, "The Brooklyn Bridge as Monument," in W. Jordy and R. Coe, eds., *American Architecture and Other Writings,* Atheneum Publishers, New York, 1963.

H. S. Smith, *The World's Great Bridges,* Harper and Brothers, New York, 1953.

D. B. Steinman, *Bridges and Their Builders,* G. P. Putnam's Sons, New York, 1941.

D. B. Steinman, *Famous Bridges of the World,* Random House, New York, 1953.

A. Tractenberg, *Brooklyn Bridge: Fact and Symbol,* Oxford University Press, Inc., New York, 1965.

KINGSTON W. HEATH, Ph.D.
University of North Carolina
Charlotte, North Carolina

TWENTIETH-CENTURY BRIDGE DESIGN

This portion of the article investigates the relevance of bridge construction in the twentieth century. To do so, bridges from the early 1900s to 1987, considered to be significant examples of design achievement and technological advancements through this period, are analyzed here.

Queensboro Bridge, 1909

The Queensboro Bridge (also known as Blackwell's Island Bridge and the 59th Street Bridge) spans the East River in New York and was completed in 1909 (Fig. 1). The Queensboro, although famous for having the largest and heaviest cantilevers in the United States, and supposedly the first U.S. bridge for which architectural counsel was retained, has been criticized from the day it opened because of its massive steelwork. (A highway and streetcar bridge built by Pittsburgh and Lake Erie in 1911 over the Ohio River between Sewickley and Coraopolis, Pennsylvania (Fig. 2), is the second heaviest [dead weight] cantilever in the United States.)

The Queensboro Bridge was designed by Gustav Lin-

Figure 1. The Queensboro Bridge, East River, New York City. Courtesy of Peter Bickford.

denthal, New York City's commissioner of bridges, and its design was the subject of much controversy. Originally, the bridge was designed to carry 16,000 pounds per linear foot load, which consisted of four streetcar tracks, four elevated railway tracks, a roadway, and two footwalks. Just before the design was completed, the Quebec Bridge, the design of which was similar to the proposed Queensboro Bridge, collapsed. The Quebec Bridge was to span the St. Lawrence River in Quebec. The bridge's design called for a 1600-ft cantilever main span, which would have made it the longest span in the world. The failure of the bridge was due to a lack of communication between engineers and workmen, incompetent engineering, and faulty workmanship. The Quebec disaster occurred in 1907, while the bridge was still under construction, killing 80 workers. The Quebec Bridge had failed because the dead weight of the cantilever was too heavy to hold itself up. The engineers discovered that the proposed Queensboro Bridge was subject to even heavier loads than the Quebec Bridge had been. The design was revised to reduce the dead weight of the bridge and the live load it would carry by removal of two of the four elevated railway tracks and heavy concrete paving.

One critic, Henry Hornbostel, who later became the architect of the bridge itself, was so shocked when he saw the bridge for the first time that he exclaimed, "My God—it's a blacksmith shop!" (1).

Whether or not the Queensboro Bridge is aesthetically pleasing, it cannot be denied that its construction was truly an innovation in the field of structural technology.

Soo Line's Railway Bridge, 1911

The Soo Line's Railway Bridge, which crosses the Saint Croix River near New Richmond, Wis., was completed on June 3, 1911. The Soo Line's Bridge is a rare and outstanding example of a multispan steel railway arch and has been considered one of the world's most beautiful steel structures. It is novel in that it was a rarity for a multispan steel superstructure to be of a three-hinged variety. Other

Figure 2. Old Sewickley Bridge over the Ohio River, between Sewickley and Coraopolis, Penn. Courtesy of the Sewickley Valley Chamber of Commerce. Photograph by James Sweterlitsch.

three-hinged arched railway bridges include: a bridge for the Milwaukee Road Railway that spans the Menominee River in Wisconsin, and one designed for the White Pass and Yukon Railway in Alaska, completed in 1900.

The Soo Line's Bridge is the work of C. A. P. Turner, a brilliant engineer who was best known for his work in concrete construction. The bridge is 185 ft high and composed of five arches, each with a span of 350 ft. Steel was chosen over concrete for the construction of the bridge for two reasons: first, the delays while using concrete during winter construction would be too costly; and second, the availability of solid rock foundations on both banks of the river suggested that an arch-type spanning system would be more effective in the long run, as opposed to sinking large, expensive concrete piers in a river that experienced severe flooding yearly.

Despite its great beauty, the Soo Line's Bridge is probably one of America's least known and most unappreciated structures because of its placement in a remote section of the Saint Croix River.

Hell Gate Railway Bridge, 1917

The Hell Gate Railway Bridge, which crosses the East River in New York, was begun in 1912 and opened in April 1917. The bridge was significant in that the steel members that comprised the arch ribs were the largest ever put together. The overall length of the bridge makes it one of the longest steel bridges in the world, and the heaviest arch bridge of all. (The Huey Long Bridge, completed in 1936, is currently the longest railroad bridge in the United States. Located just north of New Orleans, the bridge is 22,996 ft long.)

The Hell Gate was designed and built by Gustav Lindenthal, who also acted as chief engineer on the project. Of the five designs submitted, the one chosen was a two-hinged spandrel-braced arch. The bridge is 17,000 ft from its eastern abutment in Long Island to the western one in the Bronx.

The Hell Gate supports four railway tracks on a solid-deck floor. Two lower chords of the arch carry both the dead and live loads and also the compressive forces of up to 15,000 tons. Practical rather than aesthetic concerns dictated the form of the bridge; for example, the top chord at either end is reversed to provide the greatest depth at the point where it would undergo the greatest bending. The reversal of the chords also provided sufficient clearance for the trains. The one attribute about which Lindenthal was unyielding was the appearance of the towers, which he said were an architectural necessity.

The only major problem Lindenthal encountered during the construction of the bridge was the discovery of a 100-ft fault in the bearing rock beneath the site of the Wards Island tower. To overcome this obstacle, Lindenthal built a huge concrete arch over the fissure upon which solid reinforced concrete walls became the foundation for the towers.

The Hell Gate Bridge is a fine example of sheer monumentality. The massive, solid towers express strength and immortality. The bridge is a tribute to railway bridges in the United States.

Movable Bridges, 1919–1940

Movable bridges were common in the early part of the century, mostly in large urban centers, where a high-level type of bridge construction was not feasible. Movable bridges can be categorized according to the manner in which they open. The most common type is the bascule, a modern descendant of the medieval drawbridge. It consists of one or two counterweighted leaves, or bascules, that work on horizontal pivots.

One of the best-known bridges in the United States has a double-leaf bascule span in the center. The Arlington Memorial Bridge in Washington, D.C., is generally considered the capital's most beautiful and successful bridge. It spans the Potomac River from the Lincoln Memorial to the gates of Arlington Cemetery and stands as a monument to formal urban design. Although originally proposed in the mid-nineteenth century, the granite-veneered, nine-space, neoclassical structure was not begun until 1926 (2).

President Andrew Jackson suggested that a permanent bridge be built as a symbol of union between the North and South. A design competition attracted a dramatic series of monumental designs, and the submission of the engineer William H. Burr, working in conjunction with architect Edward Casey, was selected. However, the design was unsuccessfully presented to Congress in 1900, and the project abandoned for some years (3).

In the early twentieth century, as a revitalization of the L'Enfant Plan and improvement of the city were getting underway with the McMillan Park Commission, construction of the bridge was again discussed. The Commission recommended that designers be chosen by direct selection. In 1926, the firm of McKim, Mead & White of New York, with their proposal of a low neoclassical scheme compatible with the styles of the Lincoln Memorial and Union Station, was awarded the project.

The structure is 2138 ft long; it consists of eight low reinforced concrete arches and an electrically operated center draw span, which is the longest, heaviest, and fastest such draw span in the world. The span is 216 ft long and takes only one minute to be lifted (4). The bridge is faced with dressed North Carolina granite ashlar and terminated at each end by sculpture-topped pylons. The basic superstructure is of steel and has all-applied veneer of classical stone details which have led some to criticize the bridge as being eclectic or artificial. The bridge is architecturally and geometrically simple, giving most of its design emphasis to its shape and location as part of the city's monumental place. Construction was not finished until February 1932 (Fig. 3).

Mention also should be made of two other bascule span structures in the United States: the St. Charles Air Line Railway Bridge in Chicago, built in 1919, with a single-leaf bascule span 260 ft long, and the double-leaf type of the Canadian Pacific Railroad Bridge in Sault Ste. Marie, Mich., built in 1941, with a span of 336 ft.

Other types of movable bridges include vertical-lift space and pontoon bridges. The vertical-lift space bridge also had its chief development in the United States, where it almost completely replaced all other types of movable bridges. The Marine Parkway Bridge, between Brooklyn and Rockaway in New York, was built in 1937 with a vertical-lift span of 540 ft.

Pontoon bridges, basically "floating" bridges, have been used mostly for military purposes since ancient times (see Trajan's Bridge over the Danube in Bridge Design Through the Beginning of the Twentieth Century). The Lake Washington Bridge in Seattle is a pontoon type, built in 1940. It is 6560 ft long, and a central opening for navigation crossing is provided by a sliding floating span (5).

George Washington Bridge, 1931

The George Washington Bridge, also known as the Hudson River Bridge, was completed in 1931, five years after the

Figure 3. The Arlington Memorial Bridge, Washington, D.C.

plans were approved. The bridge crosses the Hudson River, connecting Manhattan and Fort Lee, N.J. At the time, the George Washington Bridge was to be the world's longest suspension bridge. It is an engineering masterpiece which was double the length of any other bridge at that time. Through the use of toll revenues to pay for the public sale of the Port Authority's bonds, the George Washington Bridge was to set the precedent for future financing methods in bridge building. The architectural significance of the bridge is somewhat controversial. Whereas one source states that it is ". . . a structure of remarkable grace and beauty . . . the huge towers [were] designed with a simplicity of line and decoration that admirably suited the enormous length of the cables . . ." (6), another source maintains that "the debate as to whether or not the towers of the George Washington are architecturally successful continues . . . the towers themselves reflect the ambivalence of their designers" (7).

The engineering staff was virtually a Who's Who of the engineering profession. Headed by Othmar H. Ammann as chief engineer, it included George Washington Goethals, Joseph B. Strauss, Daniel Moran, Gustav Lindenthal, William Burr, E. W. Stearns, and Cass Gilbert as architectural consultant.

A unique feature of the bridge was the absence of a stiffening truss. All suspension bridges before had had one, but rigidity in the George Washington was due to the great length, the weight of the roadway and enormous cables, and short side spans. Foreseeing that a lower deck would one day be needed, the designers provided for the addition of a stiffening truss to support it. By using eyebar-cables, which are two and one-half times heavier than wire cables, the rigidity of the structure was also increased.

The George Washington Bridge was built in two stages; the first took care of present needs, and the second would accommodate the anticipated increase in use and loads.

The two steel towers were originally designed to be encased in concrete for structural as well as aesthetic reasons, but the public outcry over its structural, economic, and design merits was so great that the engineers finally redesigned the steel towers to carry the loads themselves. Provisions were made for the concrete encasements to be built at a later date, but they never were.

Questions remain as to whether or not the aesthetic quality of the bridge would have been improved with the use of the proposed concrete encasements, but there are no arguments as to the significance of the George Washington Bridge as a structural work of art (Fig. 4).

Oakland Bay Bridge, 1936

The Oakland Bay Bridge has always been overshadowed by the Golden Gate Bridge because (1) they were built at approximately the same time, and (2) all of the problems that were inherent in the Bay Bridge were amplified manyfold when it came to the Golden Gate. However, the Bay Bridge still has its merits.

Construction of the Bay Bridge was seriously considered in 1921. By 1928, 38 proposals had been submitted, of which one was finally picked—a large cantilever span which, at the time it was built, was the largest cantilever span in the United States. It also held a record for the depth of its piers, which had to be sunk 300 ft.

Construction of the bridge started in July 1933 under the supervision of chief engineer C. H. Purcell, and was completed in November 1936. Today, the Bay Bridge with its overall 43,500-ft length, including its approaches, remains the longest high-level bridge in the world.

Although the Bahia Honda Key Marathon Bridge and the Seven Mile Bridge, both part of Henry Flagler's Florida Coast Railroad exploit, are longer, they cross comparatively shallow bodies of water with a series of low-level short spans.

Golden Gate Bridge, 1937

The Golden Gate Bridge, designed by Charles Ellis, spans the distance between San Francisco and Marin County

Figure 4. The George Washington Bridge seen from New York City. Courtesy of the Port Authority of New York and New Jersey.

Figure 5. The Golden Gate Bridge, San Francisco. Courtesy of Peter Bickford.

in California and was completed in May 1937, four years after construction began. The Golden Gate is truly a masterpiece of modern American suspension-bridge design. Its combination of beauty and engineering achievements has yet to be surpassed (Fig. 5).

The Golden Gate's main span is 4200 ft, making it the second longest suspension bridge in the world. (The first is the Verrazano Narrows Bridge in New York City.)

Chief engineer of the project, Joseph Strauss (also known for the invention and design of the bascule leaf-type bridge), overcame many obstacles in the years prior to the actual construction of the bridge. The first proposed design in 1921, given by Strauss to the City of San Francisco, was a monstrous cross between a cantilever and a suspension bridge. San Franciscans were aghast and so Strauss went to Marin County to get support for the bridge. Strauss needed to get permission from the War Department to build a bridge across the bay. After many negotiations with the Department, Strauss finally got the go-ahead in December 1924. By this time, the design had been changed from the combination of a cantilever/suspension bridge to that of a suspension bridge; Strauss had determined through numerous tests and surveys that the design was feasible. Bond issues were voted on and passed, and contracts were awarded before ground was finally broken in January 1933.

The project was riddled with problems, the most complex of which was the sinking of the south pier that lies 1125 ft offshore. The construction of a seawall in the form of a fender was needed to protect the south pier during construction. This procedure was unique in engineering history and, despite many difficulties, the idea finally worked.

Strauss was obsessed with the safety of his men. Among the many precautions taken to protect the workers' health and lives was the design and use of a large safety net that cantilevered out below where the men were working.

The net saved 19 lives but broke at one point when a large piece of steel fell off the deck and crashed through the net into the bay, taking 12 men with it. Of the 12, only two men survived; although a tragedy, this was still a vast improvement over the average loss of life for bridge construction of this size.

Tacoma Narrows Bridge, 1940

The Tacoma Narrows Bridge of Tacoma, Wash., was opened on July 1, 1940, and remained standing approximately four months until its collapse on November 7, 1940. After completion of the project, the Tacoma Narrows Bridge, the third longest bridge of its time, was best known for its beauty and simplistic grace. Today, the bridge is significant because it serves as an example of faulty design. The engineers of the time did not understand the true nature of the dynamics of the suspension bridge. The collapse of the bridge forced the engineering profession to take a closer look at suspension-bridge design. After the incident, a damper was placed on suspension-bridge design which was not lifted until after World War II, around 1950.

The bridge was the work of Leon Moissief, the consulting engineer of the project, and the chief engineer was Lacey V. Murrow. The main span of the bridge was 2800 ft and the width a mere 39 ft. The stiffening member had a ratio of 1:350 (depth to length), although the rule of thumb at that time was 1:50 or 1:100. The principal cause of failure was the change of shape of the structure due to wind load. When the wind blows against an obstacle, its wake takes the form of a vortex street. The exuding vortices on the leeward side of the obstacle cause forces to act at right angles to the direction of the wind, so the bridge started twisting up and down on both sides. The wind was blowing at 42 mph when the Tacoma Bridge twisted 45° from the horizontal in both directions and broke (Fig. 6). Amazingly, no lives were lost.

The failure of the Tacoma Narrows Bridge led to extended research into suspension-bridge failure and to the evolution of proper aerodynamic design. After its collapse, additional stiffening members were added to the Golden Gate Bridge, which had been completed in 1937.

Verrazano Narrows Bridge, 1965

The Verrazano Narrows Bridge connects Brooklyn with Staten Island across New York's Narrows (Fig. 7). The bridge, completed in 1965, is currently the longest suspension bridge in the world, with a main span of 4260 ft. It also holds a record for cost of construction ($325 million) and materials consumed. The wire used for its cables would encircle the globe 55 times.

The Verrazano's towers are 690 ft high and the deck rises 228 ft above the water. Designed by Othmar H. Ammann, it was his last work; he died a year after the bridge was opened.

Although the Verrazano holds records for size, cost, and materials, it is really only a super-version of Roebling's basic suspension bridge: "It represents nothing new and

Figure 6. Tacoma Narrows Bridge Disaster, Tacoma, Wash., November 7, 1940. First section of the span as it broke in two and fell 190 ft into the waters of the Puget Sound, after a 42-mph wind had caused the bridge to swing on its foundations for the last time. Courtesy of UPI/Bettmann Newsphotos.

is not nearly as spectacular as the George Washington or the colossus [sic] of the thirties in San Francisco" (8).

The Luling–Destrehan Bridge, 1983

The Luling–Destrehan Bridge just north of New Orleans is the first high-level, long-space, cable-stayed bridge in the United States. It was completed in October 1983 to carry a four-lane highway over the Mississippi River, and in 1984 was chosen as the Outstanding Civil Engineering Achievement of the Year.

At a cost of just under $90 million, the bridge clears the river by 133 ft through the central navigation channel. The deck is placed on twin steel box girders and is supported by two A-frame towers that soar 250 ft above the

Figure 7. The Verrazano Narrows Bridge, Brooklyn, New York. Courtesy of Bethlehem Steel.

roadway. Each tower supports 12 cable stays, 6 at each side, with a span of 1222 ft (9).

The significance of the Luling–Destrehan Bridge lies in the fact that it is the first of its kind to be designed to withstand the severe hurricane wind loads of the Gulf Coast. Because cable-stayed bridges are inherently flexible and subject to undesirable oscillations under wind currents, extensive wind-tunnel tests were performed with sectional models to determine the actual aerodynamic behavior of the structure. The tests were intended to measure the motion of the towers and the vibration on the cables and deck.

The project is an example of collaboration between several different groups of people in order to pool the latest technological knowledge in bridge construction. Monitoring instruments placed on the bridge by Tulane University researchers will evaluate the validity of this new technology in bridge construction.

Sunshine Skyway Bridge, 1987

The Sunshine Skyway Bridge, the longest precast concrete segmental bridge in the world, was opened to traffic in February 1987. It has a single plane of stay cable which supports a 1200-ft clear span (10). The bridge links St. Petersburg with Bradenton across lower Tampa Bay in Florida and is 4.1 mi long. The box girders comprising the center span are a record 95 ft wide and weigh as much as 220 tons (10). The Skyway piers had to be designed for as much as a 12,000 kip impact per pier because of recent accidents involving boats ramming into the previous bridge. (The original twin-truss bridge was destroyed in 1980 when a ship rammed the southbound span during a heavy rainstorm, killing 35 people and taking out 1300 ft of span.)

The new bridge carries two lanes of traffic, with full emergency lanes in each direction. Northbound and southbound traffic merge at the central 4000-ft point, where single trapezoidal box sections carry all lanes plus a median barrier (10). The 333 95-ft-wide boxes had to be cast with utmost precision since they made up the riding surface of the deck. The cable-stayed spans were erected using winches on self-advancing beams, with the stays replacing the longitudinal post-tensioning required in the shorter spans (11). The central pylons are 242 ft above the roadway; their piers rest on foundations drilled 100 ft into the bay bottom. Each pylon carries 21 stays, anchored in every other segment (every 24 ft) (11).

The Sunshine Skyway Bridge is not only structurally sound, with much thought to the recurring hazards in Tampa Bay, but also aesthetically pleasing.

In addition to the many fine examples of bridge design in the United States, there are numerous European bridges built in the last 25 years that also deserve mention.

Gladesville Bridge, 1964

The Gladesville Bridge, located in Sydney, Australia, spans the Parmatta River. When it was completed in 1964, it was the world's longest concrete span. The 1000-ft arch, made up of 512 hollow concrete boxes, weighing up to 50 tons, was constructed by casting the boxes on the shore of the river, barging them to midstream, and then winching them up to the point of the arch. They were then rolled down the form, one on each side, to form four voussoir ribs. The ribs were then tied together by transverse stressing through diaphragms (12). The Gladesville Bridge, 1900 ft long and 72 ft wide, has six lanes for traffic and two pedestrian walks.

Firth of Forth Bridge, 1964

At the time of its completion, the Firth of Forth Bridge in Scotland, near Edinburgh, was the largest bridge and the only major suspension bridge to be opened outside the United States. This record was not to last long, as the Tagus River Bridge (discussed later), with a main span 23 ft longer than the Firth of Forth, opened soon after. Economy of design, the use of tall, slender towers to achieve maximum visual effect, and the difficulties encountered during construction were three important factors that made the Firth of Forth stand apart from other bridges that were being constructed at the time. The main span of the bridge is 3300 ft, with two side spans of 1340 ft each, making the total length of the bridge 5980 ft. The two steel towers are 492 ft high, and the deck carries four traffic lanes, two cycle paths, two sidewalks, and is also used by trains (13). The effectiveness of the cables is increased by the fact that they are constructed in tunnels, anchored in rock, and prestressed. Their 42,000-ton mass is less than the 48,800-ton dead weight of the suspended structure, but the three factors listed above more than compensate for this difference (14). The total length of the cable used is 30,000 mi. The substructures of the tower piers are dissimilar in design and construction. The south tower is supported by concrete cylinders cast within caissons and sunk 80 ft through silt and mud until they hit bedrock (elevation 98 ft). The north tower stands on a slab that was cast directly onto an underwater rock that had to be blasted just to make room for the footing (15).

The construction of the bridge was delayed by a severe storm which had winds up to 100 mph and caused the cables to deflect as much as 80 ft in some places. Some cable wires were damaged, but overall, the storm proved that the bridge could survive extensive dead loads. The Firth of Forth Bridge is owned by the Forth Road Bridge Joint Board and was designed by two London firms: Mott, Hay and Anderson and Freeman, Fox and Partners. (Both of these firms worked on the design of the Severn Bridge between England and Wales.)

Alno Bridge, 1965

In 1965, the longest bridge in Scandinavia was opened to connect the island of Alno with the mainland near Sundsvall in Northern Sweden. The Alno Bridge spans 3420 ft and consists of seven prestressed spans cantilevered from six piers made of hollow slipform concrete (16). The Alno Bridge replaced a local ferry which carried 2500 cars per day, greatly reducing traffic congestion. The bridge was built by Skanska Cemetagjuteriet, a Swedish contractor from Stockholm, and cost $3.4 million.

Tagus River Bridge, 1966

The Tagus River Bridge connects the Lisbon area in Portugal with the southern Setubal section. At the time it was constructed, the Tagus River Bridge boasted the longest continuous truss, and rested on the deepest caisson in the world (17). Its main span of 3323 ft was the longest in Europe, just ahead of Scotland's Firth of Forth Bridge. The building of such a bridge was studied in 1876 by a Portugese engineer. This led to a number of surveys and plans, and a proposal was nearly settled upon with U.S. Steel International in 1939. Unfortunately, Hitler's activities in Europe at that time interfered with the plans for the bridge, which were postponed until 1953. After receiving four proposals from various combines, the Bridge Cabinet finally chose U.S. Steel International, a selection based on both design and financing considerations (18). The bridge was designed by the firm of Steinman, Boynton, Gisonquist and London of New York City (although D. B. Steinman died in 1963, just after the preliminary design of the bridge was completed).

The Tagus River Bridge is designed for high earthquake resistance and the possible addition of a railroad in the future. The steel towers are 625 ft above the water line and carry the 23-in.-diameter cables that make up the bridge's suspension (17). The open-caisson airdome method of foundation construction (first used on the San Francisco Bay Bridge) was necessary due to swift currents, rock depth, and high earthquake potential. The caisson, made up of a rectangular steel box, contains a cylindrical well open at top and bottom and topped by domes (17). The caissons were assembled in the water, barged by boat to the correct position, then sunk using concrete lifts. When the caisson hit bottom, cranes then dredged mud out of the well until it hit bedrock.

The primary reasons for building this bridge across the Tagus River were to help promote development of the southern Setubal area and to reduce traffic load on the ferries.

Felsenau Bridge, 1974

The Felsenau Bridge in Bern, Switzerland, was designed by Christian Menn for a design competition in 1970. Its design was a fully prestressed cantilever bridge, to be built without ground scaffolding to help reduce construction cost (19). This type of bridge construction was pioneered by Ulrich Finsterwalder and is built out upon itself. Small sections of the form are attached horizontally to already-built columns, cast and allowed to harden, and then prestressed by adding tendons, tying them to the existing sections (19). Three features make the Felsenau Bridge a unique and expressive structure: (1) a curved roadway; (2) the profile of the bridge, which gives each girder a slightly bowed appearance as it terminates at the columns; and (3) the use of a single box for a wide roadway, requiring less material and providing a better view (19). Menn was known for his use of partial prestressing in the decks of previous structures, and Felsenau Bridge is no exception. The slabs are prestressed for dead load only and additional nonprestressed steel resists the live load (20). The Felsenau is a beautiful example of bridge design in the twentieth century, and at the same time is economically appropriate.

Ganter Bridge, 1980

The Ganter Bridge on the Simplon Road, above Brig, Switzerland, was designed by Christian Menn, who was just finishing up work on the Felsenau Bridge, also in Switzerland. The Ganter Bridge is unique in that the cables were encased in concrete walls. The roadway is straight in the middle section, but curves at both ends. The supports, initially based on foundation conditions, were adjusted to give the entire bridge an overall symmetrical appearance and to allow for reuse of deck girder forms (21). With the use of single hollow-box pillars approximately the same width as the roadway, Menn was able to achieve a feeling of openness and expanse. The Ganter Bridge is an excellent example of the successful combination of engineering technology and true aesthetic understanding.

Humber Estuary Bridge, 1980

The Humber Estuary Bridge, located in western England, has a main span of 4626 ft, currently the longest in the world. The peaks of the bridge towers (533 ft high) are slightly out of vertical parallel to allow for the curvature of the bridge. With the inclusion of the Hessle and Barton side spans, the bridge covers 1.37 mi.

In addition to the few European examples of recent bridge design cited, the following is a list of bridges that appeared in an exhibition of twentieth-century engineering held at the Museum of Modern Art in New York (in chronological order):

1922	Bridge over Seine Saint Pierre du Vauvray, France
1977	Gueroz Bridge (over Trent Glacier) Gueroz, Switzerland
1933	Schandbach Bridge near Schwartzberg, Switzerland
1943	Sano Bridge (over Angerman River) Sweden
1955	Garibaldi Bridge (competition project) Rome
1957	Theodor Huess Bridge Knie Bridge Oberkasseler Bridge Düsseldorf, FRG
1959	Severn Bridge (over Rhine River) Cologne, FRG
1960	Poggettone and Pecora Vecchia Viaducts Autostrada del Sole Bologna–Florence section, Italy

1960	Savines Bridge (over Durance Reservoir) Savines, France
1961	Wentbridge Viaduct near Doncaster, UK
1962	General Urdaneta Bridge Laguna de Maracaibo, Venezuela
1963	Europa Bridge (over Sill River) Innsbruck–Schoenberg, Austria
1963	San Giuliano Viaduct Autostrada del Sole Florence–Rome section, Italy

Conclusion

Structure has been the dominant factor in bridge construction for thousands of years. It is only recently that man's knowledge of structural analysis has enabled the prediction, with a good degree of accuracy, of the behavior characteristics of such complex structures.

With the decline of the railways in the early 1900s, the monumental bridges of the twentieth century have been built mainly for motor traffic. Some of these older bridges in the cities are now becoming inadequate for modern vehicular loads and traffic flow and are being strengthened or replaced. The rapid development of transport systems in major urban centers means that time is an increasingly important factor in the overall economics of bridge construction. Furthermore, the tendency toward minimum-weight design will, in the future, require that even more sophisticated structural systems and materials be developed.

BIBLIOGRAPHY

1. D. Plowden, *Bridges: The Spans of North America,* The Viking Press, New York, 1974, p. 181.
2. F. A. Emery, "Washington's Historic Bridges," *Records of the Columbia Historical Society,* Vol. 38, Columbia Historical Society, Washington, D.C., 1937, p. 17.
3. *Ibid.,* p. 19.
4. D. B. Myer, *Bridges and the City of Washington,* U.S. Commission of Fine Arts, Washington, D.C., 1974, p. 21.
5. D. B. Steinman, *Famous Bridges of the World,* Random House, New York, 1953, p. 88.
6. R. S. Holland, *Big Bridge,* MacRae-Smith Co., Philadelphia, 1934, p. 252.
7. Ref. 1, p. 249.
8. Ref. 1, p. 292.
9. "Bridge," *Civil Engineering* **54,** 31 (July 1984).
10. A. Garcia and R. Robison, "Sunshine Skyway Nears Completion," *Civil Engineering* **56,** 32 (Nov. 1986).
11. *Ibid.,* p. 33.
12. "Record Concrete Span Opens," *Engineering News Record* **173,** 31 (Oct. 1, 1964).
13. "Firth of Forth Bridge Open," *Engineering News Record* **173,** 27 (Sept. 10, 1964).
14. "Firth of Forth Bridge Combines Beauty with Economy," *Engineering News Record* **172,** 26 (May 28, 1964).
15. *Ibid.,* p. 27.
16. "Scandinavia's Longest Bridge Open," *Engineering News Record* **174,** 40 (Feb. 25, 1965).
17. "Portugal Builds the Longest Suspension Bridge in Europe," *Engineering News Record* **171,** 26 (Dec. 12, 1963).
18. *Ibid.,* p. 34.
19. D. Billington, "Bridges and the New Art of Structural Engineering," *American Scientist* **72,** 29 (Jan.–Feb. 1984).
20. D. Billington, "Swiss Bridge Design Spans Time and Distance," *Civil Engineering* **51,** 43 (Nov. 1981).
21. Ref. 19, p. 30.

General References

Refs. 1, 5, and 6 are good general references.

D. Beckett, *Great Buildings of the World—Bridges,* Hamyln Publishing Group, London, 1959.

H. Escale, "New Chicago Type Bascule Bridge," *Journal of Structural Engineering* **109,** 2340–2354 (Oct. 1984).

Holly Hulse

Edimir Rocumback
Bozeman, Montana

BROCHURES.   See Communications in Architecture

BUILDING CODES.   See Regulations–Building and Zoning

BUILDING SYSTEMS.   See Construction Systems

BUILDING TEAM

Building team is a term generally but somewhat loosely used to describe the group of professional and commercial enterprises which design and construct a building project. The term construction team is sometimes used as a synonym for the building team but is more properly reserved to designate the set of enterprises involved in civil engineering or public-works projects. Many of the characteristics of the building team apply except that, due to the greater size of construction works, the participating firms operate with greater continuity in a climate of reduced uncertainty.

Principal members of a building team include the project architect, consulting engineers (typically structural and mechanical), building contractors, and sub- or specialty contractors. Sometimes, building-product suppliers and manufacturers are covered by this term; other times, consultants to these principal members, such as sociologists, ergonomists, architectural programmers, landscape architects, urban designers, and cost planners (who advise the architect), sanitary engineers, and soil mechanics, earthquake, and other consultants (who advise the engineers), are also included.

Depending on the nature of the building project, various highly specialized consultants may be involved, such as food-service and restaurant consultants, interior designers, consultants on operating theater design, urban designers, acoustic or lighting consultants, and seating or parking designers; for certain special building projects, specialists in historic restoration, transportation systems, computer facilities, or stage design can also be retained, depending on both the needs of the project and the experience and skills of the principal members of the building team.

The relationships between these consultants can be established in a variety of ways. For example, sometimes the consulting engineers may be retained by, and act as advisers to, the architect; in other cases, consultants such as the landscape architect may be retained as principal members of the building team.

As they carry out their mission of designing and constructing a particular facility, the building team members must, in all projects, cooperate with other parties, among whom are the controlling and approval agencies and resource enterprises (municipal planning and code authorities, utility companies, government safety inspectors, representatives of financial institutions, etc). These institutions and enterprises, together with the social, technical, and economic forces that have an impact on building, constitute the environment within which the building team operates (Fig. 1). Sometimes, members of the building team cooperate with the controlling and approval agencies in a teamwork situation to resolve particular problems stemming from the project under study; similarly, the public at large can become involved, through processes of public hearings or environmental impact studies.

The person (an individual or an institution of some sort) who initiates the building project, variously called the building owner or simply the client, is sometimes considered to be a member of the building team and at other times not; the term can be used with either connotation (Fig. 1).

MISSION OF THE BUILDING TEAM

The main tasks that comprise the mission of the building team fall into two categories: design and construction. They are usually carried out separately and by different enterprises because of the nature of the contracts that govern the execution of the tasks that are needed within each. This separation of design from construction is often said to be the special characteristic of the building team, one that distinguishes it from most other industries.

Specifically, the designing part of the building team's mission (carried out by firms often grouped under the term project team) includes: (1) preparing the brief or architec-

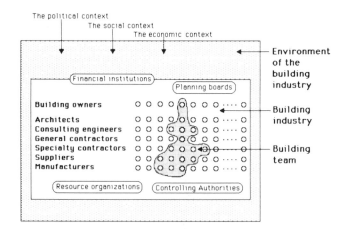

Figure 1. The building team in the building industry and the building industry within its environment. Members of the building team are selected from among the many enterprises in each category which exist within the building industry; they come together to carry out a particular building project.

tural program (namely, listing the activities that the intended building is to house, together with their functional requirements, and establishing an upper limit of acceptable costs); (2) developing this brief in terms of the performance criteria that the about-to-be-designed building must satisfy if these activities and functions are to be housed adequately; (3) proposing outline architectural designs and checking their predicted performance characteristics against the performance criteria; (4) estimating likely costs and comparing them with the upper-limit budget established previously (and making any consequential changes to the design if it is to respect that budget); (5) selecting the design that seems to meet the requirements and budget constraints best and developing it in detail; and (6) preparing all of the technical communications about this design for contract purposes, ie, working drawings and specifications.

The construction part of the building team's mission includes: (1) planning the construction operations (scheduling of required tasks); (2) organizing the building site (including placing the various temporary equipment and machinery, eg, scaffolding, hoists, etc, required to carry out the building operations); (3) establishing contracts with the various specialty trades required; (4) purchasing and arranging timely deliveries of the necessary materials and components; (5) coordinating and carrying out fabrication and assembly operations on the materials and components so that the building takes form in accordance with the finalized drawings and specifications and respects the requirements of the controlling authorities; (6) handing the building over for acceptance by the building owner in a pre-established sequence. The construction part of the mission also includes, by implication, the manufacture and supply of the materials and components, whether to standard or special designs for the particular project. It is because manufacturers are generally supplying materials and components to a very large number of projects at any one time that there is no agreement as to whether they should be counted as members of a particular building team or not, even if they are usually considered to be members of the building industry.

It is the necessary combination of the two parts of the building team's mission that enable functionally and aesthetically appropriate buildings to be designed and constructed. During the design phase, the project team members define the functional objectives which the building is to satisfy (in other words, they identify what the building client's problem really is, often having to investigate factors not made explicit in the brief); on this basis, a design can then be proposed. The passage from this formulation of the problem to the finished building design involves (1) analyses of the qualities that are required of the various parts of the future, and as yet undesigned, building (expressed as performance requirements, ie, the nonmaterial spatial and physical attributes to be provided by the future building if it is to ensure comfort and satisfaction, with no reference as yet to actual materials and their arrangements); (2) syntheses of these performance requirements into the design, expressed in terms of propositions for materials and their arrangements (a satisfactory design is one in which the set of inherent performance characteristics of these materials and arrangements comes at least up to the levels of the performance requirements). The synthesis phase leans on a number of organizing principles, such as the artistic talent of the designers, the fashions of the time, and the anticipated strengths and weaknesses of the construction members of the building team.

During the construction phase, a number of important decisions must be made concerning the optimum combination of processes for executing the designs. Two processes are involved: fabrication (manufacture) of the various components and elements of the building, and their assembly into the finished building. Many components are manufactured off the building site (either to broadly accepted standards, such as bricks or bathtubs, or to building-specific purpose designs, such as curtain walls or elevators) and are assembled in their final locations on site; others are constructed directly on site at their final locations (eg, poured-in-place concrete walls or frames) and require only certain finishing operations. How the breakdown is made between the two processes depends to a large degree on the particular skills of the members of the construction part of the building team but also to some extent on the prevailing industrial environment (as, for example, when prefabrication was used in postwar Europe).

These two parts of the building team's mission are linked to the building owner after phases of contract negotiation; a variety of arrangements are possible, reflecting the way the building owner wishes to spread responsibility and risk between himself on the one hand and the designers and builders on the other, and the importance to him of bringing design and construction members of the team together early on.

REMUNERATION OF THE MEMBERS OF THE BUILDING TEAM

The members of the building team are traditionally selected and remunerated in different ways, depending on

the part of the mission with which they are to be involved.

The building owner negotiates and signs service contracts with the firms required to carry out the design part of the mission. This can be done either separately with each or by a hierarchy of contracts where the architect assumes the prime role and centralized coordination responsibility for other consultants, such as the professional engineers; they are remunerated on a declared-fee basis, sometimes calculated as a percentage of construction costs. For the construction part of the mission, the building owner signs construction contracts, where the profits of the contractor(s) are included in their prices, but are usually not declared as such in the contracts. Again, the contracts may be signed separately with each contractor (then called "multiple prime contractors"), but more commonly they are arranged in a hierarchy, where a general contractor assumes the prime role and centralized responsibility for all construction activities. The contract may be on a fixed-price basis, may include various adjustment clauses, or may be on a cost-plus-fee basis, where the fee includes some allowance for overhead and contingencies as well as profit.

The contract of the designers may, and often does, include responsibility for site observation; this responsibility used to be, and sometimes still is, called site supervision, in the restricted sense of ensuring that the construction work (carried out under the terms of the construction contract(s) arranged separately) actually corresponds to the descriptions of the working drawings and specifications (Fig. 2).

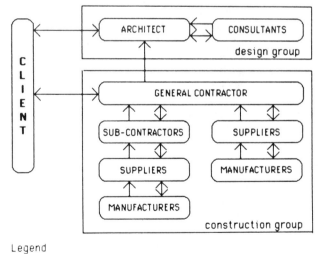

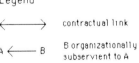

Figure 2. Organigram of the traditional building team, showing the links that exist between the various participants. Note that if this team is not formed at one time but is gradually constituted as and when participants are required to intervene and then progressively dissolves as their participation is completed, it is a "discontinuous" team; if the links shown only actually exist formally and other plausible ones only occur informally, it is a "dispersed" team.

CHARACTERIZATION OF THE BUILDING TEAM

The traditional building team is a temporary grouping of independent entities brought together by certain contracts to carry out tasks of design and construction which comprise its mission. It is characterized by its dispersion and its discontinuity. The building team is dispersed because of the nature of the contracts which establish direct links between certain participants only. As a consequence, communications within the building team fall into two categories: formal, which only allows instructions to be given and authority to be exercised along the clearly defined contractually specified paths; and informal, which permits problems to be discussed as the need arises, and, in point of fact, enables the day-to-day business of design and construction to be carried out. Any discrepancies between these two categories of communication can, and often do, lead to difficult legal problems at the end of the contracts. In a discontinuous team, the building team is also discontinuous because it exists only for the duration of the design and construction process, after which team members become involved in other projects with other firms. Members join the team at different times, in a sequence that corresponds to their required involvements, and then leave it as soon as they have completed their allotted tasks.

The building team is, therefore, a temporary multi-organization; it exists within the building industry, defined as the set of all firms and enterprises in all categories which are involved in one or more projects at any given moment (Fig. 1). (The building industry is called a multi-industry, reflecting its heterogeneous nature and the plurality of its member firms and of their objectives.) The individual firms and enterprises (architects, engineering offices, contractors, specialty subcontractors, etc) that come together for any one project also operate over a long period of time by becoming involved in a succession of projects, as has just been shown. Consequently, each firm or enterprise has its own long-term objectives and experience, which distinguish it from its competitors. When these enterprises choose to work on a given project, they accept the conditions and objectives that are both explicitly and implicitly associated with that project, and, in doing so, they accept that they are expected to subordinate their own long-term objectives to the project-specific conditions and objectives established by the building owner (each firm hopes that any incompatibilities that may arise between the project-specific short-term objectives and the firm-specific long-term objectives will not be too damaging).

CURRENT CHANGES IN THE BUILDING TEAM

From this, it can clearly be seen that the way the building owner organizes his contracts with the various members of the building team considerably influences the extent to which any discrepancy between short- and long-term objectives may arise. In other words, the building owner's procurement strategy largely determines whether there will be outbreaks of conflict within the building team or not (and thus establishes the extent to which any one

firm may feel it has to protect its long-term objectives in the face of problems stemming from the short-term project objectives); if there is conflict, it nearly always leads to productivity losses during the design and construction process, and thus to reductions in the value-for-money obtained by the building owner, as well as to lower profits or to other marketplace disadvantages experienced by the concerned parties.

In general, as long as the building owner is able to follow traditional, well-known procedures in making his procurement decisions, the members of the building team find themselves in relatively familiar situations (even if their fellow team-members are new to them) so that the eventual discrepancies between long- and short-term objectives fall within limits that are considered to be acceptable because they could be predicted from the outset.

However, these traditional procedures correspond to traditional techniques of building for traditional sets of requirements. For example, the traditional separation of design from construction is generally acceptable as long as the technical expectations embodied in the contract documents produced at the end of the design phase correspond to the contractors' and manufacturers' technical potential. Conversely, where project requirements are particularly complex (eg, if available time is limited or functional criteria are unfamiliar), some ways must be found to reduce the impact of this separation while providing for overall control of time, cost, and quality by the building owner.

A number of circumstances now arise in which traditional practices are found to be unsuitable, requiring rationalization and/or industrialization of the design and construction process. These circumstances may be technical (eg, the projected building is to meet unusual quality requirements), social (eg, a vast quantity of economical building is required), or commercial (eg, some facilities are required very quickly). In all of these cases, the organization of the building team changes. For example, if the aim is rationalization, a coordinating or management function or service is introduced, either as project manager or construction manager; the former acts as coordinator of design and construction for the building owner, and the latter as adviser during design and coordinator of construction (Fig. 3). If overall speed is important, it becomes possible (when a management service is available to ensure adequate control) to fast-track the design and construction operations, ie, to move away from the strictly linear sequencing of designing and constructing, working instead with semisimultaneous construction packages. Alternatively, when, for example, speed of construction is important, the design and construction parts of the team's mission are assumed by one integrated organization which offers complete "design–build" (design and construction) services to its clients (Fig. 4). If the aim is industrialization and technological innovation, eg, to obtain a broadly based increase in productivity, a number of individual building projects are coordinated and brought together by the concerned building owners to form an aggregated market. This is usually done by establishing some consortium arrangement, grouping the building owners' purchasing power together over a period of time. It is then possible for the building team to respond to this aggregated market

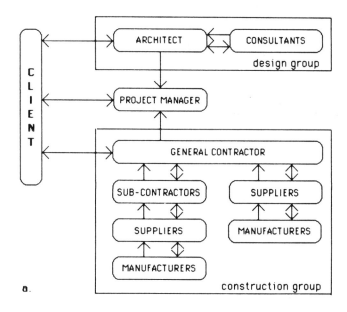

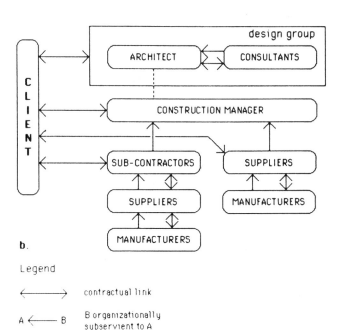

Figure 3. Changes in the organization of the building team if rationalization is desired **(a)** when a project manager is introduced to coordinate design and construction; or **(b)** when a construction manager is required to coordinate construction and, possibly, advise during design.

and develop the appropriate innovative technique by closely associating the design part of the team either with the consortium of building owners or through a joint venture of the involved manufacturers or contractors (Fig. 5).

CONCLUSION

It can therefore be seen that the term building team, despite its linguistic connotations of a team, implying a num-

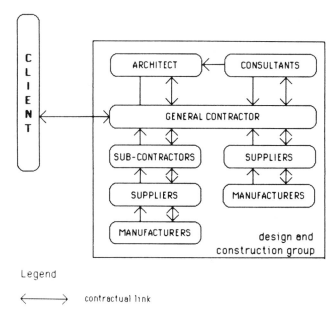

Figure 4. Changes in the organization of the building team when construction is entrusted to an integrated design–build organization.

ber of parties collaborating to attain some commonly agreed-upon objective, actually covers a loose grouping of independent enterprises which works on a particular building project and the various aspects of its design and construction. Moreover, the organization of this team is changing, moving in the direction of closer coordination and integration as current demands placed on the building industry increase in complexity and as the technological potential of that industry evolves to meet them.

BIBLIOGRAPHY

General References

J. R. Blau, *Architects and Firms, a Sociological Perspective on Architectural Practice,* The MIT Press, Cambridge, Mass., 1984, 189 pp. A study of the social context in which the design and production of architecture takes place; a comprehensive bibliography, including references on organizational design, is provided.

M. Bowley, *The British Building Industry,* The University Press, Cambridge, UK, 1966, 488 pp. An explanation of the organization of the building industry of an industrialized country, with systematic references to the economic context within which it operates.

D. Burstein and F. Stasiowski, *Project Management for the Design Professional,* Whitney Library of Design/Billboard Publications, Inc., New York, 1982, 160 pp. A practical presentation of the principles and practices of project management and the project team and its organization.

C. Crichton, ed., *Interdependence and Uncertainty: a Study of the Building Industry,* Tavistock Publications, London, 1967, 84 pp. A seminal report of a study of the circumstances under which individual firms cooperate on building projects, of the

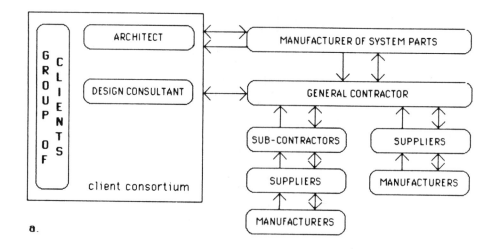

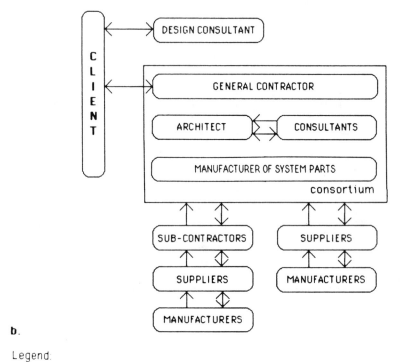

Figure 5. Changes in the organization of the building team when a market is aggregated to take advantage of innovative building technologies, such as industrialization: **(a)** when building owners form a consortium; or **(b)** when the initiative is entrusted to a consortium (or joint venture) of manufacturers and contractors. Note the corresponding changes in the allegiance of the designers.

Legend:

⟵——⟶   contractual link

A ⟵—— B   B organizationally subservient to A

communications and the conditions under which decisions are made, and of the repercussions of these decisions on other participants.

C. Foster, *Building with Men: an Analysis of Group Behaviour and Organization in a Building Firm,* Tavistock Publications, London, 1969, 217 pp. A systematic analysis of the lessons to be learned from the daily events and activities of a small building enterprise.

M. Glover, ed., "Building Procurement; Proceedings of a Workshop," *IF Occasional Paper Number One,* the IF Team, University of Montreal, Montreal, and the Construction Engineering Research Laboratory, Champaign, Ill., 1974, 72 pp. A study of the importance of the strategic decisions made by building

owners as they proceed with their procurement options and of the circumstances most likely to favor a particular approach; the implications on the participants' roles are analyzed.

M. Glover, ed., "Alternative Processes; Building Procurement, Design and Construction," *IF Occasional Paper Number Two,* the IF Team, University of Montreal, Montreal and the University of Illinois, Champaign, Ill., 1976, 168 pp. A report on the consequences of current preoccupations, eg, with life-cycle costing, on procurement, with suggestions as to strategies that should be used.

D. Haviland, *Managing Architectural Projects: The Process,* The American Institute of Architects (AIA), Washington, D.C., 1981, 112 pp.

D. Haviland, *Managing Architectural Projects: Three Case Studies,* The American Institute of Architects (AIA), Washington, D.C., 1981, 3 vols.: 35, 36, and 28 pp.

D. Haviland, *Managing Architectural Projects: The Effective Project Manager,* The American Institute of Architects (AIA), Washington, D.C., 1981, 42 pp.

D. Haviland, *Managing Architectural Projects: The Project Management Manual,* The American Institute of Architects (AIA), Washington, D.C., 1984, 160 pp. A series stressing the roles and responsibilities of the project team in its relationship to the complexities of the building process and its participants.

C. U. Merten, *A Study of the Building Process,* London, University College, 1968, unpublished report. A research report showing the importance of certain milestone decisions in building project design and of their effects on the design process and its participants.

E. J. Miller and A. K. Rice, *Systems of Organizations,* Tavistock Publications, London, 1967. A fundamental study of organizational principles, communications, and management potentials in industries possessing more or less integration and task differentiation.

A. Norsa, ed., "Answers for the Building Community: Optimizing the Choices," *IF Occasional Paper Number Three,* the IF Team, University of Montreal, Montreal, and the University of Illinois, Champaign, Ill., 1976, 68 pp. A report on patterns of strategic decisions available for public- and private-sector building owners, relating procurement options to environmental and industry conditions.

C. J. B. Roberts, *Project Analysis and Organizational Design in Building—an Investigation into the Performance of Building Projects,* Washington University, St. Louis, Mo., available from the IF Team, University of Montreal, Montreal, 1972, 219 pp. A research report showing the relationships between procurement strategies, building team organization, and the productivity of building team members.

P. Trench, "The Future Structure of the Building Industry: Bridging the Gap between Design and Construction," *Building* **216**(6561), 103–104 (1969). An argument for adopting organizational approaches to contracting for the building team's services that simplify interenterprise relationships.

Government Policies and the Cost of Building, United Nations, Geneva, 1959, 165 pp. A report on public-sector procurement strategies and their impact on the scope for technological innovation in a social and economic context of major building requirements.

See also Construction Documents; Construction Equipment; Construction Funding; Construction Industry; Construction Management; Contract Administration; Entrepreneur/Architect Relationship; Estimating, Cost; Fees, Architectural.

Colin H. Davidson
Université de Montréal
Montreal, Quebec, Canada

BUILDING TYPES

This *Encyclopedia* contains articles describing many of the more common building types. The articles trace the development of the building type from its earliest examples to the present. Articles are illustrated by the use of plan and section drawings and perspectives or photographs of outstanding representative buildings and, in many cases, statements of the philosophy of the designers.

The following building types are included:

Adobe Construction
Airports
Amusement Parks
Apartment Buildings—High-rise
Aquariums
Atrium Buildings
Banks
Bridges
Bus Maintenance Facilities
Cathedrals
Church Architecture
Condominiums
Convention Centers
Day-care Centers
Department Stores
Elementary Education
Embassies
Government Buildings
Health Care Facilities—Acute/Intensive
Health Care Facilities—Ambulatory
Health Care Facilities—Continuing Care
Health Care Facilities—Psychiatric
Health Care Facilities—Rehabilitative
Hotels
Housing, Self-help
Justice Buildings—Courts and Correctional Institutions
Laboratories
Libraries
Marine Facilities
Membrane Structures
Mixed-use Buildings
Mosques
Multifamily Housing
Museums
Museums—Architectural
Music Halls
Office Buildings
Opera Houses and Theaters
Physical Education, Athletics, and Recreational Activity Facilities
Planned Communities—New Towns
Postal Facilities
Power Generation Facilities—Fossil Fuels
Power Generation Facilities—Geothermal
Power Generation Facilities—Nuclear
Power Generation Facilities—Wind, Tidal
Rapid Rail Transit Systems
Religious Architecture

BIBLIOGRAPHY

General References

Refer to the listed articles for books and periodicals relating to specific building types.

N. Pevsner, *A History of Building Types, The A. W. Mellon Lectures in the Fine Arts 1970, Bollingen Series XXXV-19*, Princeton University Press, Princeton, N.J., 1976.

BULFINCH, CHARLES

Charles Bulfinch was born on August 8, 1763 in Boston into a well-to-do and educated family. During the Revolution, he was educated at the Boston Latin School, and entered Harvard in 1778, earning his degree in 1781. Because of the disturbances to commerce caused by the Revolution, he was able to spend considerable time in the study of architecture, including additions and repair of buildings whose maintenance had been neglected during the war. With the help of a bequest, he traveled to Europe in 1785, and returned to Boston in 1787. In England, he had the opportunity to study the work of the aging Robert Adam and William Chambers, both of whose work influenced the later Bulfinch designs. Boston at the end of the Revolution was far behind the European experience of architecture, and the younger generation of English architects were not yet famous at the time of Bulfinch's visit to England. Such men as John Soane and James Wyatt were unknown to him.

Bulfinch's intent, revealed by the family papers, was a gentlemanly interest in architecture and a dedication to public service. He was married to Hannah Apthorp in 1788. In his leisurely approach to architecture, he designed in his early married years two state capitols and three churches, as well as a number of other projects. The design of a development of a crescent of houses in which he had

personally invested led to personal bankruptcy during the depression of 1796.

Several of these early projects survive. Perhaps the most famous is the State House, Boston, 1795–1797. Despite many additions, restorations, and changes in use, the central section of the original building is easily identified. Bulfinch's original drawings still survive.

The State House, Hartford, Conn. (1793–1796), also survives, having been restored in 1918–1920 and 1961. It now serves as a museum.

After 1796, Bulfinch depended on his architectural practice for income. The seven surviving children and other relatives made a close social group, and despite later financial problems he was able to survive comfortably until 1844.

The other aspect of his life, public service, was to provide the impetus for the construction of many public works which changed the aspect of Boston into a Federal-style city. Elected in 1793 to the Board of Selectmen, it was not until 1796 and his election as chairman that Bulfinch became seriously involved in government of the city. He held the position of chairman and superintendent of police for almost 19 years. The salary from these offices supplemented the income from architectural projects.

The success that he achieved and the respect earned from his public position led to his appointment by President James Monroe as Architect of the Capitol upon the resignation of Benjamin Henry Latrobe. Bulfinch and his family lived in Washington, D.C. until June 1830, at which time they returned to Boston.

The list of his projects is extensive. His Boston work included three houses built for Harrison Gray Otis in 1795, 1800, and 1805, respectively. These famous buildings, which still survive, typify the Federal style as developed by Bulfinch.

Faneuil Hall, Boston, owes its present appearance to Bulfinch's expansion of the earlier smaller building. The interior shows the Bulfinch design, and the exterior was derived from the design of the older building.

The New North (now St. Stephen's) Church in Boston (1802–1804), restored in 1964–1965, is the single extant Bulfinch church in the city. The other Bulfinch church which has survived is the Church of Christ, Lancaster, Mass. (1816); still in excellent condition, it has been much photographed in its setting of lawn and trees.

Bulfinch generally produced plans and elevations, expecting the builder to work out the construction. As a result, many drawings survive which may be compared with the executed work. In the Lancaster church, for instance, there is reason to believe that the three arches on the front portico were changed from the Bulfinch design.

His work on the United States Capitol was required to repair the fire damage from the British burning of the building during the War of 1812. Bulfinch was charged with completing the buildings as previously designed. However, many planning changes were made, including those to the West Front, the original dome, the old Library of Congress, and the Capitol grounds. The major surviving portion of the U.S. Capitol construction is the West Front, restored to its original condition in 1985–1987. Bulfinch's character was such that he was able to achieve construction under criticism, indecision, and abuse. He was known for his civility and calm under difficult circumstances.

In one of his last projects, Bulfinch provided designs for the State Capitol in Augusta, Me. Under the terms of the Missouri Compromise of 1820, Maine was separated from Massachusetts, and eventually Augusta was designated the capitol. The design of 1829–1832 was altered in 1851 and enlarged and rebuilt in 1909–1911; the original design is mostly known from drawings and correspondence.

Just before the age of 66, Bulfinch returned to Boston, where he lived another 14 years in retirement.

BIBLIOGRAPHY

General References

H. Kirker, *The Architecture of Charles Bulfinch,* Harvard University Press, Cambridge, Mass., 1969.

C. A. Place, *Charles Bulfinch, Architect and Citizen,* Da Capo Press, New York, 1968, reprint of 1925 edition published by Houghton Mifflin Co.

E. S. Bulfinch, *The Life and Letters of Charles Bulfinch, Architect,* Houghton Mifflin, Boston, 1896.

ROBERT T. PACKARD, AIA
Reston, Virginia

BURGEE, JOHN

At present, John Burgee is a partner in the office of John Burgee Architects with Philip Johnson, recently moved from the Seagram Building to one of the firm's newest office buildings in New York City, located at 53rd Street and 3rd Avenue.

Burgee was born on August 28, 1933 in Chicago, Ill. Upon graduation from the University of Notre Dame in 1956, John Burgee became associated with one of the oldest Chicago-based firms, Holabird & Root, where his father was a partner and his brother was working, continuing the family architectural tradition.

After service in the U.S. Army, Burgee became associated with the Chicago firm of Naess-Murphy, later known as C. F. Murphy Associates. As a partner, he contributed to several major projects, including O'Hare International Airport, the Chicago Civic Center, the First National Bank of Chicago, Student Union Buildings at the University of Illinois at Chicago Circle, and the J. Edgar Hoover Building in Washington, D.C.

In 1965, when Philip Johnson was being considered as architect for the Philadelphia Airport, he approached Carter Manny, a former classmate from Harvard and at that time attached to Murphy's office, for collaboration. Manny recommended John Burgee, who had worked with him on the O'Hare project. Thus, Johnson and Burgee joined forces for this competition, the magnitude of which was such that it could not be handled by Johnson's limited staff at the time. Johnson and Burgee did not win the commission, but Johnson invited Burgee to join him in practice.

The Burgee–Johnson partnership worked well (1). Many critics agree that Burgee, a generation younger, became "a strong stimulus and calming influence for the enigmatic Johnson" (2). He brought discipline to Philip, clients oberved. Even Johnson confessed that "Burgee sets it right when I create problems" (3), and Burgee admitted, "we can edit each other without any feelings of jealousy" (2).

Some of the best work the office produced, it is generally agreed, has been since Burgee joined forces with Johnson. In fact, it is very difficult to separate the contributions made by each. Burgee has reaffirmed that the different responsibilities are not split up as they would be in other firms: "We work on all projects together. . . . We talk it out, though, even before that. Should it be a tall building? Should it stand out on the skyline? Should it have a tile roof? How should it relate to the street?" (4).

Since moving to New York City in 1967 to join Johnson, Burgee has contributed his creative talent to many joint projects. It began with the last stages of the Boston Public Library addition. Several major designs followed in 1968, among them the I.D.S. Center in downtown Minneapolis (consisting of a 51-story faceted tower, an 18-story annex, a 16-story hotel, and a 2-story retail building, all enclosing a year-round weather-protected "crystal court") and the Convention Center for the City of Niagara Falls (a multipurpose center). In the following year, the Art Museum of South Texas in Corpus Christi was built. Conceived as a pure abstract aesthetic object, irregular in form, the Art Museum mediates between the landscape and cityscape while accommodating versatile exhibitions and events.

In 1970 came the unusual design for an urban plaza known as Fort Worth Water Garden in Texas. This was followed by a group of medium-sized curtain-wall office buildings in Houston known as Post Oak Central, and an unusual oasis of greenery, water pools, fountains, cascades, and a small shrine occupying a three-acre site in downtown Dallas known as Thanks-Giving Square.

The building of Pennzoil Place, however, created a major landmark for Houston (1972–1976). The city's strongest and most identifying symbol, these twin towers, 36 stories high and trapezoid in form, are juxtaposed at sharp angles, making an abstract sculpture against the skyline. As Ada Louise Huxtable wrote in *The New York Times,* the building becomes a "statement that the public recognizes—a critical bridge between the art of architecture and its popular use and understanding" (5).

The past decade (1975–1985) has been the most productive for the firm, which recently changed its name from Johnson/Burgee to John Burgee Architects with Philip Johnson (and grew substantially in size). The impressive output of this last period includes Garden Grove Community Church, better known as the "Crystal Cathedral," in Garden Grove, Calif.; Peoria Civic Center in Peoria, Ill.; Dade County Cultural Center in Miami; AT&T Corporate Headquarters in New York City (Fig. 1); 101 California Street and 580 California Street in San Francisco; PPG Corporate Headquarters in Pittsburgh; Transco

Figure 1. AT&T Corporate Headquarters, New York City. John Burgee Architects with Philip Johnson. Courtesy of Richard Payne, The American Institute of Architects.

Tower and Park (Fig. 2), RepublicBank Center, and the University of Houston College of Architecture, all in Houston; United Bank Center Tower and Plaza in Denver; the New Cleveland Play House in Cleveland; the Crescent and Momentum Place, both in Dallas; Two Federal Reserve Plaza and 53rd At Third in New York City; Tycon Towers in Vienna, Va.; International Place at Fort Hill Square in Boston; and, now under construction in Chicago, Burgee's native town, 190 South LaSalle Street. Two major projects now in design development include the urban design and revitalization of Times Square and 42nd Street, the world-renowned crossroads, and PortAmerica, a new town development just outside Washington, D.C., on the banks of the Potomac.

Figure 2. Transco Tower, Houston, John Burgee Architects with Philip Johnson. Courtesy of Richard Payne, The American Institute of Architects.

Despite variations in the size of the projects, vocabulary, and imagery, the office remains committed to the great classical tradition of the logical plan as a generator. The unveiling of the plan follows the sequence of a processional from the approach, arrival, entry, and final experience of the building. The success of the major projects is due not only to the dynamic interaction between Johnson and Burgee and their commitment to classical principles of architecture, but also to their special vision of their client, program, and site. Gerald Hines, whose buildings shape the skyline of many American cities, is a frequent client committed to craftsmanship. The chairman of AT&T, John de Butts, insisted at the time of planning for their corporate headquarters in New York, "I simply want the finest building in the world" (6). Most of the people at AT&T who responded to a questionnaire on the project building said, "don't give us a glass box" (6).

In this case, not only was a common goal met between architect and client, but the public has reacted positively to a quality building. Even the most vehement critics of AT&T Corporate Headquarters have come to acknowledge its strong presence and polished beauty, not to mention the public amenities it offers: public spaces with tables, chairs, planters, and a shopping arcade. The same could be said for PPG Headquarters with its atrium, plaza, and winter garden, or for Transco with its fountain and park.

At one time firmly rooted in Chicago, John Burgee has now accepted the advantages of living in New York City with his family. This does not mean that he has ceased to build in Chicago; now underway is the first Johnson–Burgee building in that city, at 190 South LaSalle. But Burgee likes to cite Philip Johnson's words of advice to him when he first came to New York City: "Being an architect in Chicago means to build in Chicago. Being an architect in New York means building in the world" (1).

BIBLIOGRAPHY

1. B. Diamonstein, "John Burgee," in *American Architecture Now, II,* Rizzoli International Publications, Inc., New York, 1985, p. 29.
2. C. Knight III, "Introduction," in I. Zaknic, ed., *Philip Johnson/John Burgee Architecture 1979–1985,* Rizzoli International Publications, Inc., New York, 1985, p. 8.
3. *Ibid.,* p. 10.
4. "Interview: Philip Johnson/John Burgee," *Blount Portfolio,* **1**(3), 8–9 (1984).
5. A. L. Huxtable, "Skyscrapers, A 'New' Esthetic and Recycling," *The New York Times* (Dec. 26, 1976).
6. Ref. 1, p. 32.

IVAN ZAKNIC
Lehigh University
Bethlehem, Pennsylvania

BURNHAM, DANIEL

Daniel Hudson Burnham, architect, was born Sept. 4, 1846 in Henderson, N.Y. to Elizabeth Weeks Burnham, daughter of a Congregational minister, and Edwin Burnham,

a storekeeper. In 1855, the family moved to Chicago, where Edwin Burnham undertook several unsuccessful commercial ventures before establishing a wholesale drug business. He died in 1871, when Daniel was 26. Mrs. Burnham lived until 1893 and was able to see her son's work at the Columbian Exposition.

After a period of schooling at Chicago's Central High School and with a private tutor in Bridgewater, Mass., Burnham, failing entrance at Harvard and Yale, returned to Chicago to work for the architectural firm of Loving and Jenney. He was involved briefly and unsuccessfully in a mining venture in Nevada, a candidacy for the Illinois state senate, and a plate-glass business.

His commitment to the field of architecture came when he went to work, at his father's behest, for Peter B. Wight of the firm Carter, Drake and Wight. There he met John Wellborn Root, who had come from New York to Chicago to work for Wight after the 1871 Chicago fire. The two men formed a partnership in 1873, and the new firm of Burnham and Root prospered for the next 30 years.

In 1876, Burnham married Margaret Sherman, daughter of John B. Sherman, an influential Chicago businessman and client of the firm.

One of Burnham and Root's early works was the Montaub Block in Chicago, which had the distinction of being the first real skyscraper and successfully fireproof building. This was followed by the Rookery, in which the firm set up its offices, the Insurance Exchange, the Rand McNally Building, and the Masonic Temple, then the world's tallest building. The rebuilding of Chicago after the great fire, and the dominance of the "Chicago Style" in the new era of the skyscraper provided impetus for Burnham's firm. Another important factor was the ideal relationship of the two partners; Root was a talented, meticulous designer, and Burnham an enthusiastic, outgoing personality.

In 1890, 43 years old and principal of one of the most financially successful architectural firms in the country, Burnham became involved in the planning of the World's Columbian Exposition in Chicago. This project became perhaps his most notable achievement and brought him in contact with several distinguished professionals with whom he associated in later years: sculptor Augustus Saint-Gaudens, landscape architect Frederick Law Olmsted, architects Charles McKim of McKim, Mead and White, and Richard Morris Hunt.

John Root died of pneumonia in 1891, during negotiations for the Fair, and Burnham carried on alone as chief of construction. At that time, the firm of Burnham and Root had designed almost 200 buildings in Chicago and 50 in other U.S. cities. Architect John Atwood from New York came to work in Burnham's office and in the end designed 60 buildings for the Fair. The idea of the Fair as the "white city" in neoclassical form was Burnham's.

This experience established Burnham as the promulgator of the City Beautiful movement which swept the country in the early twentieth century, and as the father of modern city planning. His expression, "make no little plans," became the motto for new city-planning programs throughout the United States.

In the spring of 1893, Burnham was honored for his

work at a dinner in New York attended by many eminent guests, and in June was awarded honorary degrees at Yale and at Harvard, the two schools he had failed to gain entrance to earlier in life. The same year, he was elected president of the American Institute of Architects.

In 1896, at age 50, Burnham took his first trip abroad, accompanied by his wife. An entry in his diary, made at his first sighting of the Spanish coast as the liner Bismarck entered the Mediterranean Sea, indicates the impact of this experience: "O, day never to be forgotten! You bring glory to eyes that never saw you except in dreams, and dreams shall hereafter be wider and richer because of you" (1).

The next major stage in his career occurred in March 1900, when he was summoned to Washington by Senator McMillan of Michigan and offered the chairmanship of a commission to redesign the nation's capital. With the assistance of Frederick Law Olmsted, Jr., son of the landscape architect, he formed the United States Senate Park Commission under the auspices of Senator McMillan, consisting of himself, Olmsted, Charles McKim, and Augustus Saint-Gaudens. The group created the 1902 plan for Washington which confirmed Burnham's reputation as a foremost city planner. Between 1902 and 1908 he was responsible for city plans for Cleveland, San Francisco, Manila and Baquio in the Philippine Islands, and his greatest planning work, the 1908 plan for the city of Chicago.

Between 1896 and 1912, D. H. Burnham and Co. designed some 60 buildings and 11 parks in Chicago, and 90 buildings in other U.S. cities, among these Filene's Department Store, Boston (1912), Pennsylvania Station, Cleveland (1902), Union Station, Washington, D.C. (1908), Selfridge's, London (1906), the Flatiron Building, New York (1901), Mt. Wilson Observatory, Pasadena, Calif. (1909), and the San Francisco Chronicle Building (1907). Burnham died in Heidelberg, Germany, in May 1912 while on tour with his wife; he is buried in Graceland Cemetery in Chicago.

BIBLIOGRAPHY

1. C. Moore, *Daniel H. Burnham, Architect, Planner of Cities,* Vol. 1, Houghton Mifflin Co., Boston, 1921, p. 121.

General References

C. Moore, *Daniel H. Burnham, Architect, Planner of Cities,* 2 Vols., Houghton Mifflin Co., Boston, 1921.

P. Wight, "Work of D. H. Burnham," *Architectural Record* (July 1915).

T. S. Hines, *Burnham of Chicago, Architect and Planner,* Oxford University Press, New York, 1914.

DAVID P. FOGLE
University of Maryland
College Park, Maryland

BUS MAINTENANCE FACILITIES

Facilities dealing with buses are categorized to include those providing service to the passengers using a bus or to the maintenance and storage of a bus. This article focuses on the aspects relative to the maintenance and servicing of buses.

Few people spend much time thinking about where a bus goes at the end of the day, or where it is cleaned, fueled, stored, or repaired; however, these are all important functions of a bus maintenance facility. Essential to any bus company, this facility allows it to provide prompt, efficient, and reliable service.

HISTORY

The bus is very much an institution of the twentieth century. The name is a shortened version of the word omnibus, which means a large motor-driven vehicle that carries passengers. Presently, buses are powered by either gasoline or diesel engines and do not include taxicabs or limousines.

In England, the first recorded bus service was established in 1904 in London. Shortly thereafter, in 1905, regular bus service was provided in New York City on Fifth Avenue, and was called the Fifth Avenue Coach Line.

This era of bus transportation was preceded by the horse-drawn vehicle. Stagecoaches, buggies, and hacks carried up to 25 people on both improved and unimproved roads.

A bus maintenance facility, or "barn," as it is called, derives its name from the historical reference to the bus' transportation predecessor, the horse and buggy. The horse barn was where the horses were fed and groomed and included stables. The blacksmith's shop associated with the horse barn provided necessary repairs to the buggies, rigging, and shoeing. A bus maintenance facility provides all of the analogous functions of the old horse barn, including the storage, fueling, and service of a modern bus fleet.

CLASSIFICATION

A modern bus maintenance facility is classified as a Level I, II, or III, depending on the kind of maintenance and servicing provided:

Level I. A primary service facility providing running maintenance and storage. Activities include fueling, washing, fare collection, light-bulb replacement, wiper-blade replacement, fuel-level checks, etc.

Level II. A secondary maintenance facility, sometimes called an inspection garage for light maintenance, ie, engine tune-ups, lubrications, inspections, tire changing, brake repair, and minor body work, as well as unit change out (Fig. 1).

Level III. A tertiary maintenance garage that is basically a full maintenance garage. Activities include engine and transmission rebuilding, major body repairs, painting, etc (Fig. 2).

Most modern bus maintenance facilities are a combination of Levels I, II, and III. A typical large city or regional bus transportation system generally has a large central Level III shop served by satellite combination Level I and

Figure 1. Level II bus maintenance garage in Tonawanda, N.Y. (note controlled access and site separation of automobiles and buses).

II garages. The central shop provides major component repair and overhaul of units shipped to it from the satellite garages. The secondary garages provide all Level I and II operations as well as unit replacement, but no major maintenance.

On the other hand, a small local transit company is most efficiently served by a Level I or II garage, with major maintenance sent out to contract garages.

Classification is further defined by the kinds of buses served. This identification should first deal with whether the buses are gasoline- or diesel-powered. Secondly, the vehicle mix is important. The fleet may consist entirely of school buses, intracity transit buses, or intercity coaches. In addition, they might vary in size and capacity. These include passenger vans, double-decker buses (used mostly in Europe), articulated buses up to 65 ft (21 m) long, or the standard size bus, 40 ft (14 m) long. Very often, the fleet consists of a mixture of vehicle types; however, it is important to classify these at the outset of a design.

SYSTEMS APPROACH

A systematic approach to the design of a bus maintenance facility is best accomplished through a recognition of the basic systems evident in a garage and how they relate to one another.

The three basic systems, illustrated in Figure 3, are as follows:

System A: fueling/cleaning/storage

System B: maintenance/parts/storage

System C: administration/drivers/storage.

System A consists of the fueling of a bus, including a check of oil and consumable levels, ie, windshield-washing fluid, engine coolant, air, etc. In addition, the bus is cleaned both inside and out and then sent to a storage area. It is in this phase that vehicle receipts are usually removed from the bus in a coin room or vault pulling area and also where brake inspections are often made.

System B is the maintenance area and can either be on site or in a different location. Maintenance is a result of programmed maintenance based on the vehicle miles or breakdown maintenance because of vehicle failure. In either case, the need is identified in the servicing area of System A and the bus is then sent to a storage area to await maintenance. The maintenance area is the heart of any well-run transit operation. It is here that building

Figure 2. Modern Level III bus maintenance facility in Rockville Center, N.Y.

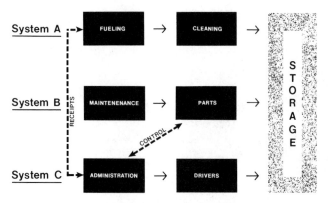

Figure 3. Bus maintenance servicing systems.

design can effect great savings in lost time. A maintenance area consists of vacant parking bays, some with pits and others with lifts for doing maintenance work. Specialized areas are usually devoted to tires, air conditioning, degreasing, upholstering, body work, painting, machine shop, carpentry, electronic fare boxes, batteries, testing, etc. The maintenance areas should be readily accessible to the parts area because the mechanics must be constantly working with the parts department; much efficiency is lost if this element is not considered. Finally, the maintenance area should be convenient to the storage area, both for retrieving buses to work on as well as returning repaired vehicles to service (Fig. 4).

System C deals with the administration of the garage and the drivers who operate the buses on the road. This system has the most interrelationship with the other systems because of the need to know and control the activities in the other systems. This is particularly true of the money removed from the buses in the servicing system and, because of the large financial investment, of parts inventory associated with the maintenance area. Typically, drivers

pick up their route and bus assignments in this area or relax between routes.

In reviewing the three systems, it is important to note the juxtaposition of key elements as well as the elements common to more than one system. For example, the receipts, although removed in System A, are controlled by System C. On the other hand, the storage area is common to all three systems.

COLD- AND WARM-WEATHER FACILITIES

It is important to recognize that difficulties may arise when a modern diesel engine is stored in air temperatures below 40°F (4°C). As a result, special precautions must be taken for buses that operate in cold climates. Storage should be inside at controlled temperatures of 50–55°F (10–13°C), or electric engine block heaters must be utilized. For optimum performance, inside storage is preferable.

Cold-climate operations should have covered circulation areas. These prevent the necessity of constantly having to open and close overhead doors, minimize the number of overhead doors required, and substantially reduce building heat loss.

Warm-weather operations are significantly different. Since circulation patterns can be outside, the system elements are very often in separate buildings. One building might be for servicing and another for maintenance and administration. Also, the storage elements are generally outside. The need for shading and protecting the buses is of concern. A bus parked in the sun heats up and requires substantial running time of the engine and the air-conditioning unit to cool it. Bus-shading elements reduce the start-up time and associated fuel usage.

The costs and benefits of covered versus uncovered storage or shaded versus unshaded storage should be evaluated on a case-by-case basis. Consideration must be given

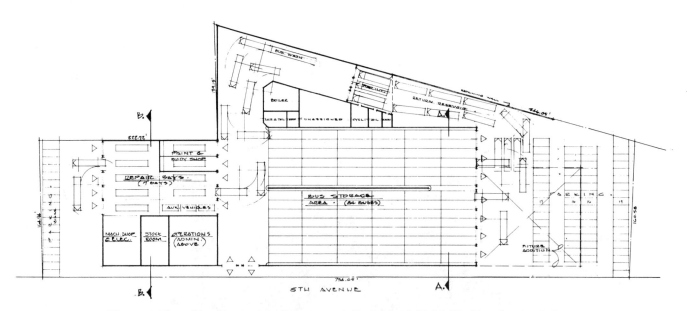

Figure 4. Floor plan of bus maintenance garage in Rock Island, Ill. Modified interior circulation plan highlighted by major servicing in the rear.

to the prevailing climate (temperature, hours of sunshine, etc), frequency of pull-in and pull-out, and building orientation.

EXTERIOR AREAS

The starting point for design is the selection of a proper site. Many factors enter into site selection; however, the first and foremost is that it be large enough to facilitate an efficient operation. A site equivalent to 2.1 times the building area is a good estimate if on-site automobile parking and ample maneuvering are desired.

The second key element is that the facility be near the system's operational center. Proximity to this center, commonly called the pulse point, eliminates deadheading, ie, driving a distance when passengers are not on the bus. The cost of deadheading, including the operator, fuel, insurance, etc, is the single largest expense associated with the operation of a bus maintenance facility, and should be minimized.

Traffic flow on and off the site should be convenient and not adversely affect existing traffic volumes. The site should be compatible with the character of the surrounding areas; if not properly addressed, the noise, smell, sight, and congestion of a bus garage can be objectionable.

The topography should be fairly level in order to avoid costs associated with leveling the site, and utilities (electric, gas, water, sewers) should be convenient. Bus washers use a high volume of water over a short period of time. Likewise, the power and fuel consumptions can, at some peak intervals, be fairly high.

Site access is also very important in an efficient bus maintenance facility. Existing traffic flow around a facility must be studied in order to minimize the impact of the buses on surrounding streets. Queuing areas entering and exiting the garage are necessary, and the right- and left-turn access across existing traffic patterns is important. Once on the site, the circulation patterns should be designed to avoid having the bus driver turn into a blind spot. For left-sided steering, the circulation should be counterclockwise and for right-sided steering, clockwise.

Vehicle types should be segregated as much as possible. Automobile parking should have separate ingress and egress from the buses and be completely separated from bus activity. Likewise, delivery trucks for parts and fuel should not interfere with normal bus operation.

SERVICING

A modern bus servicing operation is shown in Figure 5. It should be immediately accessible upon entering the facility. The first activity in servicing should be the receipt removal. For security reasons, buses should never be parked with the fare box full. Many times, the receipt removal is done in conjunction with servicing; however, where different drivers called hostlers take a bus through servicing, the bus is often parked after the receipts are removed and then is systematically serviced during off-peak hours.

Figure 5. A modern bus servicing station (note the automatic vacuum-cleaning system and fueling island).

The servicing lanes should be flexible enough to handle all of the different model and size buses in the fleet. Service islands should be long enough to handle an articulated bus and have fueling hoses long enough to reach all of the filler-neck locations. This is particularly important where an automatic vacuum-cleaning system fixes the location of the bus' front door. Additional consumables, including air, water, oil, and windshield-washer fluid, should also be available.

The floor area should be well-drained and have a non-skid surface to protect the people performing the service work. Service islands should be elevated at least 6 in. (15 cm) and be 6 ft (2 m) wide. Proper color-corrected lighting is important in order to read the fuel levels, meters, and recording equipment.

Vehicle cleaning usually follows fueling. In large garages, interior cleaning can be done while the bus is being fueled using a specially designed automatic vacuum-cleaning system. Exterior cleaning can efficiently be accomplished by automatic bus-washing equipment. Brushes should be carefully selected and controlled to minimize damage to the exterior finish and scratching of the windows.

In smaller facilities, these cleaning functions are done manually. In either case, considerations must be given to trash collection and storage, a quickly drained floor, wall and electrical protection for overspray, and grit removal from the drainage sewer.

MAINTENANCE

The maintenance area is a section of bus parking bays for doing repair work on a bus. A typical maintenance facility is depicted in Figure 6. Bay sizes for standard coaches should be about 65 × 20 ft (20 × 6 m) and 80 × 20 ft (24 × 6 m) for articulated vehicles.

Maintenance bays consist of either open bays for general maintenance or bays with pits, axle lifts, or wheel lifts. A mixture of pits and lifts is most desirable; however, the exact number is a function of the actual maintenance

Figure 6. Vehicle maintenance area with bus hoists, pits, and overhead delivery systems.

which takes place and the operator's maintenance philosophy. The more third-level activities done, the more lifts are required. With more second-level activities, pits play a larger role and a one-to-one ratio is the most desirable.

Special maintenance areas or bays may be designated. Some of these include tire bay and rack, steam clean, body shop, painting, and air-conditioning repair.

The maintenance areas should be designed with consumables available. Overhead or underfloor delivery systems for grease, torque fluid, oil, coolant, etc, make maintenance more convenient. Also, in addition to the work bays, the pits should receive electrical explosion-proof outlets, as well as air and water. Special lighting and ventilation are also prime considerations in the pit areas.

Ancillary maintenance shops should be adjacent to the maintenance bays. These include the injector room and machine, upholstery, glass, carpentry, and electrical shops. These should be organized in an efficient manner for assembly-line component repair. Since a bus is manufactured in a systematic assembly-line process, it only makes sense to simulate this in the repair procedure.

Testing is a major activity in the maintenance area. A completed repair and/or the need for repair can only be identified through testing. Some of the testing areas include chassis-, engine- and transmission-dynamometers, oil-testing, and injector rooms.

A primary consideration in the design of the maintenance area should be safety. The space should be well-lit, and the lifts and pits should be emphasized by lighting and floor stripping. Adequate space should be allowed for working around vehicles. The floor should be well-drained and not slippery. General ventilation as well as a mechanism for elimination of tail-pipe exhaust should be provided.

With engines running and tools being used, the maintenance area can be noisy. Acoustical treatment should be considered for walls, floors, and ceilings.

PARTS

As noted in the systems discussion, the parts area relates to both the maintenance and the administrative areas.

Two primary parts areas are necessary; these are segregated by part size. An area is necessary for small parts which can be placed on shelves or in bins. Also, a large parts area is required for bulk objects such as fenders, wheels, body sections, and glass.

The parts section should be easily accessible for delivery from either an outside loading dock or an inside maintenance bay. Security of this area is vital because of the large financial investment.

Computers have begun to play an important role in bus maintenance facilities, particularly in the parts area. Inventory control is accomplished efficiently through the use of input/output computers. Consumables throughout the facility, including the fueling/servicing islands, can be monitored through the computers at the parts counter. These can provide information on usage, repair frequency, inventory, and ordering of additional items.

ADMINISTRATION AREA

The administration area should be easily accessible to both visitors and employees. The predominant area is the drivers' room, in which the drivers receive their routes and bus assignments and can relax. It usually features recreational activities, tables, chairs, and vending machines. The station office generally opens into the drivers' room, with the manager's office and general offices nearby. Training rooms, locker rooms, toilets, and showers should be adjacent to the drivers' room. Separate locker and toilet facilities are usually provided for drivers and mechanics.

STORAGE

The space allotted for storage is the largest area of any bus maintenance complex. As previously noted, the kind of storage required can be significantly different for warm and cold climates; however, certain design features are important regardless of the climate.

The parking areas for standard transit buses should utilize a stall space of 12 × 40 ft (3.7 × 12 m). The most efficient parking from a space-utilization standpoint is with an in-line arrangement; however, additional flexibility can be obtained from 45 or 60° angular parking. The parking arrangement should minimize the amount of maneuvering and backing up necessary. The parking surface should be a well-drained area so that it is not slippery and has no standing water. Lighting, whether interior or exterior, should easily and safely allow the driver or mechanic to find his or her bus.

Security of the storage area is essential. Exterior lighting, fencing, alarms, and detectors can be used.

For interior storage, in addition to heating, the ventilation and make-up air requirements are of primary importance. This is particularly true at peak hours of pull-in and pull-out. A ventilation design of 1.5 cfm/ft^2 is a minimum, with 3.0 cfm/ft^2 desirable.

DESIGN

The programming or design of a facility should not be completed until a detailed analysis is made of the entire operation. A checklist of some of the pertinent information follows:

- Number of buses.
- Sizes and dimensions of buses.
- Projected fleet size for at least 10 years.
- Average bus age and mileage (km).
- Maintenance philosophy (preventive or occurrence).
- Number of nonrevenue vehicles (ie, trucks, wreckers, vans, etc).
- Number of drivers.
- Number of mechanics.
- Size of administrative staff.
- Servicing procedures.
- Revenue control.
- Cleaning procedures.
- Existing operation if currently in use.
- Site configuration.
- Environmental regulations.

Parameters vary from location to location; however, from a space-planning perspective, these guidelines are useful:

Level I Facility (inside storage): 500 ft²/bus (47.3 m²/bus)

Level II Facility (inside storage including Level I activities): 800 ft²/bus (75.7 m²/bus)

Level III Facility (no bus parking): 200 ft²/bus (18.9 m²/bus).

These figures include servicing lanes, fueling operations, and cleaning, circulation, and administrative areas. The actual number of lanes and maintenance bays and actual sizes should only be decided after the site and complete operation are considered.

The key to designing a bus maintenance facility is to recognize that, in many cities, it operates 24 hours per day and that no matter how thoroughly a bus is serviced or maintained, sooner or later the process must be repeated. Fueling and washing must be done every day, brakes every month, and engines every year or two. The challenge to the designer is to ensure that the building plans allow for an efficiency of operation that will benefit both the owner and the facility and, ultimately, the user of the bus.

BIBLIOGRAPHY

General References

G. Dallaire, "The Challenge of Designing a Bus Garage," *Civil Engineering,* 54–56 (Jan. 1982).

D. C. Duchscherer, "The Case for Pits vs. Lifts," *Bus Ride Magazine,* 54–56 (Oct. 1980).

C. L. Feiss, *Vehicle Maintenance, A Study of Vehicle Maintenance Practices Among Grantees,* Washington State Department of Transportation, Washington, D.C., Aug. 1981.

Fleet Owner's Maintenance Shop Design Book, McGraw-Hill, Inc., New York, 1982.

J. Foerster and co-workers, *Management Tools for Bus Maintenance,* Urban Mass Transportation Administration, Washington, D.C., May 1983.

R. G. Gunderson, *Technology of Articulated Transit Buses,* U.S. Department of Transportation, Washington, D.C., May 1982.

Jack E. Leisch & Associates, *Turning Vehicle Templates and Instruction Manual,* Transportation Design Techniques, Inc., Evanston, Ill., 1977.

Mitre Corp., *Bus Maintenance Facilities, A Transit Management Handbook,* U.S. Department of Transportation, Washington, D.C., Nov. 1975.

Transportation Energy Management, Energy Efficiency in Transit Buildings, U.S. Department of Transportation, Washington, D.C., Jan. 1984.

See also Transportation Facilities.

David C. Duchscherer
Duchscherer Oberst Design
Buffalo, New York

C

CABLE STRUCTURES.   See Suspension Cable
Structures

CADD/CAE.   See Computer-Aided Design and
Drafting (CADD); Computerization

CAISSON.   See Foundation Systems

CAMBRIDGE SEVEN ASSOCIATES

Cambridge Seven Associates, Inc., founded in 1962, is an
architectural firm based in Cambridge, Mass., with an
associated office in New York. The firm has achieved international recognition with a collaborative practice based
on individuals with varied backgrounds and interests.
Cambridge Seven has done innovative work in architecture, urban planning, graphics, interiors, and industrial
design. Founding partners include Peter Chermayeff,
Louis Bakanowsky, Paul E. Dietrich, and Terry Rankine.

Projects of note include the New England Aquarium
at Boston, Mass., which received a Design Citation from
Progressive Architecture in the Recreation Category in
1967; the National Aquarium in Baltimore, Md. (Fig. 1),
winner in the Architectural Design Category in *Progressive
Architecture*'s 16th Annual Awards, 1979; the U.S. Pavilion
exhibit at Expo '67 in Montreal, which received the 1967
Honor Award from the American Institute of Architects
(AIA); and the San Antonio Museum of Art in Texas (Fig.
2), winner of the 1982 Honor Award from the San Antonio
Chapter of the AIA.

The waterfront development at Harborplace in Baltimore, Md., includes the National Aquarium. The design
of this landmark building is an appropriate scale for the
waterfront location. The colorful mural and triangular-
glazed entrance and rooftop give the city an appealing
landmark. The building was designed by Peter Chermayeff
as an exhibit of water and aquatic life, and is marked by
careful integration of circulation within major architectural spaces. The climax is the glazed rooftop rainforest,
with its views of the Baltimore inner harbor. The aquarium, owned by the city of Baltimore, has become a popular
and much visited building.

Figure 1. The National Aquarium, Baltimore, Md. Courtesy of Cambridge Seven Associates,
Inc.

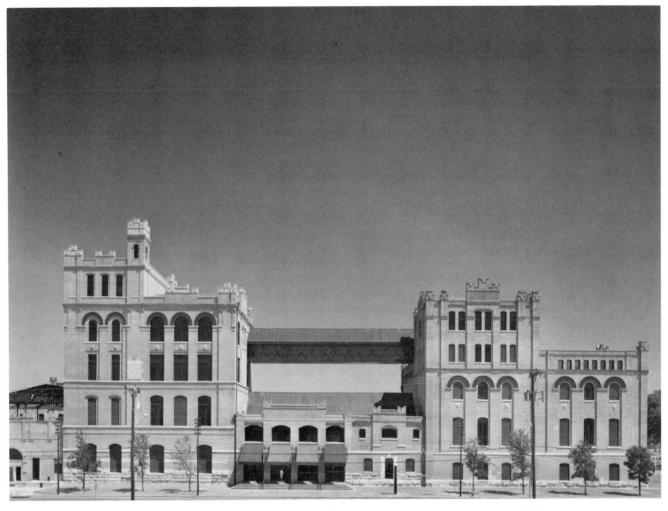

Figure 2. The San Antonio Museum of Art, San Antonio, Tex. Courtesy of Cambridge Seven Associates, Inc.

CAMPUS PLANNING

Campus planning has traditionally involved the art of providing an appropriate physical setting for colleges and universities, through the thoughtful arrangement of land uses, buildings, grounds, landscape, and pedestrian and vehicular systems, and, in recent years, also those procedures and policy determinations, such as building renewal, which affect the long-range building environment.

As an end product, a campus plan has measurable dimensions. Typically, it is an air view of the campus as it would appear when the buildings and open spaces were completed, the landscape matured, and the infrastructure working. The drawing would be overlaid with a phasing diagram, showing the sequence of events, ie, major projects, that lead up to completion. The plan would be accompanied by supporting documentation that explained the plan's functional rationale, as well as the reasoning that undergirds its aesthetic expression (Fig. 1).

All campus plans are campus designs: elemental when they are shaped essentially by locational decisions, and advanced when they depict the desired future three-dimensionally. In either case, as creative works, such plans are best prepared with design methods that are open and cooperative, with strong client involvement, unshadowed by ephemeral styles, or fashioned paternalistically by the arrogance of the aesthetically self-initiated.

What follows now in the way of further definition and discussion of campus planning is derived from U.S. experience. In general, however, the comments and suggestions are nonetheless universally applicable.

APPROPRIATE AND EFFECTIVE CAMPUS PLANS

Few design commissions offer greater challenge than preparing a campus plan. Academic institutions explain a society's heritage, understand present circumstances, and

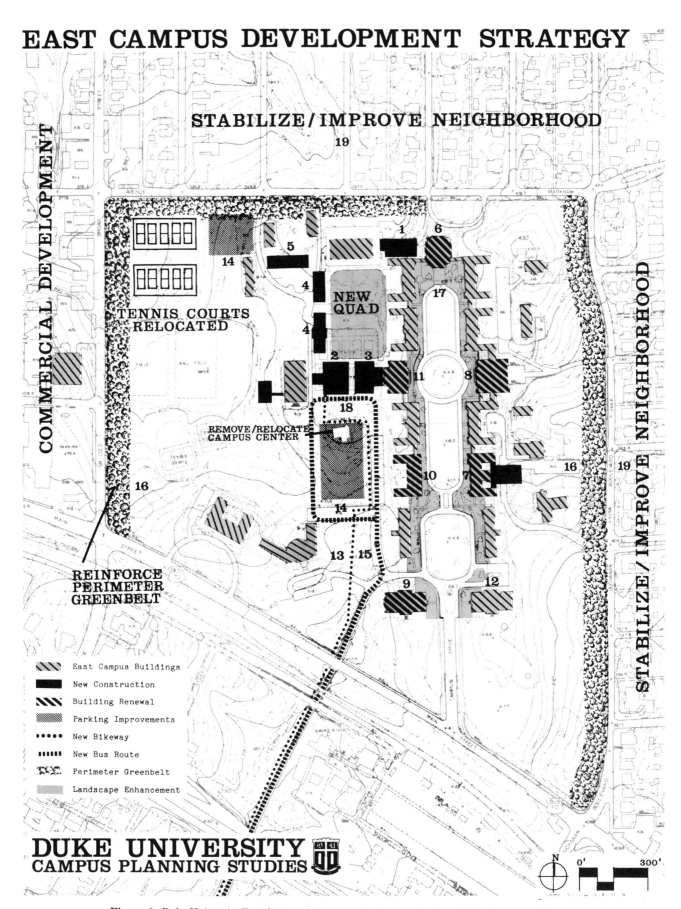

EAST CAMPUS DEVELOPMENT STRATEGY

STABILIZE/IMPROVE NEIGHBORHOOD

19

COMMERCIAL DEVELOPMENT

STABILIZE/IMPROVE NEIGHBORHOOD

TENNIS COURTS
RELOCATED

NEW
QUAD

REMOVE/RELOCATE
CAMPUS CENTER

REINFORCE
PERIMETER
GREENBELT

East Campus Buildings
New Construction
Building Renewal
Parking Improvements
New Bikeway
New Bus Route
Perimeter Greenbelt
Landscape Enhancement

DUKE UNIVERSITY
CAMPUS PLANNING STUDIES

N   0'   300'

Figure 1. Duke University East Campus Development Strategy, Durham, N.C. Courtesy of Dober and Associates, Inc.

invent the future. Their physical forms are charged with symbolic meaning, as well as being unique functional architecture. Further, where higher education once served a select population involved in settled and predictable academic routines, institutions today vary considerably in their educational missions, research, and service roles. Even within their fundamental descriptive categories, universities, four-year colleges, and community colleges, individual schools will differ in role, size, resources, traditions, and outlook. Obviously, campus plans and planning must be tailored to accommodate this diversification, which is also the taproot of campus design.

Campus plans may be divided into two categories: those that guide development on existing sites and those prepared for a new campus. In both instances, many technical factors and judgmental considerations must be weighed and balanced, some of which lie outside the campus planner's scope, but which nonetheless must be understood and integrated in the eventual plan. Fortunately, the professionalization of campus planning in recent years has generated techniques and skills that have strengthened these procedures as ideas are exchanged and experiences evaluated. This is exemplified by the incorporation of the Society of College and University Planning (1965), and the place campus-planning issues have on the agenda of workshops and annual conferences sponsored by educators, fund-raisers, governing boards, physical plant directors, and administrative officers.

From those discussions two words emerge that intrinsically mark successful contemporary campus plans: appropriate and effective. For a campus plan to be appropriate, it must reflect genuine, detailed institutional distinctions such as mission, goals and objectives, maturity, and geographic location. Searching out, clarifying, and articulating those characteristics that distinguish one institution from another is thus an essential beginning point in campus planning. The results can be summed up in an institutional profile, the program for the campus plan and the physical analysis of site factors and influences. As discussed below, each of these pieces of information has an important place in campus planning methodology.

Participatory Planning

For a campus plan to be effective, it must be prepared through a process that involves those who use the campus and those who are responsible for its physical development, management, and operations.

Arguably, participatory planning could be considered the mid-twentieth century's significant contribution to campus planning procedures. Historically, ie, in the eighteenth and nineteenth centuries, many campus plans were developed without such participation. Often, they were architectural concepts imposed by strong-willed administrators and trustees, using fashionable designs or hoary images to encapsulate educational ideas or to announce institutional advancement.

However deficient these paternalistic methods may seem today, their single-mindedness has left later generations with many extraordinary campus buildings and landscaped grounds, which only in recent years have been so recognized; in turn, this special heritage is (in the main) protected, enhanced, and adapted as an architectural legacy deserving preservation.

Important exceptions to this generalization of plans imposed, in contrast to plans derived through participation, substantiate the difficulties of putting any generalizations about U.S. higher education in a singular mold. For example, historian Helen L. Horowitz traced the faculty pressure on an early governing board at Wellesley College to insure that a "concern for economy and business as usual" in rebuilding after a disastrous fire would not lead to a "petty design (that) can never afterwards be enlarged." Such intercessions were *ad hoc* and certainly not provided for in the college administrative routines. However, in this and other instances that Horowitz cites in her seminal work on the architecture of women's colleges, the results were no less splendid a legacy (1).

Whatever their merits might have been, campus plans thus developed, without widespread campus participation, would be viewed today as visionary schemes, folly, fantasy, or expedient, and quickly shelved, lacking the necessary psychopolitical realities of collegiality and shared governance which higher education has come to value so highly.

In summary, the campus plan as a product and campus planning as a process are inextricably interwoven. Consequently, a useful discussion of campus planning must begin with an outline of methodology. The description of methodology is also a convenient way to discuss contemporary campus planning issues.

Method. As campus plans are tailored to the individual institutions, so are the methods of campus planning. For example, campus plans for new institutions will involve different procedures from those applied to existing institutions. Ideally, decision making at the latter might be riverlike—where riverlike is defined as a continuous, integrated flow of information, evaluations, initiatives, and decisions at those institutions where campus plans, once formulated and accepted, became working documents, adjusted and adapted in response to changing circumstances and opportunities, and the planning accordingly adjusted.

Laudable as such planning might be, by observation, apparently few institutions can maintain a continuing planning process; hence, tidal, or episodic, campus planning is more typical.

Figure 2 diagrams an eight-phase procedure that covers the essential steps in preparing a campus plan for either a new or existing institution. As the decision-making and planning process varies, each of the phases can be elaborated or simplified, but none should be neglected.

Organizing for Planning. Effective campus planning must be a disciplined activity. Time spent in organizing the effort, in orchestrating participation and communications, is a necessary prelude for good results.

A scope of work for preparing the campus plan should be drafted in written form. Time and resources permitting, the prospectus will state the purpose of the planning, indicate the circumstances that give cause for the undertaking, suggest the kinds of decisions expected, establish the schedule, and identify the participants, their roles, and

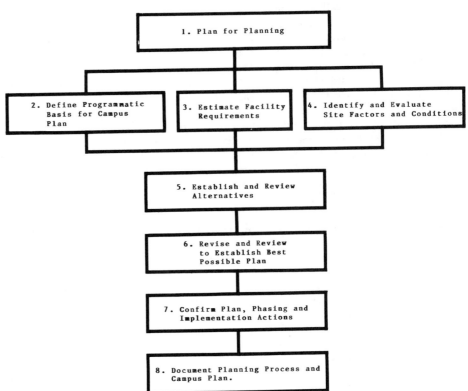

Figure 2. An eight-step procedure for campus planning.

the manner in which they will be organized to carry out specific tasks and responsibilities; for an existing campus, an institutional profile should be included.

The profile should contain a brief history of the institution, its organizational structure, demographic information, and other statistics that help depict the size and character of the institution, especially its physical resources. The latter might include building data: size, function, age, condition, utilization, history, and special features. References to earlier planning studies are also helpful. Most academics are veteran committee members. Information, the basic currency of campus planning, is highly prized. Having the profile available at the start of the effort raises faith and confidence in the process, the products, and the conclusions.

CAMPUS PLANNING COMMITTEE AND STAFF

Typically, the campus planning effort would be monitored by a committee representing the various campus constituencies: senior administration, trustees, faculty, staff, students, and alumni. The committee would review and sanction the initial scope of work, receive and discuss progress reports, serve as an information conduit to and from their peers, direct such revisions as consensus would indicate, and endorse the preliminary and final results.

The process established in this first step of the methodology would take into account various styles of governance, as appropriate for an independent or public institution. However, whatever process is used, the institutional leadership must be kept aware of what is transpiring. Those directing the campus planning effort should conduct periodic briefing sessions for the senior administration, if the administrators are not otherwise directly involved in the committee meetings.

Progress reports to the trustees or regents buildings-and-grounds committees, and the faculty senate or their equivalent, are equally beneficial. Such reports are not only politically expedient, but also give occasion for obtaining information, ideas, advice, and expression of concern, which otherwise neglected could be injurious to the final outcome. Tedious as an elaborate reviewing process may seem, the campus plans with longest life are those that hold no surprises to those reviewing and acting on their conclusions.

From the campus-plan committee, the endorsed plan (drafts and final) makes its way through various institutional reviews, to be ultimately received and acted upon by those legally empowered to do so: the institution's trustees, regents, or coequals. Along the way, discussions and judgments by the campus-plan committee or reviewers may give additional cause for revisions. The schedule should be arranged for these decision-shaping discussions and events to occur in a timely and orderly fashion.

The professional and technical effort that produces the plan and supporting documentation is best undertaken as a team effort. The team might be formed by assigning qualified staff from within the institution, by engaging consultants, or by some combination of the two. In most instances, the campus-plan committee does not play a staff role, although individual committee members may make substantive contributions through their other positions in the institutional hierarchy by providing information, defining needs, establishing criteria for assessing the plan, and judging programmatic, operational, and financial feasibility.

The team should be directed by an experienced campus planner, usually a qualified architect, landscape architect, or physical planner. Obviously technically knowledgeable, the director should also possess those skills necessary to manage and coordinate the campus planning sequence, to work with committees, and to communicate the results of the efforts to others, formally and informally, at each phase of the planning.

PROGRAM FOR THE CAMPUS PLAN

The program for the campus plan should begin with the formulation or reaffirmation of the college or university's missions, and then articulate the goals and objectives that will help the institution accomplish those ends. This information is often summarized as an academic or strategic plan. Such documents provide the programmatic descriptions and prescriptions without which the campus plan has little significance, addressing as they do organizational complexity, uniqueness, strengths, and weaknesses, both for the institution as an entity and for its subdivisions. They may be elaborate or simple statements, modulated as they would be by the institution's ability to define its present and future position in higher education and its anticipated resources, as well as its priorities. The future may be described as an enrollment level, a target year, or a cluster of specific programmatic achievements yet to be realized. Thus, some campus-plan documents are titled *A Campus Plan for Eight Thousand Students, The 1995 Campus Plan,* or *A Plan for the Renewal Of Academic Excellence.*

In the instance of the University of Miami, the *1986 Campus Plan* is the physical manifestation of the university's 10-year strategic plan and thus covers all of the essential factors, considerations, and expectations.

Having stated their overarching reasons for being and institutional objectives in the introductory paragraphs of an academic plan, institutions typically would then describe more specific expectations for the time period covered by the campus plan. These might include the degree programs offered; the number, mix, and qualifications of full-time and part-time faculty and staff; enrollments by level of academic standing, such as various categories of undergraduate, graduate, and professional-degree students; and the manner in which the institution and its suborganizations may enlarge the world of knowledge through the discovery, explication, and application of research. These descriptions will spawn the justification for facility requirements, including function, size, and sequence, and the desiderata for campus land uses.

Depending on the type of college or university, the academic plan might also define the institution's involvement in community service, such as health care; assistance to special groups such as teachers, educators, farmers, and professionals via extension services and continuing education; its role as economic stimulant through research and development institutes; or direct contracting for consulting help through individual faculty and departments. These programmatic activities will also have physical consequences when arranging the campus plan.

The extent to which the institutions will provide residential- and campus-life facilities for students, faculty, and staff; the institutional sponsorship and participation in cultural, recreational, and athletic activities for themselves and the communities they serve; the renewal of aged and obsolete buildings, particularly those used for science and technology; the introduction and integration of computer and communications facilities; energy conservation; access for the handicapped; changes in the social and cultural profile of students and faculties, and the consequences these have for facilities—these are current examples of programmatic issues that need to be addressed and possibly represented in the campus plan.

BUILDING TAXONOMIES

In the suggested campus-plan methodology (Fig. 2), the programmatic descriptions are next translated into facility requirements. The individual entries on the facility list become the featured physical elements in the campus plan. The list is usually arranged by buildings and outdoor areas, and by function. Functional differentiation is important because not all buildings and outdoor areas are equally suited for all locations.

As higher education has diversified over the past century, so too have building types. Libraries have become information centers, with increasingly specialized communications, media, and computer technologies, as well as provision for books, journals, readers, and professional staff. Multipurpose classroom laboratory and faculty office buildings are now commonplace, as well as single-purpose research facilities, sometimes covering several acres. The campus housing inventory may include residential halls, apartments, houses, and cottages. Athletic complexes may include field houses, indoor tennis courts, and swimming pools, as well as the more traditional gymnasium floors, locker rooms, and support spaces.

This overview of diversification exemplifies the many ways that colleges and universities have evolved to serve society. To reiterate, not all colleges and universities are equally structured and engaged in similar activities. Campus planning must search out distinctions and differences, as well as commonalities.

Building needs can be described and listed in an architectural taxonomy, such as the functional groupings established in the Higher Education General Information Survey in Table 1. In the main, universities, being multipurpose, will yield a more intricate and lengthy list of facility requirements than colleges. See Table 1 also for a comparison of the space profiles of several categories of institutions in the United States.

ESTIMATING FACILITY REQUIREMENTS

There are several estimating techniques available for translating information in the academic plan into facility

Table 1. Net Square Feet per Full-time Equivalent Student by HEGIS Category of Room Use[a]

	Public University	Private University	Public 4-Yr	Private 4-Yr	Public 2-Yr	Private 2-Yr
No. of campuses	552	65	456	1,272	901	248
Total NSF	713,719,800	138,457,400	353,054,700	322,486,300	148,956,100	24,366,500
NSF/FTE						
Classroom	12.1	15.5	13.1	22.3	11.4	25.6
Laboratory	27.5	34.8	22.2	24.3	19.0	15.9
Office	26.4	39.2	21.6	25.6	9.4	17.2
Study	12.7	18.8	5.5	18.8	5.5	13.4
Special Use	18.5	22.0	7.8	22.0	7.8	17.8
General Use	21.7	40.7	8.5	40.7	8.5	32.7
Support	17.9	13.8	3.6	13.8	3.6	10.1
Health Care	3.0	2.4	0.1	2.4	0.1	0.9
Residential	55.0	91.8	4.6	91.8	4.6	84.0
Unclassified	4.2	6.5	1.9	6.5	1.9	4.6
Total NSF/FTE	*199.0*	*285.5*	*88.9*	*268.2*	*71.8*	*222.2*

[a] Adapted by Dober and Associates, Inc., from National Center for Education Statistics. Inventory of Physical Facilities in Institutions of Higher Education, Fall 1974.

requirements, such as those described in the UNESCO survey *Planning Standards for Higher Education Facilities,* or some version of the 1985 University of Minnesota Facility Model. The latter has the statistical capability of evaluating existing space sufficiency, as well as estimating future needs.

Campus planners and facility committees seek such norms, standards, and methods because they convey functional exactitude, rigor, parity, and fair play. When appropriately applied, such criteria help balance the inevitable pressures to favor the most articulate campus groups when making program assessments and allocating physical resources in the plan.

Standards vary from a single allocation of space per student enrolled to elaborate formulas that take into account the following types of differences: program diversification (economics uses less space as a discipline per student than microbiology), level of instruction (upper division and graduate programs require more space per student than lower division curriculum), room and seat occupancy rates (factors determined by schedules, curriculum offerings, enrollment choices, and physical resources available), furniture dimensions (seminar rooms require more space per seat than classrooms using tablet armchairs), and the conversion rates from assignable square feet to gross square feet.

The conversion rate is an index to design efficiency. Simply stated, assignable square footage is the usable space inside the room walls. Gross square feet is the total building area, including thicknesses of walls, corridors, stairwells, utility chases, toilets, and mechanical rooms.

Net-to-gross ratios will vary according to building type. Typical conversion ratios from net to gross: residences (1.50), classrooms (1.67), library (1.43), and athletic (1.25). These differences essentially reflect variations in the amount of interior circulation space provided per unit of usable space.

Facility requirements are estimated first as net square and then calculated as gross square feet. For campus planning, the latter number is used in determining site cover-

age, affecting as it does, for example, the building footprint.

The facility requirements thus estimated will then customarily be divided into the following categories: space continuing in use, space changing in use, new construction, and buildings to be removed. The latter rarely occurs in higher education. So-called temporary buildings, for example, lacking historic or visual merit, often have a life span that defies logical explanation or the planner's rational proscription.

VARIATIONS IN STANDARDS

In the public sector, facility requirements are sometimes based on square footage and enrollment formulas that are set by governing boards, often in response to concerns about overbuilding, which was anticipated in the early 1960s, and pork-barrel appropriations, which gave politically strong institutions advantages that newer and weaker schools feared to pursue.

Currently, the trend lines in the cost of construction, operations, energy consumption, and annual and deferred maintenance give further cause for those managing higher education to seek and emphasize the importance of project justification for any new space. Accordingly, many state agencies and boards have again turned to guidelines that establish either total net square feet per student enrolled by type of institution, or more detailed square footages per person and per type of activity. An example of the latter is the promulgation of elaborate lists of space types and sizes, ie, 50 ft^2 per student using a drafting studio, or 30 ft^2 per seat in a seminar room.

Recent experiences suggest that these formulas are generally tenable and applicable with three exceptions. Standards suggested for facilities devoted to science, technology, and engineering should be scrutinized to determine whether they sufficiently account for advances in equipment, safety factors, and the differentiated physical environments and controls necessary for certain kinds of instruction, study, and research. Faculty offices are often undersized for the productivity and work routines expected. The impact of the computer and communications technologies on space size and usage should be carefully studied, including the installation of campuswide networks.

In the private sector, more often than not, entrepreneurship is at work in setting facility requirements for the campus plan rather than tabulated space formulas agreed upon in advance. The radar of need scans the horizon of opportunity, locking into what the institutional leadership considers the best balance of institutional priorities and reasonable expectations for financing the campus plan. Such planning may precede a fund drive, be animated by the arrival of a new president or dean, reflect a sense that the competition is catching up, or be a signal from the national government that funds may be forthcoming for special purposes.

APPROXIMATIONS

Buildings to be represented in the campus plan, as discussed earlier, are usually calculated in net or gross square footage or square meters. Approximations on the order of 1000 ft^2 gross, or the metric equivalent, are sufficient for most campus plans. Where possible, optimum building heights and widths should be determined, as this information is useful in making site choices. Greater detail would be helpful, but not necessary, since the campus plan (in the main) is a general design statement, not a collated collection of schematic building plans.

OTHER CAMPUS-PLAN ELEMENTS

The campus plan will obviously include more than building elements. The very word campus conveys an image of a landscaped open space, shaped and formed by architecture. Outdoor areas have aesthetic and symbolic value, as well as a functional purpose. Accordingly, elements such as playfields, agricultural plots, storage yards, arboretums, and other specific outdoor areas should be thus described and quantified as campus-plan facility requirements.

In the United States, parking requirements and related location criteria must be also carefully elucidated and quantified. Intense discussions can be anticipated as users, committees, review groups, and decision makers struggle with defining parking needs and standards, and justifying solutions. There are few campus-planning subjects that will draw more attention. In ways unflattering to higher education, access to close-in parking is a status symbol, a privilege, occasionally an indirect form of compensation, and sometimes a perquisite that is written into contracts and tenure agreements.

For urban campuses, transportation issues will also earn special attention. Commuting patterns must be ascertained and the projected needs quantified as to mode, frequency, and desired location, especially when the routes will be incorporated physically in the campus plan.

Utility requirements must also be determined in broad outline, given suitable attention in the description of facility needs, and, in turn, represented in the campus plan.

In addition to descriptions of building requirements by function and size, the program information should also include locational desiderata, for example, clustering facilities for organizational reasons such as a law school or an engineering college; grouping buildings by discipline, such as the sciences; establishing a residential sector or outdoor athletic fields within the larger campus pattern or the preferred placement of particular buildings to achieve high utilization, encouraging contact and communication between certain disciplines; or locating certain support facilities, such as libraries or dining halls close to one another, or separating those buildings reached by foot from those that serve visitors arriving by automobile. In addition, structures having symbolic importance may be designated for the most prominent sites: the chapel, library, or meeting hall. Service buildings may be tucked out of view, yet be close at hand for everyday operations.

The obvious should not be neglected in articulating these program objectives. Sometimes unstated and assumed, these fundamental considerations may later be raised and questioned, out of context, in public discussions of the campus plan and in a manner that derails the methodical explanation of how facts, needs, and results are joined together in a rational conclusion.

PHASING PLAN

However they are derived and tabulated, the building and other facility requirements for the campus plan are then divided and organized as a phasing plan. Whether new campus or old, it is necessary to know the probable construction sequence as this will affect the timing of infrastructure improvements and other site changes.

Campus planning should not proceed further until the facility lists and the probable construction sequence has been approved by the campus-planning committee (Fig. 3).

SYNTHESIS: A CAMPUS PLAN

The facility requirements can be likened to chess pieces and the campus site a chessboard. The pieces can be arranged in many different ways to realize a successful solution, ie, the campus plan. Because it is an art form as well as a functional entity, success in campus planning may be defined in many ways. As John Venable Turner reveals in his illuminating panoramic treatise *Campus: An American Planning Tradition*, Thomas Jefferson's "academical village"; early and late U.S. versions of Oxford and Cambridge quadrangles; schemes inspired by the Olmstedian interpretations of nature; civilized, imperial plans derived from the City Beautiful Movement; and designs kindled by architectural philosophies dated modern and postmodern; all of these examples attest to different approaches and contrasting aesthetics in establishing the campus plan.

Two current campus plan concepts demonstrate the polar range of possibilities: the campus as an urban place and the campus as a gardened landscape.

CENTENNIAL PLAN ELEMENTS

3

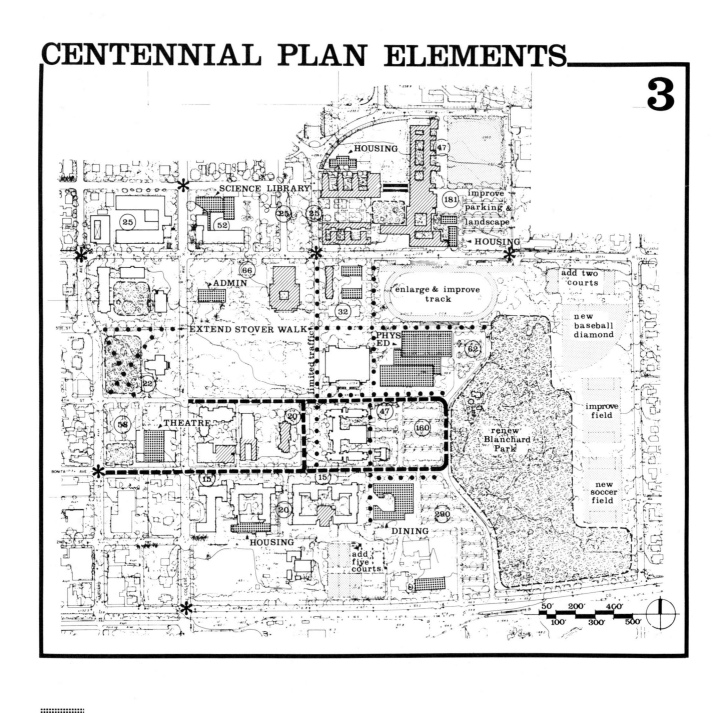

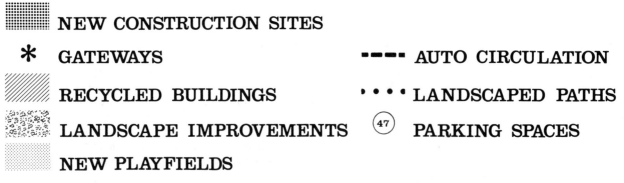

▦ NEW CONSTRUCTION SITES

✱ GATEWAYS

▨ RECYCLED BUILDINGS

▓ LANDSCAPE IMPROVEMENTS

▒ NEW PLAYFIELDS

- - - - AUTO CIRCULATION

• • • • LANDSCAPED PATHS

㊼ PARKING SPACES

Figure 3. Campus plan, Pomona College, Claremont, Calif. Courtesy of Dober and Associates, Inc.

Brown University (Providence, R.I.) is located in one of the United States' oldest settlements. The 200-year-old institution maintains intact its historic College Green. Brown encourages the conservation of eighteenth- and nineteenth-century architecture surrounding the campus, sometimes using such buildings for departmental and administrative offices. New facilities are carefully inserted into this pattern at carefully determined densities, without removing architecture listed for preservation. New buildings use the color, texture, and shape of the older surrounding architecture as design themes, as context, not direct emulation. The interaction of university and neighborhood thus creates a visually memorable campus, as well as an attractive urban design (Fig. 4).

Pomona College (Claremont, Calif.) was envisioned by its early twentieth-century president James Blaisdell as a college in a garden. Appreciating the extraordinary climate and soil in the San Gabriel Valley, he proposed that the college buildings be surrounded by open spaces and landscape that would mark the college as a unique place. Blaisdell's successors have been so faithful to that theme that some buildings are literally hanging gardens. At Pomona, the passing seasons can be tracked by trees and plants that blossom, leaf, and fade in predictable cycles. Intellectual discourse, the social graces, and outdoor recreation are enhanced by a landscape that encourages people to move through the campus on foot. Pomona buildings are sited to promote these exchanges and protect the landscape. Here, campus development is guided by design principles that, in their regard for the landscape, come close to being totemic in their application. The resulting physical and symbolic scene well approximates the mythical scriptural garden east of Eden, filled with trees of knowledge.

Paragon and paradigm campus plans may be usefully examined to discover campus-planning principles and design ideas worth emulating, useful beginning points. However, given the undergirding theme of institutional diversification and the existence of over 3000 campuses in the United States and that number again elsewhere in the world, it is unlikely that there can be a singular solution to campus planning that is applicable in all instances.

Figure 4. Air view of Brown University, Providence, R.I. Courtesy of John Foraste, Brown University.

Hence the importance of methodically examining each campus as a special place, by understanding its programmatic requirements and examining its specific physical features through an analysis of site factors and influences. Generally, the campus plan surfaces from a synthesis of these two sets of considerations.

FORMULATING CAMPUS PLANS

Programmatic information will reveal the institution's position in higher education, expectations, priorities, and physical requirements, all documented in written form, quantified wherever possible and with explanatory justification.

As to site factors and influences, as noted below, these should also be methodically ascertained and evaluated when preparing a campus plan for an existing institution. The information is best mapped and communicated in graphic formats on a campus base map, at a scale so the information and data can be seen by the campus-planning committee in their deliberations, as well as by others who will be briefed about the work and who may wish to trace the reasoning that led to the campus-plan conclusions.

CAMPUS BASE MAP

Modern photogrammetric processes can produce a useful campus base map at reasonable cost. It should be drawn at the scale 1 in. = 100 ft, less or more depending on the size of the campus. Multiple copies can then be produced from a Mylar or Sepia master on a standard copying machine, without having to paste sheets together.

At the minimum, the campus base map should show the outlines of all buildings and outdoor structures, roads, paths, parking areas, water areas such as lakes and streams, and topography. The area covered should include some of the property just beyond the campus boundaries. The master drawing should have a graphic and written scale, north arrow, institutional logo, and space for descriptive legends.

Depending on time and resources, a block model of the campus landforms and buildings might be constructed in order to sense the campus three-dimensionally as a built environment. Cross-sectional drawings of the site and air photographs can also achieve the same result and may be easier to carry than the model from meeting to meeting.

SITE FACTORS AND INFLUENCES

The following site factors and influences should be compiled, mapped, and evaluated prior to the campus-planning synthesis. The information can be gleaned from earlier planning documents, administrative reports, and field surveys.

Building use by function describes the distribution of space by size and function throughout the campus by building. In the instance of mixed functions, the predominant use is shown or the mix indicated graphically. The information can be organized by HEGIS categories and thus compared to other institutions. HEGIS (Higher Education General Information Survey) is a taxonomy describing space functions.

Building profiles express graphically building heights, predominant materials, size, age, condition, and historic and other special architectural features that the study may reveal as having an influence on campus planning decisions.

Campus growth describes the chronological sequence of campus development, illuminates earlier campus-planning decisions and is particularly helpful in planning mature campuses.

Density patterns identify the location of faculty offices, administrative offices, student contact hours, student residences, and the number of seats in public use buildings such as sports arenas, theaters, and auditoriums. This information helps rationalize location of support facilities, circulation elements, and parking.

Pedestrian-circulation routes include all walks and paths, formal and informal, mapped as major and minor routes if possible; pinpoint main entrances to buildings; and can also depict site accessibility for the handicapped.

Vehicular circulation shows all campus roads and routes used by motor vehicles, size and type of surface, origin and destination points, peak volume of traffic, service points to buildings accessible by vehicles, emergency and service routes, bicycle paths, campus transportation and bus routes and designated stops and stations, parking areas by size, campus gateways used by vehicles, and security and safety issues related to circulation, including the location of pedestrian and vehicular conflicts in traffic flows.

Campus open space and landscape features indicate the size, configuration, functions, and spatial relationships of all campus open spaces; identify significant tree and plant cover, by type and massing; and pinpoint specimens that must be protected and conditions that should be given special attention in the campus plan.

Topography includes land forms and slope analysis. Too often taken for granted as a design factor, subtle and dramatic changes in topography can be manipulated to help sectionalize campus land uses, to create attractive views and vistas, and to minimize infrastructure costs by using the land to its best site advantage.

Weather and microclimate identifies average range of temperature, precipitation, and prevailing winds by months and seasons, and locates local environmental conditions that may require special attention in siting buildings, landscape, and circulation elements.

Major utility systems are located indicating size, type, condition, and general capacity, and can strongly influence building-location decisions and project costs.

Campus design features designate and summarize special physical features that help create a sense of place. Items include overall physical form, distinctive architectural features, landscape, outdoor artworks, the image of the campus as created by the arrangement and sequence of buildings and open spaces, areas set aside for rites and rituals (commencement, homecoming, special events), and related visual and symbolic elements.

Environs are typically several maps drawn at a scale larger than the campus base map, and identify and evaluate land ownership, land use, circulation, transportation circulation, activity patterns, and special physical features that affect (or may affect) the campus plan and vice versa. Few campuses can ignore the larger physical context in which they are situated. These studies help address campus-planning boundary issues. They pinpoint areas where the municipality and university can work together to stabilize and improve their neighborhoods. They can lead to joint actions that encourage compatible physical development in the campus environs.

ARCHITECTURAL STYLE AS A CAMPUS-PLAN ISSUE

For several reasons, the sovereignty of a traditional architectural style deserves comment as a special campus-planning factor on those campuses that possess such architecture. First, the overall impressions of a campus that has been clad in a consistent style can be so visually pleasing and historically important as to deserve preservation and extension as a fundamental campus-plan objective. Second, the building style selected by the founders is often accompanied by certain site, circulation, open space, and landscape patterns, stylistic in origin. Leaving to one side aesthetics and changing tastes, these elements must be dealt with functionally as campus-planning items.

Third, whether the style is continued, adapted, or abandoned, future construction and existing construction should be sympathetically woven together in campus planning, so that certain attractive campus views and vistas are strengthened and enhanced, and the tactile and symbolic characteristics of the traditional style are appropriately respected.

A few U.S. campuses are marked by an historic architectural expression so strong and continuous in its imagery that the campuses are universally recognized as having unusual aesthetic merit. Significant examples include Dickinson University, Duke University, Harvard College (both the Yard and the Charles River Houses), Scripps College, Southern Methodist University, and Stanford University. Some comments on the Southern Methodist University (SMU) campus should be sufficient to understand how important these architectural considerations can be on some campuses.

Southern Methodist University was founded in 1915. In searching for a suitable building style for the new campus, President Robert S. Hyer chose Collegiate Georgian, seeing in it stylistic motifs and cultural memories that could be traced to the beginnings of the U.S. settlements and its colonial colleges. It was a style that was instantly recognized as being appropriate for higher education (thought Hyer). It could be applied to a broad variety of building types. It could incorporate an attractive campus landscape, such as a quadrangle, a campus design element recognized as collegiate in origin. Buildings designed as Collegiate Georgian could be economically erected, using technologies, construction practices, and materials readily at hand in Dallas, Tex., then a small town, well removed from the mainstreams of architectural thought and urbanization.

Consistently used from the beginning (with minor departures), the resulting campus is a memorable place of its kind, a picture-postcard campus. The style is now so embedded in the SMU culture that no campus plan to date would be acceptable if it were to denigrate those architectural qualities or erode the historic panoramic landscape associated with the buildings (Fig. 5).

Many U.S. campuses have clusters of buildings designed in one style and constructed in one period. Whether motivated by nostalgia, historic preservation, or an instinctive regard for aesthetic value, the desire for keeping these clusters intact has in recent years become a strong design influence on the campus plan.

ALTERNATIVE DEVELOPMENT DIAGRAMS

With the program understood and the site factors and influences identified and discussed, alternative campus-plan diagrams are then usually drawn to define and evaluate alternative physical solutions. These sketches are usually drawn on the campus base map as diagrammatic air views of a completed scheme. The information is accompanied by explanatory designs and criteria, which help sort out the positive and negative features of each scheme.

When reviewed, these diagrams may evoke questions that require program clarification or further site study, thus launching a cycle of reviews and revisions. Explanatory drawings may be generated to help describe subsections of the plan. High priority site development concepts might be illustrated three-dimensionally.

During this phase of the work, the best features of the alternatives may be incorporated into a final draft plan. In turn, the draft is exposed to campus scrutiny, discussion, and the final decision-making processes.

DOCUMENTATION

A typical campus planning effort for an existing institution would take 18 months from establishing the prospectus for planning through the publication of a final report. Significant time would be spent on technical studies, in briefing those affected by the plan, in examining and revising

Figure 5. Dallas Hall, Southern Methodist University, Dallas, Tex.

alternatives, and in reaching conclusions. The total effort should be summarized and published as a campus plan report.

As University of California Planner Albert R. Wagner noted, in advice as applicable now as it was when written in 1962, at the minimum, the report should contain written statements as to what the campus plan is supposed to achieve, a drawing illustrating the major physical planning proposals, and a description of how those proposals are to be phased.

NEW CAMPUSES

When planning new sites, the minimum information for campus planning (in addition to the academic prospectus) would include land size, configuration, site features, topography and land forms, microclimate, existing and projected vehicular and transportation routes to and from the campus, utility infrastructure, and the quality of development, existing or expected, in the areas surrounding the campus.

Here also, as a creative act, the campus plan surfaces from a synthesis of programmatic information, facility requirements, and site analysis. Preliminary plans would also be drawn as alternatives, tested through committee discussions, and reviewed and revised as necessary to reach firm conclusions. The end results would also be published in a report, with supporting documentation and reasoning.

CAMPUS RENEWAL

Campus planning in developed countries has not abated. With a predicted decline in the college-age population, and the presence of half again as many colleges and universities as there were 30 years ago, at many institutions building renewal and space-reallocation schemes, rather than new construction, have become the central topics in campus planning.

Building renewal also embraces deferred maintenance, the rocky reef which may sink many an institution's operational budgets in the coming years; for in recent times, too many colleges and universities have been balancing their budgets by neglecting their physical assets. In addition, the surge of construction that occurred in the 1950s and 1960s is now reaching maturity. Wholesale replacement and repair of building subsystems can be expected because of age and obsolescence. Without such sizable reinvestment in building renewal, campus facilities will be physically deficient and perhaps dangerous. Energy conservation opportunities will be overlooked. Cosmetic approaches to campus aesthetics will fail, for that which is fundamentally rotten will no longer lend itself further to camouflage and concealment through painting and landscape.

Since all things necessary and desired in the way of campus improvements cannot be achieved financially in the decades ahead (say many observers), building renewal priorities must be established. In this context, a comprehensive plan for building renewal can be articulated by adapting campus-planning methods. Emphasis is placed

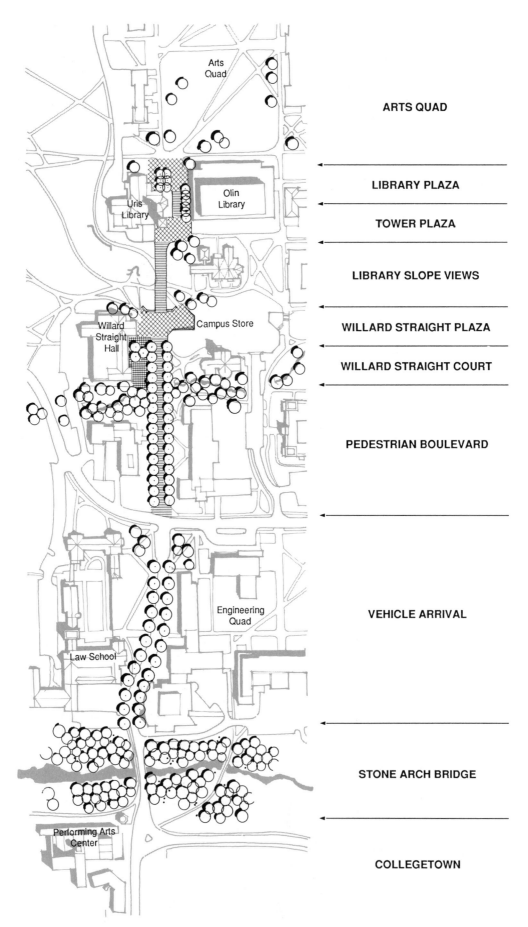

Figure 6. Cornell University Campus Guidelines, inset plan. Courtesy of the Cornell University Planning Office.

on program priorities, building condition, and utilization studies. Greater attention would be given to solving problems by using existing resources, rather than by constructing new buildings. Proposals for new construction (buildings or additions) are carefully scrutinized and approved only when program objectives cannot be met in any other way.

INSET PLANS

At mature institutions, new building construction and other site improvements, when demonstrated to be justifiable and feasible, may be positioned as inset plans, fixed in place by applying campus guidelines. The latter may be published as a functional and aesthetic compendium of site factors and influences that define the specific campus as a special place and thus establish in a physical context the equivalent of a campus plan (Fig. 6).

BIBLIOGRAPHY

1. H. L. Horowitz, *Alma Mater,* Alfred A. Knopf, New York, 1984.

General References

J. V. Turner, *Campus, An American Planning Tradition,* The MIT Press, Cambridge, Mass., 1984.

Campus Guidelines, Campus Planning Office, Cornell University, Ithaca, N.Y., 1985.

A. R. Wagner, *Campus Long Range Development Plan Outline,* University of California, Berkeley, Calif., 1962.

R. P. Dober, *Campus Planning,* Reinhold Publishing Co., New York, 1964.

S. F. Brewster, *Campus Planning and Construction,* Association of Physical Plant Administrators of Colleges and Universities; Washington, D.C., 1976.

D. H. Pylon and W. H. Bergquist, *Consultation in Higher Education,* Council for the Advancement of Small Colleges, Washington, D.C., 1979.

Higher Education Facilities Planning and Management Manuals, Western Interstate Commission for Higher Education, Boulder, Colo., 1971.

R. P. Dober, *New Campus in Great Britain,* Educational Facilities Laboratories, Inc., New York, 1966.

Planning Standards for Higher Education Facilities, UNESCO, Paris, France, 1979.

H. C. Dandekar, *Planner's Use of Information,* Hutchinson and Ross Publishing Co., Stroudsburg, Pa., 1982.

Pomona College Campus Plan, Dober and Associates, Inc., Claremont, Calif., 1978.

Southern Methodist University Campus Plan, Dober and Associates, Inc., Dallas, Tex., 1984.

University of Minnesota Facility Model, Office of Physical Planning, University of Minnesota, Minneapolis, Minn., 1985.

University of Miami 1986 Campus Plan, Dober and Associates, Inc., Belmont, Mass., 1986.

RICHARD P. DOBER, AICP
Dober and Associates, Inc.
Belmont, Massachusetts

CAREERS IN ARCHITECTURE

The architect who is expert in all fields belongs to a bygone age. Shaping today's built environment calls for the architect to have a broad foundation of knowledge supplemented by one or more specialized skills. Many of these skills present separate and distinct career opportunities that have proved to be rewarding professionally, personally, and financially to a surprisingly large proportion of graduate architects.

This article describes the two basic professional career options in architectural practice: specialties within architectural firms, and careers pursued outside the private professional office.

PRIVATE PRACTICE

Architecture has always demanded brilliant designers and always will, but firms cannot survive on design alone. The traditional practice of architecture has changed much since World War II. To prosper in today's toughened practice climate, private firms have discovered specialization. They need staff members who can contribute these specialized skills, in addition to the traditional design and delineating functions. These skills consist of marketing and marketing communications, programming, project and business management, specifications writing, estimating and cost management, construction contract administration, and proficiency in the planning and design of specialized building types such as hospitals, high-tech manufacturing plants, and high-rise office buildings.

Marketer. Attracting new work into the office has emerged as a vital skill, and many firms assign individuals to a primary (if not sole) task of bringing in clients. Whereas the main selling contact with a client prospect is an architect partner, much useful spade work, following up leads, initial contacts, and follow-through, is often done by nonarchitect staff with a marketing background.

Marketing Communicator. This position consists of preparing selling tools such as brochures, proposals, and slide presentations; developing solid relations with the media; exposing principals to audiences through public speaking; and organizing internal resources such as staff biographies, project histories, and project photo and slide collections.

Programmer. As clients become more aware that faults in buildings can often be traced to an ill-conceived program, the role of identifying the scope and nature of the client's problem before design begins has become more important. Indeed, programming is now a full-time specialty. It is often augmented by research into the needs of specialized building users, such as patients or computer operators, and combined with development of performance requirements.

Designer. Design is the ability to convert the program into a building scheme and entails such tasks as fitting the building to the site, organizing spaces, establishing proportions, and selecting materials. It consists usually of two phases: schematic design and design development.

Design is the base course, which at all architectural

schools knits together the various disciplines (such as structural, mechanical and electrical concerns, materials, professional practice, history, and theory). Design is what weighs most in the final assessment of the students, and is what they for the most part expect to pursue as they enter a firm upon graduation.

Design is what shapes buildings, neighborhoods, and cities, but the opportunity in architectural firms is limited to a few individuals due to the nature of the design–construction process and the heavy demand in all firms for nondesign skills.

Project Manager. Like marketing, management was formerly the responsibility of partners or senior staff members along with other functions. As clients and the public demand a closer accounting of a building's quality, costs, and time schedules, project management has become an important specialty in the practice of architecture. Indeed, properly managed projects can make the reputation of a firm, just as a series of poorly managed jobs can spell disaster.

Business Manager. This specialty consists of managing the business of the office, from personnel and payroll to financial matters, legal concerns, and insurance. Several schools of business administration now offer special short courses as well as joint degree programs to students with an interest in architectural business management.

Specification Writer. Specification writing has evolved into a major specialty. A good specification writer has a feel for the technical side of building materials, products, and equipment, and a good sense for the meaning of the written word. Specifications define for the contractor the desired quality of materials and workmanship for a building. Specification writing is nearly always performed by in-house staff, but there are independent consultants who prepare specifications for a fee. With the help of word processing, specifications can be prepared easier, faster, and more accurately.

Estimator and Cost Manager. The firm's estimating staff has the main responsibility for accurate cost projections. With clients insisting on facilities built within their budget, this is an important specialty. Estimating now includes cost control and cost management, concepts that go beyond estimating by combining management of building quality, scheduling, and costs to keep construction costs within the budget. The cost manager has access to current material and labor prices, a sense of the bidding climate, and knowledge of delivery times for crucial materials and equipment.

Construction Contract Administrator. This task entails processing payment certificates, material samples, shop drawings, and change order requests, but, above all, frequent trips to the building site. It attracts individuals who like the rough-and-tumble milieu of the construction site, and in larger firms is often a full-time specialty.

Other Specialties. Many architects specialize in the design and construction of particular building types such as schools, health care facilities, housing, churches, hightech manufacturing plants, or commercial structures.

As society and technology change, other specialties develop. For example, concern for distinctive existing buildings and neighborhoods has created the specialty of architectural preservation or restoration. Moreover, with older buildings deteriorating due to air pollution or sheer old age, incidents have occurred with pieces of a facade falling upon passers-by. Eventually, several cities passed laws calling for facade inspections by registered architects or engineers, and ordering to rehabilitate when required. In some cities, these laws have created the new specialty of construction evaluation.

ALLIED PROFESSIONS

Not all architects in private practice build their careers around architecture. They have discovered that other design professions also appeal to the architect's goal of creating beauty and efficiency through design. These professions include interior design, industrial design, planning and urban design, graphic design, landscape architecture, lighting design, acoustical design, and, not by any means least, the various types of engineering, with structural engineering having the greatest appeal to the architect.

Moreover, the growing accessibility of the computer and the on-again, off-again crises in energy supplies have caused a number of architects to carve out careers in computer software and energy-use consultation.

Finally, facilities management, or the process of planning, designing, inventorying, and updating corporate or government office or production space, has emerged as a career attractive to architects.

Interior Designer. Even though architects have always considered design of interiors and exteriors as part of the same professional service, with increasing specialization, architectural offices offer interior design services as a separate area of business. This has led to the growth of a new profession of interior designers, working in the residential and/or commercial or "contract" fields. Architectural firms employ either specially trained interior design staff or architects who have specialized in interior design.

Specialized services have also emerged for interior designers, such as hotel and restaurant interiors, furniture design, retail store design, expertise in historical styles and preservation, and even the design of stage sets, ships, and aircraft interiors.

In an effort to improve the qualifications for interior designers, the interior design societies require applicants to pass an examination administered by the National Council of Interior Design Qualification (NCIDQ). A listing of the interior design societies includes the American Society of Interior Designers (ASID), the Institute of Business Designers (IBD), and the Industrial Designers Society of America (IDSA).

Salaries for interior designers vary greatly, depending on talent, experience, reputation, and whether the architect works as an employee on salary or has a share in the profits. By and large, they fall into a range similar to that for private architectural firms. The salaries that major stores, institutions, industry, and manufacturers pay to their staff designers tend to be slightly higher than salaries paid by private design firms.

Industrial Designer. Architects have historically worked actively in the design of the ornament, furniture, and accessories, which together with the form of the space itself, make up the total architecture. Exterior and interior moldings, ornamental ironwork, chairs, tables, light fixtures, storage systems, even plates and cutlery have seen the influence of architects. Robert Adam, Charles McKim, Charles McIntosh, Louis Sullivan, Frank Lloyd Wright, Bertram Goodhue, George Nelson, Charles Eames, Eliot Noyes, Michael Graves, Charles Gwathmey, and Robert Venturi are among the architects who have given over part of their careers to industrial design.

Industrial design has features in common with architecture. The chief one is the need to explore many factors (in this case function, the marketplace, engineering, manufacturing, and servicing) and to assemble these into one whole that has beauty, function, safety, and value.

The industrial designer works either as a principal or staff in private practice, or as a staff designer in industry. Subspecialties have evolved, such as automotive styling, medical instrument and equipment design, furniture design, exhibit planning, and design of business and consumer electronics systems.

Many universities offer programs in industrial design (sometimes also labeled product design, design technology, etc). They are often listed as a specialty in art and design, engineering, or architectural schools.

Planner and Urban Designer. Planning and especially urban design are disciplines interwoven so tightly with architecture that they are apt to be seen as more of a variation than as distinctive careers. In fact, distinctions blur when architectural commissions require planning and urban design skills in addition to architectural skills. The difference between the two is that planning deals with the economics, demographics, and ecology of land use, whereas urban design dwells chiefly on the physical, three-dimensional appearance of outdoor spaces and the buildings that occupy them. Planning has developed into a separate career, with universities offering masters' and doctorate degrees. On the other hand, urban design has yet to emerge clearly as a career separate from planning.

A few independent planning firms exist; most larger architectural and engineering offices have planners on staff. However, the main source of employment for planners is in government at all levels, from city to federal.

Landscape Architect. Architects have always been attracted by the idea of shaping the outdoor environment in which their buildings are set. Andre Le Notre, Capability Brown, and Frederick Law Olmsted are among those landscape architects who stand out as expressions of the hope, not always realized by others, that architecture does not stop at the building's edge. Robert L. Geddes, among contemporary architects, has long made it a special concern of his firm to explore the relationship between architecture and nature.

The profession plays with variations in vista, climate, topography, and geography, as well as the excitement of observing change from season to season and year to year. Beyond that, the landscape architect is increasingly involved in the design of the urban environment, from small miniparks to the setting for billion-dollar developments.

Although many landscape architects own or work for private firms (including architectural or engineering firms), about one-third are employed by government agencies active in parks, other recreational areas, and urban planning.

Graphic Designer. Donald Holden points out that graphic designers have been called the "architects of the printed page" (1). Yet architects who think of themselves as graphic designers soon find there is a good deal more to graphic design than inventing a logotype and composing a letterhead. The subtleties of type selection and spacing, the creation of workable design grids, and the intricacies of production and dealing with typesetters, engravers, paper suppliers and printers are beyond what they learned in architectural school or picked up through experience.

Graphic designers work in a number of settings. Among the most common is the advertising agency, where they begin doing paste-ups and mechanicals at salaries that do not differ much from those of starting designers in architectural firms; they then work up to art directors who, although they make substantial salaries in the larger New York firms, have a level of job security often compared to that of a major league baseball manager.

Graphic designers are also hired by corporations to be staff designers. Fringe benefits and job security are greater than at advertising agencies. Other options include employment on the art staffs of magazine and book publishing houses. Finally, graphic designers in independent practice have carved out a highly visible niche in the nation's design community. Names such as Ivan Chermayeff and Paul Rand have influenced not only graphic design but packaging, and, through their involvement, have shaped the look of everyday objects from service stations to cereal boxes.

Education is typically through art or design school, 2–4-year programs leading to a bachelor of fine arts or similar degree.

Career advancement depends, more so than in other design professions, on personal drive, ambition, stamina, creative initiative, and ability to "sell" ideas to superiors and clients. As in other design professions, graphic designers at some point in their careers face the crossroads of getting into management, with the promise of higher income but lessened contact with design.

Lighting Designer. Whether designing with artificial light alone or mixing electric light and natural light, the lighting designer's challenge is to bring out the real quality of the architecture and, at the same time, to allow occupants to use a room so they can do their job productively. In addition, any lighting design should be energy-efficient.

Many practicing lighting designers were trained as interior designers, industrial designers, or electrical engineers. Successful lighting designers combine a sense for the aesthetics of color and form, a grasp of the technology of light (lamps, fixtures, controls, and accessories), and a feel for the computer as a design tool.

Lighting designers work either as owners or employees of private practices, as staff of electrical engineering consulting firms, or as employees of lighting manufacturers.

Acoustical Designer. The demand for proper acoustics is not limited to concert hall and church, but transcends all building types. Good acoustics counts for just as much, if not more, in the home, plant, office, schoolroom, laboratory, shopping center, or outdoor minipark. Poor acoustics stretch the nerves, endanger comfort, and impair productivity.

Acousticians, as they are often known, are usually retained by the architect, but are often called in by the owner once a building is occupied. They may have an architecture or interior design background, but more often are graduates of an engineering school. The profession demands a sense for architectural form and geometry, combined with a physicist's feel for the behavior of soundwaves. Increasingly, the acoustical designer must know how to work with the electronic systems that not only control or enhance existing sound, but also create new sounds to complement defects in existing sources.

Acoustical designers usually work as independent consultants. Some work in research and industry. Manufacturers of acoustical-absorption materials, wall materials, flooring, and ceiling systems rely on acoustical experts so their products can be specified and used to meet codes and other requirements.

Engineer. The principal building engineering disciplines are structural, mechanical, electrical, and civil. Of these, structural engineering especially is closely related to architecture. Some of the nation's best-known structural engineers, such as William Le Messurier, Paul Weidlinger, and Leslie Robertson, are either graduate architects or continually impress architects with their intuitive grasp of form and space, and their ability to reconcile exciting forms with the laws of mechanics. For centuries, most notably in the middle ages but even into the eighteenth century, the roles of architect and structural engineer were often one. The parting of the ways came about in the nineteenth century.

All states require engineers to be registered. To qualify for the examination requires a degree from an accredited engineering program, plus several years of approved experience.

Some engineering firms specialize in one discipline; some combine several. Still others provide both engineering and architectural services, and many do construction as well as design. Architectural firms often employ engineers. The options for engineers are broad; there is considerable demand for them in large corporations, especially those that build a great deal or those that are manufacturers of building products.

Construction Manager. Clients demand value for money through proper cost and schedule controls. This has led some architects (as well as contractors) into careers as construction managers. Construction managers trained as contractors know how a building is put together, how products and materials are "taken off" and ordered, and how to handle labor. Those from an architectural background know how to schedule design and construction, how to package building subsystems to obtain the best bids, and how to monitor design and construction to anticipate and forestall problems.

Construction management firms are offshoots either of larger architectural firms or of general contracting firms. To be a skilled construction manager demands experience in management or administration on a variety of building projects, computer skills, knowledge of building materials and their costs, and exposure to contractors and subcontractors. Managing building construction effectively is a crucial need in today's bottom-line economic climate.

EMERGING OPTIONS

Computer Software Consultant. There is a need for consultants who understand both the demands of architectural practice and the multipronged attributes of computer hardware and software. Architectural office business and accounting, design and drafting, engineering computations, specification writing and working drawings, cost estimating, schedule and cost management, marketing, facilities programming, research, and correspondence are all areas where computers are becoming indispensable.

Consultants have worked either on retainer to large computer hardware and software firms, or have themselves created software for sale to design firms.

Energy Consultant. Energy consultation as practiced by architects consists of two types of work: conducting energy analyses of new buildings in the design stage, and evaluating existing buildings for potential energy savings. This service is provided on a larger scale by mechanical-engineering consulting firms, but architects bring to it a special feel for the impact of energy-saving techniques on the appearance of buildings.

Facilities Manager. Facilities management consists of broad control over a company's initial and continuing facilities needs. It can cover everything from planning and design to updating and inventorying an owner's space, from furniture to rooms to entire building complexes, often in more than one city.

Some manufacturers have developed computer software to simplify facilities management, as have many architects for their own use, or for leasing or purchase by others.

CAREERS OUTSIDE PRIVATE PRACTICE

According to figures from a 1983 study that, unfortunately, are not regularly sought or methodically updated, signs point to about 11% of architects who belong to the American Institute of Architects (AIA) (and as many as 23% of those who do not belong) working at careers outside traditional private architectural practice. In 1982, a survey done by PACO (Probing Alternate Career Oppportunities) placed the ratio of nontraditional careers closer to 40%.

These careers outside of private practice are in government, industry, and education, as well as publishing, photography, research, and association and museum administration.

Architects in Government

Service in government attracts architects who believe they can best guide public planning, design and construction policy, and projects by becoming a part of the organization that makes that policy and carries it out.

In the United States, staff architects working for semiautonomous public authorities such as the Port Authority of New York and New Jersey have designed important public buildings. Mainly, however, the role of the architect in government has been more as a facilitator than as a designer, with design commissions usually going outside the agency to architects in private practice.

As facilitator, the architect in public service needs to cultivate skills unique to the milieu. One skill is the ability to work on policy and process rather than on solutions and results. The path of even a modest building, let alone a large one, is subject to constant scrutiny by public officials, the public, and the media. The staff architect must respect what may seem a cumbersome method of getting buildings built.

Another quality of successful public servants is a finely tuned sense of diplomacy. This includes the ability to recognize when to push and when to hold back, which individual is key to moving a project forward, and how to get action out of useful but balky officials, outside architects, contractors, code agencies, or vendors.

The third skill that marks the architect in government is the ability to administer construction projects so they adhere to budgets and schedules, knowing that much of the success or failure rests on the shoulders of outside consultants, including architects, who actually design and manage the work.

Benefits. *Security.* At the federal level, all but the top policy-making positions are civil service posts. Architects enter federal civil service through appointment, which entails a screening process and an examination. Requirements for entry into appointive public service at the state and municipal levels vary widely. They are best explored at these levels, with possible aid from local and state units of the AIA.

Impact on the Formulation of Public Policy. This is accomplished through special insights into the links between public policy and facilities planning.

Compensation. Most architects enter at a grade of GS-9 or lower. Roughly 60% of architects are in grades GS-11 to GS-13. Although state and local positions pay according to the size and wealth of the jurisdiction, they average 80% of federal levels.

Influence. Influence, especially by architects in senior policy-level positions, upon where to design facilities and who will design them, is another benefit.

Limitations. *Lack of Influence.* Many middle-level positions assign architects to design or technical tasks, but assign administrative tasks to a nonarchitect supervisor.

Change in Policy and Procedures. Changes in public agencies' procedures and policies are common, the result of public scrutiny, voter action, and bureaucratic shifts.

In government service, as with the corporate architect, the price of advancement and increased influence is often to pass up the traditional role of architect in favor of administration. Many architects faced with this choice decline to abandon their professional role, but they do so at a loss of status and income.

Typical positions in government service include

• Member of an agency's design or project management staff at municipal, county, state, or federal level.

• Administrator of a department concerned with planning, design, or construction at the various levels of government.
• Educational facilities specialist at the elementary, secondary, or higher education levels.
• Chief executive of a public authority charged with erecting a major city convention center.
• Researcher in a government agency.
• Facilities specialist in a branch of the armed forces.
• Elected political office.

Many architects have held high positions in the government hierarchy such as assistant secretary in a federal department, mayor of a city, associate commissioner of a major federal agency, as well as State Architect and Architect of the U.S. Capitol.

The Architects in Government Committee of the AIA is an important resource for anyone working in government or thinking of doing so. AIA headquarters in Washington, D.C. has a list of members and other resource materials.

Most architects in government first served as employees or principals in the private sector. At the federal level, about 20% come directly from school. Once they are in government, they tend to stay for an extended period of time, according to a study by the Committee. About one-third, by far the highest ratio, leave government only at retirement.

Education and Registration. A bachelor's degree in architecture is important to advancement, but not crucial to entry to some positions. Between 10 and 20% have degrees in architectural studies, and between 12 and 18% have masters', according to the study. In the higher salary ranges, those with masters' degrees have an edge over those without.

Registration is more common at the state and local levels than in federal service, no doubt because licensing is a state function and promotion is more likely to come to those with licenses. At the federal level, fewer positions require registration. Even so, at the higher salary levels, registered architects outnumber others 2:1.

Work Performed. The most common types of work reflect areas of building where the federal government is most active, such as housing administration, natural resources, environmental impact and energy matters, office buildings to house federal operations, Washington, D.C. affairs, and health-care planning. At the state and county levels, the focus changes to education, transportation, and correctional and judiciary facilities. Locally, the emphasis is on school facilities, police, firefighting, and municipal administration buildings.

To sum up, activities such as administration and management, policy development and compliance, programming and planning, and contractual matters are far more common than involvement in design, working drawings, and specification writing. It is those who carry out these administrative functions who, according to the study, report the most significant lack of degree training. Stated another way, administrative and management skills demanded at the higher levels outweigh professional architectural training, which, with some exceptions such as programs at Harvard and Florida A&M Universities, still mostly ignores management skills.

Architects in Industry

Architects in industry refers to the many architects who work as employees in the facilities, real estate, construction, or manufacturing divisions of a corporation, often as part of a company's management team. In these posts, they influence matters ranging from long-range planning, site selection, and programming to selecting the architect and other consultants, and coordinating an entire project.

Some corporations with a large volume or continuing demand for facilities have well-staffed departments. These corporations are retail chains, hotel corporations, food-service chains, large manufacturing corporations, utility companies, air and surface transportation businesses, large bank-holding companies, and building product manufacturers.

Roles. The new pattern here, as in the public sector, is to retain private architectural firms for all but minor design assignments. The scope of activities given the architect is nonetheless broad and varied. These can include the following.

In-house Designer. The architect designs and produces contract documents as in private practice. This role is less common in U.S. industry than it is in other nations.

Member of Corporate Management Team Dealing with an Outside Design Architect. In this role, the architect acts as advisor on:

- Contract negotiation.
- Innovative management techniques, including construction management, computer-based scheduling and cost-control, fast-track scheduling, and life-cycle costing.
- Replanning older company buildings for better use of space or recycling them for different uses.
- Site selection, including input on latest planning and land-use techniques.
- Dealing with constraints in getting facilities built, such as OSHA and EPA regulations.
- Selection of outside design architects, engineers, contractors, suppliers, and special consultants.
- Corporate policy such as corporate image and quality level, involving new buildings or modernization, landscaping, interior design, graphics, and lighting.

Aside from these types of tasks, the corporate architect may have a more direct managerial role such as supervising or coordinating work-in-progress at the design, contract document, bidding, or construction stages; operating and maintaining existing facilities; or in facilities programming.

Benefits. Among the benefits are

- The compensation, both as to salary and fringe benefits, which is higher than in private practice. Fringe benefits include generous vacation, insurance and medical plans, pension and profit sharing plans, and stock options.
- The satisfaction of influencing the location, program, design, construction, operation, and even recycling of a building.
- The chance to become a specialist in certain building types, such as hotels, retail stores, or banking facilities.

Limitations. A limitation is that advancement to higher rank and income often means switching course to management and abandoning traditional professional tasks. Real status often does not come with doing architectural tasks, but only with moving into management. Moreover, except in very large corporate facilities departments, compatible managerial slots are few. In some circumstances, the architect who wants to advance within the company may need to leave architecture altogether. Yet, increased pay and status within the company usually reward such a resolve. Indeed, several top leaders of U.S. industry have an architectural background. Companies often view architects as promising executive material due to special skills they develop in training for their profession, skills that call for creating order out of a host of different and often conflicting demands.

Compensation. Architects in industry generally make more money than architects working in a private firm.

Preparation. The best preparation is a professional degree in architecture that includes some business management courses, or a degree supplemented by management experience or seminars. Few design-school programs demand more than a superficial exposure to management matters, although some offer joint programs with business schools to attract mid-career executives.

Registration is useful but not essential, except for the few companies that do most of their design in-house.

The Architects in Industry Committee of the AIA is a useful source of information, such as a published roster of architects in industry and a tape–slide show citing cases of architects' activities in industry.

Architects in Education

Teaching in architectural schools has a distinguished tradition. An architect can either devote an entire career to teaching, such as the late Jean Labatut at Princeton University, or work as an established architect, teach for a number of years, then return to private practice, such as Robert Geddes, Henry Cobb, and Paul Rudolph.

Career Tracks. Architectural schools look for a teacher who is one of the following:

- A recent architectural graduate. This individual is about 26 years old and has a master's degree in architecture.
- A registered architect with a good academic record and experience with an outstanding firm, who can expect to begin as an assistant professor.

- An older architect who has spent life in practice, perhaps with some occasional teaching, looking for a complete career change.

Early in their careers as teachers, architects must decide whether they want to teach, do research, become an administrator, or do a combination of these.

To become a leader in the teaching profession, the architect must be awarded tenure. Although the "publish or perish" dictum does not always apply in architecture, the underlying thinking holds true. No one gets tenure solely for being a good teacher. The faculty committees that recommend tenure see universities primarily as places for advancing knowledge. They have viewed professional schools (such as architecture and engineering) as an anomaly, since the aim of such schools is not so much to advance knowledge as to prepare students for a career.

One way to promotion for the architect–teacher is to do scholarly research and hope to have it published either as a book or in a journal on architecture, urban or interior design, planning, or other design field.

Another way is to advance on the cutting edge of practice, with innovations in architectural form that win important professional awards.

Whereas schools do encourage their architect faculty to practice, they prefer the practice to offer insight into broader areas, such as energy conservation, historic preservation, or the sociology of housing.

The Practitioner as Teacher. Some schools of architecture accord practitioners special status as adjunct or visiting faculty. Both school and practitioner benefit from this type of arrangement. The school obtains an infusion of firing-line experience. The practitioner–teacher has the chance to gather and sort the yield of years of practice and express it forcefully in the classroom.

Teaching as a Career. Benefits include

- Intellectual stimulation.
- Chance to explore new directions in design, technology, or management.
- Satisfaction of nurturing talent among the students.
- Security on attaining tenure.

Limitations include

- Difficulty of maintaining a private practice.
- Earning potential limited to university salary scales.

Who the Teachers Are. Some 3000 individuals are primarily occupied in teaching architecture at about 90 schools with programs accredited by the National Architectural Accrediting Board (NAAB) (2). Another 300 or so teach at junior or community colleges, and in other nonprofessional programs.

Of these totals, according to NAAB, 1588 were full-time faculty (73% in public universities, 27% in private) and 1391 were part-time faculty (47% in public colleges, 53% in private).

A few schools offer a combination of teaching and re-

search through an architectural research center or laboratory, leading to some excellent work. On the other hand, at many schools, research is not given top priority, which is a hurdle to attracting research funds. Sometimes, available outside funds do not conform to the school's program emphasis or the interests of the faculty.

Other Careers for Architects

Architects who work in government, industry, or who teach make up the majority of those who work outside the traditional scope of private practice. However, there are other career options for which an architectural background is useful.

The Architect as Communicator. The architectural profession needs voices to express its goals, support or challenge its directions, inform its practitioners, and carry its message to the world at large. Architectural writers and critics have backgrounds in architecture, art history, or archaeology, or have formal training in journalism or English.

Writers, editors, and critics with a background in architecture bring a special insight into the workings of the profession. In addition, although only about 100 individuals write regularly about architecture, it is a career that serves the profession and society in a highly effective way. Typical forms such a career may take follow.

Architectural Journalist. This may include service as editor on a professional journal, as editor or publisher of books on architecture and design, or as editor or critic on a newspaper or weekly magazine. Editors and writers on professional journals are able to see the profession at work; meet its practitioners; review its buildings; take stands on aesthetic, technological, legal, and business issues involving architecture; and, by means of publication or nonpublication, reward the good projects and chastise the bad, as they see them. Architect–writers in consumer publications and newspapers reach a broader audience—the general public and the potential client—and have an important responsibility because they influence public attitudes about architecture.

Too many critics limit themselves to the aesthetics of architecture, hawking the superficial and the sensational at the expense of solid, informed analysis. This leaves an opening for critics who also review the technical and functional side of a particular project. This expanded role is often hampered by the reluctance of client and architect to talk about a building after completion.

Architectural Photographer. Photography is a natural extension of the writing medium; several members of the small group of professional architectural photographers have a background in architecture. Specialists who photograph the facades and interiors of buildings are vital communicators of architectural information to professionals and the public.

Editorial Consultant. An editorial consultant carries out special writing and editorial assignments for public agencies, foundations, corporations, and professional and trade associations. Editorial consultants also advise architects in private practice on the marketing promotion of their practices.

Many architects work more than one of these writing–editorial options. By combining roles, they develop more coherent viewpoints and augment their incomes.

The Architect as Management Consultant. A number of architects have developed careers in helping architectural firms towards better-managed practices. Either through in-house consultation or by way of seminars, they advise firms in such areas as business and project management, professional liability, ownership transition, marketing, and personnel management.

The Architect as Researcher. Architectural graduates in research serve on the staffs of governmental and private for-profit research institutes, product manufacturers, and a few architectural schools. A handful of large professional firms have full-time research staffs.

Most of the nation's research effort has been by governmental agencies, such as the Center for Building Technology of the National Bureau of Standards, and the National Institute of Building Sciences (NIBS), and by the major building product manufacturers and their trade associations.

A major challenge facing the architect thinking of a career in research is to make the findings of research applicable to day-to-day practice.

Salaries. Most researchers work on staffs of industry, government, or design schools, and salaries reflect scales in those areas.

Association Staff Administrator. The professional administrators who manage the national, state, and local societies coordinate the time contributed to the profession by practitioners. Titled, variously, as executive secretary, executive director, or executive vice-president, professional administrators are responsible for organizing, scheduling, and staffing the committees who do so much of the work of the association; managing the support activities such as document preparation and sales, library collections, and magazine subscriptions; organizing exhibits; and advising student groups about architecture.

Museum Administrator. With public interest in architecture on an upswing, many of the nation's museums are establishing collections of photographs of buildings, original drawings and models, and organizing exhibitions derived from these collections.

Positions as curators or departmental administrators, although few, can be challenging career options, as can the job of officer in charge of a museum's building program. In such a position, the architect's role is comparable to a senior staff architect in industry or government, and income is roughly equivalent.

Real Estate Developer. For the successful architect–developer, real estate development can be a highly lucrative yet highly risky enterprise. Architects can bring to real estate development a sense of design quality.

The architect–developer faces the high risk climate of development work, which calls for a cool head, a sense of adventure, and a feel for picking the right associates.

The Architect as Politician. Architects have served successfully as elected officials at local and state levels. The longevity of such careers is chancy and at the whim of the voter, but income levels are on the rise and pension benefits, after a long term in office, are attractive.

There is, above all, the challenge to introduce and pass legislation in such areas as housing, health care, education, and urban planning that benefit large segments of the population.

In summary, the goals of architecture, the creation of attractive, strong, and useful buildings and environments, are met not only through design, but through the many added activities described above. To carry out these activities professionally is the basis for many challenging and rewarding careers.

BIBLIOGRAPHY

1. D. Holden, *Art Career Guide,* 4th ed., Watson-Guptill, New York, 1983.
2. *Architectural Schools of North America,* Petersen's Guides, Princeton, N.J., 1985.

General References

PSMJ Executive Management Salary Survey, Practice Management Associates, Newton, Mass., 1986.
R. K. Lewis, *Architect? A Candid Guide to the Profession,* MIT Press, Cambridge, Mass., 1985.

Organizations

Acoustical Society of America, 335 East 45th Street, New York, N.Y., 10017.
Advisory Board on the Built Environment, 2101 Constitution Avenue, N.W., Washington, D.C., 20418.
American Association of Engineering Societies, 345 East 47th Street, New York, N.Y., 10017.
American Consulting Engineers Council, 1155 15th Street, N.W., Washington, D.C., 20005.
American Institute of Architects, 1735 New York Avenue, N.W., Washington, D.C., 20006.
American Society of Interior Designers, 1430 Broadway, New York, N.Y. 10018.
American Society of Landscape Architects, 1733 Connecticut Avenue, N.W., Washington, D.C., 20009.
American Planning Association, 1313 East 60th Street, Chicago, Il., 60637.
Association of Collegiate Schools of Architecture, 1735 New York Avenue, N.W., Washington, D.C., 20006.
Construction Specifications Institute, 601 Madison Street, Alexandria, Va., 22314.
Graphic Artists Guild, 30 East 20th Street, New York, N.Y., 10003.
Industrial Designers Society of America, 1360 Beverly Road, McLean, Va., 22101.
Illuminating Engineering Society (and the Illuminating Engineering Research Institute), 345 East 47th Street, New York, N.Y., 10017.

International Association of Lighting Designers, 30 West 22nd Street, New York, N.Y., 10010.

National Architectural Accrediting Board, 1735 New York Avenue, N.W., Washington, D.C., 20006.

National Council of Interior Design Qualification, 118 East 25th Street, New York, N.Y., 10010.

National Society of Professional Engineers, Private Practice Division, 2029 K Street, N.W., Washington, D.C., 20006.

See also BUILDING TEAM; COMPUTERIZATION; CONSTRUCTION INDUSTRY; CONSTRUCTION MANAGEMENT; CRITICISM, ARCHITECTURAL; EDUCATION, ARCHITECTURAL; ENTREPRENEUR/ARCHITECT RELATIONSHIP; PROFESSION IN CONTEMPORARY SOCIETY, THE; ROLE OF THE ARCHITECT.

STEPHEN A. KLIMENT, FAIA
New York, N.Y.

CAST IRON. See STEEL IN CONSTRUCTION

CATHEDRALS

The history of architecture is concerned more with religious buildings than any other type, because in most past cultures, the universal and exalted appeal of religion made the church or temple the most expressive, the most permanent, and the most influential building in any community, serving as a place of worship, shelter for images and relics, and holy center of a cult. Religious buildings also reveal more about a culture than any other type.

Beliefs as dissimilar as Christianity, Buddhism, Judaism, and Islam are based on communal participation in rites, so their buildings have evolved similar plans with the requirement that a maximum number of worshipers be able to face the focal point of the service. Historically, many religious buildings have been converted from one faith to another following conquest. Likewise, monasteries, convents, and abbeys that combine the practice of religion, even of different faiths, with scholarly, agricultural, and industrial activities have produced similar plans. To absorb local cults, Christian churches were often built over pagan sites.

A cathedral is the seat of a bishop, who, in the Roman Catholic Church, has the duty of attending the seasons of Advent, Lent, and the great festivals of Christmas, Easter, Pentecost, and Corpus Christi. In Protestant churches, deans or provosts and chapters manage a cathedral's affairs, and the bishop may only have the right to preach on specific occasions and to carry out ordinations of priests and deacons and confirmation services. In all cathedrals, the Bishop has a throne which in early Christian planning was placed centrally behind the high altar. This arrangement was common in Italy, but north of the Alps, Norwich, UK claims to have the only example.

When Christianity became established by the Emperor Constantine in 310, the administrative structure of the Empire was copied and cathedrals were built in the principal cities. In some cases, as at Syracuse, pagan temples were adapted to Christian use. A cathedral need not be a large building; sometimes, in the Eastern Orthodox branch of Christianity, they were quite small. However, the tendency was for cathedrals to grow in size as the population of Christendom increased. Rome was the exception, as its population shrank drastically from about 2 million to about 25,000 persons at the nadir of its fortunes in the eighth century. The growth of cathedrals was carried out in stages, a late style superseding an earlier one, as at Salerno where Baroque encases early Christian, at Cefalu where Renaissance covers Romanesque, or at Ripon where the process was halted showing Perpendicular Gothic swallowing Romanesque. The main piers of the central tower of York Minster have an eleventh-century core, surrounded by thirteenth-century, and encased in fifteenth-century work.

Essentially, the cathedral was built in a city, and in the course of time became the largest and most important building. Only in the twentieth century have the dimensions of cathedrals been exceeded by secular buildings such as office blocks and covered sports arenas. There were two types of cathedrals in Northern Europe: secular and monastic. Besides having a refectory, kitchen, dormitory, hospital and cloisters, the monastic cathedral had a hospice for guests and ran a school. In this way, the cathedrals became the basis of Western learning as established by Alcuin of York under the Emperor Charlemagne in 800 (1):

> Architecture may be defined as the art and technique of building, employed to fulfill the practical and expressive requirements of civilized people . . . without it man is confined to a primitive struggle with the elements, with it he has not only a defense against the natural environment but also the benefits of a human environment, a prerequisite for and a symbol of civilized institutions.

Cathedrals can be considered the most significant examples of historic architecture.

Architecture should have the characteristics of Firmitas, Utiltas, and Venustas, as given by Vitruvius (2) and repeated in changed order by Palladio, by way of Sir Henry Wooten as "commodity, firmness and delight." Alberti changed delight into visual pleasure, *amoettas,* and divided it in *pulchritudo,* harmonious proportions, and *ornamentum,* decorative interest given by appropriate and seemly ornament (1). Commodity deals with the spatial characteristics of architecture, with movement through a building and its use, internal arrangements, lighting, heating, ventilation, and acoustics. Firmness deals with structural stability and delight with its visual qualities. Commodity and firmness are the qualities that primarily give a building longevity. Cathedrals will last as long as they are used and wanted. Use will ensure regular maintenance, for which cathedrals were generally designed.

In time, a building acquires additional values over and above its architectural qualities. The most commonly appreciated values are that they represent continuity in a time of rapid change, cultural and social identity, and are spiritual symbols of faith; by dominating their city, they evoke the past power and prestige of the church and are focal points of urban landscape and form. They are also venerated for their age and the history they encapsulate. They have archaeological, cultural, and documentary values, and often are technological achievements. In addition to their functional uses, they act as pilgrimage or tourist attractions, generate considerable local employment, and symbolize local and national life. Hitler appreciated the significance of cathedrals when he initiated the Baedeker raid of World War II, which damaged both London's St. Pauls and Norwich Cathedrals and destroyed Coventry Cathedral.

One type of plan for an early cathedral evolved from the Roman basilica (some cathedrals are still called basilicas). These aisled halls are relatively easy and economical to build, and enabled a large number of persons to participate in a ceremony with adequate vision and hearing. Transepts were added to give the symbolic cruciform plan; aisles increased the overall area. A sanctuary was needed for priests to perform sacred rites; this area was defined by steps, rails, or screens. Screens evolved into decorative features and partitions, such as the icontasis, to enhance the mystery of the sacred rites as in the Orthodox Church.

Another type of plan evolved from the great Roman technological achievement: the domed structure. The dome, a symbol of power and perfection, was adopted by the humanists of the Renaissance and was the basis of designs for St. Peter's, Rome, and St. Paul's, London. In designing St. Paul's, Sir Christopher Wren placed a dome on top of a Latin cross plan, with aisles penetrating the central domical area, as it did not suit the clergy's requirement for processional functions.

The Orthodox Churches were built with bays, each roofed with a dome, the most important emphasized by the height of the dome. Sometimes, as at St. Basil's, Moscow, the domes are of great variety (Fig. 1).

Changes of emphasis in theology caused changes in liturgy. Indeed, the cultural unity of architecture and theology can be found in that each new mode of thinking was expressed in a change in architectural style, at least in western Europe; in eastern Europe, the Orthodox Church codified its rituals rigidly for a millennium, thereby affecting its architecture.

HISTORIC CATHEDRALS AND ABBEYS

Early Christian

Until the end of the nineteenth century, it can be postulated that the design and construction of cathedrals was based on Roman technology. The Gothic rib could be said to have an ancestor in the brick ribs in the Basilica of Maxentius ca 306. Roman technology and design, which developed out of the Greek, is well described in the *Ten Books of Vitruvius* (active 46–30 B.C.) which even today contain useful information and interesting anecdotes illustrating the role of the architect.

The Roman basilica was built to serve as a law court and civilian exchange market. Being the most economical way of covering a large space, it was adapted to church

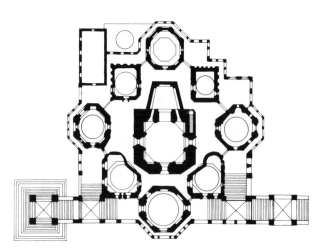

Figure 1. St. Basil's, Moscow (3). Courtesy of Birkhäuser Verlag Ag.

use by adding an apse and then a transept. The more magnificent structures had barrel vaults which used brick ribs as supports of the formwork for concrete infill. This concrete has survived in buildings, bridges, or ruins for centuries partly because it is much more elastic than Portland cement concrete.

Early churches tended to be built on the perimeter of Rome due to the hostility of the noble families to the new religion. St. Peter's was built on the site of his martyrdom, S. Paulo Fuori le Muri (St. Paul's Outside the Walls) on a site well outside the fortified area of the city. The first basilica of St. Peter's (Fig. 2) was destroyed to make way for the present great baroque structure. S. Paulo Fuori le Muri is comparable to the old St. Peter's, although mostly a reconstruction after the earthquake and fire of 1824.

The nave and double side aisles of S. Paulo Fuori le Muri of ca 380 are almost the same size as the old St. Peter's, 270 ft (82.3 m) long and 200 ft (60.9 m) wide. There is a double bema or transept, but like St. Peter's,

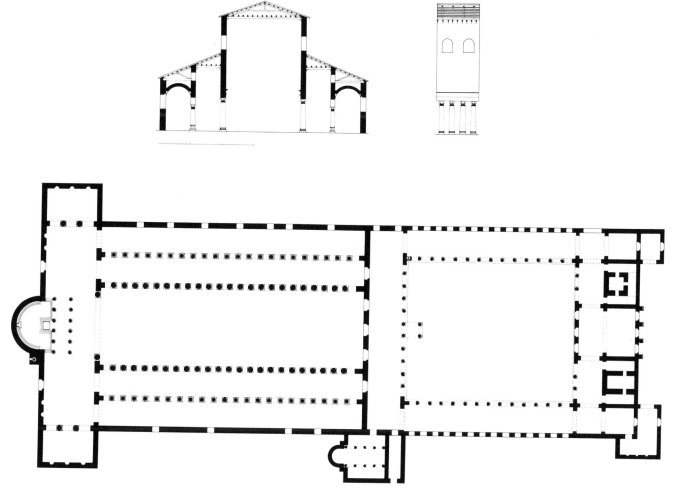

Figure 2. Old St. Peter's, Rome (3). Courtesy of Birkhäuser Verlag Ag.

it has a narthex and large collonaded atrium. The span of the nave is impressive, over 60 ft (18.3 m), requiring a sophisticated truss, probably queen post, but as the present roof is a reconstruction, this is not certain. The apse survived the disaster and has good Early Christian mosaics of the fifth century.

Walls were built of brick or tufa, an easily cut volcanic rock, laid on pozzulanic lime mortar and then plastered internally and externally. Colonnades to support the nave and inner aisle superstructure consisted of 80 marble columns with Corinthian bases and capitals linked by short span arches, which would exert very little lateral thrust. The apse with its hemidome followed Roman practice and acts as an efficient buttress.

The simplicity of basilica construction, timber roofs covered with interlocking tiles at a pitch of about 30° resting on relatively slender walls, which had windows with circular arches placed not too close to each other, could scarcely be exceeded. It has met the functional church requirements of ritual and procession very well, but is less good for preaching.

Byzantine

In spite of establishing the Church in Rome, the Emperor Constantine found it expedient to move his capital to a new site on the Bosporus named Constantinople (now Istanbul). He there built a basilica church on the site of Hagia Sophia (also called Sancta Sophia, meaning Holy Wisdom). This was replaced a century later by a similar structure. In 532, the Emperor Justinian commissioned Anthemius of Tralles and Isodorus of Miletus to build the present domed structure (Fig. 3). In dimensions, other cathedrals may exceed Hagia Sophia, but for the sense of space it is superb, as the mosaic decoration and lighting seem to dissolve the structure (4):

> The monumental interior gives the impression of one vast domed space but the detailed effect with the great hemicycles and smaller exedra is one of extreme intricacy in spite of the simplicity of the general scheme.

Scale is obtained by gradation of the various parts from the two-storied arcades of the aisles to the lofty dome which rests, with little apparent support, like a canopy over the center or, as Procpius described it, "as if suspended by a chain from Heaven" (4). The dome, 107 ft (32.6 m) in diameter, covers the central space which is extended east and west by demidomes, with an eastern exedra. The dome has 40 small windows in its lower part, which suffuse the interior with light. It is constructed of bricks 27 in.

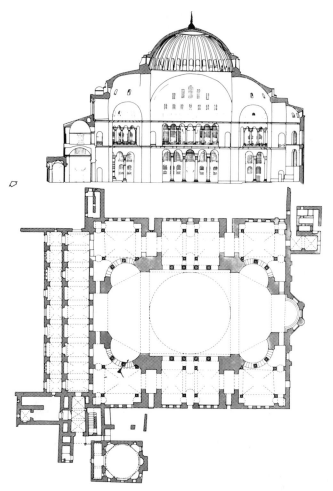

Figure 3. Hagia Sophia, Istanbul (3). Courtesy of Birkhäuser Verlag Ag.

(686 mm) square, about 2 in. (50 mm) thick in the lower part, reducing to 24 in. (610 mm) at the crown. The bricks are laid in mortar about the same thickness, at an angle to the radius in order to reduce the thrust. The dome now rises 50 ft (15.2 m) in its span of 107 ft, so it is nearly a hemicircle.

Hagia Sophia suffered damage in a severe earthquake in 556 and part of the dome collapsed during repairs. In rebuilding the dome, together with the main eastern arch, its height was raised. Since then, it has survived several earthquakes with only minor damage, in spite of being in a high risk zone with a design coefficient for horizontal shear of 0.109 g.

The dome sits on four gigantic pendentives over 60 ft (18.3 m) high, projecting 25 ft (7.3 m), and is supported by four massive buttresses measuring 60 × 25 ft (18.3 × 7.6 m). These buttresses are pierced by arches for the north and south aisles and galleries, which are two stories high and 50 ft (15.2 m) wide. With the aisles, the main building measures approximately 250 × 220 ft (76.2 × 67 m), to which the eastern apse, outer and inner narthex, which measures 200 × 30 ft (61 × 9 m) should be added. The thrusts from the dome are taken by the buttresses in the north–south direction and by the hemidomes and exedrae in the east–west direction.

The interior is clad with white, green, blue, and black marble sheets fixed with bronze, and the floor is paved with large marble slabs. There are examples of the simple sixth-century mosaics in the narthex and aisles, and some wonderful pictorial mosaics from the ninth and twelfth centuries in various parts of the building. Otherwise, the walls are covered with plaster decorated in the style of the Turkish conquerors, who converted Hagia Sophia into a mosque in 1453. Under the galleries, there are 107 marble columns with molded bronze rings circling the junctions with the capitals and at the base, which is set on a lead pad to absorb unequal loading. The capitals are cubiform with delicate incised carving and small Ionic volutes at the corners. There are 12 windows each on the north and south sides under the great arches. The dome, the immense buttresses with deeply recessed spandrel walls on the north and south sides, and the hemidomes give an effect of massiveness and symmetry.

The exterior is less impressive than the interior, for the brick walls are plastered over and distempered. The actual shapes of the dome and hemidomes are visible because the covering lead rests only on wood boarding placed immediately over the outer surface. The lead is ¼ in. (6.4 mm) thick.

When Constantinople fell to the great seige guns of the Turks, Hagia Sophia became a mosque and minarets were added. Today it is being used as a museum. Few buildings have achieved such architectural effect with such economy; Hagia Sophia must be regarded as one of the high water marks of cathedral building and architecture. The influence of Byzantine technology spread south into Islam, where the Dome of the Rock in Jerusalem is a noteworthy example, and westward, where the octagonal San Vitale (426–547) in Ravenna and the circular Cathedral of Aachen (Aix-la-Chapelle) (790–805), later with Gothic choir, are further examples.

Aisled Byzantine churches, having central domes and octagonal plans, used the buttressing effect of the aisle roof vaults to resist the thrust of the lower part of the dome with great skill. The sloping vaults to the aisles of Aachen are truly remarkable. St. Mark's, Venice (1063–1085) (Fig. 4), and St. Sophia, Novrogod (Leningrad) (1052), are developments of Byzantine architecture that produced striking silhouettes with bulbous domes, of which St. Basil's (1554) in Moscow is a well-known example.

Romanesque and Norman

Romanesque is a diverse style with simple structures and techniques based on Roman practice. After the collapse of the western Roman Empire, there were many invasions and infiltrations of races from Asia and Central Europe. Small kingdoms rose and fell; some were pagan, some were Christian like those at Canterbury or York, which would build small cathedrals that were generally burnt down so little remains. It was not until the eleventh or twelfth century that anything of great significance in terms of architectural design or construction was created. Then there was continuous development of technique for 250 years until 1350, when the Black Death struck the population (5).

The Norman Abbeys at Caen were the prototype of

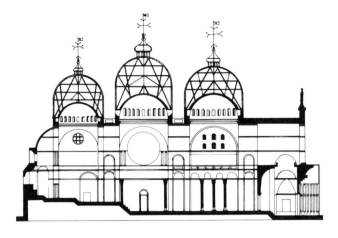

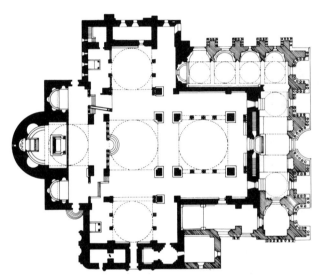

Figure 4. St. Mark's, Venice (3). Courtesy of Birkhäuser Verlag Ag.

William the Conqueror's great building achievements in the UK, where fine examples still stand as at Durham, Ely, Norwich, Peterborough, Gloucester (nave), Rochester, Worcester (nave), and Winchester (transepts only). These were all long-aisled buildings with transepts. Being associated with monasteries, they often had an enclosed choir, leaving only the nave to the laity. The cloisters were for the use of the monks. York (1080) was an exception, having a wide span of 46 ft (14.0 m), where the normal span would be from 30 to 33 ft (9.1 m to 10 m). Later, when York Minster was transformed into a Gothic Cathedral, ca 1220, aisles were added and the piers supporting a gigantic Norman tower were incorporated by stages into the present structure (Fig. 5). Durham Cathedral (1093–1133) (Fig. 6), stands together with the Bishop's Castle on a promontory almost encircled by a river. The dramatic setting is equaled by the forceful architecture, which emphasizes its strength. The piers and pillars are substantial and the vaults are ribbed (the first ribbed vaults in Europe), but it must be said that the ribs are crude compared with

later Gothic work. There are twin western towers. The nave has eight bays, the seven side aisles plus the towers. The transepts extend three bays beyond the aisles, and have aisles on the eastern side and stair turrets at the northwest and southwest corners. The choir of four bays must have been longer, but two centuries after its construction, the Chapel of Nine Altars (1242–1280) was built. The graceful central tower dates from the fifteenth century.

Mention must also be made of the three East Anglican Cathedrals which are also complete examples of Norman Romanesque: Peterborough (1170–1195), with 10 nave bays plus towers, and five bays in the sanctuary which has a curved east end (the timber roof is probably the oldest in the UK); Ely (1322–1340) (Fig. 7), with 12 bays plus towers (13 before the central tower fell and was replaced by the marvelous lantern); and Norwich (1080–1140), which has 14 bays in the nave and four bays in the sanctuary, and also has a curved end. The circular chapels at the east end of Norwich Cathedral are remarkable, but it is the central tower that can claim to be the finest of its period. Viewed internally, it could be described as the apotheosis of Romanesque, almost Gothic in spirit. Some people regard Romanesque as dull, but it has a calm, mystical spirit. The structure is heavy; walls are 6 or 8 ft thick, piers are simple and robust, arches are semicircular with heavily cut decoration, carving is stylized, and windows are without tracery. If the Romanesque cathedral were entered in the eleventh century, the crude and bizzare internal decoration would be disconcerting, judged by contemporary taste. Pale fragments of the decor remain in Norwich Cathedral, and some were also exposed in the excavations at York Minster.

The Normans were good builders and a study of specialist mason terms reveals many French words: voussoir, intrados, extrados, quion, etc, which show that these Normans taught the indigenous Saxons to build in stone. Norman masonry relied on small stones, often cut to size in the quarry using an axe with a diagonal cutting stroke. The mortar joints are wide [up to ⅝ or ¾ in. (10–14mm)] and the quality of the mortar was excellent. Being good builders, they did not skimp work on foundations, those of Norwich Cathedral tower being perfectly designed for hard gravel at 4 tons/ft^2. There are no signs of differential settlement over 900 years. At York, the problem was different; as the ground was of poor quality, an oak grillage was incorporated and initially the Minster sank about 4 in. (101 mm) to form its own foundation. In due course, the water table was lowered and the grillage rotted away; the foundations became suspect and had to be consolidated and enlarged in 1967–1972.

On the continent, Romanesque matured in a slightly different way, as can be seen from Worms Cathedral (Fig. 8) with its multiple towers, two at the east end, a central tower, two at the west end, and a lower one at the center. The vaulting was ribbed, and the exterior had shallow pilasters and a decorative cornice with arch motif.

Gothic

In the second half of the twelfth century, there was an intellectual ferment in Europe that centered on Paris,

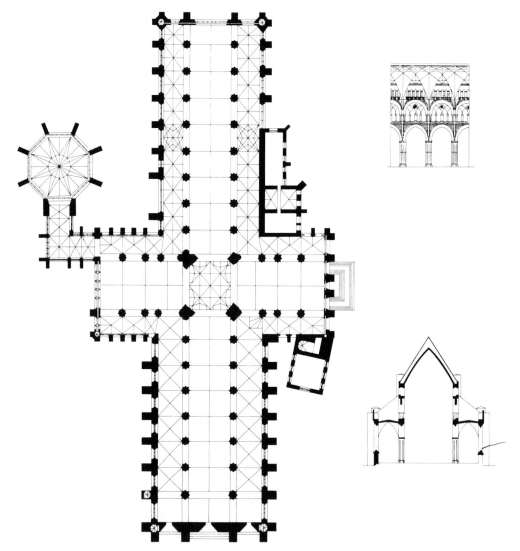

Figure 5. York Minister (3). Courtesy of Birkhäuser Verlag Ag.

where the great scholar Abelard taught. Roger Bacon, an English monk, wrote ca 1260 (10):

> Machines may be made by which the largest ships, with only one man steering them, will be moved faster than if they were filled with rowers; wagons may be built which will move with incredible speed and without the aid of beasts; flying machines can be constructed in which a man . . . may beat the air with wings like a bird . . . machines will make it possible to go to the bottom of seas and rivers.

He spoke for the master masons of his time.

The new spirit was that of scientific inquiry and an attempt to defy the forces of nature which ultimately defeated gravity by rocketing astronauts to the moon in 1966. This spirit manifested itself in Gothic architecture with its tall structures having thrusts and counterthrusts to ensure its stability, giving up reliance solely on weight and gravity. Gothic spread like wildfire throughout western Europe with the exception of Italy, which had an elegant version of Romanesque as shown by Pisa Cathedral

(Fig. 9), Sienna Cathedral, and San Miniato in Florence. There were also political reasons for rejecting Gothic as belonging to the Imperial party.

Gothic started in the Ile-de-France, centered in Paris where the Abbot Suger (1081–1151) was its great advocate. Notre Dame (1163–1250) (Fig. 10) was started in the Gothic style, being given a spire by Viollet le Duc in 1860. Amiens (1220–1288), Rheims (1211–1427), Chartres (1194–1260), and Rouen (1220–1230) are all fine examples of Gothic, having west fronts with final portals enriched with carving, topped with towers, naves, and choirs with side aisles and chapels, and ending with a chevet with segmental chapels. The spatial rhythm was, however, interrupted by the transepts. Bourges (1192–1275) dispenses with transepts and achieves a spatial miracle with deceptively simple means; to enhance the spatial value, the columns are made daringly slender.

Bourges Cathedral (Fig. 11) has great clarity of plan, expressed in the sections which resulted in the creation of space within an ambience of luminous light. This would and the building reveals itself in its prodigious unity. The work was continued with minor modifications to Branmer's design.

Originally, the exterior was austere, but false transepts and a flèche were added only to be removed by Viollet le Duc. The economy of the design can be appreciated when compared with Chartres, where each pier, exclusive of foundations, weighs 1000 tons, whereas at Bourges, they each weigh a mere 400 tons.

The west front has five entrances which reflect the five divisions of the plan. The south tower soon showed signs of fatigue and in 1313 was given a clumsy buttress, but it was the north tower that showed signs of movement in 1504 and fell with a frightful crash in 1506, taking one-and-a-half vaults of the high nave with it, followed later in the day by two more pillars and another bay of vaulting. The vaults were rebuilt by 1518 and the tower by 1540.

Canon Dunlop (8) in his book *The Cathedral Crusade* writes

> An architect can only form his ideas within the actual material limits of his technique. As such he must be a technician. But as an artist he makes men free of his own vision, a vision in which he sees a certain kinship between mind and matter which goes beyond the boundaries of knowledge an invitation to regard the world in a certain light penetrated with a spiritual dimension.

This is true of designers of great cathedrals in every epoch. The stupendous effort that went into cathedral building

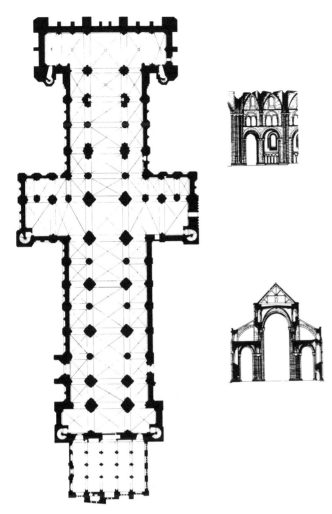

Figure 6. Durham Cathedral (3). Courtesy of Birkhäuser Verlag Ag.

not have been possible without the invention of flying buttresses. Bourges is the product of a single mastermind, Robert Branmer, *le maître de Bourges,* who started work in 1195, having the theological theme of the rapprochement between Jews and Gentiles culminating in the New Covenant and Last Judgment. Bourges influenced the design of Le Mans and Coutances, and finally Beauvais.

The immense height of the main columns and lower aisles give the effect of facades grouped behind facades. There is no transept, so nothing interrupts the all-pervading sense of unified spaces. Louis Gonse (7) writes

> The monumental grouping of high naves extending without interruption and seeming to gather monumentum towards the circular movement of the apse produces one of the most beautiful architectural compositions that it would be possible to see.

The advent of the flying buttress had opened out a new possibility, in the words of Jean Bony, "to hollow out from the interior the pyramidical mass of Notre Dame and retain only the outer shell" (11). In this great vision of wholeness and completeness, matter loses much of its substantiality

Figure 7. Ely Cathedral (3). Courtesy of Birkhäuser Verlag Ag.

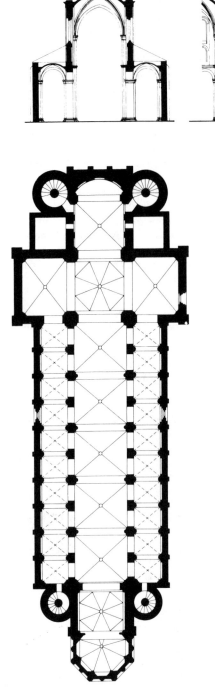

Figure 8. Worms Cathedral (3). Courtesy of Birkhäuser Verlag Ag.

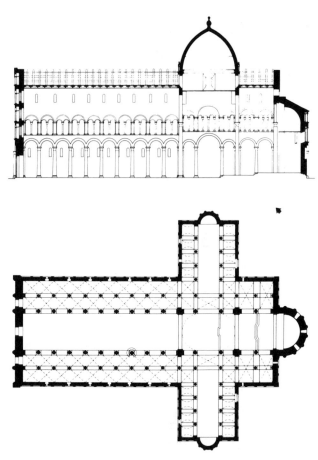

Figure 9. Pisa Cathedral (3). Courtesy of Birkhäuser Verlag Ag.

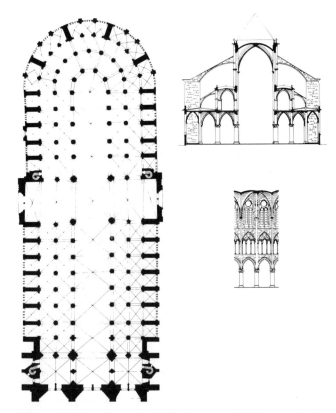

Figure 10. Notre Dame, Paris (3). Courtesy of Birkhäuser Verlag Ag.

from 1100 to 1350 can be shown by the estimate that more stone was used for this campaign than in the whole of the Egyptian architecture (including the pyramids) in four millenia.

French cathedrals were generally built by large bodies of masons working in intense programs to a unified and predetermined plan. Chartres was created in three 10-year campaigns. French Gothic was enhanced by the art of the sculptor and glazier; Chartres must be visited to experience this sythesis of the arts. Indeed, it could be

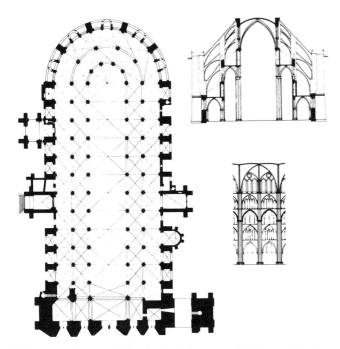

Figure 11. Bourges Cathedral (3). Courtesy of Birkhäuser Verlag Ag.

claimed that the French cathedrals rank with the classic Greek temples. It may come as a surprise to learn that all Gothic sculpture was polychromed, but so were Greek temples. Salisbury Cathedral (Fig. 12) is an exception to typical English practice, having been completed in one campaign and so achieving a stylistic unity. As the interior does not have the spatial quality of Bourges, it seems rather dull. Lincoln (Fig. 13) is one of the finest of the English cathedrals, set on a hill overlooking the city and having a fine central tower and two western towers set on top of a Romanesque west front. The Cathedral has a wealth of carved heads and details, as well as beautiful representations of Edward I and his beloved wife Queen Eleanor, who saved the lives of the burghers of Calais. Internally, the cathedral is magnificent with its angel choir and original type of vaulting. The plan is one of the most complex, having extra chapels at the west end, a Galilee porch to the south transept, a choir transept with semicircular apsed chapels, and a fine Chapter House with magnificent flying buttresses, as well as cloisters.

Renaissance and Mannerist

Brunelleschi's San Lorenzo (1421–1460) in Florence (Fig. 14) is one of the earliest and an almost perfect example of a large, albeit basilican church, in the style of early Renaissance. As Florence was the starting point of this intellectual and humanist cultural movement to which architects, eg, Panofsky, were the first to give visible expression, it was not surprising to find such a church in such a city, yet to compare it with contemporary North European designs, such as King's College Chapel (1446–1515) in Cambridge (Fig. 15), would show a great contrast. This early development could happen because Gothic never took deep root in Italy, where it symbolized the German Emperor's claims to dominion established by Charle-

magne. The story of the building of the cupola of St. Maria dei Fiore (cathedral) (Fig. 16) was also affected by this political factor. As the external buttresses typical of Gothic architecture would have had imperial connotations, so Andrea Pisano and Francesco Talenti were instructed by a Commission of Artists to build the drum of the dome without buttresses. It needed the structural genius of Brunelleschi to solve the problem of building a cupola with no lateral thrusts. He designed a double dome, possibly following Islamic examples with diagonal layers of brick together with stone and wooden ties, so reducing the width and counteracting the thrusts from the cupola.

The pronounced ribs of the cupola at the eight points of its octagon are expressed externally, being finished in white marble, whereas the roof is tiled. He also invented a suspended centering as well as numerous lifting machines. His inventiveness was remarkable and perhaps contradicts the general impression that Renaissance architecture made practically no contribution to building technology.

Another example of a Rennaissance church can be found in the choir and central dome, transepts, and crossing in St. Maria delle Grazie (1485–1494) in Milan (Fig. 17) by Bramante, and the mature Renaissance style is expressed in his small Tempieto in San Pietro in Montorio in Rome (1502–1510). S. Maria della Consolazione in Todi (1508–1602) (Fig. 18) has the perfect Greek cross plan; however, Bramante's centrally planned cathedral to replace the early Christian basilica of St. Peter's is the most significant document for the new type of church required by humanist intellectuals. Although the next plan by Sangallo had an extended nave, the emphasis was still on a central dome; this was followed by Michelangelo's design (1456), which was built over earlier foundations using massive piers and brick walls some 33 ft (10.1 m) thick faced with huge travertine blocks. The effect of this masonry, best seen in the transepts, is breathtaking, and even today it is in practically perfect condition. Following the precedent of Florence, a double dome was built, finished in a rush with hundreds of workmen under Giacomo della Porta in 1583–1590.

However, the central plan did not give the congregation enough space and was unsuited to festal processions, so Carlo Maderno had to lengthen the nave (1606–1612), forming a Latin cross and using much lighter construction than Michelangelo. Maderno's work spoils the view of the dome from the Piazza, particularly as the drum seems relatively squat, especially when compared with St. Paul's in London.

Finally, St. Peter's was built with a span of 84 ft (25.6 m), an internal length of 600 ft (182.7 m), and 450 ft (137 m) across the apsed transepts. The dome at peristyle level is 137 ft (41.7 m) in diameter (less than the Pantheon, or Florence). The nave is 150 ft (45.7 m) high with giant Corinthian orders 83.5 ft (25.4 m) and entablature 20 ft (6.1 m) deep, aisles were 76 ft (23.1 m) high, and the dome reached 452 ft (137.7 m) above the church floor. In spite of its size, it does not have the spatial impact of Hagia Sophia built nearly 1000 years earlier.

Bernini, besides designing the throne of St. Peter's and the 100-ft high baldacchino, created the marvelous piazza with fourfold Tuscan colonnades in front of St. Peter's

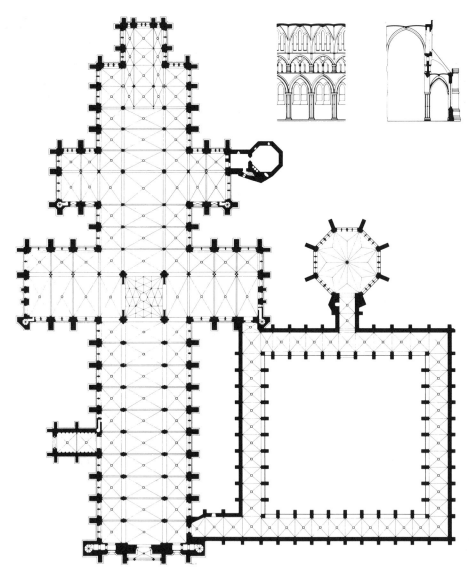

Figure 12. Salisbury Cathedral (3). Courtesy of Birkhäuser Verlag Ag.

(1655–1667) which was spoiled somewhat by the approach road made under the fascist regime of Mussolini. Maderno's facade is a disappointment in spite of its size. If Michelangelo's scheme with free-standing columns of 90.75 ft (27.6 m) and 9-ft (2.74-m) diameter with a 20-ft (6.1-m) entablature had been executed, this would have been one of the most impressive sights in Christendom.

Apart from the superb quality of the materials and work, Michelangelo, della Porta, Maderno, and Bernini did not contribute important technological advances. Apart from the double dome, the technology was precisely that of ancient Rome 1600 years earlier because commissions were given to artists and sculptors by humanist intellectuals. The purely intellectual basis for the Renaissance was one reason for its slow spreading. There were 200 years between Brunelleschi's church and Inigo Jones's work at Old St. Paul's Cathedral and the Queen's House, Greenwich.

Cathedral building had been brought to a climax with St. Peter's and then practically stopped until the nineteenth century. The Reformation demanded a different

sort of church, the best examples of which occur in The Netherlands, the West Church (Westerkerk) (1620–1638) in Amsterdam (then one of the richest cities in Europe), and the New Churches (Nieuwekerk) in the Hague (1649–1656) and Haarlem (1643–1649).

Baroque and Rococo

When St. Paul's in London (Fig. 19) was built, it was the only cathedral designed for the Anglican faith. Sir Christopher Wren had already designed a truly remarkable series of city churches of great variety. His early proposals for St. Paul's are interesting; the first was a preaching box, followed by a fine plan based on a Greek cross to be seen now in model form in the crypt. The next design was rather pedestrian, but King Charles in his Royal Warrant gave him permission to make variations "artistic not otherwise" so the final design evolved with a central dome and two western towers that are truly baroque in form. When foundation work started, all Wren had decided for the dome was its diameter of 112 ft and

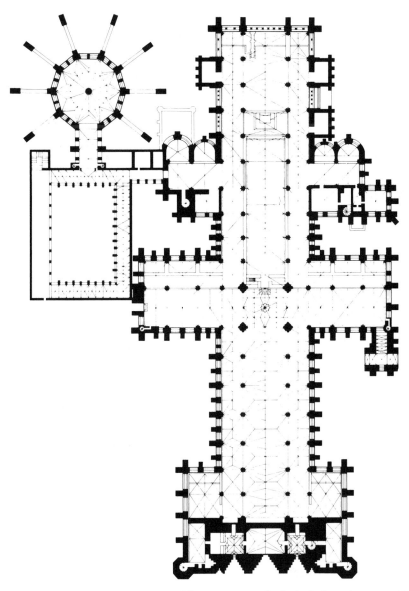

Figure 13. Lincoln Cathedral (3). Courtesy of Birkhäuser Verlag Ag.

that it was to rest on eight piers, thereby solving the liturgical demand for processions down the aisles. The dome is his masterpiece; he was determined to have this dome as a symbol in spite of the difficulties of building it on a tall drum. The geometry of the dome is perfect; for Wren, geometry was the ultimate source of beauty.

The body of the church consists of two orders and a strong rusticated plinth. The lower order has Corinthian pilasters, whereas the upper is composite. The upper is merely a screen wall to hide the buttressing of the nave and choir vaults. A balustraded parapet was added on orders from the Commission, as by 1700, the younger generation of architects such as Lord Burlington considered that the baroque style, which was to have had pairs of statues above the twin pilasters, was old-fashioned; they wanted the new Palladian style. Wren was also forced to accept cast instead of wrought iron railings. Today, this

is considered an interesting example of technological innovation.

The plan is the usual Latin cross with an apsidal end, but with chapels situated in the bay to the east of the western towers. There is a crypt under the entire cathedral. The main church is 91 ft (27.7 m) high with aisles 47 ft (10.3 m) long. The upper dome is 214.25 ft (65.3 m) above the floor, whereas the cross is 365 ft (111.5 m) above the ground level. This dimension was probably symbolic as Wren was a former professor of astronomy.

The walls are faced with ashlar and filled with lime concrete. To give the effect of very fine joints, the under surface of each stone was hollowed out except at the face so that a joint of about ⅝ in. (16 mm) would appear only ⅛- or ³⁄₁₆-in. (3- or 5-mm) wide; this has caused the spalling of most of the horizontal joints in the pilasters. Not all of the lime concrete in the 8 ft (2.43 m) thick walls was

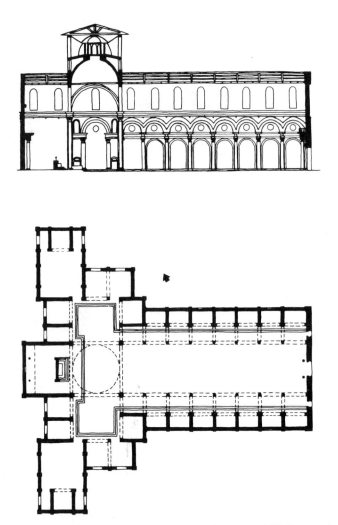

Figure 14. San Lorenzo, Florence (3). Courtesy of Birkhäuser Verlag Ag.

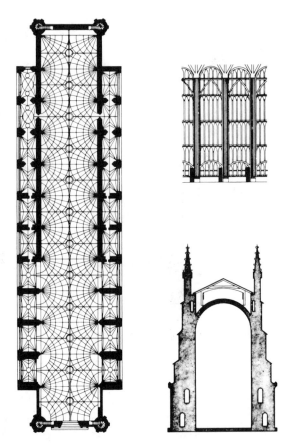

Figure 15. King's College Chapel, Cambridge (3). Courtesy of Birkhäuser Verlag Ag.

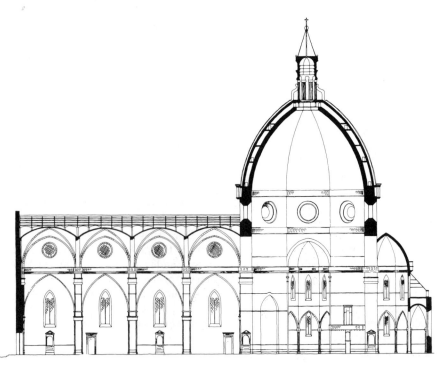

Figure 16. S. Maria dei Fiori, Florence (3). Courtesy of Birkhäuser Verlag Ag.

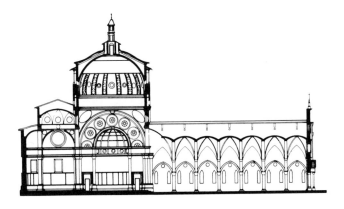

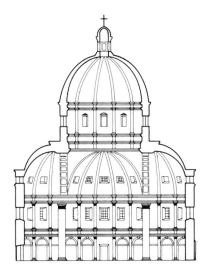

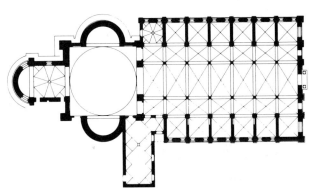

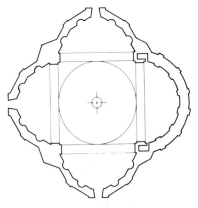

Figure 17. S. Maria delle Grazie, Milan (3). Courtesy of Birkhäuser Verlag Ag.

Figure 18. S. Maria della Consolazione, Todi (3). Courtesy of Birkhäuser Verlag Ag.

set. In important places, trass, imported from the Rhineland, was added to the lime and as this was expensive it was sparingly used. The mortar mix was rich in lime, being one part lime to two of sand, but some gypsum found its way into the mortar, perhaps as an adulteration of the lime. The stone was generally from the Portland quarries, transported by sea from a small jetty, journeys taking two days or more according to wind and tide. However, some Ketton and Burford stone was used when supplies ran short due to the harrassing activities of French privateers during the Wars of the Spanish Succession. The Burford stone came from a quarry owned by one of the master masons and could be transported down the Thames, but how the Ketton came is not stated. However, the accounts published in 1924 by the Wren Society are fascinating, complete documents throwing much light on building practices at the end of the seventeenth century. From these, there are indications of an early practice in quantity surveying, some of which are applicable today. Although some day works were paid for, most work was measured on completion. The quantities of materials are extremely accurate.

Wren divided the work between six master masons; their work had to meet accurately on center lines at the top of semicircular arches, leaving no room for mistakes. The reason for this division was that the size of St. Paul's posed an excessive demand on the capacity of the building industry of its time.

The challenge of building St. Paul's led to several innovations that later became normal contractual practice. Wren initiated some form of statics analysis which, as he was an astronomer and a colleague of the great experimental mathematician Hooke, was not surprising. As has been said, when he set out the foundations, he had no conception of how to build the dome, which weighs 67,000 tons and exerts a load of 5 tons/ft^2 on the main piers. There were at least three schemes; the final solution consisted of a brick inner dome surmounted by a steep-sided brick cone supporting the golden gallery at the top of the dome, with a tall lantern 88 ft high topped by a cross set on an orb. The downward line of thrust comes close to the geometry of the cone; lower down, the thrust from the inner dome is resisted by the abutting bastions. There were three chains in the cone, and a fourth and fifth were added, probably unnecessarily, in the Great Restoration of 1921–1931. The real problem may have been the settlement of the foundations disturbed by the building of an underground railway.

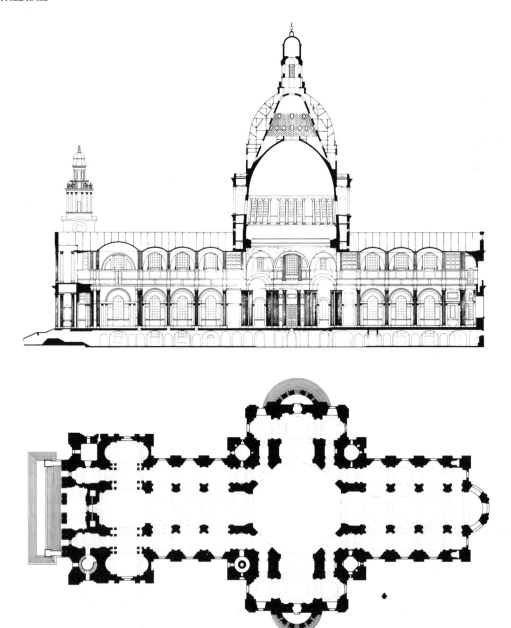

Figure 19. St. Paul's, London (3). Courtesy of Birkhäuser Verlag Ag.

The perfect hemisphere of the dome is set out with timber framing and finished with lead sheets on wooden boards, creating a considerable fire hazard. The elegance and structural economy of this arrangement is impressive even today. The dome provides London with a symbol of identity and continuity; key views from the south and west were protected by legislation in the 1930s. At that time, no one envisaged buildings taller than 10 stories; however, there is a backdrop of tall commercial buildings in the center of London.

Baroque rococo architecture achieved great splendor in the churches built in Rome, often with money from the New World, and in the Bavarian and Austrian monasteries and pilgrimage churches such as Melk (1702–1740), Veirzegnheiligen (Fig. 20), and Weiss (1746–1754). These churches are superb examples of artistic collaboration between architects, sculptors, painters, ironworkers, and craftsmen. Light is handled with consummate skill so it is hard to decide what is illusion and what is reality. The exteriors can be extremely simple as at Weiss, set on a hill in a rural landscape contrasting with the heavenly vision vouchsafed in the interior and expressed in the music of Bach, Mozart, and Haydn. The fact that it is all paint and plaster shocks those who hold puritanical scales of values.

During this period, magnificent monasteries and convents with fine churches were also built in Latin America when the fusion of Portuguese, Spanish, and Indian art took baroque architecture further than even Italy. The works of the Brazilian sculptor-architect Aleijadinho

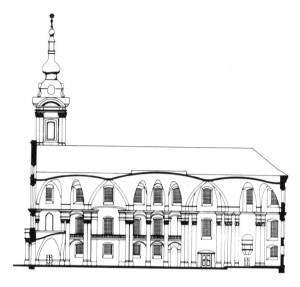

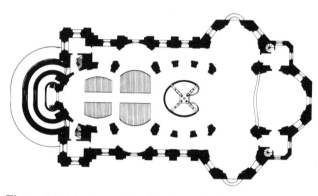

Figure 20. Pilgrimage church, Vierzegnheilligen (3). Courtesy of Birkhäuser Verlag Ag.

(1738–1814) are intensely moving, and the church at Congonhas do Campo (1800–1805) may be considered his supreme masterpiece. These buildings were built in earthquake-prone zones and accordingly suffered severe damage in spite of being strongly built. Whereas domestic architecture had several antiseismic precautions, the major public buildings do not give evidence of similar measures.

Revived Styles

The Enlightenment led to a Nonconformist movement that did not encourage cathedral building, but the romantic movement led to the revival of historic styles; with the great increase of population and wealth in the western world, there was a consequential increase in cathedral building. Most of this was inspired by a rose-tinted vision of the Middle Ages, combined with a desire to forget or at least to ignore the social problems of the Industrial Revolution. Horace Walpole started the fashion for "Gothik" in Strawberry Hill (1747–1763) whose abandoned travesty of medieval technique has since shocked and delighted its critics; light, gay, and playful, it exhibits all of the qualities associated with rococo. Scholars and ar-

chaeological researchers produced more reliable information and a generation later architects were locked in the battle of styles, neoclassicism vs Gothic; some of the greatest Victorian practitioners were equally competent in both. In his book written in 1836, *Parallels between the Noble Edifices of the Fourteenth And Fifteenth Centuries, and Similar Buildings of the Present Day: Shewing the Present Decay of Taste,* and again in the *True Principles of Christian or Pointed Architecture* (1841), A. W. N. Pugin (1812–1852) did a great deal to establish Gothic as the correct style for churches. He collaborated with Sir Charles Barry in designing the details of the Houses of Parliament (1836–1868) and built Kilkenny Cathedral in the UK.

In the UK, outstanding examples of cathedrals of eclectic design can be found at Truro (1897–1910) by J. L. Pearson in revived Gothic; Westminster (1895–1903) by J. F. Bentley, Byzantine style; and Liverpool (1903) by Sir Giles Gilbert Scott in Free Gothic style. Sir Giles Gilbert Scott's father had been a leading architect and designed the Nikolaikirche in Hamburg (1845–1863). There are also fine works by English architects working in the Commonwealth such as St. Patrick's Melbourne, and G. F. Bodley who added flying buttresses to York Minster and was responsible for the design of Washington Cathedral; by far the most significant contribution was Trinity Church, Boston (1872–1877), by H. H. Richardson. It is Romanesque in character; the plan is a Greek cross dominated by a massive central tower with round corner turrets and built of red granite with rock-faced texture. The character is essentially American. Internal decor was by John La Farge and the porch was skillfully added in 1897.

Relying on the traditional craft skills, the cathedral building of the nineteenth century produced no technological advances. Because professional men had replaced the artist craftsmen of Medieval Gothic and the baroque, there was a mechanical feeling and dryness about most of the work, which appeared contrived rather than organic and spontaneous. There were exceptions of course: L. A. Boileau (1812–1896) created an iron-framed church in St. Eugene, Paris (1854–1855), and G. E. A. de Baudot built the first church in reinforced concrete, St. Jean-de-Montmartre, Paris (1897–1905).

Another remarkable exception is the dramatic and eccentric church of the Sagrada Familia, Barcelona (1882), in the art nouveau style by Antoni Gaudi. The crypt, transept, and chevet have been built, and there is a model to indicate the architect's future intentions. The work is a fantasy profusely ornamented with flowers and figures carved with soft outlines in stone, and weird angular trees with stark branches reach upward to sustain a stalactite vault.

Cathedrals continue to be built in the latter half of the twentieth century. One example is Sir Frederick Giberd's Liverpool Cathedral built over the earlier crypt of the ambitious design by Sir Edwin Lutyens. (Construction had stopped in 1941, and the original plans abandoned because of cost.) Giberd's building is conceived so that the priest can celebrate facing the faithful. This post-Vatican II Cathedral has a central altar under a vast conical roof. Somehow the building fails to be convincing as a cathedral; everything looks as if it has been done in too much of a hurry and too cheaply; perhaps it expresses the spirit of the times too clearly.

The master of reinforced-concrete design, Pier Luigi Nervi, collaborated in the building of St. Mary's Cathedral in San Francisco which was completed in 1961. Angus McSweeny and Ryan were appointed by the Archbishop as architects, who obtained the services of Pietro Belluschi as consultant, who in turn asked Pier Luigi Nervi to assist in the realization of the project in engineering terms. The concept of a cruciform roof supported on four great pillars belongs probably to Belluschi, but the realization depended on Nervi. As is the case today, the architecture depended on the skill of structural engineers, although Nervi himself had combined the skills of designer and contractor, in the same way as a Gothic master, being an artist who makes "man free of his own vision, a vision in which he sees a certain kinship between mind and matter which goes beyond the boundaries of knowledge." As Nervi said, "The essence of contemporary architecture is not the avoidance of style or the creating of a new one but insistence on integrity of thought."

The Cathedral is a 200-ft (61.1-m) square in plan and 190 ft (58-m) high, seating only 1200 persons. Belluschi demanded a strong structural concept to be handled with a kind of simplicity that becomes both a structure and a symbol to be looked at and remembered. Priest and people were to be united with the altar, as their focus was postulated by Vatican II. The design is both dramatic and serene, and, as with all great cathedrals, the interior is the justification of the exterior.

Mention must also be made of the masterpiece of the "Great Form Giver" (Charles-Edouard Jeanneret, known better as Le Corbusier) of the modern international movement, Ronchamp (1950–1955). This pilgrimage chapel stands isolated on a lonely hill dominating the wooded landscape of the Jura. The form is compact and the walls are massive, the south wall being battered inwards and containing an intriguing pattern of slot windows of varying dimensions and proportions, some square and inert, others with vertical or horizontal trends, one with deep reveals reflecting light onto a statue of the Virgin Mary, giving it a marvelous halo contrasting with the crepuscular gloom. Round, soft, contoured-angle towers contain minor chapels lit mysteriously from above. The great billowing roof, which must have been built before the walls, is supported by the towers and a great spur buttress at the southeast corner, and is separated by a continuous narrow band of glazing which lights the ceiling. His design contradicts all of his polemic and is his final personal statement, producing architecture of this age that can stir the depths of the soul.

BUILDING TECHNOLOGY

Throughout the Roman Empire, building techniques were remarkably standardized through the work of the legions, who were armed tradesmen. Also, architecture was one of the nine recognized subjects for higher education, which any Roman administrator was required to study. A great debt is owed to Roman building technology in that it lasted in its trade practices right up to the mid-twentieth century, using methods and materials that were mutually compatible. Today, financial interest in rapid construction and space saving have led designers to explore the possibilities of an industrialized building technology compared with traditional technology (Table 1).

One of the triumphs of Roman construction technique was the Pantheon (120–124) (Fig. 21), with its dome of 146.5 ft in diameter, only equalled in Brunelleschi's octago-

Table 1. A Comparison of Traditional Technology and Industrial Technology

Traditional Technology	Industrial Technology
Few materials, often obtained locally, all well understood when used traditionally, incorporating generations of experience.	Based on theories and "standards," using many materials often imported long distances and having unknown qualities.
Simple construction, with a certain amount of overdimensioning, giving tolerance for adaptation and flexibility in use.	Complicated construction, with very little extra material or security in dimensioning.
Soft construction, with ability to breathe and absorb, and give up moisture and tolerate deformation.	Hard construction of rigid buildings, which cannot tolerate deformations or movement of vapor.
Massive heavy homogeneous constructions, with high thermal capacity and moisture "buffer" effect.	Light, multilayer specialized construction, with low thermal capacity and practically no "buffer" effect.
Built with small elements with joints and therefore easy to repair.	Big elements with rigid joints, which are often impossible to repair, eg, epoxy resin glue joints or depending on mastics.
Relying on natural light and ventilation, with simple local heating appliances, supplemented by mechanical and electrical installations in the nineteenth and early twentieth centuries.	Dependent entirely on mechanical and electrical installations.
Built on-site in open weather. Some prefabrication of joinery and small elements.	Mostly made in factories protected from the weather.
Low in energy consumption.	High in energy consumption.
Many man-hours of labor, small transportation costs.	Fewer man-hours in labor, but with high organizational and transport costs.
Designed for repair and maintenance.	Either repair-free or impossible to repair.
Ages gracefully in a predetermined and acceptable way.	No consideration given to aging.
Easy to change, can be altered if services are exposed.	Difficult to change, involving major and possibly harmful disruption.

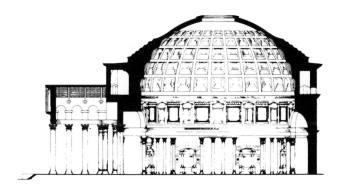

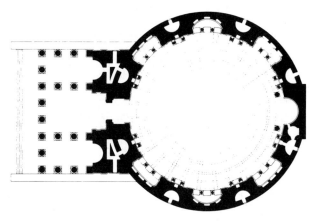

Figure 21. Pantheon, Rome (3). Courtesy of Birkhäuser Verlag Ag.

nal cupola on St. Maria dei Fiori in Florence and only substantially exceeded in size in the nineteenth century by using iron or steel and reinforced concrete. The Pantheon also had bronze trusses over the portico, and the roof was clad in bronze tiles. Only the ring around the opening at the apex of the dome remains, the valuable bronze being removed to provide metal for Bernini's baldacchino in St. Peter's. The roof is now covered with lead sheets.

CATHEDRAL BUILDING

Cathedral building needed a patron, finance, designers, artists, craftsmen, laborers, and suppliers. A program might last hundreds of years or might never be completed; for a cathedral to be finished in its designer's lifetime was, in past centuries, a rare exception. Sir Christopher Wren was one of the few historic architects to see his masterpiece completed, as he lived to the age of 91. He was commemorated in his cathedral with the terse memorial *si monumentum requiris circumspice*. It took three major campaigns, by about 250 men, of 10 years duration to build Chartres Cathedral and over 250 years to build York Minster, with about 30–40 men almost constantly employed under a succession of some 20 master masons. It might be estimated that it took some 7000–9000 man-years to build a great cathedral.

How was the need for a cathedral conceived? Often, as at York and St. Paul's, fire had destroyed the cathedral's predecessor. At Norwich, it was the result of an ecclesiastical reorganization, and at Salisbury, the need to find a better site led to the erection of a completely new building.

Funding

Funding was largely by gifts from rich clerics or the landed wealthy. Sometimes these gifts were in kind: oak trees from the Percys and stone from the Vavasours, being commemorated by sculpted memorials on the west front of York Minster. It is recorded that Romanus, the Treasurer, paid for rebuilding the north transept of York Minster, and Archbishop de Grey paid for the south transept, where his tomb stands today.

The deterioration of the early Christian basilica was given as the reason for rebuilding of St. Peter's. Funds were raised by the sale of indulgences, giving so many days relief from pain in purgatory; it was this abuse that precipitated the Reformation. Funds for this great enterprise were also raised from the Orders working in Latin America, so it can be truly said that American money contributed to the beautification of Rome. The building of St. Paul's Cathedral was funded by a tax raised on the sale of coal at 6d per cauldron. This tax had to be voted by Parliament, so Christopher Wren stood and was elected for Windsor. As funds ran out, he had to stand again. In fact, the cash flow was irregular, and Sir Christopher and the six master masons working under him had to lend money to St. Paul's to finance the continuation of the work. This great work tested the capacity of the building industry and saw the emergence of standard rates for measured work and height of masonry, and thus was the basis for many modern building practices.

Historic Drawings

Plans and evaluations of early cathedrals are rare. The notebooks of Villard de Honecourt gave some idea of what a mason would find interesting. The drawings of Sienna Cathedral can be seen, and those of the west front of Cologne Cathedral were used for the 1824–1880 restoration when the nave and 500-ft western towers were built. When completed with its cast-iron flèche over the crossing, Cologne was the highest building in the world, but this was probably exceeded by old St. Paul's before the top of the spire fell; later, the whole burned down. Medieval spires were removed from Lincoln Cathedral and never built at York. In Vienna, there are several designs by late medieval masters. It is thought that the master mason would work by angles and proportions, and set all his work to full size. This view is supported by the discovery of the tracing floor in the monks' parlor of York Minster. The exact correlation between the setting out and execution of the aisle windows in the choir and lady chapel was proved by photogrammetry. Engraved tracings can also be seen at Bourges. The masons' wooden templates were found at York.

There are plentiful drawings of St. Paul's, all to differing scales, as the size of the paper dictated the scale found on the masons' setting-out compasses. Wren would always insist on seeing and approving a mock-up of any new detail or carved capital. Scale models that were frequently used for smaller buildings would have had great advantages over drawings, as they would be easier for unlettered builders to understand and translate into reality.

Drawings were necessary for making a statics analysis. There is evidence that Wren made initial attempts at analysis. These may have gone further, as he was closely associated with Dr. Hooke and was also a mathematician himself. However, the great credit for a full statics analysis must be given to Poleni, whose study of the dome of St. Peter's, which had serious cracks and gave evidence of progressive failure, was the turning point in this science, as was Coulomb's memoir in the science of soil mechanics. It is a sobering thought that engineers have lost most of their acquired practical knowledge of arched construction since the introduction of framed structures at the end of the nineteenth century. Today, only a few engineers have the correct approach to historic buildings, an approach that should be based on careful examination and the application of judgment assisted by calculations. Cathedrals were built long before codes of practice were devised and will outlive most regulations; however, with respect to wind loadings on tall towers and spires, design of rainwater disposal, and earthquake and fire precautions, higher standards than given in codes should be adopted as the hazards increase with longevity. The designer working on a cathedral works in four dimensions: length, breadth, height, and time.

Designers

The status of the medieval master mason has been established by John Harvey, who shows that the leaders of the profession acted very much like modern architects and were constantly traveling, often with their patron. They were well paid and honored with gifts of fur gowns. There are records of their seeking each other's advice, as did John Morton who asked John Everard, the builder of Norwich Cathedral's 325-ft high spire, to give him the batter (ie, the angle of slope) so that he could use this for St. Mary Redcliffe in Bristol.

Artisans

The masons and laborers traveled from project to project and worked hard. A mason was given a mark to indicate the stone he had prepared and for which he would be paid. This mark would be operative throughout the project, but would not necessarily be used on the next project. The York Minster fabric rolls give an insight into conditions of employment and working hours. The main tradespeople involved in building a cathedral were masons and brick layers, mortar makers, carpenters, and blacksmiths.

Two important sets of regulations for the craftspersons employed at York Minster have survived. The earlier of them, compiled in about 1352, is written in Latin and runs, in translation, as follows (9):

> That the masons, carpenters and other workmen ought to begin to work, on all working days in the summer, from Easter

to Michaelmas, at sunrise and ought to work from that time until the ringing of the bell of the Blessed Virgin Mary, and then they should sit down to breakfast in the lodge of the works, if they have not breakfasted, for the space [of time that it takes to walk] half a league; and then the masters, or one of them, shall knock upon the door of the lodge, and all shall at once go to their work; and so they shall diligently carry out their duties until noon, and then they shall go to their dinner [prandia]. Also in winter, from Michaelmas to Easter, they shall come to their work at dawn and everyone when he comes shall immediately start work, and so continue in the said way until noon. From the feast of the Invention of the Holy Cross [3 May] to the feast of St. Peter's Chains [1 August], they ought to sleep in the lodge after dinner; and when the vicars come out from the canons' hall [mensa] the master mason, or his deputy, shall cause them to rise from slumber and get to their work; and so they ought to work until the first bell for vespers, and then they shall sit and drink in the lodge, from the said first bell to the third bell, both in summer and winter. Also from the [1 August] to the [3 May], they shall return to their work immediately after their dinner, for which a reasonable time shall be taken, without waiting for the return of the vicars from the canons' hall; and so they shall work until the first bell for vespers and then they shall drink in the lodge until the third bell has rung, and shall return to their work, and so they shall work until the ringing of the bell of St. Mary's Abbey which is called le Langebell, namely, every working day from the feast of St. Peter's Chains to Michaelmas, and from Michaelmas to the said feast of St. Peter, they shall continue to work as long as they can see by daylight. Also each mason shall take less for the week in winter, that is from Michaelmas to Easter, than in summer by one day's wage. Also when two feast days happen in one week, each loses one day's wage [dietam] and when three occur, half that week. Also on vigils and on Saturdays, when they rest after noon, out of respect for the next day, then they shall work until noon strikes. Also the said two master masons and the carpenter of the works shall be present at every pay-day [pacacione], and there shall inform the warden and controller of the works of any defaults and absence of masons, carpenters, and other workmen, and according to his lateness [moram] or absence deductions shall be made from each man's wages, both for a whole day and a half day, as is reasonable. Also the said two master masons and carpenter, for the time being, ought faithfully to observe the said regulations, in virtue of the oath which they take, and they shall see that they are kept by the other masons and workmen working there, on pain of dismissal. And if anyone refuse to work in the said manner, let him be dismissed at once and not taken back again on to the works until he is willing to keep the rules in every detail.

Cathedral Structures

Every building is individual, unique in some way; nevertheless, families of buildings exist, and although generalizations cannot be made, they may contain some useful hints. Where good timber was available the earliest constructions may have been wooden post and lintel, which was translated into the stone column with short-span stone lintels as in the Greek Doric. The most common family is that of mass walls with timber beam roofs; when heavier loads had to be carried, mass vaults were introduced. When wider spans had to be bridged, trusses were devised and means developed to spread any point loads. The next family used barrel vaults together with mass walling; this was developed into domical construction. The fourth family consisted of the stone skeleton frame, a daring innovation as it did not simply rely on weight for its stability. Later, the use of iron and steel enabled framed structures with stiff joints to be developed using structural continuity; such frames are also used with reinforced concrete. Lastly, suspended tentlike structures were developed; these too have been used in churches.

Structures must be considered at three levels: first, the total system; second, the structural elements and their interactions; and third, the strength, durability, and compatibility of the materials. As Pier Luigi Nervi said, it is not a coincidence that those historic buildings that are generally regarded as beautiful are also good examples of building technology considering the materials available at the time.

Post and lintel construction is one of the most elementary techniques. Concealed in every stone lintel is an arch, so if it cracks, there is no need for alarm. Walls and slabs are merely an extension of post and lintel as the slab may be considered a series of beams if made of stone or wood. If the posts are made of wood, they are vulnerable to decay as a result of moisture in the ground, unless protected by a damp-proof course, which would be quite exceptional in an historic building.

Trusses developed from a single king post with one vertical member, to the queen-post truss with two verticals into scissor trusses, to many more complicated types, often redundant. With wood, the problem was always at the joints; designers tried to avoid more than two members meeting at a point, as otherwise the joint became too weak. Unfortunately, decay from fungal and insect attack always seems to seek out this vulnerable point.

There are 35 distinct shapes of arch, of which the following may be found in cathedrals: semicircular, segmental, round horseshoe, pointed horseshoe, horseshoe lancet, equilateral, drip, pointed segmental, three-centered depressed, three centered, pseudo three centered, four centered, pseudo four centered, rampant, elliptical, parabolic, round trefoil, pointed trefoil, round trefoilated, pointed trefoilated, cinquefoil, multifoil ogee, Italian pointed, Venetian, Florentine, shouldered, flat, or straight.

The most important characteristic of the arch is that it always thrusts outward on its supports as well as weighing down vertically upon them. The thrust can be effectively contained by a tie between the feet of the arch; without such a tie, an arch has a tendency to spread, a flat arch having the tendency to push out most. The load capacity of an arch depends on the ratio of its rise to span, the depth of the voussoirs, and the strength of its abutments. The pointed arch is ideal for taking a load at its apex. Arches can be strengthened by repointing mortar joints, followed by grouting. Rebuilding is sometimes necessary.

Barrel vaults are merely arches extended laterally and behave like arches, but have the capacity to distribute loads sideways. Roman vaults incorporated hidden arches, anticipating Gothic ribs. Where used as floors, they also brace adjacent walls. In post-Roman construction, it is unusual to find heavy barrel vaults used in upper stories

of buildings. Hollow clay pots were used, and in the eighteenth and nineteenth centuries, light tile vaults were used. Groined vaults were a refinement on simple barrel vaults and greatly reduced dead loads. Bearing in mind the collapse of Beauvais, the long-term ability to contain the thrust from a high central vault, due to problems caused by deformations and cumulative thermal movement, is critical to the survival of a cathedral.

Provided that the outer thrusts developed in the upper part of a dome can be contained by circumferential tensions lower down so that it develops purely vertical loads on its supports, a dome is ideal from the theoretical point of view of strength and stability. Its form is also well fitted for resisting side loads from wind or earthquake. However, the masonry of a dome certainly lacks the required tensile strength, so ties of timber or iron were introduced. Transition elements, basically either pendentives or squinches, were needed to transform the circle of the dome to the square or polygonal plan of the base; these too add to the outward thrusts. The semidome is potentially an excellent buttress, as is shown in Hagia Sophia.

Margins of safety in a historic building diminish with time, not only as a result of ill-considered additions to the structure. Weathering of masonry and mortar, rotting of timber, high atmospheric pollution, corrosion of metals, erosion by crystallization of ground salts, and changes in ground water level are among the extrinsic causes of decay. Poor workmanship, faulty design, and progressive increase of deformations due to thermal movement or traffic vibration are intrinsic causes. Differential foundation settlements due to consolidation of the ground should diminish with time, unless the settlements significantly change the distribution of pressures on the ground as can happen with a leaning tower or column. Settlements should have reached their final values within the first 100 years. However, further diffential settlements may occur at any time, due to the rotting of wooden piles or bodily ground movements. Also, a cathedral may have suffered several severe fires in its lifetime, which may have weakened the structure. All relevant details of construction must be taken into account, particularly the nature and condition of masonry or brickwork throughout its thickness and the condition of joints in timber trusses and frames. Only when all of these have been considered can a useful quantitative analysis be made.

BUILDING MATERIALS

Supplies of stone and burnt lime came from the quarries, and the cost of transport was such that heavy materials could not be carried more than 12–15 mi unless water transport was available. For example, a shipload of Caen stone was brought from a quarry in Normandy for £1.6/8d ($1.33), shipped to Great Yarmouth for £2.10/8d ($2.53), loaded into barges there for £2/2d ($0.108), ferried 20 miles up river for £7/2d ($0.36), and unloaded near Norwich Cathedral for £2 ($0.10). Transportation accounted for 75% of the cost (9). It might be estimated that the load was 30–40 t and surmised that the stone was already dressed, making it easy to handle and thus economical to purchase.

In contrast, long-distance road transportation today may account for no more than 25% of the cost. The stone was extracted from the quarry by drilling and driving in metal wedges called feathers; these split off sizable blocks which would then be hand sawn to a workable size and left to harden as the quarry sap dried out, preferably over a winter as the frost would seek out weak stones.

Stone

On arrival at the cathedral workshop, the stone would be shaped by mallet with various types of chisels to dimensions given by the master mason and marked by the mason. It would then be taken up the scaffolding and built into the face of the wall in regular courses. Shafts and voussoirs would be of molded stones and carved features such as crockets, finials, gargoyles, capitals, urns, and swags would be prepared by the carvers and built in by the masons. The tools of the masons and carvers were much the same as today. However, standards of workmanship and finish evolved. The Romanesque masons gave their stones a slanting diagonal cut as they used an axe. The rough dressing was probably excused by the fact that their work was to be finished with a fine lime plaster painted with bright decorative colors. The thirteenth-century Gothic masons left their stones with a henpecked finish from a fine chisel, whereas in later work, the surface was rubbed smooth. Also, although the size of stones tended to increase in later periods, the thickness of the joints decreased from as much as ⅝–¾ in. (16–19 mm) in the eleventh century to 3/16 in. (4.8 mm) in the seventeenth century at St. Paul's, London, and 1/16 in. (1.6 mm) in the nineteenth century at St. Giles, Edinburgh. These fine joints made maintenance difficult and did not allow the building to deform comfortably by compressing the soft lime mortar; instead, the stones themselves tend to crack or spall under pressure.

The mason relied on the blacksmith to keep the tools sharp and tempered to the degree that suited the stone they had to cut. Today, much of the mason's work has been mechanized with hand power tools, planing machines, and large circular saws, with diamond-tipped cutting teeth. Machine work gives the face of the stone a different finish.

Scaffolding was necessary for the works. Often the putlocks were built into walls and projected on both sides to support horizontal hurdles from which the masons worked. Otherwise, poles would be necessary, with horizontal ledgers all connected by ropes; this was liable to stretch and slip, and was therefore kept wet by an apprentice. Ramps of hurdles were constructed for laborers to bring up the materials which could also be lifted by a jenny wheel or block and tackle and on a large project by a treadmill. Scaffolding always presents problems and may control the way projects were executed. In the case of Salisbury Cathedral, the spire of 404 ft was built of stone 9 in. thick, set overhand from internal staging. In the case of Norwich, spire building stone had to be transported at least 100 mi, so economy was at a premium; the spire was built of 4½-in. (114-mm) brickwork for the top 120 ft (36.4 m), cased with 3-in. slabs of stone. Again, it was built overhand

from an internal staging until the space was so narrow at the top that an external scaffold was constructed on two stout members projecting through the uppermost windows.

In Italy, the putlock holes left in buildings are often seen; these must not be confused with fixing holes for marble decoration of a facade. Putlocks that had been built in had to be sawn off flush with the wall; in due course these rotted, leaving a row of holes as may be seen at Fountains Abbey.

Brick

Brick was considered by Vitruvius to be the most durable of building materials; this is true if it is well burnt and has a porous structure able to resist frost and ground salts. Brick is made by burning a sandy clay in kilns or clamps, which can be done close to the cathedral provided sufficient fuel is available. Wood is the historic fuel for burning and gives a different color from coal or oil.

Roman bricks were used in early Christian buildings and even recycled for the building of St. Alban's Cathedral in the eleventh century. In fact, the recycling of masonry and timbers was common practice; Roman masonry is found in the foundations of York Minster. Full Roman bricks are more like tiles, measuring 9 × 9 × 1¾ in. and laid with thick mortar joints. In Northern Europe, the art of brickwork seems to have been lost after the Roman withdrawal, although the impressive Saxon Church at Bricksworth poses questions, and was not revived until the twelfth or thirteenth century in The Netherlands, when bricks were imported for royal works on the Tower of London in 1238. However, in Lombardy, the brick tradition seemed to survive; in The Netherlands and northern Germany, cathedrals were built of brick. Some of these used bricks of gigantic size, about 16 × 6 × 4½ in. (406 × 152 × 144 mm) for a ⅜-in. (9.5-mm) joint. The thickness could and did vary from 1¾ in. (44 mm) to a full 3 in. (76 mm) in the eighteenth century. The manufacture of bricks was taxed; this tended to encourage thicker bricks, which are aesthetically undesirable.

Mortar

Stone and brick need mortar as a binder. Mortars were generally one part slaked lime to two or, more usually, three parts sand. It would take lime mortars up to five years to harden fully and the quality of the lime would inevitably vary with the chemical content of the stone from which it was made. The setting qualities of lime were improved by the addition of pozzuolanas. Pozzuolanas are the secret of the success of Roman building technology; they were in the first instance volcanic earths found near Pozzuoli, but any earth that has been subjected to intense heat obtains pozzuolanic qualities; these improve the strength and setting of lime mortars as well as having sufficient elasticity to resist daily thermal changes and stress. Ground brick or tiles are good pozzuolana; Wren imported German volcanic earth, called trass, for St. Paul's and used it sparingly as it was seven times as expensive as lime.

By modern standards, cathedrals were built slowly to

allow lime mortars time to set and foundations time to settle as the loads increased year by year. Viollet le Duc, in his long monograph on construction, was of the opinion that buttresses would be built before walls so that when the wall was built and bonded to the buttress and tended to settle the buttress would receive some prestressing, inclining it inwards rather than outwards (11).

Wood

Wood, generally oak or sweet chestnut, is a vital material for the pitched roofs of cathedrals. Unfortunately, it is liable to destruction by fire and decay from fungi and insects. The dimensions of trees available for structure were determining factors in design as specially long members would be required to span cathedral roofs. The timbers in the lantern of Ely Cathedral are probably the largest ever used in the UK, measuring 62×2.5 ft (18.9×0.761 m). If they had to be replaced today, it is probable that such timbers could not be found. The design of trusses overcame the problem of obtaining extra large and long timbers, but even so supply of suitable timbers for the restoration of cathedrals is likely to be an acute problem.

Iron and Steel

Iron and steel were rarely used in cathedrals until the nineteenth century when cast and wrought iron became structural materials. Apart from Norwich Cathedral, which has small iron ties about $\frac{3}{4} \times \frac{3}{4}$ in. (18×18 mm) in the Norman Romanesque clerestory arches, the earliest use, apart from tools and cramps, is also found in Westminster Abbey which has 2×2 in. (50×50 mm) ties linking the capitals in the Early English arcade. Iron was used extensively for cramps and embedded in masonry where tensile stresses were anticipated, as in the dome of St. Paul's where there are five rings of wrought iron and stainless steel. Where exposed, these were found embedded in linseed oil putty which had prevented rusting. However, the rusting of iron ties is a major problem for cathedrals, caused by the increased aggressiveness of the modern polluted industrial atmosphere. Iron has been used extensively as tie bars in windows and for ferramenta, and again the rusting has caused problems solved only by replacing iron with bronze or stainless steel.

Where ancient masonry lacks tensile resistance, stainless steel belts of stranded stainless steel wire in horizontal joints of masonry have provided useful antidotes and prevented structural failure. Two stainless steel chains were inserted in St. Paul's Cathedral during the restoration works of 1921–1925, and 400 stainless steel tension rods were inserted into the foundations of York Minster (1967–1972).

Concrete

Roman mass concrete with brick facings and brick ribs was the forerunner of today's modern reinforced concrete using Portland cement and steel. Whole structures have been made of this relatively new material which is tremendously strong but introduces new problems into building technology, because it is relatively impermeable; produces salts on setting; shrinks and creeps, cracks or crazes if workmanship or design is faulty; and gradually loses its alkaline protection for the embedded steel. Some cathedrals have been built of this material; only time will show whether the decision to use it was correct.

Glass

Glass is an important material in most cathedrals, although some may use translucent stones such as onyx or alabaster to admit light. The whole handling of light is a vital question in the design of a cathedral, as well as interpretation in a restoration scheme. Sir Basil Spence's design for the new Coventry Cathedral suffers on this point because the bright light from the large west window of clear, or white, glass kills the tapestry at the east end and the delightful idea of a progressive spectrum of colored glass windows can only be appreciated by the celebrant; only the Baptistry windows by John Piper are truly effective.

Glass tempers the light that enters a cathedral, and it is this quality of light that affects the whole interior. The handling of light in the Transparente in Seville Cathedral, the Church at Weiss, or Le Corbusier's Ronchamp is masterly. That the nature of the sky-light source differs radically between the Mediterranean and northern Europe, which is so affected by pollution, does not seem to have been appreciated by modern architects. The nature of light affected Gothic cathedral design radically; for this reason, Italian Gothic is different from Northern Gothic. In Italy, windows were small; wall spaces dominated and could therefore be filled with frescoes. In the north, windows were large and filled with painted and stained glass.

Painted and stained glass has its greatest achievements in cathedrals. Outstanding examples are Bourges, Chartres, Canterbury, Strasbourg, and York Minster. Earliest examples date from the eighth century. Generally, the glass was designed in square panels which filled the vertical lights; specially shaped pieces were assembled to fill the tracery. Appropriately, colored glass was chosen and then painted over with black ground-glass powder with lines and hatching to delineate the subject. Each piece was then fired in a kiln until the glass powder fused with the background. Then, the pieces were assembled and leaded with cames soldered together. Early work had cames about $\frac{1}{2}$ in. (12 mm) wide, whereas Victorian work reduced this to $\frac{1}{4}$ in. (6 mm) needlessly, because the visual halation when viewing a stained glass window dissolves the width of the cames. In repairs, fine leads of $\frac{1}{8}$-in. (3-mm) thickness are used; these are virtually invisible at the distance of viewing, at least in a cathedral. Old glass can be crazed, cracked, and pitted and have lost some of its thickness, in which case it is plated with new glass externally and sometimes internally as well. Considering the artistic value of most medieval painted and stained glass, it is amazing that it continues to be displayed in situations where it is subject to decay and even vandalism.

Roofing Materials

In southern Europe, the tradition of tiled roofs was certainly maintained, using either half-round tapered tiles, or larger flat tiles with half-round capping. Glazed tiles were used in Burgundy, Switzerland, and Germany, forming bold patterns in green, red, and yellow on the roofs. In northern Europe, thatch or wooden shingles were probably used and found to be all too vulnerable to fire. Plain tiles replaced shingles, and later in the nineteenth century slates were used. Lead sheets weighing 7 lbs/ft² were common in the UK, which at that time produced at least half the lead in Europe. Generally, lead roofs may last somewhat over 100 years. If maintenance costs are taken into account, a lead roof is one of the cheapest over 100 years of use, provided it is correctly designed and laid.

CAUSES OF DECAY IN CATHEDRALS

Cathedrals are often neglected; it is only when some disaster is imminent or actually occurs that the authorities responsible take action. It needed a "Dangerous Structure" notice to galvanize the Dean and Chapter of St. Paul's Cathedral, London, into action, now known as the Great Restoration (1921–1925), but the district surveyor who served this notice was not thanked for his zeal.

All historic buildings are subject to decay, which is a law of nature; however, by analyzing the causes, decay can be slowed down considerably and neglect can be eliminated. The external causes of decay fall into five categories:

1. *Intrinsic*. Originate in defects in design and workmanship.
2. *Climatic*. Wind, including hurricanes and tornados, rain, frost, ice and snow, dust, and continual change of temperatures which has daily and seasonal variations.
3. *Biological*. Insects, fungi, mold, lichens, algae, plants, and so on.
4. *Disaster hazards*. Fire, lightning, earthquake, and flood.
5. *Man-made*. War, pollution, vibration, vandalism, tourism, and fashion.

Intrinsic causes of decay in a cathedral originate in defects in design and workmanship. The reasons for the collapse of Beauvais Cathedral are debated even today; nevertheless, the daring and skill of the great builders of the past must be respected. They did not possess today's skills of structural analysis, yet they created buildings beyond the powers of such analysis. They were outstanding designers of genius, and the task attracted the great talent available among those who wanted to become neither clerical bureaucrats nor soldiers. Master masons certainly ranked above mere knights in royal favor and patronage; their skills were learned by working with their hands and giving life to stone.

Design involved work on foundations that were often built on difficult ground. The larger the cathedral, the more complex the problems; however, the slow rate of medieval building and the nature of the lime mortar allowed the building to accept quite large deformations and to consolidate its site as the work proceeded. Earthquakes introduced incomprehensible problems for the medieval master masons. They could not understand the complex combination of shock waves that would seek out every weakness in the structure.

Generally, the quality of the workmanship was first-class on cathedrals, as they were prestige buildings paid for by wealthy patrons. Nevertheless, some deliberate malpractices, or at best carelessness, have been found out centuries later, such as coffins used as stone in buttresses of York Minister or a pier with but half a foundation. The quality of workmanship reflects the prosperity of the local community. The cathedral workshops of today can equal the best medieval work and can train apprentices to carry on this tradition unbroken at Cologne, Strasbourg, and York.

Because of their great weight, wind is an abnormal cause of decay in cathedrals. Tall towers and spires will be more subject to strong winds than normal codes of practice stipulate, so at least a 100-year survey period should be used. The spire of Norwich Cathedral suffered severe decay due to wind vibration. Similarly, wind loadings slightly increased the eccentric pressures on the foundations of York Minister when the structure was in a critical condition.

Much damage is caused to cathedrals by faulty design of gutters, which are often behind parapets. Water leaks onto the feet of timber trusses or rafters below, which are then liable to insect or fungal attack, or both. Overflowing gutters and faulty down pipes can lead to many other damages, particularly if they wet a wall with a fresco or cause dry rot in woodwork.

A wanton cause of damage is the trash thrown down or discarded by tourists when they are given access to the upper parts of a cathedral, such as the Dome at Saint Paul's or Central Tower at York Minister. This trash blocks gutters; the cathedral architect, if wise, organizes an alternative rainwater outlet as a safety valve.

The characteristics of rainfall, which can have short periods of great intensity, and the runoff from large areas of the roof are the particular concern of the cathedral architect who should always check the design of rainwater disposal and collection systems, best inspected during heavy rain.

Frost is destructive of masonry unless the material has a hydrophobic pore structure and is strong enough to resist the forces generated when the water freezes. The hazard is increased by the number of freeze–thaw sequences, so temperate climates like the UK may be worse than central Siberia in this respect. Every few years, a very severe frost quickly follows a heavy rain and this can be particularly damaging to porous masonry and roof tiles, even if they have lasted decades without failing.

Snow loads can cause weakened timbers to sag or break. Snow blocks parapet gutters and so causes back flooding. Special wooden shovels are needed for clearance work; these must be kept ready. Snow in melting forms icicles and on refreezing can block rainwater outlets. To overcome these hazards, electric heating wires can be installed. In continental climates where icicles can grow to alarming proportions and be lethal if they fall, it may be necessary to knock them off before they grow, so maintenance access is desirable. Roofs can be designed with a cool underside to minimize this problem.

In Italy, fine dust carried by a sirocco wind from the Sahara is certainly a nuisance as it gets everywhere and rests on ledges and crevices in masonry. In other places, the abrasion caused by windborne particles can accelerate the decay of masonry.

Biological causes of decay are insidious. Picturesque lichens on roof tiles produce acids that destroy gutters by eroding the stone. Algae build up humus, which eventually allows plants to establish themselves in inaccessible places; these plants thrust their roots into the crevices of masonry and in growing expand with incredible strength. Although it is a sign of criminal neglect, it is not infrequent to see a tree growing out of the wall of a cathedral, and ivy is not at all uncommon. Grasses often grow in the humus found in rainwater gutters, which should be cleaned out twice a year.

Chemical sprays can be used to check the growth of lichens and algae as well as plants, but should be used with caution as some may have dangerous side effects.

Insects, especially termites together with anobium and in England and Wales but not in Scotland the deathwatch beetle *Rustofillium xenophobium,* are damaging causes of decay in wood. Termites have extended their territory northwards; some insects have been imported with foreign timber, so zones of different types of insects have been extended. There seems to be incredible indifference to identifying insects accurately by their Latin names and no general assessment of their power for damage. The so-called deathwatch beetle breeds in April and May, and the larvae may live for over 20 years inside historic oak impervious to chemical surface treatments, which have a limited life. A pair may produce 400 progeny. To eradicate insects, their life cycle must be studied. There are risks to the operatives applying chemicals in attempts to destroy insects; some of their chemicals can pollute water supplies; others affect electrical installations or dissolve some plastics.

Some woods, such as Western Red Cedar, Jacaranda, and Acacia, are resistant to insect attack, but it is found that after a given time they lose this resistance due to their natural oils having evaporated and then they are vulnerable. A constant watch against insect attack is needed; if the cathedral cleaning staff is instructed on the signs of insect attack, they may well form a first line of defense.

Cathedrals have shared with humanity the natural disasters that affect a region, floods and earthquakes with the associated dangers of landslides, avalanches, and soil liquefaction. The worst flood was probably in Florence in 1966, but it must be said that Saint Marks, Venice, gets flooded frequently when there is an *aqua alta.* If vulnerable valuables are kept above flood levels, the building generally survives.

Earthquakes are another question. Cathedrals in earthquake-prone zones, being outstanding historical monuments, deserve special studies, which are costly. The risk lies in two causes: structural weaknesses with lack of maintenance, and foundation or ground failure.

The vulnerability must be assessed and in this respect the contents must also be considered. For example, the Cathedral of Saint Tryphon at Kotor in Yugoslavia has a marvelous twelfth-century ciborium over the High Altar: if it were damaged by falling masonry, it would be a tragedy. This ciborium has some antiseismic bracing, which stood it in good stead in the Montenegro earthquake of 1979.

Lightning is best prevented by an adequate installation of lightning conductors, which must be inspected and tested by an expert annually. Bonding of lead roofs and any mass of metal such as bell frames or trusses, together with lateral linkage of all down tapes, should be normal practice. In medieval times, the lack of lightning protection caused so many fires that stone vaults were introduced to minimize the resulting damage. Nearly every cathedral has a long list of burnings.

Study of fires in cathedrals lead to the conclusion that four-hour resistance is desirable in the main structure at least and that there should be a greater reliance on passive measures such as compartmentalization of roof spaces in order to limit the lateral spread of fire. Water sprinklers could be a mixed blessing, as they might cause the vaulting to collapse if much water were trapped in the huge voids formed by the vaults, and water and most sprays could damage wall and ceiling paintings. Halogen gas seems to offer more possibilities, especially if combined with compartmentalization. Flame and smoke detectors are notoriously unreliable in large historic buildings; however, if wired together in triplets, the nuisance of false alarms can be overcome. This is an area where research is needed.

Every precaution must be taken against fire, the most elementary being provision of hydrants, hose reels, and portable extingushers. Cathedral staff should practice the use of extinguishers and there should be semiannual rehearsals with the fire department. Arson in cathedrals is not unknown, so security must be maintained with supervision of danger spots. Strict rules are necessary for workmen using flame; two must work together, each with a portable fire extinguisher, and they must stop work one hour before the supervisor makes a final check. Smoking by workmen, except in a rest room, is a legitimate cause for instant dismissal.

War has been indiscriminate in its damage to cathedrals. Ypres was almost totally destroyed in World War I. In the UK, cathedrals were the specific objectives of the so-called Baedeker raids; Norwich and Saint Paul's were hit, whereas Coventry was destroyed, not to be rebuilt but left as a memorial. Much more damage could be mentioned.

Other man-made causes of decay are atmospheric pollution due to burning fossil fuels, with the exception of natural gas. Although there is much discussion about the actual mechanisms by which pollution destroys stone, there is no doubt that the situation is serious. The only solution is to reduce pollution at its source; this means a conflict with powerful commercial interests. However, both Paris and London have imposed a limit to the sulfur content in oil for central heating plants, a reduction that will undoubtedly benefit their cathedrals. Norwich Cathedral suffered for years from the proximity of the gas works, whose emissions hastened the decay of stone on the north side; there is still a problem from the tarry oils polluting the subsoil.

Damage from vibrations is difficult to distinguish from the natural aging process caused by daily and seasonal thermal movement. Czechoslovakian research claims to prove that heavy traffic can halve the life expectancy of a building. In the case of Saint Paul's Cathedral, heavy traffic on the south side probably aggravated the bulging of the south transept wall and the splitting of stones in the walls and columns so that the decision of London to limit the weight of traffic to 3 tons was most welcome. Damage from vibrations is almost impossible to prove scientifically, as it cannot be isolated from other causes.

Tourism is both a source of money for cathedrals and a cause for decay, not least because visitors wear the floors out and are liable to remove things as mementos. Tourism needs guidance and interpretation, visitors should be given time to appreciate a cathedral; tour operators frequently rush tourists through at an unreasonable speed and the guides jump onto the chairs and shout, which creates an un-cathedral-like atmosphere.

It may seem strange to list fashion as a destructive force in cathedrals, yet much value has been lost due to alterations caused by either religious or archaeological fashions. There is a fashion for modernizing out-of-date religious "plant," which leads to a continuous reordering of cathedrals; this is all very well as long as it is reversible. It was a fashion in the nineteenth century to seek a view of the high altar from the moment the entrance to the cathedral at the west door was reached, so screens and organ lofts were removed to create a vista. This destroyed the sense of mystery in a cathedral and, in the case of Saint Paul's Cathedral, ruined its acoustics, as the choir now sings into the dome.

Work on cathedrals presents a challenge to modern architects because they must respect the structure and yet be brave enough to create something of their own time where appropriate. There are principles and ethics that help to guide this work, which is now thankfully free of revivalism. The principles are contained in the Venice Charter, which emphasizes the need for full documentation before and after any work and insists on authenticity and cultural integrity.

Feilden (12) summarizes the ethics that should guide all interventions to historic buildings as follows:

1. The condition of the building before any intervention and all methods and materials used during treatment must be fully documented.
2. Historic evidence must not be destroyed, falsified, or removed.
3. Any intervention must be the minimum necessary.
4. Any intervention must be governed by unswerving respect for the aesthetic, historical, and physical integrity of cultural property.

Any proposed interventions should be reversible, if technically possible, or at least not prejudice a future intervention whenever this may become necessary; not hinder the possibility of later access to all evidence incorporated in the object; allow the maximum amount of existing material to be retained; be harmonious in color, tone, texture, form, and scale, if additions are necessary, but should be less noticeable than original material, while at the same time being identifiable; not be undertaken by conservators or restorers who are insufficiently trained or experienced, unless they obtain competent advice. However, it must be recognized that some problems are unique and must be solved from first principles on a trial and error basis.

There are several fundamental differences between architectural and arts conservation, despite similarities of purpose and method. First, architectural work involves dealing with materials in an open and virtually uncontrollable environment, the external climate. Whereas the art conservator should be able to rely on good environmental control to minimize deterioration, the architectural conservator must allow for the effects of time and weather. Second, the scale of architectural operations is much larger, and, in many cases, methods used by art conservators may be found impracticable due to the size and complexity of the architectural fabric. Third, and again because of the size and complexity of architecture, a variety of people such as contractors, technicians, and craftsmen are actually involved in the various conservation functions, whereas the art conservator may do most of the treatment alone. Therefore, understanding of objectives, communication, and supervision are most important aspects of architectural conservation. Fourth, there are those differences that are due to the fact that the architectural fabric must function as a structure, resisting dead and live loadings, and must provide a suitable internal environment as well as be protected against certain hazards such as fire and vandalism. Finally, there are further differences between the practice of architectural conservation and the conservation of artistic and archaeological objects in museums, for the architectural conservation of a building also involves its site, setting, and physical environment.

The scale of work on cathedrals imposes certain restrictions with regard to untested experimental innovations and affects decisions as to how much restoration should be done. The cost of scaffolding means that items such as towers and spires are only maintained once in 100 years, whereas lower down, once in 60 years may be the norm. Once in every 30 years should be possible at ground level.

Engineering interventions require the greatest skill in design and a consciousness of the fourth dimension: time. Unless the history of evolution of the structure and its phases are fully understood, serious mistakes can be made. The engineering problems are different from contemporary practice because the cathedral fabric is made from weak materials and is always liable to movement. A full appraisal of any structural distress must be made; it is desirable to monitor movements for several seasons by accurate measurements. Saint Paul's Cathedral has over 50 years of such measurements, which enable the health of the structure to be studied and the continuing downward movement of the dome to be monitored.

Before any intervention is planned, there must be a full inspection of the fabric of the cathedral and a formal report on all visible defects. This duty, which falls to an architect, requires an objective approach; the report must keep observed facts and opinions quite separate. It is a time-consuming task for an experienced professional. The inspection of York Minister took 2000 man-hours and Saint Paul's 1400 man-hours; yet, without this inspection, it is impossible to understand a great building in its totality. It is also necessary to study all previous reports and available literature to achieve this understanding. This visual inspection can lead to further studies and investigation of doubtful or critical points. Foundations should always be checked, but only with archaeologists in attendance. Borings may be necessary to ascertain the structure of the subsoil or to explore the nature of the masonry. The strength of masonry may be tested in situ as a basis of antiseismic studies, if the cathedral is in an area threatened by earthquakes.

The inspection should also be used as a basis of devising a maintenance strategy. In the report, defects should be listed in five categories backed up by approximate estimates:

Immediate. Items causing danger.

Urgent. Items causing rapid decay.

Necessary. Items needed to maintain the fabric.

Desirable. Items needed to improve the fabric.

Keep under observation. Items that should be reported on in the next regular inspection.

Estimates should express the range of doubt by giving a reasonable figure and a pessimistic figure; no one should complain if the actual cost comes out between these two figures. The financing of cathedral maintenance varies from country to country. In countries with bureaucratic centralized structures it is easier to organize the complete restoration than deal with plant growth or blocked rainwater gutters, as there is no political mileage in essential maintenance. The development of a preventive maintenance strategy demands rare skills and can greatly reduce costs; sadly, however, those paying the professional's fee only see what this costs them and not the large sums that have been saved.

The alternative is the laissez-faire approach, which depends on a crisis of sufficient proportions to precipitate gifts from those who care about the cathedral. The giving is to save the fabric. These appeals occur at 15–20 year intervals unless those responsible for the fabric of the cathedral appreciate how much more efficient continuous maintenance on a 30-year cycle can be. A 30-year cycle of maintenance should be followed because it is the duty of the community to hand the cathedral on to their successors in the same or better condition than they inherited.

The system of responsibility divided between church and state has some serious defects, as it aggravates their different approaches to the fabric and can cause sad disasters. Either the representative of the state treats the cathedral as an archaeological site, as at Salerno or Cefalu, or the priest destroys the aesthetic harmony by inserting discordant "plant."

Having analyzed the causes of decay and made a diagno-

sis and proposals, the cathedral architect will suggest a program of repairs and improvements. At this moment, the archaeologist and art historian must be consulted. Often, repairs present unique opportunities for archaeological exploration of the interior, and it is better for the art historian to comment before the event than criticize afterwards. In all of these works, full documentation is essential, which should be a separately budgeted item in all projects.

One of the problems of cathedral archaeology is the fact that numerous burials will be encountered. There is a developing field of medical archaeology, which can contribute greatly by its study of human remains; however, this must be done within the law of the land and customs of the church, both of which will probably be fairly flexible if consulted in advance.

Under the heading of desirable works, the cathedral architect must face the problems of alterations and upgrading of mechanical and electrical services. Here, understanding of the fabric as a structural/environmental/spatial system is essential. Changes can have unexpected effects. Most typically, improvements of heating can increase the vapor pressure internally and lead to condensation in roof spaces, which, in turn, causes the corrosion of metal roof coverings or encourages insect attack.

Inserting new lighting into a cathedral is one of the most exciting architectural tasks, as light that is both scalar and vector can be used like music both to interpret the building and express the liturgy. There are many obstacles to be overcome, such as difficult shadows and strange reflections that could never be envisaged unless work was done with temporary wiring and fine adjustments were made. In general, simple functional, almost industrial, fittings are best because they are efficient.

BIBLIOGRAPHY

1. L. B. Alberti, *De re Adeificatoria,* 1485, English translation by James Leoni, London, 1755–1758.

2. Vitruvius, *Ten Books of Architecture* (translated by M. H. Morgan), Harvard University Press, Cambridge, Mass., reprinted by Dover, New York, 1960.

3. W. Blaser, ed., *Drawings of Great Buildings,* Birkhäuser Verlag, Boston, Mass., 1983.

4. B. Fletcher in J. C. Palmes and co-workers, eds., *A History of Architecture,* 18th ed., University of London Athlone Press, London, 1975, p. 383.

5. J. Gimpel (translated by T. Waugh), *The Cathedral Builders,* Michael Russell (Publishing) Ltd., Wilton, Salisbury, UK, 1983.

6. L. White, Jr., *Mediaeval Technology and Social Change,* Clarendon Press, Oxford, UK, 1962, p. 134.

7. L. Gonse, *L'Art Gothique,* 1890.

8. I. Dunlop, *The Cathedral Crusade,* Hamish Hamilton, London, 1982.

9. L. F. Salzman, *Building in England Down to 1540: A Documentary History,* 2nd ed., Clarendon Press, Oxford, UK, 1967, pp. 56 and 57.

10. *Ibid.,* p. 119.

11. E. E. Viollet le Duc, *Lectures on Architecture,* translated by S. Low, 2 Vols., Marston, Searle and Rivington, London, 1881.

12. B. M. Feilden, *Conservation of Historic Buildings,* Butterworth & Co. (Publishers) Ltd., London, 1982, p. 6.

General References

Refs. 4 and 8 are good general references.

R. Di Sephano, *La Cupola di San Pietro,* Edizione Scientifione Italiane, Napoli, 1975.

J. Heyman, *Coulombs Memoir on Statics: An Essay on the History of Civil Engineering,* University Press, Cambridge, UK, 1972.

M. Charles and F. W. B. Charles, *Conservation of Timber Buildings,* Hutchinson, 1984, p. 47.

D. Knoop and G. P. Jones, *The Mediaeval Mason,* 3rd ed., Manchester University Press, Manchester, UK, 1967.

D. J. Dowrick, *Earthquake Resistant Design: A Manual for Engineers and Architects,* John Wiley & Sons, Inc., New York, 1977.

R. Mark, "The Structural Analysis of Gothic Cathedrals" *Sci. Am.* (Nov. 1972).

"St. Mary's Cathedral, San Francisco," *Archit. Rec.* **150**(3), 113 (1971).

Sir Bernard Feilden, CBE,
FSA, FRIBA, Hm, FAIA
Norfolk, United Kingdom

CAUDILL ROWLETT SCOTT SIRRINE

HISTORY

The architectural firm of Caudill Rowlett Scott Sirrine (formerly Caudill Rowlett Scott) has achieved recognition for its professional managerial style and client-oriented design processes, as well as its buildings. Founded in March 1946 by AIA Gold Medalist William W. Caudill, FAIA, and John Rowlett, the firm has grown into one of the largest architecture, engineering, construction, program management, and project financing firms in the world. Early proponents of the concept of "architecture by team," Caudill, Rowlett, and subsequent founding partners, Wallie Scott (1948), William Peña (1949), Tom Bullock (1954), Edward Nye (1956), Charles Lawrence (1958), and Herb Paseur (1961), were adept at specialization, which gave CRS a strength in diversity from the perspectives of design, management, and technology. Processes and techniques such as "architecture by team," "squatters" sessions, and "problem seeking" methodology were developed and articulated by CRS. These practices have become professional standards and are still an integral part of every CRSS project.

Caudill Rowlett Scott made its mark in the early 1950s by designing innovative schools. The postwar baby boom created a demand for more and better school buildings. CRS brought modern architectural design to educational facilities, supported by innovations through research.

As a graduate student at MIT, founder Bill Caudill wrote *Space for Teaching* (1), the first of 12 books and 80 articles on functional, low cost, energy-efficient school design. While teaching at Texas A&M University (1946–1949), Caudill continued his research effort, investigating school lighting, ventilation, construction, and curriculum. His books intrigued educators and architects by putting forth what were then revolutionary concepts: that schools should be designed around the curriculum and designed for children, with stimulating lighting, air movement, comfort, and color.

Space for Teaching, along with the founders' background in research and education, led to Caudill Rowlett Scott's first educational project, an elementary school in Blackwell, Okla. (Fig. 1). This 1948 design was acclaimed for its many innovations (2). The publicity not only put the fledgling firm on the map, it also gave CRS a speciality, one developed in over 1000 educational facility projects in 26 states and eight foreign countries. CRS's first AIA award winners were for high schools in Norman, Okla. (1954), and San Angelo, Tex. (1959).

The research, innovation, and commitment to "logical" people-oriented facilities, which gave CRS its reputation as one of the leading school architects in the United States, helped it to grow into other markets. The firm grew with children from the postwar baby boom, from elementary and high school projects to junior colleges and universities. Concepts developed in the 1950s for schools, such as open planning, eventually became widely utilized in other institutional and commercial facilities. Diversification led to work in commercial, civic, and manufacturing facilities. In the 1960s, CRS also expanded into the health care market. Responding to each client's needs and environments, CRS designed hospitals as diverse as Desert Samaritan Hospital in Mesa, Ariz., and Yukon Kuskokwim Delta Regional Hospital in Bethel, Alaska.

To fuel its growth both geographically and in service capabilities, CRS became the first architecture–engineering firm in the United States to go from private to public ownership in 1971. The corporate structure gave rise to a family of affiliate companies as a response to CRS innovations in construction management, building systems, and

Figure 1. Blackwell Elementary School, Blackwell, Okla. Photograph by Julius Shulman.

computing services. Most notably, CRS advanced the idea and implementation of fast-track scheduling. Again, this management technique to save both time and expense by overlapping design and construction activities was the by-product of a CRS study and practical project experience.

Growth in the 1970s expanded internationally. The firm's expertise in educational facilities led to a commission to master plan and design the University of Petroleum & Minerals in Dhahran, Saudi Arabia (Fig. 2). CRS leveraged this experience to become one of the leading architecture firms working in the Middle East. Project scopes expanded to include entire campuses and housing complexes, with complete requirements for planning and infrastructure as well as architecture. Throughout the decade, international projects became an increasingly important segment of CRS business.

In 1972, the American Institute of Architects conferred its Architectural Firm Award on CRS, citing it as a firm that has added significant new dimensions to the vitally important design process. Throughout CRSS's history, the design process has been as important as buildings. The approaches and techniques developed by CRS that fostered its growth to international prominence continue to form its philosophical core. The company's most basic belief is that complexities of twentieth-century architecture demand a team approach, one sensitive to human needs and values. Underscoring this concept to produce better buildings is the inclusion of client–users as integral members of the project team. CRSS specialists in design, management, and technology build the team, which may expand to include sponsors from other disciplines as necessary to the success of the endeavor. *Architecture by Team* (3) by William W. Caudill gives insight into the concept and practice of architecture by team at Caudill Rowlett Scott.

"Squatters," a CRSS trademark of intensive on-site work sessions with a client to produce a design, was invented on CRS's first school project as a means to solve a long-distance communication problem. The focused interaction not only improved client–architect communication, it also significantly increased user satisfaction by their having direct participation in settling design objectives. Over the years, the squatters idea has been expanded in both timing and intent. The evolution has taken the idea back in the project timetable to programming, and may occur several times during design, construction documents, move-in, or post-occupancy.

Architectural programming is a process leading to the statement of an architectural problem and the requirements to be met in offering a solution. Like other practices, programming at CRSS involves a high degree of client input, scrutiny, and decision making. CRS pioneered an organized method of inquiry to uncover and define a client's facility needs and design criteria. Characteristically, CRS published the methodology that had been tested over many projects. *Problem Seeking* (4), now in its third edition, by CRSS senior vice-president and founder William M. Peña, FAIA, has become the standard text on architectural programming in colleges and universities nationwide. The process is best understood as an information framework covering a five-step procedure (goals, facts, concepts,

(a)

(b)

Figure 2. (a) and **(b)** University of Petroleum & Minerals, Dhahran, Saudi Arabia. Photograph by Balthazar Korab.

needs, problem) involving four considerations (function, form, economy, time). Based on a combination of interviews for data gathering and work sessions for decision making, the information is graphically displayed by analysis cards and brown sheets. The prelude to good, responsive design, this problem-seeking method of analysis is well suited to any building type.

In 1983, in an effort to further strengthen its technological capabilities, the CRS Group merged with J. E. Sirrine, an industrial and power engineering firm from Greenville, S.C. This, along with other acquisitions, gave the newly formed CRS Sirrine the ability to perform any, or all, roles on any type of construction project, including complete turnkey responsibility.

Today, under the leadership of president and design principal Paul Kennon, FAIA, the architecture group is best known for a wide range of complex, technologically demanding projects. The spectrum includes new research technology centers (the Austin Center/3M, Fig. 3), sports arenas (Carver Hawkeye Arena, University of Iowa), and performing arts centers (Orange County Performing Arts Center). Educational and health care facilities continue to be important design opportunities for the firm.

The 1980s have seen CRSS expand its interior architecture capabilities, specializing in corporate interiors, law firms, and renovation–retrofit work. Consulting services that merge CRSS client-oriented decision-making methods with new technologies play an increasingly larger role in CRSS business. Planning, programming, facilities management, and program management assistance broaden its spectrum of design-support services as CRSS responds to clients' growing complexities in facilities' needs.

The firm has never neglected its commitment to quality design and innovation through research. In addition to the 1972 AIA Firm Award, CRSS has won over 300 awards for design excellence. In 1978, the company formally organized a research department to explore new applications for its growing flexibility. CRSS Research is now headquartered in a "living" laboratory to investigate how the application of technology can facilitate the process of doing knowledge work. The firm calls this "officing."

The evolving design philosophy focuses on three significant forces that shape architecture: people, context, and spirit.

1. *People.* Involving and understanding their aspirations, institutions, activities, program needs, humanistic values, associations, and references.
2. *Context.* Designing for the appropriate fit within an existing environment: the primacy of place—a building is always a part of a larger order of things.
3. *Spirit.* That life-giving quality given by the architect, the conceptual thinking that is transmitted by aesthetic systems for the intangible through the tangible act and transcends to an intangible presence, or formal order that radiates and moves intellectual, physical, and emotional being.

CRSS has evolved in many directions since its inception. From a small two-man specialized practice to a large multifaceted corporation, CRSS has sustained its early values

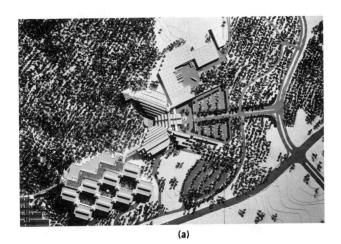

(a)

(b)

Figure 3. (a) and **(b)** Austin Center/3M, Austin, Tex. Photograph by Ralph Smith.

in team concept, problem solving, and humanistic response to facilities. As with the founders' specializations in research, design, engineering, and management, the firm retains a multidisciplinary approach to architecture. Ultimately, CRSS's problem-solving approach to design, using the team concept including the client, may be its most significant contribution to the profession.

BIBLIOGRAPHY

1. W. W. Caudill, *Space for Teaching,* Series No. 59, Vol. 12, Texas Engineering Experiment Station, Texas A&M University, Aug. 1941.
2. W. McQuade, "The Little Red Schoolhouse Goes Modern," *Collier's,* 65 (Sept. 9, 1950).
3. W. W. Caudill, *Architecture by Team,* Van Nostrand Reinhold Publishing Co., New York, 1971.
4. W. M. Peña and co-workers, *Problem Seeking: An Architectural Programming Primer,* 3rd ed., AIA Press, Washington, D.C., 1987.

General References

W. W. Caudill, W. M. Pena, and P. A. Kennon, *Architecture and You: How to Experience and Enjoy Buildings,* Whitney Library of Design, New York, 1978.
C. Estes, "Gaming at CRS," *J. Archit. Ed.* (Sept. 1979).
J. M. Kraker, "CRS Sirrine's Tradition is Change," *Eng. News Rec.,* (June 26, 1986).
C. Lawrence, *Saudi Search,* CRSS, Houston, Tex., 1986.
W. M. Peña, ed., *TIBs of Bill Caudill,* CRSS, Houston, Tex., 1984.
W. M. Peña and S. Parshall, "Squatters Revisited," *Tennessee Archit.* (Winter, 1980).
W. W. Caudill, C. Schorre, and J. Conroy, *From Infancy to Infinity,* Herman Miller Inc. and CRS, Houston, Tex., 1977.
W. W. Caudill, F. D. Lawyer, and T. A. Bullock, *A Bucket of Oil: The Humanistic Approach to Building Design for Energy Conservation,* Cahner Books, 1974.
W. W. Caudill, *In Education the Most Important Number is One,* CRS, Houston, Tex., 1964.
W. W. Caudill, *Toward Better School Design,* F. W. Dodge Corp., 1953.

PAUL A. KENNON, JR., FAIA
CRSS, Inc.
Houston, Texas

CAULKING. See SEALANTS.

CEILINGS

A ceiling is often thought of as a simple plane surface at the top of a room or space. It is, however, much more complex than that. Ceilings are the primary source for air distribution, air return, lighting, fire-protection systems including smoke detectors and sprinklers, public address and music distribution, and acoustic control. Historically, the ceiling has been diligently designed as a major element defining a space; many spaces today deserve the same attention to ceiling design.

CEILING DESIGN

The purpose of ceilings is both visual and functional. The acoustic, mechanical, and electrical items listed above must be properly arranged to perform efficiently, without conflicting with any of the other items. For example, supply-air diffusers are required to distribute a specific volume of air in a space, necessitating a particular pattern of diffusers. Simultaneously, lighting must also be delivered at a specific level evenly throughout the space, requiring a particular luminaire pattern. Both patterns are invariably different, but must mesh in the same plane. Smoke detectors, fire-protection sprinkler heads, return-air grilles, and speakers also require individual patterns for distribution and must share the same plane with the lighting fixtures and supply-air diffusers. In addition to these systems, there must be enough ceiling left to perform the acoustical task required, either sound absorption or prevention of sound transmission to adjacent spaces, and occasionally both. Good ceiling design deals with all of the above issues and in addition presents visually pleasing surfaces. The appearance of a ceiling is important in most spaces, and extremely important in assembly and public areas such as churches, lobbies, and auditoriums.

Mechanical and electrical systems require space within the plenum, which is the space between the ceiling and the structure. It is often desirable to keep the height of the plenum to a minimum, particularly in high-rise buildings or buildings with a large perimeter, because every inch added to the plenum means an additional inch per floor added to the exterior skin, elevators, and fire walls, as well as increased interior-air volume to condition. Careful coordination is therefore required between the design and technical people involved in a building project.

HISTORICAL BACKGROUND

Throughout history, the ceiling has been a major element in the design of an important space, whether that ceiling was a carefully articulated exposed structure, or frescoed or fancifully decorated plaster.

Many Egyptian, Greek, and Etruscan tombs were carved out of rock or, as in the pyramids, were built out of solid stone. The ceiling was generally vaulted, although in the rock-cut Etruscan tomb at Corneto, the stone ceiling was carved to resemble a wood beam structure (1).

The ceilings of Egyptian temples were exposed stone structures consisting of stone slabs spanning a narrow room or supported by stone beams resting on columns. Other Egyptian buildings used brick vaults, either left exposed or plastered, or timber structures (1).

Greek temples generally had wood board ceilings resting on timber beams, which spanned stone architrave beams on relatively closely spaced columns and column rows. Often the wood ceiling was decorated with lacunaria (or coffers) and decoratively painted. In the peristyles, or outer collonades and porches, the ceiling was often of stone slabs carved into coffers (1).

Concrete vaulted and domed ceilings developed by the Romans to create large clear-span spaces in public buildings were frequently decorated with coffers, both as decoration and to reduce the weight of the structure. Smooth vaults were often covered with marble or plaster, which was often shaped into low-relief coffers (1).

The huge brick domes of Byzantine churches were usually covered with marble and richly colored mosaics, which continued uninterrupted over the pendentives, piers, arches, apses, and wall surfaces (1).

The exposed, vaulted stone-roof structure of Romanesque and Gothic cathedrals is one of the greatest aspects of their overall designs. Particularly in the Gothic, the design relied, according to Sir Banister Fletcher, on the "evident truthfulness of its structural features, which . . . are component parts of the artistic scheme." The open timber roofs of English Medieval churches and halls were wonderful combinations of function and beauty (1).

Plastered surfaces probably date back to before recorded history, and were usually used in more humble building types; however, as indicated previously, decorative plaster was used extensively by the Romans. Decorative plaster ceilings with geometrical or pendant designs were used during the Tudor period of English Medieval architecture. Plaster was exploited to its fullest for fanciful and intricate decoration during the Renaissance and baroque periods and was often gilded and frescoed. From then until about the first third of the twentieth century, nearly all ceilings were of plaster.

Acoustical materials did not begin to be applied to ceilings until the early part of this century. Following acoustical research during the last half of the nineteenth century by Joseph Henry, Lord Rayleigh, and Wallace Sabine, commercial companies developed acoustical materials from wood, asbestos fibers, and cork. By the 1930s, prefabricated acoustical panels and tiles were being applied to the ceilings of a wide variety of assembly or otherwise noisy spaces, including churches and synagogues, offices, schools, and gymnasiums (2).

Suspension systems were developed to create a smooth plaster or acoustical panel or tile surface without regard to "messy" structural systems. This was particularly true of cast iron- (and later steel) framed buildings, which were developed about the middle of the nineteenth century. The development of central-ventilation and air-conditioning systems, and all of the metal ductwork thus required, furthered the use of suspended ceilings. Lighting fixtures were designed to fit in suspended ceilings, allowing a smooth ceiling plane. Finally, during the second half of the twentieth century, other building services found their way into the ceiling space, including speakers and paging systems, fire-protection sprinkler systems, smoke-detection devices, pneumatic tubes and other transportation systems, and telephone, power, and computer distribution systems. Without a means of access to all of these pipes, ducts, and wires, they could not all be located in the ceiling. The lay-in acoustical panel ceiling provided complete access at an economical price and today is used in nearly every nonresidential space in the modern world. Most other ceiling systems are a result of a need for a special appearance, or specialized functional or acoustical requirements.

ACOUSTICS

Ceilings generally must either absorb sound or prevent sound from being transmitted to adjacent spaces. Acoustical materials absorb sound by converting the sound energy to heat. Heat is created through friction as the sound waves make the fibers in the material vibrate and rub against one another. Sound absorption is measured in a test that provides the noise reduction coefficient (NRC), which is an average of the material's absorption of sound at frequencies of 250, 500, 1000, and 2000 Hz (hertz) or cycles per second. An NRC value of 1.00 is considered to be equal to that of the open sky, that is, no sound is reflected back into a space. A material with an NRC value of 0.85 absorbs 85% of the sound hitting it. Because human speech is generally in the range of 1000–3000 Hz, sound-absorbent materials utilized to reduce noise generated by people talking should be selected based on their noise-reduction characteristics in that specific frequency range, not just on a simple NRC value. Although some degree of sound absorbency is desired in most spaces, highly absorbent ceiling materials are frequently used in athletic spaces, manufacturing areas, cafeterias, and open office areas.

Sound transmission is reduced by installing a dense material between a sound source and its receiver. The ability of a barrier to stop sound from passing through it is measured in a test that provides its sound transmission class (STC). A material with an STC of 21 will prevent 21 dB from passing through it. As opposed to ceiling materials which absorb sound, sound that is prevented from passing through a material is reflected back into a space and may need to be dealt with by sound-absorbent materials elsewhere in the space. Ceilings with high STC values are generally used to reduce sound transmission between adjacent spaces such as private offices, conference rooms, exam rooms, and classrooms.

Because of the opposite characteristics of soft absorbent materials and dense reflective materials, ceilings with high STC values usually have low NRC values and vice versa. For special situations, there are lay-in ceiling panels composed of both types of materials, which are effective in treating both acoustical problems. In most cases, the use of a space is such that either one or the other type of ceiling material is needed.

CEILING TYPES

Suspended Acoustical Lay-in Panel Ceilings

Suspended acoustical lay-in panel ceilings are, by far, the most frequently used ceiling systems. Panel systems are manufactured to answer nearly every ceiling need, including appearance; acoustical control; fire resistance; abuse resistance; cleanability; and chemical, stain, and grease resistance. Panels are available in a large variety of textures, from mirror-finish metal and plastic overlays to some that resemble a heavy dash stucco; patterns including linear systems and grids; and even a variety of soft colors, fabrics, and real wood veneers. Acoustical lay-in panel systems provide complete accessibility to the plenum and accommodate a broad array of luminaires and air-supply diffusers. Acoustical panels are available with excellent noise-reduction characteristics (high NRC values) or with the ability to reduce sound transmission through the ceiling (high STC values). There is a wide variation in both NRC and STC in the various materials. Each should be closely investigated. Table 1 summarizes most available panel characteristics.

Table 1. Acoustical Panel Ceilings

Materials	Thickness, in. (cm)								Size, in. (cm)								Edges		Fire Rating Available	NRC Range						STC Range				Special Applications				
	1/2 (1.27)	5/8 (1.59)	3/4 (1.91)	7/8 (2.22)	1 (2.54)	1½ (3.81)	2 (5.08)	3 (7.62)	24 × 24 (61 × 61)	24 × 48 (61 × 122)	20 × 60 (51 × 152)	30 × 60 (76 × 152)	60 × 60 (152 × 152)	48 × 48 (122 × 122)	24 × 60 (61 × 152)	30 × 30 (76 × 76)	Square	Reveal	Fire Rating Available	0.40–0.50	0.50–0.60	0.60–0.70	0.70–0.80	0.80–0.90	0.90–1.00	25–29	30–34	35–39	40–44	High Abuse–Impact	High Humidity	Food Service	Exterior Soffits	Chemical or Stain Resistance
Mineral fiber board																																		
Painted	•	•	•	•				•	•	•	•	•					•	•	•				•			•	•	•	•					
Plastic face		•							•	•							•	•	•			•						•	•	•				•
Aluminum face		•								•							•	•	•		•	•							•	•	•	•[a]	•	•[a]
Ceramic		•							•	•							•		•		•	•							•		•	•	•	•
Mineral face		•	•						•	•							•	•	•	•	•							•	•	•	•		•	
Mylar face		•								•							•		•		•							•	•			•		
Cloth face				•					•									•				•	•					•	•					
Wood veneer			•						•									•																
Glass or mineral fiber																																		
Glass cloth face					•	•	•	•	•	•	•	•	•	•	•	•	•	•					•	•	•	•	•							
Vinyl face					•	•			•	•	•	•	•	•	•		•						•	•										
Gypsum	•								•	•							•		•										•				•	
Tectum					•	•			•	•		•		•		•	•	•		•	•									•				
Metal									•	•							•		•				•[b]	•[b]				•[c]	•[c]		•	•	•	
Wood									•								•																	

[a] With vinyl facing.
[b] Perforated metal panel with sound-absorbing pad.
[c] With 28-in. gauge metal or cement asbestos attenuation panel insert in perforated metal panel.

577

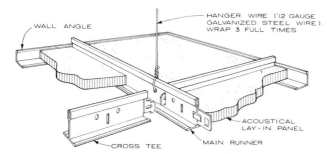

Figure 1. Acoustical lay-in panel-suspension system (3).

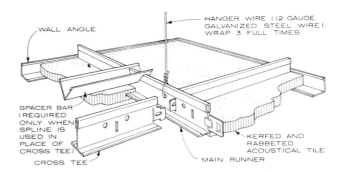

Figure 3. Concealed grid, acoustical tile-suspension system (3).

Lay-in panels are suspended by a grid system (Fig. 1). The most common is an inverted T-bar grid which has a 15/16-in. (2.38-cm) face. Other grids provide special profiles for ease of partition attachment, narrow regressed appearance, or special wide profiles with gaskets for areas such as clean rooms. Suspension systems may be of roll-formed steel or aluminum, extruded aluminum, or fiber glass-reinforced plastic. The module and edge detail of the panel is determined by the grid profile and size (Fig. 2).

Weight carried by the ceiling should be coordinated with the proper grid. Each supplier has tables listing the load limits of each type of suspension system. These should be coordinated with the total weight in mind.

Uses of suspended acoustical panel ceilings include nearly every imaginable type of space where a suspended ceiling is needed.

Suspended Concealed Grid Acoustical Tile Ceilings

Made of mineral fiber in a variety of textures and colors, acoustical tile ceilings are very similar to acoustical panel ceilings, but without the exposed grid (Fig. 3). Plenum access is limited to designated areas unless an accessible grid system is installed to allow the required access (Fig. 4). The individual tiles are generally 12 × 12 in. (30.5 × 30.5 cm), but other sizes are available. They are supported by a kerf (or groove) on all sides that has a steel-suspension component inserted into it. These ceilings accommodate a variety of luminaires and air-supply diffusers. The major advantage to acoustical tile ceilings is the uniform plane-ceiling surface appearance. Therefore, this ceiling type is used primarily in areas where a dominant grid is not wanted, such as lobbies, corridors, private offices, and con-

ference rooms. Acoustical tile characteristics are summarized in Table 2.

Integrated Ceilings

Integrated ceilings are systems of components including ceiling, suspension system, lighting, and air-handling components, which are all provided by one manufacturer (Figs. 5 and 6). The acoustical, mechanical, and electrical performance characteristics of the ceiling have all been engineered and tested as part of an assembly to provide a system that functions at predetermined performance criteria. The components have also been designed to function together aesthetically and to accommodate subsequent changes without damaging or altering the appearance of the system (Figs. 7 and 8). One major advantage of this

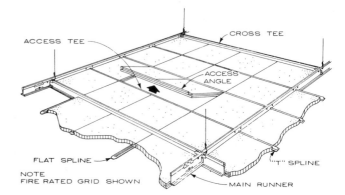

Figure 4. Concealed grid, acoustical tile-suspension system with upward access (3).

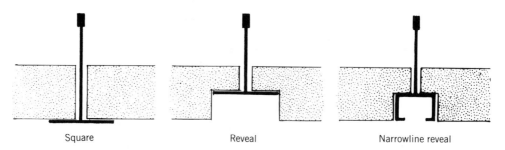

Figure 2. Acoustical lay-in panel-suspension grids and panel-edge configurations.

Table 2. Acoustical Tile Ceilings

Materials	Thickness, in. (cm)			Size, in. (cm)	Edges				Fire Rating Available	NRC Range			STC Range						Special Applications	
	9/16 (1.43)	5/8 (1.59)	3/4 (1.91)	12 × 12 (30.5 × 30.5)	Kerfed and Rabbetted, Square	Kerfed and Rabbetted, Beveled	Tongue and Groove, Square	Tongue and Groove,[a] Beveled		0.50–0.60	0.60–0.70	0.70–0.80[b]	20–24	25–29	30–34	35–39	40–44	45–49	High Abuse–Impact	Food Service
Mineral fiber board	●																			
Painted		●	●	●	●	●	●	●	●	●	●	●	●	●	●	●	●			
Aluminum face				●		●				●	●						●		●	
Mineral face		●	●	●		●			●	●	●							●	●	
Mylar face		●		●		●				●	●					●				●

[a] Tongue-and-groove tiles are usually used for direct glued application or stapled to wood furring strips.
[b] Ceiling tiles with high NRC values usually have low STC values.

579

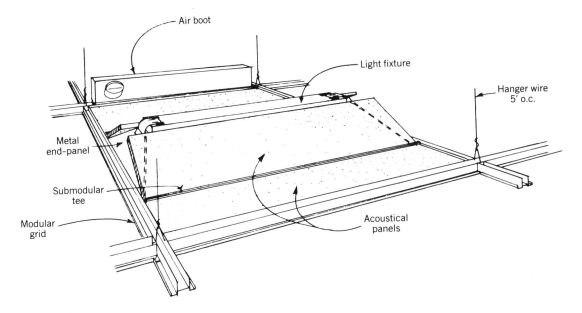

Figure 5. Integrated ceiling suspension-system components (acoustical lay-in panel type). Reprinted by permission of Armstrong World Industries.

type of system is that one supplier has single responsibility for all of these items. Integrated ceilings are generally available in either acoustical panel or linear metal systems; see those sections for more specific information. They are most frequently used in office buildings and schools.

Metal-Pan Ceilings

Metal-pan ceilings are used for cleanability, resistance to humidity, or for the drama of reflective or special-finish metal surfaces. Complete accessibility to the plenum can be provided, and sound absorbency is quite high when perforated panels are used with an acoustical backing. NRC values vary from 0.70 to 0.90, depending on the type and thickness of the sound-absorbing pad and perforation size and pattern. Depending on the manufacturer, individual panels are usually either 24 in. (61 cm) square or 12 in. × 2 ft (30.5 × 61 cm); 3, 4, or 5 ft (91, 122, or 152 cm) long; and scored at 1-ft (30.5 cm) increments to resemble 12-in. (30.5 cm) squares. Metal-pan ceilings may be either lay-in or concealed suspension (Fig. 9). They may be painted steel, stainless steel, aluminum, or specialty-finish metals. Some panels are totally enclosed in metal, others are face panels only.

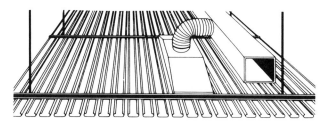

Figure 6. Integrated ceiling-suspension system (linear metal type). Copyright 1983, Alcan Aluminum Corp. Reprinted with permission of Alcan Aluminum Corp.

Figure 7. Integrated ceiling with flat module and rectangular luminaire (acoustical lay-in panel type).

Metal-pan ceilings are most frequently used in lobbies, cafeterias, commercial kitchens, and swimming pools.

Linear Metal Ceilings

Linear metal ceilings are a fairly economical means of providing color, form, or visual interest to the ceiling plane. Linear metal panels are usually roll-formed aluminum in a variety of sizes and configurations clipped to a suspended carrier channel or tee (Figs. 10 and 11). They are

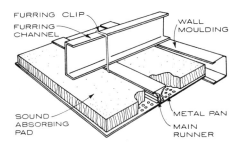

Figure 9. Metal-pan ceiling suspension system (3).

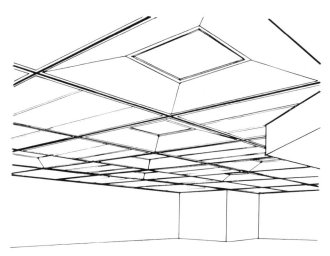

Figure 8. Integrated ceiling with vaulted module and square luminaire (acoustical lay-in panel type).

available in a large variety of colors, as well as bright or brushed chrome, brass, or copper, and may be used to create curved ceilings, either parallel or perpendicular to the panels. Some degree of plenum accessibility is provided by simply removing individual panels, although items that require regular maintenance should be provided with access doors that match the ceiling. Sound absorbency is achieved by means of black sound-absorbing insulation

blankets laid over the ceiling with no filler strips used between panels. Typical NRC values range from 0.70 to 0.90, depending on the type of sound blanket used and space between panels. Panels may also be perforated for higher absorption rates.

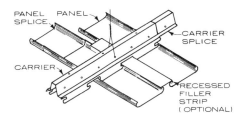

Figure 10. Typical linear metal ceiling suspension system (3).

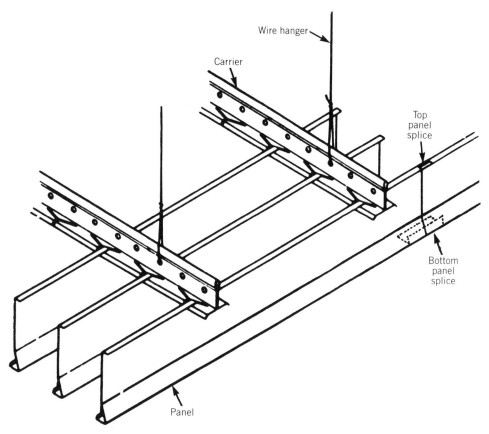

Figure 11. Linear metal ceiling suspension system with vertical panels. Copyright 1984, Alcan Aluminum Corp. Reprinted with permission of Alcan Aluminum Corp.

Because of the strong linear character of the ceiling, particular attention must be given to type and location of luminaires and air-supply diffusers. Most manufacturers have compatible components designed to fit their particular systems; see the paragraph on integrated ceilings. As most systems are made entirely of aluminum, they are suitable for high humidity environments such as swimming pools and exterior canopies and soffits. Linear metal ceilings are typically used in lobbies, transportation facilities, shopping malls, cafeterias, and conference rooms.

Open-Cell Metal Ceilings

Open-cell metal ceilings are suspended open-square or -rectangular aluminum grids used to define a ceiling plane, where the space below is still primarily open to the plenum space above (Fig. 12). Finishes are available in a large variety of standard and custom colors, as well as chrome and polished brass. Air-supply and -return speakers, smoke detectors, and fire-sprinkler systems may be located above the ceiling, without regard to how their locations relate to the finished ceiling's appearance. This is also a cost-saving feature. Everything above the ceiling plane should be painted a dark color. Luminaires may be integrated into the system, and tracklighting systems may be used by installing the track immediately above the ceiling and inserting the fixtures through individual cells into the track. Acoustical control is provided by installing sound-absorption material in the plenum space. Individual cells are usually 3 to 6 in. (7.62 to 15.2 cm) square, and may be as large as 48 in. (61 cm). Variations include rectan-

gular cells and systems in which some grid elements are deeper than the others to develop either a linear pattern or to define small cells within a larger cell. Typical uses include shopping malls, retail stores, transportation facilities, and auditoriums. Being all aluminum, they are also used for exterior soffits and canopies.

Baffles

Baffles are vertically hung metal or fabric acoustical panels, which may be arranged in linear or large grid patterns. Hung below exposed mechanical and electrical systems, they may form an open-ceiling plane by themselves or they may be suspended directly below an acoustical panel ceiling. Baffles can be an excellent acoustical material. Because of the large surface area available, NRC values for the ceiling can exceed 1.0. The product range includes fabric- or perforated vinyl-wrapped acoustical panels, as well as flat or perforated metal systems with special connectors (Figs. 13 and 14). Perforated vinyl-covered, glass-fiber "cushions" with grommetted holes along one edge for hanging are also available for industrial noise control. Typical baffle installations include open-office areas, classrooms, cafeterias, manufacturing areas, transportation centers, malls, and recreation areas.

Luminous Ceilings

Luminous ceilings are generally expanses of ceiling, sometimes an entire room, that provide an even source of illumination. The ceiling plane may be a smooth or molded plas-

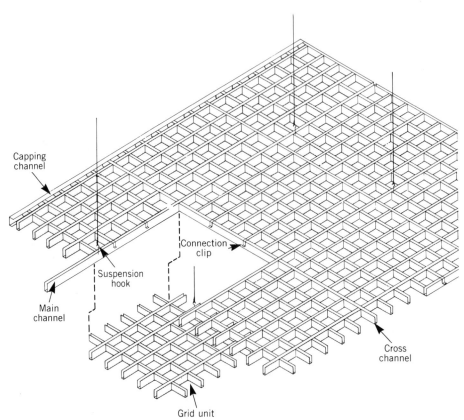

Figure 12. Open-cell metal ceiling suspension system. Courtesy of Forms & Surfaces.

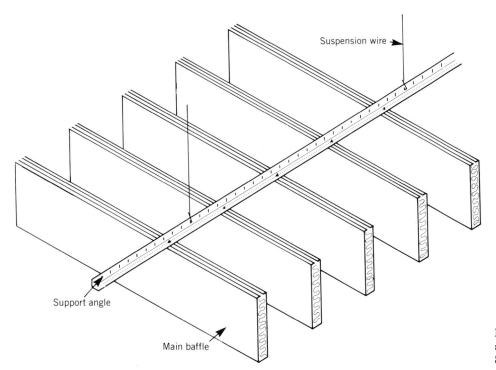

Figure 13. Linear baffle suspension system. Courtesy of Forms & Surfaces.

tic-lens material set within a suspension grid or suspended from special hangers (Fig. 15), suspended aluminum grilles, or a system of metal "leaves" hung from a special suspension system (Fig. 16). Parallel rows of fluorescent lighting fixtures are hung from the structure at a specified distance above the ceiling plane, ie, the spacing of the lamps must not be less than the distance to the lens. Note that lamp spacing and their distance from the floor determines the lighting level. Luminous ceilings have no positive acoustical values; thus, other acoustically absorbent materials may be needed. Luminous ceilings are typically used for dramatic effect in lobbies, retail shops, con-

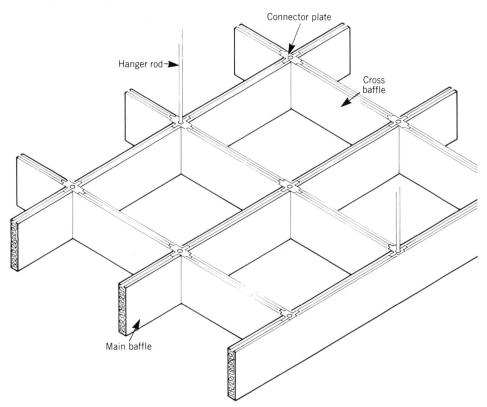

Figure 14. Square baffle suspension system. Courtesy of Forms & Surfaces.

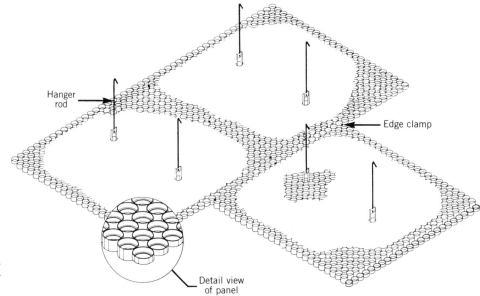

Figure 15. Luminous ceiling, plastic cell suspension system. Courtesy of United Lighting & Ceiling.

ference halls, and large public spaces. Lens and frame systems are also designed to simulate skylights or may be used in small areas such as elevator cabs or residential kitchens.

Wood-Ceiling Systems

There are occasions when wood ceilings are desired to add warmth and texture to a space. Available systems include grilles (Fig. 17), grids (Fig. 18), and linear wood (Fig. 19). Excellent sound absorption characteristics are obtained by means of black sound-absorbing insulation laid over the ceiling or installed in the plenum. Wood ceilings may be adapted to fit a variety of luminaires and air-supply diffusers, and, similar to metal grid ceilings, wood grids and grilles permit air supply and return, speakers, smoke detectors, and fire-sprinkler systems to be located above the ceiling, without regard to how their loca-

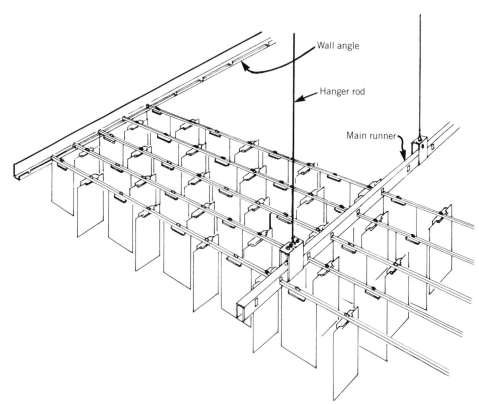

Figure 16. Luminous ceiling, leaf suspension system. Courtesy of Intalite Ceilings, Inc.

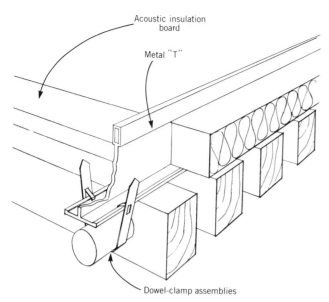

Figure 17. Wood-grille suspension system (Ventwood Registered).

tions relate to the finished ceiling's appearance. Wood grids and grilles may also be used to create a luminous ceiling. The wood may be field-finished, but a factory finish is generally preferred because of the configuration of the pieces. Class I flame-spread treatments may also be required in some locations. Uses include lobbies, dining rooms, cafeterias, conference rooms, and auditoriums.

Suspended Lath and Plaster Ceilings

Plaster ceilings are used where a dense, smooth ceiling is desired and where limited plenum access is required.

Plaster is usually applied in three coats (scratch coat, brown coat, and finish coat) over metal lath attached to a suspended metal-framing system (Fig. 20). The various spacings of hanger wires, runners, and cross-furring channels are all dependent on each other and on the type of metal lath used. Tables are available to establish the required spacings. Access through the ceiling is provided using metal access doors, flush with and painted to match the ceiling. The dense quality of plaster provides a ceiling with a high STC rating, but virtually no sound absorption. Plaster ceilings contribute to the fire retardancy of floor–ceiling and roof assemblies, and have been tested with a large variety of structural systems to provide 1-, 1½-, 2-, 3-, and 4-h fire ratings. If the ceiling is part of a fire-rated assembly, fire-rated luminaires, air-supply diffusers, and return-air grilles must be utilized. When used in large spaces, control joints should be used to divide the ceiling into panels that do not exceed 2400 ft² (220 m²) in area or 60 ft (18 m) in any dimension. Because of its plastic nature and hand-crafted construction, plaster may be used to form almost any conceivable shape of ceiling, including vaults and domes, or for cornice moldings and other decorative shapes and designs. Plaster ceilings are naturally used in restoration projects. Other uses of plaster ceilings include hotel rooms, apartments and condominiums, private offices, lobbies, and other public spaces.

Suspended Gypsum Drywall Ceilings

Suspended gypsum drywall ceilings are similar in use and function to suspended lath and plaster ceilings, but with less durability and density and at a lower cost. Gypsum board is screwed to a suspended system of light-gauge

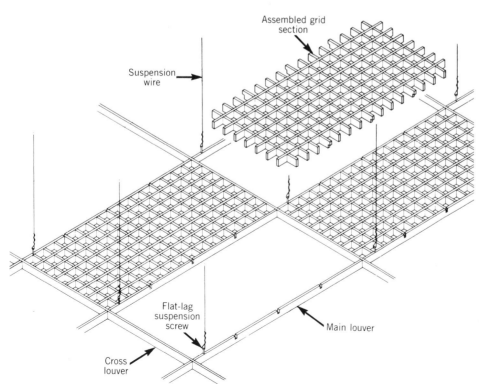

Figure 18. Wood-grid suspension system. Courtesy of Forms & Surfaces.

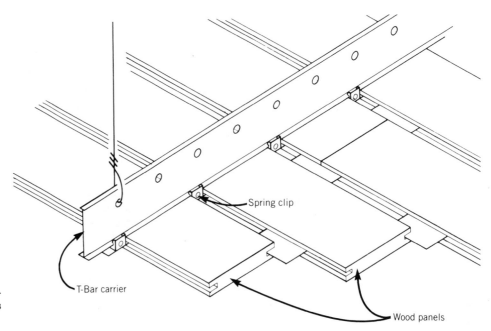

Figure 19. Linear wood-panel suspension system. Courtesy of Forms & Surfaces.

metal framing (Fig. 21). As with gypsum drywall walls, joints are then taped, and joints and screw holes are filled with joint compound and sanded.

As with plaster ceilings, access through the ceiling is with metal access doors. Drywall ceilings also contribute to the fire retardancy of floor–ceiling and roof assemblies, and have been tested with various structural systems to provide 1- and 2-h fire ratings. Control joints should be provided to break the ceiling into panels, with a 50-ft (15 m) maximum dimension where the ceiling has perime-

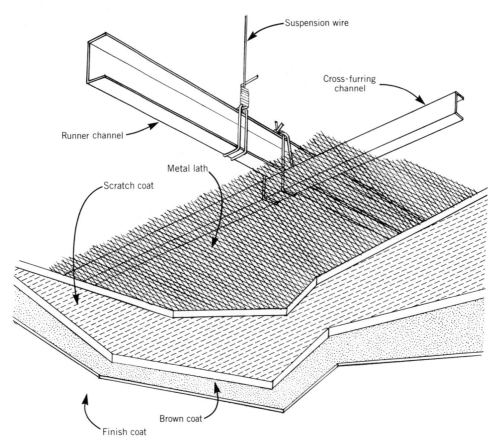

Figure 20. Suspended metal lath and plaster ceiling system. Reprinted with the permission of National Gypsum Co. which owns the copyright.

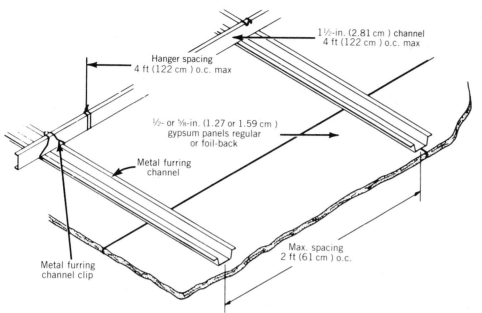

1½-in. (2.81 cm) channel
4 ft (122 cm) o.c. max

Hanger spacing
4 ft (122 cm) o.c. max

½- or ⅝-in. (1.27 or 1.59 cm)
gypsum panels regular
or foil-back

Metal furring
channel

Metal furring
channel clip

Max. spacing
2 ft (61 cm) o.c.

Figure 21. Gypsum drywall ceiling—metal furring channel suspension system. Courtesy of United States Gypsum Co.

ter relief or with a 30-ft (9 m) maximum dimension where there is no relief at the perimeter. Decorative cornices and other special shapes can be added to drywall ceilings by means of glass fiber-reinforced gypsum components. These are factory-fabricated products that are available in a large variety of standard shapes and may also be custom fabricated.

Furred Ceilings

Where there is a limited number of mechanical and electrical services located above the ceiling, the ceiling, usually gypsum drywall, may be mounted on furring strips anchored directly to the structure (generally, wood or metal joists) (Fig. 22). The most frequent use of furred systems is in multifamily residential buildings, although furred systems may also be used in small-scale office or educational buildings.

Exposed Structure

There are occasions when it is desirable to expose the structural system of a building. Large-volume spaces such as church sanctuaries, atria, and exhibit halls frequently have exposed structures. When a ceiling is very high, it is no longer necessarily the best location for mechanical and electrical services and acoustical control. Sometimes a designer simply wants the structure, as well as possibly mechanical and electrical systems, to be a part of the building design.

Exposed-wood structure is well suited to places of worship, small offices and other commercial buildings, park and camp buildings, and residential buildings. The rehabilitation of old timber-framed buildings provides a natural opportunity to use natural wood-beam ceilings.

Exposed concrete structure is appropriate to a variety of building types, including schools, offices, public build-

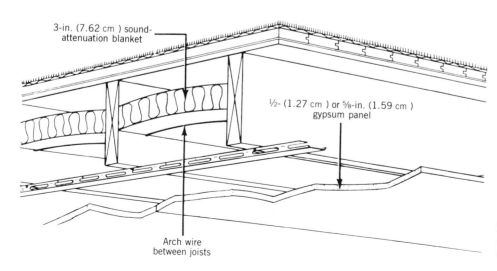

3-in. (7.62 cm) sound-
attenuation blanket

½- (1.27 cm) or ⅝-in. (1.59 cm)
gypsum panel

Arch wire
between joists

Figure 22. Furred drywall ceiling. Courtesy of United States Gypsum Co.

ings, athletic facilities, and churches. Of particular importance in an exposed concrete system is the quality of the concrete finish, which is a direct result of the formwork used.

Exposed-steel structure is restricted in use by building codes to limited functions and/or to a minimum height above the floor. Atria and large athletic and exhibit halls are places where an exposed-steel structure can be used.

With the decision to expose a structural system comes the challenge not only to coordinate the structure with the design, but also to deal with acoustics and mechanical and electrical services in a creative manner. Depending on the size of the space, some of these systems, such as acoustical absorption, air supply and return, and loudspeakers, may be located in the walls. Other systems, such as lighting, sprinklers, and smoke detectors, usually must be ceiling mounted. All of the elements chosen to be exposed must be well organized, and relate to each of the other elements and to the structural system.

BIBLIOGRAPHY

1. B. Fletcher and co-workers, *A History of Architecture on the Comparative Method,* 17th ed., Charles Scribner's Sons, New York, 1963.
2. W. Connelly, *Interior Constr.,* 8 (Dec. 1986–Jan. 1987).
3. C. G. Ramsey and H. R. Sleeper, *Architectural Graphic Standards,* 7th ed., John Wiley & Sons, Inc., New York, 1981, pp. 473–475, 477–479, 484–486, 594–595.

General References

H. Lefer, *Prog. Archit.,* 76 (Mar. 1977).
R. Rush, *Prog. Archit.,* 220 (Sept. 1980).
R. M. Woertendyke, *Corporate Des. Realty,* 82 (Jan. 1986).
C. Olson, *Build. Des. Constr.,* 98 (Feb. 1986).
"Ceilings," *Sweet's Catalog File SD,* Vol. I, Products for General Building and Renovation, Sweet's Division, McGraw-Hill Information Systems Co., New York, pp. 2–57 to 2–84.

Organizations

Alcan Building Products, Division of Alcan Aluminum Corp., Warren, Ohio
American Luminous Ceilings, Cleveland, Ohio
Architectural Products, Nichols - Homeshield, St. Charles, Ill.
Architectural Surfaces, Inc., Minneapolis, Minn.
Armstrong World Industries, Inc.
Celotex, Building Products Division of The Celotex Corporation, Tampa, Fla.
Chicago Metallic Corporation, Chicago, Ill.
Craxton Products, Inc., Minneapolis, Minn.
Decoustics, Rexdale, Ontario, Canada
Donn Corp., Westlake, Ohio
Eckoustic Division, Eckel Industries, Inc., Cambridge, Mass.
Forms & Surfaces, Santa Barbara, Calif.
Gold Bond Building Products, Division of National Gypsum Co., Charlotte, N.C.
Howard Manufacturing Company, Kent, Wash.
Hunter Douglas, Inc., Maywood, N.J.
Intalite Louvers & Ceilings, Inc., Northbrook, Ill.
Levelor Lorentzen, Inc., Lyndhurst, N.J.
National Cellulose Corporation, Houston, Tex.
Owens Corning Fiberglas Corporation, Interior Products Operating Division, Toledo, Ohio
The Proudfoot Company, Inc., Greenwich, Conn.
Rulon Company, Division of CRF Industries, Inc., Souderton, Pa.
Simplex Ceiling, Hoboken, N.J.
Simplex Ceiling Corp., New York, N.Y.
Sound Reduction Corp., Cleveland, Ohio
Steel Ceilings, Inc., Conshocton, Ohio
Technical Ceiling Systems, Inc., Fenton, Mo.
Technical Services, Mitsubishi Chemical Industries America, Inc., White Plains, N.Y.
Tectum, Inc., Newark, Ohio
United Lighting & Ceiling, Architectural Products Division of United Plastics Corp., Oakland, Calif.
United States Gypsum Co., Chicago, Ill.
Vicrtex Division of L. E. Carpenter and Co., Wharton, N.J.

See also ACOUSTICAL DESIGN—PLACES OF ASSEMBLY; ACOUSTICAL INSULATION AND MATERIALS; ACOUSTICS, GENERAL PRINCIPLES; ELECTRICAL EQUIPMENT; MECHANICAL SYSTEMS; OFFICE INTERIOR DESIGN.

F. JOHN BARBOUR, FAIA
Setter Leach & Lindstrom
Minneapolis, Minnesota

CELLULOSE AND CELLULOSE DERIVATIVES

Cellulose is the most abundant of all naturally occurring organic polymers, and probably makes up at least a third of all vegetable matter on the earth. Cellulose is present as paper in books, periodicals, and wall coverings; as textiles in clothing, carpets, upholsteries, and drapes; and as the most important ingredient in the wood of houses, furniture, and art objects. Currently, at least 80% of the natural fibers produced in the world are cellulosic, primarily cotton (1). In addition, it appears in some bacteria, fungi, algae, and lichens. A closely related polymer, chitin, is the important structural unit in the exoskeletons of insects and crustaceans, and in fungi.

At the end of this chapter is a short list of general references for those who want to know more about cellulose. The isolation, analysis, and characterization of cellulose was carried out by the French industrial chemist Anselm Payen (1795–1871) around 1838 (2). The term cellulose first appeared in a report by a committee of the French Academy in 1839 (3). Whether or not Payen coined the word is of little consequence, since he is credited with the discovery of cellulose.

CHEMICAL STRUCTURE

Cellulose is known to be a polymer of anhydroglucose units, ie, a chain of glucoses from which molecules of water have been removed to form the linkages between the original glucose units. The conventional written structure is shown in Figure 1a. The brackets enclose what is known as the repeating unit, composed of two glucose units, one of which is facing up and the second of which is facing down. The third unit added to the right side would face up, and the fourth would face down, etc.

This molecular structure depicts two of the important chemical aspects of cellulose: the acetal linkage between the glucose rings, and the presence of the three hydroxyl (OH) groups that furnish the chemical reactivity of the molecule. However, it is necessary to look at the molecule in three dimensions. Figure 1b is a view of this three-dimensional conformation. Notice that the individual rings are not planar, but are buckled in what is known as the chair configuration. To further understand cellulose, it is necessary to look closely at the acetal linkage between the glucose rings. Consider that one of the carbon atoms that is connected by the oxygen in the acetal linkage is optically active; ie, it is connected to four different groups: another carbon, a hydrogen, the oxygen in the ring, and the oxygen in the ether link. This configuration implies the existence of an optical isomer that bears the same mirror-image relationship to the original as a left glove does to the right. Figure 1c shows the linkage as it exists in cellulose, known as the beta link; Figure 1d shows the isomeric linkage that appears in the starch molecule that also contains two glucose rings connected by the acetal

linkage known as the alpha type. This difference in linkage causes profound differences in behavior (4,5).

Fine Structure

The beta connection in cellulose allows the chain to grow in an approximately straight line, and the chair conformation of the ring places the functional OH groups along the side of the chain so that they are readily accessible to similar OH groups in adjoining chains. The H atoms in these OH groups can then form hydrogen bonds with the electron pairs of the oxygens, either in the ring or in another OH group in the adjoining chain. The symmetry of the chains allows a large number of such matchings, and although the hydrogen bond is relatively weak compared to a covalent C–C bond, the total force developed is enough to hold the chains together.

The alpha connection in the isomorphic starch molecule causes the chain of glucose units to assume a spiral configuration that prevents the formation of large numbers of hydrogen bonds in starch, and thus prevents the formation of useful fibers.

In cellulose, the hydrogen bonds between adjoining chains can form agglomerates of these chains, and if these are orderly enough, oriented in the same direction, and densely packed, they may be classified as crystallites because they exhibit some of the properties of crystals. The

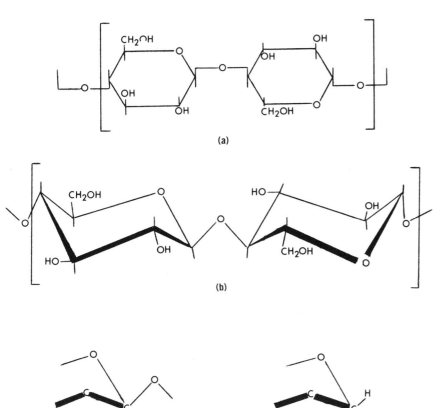

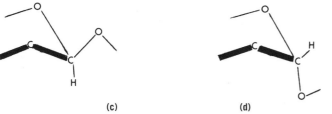

Figure 1. Chemical structure of cellulose: (a) conventional written structure; (b) three-dimensional configuration; (c) beta linkage in cellulose; and (d) alpha linkage in starch.

noncrystalline areas are called amorphous. There is no sharp, well-defined separation between crystalline and amorphous, but the ratio is used as a quantitative characteristic of fibers. For example, native cotton fibers are considered to be about 70% crystalline. Wood pulp fibers are thought to be about 65%, and rayon, made from regenerated cellulose fibers, has about a 40% crystalline content (6).

The length of the cellulose chain is usually reported as the degree of polymerization (DP), or the number of monomer units connected to form the polymer chain. Native cellulose, such as in cotton, has been shown to contain about 10,000 glucose units in a chain. Harvesting, ginning, and further purification reduce this to about 2000–3000 in ordinary cotton cloth. Rayons contain about 300–500 units in their molecules. Ancient cotton fabrics, as old as 1000 years, have DPs of about 200, which seems to be the lower limit for fibers that still maintain some shape (7).

Gross Structure of Fibers

Natural cellulosic fibers appear in various parts of the plant. Cotton, kapok, and milkweed are seed hairs; flax, hemp, jute, and ramie occur in the stems and are known as bast fibers; and abaca (Manila hemp), raffia, and sisal are obtained from the leaves of the plant.

All of these fibers exist as hollow tubes. In cotton and ramie, the length of these single cells varies from about 12 to 250 mm. All of the other species mentioned produce hollow tubes of much shorter length, and in most cases, these short tubes are cemented together in aggregates by plant resins similar to lignin. The hollow space in the center of the fiber is called the lumen and is characteristic of all cellulosic fiber. The familiar bast and leaf fibers are actually several ultimate cells assembled into a useful length; the harvesting and purification methods allow for the control of this length.

In wood, the cellulose tubes are very short and covered by a matrix of lignin containing other related polymers. The cellulose (about 40% of the total wood) cannot be freed from the matrix without separating the fibers into the ultimate cells that vary in length from about 1 to 8 mm.

The approximate dimensions of the cellulosic fibers mentioned previously are given in Table 1. More information on these and other fibers will be found in Ref. 8.

Table 1. Approximate Dimensions of Natural Cellulosic Fibers

Fiber	Ultimate Cell		Composite Fiber	
	Length, mm	Width, μm	Length, cm	Width, μm
Abaca	3–12	12–46	180–450	10–280
Cotton	12–64	12–25	none	none
Flax	4–66	12–76	20–150	40–620
Hemp	5–25	15–50	100–300	
Jute	1–5	10–25	150–350	30–150
Kapok	10–30	10–30	none	none
Ramie	50–250	15–125	10–200	60–9000
Sisal	1.5–5	15–30	75–120	100–450

Man-Made Cellulosic Fibers

The cellulose-based fiber rayon, the first commercial man-made fiber, was pioneered in 1891–1892. Pure cellulose is solubilized by reacting it with carbon disulfide and sodium hydroxide. The resulting solution, called viscose, is extruded through spinnerets into a dilute acid bath that coagulates the cellulose xanthate, decomposes it, and regenerates the cellulose. The fiber is stretched to align and orient the molecules, and produce the necessary crystalline regions. Today, there is renewed interest in versions that are more environmentally acceptable.

The three OH groups, which are the chemically active sites on the cellulose molecule, make it react like an alcohol. This means that acids under the proper conditions will react with cellulose to produce esters. The most common ester, and the only one having usage as a fiber, is the acetate, formed from cellulose, acetic anhydride, and a trace of sulfuric acid. It is possible to substitute some or all of the three available OHs on the cellulose with the acetate group. The first acetate produced in the early 1900s had about 83% of the hydroxyls substituted. This fiber is generally referred to as secondary acetate. In 1954, the so-called triacetate fiber, in which at least 92% of the hydroxyls were acetylated, became a commercial success.

Like all man-made fibers, including viscose rayon, acetate fibers are infinitely long, or filaments, as opposed to the short or staple natural cellulose fibers.

INDIVIDUAL CELLULOSE FIBERS

Cotton

About six billion pounds of cotton fiber is harvested each year in the United States, making it an important fiber (9–12).

With the exception of kapok, cotton is the only seed hair to be used in ordinary consumer products. The fiber is a single cell that gradually tapers from its root at the seed to its tip, for a distance of 12 mm for short, coarse cottons, to 64 mm for long, fine cottons. The cell is circular in cross section when it is alive and developing, but when it is harvested and dried, the hollow tube collapses so that the cross section is kidney shaped, with the prominent lumen, or hole, in the center (Fig. 2).

When a cotton fiber is viewed longitudinally under low magnification, it can be readily recognized and easily distinguished from other cellulosic fibers because of its twisted or convoluted shape (Fig. 3). Although other fibers have a visible lumen, none of them twist and turn like cotton.

The overall composition of the fiber is at least 95% cellulose, the remainder being small amounts of protein, pectins, and wax.

The relatively high crystallinity and the presence of strong hydrogen bonds in cotton make the fiber a moderately strong one, with a tenacity of about 2–5 g per denier. Tenacity is the breaking load expressed in grams per unit of linear density, an approximation of diameter. The most

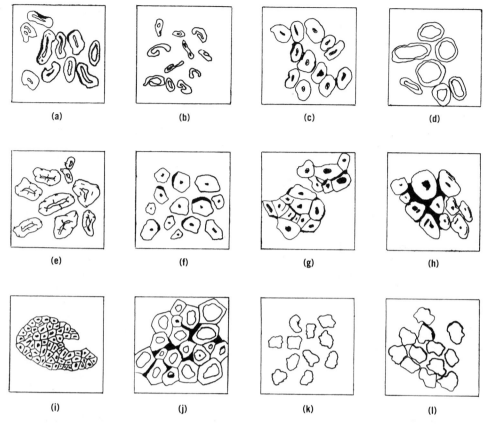

Figure 2. Cross sections of cellulosic fibers: **(a)** raw, mature cotton; **(b)** raw immature cotton; **(c)** mercerized cotton; **(d)** kapok; **(e)** ramie; **(f)** flax; **(g)** jute; **(h)** hemp; **(i)** sisal; **(j)** abaca; **(k)** viscose; and **(l)** acetate.

useful unit of linear density for fibers is denier, defined as the weight in grams of 9000 m of fiber or yarn.

Water is adsorbed in quantities up to 8% by weight in standard humidities. The adsorbed water causes wet fibers to have higher breaking strengths but lower recovery from distortions such as wrinkling. At 65% rh, cotton has a breaking elongation of about 7–8%, and an elastic recovery of only about 75% after 2% stretch.

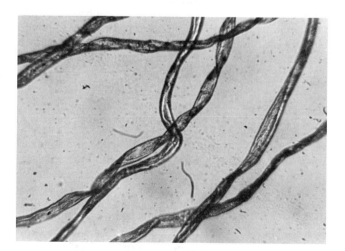

Figure 3. Longitudinal view of cotton fiber.

For a fiber, cotton has a relatively high specific gravity of 1.54 and readily conducts heat, so that cotton fabrics feel relatively heavy but cool to the touch. Its ability to absorb water makes it a popular fiber in moist conditions, and the moisture reduces the possibility of static buildup in the fabric.

Like all cellulosic fibers, cotton decomposes at about 300°C and ignites at about 400°C. Other conventional apparel fibers decompose in the range of 230–400°C and ignite at 400–600°C. It can be treated readily to prevent propagation of ignition beyond the starting point, ie, it can be made flame retardant.

Exposure to sunlight, particularly the shorter uv wavelengths, causes very slight direct photolysis, but does promote oxidation in the presence of moisture and heat, and of course, oxygen.

Cellulose resists attack by cold dilute acids, but is destroyed by hydrolysis with hot dilute acids or cold concentrated acids. The chain is disrupted by the hydrolysis of the acetal link to produce separate glucose residues with their original hydroxyl groups.

Alkalies have very little degrading effect on cellulose in the absence of oxygen. Strong sodium hydroxide has a beneficial effect on cotton known as mercerization that swells the fibers so that their cross-sectional shape is more circular. This swelling makes the yarn or fabric slightly stronger and much more lustrous, and causes the fibers to dye more evenly.

Cellulose is attacked by fungi and bacteria. The stains produced by mildew on cotton fabrics are a common annoyance. Most microbiological attacks on cotton seem to be promoted by the presence of more acceptable foods for the microorganisms such as starch, glue, or food stains (13).

Most insects do not harm cotton unless it presents a barrier to their passage, but roaches and silverfish will consume cotton if it is contaminated with other foods.

Kapok

Kapok is the only other seed fiber of commercial value. Although some of the fibers may be as long as 32 mm, they are too brittle to spin into yarns, and so are not used for making fabrics. The fibers are very lightweight and thin walled, and have large lumens. They are used for the padding and stuffing of upholstery, and for filling life belts or other floating marine equipment (10).

Ramie

Ramie, also known as China grass, is obtained from the stalk of a perennial plant that grows as high as 2 m. The individual cells, which are as long as 250 mm, are freed from the stalk by first removing the bark and then soaking the inner part of the stalk in dilute caustic solution. A great deal of scraping and manipulation is required to finally rid the fiber of gum and other surrounding materials. The resulting cells are stiff and fairly coarse, but have been used in clothing in the East and in Europe for many thousands of years (10,11).

Flax

Flax is probably the oldest textile fiber known. It is derived from the inner bark of an annual plant that grows to about 1.5 m in height. The fibers are freed from the stalk by a fermentation process known as retting, after which the woody core is mechanically removed (scutching) and the long, slender, thick-walled groups of cells are separated by combing (hackling). The resulting composite fibers (Table 1), which may be as long as 150 cm, are composed of many shorter ultimate cells. The fibers do not show any of the convolutions that are so characteristic of cotton. Probably the most characteristic feature of the cells is the squared-off or polygonal appearance of their cross sections (Fig. 2) (10,11).

Because the flax fiber is practically 100% cellulose after it has been purified, it has many of the same properties as cotton. The specific gravity is 1.54. The fiber is slightly stronger than cotton; it has a tenacity as high as 7 g per denier. Its breaking elongation is a little less than 2% dry, and therefore, it is classifed as a stiff fiber.

Linen fabrics made from flax fibers have very good heat transmission and are well known for their cool feel. Their high moisture regain makes them comfortable for clothing in warm, moist climates.

As one would expect from its cellulose content, flax undergoes the same chemical and biological reactions as cotton.

Modern interest in linen seems to be restricted to a small amount of imported clothing, much of which is made of linen–polyester blends, to household items such as drapes and napery, and particulary to towels used for drying, as the fiber does not leave lint.

Jute

Jute is a bast fiber that has been grown in very large quantities for thousands of years; it is an annual plant with a height of 7 m. It is probably the second largest fiber crop in the world after cotton (10,11).

The fiber is freed from the plant in the same manner as flax. Individual cells are too short for any kind of processing, so the fiber is always used in the form of long composites containing as much as 20% lignin by weight as a natural binding agent.

Jute fibers are stiff and have very low elongations, so that yarns and fabrics known as burlap have good dimensional stability, and are desirable for sacks and for backing fabrics for carpets. Because the fibers are stiff, spinning is difficult; it is not unusual to add as much as 5% oil to make them more flexible.

Although the cellulose in jute has the same chemical resistance as cotton, the 20% of binding agent, lignin, does not, and burlap fabrics can be easily destroyed by alkaline materials that reduce the composites to very short, useless single cells.

Cross sections of jute show polygonal cells in groups, each cell having an obvious lumen that is usually larger than those in hemp, which has a very similar cross section (Fig. 2).

Hemp

Hemp is also a bast fiber, closely resembling jute in its physical characteristics. The fibers are freed from the woody residue by the same methods used for flax and jute. Like jute, the hemp-fiber composites contain much lignin and are, therefore, stiff and have low elongations (10,11).

In the cross-sectional view, hemp appears quite different from jute if the viewing is done patiently. The major difference is in the appearance of the composites, which have prominent lumens in jute and more diffuse ones in hemp. Also, individual hemp cells, not in composites, have lumens approaching those of cotton in appearance (Fig. 2).

Sisal

Sisal is a fiber derived from the large leaves of the Agave species of cactus or century plant indigenous to Central America. Mechanical beating and scraping are sufficient to remove the woody portion of the leaf and free the composite fibers which may be as long as 120 cm. The ultimate cells of sisal are about 2.5 mm long on the average and are of little value as single fibers. The composites, like those in the bast group, are held together with natural gums and lignin. These binders can be attacked by chemicals and water, but the remaining fibers are cellulosic and have the same properties as other fibers containing cellulose (10).

Sisal is used primarily in the manufacture of cords and twine in the United States. The cross section is unusual in that it has C-shaped sections of composites containing a relatively large number of ultimate cells.

Abaca

Abaca or manila, sometimes called Manila hemp, is the the cellulosic fiber from the leaves of a plant closely related to the banana; it is derived by scraping away the pulpy portion of the leaf. The resulting fiber composites may be as long as 4.5 m (10).

Abaca is used for rope, cordage, and twine in the United States. Cross sections show that abaca generally has cells with thinner walls and much larger lumens than sisal, hemp, and jute.

MAN-MADE CELLULOSIC FIBERS

Rayon

The cellulosic man-made fibers, like all other manmades, are infinitely long filaments upon manufacture; the filaments can be cut or broken into shorter fibers on demand. Using ordinary methods, they are capable of being spun into fibers with cross-sectional areas about the size of cotton, about 1.5 deniers (10–12).

The most common kind of rayon is viscose, made through the intermediate cellulose xanthate from which cellulose is regenerated in acid. The resulting fibers have breaking tenacities up to 7.5 g per denier (12) for those fibers that are most crystalline, most highly oriented, and that have the highest DPs. Those fibers with low crystallinity, low orientation, and low DPs have breaking tenacities of about 3 g per denier, but have higher breaking elongations—35% compared to about 15% for the stronger fibers. Because viscose rayon is less crystalline than cotton, it will generally have a higher moisture content.

The cross sections show a shriveled skin, which can be assumed to be characteristic of most of the fibers that are wet spun, ie, spun from solvents or into a solution such as viscose.

Cellulose Acetates

There are two recognized names for these fibers: cellulose acetate and cellulose triacetate, or simple acetate and triacetate. Both are derived by substitution of the OH groups of cellulose by the acetate group, CH_3COO. The acetate fiber, sometimes called secondary acetate, has about 2.5 of the hydroxyl groups replaced, whereas in the triacetate fiber, virtually all three are converted to the acetate (10–12).

Both fibers have tenacities of about 1.5 g per denier, and breaking elongations of about 40%. Both fibers are very lustrous and have specific gravities of 1.32. The main differences are solubility and thermal characteristics. Acetate dissolves in acetone but historically newer and more expensive solvents such as methylene chloride are required to dissolve triacetate. Acetate melts at about 260°C and triacetate at about 300°C. Acetate picks up about 6.5% moisture at standard conditions, triacetate about 3.0%. The acetate fiber is widely used in lingerie and robes, the triacetate in more formal clothing. The major difference is in the ability of the triacetate to be heat-set, ie, annealed so that it has excellent recovery from wrinkling. Acetate fibers have good resistance to sunlight.

IDENTIFICATION

None of the natural cellulosic fibers will melt when a tuft of fibers is held near to a flame. The fibers will ignite and continue to burn if the igniting flame is removed. The burning fibers give off a characteristic odor with which most people are familiar. The acetate fibers will melt, ignite, and continue to burn, and will have a characteristic odor different from that of pure cellulose (14,15).

Acetate and triacetate, but not the other cellulosic fibers, will dissolve in 85% formic acid at room temperature. Acetate, but not triacetate, will dissolve in acetone.

Distinctions between the natural cellulosic fibers can best be made by microscopic examination (15,16). Figure 2 shows some sketches of the prominent characteristics of cross sections of the various fibers that will help in making these distinctions.

DYES

Natural cellulosic fibers and rayon can be readily dyed with a number of dye classes. Direct dyes are attached to the cellulose chain by hydrogen bonds. Fiber-reactive dyes form covalent links through the hydroxyl groups. Vat and sulfur dyes are applied in the reduced, water-soluble state and are allowed to penetrate the fiber. They are then oxidized to the water-insoluble condition inside the fiber where they become durable. Azoic or naphthol dyes are formed inside the fiber by the reaction of two water-soluble reagents that produce a colored, water-insoluble product. Cellulosic fibers can also be colored using pigment-binder systems (11).

Acetate and diacetate fibers can be dyed using disperse dyes. Selected direct and acid dyes may also be used in special cases. Addition of pigments or special dyes to the spinning solution of these cellulose derivatives leads to colored fibers with excellent colorfastness.

FIBER ASSEMBLIES

These fibers are normally of little use as single fibers or as unorganized masses, so they are assembled into some kind of structure that can be used to produce an object such as a drapery, an upholstered seat, or a carpet. The simplest of these useful structures is a mass of fibers entangled with each other such as a felt or a nonwoven sheet. Occasionally, short or staple fibers may be assembled into a parallel, untwisted rope called a sliver that can be incor-

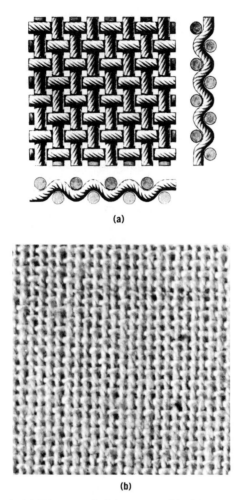

Figure 4. (a) Diagram of plain weave; (b) plain weave fabric (17).

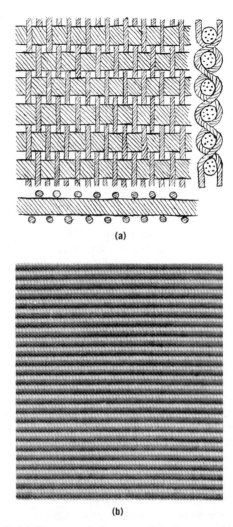

Figure 5. (a) Diagram of rib weave; (b) rib weave fabric (17).

porated into a knitted fabric to produce a fleece or fur-like surface useful for clothing or decoration. Most of the short fibers produced in nature and by breaking or cutting the man-made filaments are carefully twisted into uniform structures known as yarns.

Yarns produced by twisting staple fibers such as cotton or flax are called spun yarns. Those produced by twisting filaments are known as thrown yarns. In either case, the yarns are then assembled into fabrics, usually by weaving; weaving involves two sets of yarns that are interfaced at right angles to each other. The warp yarns, which run the length of the fabric, are arranged according to some plan and the filling yarns, which run from side to side, are then inserted one at a time. The arrangement of the warp yarns, which can change with each filling insertion, as well as the size of the yarns involved, produce a characteristic pattern (Figs. 4 and 5).

Yarns may also be assembled into fabrics by knitting, which involves pulling a loop of yarn from the middle of a continuous piece and from the organized entanglement of this loop with the same or with another yarn.

Although natural fibers have gradually given ground to man made replacements, cellulose remains a dominant fiber in the environment. Its fibers, yarns, and fabrics contribute to the beauty and comfort of living and working spaces.

BIBLIOGRAPHY

1. *Text. Organon* **55** (11), 213 (Dec. 1984).
2. E. Farber, ed., *Great Chemists,* John Wiley and Sons, Inc., New York, 1967, p. 497.
3. A. Brogniart, M. Debuze, and A. B. Dumas, *C. R.,* **8,** 51 (1839).
4. J. Blackwell, F. J. Kolpak, and K. H. Gardner in J. C. Arthur, Jr., ed., *Cellulose Chemistry and Technology,* American Chemical Society, Washington, D.C., 1977, pp. 42–55.
5. J. Blackwell in R. M. Brown, Jr., ed., *Cellulose and Other Natural Polymer Systems,* Plenum Publishing Corp., New York, 1982, pp. 404–417.
6. F. Happey in F. Happey, ed., *Applied Fibre Science,* Vol. 1, Academic Press, Inc., Orlando, Fla., 1978, p. 13.
7. G. M. Berry, S. P. Hersh, P. H. Tucker, and W. K. Walsh in J. C. Williams, ed., *Preservation of Paper and Textiles of Historic and Artistic Value,* American Chemical Society, Washington, D.C., 1977, p. 237.
8. M. Harris, ed., *Handbook of Textile Fibers,* Harris Research Labs, Inc., Washington, D.C., 1954, pp. 37–41.

9. M. L. Rollins in D. S. Hamby, ed., *American Cotton Handbook,* 3rd ed., Vol. 1, Wiley-Interscience, New York, 1965, pp. 44–81.

10. J. G. Cook, *Handbook of Textile Fibres,* Merrow Publishing Co., Durham, UK, 1984.

11. H. L. Needles, *Handbook of Textile Fibers, Dyes, and Finishes,* Garland Publishing, Inc., New York, 1981.

12. M. E. Carter, *Essential Fiber Chemistry,* Marcel Dekker, Inc., New York, 1971.

13. J. A. Gascoigne and M. M. Gascoigne, *Biological Degradation of Cellulose,* Butterworth & Co. (Publishers) Ltd., Kent, UK, 1960, pp. 207–215.

14. *Identification of Textile Materials,* 7th ed., The Textile Institute, Manchester, UK, 1975.

15. *Technical Manual,* Test Method 20, American Association of Textile Chemists and Colorists, Research Triangle Park, N.C., 1984, pp. 81–103.

16. J. W. Weaver, ed., *Analytical Methods for a Textile Laboratory,* 3rd ed., American Association of Textile Chemists and Colorists, Research Triangle Park, N.C., 1984, pp. 29–33.

17. D. S. Lyle, *Modern Textiles,* 2nd ed., John Wiley & Sons, Inc., New York, 1982.

General References

D. S. Hamby, ed., *American Cotton Handbook,* Vols. 1 and 2, Wiley Interscience, New York, 1965 and 1966.

N. M. Bikalis and L. Segal, ed., *Cellulose and Cellulose Derivatives,* John Wiley & Sons, Inc., New York, 1971.

R. M. Brown, Jr., ed., *Cellulose and Other Natural Polymeric Systems,* Plenum Publishing Corp., New York, 1982.

T. P. Nevell and S. Haig Zeronian, eds., *Cellulose Chemistry and Its Applications,* John Wiley and Sons, Inc., New York, 1985.

J. W. WEAVER, PHD
University of Delaware
Newark, Delaware

CERAMIC TILE

The use of ceramic tile as a construction material cannot be properly understood or appreciated without a good knowledge of the chemistry and physics of materials. All materials may be classified into one of three groups: the metals, the oxides of the metals, and the organics or compounds of carbon. Ceramics is the field of the oxides.

Each of the three main classes of materials has distinct and characteristic properties that set it apart from the other classes and make it unique. The metals are characterized by such physical properties as ductility, high strength in tension, moderate hardness, high modulus of elasticity, and resistance to impact. Chemically, they have moderate to low resistance to acids and alkalies and the chemical agents of weathering such as oxygen, carbon dioxide, and water. Ceramic materials, on the other hand, are brittle and rigid and have only moderate strength in tension but a high resistance to compression, low creep characteristics, and high scratch hardness. Chemically, they have high resistance to the action of water, acids, and alkalies (except hydrofluoric acid). Ceramic materials have low interfacial tension with water and hence are readily wet and easily cleaned with water solutions. Ceramic materials have high melting points and high softening points and are resistant to the action of high temperatures and oxidation (burning). Organic materials are characterized by such physical properties as softness, low scratch resistance, low tensile and compressive strength, and pliability. Chemically, they generally have moderate resistance to chemical action and water vapor, but not to organic solvents. They are not easily wet with water and require detergent action. They are not resistant to high temperatures or to high-temperature oxidation.

The term ceramics comes from the Greek *keramos,* meaning "burnt stuff." The ancient Greeks applied the term to metals as well as ceramics, for they also were products of fire. Gradually, because of their distinct properties, the metals were recognized as a separate class, and the term *keramos* referred to fired clay products. The modern term ceramics has a much broader connotation and now refers to such materials as glass, refractories, porcelain enamel, abrasives, and cements as well as pottery, porcelain, tile, brick, and other commonly recognized materials. Certain so-called new ceramics consisting of silicon carbide, aluminum oxide, boron nitride, and graphite further extend ceramic materials into the so-called high-tech areas.

DEFINITION OF TILE

Tile is defined officially as follows (1): a ceramic surfacing unit, usually relatively thin in relation to facial area, made from clay or a mixture of clay and other ceramic materials, called the body of the tile, having either a glazed or unglazed face and fired above a red heat in the course of manufacture to a temperature sufficiently high to produce specific physical properties and characteristics.

This definition restricts the term tile to a ceramic product and requires that products other than those ceramic in nature have a modifying term such as plastic, vinyl, asphalt, metal, or other used to describe them. The definition further restricts tile to a surfacing material rather than a structural material such as brick or structural clay tile.

The term ceramic tile is of recent origin, having first been used about 1955 to describe the product formerly called clay tile or real clay tile. The term was conceived by the Tile Council of America, Inc., an association of tile manufacturers, as a modern term to describe its product. As a matter of fact, many types of tile do not use clay as the principal ingredient. Most wall tile made in the United States has as its principal ingredient either talc or pyrophyllite, whereas the main ingredient of porcelain ceramic mosaic tile is feldspar. The term ceramic tile was so successful that by 1960 it was used almost universally in the United States and in most foreign countries that were interested in the U.S. market.

HISTORY OF TILE

Tile is a very old material in terms of civilization. Because of the chemical and physical properties of ceramic materials, namely, resistance to weathering, the history of tile is well preserved in the oldest works of man. It is probably true that broken bits of crudely fired pottery vessels were used to pave or surface areas in place of stone chips, hence the earliest form of ceramic mosaics. When glazes and colors were developed, this treatment became more desirable. As the techniques of glassmaking were developed, bits of glass found similar use.

The techniques of making tile were derived from pottery making; the earliest tiles were made by potters. The same raw materials, glazes, and colors were used as well as the same forming and firing practices. This condition existed into the eighteenth and nineteenth centuries, when the earliest attempts at mechanization led to the development of manufacturing organizations devoted solely to tile. The techniques of extrusion and pressing found favor in producing tile, although they were of little interest to the manufacturers of porcelain and china dinnerware and sanitary ware.

In the history of tile development, the easiest sizes, shapes, and colors came first. Ceramic mosaics, which are the small tiles, often arranged in decorative and interesting designs, were the earliest produced. As manufacturing techniques were developed, larger pieces were developed for paving floors. From this, the quarry and paver tile industry developed. As ceramic mosaics were glazed and colored, they found application as wall coverings. Later, larger sizes and colored glaze found application as decorative and utilitarian surfaces.

By the end of the nineteenth century, the manufacture of tile had reached a fairly advanced stage in Western Europe. The various sizes, shapes, and colors that form the basis of present-day tile making had been developed. The U.S. manufacturers were established in the latter half of the nineteenth century, and they borrowed largely on the technology of Western Europe. This condition prevailed up to the period of World War I.

During the 1920s and 1930s, the industry expanded greatly to accommodate the building boom of the 1920s. During this same period, the product pattern of the industry was established. This consists of three main classes of tile, namely, ceramic mosaic tile, glazed wall tile, and quarry tile or pavers. Likewise, during this period the first product specifications were adopted by the industry.

Ceramic mosaic tile is made from a hard, dense body of low porosity, high strength, and exceptional wear resistance. Glazed wall tile is made from a porous body, usually white in color and having water absorption of 10–15%. It is covered on the exposed surface with an impervious glaze. Until about 1930, the glazed wall tile was covered with a clear glaze, and a white product resulted. Also, these glazes were subject to crazing, which is a pattern of fine cracks caused by a mismatch in the thermal expansions of the body and glaze and by moisture expansion of the body. The decade of the 1930s saw two very important develments in glazed wall tile. The first of these was the development of colored glazes. The second was the development of talc and pyrophyllite bodies, which have a high coefficient of thermal expansion. This places the glazes in strong compression and low moisture expansion, which prevents the loss of this compression. This development eliminated crazing.

During the period of World War II, new construction was at a minimum, and technical development was nonexistent. Many tile producers actually ceased production for the duration of the war, and a few were permanently closed. In 1946, U.S. production of tile was approximately 5 million m^2 (50 million ft^2).

The industries of Japan and Western Europe were destroyed. The countries were faced with a huge demand for all types of building materials, including tile. During this period, there were many substitute materials introduced in an attempt to fill the gaps in building materials. In the tile field, these took the form of plastic tile, porcelain-enameled steel tile, painted steel tile, and even hardboard, with the outline of tiles printed on the face. Time and the action of continual water exposure proved the inadequacies of these materials. By 1950, the U.S. industry had a production of over 20 million m^2 (200 million ft^2), but the supply was still for the most part inadequate.

In 1946, the Tile Council of America was formed (2). This organization, devoted exclusively to promoting greater use of tile in the construction industry, was well supported by the great majority of manufacturers. The Tile Council organized a very extensive program consisting of design prizes in the architectural schools, designs by leading architects, and advertising in the leading professional periodicals and shelter magazines. Extensive stories featuring ceramic tile appeared in magazines and newspapers. By the late 1950s, ceramic tile was a household term familiar to everyone, whereas in 1950 the product called clay tile was relatively unknown to the general public. By 1986, the consumption of tile in United States approached 100 million m^2 (1 billion ft^2). Consumption in the United States is approximately 0.4 m^2 (4 ft^2) per capita (3). The worldwide consumption of tile varies widely, being as high as 1.0 m^2 in some countries of Western Europe. Predictions for consumption in the U.S. market are that it will approximate the consumption of Western Europe as the idea of tile as a decorative material of permanence becomes more widely accepted by architects and the general public.

HISTORY OF TILE INSTALLATION

An important aspect of tile is the installation method. Prior to World War II, the method of installation with a bed of conventional Portland cement mortar was the only one in use. It required a high degree of skill, and tile setting was a recognized trade. Following the war, there was an acute shortage of tile setters, and the industry turned to other options. The first of these was organic mastics, with the tile applied over gypsum wallboard or plywood. This method proved unsatisfactory because of the lack of water resistance of the underlayment and adhesive. It was not until 1952 that a standard was adopted by the tile industry. Although most organic adhesives could not comply initially with this standard, the standard did set forth the necessary properties for them, and by 1965, very satisfactory adhesives were produced.

The Tile Council organized a research program in 1952 that addressed the problems of installation from the standpoint of materials as well as that of procedures and techniques. By involving all facets of the industry, including architects, tile contractors, distributors, tile layers, mortar manufacturers, adhesive manufacturers, regional tile institutes, and so on, in the problem, great progress was made. By 1970, installation specifications were formulated as American National Standards and approved by the industry.

One of the outstanding developments of the Tile Council of America was the development of dry set mortars. These mortars require no prolonged curing with water, even though they are based on Portland cement. Also, they do not require presoaking of porous tile before setting. Another feature of these mortars is that they may be spread in a thin coat by means of a notched trowel. The mortars are completely formulated in factories under license, thus eliminating variations in mixing by tradespersons. This remarkable development is estimated to have saved billions of dollars in tile-setting costs, and during the 1960s and 1970s their use under license spread worldwide. Likewise, dry set mortars revolutionized the techniques of underlayment surfacing to receive tile.

CLASSIFICATION OF TILE

For many years prior to World War II, tile was classified according to its usual applications: floor tile, wall tile, and quarry tile or paver tile. The tile was manufactured specifically for the purpose described, except for quarry tile, which was used to pave areas of high traffic or other difficult conditions. The methods of installation, although generally similar, were tailored specifically to walls or floors. Floor tile was made of a hard, dense, unglazed body suitable for heavy floor traffic. Because of the difficulties of manufacture, it was necessarily of small size, usually less than 7.62×7.62 cm (3×3 in.). The individual tiles were mounted in sheets on paper with the proper space for grout between them. Round and hexagonal shapes were popular. Wall tile was a porous body covered with a transparent glaze. It was not intended for hard usage, and the body of the tile was quite weak. Because of the porous body, the tile could be made in larger sizes, 15×7.5 cm (6×3 in.) and 15×15 cm (6×6 in.) being popular. Quarry tile was an unglazed hard body, usually red in color. The standard size was 15×15 cm; it was used where conditions were severe, on floors and walls. The method of manufacture caused considerable size variations, necessitating wide joints for good appearance.

As the use of tile became more widespread and new applications were developed, the traditional use of tile was no longer followed. Unglazed floor tile was made in a wide variety of colors and was used on walls, countertops, and exterior surfaces as well as floors. Both clear and colored glazes were applied to ceramic mosaic tile, thus greatly extending its use. Glazed wall tile, heretofore considered unfit for floor use, was covered with a crystalline-type glaze suitable for use on light-duty residential floors. The most popular size was 10.8×10.8 cm (4.25×4.25 in.), and at one time, perhaps 95% of all glazed tile in the United States was of this nominal size. Originally, the facial surfaces of both glazed tile and ceramic mosaic tile were 90° to the vertical sides of the tile. This is com-

monly known as square-edged tile. Gradually, it was replaced by cushion-edged tile, which has a radius at the intersection of the faces with the edge surfaces. This radius improved the appearance of the installation by minimizing the difference in thickness between tiles. It also removed the sharp edges, which had a tendency to chip, particularly with tile that had a porous body. Quarry tile and pavers, which originally were strictly utilitarian products, took on a new style, with various colors and sizes, such as 10 $\times$ 10 cm (4×4 in.), 20×10 cm (8×4 in.), 20×20 cm (8×8 in.), and larger, in addition to the traditional 15 $\times$ 15 cm (6×6 in.). Grinding the four sides of 15×15 cm (6×6 in.) quarry tile greatly improved the appearance of the joints and the ease of tile setting.

Tile may be classified in another manner, that is, by porosity or water absorption of the body. Tile is designated as nonvitreous if it has a water absorption of more than 7.0%. It is semivitreous if its absorption is between 3.0 and 7.0%. It is vitreous if it has an absorption of 0.5–3.0%. It is classed as impervious if the absorption is below 0.5%.

The current method of classification of ceramic tile (1) is a combination of end use, form, and physical properties. At present, specifications recognize several types of tile as follows.

Ceramic Mosaic Tile

This tile (Fig. 1) is formed by either the dust-pressed or plastic method, usually 0.635–0.952-cm (0.25–0.375-in.) thick, and has a facial area of less than 6 in.^{2}. Ceramic mosaic tile may be either of porcelain or natural clay composition and may be either plain or with an abrasive mixture throughout. This class of tile may be either unglazed or glazed. The unglazed version is produced in a wide variety of colored bodies, and the color is uniformly distributed throughout the thickness. The glazed version of ceramic mosaic is usually produced from a white body and covered on one face only with a glaze that is offered in a variety of colors. Unglazed ceramic mosaic tile is normally produced with a cushion edge on both faces so that either side may be used as the exposed face. In the process of manufacturing, this facilitates the mounting or assembly of the individual tiles into large sheets for ease of installation. The unglazed ceramic mosaic tile is normally produced in the porcelain-type body, which lends itself to the production of a wide variety of colors. This body is normally in the impervious class (absorption less than 0.5%), which renders it very hard and nonabsorbent. The glazed ceramic mosaic tile may be produced from a vitreous body (absorption 0.5–3.0%). This class of tile is used only on walls or light-duty floors since the glaze is subject to scratching and wear. Manufacturers offer tile in mounted sheets in a combination of unglazed and glazed tile, which provides the architect and designer with an almost unlimited variety of effects. Beautiful murals may be made from this material at a relatively low cost. Natural clay ceramic mosaics are made from a single colored clay or a mixture of clays. The colors are usually earthy tones, although many interesting color textures can be produced. This class of tile is usually produced in the vitreous range of absorption (0.5–3.0%), and its use may be on walls or floors.

Figure 1. Entryway in ceramic mosaic tile. Courtesy of American Olean Tile Co.

Glazed Wall Tile

This tile (Fig. 2) is formed by the dust-pressed method, is usually nominally 0.793-cm (0.313-in.) thick, and has a facial area greater than 38.7 cm² (6 in.²). Glazed wall tile is made from a nonvitreous body and has an impervious white or colored glaze covering the face. It is made in a variety of sizes and shapes and commonly has spacer lugs or projections on the sides, which provide uniform spacing of the tile. Normally, the tiles have a radiused edge. This class of tile is produced in a great variety of colors, and great care is given to shade control. Likewise, great care is exercised over the size variation of the individual tiles. Glaze textures varying from bright glossy to matte and crystalline are produced. The porous nature of the body lends itself to easy glazing and uniform size control. The nonvitreous body is not as strong as the semivitreous and vitreous bodies, and for this reason it is mostly confined to use on walls and countertops.

Quarry Tile

Glazed or unglazed quarry tile (Fig. 3) is made by the extrusion process from natural clay or shale and usually has 38.7 cm² (6 in.²) or more of facial area. This class of tile was originally derived from brick and was used exclu-

sively for floors in areas of heavy use. By definition, the term is confined to tile manufactured by the extrusion process to differentiate it from paver tile, which is made by the dust-pressed method. The extrusion process gives the quarry tile a unique "skin effect" on the surface, which renders it more resistant to penetration by liquids. Because it is primarily intended for heavy-duty use, it is commonly offered in two thicknesses: 1.27 cm and 1.905 cm (0.5 in. and 0.75 in.). Popular sizes are 15.24 × 15.24 cm (6 × 6 in.), 20.32 × 15.24 cm (8 × 4 in.), and 20.32 × 20.32 cm (8 × 8 in.). Hexagonal and other decorative shapes are also manufactured. Quarry tile now finds numerous applications other than for heavy-duty floors. It is extensively used for patios and roof decks. One of the major uses of this product is as a chemically resistant surfacing material in food manufacturing, preparation, and serving areas such as in breweries and kitchens where a variety of food acids are encountered and where frequent cleaning with strong alkaline cleansers is required. Because of the natural clay raw material, quarry tile is offered in a limited line of colors. Buff, gray, green, and various shades of red are common. The specification for quarry tile allows 5.0% absorption, although most manufacturers produce a denser product. Most quarry tile today is ground to exact facial dimensions on all four sides. This, and the fact that quarry tile is extruded, requires that it be square edged.

Paver Tile

Glazed or unglazed porcelain or natural clay paver tile is formed by the dust-pressed method and has 38.7 cm² (6 in.²) or more of facial area. The most popular sizes of this class of tile are 10.16 × 10.16 cm (4 × 4 in.), 15.24 × 15.24 cm (6 × 6 in.), 20.32 × 10.16 cm (8 × 4 in.), 20.32 × 20.32 cm (8 × 8 in.), and 30.48 × 30.48 cm (12 × 12 in.). The most popular thicknesses are 0.952 cm (0.375 in.) and 1.27 cm (0.5 in.). Paver tile made from a porcelain body is impervious, whereas the natural clay paver tile may be either vitreous or impervious. Porcelain paver tile may be made in a wide variety of colors, with the color being solid throughout the body. Natural clay paver tile, because of the earthy nature of the clay color, is limited to a range of buffs and reds. Grays and dark greens are also produced. Paver tile, because it is pressed, tends to be of more uniform size than quarry tile, and therefore is not normally ground to exact size, but may be sorted into uniform size ranges. When glazed pavers are produced, a wide variety of glaze colors and textures may be obtained. Also, textures may be pressed into the face of the body. This is normally impossible with quarry tile, which is made by the extrusion process. Both unglazed and glazed pavers have gained wide acceptance for use in entryways and in rooms where special surface effects or colors are desired. Because of the greater thickness and the hard bodies used, this class of tile has superior resistance to impact and wear. In normal moderate-duty use, it is practically indestructible.

Monocottura

This is a relatively new type of glazed tile that originated in Italy; its production has now become worldwide. It may

Figure 2. Glazed wall tile in shower room showing extensive use of trim tile. Courtesy of American Olean Tile Co.

be considered a glazed paver tile. It is somewhat less thick and is produced by the one-fire process in fast-fire kilns. It came into popular use during the 1960s and 1970s. It is produced by the dust-pressed process from a natural clay body, is generally red in color, and is impervious or vitreous. The glazes are very opaque to mask the red color of the body and are produced in a wide variety of colors and textures. Like the other types, it is made in several facial dimensions, the most popular being 20 × 10 cm (8 × 4 in.), 20 × 20 cm (8 × 8 in.), 30 × 20 cm (12 × 8 in.), and 30 × 30 cm (12 × 12 in.). In addition to square and rectangular shapes, a variety of hexagonal and octagonal shapes are offered. Spacer lugs are not popular in this product because it is manufactured primarily for non-U.S. markets where the cost of installation is not a major consideration. Its thickness is in the range 0.5–1.0 cm (0.197–0.394 in.). Because of the hard, dense body, the product is quite durable and is resistant to impact. It is

also resistant to frost action, particularly when the body is impervious. Although it was originally intended for use on residential and light commercial floors, it now finds extensive application on walls and countertops as well.

Split Tile

This is a class of tile made by the extrusion process, usually of a natural clay or shale. It may be either glazed or unglazed. The unglazed tile has a limited range of color but the glazed split tile is produced in a wide variety of glaze colors. Because of the nature of the clay body, the colored glazes must be quite opaque. The tile gets its name from the fact that two tiles are extruded back to back and joined by a thin web of clay, which is part of the extrusion. This web is strong enough to hold the tiles together during the manufacturing processes, but fragile enough to be easily split apart by a sharp blow after firing. This leaves

Figure 3. Unglazed quarry tile on both floors and walls. Courtesy of American Olean Tile Co.

an irregular projection on the back of each tile, which must be removed by grinding to make the tile suitable for setting by a thin set method.

TRIM TILE

The most common classes of tile are made with some form of trim shape (Fig. 4) to finish the installation properly. The use of trim shapes varies greatly with the class of tile and the architectural practice in the area. In the United States, trim shapes are used extensively, and all major producers of tile offer a wide variety of shapes. In Western Europe, the use of trim is much less extensive, and in some areas of the world it is not produced at all. To compete in the U.S. market effectively, it is necessary to offer at least a limited number of trim shapes. The original U.S. tile installations were confined to bathrooms and kitchens. Wainscots were used extensively, and the tile was not an integral part of the wall structure. This condition called for extensive use of trim shapes to finish installations properly. In Europe, where tile was used extensively and masonry was the principal method of construction, it was common practice to tile from floor to ceiling; the tile installations were flush with the finishing plaster. Many installations required no trim. Trim tile is very expensive to make compared with the flat pieces. It is common practice to make a line of trim shapes corresponding to each size of flat tile (Fig. 5). All pieces are the same thickness as

the flat tile, and the line of trim consists of stretcher pieces to finish out-corners known as "bullnoses" and for in-corners known as "coves." Left- and right-hand angle pieces are provided to allow for the intersection of corners. A uniform system of numbering trim shapes was developed by the U.S. tile industry in 1921. The method of assigning

Figure 4. Trim tile showing use of bullnose and cove angles and stretchers. Courtesy of American Olean Tile Co.

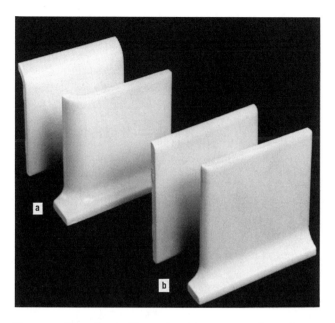

Figure 5. Trim shapes illustrating **(a)** conventional type for use with thick mortar beds, and **(b)** surface type for use with thin mortar beds and organic mastics. Courtesy of American Olean Tile Co.

numbers to shapes is described in Bulletin K-400, "Glazed Tiles and Trimmers" (4), published by the Associated Tile Manufacturers in 1921. The Tile Council of America has a numbering and shapes committee, which updated the description of trim shapes in 1958; the committee assigns standard numbers to new shapes and keeps the numbering system current. The non-U.S. producers of tile have always avoided and discouraged the use of trim unless absolutely necessary. Therefore, little trim is used on a worldwide basis. In the U.S. market, architects have always demanded a high degree of attention to detail and appearance; this has led to the extensive use of trim shapes. With the greatly expanded use of tile, attention to the cost of tile, and installation and influence of imported tile in the U.S. market, the use of trim is greatly reduced. An exception to this is the use of tile on countertops in the western United States. This application depends on the use of several unique shapes, and new ones are constantly being developed.

MOUNTED TILE

This is a product that may be made from almost any class of tile. It consists of joining, by various means, individual tiles to form relatively large sheets. The earliest process of mounting, which has been in use for hundreds of years, is the so-called face mounting of ceramic mosaics, glass mosaics, and marble mosaics. In this process, the individual tiles, or stones as they are referred to, are placed face up on a board with thin strips of metal separating the individual tiles. The tiles are then glued to a sheet of paper with water-soluble glue. When the glue has dried, the sheets of paper with tile attached may be easily handled by the tile installer and placed in the setting material (mortar or adhesive). After the setting material has become firm or set, the paper is saturated with water, and the water-soluble glue releases the paper from the tile faces. In recent developments, the face paper has been replaced with a permanent backing material, which becomes part of the installation. This backing may consist of punched paper impregnated with a waterproofing plastic, a woven mesh of paper or cloth sufficiently waterproof to render it free of shrinkage, or a similar material that provides the setting mortar or adhesive direct access to the back of the tile. Another method of mounting tile is to join the individual tiles together at the joints by applying small buttons or dots of rubber or plastic to the back of the tiles. Tile mounting is usually confined to ceramic mosaic tile where square sheets of 144 pieces or rectangular sheets of 288 pieces are mounted for installation as one piece. Most manufacturers of ceramic mosaic tile are equipped to mount tile in patterns, and endless combinations of color are possible. Glazed wall tile is also mounted to a limited extent in the 10.8×10.8 cm (4.25×4.25 in.) size in sheets of 12 pieces, thus enabling 0.139 m² (1.5 ft²) to be installed at one time. Larger and heavier tile such as quarry and pavers become impractical to handle.

PREGROUTED TILE

This is a modern variation of mounted tile. In addition to the individual tiles being held together in a sheet, the joints are also filled with a flexible plastic material such as silicone rubber. In this manner, when the sheet is installed in the wall or floor, no grouting of joints is necessary, except for the joint that surrounds the entire sheet. In this product, the grout composition is non-Portland cement.

MODERN TILE INSTALLATION

Of nearly equal importance to the tile itself is the method of installation. In order to have a lasting and trouble-free installation, great care must be taken in the preparation of the backing surface or underlayment as well as in the selection of bonding coats and joint fillers (grout). This is a very complicated field and one of rapidly changing technology and practice. The Tile Council of America publishes an annual edition of the *Handbook for Ceramic Tile Installation* (5). The reader is referred to the current edition of this handbook. It is exceptionally complete and is constantly revised and updated. Included are charts relating performance levels or service requirements to installation methods and choice of materials. In addition, it contains over 50 detailed drawings of typical tile installations. For each specific installation detail, the *Handbook* also lists the ANSI installation specifications and the ANSI material specifications that apply.

Grouts

The traditional method of filling the joints between tiles is known as grouting; the most widely used grout is a mixture of white or gray Portland cement with either ground limestone or fine sand. This is the most vulnerable part of a tile installation because the Portland cement is easily attacked by dilute acids such as acetic acid (vinegar) and citric acid (lemon juice). For this reason, a number of chemical grouts have been developed and are commercially available. For the most severe service, furan and epoxy grouts are available (6). These materials require special techniques for application and involve additional cost. Grout additives for mixing with Portland cement grouts are available. These improve the hardness of the grout by aiding the curing of the Portland cement. A so-called mastic grout developed by the Tile Council of America is available from licensees of the Tile Council. This material is a single-component material that does not require curing and has excellent hardness and resistance to mild acids and alkalies such as those encountered on countertops. The reader is referred to the *Handbook for Ceramic Tile Installation* (5).

BIBLIOGRAPHY

American National Standard Specifications are frequently revised, and hence no date of publication is given. The reader should always refer to the most recent edition. The same applies to the *Handbook for Ceramic Tile Installation*.

1. American National Standard Specifications for Ceramic Tile, ANSI A 137.1, Tile Council of America, Inc.
2. J. V. Fitzgerald, "Profile of the Ceramic Tile Industry," *Ceramic Ind.* **111**(1), 28–29 (1978); *ibid.* **111**(2), 24–25 (1978); *ibid.* **111**(3), 46–48 (1978).
3. J. H. Schott, "Consumers Drive Tiles Upward Trend," *Ceramic Ind.* **126**(6), 33 (1986).
4. "Glaze Tile and Trimmers," Associated Tile Manufacturers, Bulletin K-400, 1921.
5. *Handbook for Ceramic Tile Installation,* Tile Council of America, Inc., Princeton, N.J. (refer to latest annual edition).
6. American National Standard Specifications for Chemically Resistant Water Cleanable Tile-setting and -grouting Epoxy, ANSI A 118.3, Tile Council of America, Inc.

General References

Refs 1–6 are good general references.

American National Standard Specifications for the Installation of Ceramic Tile with Portland Cement Mortar, ANSI A 108.1, Tile Council of America, Inc.

American National Standard Specifications for the Installation of Ceramic Tile with Water Resistant Organic Adhesives, ANSI A 108.4, Tile Council of America, Inc.

American National Standard Specifications for the Installation of Ceramic Tile with Dry Set Portland Cement Mortar or Latex–Portland Cement Mortar, ANSI A 108.5, Tile Council of America, Inc.

American National Standard Specifications for the Installation of Ceramic Tile with Chemical Resistant, Water Cleanable Tile-setting and Grouting Epoxy, ANSI A 108.6, Tile Council of America, Inc.

American National Standard Specifications for the Installation of Ceramic Tile for Electrically Conductive Ceramic Tile with Conductive Dry-set Portland Cement Mortar, ANSI A 108.7, Tile Council of America, Inc.

American National Standard Specifications for Dry-set Portland Cement Mortar, ANSI A 118.1, Tile Council of America, Inc.

American National Standard Specification for Conductive Dry-set Portland Cement Mortar, ANSI A 118.2, Tile Council of America, Inc.

American National Standard Specifications for Latex–Portland Cement Mortar, ANSI A 118.4, Tile Council of America, Inc.

American National Standards for Organic Adhesives for Installation of Ceramic Tile, ANSI A 136.1, The Adhesive and Sealant Council, Inc.

"Ceramic Tile Shapes and Sizes," Tile Council of America, Inc., 1958.

R. V. Tailby, "TCA Moves to Resolve Standards Confusion," *Ceramic Ind.* **126**(4), 52–53 (1986).

EDWARD P. McNAMARA, PhD
San Angelo, Texas

CHAMBERS, WILLIAM

Sir William Chambers was one of the two preeminent British architects of the second half of the eighteenth century. With his rival, Robert Adam, he shared the post of Architect to the King in 1761 (succeeding to the sole Comptrollership of the King's Works in 1769 and finally to Surveyor General) and obtained roughly his fair half of the most important public and domestic commissions of the time. He is justly regarded as a master of monumental classical architecture, both for his concise and elegant *Treatise on the Decorative Part of Civil Architecture,* first published in 1759 (1), and for the power and dignity of his greatest building, Somerset House on the Strand, begun in 1776.

During an age of English dominance in world trade and a sharing of cultural ideas with Europe and the East, Chambers was a cosmopolitan artist and a gentleman, fully representative of the new pluralism of his time. The son of a Scottish merchant, he was born in Göteborg, Sweden, and through extensive travels became versed in several languages. After an English education, he joined the Swedish East India Company, making voyages to India and China (1743–1749) and studying Chinese architecture and culture. He received his architectural training in France, at the renowned studio of Jacques-François Blondel, and was acquainted with several of the leading Parisian architects of the day. This gave him a thorough grounding in precepts of French academic classicism as well as a taste for the more forward-looking neoclassical abstraction of the 1770s. Although he also spent five years in Italy (1750–1755), receiving instruction in drawing from Adam's friend Clérissau and from Pécheux and studying Italian classical monuments, his predilections remained tied to French architecture—in contrast to his nemesis, who was a committed Italophile. He married in 1753, settled in London, and was well established as a practicing architect by the end of the 1750s.

Chambers began his career with the patronage of the

Prince of Wales, later to become George III, and benefited handsomely thereafter from the graces of royalty. In designing numerous garden structures at Kew Gardens for the Dowager Princess, he made two significant contributions to the architecture of his time. The first was the introduction of oriental buildings and gardening features to England, and the second was the publication of books to popularize the style—in 1757, he published *Designs of Chinese Buildings, Furniture, Dresses, etc.*(2), and in 1763, he published a book documenting his work at Kew, in both classical and exotic styles (3). His 1763 Chinese Pagoda still towers over the public gardens and is one of Kew's popular landmarks.

One of the intriguing paradoxes of Chambers's work and personality was his dual nature: How could one of the most severe, robust, and exacting classical architects in England also design works with the delicacy of the oriental styles? Chambers demonstrated his commitment to the abstract principles of classical architecture in his *Treatise,* admired for its clarity by Walpole, while making his equally strong distaste for Capability Brown's English landscape gardening principles known in the controversial 1772 *Dissertation on Oriental Gardening* (4), a work that Walpole attacked.

The *Treatise,* modeled in form on Isaac Ware's *Complete Body of Architecture* (5), is written in a cool, rational style perfectly in tune with Chambers's architectural taste. It deals with the origins of architecture in the manner of Laugier, with particular reverence for the Greeks and Romans, whose achievements were just being recognized by archaeology. Although less verbose than a typical French treatise of the time, it has the scholarly and empirical quality associated with such works as J. F. Blondel's *Cours d'Architecture* of nearly the same date (6). In the matter of the orders, Chambers distilled his own preferred version of each genus from Roman and Renaissance sources. On the whole, they are richer and more complex than those of Gibbs, whose popular book 30 years earlier was a standard for English builders. The remainder of the book, like that of Gibbs and Ware, is devoted to specific elements and ornamental problems, such as doorways, niches, and pediments, and finally concludes with designs for small monumental buildings and decorative motifs.

Chambers's architectural works cover all categories and building types. His Royal Bank of Scotland on St. Andrew's Square in Edinburgh ranks with the UK's stateliest public buildings, and his classical villa-type country houses, such as nearby Duddington Hall (1762–1763), are among the most disciplined and innovative of their genre. One of his most admired works, the Casino at Marino Clontarf near Dublin (1758–1776) (Fig. 1) demonstrates his absolute mastery of the classical language as well as a flair for designing in miniature, as required of garden pavilions. In it, the formal theme of the Greek cross is superimposed on a square plan at entablature level, producing a void at the corner unusual in classical buildings. There were also numerous designs for monuments and public buildings done for exhibitions and academic purposes. Cham-

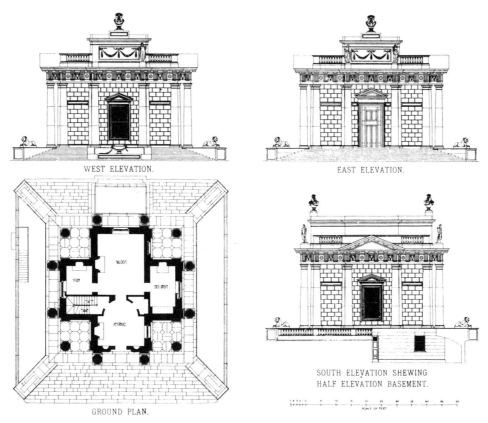

Figure 1. The Casino, Marino Clontarf (1758–1776) (7). Courtesy of W. W. Norton & Company.

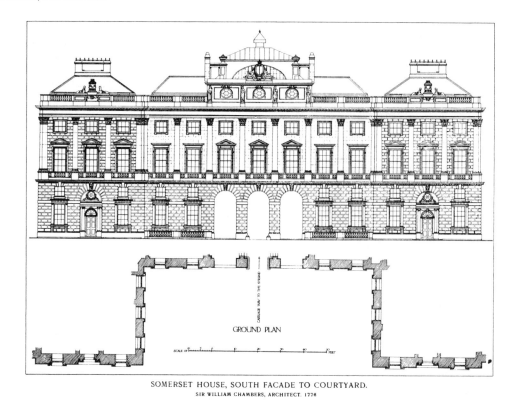

SOMERSET HOUSE, SOUTH FACADE TO COURTYARD.
SIR WILLIAM CHAMBERS, ARCHITECT. 1776

Figure 2. Somerset House, South Facade to Courtyard (1776) (7). Courtesy of W. W. Norton & Company.

bers was a founder of the Royal Academy of Arts in 1768 and a respected teacher.

With Somerset House (Fig. 2), the rebuilding of an old palace off Waterloo Bridge on the Thames, Chambers received the signal opportunity to demonstrate his skills in monumental design in the tradition of Michelangelo, Perrault, Vanbrugh, and Vanvitelli. London had no Louvre or Versailles. The projects of Jones, Webb, and Wren for large public palaces and planning had come to nought. Thus, Chambers was building London's largest and grandest structure on one of its most prominent sites. The project took nearly all of his energies during the last 20 years of his life.

His design, understated and full of repose, incorporated a panoply of formal elements, motifs, and devices from Roman, Palladian, French neoclassical, and even Italian baroque sources. Although the riverfront, some 500 ft long, is somewhat mute and reserved, it handles its vast length deftly. Unlike Adam, whose works strive for movement and drama, Chambers's architecture bespeaks a kind of frozen intensity, no better demonstrated than in the Strand gate and south courtyard of Somerset House. The building saves its best for these great interior spaces, where the sculptural interplay of the orders against the undulating rustication of the wall is effectively capped by a variety of roof elements. The building's many staircases and monumental passages are also noteworthy. In this masterpiece, the architect epitomized his taste for the "chaste and simple" manner of what A. E. Richardson called Roman–Palladian classicism, in contrast to all that was "bold, luxuriant, and licentious" (7).

Chambers achieved considerable wealth, social prestige, and honors during his career. By expanding the public roles and prestige of the architect, he helped to achieve a professionalism that altered the public's perception of the architect as merely a gentleman artist without talent for administration, political maneuvering, or business. Indicative of his stature were his elevation to Knight of the Polar Star by the King of Sweden and his subsequent English peerage. He died in London on March 8, 1796 and was buried in the south transept of Westminster Abbey.

BIBLIOGRAPHY

1. W. Chambers, *Treatise on the Decorative Part of Civil Architecture,* London, 1759.
2. W. Chambers, *Designs of Chinese Buildings, Furniture, Dresses, etc.,* London, 1757.
3. W. Chambers, *Plans, Elevations, Sections and Perspective Views of the Gardens and Buildings at Kew in Surrey,* London, 1763.
4. W. Chambers, *Dissertation on Oriental Gardening,* London, 1772.
5. I. Ware, *Complete Body of Architecture,* T. Osbourne and J. Simpson, London, 1756.
6. J. F. Blondel, *Cours d'Architecture,* Desaint, Paris, 1771–1777.
7. A. E. Richardson, *Monumental Classic Architecture in Britain, Scotland and Ireland,* W. W. Norton & Company, New York, 1982.

General References

Refs. 1 and 3 are good general references.

T. Hardwick, "A Memoir of the Life of Sir William Chambers," in J. Gwilt, ed., *A Treatise on the Decorative Art of Civil Architecture,* London, 1825.

A. E. Richardson, *Monumental Classic Architecture in Great Britain and Ireland During the Eighteenth and Nineteenth Centuries,* Scribner's, London, 1914.

J. Summerson, *Architecture in Britain 1530–1830, Pelican History of Art,* 5th rev. ed., Penguin Books Ltd., Harmondsworth and Baltimore, 1959, pp. 415–441.

J. Harris, *Sir William Chambers,* Zwemmer, London, 1970.

H. Colvin, *A Biographical Dictionary of English Architects 1600–1840,* John Murray, London, 1978, pp. 204–209.

J. Rykwert, *The First Moderns, The Architects of the Eighteenth Century,* MIT Press, Cambridge and London, 1980.

J. Harris, "Chambers, William," *Macmillan Dictionary of Architects, Vol. 1,* Macmillan, New York, 1981, pp. 403–406.

Mark A. Hewitt
Columbia University
New York, New York

CHICAGO SCHOOL

The term Chicago School refers to the architects and engineers who were active in Chicago from the time of the great fire of 1871 to ca 1912. Their activity resulted in the application of new technology to the high-rise commercial office building. The shift from masonry bearing walls to steel framing on concrete footings and foundations with lightweight curtain walls, and the introduction of fire-protected steel were hallmarks of the school. Many of the advances were developed by William Le Baron Jenney (1832–1897), but the design implications, including the "Chicago window," the use of ornament, and the handling of the grid of vertical and horizontal members on the facades, were worked out by a number of firms.

The scale of building after the fire was immense, and several firms became successful:

William Le Baron Jenney (from 1868–1891); Jenney and Mundie (1891–1895); and Jenney, Mundie and Jensen (1895–1897).

Burnham and Root (1873–1891); and D. H. Burnham and Company (1891–1912).

Kinney and Adler 1869–1871; Burling and Adler (1871–1878); Dankmar Adler, Architect (1878–1883); Adler and Sullivan (1893–1895); and Louis Sullivan (1895–1922).

Holabird and Simons (1880–1881); Holabird, Simons and Roche (1881–1883); Holabird and Roche (1883–1927). Holabird Sr. died in 1923, but the firm was carried on by Holabird Jr. until the death of Marin Roche in 1927, when the younger Holabird formed a partnership with the younger John Wellborn Root to form the firm of Holabird and Root.

Frank Lloyd Wright was employed by Adler and Sullivan from about 1888 to 1893, before starting his own firm.

BIBLIOGRAPHY

General References

S. Giedeon, *Space, Time and Architecture,* Harvard University Press, Cambridge, Mass., 1949.

C. Condit, *The Chicago School of Architecture,* University of Chicago Press, Chicago, Ill., 1964.

See also Burnham, Daniel H.; Holabird and Roche; Root, John Wellborn; Sullivan, Louis; Wright, Frank Lloyd.

CHROMIUM PLATING

Chromium plating is used extensively wherever a metal's brilliance is suitable and wherever corrosion, wear, and abrasion resistance are necessary. Electroplated chromium is unique in its combination of desirable properties. In particular, two functional properties of bright chromium make it useful to the architect: its hardness and its corrosion or tarnish resistance. Figure 1 compares the relative hardnesses of several electroplated metals.

This hardness makes bright chromium especially useful on items that might be cleaned with the common abrasive cleaners. Bright chromium is unique in its ability to resist scratching and dulling.

Hard or functional chromium is deposited for its low coefficient of friction and high hardness, which lead to good wear resistance for varied uses, such as for automotive shock rods, McPherson struts, piston rings for aircraft engine parts, crankshafts, gun barrels, gauges, and many others. These hard chromium deposits differ from the typical decorative chromium deposits mainly in two ways. They are thicker, usually over 1 μm (40×10^{-6} in.), and they are frequently deposited directly onto the basis metal, usually a hardened steel.

Decorative chromium deposits, on the other hand, are relatively thin, approximately 0.2–0.6 μm (8–24×10^{-6}

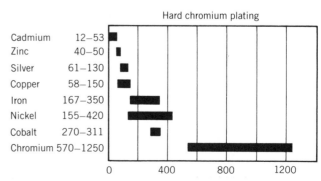

Figure 1. Variations in hardness of various electroplated metals. Courtesy of Gardner Publications, Inc.

in.), and are almost invariably deposited onto an intermediate electrodeposited layer of nickel. An exception is the deposition of chromium directly onto polished stainless steel. Decorative deposits are notably used for automotive bumpers and trim. In the building trade, these deposits are most common on plumbing and plumbing hardware, light fixtures and switch plates, door hardware, trim, and handrails, which all encounter rubbing wear and corrosive wear.

Special decorative effects can be obtained by varying the chromium plating conditions (eg, high-temperature chromium has a milky rather than bright appearance) or by treating the basis material. Blasting the basis material with an abrasive before chromium plating can produce a novel matte appearance. By the judicious use of masks, both bright and satiny finishes can be obtained in the same piece at, of course, higher costs of processing.

Black chromium, actually a codeposit of chromium metal and its oxides, may be used for a "telephone" finish and has been established as an excellent solar absorber material. In the latter case, the finish is not as abrasive resistant as the standard bright chromium, but this is no problem since solar absorbers are usually encased with glass to make use of the greenhouse effect to trap the radiant energy as heat.

HISTORY

Although chromium was plated as early as the mid-1800s, such plating was sporadic and irreproducible until the work of C. G. Fink at Columbia University. He made commercial chromium plating a reality in the early 1920s by showing that chromium can be reproducibly plated by using an aqueous solution of chromic acid (chromium trioxide, CrO_3) and an optimum amount of a catalyst (1).

The first catalyst, the sulfate anion, is still used extensively today, either by itself or in combination with adjuvant catalysts. An aqueous solution containing 250 g/L of chromic acid and 2.5 g/L of the sulfate anion makes a good general-purpose plating solution and is still widely used. Unfortunately, this bath has a current efficiency of only up to ca 16%. That is, 16% of the electrical current passing through the plating bath produces chromium metal; the other 84% is wasted by producing hydrogen and some trivalent chromium. Fink's original work disclosed that complex fluorides could also be used as catalysts and that these fluoride catalysts could produce cathode efficiencies on the order of 25%.

Thus, the chromium could be plated almost twice as fast and with the power costs reduced proportionately. For further historical information, see Refs. 2 and 3.

CORROSION

It is impossible to discuss decorative plating without also discussing nickel plating. The only basis metal commonly plated directly with decorative chromium is stainless steel (eg, automotive trim and wheel covers). In virtually every other case, the electrodeposited chromium is preceded by a layer of electrodeposited nickel. When nickel was in short supply (during the Korean War), attempts were made to plate directly onto steel, copper, or brass, or to substitute a brass electrodeposit for the nickel. The corrosion results were seldom favorable.

A chromium plate should provide wear and corrosion resistance for the normal life of the product. It must be appreciated that, like every other complex manufactured product, only the ideal electrodeposit is free of flaws. Because ubiquitous flaws provide pathways for corrosion, the plating processes must be chosen to anticipate corrosion and minimize its effects. Basically, this means that the thickness of the electrodeposits must exceed certain minima. Although this is complicated by the use of duplex nickel and microdiscontinuous chromium, there is no substitute for a thick, well-plated layer of nickel under the chromium. Specifications like those developed for the automotive industry could prevent pitted electrical fixtures and worn and tarnished plumbing fixtures. "Fingerprint" acids are extremely corrosive. Abrasive household and industrial cleaners do accelerate wear, a good reason for relatively thick chromium deposits. It is obvious that fixtures in humid atmospheres, such as in kitchens and bathrooms, will meet corrosive conditions.

Very thick chromium deposits, on the order of 2.5 μm (100×10^{-6} in.) and greater, have been shown to be very corrosion resistant and may resist outdoor corrosion almost indefinitely. Such thicknesses are usually uneconomical. A thin flaw-free chromium deposit over nickel could be very corrosion resistant, if there were no flaws in the chromium. Early attempts to produce flaw-free chromium layers soon failed because the inevitable occasional pore or crack became a center for accelerated corrosion and failure. The opposite tack has proven to be a more successful one. When a high density of pores or cracks, so small or so thin as to be invisible, is formed in the chromium plate, the onset of corrosive failure is postponed. Microcracked and microporous chromium have been given the general name microdiscontinuous. Microdiscontinuous chromium successfully reduces corrosion by spreading the inevitable corrosion over a wide area. Because the corrosion reaction is limited by the cathodic reaction, the availability of dissolved oxygen in the corrosive solution, and because the corrosion reaction is spread over a wide area, its visible effect becomes negligible because the corroded areas are so widespead and microscopically small. These considerations may be summarized by the electrochemical corrosion reactions:

| Anodic | Ni | $-2e^-$ | $= Ni^{2+}$ |
| Cathodic | $\frac{1}{2} O_2 + 2H^+$ | $+2e^-$ | $= H_2O$ |

The actual physical situation for the contrast between microdiscontinuous chromium over nickel and ordinary chromium (with the inevitable pore or flaw) over nickel is illustrated in Figure 2. Figure 2a illustrates the electrochemical process when a corrosive solution containing oxygen is in contact with the electrodeposit; Figure 2b illustrates the results.

The combination of a duplex nickel deposit with microdiscontinuous chromium can extend the life through nor-

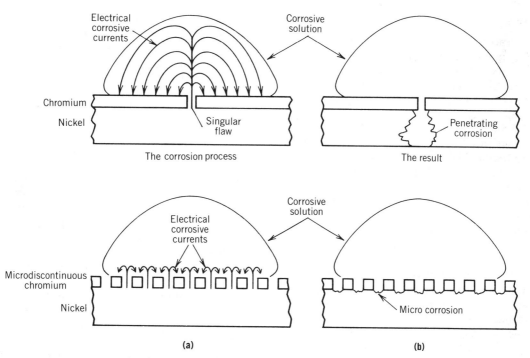

Figure 2. The contrast between microdiscontinuous chromium over nickel and ordinary chromium over nickel. **(a)** The electrochemical process occurring when an oxygen-containing corrosive solution contacts the electrodeposit. **(b)** The results of the process outlined in **(a)**.

mal automotive use for three to five years. The thicker the nickel deposits, the thicker the chromium deposits, and the longer the life. Long life can be obtained from the combination if the semibright underlayer of noble nickel is on the order of 25 μm (1×10^{-3} in.) with an overlay of bright (more active, sulfur-containing) nickel ca 8-μm (0.3×10^{-3}-in.) thick followed by a final layer of microdiscontinuous chromium ca 0.75-μm (30×10^{-6}-in.) thick.

BASIS MATERIALS

Functionality and economics dictate the basis material to be chosen for processing.

Plumbing fixtures such as faucets are made of leaded brass because of the ease of casting, machining, and polishing. Considerable buffing is required to provide enough polish that the final brilliance is obtained with a relatively thin, ca 5-μm (0.2×10^{-3}-in.), layer of bright nickel. A flash of chromium, up to perhaps 0.25 μm (10×10^{-6} in.), often suffices to complete the process. (Thicker deposits would last longer. See Corrosion.)

Light fixtures, switch plates, and some tubing are of steel, usually formed by stamping. Buffing and polishing requirements are not as stringent, and the bright nickel deposit provides the necessary brilliance.

Attempts to use zinc base die castings, or more recently plastics, for the basis materials have not produced items of equal quality. Stainless steel tubing may be plated directly with chromium for handrails to provide good wear and corrosion resistance. Plain steel, with nickel and chro-

mium, is cheaper. Decorative trim can be processed by many plating shops. The processing of large panels may be limited to fewer shops, but the sizes handled can be larger, even 1.25 × 2.5 m (4 × 8 ft) and more.

The design of parts to be plated is an art requiring an understanding of the plating process. Generous radii are a necessity. Recesses tend to get less electrodeposit; protuberances get more. Sharp edges are like lightning rods in drawing electrical plating currents and may build up or even burn, whereas the hollows get little or no plated metal. Sometimes the placement of workpieces on the rack can help distribute the plating current more evenly, but odd rack designs may add to the cost of processing. Another important requirement of the part design and its racking is the necessity for good drainage of the solutions as the plating rack proceeds from one solution to another. Hollows that trap processing solutions present serious problems, which may be overcome with proper drainage holes. It is important that the designer of new items be aware of the desirability of smooth contours for ease of plating. Items that are easily racked and plated are processed more economically, and the result will be pieces with enhanced corrosion and wear resistance.

THE ELECTROPLATING PROCESS

Suppliers of proprietary materials predominate in the electroplating industry. This is largely because, with the exception of some sparse work from academia, most research and development has been done by these suppliers. This is true for every stage of processing.

The Plating Line

As a first and rather imprecise criterion, the thicknesses of the electrodeposits, nickel, and chromium determine the quality of the combination. These thicknesses may be limited by the physical plating setup. The most flexibility is obtained from the "hand" line. A group of tanks in a central location is used. Work is placed on small racks, which can be hand carried from one tank to another. The work can be left to plate for as long as is necessary to build the minimum thickness of deposits. This type of flexibility is necesary for job shops that plate a miscellany of work on a contract basis. Labor costs are high. Job shops are quite common in the plating industry. There are job shops that can plate all sizes of work from tiny eyelets and screws to mold bodies 1.25×2.5 m (4×8 ft) and larger. Such shops have the facility to plate decorative grilles and architectural panels also.

As the work gets larger, it is handled by hoists. It is only a step to the automatic or programmed hoists, which process greater volumes of parts on large racks in appropriately large tanks. Hoist lines are, of course, more labor efficient at the expense of lost flexibility.

Flexibility in processing is almost entirely sacrificed to efficiency when an in-line automatic plater is used. This type of machine is used when large volumes of the same or similar work with the same plating specifications are being processed. A conveyer carries the work through a series of tanks in a line. The speed of the conveyer and the length of each tank determine the processing time in each tank. The thicknesses of the deposits as well as the time of cleaning, activating, and rinsing are largely fixed by the speed of the conveyer and the length of the processing tanks.

Cleaning and Activation

A proper electrodeposit adheres to the basis metal or to the preceding electrodeposit with true atom-to-atom bonding. This is at least an order of magnitude greater than the adherence reported from any adhesive or from processes like metal spraying, which adhere by keying into micro and macro roughnesses. Proper cleaning is an absolute necessity. This necessitates superior cleaning and activation.

Solvent cleaners may be used in precleaning, but aqueous cleaners are invariably used with or without this precleaning. Frequently, particularly for steel, a strongly alkaline solution is used, perhaps close to boiling, as a precleaner.

Final cleaning is done most often from milder alkaline solutions containing high concentrations of surfactants. The removal of buffing compounds is especially difficult, and ultrasonics may be used in the final cleaner, which is invariably an electrolytic cleaner. The electrolytic current forms gas bubbles at the metal–cleaner solution interface, which helps in the cleaning action. Because alkaline cleaners tend to leave an oxide film on the basis metal, it is usually necessary to follow the alkaline cleaner with an acid activator, which dissolves oxide layers. In the case of most steels, this may be a solution containing sulfuric acid or its acid salts, surfactants, and even, sometimes, halides such as fluorides or iodides.

Sulfates cannot be used with leaded brasses because of the insolubility of the lead sulfate. In this case, more esoteric acids such as fluoroboric or citric will form the basis of the activator.

Good water rinsing before (and after) the activator is necessary to minimize dragover of the solutions.

Nickel Plating

In the past, cleaning and activation were most often followed by a "strike" of copper from a copper cyanide bath. Because of the toxicity of the cyanide, the plating industry has tended to try to eliminate the copper cyanide strike, often without success.

Nickel may be plated directly onto the clean and active basis metals quite successfully. Commercial nickel plating has had a long and varied history, starting in 1869 with the plating of Adams (4). Modern nickel plating baths are almost always a variant of the bath described by Watts (5). A typical composition of the basic bath is given in Table 1.

Nickel sulfate is the main source of nickel ions that are in high enough concentration to reduce concentration polarization and burning of the deposit. Nickel chloride provides the chloride ions necessary for good anode dissolution. In addition, the chloride ions increase the electrical conductivity of the solution, thus reducing power costs. Buffering in the cathode film is attributed to the boric acid, but its action goes beyond this to make the deposit both lighter and smoother.

Various organic additives are used in the nickel bath to modify the action of the bath and the properties of the deposit. Every nickel bath has a surfactant to lower the surface tension and permit the release of gas bubbles. Semibright nickel deposits are corrosion-resistant nickel deposits containing little or no sulfur. The addition agents are chosen to produce a deposit that is relatively noble. In contrast, bright nickel deposits are deposited from baths containing sulfur-producing additives. These additives are formulated to produce a bright banded structure, which results largely from the presence of codeposited nickel sulfide. The use of these bright nickels minimizes the amount of buffing necessary to obtain sufficient brilliance, and thus reduces processing expense.

In nonspecification plating, the bright nickel is always the only nickel deposit. In contrast to the electrochemical

Table 1. Typical Composition of a Modern Nickel Plating Bath

Compound	Concentration, g/L
Nickel sulfate, $NiSO_4 \cdot 6H_2O$	300
Nickel chloride, $NiCl_2 \cdot 6H_2O$	45
Boric acid, H_3BO_3	40
Temperature, °C (°F)	50–60 (130–140)
pH	3–4
Current density, $A/dm^2 (A/ft^2)$	5.5 (50)
Additives	

nobility of the semibright nickel deposit, the bright, sulfur-containing nickel deposit is electrochemically more active. Its corrosion resistance is not as good. This is the type of deposit ordinarily encountered outside the automotive field.

Specification plating for automotives calls for a bright nickel layer, ca 8 μm thick, over a semibright nickel deposit 20-μm thick. The combination is superior for corrosion resistance and appearance because the bright nickel, acting as a sacrificial electrochemical element (like zinc on steel), prevents penetrating corrosion.

CHROMIUM PLATING

Chromium plating differs from the plating of most other metals in several respects. In most cases, the metal being plated out at the cathode, the negative electrode, is replenished by an equivalent amount being dissolved at the anode, the positive electrode. When acid solutions of nickel, copper, or zinc are used for plating, the anodes are made of nickel, copper, or zinc, and the metal content of the bath tends to remain constant. Conversely, the chromium metal from the plating bath is replenished by the addition of more chromic acid because the anodes are inert alloyed lead, and the main anode reaction is the release of oxygen gas, not the formation of chromium ions.

Chromium plating requires rectifiers with larger capacities than the other plating baths. For example, nickel is plated with current densities of 4.5–5.5 A/dm^2 (40–50 A/ft^2). Decorative chromium plating requires ca 15 A/dm^2 (140 A/ft^2). Heavier bus bars are necessary to carry these higher currents.

Because so much of the applied current goes to make hydrogen gas at the cathode and oxygen gas at the anode, and toxic sprays are produced, higher-velocity exhaust systems are necessary for chromium plating tanks than for nickel plating tanks, where only slight amounts of gas may be discharged.

In addition to strong exhaust systems, two auxiliary means have been employed to help control the generated gases. A layer of polyethylene or polypropylene balls (solid, or hollow like ping pong balls) on the surface of the plating solution helps the gases escape without the concomitant liquid bubble films. Because these balls are trapped on the entering and exiting racks and because they degenerate chemically, they are not recommended. Surfactants are used in decorative chromium plating. These may be organic sulfonates. Only the perfluorinated ones have enough oxidation resistance for long life. These surfactants reduce liquid entrainment on the gases by reducing the surface tension so that the bubbles do not implode. Also, the foam layer on the surface of the plating bath is a physical barrier, much like the plastic balls.

The materials of construction for all equipment must be chosen to resist the strongly acid oxidizing power of the chromic acid solution. Engineering of plating lines and materials of construction are described in Ref. 6.

In general, nonconductors are formed of the plastisols, chlorinated poly(vinyl chloride), and fluorinated plastics. Few metals are resistant to chromic acid solutions, and

uncoated conductors steal plating current and plated metal.

The bright plating range for chromium plating is limited. For the bath containing 250 g/L of chromic acid and 2.5 g/L of sulfate, at 35°C the bright current density range is ca 2–12 A/dm^2 (19–112 A/ft^2); at 45°C it is ca 4–24 A/dm^2 (37–223 A/ft^2). Thus, decorative plating (6) is usually at 45–50°C. Since it is often the bright plating range of the chromium plating bath that limits the success of plating a given workpiece, conditions are chosen to obtain the maximum bright range.

Although plating cylinders and other simple shapes present few problems, shapes as complex as faucets can be difficult to plate acceptably. It is characteristic of any electroplating bath that recesses are more difficult to plate, because it is more difficult to reach them with plating current. Chromium has less ability than nickel to "throw" into these recesses even when special precautions are taken; that is, the ratio of chromic acid to catalyst is raised to increase this throw. The difficulty is compounded by the preplate problems of reaching all recesses with the buffing wheel. Thus, the nickel electroplate may be rougher in the recess, which makes coverage with chromium even more of a problem.

These types of considerations make racking, that is, the placement of workpieces on a rack to go through the plating processes, an art, one requiring experience and an understanding of the principles of plating current distribution. Even though the throw of the plating bath can be increased by increasing the ratio, there is a limitation. As the ratio of the chromic acid to the catalyst in the bath is increased, the activating ability is decreased; too high a ratio can result in nonplated areas because the nickel becomes passivated. Proprietary chromium plating baths may contain better activators than the sulfate of the ordinary bath and so combine a better plating range with better activation.

Chromium plating baths have more tolerance for foreign metal impurities than most plating baths. For example, a nickel or zinc plating bath may tolerate only a few parts per million of copper before deleterious effects are noticed in the deposit; chromium plating baths, on the other hand, have been known to operate successfully with up to 2–3 g/L of iron, nickel, or copper. Still, there is a limit, and dragover from the nickel bath also contains the ions of sulfate and chloride, both of which are catalysts, as well as boric acid. Good rinsing, then, is required between nickel and chromium plating. In modern installations, the rinsing after the nickel plating is done with two or three tanks in series utilizing cascade, counterflow rinsing. This most efficient type of rinsing in which the rinse water flows counter to the direction of work flow uses the least water to accomplish the best rinsing. In this day of EPA-mandated impurity levels for waste, efficient rinsing is essential both within the process and at the end of the process.

EFFLUENT AND PURIFICATION

The days of dumping rinses, spills, and even inoperative plating solutions directly into the sewer are over. Stringent limitations on the amounts of metals such as nickel, chromium, and lead that can leave a plant in the effluent stream are mandated by the law, and violations can lead to heavy fines, even jail terms.

Metals that cannot be returned to the plating tank must be made insoluble, collected, and sent to hazardous waste sites. Because the expense of these sites is so high, considerably more effort is going into returning the metals to the plating tanks. The return of a great proportion of the dragout means, however, that there is a buildup of impurities, impurities that can be catastrophic in their effect on the process. These impurities arise from various sources: from dragover, from leaching of tank linings and coatings, from dissolution of the racks, from the makeup water, from attack of pipes, from steam and oil leaks, from grease from the conveyer, and even from foreign metals in low concentration in dissolving anodes. Thus, the loss of the ability to keep impurity concentrations low and tolerable by discarding dragout to the waste stream is gone. It is necessary, then, to be able to purify the dragout and rinse water before it returns to the process tank, to purify the process tank itself, or both.

Recycling is the ideal approach, and it is being done successfully. In the case of nickel-containing solutions, electrodialysis is being used to separate the impurities from the nickel ions.

Most impurities in chromium plating are cationic metals in the acid solution, that is, nickel, iron, copper, and zinc. Chromic acid is in the anionic form in solution. The cationic impurities are removed from the anionic solution by using an oxidation-resistant cation-exchange resin. The cations are trapped on the resin while the chromic acid solution proceeds through. In the case of dilute rinse waters, it may be necessary to concentrate this treated solution before it returns to the plating tanks. The heated tanks themselves tend to act as evaporators. The impurity metals, recovered as the sulfates on regeneration of the resin bed, are appropriately treated to make them suitable for waste.

BIBLIOGRAPHY

1. U.S. Pat. 1,581,188 (1926), U.S. Pat. 1,802,463 (1931), C. G. Fink.
2. G. Dubpernell, "Chromium Plating," in F. A. Lowenheim, ed., *Modern Electroplating,* 3rd ed., John Wiley & Sons, Inc., New York, 1974.
3. G. Dubpernell, *Electrodeposition of Chromium from Chromic Acid Solutions,* Pergamon Press, Elmsford, N.Y., 1977.
4. I. Adams, *Trans. Am. Electrochem. Soc.* **9,** 211 (1906).
5. O. P. Watts, *Trans. Am. Electrochem. Soc.* **23,** 99 (1913).
6. A. K. Graham, *Electroplating Engineering Handbook,* 3rd ed., Van Nostrand Reinhold Co., Inc., New York, 1971.

Hyman Chessin, PhD
Brick, New Jersey

CHURCH ARCHITECTURE

Church architecture is the architecture that best describes the places where Christians assemble to worship God, or buildings that were designed and built for this specific purpose. With a few possible exceptions, the design and construction of churches did not occur until after the Roman Empire adopted Christianity as the state church in the fourth century. The history of church architecture is, to a large degree, the history of architecture itself since the fourth or fifth century. It embraces the science of construction, the highest levels of design and execution in the use of various materials, the development of visual art forms, and music. For over a thousand years, churches and cathedrals were the most significant buildings built; they were the center of the social structure and by their magnificent presence influenced many other forms of architecture.

Until after the Reformation, most churches were arranged in a basilican plan, with the design being influenced by geography, climate, and social conditions. After the Reformation, the worship services of many different denominations began to change; this had an impact on the internal arrangements and the architecture. In recent years, the major changes in church architecture have been in direct relation to the changes in the form of worship by and within each denomination; the expansion of the churches' participation in many different levels of community life and changes in the social structure have also been influential.

Unlike that of most other types of buildings, church design may incorporate a variety of art forms and specialized technologies to meet requirements unique to it. There is no single set of standards that would be applicable to more than a single denomination; at best these standards can only be used as guidelines.

The single factor that can be used to define what a church should be is that it is a place where people assemble to worship God. Beyond this, the spaces themselves vary dramatically. For instance, there is no similarity whatsoever between a Greek Orthodox church and a U.S. Baptist church. The internal arrangements of the space, furnishings, and appointments are poles apart. The reason for these differences is that the Greek Orthodox church is a liturgical and highly ritualistic church, whereas the Baptist church is primarily an evangelical church with little liturgical or ritual emphasis.

Churches, like any other building type, are designed for an intended use of space. Whatever the function, if the building does not provide the types and juxtaposition of spaces and the elements needed within those spaces, then it can be stated most emphatically that the building was not designed, as a result of the architect's inability or lack of knowledge. In addition to having talents in art and building technology, the architect must be able to analyze the client's needs, even though they may not be clearly defined.

The architect who is commissioned to design a church building should make it a point to learn as much about the religion of the denomination as possible. What is important to the particular body of people must be understood, through both contact with the client and research. Armed with this knowledge, the architect, having all of the other required talents, should be able to design a church building of outstanding merit.

Many architects have emphasized the importance of a scholarly understanding of the history of architecture. This is the very basis for being well educated and equipped to design buildings that relate to the present or future. *A History Of Architecture on a Comparative Method* (1), written by Sir Banister Fletcher, is perhaps the most complete examination of the history of church architecture in print.

HISTORY

In the first years of Christianity, small groups joined in the worship at Jewish synagogues. This practice did not last very long, as these Christian groups were soon excluded from teaching and preaching in the temple. For their own services, they met in private homes to pray and break bread. The apostle Paul established many Christian communities in his missionary travels in Italy, Syria, Africa, and Greece; he preached, "We are the temple of the living God." The early Christians did not attempt to establish facilities solely for worship. "Jesus, as everyone knows, didn't ask his followers to build anything. Indeed, on the Mount of Transfiguration, he persuaded his disciples not to build some shrines they thought appropriate" (2). Unlike the pagan gods who were sheltered in great temples, this God was an unseen deity and did not need a temple. Until Christianity was permitted as the recognized religion of the Roman Empire, most services were held by small groups in secret. It was not until after Constantine's decree in 313 A.D. recognizing Christianity, which soon after became the official religion of the Roman Empire, that Christians gathered in public. As their numbers increased, they were forced to abandon meeting in homes and to find structures that would house larger gatherings.

History is unclear about when the first church building was built for Christian worship, but there is evidence that Christians were permitted to use Roman halls of justice, which were called basilicas. Believed to be the oldest, Basilica Porcia was constructed in Rome about 184 B.C. From that time onward, the Romans built basilicas for the administration of justice throughout the Roman Empire. These halls of justice were always a prominent feature in Roman town planning.

Since they were the most suitable public buildings, it is understandable that Chrisitans borrowed basilicas for places of worship rather than pagan shrines or temples. The use of basilicas prior to the construction of churches for worship has had a profound and lasting influence on church architecture, particularly in Western Europe and later in the United States. The basilican churches built by the Roman Church followed the basic architectural style of the Roman law courts with little change until the Middle Ages; the basilica was usually built over the grave of a saint.

When Christians first started to use basilicas, they adopted the internal arrangement of the hall of justice, which shaped the arrangement for worship. In many older liturgical churches, the basic interior arrangement still exists, with some modifications (Fig. 1). The altar, which in the basilica had been used for sacrificial offerings to the gods, was adapted to the celebration of the Mass, which emphasized the sacrificial death of Christ. The apse, a recess behind the altar, which had been where the praetor sat in the Roman basilica, now became the seat of the bishop.

To either side of the central bishop's seat, often referred to as the bishop's throne, sat the presbyters or members of the church council, replacing the earlier use of the same by the Roman assessors. The growth of the ritual resulted in the addition of a choir, which was enclosed by low screen walls called *cancelli,* the Latin word for chancel.

At the same time, an ambo, now referred to as a pulpit, was incorporated in or as a part of the screen walls on either side for the reading of the Epistle and the Gospel. The addition of the choir and pulpits took place in the fourth century. Prior to this time, it is assumed that the music, if any, was provided by a cantor, a carryover from the singer of liturgical solos in the synagogue.

The nave, derived from *navis,* the Latin word for ship, was divided by a wide central aisle, and it is thought that women and men gathered separately at either side following the Jewish tradition, which is still practiced in orthodox synagogues. Originally, the early basilicas had an atrium, which one entered before entering the nave. In the center of this walled and columned enclosure was a fountain for ablutions, which in the Roman Catholic church is still symbolized by the holy-water basins placed within the church at the main entrance.

The narthex, or enclosed vestibule at the main entrance, had its origin in the covered part of the atrium or porch, which leads into the nave. The sanctuary is a derivative of the Latin word *sanctuarium,* which means a sacred or holy place. The sanctuary was a term that was used for the area in or near the apse, where the altar stood. In many denominations, the word sanctuary is now used in reference to the entire interior of the place of worship, or a place of refuge.

The addition of transepts or wings to the original rectangular shape of the basilica did not evolve until the Middle Ages; thus, the plan then became the shape of the Latin cross. Others contend that the cruciform plan had its origin as early as the fourth century when these transepts were used as sepulchers or burial vaults. In comparing the plan of the early basilican church with that of what is commonly referred to as the traditional church floor plan, the similarities become evident.

As the Christian faith grew and became more widespread, certain embellishments were added. These embellishments were typified by the introduction of religious art and music that reflected local culture. It was during this period of growth that the basic precepts of worship and communion in the Roman Catholic and Eastern Orthodox churches became influenced by the development and growth of the liturgy. Some scholars do not agree with

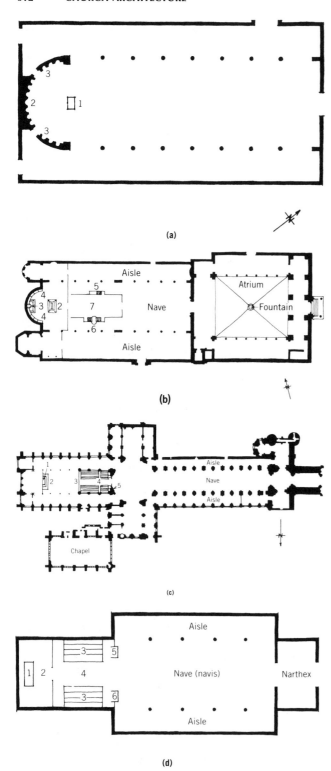

(a)

(b)

(c)

(d)

Figure 1. Interior arrangements. **(a)** Basilica or hall of justice in the Palaces of the Emperors on Palatine Hill, Rome, 200 A.D. 1, altar; 2, praetor seat; 3, assessors. **(b)** Basilica Church of Saint Clement, Rome, 1108 A.D. 1, altar; 2, sanctuary; 3, bishop's throne; 4, presbyters; 5, Epistle ambo; 6, Gospel ambo; 7, choir. **(c)** Ely Cathedral, Cambridgeshire, England, 1081 A.D. to 1349 A.D. 1, altar; 2, sanctuary; 3, presbytery; 4, choir; 5, pulpit (Gospel ambo). **(d)** Typical church, 12th to 20th century. 1, altar; 2, sanctuary (*sanctuarium*); 3, choir; 4, chancel (*cancelli*); 5, lectern (Epistle ambo); 6, pulpit (Gospel ambo).

the growth of liturgy and feel that the way in which the early Christians prayed and met is the only valid approach to worship. Others believe that the development of the liturgy gave great meaning and inspiration to those who gathered in Christ's name.

As the clergy had some education, it became very influential in the affairs of the church and in the conduct of services. The development of the liturgy did not have a negative impact on the growth of Christianity; rather, it may have had its part in the growth of the church. It is very clear that the history of humanity and its belief in God or gods have always contained elements of liturgy or ritualism. The growth and development of the liturgy seems to have been a very natural evolution, as these embellishments of the worship service gave great meaning, inspiration, and a sense of awe to those who often traveled great distances to come and worship.

E. A. Sovik (2) makes a point that three factors were of profound influence on the growth of the church. First, the church compromised some of its distinctive qualities when Christianity was made the public religion of the Roman Empire. Prior to this time, the practice of Christianity was private. This development resulted in the institutionalization of the church. Second, the rather sudden and vast increase in the number of Christians throughout the empire then required that special structures for worship be built. The third factor is that those who had been martyred during the persecution were then honored by buildings built over their graves or by having their relics incorporated into church structures. Thus, the church became not only a church, but also a shrine to holy persons. It is argued that these influences changed the conception of people as the temples of God, to the idea that the building itself was the house of God.

There is no doubt that these and other factors tended to shape the church from a very private religion into a public religion. When the early Christians abandoned the idea of using homes and moved into basilicas, they adopted the internal arrangement and adapted that to the form of worship.

During the Reformation, many images and relics were destroyed in an attempt to break from the influences that shaped the church up through the Middle Ages. The new churches that appeared soon after the Reformation were quite different, but they did not discard all of the traditions that had been adopted by Christians from the fourth century through the Middle Ages (3):

The lesson to be learned here is that architecture is a more influential factor in the life of society than most people suppose. The incompleteness of the Reformation in terms of architecture was no doubt the result of the longevity of architecture. Buildings stand, and are not easily removed or changed. The "houses of God" from medieval times continued to stand, continued to assert themselves as "houses of God" because of their strong ecclesiastical character, and continued to teach the people around them that there ought to be such a place as a "house of god." Despite what people read or heard of the words of Jesus or the apostles or the Early Fathers, the silent voice of architecture spoke more persuasively.

As far as the environment of worship is concerned, the last four centuries have been the children of the Middle Ages, not the Reformation. And most of the churches have continued to establish "holy places," more or less on the medieval patterns.

After the Reformation and the formation of those denominations that protested the authority of Rome, there was no immediate or significant change in the liturgy or the architecture of the newly created Christian denominations. It was not until the founding and growth of the evangelical denominations, which departed from the traditional forms of worship, that the traditional interior arrangement began to change.

Since the Reformation in the sixteenth century and the dispersal of the church into many denominations and individual congregations, the character of the architecture of churches has been vastly affected by the forms of worship acknowledged by various groups of Christians. Many denominations attempted to reassert the teachings of the New Testament and cast aside those traditions incorporated into the church buildings. Many denominations built meeting houses, which were used for both worship and public assembly. These buildings were quite simple and secular in appearance. In many instances, it was thought that the building itself was not a house of God and there was no divine presence except when the Christians gathered; as Paul wrote, "We are the temple of the living God."

It would seem that the building and worship service were then in conflict, or that the traditional structure inhibited the return to simpler forms of worship. Today, there is a universal movement among the institutional churches and independent congregations to reform the church. This movement is having a profound effect on the design of church buildings. Depending on the denomination, and often on the individual church, the difference in church environments is vast. The current era of reformation has had its impact on the liturgical churches as well as the evangelical churches. Some of the denominations that have been known as liturgical churches have become more evangelistic, and some of the evangelistic denominations have become more liturgical. Thus, at the present time, the church is in a transitional era (4):

At the present time, the churches of this country are at the beginning of what may be a great new reformation. Indeed, historians of subsequent centuries may look back upon our period in time as one of great renewal and strengthening within the church just as we now consider the previous century as one of tremendous work in the expression of the faith.

Since the 1920s, there has been a growing recognition among theologians and educated laypersons that the church, Roman Catholic and Protestant, needed to reexamine both biblically and theologically the design of the worship space. Vatican II recognized this psychological fact in the age of "postliterate man" when it declared, "In the restoration and promotion of the Sacred Liturgy . . . full and active participation by all the people is the aim to be considered before all else"(5). At the same time, many of the Protestant churches were beginning to recognize that the emphasis should be placed more on the corporate worship and the involvement of the people rather

than on having the priest or minister perform for an audience. As a result of this thinking, many church buildings are taking a different shape and departing from the long rectangular places of worship to those that allow the worshipers to gather around the central point of worship.

CURRENT TRENDS IN CHURCH ARCHITECTURE

Sovik makes a strong statement for a return to the "nonchurch" which could be a meeting place that becomes a church as the faithful gather. He suggests that the room be called "the centrum" so that the name of the space would be sufficiently free of ecclesiastical connotations. The centrum would then become a multipurpose space so that the secular and the sacred would not be separated and the place could become sacred when a liturgical event is brought into the space. There is clearly an historical basis for this approach, and it also makes sense from an economic viewpoint. Whatever the validity, the most important factor is the quality of the personal worship experience of individuals and congregations. Worship is both a spiritual and an emotional experience. Both may be related to the sense of tradition or roots that provide or help to provide an uplifting of the spirit. The return to the nonchurch would not be readily accepted by all. The great cathedrals in Europe as well as the monasteries and parish churches are visited by millions of people every year. The average layperson is not interested solely in the architecture itself. There is also an appreciation for the roots and tradition of the church. Few people would support the notion of letting these edifices of the past disappear; on the contrary, a large portion of the funds that support the cost of upkeep come from those who make pilgrimages to these places. The sense of roots relates interdependently to religion, history, and architecture.

Future changes in the church are as inevitable as those in the past. The changes occurring in the past resulted in great and irreplaceable works of art and music, all of which are related to the Christian faith and cannot be pushed aside or dispelled as now unimportant, as if those extravagances were misdirected. If, in fact, the Christian church had departed from the teachings of Christ and put too much emphasis on places that incorporated the most significant developments in art and music, all to the glory of God, is it reasonable to assert that these developments no longer have any meaning in religious heritage?

If a group of clergy representing a number of different denominations was gathered together and asked, "If you and your congregation were building a church today, how would you arrange the worship space?" the answers may or may not be similar, but in examining the subject with each, one would find a great deal of variation of opinion. Some clergy and congregations would still opt for the traditional styles of architecture, where others would desire to break with all traditions and create a space around what they believe to be important in the worship experience.

One should recognize that the church building is not only a worship space, but may also contain many other elements of building to serve the needs of the church.

Depending on the size of the congregation and its activities and programs, these other needs must be given proper recognition as they support the total program in the church. Unlike the churches of the Middle Ages, many churches conduct or sponsor numerous activities throughout the week. First, there is the administrative office, which is engaged in operating the programs and business of the church and communications to its congregation and others. Larger congregations have a number of staff persons, each responsible for some activity or program in the church or related outreach programs. Second, it is not uncommon for churches to provide counseling or space for counseling within the building. This activity usually takes place during the week, which makes it possible to use the same space for other purposes on weekends. There are also other weekday programs for groups within the church, including activities such as meetings and in some cases the provision of food and clothing for the elderly or those in need. Other types of spaces that serve the varied programs might include libraries, conference rooms, and other spaces for special needs. Third, as a response to community needs and the economic infeasibility of building classrooms that are used only once a week, many churches utilize educational spaces for weekday preschool and/or school-age educational programs. The type of facilities for education vary considerably, depending on a number of factors related to the emphasis on Christian or secular education. The space per person, the arrangement of this space, and the sizes of the rooms, are all related to methods of teaching and whether or not spaces will be used by different groups having different requirements. Fourth, fellowship programs usually require a large open room for the gathering of a number of people, and this must be a truly multipurpose area. In smaller communities, the fellowship hall or the parish hall may also be used by groups within the community that have no direct association with the church; thus, the space is also a community room. The facilities required, such as stages, kitchens, projection booths, or other ancillary facilities, depend entirely on the type of program that must be accommodated in the space. A number of churches do not plan the community room as a separate space, but adapt the same space for the worship services, as suggested in Sovik's use of the term centrum. If a single room is to serve both sacred and secular activities, then extreme care must be exercised in providing a space that is easily adaptable and physically suitable to provide the right environment for all activities. The conversion of a single space from one for secular programs to one for worship requires a rearrangement of furniture and presents many challenges in acoustics, lighting, music, and other factors relating to the environment required for each type of use.

The functional relationship of the various elements or parts of the church building requires careful consideration. The flow of people entering and leaving the church facilities on Sunday may be totally different than the flow of people using the building during the week. Most buildings have front doors because, until the advent of the automobile and parking areas placed to the rear of a facility, people always approached a building from one direction. There are churches today whose front doors are rarely used be-

cause they are the farthest removed from the parking areas. Ideally, the entire family should be able to enter the facility at one point and then easily break off to the part of the building to which each will go. For example, the children may go to Sunday school, one parent to choir, and the other parent to a classroom. It would not be appropriate for a facility to require a family to disperse through doors and go into different entrances to get to their designated activities. Consideration should be given not only to security, but also to informing strangers entering the building. It is surprising how much time is lost by strangers trying to find the church office during the week. Ideally, the church office should be located at a primary entrance to the building so that someone from the staff can control entry to the building and can also be available to assist anyone entering the facility. The primary entrance should be of a generous size, as people will naturally gather together just before leaving the building (Fig. 2).

The dispersal of various facilities by type of use will, for the most part, make it unnecessary to open all parts of the building for a single type of use. It may also be possible to isolate the unused portions of the building from the part of the building in use. As a result, money will be saved in the operation of the heating and air-conditioning systems, and in maintenance.

THE WORSHIP SPACE

As mentioned previously, there is no totally acceptable arrangement of space that would suit all denominations. The churches that can be broadly identified as liturgical are more likely to have established forms of worship that, to varying degrees, include ritualism. In these types of settings, the altar or table is the chief focus of the worship environment. Generally, in the evangelical churches, the

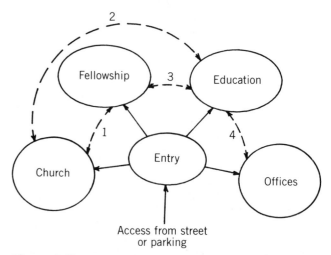

Figure 2. Functional relationship of building elements. Solid arrows illustrate access, dashed arrows refer to internal relationship. 1, Movement from church to fellowship for after-service reception; 2, movement from church to Sunday school education or vice versa can be a requirement; 3, use of fellowship area for extension of weekday educational programs; 4, access for school staff using office facilities.

altar or table is not as prominent; greater emphasis is given to the placement of the pulpit for the preaching of God's word as revealed in the New Testament. Most, but not all, denominations have some kind of music as a part of the worship service, which could include organ, piano, solo, and/or choir music. The choir is more prominent as a performing body in the churches giving little emphasis to an established form of worship, that is, to liturgy. Far less emphasis is placed on the location of the choir in liturgical churches because the purpose of the choir is to enrich the liturgy and not to supplant or dominate it. For this reason, it is not unusual to find a choir and organ in the balcony of some liturgical churches. The argument for this location is that the choir can provide music to enrich the liturgy and back up the congregation in the singing of hymns. The opposing argument is that the choir members are too far removed from participation in the services with the rest of the congregation.

It is interesting to note the changes taking place in the forms of worship. The liturgical churches, the Roman Catholic Church included, are placing far more emphasis on the gathering and participation of the worshipers. In the past, these churches were severely criticized for "putting on a show" instead of involving the people in the service. At the same time, some are drawn to watching religious television shows such as talk shows and musical extravaganzas.

As a result of these and other differences, the question of the focal point arises. Whether it be the altar or the pulpit, this decision is based on the practices of each particular denomination or congregation. It is impossible to emphasize the degree of importance to be given to locating the altar, pulpit, lectern, baptismal pool, font, or choir, as these factors depend entirely on the emphasis that each denomination or congregation places on any one or several of these principal elements. It is also impossible to make a brief examination of the chief emphasis in each church. The architect cannot make any assumptions about these matters unless guidance in planning the worship arrangement is reasonably well defined, as in the case of the Roman Catholic Church, whose requirements are published by liturgical commissions. Other denominations have similar publications that provide guidance, but not absolute direction.

These influences will be discussed in general terms, but cannot be applied to all denominations and independent congregations.

At this time, a number of independent congregations, not associated with organized or institutionalized denominations, are surfacing. These "assemblies of the faithful" find it impossible to identify with the politics and policies of established denominations. Many of these congregations are basing their credence on a literal interpretation of the Bible and often use the word covenant in defining the emphasis of and reason for their assembly. They seek to give emphasis to the promises made by God to man. The nature of this emphasis within established denominations and independent groups is to establish or reestablish that the basic beliefs and practices are in concert with the New Testament, that is, the "new covenant."

Even those who have formed new associations, all seeking the true meaning of the New Testament, do not agree on all matters. So it is essential to recognize these differences when designing a building. The building must respond to the congregation's primary thrust. It must provide an environment that matches its physical and environmental needs.

The designer of churches must be sensitive to these factors and, regardless of personal convictions, be responsive to the needs of others to provide facilities that emphasize what they feel is important or essential.

The only factors that are common to all churches, regardless of denomination or individual differences, are the following:

1. One usually enters and leaves the auditorium or church by means of a main door.
2. When seated, everyone is usually facing the location of the action; there is always a focal point, even though the point of focus may change during the course of the worship service; that is, if the font is at the rear of the church and a baptism takes place during the service, then it will be necessary for the participants to turn around.
3. When a service is over, people usually wish to be greeted by the minister or priest or to greet each other. Many consider this postservice time very important in bringing people together in an atmosphere of family or community gathering. To slow down the exodus, coffee is sometimes served to encourage this type of fellowship. These gatherings usually take place in a large area easily reached from the worship area.

Other similarities may be evident in liturgical churches as well as in evangelical churches. It is important to recognize that there is no absolute division between liturgical and evangelical churches. In differing degrees, there is an evangelical emphasis in those churches that are usually identified as liturgical. Also, some evangelical denominations have an adopted form of worship that could be referred to as a liturgy. These similarities and dissimilarities make it impossible to design a single building that would be suitable for all forms of worship. The interior arrangement of the space must respond to what a single congregation may wish to accomplish in its worship experience. Departing from the traditional rectangular arrangement, the space could be round, square, triangular, hexagonal, or any other shape or form to enclose the internal arrangement. The point of focus should be located, and the arrangement of people will often dictate the shape of the building, rather than the shape of the building dictating the internal arrangement. The shape of the building must not only create a comfortable envelope around the congregation, but it must also provide for all of the necessary lighting, acoustics, and other environmental considerations.

THE PLATFORM OR CHANCEL

In the traditional church, which grew out of the influence of the early basilicas, the chancel was placed at the end of a long rectangle. In the cathedrals and monasteries built during the Middle Ages, the chancel was raised above the public area of the building, in some cases by as much as a full story. It is almost universally true that the chancel is no longer a remote area; it has been brought in closer proximity to the worshipers. The chief purpose in raising the platform or having steps is to permit better visual contact. In many cases, the choir is also on this raised platform and is sometimes elevated in tiers so the choir members will see the director and also have eye contact with the congregation.

In addition to the normal worship functions taking place in this location, it is often requested that the furnishings be movable so that the platform or chancel can be used for pageants, plays, concerts, and so on. In the liturgical churches, the altar or eucharistic table is the point of focus on the chancel platform. In the evangelical churches, the pulpit will normally be the center of focus, with the table being on floor level with the congregation. The size, shape, and extent of any platform or platforms is directly related to what space needs to be provided for the various functions. Obviously, if the choir were to be located in the chancel and elevated for eye contact, the platform would be much larger than if it were only for an altar or pulpit.

CONGREGATIONAL SEATING

Seating was not provided for the worshipers until sometime in the Middle Ages. They stood or sat on the floor and often moved about during the service. The first seating was probably benches, which gradually evolved into more elaborate structures with boxlike enclosures. These enclosures were usually paid for by and reserved for a family. The enclosure did tend to reduce the amount of cold draft across the floor in unheated churches.

In this era, pews became commonplace and were very often elaborately carved and shaped as part of the decor of the building. Pews are more commonly identified with churches than with cathedrals as many cathedrals are furnished with chairs, which usually can be linked together to form rows of fixed seats. Renovations to some older church buildings have resulted in all of the fixed seating being removed and replaced with movable seating to permit flexibility in arrangement for different types of experimental services. Pews are adaptable only to the type of space that will not require rearrangement of the seating for other type of functions. In fixed seating arrangements where pews are used, open areas for circulation within the seating area might be considered overflow space for the introduction of chairs on those few occasions when maximum seating is necessary.

The arrangement of seats, whether fixed or movable, is usually set so people are faced toward the center of worship. There is a general trend to bring a greater number of people closer to the point of worship to encourage a feeling of communal participation. Thus, the shape of the worship space has become wider and shorter in length. Seating is arranged in radial or segmented arcs perpendicular to the desired line of focus. Segments or sections

of seating are interrupted with aisles for access and egress. Main or center aisles are often made wider than required by code to provide a generous passage for processions, wedding parties, and funeral services. Added width may be desirable to provide a more comfortable departure after a service. It cannot be assumed that all churches need or want a center aisle or that all churches conduct marriage or funeral services; some churches have processions, whereas others do not. Spatial arrangements of groups of seats, aisles, direction of focus, and sloped or level floors are all design considerations that must be responsive to the specific, and sometimes unique, requirements of a congregation.

THE ALTAR OR TABLE

In the pre-Christian era, the altar was the place where sacrifices and offerings were made to a god or an ancestor. This term was adopted by the early Christian church, probably at the time when Christians started using the Roman basilicas. During the Reformation and since, many have preferred to associate the table with the Last Supper and feel it should be called the Eucharistic table or Communion table.

In most denominations, the altar or Communion table becomes the chief focus during the Mass or Communion service. Until very recently, this service was conducted with the clergy's back to the congregation. Now the clergy faces the congregation to elicit its participation in the service.

The participation of the congregation in taking Communion varies considerably. In the Roman Catholic Church, the priest, or priests, stands in the front of the church, and the congregation passes by and receives wafers. Serving the wine or the "blood of Christ" in a cup or chalice was discontinued during the great plague in Europe. Other liturgical churches frequently have a Communion rail where congregational members come to stand or kneel to receive the Communion, which consists of bread and wine administered by the clergy and/or appointed laypersons. In others, they have the bread in trays and grape juice in small plastic or glass cups. In still other churches, the bread and the grape juice are passed around to the people as they sit in the pews or chairs. Far more circulation space is needed in the chancel area when the congregation comes forward to receive Communion. Where the people gather, a Communion rail often completely encircles the altar or Communion table, symbolizing the Last Supper. In some liturgical churches, the space around the altar that is enclosed by the Communion rail is called the sanctuary. There has been some experimentation with using a large table where people come and stand, or sit around a number of large tables, for the taking of the bread and wine. The significance of this rite or "act of remembrance" differs considerably, and these differences have a direct effect on the arrangement and size of the space in and around the altar or table. The use of candles on or near the altar may have symbolic importance or may simply be a continuation of the tradition prior to electricity. In a well-lit church, candles are no longer needed solely for illumination.

THE PULPIT

Prior to the addition of the choir and chancel area in the Roman basilica (probably in the fourth or fifth century, when the ambos were also added), there was probably no such thing as a pulpit. The clergy must have had to depend on its education to relate stories from both the Old and New Testaments as it was not until the monastic era that great numbers of manuscripts were copied by monks and made available to the clergy. The placement of the pulpit had little theological significance, except that it is a location where the priest or minister stands to give a sermon or homily. The pulpit must be located so that the speaker can have eye contact with most of the congregation; except in rare instances, the speaker's back should not be turned to anyone. The lectern, also called an ambo from basilica tradition, is a reading stand and resting place for the Bible. From this location, portions of the Old and New Testaments are read. In those denominations where the pulpit is the key focal point, the lectern is often omitted.

BAPTISM

Baptism in some churches is done by immersion, whereas in most of the liturgical churches baptism is performed by sprinkling water on the head from the font or a bowl. Some believe that the fountain or pool in the atrium of the basilica was used for baptism and that no one could enter the church until baptized. Perhaps it is to symbolize this practice that older churches and cathedrals have placed the font at the rear of the church.

In the case of a baptismal pool provided for immersion, it is preferable to locate this near or in the chancel area or where it can be easily viewed by the congregation.

The font is usually of stone or wood, into which a bowl is placed to hold the water for this sacrament. The font can be a large, immovable object, or it can be a simple bowl, which can be placed anywhere in the church. In many churches, the location is not dictated by the denomination; therefore, the choice is often made by the congregation. If it is important that the people in the church participate in the baptismal service and renew their own vows, then the place for baptism is usually near or in the chancel area. If the font, which could also be a small fountain, were to be given more prominence, then a special place could be incorporated in the architecture.

CHOIR

In any church, the choir should ideally be located where the voices can be heard by those present. With few exceptions, either an organ or a piano is used with the voices in the choir. Even in liturgical churches, where the primary purpose of a choir is to take part in the liturgy and to lead the congregation in the singing of hymns, it is usual at some point in the service for the choir and musicians to perform for the congregation. The location of the choir within the church is often bitterly contested. The chief reason for this is that musicians often desire the church to be a concert hall; they are partly correct. The other side of this argument relates to the fact that a church is where people come to worship God, and if the choir or its instruments dominate the scene, then the emphasis is away from worship. In liturgical churches, there are certain services that have no music.

The traditional location of the choir, between the people and the chancel, has disappeared in response to bringing the point of worship into the midst of the people. The location of the choir then depends on its purpose and presence as an important element in the worship service. Locating the choir on the center axis facing the congregation, although possibly ideal for concerts, is not the best solution in liturgical churches. Some recent churches have actually located the choir on the main floor of the church in seats or chairs that would otherwise be occupied by worshipers. If the choir is to be located in the chancel, then it could be placed to one side of the chancel (not both sides), and the chancel itself could be extended at a right angle or on a diagonal to provide a wraparound raised platform (Fig. 3).

There are several key elements that must be considered in relation to the music:

1. To accomplish well-blended and modulated voicing, it is desirable that the entire choir be located together in a single group. This is not any different than for any other singing group.
2. The director is almost always in front of the choir, unless the director is also the organist. In that case, the location of the organ console is important. Many who come to worship are disturbed by the prominence of the director during choir performance.
3. The floor and wall surfaces surrounding the choir and instruments should be hard, reflective surfaces.
4. Ideally, the pipe organ should be located directly behind the choir to ensure that all of the music, vocal and instrumental, is coming from the same source. This also provides the director with the advantage of hearing the blend of the instrument and voices. If an electronic organ is used, the speakers can be located similarly.
5. Many churches use a piano in combination with an organ. In these cases, there needs to be eye contact among the director, the organist, and the pianist.
6. If other instruments are used on a regular or irregular basis, space should be considered so that the entire musical assembly performs in a group.

ORGANS

The pipe organ is basically an assembly of metal and wood whistles. These are arranged in ranks, and the wind is produced by a blower, which is often placed in a remote location and connected to the pipe organ by welded sheet

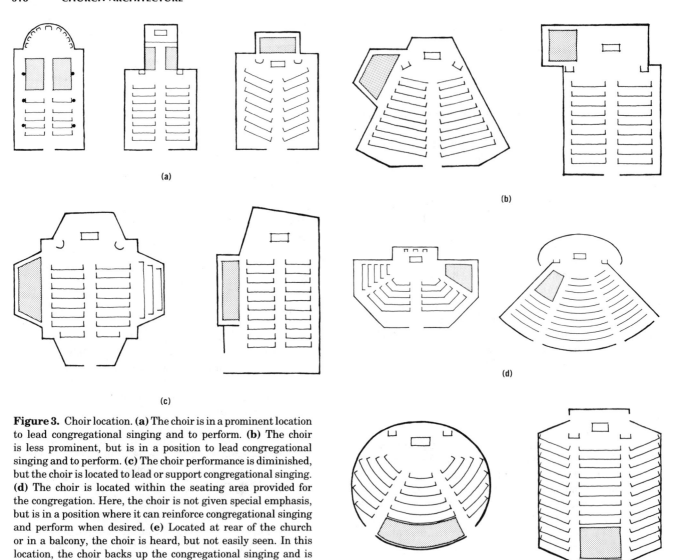

Figure 3. Choir location. **(a)** The choir is in a prominent location to lead congregational singing and to perform. **(b)** The choir is less prominent, but is in a position to lead congregational singing and to perform. **(c)** The choir performance is diminished, but the choir is located to lead or support congregational singing. **(d)** The choir is located within the seating area provided for the congregation. Here, the choir is not given special emphasis, but is in a position where it can reinforce congregational singing and perform when desired. **(e)** Located at rear of the church or in a balcony, the choir is heard, but not easily seen. In this location, the choir backs up the congregational singing and is not in a position to perform visually. Paid musicians who are not necessarily members of the congregations are often located in a rear balcony.

metal or PVC pipe. A small organ can have as few as five or six ranks, whereas larger organs may have as many as 50 or more ranks. The number of pipes in a rank depends on the number of keys on a console. Smaller churches seating 300–500 people can usually manage quite well with an instrument containing 15–20 ranks. Some of the ranks are enclosed in a swell box, which is louvered to open and close to control the volume. Prior to the advent of electricity, manually operated bellows were used to produce the wind.

The organ was first used for liturgical music in the monastic orders around the eighth or ninth century A.D. Pipes at that time were made from brass, copper, and wood. Prior to that time, other instruments may have been used, but most of the music was provided by cantors or voices singing a cappella (without musical accompaniment).

There was also a reed organ, which produced sound by reeds that vibrated, similar to an oboe or bassoon. Reed organs are currently used only in certain types of music.

The mechanical functions of a pipe organ or the uses of electronics to control the action of the organ vary considerably. Tracker organs were usually consoles, where the keys mechanically controlled the amount of wind that escaped into a pipe. These mechanical devices, which were wood rods or wires, required the pipe assembly to be in close association with the console. This can be seen in organs where the console and pipes are together as a single piece of equipment.

The controls from the console directing the wind into the selected pipe or pipes can be activated by wind or mechanical or electronic devices. There are stops and couplers, which control the selection of the pipes that will receive wind to activate whistles by depressing a single key.

Thus, provisions for mechanical, wind, or electronic controls from the console to the organ are of importance. If a church requires mobility for the console, such as may be required for concerts, then this can only be accomplished by an electronic command from the keyboard, which can be transmitted via a flexible cable containing a number of low-voltage wires.

Many highly accomplished organists prefer a tracker-action organ, which gives them ultimate control that cannot be achieved by mechanically or electronically controlled devices; such purists are scarce.

A complete pipe organ can simulate, with a single musician, many of the sounds that would come from a symphony orchestra. Artfully arranged, a pipe organ can be a work of art that need not be hidden in a chamber.

Electronic organs generally produce sounds to imitate a pipe organ by electronic components that produce sounds through artificial means; some manufacturers have been able to produce reasonably good imitations, which, to the unskilled listener, sound authentic. Generally speaking, rank by rank, the electronic organ can provide a greater range of tonal selection for a smaller initial investment.

A pipe organ, with reasonable care and maintenance, has an unlimited lifetime. The pipes that produce the sound never wear out. Electronic components do have a limited lifetime, as do circuitry and speakers that produce artificial sounds.

The surfaces around the pipes or speakers, whether in the open or in a recess or chamber, require a highly reflective, hard surface to project the sounds from the instrument into the building.

ACOUSTICS

The role of acoustics in the worship place is often misunderstood and is debated among architects, musicians, acousticians, ministers, and laypersons. There is a popular misconception that any acoustical surface in a church is detrimental to the reverberation. Too much reverberation is just as bad as no reverberation at all. Laypersons frequently confuse the terms echo and reverberation. Echoes are sharp reflective sounds that can be heard, whereas reverberation is the persistence of sound in a space after the original sound source has been stopped.

The tempo of music in cathedrals is fairly slow to allow the reverberating sound to dissipate. Lively music is generally not played in buildings with long reverberation periods. Most liturgical music was composed for large cathedrals or churches where the reverberation period was at least 2 s at midfrequencies and up. Chanted music, such as plainsong, was composed for large cathedrals and monasteries having reverberation periods of up to 5 s. Churches with long reverberation times make it extremely difficult for the speaker unless the rapidity of speech is perfectly tuned to the reverberation time. Most speakers are not trained to speak in a slow and deliberate manner. In a reasonably live room of 3000–4000 ft^2, amplification for the spoken word should not be needed, provided a speaker is well trained in articulation and modulation. With the advent of laypersons participating in the service, untrained speaking voices have been introduced. As the average church cannot depend on having well-trained speakers at all times, it is best to plan for a public address system

with speakers located either high over the microphone or at strategic points throughout the church. In providing such a system, at least two other aspects should be considered:

1. An audio loop, usually installed in or on the floor, should be a part of the audio system. This will broadcast the service to receivers, which can be picked up by the hard of hearing.
2. Many churches wish to record the service, either for their files and records or for distribution to people who are shut-ins. Some churches wish to record the music in stereo. If this is the case, an independent audio system will be required for this purpose. One often hears the demand for a microphone for the soloist, but any trained singing voice within a church with reasonable reverberation should not need any amplification. If the organ or the other voices in the choir drown out the soloist, then the music director is at fault.

It is true that the floor surface under those people who are "making the joyful noise" should be a hard, reflective surface. This also relates to the people within the congregation who are standing and singing. An individual singing in a group on an absorptive surface can only hear the voices of others in the immediate area. Many people overlook the fact that people, their hair, and their clothes absorb sound. Therefore, the acoustics in an empty church with upholstered pews should not be vastly different from that of a packed church with solid wood pews. Other than the people, who are acoustical units, and carpeting in aisle spaces, other acoustical absorbing materials should only be considered after careful analysis. The beauty of the reverberation factors in cathedrals results from the dispersion of sound waves reflected by the many facets of the architecture and the openings permitting the sound to bounce around in the recesses of side aisles, chapels, and clerestories. It is a fact that a single boy soprano placed in the choir stalls of any great cathedral can be heard all over such an expansive building, even if it has a reverberation time of up to 4 or 5 s.

The science of acoustics is, in some respects, an exact science. The perfectly tuned church must sacrifice some of the qualities desired for the music program in order to achieve the type of acoustics best suited for the projection of the human speaking voice.

Churches that decide to build a multipurpose room for both sacred and secular purposes will encounter great difficulties in adapting the acoustical quality of the space for all programs. Certainly, during a church dinner, the noise associated with the clatter of dishware, glasses, and silverware would lead one to hope that there is a considerable area of acoustical absorptive material. Also, during movies, speakers, or pageants, a "live" room with reverberating qualities would be detrimental to the program. If the room is acoustically treated for the programs requiring larger areas of absorptive material, then it is not easy to "push a button" to make these materials disappear to convert this area into a place for liturgical music. The acousti-

cally treated space that incorporates large areas of acoustically absorptive material may not present as many
problems in those churches that have lively music with
a faster tempo than liturgical music.

ILLUMINATION

Illumination requirements differ from church to church.
Generally, the basic requirement for lighting is to provide
ample quantity and quality of light for reading while either
seated or standing in the worship area. Those churches
that are generally classified as evangelistic congregations
usually require a higher level of light than liturgical
churches. The reason for this is that there are often long
periods of reading on weekday evenings. Requirements
vary. However, at least 215.2 lx (20 fc), perhaps as much
as 430.4 lx (40 fc), is appropriate on the reading surface.

In liturgical churches, periods of reading usually consist
of following the service in the prayer book and singing
hymns. Except for those who may have sight difficulties,
58.8–107.6 lx (5–10 fc) of light on the reading surface is
usually adequate for short periods of reading. However,
higher levels of light are needed for other occasions, particularly weddings. For a quick, rough calculation, it is comparatively safe to figure approximately 4–5 W/ft^2 to illuminate an area at approximately 166.4–215.2 lx (15–20 fc)
as an average level at the point where the reading material
is held.

It is generally accepted that the illumination in the
seating area should be operated by dimmers so that the
level of lighting can be adjusted to suit the occasion. Floodlighting and spotlighting are normally required in the
chancel or platform area. Separate dimmer controls should
be provided for changing the emphasis or focus depending
on what is going on. If the choir is performing, obviously,
it should be well illuminated, not only to be seen, but
also for reading music. If the emphasis is on the pulpit,
then dimmers can accentuate this area. Pinpointing and
accent lighting may be required for special effects. The
quality of light is every bit as important as the quantity
of light. The quality refers to achieving a uniform level
of lighting and light of the right color to provide the distinct
atmosphere that is most suitable for the occasion. It should
be remembered that lighting is a very important element
in creating a certain atmosphere within a certain space.
Illumination from natural light sources should also be a
consideration for the daytime use of the facility. Controlling the influx of exterior light is often necessary for the
general comfort of occupants. Churches that incorporate
stained glass often wish to illuminate these windows at
night; this aspect will be discussed under Stained Glass.

It is understandable that few electrical engineers, those
who usually design the electrical and the illuminating
systems, understand what church illumination should be.
The reason for this is that most electrical engineers are
not specialists in the illumination of churches. The chief
designer, the architect, should first understand the needs
of the church and then must be certain that the engineer
understands the requirements.

STAINED GLASS

Stained glass is a glass that is colored in various ways
by fusing metal oxides into it or by painting and/or burning
pigments into its surface.

Until the seventeenth or eighteenth century, it was
impossible to manufacture large sheets of glass. As a result, the earliest glass was made in small pieces, which
were held together by lead cames, resulting in a unit to
fill in larger openings. This limiting factor existed when
stained glass was in its infancy. Starting in about the
eleventh or twelfth century, there was a predominance
of stained glass in cathedrals and monasteries. These windows used colored glass and paint fused on the surface
to depict scenes from the Bible and figures of martyrs
and saints as an educational tool. Most people were illiter-
ate; thus the clergy would point to the windows and tell
the story so the people would have a better understanding
and remember their lessons. Even in these early periods,
those artists and craftsmen designing and building these
windows gave careful consideration to which colors and
densities of colors to use, depending on the orientation
to the sun.

The two major types of stained glass used in churches
today are leaded glass and faceted glass. Stained glass
is still fabricated with different types of lead cames and
is made in rather small sections, which are either installed
in a frame or are supported by a series of reinforcing
rods to hold the panels together in a uniform plane. This
type of glass should be protected on the outside of the
building by another layer of glass or by some type of clear
acrylic sheet; the protective glass also reduces heat loss.
Glass manufactured for faceted glass windows is usually
about 1-in. thick and is cast in slabs no larger than 1
ft^2. The range of colors is almost unlimited; the surface
of the slabs usually has deformations similar to those in
handblown glass. These units are either cut or sawed into
smaller segments of glass to be fit into the pattern in
the design of the window. The pieces of glass are held
together by an epoxy cement, which can vary in thickness
from 0.25 in. to several inches. The edges and/or surfaces
of these chunks of glass are faceted by using a sharp tool
to chip off pieces or layers of the glass to achieve a sculptured appearance. The most accomplished craftsman can
select a piece of glass and chip it in such a way that it
gives expression to what began as a flat, uninteresting
surface.

Generally, faceted glass is less expensive than leaded
glass simply because it requires less labor and time to
fabricate. Independent panels of faceted glass can be made
up to about 5 ft^2. In smaller openings, panels can be stacked
up to about 12 ft without structural supports and can
also be installed directly in masonry openings without
the use of window frames. In larger windows, window
frames and structural supports are required to hold these
panels together and also to provide the necessary wind
bracing.

In a literate society, it should not be necessary to use
scenes in the glass as an educational tool, yet many
churches still desire to continue the traditional and origi-

nal purposes of stained glass. Stained glass is frequently used without symbolism or to depict saints or martyrs simply by designing a window that has a symphony of color and design. The facets, or pieces that have been chipped away, bend the light like prisms and introduce a jewel-like quality that cannot be achieved in a flat piece of colored glass. The use of stained glass in buildings is not limited to churches; it has become a recognized art form that is frequently used in secular buildings.

The quality of the artwork is entirely dependent on the abilities and talents of the artist. The artist must not only design, but also select the palette of colors to be used, and must cut and facet the glass where needed to carry out the design concept. Careful consideration should be given to the selection of the artist or studio employed to do the work.

FURNISHINGS

The construction of chairs and pews has become largely standardized in the church furniture manufacturing industry. Veneers are frequently used because of the competitive nature of the market. Solid wood construction is still available at a somewhat higher cost. Although other wood furniture, such as pulpits, altars, and so on, can be purchased from stock design, unity in design can only be achieved by designing the furniture as a part of the total concept.

Too often, furnishings are treated as an afterthought; the architect fails to assume responsibility as the designer and leaves the choice to a committee. Frequently, a committee is inexperienced and selects furniture that is of lesser quality than custom-made furnishings available at very little additional cost.

There are studios that specialize in the design and production of furnishings and total interior church design. Working with the architect and committee, these firms can assist in developing the most appropriate appointments.

OTHER ART FORMS

The inclusion of other art forms may or may not be appropriate. Liturgical churches are more likely to incorporate certain art forms such as sculpture and paintings. Paintings, mosaics, sculpture, and other media may become a part of the structure or may be independent. Art forms such as wood carvings are often incorporated in ecclesiastical furnishings such as the altar, reredos, pulpit, and so on.

Art forms of any kind are at their best when the building is planned to give appropriate attention to art rather than art being added as an afterthought. The selections of the art, materials, color, and texture are a part of the total design concept. All of these factors are essential in achieving a sense of design unity. It is not suggested that order

in the design should be so rigid that the environment is engineered and becomes a regimented, or sterile, environment.

There are often opportunities to provide a gallery setting in some part of the building where traveling art exhibits can be displayed. A well-designed and orderly environment can often be sterile; however, the introduction of a single piece of art can often breathe life and vitality into it. An example of this is the beautifully designed Georgian Cathedral in Birmingham, UK. The stained glass windows designed by Burne-Jones in the late nineteenth century are world famous. The bold use of color projects vitality and energy into the entire structure.

The creative abilities and imagination of the architect can, with the understanding and appreciation of the congregation, do much to make a simple building a beautiful and interesting place. One other method for converting a sterile building into a special place is the use of colorful banners incorporating symbolic patterns. Even though the pageantry normally associated with the use of banners may be nonexistent, a rather nondescript room can be converted into an "alive" space.

In one short interval in the 1960s, some theologians, artists, and architects espoused the use of disposable art, on the premise that people tire of anything permanent. This was an era when changes were taking place within the church; it was also a time of political and social reexamination. Disposable art such as posters and graffiti attracted those who sought temporary expediency during periods of change. The idea of using disposable art is no longer commonplace.

THE FORM

In this context, it is suggested that form follow function. This is a rational approach to creating an envelope of building walls to enclose the internal spaces. From a purely logistical viewpoint, if the functions within were to dictate the external form entirely, then the end result could be an architectural disaster. Although there is significant merit in design based on function, and the idea that form is to follow function, one should not ignore how the internal function may present unsolvable problems with respect to structure and external form. The creative ability of the architect should give equal consideration to achieving a well-designed building without compromising either internal function or the elements that result in a well-designed building.

Historically, churches have had a quality that is identifiable. A church is not a recreational building, a clubhouse, or just any secular building. Its form should be unique so that it can be identified.

Figures 4–7 are examples of the centrum, a worship space that serves both sacred and secular needs. Figures 8–10 are other churches where the worship area is less flexible for uses other than concerts, pageants, and teaching.

(a)

Floor Plan

centrum

mechanical · choir · sac. · m · w

classroom · classroom · classroom · classroom

infants · toddlers · nursery · jan · stor.

memorial garden

courtyard · junior high · play yard

concourse

library · imc · m · w

storage · fellowship hall

kitchen

off · wk · pastor · pastor · senior high

terrace

0′ 8′ 16′ 32′

n

(b)

Figure 4. Trinity United Methodist Church, Charles City, Iowa. Architects: Sovik, Mathre & Madison; Northfield, Minnesota. (a) Interior; (b) Plan.

(a)

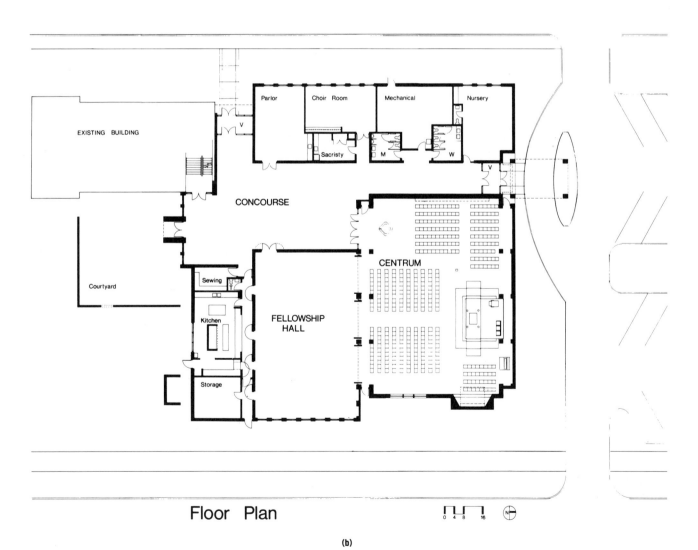

Floor Plan

0 4 8 16 N

(b)

Figure 5. Our Savior's Lutheran Church, Jackson, Minnesota. Architects: Sovik, Mathre, Sathrum, Quanbeck; Northfield, Minnesota. **(a)** Interior; **(b)** Plan.

(a)

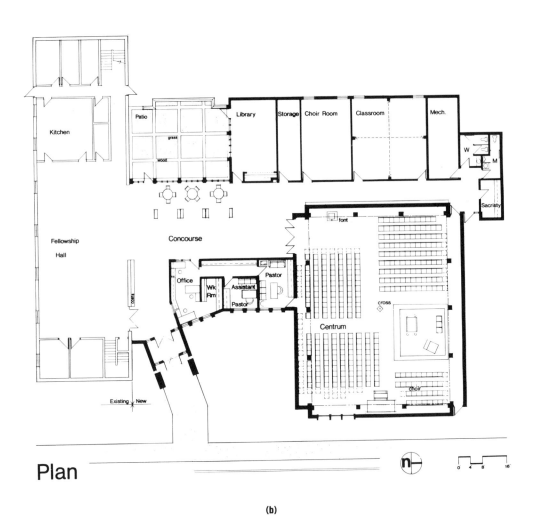

Plan

(b)

Figure 6. Trinity Lutheran Church, Princeton, Minnesota. Architects: Sovik, Mathre & Madison; Northfield, Minnesota. **(a)** Interior; **(b)** Plan.

(a)

Figure 7. Interior of St. Michael's Catholic Church, Sioux Falls, South Dakota. Architects: Sovik, Mathre, Sathrum, Quanbeck; Northfield, Minnesota. Photograph by Joel Strasser.

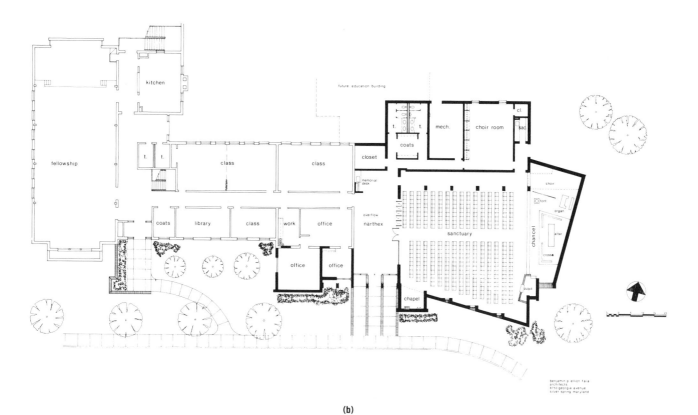

(b)

Figure 8. St. Matthew's United Methodist Church, Bowie, Maryland. Architect: Benjamin P. Elliott, FAIA, Rockville, Maryland. Photograph by J. Alexander. **(a)** Exterior; **(b)** Plan.

(a)

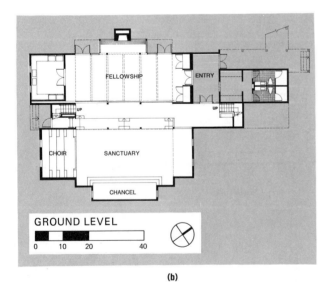

GROUND LEVEL

0   10   20   40

(b)

Figure 9. Immanuel Presbyterian Church, McLean, Virginia. Architects: Hartman–Cox, Washington, D.C. Photograph by Lautman Photography. **(a)** Exterior; **(b)** Plan.

BIBLIOGRAPHY

1. B. Fletcher, *A History of Architecture,* The Butterworth Group, Boston, Mass., 1987.
2. E. A. Sovik, *Architecture for Worship,* Augsburg Publishing House, Minneapolis, Minn., 1973, p. 9.
3. Ref. 2, p. 19.
4. J. White, *Protestant Worship and Church Architecture,* Oxford University Press, New York, p. 143 (date unknown).
5. *Constitution on the Sacred Liturgy,* (Sacrosanctum Concilium), Guild Press, New York, 1966.

General References

Ref. 1 is a good general reference.

T. D. Atkinson, *A Key to English Architecture,* M. S. Mill Co., Inc., New York, 1936.

C. J. Cormick, *Adventures in Light and Color,* Random House, New York, 1937.

E. Short, *Post-war Church Building,* Hollis and Carter, London, 1947.

E. D. Mills, *The Modern Church,* Frederick A. Praeger, New York, 1956.

A. Christ-Janer and M. M. Folley, *Modern Church Architecture,* McGraw-Hill Inc., New York, 1960.

P. Hammond, *Liturgy and Architecture,* Columbia University Press, New York, 1961.

Building New Churches, Church Information Office, Church House, London, 1962.

G. E. Kidder Smith, *New Churches of Europe,* Holt, Rinehart & Winston, New York, 1963.

D. J. Bruggink and C. H. Droppers, *Christ and Architecture,* William B. Eerdman's Publishing Co., Grand Rapids, Mich., 1965.

E. C. Lynn, *Tired Dragons,* Beacon Press, Boston, Mass., 1972.

C. E. Hiller, *Caves to Cathedrals,* Little, Brown and Co., Boston, Mass., 1974.

R. G. Kennedy, *American Churches,* Steward, Tabori & Chang, New York, 1982.

G. Randall, *The English Parish Church,* B. T. Batsford Ltd., London, 1982.

B. Hayes, *Tradition Becomes Innovation,* The Pilgrim Press, New York, 1983.

T. F. Bumpus, *Cathedrals and Churches of Rome and Southern Italy,* E. P. Dulton & Co., New York (date unknown).

The following periodicals are good general references:

Faith & Form
Stained Glass

See also ACOUSTICAL DESIGN—PLACES OF ASSEMBLY; ARCHITECTURAL STYLES; CATHEDRALS; GLASS IN CONSTRUCTION.

BENJAMIN P. ELLIOTT,
FAIA
Duane, Elliott, Cahill,
   Mullineaux & Mullineaux
Rockville, Maryland

(a)

(b)

Figure 10. Forcey Memorial Church, Silver Spring, Maryland. Architect: Benjamin P. Elliott, FAIA, Rockville, Maryland. Photograph by J. Alexander. **(a)** Exterior; **(b)** Plan.

CIVIL ENGINEERING.   See Engineering, Civil

CLIMATE AND DESIGN

The earliest man evolved in a tropical or semitropical climate. He lived an animal-like life without clothing or shelter, for in such a climate he needed neither. At first, he was without fire but, after he learned to control it, he wandered away from the tropical area and began to feel the need for protection and shelter from the elements. The very earliest archaeological artifacts are remains of campfires that had been built under ledges or overhanging cliffs where man found protection from the rain and from his enemies or wild animals. The climate not only created the need for shelter, it also determined the materials and type of shelter that he built. In some areas, there was ample vegetation, branches of trees, reeds, and grasses, while in others, stones and mud from the river bottom were the primary ingredients. As he gradually moved into the more severe climate of the north, animal hides and ultimately the snow itself provided material for shelter.

The shelters that were developed over periods of thousands of years slowly became adjusted to a particular climate. In the Caribbean Islands, up until the middle of the twentieth century, some of the isolated housing was still in its earliest primitive form, a series of poles with a simple thatched roof and no walls of any kind (Fig. 1). Cooking was carried out on small raised platforms that stood outside the roofed area. This shelter not only gave protection from the rain but was also open to the welcome breezes that provided comfort and kept away the insects. Cold was not a problem and there were no wild animals or enemies to fear. The scattered shelters did not need walls for privacy. In the southwest region of the United States, where the climate and materials were totally different, the choice building site was still, as it was for the earliest campfires, under overhanging cliffs. The best faced south to take advantage of the warmth of the winter sun and provided protection from the cold northwest wind in

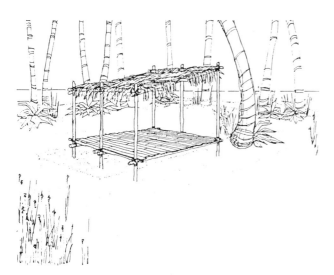

Figure 1. Island shelter in the Caribbean, ca 1956.

the winter. The building materials were mud, rock, and later sun-dried brick. Many of these still stand as monuments to the early builders (Fig. 2). At the other extreme, the barren Arctic wastes provided no normal building materials. In winter, the structures were built simply of snow and often lined with animal skins. In summer, the skins were used for tents. Yet even these were designed for the climate and the material. The domelike shape was simple to build from cut blocks of snow, the raised floor (or depressed tunnel entrance) helped conserve heat and cut off the wind. During the total darkness of the Arctic winter when these were used, windows were of no value.

Today, the ease of transportation, wide availability of building materials, and ability to provide artificial heat, light, cooling, and ventilation have caused some designers to ignore the climate in which building is undertaken.

Climatologists have many classifications for different climates. One, for example, has listed approximately one hundred different climates in the United States alone. Each one of these varies from all of the others by 10% in at least one of ten different characteristics. Such fine classifications are not needed here. The primary questions are: Is it too hot or too cold, or is it too wet or too dry? Although these classifications may be convenient, the divisions between these different areas are not sharp. No one location is consistent all year. In fact, in some locations, such as Chicago, all of those conditions exist at one time or another during an average year. It may be necessary to choose which classification predominates, or, in some cases, which ones to ignore, perhaps because of something not related to climate.

HOT DRY CLIMATE

The outstanding characteristics of a desert or hot dry climate are long, high temperature days with little or no rainfall, low humidity, dry ground, clear skies, and intense sun. Over a hundred days of temperatures over 38°C and twenty days of temperatures over 44°C can be expected. Nighttime temperatures vary drastically from daytime temperatures, running from 19 to 25°C in the middle of the summer season. Because of the intense sun and low rainfall (averaging just under 200 mm per year), vegetation is sparse except along the banks of seasonal streams, or around pools that collect during the rainy spells; the consequently bare ground produces an unpleasant glare.

Scattered thundershowers provide most of the precipitation in the summer; these occur in the afternoon. The total precipitation may average 10 mm for the month of June, may increase to 25 mm for the months of July and August, and decrease only slightly in September. As the rainfall increases, the humidity starts to build up. The relative humidity at about 4:00 in June will be about 40%, building up to 60% at the same time in August. The low relative humidity at about 16:00 hours varies from a very pleasant 10% in June to 40% or more in August.

Winds are consistently from the east and southeast in the morning, changing to west and southwest in the afternoon, and are mild. Through ventilation is thus in an east-west direction during the milder months. When

Figure 2. Cliff dwellings in Arizona, ca 1100 A.D. They were abandoned in 1475 A.D., perhaps because of change in climate and rainfall.

the occasional strong winds occur, they stir up great quantities of dust and may sometimes cause damage.

There was a time when it seemed that the dams on the natural rivers in areas of hot, dry climate produced an unlimited supply of water for irrigation. Water conservation methods are now necessary because of the population growth in most desert cities.

Exterior Walls and Openings

All of the many functions of exterior walls except visual privacy are related to the sun. The primary function is to control the difference between the high exterior temperature and the desired interior temperature. In addition, exterior walls should control solar radiation and reflected radiation from the hot ground and withstand driving rain and dust.

The walls reflect part of the sun's radiant energy, and absorb the rest along with the heat from the air itself. Heat absorbed by the wall during the day must be dissipated during the night. Adequate ventilation must be provided to cool from the interior, as cooling from the outer surfaces alone is not enough. Windows should be as small

as possible during the day because they will allow more heat to enter than does a thick, heavy wall. At night, windows should be as large as possible for ventilation. Larger openings with massive shutters are an effective compromise.

The ideal exterior wall would consist of a massive masonry wall with a layer of lightweight insulation on the exterior of the building. As with all other compromise solutions, there are problems. The insulation prevents the heat buildup in the masonry, but also prevents the heat dissipation at night. If heat is allowed to collect in the heavy material, in the absence of proper ventilation and cooling, the result will be worse than having no insulation.

The upper part of the wall can be protected by an overhanging roof on the south side; its effectiveness depends on the width of the overhang and the sun's angle. The east and west walls can be extended to protect against the low early morning and late afternoon slanting rays of the sun. Windows should not be put on the west because it must bear the heat of the late sun at low altitude during the hottest time of the day. When properly protected with shading devices, east-facing windows are acceptable.

Floors, Foundations, and Basements

Basements are traditionally not common in areas of hot, dry climate; because of the lack of frost, there was no need to dig deep foundations or to bury utilities at great depth. A properly designed basement can, however, be very desirable, as the ground at basement level has an annual average temperature of approximately 21°C. Basement walls exposed to such a temperature would be almost ideal. The condensation problem found in basements of more humid areas is not present because of the low humidity.

Buildings built with one side exposed and three sides buried in a hillside, underground in effect, and the use of arcades or open central courts appear to be successful solutions. However, in the latter case, if the court is too large, allowing the sun to strike its floor, it loses its value as protection. Arcades keep the walls shaded and aid in shading the floor. Pools of water and fountains are functional as well as decorative; they cool and humidify the dry air.

The rooms in the house surround the court; many arrangements are possible with roof overhangs to provide all of the protection needed for circulation between rooms.

The foundation wall itself can be made of any of the usual materials, but the portion in contact with the ground should be protected against the occasional, but sometimes very heavy, rain. Some of the requirements of basement design are: positive drainage away from the building wall; a surface-applied waterproofing material on the wall itself; membrane waterproofing (in some cases); and a drain at the base of the wall to carry away what water does seep down to that level.

Basement rooms with no windows are not generally acceptable and are often prohibited by building codes. An areaway or basement window well can be used to provide for a full-size window. The well is generally made of the same materials as the foundation wall, with a gravel floor connected with the drain around the foot of the basement wall.

A concrete floor or slab-on-ground is exposed to the uniform temperature of the soil and is protected from the heat of the sun. Carpets or heavy rugs can be used to insulate the floor and help maintain constant living conditions. The surface may be densely packed earth, concrete, terrazzo, brick, tile, or marble, depending on the region and the economy. The low humidity prevents the surface condensation, common in humid climates; there should be no deterioration caused by mold or mildew.

A raised floor does away with the cooling and thermal storage provided by a slab-on-ground. It must be well ventilated and protected from termites, and have means to prevent surface water from entering or collecting in the space.

Paved terraces or patios below windows on the east or west sides, and on the south side, unless protected from the sun, as well as hard, smooth surfaced walks or driveways, should be avoided; they will not only heat the surface, but the heat will be reflected to the walls as well. Exposed aggregate concrete or some other material should be used to break up the reflection.

Roof Construction

The roof is the most exposed surface of a house and the largest; an exposed roof under summer conditions may reach a temperature of 75°C or more. It is subject to the sudden chilling of a summer thunderstorm, and the regular stress of changing from day- to nighttime conditions. Although seldom seen or noticed, the roof is the most important surface in one of the most difficult climates in the world for roofing materials. The sun commonly causes roofing problems, not the rain as in other climates. The roof is exposed to the sun for a greater length of time than the walls. A roof where roof and ceiling can be separated and the space between ventilated is more desirable than a flat or shed roof.

As much radiant heat as possible should be reflected by the roof surface. The ideal roof, a polished metal surface, is difficult to obtain, and also impossible to maintain. The best and common choice is a white surface. Shading the roof surface is desirable, although it is seldom attempted except through the use of trees.

Insulation should be at the ceiling level and lightweight; it should have low conductance and be as thick as possible. Air conditioning is desirable for the rooms below the roof when insulation is placed directly below the roofing without a ventilated space. In the case of a separated roof and ceiling, the space between should be well ventilated. A fan should be used to provide positive air movement when there is any question of the amount of air moving through the space because of the roof configuration, as in a hip roof, or because of the restriction of air movement caused by other buildings or trees. The fan can be controlled by a thermostat that sets it to operate whenever the air temperature in the space is higher than the outside air.

HOT HUMID CLIMATE

The hot, humid climates are more prevalent throughout the world than are the hot, dry climates; there are three of them. The first is the island climate, where the temperature is high because of its location relatively near the equator and changes little all year. The rainfall is heavy but seasonal, with very pronounced rainy and dry seasons. The winds are steady, both in direction and in intensity. The second, the coastal climate, because of its location, has relatively high temperatures also and, while there is some change, there are no marked seasons. The rainfall is heavy and more evenly distributed throughout the year with no dry season. The winds may be subject to local conditions but have an overall pattern of reversing direction daily, from offshore during the night and from land during the day. The third, the inland climate, is found in low-lying areas along major rivers; the temperature here is markedly seasonal. This area covers a considerable distance north and south; those in the north may not only have major periods of hot, humid weather, but equally major periods of cold weather. They share enough with the milder temperatures to be included in the hot weather discussion, but the cold weather period cannot be ignored.

The Island Climate

Designs for this area do not feature protection from the elements as do the hot, dry designs, but rather they emphasize ventilation as the most essential factor, with shading from the sun being secondary. Architectural features include large floor-to-ceiling openings with louvers or awning-type windows, or entire screened and louvered walls. Floors may be elevated above the ground level, and a wide overhanging roof may run entirely around the building.

Site and Building Design. With the average daily temperature seldom going below 25°C, the average daily high temperature rarely going above 27°C, and the equally steady and high humidity throughout the year, the climate can only be described as monotonous. There is nothing about it to be feared or against which major protective measures must be taken. The vegetation, as might be expected, is lush. The island's origin may be either volcanic or based on the growth of coral, and in either type, there is enough topsoil to support vegetation. Some of the volcanic islands are large and have enough altitude to produce a variety of climates, but most of them are low.

Exterior Walls and Openings. In many cases, the exterior walls are the openings. The entire wall is screened and often fitted with shutters. When these are fixed, the shutters are often panelized, and may be hinged at the top and propped open at the bottom to allow light and an even greater opening for air movement (Fig. 3).

Where greater privacy is desired, conventional walls may be built of any convenient material. Windows are still large and generally run to the ceiling to provide for adequate air movement. Protection against the occasional hurricane may be provided in the form of a demountable panel. Planting close to the building is avoided to allow free air movement. Ceilings are high for the same reason.

Roof Design. The roof surface should be light colored, even though the solar intensity here is not as great as it is in the dry countries. Some insulation is desirable to reduce the reradiation into the building. In those areas where rainwater is collected for domestic use, the so called Bermuda tile is very effective. It is usually light colored and provides a degree of insulation.

Floors and Foundations. Basements in this area are almost unknown, as is the slab-on-ground floor. The desire

Figure 3. Louvered wall house in hot, humid climate.

is to get up into the flow of air rather than to go down and avoid it. The raised floor may be built on masonry piers or on wooden piling. The wooden piling base has the advantage of yielding somewhat during the high tides and winds that accompany the hurricanes. In any case, the area under the floor is left open for ventilation.

The Coastal Climate

A greatly simplified description of the coastal climate would be similar to the island climate, except for greater extremes. The average monthly high for the three hottest months is above 30°C with a maximum of 33°C. Similarly, the low daily average temperature for the same three months is 10°C with the lowest daily average at 8°C. In the months of October, November, and December, the average rainfall is less than 100 mm per month; the rest of the 155 mm annual total is divided throughout the balance of the year. The winds are reliable and the sea breeze from the south blows during the day and reverses from the north by night. It is the breeze that makes this climate habitable.

Walls and Openings. In order to take advantage of the cooling breezes, openings are large and extend from floor to ceiling. Because of cold winters, however, the louvered opening is replaced by a tightly fitted window sash, particularly when heating and cooling are provided.

Roof Design. Because the outdoor climate is pleasant for many months of the year, roof structures are extended into wide overhangs to provide protection for outdoor porches and paved terraces that may run entirely around a building. The roofing material should reflect the solar heat. The roof should be insulated and the space between the roof and the ceiling should be well ventilated. Gutters are desirable, not only to help protect the wall, but also to protect the ground from erosion. Care must be taken around chimneys and other penetrations through the roof or on the intersections of various planes to provide adequate flashing. While no freezing action is expected, the continuous high humidity and the fact that surfaces may not dry for long periods of time may lead to the development of mold and rot. Wood should be painted with a mildew-resistant paint, and sheet metal should be either well painted or selected to resist corrosion. Careful detailing of all exterior wood and trim is essential to prevent leaks and standing water.

Floors, Foundations, and Basements. The heavy rainfall results in a high water table. This, combined with high humidity, makes basements very undesirable. The breeze, which produces comfort in this climate, must be given every opportunity to flow. Living quarters then can be raised above the ground on stilts or on an artificial knoll. When the building is on stilts, it allows the strong winds from hurricanes to pass under the building and reduces the effect of the negative-pressure area that develops behind buildings during such storms.

Mechanical. Mechanical refrigeration is highly desirable. Its use to control temperature and humidity extends over a four-month period. Heating is limited to the use of fireplaces often found not only in the main room of the house but also in minor rooms such as bedrooms. With the increased use of central air conditioning, heating systems using the same ductwork are common.

The Inland Climate

This climate is similar to the coastal, hot, humid climate except that the rainfall is not as heavy, although it is distributed throughout the year. The high temperatures are not quite as high, but the low temperatures are much lower. The changes from hot to cold are often frequent and quite sudden. A drop of 10°C in an hour is reasonably common as a cold front moves through the area.

The problem facing the designer is whether to work with the climate or against it. In the hot, dry country, design is counter to the climate: everything is done to ensure protection from the sun. In the coastal climate, one works with the climate, utilizing winds for through ventilation and placing the living and occupational functions so they are protected from the sun and exposed to the breezes. Here, the hot afternoon sun is unpleasant but the breezes come from the same direction, the southwest. The design objective is to exclude one and admit the other.

Wall and Window Design. Sudden changes in temperature and relative humidity after a storm produce stresses that crack surfaces and damage many materials. High wall openings and windows help move the volume of air immediately below the ceiling. Glass should be protected from the summer sun by overhangs or awnings; in winter, double glazing is desirable. Heavy masonry walls are not desirable because of the storage of heat in the wall and the heat lag that carries well into the night. Properly oriented windows may provide sufficient heat for daytime purposes during the spring and fall. In the winter, they are of little use because of the heavy cloud cover.

Roof Design. In this climate, rooftops and pavements during the summer months will reach a temperature of 65°C, and the relative humidity may drop as low as 10%. This is similar to the temperature and humidity found in the hot dry climate. On the other hand, the freeze–thaw cycle occurs at least 60 days of the year, and the combination produces extreme stress on building materials. Wide overhangs are desirable, and gutters are almost a necessity. The roof surface should be light in color and reflective if possible. Insulation material should be of the low, thermal capacity type and have low conductivity. A vapor barrier is needed on the warm-in-winter side of the insulation. The gutters should be designed to take care of the heaviest rains, during which 50 mm may fall within a 30-min period.

Foundations and Basements. A basement is considered a liability in this climate as there will be condensation of moisture from the air because of the cool walls and floor. This condition could exist for as much as 75% of the time during July and August. However, when proper dehumidification is provided, it can be a very pleasant area. Chemical dehumidifying agents are seldom adequate. A sloping site or windows to admit the sun and light will help control interior humidity. Frost penetrates as much as 600 mm, making a raised floor and a shallow basement worth considering. When a concrete slab-on-ground is used, the exterior grades should fall sharply in all directions from the slab, and the slab itself should be poured over a well-drained gravel fill. A vapor barrier over the fill is a simple method of preventing concrete fines from penetrating into the fill and destroying the fill's usefulness. When a wood floor is used over a crawl space, protection must be provided to prevent the entrance of termites, which are active in this area, and to prevent water from standing or collecting in the crawl space area. The floor should be insulated when the vents in the wall are left open in the winter. When unvented, the exterior wall of the crawl space and the edge of the floor construction should be insulated. When vents are closed, some heat may be introduced into the crawl space. In either case, a moisture barrier over the ground, such as lightweight roofing felt, is desirable.

Mechanical. In this climate, a central heating system and a central cooling system are almost mandatory. All of the precautions taken, as described previously, help make the mechanical system more efficient and easy to operate.

THE COLD CLIMATES

The cold climates are difficult and more demanding in design than are the hot areas, and they inflict greater punishment if ignored. Temperature ranges are extreme; lows of −40°C are not unknown, nor are highs of 40°C or more. Periods of high temperature are brief, but the brutal cold lasts for a long period of time. The monthly average for each of the winter months, December, January, and February, is below −10°C. Other features of the climate are equally extreme. There is not enough sun in the winter, and the sun is intense in the hot summers. The winter winds are severe and consistently from the northwest. The rains in summer are irregular and heavy. In winter, there is little moisture in some areas and the result is a very dry, fine snow. In other areas, the snowfall is heavy and full of moisture.

In dry parts of cold areas, the annual precipitation may be as low as 280 mm. It is lowest in the three summer months, averaging 13 mm per month; the other months average less than 26 mm. (This is almost as low as the rainfall in the desert or hot dry climate.) The rate of evaporation is much less than in the desert, so there is more vegetation. The snow is not heavy and creates no roof-loading problems, except when accumulated by wind action.

In areas of heavy snowfall, the annual total precipitation may average 1 m or slightly less, and it can be many times that in the ski areas in the mountains surrounding the recording station in the valley. These represent special conditions, or microclimates, and must be investigated individually.

Where snowfall is light, the winds keep the roof surfaces clear, but parapets, which create turbulent wind patterns and drifts, should be avoided.

Buildings are inclined to be extremely dry when heated in the winter and equally inclined to be damp during the summer. The ground often freezes to great depth below the surface.

Building Design

Man's earliest structures provided protection, and in cold areas, protection is still the first requirement in designing any part of a building. Faced with the prevailing northwest winds, it is quite probable that the ideal house would turn its back to the northwest and have no openings at all on the north, and very few on the west side of the structure. The south would have windows to welcome the sun, but they would not be as large as in the hot humid area where they also provide ventilation. The east side would also be more open to face the welcome morning sun. The typical house illustrated in Figure 4 with only slight modifications would be acceptable here.

The ground floor, instead of being totally open, could be entirely enclosed but should still provide parking for automobiles, a utility area, and probably a play area for children or a family room; Figure 4 shows such a house. The raised floor should contain the living portion of the house and possibly a balcony to be used during the very brief but pleasant period of the summer. (The balcony floor should be designed so it does not hold snow, preferably, or should have structural supports to hold snow.) In the cold climate, the house should be compact, presenting a minimum of exterior wall surface, and windows should be double or triple glazed, with provisions for heavy wall-to-wall, floor-to-ceiling curtains or draperies to cut off the glass area at night. The ceiling area should similarly be very well insulated; a ventilated space between the insulated ceiling and the roof is desirable. A vapor barrier on the warm-in-winter side of the ceiling insulation is an absolute requirement.

The entry into a building in a cold climate should be through a protected vestibule. It should be large enough to be comfortable, well lighted, and with ample storage space for heavy outdoor clothing. The floor should withstand not only traffic but the water from melted snow.

Because of the low temperature, the ground often freezes to a depth of 2 m. Utilities should be placed below that depth. This means that the foundation footings for

a building should be below that depth, which makes a basement so practical as to be almost mandatory.

In areas of heavy snow, a roof with a higher pitch (to shed the snow) is traditional. If the roof is lower pitched, even if it is properly designed to support the heavy snow load, there may be a problem with leaks from the buildup of ice dams. These are simply blockades created by water from snow melting and running down the roof until it reaches an overhang, where it freezes because of the cold from below as well as from above. This builds up, and in time, forces water back up the roof until it penetrates the roof and appears as leaks in the space below.

In some areas of Ontario, Canada, where the heavy snow is common, the tradition is to apply a metal roof over the lower four feet or so of the sloping surface to prevent leaks. If the attic space is properly ventilated and the ceiling insulated, the roof will remain cold and the danger of ice dams can be eliminated.

Walls and Openings. Walls in this climate are subject to great extremes. The high air temperature may be as high as 40°C in the summer and as cold as −40°C in the winter, and may also be subject to intermittent cycles in a range of 55°C or more because of sudden showers. This temperature range makes it mandatory to select exterior wall materials that are not subject to stress from expansion and contraction, and should be free from cracks or ledges where wind-driven snow could penetrate.

Wall insulation is required and should be protected on the warm side by a carefully sealed vapor barrier. Without this protection, moisture will migrate from the warm interior of the building through the insulation and condense and freeze in the outer wall, thus destroying the insulation value of the material and probably the material itself.

Windows should be double or triple glazed and weather stripped. When a separate storm sash is installed outside a regular window, the interior sash should be weatherstripped, otherwise moisture will condense on the inside of the storm sash. In sealed double-glass units, the air space is dehydrated to prevent condensation. Water pipes and plumbing drain lines should not be located in the exterior walls where they are difficult to insulate. If water lines servicing a kitchen sink, for example, are to be located in a wall under a window, they should be on the warm-in-winter side of the insulation rather than in the center of the wall. Exterior doors should be weatherstripped, fitted with automatic closers, and protected by a storm door.

Floors and Basements. Since the foundation walls must extend to nearly 1.25 m below grade because of the deep penetration of frost, basements are almost universal. They provide ideal places for heating systems and with proper lighting, can become useful spaces as playrooms, recreation rooms, hobby rooms, storage areas, or other uses. The basement in this climate has serious drawbacks, however.

The earth temperature outside the basement is approximately 15°C in the summertime. This, combined with high humidity in the outside air, causes heavy condensation. Additional ventilation only makes the matter worse, bring-

Figure 4. House in cold, dry climate.

ing in more moist air. One solution is to heat the space to a temperature of about 25°C, which will dry the basement. Another is to provide mechanical dehumidification; for that to be effective, the basement should be sealed to prevent possible infiltration of outside humid air. An areaway is equally effective here for providing light, but it does little to reduce condensation and may fill with snow. If a greenhouse-type glass roof is installed over the areaway, it becomes a very useful cold frame, or place for plants in the wintertime, but is of no help in the summer. An ideal solution, again, would be a hillside building site where three sides of the structure are protected by the earth and the fourth side is open to the south to admit warmth and sun in the summer as well as what little sun is available in the winter.

Drainage should be sharply away from the building, and the exterior wall of the foundation should be protected; drainage should be provided as in other climates. Concrete slab-on-ground construction for residential buildings is not common or popular in this area. Without proper insulation and heating, frost may actually form on the floor next to the outside walls and particularly in either corners or the backs of large pieces of furniture. Insulation should be provided at the edge of the slab and back under the slab for several feet. It should be of a type that does not absorb water or deteriorate in the presence of water. The heat should be provided through a radiant heating system in the floor, circulated warm air ductwork in the slab, or a baseboard-type radiator with circulated hot water.

Roof Design. The roof is subject to the same temperature extremes and the same cycles as the outside wall. It should be of a light-colored material that is desirable in the summertime, and should not be of a material that deteriorates rapidly from the stress of contraction and expansion. Expansion and contraction and the freezing of moisture can be very destructive, particularly around flashing at chimneys or intersecting roof planes. The ceiling should be heavily insulated and protected by a vapor barrier. Dry snow driven by the wind can penetrate the smallest cracks or openings.

THE MODERATE CLIMATES

All climates are not as severe or as extreme as the ones that have been described, nor are the extremes as precisely defined. Moderate climates share features with both the hot and the cold and with the wet and the dry. The temperatures, humidities, and rainfall are much the same and they can be found not only in the United States, but in northern Europe, Russia, and in the Pampas of South America.

As with all climates, the designer must weigh each factor and establish a graded scale. This weighted scale is necessary since the solutions of some problems may be in direct conflict with each other.

The two areas chosen to represent the moderate climates are the central Ohio area in the East, and western Missouri in the West. Although these two areas are separated by 1000 km, they are remarkably alike in their major climatic factors. The average annual temperature for the eastern area is 20°C; for the western, it is 20.4°C. The rainfall for the east is 900 mm; for the west, it is 861 mm. The relative humidity in the east averages 70.9%, and in the west, 68%. The design for this area is a compromise between the hot and the cold. In winter, there will be freezing, thawing, snow, drizzle, and mud; the cold will not be extreme. The snow will not build up to a great depth, and it will not last too long. The summer's rain is about evenly distributed, and extended dry periods occur only very rarely.

Foundations and Basements

With the ground freezing to a depth of approximately 1 m, and thus requiring foundations at least that deep, a basement is quite reasonable to consider, and with adequate light and ventilation, it can be a most delightful part of the house. There is the problem, however, with condensation during the summer months. Some choose to ignore the condensation and merely surrender the basement for the summer months. In that case, they utilize flooring materials and wall materials that will not be damaged by the summer humidity. In some areas, ventilation along with adequate windows will keep condensation under control.

Slab-on-ground construction is acceptable but should have edge insulation, and the insulation should turn back a short distance under the floor slab. There may be condensation on the floor surface during occasional periods of excess humidity in the summer. A crawl space or raised floor should add adequate ventilation.

Wall Design

Exterior walls require insulation. When energy for heating purposes was cheaper, designers would reduce the insulation in the exterior wall to one-half of that used in extreme cold climates. With the current prices, full, thick wall insulation is justified. Windows should be weather-stripped, and double glazing is desirable.

Roof Design

The roof's surface will be exposed to temperatures as high as 65°C and as low as −30°C, so the selection process is the same as for cold climates. The snow may be dry and light and blow off the roof surface, or it may occasionally be wet and cling. The roof should be well drained and able to withstand being wet for long periods, as the evaporation may be slow. Ceilings require insulation and a vapor barrier on the warm-in-winter side. The space above the ceiling should be well ventilated.

Mechanical

Central heating systems are mandatory, and central air conditioning would be highly desirable because of the summer humidity. Solar heat gain is pleasant in the winter months but frequent cloud cover prevents the designer from relying on it too extensively.

SOLAR SHADING DEVICES

Glass for windows is available in a variety of types, many of which are formulated to reduce the transmission of not only visible light but uv and ir light. They come in a variety of colors, thicknesses, and coatings with a variety of transmission coefficients, and should be considered by designers working in a climate requiring protection from extreme heat or cold.

Metal screening material is made to provide shading from the sun as well as protection from insects. It is available in several types of metal and consists of either small flat 2-mm wide strips of metal woven with round wire verticals, or of sheets of stamped thin metal. The result is very similar to a tiny venetian blind. They are very effective on east and west exposures when the sun is close to the horizon.

Vertical Shading Devices

Vertical shading devices are common and their size depends on how far they project from the wall or glass surface. They may be made from any material, from wood to stone or concrete.

A combination of vertical and horizontal shading is often called eggcrate. It is extremely effective since it protects from the low angle setting and rising sun as well as the overhead sun. Again, it can be made of almost any material. Stone, precast concrete, clay tile, metal, and wood are all common in the southwest area.

BIBLIOGRAPHY
General References

C.E.P. Brooks, *Climate in Everyday Life*, Philosophical Library, Inc., New York, 1951.

R. Clayborne, *Climate, Man and History*, W.W. Norton & Co., Inc., New York, 1970.

J. R. Engleman, *The Visualization of Climate*, D. C. Heath & Co., Lexington, Mass. 1973.

E. L. Fenton, *California's Many Climates*, Pacific Books, Publishers, Palo Alto, Calif., 1965.

J. F. Griffiths, *Applied Climatology*, 2nd ed., Oxford University Press, Inc., New York, 1976.

Koenigsberger, Ingersoll, Mayhew, and Szokolay, *Manual of Tropical Building and Design*, The London Group, Ltd., London, 1974.

V. Olgyay, *Design with Climate*, Princeton University Press, Princeton, N.J., 1963.

All data on rain, snow, temperature, and humidity, including summaries, averages, etc, are taken from publications of the National Oceanic and Atmospheric Administration, National Climatic Data Center, Asheville, N.C.

See also COLD DRY CLIMATE CONSTRUCTION; COLD WET CLIMATE, BUILDING IN; HOT DRY CLIMATE CONSTRUCTION; HOT WET CLIMATE, BUILDING IN.

JAMES T. LENDRUM, FAIA
Phoenix, Arizona

CLINICS, MEDICAL. See HEALTH CARE—AMBULATORY.

CLUSTER DEVELOPMENT AND LAND SUBDIVISION

The essential attribute of clusters is the grouping of houses around a common area that is usually jointly owned. A true cluster is not only physically defined, but incorporates an element of communal interaction in its definition. By this interpretation, only a relatively small number of houses can adequately form a cluster, with the strength of interaction varying according to the culture and the physical arrangement.

Clusters are praised as a more effective and economic land development pattern, and, generally in the Third World, are used to encourage community interaction and provide protected open space.

Cluster layouts have been known by many names: cul-de-sac layouts, closed-court layouts, grouped houses and, in larger developments, group house neighborhoods, and density or cluster zoning planning. They range in size from a single group of houses to the repetitive groupings in large-scale land development. In the United States, clusters are generally associated with single-family, detached housing, but the trend is increasingly toward town houses and three- to five-story apartments.

HISTORY

People have traditionally organized their housing in clusters. Clusters have been found in high density urban areas and in lower density rural settings. In parts of urban India, they are known as *pols* or *mahalla* as in northern India; while in the Arabic urban cultures, they are known as *harahs* or *atfahs*. In the rural areas of Sri Lanka (formerly Ceylon), they are known as *gamgodas*. In Africa, the tribal groupings are familiar to everyone. In the fourteenth and fifteenth centuries in Europe, the Beguine houses could be classified as cluster developments. In a later example, the mews in England are clusters that arose out of a change in use.

Planned clusters in the United States were associated with the garden city movement by Clarence Stein and others, with Radburn in the late 1920s, and with some early New Deal Greenbelt towns following the British Garden City concept (Fig. 1). In the late 1930s, Baldwin Hills in Los Angeles also exhibited a type of clustered layout of houses. Earlier, in 1910, bungalow courts appeared in southern California and spread throughout the United States. These were small houses grouped around a common court and promoted as the modern living environment.

In the United States, as a reaction to the land sprawl from developments driven by Federal Housing Administration (FHA) funding, builders rediscovered clustered layouts in the 1960s to break the monotony of gridiron layouts, to lower increasing site development costs, and to provide useful open areas. More recently, the planned unit develop-

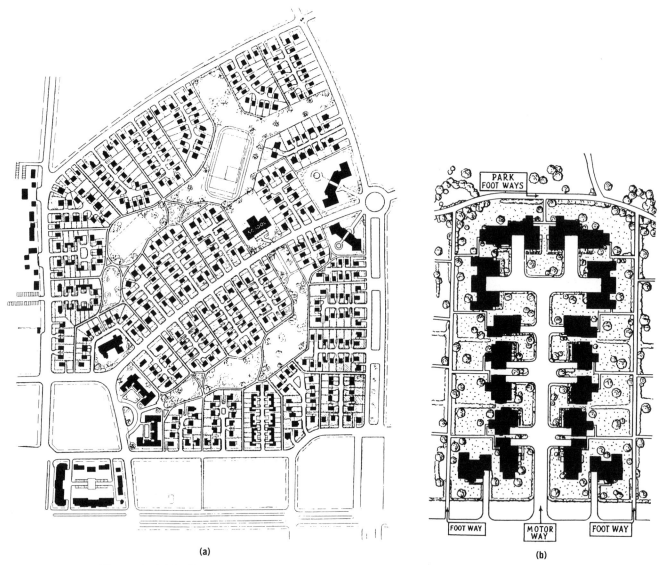

Figure 1. **(a)** Radburn development, 1929, an early example of the large-scale use of clusters; **(b)** In this example, the cluster units face outside.

ment (PUD) approach is often characterized by its use of a cluster geometry.

PHYSICAL PATTERN

A cluster geometry has three basic elements: the house lot, the circulation access, and the common shared spaces (Fig. 2). The house lot may contain a variety of house types: detached, semidetached, and town houses. Market conditions, target groups, and local acceptance dictate the type.

The most common circulation arrangement is the cul-de-sac, which prevents through traffic from disrupting residential areas, and offers greater safety for children. Small, looped streets have also been used for clusters, but must be carefully designed to be effective in contributing toward social interaction (Fig. 3).

The jointly used common area is a particular attribute of clusters, and its sizing is critical. There are two types: the common shared space around which houses are clustered, and the open land gained from repetitive clusters by the accumulation of backyard segments, and the reduction of the individual lots to economical yet functional sizes (Fig. 4). In the United States, functional considerations influence the size, ie, fire truck access, circulation, and parking, whereas in the Third World, size is often determined by the number of families sharing a space, particularly because of the emphasis on communal participation among low income families living in relatively small lots. In a group of clusters, the open space gained is often designated a park, as idealized in early schemes like Radburn that separated vehicular from pedestrian movement. These areas may also include other shared amenities, eg, a swimming pool and golf course.

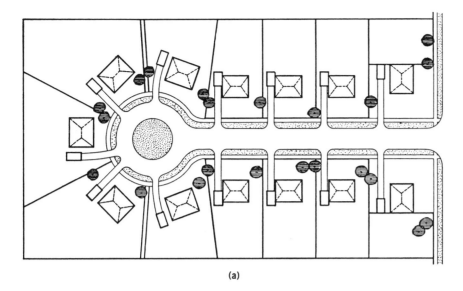

(a)

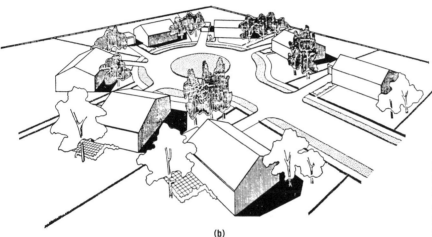

(b)

Figure 2. Basic physical pattern. **(a)** Three basic elements make up the cluster: the house lot, the circulation access, and the common shared space; **(b)** The example shown is a typical cluster in the United States (1). Courtesy of the Appraisal Institute of Canada.

ADVANTAGES

A variety of advantages arise out of the inherent geometry of clusters.

Economic. Substantial savings are accumulated in site development costs. To begin with, there is less land clearance and grading. There are shorter utility lines that serve a greater number of houses and a simplified storm drainage plan because of the less paved area, the use of the open common areas that provide a space for runoff, and less area for streets and sidewalks. Housing can be offered to a wider range of income groups because of the lowered costs.

For civic authorities, cluster subdivisions relieve them of many administrative burdens, and lower maintenance costs. They remove land and streets from public responsibility and reassign it to private groups (eg, to cluster associations) where the installation and maintenance of streets, utilities, and open spaces are borne by the direct users.

The reduction in street lengths also allows more economical and effective delivery of services, eg, garbage collection, mail delivery, and quicker response to police and fire protection.

Social. Clusters define and reinforce smaller social groups, increasing the potential for a sense of belonging and identity. The pattern provides a setting in which cooperation of the families may be encouraged, which, in turn, may lead to joint efforts in other endeavors. For example, lower crime rates have been attributed to cluster developments because of increased awareness by the residents and their identification with a defined territory.

At the larger neighborhood scale, the cluster focuses transportation routes and more clearly defines streets with shopping potential. It helps in defining neighborhood centers and focusing social activities.

Evidence suggests that the size of the house lots and the number of families is a key to social interaction of the residents. In the larger lot situations, the economic advantages in shortened infrastructure lines remain, but effective communal interaction is less likely to occur.

Cultural. Clusters represent traditional forms of land development, particularly in the Third World in the search

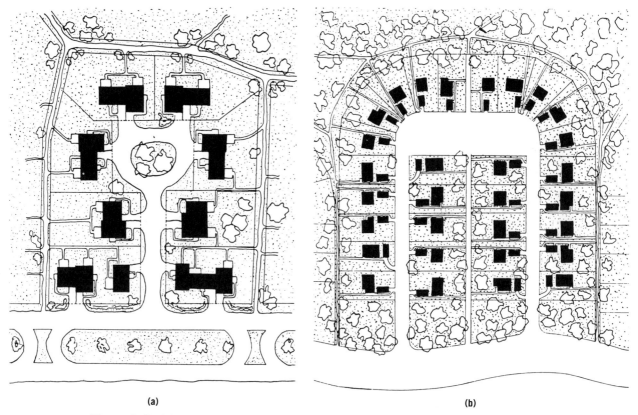

(a)   (b)

Figure 3. Basic arrangements of two individual clusters: **(a)** the cul-de-sac and **(b)** the loop. The cul-de-sac has potentially the better social interaction and cohesion (2). Courtesy of the Urban Land Institute.

for more culturally appropriate solutions. In the industrialized world, they have been used in reaction to the anonymous gridiron pattern.

Administrative. The cluster grouping has the potential for simplified administration, for each cluster may be handled as a single unit. Depending on local regulations and practices, common utility billing, common tax billing, and simplified title allocation may be incorporated. It is suggested that clusters allow better control and direction of development since the preplanning of large sections could

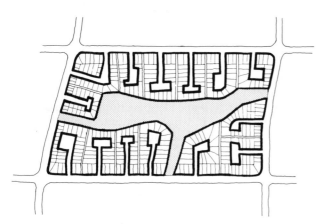

Figure 4. Two types of common areas: the common shared area in each individual cluster, and the open land gained by the more effective land development pattern.

control premature wildcat subdivision. In the rapidly exploding urban areas in the Third World, the simplified administrative framework allows some degree of organization and direction by overburdened municipalities. Control is achieved through its cul-de-sac layout, constricted entrance designs, and gates, as often noted in historical examples.

Flexibility. Proponents argue that future change can more readily be accommodated because of the single title for many smaller land holdings and because land assemblage is simplified when changing land use. The common areas provide open space that can be more effectively used, as opposed to the gridiron alternative of dividing the land into individual lots.

Environmental. The common shared areas can easily incorporate irregular topography as a desirable natural feature. Streams, ravines, and rock outcroppings may be accommodated, and stands of trees and larger wooded areas can be maintained, which would be difficult in the traditional subdivision pattern of individual house lots.

PLANNING CONSIDERATIONS

Designers may approach designs from larger scale urban issues while still being sensitive to smaller scale grouping. A large ordering framework (LOF) may be designed first, while decisions concerning the lots can be made independently. This approach parallels the superblock concept,

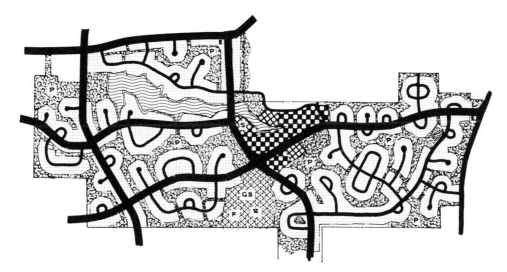

Figure 5. Superblock development: Parkwood in Durham, N.C., 1960. The use of clusters facilitates a superblock approach in land development, and allows clear separation of large-scale circulation networks while still being sensitive to small-scale residential concerns (3). Courtesy of the Urban Land Institute.

where the community is a physically defined entity, and details of the residential areas are developed independently inside this framework (Fig. 5). The preplanning of large areas, without knowing, or needing to know, details of lot areas and dimensions, allows greater flexibility in land development and parallels market changes more closely.

Clusters can also be more flexible since lot size and area can vary considerably, and designers have more freedom in providing a greater variety of sizes. The more critical cost dimensions are now the cluster frontage and the cluster depth, and subdivision costs are no longer dictated by individual lot frontage. This grouping of lots mimics large-lot geometries with the lower infrastructure network costs.

The cluster geometry allows clear separation and definition of the responsibility of the municipality and the developer. It allows concentration of the main utility networks along these primary streets, which facilitates installation and maintenance. Effective joint development efforts may be possible, with the municipality taking the lead in installing the overall structure, and private developers working within this framework (Fig. 6).

Legal Considerations

The rights of the individual homeowner, the legal aspects of the common shared areas, and the relationship between the two must be clearly defined. House lots are usually individually owned, and the common shared space is controlled through a joint arrangement, eg, as a cooperative or condominium.

In the larger land developments, the open space may be deeded to the local government, but it is then treated as public space. Alternatively, a special government district may be established that coincides with the open space area. This is a nongoverning entity and only administers this specific service. In both cases, the burden of mainte-nance remains with the public authorities. More commonly, the land is deeded to a mandatory homeowners' association generally set up as a nonprofit corporation responsible for regulation, protection, and maintenance of the area. More control is retained by the users, and the direct costs to the public authorities are eliminated.

In large developments, it may be advantageous to set up a separate legal entity for each individual cluster to reinforce social identity. Each would be represented in an association responsible for the larger common open area, as in Reston, Va., and Columbia, Md.

In all cases where the land is not deeded to the public authorities, a fee, which can become a lien on the properties, is levied against the homeowners. This fee covers maintenance costs, liability insurance, local taxes, and when provided, expenses for special facilities such as a swimming pool, golf course, etc. When set up as a special district, a special levy is charged by the municipalities.

Difficulties normally stem from individual and group tensions. These may include lack of management expertise of the homeowners' associations, community apathy, and ambiguous enforcement procedures. Experience suggests less difficulty in most of these aspects in larger developments.

Maintenance

Regardless of the legal arrangement, the homeowners share in the costs of maintenance, liability, and security for the common areas. Families who identify with their cluster generally assume a degree of control and responsibility, which is believed to result in better kept, cleaner, and safer areas with lower costs of upkeep. In the larger common areas, maintenance and security have been particularly critical issues. Often replacement costs and control mechanisms have not been adequately considered, and the large common areas become a no-man's-land.

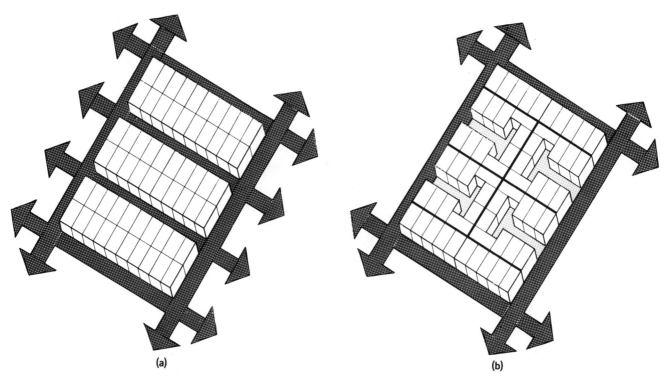

(a)

(b)

Figure 6. **(a)** Cluster layout vs **(b)** gridiron layout. A cluster approach minimizes public streets, focuses circulation, and reinforces neighborhood identity.

Zoning

Conventional zoning ordinances often do not permit cluster subdivisions; a special review is required. Large developments are more readily approved under cluster or density zoning regulations, which allow many restrictions to be modified; for example, houses may be more tightly grouped but with average density requirements remaining the same.

Some critics have challenged large-scale cluster developments as a form of snob zoning.

Planned Unit Development

A planned unit development (PUD) is a legal definition of a development approach in the United States geared toward larger land developments and more flexibility for developers. The FHA defines a PUD as a subdivision that is planned as a unit, allows reduced lot sizes, and includes some common open space, considerations ideal for a cluster-type development. Most PUDs use a cluster geometry to bring down site development costs.

CLUSTERS IN THE THIRD WORLD

Cluster approaches are contemporary throughout the Third World, but special use has been made of them for the lowest income groups, in contrast to the generally

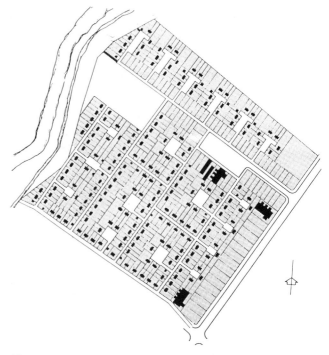

Figure 7. Cluster developments in the Third World: Sensunapan Site and Services Project, Sonsonate, El Salvador. A project for low income families prepared by the Fundación Salvadoreña de Desarrollo y Vivienda Mínima. Families build their houses around an initially provided utility core. Courtesy of George Gattoni.

Figure 8. Model cluster development. A model neighborhood for high density urban situations as frequently found in the Third World. A superblock approach defines major through streets on the perimeter, leaving the interior free for residential uses with a variety of cluster types (4). Courtesy of The MIT Press.

middle- to upper-income groups in the United States. Clusters were actively encouraged in the early 1970s in government designed site and services projects, initially in Central and South America, but they are now used in most countries (Fig. 7).

Clusters are found to be particularly appropriate in the context of the small lots that are eventually completely covered by dwellings despite prohibitive regulations. For example, 45-m^2 lots are not uncommon, and in extreme cases, as in a project in India, 14.5-m^2 lots are noted. The advantages of lower infrastructure costs and less land under public responsibility still apply and become more important in this context (Fig. 8).

A common characteristic is the expanded use of the shared area inside each cluster, whereas emphasis in the United States has been on the common open areas gained by the repetitive use of clusters. In many cases, the shared courts provide the only ventilation space and access to light, secure play areas for younger children, and additional space for cooking and socializing. From a developmental standpoint, the common area provides a logical location for shared water and communal toilets, which readily allows staged upgrading of the services (Fig. 9). A recent focus on community participation has further encouraged the use of clusters because of the potentially

strong social interaction that the physical pattern reinforces. The allocation of families to the clusters must be sensitively handled, with particular awareness of class, kinships, and ethnic issues.

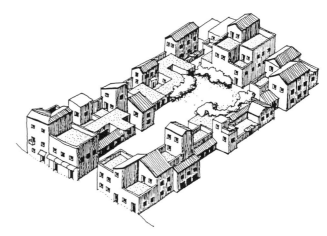

Figure 9. High density clusters in developing countries. A small-lot situation where the lots are completely covered with dwellings. The common shared court often provides the only ventilation and light, as well as being a play area for younger children.

BIBLIOGRAPHY

1. J. Kostka, *Planning Residential Subdivisions,* Appraisal Institute of Canada, Winnipeg, Canada, 1957, pp. 107–108.

2. Harman, O'Donnell & Henninger Assoc., Inc., *New Approaches to Residential Land Development: A Study of Concepts and Innovations,* Urban Land Institute, Technical Bulletin 40, Washington, D.C., 1961, pp. 97 and 102.

3. B. R. Hanke and others, *The Homes Association Handbook, A Guide to the Development and Conservation of Residential Neighborhoods with Common Open Space,* Urban Land Institute, Technical Bulletin 50, Washington, D.C., 1966, p. 68.

4. H. Caminos and R. Goethert, *Urbanization Primer,* The MIT Press, Cambridge, Mass. 1978, p. 29.

General References

T. Adams, *The Design of Residential Areas: Basic Considerations, Principles, and Methods,* Harvard University Press, Cambridge, Mass., 1934.

J. De Chiara, ed., *Time-saver Standards for Residential Developments,* McGraw-Hill Inc., New York, 1984.

J. Kostka, *Neighborhood Planning,* Appraisal Institute of Canada, Winnipeg, Canada, 1957.

Land Design Research, Inc., *Cost-effective Site Planning: Single-family Developments,* National Association of Home Builders, Washington, D.C., 1976.

R. Posada, *Apuntes sobre agrupaciones de vivienda,* Centro Interamericano de Vivienda Y Planeamiento, Unión Panamericana, Bogotá, Colombia, 1963.

R. Untermann and R. Small, *Site Planning for Cluster Housing,* Van Nostrand Reinhold Co., Inc., New York, 1977.

Harman O'Donnell & Henninger Assoc., Inc., *Innovations vs Traditions in Community Development: A Comparative Study in Residential Land Use,* Urban Land Institute, Technical Bulletin 47, Washington, D.C., 1963.

J. Rosenthal, *Cluster Subdivisions,* Report No. 135, American Planning Association, Planning Advisory Service, Chicago, Ill., 1960.

W. Sanders, *The Cluster Subdivision: A Cost-effective Approach,* Report No. 356, American Planning Association, Planning Advisory Service, Chicago, Ill., 1980.

See also Planned Communities (New Towns); Urban Design–Architecture at Urban Scale; Urban Design–Creation of Livable Cities.

Reinhard Goethert, PhD
Massachusetts Institute of
Technology
Cambridge, Massachusetts

COATINGS.   See Paints and Coatings

CODES.   See Regulations—Building and Zoning

COLD DRY CLIMATE CONSTRUCTION

A cold, dry climate is where temperatures can be, for a considerable length of time, extremely cold without thaw, a condition found in the more northerly or extreme southern latitudes of the world.

Within the locations that have extreme cold, there have been both permanent and transient settlements and exploration. These have established an indigenous or cultural response to the cold, dry climate in their built environment.

Construction in regions of cold, dry climate requires multidisciplined awareness of the physical, economic, sociological, and environmental requirements. There are magnified demands upon facilities because of the extremes that exist in such regions. These are the extremes of temperature, winds, darkness, ground conditions, transportation and communication, and remoteness or isolation.

Special attention and analysis must be paid to foundation, structure, weather protection, flexibility of interior spaces, compactness of facilities for efficiency, general safety of facilities and personnel, and environmental control systems. Foundations may be complicated by conditions of permafrost. The structure must be considered for seismic as well at heat-transfer conditions. The cost of transportation and labor may dictate construction types and methods. Building envelopes or skins require minimal openings and joints, minimum heat loss, and special consideration of connections to utilities, utilidors, and air intake and exhaust openings. It is also necessary to consider the extreme effects of infiltration, the solar effect of low sun angles, and the large relative humidity differentials.

Site planning criteria must consider aerodynamics of structures and the subsequent variations of wind and snow accumulation, as well as the reflectance and radiation of exterior surfaces.

Additionally, experience has shown the need for more complete analysis of social and psychological requirements for occupancy due to unique working schedules, harsh weather conditions, and often isolation.

Design considerations beyond the technical solutions, use of materials, and construction techniques should include the assurance that life-support systems are of a quality that will provide a healthy and constant interior environment with provisions in case of mechanical failure for alternate systems to be activated, and that areas and spaces will be of sufficient shape, texture, and color to provide relief from the routine. A visual as well as a physical sense of protection from the extremes of the exterior climate should be provided. Flexibility for changes in the function of spaces should be ensured, and privacy for the individual with a sense of transition from public areas to private retreats should be provided.

Design, engineering, and construction for cold climates must respond to a wide range of built-environment determinants because of the great range of conditions imposed. Severe design criteria of long winters give way to opposite extremes for short summers (cold, dark, windy winters vs warm, light, sunny summers). The psychological as well as the physical design criteria change with the seasons, as does the degree of extremes imposed.

Most areas of cold, dry climate in the northern hemisphere are in the far north or at very high altitudes. High altitude design, engineering, and construction is quite limited and largely restricted to small resource exploration and resort facilities. Areas in the south that would be classified as cold, dry climates are on the antarctic continent. Areas in the northern hemisphere include much of Alaska, the northern half of Canada, the arctic coast of Siberia in the USSR, and the islands of Spitsbergen and Greenland.

Design and construction criteria or parameters within these areas vary only in degree. Each location, of course, varies from any other, and the specific microclimate data must be investigated individually.

Cold, dry regions are defined by temperature, permafrost, treelines, and the arctic circle. Common definitions are also arctic and subarctic. Several delineations of cold regions in the northern hemisphere are shown in Figure 1.

The arctic circle is at 66° 33' north latitude and defines those regions that have 24 hours of sunlight or darkness sometime during the year. Thirty-two degrees Fahrenheit mean annual temperature is shown as an often used identi-

fication of the southern boundary of very cold regions. This does not give any indication of extremes of temperature (1). The southern limits of continuous permafrost and the southerly limits of discontinuous permafrost indicate areas where frozen and partially frozen ground will create foundation concerns (2). The northern boundary of trees is the demarcation between forested areas (Tiaga) and the tundra of the arctic. It represents a physical change in light, wind, soil moisture, and vegetation (2). In Figure 2, cold, wet and cold, dry climates are differentiated in the northern hemisphere.

The arctic and subarctic are considered to be cold, dry climates primarily by temperatures and length of the freezing period that would eliminate precipitation except in a frozen state. The arctic is that region in which the mean temperature for the warmest month is below 50°F (10°C) and the average annual temperature is no higher than

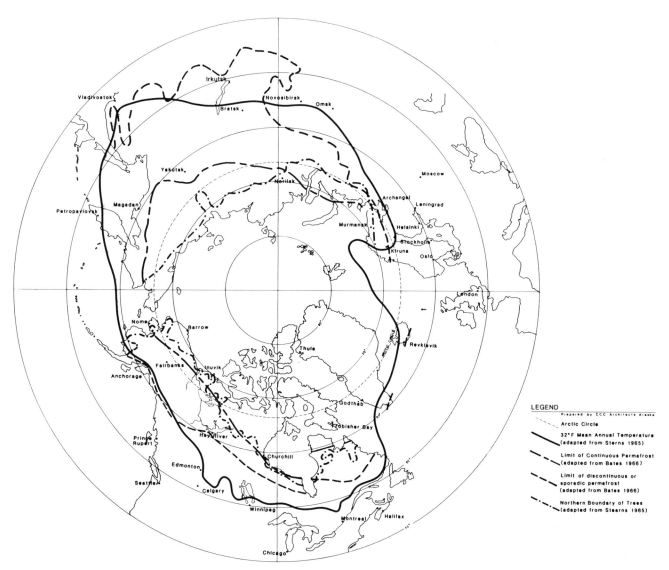

Figure 1. Map of the cold climate regions of the Northern Hemisphere showing the demarcation of critical climatic zones. These include the arctic circle, the northern boundary of trees, the southern boundary of continuous permafrost and discontinuous permafrost, and the line of 32°F mean annual temperatures (1,2). Courtesy of Cold Regions Research Engineering Laboratory.

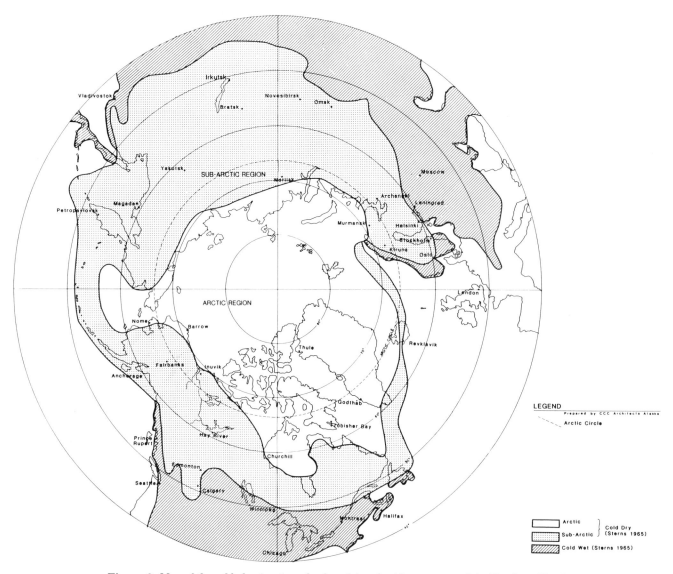

Figure 2. Map of the cold, dry (arctic and subarctic) and cold, wet areas of the Northern Hemisphere (1,2). Courtesy of Cold Regions Research Engineering Laboratory.

32°F (0°C). The subarctic is that region in which the mean temperature for the coldest month is below 32°F (0°C), where the mean temperature of the warmest month is above 50°F (10°C) but where there are less than four months with a mean temperature above 50°F (10°C).

The cold, wet climate is considered to be that area below the subarctic that has cold winters. This is defined as the 32°F (0°C) isotherm for the coldest month and as having a mean temperature for that month between 32°F (0°C) and 0°F (−17.8°C) (2). Areas south of this isotherm may on occasion be subject to cold, wet conditions. The 40° north latitude in North America approximates a southern boundary for the cold wet climate except for high elevations.

In indigenous native cultures, shelters were built to provide maximum use and retention of available energy. They were small, compact structures constructed from sod and other indigenous materials. They were entered through a subterranean hallway in the cold winter months.

The hallway or tunnel prevented heat loss from the main living area and provided a storage area. A hole in the roof provided ventilation and, in summer, light for the house. For this kind of house, two or three seal-oil lamps would keep the temperature at 60–70°F throughout the winter (Fig. 3).

When the white man entered the north, he brought with him his culture and his particular form of built environment. His houses were normally unsuited to the severe arctic climate, as they had evolved under more temperate conditions.

The contrast in housing from the aboriginal to that imposed by the white man shows conflicts. There is an extreme need for designers to understand the cold climatic conditions and respond with the technology now available. Neither the old way nor the introduced new way suffices.

The old provided adequately for the minimal shelter requirements of the society and was adapted to the climatic conditions. Wind blew over, not against; heat loss was

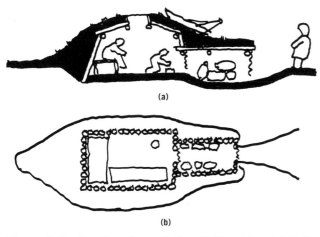

(a)

(b)

Figure 3. Section through an Alaskan Eskimo igloo. **(a)** Driftwood logs were placed vertically in the ground and covered with slabs of tundra. Lower entrance tunnel served as a cold trap and for storage. **(b)** Interior consisted of sleeping and sitting benches and a seal oil lamp.

minimized by the natural sod insulation. Movement caused by thawed permafrost did not affect the shelter. Drainage at breakup was not a problem because the inhabitants moved to a tent, sometimes on top of the igloo, and enjoyed the outdoors after a winter below ground.

That is the challenge to designing for cold regions. Right and wrong are subjective terms influenced by the whole range of modern man's society. The prefabricated box first used in the eastern arctic was right under the conditions of transportation, expediency, and wartime need. The sod igloo and the log cabin were right in time and culture; the temporary ice igloo is still appropriate in an emergency on the open ice.

TEMPERATURES

Extreme cold is the most inhibiting climatic factor. It is the most demanding upon man and equipment, and requires both the most consideration and the most protection in providing built environments for human activities.

A measure of temperature in terms of heat required to overcome the cold and provide for human habitation is the number of degree days of heating required (Table 1). The duration of cold in the higher latitudes causes drastic increases in heating requirements. Fairbanks has a 75% increase, and Point Barrow a 150% increase, over Minneapolis.

Table 1. Temperature in Terms of Degree Days

Location	Degree Days
Minneapolis	8,383
Anchorage	10,864
Fairbanks	14,229
Barrow	20,174
Edmonton	10,285
Winnipeg	10,980
Dawson	15,355
Churchill	17,148

A wind chill equivalent temperature is often used to describe local weather conditions. It is the temperature that will produce the same cooling effect with a wind of 5 mph as is produced with the actual temperature and wind speed. A $-20°F$ temperature with a 20 mph wind will produce a wind chill factor of $-67°F$. An experienced and properly clothed person can normally function in wind chill temperatures down to -20 or $-30°F$. Wind chill factors below that present a serious danger of freezing of exposed flesh, loss of body heat due to inadequate clothing protection, and a consequent reduction in the ability to perform.

Facilities for protection from cold are the primary design and construction elements. Concentration of facilities is an obvious answer, both by eliminating perimeters and minimizing openings, and by simplicity of utilities. Concentration causes more disruption to blowing snow and therefore more drifting problems, and a potential increase in fire hazard.

The importance of minimizing building heat loss is increasingly critical as the heating index increases. As indicated previously, required energy consumptions exclusively due to lower temperatures and longer periods of cold increase radically in the far north. Additionally, the cost of energy increases the farther fuel must be transported. Many areas of the arctic can only be supplied once a year by ship or by air. Others have long transportation routes.

The technology for minimizing heat loss, moisture penetration, and thermal bridging is the same in cold climates as in any other area.

Without adequate insulation in the walls or the windows, condensation in the form of frost builds up on interior surfaces. Frost can accumulate on windows, door knobs, masonry, and thermal bridges through the wall or roof structures.

The high humidity of smaller spaces for human habitation can be countered by providing adequate exhaust to reduce the high humidity, but this increases heat demand. Ventilated roof structures or cold roofs are advisable to avoid damage to insulation by freezing of condensation.

The danger of cold and the fear of cold are primary design parameters. Living accommodations, communities, and work places must be designed for security and redundancy for emergencies. The degree to which this is accomplished responds to the psychological needs for humans living and working in extreme cold. This extreme cold, as well as the isolation, fear for one's safety, and continuous darkness, must be considered in design (3).

SUN ANGLES

Low sun angles and long periods of darkness are additional factors usually found in cold, dry climates. Both factors are caused by the high latitude and are contributory to the cold temperatures. The arctic circle separates the area to the north that receives continuous sunlight during part or all of the summer and no sunlight during part or all of the winter, from the area to the south. The sun at Barrow reaches 43° altitude at noon on the longest day.

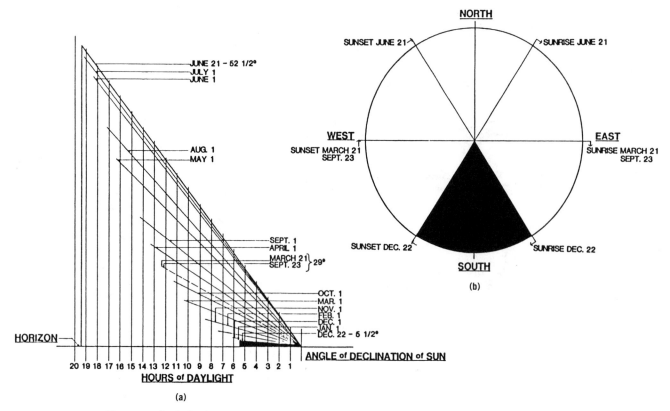

Figure 4. Sunlight data for Anchorage, Alaska (latitude 61°10′): **(a)** sun angle in elevation; **(b)** sun angle in plan. The graph shows the hours of sunlight, the declination of the sun, and the location of sunrise and sunset.

It is 22° above the horizon at both 6 A.M. and 6 P.M., and 3.5° above the northern horizon at midnight. At Minneapolis, the noon sun altitude is 68° on June 21, and 16.5° at 6 A.M. and 6 P.M., and, of course, there is no midnight sun. The data for each specific location can be obtained from government weather charts, and local calculations should be made (Fig. 4).

During the summer months, higher latitudes experience more potential sunlight hours because of the large solar azimuth travel. For 55° north latitude, there is 63% sunlight in summer, and 37% sunlight in winter; for 70° north latitude, there is 79% sunlight in summer, and 21% sunlight in winter.

There are other factors that affect sunlight. One, called alvedo, is sunlight going through multiple reflections between snow and clouds, giving high intensities of diffused light during the short winter and spring days. Cold, dry climates, particularly in the arctic, experience considerable high cloud cover.

Both the long winter nights and the long summer days affect design and construction primarily in responding to the psychological needs of the inhabitants. A response to this would affect siting and orientation of facilities, as well as interior design and maximum exposure to the south.

To provide for south-faced exposure to sunshine in a community, one-story buildings in the northern part of the United States can be spaced as close as 25–34 ft apart, whereas in mid-Canada and farther north, the sun angles are so low that similar exposure could require 150–300 ft, depending on the latitude (Fig. 5).

In the summer, it is desirable for residential facilities to open out to the landscape to allow sunshine to penetrate. In the darkness of winter, the monotony and the impression of cold suggests a drawing in and protection from the outdoors that is consistent with protection from the extreme temperatures and high winter winds. The months of darkness contribute strongly to the feeling of isolation and boredom and suggest interior circulation patterns to provide maximum human contact and alternative vistas,

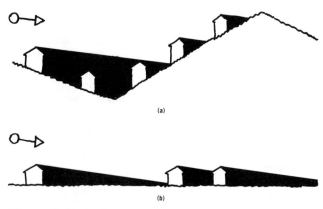

Figure 5. South slope orientation: Diagram shows the extent of shadows cast from a low sun angle on **(a)** a hillside site and on **(b)** a flat site.

Table 2. Duration and Amount of Snowfall

Location	Yearly Precipitation, in.	Period of Snow Coverage On Ground, mo	Mean Yearly Snowfall, in.
Minneapolis	26	3.0	45.0
Anchorage	15	5.0	64.0
Fairbanks	11	6.5	70.3
Point Barrow	5	10.0	35.0

forms, and colors for relief. The long periods of darkness require extreme consideration of the lighting systems, both interior and exterior, for safety and a sense of scale on the exterior, and for a variety of activities and privacy on the interior.

In site selection and placing of facilities, a south slope obviously overcomes some of the extremes of spacing to allow sun penetration, and suggests the construction of lower buildings to the south and taller buildings to the north (Fig. 5). These site planning factors need to be considered in conjunction with a katabatic drift, which is the flow of air down a slope as it is cooled by radiation, as well as prevailing wind directions and problems of snow drifting.

PRECIPITATION AND SNOWFALL

Precipitation and snowfall in cold, dry climates are considerably lower than in the coastal and more southern cold, wet, and moderate zones. Because of prevailing high winds, snow accumulation and drifting does occur, necessitating design parameter responses similar to those in other, more moderate zones.

Precipitation can be rain or snow. The conversion factor is usually about one to ten. Maritime or coastal areas are expected to have considerably more moisture than interior areas. The major exception is the arctic coast where precipitation is minimal. In fact, much of the arctic, where precipitation is only 5 in. or less, is sometimes called the arctic desert. Of more critical importance is the duration and amount of snowfall (Table 2). Most concerns for precipitation, including rain and snow in the areas of lesser precipitation, relate to the movement of that moisture by relatively high winds.

In areas of permafrost and where the seasonal frost on the ground lasts late into the summer season, drainage can be a major concern, even though the precipitation is light. Obviously, drainage away from buildings is advisable, but it is critical in permafrost areas because the warmer moisture will cause thaw to considerable depths.

With careful planning, snow can be used as insulation around foundations, banked against the north side of buildings, and even held onto roofs, if they are designed for this loading.

Windblown, dry, fine snow can penetrate the most minute cracks or openings. Air exhausts and intakes, plumbing exhausts, and even key holes and air vents must be carefully designed and protected to avoid snow penetration (Fig. 6).

The long duration of snow cover emphasizes the remoteness and isolation. Additionally, the often flat environment distorts perspective and judgment of distances. Uniformity of color and forms that are leveled out by drifting snow emphasize the bleakness (3).

White-out and ice fog conditions near the ground can, even on otherwise perfectly clear days, wipe out all sense of scale and distance.

Humidity can be a particular concern in cold climates because of the extreme difference in pressure between a warm interior and a cold exterior. The necessity for tight vapor barriers becomes more extreme the colder the exterior becomes.

WINDS AND DRIFTING SNOW

High winds, blowing snow, and drifting snow can occur in all areas of cold, dry climates. The coastal regions of

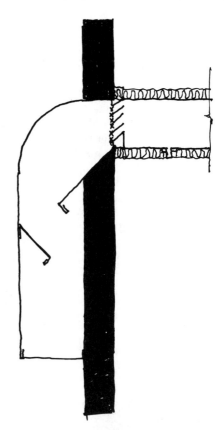

Figure 6. Air vent for cold climate. An air intake for combustion air or fresh air must be designed to avoid blockage by snow and allow for drainage of moisture.

the arctic and the open plains of the subarctic are more subject to disturbance by wind than the forested areas south of the tree line.

Wind speeds and directions for both winter and summer must be analyzed for each location because they are affected by the topography. Often in the flatter areas, wind directions are relatively constant and can be uniform in force.

Design for wind must give concern to the wind chill factor, the heat loss, snow drifting, and the structural requirements for buildings. The arrangement of the structures also influences wind patterns in the microconditions of the community, where it may either increase or decrease problems encountered.

Katabatic wind is the cold air flow from higher elevations to low areas that causes a wide difference in temperature between upland and low, flat terrain. A moderate wind may relieve these conditions and can break up ice fog created by inversion over low-lying communities (Fig. 7).

As the amount and type of snow and the wind velocity are predictable, drifting snow about a single structure is also predictable. The effect, however, of adjoining structures, trees, hillocks, road berms, etc, is less predictable and must be studied carefully.

When wind speeds near the ground approximate 7–10 mph, fresh snow particles can be picked up and carried along over smooth surfaces until they are deposited in any area where the wind speed is reduced by interaction with an object such as a building. In exposed areas, there can be a large supply of snow collected, even though there is minimal snowfall.

Where there is a relatively isolated structure, snowdrifts will form on both the windward and the leeward sides. The windward drift can grow to a maximum height, not exceeding the height of the structure. Usually, there will be a scoured region between the drift and the building. On the leeward side, the wind speed is reduced. However, the drifts can reach the height of the building and ultimately extend horizontally to a maximum of ten times the height of the building (Fig. 8). Obviously, if wind blows at an angle, the shape will be changed and probably shortened (4).

In terms of design for foundations in permafrost, buildings are often built off the ground to maintain a cooler or freezing condition below the building. This may allow the wind to blow snow under the building, causing drifts

Figure 8. Snow drifting about a structure on grade showing the scooped-out area to windward and the pileup of snow on the leeward side caused by the slowdown of wind after sweeping the roof.

on the leeward side only. Depending on the building width, this may also create a venturi effect, sweeping the snow from under the building (Fig. 9).

Roof shapes affect the drift, and a break on the leeward side can fill to a depth that may be structurally unsafe (Fig. 10).

Major access routes, pedestrian walkways, and building exits should have priority in planning for drifting snow and wind. Wind, when funneled between buildings or forced through a narrow space, can develop considerable force and become a serious problem. Upwind barriers such as snow fences or a line of buildings can provide some control by collecting drifts.

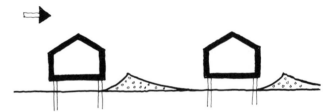

Figure 9. A structure raised on piles allows wind to pass under, creating a venturi effect that carries snow under and creates drifts only on the leeward side.

Obviously, the minimum building area perpendicular to the wind will have the least effect on heat loss and on drifting snows. This orientation must be weighed against the desirable orientation for other reasons, such as penetration of sunshine and vistas.

An aerodynamic shape with rounded or diagonal corners, both vertical and horizontal, helps reduce turbulence and decreases the impact of high winds (Fig. 11). Wind has a considerable heat loss influence on exterior skins, particularly on window areas, by reducing the insulating air film that is close to the surface. Wind can penetrate

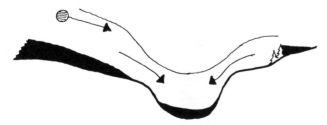

Figure 7. Section through a valley showing the cold air flow (katabatic wind) to the valley floor and the subsequent stratification of temperatures.

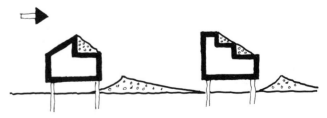

Figure 10. Broken roof forms create drifting conditions on the leeward side that can overload the structure.

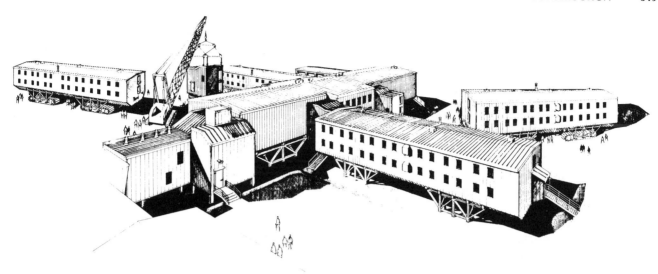

Figure 11. Placing modules for the Arco–Exxon operations center at Prudhoe Bay, Alaska.

cracks around windows, doors, and other openings, increasing heat loss. On the leeward side, high winds can draw warm air out of buildings through cracks and openings. Triple-glazed sash and the use of modern sealants and caulking greatly reduce this loss.

PERMAFROST

Permafrost and deep frost layers are the least understood and perhaps most significant special condition of some cold, dry climatic regions. About one-half of the land area of Canada and the USSR, more than 60% of Alaska, 22% of China, as well as most of Greenland and Antarctica are underlain by perennial frozen ground, more commonly known as permafrost. Permafrost is also encountered in isolated locations related to lakes and streams at high elevations, and in shaded and extremely wet locations considerably farther south.

There are many types and conditions of permafrost. Basically, it is a thermal condition in soil or rock with persistent temperatures below 0°C. Continuous permafrost is that which occurs throughout a large region. Discontinuous permafrost is that which occurs in some areas below the ground surface, while other areas are free of permafrost. Dry permafrost is perennially frozen soil or rock without ice, which does not yield excess water upon thawing. Ice-rich permafrost is frozen ground containing ice in excess of that required to fill porous spaces. Thaw-stable and thaw-unstable permafrost are critical descriptions related to the strength of the soil when thawed. Well-drained, granular materials may have no change in bearing strength when thawed, whereas many frost-susceptible materials may allow significant settlement (5).

Permafrost forms an impervious layer to moisture and all water from rain and snow thawing that accumulates above. This condition gives swampy characteristics to the northern tundra in the summertime. The vegetation forms an insulating blanket that effectively maintains a small active layer of soil generally less than a meter in thickness in the far north. Disturbance of that vegetated mat increases thaw rates, raises soil temperatures, and causes the permafrost to melt, thus altering the character of the surface.

Since permafrost is a phenomenon of temperature, any change in the thermal regime of an area can lead to thawing resulting in slumped banks and cliffs, and topography consisting of mounds, sinkholes, caverns, and ravines. The local melting of ground ice and subsequent settling creates this topography.

Man-made disruption of the natural regime seriously affects the delicate thermal equilibrium. Clearing, digging of trenches, and erection of buildings may result in the thawing of the frozen ground or even the raising of the permafrost table.

The mechanical problem associated with the degradation of permafrost is that, upon thawing, the material loses its capacity to support the overburden. The amount of ice present in permafrost may vary from a small number of minute particles to as much as 90%.

Large lakes and rivers do not freeze solid in winter, producing significant thaw bulbs in the permafrost beneath. Many of these thaw lakes can extend for several miles in length and are seldom deeper than 10 ft.

Polygonal or patterned ground characteristic of permafrost regions results from ground contraction during extremely low temperatures. Water and snow collect in the contraction cracks, eventually turning to ice and producing ice wedges that surround each polygon.

The soil overlaying permafrost can vary in depth from as little as several feet in the far north to 10 or 12 ft in sporadic permafrost zones. This is the level of annual frost or the active layer that freezes and thaws seasonally.

This active layer often consists of frost-susceptible soils and is generally saturated because of poor drainage. This high moisture content, in turn, causes frost heaving. The differential heaving as a result of frost action is a serious cause of damage to foundations and buildings. There are numerous examples of buildings settling with their floor levels well below the original ground surface, and others

Figure 12. Permafrost thaw created by heat from a building can cause serious settlement or differential settlement and breakup of the structure when an ice lens in the permafrost is also thawed.

with differential settlement and heaving that can completely destroy the building (Fig. 12).

Adequate site investigations are essential prior to design and construction. This investigation should identify the distribution of permafrost, the conditions of the subsurface, including the physical and mechanical properties of the soils, and the thermal regime of the ground.

In the extreme north, where the permafrost is stable and there is a minimal active zone such as at Prudhoe Bay in Alaska, many structures are built on piles driven or thawed into permafrost and shaped or banded to avoid uplift in the active zone. Structures built on piles are usually constructed four to eight or more feet above the natural grade to minimize disturbance of the natural regime and to allow continuous air movement and refreezing of summer thaw during the cold winter. Only the piles, often wooden piles, and the utility connections should transmit heat to the frozen ground (Fig. 13). This method is sometimes used in less stable areas, with additional precautions such as layering of gravel for insulation over the existing active zone to eliminate any thaw cycle.

Permafrost conditions can be neglected on well-drained and thawed granular soils or solid rock. This condition may exist on south slopes that are well drained. Conventional designs and construction methods are then possible.

Where piles may be difficult to place or unavailable, structures that will not require much heat can be placed on insulated fills. This is a common practice for the building of roadways and parking surfaces. The depth of fill depends on the loading requirements and on the heat load from the structure. This may range from 3 or 4 ft to 6 or 8 ft. Additionally, layers of rigid nonabsorbent insulations can be placed in the fill and extended out considerable distances on each side of the actual structure.

A relatively expensive and perhaps not fully permanent method used in sporadic zones is removal and replacement with compacted, well-drained, non-frost-susceptible mate-

Figure 14. A thermopile is a tube completely sealed and used as a structural pile. Fins at the top radiate off the heat brought up by convection.

rial. The depth of excavation and fill required to avoid further thawing would depend on the estimated rate of subsidence, the changes to the surrounding thermal regime, and the success of drainage. In some areas, design must anticipate settlement because of the size of structures or the cost of other means of avoiding thaw. Flexible foundations providing jacking devices or adjustments to pile caps can be used. Also, settlement joints permitting individual sections of the building to move differently may be designed.

Recent developments of thermal or heat valves have eliminated a considerable amount of the uncertainty of other methods of supporting structures on permafrost.

The devices are designed to withdraw heat from the underlying soils and radiate it to the atmosphere. They are usually tubes filled with a gas or liquid that flows because of temperature differential. The earlier systems of thermopiles used pipe piling placed as a structural foundation system that maintained or refroze the supporting bulbs of frozen soil; the bulbs were either integral with the permafrost or large enough to provide adequate bearing (Fig. 14).

Newer systems use smaller pipes called thermoprobes that can be placed alongside foundations or piles, placed horizontally under the slab and foundation, or even driven in later as repair methods to achieve the same goal. Instead of fins on top of the pipe piles, these pipes or tubes are connected to fin-type radiators located either on the building or free standing to disperse the heat drawn from the foundation conditions (Fig. 15).

Figure 13. Buildings separated from the ground by piles usually do not degrade the permafrost. Where gravel fill and insulation are used, the line of permafrost may rise.

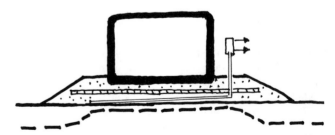

Figure 15. Horizontal heat valve. A thermoprobe is not structural and is placed or driven under a slab on grade or alongside a foundation.

These systems have been used so successfully in preservation of aboveground piping as well as buildings that they have become a common method in almost all permafrost conditions. The advantage of the heat valve is that it can maintain or refreeze soils of almost any water content and requires no mechanical system or power source.

UTILITIES

Adequate utilities in cold climates are often the most difficult and costly service to construct and maintain. Domestic and fire-protection waters and disposal of wastes and sewage are usually water borne and consequently must be protected from low temperatures.

Individual wells and septic tanks are generally prohibited by permafrost or by deep seasonal frost, sometimes to 12 ft. Conventional piped-water supplies and sewage systems in unheated and uninsulated pipes buried in permafrost quickly freeze. Service lines can be placed on or above the ground surface in insulated arctic pipes (Fig. 16). This exposes the lines to damage and creates obstructions to traffic. The alternative is insulated and heated pipes in utilidors (Fig. 17).

Utilidors are insulated conduits that house water, wastewater, and sewage pipes and, in some instances, steam or hot water-lines for heating and electric and communication system distribution. Heating of the utilidor must be achieved by supplying heat to the air within the utilidor, by heating the water that is circulated, or by electric heat tracing. Insulation is provided not only to protect the waterlines from freezing, but to protect the permafrost from thawing. The lines are looped so that

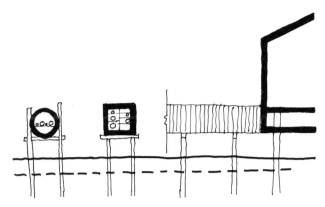

Figure 17. Utilidors may be made of wood as an insulated box or of insulated metal panels. They may be placed directly on the ground or raised high enough for passage below.

the water can be continuously circulated when supplies are not being taken from the line.

Reservoir construction in the arctic is an expensive operation, but is often necessary where natural water supply storage is not adequate. Lakes are the usual source of water if the depth is great enough to provide unfrozen water below the ice. Water can also be found in underground strata below streams. Wells can be used in permafrost areas where water strata can be found below the permafrost.

Water can be distributed in three general ways within arctic communities: by tank trucks; by summer piping systems supplemented by cold weather tank truck delivery; and by waterlines in insulated utilidors.

In addition to normal sanitary safeguards, there are heating, insulation, and circulation requirements needed to ensure adequate functioning.

Piped systems are superior to haulage systems because there is less chance of contamination during distribution. They allow a greater amount of water consumption; interruption of service is less frequent; fire protection is available; and inspection and control of water quality is possible.

Sewage disposal is one of the major physical difficulties facing arctic communities. The need to maintain sanitary surroundings requires that the disposal system be on a community-wide basis.

One of two general approaches is used for the solution to this problem: the use of tank trucks to remove sewage and wastewater from household storage; or the use of a piped system for collection. Tank trucks are prone to problems similar to those of hauled-water distribution systems: operating and maintenance costs are high; danger of spillage exists during pumping; service may be limited and sporadic because of adverse weather; and valuable indoor space must be utilized for storage facilities. The piped systems are not limited by storage problems and are ultimately more satisfactory although more costly to install. When used in conjunction with a piped-water supply system, the same utilidor can be used to keep the sewer line from freezing.

Treatment of sewage wastes can be done in several ways, including outfalls directly to a large body of flowing water. Biological treatment can be either aerobic or anaero-

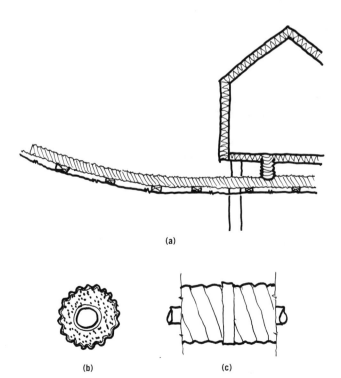

(a)

(b)   (c)

Figure 16. (a) Arctic pipe on ground is prefabricated with (b) foamed insulation and (c) a metal protective skin.

bic. Physical chemical treatment can be used to break down the impurities, and incineration, which oxidizes the waste, can be used with solid waste.

Biological treatment is the most common, and can be handled by stabilization lagoons and a variety of proprietary extended aeration systems.

The sewage lagoon is the simplest, most common, and most economical biological system to operate. Wastewater is ponded in a shallow reservoir for an allotted period of time, allowing the growth of aerobic bacteria, which consumes 95% of the organic wastes. During long periods of ice cover, the lagoon serves primarily as a holding tank with minimal anaerobic action occurring. The primary action is in the summer with its long periods of sunlight.

There are manufacturers with patented equipment for biological treatment that do a very creditable job for smaller installations. This consists of activated sludge and extended aeration processes.

Power generation and distribution can be most critical from a life safety point of view. In extreme cold, a breakdown of power sources for periods of even an hour or two can be disastrous. Generation and distribution systems differ only slightly in cold climates from those in more moderate zones. However, the cost of fuel and the need for redundancy in equipment to avoid lengthy shutdowns increase the operating and maintenance costs. Waste heat from generation units is commonly reused in heating systems. Electrical power requirements are considerably increased on a per capita basis by the increased lighting demands and use of electrical heat in remote locations where normal utility service and heating would be difficult and expensive.

Heating and ventilation systems for human habitation in extreme cold are based upon design criteria such as that indicated previously for the degree days. Similarly, design temperatures for heating and ventilating are substantially increased. An extreme example is Fairbanks, Alaska, which has a design temperature differential of 140°F (Table 3). Only in the interior and extreme northern areas, however, are design temperatures greatly in excess of those recognized in the northern plains states of the United States.

In summer, the effect of solar radiation is intensified by the lower sun levels with resultant reduced reflection and increased solar heat gains, particularly on the east and west exposures. There is a more continuous sun effect resulting in almost round-the-clock solar gain. The intensity, however, is generally considerably reduced because of the low sun angle and sky haze.

In permafrost areas, the floor must be insulated as heavily as walls and ceilings because of the air space and air movement below the floor required to keep the underlying permafrost frozen. Generally, a 6-mil polyethylene or other low perm-rating vapor barrier should be used in cold conditions. In high humidity, a metal foil type with minimum perm rating should be used.

At low temperatures, humidity control can become very expensive because of the need to keep surface temperatures above the dew point. Without humidification in a design temperature of −40°F or colder, ten percent relative humidity or less can be expected, causing excessive drying of the structure itself as well as furniture. With low humidities, dry-bulb temperatures as high as 78–80°F may be necessary for personal comfort. Low humidity also allows for a buildup of static electricity, which can be uncomfortable.

In extreme cold, the use of operable windows should be discouraged. Closed storm vestibules (arctic entrances) should be provided to reduce vapor condensation that can build up on door frames, freezing them shut or forcing off the door butts, as well as for personal protection and reduction of heat losses.

Exposed equipment, such as HVAC (heating, ventilating, and air conditioning) units and exhaust fans, should be avoided because of the extreme temperature differences to which the equipment is exposed, particularly if the equipment is on a controlled cycle with night shutdown. Outside air intakes and exhaust outlets require baffles to trap the windblown snow, preventing it from entering into the ductwork or thawing and causing leaks.

In remote areas, mechanical design and controls should be as simple and maintenance free as possible since personnel generally are not familiar with more complicated systems. Standby equipment should be considered because of the difficulty of obtaining service and parts.

A heating system should normally deliver its heat around the perimeter of a building to be effective. Warm air systems with perimeter ductwork, a manual control, and interlocking return air and outside air dampers can be quite simple for systems with one to three heating zones. In larger systems, make-up air should be heated through a heat exchanger from the central system. Systems with perimeter baseboards and fan coil units using boiler water should use a 50–50 solution of ethylene glycol to prevent freeze up.

Several facilities have been built with double walls using return air to warm the inner walls, avoid downdrafts, and draw off any moisture that might penetrate the vapor barrier (Fig. 18).

Where spaces for access to plumbing and ductwork are not feasible because of permafrost conditions, insulated and heated crawl space hung from the structure and above the ground level becomes practical. The alternative is to highly insulate and protect all water-carrying piping directly below the floor.

The advantage of the insulated crawl space is that repairs and maintenance can be undertaken in the wintertime more easily than having to build a temporary enclosure around a faulty connection.

COSTS

Many factors contribute to the high cost of construction in the north. In addition to the harsh climate and the

Table 3. Design Temperatures in °F

Location	Heating	Cooling
Seattle	+15	+85
Minneapolis	−20	+90
Anchorage	−30	+73
Fairbanks	−60	+80
Point Barrow	−50	+58

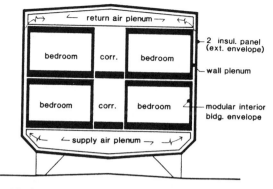

Figure 18. A section through permanent housing units on the Alaska pipeline shows double-wall construction.

remoteness of development sites, unskilled local labor plays a significant role in escalating total costs. The development of construction techniques specifically for the extreme cold has evolved into a technology unlike that found in subarctic or temperate climates.

Because of the limited size and number of communities, contractors are often required to furnish living accommodations for their employees. These are usually portable, temporary, and small with limited recreational facilities. Trailers and modular building units are most commonly used. Government and trade unions have set minimum standards for camp facilities. Temporary sewer and water systems are required. An adequate water supply is essential and, in most cases, is readily available from a nearby river or lake.

The absence of a nearby wholesale trade sector increases construction costs. One of the most frustrating problems is maintaining optimum inventories of materials. Careful planning and good logistical control are required to ensure that materials are at the site when needed but not stored any longer than necessary.

A primary concern of arctic construction is protection of construction materials and stored equipment, both during shipment to the job site and while in storage. Damage in transit not only raises costs but can also result in a shortage of materials or equipment needed at a crucial time. Such shortages drastically increase costs by disrupting job progress.

Costs are seriously affected by the factors of equipment, labor, and transportation discussed in the following section.

EQUIPMENT, LABOR, AND TRANSPORTATION

The most common methods of handling construction material and equipment in transit and on the job are palletization and containerization. These must be reduced to the size that available equipment can handle. A Hercules aircraft is limited to $8 \times 8 \times 52$ ft and to 14,000 lb. Materials vulnerable to weather extremes, such as gypboard or plywood, are covered with watertight envelopes. Grease, oil, and other hydrocarbon products are sealed tightly to prevent contamination by ice, snow, or dirt. Material wastage is sometimes increased from a norm of 5% to 15 or 20%.

Construction equipment must be modified to protect

it from temperature-related failure and to protect the operator from weather extremes. Extreme subzero temperature places a heavy burden upon operating equipment, thereby significantly reducing its life expectancy. Maintenance costs can be seriously increased. Engine overhaul is increased because of long idle times. Tires become brittle from cold. Cold increases metal failure. Cable insulations crack, and hydraulic systems have increased failure.

The problem of maintaining equipment in remote job sites centers around one basic consideration: that of replacing parts and providing special-purpose tools. An inventory of easily accessible replacement parts must be available. When a key piece of equipment is involved, delays can become very expensive. Whenever possible, equipment with identical component parts that require a smaller inventory of repair parts (eg, engines, hydraulic systems, etc) should be used.

Tying job production to single-purpose equipment is a practice to be avoided. For instance, loading belly dump trucks with a single loader or dragline may appear to be a more efficient operation than using self-loading scrapers and pusher cats. However, if the single piece of loading machinery fails, the job will be interrupted until the equipment is repaired or replaced.

The high cost of labor in the arctic plays a significant role in escalating total costs of construction projects. Problems compounding this are monetary differentials arising from higher living costs, exceptional recruitment cost, and termination cost due to seasonal and cyclical instability in employment. The cost of manpower is also increased because of a lower productivity rate compared to that of temperate-zone working areas. Physical productivity is reduced for a variety of reasons: adverse climatic conditions, psychological stress, construction methods, and equipment unsuitable for arctic conditions. This can mean an increase in labor costs of from 33 to 50% for winter construction.

In both Canada and Alaska, the contractor generally attempts to hire local labor as much as possible, although this practice varies. Some contractors feel that native (Eskimo or Indian) labor is unreliable, while others praise the skills and aptitudes of the native. During times of extreme winter weather when work must be performed outdoors, the native frequently outproduces his white counterpart. This difference in work production under adverse weather conditions can be attributed in part to pride on the part of the worker, physiological traits peculiar to the native, and adaptability to severe conditions developed by a lifetime of experience in cold regions. It would be desirable for a large percentage of the labor force to be experienced in working in the cold, since isolation and extreme working conditions are the most frequent causes of labor force turnover. The worker who knows what to expect will be less likely to develop morale problems or terminate employment before the project is finished.

Transportation of construction materials and other supplies to arctic sites is often the determining factor in the final cost of the project. Damage to materials and supplies in transit also contributes to cost. Food supplies are especially vulnerable. Delivery of materials can be accomplished by marine, land, or air transportation. At times, more than one of these methods may be necessary. In

Alaska, for example, materials for the development of oil-drilling facilities at Prudhoe Bay were shipped to Seward, freighted to Fairbanks by train, and trucked to Prudhoe Bay over ice roads in the winter or air freighted in the summer.

Because of seasonal ice conditions and shallow near-shore waters, marine transportation to the Arctic is limited. The coast is usually free of ice in the summer. The ocean route around Point Barrow is open for only six weeks during August and September.

Roads are extremely limited. Except for the trans-Alaska pipeline haul road, there are no overland routes to the arctic in Alaska. Most villages have minimal internal road systems connecting them with their airstrips.

Snowmobiles and tractor trains are used for overland travel in winter. In summer, heavy equipment can seriously damage the very sensitive tundra with its thawed soils and standing water, effectively prohibiting overland travel in summer except on foot.

Truck freight costs are roughly the same as those incurred by air shipment; trucks do have the advantage of being able to deliver goods without extra handling costs from airport to work site.

Air transportation plays a major role in arctic activities. Aircraft can operate year round and provide the fastest means of transporting supplies. To inland communities, air is often the only means of freight transportation. Many improved airports exist in the arctic. Some have navigational aids and are capable of accommodating commercial jets.

Construction methods can adapt to weather conditions and site location by modifying facility design or by providing protection from the cold. The oil-gathering stations, as well as operations centers at Prudhoe Bay, were completely fabricated in the continental United States. They were barged in maximum-size modules to the North Slope where, with a minimum crew, the modules were carried on crawlers to the site and jacked onto pilings (Fig. 11). Over the past years, a large percentage of the construction projects in Greenland were prefabricated in Denmark. Much of the housing in the Canadian eastern arctic is prefabricated in the south and shipped to various locations for erection. Housing in Bethel, Alaska, was completely fabricated in an enclosed shop in the community and skidded to location. Housing units for one project in the north were panelized throughout the winter in one building which was constructed the previous summer. An estimated two months of cold weather construction time was saved. Numerous structures in the arctic and subarctic have been temporarily enclosed with double plastic film on a light wood frame, allowing continual job progress in a protected structure throughout the cold months.

Economics and the social and political climates affect available materials and equipment and methods of construction. The information in these sections applies primarily to North America.

MAN IN THE NORTH

The natural and climatic conditions of the north were largely responsible for the physical, psychological, and so-cial responses of the early native cultures. These same conditions must be faced by the modern immigrant to the north. These are identified by Zrudlo as (3):

1. Temperature, related to isolation.
2. Long duration of snow, related to isolation and poverty of stimuli.
3. Polar night, related strongly to unfamiliarity and poverty of stimuli.
4. High wind velocity, related indirectly to isolation and directly to unfamiliarity.
5. Remoteness in general, strongly related to isolation.
6. Lack of scale (flat tundra), related to unfamiliarity and poverty of stimuli.

Isolation is both the cause and effect of low populations in the cold climates. It is largely lack of contact with the outside world caused by remoteness of high latitudes. Low temperatures, high winds, and remoteness from major population zones accompany the high latitude. For the indigenous peoples, this was largely an isolation from other small villages or family units. Today, remoteness is more lack of contact with the familiar and is a result of the time, cost, and means of transportation available. Of all of the deprivations experienced in northern living, the greatest is the sense of confinement and the inability to get away.

The high latitude, with its long summer days and winter nights, causes a disruption of the normal habits of a southerner, and because of his unfamiliarity with the natural environment, conditions of insomnia and boredom have psychological as well as physical effects upon individuals. The long periods of darkness cause more psychological problems than do the long days.

Long periods of extreme cold slow down or halt outdoor activity, increase the feeling of isolation and confinement, create a need for vigilance to maintain personal and facility safety, and slow down normal motivation. Low temperatures can also create visual distortion and limitation resulting from low visibility.

High winds, combined with low temperatures, produce extremely dangerous conditions—increasing the risk involved in outside activity, emphasizing the isolation, increasing the potential of severe loss due to fire, reducing visibility, and having a leveling effect on the landscape.

The topography and general geographic features are varied and seem strange to the newcomer. They lack scale and tend to be monotonous, emphasizing again the feeling of isolation. Landscape of the arctic and the effects of the low sun angles can be extremely beautiful, but with solitude and silence, the result for many is monotony.

Responses of the indigenous people to conditions in the north in the past obviously differed in the extreme from that possible today with the input of the southern culture and technology.

Native communities were small, often consisting of a single-family group. They were in balance with the ecology and natural food supply. Villages were far apart and located next to hunting grounds. Overpopulation meant starvation, as did disruption of the natural environment.

Lack of materials for building and the extremes of the climatic conditions caused overcrowded, minimal-sized structures, often partially below ground and, in winter, generally covered with snow. Lack of fuel, other than animal oil, required compactness and overcrowding.

Prior to outside contact, the Eskimo developed his entire social structure and psychological needs around the gathering of food supplies and protection from the climatic conditions. Remoteness and isolation were advantages. Physical and psychological conditions that are most difficult for southerners are the conditions in which the Eskimo survived.

Social, psychological, and economic needs of the southern culture transposed into the far north have created a major conflict between the indigenous people and the outsiders. Most Eskimo communities today still cling to some of the social and subsistence structure of the native culture, but are dependent upon the social and economic structure of the southern culture. Most indigenous people no longer live in their old ways after the introduction of social services, transportation means, and a monetary economic base.

Some of the change has been gradual, through early contact with whalers, freighters, miners, missionaries, and government officials. For many, however, the shift has been rapid, starting with contact with the military in World War II and today's oil and gas exploration.

Schools and community centers have been built with government funds and imported labor. Disposal and water systems have been provided, not just to communities, but to individual homes. Food and other provisions are available at community stores. The cash economy is there. The younger generation is making the complete shift to the white man's culture. The needs of built environment for the cold regions in the far north, and the responses to the physical, psychological, and social conditions, are now those of the southerner transported to the north.

Throughout the north, technological response to physical conditions has been rapid. The military, oil and gas companies, and federal and state governments are providing facilities with physical standards nearly equal to those provided in the south. A time no longer exists when less-than-equal standards for the north are considered adequate. If southerners and northerners are to live in harmony with the conditions of the north, consideration within the built environment must be given for protection from the elements; for the feeling of isolation and loneliness; for privacy as well as social intercourse; for sensory stimulation; and for an environment conducive to enjoyment of the northern conditions.

The economic and political structure of nations dictates varied solutions in the construction process. It is hard to believe that design for indigenous peoples' housing in Alaska, in the arctic islands of Canada, Greenland, northern Scandinavia, and on the arctic rivers of the USSR could be similar. There are differing delivery systems, materials, and transportation available as well as social and political requirements of each. With the consideration of the varied conditions, exchange of information can be invaluable to policy, program, and design–construction.

Normally, housing in the cold regions of North America is based on traditional modes of construction, largely wood frame and on-site construction. Variations of the stick-built construction methods have been tried, including pre-

cut lumber, prefabricated sections, and even complete modules. The use of foam insulations in wall, roof, and ceiling panels has appreciably increased the thermal value and reduced loss through infiltration. The adaptation of more industrialized components to housing has not, as yet, been successful, nor has it been adequately tested.

In contrast, industrial facilities related to oil and gas have successfully demonstrated the value of huge modular construction, steel framing, and insulated skin panels. The extreme of modularization is represented at Prudhoe Bay where housing, operations centers, and flow and pumping stations have been completely fabricated thousands of miles from the site and transported by barge and crawler in better than 99% finished condition. Size is largely restricted by the practical conditions of offloading and access, which limit larger modules to only certain coastal regions. Modules of air-shipment size, combined in various configurations or stacked, and either bearing one on the other or within a structural frame, provide an alternative that reduces cost of labor and increases quality of construction.

The communities of Barrow, Alaska, and Inuvik and Frobisher Bay in the Northwest Territories are regional centers developed to serve the growing concentration of people moving from the smaller villages and to accommodate regional government and social services.

Barrow is an example of the haphazard growth of communities where housing has expanded and been interspersed as the time and the funding allowed, with public facilities, stores, warehouses, and more recently, apartments. Barrow has been provided with a gas distribution system built above ground and looped over existing pedestrian and vehicle trafficways. Provision of utilities other than power has proven difficult because of the cost of servicing such a haphazard development. Recently, very costly belowground utilidors have been constructed.

Inuvik is a planned community providing for dispersed settlement. Utilities, other than power, are limited to defined areas, providing for government workers in apartment-type structures, a government complex, a community center complex, and a school complex. These utilities are enclosed in above-grade utilidors that also unintentionally create physical and social barriers.

Frobisher Bay is a dispersed community developed largely by government programs. The government center was constructed with the intention of providing commercial and recreational facilities as well as apartment structures. It does not serve the large number of the population spread out on the flats below. Utility services are provided to the government facilities, and an effort has been made to tie in the housing areas as they have developed. Kotzebue, Alaska, and other communities edged along the water have a linear dispersion with the similar problems of utility services and long distances.

These examples of dispersed-type communities have not been built with consideration of the climatic conditions (the low temperatures, the high winds, and the drifting of snow), but rather are based on the early, indigenous, single-family needs without consideration for a modern physical infrastructure.

In contrast to these examples of dispersed and nonresponsive design are the extremes of megastructures such as the apartment building in Hammerfest, Norway (Fig.

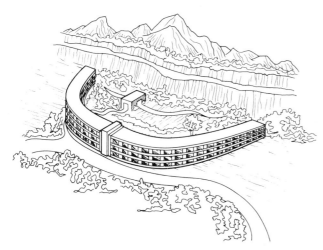

Figure 19. Apartment complex in Hammerfest, Norway. The structure curves into the south sloping hill to provide maximum southern exposure.

Figure 21. Accommodations units at Polaris Mine on Little Cornwallis Island in the Northwest Territories, Canada. The housing units were designed to be built within the largest module and then rolled on tracks to their position in this linear complex for single persons.

19), operations centers at Prudhoe Bay for ARCO–EXXON (Fig. 11) and Sohio–BP (Fig. 20), and the government complex at Frobisher Bay. These megastructures provide nearly all services and facilities within single or connected structures. They are compact with total environmental control, reducing the necessity to go outside to a minimum, unless to work sites. Except for Frobisher and Hammerfest, they provide for specific requirements and total control by the operating entity, either the governing agency or a resource development corporation. The facility at Frobisher does provide for some community recreation and commerce. Megastructures have a higher initial cost than

dispersed facilities. This is offset by lower maintenance costs.

The mining complexes by Colin Bent for Nanisivik and Polaris (Fig. 21) in the Northwest Territories are additional examples. Nanisivik provides a community center including school, recreational, and administrative facilities, and a fire hall to serve dispersed family housing. Polaris, on Little Cornwallis Island, is a linear megastructure serving all of the needs of a bachelor work force.

In the USSR, designs have been developed for highrise housing attached to and sometimes surrounding

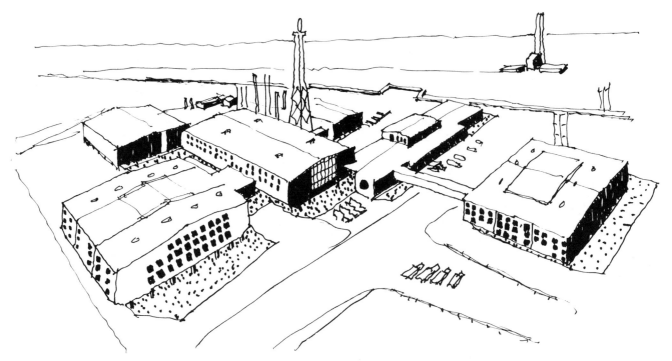

Figure 20. The Sohio (Standard Alaska) operations center, Prudhoe Bay, Alaska. Buildings were shipped by barge in large sections that were assembled on the site.

Figure 22. A proposed design for a community of 2500 in the USSR. This design, presumably on bedrock rather than permafrost, provides apartments in the towers and community facilities under the dome.

domed enclosures serving as community centers (Fig. 22).

The psychological response of the inhabitants has not been scientifically researched. It would appear that living within a megastructure would cut the inhabitant completely from his outside environment, and instead of adjusting to the northern conditions, he would be isolated from them.

A third type of community is that proposed for Resolute Bay in the islands of the Northwest Territories. The small community of Resolute Bay has all of the physical and psychological conditions of the far north in the extreme. The design developed by Ralph Erskine provided for a megastructure containing the town center, community facilities, schools, administrative facilities, and commercial needs. Attached to this are two long, linear arms of apartment structures allowing access to the town center within closed connection or outside access to the center and the remainder of the community. Isolated housing and other facilities are located within the arms. Only in Resolute, which is an entirely new town, have full consideration to orientation, terrain, wind direction, and vistas, as well as economy of infrastructure, been used as controlling determinants of the design.

The plan of Resolute follows the studies by Erskine for other cold climate communities and the planning of Svapavarra in Sweden (Fig. 23).

There was considerable community participation in Resolute in developing the program of needs and input into the planning and design process. The extent of local community participation in facility or community design can be critical to the acceptance of the facility, as well as providing the determinants used by the designer.

In planning for the proposed mining community of Lost River, Alaska (Fig. 24), an extensive questionnaire of potential inhabitants was taken to identify what they liked and did not like about their own communities, residences, neighbors, social services, and community structure, and also pertaining to any hopes and desires for a community they would wish to move into.

The resulting design has not been built. The design provided for a linear add-on, central enclosed mall with social service facilities, and school, recreational, commercial, and administrative facilities plugged into the mall as separate buildings. Housing stretched in arms toward the water, providing a mix of apartments and single-family residences in smaller compoundlike groups. The community center was backed up to the hills in the effort to protect as much of the community as possible from the high winds and to avoid the snow dropout that blew over the hills. A similar approach has been built at Fremont, Quebec (Canada).

Both the Resolute Bay design and the Lost River design tried for a combination of megastructure and dispersion.

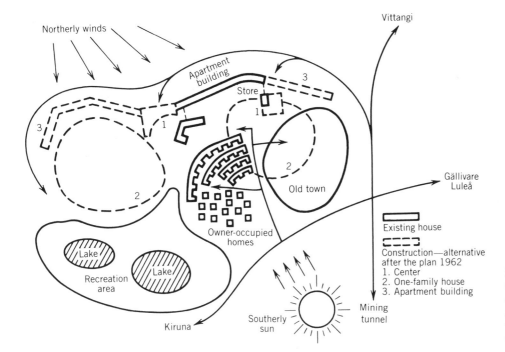

Figure 23. Plan for Svapavarra, Sweden, by Ralph Erskine. The plan orients the community on a south slope, protected from the north winds. The taller structures are to the north, giving added protection.

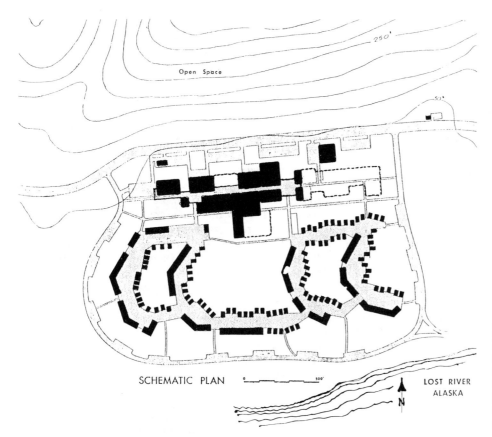

SCHEMATIC PLAN

LOST RIVER
ALASKA

Figure 24. A sketch plan for Lost River, Alaska, shows a strong, linear enclosed street on the north with a school, hospital, shops, entertainment, and administration buildings plugged on. To the south and toward the water are apartments and single units.

Both gave consideration to orientation of the community, wind conditions, and snowfall. Both provided for indoor and outside circulation, sheltered outdoor recreation, and social areas. The concern evident in both plans is demonstrated on a smaller scale in a military facility at Cape Lisburne and the two facilities at Prudhoe Bay, which allow for varying degrees of privacy and contact between individuals and groups. Studies of military facilities in Alaska have indicated a need for central meeting places where individuals can come into contact with each other or are forced to do so by the circulation patterns.

The design determinants for the built environment derive from the physical and psychological needs of the inhabitants, including economic needs. A viable economic base requires a viable human environment to maintain its balance. The designer must be aware of these determinants and program them into the designs he creates.

BIBLIOGRAPHY

1. S. R. Sterns, *Selected Aspects of Geology and Physiography of the Cold Regions,* Cold Regions Research Engineering Laboratory, 1-A-1, Hanover, N.H., 1965.

2. R. E. Bates and M. A. Bilello, *Defining the Cold Regions of the Northern Hemisphere,* Cold Regions Research Engineering Laboratory, TR 178, Hanover, N.H., 1966.

3. L. R. Zrudlo, *Psychological Problems and Environmental Design in the North,* Collection Nordicana, Université Laval, Montreal, Canada, 1967.

4. C. J. Williams, *Arctic Snowdrifting,* Report No. 48412381, Department of Public Works, Northwest Territories, Yellowknife, Canada, 1984.

5. G. H. Johnston and co-workers, *Permafrost Engineering Design and Construction,* John Wiley and Sons, Inc., New York, 1981.

General References

T. Armstrong, *Russian Settlement in the North,* Cambridge University Press, Cambridge, Mass., 1965.

R. B. Bechtel and B. Ledbetter, *The Temporary Environment, Cold Regions Habitability,* Special Report No. 76–10, Cold Regions Research Engineering Laboratory, Hanover, N.H.

D. Carriede, *Solar Houses for a Cold Climate,* Charles Scribner's Sons, New York, 1980.

P. B. Crews, "Wall Plenums for Cold Climates," *Air Cond., Heat., Vent.* (March 1969).

E. B. Crittenden and co-workers, *Arctic Engineering and Construction Techniques,* U.S. Army Corps of Engineers, Anchorage, Alaska, 1972.

E. B. Crittenden and co-workers, *Arctic Community Design,* Institute of Social and Economic Research, University of Alaska, Anchorage, Alaska, 1979.

B. Culjat, *Climate and the Built Environment in the North,* Avdelningen for Arkitektur, Kth., Stockholm, Sweden, 1975.

M. Devine, ed., *NTW Databook 1982–83,* Outcrop, Ltd., Yellowknife, Canada, 1982.

R. Erskine, "The Challenge of High Altitudes," *J. R. Can. Inst. Archit.* (Mar. 1964).

P. Freuchen and F. Salomonsen, *The Arctic Year,* The Putnam Publishing Group, Inc., New York, 1958.

P. R. Johnson and C. W. Hartman, *Environmental Atlas of Alaska,* University of Alaska, Fairbanks, Alaska, 1969.

G. H. Johnston, ed., *Permafrost, Engineering Design, and Construction,* John Wiley & Sons, Inc., New York, 1981.

V. Jorgensen, *Native Housing in Alaska,* Alaska State Housing Authority, Anchorage, Alaska, 1968.

V. Jorgensen, *Housing in Greenland,* Alaska State Housing Authority, Anchorage, Alaska, 1968.

A. Koerte, *Towards the Design of Shelter Forms in the North,* Series 2, No. 20, Center for Settlement Studies, University of Manitoba, Winnipeg, Canada, 1974.

E. F. Lobacz and H. E. More, eds., *Building Under Cold Climates and on Permafrost,* U.S. Department of Housing and Urban Development, Washington, D.C., 1980.

V. J. Lunardini, *Heat Transfer in Cold Climates,* Van Nostrand Reinhold Co., Inc., New York, 1981.

D. D. MacInnes, "Designing for Alaska," *Air Cond., Heat., Vent.* (March 1969).

R. St. J. MacDonald, ed., *The Arctic Frontier,* University of Toronto, Toronto, Canada, 1965.

National Reserach Council of Canada, *Problems of the North,* No. 10, National Research Council, Ottawa, Canada, 1966.

Nazaroma and co-workers, *Design and Construction Experience in Cities in the Extreme North,* Cold Regions Research Engineering Laboratory, Hanover, N.H., 1973.

V. Olgyay, *Design With Climate,* Princeton University Press, Princeton, N.J., 1963.

D. Oppenheim, *Small Solar Buildings in Cool Climates,* The Architectural Press, Ltd., London, 1981.

T. L. PeWe and R. L. MacKay, eds., *Permafrost, Second International Conference, Yakutsk, U.S.S.R.,* National Academy of Science, Washington, D.C., 1973.

A. Phukan, *Frozen Ground Engineering,* Prentice-Hall, Inc., Prentice Hall Press, Englewood, N.J., 1985.

E. B. Rice, *Building in the North,* University of Alaska, Fairbanks, Alaska, 1975.

J. F. Ross, *Arctic–Subarctic Urban Housing,* School of Architecture thesis, University of British Columbia, Vancouver, Canada, 1977.

J. E. Slater, *The Arctic Basin,* Arctic Institute of North America, Washington, D.C., 1969.

R. C. Speers, *Preliminary Work Towards Building Form and Orientation in Subarctic Communities,* Series 2, No. 14, Center for Settlement Studies, University of Manitoba, Winnipeg, Canada, 1976.

S. R. Sterns, *Selected Aspects of Geology and Physiography of the Cold Regions,* Cold Regions Research Engineering Laboratory, Al, Hanover, N.H., 1965.

H. Strub, *Arctic Habitation,* School of Architecture thesis, University of British Columbia, Vancouver, Canada, 1971.

T. S. Vinson, ed., *The Northern Community, Conference Proceedings,* American Society of Civil Engineers, New York, 1981.

C. J. Williams, *Arctic Snowdrifting,* Report No. 48412381, Department of Public Works, Yellowknife, Canada, 1984.

See also CLIMATE AND DESIGN; COLD WET CLIMATE, BUILDING IN; INDUSTRIAL BUILDINGS.

EDWIN B. CRITTENDEN, FAIA
Anchorage, Alaska

COLD WEATHER CONSTRUCTION.   See COLD DRY CLIMATE CONSTRUCTION; COLD WET CLIMATE, BUILDING IN

COLD WET CLIMATE, BUILDING IN

Building in a cold wet climate means building in an area where heavy snow accumulates in winter. Designing for heavy snow loads in flat country can be as serious a consideration and as extreme a determinant of building type and form as site location in mountainous country.

Safe design of roofs in snow country means not only designing for the loads imposed by a uniform snowpack but being aware of how, under certain conditions, roof snow loads can be increased by drifting in the case of a pitched roof or a roof in the lee of another building, or from sliding from a higher roof. It is also important to detail the roof so that ice dams will not form on the eaves. Ice dams cause problems of water leakage into the interior of the structure and the formation of icicles on the exterior. In mountainous areas of North America, particularly in the Sierra, Cascade, and Rocky Mountains and ranges in Alaska and British Columbia, large avalanches occur. Building sites in these or similar areas should always be checked for avalanche danger—not just for evidence of avalanches that came down within the last year or five years ago, but also for evidence of avalanches occurring as many as 50 years ago. The architect should also consider future human activity and how this activity might cause avalanches to occur in places where there have never been avalanches in the past. There are a few occasions when a transmission tower or some essential facility must be located in a known avalanche path. In this case, it is necessary to either build a direct protection avalanche barrier or deflection barrier uphill from the structure or to provide enough strength and form resistance in the building structure itself to resist an avalanche. A better solution to the avalanche problem in many instances is to build structures to prevent avalanches in their starting zone. This has been done extensively in Europe and may become a popular method in inhabited mountainous areas of North America in the future.

Downslope creep and glide of the mountain snowpack can cause damage to buildings. Structures that are located below even comparatively gentle slopes and are unheated in winter are affected by these pressures. Careful attention to understanding snow and its effect on buildings and their surroundings is essential to successful building in snow country, the winter aspect of a cold, wet climate.

VERTICAL SNOW LOADS

Prudent designers working in a cold, wet climate have always included a snow load along with roof dead loads in their design process. Before statutory minimum snow loads were established by local building officials or model codes, snow load values were obtained from weather service information, local snow depth data, or pure judgment. Occasionally during very severe storms, actual snow loads on roofs have been recorded considerably in excess of the recommended minimum for some particular area. This was the case for the winter of 1978–1979 in the Chicago area. The record snowfall of 88.4 in. (2.25 m) was accompanied by severe winds and cold temperatures. The dense deep snow and heavy drifts caused several major roof failures, as well as numerous partial collapses (1). Roof structures with the highest rate of failure consisted of wood and steel trusses. This high failure rate was partly because of the lack of redundancy in simple trusses and the fact that the pitched roofs promoted drifting and unbalanced loadings, as well as having a low dead load to snow load ratio. Recent revisions of the National Building Code of Canada (NBCC) (2) and the American National Standards Institute (ANSI) Code (3) have extensive provisions for the consideration of drifting snow, which appears to be a major cause of winter collapse (4). Figure 1 shows the collapse of a metal building near Moscow, Idaho, under snow loads that were much heavier than the design loads of the structure.

Snow loads on roofs vary according to geographical location, site exposure, shape and type of roof, and from one winter to another. Both the NBCC and the ANSI Code are based on measured ground snow loads. The wide climatic variations existing throughout North America produce wide variations in snow load conditions across the continent. In the coastal regions of both the Atlantic and Pacific oceans, frequent thaws throughout the winter result in snow loads of relatively short duration. One exception is a portion of the coast of Alaska where snow loads can be of six months duration. The mountainous regions of North America experience the heaviest snow loads, lasting the entire winter and varying considerably with elevation. The plains and the northern regions frequently have very cold winters with strong winds causing considerable drifting snow, both on roofs and on the ground. Finally, the central region around the Great Lakes is marked by varying winds and snowfall and sufficiently low temperatures in many places to allow snow accumulation during the entire winter. In this area, high uniform loads as well as high drift loads occur.

As soon as a snow crystal reaches the ground, it experiences a change in environment. No longer falling freely through the air, it suddenly becomes a small part of a snowpack. Immediately each crystal begins to undergo

metamorphism. Because the flakes reaching the ground are essentially unstable crystals, the fine points of the stars immediately begin to sublime. This is called destructive metamorphism. The resultant water vapor resublimes nearer the center of the crystal, tending to deform the stars into rounded granules. These granules have a smaller surface area than the original granules, causing the new snow layer to gradually settle (5). The average specific gravity of newly fallen snow is 0.06–0.10, while the ice in a snowflake has a specific gravity of 0.9. Destructive metamorphism transforms the original snowfall into a layer of snow containing about 70% air and having a specific gravity of between 0.2 and 0.3. Since a portion of any given snowpack usually consists partly of recently fallen snow and partly of old snow, a specific gravity of 0.2 is commonly used for calculations involving ground snow cover (6). This value is now considered to be too low. Revisions of codes based on this value will probably use a somewhat higher value.

Because snow is a plastic material, it has the ability to flow or creep under certain conditions. Its plasticity is a result of its constantly changing nature; its crystals continually respond to forces of gravity, wind, and temperature. It exhibits the characteristics of a viscous liquid with its viscosity varying inversely with the temperature. Snow will creep whenever it lies on an inclined surface. The amount of creep is directly related to the slope angle, snow depth, temperature, and water content. Friction between the supporting surface and the snow causes the snow closest to the ground to move more slowly.

When considering the effect of vertical snow loads on the roof of a building, attention must be given to the temperature and wind conditions during and after snowfall, roofing materials and texture, sun orientation, proximity of timber stands or other buildings, ground contours, and even the possibility that snow removal equipment might deposit snow on the building. In alpine and some northern areas where heavy snow occurs and is retained throughout the winter, snow load must be considered as a long-term loading in the same way that dead load is considered such. This negates the use of reduction factors permitted for temporary loading situations. Because differential loading conditions can occur when other influences such as wind or sun act upon snow, loads other than an evenly distributed balanced load must be considered in many instances. For example, snow might slide off the sunny side of the roof creating a full load situation on only one-half of the structure and no load on the other (Fig. 2). It is imperative that in the analysis of snow load-resisting systems all combinations of eccentrically loaded conditions be considered.

In addition to being a major consideration in the design of vertical load-bearing systems, as stated in Section 2312(c) of Ref. 7, when snow loads are greater than 30 psf (1.43 KN/m^2), they must be added to roof dead loads for calculating lateral forces due to earthquakes.

EXISTING CODES

Uniform Building Code (UBC). This is the legally adopted code in many areas of the United States. In its

Figure 1. Roof collapse due to snow. Courtesy of R. L. Sack; University of Idaho.

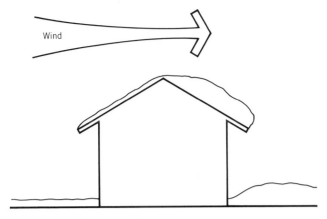

Figure 2. Unbalanced snow load.

1985 edition, the UBC defers to local building officials for the magnitude of roof snow loads. It states that the accumulation of snow in valleys, parapets, and roofs of uneven configuration shall be considered (7).

National Building Code of Canada. The basis for the NBCC is the accumulation of snow depth records from about 480 stations throughout the country for periods of from five to 31 years with about one quarter of the stations having records of at least 20 years. A density represented by a specific gravity of 0.2 is assumed for the whole snow cover. Because it is possible to get a heavy rain on top of the maximum snow depth, an equivalent weight of a 24-h rain is added to the calculated weight of snow to determine the ground snow load at any location.

American National Standards Institute. The 1982 edition of the ANSI Code provides a way of obtaining design snow loads for many parts of the contiguous 48 states and Alaska. This standard is based on estimated ground snow loads and takes into account the exposure of the roof, the slope of the roof, and the thermal conditions under which the building is expected to exist.

The ground snow loads with a 2% annual probability of being exceeded correspond to a 50-year mean recurrence interval. To establish these values, snow depth and snow load on the ground were measured at 184 National Weather Service (NWS) stations at different locations throughout the country, with a minimum of 20 years of records, including the severe winter of 1980. This data then provided the basis for interpretation of the information from 9000 other measurement sites where snow depth only was recorded. A snow load contour map for the contiguous 48 states and a table of ground snow loads for specific locations in Alaska were developed from this data and is a part of the ANSI Standard. Mountainous areas and some areas around the Great Lakes are shaded on the snow load contour map, and show no snow load contours in these areas because the ground snow loads change too rapidly for mapping at this scale. Snow load information for the shaded areas must be obtained from local sources. For these same reasons, Alaska ground snow loads are not shown in contour map form, but are given in table form for specific sites similar to the tabular presentation of Canadian ground snow loads.

Unbalanced loadings on gabled roofs, multiple folded plate, sawtooth, and barrel vault roofs and drifting on

lower roofs are considered. The problem of increased snow loads due to drifting probably contributes to snow load-induced roof failures more than any other single factor.

Ground snow loads with recommended ground-to-roof conversion coefficients for much of the mountainous regions of the western United States are available from local sources listed in Table 1. The same care in dealing with drifting should be exercised as when using the ANSI Code or the NBCC. These sources give information for much of the shaded area in ANSI where no ground snow loads are given.

Table 1. Local Sources for Information on Ground Snow Loads with Recommended Ground-to-roof Conversion Coefficients

Alaska:	L. D. Leslie, *Snow Loads in Alaska,* Alaska Climate Center, Technical Note 4, Anchorage Alaska, 1987.
Arizona:	*Snow Load Data for Arizona,* Structural Engineers Association of Arizona, 1973.
California:	C. B. Reed, Jr., *Snow Load Report for Nevada County,* 1980.
	C. S. Hayes and D. Edson, *Snow Load Study: Sierra County, California,* Apr. 1977.
	Snow Load Design Data for the Lake Tahoe Area, Structural Engineers Association of Northern California, Dec. 1964.
	C. Coen, *Placer Country Snow Design Ordinance,* Mar. 1985.
Colorado:	*Snow Load Design Data for Colorado,* Structural Engineers Association of Colorado, 1971.
Idaho:	R. L. Sack and A. Sheikh-Taheri, *Ground and Roof Snow Loads for Idaho,* University of Idaho, Moscow, Idaho, 1986.
Montana:	P. Stenberg and F. Videon, *Recommended Snow Loads for Montana Structures,* Dept. of Civil Engineering—Engineering Mechanics, Montana State University, Bozeman, Mont., Mar. 1978.
Oregon:	*Snow Load Analysis for Oregon,* Structural Engineers Association of Oregon, June 1971.
Washington:	*Snow Load Analysis for Washington,* Structural Engineers Association of Washington, Dec. 1981.

In addition to using codes or standards, an architect designing a building in snow country should inquire whether the measured ground snow loads in the area have been noted to be heavier than those stated in a national code or standard or by local building officials. A source of excessive loads on a roof structure in the mountains can occur when snow drifts over the top of the building. In this situation, the roof snowpack is physically connected to the ground snowpack. When the ground snowpack settles, part of it is supported by the roof, thus increasing the roof loads, possibly by several times.

ROOF DETAILING

In heavy snow country, one of the main concerns should involve the design of a roof that functions well in a number of important ways. This means not only a roof structure and supporting vertical and horizontal members that will carry the weight of the snow and provide a cover for the building, but also a roof form and thermal regime that acknowledge the nature of snow and how it acts on a building. In heavy snow country, the designer must think not only of basic human needs, but must also successfully deal with the proper location of chimneys and other protuberances in order that sliding or creeping snow does not shear them off. The protection of windows from falling icicles or dumping snow, the prevention of ice dam formation at the eaves that can cause water damage inside the building and damage to roofing and gutters outside the building, and the protection of people who are outside the building from falling snow or ice should be major considerations. The designer will find very little direct help from documents such as the UBC or past experience in designing buildings in nonsnow country. Only by direct experience in heavy snow country, or by the interpretation and understanding of the experience of other designers, can successful designs be accomplished.

ICE DAMS

A major source of snow-related problems on sloping roofs is the ice dam. Ice damming, as commonly used in snow country design literature, indicates the blockage of water by an obstruction of ice. Ice dams are a common and vexing difficulty, causing problems with pitched roofs in snow country. Ice dams are formed when heat from the attic or other space below the roof warms the roof and melts the snow at or near the ridge areas and along the entire roofline above the eaves. Melting of the snow occurs at the snow–roof interface and runs down under the snow as water. The water does not refreeze as it runs along the roof because the snow pack acts as insulation. At the eaves or lower edge of the roof, colder conditions normally exist. If the air temperature is below freezing, the snow water freezes as it exits the snow pack, thus forming an ice dam. Figure 3 provides an illustration of a typical ice dam. Subsequent melting of roof snow accumulates as a pond behind the ice dam. "Ice dams develop on buildings whenever or wherever roof snow accumulates on roofs to a depth of an inch or two and when weather turns or remains below freezing for three or four days"(8). If shingles are used as a roofing material, water eventually backs up under them and over time can cause major damage to the plateline area. This damage can take the form of soaked and therefore inefficient insulation in the wall, cracked and spalled plaster and Sheetrock, damp, odorous, rotting wall cavities, and stained, blistered, and peeling wall paint (8). "On a 40-ft-(12-m-) long, R20 sloping roof covered with 3 ft (1 m) of snow, roughly 2 gal (8 L) of water will be deposited for every lineal ft (3.07 m) of eave every day if the interior is 70°F (21°C). . . . On a roof pitched 4 in 12 (15°), an ice dam 3 ft (1 m) thick will back water more than 9 ft (2.8 m) up the roof. This produces hydrostatic pressure that will cause a conventional shingle roof to leak. None of the building codes used in the United States today considers this a problem, yet it is the most frequent defect of sloping roofs in cold country"(9). "Continuous roofings, metal or bituminous, are not as bad, but

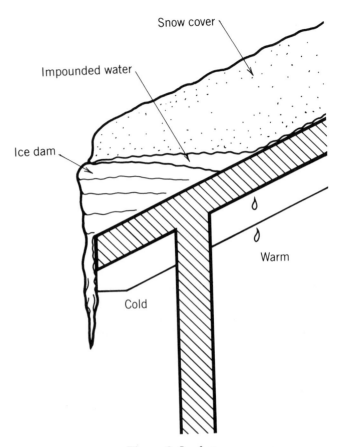

Figure 3. Ice dam.

the ice dam will form anyway and cause damage to the roof"(10).

One very great problem for the owner of a building in snow country with a sloping roof on which ice dams can form is the danger to persons outside the building. Falling icicles formed below the ice dam (Fig. 3) or falling portions of the ice dam itself can be an extreme danger to life and limb for persons outside the building. "An ice dam may hold ice and snow through several storms until a great mass is accumulated. When it at last falls, it can crush anything in the way"(9). Figure 4 shows icicles resulting from extensive ice dams on a condominium at Sun Valley, Idaho.

Different ways of solving or eliminating the ice dam problem have been tried over the years. Most of the following methods described are not very effective:

1. Shoveling, chipping, or chopping ice dams. These methods, often used in snow country, mainly cause damage to the edge of the roof. They do not solve the problem because the ice dam continues to form.
2. Heat tapes (electrical cables) installed on the eaves. The effectiveness of heat tapes is limited to the area only a few inches from the cable as seen by the zigzag melting pattern of installation. Secondary ice dams often form above the heat tapes causing the problems of the ice dam to be recreated a little further up the roof. In addition, heat tapes are easily damaged by snow sliding and snow creep.

Figure 4. Ice dam on Edelweiss Condominium in Sun Valley, Idaho.

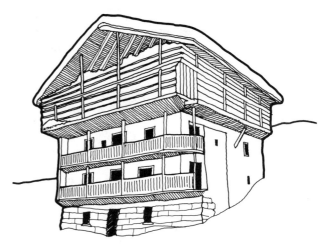

Figure 5. Swiss chalet. Courtesy of Ronald Wright

3. Eave flashings. In the snow country near the Canadian border, from Maine to British Columbia, many houses can be observed with eave flashings of sheet metal. These flashings are about 3 ft (1 m) in width and extend all along the edge of the eave. The smooth edge band (usually aluminum) eases the slough-off of eave snow and ice along the eave projections where attic heat is sufficient to sustain flows of snow water farther down the roof. It is quite common to have secondary ice dams form above the metallic flashings.

4. Metal roofs are common from the Cascade and Sierra mountains to New England—good metal roofs with interlocking edges of the metal sheets serve as a total roof flashing. They are directed toward leak protection and serve well, especially on steeply pitched roofs by sloughing off troublesome roof snow. Ice dams have been observed on metal roofs where the pitch is less than 50%.

A satisfactory solution to the ice dam problem requires that the designer have a rational concept of the causes of ice dam formation and follow this concept throughout the design and detailing phase. As Hendrik Bull, a noted architect and designer of mountain buildings has pointed out, "The only right way to deal with ice dams is the expensive way. The entire surface must be kept either cold or warm so there is no temperature differential"(10).

TYPES OF ROOF CONSTRUCTION

Cold Roof. For hundreds of years, the Swiss have used what is now called a cold roof as part of their traditional mountain farmhouse known as a chalet. These chalets, as shown in Figure 5, were divided into three zones of use. The top level directly below the roof was somewhat open on the sides and was used for hay and grain storage. The outside air was free to circulate in this space and kept the undersurface of the roof cold. When the outside

air temperature was below freezing, the snow on the roof did not melt and ice dams did not form. The family lived in the middle zone of the chalet while the lower level was used for the cows. The European cold roof is still used in Europe and North America for houses, ski lodges, and other snow country buildings. It consists of two separate roof layers with outside air flowing between them. With this kind of roof, there is little heat transfer between the inside of the building and the surface that supports the snow. Just as with the chalet, when the outside air is below freezing, the snow on the roof does not melt and ice dams do not form. When the outside air fluctuates between thawing during the day and freezing at night, it is possible for icicles to form but they will usually not be as large as when they are a product of ice dam formation.

Katharine Kennish shows examples of two successful cold roof designs in the Sun Valley, Idaho area in her book *The Mountain House* (11). Numerous successful cold roofs can be seen in the Sun Valley area in winter. A typical example is shown in Figure 6. Cold roofs are especially well suited for this area because the winter air temperature normally stays below freezing both day and night.

An architect who has addressed the problem of mountain building construction in heavy snow country is Philippe Delasalle of Canmore in Alberta, Canada. Among many other buildings, he has designed three ski lodges for Canadian Mountain Holidays' helicopter skiing bases in British Columbia, Canada. These buildings share two roof design features: they have a slightly sloping shed roof and cold roof construction. According to Canadian Mountain Holidays' president, Hans Gmoser, the cold roof design has been very successful. Examples of Delasalle's Bugaboo lodge and its cold roof venting are shown in Figures 7 and 8. These cold roofs have been successful in preventing ice dams and icicle accumulation even though winter daytime temperatures are sometimes above freezing (12).

Cold Attic. The cold attic has been used as a method of eliminating the problems of ice dam formation in residential construction in snowy areas of North America for some time. The cold attic achieves many of the advantages of the double European cold roof without the added expense

Figure 6. Cold roof in Sun Valley, Idaho.

of building a double roof. The cold attic requires the following elements:

1. Uninsulated rafters. The construction at the rafter level consists of roofing, waterproof membrane, roof sheathing, and rafters.

2. Insulation applied and supported by the ceiling joists (rafter ties). At this level, the ceiling consists of insulation (preferably R30) and ceiling material such as Sheetrock.

3. Extensive venting of the attic space, usually at both gable ends.

Heavily Insulated Semicold Roof. As shown in Figure 9, a heavily insulated semicold roof seems to have many

Figure 8. Bugaboo lodge, British Columbia, Canada.

of the advantages of the double European cold roof (including cold overhangs) without the expense of having an actual double roof. In addition, it has the advantage of being able to use wide overhangs. This roof has been used on the John Droege residence in Ketchum (Sun Valley), Idaho. The photograph in Figure 10 was taken in March after a very heavy snow winter. The absence of ice dams and icicles can be seen. The owner–designer is very satisfied with the roof shown.

Superinsulated Warm Roof. Architect Ian MacKinlay, who has considerable experience in designing mountain buildings and who has authored worthwhile publications on the subject (9,13), has written (9):

In most locations where there is a significant daily temperature swing through the freezing point, the best way to control ice dams is to use a warm roof with additional insulation (R30 or more) so that the building heat melts the snow at a slower rate. In fact, if the snow blanket is thin and the air is cold, there may be no melting from building heat.

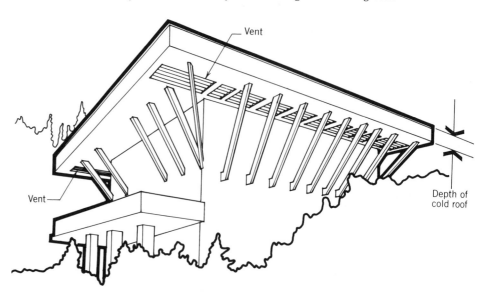

Figure 7. Bugaboo lodge cold roof.

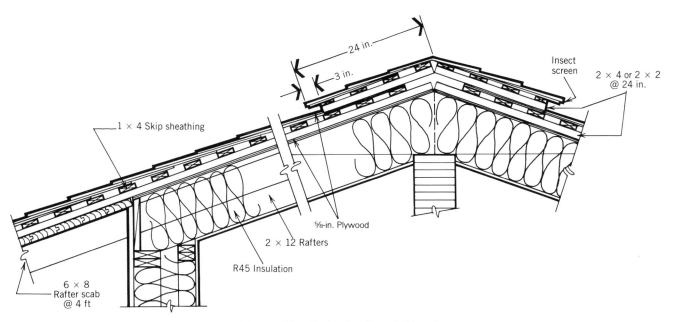

24 in.

3 in.

Insect screen

2 × 4 or 2 × 2 @ 24 in.

1 × 4 Skip sheathing

⅝-in. Plywood

2 × 12 Rafters

R45 Insulation

6 × 8 Rafter scab @ 4 ft

Figure 9. Heavily insulated semicold roof.

MacKinlay points out that the insulation thickness should be reduced at the roof edge to create a natural temperature gradient so that water at the eave line is less likely to freeze. Hendrik Bull also indicates that a "very carefully detailed warm roof" should be considered (10). A sketch of a superinsulated warm roof with eaves is shown in Figure 11.

Flat Roof. Ice dams will normally not form on a flat roof as long as the interior of the building is kept warm and as long as the roof can drain through the interior of the building. The advantageous use of flat roofs to control ice dams in snow country has been pointed out by a number of authors (11,13,14). In addition to ice dam control, there may be a number of other advantages to using a flat or nearly flat roof in snow country and especially in the mountains. Some advantages to a flat roof may be the following:

1. The snow loads are more or less uniform, except at protuberances.
2. In windy or mountainous country, much of the roof snow may be blown off.

3. Views from the top floor rooms are not obstructed or partially eliminated by the structure of a steeply pitched roof.

BUILDING IN THE MOUNTAIN ENVIRONMENT

To design well for the mountains, one must understand the harsh conditions imposed. In the mountains, there are tremendous forces at play that are unknown elsewhere. These environmental forces should be viewed as form-gen-

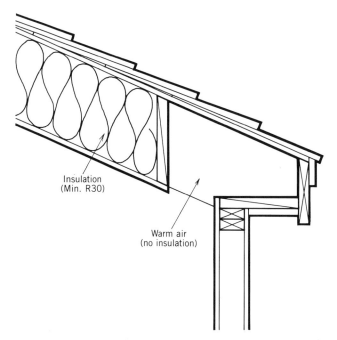

Insulation (Min. R30)

Warm air (no insulation)

Figure 11. Superinsulated warm roof (9). Courtesy of *AIA Journal*.

Figure 10. Superinsulated roof in Ketchum, Idaho. Courtesy of John Droege.

erating characteristics that will be of paramount importance in the morphology of the design, from its site orientation and the overall character of the building down to the smallest detail. For example, lateral snow pressure caused by snow creep and glide and static pressure is of sufficient magnitude to crush or laterally displace structures of wood, steel, or concrete. The destructive capabilities of avalanches are devastating, as the total energy release occurs almost instantaneously. In the mountains, building materials are subjected to daily and seasonal changes in temperature that are seldom realized in most lowland areas.

Roof shapes can have dramatic effects not only upon the comfort and safety of the occupants and the prevention of damage to the building itself, but also to the pedestrian who may be forced unknowingly into areas where he could be injured or even killed by falling icicles or roof avalanches. Site planning in the mountains can have similarly catastrophic consequences. The architect must be observant in the study of the site to avoid trespassing upon existing avalanche paths, as well as taking care not to produce conditions conducive to the formation of new ones. Designing a building to be located in the mountains is not only different from designing a building for another site, but it can be extremely dangerous if the architect is unaware of the forces with which the structure will have to contend once the snow begins to fall (15).

Avalanche

Qualitatively, the basic requirements needed to cause snow to avalanche are very simple to describe, ie, a steep enough slope covered with a deep enough layer of snow. It is quantifying the terms deep enough and steep enough that makes avalanche prediction complicated. The architect designing buildings for mountainous regions should be familiar with the following conditions. The majority of avalanches occur on slopes from 25 to 55° from the horizontal. At angles under 25°, the frictional and cohesive forces usually exceed the gravitational forces, and the snow remains stable. On slopes over 55°, snow adheres poorly to the surface of the slope, slides continuously during storms, and rarely builds to menacing proportions. This is termed sluffing. Wind, however, can pack snow onto slopes steeper than 45°. Another dangerous situation can occur on steep slopes when wind coming from directly behind the crest forms a cornice. This cornice not only represents a danger in itself but could trigger an avalanche in unstable snow below, thus magnifying its destructive potential many times. An example of an existing avalanche path is shown in Figure 12.

In mountainous areas of the western United States, there are many instances where buildings are constructed directly in avalanche paths (places where avalanches have come down in the past). Unless adequately designed control structures are built in the avalanche starting zone, avalanches will eventually come down that same path at some time in the future. However, in most cases, neither avalanche control structures in the starting zone nor barriers to directly protect the building are constructed. Special strengthening of the structure of the building for protection

Figure 12. Avalanche path.

from direct avalanche forces is seldom designed. In Switzerland, many towns have ordinances against construction in known avalanche paths. Such regulations do not exist in most other countries. For example, in the state of Washington, a condominium in the Alpental ski area near Snoqualmie Pass is located very close to a 50-year avalanche path; at Crystal Mountain near Mt. Rainier, a ski club cabin is located in an old avalanche path. In Juneau, Alaska, one subdivision along Barents Avenue is at the base of an active avalanche path. The residents of this threatened subdivision seem to be apathetic about the probability of avalanche disaster (16). Montgomery Atwater, in *Avalanche Hunters,* noted that there are lots in Squaw Valley, Calif., swept by a major avalanche as recently as 1958, upon which houses were constructed at the time of the 1960 Winter Olympics. Atwater described this as a "sleeper avalanche, one that lies quietly for years and then erupts like a volcano"(17). At the now defunct Yodelin ski area on the east side of Stevens Pass in the state of Washington, private cabins were located at the base of an active avalanche path and were subsequently destroyed with loss of lives (Fig. 13). Locating a building in an avalanche path is definitely very hazardous.

The Destructive Forces of Avalanches. As a destructive force, avalanches rate very high among natural phenom-

Figure 13. House destroyed in avalanche in Yodelin, Wash. U.S. Forest Service Photo by Roland V. Emertaz.

ena: "Like wind, flood, earthquake, and fire, the avalanche has played its part in the history of the Americas. It is inferior to none of these natural forces" (17). Calculations based on measurements of avalanche damage that occurred in the Vorarlberg (Austria) on January 11, 1954 have been made. The results of these calculations can be thought of as giving the lower bound forces against stationary objects for a cohesionless snow avalanche occurring on relatively slight slopes (30°). The pressure estimated to act upon walls or other obstacles to the flow of the avalanche seldom exceeded 470 lb/ft^2 (22,473 N/m^2). The upward vertical forces acting on the uphill wall of a building or obstruction hit by an avalanche was estimated to be about one-half the horizontal force. Structures overrun by the avalanche were loaded vertically by the dammed up depth of the snow. The destructive action of the air blast, which often precedes an avalanche, was estimated to be about 103 lb/ft^2 (4925 N/m^2)—high as compared to normal design wind forces of 30 lb/ft^2 (1434 N/m^2)—but relatively low compared with the force of the avalanche itself. In three cases in Switzerland where an avalanche was traveling on a relatively steep inclination (45–100% slope), calculations based on observed damage estimated pressures of from 2069 to 4138 lb/ft^2 (478 to 956 kN/m^2). These forces are clearly much too high to design ordinary buildings for, but could be applicable to an essential structure that must be located in an unshielded avalanche path or to special avalanche barriers designed to protect structures. Along with this empirical data, a series of equations

has been derived and presented in *On the Destructive Force of Avalanches* by A. Voellmy, which, in view of substantiating evidence, provides a reasonable estimate of the forces due to avalanches under varying weather, snow, and ground conditions (18). In this same publication, many useful observations are made:

1. For structures of any kind, an important part of their potential to resist avalanche force is their resistance to tipping, which requires very strong anchorage of the uphill wall to the foundation.
2. An existing building located in an avalanche path can be significantly reinforced in its ability to resist avalanche forces if its uphill wall is strengthened to resist vertical forces.

Architects who are designing buildings for mountainous areas with cold, wet climate should understand that avalanches can be extremely destructive, with potential forces so large as to make it impractical to design ordinary buildings against them. Therefore, avalanche paths should be avoided when selecting a building site in the mountains. The architect must not only suspect the existing mountain environment, but also any alterations he makes to it that could result in new avalanche situations. In order to do this, the architect must become familiar with the way avalanches behave in the area in which he plans to design. Academic study should be supplemented by firsthand observations in the field. This need not be a dangerous endeavor, as avalanche paths may be safely observed in spring or even summer, once the architect is able to recognize the signs that constitute evidence of past avalanche activity. These field trips will not only help to give the architect an understanding of the ways of avalanches, but also develop respect for a force that could create a threat to the lives and property of people who put their trust in the architectural professional.

Protection Against Avalanches. The best protection for a building against avalanches is to locate it well away from potential avalanche paths. It is possible for inhabited areas once protected from avalanches by forests to become highly endangered by the cutting of these forests. The role of forests in preventing avalanches has been realized in Europe since the fourteenth century and before; yet when tree cutting was not prevented by law, the forests were cut and new avalanche paths formed.

Early attempts at avalanche protection for houses located on a slope consisted of placing an earth fill level with the roof against the uphill wall, hoping that an avalanche would pass completely over the building without doing any damage. Subsequently, a mound of earth in the shape of a wedge was placed on the slope above the building so that the avalanche would split and pass by each side. Sometime later, the wedge-shaped avalanche protection structures began to be made of masonry, and are currently known as *Spaltkeile*—splitting wedges. The church at Oberwald in the Valais of Switzerland has a masonry splitting wedge on the uphill side that is 25 ft (7.7 m) high and 5 ft (1.53 m) thick. There were also cases where the uphill wall of the building was constructed like the prow of a boat, thus acting as its own splitting wedge; one example is the church in the village of Davos-Frauenkirch, Switzerland (Fig. 14). One of the largest splitting wedges ever built protects almost the entire village of Pequerel in the Val di Chisone of Italy (Fig. 15). The original part of this wedge was built about 269 years ago. It is now 6 ft (1.84 m) thick and about 16 ft (4.9 m) high; each branch of the V is about 300 ft (92 m) long. Splitting wedges are still built to protect highly vulnerable structures such as electrical power or cable car towers. The advantage of avalanche wedges and diverting walls is that they can provide direct protection specific to one structure. The disadvantages of these direct avalanche defenses are:

1. During heavy snow winters, when avalanche danger can be very high, the uphill side of the defense wall is often snowed in so that the avalanche can shoot right over the top of the defense.

2. The inhabitants of the houses protected by defense walls are safe only when inside or away from their house; while coming or going, they are at great risk. As Colin Fraser has pointed out in his book *The Avalanche Enigma,* "In reality, all methods covered so far have been passive in nature, allowing the enemy to reach the door before offering any resistance. The better solution seems to be to attack the enemy in his lair—that is to say to erect structures in the avalanche breakaway zone which will support the snow cover and prevent an avalanche ever starting" (19).

These breakaway areas or avalanche starting zones are often, but not always, above timberline areas near the top of ridges—well above the inhabited areas that are usually in the valley, at or near the base of the ridge. The first attempts at preventing avalanches in the starting zone were made over 100 years ago with the construction of stone walls. These starting zone defenses proved fairly

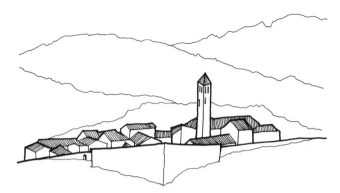

Figure 15. Splitting wedge that protects the village of Peguerel, Italy. Courtesy of Ronald Wright.

successful but they suffered from the disadvantage that snow drifted behind them as it will any solid wall, and in some exposed locations, cornices formed on top of them, providing an added danger. Major efforts at preventing avalanches in the starting zone began in Austria, Switzerland, and France in the early years of the twentieth century. The most successful type of starting zone avalanche control structure has proven to be a braced open structure built in the form of a snow bridge or snow fence. This type of starting zone defense provides the strength to prevent the snowpack in this area from sliding, while because of its open nature, it does not cause drifting behind the fence. An English translation of a Swiss design manual (*Lawinenverbau im Anbruchgebeit*) for starting zone avalanche control structures has been published by the U.S. Forest Service. This manual, *Avalanche Control in the Starting Zone,* is an indispensable reference on this subject (20).

Lateral Pressures Due to Snow

Because of the plastic qualities and sometimes semiliquid nature of snow in a deep snowpack, it is possible for snow to exert significant pressures against the walls of buildings. This phenomenon is most common where buildings are sited on or near moderate-to-steep slopes and where the snow is deep enough to extend some distance up the wall. "Many more buildings are destroyed in the snow country by inward buckling of their walls than by sudden collapse of the roof"(13).

There are three types of lateral pressure acting on structures exposed to snow loading. These are static pressure, creep pressure, and glide pressure. Static pressure is lateral pressure that occurs on an object or structure against which a liquid or semiliquid substance (eg, soil or snow) is resting. For example, just as a dam prevents water from moving laterally and thereby is subjected to lateral forces, the wall of a building against which the snow is deeply piled receives lateral pressure as it prevents the snowpack from moving laterally. If a building is entirely surrounded by snow, there is no resultant lateral pressure tending to push the building off its foundation or overturn it. However, if the snow is higher on one side of a building than another, a resultant lateral force acts on the building. There is investigative evidence that both the Paradise

Figure 14. Church as Davos-Frauenkirch, Switzerland, with the uphill wall designed to split avalanches. Courtesy of Ronald Wright.

Inn located at the 5000-ft (1533-m) level of Mt. Rainier in the state of Washington and the new wing of the Timberline Lodge located at the 6000-ft (1840-m) level of Mt. Hood in the state of Oregon have experienced lateral displacements in part because of static pressure.

Creep pressure is pressure acting on a structure due to downhill movement within the snow cover. It is caused by more rapid movement of the upper layers of the snow cover with respect to the lower layers. Creep occurs in the snowpack whether or not the snowpack is sliding over the ground. Creep increases with increasing slope and is related to the density of the snow and its temperature. Investigations have shown creep of the snowpack to be a factor in the lateral displacement of the upper portion of the Paradise Inn at Mt. Rainier where the average slope on the uphill side of the building is only 11.5°.

Glide pressure is that pressure acting on a structure due to downhill movement of the snow cover with respect to the ground. Glide pressure varies both with the slope and the roughness of the terrain and usually consists of a glide factor applied as a multiplier to the creep pressure. A wet and relatively smooth ground surface is generally required for significant glide to be present and does not usually occur unless the slope angle exceeds 15°.

A commonly used method for calculating creep and glide pressures is to employ the formulas and tables presented in the *Swiss Guidelines,* translated as mentioned previously, by the U.S. Forest Service as *Avalanche Control in the Starting Zone* (20).

The calculated creep, glide, and static pressure forces on building sites at the base of snow slopes can be high. The cost of a structure required to resist such forces could be considerable. Structural costs can be greatly reduced by decreasing the width of the uphill wall of the building. Snow static pressure, creep, and glide do not appear to affect buildings kept continuously heated. Where heat can escape through the uphill wall, the snow melts back from the wall faster than it moves toward the walls.

BIBLIOGRAPHY

1. I. R. Chin, A. J. Gouwens, and J. M. Hanson, *Review of Roof Failures in the Chicago Area Under Heavy Snow Loads,* ASCE Reprint No. 80–145, American Society of Civil Engineers, New York, 1980.

2. *National Building Code of Canada,* National Research Council of Canada, Ottawa, No. 17724, 1980 Supplement.

3. *American National Standard,* American National Standards Institute, New York, 1982, pp. 16–64.

4. A. Seltz-Petrash, *Civ. Eng.,* 42 (Dec. 1979).

5. U.S. Forest Service, *Snow Avalanches,* U.S. Government Printing Office, Washington, D.C., 1961, p. 8.

6. C. G. Souster, *A Study of the Existing Data on the Physical Characteristics of Snowfall,* University of Sheffield, Sheffield, UK, 1975, p. 6.

7. International Conference of Building Officials, *The Uniform Building Code,* International Conference of Building Officials, Whittier, Calif., 1985, p. 110.

8. H. L. Grange and L. T. Hendricks, *Agricultural Extension Service, University of Minnesota Extension Bulletin No. 399,* Rochester, Minn., 1976.

9. I. Mackinley, *AIA J.* **72**(2), 49 (Feb. 1983).

10. H. Bull, *Ski Area Manage.,* 49 (Spring 1973).

11. K. Kennish, *The Mountain House,* 1st ed., Northwood Institute Press, Midland, Mich., 1981, pp. 62 and 185.

12. R. G. Albrecht, *North. Eng.* **14**(3), 11 (Fall 1982).

13. I. Mackinley and W. E. Willis, *Snow Country Design,* National Endowment for the Arts, Washington, D.C., 1965, p. 8.

14. M. Cereghini, *Building in the Mountains,* Edizione del Milione, Milan, Italy, 1957.

15. J. Hartman, *Architectural Design in Heavy Snow Country,* Master's degree thesis, University of Washington, Seattle, Wash., 1976.

16. D. Cupp, *Nat. Geographic* **162**(3), 290 (Sept. 1982).

17. M. Atwater, *The Avalanche Hunters,* Macrae Smith, Philadelphia, Pa., 1960, pp. XIII, XVII.

18. A. Voellmy, *On the Destructive Force of Avalanches,* U.S.D.A. Forest Service, Washington, D.C., 1964.

19. C. Frazer, *The Avalanche Enigma,* Rand McNally and Co., Chicago, New York, and San Francisco, 1966, p. 260.

20. F. Frutiger, translator, *Avalanche Control in the Starting Zone,* U.S. Forest Service, Fort Collins, Colo., 1962.

See also CLIMATE AND DESIGN; COLD DRY CLIMATE CONSTRUCTION.

ROBERT ALBRECHT
University of Washington
Seattle, Washington

COLLEGES.   See CAMPUS PLANNING

COLOR IN ARCHITECTURE

FROM CAVES TO CATHEDRALS

As the eye wanders up the vistas, the three primitive colors . . . red, yellow, and blue, strike the eye by the intensity of their brightness; but by blending in the distance, by the effect of parallax and diminished visual angle, the whole as in nature disappears into a neutral gray. To appreciate the genius of Owen Jones, one must take his stand at the extremity of the building . . . Looking up the nave, with its endless rows of pillars, the scene vanishes from extreme brightness to the hazy indistinctness which Turner alone can paint. . .

This extract from an article in the May 17, 1851 issue of the *Illustrated London News* (1) described the impression of the interior decoration of Joseph Paxton's Crystal Palace erected that year in London. Paxton had appointed the designer Owen Jones to supervise the internal and external decoration of his iron and glass structure—a commission that gave Jones the opportunity to apply a theory of architectural color based on his initial study of the colors of the Islamic Palace of the Alhambra published in 1845. Jones's restoration had illustrated its columns as painted in red, blue, and gold, the primitive colors referred to in the article (Fig. 1). His subsequent research, later published in his monumental *Grammar of Ornament* (1856) (2), provided an exhaustive and scintillating handbook of the color and form in Egyptian, Greek, medieval, Renaissance, and Far Eastern architectural decoration. In graphically reconstructing the color and decoration of 19 historical styles, Jones had produced a design manual containing 37 axioms of color and form from which nineteenth-century designers could create an architecture worthy of the machine age (Fig. 2).

However, Jones's color application in the Crystal Palace was also tempered by a developing interest in the science of color vision because his color system followed Chevreul's rules of color clarity and Field's laws of proportion. For instance, the slim iron columns were painted with narrow stripes of red, yellow, and blue, each separated by a white field. The color application also responded to a proportional harmonic that related three parts yellow to five parts red to eight parts blue. Close by, the colors were perceived as distinct but, as the *Illustrated London News* confirms, over distance an optical mixing of atmospheric perspective caused his hues to progressively fuse into a vibrant blue-gray haze, a visual phenomenon first noted by Leonardo da Vinci, which was later to be exploited in the Neo-Impressionist Divisionism of Suerat's paintings and, again, in the color interaction experiments of Joseph Albers.

This review of architectural color begins inside the Crystal Palace because there is no doubt that it functioned as an important landmark in the evolution of architectural polychromy. Having embodied the whole history of architectural color through Jones's studies, it not only stood as a model of Victorian polychromy that exhibited its own identity and one uniquely befitting its time, but it also created a point of reference for many ensuing buildings, including modern structures, such as the Pompidou Center in Paris. Furthermore, in utilizing the three primitive colors, it represented a link in a chain of polychromy that begins in the prehistorical caves of southern Europe.

Painted Caves

The story of architectural color is closely allied to its use in painting and sculpture. Color was appreciated by the primitive caveman, and its application in a painted decoration played an important role in his struggle to survive. He projected his perception of this struggle onto the walls of the more secret recesses of his cave in the form of painted images using three basic colors: red, yellow ocher, and magnesium. However, earlier accounts of a great variety of hues used in the primitive palette stem from the considerable variation in the quality of the deposits used for paint-making. For instance, depending on its unpredictable variation due to oxidization, magnesium can turn blackish, brownish, or bluish.

Many questions still surround the existence of cave paintings. For example, it has been suggested that they embodied a magical power to ensure success in the hunt for food—but we now know that their authors ate the meat of species that are rarely depicted in the art of Paleolithic man. Another explanation has suggested that they represent the earliest form of artistic expression, but this theory is considered to be too simplistic. What is of interest is the variation of color and style during the 25,000-year cycle of cave art—earlier and later periods of painting using more color—with a middle phase in which the use of black for a time replaced that of red. Also of interest is the mode of representation; paintings were often composed of both figurative animal forms and abstract patterns that seemingly documented primitive man's perception of the fauna in his landscape, and also expressed early forms of symbolic graphic structures using the grid, the dot, and the phallus. What is even more significant is the spatial organization of some paintings in relation to the interior architecture of the caves, for these are composed purposefully to create wall and ceiling murals and friezes. Furthermore, the later paintings, notably those at Altamira in northern Spain and Lascaux in the French Dordogne, also incorporated the existence of calcite crystal into their design as a subtle means of introducing white into their color impression.

However, it is the as yet undeciphered symbolic contents of cave paintings that possibly provide the clue to their meanings. Later theories—namely that by the French anthropologist, André Leroi-Gourhan—point to the idea that cave art was a focus of primitive rites and that these provided a backdrop to a totemic system in which the kinship of tribal membership was believed to hold a common ancestry with an animal species or an object.

Many such caves have been discovered—mainly in France, Spain, and Italy—but these are obviously only a small fraction of the colorful underground spaces containing an art whose demise coincided with that of the Ice Age.

As man emerged from the caves into the sunlight, and as knowledge of pigments increased, it was natural that the significance of color should turn to symbolizing the wonders of the cosmos and be applied to the first crude hut and tent shelters. Later, in the deserts, the concept of sublimating a religious ritual by elevating the shrine on which it took place led to the appearance of giant towers and man-made mountains above the dune-colored plains of Sumeria and Mesopotamia. These appeared around the fifth millenium B.C. and were built of mud bricks, but were occasionally plated with metal and decorated with the three primeval hues: the red of clay and sandstone, the black of shale and bitumen, and the white of mother-of-pearl.

Red, black, and white present the three basic anthropological colors, and are the only ones found in every civilization. Apart from their chromatic value, these three colors embody archetypal notions that date back to the darkest origins of human life: colorless and pure (white); colorless and sullied (black); and colored (red).

It is now thought that color was used purely symbolically throughout ancient civilizations as it is today in surviving primitive cultures. Among the primitives, there still exists no real difference between building and image making so far as usefulness is concerned. Their shelters simply function to protect them from spiritual powers they feel to be as real as the forces of nature. It is interesting to note that this use of color occurs in almost all primitive and ancient cultures of the world, and that always the same type of strong, saturated hues are used: notably, red, blue, yellow, green, black, and white, together with the precious metals of silver and gold. It has been speculated that the psychological primaries of red, green, blue, and yellow are related to the primary emotions. This might explain their overwhelming use as symbolic colors. However, the main factor confusing any comparison of symbolism between cultures is that colors can be used to signify so many different concepts, and that these concepts are dependent on the availability of pigments and the structure of a given society. The uses of symbolic color functioned mainly in areas of religion; mythology and astrology; ritual; for healing purposes; and to denote status, race, the elements of science, and the points of the compass.

China and South America

The civilization and culture of China precede that of the Western world; its language and literature, poetry and calligraphy, and art and architecture are steeped in symbolism. The Chinese primary colors were red, yellow, black, white, and green, and these were assigned respectively to the elements of fire, metal, wood, earth, and water and, in turn, to the five virtues, vices, and precepts of faith. Red and yellow respectively symbolized the essence of positive and negative—positive being heavenly and masculine, negative earthly and feminine. For this reason, the walls of ancient Peking were painted red, symbolizing south, sun, and happiness under yellow-colored roofs—the symbol of earth. Color symbolism was bound up in a belief in the existence of good and evil spirits, and color was often architecturally deployed either as protection or to gain their favors; the yellow roofs of Peking functioned as a kind of camouflage that might confuse evil spirits as they passed overhead.

From the archaeological evidence, much early architecture involved a color symbolism corresponding to the sun and planets for, when people looked skyward, they all saw the same hues, ie, a red Mars, an orange Jupiter, and a yellow sun. The ancient Egyptians, for example, actually idolized color and assigned hues to the sculptured manifestations of a deity system that centered on the worship of the sun, as did earlier religions. For instance, in the far-flung rain forests of Central America, the sun-worshiping Mayans were also masters of stucco and adorned their magnificent pyramidlike temples with carvings and designs covered in intense mineral colors. An example of brilliant color use in the classical period (200 B.C.—900 A.D.) can be seen on the replica of the Temple of Quetzalcoatl from the citadel at Teotihuacán exhibited in the National Museum of Anthropology in Mexico City. Inside, there were murals with religious motifs, such as the one under the Palace of Quetzalpapolti, comprising vivid oranges, reds, golds, greens, and blue-greens.

The awe-inspiring city of Palenque, also in Mexico, was discovered in conditions of almost pristine color by successive expeditions in the seventeenth and eighteenth centuries. Eager to expose its brilliance more fully, the members of one expedition hacked and burned down the surrounding jungle; as they disturbed the delicate and preservative microclimate, the colorful stucco they had intended to preserve perished.

Mesopotamian Ziggurats

The Mesopotamian civilization was dominated by the study of astrology, and color, being assigned to the solar system, was also related to the horizontal stratification of its buildings. In his book, *Ur of the Chaldees* (3), Dr. C. Leonard Woolley describes his expedition that unearthed the ancient ziggurat, the Mountain of God. Dated 2300 B.C. and located between Baghdad and the Persian Gulf, it represents one of the oldest buildings in the world and is thought to be the original home of Abraham. This mud brick edifice was constructed in four stages to achieve a height of 70 ft from a base 200 ft long and 150 ft wide. Woolley describes its lowest stage as black and representing the dark underworld, with the upper stage colored red to signify the habitable earth. At the very top was a blue-tiled shrine with a gilded metal roof, signifying the heavens and the sun.

Another example of the architectural layering of symbolic color is found in descriptions of the Chaldean city of Ecbatana as a conurbation of great size fortified by concentric walls springing from a circular plan, with each designed so that the battlements of successive walls were higher than the wall below. There were seven such walls built on a hill that exaggerated the cuneiform appearance of the city. The inner wall contained the royal palace and treasury and its battlements were plated with gold. According to Herodotus, the battlements of successive walls were plated with silver, painted in orange, blue, crimson, black, and, the outer wall, white.

It is thought that Herodotus had referred to the great Temple of Nebuchadnezzar at Barsippa, which was excavated in the twentieth century. Hitherto, apart from a superficial ornament and facings, Mesopotamian buildings had been constructed of solid mud brick. However, under Nebuchadnezzar in the seventh century B.C., there was a great revival of building activity and everywhere ancient temples were reconstructed by him on a pretentious scale. There was little available stone for sculptured reliefs but the technique of glazed faience, which was nearly as old as the earliest cities, was known to his builders. Therefore, they used this material to sheath large areas of outer facades. Accounts of the coloration of Nebuchadnezzar's temple that confirm a similar color sequence described by Herodotus are contained in the respective books by George Rawlinson and James Fergusson. In his book *History of Architecture in all Countries*, Fergusson suggests that the layered walls of the ziggurat were dedicated to the seven planets (4):

> . . . the lower, which was richly panelled, was black, the color of Saturn; the next, orange, the color of Jupiter; the third, red, emblematic of Mars; the fourth, yellow, belonging to the sun; the fifth and sixth, green and blue respectively, as dedicated to Venus and Mercury, and the upper probably white, that being the color belonging to the Moon, whose place in the Chaldean system would be uppermost.

In his book *The Five Great Monarchies of the Eastern World*, Rawlinson described the means of color application. He suggested that the basement stage was blackened by means of a bitumen coating; orange was achieved using a facing of burned bricks, while a blood red resulted from half-burned bricks of red clay. The fourth stage appeared to have been actually plated in a thin sheave of gold, while the fifth stage (described as green by Fergusson) received a pale yellow tint from a use of bricks of that color. The sixth stage was given an azure tint by vitrification—the whole level being subjected after it was erected to intense heat in which the bricks were transformed into a mass of blue slag. Finally, as in the fourth, the seventh stage was probably coated with actual plates of metal (5).

Although conflicting, each description maintains that color existed as an important feature of the city of Ecbatana. Against the monotonous geometry of otherwise undecorated clay buildings in its vicinity and the monochrome of an alluvial landscape, the glittering facades of this structure must have acquired an exaggerated brilliance, like the gilded domes and ceramic facades of mosques in a modern Islamic city. Rawlinson also observed that the horizontal bands of color were apparently arranged ". . . almost as Nature's cunning arranges the hues of the rainbow"(6).

There were many buildings like this in ancient Babylon, each following color principles similar to those at Barsippa. For example, another ziggurat described by Fergusson is the Temple of Khorsbad. This provides a further model of a seven-stage edifice, again with stages corresponding to the colors ascribed to Ecbatana and, possibly, the type of building mentioned in the Bible as the Tower of Babel.

Several ziggurats have survived, but their brilliant mosaic patterns formed from thousands of copper-faced, clay-fired cones, their gilding, and their blue tiling have long since disappeared. However, it is known that their interior halls were similarly decorated using mosaic, molded bricks, and painted frescoes to form ornamental dadoes around whitewashed stucco walls.

Thus, in the beginnings of civilization, the art of building and the art of color were as one. According to the eminent color consultant, Faber Birren, "The ancients were, essentially, realists. For them, astrology represented a practical system in the fusing of heavenly and earthly kingdoms"(7).

Egypt

Color also played a central role in the life and religion of ancient Egypt. However, in contrast to the lack of masonry in Babylon, one important aspect of the Egyptian environment was the abundance of building stone in the Nile valley. The Egyptians had also evolved a language of color that was very precise in meaning; this hieroglyphic picture writing was applied in the form of pigment to embellish their low relief carving on the interiors and exteriors of their buildings.

The Egyptian artist had available to him only a simple and restricted palette. A paint box dating from around the fifteenth century B.C. was found to contain seven colors: terra cotta, light and medium yellow ocher, turquoise blue, green, white, and black. An eighth compartment was empty, but was thought to have contained a blue or a purple. The pigments were composed of mineral pigments mixed with a tempera base of gum, egg, or other binding agent. Many types of pigment were used to produce different colors; most were indigenous but a few rarer hues, such as the highly prized lapis lazuli, were imported from Central Asia. Carbon was used for black; cobalt, copper sand, and subcarbonate of soda for bright blue; lapis lazuli for ultramarine; ocher earths for reds, yellows, and browns; iron oxide for pinks and reds; arsenic trisulphide for bright lemon yellow; malachite for greens; lime and gypsum for whites; and vegetable dyes for indigo.

Apart from the fact that the ancient Egyptian way of life revolved around the worship of the sun, it was the dazzling quality of sunlight that had a profound effect on their architectural polychromy. Their environmental color sense was extremely lively, and hues were expressed in even, decided, and sometimes quite violent tones, but could also be delicate and faint. They loved to juxtapose contrasting colors in a manner that reveals a deep feeling for the unique quality of each particular hue. For instance, black and white were used mainly to delineate and separate larger areas of red, blue, or yellow. This was a most deliberate color deployment because, apart from the precision of its symbolic content, polychromy was used to accentuate architectural detail in a climate where plastic form, if softly modeled, would appear diffused. Such color use can be seen in the temples at Luxor and the Tomb of Sennefer at Thebes. Often the temples contained blue-painted ceilings to symbolize the heavens above green-colored floors representing the meadows of the Nile.

However, a more spectacular record survives today in the ruins of Karnak at Thebes. Constructed some fifteen centuries before Christ, it was perhaps the most colorful edifice ever built by man. James Fergusson wrote of it (8):

> No language can convey an idea of its beauty, and no artist has yet been able to reproduce its form so as to convey to those who have not seen it an idea of its grandeur. The mass of its central piers . . . are so arranged and lighted as to convey an idea of infinite space; at the same time, the beauty and massiveness of the forms, and the brilliance of their colored decorations, all combine to stamp this as the greatest of man's architectural works. . . .

The colors of the pigments at Karnak were red, yellow, green, and blue, hues that held a particular significance for the Egyptians. For instance, red, the color of the sunset, was the color of Shu, the god who separated earth from sky; it also represented the color of mankind. Yellow was the color of the sun god Ra, and green, the color of Osiris and the hue of time, often addressed as the everlasting green one. The wife of Osiris, Isis, was colored blue, the hue of divinity and the union of the soul of truth with the infinite.

Ancient Greek Cosmetics

The Egyptian use of symbolic color and that of Mesopotamia was passed on via Asia Minor to Greece, where it became adapted to suit a new form of religion. Although the culture of the ancient Greeks had more influence than any other on present-day Western civilization, and much is known about their architecture and society, little was known about their use of architectural polychromy until the detective work that began in the 1830s. However, if Athens had suffered the fate of Pompeii and Herculaneum, its emergence from the preserving action of the volcanic ashes would have changed the concept of the visual appearance of the ancient Greek capitol. A walk along one of its streets would prove to be something of a colorful experience, for most of the houses and temples would be found to be painted in symbolic, and sometimes cosmetic, coloration—some statues even wearing lipstick, false eyelashes, and possibly precious stones simulating flashing eyes in their flesh-colored stone heads. Only gold and silver would be seen to be unpainted within this predominantly white, blue, red, and yellow environment.

The ancient Greeks covered their architecture with color washes almost entirely in the belief that the natural coloration of wood, marble, ivory, and bronze was no substitute for the artistic creation of the city as a total art form. Many scholars had thought that early Greek architecture used little applied color. This is easy to understand as there was very little evidence of it due to the fact that the climate of Greece is much wetter than that of Egypt; the exposed pigments deteriorated quickly. In Greek architecture, color was mostly applied on stucco and in fresco form and was limited to a palette comprised of chalky red, dark brown, pale yellow, bright blue, black, and white.

Evidence of the earthy pigments of ancient Greece came with informal excavations carried out at Aegina, Bassae, and Selinus in the early nineteenth century. Architectural fragments were drawn out of the earth and displayed traces of vivid, flat-painted colors. These traces faded rapidly upon exposure to the air and were thus known only to their excavators and recorded only in their observations and quick color sketches.

C. W. Ceram's description of freshly unearthed remains perhaps best illustrates the Greeks' love of color (9):

> The plastic works of the ancient Greeks were gaily colored. Statuary was deeply dyed with garish pigments. The marble figure of a woman found on the Athenian Acropolis was tinctured red, green, blue, and yellow. Quite often, statues had red lips, glowing eyes made of precious stones, and even artificial eyelashes.

Again with regard to statuary, an unknown author describes an excavated pediment (10):

> Flesh, reddish in tone; globe of eyes yellow, iris green, with a hole in the center filled with black. Black outlines to eyebrows and eyelids; hair and beard bright blue at the time of excavation, which disintegrated later into a greenish tone; circle of brown around the nipples.

The portrait painter Sir William Beechey (1753–1839) offers one clue as to the significance of the Greek love of architectural polychromy. He observed that the lost colors were not simply a capricious decoration but appeared to respond to an established code of practice that assigned individual hues to specific components of a building. The

archaeologist Frederick Poulson (1876–1950) developed this observation when remarking on the striking similarity between the richly painted treatments of reliefs on the Acquinetum pediment and the metopes of the Sicyonian Treasury. Helmets and clothes were blue and red, respectively, but each edged with a line of the other color; whenever two or more articles of clothing or armor were worn, these were counterchanged. Similarly, the borders of overlapping shields signaled an alteration of red and blue. The tails and manes of horses and lions were also in red, but when several were superimposed, blue was used to alternate the color scheme.

A picture rapidly emerges of a color system that deployed contrast as a means of visual emphasis and clarification. This seems entirely logical when, on the one hand, it is considered that much of the elaboration was elevated high above eye level and, on the other hand, that the Greeks were masters of the optical illusion, a skill which their use of entasis (the subtle curving of architectural forms to correct perceptual distortion and reduce apparent weight) clearly demonstrates. The polychromatic extension of a three-dimensional experience, therefore, seems to have existed in classical Greek architecture as a device to intensify form. It is found in the use of blue to underline the shadows on limewashed Ionian capitals, and the use of two blues on the indentations of triglyphs—a lighter on the face and a darker on the indented facet—to accentuate their shape. A similar color use can also be found in Crete where the wall paintings of Knossus date from 1600 B.C. These depict abstract designs and scenes with flowers, hunters, and girls. The colors used were much the same as those on the mainland: red oxide, yellow ocher, blue, brown, and black. However, it is the structural diagramming of form that is of interest, for here, against the blue of the Aegean, red, yellow, ocher, and black columns supported the blue of pediments.

However, if a second look at the colors of ancient Greece is taken, another more deep-rooted function can be found, for the pediments and friezes, such as those on the Parthenon, functioned as gigantic billboards narrating the mythology of a Golden Age, a legendary and social state of perfection toward which (aided by a clearly defined color and precious metal symbolism) the Greeks strived. Here, a strong color played a highly significant role much as it does in modern advertising. Blue, for example, was associated with truth and integrity, color attributes that—worn earlier on the breastplates of Egyptian priests to signify the holiness of their judgments—were to later reemerge in the cloaked Madonna of a Christian symbolism. White was the basic color of the Parthenon and of Athena's statue. The meaning of the Greek word parthenon is synonymous with virginity, and white is still displayed by blushing Western brides. Red was ascribed to love and sacrifice, the latter accounting for Dionysius's red face during the period of the annual wine festival. Like the Egyptian gods before them, other Greeks gods were also vested in their appropriate colors; some were painted different hues to reflect the changing cycles of seasons. However, the reddening process is at the very root of symbolism; to learn more, the potency of red must be viewed in the perception of today's forebears.

Red was seen to embody a power capable of influencing events; the daubing of a corpse with red ocher, for instance, could prepare the deceased for a life beyond the grave. This use of red is practically universal throughout the diverse structures of color symbolism in both ancient and primeval societies, and it is still evident today among primitive tribes. Apart from its widespread availability as a pigment, red is a hue common to all races as the life-giving color of blood. It is the color of passion—a color to be summoned from within to the surface of the skin in order to convey emotion via the blush of love or the flush of anger. It is also the color to be artificially applied to the exterior surface of the skin, as in the case of war paint, a kind of heraldic anger intensifying and prolonging the heat of the moment. The facial reddening of the living, the dead, and the inanimate was practiced in ancient Egypt where extremes in complexion were highly prized. In order to enhance the redness of their own pigmentation, the Egyptians used body cosmetics, and red was also applied to the faces of their mummies, and to that of the Sphinx. Red paint, in one form or another, has been used as a symbol of man's aspiration to a continued existence—from the fertility icons and wall paintings of prehistoric man to the exterior facades of Greek temples and medieval cathedrals.

Red was also used on the Parthenon frieze as a background for the flesh tints and gilding of the metopes, and also to function as a counterchange color with the blues of the triglyphs. Unlike the painted stucco on the rough limestone of other Greek buildings, the Pentallic marble of the Athenian monuments received a direct coloration—the brilliance of color and gilding on the interior friezes and the Elgin marbles contrasting against the columns of a completely limewashed Parthenon.

The fact that the Parthenon was completely coated in paint, and not the pristine marble edifice in the mind's eye of scholars, first became public in France when a portion of its east frieze—acquired by the Louvre from the collection of Choiseul-Gouffier—was seen to have traces of color still visible on its marble. The original idea that Greek color might have been exclusive to sculpture was to change and, apart from the disbelief of some idealists, there followed an enthusiastic program of architectural color restoration. In 1822, the historian, F. W. J. Schelling, after his study of the pediments of the Temple of Aegina, concluded that painting in Greece derived from painting primitive wooden temples.

Rome

Much of the Greek deployment of architectural color has been described as Egyptoid in nature, but its symbolic content can be traced through the cultures of Persia, Assyria, and Babylon. The Greek use of polychromy was eagerly adopted by the Romans, whose overriding interest in colored buildings was displayed in their use of materials: brightly colored paints and marbles, gold, bronze, and mosaics. However, being a more practical people, the Romans restricted the application of color to buildings and left statuary unpainted. The discovery of Pompeii and Herculaneum almost intact beneath Vesuvius's ash in the early

eighteenth century unearthed a new degree of brilliance in colors that would change forever the perception of Roman architecture. Between 1762 and 1767, Johann Wincklemann uncovered undisturbed evidence of free use of bright and deep colors, including large areas of black sometimes covering entire internal walls and relieved only by paintings and ornamental decoration. Other background colors included vivid green, vermilion, red oxide, orange, yellow ocher, and azure. The Pompeii wall paintings have been classified into four successive periods, the earliest dating from the second century B.C. They were executed directly on the plaster in fresco, tempera, oil, or pigments mixed with melted wax. Early decoration imitated marble veneers and paneling but, during the Empire period, motifs became more complicated in their simulation of an illusory architecture—the elaborate framework of improbably accentuated classical shapes sometimes incorporating an elementary form of perspective. Figurative scenes contained within the enclosed panels were even more remarkable because they were often depicted as though seen through a window.

Like their Greek prototypes, the floors of Pompeii houses were initially decorated with delicate mosaics using a border of floral or geometric design to frame a central picture. However, a growing naturalism, which was to foreshadow the advent of the Renaissance, led to freer and more humanist designs that coincided with the decline of the empire. This gradual movement away from the symbolism of architectural polychromy was also noticeable in fifth- and sixth-century Byzantium where color expressed a more emotional stimulus. The interior of St. Sophia at Constantinople was richly decorated with paintwork in red, green, blue, and black, with colored marbles, gold leaf, jewels, carved cedar, amber, ivory, mosaics, and cast metal. The total effect of this color experience conveyed a feeling more of religious mystique than of ritualistic or pagan attitude.

In discussing the Roman importation of the Greek pigments, Pliny had first described the color-making compounds in terms of their healing properties, for their sources were the same as those of medicinal potions (11). However, the colors of Pompeii represented major advances in a new state of the art in a developing color technology. Developments in binders for pigments together with advances in fresco painting (the addition of pigment to damp plaster) had increased their permanence.

Fired clay and glaze came together in Egypt during the fifth millenium B.C. By the first millenium B.C., a transparent lead glaze was in use in the Middle East, and in China by 300 B.C. As a result, ceramics became the color medium for a scintillating architecture of the East, a development that simply fused the potter's art with the scale of the mosque.

Islam

Before Suleyman the Magnificent undertook the refurbishment of the mosques in Istanbul in 1546, Islamic architecture was decorated inside and out with massive displays of tiles. These projected complex floral patterns together with calligraphic texts, which, apart from tracts from the

Koran, inscribed poems and proverbs on the facades. Tile mosaics were a means of creating colorful displays without the problem of mixing glazes on one tile. The fluted lines of the dome of the Sir Dar at Samarkand is covered by a mosaic of small tiles and, at Isfahan, polychromatic tiles, each forming a precise module in an intricate pattern, cover walls, arches, and cornices as effortlessly as a coat of paint.

In twelfth-century Persia, the combination of quartz with alkaline glazes provided a new and brilliant architectural palette that became dominated by the rich turquoise and deep cobalt blue so beloved by the Islamic potters, and that coats the Blue Mosque at Tabriz. The palette of glazes was also extended by the greens, browns, and purples obtained from iron and manganese, and a red, known as Armenian bole. Furthermore, the admixture of sulfur, silver, and copper oxides provided metallic finishes that could simulate gold.

Gothic Cathedrals

Such advances in the technologies of pottery glazing and glassmaking combined to extend the architectural color range. However, it was glass that gave a luminosity so beautifully exploited in Greek, Roman, and Byzantine mosaics and that was to eventually color the stained glass of the medieval cathedrals. The immense influence of the Roman Empire extended over almost the whole of western Europe, and following its armies came the early Christian missionaries, bringing with them their brand of color symbolism whose roots had begun in ancient Egypt. These symbolic hues again became tempered in their adaptation to local materials and merged with those of the pagan religions, such as that of the Druids. Ultimately, these primitive colors became part of the religious architecture of the Romanesque and Gothic periods.

Rich color was an intrinsic element of glassmaking because, until the Renaissance, clear glass was much more difficult to achieve. Therefore, a multicolored sunlight poured into medieval cathedrals, but it also illuminated the brightly painted surfaces of their interiors—a color experience that was matched and, according to James Ward, often overshadowed by a corresponding application of pigment and gilding to external facades. Traces of medieval colors are still distingushable on the exteriors of many French cathedrals, such as the flecks of red, blue, and green pigment at Angers, and the red stain on Notre Dame. With reference to Notre Dame, James Ward writes (12):

> The coloring occurred principally on the moldings, columns, sculptured ornaments, and figurework. The outside coloring was much more vivid than the inside work. There were bright reds, crude greens, orange, yellow ochre, blacks, and pure white, but rarely blues, outside, the brilliancy of light allowing a harshness of coloring that would not be tolerable under the diffused light of the interior. . . . There is also evidence that the greater portion of similar edifices of the thirteenth, fourteenth, and fifteenth centuries in France were decorated in color.

There is strong evidence of similar decoration used in England during the Middle Ages. For example, when dis-

cussing the great west front of Wells Cathedral in *Gothic Architecture,* Cecil Stewart states (13):

> . . . its one hundred and seventy-six full-length statues were brilliantly colored. The niches were dark red, and the figures and drapery were painted in yellow ochre, with eyes and hair picked out in black and the lips in red. In the central group of the Virgin and Child, the Virgin's robe was black with a green lining, while the Child's robe was crimson, the composition being set on a background of red and green diaper. There is evidence, from plugholes, that the statues were further enriched with gilded metal ornament. Above, the row of angels were painted rosy red.

Basically, the color of religious architecture in medieval Europe occurred in three main forms: stained glass, applied paint, and a decorative use of intrinsically colored materials. The natural colors of building materials were greatly exploited in Italy and England, but rarely in France and Germany. Throughout the Middle Ages, tempera and fresco painting were practiced across Europe. Up until the end of the thirteenth century, only the early pigments of reds, browns, and yellows were used before the introduction of an oil medium that enabled the introduction of more blues and greens. Although the basic pigments were crude in quality, their color quality—although possibly mellowed slightly by a protective coat of linseed oil—must have been strong and brilliant. Furthermore, judging from their orchestration of color in the surviving illuminated manuscripts, the overall effect of architectural polychromy would not have been crude.

The spontaneity of a medieval color application is preserved in stained glass. Medieval glass makers could color their glass in different ways. For instance, the glass itself could be colored or a silver stain applied to white glass to give gradations from pale yellow to deep orange. Flash glass was also used, in which a film of blue or red was fused to white glass film. In the flash glass process, one colored layer could be ground away to expose the other and thus achieve two colors on a single sheet. Furthermore, additional detail and shading could be worked into a design by the use of an oil or gum-based iron oxide enamel that fired onto the glass.

It was as an extension of an aspiring Gothic architecture that the ancient and symbolic colors appeared on buildings for the last time. Due to the crudity of pigments, both their meaning and impression were to fade and later to almost completely disappear under the Reformation scrubbing brush and the Puritan whitewash, instruments of a new brand of religious fervor that set out to rid religious buildings of their sensuous, vulgar, and pagan overtones in a fierce reaction against materialism.

However, some evidence of the lost symbolic colors occasionally flickers and dances in the light of the modern environment, kept alive by the undercurrents of a folk art tradition, vestiges of heraldry, the ceremonies of pagan festivals, and the symbolism of primitive religious rites. English Morris dancers, for example, still carry the spring green of fertility around their maypole. The Pope remains cloaked in the precious purple of the ancients—a pigment so difficult to achieve that it was reserved by the Romans (and the Greeks before them) only for those of the highest rank. Although deprived of much of their original meaning, some of the ancient reds, yellows, blues, and greens escaped the puritanical purge by keeping on the move. They remain in currency with the British bargeman's art of longboat decoration. Also, they are still meticulously painted over the trappings of other portable environments, such as the circus, gypsy caravans, and the traveling fairground. It is the sheer, uninhibited exuberance of fairground paintwork and gilding that possibly represents a reasonable simulation of the form-following coloration of an ancient Greek city. Its decoration comes close to reflecting the methods used by the ancient designers who used polychromy not only as a language, but also as a medium for extending the perceptual experience of their architectural and sculptural form.

One aspect of the use of architectural color by the ancients should be kept in mind; namely, that the desire to decorate with color or the potency of color symbolism was much stronger than the pigments at their disposal. If a more complete documentation of their color systems had survived, there would be more clues to its meaning. From this point in time, it can only be surmised that the colors of an ancient polychromy held deep-seated meanings because the experience of a city, temple, or cathedral was not merely that of an architecture, but of a structure that communicated concepts, possibly as did the primitive cave paintings, about survival.

COLOR REVOLUTIONS AND REVIVALS

Glass, first developed in a crude form by the ancient Egyptians, was a technology that was to further the movement toward humanism during the early Italian Renaissance as it was to affect concepts of color and spatial visualization. Lewis Mumford has indeed described this transition between the philosophies of the medieval and Renaissance periods in terms of the gradual purification and subsequent clarification of window glass (14). As clear glass had not yet been perfected, medieval symbolism was represented by the brightly colored stained glass of cathedral windows that began to dissolve into the clear glass of the fourteenth century, thus allowing an unimpeded view through to the hues and forms of nature. This was a naturalistic perception characteristic of the beginning of new thought in Europe. This new and sharply focused world was also framed by the glass of spectacles that, in adding additional years to eyesight, had boosted the revival of learning. The later invention of microscopics and the simultaneous improvement of telescopics had shattered man's naive conceptions of space and color and extended his perception of an expanding world. However, a world viewed through the glass of windows, spectacles, and optical instruments is a framed perception similar to that of viewing a painting in a picture frame as distinct from viewing a painted building.

The Rebirth of Color (The Renaissance)

Up until the Renaissance, buildings had been conceived as total works of art created by artist–craftsmen who had orchestrated the urban environment as a fusion of habit-

able space (architecture) and as the elaboration of form (sculpture) and planes of color (painting). With the advent of humanism and the resultant thirst for knowledge during the quattrocento came a creative outburst that led to the gradual separation of architecture and art into distinct avenues of study. Each branch of intellectual activity became isolated from the others and a building, a piece of sculpture, and a portable painting existed in their own terms. Not only was the artist's identity separated in this way, but his work and color expertise became divorced from their hitherto architectural context and for the first time artists formed themselves into groups or schools. Initially, carved objects and painted images were designed for specific buildings but, as the idea of art for art's sake grew, built spaces became tailored to house them.

A further cause for the divorce of art and architecture appears to stem from the beginnings of archaeology. This newfound interest in the relics of the past began earlier in the 1440s when Flavio Biondi, who has been described as the father of archaeology, systematically catalogued the surviving remains of imperial Rome. Up until that time, the architectural glories of the ancient Roman culture had been left to rot. The Forum, for instance, was partially buried and used both as a grazing field for cattle and as a convenient city quarry for building materials.

The subsequent excavations in the city transformed Rome into a vast museum and a fashion was started for the collecting of relics as *objets d'art*. Both Filippo Brunelleschi and Donato Donatello compiled private collections of found objects that were to have a profound influence on the direction of their work and, indeed, on the subsequent development of sculpture and architecture as separate art forms.

From the ranks of an emerging and wealthy merchant middle class, patrons not only collected the archaeological finds but also actively commissioned sculpture and painting by contemporary artists. This, for the first time, isolated the artist's products as entities or works of art to be viewed out of the context of their original architectural settings.

The Renaissance caused creative men to reject the almost redundant idea of symbolic color as part of an environmental language and turn instead toward an individual translation of the colors of nature. Leonardo da Vinci meticulously began to examine the spatial behavior of color, recording in words and paint the effect of changing light and distance on the hues of objects in space.

Thus, man's newfound individuality had spawned a self-expression that required a new and creative color sense. The colors of humanism evolved not only to overshadow the restrictive palettes of symbolism, but to form the basis of modern color sensibilities. For example, the legacy from the Renaissance is the twentieth-century notion of form and volume that has developed from an understanding of space as defined by the visual elements—form, shape, line, texture, and color. Most present-day design courses are founded on this principle, which would later be expounded at the Bauhaus by the teachings and writings of Johannes Itten, Paul Klee, and Wassily Kandinsky.

However, the last remants of an antiquarian color symbolism could still be found in Renaissance Rome. For in-

Figure 1. "The Transept from South," one of the series of sumptuous chromolithographs produced by Joseph Nash for Dickinson's *Comprehensive Pictures of the Great Exhibition,* 1981-1983, which document the impact of Owen Jones's color system on the interior of Joseph Paxton's Crystal Palace in Hyde Park, London. Courtesy of Henry Sotheran Ltd.

Figure 2. A chromolithographic plate from the Egyptian Ornament section of *Grammar of Ornament,* Owen Jones, 1856. Jones suggested that the Egyptian builders painted everything on their architecture using a range of flat, diagrammatic hues in which green symbolized the lotus leaf.

Figure 3. The lavish ceiling of the banqueting room inside The Royal Pavilion at Brighton, England. Restored by Prince Regent in 1812, its bizarre, deep-colored interior was much influenced by Islamic, Indian, and Chinese decoration and contains this huge metal palm tree and "bedragonned" chandelier. Courtesy of The Royal Pavilion.

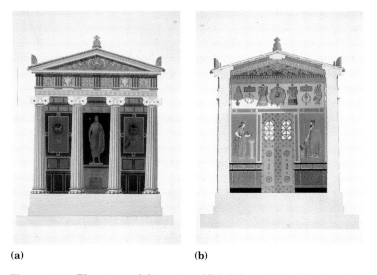

(a)   (b)

Figure 4. (**a**) Elevation and (**b**) section of Jakob-Ignaz Hittorff's watercolor reconstruction of the Temple of Empedocles at Selinus, published in his *Restitution du Temple d'Empedocle a Selimonte, ou l'Architecture Polychrome chez les Grecs,* 1851. Being derived from a wide variety of different sources, Hittorff's proposal of a Greek system of architectural color met with fierce controversy when it was first published. Courtesy of Henry Sotheran Ltd.

Figure 5. Louis Sullivan, The National Farmers Bank, Owatonna, Minn. Sullivan's delicate arrangement of bands and borders of subtly variegated terra cotta faience to brace the brickwork of facades and frame windows and entrances exhibit certain characteristics of art nouveau and became the hallmark of his midwestern bank buildings. Courtesy of Sandak, Inc.

Figure 6. Gerrit Reitveld, Schroder House, Utrecht, Holland, 1924. Reitveld's architectural polychromy drew from artist Piet Mondrian's stark Neoplastic palette of primary hues with black and gray against a white ground and was deployed on both the interior and exterior of this private house to modify perceptually the impression of its three-dimensional form. Courtesy of the Reitveld Archive.

Figure 7. The Le Corbusier Center, Zurich. Originally designed as a house, and now a museum, this was among Le Corbusier's last projects, built three years after his death in 1968. Courtesy of Preben Holst.

Figure 8. Wallis, Gilbert & Partners, Hoover Building, Perivale, London, 1932. The art deco revivalism of this factory building enlists a cocktail of color decoration sources to brighten up the workplace. Its architects believed that a colorful industrial environment would both improve the attitude of employees and promote the image of the product.

Figure 9. Frank Lloyd Wright, "Falling Water" (Kaufmann House), Bear Run, Pennsylvania, 1936. By architecturally extending the water-course rock formations above which it is perched, the earth-tinted horizontal planes of this example of Wright's later work is widely accepted as a supreme statement of architectural integration based on organic principles. However, Wright had originally planned for this house to be colored gold. Courtesy of Sandak, Inc.

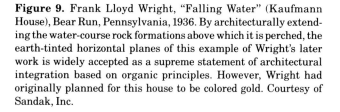

Figure 10. Richard Rogers and Renzo Piano, Pompidou Center, Paris, France, 1976. In order to tackle the problem of scale on this huge building, the Anglo-Italian design team employed a color-coding system using the latest technology in pigments, such as vinyl plastic coatings, to diagram its exposed ducting and structural members. Courtesy of Richard Rogers. Photograph by Paul Wakefield.

(a)

(b)

(c)

Figure 11. Jean Philippe Lenclos's **(a)** gathered environmental samples form the basis of **(b)** a palette of proposed facade colors for the new town of Le Vaudreuil in Normandy, France. Lenclos's system of environmental color "mapping" begins with the meticulous identification of regional hues. Soils, vegetation, and traditionally applied pigments are faithfully recorded before being classified into regional palettes. In order to instill a sense of place, these are then reapplied to existing and future buildings. **(c)** Apartment buildings in Le Frioul in the south of France demonstrate the reflection of the colors of the landscape in the building. Courtesy of Jean Philippe Lenclos.

Figure 12. Color-restored facade in the Piazza della Republica, Turin, Italy. Giovanni Brino's restoration of over 7000 facades in Turin's main piazzas and processional streets reinstates the vibrant pattern of polychrome pathways first conceived and installed by the city's Council of Builders in 1850. Courtesy of Giovanni Brino.

Figure 13. Charles Moore, Piazza d'Italia, New Orleans, 1978. In collaboration with August Perez & Associates, Charles Moore's distinctive design for a small plaza and fountain in the heart of New Orleans uses rich red and yellow ochers with off-white and pale blues to etch the arches and columns of this seemingly flimsy but solidly constructed stage-like environment. Nightfall sees the function of delineation replaced by more intense glow of neon strip lighting. Courtesy of Norman McGrath.

Figure 14. Michael Graves, Humana Building, Louisville, Ky. (1982). View from Main Street. Courtesy of the architect.

stance, the ceiling of the Apartomento Borgia in the Vatican was painted scarlet, emerald green, cobalt blue, and gold. Coincidence is hardly likely because, according to Vasari, the ceiling, with its centaurs, mythological birds, and animals, together with signs of the zodiac, included much Greek and Roman symbolism. Its survival in the Vatican is not surprising, as color symbolism was still important within the ceremony and ritual of Catholicism. Even so, the use of applied color on religious as well as secular buildings had begun to decline into insignificance.

Now stripped of raw pigment, a new and uninhibited architecture and sculpture emerged that glorified man rather than gods and saints in the exploited natural colors of stone and metal. Symmetrically proportioned and arranged around the central vanishing point of Brunelleschi's newly refined perspective drawing, an essentially theatrical architecture functioned as backdrop, frame, and stage set for works of art. Color was now taken inside to heighten a contrast between urban and interior space. Rooms were filled with a lavish use of sculpture, carving, inlaid woods and marbles, gold, and, of course, paintings, all set against walls of rich, dark hues, or walls painted off-white.

Oil painting, which was first applied to portable wooden panels and then to canvas, became the focus of an adventure into creative color expression. The medium had evolved from mixing pigment directly with the varnish that had, hitherto, been applied to protect the egg-bound medium of tempera. Meanwhile, fresco painting—first used by the Egyptians over 4000 years earlier—had also been refined and was being applied to the drying plaster of interiors. However, although fresco remained an integral part of buildings, its skillful enlisting of perspective in the creation of trompe l'oeil effects brought a naturally tinted illusion to the walls and ceilings of interiors that, in the masterful hands of artists such as Michelangelo, Mantegna, and Veronese, dissolved into images of populated landscapes and skyscapes.

France

The creative color of a humanist Italian Renaissance was to have a profound effect on a Europe still in the grip of Gothic polychromy. Its impact, felt initially in France, was to spread gradually, with its wave of influence, in turn, causing a succession of waves of architectural color that, in the stately interiors of the rich and powerful, alternately flickered and darkened. While the medieval pigments faded on the facades of cathedrals, successive French monarchs began their interpretation of the spirit of the Renaissance. First came Francis I, who imported some of the Italian masters to the French court. His expression of a new individualism began in the middle of the sixteenth century with the fabulous stonework of palaces such as the Louvre and Fontainebleau, whose interiors flashed with gilt against the introduction of a subtle and neutral gray. Under Louis XIII in the first half of the seventeenth century, work began on the magnificent palace of Versailles, which was enlarged in the second half of the century by Louis XIV into a Baroque treasure house

with its riches set against walls of gilded, crimson, and green-painted woodwork.

A synthetic and applied architectural polychromy was now a significant aspect of interior design, but a more sophisticated and intimate sense of color that paralleled that of a French court pomp emerged from the tastes of successive wives and mistresses of the French rulers. This feminine revolution in interior decor began with the mistress of Louis XIV, Madame de Pompadour, who patronized the arts and promoted the fashion for chinoiserie. Her taste for oriental pastels and muted hues caused the royal apartments and boudoirs to be painted in soft pinks, pale blues, and lilacs, hues that coincided with a sinuous rococo style. During the ensuing neoclassical revival that began in the reign of Louis XIV, Marie Antionette continued to favor an even more subtle pastel range while a concurrent and mainstream classical revivalism preferred the pure, simple, and symbolic hues. Again, even after the French Revolution at the beginning of the nineteenth century, and while Napoleon's favorite reds, greens, and yellows symbolically decorated the deteriorating neoclassicism of an eclectic Empire style, Josephine's influence on interior color schemes—in promoting gray and muted colors with accents of blue, silver, mauve, and pink—followed the previous fashion of the French queens.

The United Kingdom

Across the channel, the initial effects of the Renaissance arrived in sixteenth-century Tudor, Elizabethan England to cause the decline of medieval influence. While trade and literature flourished, an architecture of patterns constructed from the hues of wood, brick, and stone enclosed oak-paneled or white-painted rooms in which hanging tapestries provided the main color focus. Outside, the earth and straw stucco of in-filled, half-timbered facades is now thought to have been daubed with red or yellow ocher; the conception of a black-and-white half-timbering resulted from a much later Victorian pitch and limewash that, in following a nautical tradition, applied a protective skin to Tudor buildings in coastal areas.

However, the full impact of the Renaissance had to await the House of Stuart when, in the early seventeenth century, Inigo Jones returned from his Italian tour with notions of a classical and simple proportion. These became expressed in his ensuing architecture, but particularly in his design for the Banqueting House in London for James I, which contained off-white walls and ornate gilded moldings under the brilliant colors of a Rubens ceiling. In this building, an animated color was intended via the costumery of the masques and balls it was designed to accommodate. Later in the century, after taking refuge in France from the Plague of London, Christopher Wren also returned, bringing with him the full flowering of the French Renaissance and an architecture of confidence and colored stone. He arrived in time to supervise the replanning and rebuilding of a Renaissance-inspired London; the white stonework of St. Paul's Cathedral symbolizes the city's phoenixlike resurrection from the ashes of the Great Fire of 1655.

A further wave of continental influence came in the

Dutch taste of King William who, with his queen, Mary, acceded to the English throne at the end of the seventeenth century and imported a passion for the subtlety of chinoiserie in paint and wallpaper. The House of Orange was also to favor a pale green paintwork, the popularity of which (according to Faber Birren) was to survive and hallmark the interiors of an ensuing English style that was to have an enormous influence on the U.S. during the Georgian period.

With Johann Wincklemann's unearthing of a color-preserved Pompeii and Herculaneum in the mid-eighteenth century came a revival of interest in the rich colors of the ancient world. Proliferated by a new flourishing grand tourism and a greater continental trade, the Georgian period saw the reappearance of symbolic hues incorporated into the Greek motifs of a neoclassical interior design with the Adam brothers as its leading practitioners in Great Britain. However, inside the white-painted and elegantly proportioned houses, there was a livelier color than can be imagined today. Based on pigments remixed by restorationist Ian Bristow in 1977 to their eighteenth-century formulas, the Georgian greens, blue-greens, creams, and tans appear far more full-blooded than the pastel tints commonly associated with the now faded schemes of the period.

The decline of the English neoclassical clarity of color paralleled the deterioration of the architectural style, a shift that was to coincide with the demise of the classical revival in France during the Empire period. Its final dissipation came with the Regency period in which, as in France, the mood shifted toward a predilection for excess, coarseness, and a kaleidoscope of style and sullied color. As the UK approached the twentieth century, interior colors darkened while a renewed interest in a painted, external polychromy was to reappear. As the Victorian era dawned, the frivolously striped paintwork on and in George IV's Brighton Pavilion, although superficially inspired, seemed to signal yet another revival of the antique hues (Fig. 3). However, the revival that was to follow in the 1830s was a more rigorous and serious resurrection.

The United States

While an exuberant Europe had adopted and evolved its own expression of the rebirth of art and architecture that had mushroomed in the Italian quattrocento, the American continent was busy being colonized by a transplanted patchwork of clustered communities from the Old World. As if to reaffirm its own cultural identity in a new setting, each settlement brought a version of its own vernacular expressed in crude wood and clay shutters, with occasional patches of exterior architectural color, such as a Spanish earth-colored adobe in the south and a German folk decoration in the north. Meanwhile, a peep inside an early Colonial house in New England would find a simple space painted in a Puritan limewash. Apart from the occasional variegation supplied by needlework and quilts, there was little color, except that which might later be added to walls in the form of stippled paint applied through the stenciled patterns of itinerant decorators.

The United States had to await an eighteenth-century affluence before it was ready to assume an identifiable and classical brand of architecture and color. This arrived with a strong early Georgian influence that inspired a local palette of bright paints and wallpapers for interiors and a distinctive spectrum of facade colors for cities like Williamsburg, Charleston, and Savannah.

However, the revolution in America was to sever the alliance with Great Britain and, in turning to France for its political model, a Louis XVI taste for style and color was imported by Thomas Jefferson. Under this patriotic zeal, a French version of the classical ideal had, by the end of the eighteenth century, established the Federal style as the first truly authentic breed of U.S. architecture. This was to spread across the continent and, in its wake, leave the now familiar white-painted columns of churches, plantation villas, and bureaucratic monuments, each decorated with motifs drawn from a Greco-Roman source. Later, just as the recycled classicism had degenerated in Europe, and as the U.S. entered the nineteenth century, the simplicity and clarity of colors and forms began to darken and become heavy. This shift accompanied the fading of the Federal style as it shadowed Napoleon's preference for the more cluttered Empire style.

Thirty years before the United States plunged into a bloody civil war, yet another important color revolution was to take place in Europe.

European Revivalism

During the years around 1830, there was a sudden outburst of European interest in restoring the original appearance of the exterior painted ornamentation of ancient Greek temples. Based on new and archaeologically motivated research into the symbolic colors of antiquity, this was an event that was not only reminiscent of an early Renaissance passion for the past, but it was to open a heated European debate between a painted polychromy and one derived structurally from the natural colors of building materials.

Most influential of a new breed of applied color evangelists were the French artist, Jakob-Ignaz Hittorff, and the German architect Gottfried Semper who, combining speculation with fact, began to publish their respective reconstructions of Greek polychromy. However, this general interest was largely dominated by architects and characterized by the production of colored drawings almost as works of art, an activity that was later to occupy an initially suspicious body of faculty and students at the Ecole des Beaux Arts. Both Hittorff and Semper had developed a personal approach to the use of color in restoration based on their respective discoveries. For example, Hittorff had studied the colors of Pompeii and personally excavated painted architectural fragments at Selinus (Fig. 4). Meanwhile, taking advantage of repair work to the Trajan Column, Semper had climbed the scaffolding and his close inspection had detected traces of red, yellow, and blue paint.

In Hittorff's reconstructions, architectural form functioned merely as a two-dimensional framework to receive a system of related painted patterns. Semper, on the other hand, approached architecture as the starting point for a complex color deployment that would modify its spatial impression, a system in which shadowed areas of facades received a positive color.

During the 1830s, a number of buildings were designed and painted externally by Hittorff and Semper together with other enthusiasts, such as Bindesbøll and von Klenze. However, following the publication of his sumptuous chromolithographic reconstructions in 1829 (15), the reality of Hittorff's exuberant reds, yellows, and blues on the Cirque d'Ete were much criticized because, as they were derived from a light quality far removed from that of northern Europe, they seemed inappropriate for the Parisian climate.

Victorian England

Despite the later success of Owen Jones's blue-and-white-painted Crystal Palace in the UK (visited by both Hittorff and Semper), the instability of high Victorian paintwork was overtaken by the search for a more permanent form of architectural color. This new phase stemmed from the fact that painted polychromy cracked, flaked, and washed away—a lack of durability that a Victorian obsession with permanence could not tolerate. Eventually in the UK, a Ruskinian preference for colored stones prevailed. Meanwhile, limestone came to replace stucco in Paris, terra cotta replaced plaster in Germany, and granite replaced brick in Boston. This desire for durability led to the resurrection of old techniques of architectural polychromy together with the innovation of new ones. For instance, for the painting of exposed and interior stonework, the forgotten Renaissance technique of fresco, lost behind the white marble of a classical ideal, was revived, but this time using cement. New processes included an encaustic technique in which, under heat, a mixture of pigment was baked onto building materials, and a French use of enameled lava that proved virtually indestructible. Influenced by oriental architecture, there was also widespread use of painted terra cotta, glazed tile, and enameled brick, the latter becoming a common feature of continental architecture.

It was during the 1850s that a high Victorian style had emerged with its use of colored materials; it was practiced by designers who had no direct links with the architects who had experimented with a painted polychromy in the 1830s. In the UK, William Butterfield was exploiting a glazed brickwork and stone to create colored patterns and banding on his All Saint's Church for the Ecclesiastical Society in London completed in 1859, and was also counterchanging the natural vegetation of brick on Oxford's Keble College. Meanwhile, George Edmund Street had used an orange-and-black-tarred brick with white limestone for the design of another All Saint's Church in Maidenhead, which was finished two years before its London counterpart. Both had pursued the concept of a structural polychromy in which color was seen as inextricably linked with the reality of construction, a concept preached by the Ecclesiologists and also practiced by Pugin.

Under the pressure of dogmatic Ruskinian views of what, in the UK, constituted bad taste, the Victorian excursion into a painted polychromy had also been brief.

Instead, the resurrected ancient colors became delegated to the embellishment of the cast iron of Brunel and Stephenson's machine age, and an eye-catching protective paintwork was applied to iron structures such as bridges, to the coachwork of steam engines, and to the working parts of industrial and agricultural machinery. This was a tradition that, over a century later, was to keep alive the ancient hues for their reapplication as industrial colors over the high tech architecture of the 1960s and 1970s.

Nevertheless, during these experiments with both applied and intrinsic polychromy, the realization that the ancients had used brilliant colors continued to meet a lingering skepticism. As late as 1863, 12 years after the Great Exhibition, Sir Lawrence Alma Tadema triggered a minor scandal in London with the unveiling of his painting "Phideas and the painting of the frieze of the Parthenon." The fact that he had realistically portrayed its codesigner in the process of applying the paint was to cause a storm, inciting protestations from the sculptor Auguste Rodin who exclaimed that he believed in his heart that such buildings were never colored.

During the growth of the Industrial Revolution, there was an influx of labor that moved out of the poorly lit houses of the countryside into the smoke-blackened dwellings and factories of the cities. City housing tended to be drab, built of brick and stone, and decorated inside by their landlords in dark green and brown paintwork relieved only by the occasional flashes of color from wallpaper, chintz drapes, Turkish carpets, and patchwork quilts. However, the transition from oil lamps to gas lighting threw a stronger light into the murky corners of the rooms and, as a result, a stronger need for color, such as olives, wines, and rose pinks, developed. Also, the discovery of nonfading aniline dyes by William Henry Perkins in 1856 added magenta, purple, and violet, colors popularized by Queen Victoria that were to later become associated with the Gay Nineties, also known as the Mauve Decade.

At this point, it would be worthwhile to review the traditional colors of ordinary dwellings because, as shall be seen, color choice tended to be a prerogative of the rich.

TRADITIONAL COLOR AND RESTORATION

Until the early nineteenth century, European towns and cities developed by a slow process of organic growth, usually employing materials indigenous to their regions. Architectural styles evolved within the limitations of available materials and this disciplined the form of the buildings, which were related to human scale. The constant use of local materials produced urban settings with visual harmony despite a diversity of forms. For example, the buildings on High Street in Oxford reflect several hundred years of stylistic change, but all are unified by scale, material, and, especially, color. Color in Oxford responds to the warmth of local sandstone and is deployed with apparent coordination. The predominant ochers (now replaced by synthetic equivalents) originally had only to be transported from Shotover Hill at the city's edge, a famous source of highly prized yellow ocher.

Outside the conurbations, the colors of agricultural buildings were either blended with or perceptually detached from the color of their landscape settings. Where an ocher was used, it would be the same as the earth on which the farm building stood, offering a camouflaged security. Where farms were whitewashed, the resulting contrast identified the farmer's place of refuge from a distance. Normally, the color decision was disciplined simply by the cheapness of applying local deposits of colored earth or using them to tint or stain distemper and limewash. In turn, this process created architectural color maps in which certain colors became identified with particular regions. In the rural United Kingdom, for instance, the national palette contains pinks and reds in the east and west, with umbers to the north and south surrounding a hinterland of yellow ocher.

Meanwhile, back in the towns and cities where an architecture creates its own backdrop, there was always access to the deposits of local earth pigments for painting stucco facades. For those who could afford the protection of oil-based paints for exposed woodwork and the status of foreign colors, there was the diversity of imported pigments. Today, the designer can select colors for external use from an assortment of similarly priced and stable paints, but this was not the case in the past when pigments varied widely in both cost and quality. For example, in the early nineteenth century, the association of the brighter colors with wealth stemmed from the fact that blues, organic yellows, reds, and some greens were ten times, and often 100 times, the price of the common earth pigments.

It is through such limitations of selection that the architecture of cities and regions all over the world has come to be associated traditionally with particular ranges of color. For instance, the ochers and reds of Lyons; and, among the blues and reds, the predominance of a Maria Theresa yellow in central Vienna. There are also the brick dust reds and distinctive Georgian greens of a revamped Savannah, the pinks of Suffolk and Devon cottages, and the brilliant reds, blues, and yellows of the houses of Burano, Italy, and of the housefronts of Mexico, Venezuela, and many other parts of Latin America.

In order to protect color traditions, certain cities, such as Venice, exercise legislative control. In other places with a color-conscious heritage in Europe, as well as in U.S. towns such as Salem, Mass., Williamsburg, and Charleston, architectural color is preserved and protected. However, a supreme example of architectural polychromy on a city scale is to be found in Turin where, in 1800, a Council of Builders was established to develop and apply a unique color plan for the entire city. Their concept was to invest principal streets and piazzas with colors according to a coordinated system and based on hues already popular and in widespread city use.

The council advised a series of chromatic pathways that followed the major processional approaches to Turin's ideal center—the Piazza Castello. The major routes were interconnected by a network of small streets and squares for which a secondary and more variegated color sequence was prescribed. The basic scheme enlisted around 80 different hues, which were deployed to form a continuous and, at the same time, changing progression of experience.

After surviving a series of bureaucratic changes, the council was abolished in 1845. No one knows just how long the original color scheme survived, but it existed as one of Turin's distinguishing features, praised by such illustrious visitors as Friedrich Nietzsche in the late nineteenth century and Henry James in the early twentieth century.

COLOR AND THE MODERN MOVEMENT

Meanwhile, in the mainstream of design, two distinct philosophies of style had begun to emerge toward the end of the Victorian period. On the one hand, there was an arts and crafts movement in the UK that, seeded by John Ruskin and William Morris, began as a protest against the eclecticism of nineteenth-century neoclassicism. In reaction to the brashness of the synthetic purples and violets, Morris sought to reinstate the hues of natural dyes for wallpapers and interior furnishings, and his doctrine formed the basis of a new style of interior design led by the Glasgow School. In 1904, Charles Rennie Mackintosh designed his first and influential art nouveau interiors in off-white with a pale green and pink decoration. Led by a small group of intellectuals, art nouveau became a fluid and elegant style that, combining form, ornament, and color, spread throughout Europe until its collapse at the outbreak of World War I.

The second brand of design philosophy was to have more far-reaching influence on the development of architectural design and color and it, too, was born of a dislike for the excesses of Victorian style. In 1892, Louis Sullivan's essay *Ornament in Architecture* was published in which he suggested that "... ornament is mentally a luxury and not a necessity"(16). The following year in England, Charles Voysey expressed much the same opinion when he wrote "... discarding the mass of useless ornaments ..."(17) would be both healthy and desirable. Those early rejections of an architectural bric-a-brac heralded yet another stylistic metamorphosis in which a shift toward a forthcoming Miesian and function-following architectural form preoccupied with integrity of material and an expression of pure, simple shapes was to give birth to the modern movement. This new philosophy was later to polarize at the beginning of the twentieth century in the founding of the Bauhaus design school in Germany and the formation of the Dutch de Stijl movement.

Under the directorship of Walter Gropius, the Bauhaus was established in Weimar in 1919 with an international faculty comprising architects, craftsmen, and artists. However, although the study of color based on the systems of Philipp Otto Runge and Wilhelm Ostwald was an important aspect of its curriculum, and although artists such as Wassily Kandinsky, Johannes Itten, and later Joseph Albers had evolved personal color theories, an architectural polychromy was not developed. This was because of a Bauhaus preoccupation with functionalism and a state-of-the-art technology and construction in which large areas of exposed concrete, steel, and glass were difficult to color.

The subsequent closure of the Bauhaus as a result of

Hitler's purge five years before the outbreak of World War II scattered its teachers into more stable areas of Europe and beyond. As a consequence, two of the leading champions of a monochrome modern movement, Walter Gropius and Marcel Breuer, together with two of the polychromes, artists Johannes Itten and Joseph Albers, eventually settled in the United States. However, compared with the enormous and immediate influence of Gropius and Breuer, the impact of the two artists was not to be felt until later by a young generation of designers who, as students, had been weaned by Itten's *The Elements of Color* (18) and, especially, Albers's *Interaction of Color* (19).

While a modern movement philosophy was being fashioned in Europe, American cities were being fashioned by the versatile and plastic attributes of terra cotta. According to Darl Rastorfer, terra cotta's widespread popularity in the architecture of the time resulted from its ability to be produced in fireproof building block form and to be fired with glazes to simulate the colors of natural stone. During his heyday, between 1880 and 1920, Louis Sullivan used areas of terra cotta in relief to create a high contrast against the burnt earth of brickwork. Among Sullivan's finest examples are the rich displays of green, blue, yellow, and cream-glazed borders and frames that decorate and define the facades of his midwestern bank buildings with delicate filigree of faience (Fig. 5). Frank Lloyd Wright was also to find terra cotta ideally suited to his organic philosophy, suggesting that its plasticity was ". . . in the hands of the architect what wax was in the hands of the sculptor"(20).

Meanwhile, in The Netherlands during the 1920s, another important turning point in the evolution of modern architecture occurred. Suddenly, primary colors on buildings reappeared, but this time as part of a de Stijl reexamination of their basic spatial effects and on a Dutch brand of architecture that was also stripped of ornamentation.

While Piet Mondrian attempted to tame pure colors on canvas by containing them in grid plan abstractions reminiscent of the crisscrossing of Dutch dykes, Gerrit Reitveld projected them as a means of spatial control onto the internal and external planes of his architecture. Through a use of red, blue, and yellow against white, he fixed the elevation modulations of the Schröder House in space (Fig. 6). When necessary, he articulated the visual pushing and pulling qualities of color to induce illusions of increased depth.

During the birth pangs of the modern movement, there had been philosophical clashes between another de Stijl proponent, Theo van Doesburg, and the Swiss architect, Le Corbusier. Despite their differences, both had employed pulsating colors in their designs—the former carrying them into interiors as had art nouveau designers, such as Victor Horta, before him, but this time to define the hard edges of a modernist geometry rather than as a sensuous adjunct to the curve. Theo van Doesburg believed (21): "Colored surfaces form an organic part of the new architecture as an element which directly expresses its own space-time relationships. Without color, these relationships are not living realities; they are not visible." Also, and as if to appeal to those functionalists who had scoured ornament and bleached color from their buildings, he wrote (22):

"The new architecture is against decoration. Color (and whoever distrusts color must realize it!) is not ornament or decoration, but an organic element of architectural expression."

In contrast to a popular misconception proliferated by an achromatic publication of his work, Le Corbusier loved the powerful hum of color, especially as stabs of bright paintwork against the white concrete of his facades (Fig. 7). In his large-scale housing projects, such as Unité d'Habitation in Marseilles, he employed primary color to emphasize the indented rhythms of external walls, employing paint to separate inside from outside in the transitional space of balconies and deep recesses. Additionally, the relationship between Le Corbusier's interior and exterior color use is fascinating because, by contrast to the sheer white and primary hues of facades, his interior schemes became earth, muted with umbers, burnt siennas, and green-grays reflecting those of his Purist paintings; he created these in collaboration with his artist and colorist colleague, Henri Ozenfant.

For Le Corbusier, color was a means of spatially modifying the existence of architectural form. It could be used at the end of the design process to cause ". . . a lightening of the volume and enlarging [of] the surfaces"(23). In 1927, he wrote (24):

This polychromy is absolutely new, it is essentially rational. To the architectural composition, it adds elements of extreme physiological power. By harmoniously arranging the physiological sensations of volume, surfaces, surroundings, and colors, it is possible to achieve an intense lyricism.

Another great color pioneer and practitioner was the German architect Bruno Taut. In 1919, he, together with several militant architects of the time, such as Peter Behrens and Hans Poelzig, had endorsed the text of "A Call for Color in Building" published in *Die Bauwelt* that sought to reinstate a liberated, colorful townscape after the terrors of World War I (25). Later, in the twenties, Taut continued to battle for color while a councilor for Magdeburg, and later when he built his low cost housing projects in Berlin. One of them, the Onkel Tom Hütte estate (recently restored to its original facade colors of Pompeii reds, yellows, and lilacs with their distinctive, tricolored window frames), used color combinations based on a complex musical harmony. As part of his well-publicized battle against drab streets, Taut had commented that in an old Magdeburg street that was half-painted and half left gray, it was possible on a rainy day to see how the painted section possessed a "plastic and truly material life," while the gray part seemed a "disturbing abstract ghost"(26).

Taut's approach to architectural color was, essentially, uncomplicated. To Taut, color simply represented a postwar *joie de vivre*. In 1925, he wrote (27):

Color, with its appealing qualities of freshness, gaiety, of liberty, is the best thing we have in the current mess. . . . As soon as you clear away the superfluous junk and start with a clean slate, color clearly shows itself to be the only natural way of defining space. . . .

By contrast to the more psychologically aware and scientifically controlled color schemes of the modernists, remnants of a more revivalist and decorative color can be found on art deco shrines, ie, modern temples, such as those by Wallis, Gilbert & Partners that, designed for an outer London of the late twenties and early thirties, were invested with a fusion of Egyptian and American Indian inspired decoration, and dedicated to the glory of Firestone tires and Hoover vacuum cleaners (Fig. 8). Also dotted around London were the movie theaters of Oscar Deutsch. His Odeans and Gaumonts were temples to Hollywood, and each was given an antiquarian character derived from ancient Egypt, Greece, and China.

Influenced by the new ideas that had crossed the Atlantic from France in the mid-twenties, it was Hollywood movies that were to glamorize the art deco style and cause glitter to invade the home. Gold, silver, bronze, steel, and chrome were combined with marble and glass to provide, for the rich, a new gloss. However, the development of a new and nonyellowing paint made possible with titanium dioxide had, by the thirties, replaced the silver and black decor of the twenties.

In the U.S. during the thirties and forties, Frank Lloyd Wright was designing his low cost Usonian houses. Based on his principles of an organic and natural architecture, their appearance as an integrated part of the landscape was in complete contrast to an architecture as center of attention, as practiced by his contemporaries. They were built from a careful orchestration of the polychromy of natural materials—the only unnatural color being a red coloring introduced to the concrete mix of his polished concrete floors to coordinate with the red of exposed brick and cypress. When Wright used synthetic colors, they occurred as an integral element of a building material, such as in his designs for stained glass windows and his widespread use of pigmented concrete. Wright had said that he had begun to ". . . see brick as brick. I learned to see concrete or glass or metal each for itself. . ."(28). However, an exception to his organic philosophy and its terrain-tinted architecture almost appeared with his intention for a gilded house at Falling Water, a plan scotched by a client who insisted upon its existing parchment-pigmented concrete (Fig. 9). Wright also cherished a particular red he named Cherokee red; it is found at Taliesin and also on several of his buildings in the form of a single square of glazed tile functioning as his architectural signature.

1950–1980

During the post-World War II years of austerity, slabs of blue, maroon, turquoise, and green-gray appeared to occasionally soften the impact of a Bauhaus-spawned curtain wall architecture used to rebuild war-torn cities. This caused the spread of a neutral raw concrete, metallic, and glass urban environment whose universality, brutalism, and scale began to erode the traditional colors and materials of the city. However, the postwar period brought technological advances, the coloring of fabrics and finishes, and, via cheaper color printing techniques, a growing fascination for interior design fueled by a do-it-youself craze. In the early fifties, a two-tone coloration became popular for products and clothes; interiors would often incorporate two patterned wallpapers in the same room, or be completely off-white with one wall painted in a strong accent color. This emphasis on an eye-catching impact was a phenomenon simultaneous with events in U.S. industry. Here, the founding of the Institute for Motivational Research and the Color Research Institute of America had initiated the examination of the potential of color in psychological marketing techniques based on the pioneer research into the effects of color at the beginning of the century. Consequently, the role of the color consultant was born; it was epitomized in the work of Faber Birren and his application of color research findings to commerce, industry, and architectural design.

However, a lull before the oncoming storm of color is represented by the late fifties. This was a period influenced predominantly by Scandinavian designers, such as Alvar Aalto who, together with the development of polyurethane sealants, brought for a time the elegance and simplicity of plywood to interiors and exteriors accompanied by clearer warm pinks, reds, oranges, and neutrals, which had replaced the patterned fussiness that had heralded the beginning of the decade.

The dawn of the Swinging Sixties was to witness yet another explosion of bright, spectral hues into the urban setting. This was an upsurge reminiscent of Hittorff's revival of polychromy in the 1830s that, while also recycling Taut's liberation of color from the gray-greens of militarism in the 1920s, was a reaction to a wartime khaki and camouflage, and a rejection of an inherited, urban drabness. It was triggered by a hallucinogenic-inspired, psychedelic American art and a pop art culture, with its blurred edges between painting and sculpture, that had emerged simultaneously in New York and Los Angeles. In drawing its images from mass culture, its departure from formal channels of art—dislodged by the happenings of the fifties—heralded the return of primary colors, this time in the form of supergraphics and megamurals that appeared in the street to take their place alongside billboards and traffic signs. The increasing size of pop art objects helped to accelerate the move away from the studio–gallery situation; this was also influenced by a growing concern by artists who realized a pressing need to enhance the gray urban environment.

This resurgence of wall painting derived from an age-old tradition. The use of architecture as a support on which to hang a narrative or an abstract paintwork did not originate in New York or Los Angeles or even with the Mexican protest murals of Rivera, Orozco, and Siquerieros in the 1920s; it is a practice as ancient as building itself. In central Europe, the art has survived from the Middle Ages, with superb examples to be found in towns near the German-Austrian border like Mittlewald and Oberammergau, on the painted churches of northern Romania, and in many Italian cities.

Encouraged by the favorable reactions from both public and psychologists alike, and fired by the publication of Charles Moore's vibrant supergraphics inside Sea Ranch and by Minoru Takeyama's towering architectural answer to wall painting in Tokyo, architects gradually turned to a peacock architecture. By the seventies, designers had a whole new range of building materials to experiment with and many of them, such as anodized and plastic-coated metals, glass-reinforced plastics and concrete, plasticized stucco, and an extended palette of pigments for concrete, demanded a color decision for their formulation. Architects, now fully aware of Albers's teachings, and knowledgeable of the researched relationship between color and space and between pigment and illumination, began deploying simple but brilliant arrangements of color in the built milieu.

At the center of this new awareness of color was the universally adopted and sophisticated system of color notation devised in 1905 by Albert H. Munsell (29). Munsell had given Sir Isaac Newton's color circle (invented in 1660) a finer calibration to accommodate a more sophisticated spectrum of visible hues. In charting the world of color, a world first mapped in different ways by, among others, Philipp Otto Runge (1810), M. Eugéne Chevreul (1839), and Wilhelm Ostwald (1915), Munsell arranged the three attributes of color (hue, value, and chroma) into scales of equal visual steps. The scales are used as dimensions or parameters for the accurate analysis or description of color under standard viewing conditions. However, the uniqueness of Munsell's system is expressed in the irregular shape of his conceptual color solid; its bulging sides account for the increased chromatic strength of reds and yellows in comparison to that of blues and greens.

The early seventies also gave rise to an awareness of another color system, based on the theories of Ewald Hering (1878) and on Sven Hesselgren's color atlas (1952), that was developed in Stockholm by Anders Hård as director of the Swedish Color Center Foundation. Hård's work resulted in the refinement of the Natural Color System (NCS), a system that is different from Munsell's system because, rather than describe color as a physical stimulus, it measures its perceived experience in the eye. This innovation is important because it accounts both for individual colors as seen and also how they appear when viewed in the context of different colors. The ability of the NCS to monitor the changing impression of color due to interaction and also to distance has led to its adoption as a research tool by various institutions, including the University of Göteborg, where the effects of color on interior and exterior built space are studied.

Much of the architectural color display of the early seventies performed acts of aggression, ie, blasts of color against a lingering postwar austerity. For instance, the blue, yellow, and pink fantasy of Ludwig Leo's University and Engineering Building in West Berlin, Aldo van Eyck's scientific rainbow colors on his Mother's House in Amsterdam, Stanley Tigerman's heraldic diagramming of the Illinois Regional Library for the Blind and Physically Handicapped, and, especially, Richard Rogers and Renzo Piano's primary-color Pompidou Center in Paris each landmarked a revolution of color, recalling that of Owen Jones in 1851 (Fig. 10). Each had also represented a synthesis between a high style and a celebration of an advanced technology known as high tech. Now color had returned to diagram with paint and self-colored materials a dismembering of form in which the hitherto private parts of buildings were now multicolored and disgorged into the street. This new revolution of an industrial color had also restored a degree of color symbolism, spawning Gunnar Birkerts's blazing red fire station in America, the aqua blue Thames Water Research Station in Slough, England, and the nearby butter-colored margarine warehouse.

Alongside the color coding of a high tech architecture, there were also other experiments that, in the manner of Le Corbusier and Taut, simply applied paint to the stucco of both small and large buildings. For instance, in Mexico, Luís Barragán was demonstrating his masterful handling of pinks, purples, ochers, and red oxides on the external planes of his ranches to create colorful outdoor rooms, thus singlehandedly illustrating the thrilling potential of a truly polychromatic modern movement architecture. In Spain, headed by Ricardo Bofill, the Taller de Arquitectura had painted large-scale apartment buildings with bright reds, blues, purples, and greens. Both Barragán and Bofill had discussed their love of paint in terms of a necessary skin that, when applied, allowed their respective forms to breathe, thereby investing their buildings with life (30).

Another kind of colored skin is found on the walls of the five inner courtyards of Waldren Seven, a large housing project in Barcelona. Here, Ricardo Bofill had revived Moorish tradition in the patterns of blue tiles that clad and psychologically cool each of the cathedral-like spaces. This use of a ceramic immediately reminds one of his countryman, Antonio Gaudi, who sheathed the art nouveau towers atop his Sagrada Familia cathedral in Barcelona with a scintillating potsherd mosaic, a technique involving fragments of glass, porcelain, and china, which he also used to decorate his serpentine seating in Guell Park situated in the same city. Glass and ceramics have performed as a kind of architectural jewelry throughout history, with obvious roots in the jackdawlike assembly of glittering fragments in the art of mosaic. More modern examples include the cobs of green-blue glass dotted about the external stonework of Bavanger House in Norman, Oklahoma, and the breathtaking mosaic mural by J. O'Gorman that completely envelops the windowless library building in Mexico's Ciudad Universitaria.

The seventies were also to witness the emergence of a new kind of environmental designer, the colorist, who specialized in identifying the traditional patterns of color in the built landscape. In France, colorist Jean Philippe Lenclos had begun to classify systematically the regional palettes of his native country, a vast project that, before its publication in the mid-eighties, was to have a major impact on the site-related coloration of new towns both in France and Japan (Fig. 11). Simultaneously in Italy, Giovanni Brino had begun to restore the faded and forgotten facade colors of Turin. Guided by the discovery of the city's 1850 color archives, he led a massive restoration program that was to spread to many other urban centers in the Piedmont region (Fig. 12). This new interest in the preservation of a local color that signaled a sense of place had already been exemplified in the success of the face-lifted Victorian "Painted Ladies" in San Francisco (inspired by a Haight-Ashbury hippie house painting in the sixties), and the award-winning restoration of the medieval quarter of Höchst in Darmstadt, West Germany by Gerhard Schweizer.

1980s

By the eighties, the fascination with primary colors faded into a preoccupation with pastels, a chromatic shift that became associated with a focus on yet another neoclassical revival. In rebelling against the stylistic constraints of international modernism, a so-called postmodernism moved toward an eclectic and indiscriminate classicism that celebrated ornament, historical allusions, and color. Running parallel with this shift of interest was the Milan-based design group, Memphis, led by Ettore Sottsass. He, together with another Milanese, Andreas Branzi, had begun to seriously pursue the relationship between a brazen color and a questioning form in their highly influential designs for interiors and furniture. However, its leading practitioners, Robert A. M. Stern, Charles Moore, Stanley Tigerman, Michael Graves, and the Italian Paolo Portoghesi, began to handle architectural color to make obvious and sometimes overt references to nature and to the past. In so doing, their widely published works not only attracted the disapproval of old guard and achromatic modernists but also influenced a younger and international generation of architects, including Mario Botta, Mark Mack, Thomas Gordon Smith, and the Miami-based design group, Architectonica.

One of Charles Moore's first excursions into a painted external architecture occurred near Santa Monica when he introduced approximately 17 subtle variations of an earthy range of ochers, oranges, reds, and mauves to the stucco of the Burns House. His color system, while breaking rules of formal integrity by changing hues at the intersection of vertical planes, appears to echo Barragán's approach but uses a muted Mexican palette. This is not surprising, as Moore's colors borrow from a Californian tradition of Spanish mission colors. It is also a color range that he was to later heighten to diagram the vertical components of his celebrated outdoor stage set, the Piazza d'Italia in New Orleans. Here, Moore uses rich variations of red and yellow ochers against backgrounds and recessed planes of off-white to contrast columns of stainless steel and marble and the modulations of an achromatic floor-scape (Fig. 13).

Throughout history, color has been used to instinctively modify the appearance of size, shape, and form. During the Renaissance, it was not uncommon to use horizontal bands of red, orange, and deep yellow to give an illusion of added girth to buildings; it is also a device common in the work of Botta, Graves, and Mack. The use of stripes is also thematic in buildings by Paolo Portoghesi who, with Vittorio Gigliotti, designed the Casa Papanice in Rome. The architects explain that their colors for this private residence carry on a dialectic with nature. Over a mostly white facade, glass mosaic stripes of green emerge vertically from the undergrowth and, together with an earth brown, travel skyward. These alternate with blue stripes that descend from the heavens. All are mixed with ribbons of gold, bringing light to a color modulation set amidst the monotonous panorama of modern Rome. By

comparison, the horizontal color bands of their elementary school at Asti brace a white, prefabricated structure with green (grass) at the base, gold (light) at its middle, and blue (sky) under the eaves. Bound up in the postmodernist symbolism of Portoghesi and Gigliotti, and also in the early work of Michael Graves, is a movement toward natural color.

The earlier colored buildings of Michael Graves appear to make references to the historically recycled hues of the ancients. For example, his space frame delineations of blue, yellow, and red against the white background of his addition to the Benacerraf House not only reflect the basic colors of the Parthenon, but also extend a distinct genealogy of color practiced by Owen Jones, Gerrit Reitveld, and Le Corbusier. However, the later color harmonies of both his interior designs, such as those for the Sunar showrooms, and the much-publicized facades of his later buildings, become paler and more subtle, developing his distinctive range of blue-greens, viridians, creams, and browns, that have also become the hallmarks of postmodernist polychromy. These he used to elaborate his huge and controversial Public Office Building in Portland, Oreg., a monumental project that serves to reinstate architectural color on a scale not witnessed since ancient times.

Graves's philosophy of color is fascinating because, in shunning the purists' dislike of a painted cosmetic, he extols its power to modify the physical appearance of building materials. He suggests that "No matter how one might know color to be an application to a surface, we see color first as representational"(31). In other words, if a concrete wall or gypsum board is painted terra cotta in order to allude to brick, the first perceptual reaction to that surface is of brick. The symbolic function of a skin of paint to transform magically the impression of building materials forms the basis of a postmodernist color language. In this manner, conversations between a building and its history are introduced—a colored paintwork playing an historical game by nudging the memory into recalling a mixture of past images and creating echoes of materials with classical roots. This particular color function reflects that of a traditional Italian trompe l'oeil decoration where paint was applied as a substitute for expensive building materials and a lavish exterior decoration.

Graves's representational use of color on the Portland Office Building reappears on subsequent projects and buildings, another major color statement finding expression on the Humana Building in Louisville, Ky. (Fig. 14). Graves's use of color also represents one aspect of an architectural tradition that has occupied designers throughout the history of building. This is the deliberate and symbolic placement of a man-made object in the landscape. Conversely, a second tradition concerns the careful integration of a built form that is more akin to the earth, ie, either constructed from the same materials on which it stands or colormatched to blend in to the surrounding landscape. The first approach is aggressive, the second, passive; compare, for example, a Le Corbusier white house or a Richard Meier museum in a green field with a Frank Lloyd Wright house of the same color as the earth, or in ancient times man living in a cave at the same time as he built temples. Both traditions represent a fundamental color decision—

a decision that will continue to preoccupy those designers who do not practice architecture as a colorless science.

CONCLUSION

This review of architectural color began by experiencing the interior of the Crystal Palace through the eyes and words of a nineteenth-century journalist from the *Illustrated London News;* it will be concluded with the observation of the man who was responsible for its painted decoration, Owen Jones. Jones had always maintained a belief that it was only the cultural high points of art that were hallmarked by the presence of the unsullied primary colors, decadent periods being synonymous with a descent into the secondary and tertiary hues. If Jones's observation is applied to the historical evolution of architectural polychromy, it can be seen that a spectral display of hues did, indeed, seem to accompany the dawn of each new philosophy of environmental design, and that its dilution preceded a decline into heavier and darker hues. Furthermore, a reduced saturation appears throughout history to attend the demise of aspirations, empires, and styles. In seemingly reinstating the colors of antiquity, each high point also coincided with the need for designers to apparently rediscover the palette of architectural polychromy. Each color cycle began with a renewed investigation of the symbolic and spatial significance of saturated chroma and, as the cycle progressed, there followed an exploration of the effects of their admixture before an ensuing experimentation of desaturation by the effect of white and that of black.

However, as each successive revolution of color completes its cycle, its dynamic, expressed in the buildings down through the ages by those who have orchestrated a conscious polychromy, seems to reaffirm man's belief that color is a sign of life.

BIBLIOGRAPHY

1. *Illustrated London News,* (May 17, 1851), pp. 424–425.
2. O. Jones, *Grammar of Ornament,* Bernard Quaritch, London, 1856.
3. C. L. Woolley, *Ur of the Chaldees: A Record of Seven Years of Excavation,* Faber, London, p. 122.
4. J. Fergusson, *History of Architecture in All Countries, From the Earliest Times to the Present Day,* John Murray, London, 1865, p. 140.
5. G. Rawlinson, *The Five Great Monarchies of the Eastern World,* John Murray, London, 1862, p. 467.
6. *Ibid.,* p. 448.
7. F. Birren, *The Story of Color,* The Crimson Press, Westport, Conn., 1941, p. 29.
8. Ref. 4, pp. 107–108.
9. C. W. Ceram, *Gods, Graves, and Scholars,* Alfred A. Knopf, New York, 1952.
10. Ref. 7, p. 120.
11. Pliny, *Natural History,* Henry G. Bohn, London, 1857.
12. J. Ward, *Colour Decoration of Architecture,* Chapman and Hall, Ltd., London, 1913, pp. 74–75.
13. C. Stewart, *Gothic Architecture,* Longmans, London, 1961, p. 65.
14. L. Mumford, "Agents of Mechanization and the Eotechnic Phase," in S. Friedman and J. B. Juhasz, *Environments: Notes and Selections on Objects, Spaces, and Behavior,* Brooks/Cole Publishing Company, Monterey, Calif., 1974, pp. 184–191.
15. J. I. Hitorff, *Architecture Antique de la Sicile,* Paris, 1827–1830.
16. L. Sullivan, *Kindergarten Chats,* George Wittenborn, Inc., New York, 1947, p. 187.
17. "An Interview with Mr. Charles F. Annesley Voysey, Architect and Designer," *The Studio,* Vol. 1, London, 1893, pp. 321–327.
18. J. Itten, *The Elements of Color,* Van Nostrand Reinhold, New York, 1970.
19. J. Albers, *Interaction of Color,* Yale University Press, New Haven, Conn., 1976.
20. D. Rastorfer, "Terra Cotta: Past to Present," *Architectural Record,* 110–111 (Jan. 1987).
21. T. van Doesburg, "Verso un'Architettura Plastica," *De Stijl* **6/7,** 78–83 (1924).
22. *Ibid.*
23. Le Corbusier, "Pessac," *l'Architecture Vivante,* 30 (Autumn–Winter 1927).
24. *Ibid.,* p. 30.
25. B. Taut, "A Call for Color in Building," *Die Bauwelt* (Sept. 18, 1919).
26. P. Portoghesi, "Color in Town," *Domus* (602), 20–21 (Jan. 1980).
27. B. Taut, "Zur Farbenfrage," *Das Schlesische Heim,* 55 (1925).
28. H. Varley, ed., *Color,* The Knapp Press, Los Angeles, 1980, p. 123.
29. A. H. Munsell, *A Color Notation,* Ellis, Buston, 1905.
30. T. Porter, *Colour Outside,* The Architectural Press Ltd., London, 1982, p. 67.
31. *Ibid.,* p. 72.

General References

E. Ambasz, *The Architecture of Luís Barragán,* The Museum of Modern Art, New York, 1976.
F. Birren, *Color for Interiors,* The Whitney Library of Design, New York, 1963.
F. Birren, *Color Psychology and Color Therapy,* McGraw-Hill Inc., New York, 1950.
F. Birren, *Light, Color & Environment,* Van Nostrand Reinhold Co., Inc., New York, 1969, pp. 103–123.
G. Brino and F. Rosso, *Colore e Città—Il Piano del Colore di Torino 1800–1850,* Idea Books, Milan, 1980, pp. 11–15.
I. Bristow, "Ready-Mixed Paint in the 18th Century," *Archit. Rev.* (963), 246–248 (Apr. 1977).
R. Darl, "Terra Cotta: Past to Present," *Archit. Rec.* (Jan. 1987).
S. Goodman, *Color,* Department of Architecture thesis, Oxford Polytechnic, 1973.
N. Miller and co-workers, "Color in Architecture," *AIA J.,* 40–55 (Oct. 1978).
T. Porter and B. Mikellides, *Color for Architecture,* Van Nostrand Reinhold Co., Inc., New York, 1976.
T. Porter, *Architectural Color,* The Whitney Library of Design, New York, 1982.
T. Porter, *How Architects Visualize,* Van Nostrand Reinhold Co., Inc., New York, 1979, pp. 1–14.
J. Ruskin, *The Seven Lamps of Architecture,* George Allen, London, 1906.

D. Van Zanten, *The Architectural Polychromy of the 1830's,* Garland Publishing, Inc., New York, 1977, pp. 6–65.

See also PAINTS AND COATINGS.

TOM PORTER
Cornfield
Sunningwell, United Kingdom

The author acknowledges a special debt to Faber Birren who graciously extended his help and expert guidance throughout the preparation of this material. The author would also like to thank Nancy Lambert, the librarian of Yale University's Art and Architecture Library and the Faber Birren Collection of books, for her invaluable assistance.

COMMUNICATIONS IN ARCHITECTURE

COMMUNICATIONS: THE ARCHITECT'S JOB

Buildings are often interpreted as communications media, as implicit footprints of cultural values and explicit billboards of symbol and image. But communications are basic, not just to what architecture is, but also to what architects do, starting with getting the job.

Management does not merely support a firm's design goals, but effectively delimits them and probably defines them (1). One of the most important goals of architectural management is to keep convincing the client—at first via marketing communications and a well-cultivated reputation for design excellence, later through effective communication of the design team's ideas—to support the design proposal. Often the ability to do this is the difference between good and bad design.

Architecture and its allied professions have pioneered the relatively new field of professional services promotion. The broadly named Society for Marketing Professional Services (SMPS) is almost wholly made up of design professionals. The dramatic growth of organized marketing since the early 1970s has made marketing communications the most visible category of architectual communications, so that at times the two ideas seem virtually synonymous.

Beyond getting and keeping the job, the architect's communications center on the proposals, meetings, messages, and documents needed to get a project designed and built. In using these tools, architects and staff function as researchers, authors, editors, illustrators, and publishers, and often as producer-directors and actors as well. Much of this effort is conventionalized and not considered creative, but it is really much more than administrative. Thoughtful observers acknowledge that the creative process is rarely confined to the tip of a designer's soft pencil, but more often grows out of a dialogue among many people and forces, which the successful architect understands and orchestrates.

Architecture is a public art, and this presents the profession with a demanding communicative front. Allowing people to imagine and discuss inhabiting objects and spaces where nothing exists is an extraordinary task, but one that architects take on with remarkable (and sometimes unjustified) confidence. The audience can range from an individual homeowner to an entire city (via a televised hearing or design charrette, for example). In between is a confusing array of building committees, review boards, citizens' groups, and boards of directors, each making its own communications demands.

At the same time, architecture's dialogue with both general and specialized publics goes beyond individual projects to encounter a larger world of ideas. Architectural education, theory, and practice are linked to such fields as art and intellectual history, the social sciences, economics, urban politics, and the fine arts, as well as mathematics, the applied sciences, and hundreds of technical disciplines, industries, and crafts. Compared with other professionals, architects regularly step out of their roles as technicians to do more than "talk shop."

This minding of others' business becomes a survival skill when it comes to architecture's position within the real estate and construction industries. Despite many good relationships between architects and owners, contractors, suppliers, and brokers, the country's largest industry has become a guarded, adversarial game. "Fragmented" is a favorite but understated description, both of the business and its way of communicating. The U.S.'s roughly 60,000 practicing architects constitute a minority party in this uncommunal community. Simply to be heard, never mind to fulfill some professional, political, or business agenda, requires formidable communications skills.

The architect's leadership of the construction industry is perennially found to be eroding. In fact, that role has never been one to be taken for granted. In the United States at least, it has always depended on allies and consensus-building. More than their counterparts in law or medicine, architects rely on the cooperation of people well outside their own professional sphere in order to accomplish anything, whether the goal is to complete a single building on time, cause a city to adopt enlightened urban design standards, or get a new architect–engineer procurement bill through Congress. In place of absolute, legislated authority (and the weight of alternatives such as jail or death), architects must rely on persuasiveness, the power of clearly presented ideas, and an understanding of the principle of leverage.

Design is the distinctive activity of architecture, but communications, in the broadest sense, power and sustain the profession. On a mundane level as well, architects spend most of their working hours documenting, writing, and talking. To a perhaps unacknowledged extent, communicating is really "what architects do."

ARCHITECTS AS COMMUNICATORS

It is a common perception among those who claim to know the profession that architects are poor communicators. The problem is said to be that architecture is a visual medium and that most architects are therefore more or less nonverbal.

As we have already seen, the myth of the uncommunicative architect is illogical at best. From the most basic marketing and selling to specifications and contracts to punch lists and publicity, architects must use words at least competently just to survive. Mies van der Rohe's "Don't talk, build" expresses the way many practitioners, frustrated by the constant need to explain, feel at times. But on closer scrutiny, the designer who insists that "the work must speak for itself" regularly proves to be an effective one-on-one salesman, a forceful writer, an inspired community organizer, or a lion of the lecture platform.

The words-and-graphics presentations that business schools praise for being highly memorable derive as much from architects' presentations as from advertising or computer software. Long before electronic, or even electric, media, students at the Ecole des Beaux Arts were learning to make fast, effective visual presentations and to think on their feet in defending them before a jury. This audio-visual pioneering derived in part from theater (architects have long experimented with what we now call production design). With the advent of CADD and reasonably priced video, architects have begun to leave homemade slide shows to reassert their leadership in audio-visual technique.

Meanwhile, the profession's journals consistently win publishing awards. Compared with most professional and trade groups, the American Institute of Architects and its components, along with such enabling groups as the Boston Foundation for Architecture, do a creditable job of public outreach. Despite mixed reviews for such examples as Robert A. M. Stern's "Pride of Place," architecture seems to be coping about as well as the other traditional arts with the confines of television.

When architects themselves feel inept at writing, it may be because their predecessors have set high standards. As Thomas Hines has shown, U.S. architects from Jefferson to Sullivan and Wright to Charles Moore claim an impressive literary tradition. Their writings go beyond communications as defined here, that is, beyond messages primarily instrumental to building a building or promoting a practice, to "explicate their own and their fellows' work [and] to comment philosophically on the larger meaning of architecture and its relation to society"(2).

In the *New York Times Book Review*, Hines confesses that in this profession the line between literature and communications is not hard and fast (2):

> The complex process of "getting the job" has been more competitive [for architects than] for lawyers and doctors and considerably more market-oriented than for most other artists. One dominant motive, then, for the architect's frequent resort to words has been the ingrained, though partly unconscious, need for subtle self-promotion. For this reason architectural self-analysis has often seemed suspect.

Books by architects often become part of a firm's marketing communications materials. Conversely, much practice-oriented material and architectural journalism eventually appears in book form. Although it is arbitrary to exile books from a discussion of communications in architecture, communications implies contemporaneousness and the possibility of two-way exchange; according to that distinc-

tion, bound material, and anything designed for a long shelf life, has been consigned to another article (*see* LITERATURE OF ARCHITECTURE).

COMMUNICATIONS, MARKETING COMMUNICATIONS, AND PUBLIC RELATIONS

Communications can be defined as the art and science of exchanging information and ideas. But the word is problematic because of its changing and multiple meanings. The general press has used the plural noun interchangeably as shorthand for telecommunications business or technology, as a catchall for message-sending by any means, and as a euphemism for public relations.

In consumer goods marketing, marketing communications describes a large category that includes advertising and sales promotion (giveaways, for instance) as well as public relations. The public relations component here is usually minor, although increasingly it has been given the dominant marketing role.

In the professional services world, however, almost all planned communications (including advertising, which usually conforms to the notion of institutional advertising as done by public relations firms) are some form of public relations. Public relations is the planned, continuing use of communications tools to promote a desired understanding between a client and its audiences or public. Compared to advertising, it is much broader in scope, generally using a mix of tools other than paid time and space, and is relatively inexpensive; it offers less control of the message, but, generally, more believability. In a reverse of the consumer situation, marketing communications for professional services firms is a subcategory of public relations. It describes, primarily, materials and messages aimed at prospective clients or client groups.

The difference between marketing and selling deserves mention here. Technically, "marketing communications" means the process of identifying prospective clients and establishing qualifications and interest. When the emphasis shifts to personal, usually face-to-face, selling, "sales communications" takes over to describe the techniques and tools the architect uses to get a particular job. The distinction is more than pedantic: messages that confuse marketing and selling (such as a cold call that suddenly turns into a pitch for a job interview) often fail. But marketing, like the older euphemism "business development," is inevitably stretched to cover selling as well.

Again, since the 1970s, architects' interest in marketing has often made marketing communications seem to be pretty much the whole of communications. This is the impression given by "The Architect's Communications," a section of the American Institute of Architects (AIA) *Architect's Handbook of Professional Practice* by Stephen A. Kliment (3).

Kliment defines three communications categories. Project communications (construction documents plus conversations and correspondence among the project team, building officials, lenders, etc) and internal communications (in-house information also shared with out-of-house lawyers, accountants, and insurers) he regards as essentially parts of normal office practice, covered elsewhere in the Handbook (although not with Kliment's perspective on communications technique, unfortunately). "The Architect's Communications," it turns out, is really about the third category, marketing communications.

Kliment gives a lucid review of the three communications program essentials:

1. *Message.* This ought to derive from the firm's stated goals and business plan; it can be basic ("we're here"), but ultimately should develop a unique marketing proposition.
2. *Target/Audience.* Usually, the firm's marketing plan sets priorities among client groups. There may be many secondary audiences (for instance, the local AIA chapter as a source of referrals), including some not directly linked to marketing.
3. *Tools/Media.* The main classes are print, audiovisual, and speech; each has its pluses and minuses for use with a particular audience.

The article then suggests criteria for selecting media to reach various audiences and provides a good critical checklist of possible marketing communications tools:

- Proposals.
- Brochures (and the option of no brochure).
- News releases.
- Advertisements.
- Correspondence.
- Direct mail.
- Newsletters.
- Award submissions.
- Clients' interviews.
- Seminars.
- Speaking forums.

A more extensive rundown of tools and techniques can be found in Ref. 4.

Kliment warns against equating tools and techniques with actual marketing or selling (3):

> . . . much misunderstanding [has] developed over the role of public relations in developing new architectural business. Only in rare cases can an architect rely entirely on public relations activities to bring in work. . . . activities that project the image of the firm, chiefly through press publicity and community involvement, all help create a receptive environment when the architect makes an inquiry or a solicitation.

Kliment's basic formula—define message, identify audiences, select and employ appropriate media—is essentially that of a classic public relations program. The need to pay attention to all three elements is often forgotten in the heat of planning a marketing communications project. Likewise, the formula can profitably be applied to Kliment's other two categories, project communications and internal communications.

Unfortunately, to some design professionals, public re-

lations suggests a useful but distasteful species of "hype" basically external to their practice. The AIA, ever wary of the wrong appearance, changed the name of its own public relations department to "Communications" in the mid-1980s. On the contrary, successful public relations practitioners seek to align their function with the daily life of the design firm in order to gain accurate information that, when clearly presented, will be credible and effective. Jones (4) quotes journalism professor John E. Marston on the essentially integral (and understated) quality of good public relations:

> Public relations communications is not debate. It is not advertising in which something *must* be said in order to convert someone because something must be sold. Public relations ideas do not have to be sold—they must be *bought*. Public relations is . . . the discovery and exposition of facts that are to the common interest of two or more parties . . . .
>
> Conclusions develop from facts and are best achieved when seen by the reader himself. Psychologists say that, especially for less well-informed readers, conclusions need to be stated, but this can be done modestly and in terms of mutual benefit. In the end it is not what the speaker wants, but what the hearer wants that will be remembered.

Choose "public relations" or "communications"; either should describe a firm's inclusive effort to establish and maintain good relationships with all of its publics, including neighborhood groups, friends of the firm, employees and professional peers, as well as prospective clients. Public relations may support marketing quite indirectly, through raising an architect's visibility in the community, for example. It can also be valuable in areas with no direct link to marketing—in attracting talent to the firm or in presenting the firm to investors or lenders. Ultimately, architectural firm communications is not a marketing function, but a management function.

PROPOSALS

Of all marketing communications tools, the proposal is probably the most essential and perhaps the most misused. From simple letters of interest, to government SF 254/255 forms, to elaborate, detailed responses, almost every project requires one. The proposal is neither a polished promotional message nor a practical, ad hoc piece of client correspondence—it is both, a shifting of gears between generalized qualifications for doing similar jobs and specific approaches to doing a particular one. Michael Hough in *A/E Marketing Journal* provides one of the best guides to proposal preparation (6), and several main points deserve repeating.

A proposal can be defined as a written document clients use to qualify a firm for further consideration. Although it contains information that may later become the basis for an architect–client contract, it is essentially a marketing message; "some puffery is allowed." In a good proposal, however, self-praise is crowded out by essential information for the client:

- A specific discussion of the client's needs that demonstrates the architect's understanding (and, implicitly, the architect's interest).
- A summary of special qualifications of people who will work on the project, showing how they fit their proposed roles.
- Clear evidence that the architect will fulfill the client's requirements; time, budget, and quality are endlessly repeated, but usually prime concerns.
- A list of past projects convincingly related to the client's current needs.
- A precise answer to each item in the client's request for proposal/qualifications.

Successful proposals often present more than a literal fulfillment of requirements, however. They are often the result of considerable research and decision-making as to whether to go after the job in the first place, and reflect more or less inside information. Marketers talk about "hot buttons," very specific needs not necessarily present in the request for proposal (RFP). They may be too urgent or embarrassing to state in a formal RFP (an impossibly short deadline, for example, or a building that has been exceptionally slow in leasing), or they may be as yet unknown to the client (the likelihood of opposition by a citizens' group). Uncovering hot buttons is an example of the holistic nature of architectural communications at work (see Architects in Context). In addition to talking to the prospective client and visiting the site, the architect may get information from current clients and other business contacts, from friendly consultants, and from regulatory agencies and city officials. Finally, in-house technical people not ordinarily involved in marketing can often spot hot-button needs.

Just as hot buttons stand for very specific problems, so the proposal's solutions must be equally pointed. It is not enough simply to say that the firm can perform within a very tight schedule (if completion date proves to be the client's main concern); there should be references, case histories, and staff resumes documenting the firm's on-time performance, a critical path chart for the proposed project, and similar evidence of the firm's scheduling ability throughout the proposal. "Each proposal must scream out what unique expertise your firm has to solve the client's problem. Anything not directly supporting this message must be left out"(5).

Everyone who has looked through a stack of architects' proposals or brochures has come across language more or less like this:

> Quality design has long been our hallmark, due to a long-standing commitment to an innovative, interdisciplinary team approach that maximizes the personal involvement of firm principals. We set clean-cut goals—then implement them through an overall action plan sensitive to your specific needs.
>
> Beyond the bottom line, our responsiveness to user needs creates people places . . . places that are also highly cost-effective, energy efficient, and uniquely creative, yet responsive to the overall environment as well as cost and time constraints—without sacrificing present or future flexibility. At the same time, a meaningful programming concept is ulti-

mately the product of user input, careful assessment of all primary forces, and the proactive establishment of a clear-cut overview within time and budget parameters.

Step Two: A well-defined task cycle. Implementation of a highly integrated organizational network ensures that team involvement at every stage is responsive to your specific needs.

The problem here is not so much self-praise or polysyllables (or even "boilerplate" language, some of which is necessary in all business communications) but, despite the insistent reference to client needs, the lack of any sense of the architects as real humans bringing special abilities to bear on real problems. A proposal that seems canned, with no connection to anything else the firm knows, does, or is, conveys precisely the opposite of enthusiasm. It is enthusiasm that, today, most consistently wins jobs and keeps clients.

ARCHITECTS IN CONTEXT

Architects' tendency to communicate surprisingly well, as well as their chronic need to communicate better, grow out of the profession's peculiarly holistic relationship to society. Doctors and lawyers are notoriously opaque communicators, except when they dip into their work for a popularizing best seller. Architects, although scarcely jargon free, by and large address their publics in much the same terms they use with other professionals. This is possible not just because building is relatively dumb, brick-on-brick stuff compared to medical technology or legal reasoning. It also happens because, although sickness and lawsuits are more urgent events in peoples' lives than leaky roofs, buildings involve more people, more constantly, in more ways.

A reporter, however, looking for the big news from the architectural industry, is likely to see political deals being made, money changing hands, and steel being topped out. The architect's message in all this, although hardly unimportant, rarely plays stage center. Newspapers persist in featuring building projects without mentioning the architect. Fair or not, the reporter's view reflects that of many of the architect's publics, including some clients. "Name" architects are sometimes thought to confer distinction on a project. More reliably, it is still the project that reflects credit on the architect.

Architects who understand this reality, and greet it with humility, know they are nonetheless strategically placed near the center of the building process, with leverage for getting their ideas across. In exchange for sacrificing some control of the message, for example, architects can often convince owners to support promotional events and publicity programs that benefit the design firm.

This realistic self-view, whether called holistic, client-centered, or contextual, is not automatic, however. The members of any specialized field can easily come to see themselves as a part of an already enlightened cadre that primarily (it believes) needs to get the word out, to educate the public rather than talk with and listen to its own publics.

Meanwhile, competitive pressure can fix a firm's gaze

on new business, with an accompanying tendency to equate communications with architect-to-prospective-client promotion. Again, it should be clear that massive popular promotion is not only too expensive for architects, but almost certainly too blunt for a product as complex and specialized as professional services.

To say that the architect's communications are about more than marketing does not deny that, for most firms, marketing goals provide the impetus for a communications program. However, experience suggests that professional services, unlike products, are best marketed in an interactive way that makes use of all of the formal and informal communications systems professionals already have in place.

In a holistic view, communications that support smooth project delivery, professional development, and interaction with other professionals can and should be integrated with messages that support finding prospective clients and selling services. The architect's project manager, for example, can routinely take a few minutes from the construction documents process to do statistical takeoffs, which can later be used in a case history or press release. The firm's research on the tax advantages of reusing an historic building can be published in a community newsletter or professional journal and then reprinted as a mailing to selected prospective clients (a technique called content-oriented public relations). A balanced program allows activities like these to support each other and creates opportunities for clients, friends of the firm, and other professionals to become supportive as well.

A recent SMPS roundtable of design firm marketers considered the relationship between marketing and delivery of design services, especially clients' perception of being deluged with material during the marketing courtship and then left relatively uninformed after the contract has been signed. They agreed that an integral public relations plan is the key to smoothing this transition. The architect, they concluded, should maintain a flow of information to and from the client, both before and after the sale. Ideally, this would mean the disappearance of marketing from the client's point of view. Getting and doing the job would be a seamless, well-communicated process, with the client's decision to hire an almost minor incident along the way (6).

If this concept seems idealized, at least it remains focused on getting a particular job. Martin McElroy argues for an even higher use of communications, and for higher marketing goals, in his 1985 essay "Marketing: Has It Benefited Architecture?"(7):

> The marketing era has been misnamed. Its focus has been sales or business development. . . . missionary work to expand demand for better buildings has not really occurred . . . We need to acquire and then articulate a better understanding of the value of the design in balance with other owner objectives. At this level, market research is not just finding out where the action is, but where it can [be] or ought to be, and developing client awareness of this potential.
>
> This kind of marketing is not done on our turf, but rather on the client's home ground . . . John A. Seller's article in the July–August 1984 *Harvard Business Review,* "Architecture

at Work," linked environmental planning to employee performance. That is marketing.

Whether architects are setting out to pioneer new markets, or simply trying to improve their chances of getting the next job, the truth remains that the total dialogue about architecture, including who will be hired, is much larger than the communications they themselves can initiate and control. Nonarchitects as well as architects carry on architectural communications. This is true not only of informed criticism by a newspaper writer, but also of a building owner's discussion of program or corporate image, a building user's reaction to lighting quality or closet size, or a prospective client's reply to a direct mail publication. The conversation does not have to be carried on by professionals, or even those well informed about building and design, to make a difference in the built result or in the architect's reputation, commissions, and profits.

All of this reminds architects to look again at a variety of answers to the question, "Why communicate?":

- To gain the attention of past, present, and future client groups.
- To clarify the architect's contractual role to avoid liability.
- To promote understanding and cooperation within the building project team.
- To build firm morale and promote professional development.
- To attract good employees, both graduates and experienced professionals.
- To gain visibility and rapport with architects and critics who serve on juries, give referrals, and recommend joint venture partners.
- To promote the interests of the firm and the profession with legislators, regulators, and other public officials.
- To reach decision makers in the private sector.
- To foster trust and understanding of the architect's role with citizens' groups and other users of buildings.
- To expand the public's thinking about who architects are and what they can do.

Architects need not believe their reputation as communications novices, but they should be realistic about their numerically small and sometimes less than newsworthy place in a big industry. They should look for ways to use their strategic position and understanding of the building process to gain leverage in publicity, promotion, and management. Perhaps most difficult, even when focusing on urgent marketing specifics, they should step back and see the larger context of planned and unplanned, business and nonbusiness messages that surround every architectural practice, and use that context, also, to maximum advantage.

ARCHITECTS AND MEDIA

For roughly 100 years, U.S. professional journals found a small audience for architectural theory and criticism, news, and features. Meanwhile, trade and business journals and local newspapers picked up occasional stories about architecture, although usually with some other news peg (historic preservation, real estate, emerging technology).

In the last two decades, however, this sedate picture has changed decisively. The general media—large circulation magazines and newspapers and occasionally television and radio—have taken an interest in architecture, more or less on its own terms, and given communications in architecture still another dimension.

The only recognized popular critics of architecture as recently as 1965 were in New York, Washington, D.C., and California. Today, nearly 40 newpapers publish informed articles about architecture and urban design. "Shelter" magazines that once took a cosmetic approach to home design now compete with professional journals for writers and photographers. Serious, or at least well-informed, articles about architectural personalities and major buildings now turn up everywhere, from airline in-flight magazines to *Vanity Fair* and *Parade*.

The reasons for architecture becoming "hot" in the late twentieth century are worth pondering in any discussion of the profession's communications. One reason has been an expanding market for culture in general. More art and art history students, more corporate sponsors and curators, and a surfeit of Postimpressionist blockbuster shows and Mozart festivals all seem to have led to the discovery of architecture as a largely unexploited corner of the art world. Concurrently, advertisers have sought affluent customers through a growing number of publications and shows devoted to quality. Architecture, despite being promoted by architects themselves as a tool of social change, has been pegged by Madison Avenue's unerring eye as the gilt-edged taste it generally is.

Architectural postmodernism brought newsworthy controversy plus a revival of fine drawing and architect-designed craft objects that allowed architecture to enter the art gallery. The real estate market mandated such stylish building types as beach houses, megaboutiques, and skyscrapers, and political conservatism fostered a climate where display of wealth was acceptable. Meanwhile, architecture offered more substantive help for America's continuing uncertainty about energy, the transformation of the workplace by computers and telecommunications, and the continuing atomization of cities and their regions.

One more factor, whether cause or effect, was the lifting in these years of architects' own ethical ban on advertising and firms' growing interest in organized publicity and promotion efforts. Growing competition from both within and outside the profession, plus a boom-and-bust construction economy, explained much of this activity. But the availability of new media and hardware, from videotape to laser printing, have undoubtedly also played a part, as has the supply of journalism and marketing graduates attracted to design firms.

The spread of stories about architects and architecture—and related stories about the other design professions, historic preservation, real estate, and construction—into a widening range of media has, in effect, opened up many choices for architects planning a communications program. As in design, having many choices is not always a blessing. A firm may find it difficult just to research all of the local, regional, and national media linked to the audiences it wishes to reach; continuing contact with the whole list may prove impossible. The challenge is to set criteria for selecting a manageable roster of media targets.

The basic measure remains that of any public relations action: Is this medium (or tool) the best one for conveying the firm's message (image, identity) to a particular audience? Does it really make the connection?

A complication here is that, unlike many readers of advertisements or public-relations-developed articles, the architect's audiences will seldom act directly on what they see. A captioned magazine photo of a new project may cause a city official to remember the firm's name or a prospective client to recall a link with an earlier project. Visibility and image are strengthened. But the reader will rarely lift the telephone and schedule an interview. That may result, however, from the architect's having mailed (or handed) a reprint to the target person, perhaps with a note that connects the article to some remembered interest or project.

What kind of publication yields a good reprint? (The question can also apply to TV programs and videotapes.) Often, it is a newspaper or magazine a public relations practitioner would pick in any case, a publication the audience normally reads and finds credible.

If the firm's goal is to design wicket factories, an article on wicket factory design, bylined by one of the principals, in *Wicket World* is probably a more valuable marketing tool than a cover story in *Architecture*. A news item in *Forbes* will convince a community group of the firm's national importance, but a story about a design charrette in the local weekly paper will say more about its interest in their neighborhood.

This trade, business, and local publicity, like participation in trade shows, business organizations, and local activities, is an extension of the architect's most basic communications task: keeping in touch with its own community of clients, friends, and employees. In general, the closer the medium is to this home, the better.

There are exceptions, however. Sometimes the third-party endorsement provided by publication carries more weight, especially with a more sophisticated audience, if it comes from a perceived expert such as a critic, a professional journal editor, or another respected architect. Recognition coupled with an award or a successful competition is even better. Existing clients may find these kinds of honors particularly useful for their own marketing and public relations purposes and may join with the architect in going after them. Professional allies and the firm's own employees are also a rewarding audience for this kind of exposure.

The architectural press, in short, although deprecated by publicists as "architects talking to themselves," has its uses. Reprints from the three major professional magazines are handsomely produced, for one thing.

A tight definition would limit the architectural press in the United States to three national professional journals (*Architectural Record, Progressive Architecture* (*P/A*), and

Architecture), plus several roughly similar regional journals and a group of "little magazines," most of them linked to architecture schools. Alternatively, architectural journalism can be anything written about architecture. For a more detailed listing of periodicals in architecture and related fields, see Table 1.

Taking a broad middle road, the first national conference on architectural journalism, "The Architectural Press:

Table 1. Periodicals in Architecture and Related Fields[a]

U.S. architecture publication with circulation

Architectural Record	76,500	*Blueprints* (National Building Musuem)	25,000
Architecture	39,706	*Frank Lloyd Wright Newsletter*	3,000
Progressive Architecture	66,825	*Historic Preservation*	140,000
		New Orleans Preservation	6,000
Arts & Architecture	32,000	*Preservation News*	140,000
Inland Architect	4,700	*Preservation Perspective*	3,000
Metropolis	8,400		
		Society of Architectural Historians News	4,500
A-E-C Automation News	4,200	*Society of Architectural Historians Journal*	4,500
AUA Newsletter			
Corporate Design	25,000	*Architectural Design*	
Design Cost & Data	25,000	*Home*	500,000
Faith and Form	37,500	*Land*	7,500
Guidelines Letter	3,000	*Landscape Architecture*	17,250
Journal of Architecture & Planning Research		*Places*	
Memo (AIA)	42,000	*Space & Society*	800
National Center for Barrier-free Environment Report	13,500		
Underline	1,500	*Architecture California*	8,329
ACSA News		*Architecture Minnesota*	7,000
Crit (AIA)	3,800	*Architecture New Jersey*	4,300
Design Book Review	30,000	*Iowa Architect*	5,600
Design Methods & Theories	7,000	*North Carolina Architect*	3,200
GSD News	1,000	*Texas Architect*	10,400
Journal of Architectural Education	10,500	*Wisconsin Architect*	1,700
	4,000		

Selected U.S. building and construction publications

Building Design & Construction			
Building Design Journal	72,669	*Construction Specifier*	17,400
Building Operating Management	50,000	*Construction Times*	14,500
Buildings	65,694	*Constructor* (AGC)	20,000
Commercial Renovation	34,659	*Contractor*	45,344
	40,255		

Selected U.S. housing and urban planning publications

American Planning Association Journal	13,000	*Planning*	24,000
Apartment Owner–Builder	58,000	*Shelterforce*	3,000
Neighborhood	4,000	*Urban Land*	7,000

Selected U.S. design and decoration publications

Contract	21,000	*Architectural Digest*	450,000
Designer	18,000	*Better Homes & Gardens*	8,000,000
Industrial Design	10,000	*House & Garden*	1,111,539
Interior Design	10,000	*House Beautiful*	800,000
Interiors	29,200	*Metropolitan Home*	750,000

Selected foreign architecture periodicals with circulation

A&U (Japan)	25,000	*Building* (UK)	25,000
Abitare (Italy)	120,000	*Building Design* (UK)	25,389
Architects Journal (UK)	20,000	*Casabella* (Italy)	48,000
Architectural Design (UK)	12,000	*Deutsche Bauzeitung* (Germany)	34,500
Architectural Journal (PRC)		*Domus* (Italy)	57,000
Architectural Review (UK)	17,000	*Japan Architect* (Japan)	15,000
Architecture d'Aujourd'hui (France)	26,054	*Lotus International* (Italy)	
Architektura (Poland)	15,000	*Mimar* (Islamic/Third World)	
Architektur und Wohnen (Germany)	220,000	*RIBA Journal* (UK)	29,000
Arkhitektura S.S.S.R. (USSR)	14,250	*Summa* (Argentina)	10,000
Arkitektur (Sweden)	6,016	*UIA International Architect* (UK)	6,000
Arquitectura (Spain)	8,200		

[a] Ref. 8.

Forming an Architectural Culture," held in 1985 at Virginia Tech's Washington/Alexandria Center, included the major and little journals plus newspaper and popular magazine critics, student editors, representives of technically oriented building industry publications (for example, *Building Design and Construction* and *Corporate Design*), and representatives from AIA headquarters, itself a major publisher and communications forum.

A 1986 symposium at Columbia University's Buell Center, "American Architecture Through American Eyes: Magazines and Journals, 1850–1986," followed with a scholarly review of professional and popular magazines. If these and later conferences did not succeed in setting precise limits to the U.S. architectural press, at least they began to give it some sense of its own power as an institution and raised persistent questions about its role as a maker of reputations and its ability to deal in serious criticism.

THE COMMUNICATIONS FUNCTION

In *The Architect's Handbook of Professional Practice*, Kliment has outlined alternative roles for the architect as a more or less full-time communicator within the architectural profession (9). Consistent with his definition of the architect's communications, he separates "Marketing Communications" from such other choices as "The Architect as Writer/Editor, Photographer, and Critic."

Marketing communications, he says (10),

> . . . consists of preparing such selling tools as brochures, proposals and slide presentations; developing productive relations with the professional, business and general press; exposing principals to audiences through public speaking; and organizing internal resource files. Marketing communications has become a special function in many medium to large firms, as well as a consulting specialty offered to firms too small to take on a full-time expert.

Although this is a typical job description, it again separates marketing communications abruptly from the firm's larger need to communicate with present clients, project teams, and employees, as well as with audiences beyond immediate prospective clients. The answer to broadening the definition may be to get more professionals involved in various aspects of public relations, client contact, and selling.

Meanwhile, a consultant in public relations and marketing communications can also be useful to a larger firm, where some communications projects may be too complex or politicized to handle entirely in-house and where the crush of proposal writing and ad hoc sales support may make it desirable to transfer some long-term functions to an outside specialist. In general, a combination of one or more principals and project managers, an in-house specialist to handle scheduling and day-to-day needs, and an outside consultant to carry out continuing or especially demanding programs can provide a flexible mix, allowing communications to be managed effectively.

BIBLIOGRAPHY

1. B. Perkins, *Architectural Record* **172,** 33 (Apr. 1984).
2. T. S. Hines, *New York Times Book Review,* 1 (Sept. 8, 1985).
3. S. Kliment, "The Architect's Communications," in *Architect's Handbook of Professional Practice,* American Institute of Architects, Washington, D.C., 1986, sec. B-9.
4. G. Jones, *Public Relations for the Design Professional,* McGraw-Hill, Inc., New York, 1980.
5. M. Hough, *A/E Marketing Journal* **13,** 3 (July 1986).
6. Society for Marketing Professional Services, 1984 Roundtable, SMPS, Alexandria, Va., 1984.
7. M. McElroy, *Architectural Record* **173,** 51 (July 1985).
8. Ulrich International Periodical Directory, 24th ed., R. R. Bowker, New York, 1985.
9. Ref. 3, Sec. A-4.
10. *Ibid,* p. 3.

General References

F. Ventre, "An Introductory Comment on the Periodical Literature in Architectural Design and Construction," *Journal of the AIP,* 359 (Sept. 1967). Pioneering article on architectural journalism.

S. A. Kliment, *Creative Communications for a Successful Design Practice,* Whitney Library of Design, New York, 1977. A pioneering book on publications design, among other topics.

P. E. Pace and J. Culberton, *Successful Public Relations for the Professions,* Professional Publishing, Edwardsville, Kans., 1982.

W. Coxe, *Marketing Architectural and Engineering Services,* 2nd ed., Van Nostrand Reinhold Co., Inc., New York, 1983. A standard reference.

S. D'Elia, J. Ricereto, and M. Spaulding, *The A/E Marketing Handbook,* MRH Associates, Newington, Conn., 1983.

G. Jones, *How to Market Professional Design Services,* McGraw-Hill Inc., New York, 1983. A good complement to Coxe.

A. Saint, *The Image of the Architect,* Yale Press, New Haven, Conn., 1983. A meditation on art versus business messages.

J. R. Blau, *Architects and Firms: A Sociological Perspective on Architectural Practice,* MIT Press, Cambridge, Mass., 1984. Insight on the profession's self-image, based on a study of New York firms.

The following are good bibliographical references:

M. Spaulding, "A/E Marketing Resource Directory," *A/E Marketing Journal,* supplement published each August. An excellent, informed, annual bibliography available to subscribers.

American Institute of Architects Communications Center, "Periodical Articles on Public Relations," p (337); "Periodical Articles on Brochures," p (449); "Periodical Articles on Newsletters," p (505); "Periodical Articles on Proposals," p (323)." These list publications in the library at AIA's Washington, D.C., headquarters; available at nominal cost. Updated regularly.

A/E Marketing Journal, Professional Marketing Report, the Society for Marketing Professional Services (SMPS), Practice Management Associates (Newton, Mass.), and the AIA regularly publish articles and handbooks of interest.

See also ARCHITECTURAL PRESS, U.S.; LITERATURE OF ARCHITECTURE; MEDIA CRITICISM.

ROBERT L. MILLER, AIA
Robert L. Miller Associates
Washington, D.C.

COMPENSATION.   See FEES, ARCHITECTURAL

COMPETITIONS, ARCHITECTURAL DESIGN

An architectural design competition was once defined by the American Institute of Architects (AIA) by this statement (1):

> An architectural design competition exists when two or more architects prepare designs for the same project, on the same site, at the same time, for the same client.

This simplistic definition describes a basic type of project competition. An architectural design competition of this type has two goals: a search for excellence in design and the selection of an architect for a project. The architect commissioned for the work must have the design talent and all other capacities required for the successful realization of the final project. If there are only two competitors, a possibility suggested by the AIA definition, the search for architectural excellence may not be well served, unless the invited two are carefully selected from among the acknowledged great form givers of the time.

Usually a carefully prepared statement of project requirements is developed and issued to a larger group of architects, with an invitation to submit conceptual designs responding to these requirements. In a properly organized important competition open to all architects, several hundred architects may respond. Such a competition offers the maximum opportunity for the discovery of new or relatively unknown design talent. The very fact that a previously unknown architect may be the winner may raise questions concerning the continuing design process. Will the personal relationship between the unknown architect and the owner be conducive to continued creativity? Will the architect have the organizational ability to carry the project through to a successful conclusion? Although the competition process provides solutions to both of these questions, the sponsor may wish to limit participation in the competition to firms of known talent and management capacity. In this case, a relatively small number of architectural firms are invited to enter the competition, and the number of competitors is limited to those who agree to compete under the terms offered.

There are a number of types of competitions not described by the quoted AIA definition. Some of these may be combined to suit specific competition goals. The competition process is unusually adaptable to a variety of situations in which a search for design excellence remains the primary objective and the completion of actual project construction may or may not be involved.

TYPES OF COMPETITION

Project Competitions

This type of competition is intended to lead directly to construction of a specific project. The program for such a competition will generally provide prizes for the winning designs and the award of the architectural commission for the project to the first-prize winner. The project may be a single building, a group of related buildings, a monument, a bridge, or any definable work of architecture, but is not necessarily limited to these. Industrial design, graphics, furniture, and interior design are suitable subjects for competition. Successful competitions have also been focused on regional and city planning, urban design, and landscape design.

There are circumstances that may prevent the award of an architectural commission at the conclusion of a competition. For example, requirements for enabling legislation by a public body may inhibit immediate progress. If these circumstances exist, the competition program should state them and outline equitable alternatives to the commissioning of the work if the project is delayed. Planning projects may address long-range goals requiring incremental development, future adjustments, and continuous guidance. In such cases, the architectural or planning commission may be limited to completion of the design of initial elements or specific features of the plan, or the commission may provide for extended consulting service, or both, as most appropriate. Competitions in the field of industrial design, furniture design, and graphics may provide for the award of contracts for final design, additional research and development, royalty agreements, or other suitable prizes and rewards. In any case, if prolonged delays are anticipated for a building project or other difficulties are likely to limit realization of the final work, the competition process is sufficiently flexible to provide equitable treatment for all parties. Under some circumstances, the sponsor may elect to conduct a competition of ideas rather than one intended to result in immediate project construction.

Idea Competitions

Idea competitions are focused on the generation of ideas and cover a wide variety of design issues. They may be concerned with the improvement of building types and specify either real or hypothetical sites. They may investigate creative uses of material and construction methods or be concerned with improvement of building products. City planning and urban design provide suitable subjects for idea competitions.

This type of competition can be of value in stimulating interest in quality design, in investigations of unexplored or untried design areas, and certainly in uncovering fresh design talent. The subject and scope of idea competitions must be carefully selected and defined to attract the fullest participation by architects and designers. Rewards to the participants are generally substantial prizes and always the enhancement of professional reputation and prestige through widespread publication of the competition results. Idea competitions have on occasion had a positive impact on industrial products. The published results of a competition sponsored by Chicago Bridge and Iron for the design of an elevated water storage tank have had a profound effect on the design of such structures for many years. The elliptical bottom tank featured by several of the competition designs was introduced as an alternative to the hemispherical bottom tank, and the giant "golf-tee" form of elevated water storage tank featured by at least one competition entry began to appear as a part of the suburban landscape.

Eligibility

Competitions in the United States may be further classified in terms of the eligibility requirements for entrants. The terms used hereinafter and the process described conform to U.S. usage.

Open Competition. In an open competition, the invitation to compete is addressed to the entire architectural profession. Any licensed architect may enter. In some cases, designers and students may also enter, either independently or in association with a licensed architect. In the event a designer, student, or unlicensed professional participating independently wins a project competition, a later association with an experienced and talented architect acceptable to the sponsor will be required in order to assure realization of the completed work. Association with a firm, frequently a local one, may also be required if the competition winner is a relatively inexperienced architect or lacks the organizational resources needed for completion of the final design and provision of the related architectural services.

Cash prizes are generally awarded to the winners, and additional designs may receive special recognition in the form of an honorable mention, award of merit, or similar citation. The results of important competitions are generally published in brochures issued by the sponsor and in the architectural press. Although the memorial has not been built, the majority of the designs received in the Franklin Delano Roosevelt Memorial Competition were published in a valuable book by Thomas Creighton, *The Architecture of Monuments* (2), providing illustrations and identifying the competitors. Inclusion of architects' work in such publications adds significantly to their reputations for design talent. The opportunities for this form of recognition are an important incentive encouraging the architect to invest time and talent in design competitions.

Limited Competitions. A limited competition is similar to an open competition, except that it may be open only to a portion of the architectural profession. For example, entrance to the competition may be restricted to those professionals living or practicing in a given geographical area. A desire to attract only those architects who are fully aware of building requirements and construction practices in the region may influence the sponsor to select this form of competition.

Invited Competitions. If the sponsor wishes to select a small number of firms whose talents and capacities are well known and particularly suited to the project requirements, several firms may be invited to submit design concepts. The usual practice is to commission each of the selected firms to prepare conceptual designs for the project in accordance with a uniform program. As in other competition types, the program defines project requirements and

goals, specifies the form and extent of presentation materials, and establishes other basic rules and agreements. The submissions required in an invited competition may be somewhat more complete than those generally requested in an open competition, as the fee paid to each competitor can be designed to compensate for the form and completeness of the presentation.

Student Competitions. Architectural students are able to compete in student competitions. These may be restricted to students in a single school or a group of schools. Winners may receive special prizes, scholarships, or other awards. A number of traveling fellowships have been awarded on the basis of such competitions.

Competitions in Stages

The majority of open architectural competitions are conducted in a single stage. Architects are invited to submit designs responding to specified program requirements and to deliver their entries on or before an established time and date. The required presentation is generally limited to drawings and brief statements sufficient to illustrate and describe the design concept. It is considered good practice to place limits on the form and scope of the entry exhibits in order to avoid undue expense and waste of design talent and to encourage widespread participation. The entries are evaluated by a professional jury, the majority of which is generally composed of design professionals capable of judging the value of the design concept and the creative skill of the architect. After the judging, the final jury report is issued, winners are announced, prizes are awarded, and, when applicable, the architectural commission is awarded.

For complex projects, and particularly if it is deemed important to have the final judgment based on more than a conceptual presentation, a two-stage format may be followed. In the first stage, a limited number of entrants are selected to compete in a second stage. This selection is made in the same fashion as that in a single-stage competition. The first-stage winners are then invited to develop their designs further and to present additional drawings, sometimes models, and other materials for judgment in the second stage. The first-stage winners receive substantial prize money in recognition of their performance and to help defray at least a portion of the expense involved in the preparation of the more elaborate second-stage submission. A two-stage competition is most appropriate for large and specialized projects requiring extensive study and research and those in which additional testing of the feasibility of conceptual designs may benefit the quality of the final work. The first-stage submissions can be made relatively simple, thus attracting a larger number of entries. The more specific and detailed requirements for the second stage provide the architect with the opportunity for further study of the problem and the jury with a more reliable basis for judgment. A modified form of this type of competition has been used in recent years for important federal (U.S. Government) projects. The General Services Administration (GSA) refers to their version as a two-level competition. The first level involves the selection of a limited number of firms on the basis of an evaluation of their general professional competence. Those selected for participation in the second level are then paid a fee for the presentation of conceptual designs in a stipulated form and responding to a detailed statement of project requirements. These designs are evaluated by a jury appointed by the GSA, but not necessarily identified in advance or composed of registered architects in a majority.

International Competitions

International competitions are those in which architects, planners, and designers from more than one country are invited to participate. International architectural design competitions are usually conducted in one or two stages and in compliance with applicable international codes and guidelines.

Quasi Competitions

Quasi competitions are defined as architectural selection processes that bear a resemblance to the traditional architectural design competition. Urban renewal competitions, as practiced in recent years, provide an example. Developer groups including builders, architects, planners, financiers, and others are asked to submit proposals under a variety of situations. The proposals generally show the proposed use of the urban renewal area, the conceptual design of buildings and other improvements, and the price the proposer is willing to pay for the land. Proposals are evaluated on the basis of broad and variable criteria including design, social benefits, price offered by the developers, and total financial impact on the development agency or local government. Such contests cannot be considered design competitions, as there is no assurance that the offer proposing the best design will be chosen. It is highly likely that the proposal meeting the bare minimum project requirements and offering the best price will be accepted.

HISTORY OF COMPETITIONS

The Development of Rules

Competitions have a long history. Judith Strong, in *Participating in Architectural Competitions,* notes that "as early as 448 B.C. . . . the Boule (senate or council) of Athens invited designs from architects for a war memorial on the Acropolis"(3). She also lists numerous architectural achievements resulting from competitions: Brunelleschi's cupola for the Florence Cathedral, the completion of the Louvre in Paris, and many churches and city halls resulting from competitions held at the rate of over 100 per year in Victorian England. At this rate, it is not surprising that some competitions were subject to abuse and bad management, and that the conduct of competitions came under severe criticism. After the formation of the Royal Institute of British Architects (RIBA) in 1834, the clamor continued for the development of rules that would assure fairness in the conduct of design competitions. It was in 1872 that a special RIBA committee issued regulations asking for qualified judges to evaluate competition submissions, reasonable prizes, and other rewards to the winners. RIBA's *Regulations for the Promotion and Conduct of Competitions* (4) was adopted, but did not become mandatory for its members until 1907.

As early as 1870, the AIA recognized that a uniform set of competition rules was needed if such contests were to be conducted with equity and fairness and in the best interests of the owners, the public, and the profession. Accordingly, it issued its first "Schedule of Terms" regulating the conduct of architectural competitions. This code, reflecting the policy of the AIA at that time, has been subjected to study, revision, and improvement for over a century. The last official *Code for Architectural Design Competitions* (1) of the AIA, published in 1972, was the product of long experience with the conduct of competitions and a continuous search for techniques that would assure equity and the best possible results. Although rules were changed and improved, the basic objectives remained unchanged. The preface to the 1972 code states, in part (5),

> The selection of an architect by competition involves the observance of the processes which will insure fair conduct on the part of all participants, establish equitable relationships between owner and competitors, and insure the results are in the best interest of the owner, the public, and the profession.

Amendments to the code, for the most part, have been focused on improvements of the competition techniques. The perfection of methods for assuring that entries are submitted and judged anonymously has provided the greatest protection against the selection of an architect on the basis of improper influences or favoritism. Other important improvements developed over the years include

- The requirement for employment of a professional adviser, who must be a qualified architect and who serves as a consultant to the owner. The professional adviser plans, organizes, and conducts the competition and prepares all program documents and rules of the competition.
- The requirement for the evaluation of entries by a professional jury composed of at least three members, a majority of whom must be architects. For competitions including requirements featuring planning, landscape design, sculpture, or other creative work, representatives of other design disciplines are frequently added to the jury.
- The establishment of an AIA service to review and approve competition programs and the prohibition of participation by AIA members in competitions not reviewed and approved by the Institute. It became the professional adviser's duty to submit a draft of the competition program to the AIA's Committee on Architectural Competitions and to work with that committee to make amendments and additions as necessary. When approved, a statement was added to the program indicating that the program had been reviewed by the AIA and was approved for participation by its members.

In November 1976, the 1972 AIA code was withdrawn and replaced by *Guidelines for Architectural Design Competitions* (6). This action was taken after advice from the federal government that elements of the competition code were in violation of laws relating to restraint of trade. All mandatory requirements governing the conduct of competitions and the participation of AIA members ended with the withdrawal of the code. The guidelines were issued as an advisory document to those who wished to sponsor competitions. Compliance became voluntary. Under this new procedure, the Institute offered to review programs and suggest improvements, which the sponsor was free to accept or reject. If the institute's committee found the competition to be in compliance with its guidelines, it would so state, and the sponsor was free to use this statement in announcements and program documents as a means of attracting increased participation.

In 1982, the AIA issued a more complete document, the *Handbook of Architectural Design Competitions* (7). This booklet, prepared by a task force of the Institute, provides more detailed advice to the sponsors, architects, and others who have an interest in the conduct of design competitions. This publication was supported in part by a matching grant to the AIA from the Design Arts Program of the National Endowment For the Arts. An excellent discussion of competitions and the competition process, including the roles of the sponsor, professional adviser, and jury, is provided.

The preface to the handbook lists the following as essential to a well-run design competition:

- A conscientious sponsor.
- A competent professional adviser.
- A thorough and carefully written program.
- Complete graphic and other illustrative material.
- Fair and precise competition rules.
- Clearly stated submission requirements.
- A realistic schedule.
- A qualified jury.
- Appropriate prizes.
- Arrangements for publicizing the winning design.

A sponsor who wishes to attract the widest interest and participation in a design competition in the United States would be well advised to give careful consideration to the recommendations presented in this handbook. Architects who wish to be assured that their investment of time and talent will not be squandered in unfair or badly managed competitions must evaluate the program, terms, and conditions of a competition before entering.

CODES AND REGULATIONS

Multinational Codes and Guidelines

Competitions have been utilized extensively in the Scandinavian countries. Codes for the conduct of competitions have been adopted by several countries. The *Code for Ar-chitectural Design Competitions* (8) of the Federation of Danish Architects (DAL) is an interesting and very complete document. Similar rules governing Scandinavian architectural competitions have been mutually endorsed by Danish, Finnish, Norwegian, and Swedish federations of architects. The Danish code recognizes the Scandinavian code as having jurisdiction in certain multinational contests.

International Codes and Guidelines

Union International des Architectes (UIA) has developed and adopted *Standard Regulations for International Competitions in Architecture and Town Planning* (9) for the control of international competitions. The General Conference of the United Nations Educational, Scientific and Cultural Organization, in 1956 adopted *Recommendations Concerning International Competitions in Architecture and Town Planning* (10) and in 1978 issued a revised recommendation annexing the latest issue of the UIA standard regulation. Competitions are designated international if they are open to participants of different nationalities who reside in different countries. The international regulations establish principles guiding the organization of competitions and address the interests of both promoters and competitors. Provisions of these regulations are much the same as those set forth in the previous AIA code, the later AIA guidelines, and the current AIA handbook, with added requirements appropriate to the international scope. The conditions of the competition may be published in any language, but must be accompanied by a translation in one of the four official languages of the UIA (English, French, Russian, and Spanish). Designs are submitted and judged anonymously, a professional adviser is required, and the conditions must state the purpose of the competition, the nature of the problem, and the practical requirements to be met. Background information (social, economic, geographic, topographical, etc) essential to an understanding of the problem is supplied to competitors. The metric scale is generally used. If not, a table of metric equivalents is made part of the conditions. When the furnishing of documents to competitors is conditioned on payment of a deposit, provision is usually made for return of the deposit to competitors who submit designs. The name of competitors selected to compete in the second stage of a two-stage competition are not revealed publicly or to the jury until the conclusion of the competition, except under special conditions established in advance and agreed to by competitors and the jury. Prize money related to the size and importance of the project is stated in the conditions, and the promoter is obligated to entrust the design of the project to the author of the winning design. If the jury is not satisfied that the winner has the ability and resources to carry out the work, it may require collaboration with another architect or town planner. In the event no contract for carrying out the project is signed within 24 months, the competition regulations provide for payment to the winner of a further sum equal to the first-prize money. In this case, the promoter may not carry out the project except in collaboration with the author of the prize-winning design. The jury is required to be appointed prior to the competition and is named in the regulations for the competition. The jury for UIA-approved competition must be composed of not more than seven (preferably three or five) persons who are architects, town planners, or, under special conditions, other professionals working in association with them. At least one member of the jury must be appointed by the UIA. Provision is made for reserve jury members, who are nonvoting except when a voting member is absent, in which case the reserve member acquires a vote and may, under specified conditions, retain such vote throughout the judging. The jury must make all awards. Provisions are made for the public exhibition of all designs, and photographs of the winning designs are furnished to the UIA for possible publication.

Reciprocity Between Code Authorities

Cooperation between the several code authorities has been cordial and extensive. The Danish code recognizes the UIA code as governing international competitions. The UIA has in the past endorsed international competitions originating in the United States and conducted under AIA rules. Similarly, the AIA has recognized the UIA code as controlling the conduct of international competitions originating outside the United States and has approved such competitions for participation by its members. As previously explained, there is now no AIA code governing the conduct of competitions in the United States. Previous reciprocal agreements relating to the conduct of international competitions may be subject to reconsideration by the UIA or other code authorities. An architect's decision to participate in a competition conducted in the United States must now be based on a personal evaluation of the terms and conditions of the competition program rather than on its compliance with an established code.

IMPORTANT COMPETITIONS IN THE UNITED STATES

The United States Capitol

One of the earliest competitions in the United States was that for the design of the U.S. Capitol. The location and boundaries of the Federal City had been established, the site for the Capitol had been acquired, and the basic map had been prepared by Pierre Charles L'Enfant by 1791. It was at least partially to stimulate interest in the development of the Federal City that Washington agreed with Jefferson's recommendations for a competition for the design of two major buildings, the "President's House" and the "Congress House." Jefferson prepared a "sketch or specimen of advertisement," and ads were placed in newspapers announcing, in part, as follows (11):

A PREMIUM

of a lot in the city, to be designated by impartial judges, and $500, or a medal of that value, at the option of the party, will be given by the Commissioners of Federal Buildings to persons who before the 15th day of July 1792, shall produce them the most appropriate plan, if adopted by them, for a

Capitol to be erected in the city and $250 for the plan next in merit to the one they shall adopt; the building to be of brick and to contain the following . . .

Drawings, will be expected of the ground plat, elevations of each front and sections through the building in such directions as may be necessary to explain the material, structure and an estimate of the cubic feet of brick work composing the whole mass of the wall.

Thos. Johnson
Dd. Stuart
Danl. Carroll
Commissioners

The drawings received by the Commissioners provided evidence of the limited capacities of the architectural profession in the United States at that time. Stephen Hallet was the only professional architect to enter the competition. The rest were amateur designers or skilled master builders who had an acquaintance with the available plan books and builder's guides. The design by James Hoban for the President's House was accepted, but all designs for the Capitol were rejected by the Commissioners. Hallet's design received some favor as evidencing good taste, but was not acceptable on several counts. During the summer and early fall of 1792, there was an effort to find, among the plans submitted, the basis for an accepted design. Hallet was invited to improve his design and make a revised submission under at least an implied agreement that he was being retained for the work. Hallet's work went slower than either he or the commissioners had anticipated, and in January 1793, he asked for additional time to complete his drawings.

Meanwhile, William Thornton, a physician living in Tortolla in the Virgin Islands, wrote to the Commission on July 12, 1792, saying that he had not heard of the competition until the time was almost expired, but that he was nonetheless making drawings that might be of value if none of the plans submitted by the original deadline were adopted. He again wrote to the Commissioners on November 9, 1792, saying that he had learned through a friend that all designs were rejected and asking permission to submit his entry. The Commissioners responded that the Hoban plan for the President's House had been accepted, but that Thornton's plan for the Capitol would be reviewed. It appears that after some personal investigation, Thornton became convinced that his in-progress design would not be acceptable. In any case, he started anew, and finally, on January 31, 1793, submitted his still unfinished plan to the President. Both Washington and Jefferson were impressed by the design and paid it such high praise that acceptance by the Commissioners was assured. Feeling some obligation to Hallet, the Commissioners appointed him to develop Thornton's designs to meet more precisely defined requirements. This attempt at appeasement had results that could have been expected. Hallet's efforts resulted in changes to the building exterior and in inevitable controversy. Hallet was highly critical of the Thornton design and sought to substitute details of his own, to the point where he stated in a letter dated June 28, 1794, to the Commissioners (12):

In the alteration I never thought of introducing in it anything belonging to Dr. Thornton's exhibitions. So I claim the original invention of the plan now executed and beg leave to lay hereafter before you and the President the proofs of my right of it.

Following this, Hoban was named Superintendent of Construction on the Capitol as well as the President's House, with Hallet as Assistant Superintendent and Draftsman for the Capitol. Hallet's actions continued to earn him disfavor in several quarters, and he was formally discharged in 1794. Thornton was then given more control of the work when President Washington appointed him one of the three commissioners of the District of Columbia. Although the early development of the Capitol was plagued by controversy, there can be little doubt concerning the importance and value of Thornton's competition designs or his later developmental work. Figure 1 shows an elevation of the Capitol as redesigned by Thornton after his appointment as Commissioner in 1794. Thornton's work as Architect of the Capitol continued until the Board of Commissioners was abolished. Benjamin Latrobe became the second Architect of the Capitol and executed some of Thornton's original designs. Charles Bulfinch became the third Architect of the Capitol and supervised construction of the central section, increased the height of Thornton's dome, and restored the wings burned by the British in 1812. The present dome was added by Thomas U. Walter in 1850. The Capitol now stands as the work of many dedicated men. It has been expanded and reshaped with great care to satisfy the needs of a growing democracy. The miracle of the Capitol is that in its maturity it has managed to respect the basic concepts of Washington and Jefferson and the talents and efforts of its first architect.

After Thornton's official connection with the Capitol was terminated, he remained in Washington, D.C. A man of many talents, he is remembered not only as the first Architect of the Capitol, but also, among architects, as the designer of the Octagon House, now the home of the AIA. Upon completion of his work on the Capitol, President Jefferson appointed Thornton as a clerk to undertake the issuance of patents. Thornton's policies provided the early regulations for control of patents, and he is generally regarded as the founder of the United States Patent Office.

The Chicago Tribune Administration Building

This international competition was sponsored by the *Tribune* to commemorate its 75th anniversary, June 10, 1922. An analysis of the aims of this competition stated (13):

> It had for its prime motive the enhancement of civic beauty; its avowed purpose was to secure for Chicago the most beautiful office building in the world.

The program asked for a worthy structure to efficiently and conveniently house the newspaper's operations and to inspire its workers.

The competition program announced that not more than ten architects or firms of repute in the United States were to be extended a special invitation to compete. The invited competitors were to receive remuneration. All other architects in the United States and all other countries were invited to submit entries in an open competition. Rules of anonymity were established, and each entry was given an identifying number as it was received. Prizes were established, with $50,000 as the first-place award, $20,000 as the second-place award, and $10,000 as the third-place award. The first-place winner was promised the architectural commission for the project, with the $50,000 prize being the initial payment of the architect's fee.

The jury included four managers of the Tribune Building Corporation plus a distinguished architect who was to advise and assist other members of the jury. The closing date for receipt of entries was November 1, 1922, with one month's grace period given to drawings coming from distant points. The competition was given extensive publicity in the United States and in the international press beginning in June 1922 and extending throughout the year. By December 1922, a total of 204 entries had been received, with 25 countries represented. The jury began its examination of designs shortly after the November 1 closing date and by November 23 had selected 12 designs for additional consideration. On November 29, an additional design (number 187) was cleared through U.S. Customs from Finland. Upon review of this entry, the reassembled jury was so impressed by its value and beauty that it was immediately included in the group of designated

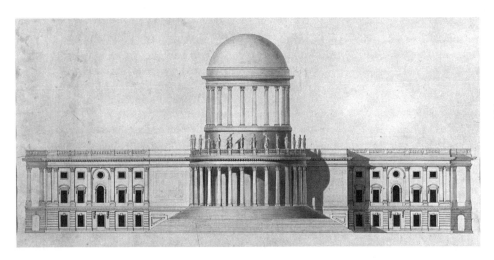

Figure 1. West elevation of the U.S. Capitol showing Thornton's revised design (1795–1797). This drawing shows the temple which was intended to surmount the circular conference room. The temple is sometimes misinterpreted as one of many alternate designs for the dome. The original drawing is in the Library of Congress. Courtesy of the Architect of the Capitol.

finalists. On December 3, the final selections by the jury were announced: Entry 69 by John Mead Howells and Raymond M. Hood of New York ($50,000), Entry 187 by Eliel Saarinen of Helsingfors, Finland ($20,000), Entry 90 by Holabird and Roche of Chicago ($10,000).

Each of the ten invited American architects received $2,000. The publication of the winning designs gave rise to a substantial voice from the architectural profession in praise of the Saarinen design over the Howells and Hood first-prize winner. The freshness of the Saarinen design clearly expressed the essentials of the steel construction of skyscrapers (Fig. 2). It was in sharp contrast to the more ponderous forms, the decorative elements, and structural expression that suggested a relationship to Gothic architecture in the Howells and Hood solution (Fig. 3). The force of this evaluation is attested to by the influence the Saarinen design has had on the design of later skyscrapers. Louis Sullivan, writing on the design of Eliel Saarinen in the *Architectural Record*, said (14):

> . . . it is a voice, resonant and rich, ringing amidst the wealth and joy of life. In utterance sublime and melodious, it prophe-

Figure 3. The Chicago Tribune Competition First Prize Design. This perspective by Howells and Hood presents a building with its steel frame clothed in forms of Gothic derivation. The building constructed in Chicago represents the final development of this design. From *Competition for a New Administration Building for the Chicago Tribune*, 1923. Courtesy the AIA Archives.

Figure 2. The Chicago Tribune Competition Second Prize Design by Eliel Saarinen. The design, presented in this perspective, was acclaimed by many architects who recognized in it a new expression of the verticality and lightness of steel framed high-rise buildings. From *Competition for a New Administration Building for the Chicago Tribune*, 1923. Courtesy the AIA Archives.

sies a time to come, and not so far away, when the wretched and the yearning, the sordid, and the fierce, shall escape the bondage and the mania of fixed idea. . . . Qualifying as it does in every technical regard, and conforming to the mandatory items of the official program of instructions, it goes freely in advance, and, with the steel frame as a thesis, displays a high science of design such as the world up to this day had neither known or surmised. In its single solidarity of concentrated intention, there is revealed a logic of a new order, the logic of living things; and this inexorable logic of life is most graciously accepted and set forth in fluency of form. Rising from the earth in suspiration as of the earth and as of the universal genius of man, in beauty lofty and serene . . . until its lovely crest seems at one with the sky.

Possibly, the judgment by this jury composed of four corporate executives and only one architect provided at least one argument for the change in the AIA code that required that a jury for such a project competition have a majority of architects.

It should be noted that competitions have been more widely used in Europe than in the United States and that Saarinen had already gained considerable prominence through his success in a number of European competitions.

However, it was the *Tribune* competition that brought him to prominence in the United States and resulted in his move to the U.S., where he first taught at the University of Michigan and later headed the Cranbrook Academy of Art, teaching and practicing architecture in Bloomfield Hills, Mich. The *Tribune* competition not only introduced new and fresh architectural forms, but added strength and talent to the profession of architecture in the United States.

The Jefferson National Expansion Memorial: The Gateway Arch, St. Louis, Missouri

This two-stage architectural design competition was won by Eero Saarinen, who stands with his father, Eliel, as a great competitor. The building of this memorial must be credited to the imagination and energies of a private group, the Jefferson National Expansion Association. This group, under the leadership of Luther Ely Smith, conceived the project and, through years of organized effort, enlisted support from numerous governmental and private sponsors until the project developed sufficient strength and financing to make the competition and final construction possible. The purity of this gleaming steel arch, its scale, and its grandeur make it one of the most moving of all monuments. The nicety of its relationship to the little

courthouse in which the Dred Scott case was tried, seen directly on axis when looking west through the arch, adds significantly to the symbolism of the gateway concept (Fig. 4). From initiation of the competition, this project required approximately two decades to complete. For those involved, the rate of progress must have been frustrating at times, but the final work was accomplished in much less than the time required for many projects of similar magnitude.

The effect of the *Chicago Tribune* competition in bringing Eliel Saarinen to the United States appears all the more important when the architectural and artistic contributions of his family and associates are considered.

The Viet Nam Veterans Memorial, Washington, D.C.

This recent, successful competition was made possible by a private organization, the Viet Nam Veterans Memorial Foundation. This group not only sponsored the competition, but raised the money needed to accomplish the final construction. The project stands as an important national memorial, completed entirely with private funds (Fig. 5). The competition was conducted under the able direction of Paul D. Spreiregen, FAIA, who served as professional adviser. This was a single-stage competition, open to architects and other design professionals, as well as students. Entrants were required to compete as individuals rather

Figure 4. The Jefferson National Expansion Memorial, St. Louis, Mo., also referred to as the Gateway Arch, as viewed from the Illinois side of the Mississippi River. Courtesy of the National Park Service, Department of the Interior.

Figure 5. The Sydney Opera House as seen when facing the end of its peninsular site. Courtesy of Promotion Australia. Australian Information Service photograph by Alex Ozolins.

than as firms. This requirement was designed to develop broad participation, particularly to encourage young and as-yet unknown talent to enter the competition. The success of this strategy was fully demonstrated by the final results. The winning entry was submitted by Maya Ying Lin, a student at Yale University, who completed her competition design as a class project in funerary design. The firm of Cooper, Lecky Architects of Washington, D.C., was selected by the Foundation as the architect for the project, with the concurrence of the competition winner. Maya Ying Lin was then employed by the architectural firm as a student-intern for approximately a year and a half and was thus able to participate in the full development of the final design, working as well on other firm projects. The designer's statement accompanying her competition submission stated, in part (15),

> . . . the memorial appears as a rift in the earth—a long polished black stone wall emerging from and receding into the earth. . . . At the intersection of these walls, on the right side of the walls' top, is carved the date of the first death. It is followed by the names of those who died in the war in chronological order. . . . As we turn to leave, we see these walls stretching into the distance directing us to the Washington Monument, to the left, and the Lincoln Memorial to the right, thus bringing the Viet Nam Memorial into historical context. . . .

The quality of these great national memorials thus brought into association provides convincing demonstration of the value of the competition process in the continuing search for design excellence.

INTERNATIONAL COMPETITION

The list of competitions in the United States alone is extensive. The international list is even more impressive. Some of these have attracted widespread participation, generated lively controversy, directed public interest to good design, and resulted in the completion of architecture of great quality. One of these is worthy of special attention

here, as it demonstrates many aspects of the total design process.

The Opera House, Sydney, Australia

That this competition has been the subject of controversy in the public as well as the architectural press is not surprising when one considers the scope of the project. The owner, the Government of New South Wales, visualized an opera house of a scale that would have been astonishing in any of the world's largest cities. Seventy acres of land on Benelong Point, a peninsula extending into Sydney harbor, was provided as the site. The building was to contain a major hall, a minor hall, restaurants and bars, a large parking facility, and all of the support facilities for opera and theater. It was even speculated that in this structure everything from boxing matches to political meetings might take place. This attitude led to the development of a program statement that encouraged competitors to produce concepts having the widest possible scope with relatively few mandatory requirements.

The conditions (the "program" in U.S. usage) emphasized that it was unlikely that the winning scheme would be built without alteration and that the goal of the competition was to select a sound basic scheme and a competent architect. The jury ("assessors" in international usage), composed of Prof. J. L. Martin, Eero Saarinen, Cobden Parker (the New South Wales government architect), and Prof. H. Ingham Ashworth (Dean of the Faculty of Architecture at Sydney University), was therefore forced to make many of its own assumptions in the judging. It was recognized that a much more precise program would be worked out with the winning designer at a later date. The jury stated that its first intention was to select a design appropriate to the Benelong Point site. It rejected a building presenting a massive image as inappropriate to this harbor site. In its report, the jury stated that its attention had been focused first on proper use of the site, second on internal circulation and planning, and third on selection of a scheme that gave promise of a building of architectural significance. It concluded that, among the 220 schemes submitted, the design by Jorn Utzon best met these objectives (Fig. 5).

The jury made clear its realization that there were many points of detailed criticism and numerous corrections to be made during the design development process. It should be recalled that the conditions of the competition made provision for such alterations. Finally, it was the jury's conclusion that the winning design gave promise of becoming one of the great buildings of the world.

The winning design by Jorn Utzon, a pupil of Alvar Aalto, proposed a platform gradually ascending from the mainland with provision for an important pedestrian approach as well as automobile access with parking. The building was to house a major hall for concerts and opera plus a second hall for somewhat smaller audiences. An auditorium suitable for chamber music was also included. An experimental theater was added later, during the design development stage. The entirety was to be covered by an interlocking series of shell vaults of such form and lightness of expression as to resemble the wind-filled sails of great yachts natural to the harbor setting. The designer stated, in his explanation accompanying the submission, "the whole exterior radiates lightness and festivity and is standing in clear contrast to the square buildings of Sydney" (16).

The structural engineering firm of Ove Arup and Partners collaborated with the architect on this project, which presented many structural problems, ranging from the foundations to the design and construction of the shell vaults. The spectacular design of the shells or "sails" was completed by the architect and worked out in concert with the engineers. After poured-in-place thin-shell concrete vaults were considered, precast concrete sections were decided on. These were raised and placed in position using the largest available cranes. Poured-in-place concrete was then used to anchor the entirety. Problems relating to structural design, construction technology, acoustics, seating, and a multitude of systems were severe and remained to be solved in a design process that in some cases gave rise to public and professional debate characterized by an understandable degree of acrimony. All of this gave support to those who deride the architectural competition process as impractical and uncontrollable. Under any circumstances, the design of a building of such complexity and responding to such a courageous concept could not be expected to reach completion without more than the normal pains of creativity. It is hard to believe that such a fresh and creative design solution as that now seen in the completed Opera House would have emerged through a normal government agency–architect relationship. Photographs of the Sydney Opera House appear frequently in advertising intended to attract tourists to Sydney and Australia. Hotels call attention to their desirable location overlooking the opera. Promoters of the project saw great orchestras, singers, soloists, and conductors, as well as audiences, coming from afar to see this grand architectural expression in the natural amphitheater of Sydney harbor. Despite all of the difficulties encountered during the design development process, citizen pride in the completed work would say that the effort was worth it. The Sydney Opera stands as testimony to the creative force of architectural design competitions.

OTHER IMPORTANT COMPETITIONS

A review of any listing of projects achieved through competitions indicates that design competitions have resulted in the creation of great architecture and have added significantly to today's cultural heritage. Competitions that result in actual construction are generally regarded as the most successful. However, competitions that resulted in only paper designs have also had educational value to the profession and the public. In a few cases, the resulting controversies can be credited with the development of public interest and a growing awareness of the value of good design.

A few completed projects resulting from competitions are listed herein to illustrate the variety of competitions and their impact on the built environment. For those having a special interest in the story of these or other competitions, personal research is suggested.

1792	The White House, Washington, D.C. Architect: James Hoban
1848	The Washington Monument, Washington, D.C. Architect: Robert Mills
1862–1874	The Paris Opera, Paris, France Architect: Charles Jean Louis Garnier
1891	Union Station, St. Louis, Missouri Architect: Theodore C. Link
1897	The Public Library, New York Architects: Carrere and Hastings
1904–1914	The Railway Station, Helsinki, Finland Architects: Gesellius, Lindgen, Saarinen
1905–1922	The Town Hall, Stockholm, Sweden Architect: Ragnar Ostberg
1907	The Pan American Union, Washington, D.C. Architects: Albert Kelsey and Paul Cret
1920	The State Capitol, Lincoln, Nebraska Architect: Bertram Grosvenor Goodhue
1922	The Lincoln Memorial, Washington, D.C. Architect: Henry Bacon
1928	Tuberculosis Sanitarium, Paimio, Finland Architect: Alvar Aalto
1962	The City Hall, Boston, Massachusetts Architects: G. M. Kallman, N. M. McKinnell, E. F. Knowles
1965	Copley Square, Boston, Massachusetts Architects: Sasaki Associates
1969	The Birmingham-Jefferson Civic Center, Birmingham, Alabama Architects: Geddes, Brecher, Qualls, Cunningham

ADVANTAGES AND DISADVANTAGES OF COMPETITIONS

The evaluation of the competition process as a means of achieving high-quality design and selecting an architect involves subjective judgment to an important extent. Certainly, there are a number of equally valid techniques for the selection of an architect. Each method of selection will have some outstanding advantages to recommend it above others in a given situation. From the public view, an open competition provides the greatest protection against selection of an architect based on improper influences or favoritism. A public body or a building committee may free itself of suspicion of political patronage or conflict of interest through the utilization of the competition method. However, if relieving the owner of responsibility for architectural selection is the only goal, there is little justification for the effort and expense involved in a design competition. The search for design excellence must be at least a companion goal. Certainly, the selection of an architect on the basis of a test of architectural design skill is in the public interest.

From the professional as well as the public view, an outstanding advantage of design competitions lies in their encouragement of good design and, in the case of an open competition, the possibility for the emergence and development of new creative talent. Further, the public enthusiasm and support for improvement of the physical environment that may be generated by the publication of fresh and exciting designs acts to benefit the public. A principal advantage to the owner is the wealth of creative thought that will be directed toward achieving a solution to the specific building problem. Although a competition provides stimulus and encouragement to the profession in a continuing search for design excellence, it should be recognized that the achievement of the final work requires much more than an excellent basic design concept. The completion of the design of a truly fine building requires the efforts of a qualified and experienced design team. It is for this reason that the program for an open design competition generally provides for the association of the winner with another qualified firm when such support is needed.

The conduct of a competition involves careful observance of a process that should be fully understood by those considering the use of this method for selection of an architect. A thoughtful, complete, and accurate program must be prepared by a qualified architect serving as the professional adviser. The owner's needs are communicated to competitors through this program statement and through the usual limited provision for questions and answers funneled through the professional adviser. The rules of anonymity are specific in this regard, prohibiting direct contact between owner and competitor. The rich give-and-take of information between owner and architect during the early phase of the normal design process is thus eliminated during the conduct of the competition. It is only after the winner has been named and the contract for architectural services arranged that the owner and architect can discuss the project in greater detail. This has been cited as a weakness in the competition process, as it appears to prevent full explanation of the owner's wants at the initial design stage. In opposition to this view, it is argued that the professional adviser is able to develop a statement of requirements that is far clearer and more complete than that usually available to the architect at the beginning of the design process. This is a matter of continuing debate. An early AIA document entitled "Abstract of a Proposed Tract for Competitions" provides amusing evidence that this is an old and unsettled issue (17):

A competent consulting architect can give to even a complicated problem such preliminary investigation as will enable a committee to find out in advance what they really want and to set it forth clearly to competitors. . . . It would be as well in most cases, of course, to let the man who has so thoroughly informed himself proceed with the work, that is, to appoint an architect in the first place.

One seldom-discussed difficulty with the competition process is the limitation imposed by the available presentation methods. Designs are generally evaluated on the basis of drawings. As drawings are the medium of expression, the skilled delineator has a distinct advantage. A mediocre design presented by a drawing calculated to impress the jury is seldom successful, but a poor drawing is usually inadequate as an explanation of the fine qualities of a concept that requires further delineation and development for full appreciation. Architectural models are sometimes used to supplement drawings, but their use is generally limited to the second stage of a two-stage competition.

There is also the problem of scale. As drawings are usually presented on boards of manageable size for shipping, handling, and display, the scale of the drawing for large architectural projects may be prescribed to be $\frac{1}{16}$ in. = 1 ft or even smaller. At this scale, fine detailing and some of the most sensitive mass relationships may be obscured. Some of the most successful competitors have learned to present simple and sometimes overstated relationships in order to give emphasis to a design concept. The winning design in the Franklin Delano Roosevelt Memorial Competition provides a case in point. The proposed design consisted of a series of large monolithic upright slabs, referred to as "instant Stonehenge" and "bookends out of deep freeze" by some of its detractors. The size of these soaring slabs was indeed awe inspiring even at the small scale required for the presentation. The presentation was indeed a strong and demanding eye catcher, but the design was also of quality equal to its presentation. When subjected to the design development process, the entire complex might have been reduced in scale and the pedestrian way through the complex given full emphasis.

A further problem is the difficulty of comparative evaluation of solutions of widely varying types. The program for the F.D.R. Memorial Competition permitted solutions ranging from those having strong architectural expressions to quiet contemplative landscape solutions. Elbert Peets, one of the foremost planners of the early twentieth century, suggested a rose garden with quiet pathways and seating areas an an appropriate memorial, saying after sketching a detail, "Franklin would have loved this." The problem of presenting a rose garden using the scale and form of presentation required for this competition presented a virtually impossible situation.

Competitions do take time and are clearly inappropriate if the owner must build on a very short schedule. Projects for which an adequate development budget is not available and those for which realistic financing has not been arranged should not be the subjects of project competitions.

Much has been said concerning the cost of competitions. The sponsor should recognize that a considerable investment of money, time, and talent by the design profession is required for a successful competition. The decision to conduct a competition should not be taken lightly. Although the sponsor will incur expenses for the organization and conduct of an open competition and the award of substantial prizes, this will appear minor when compared with the total investment by the design professions.

ARCHITECTURAL AWARD PROGRAMS

The term competition is used to refer to many types of contests in business, sports, and all aspects of design and construction. Architectural awards programs are frequently referred to as competitions, but are not to be confused with architectural design competitions. An architectural awards program is conducted to honor completed buildings, whereas the architectural design competition awards prizes and recognition to designs for projects not yet built.

The AIA Honors Awards program is conducted annually by the Institute. Architects are invited to submit a photographic exhibit of their completed work. Submissions are received anonymously and are judged by an awards jury of architects. Several hundred entries are received each year, and those judged to have exceptionally high quality receive the AIA Honors Award. This award, made in recognition of design excellence, honors both the architect and the owner.

Similar awards programs are conducted under a wide variety of sponsorship and may be organized on a national, regional, or local basis. Industry groups have conducted awards programs focused on demonstration of the best and most creative uses of materials. Local governmental or civic groups may sponsor awards programs in support of related municipal goals. Awards programs have provided recognition to architects, owners, builders, craftspeople, and others who are important contributors to the successful completion of projects of merit.

BIBLIOGRAPHY

1. *Code for Architectural Design Competitions,* American Institute of Architects, Washington, D.C., Document J 331, Dec. 1972 (now obsolete).
2. T. H. Creighton, *The Architecture of Monuments,* The Franklin Delano Roosevelt Memorial Competition, Reinhold, New York, 1962.
3. J. Strong, *Participating in Architectural Competitions: A Guide for Competitors and Assessors,* Architectural Press, Ltd., London, 1976, p. 2.
4. *Regulations for the Promotion and Conduct of Competitions,* Royal Institute of British Architects, RIBA Publications Ltd., London, England.
5. Ref 1, p. 1.
6. *Guidelines for Architectural Design Competitions,* American Institute of Architects, Washington, D.C., Document J 332, Nov. 1976.
7. *Handbook of Architectural Design Competitions,* American Institute of Architects, Washington, D.C., 1982.
8. *Code for Architectural Design Competitions* The Federation of Danish Architects, Copenhagen, Denmark.
9. *Standard Regulations for International Competitions in Architecture and Town Planning,* Union International des Archetectes, Paris, France.
10. *Recommendations Concerning International Competitions in Architecture and Town Planning,* United Nations Educational, Scientific and Cultural Organization, New York, 1956.
11. I. T. Fray, *They Built the Capitol,* Garrett and Massie, Richmond, Va., 1946, p. 19.
12. *Ibid.,* p. 36.
13. *The Chicago Tribune Tower Competition,* Vol. 1, Rizzoli, New York, 1980, p. 2.
14. *Ibid.,* p. 54.
15. M. Y. Ling, statement included with competition submission—not published.
16. J. Utzon, P. Keys and C. Forman. "Progress Reports on the Sydney Opera," *Architecture in Australia* **54,** 72–92 (Dec. 1965), **57,** 301–312 (Apr. 1968), 462–468 (June 1968), 642–643, (Aug. 1968), 814–820 (Oct. 1968).
17. "Abstract of a Proposed Tract for Competitions," American Institute of Architects, Washington, D.C.

General References

Refs 3, 7, 8 and 9 are good general references.

"The Tribune Tower Competition," The Chicago Tribune Co., Chicago, Ill., 1923; reprinted as *Chicago Tribune Tower Competition,* Vol. 1, Rizzoli, New York, 1980.

Alvar Aalto, Wittenborn and Co., Scarsdale, N.Y., 1963.

L. Adams, ed., *The Birmingham-Jefferson Civic Center National Architectural Competition,* Birmingham-Jefferson Civic Center Authority, Birmingham, Ala., 1969.

Alvar Aalto, Praeger, New York, 1971.

P. D. Spreiregen, *Design Competitions,* McGraw-Hill, Inc., New York, 1979.

J. F. Butler, *Competition 1792, Designing the Nation's Capitol,* Vol. 4, No. 1, Capitol Studies, U.S. Capitol Historical Society.

F. Kimbal and W. Bennett, "The Competition for the Federal Building 1792–93," Articles in the *Journal of the American Institute of Architects,* Washington D.C., **7,** 8–12, 98–102, 202–210, 355–361, 521–528 (Jan., March, May, Dec. 1919), **8,** 117–124 (March 1920).

A. Stanley McGaughan
American University
Washington, District of
Columbia

COMPUTER-AIDED DESIGN AND DRAFTING (CADD)

In recent years, the increased use of computers in the architect's office has resulted in widespread applications for preparing working drawings and specifications. The increased power of the microcomputer and the improved quality of images produced has made this economically feasible for the firms. The development of software for both two-dimensional (2D) and three-dimensional (3D) images by the profession and computer vendors has greatly improved the application of computer usage. Networking between computer terminals has allowed more than one individual to work on the drawings at the same time. For a diagram of equipment systems to create drawings, see Figure 2 in the article COMPUTERIZATION. Typical applications for computers in the architect's office indicate the possible application of CADD drawings (1).

APPLICATIONS

Programming. Computer-generated drawings of functional relationships and room adjacencies can be useful programming aids.

Site Design. Three-dimensional images, possibly combined with video images, can be used to show the proposed development on its actual site.

Project Management. Scheduling, assignment of staff, monitoring of progress, budgets, and hours spent can be diagrammed. Problems may occur with very simple projects, or extremely large and complex projects.

Schematic Design. Computer-aided design and drafting (CADD) has limited application during the schematic design phase because computers best address complex data and repetition, not associated with the sketch quality of schematic design. One appropriate application would be early involvement of consultants electronically linked to the architect's office to provide faster, better information during this phase.

Design Development. Increasing use of CADD allows more detailed information to be recorded at the design development phase, with immediate transfer to contract document development. Electronic communication with consultants and clients results in more complete design-development documentation.

Marketing. Marketing of architectural services may make use of desktop publishing with images taken from drawings and photographs for specific client applications, and for preparation of renderings. The 3D programs allow selection of appropriate views for preparation of hand-prepared renderings.

Contract Documents. The architect's most frequent use of CADD is for the development of contract documents. This computer application has been fairly recent, based on the earlier experience in engineering and electronics. Common building elements, symbols, dimensions, and notes can be electronically stored and used in the preparation of drawings. Some manufacturers have developed details that may be entered into the architect's computer; finish schedules and door and window schedules can be generated from the computerized drawings automatically.

Contract Administration. Field changes can be prepared and integrated into contract drawings using CADD. Field location of computers allows direct communication with the architect's office.

Facilities Management. Common uses of CADD for facilities management include drawings of the location and type of equipment, reorganization of spaces, and spatial needs for future growth. Special applications include location of wiring and cabling in a building to find the most direct or least crowded path for new lines.

The development of computers has meant lower costs for greater capability and new applications in the archi-

tect's office. Among developments that can be anticipated is the improved quality of information in all phases of project development. Anticipated uses include automatic code checks and zoning analysis generated from CADD drawings and better management control based on experience and judgment supported by increased timely information, including employee skill and experience applications.

In schematic design, more data will be available and less time will be spent on unworkable schemes. Smaller firms may be able to take on larger projects. Integration of architectural practice with engineering and other specialized consultants will increase and greater electronic sharing of information will occur. Increased compatibility between equipment will improve the flow of information and the development of standard data bases.

Direct linkage with clients will result in some changes in practice, particularly with the sophisticated client knowledge derived from their own computer applications. It may be anticipated that this will encourage a marketing approach to the client based on an integrated design team with full design capabilities.

Linkages of CADD to data bases for product selection and to other data bases will allow automated specification development. Cost-estimating data bases can also be accessed by information on the CADD drawings. These data bases could be accessed for continuous update and the user could obtain access through questioning. Decisions on product selection could automatically be shared with the manufacturers involved for use in preparation of shop drawings and manufacturing scheduling. Contractors could electronically identify the least costly or most available products for use on a given project, as well as deliveries in sequence of construction.

Applications of computers for recording and diagnosing existing conditions is under development. Photographs can be reproduced on the working drawings, and existing drawings can be read into the computer using digitizing equipment. As buildings are monitored and diagnosed by application of computers, maintenance will be improved. Computers can be used to train and provide reports for facility managers.

This article demonstrates that the CADD applications now in use will become only part of the expanding utilization of computers. Experience gained in other fields, which has been adapted for architectural use, suggests that further unanticipated applications will occur.

BIBLIOGRAPHY

1. S. Doubilet and T. Fisher, "Designing Electronically," *Progress. Archit.,* 113–128 (Apr. 1987).

General References
   The architectural press consistently publishes general information for computer and CADD operations of interest to architects:

Archit. Rec., published by McGraw-Hill, New York.

Architecture, published by the American Institute of Architects, Washington, D.C.

Progress. Archit., published by Reinhold Publishing, a division of Penton Publishing, Cleveland, Ohio.

See also COMPUTERIZATION.

ROBERT T. PACKARD, AIA
Reston, Virginia

COMPUTERIZATION

Architects have two things to offer their clients: design and service. Both can be greatly enhanced by computers. Architectural practice is virtually an information business. Design professionals spend the vast majority of their time gathering, sorting, and manipulating information. The result of such efforts is an abstract and technical information product in the form of contract documents. The documents represent the design. Their development and delivery is the service. Computerization of professional design practices has a universally strong effect on the skills of architects and engineers and how they manage the processes of information handling.

THE DEVELOPING NEED FOR INFORMATION

The importance of information has historically been congruent with the rise of industrialization. As world cultures evolved from craft-based and agrarian economies to manufacturing-based economies, the associated technologies became dependent on reliable and repeatable processes of production. Standardized products that could be made in large quantities were required. The new mechanics of industry had significant social implications, particularly with regard to anxieties about human safety. As a result, labor unions were born. Construction became more complex and the jurisdiction of the various trades overlapped and became less clear. Architects were consistently being asked to differentiate the various work items in their documents as well as to indicate greater detail for accurate production of machine-made components. There was a need for much greater quantities of information.

The differentiation and expansion of information for builders, along with the growing complexity of mechanized production, gave birth to whole new professional groups, including structural, heating, ventilating and air-conditioning, plumbing, and electrical engineers. Each of these groups developed subsets of information for the architect to assemble, coordinate, and distribute. The problems associated with this were more than just intellectual. There was, for example, the simple but critical physical problem of how to distribute such large quantities of documents. The answer came with the invention of the blueprint machine. It provided large quantities of information quickly and economically. It became a critical tool that allowed the architect to provide comprehensive design documents. What was lacking was a tool or tools to develop the information quickly and precisely.

DEVELOPMENT OF COMPUTING MACHINES

The invention of machines that could tabulate large, complex quantities of data was born out of the needs of the U.S. census and other government activities. When data for the 1890 census were being collected, it was realized that 1880 census data were still not fully compiled. Thus, a suitable tabulating machine was invented (1). During World War I, the War Industries Board was interested in regulating the production of all U.S. industries as well as the control and distribution of goods. Although this was never actually achieved, it reflected the pressing need for dealing with large, complex information models. Likewise, the Social Security Act necessitated the handling of large-scale data for what has been called the world's biggest bookkeeping job. In the 1950s, the science of cybernetics and computers, in principle, came into practical use in private industry. The industries, such as utilities, were large and few. When computers became commercially available in the early 1960s, architects started experimenting with their use.

COMPUTING SYSTEMS

A computer system, whether a large mainframe costing millions of dollars or a small, inexpensive desktop personal computer (PC), is composed of several basic components. As illustrated in Figure 1, these components are a person (or persons) operating the machine, data that are put into the machine, a central processing unit (CPU), memory banks, and the information that comes out of the machine. A more detailed illustration of some typical peripheral devices used in a configuration of computer hardware can be seen in Figure 2.

ARCHITECTURAL PRACTICE AND SYSTEMS ANALYSIS

The professional field of systems analysis is quite similar in process to that of architectural services (2). Both profes-

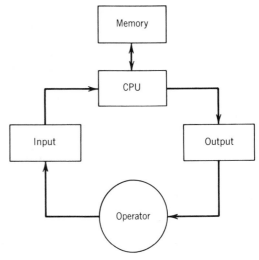

Figure 1. The basic components of a computer system.

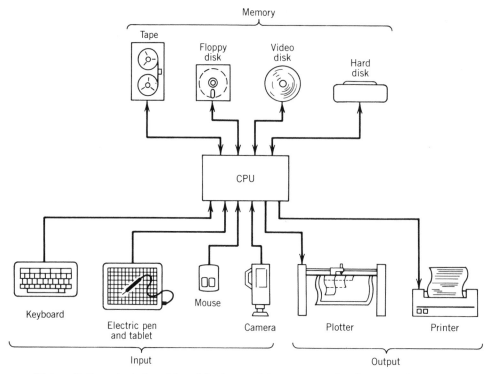

Figure 2. Some typical peripheral devices used in a computer hardware configuration.

sions are singularly creative and analytical; hence, architects are able to appreciate the way computers are used to solve problems and manipulate data. A direct comparison of systems development methodology and the development of architectural services is shown in Table 1.

INFORMATION SYSTEMS

Although the subjects of general systems theory and cybernetics are extensive, the general nature of processes, and particularly architectural practice, calls for an understanding of some basic notions of information and systems. A system is a set of objects and their interrelationships, which are ordered to a common goal. An information system is a major component of any organization. It is a metabolism for the delivery of goods or services. Information is intelligence derived by identifying data (facts) and overlaying the data with meaning, as defined by its use (3). It is interesting to note that a synergistic effect results when an organization emphasizes the totality of component entities. It is also interesting to note that as systems gain greater intelligence they require more and more information to remain comprehensive. In architectural practice, this is particularly seen in the complexity of a document production process that carries all of the anxieties of practice associated with errors and omissions. Such production processes are asymptotic to being truly complete. Design is never complete. It is shifted to the development of working drawings and specifications at some arbitrary point with respect to the design's refinement. Likewise, contract documents never reach true completion. They reach an arbitrary cutoff point where they are issued to construction

contractors. Both design professionals and contractors know that the process of construction is never complete and are left to negotiate the point where construction becomes maintenance. Maintenance is never complete until the building is demolished and the entire process begins again.

As design professionals go through the various stages of a project and its information development, they often fall prey to the phenomenon of "excess perfection," due to the open-ended requirements of the information system. Figure 3 graphically illustrates a curve typical of a work effort and its asymptotic relationship to completion. Only good information management can keep the costs of efforts from exceeding the fees agreed upon (4). But if it is a practice-based business rather than a business-based practice, the design professional will fall prey to the notion that perfection is complete information.

In order to overcome this phenomenon, good information management must include continuous control of several aspects of the work. These include services, quality, budget, and compensation (5). Maintaining an accurate accounting of contracted services, the owner's and architect's standards for a final product, and the moneys to be expended and reimbursed requires constant adjustment and tracking. The speed and precision of a computer make it an ideal tool for managing information systems, including those unique to architectural practice.

WHY ARCHITECTS USE COMPUTERS

Architects and other design professionals have turned to computers for a variety of reasons. One basic reason is

Table 1. Comparison of Systems Development Methodology and the Development of Architectural Sciences.

Systems Development Methodology	Development of Architectural Sciences
Systems analysis • definition of user needs • system scope • gathering and analyzing system study facts	*Programming* • definition of user needs • sizing of functional spaces • identification of technical requirements
General systems design • development of design blocks as work assignments • listing alternatives for user consideration	*Schematic design* • drawing functional relationship bubble diagrams • exploration of various forms and spaces
Systems evaluation and justification • employee impact analysis • cost effectiveness	*Preliminary design* • identification of suitable materials, construction techniques, and scope • construction cost estimate
Detailed systems design • precise definitions developed for each design block	*Contract documents* • production of working drawings and specifications
Systems implementation • training and education of users • system testing, conversion, and follow-up	*Construction contract administration* • monitoring construction for compliance with design intent • postconstruction evaluation

the need for a tool that can handle the complexities of design and construction information systems. As the data bases for these systems become more extensive, and as the systems become more and more integrated, the complexities of practice easily justify their use. The critical issue in the matter of practice management is quality control. This is particularly true in the production of contract documents. Any discrepancy, even a small one, can hurt the credibility of the architect with either the owner or the building contractor. Such failure quite often leads

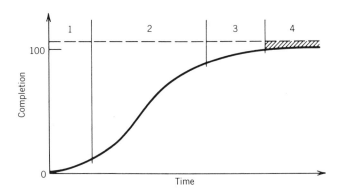

Figure 3. A typical work effort comprised of (*1*) a beginning effort, (*2*) a substantive effort, (*3*) completion, and (*4*) excess perfection (where results cannot be justified economically).

to legal action when the discrepancy, or a series of them, results in significant cost impacts. Computer applications can provide a rigorous format of procedures for adequate cross checking and detailed analysis of the entire process of professional service.

The computerization of professional design services enhances the working metabolism of the practice. Computer-aided drafting techniques and machine-plotted drawings provide tremendous precision in their applications. This is not to be confused with accuracy, however, since that depends on a conscientious effort by the system user.

Since the 1960s, the staffs of architects' offices have undergone a shift in the type of personnel who do the production drawings. Staff positions that had traditionally been titled draftsperson were filled by people who were not design professionals and were dedicated primarily to documentation. As more and more graduates of architectural schools came into the marketplace, their broader interests and capabilities created a basic change in the character of architectural practice. Although the skill of developing precise and accurate documents had been passed to the new generation of young professionals, documentation as a discrete task became limited when viewed within the context of professional practice. Today, the arduous nature of documentation is rapidly diminishing as a source of job satisfaction. There is a clear desire to increase the time devoted to design within the time available, as set by professional fees. The number of graduates of architectural schools has continued to increase, and architectural practice remains a labor-intensive industry that is sometimes awkward to manage, always the primary factor in fee proposals. Although job dislocation may or may not become a broader reality for younger architects, the entire industry faces increasing pressures of competition as other design entities gain greater market shares (6). The goal of greater efficiency is not simply based on greater profit motive, but is basic to the strategies of sales to clients who are very sophisticated in procuring services of all types, including design.

ESTABLISHING INFORMATION SERVICES IN PRACTICE

Terms such as "the computer revolution" have been popular. However, the transition from performing tasks manually to computerizing them has been an evolutionary process in several distinct areas: data processing, word processing, image processing, and network communications. These four areas can be identified as basic to any program of computer office automation. There are various ways to approach the implementation of computerized practices, as follow.

Service Bureaus. These separate and remotely located businesses offer specialized computer services for virtually any computer application. An individual service bureau's offerings are usually limited to certain types of applications, which necessitates employment of more than one bureau. They are initially relatively low in cost compared with the acquisition of in-house systems, but become very costly in the long run. Their advantages are that they allow quick bail out, low initial cost, and no hardware or software investment. Their disadvantages are that they offer relatively slow turnaround time and little firsthand experience and control.

Time Sharing. This involves the use of a remotely located business whose computer processes work either in an on-line interactive process with the customer by way of a terminal or in batch processes where data are sent to the computer facility and information is returned by messenger or mail. The advantages include dedicated responsibility, moderate costs, a range of services and costs, and preparatory experience to more sophisticated alternatives. The disadvantages include the high long-range expense and the possibility of the essential lock-in to the vendor.

Bottom-up Acquisition. This is the incremental acquisition of small, inexpensive computer systems, each dedicated to very specific tasks. The advantages of this approach are the low initial cost and relative ease of operation and management of acquisitions. The disadvantages are long-term high costs, a possible lack of system integration, and an eventual difficulty of comprehensive management control. In addition, smaller systems may not have the capacity to fulfill certain application needs, thereby frustrating the user and diminishing system credibility.

Top-down Acquisition. This is the single acquisition of larger shared-logic computer systems that have enough computing power to handle foreseeable applications. The advantages of this approach are the feasibility of acquiring any extent of software applications at any time, coherent centralized management control, long-range minimal cost, and single-source responsibility of support. The disadvantages are the high initial cost and sudden impact on a firm's organization and operations.

In general, the major benefits of computerizing an architectural practice are the improvement of quality control through better coordination of documents, greater precision, greater efficiency through higher speed, and stronger competitiveness through a state-of-the-art marketing image. The major risks are those of an unsuccessful implementation of the system and loss of financial investment.

As rapid advances continue to occur in both hardware and software development, the distinction between bottom-up and top-down approaches is becoming less clear. The trend is still toward smaller and more powerful systems, which points the way toward stand-alone workstations connected by flexible communication networks (7).

There is no foreseeable limit to industry changes in computing hardware, and so it seems quite reasonable for an architectural practice to consider a hybrid of acquisition approaches. No single system or type of approach to systems acquisition will offer total or permanent solutions to a firm's needs. A hybrid of manual techniques and shared-logic and stand-alone systems, although complex to deal with, offers positive flexibility in practice. Concerns about industrial obsolescence of systems are irrelevant as long as the systems continue to perform as intended.

OFFICE AUTOMATION IMPLICATIONS

The choice of approach and the presence of a new system in an office have significant implications for a practice's organization and operations. The impact is strong, and the commitment must come equally from top management, professional staff, and administrative support people. The impact is much more than that of technophobia, the fear of new technologies. In fact, the very personality of a firm is affected by computerization. Every organizing principle and day-to-day task will be touched by the presence of such systems. There is great truth in the proverb "software is policy," and a clear view of policies is essential for all levels of management and staff. Of course, such coherence is always desirable, but when introducing new systems, special care must be taken to realize that a fresh view of policies will probably be necessary and that the view must be nurtured throughout the firm, especially within top management.

When a large-capacity shared-logic system is installed, a distinct group must be responsible for the system's operations and management. The most positive way to distinguish such a group is to establish a subsidiary company that vends services to the parent company as well as to others. Creating such a company is a business decision. Whether separate or not, the schematic organization involves the following positions.

System Manager. The system manager oversees the day-to-day operations of the system and interfaces with the system vendor for continuing support and expanded applications. This person is responsible for troubleshooting and scheduling use of the system as well as overseeing training of future operator candidates.

Data Manager. The data manager acts as assistant to the system manager and starts, stops, and performs scheduled routine tasks associated with the system. These tasks include making backup files and verifying that operators have logged in and out. This person also has responsibility for maintaining discrete portions of the system database. In a multidiscipline firm, there is a different data manager for each discipline of interests.

Operators. The operators do the actual task applications on the system and may or may not be dedicated to this task alone. Dedicated personnel are nonprofessionals. However, professional designers may be operators, according to a firm's organizational interests, and it can be assumed that all personnel at virtually all levels will interact with the system in one way or another.

TRAINING OF OPERATORS

Training is intended to give individuals enough proficiency to continue their own self-directed development and is basically provided by system vendors or private consultants. Initial training is relatively short and intense, lasting one or two weeks. The period required to achieve a proficiency equal to that in traditional manual methods depends on the complexities of individual systems and the design disciplines involved. Architectural design and drafting applications can require learning periods of several months, compared with just days or weeks for clerical or administrative tasks. Scheduled additional training should be expected periodically to boost trainees beyond the limits of self-directed development. Selected operators implement training of future candidates under the direction of the system manager.

SYSTEM OPERATING SCHEDULE

Acquisition of a central host or shared-logic computer system suggests that a practice be operated more than eight hours per day. Architectural practices usually do, in any case, and the additional operating time of a system is desirable for two reasons. First, the system is a capital investment that should get maximum utilization. Second, various departments and individuals should have maximum operating time available, without having to compete for use of the system. Also, in terms of overall firm operations, extensive and rigorous system scheduling can have very positive benefits in general management techniques.

There are four basic daily activities to be scheduled for groups or individuals: preparation, work on the system, backup work (copying files), and lunch. It should be noted that, in contrast to what most architects believe, only about 40% of a design professional's time is spent doing drawings. Sixty percent is spent in technical reference, meetings, coordination and checking, site visits, conversation, and time off (8). Computerized design and drafting applications, which require the maximum amount of computing power, can be conveniently scheduled in shifts, as shown in Figure 4. The three-shift schedule illustrated is somewhat arbitrary with regard to the actual requirements of any given firm, but indicates how different entities' needs can be accommodated in a 12-h period.

PROFESSIONAL APPLICATIONS

As mentioned earlier, there are four general aspects of computer activity that can be applied to design profession activities. These are data processing, word processing, image processing, and network communications.

Data Processing. This includes the traditional, familiar function of numerical calculation of mathematical formulas, especially as used in matrix spreadsheet applications where different scenarios of formulated problems are quickly and easily developed. Such scenarios are usually thought of as "What if?" variations of a quantifiable situation.

Word Processing. This is the capturing, storing, and manipulation of written text. Manipulation can consist of removal, replacement, and rearrangement of individual letters, words, sentences, or paragraphs.

Image Processing. This consists of generating graphics, which may be anything from line drawings and charts to intricately detailed varying-tone drawings or photographs. Like data or words, such drawings and images can be produced in physical copies by a variety of printing and plotter devices that are peripheral to the computer.

Since medieval times, and probably before, graphic images have been central to the techniques of architectural practice (9). The advent of computer-aided design/drafting (CAD or CADD) represents one of the more intriguing aspects of computer applications in architectural practice.

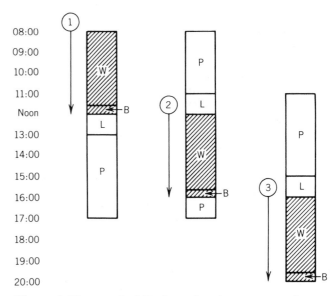

Figure 4. Three work shifts for a shared system spread over the period of 8:00 A.M. to 8:00 P.M. W, work time on the system; B, backup (copying) work; L, lunch; and P, preparation time (non-drawing activities).

Geometry is the most basic tool used in design or drafting since physical objects are most easily understood and manipulated in terms of their shapes and sizes. Circles, arcs, and curvilinear and straight lines are compiled in drawings in quantifiable relationships (10).

Computers have the capacity to store very large numbers of quantifiable relationships and permit users access to them for extensive and rapid manipulation. Such an interactive process of rapid manipulation involves the same mental processes of trial-and-judgment by the designer as have been used in the traditional design/drawing process for centuries. Such a machine-aided process also permits analysis of the same quantifiable relationships defining square footage, cubage, or listings of the amounts and costs of various construction components. Within the operations of a computer, design and drafting activities can be realized with great speed, repeatability, and precision. It should be noted that the term precision is used here and not accuracy, which is solely dependent on the judgment and instructions of the person operating the system.

In the most strict sense, design is only aided by a computer through facilitating rapid drawing. The artistic and inventive processes of design synthesis still occur in the human mind. This process will change, however, and the roles of man and machine will be obfuscated with the extended development of artificial intelligence. The so-called bionic architect will become a reality, with each individual defining a relationship to a computer system on personal rather than system terms.

Among the variety of devices used for graphic input in image processing is the electronic camera. Essentially, a TV camera device is useful in a variety of applications. For design or contract documentation, individual frames of videotape or video disk can be transferred directly onto sheets as photographic views of existing site features, buildings, and their details, which can also be combined with other elements of CAD.

The same sort of photocapturing of visual information can be applied to routine office administration tasks, such as recording all incoming project mail with a desktop camera. The only project information that needs to be digitalized and stored in a computer's memory for later retrieval is outgoing correspondence, reports, and specifications; the image processing of incoming items accounts for the other portion of the project record, resulting in virtually no need for office retention of paper records.

Network Communications. Network communications, like all forms of telecommunications, offers the most significant and exciting social and cultural implications. The complexity of the exchange of data, words, and images produced by networking, plus the tremendous capacities of computers and their storage devices, have produced a collective intelligence of profound professional consequences.

OTHER APPLICATIONS

The following indicates the range and types of professional applications for the design professional utilizing data, word, or image processing or network communications.

Marketing

Production, coordination, and filing of marketing materials result in such products as brochure narratives, resumes of key personnel, project data summaries, design drawings and renderings, sample contract documents, and consultants' credentials. Files can be classified to form libraries of photographs, slides, and videotapes. Public relations materials such as biographies, press clippings, fact sheets, speeches, published articles, and awards and honors can be input. Applications for client communications include mailing list manipulation, generation of standard letters, tracking of follow-ups, and interoffice lead processing.

Project Management

Project record items can be manipulated on the computer by maintenance of project directories, indexing of project records, summaries of project data, tracking of checklists for project management, working drawings, consultant coordination, specification coordination, logging and tracking of shop drawings, logging and tracking of construction sketches, tracking of change orders, logging and indexing of drawing documents, quantity surveying and material takeoff, cost estimating, project scheduling and labor planning, project accounting of time and expenses, budgets, and expenditures, fee planning, logging of invoices and communications via electronic mail, electronic conferences, and access to national databases.

Planning and Urban Design

Analysis of land use and its social and political consequences can be characterized by such activities as report generation, statistical modeling, optimization analysis, topography, soils, geology, climate, and water survey evaluations, environmental impact analyses of vegetation, wildlife, and flood control, analysis of local regulations for zoning, utilities, roads, and transportation, and optimization analysis of political and social trends, of public facilities, service facilities, population, and demographics.

Architectural Programming Design and Documentation

Information gathering, classification, manipulation, and synthesis into an artistically and technically detailed construction directive are characterized by such activities as functional relationship diagramming and weighted relationship analysis, code searching, sketching and solid modeling, solid model interference checking, perspective generation and sequential views, shadow analysis, illumination design and analysis, heat gain and loss analysis, volume and area calculation, integrated engineering design, construction products search and analysis, working drawing generation, reference drawing and standard detail cataloguing, specifications generation, detailed construction cost estimation, and intradocument and interdocument checking and coordination.

Contract Administration

Applications in contract administration include maintenance of submittal, shop drawing, samples, and change-order tracking logs, report generation, substitutions analysis, and generation and logging of construction sketches.

Multiple Use of Data

One aspect of computer functions should be noted here in order to explain how many of the applications listed work with each other. In principle, data compiled in one application area can be borrowed for use in another (11). This can be seen in such examples as the automatic generation of door schedules from floor plans or derivation of the building's square footage from the same floor plans for use in a marketing group's project data summary. As data are originated, they are arranged and stored in discrete formats that permit their combination and reuse with other discretely stored data. This principle is not unlike the layering of graphic information used in pin-registered overlay drafting. As databases go, there are typically hundreds of such layers. It is this highly detailed formatting of data that allows extensive manipulation in unique ways.

Facilities Management

A particularly interesting application of computers is in the field of facilities management. Until recently, when architects completed a project they would roll up the documents and put them in storage. Historically, an architect's interests in and duties to a project lasted for the life of a building or the term of the architect's career. No alteration, or even decorative change, was considered without the original architect's participation. With the advent of modern technology, such participation became more cumbersome and reverted to the owner's building maintenance department. Consequently, the facilities management tasks, including redesign and the revision and updating of drawings and other documents, did not have the benefit of professional expertise.

As the use of computers became more prevalent in the development of construction documents, engineers and architects came to realize two important things. First, in its digitized form, document information was easy to manipulate and revise. Second, the same information was an extremely valuable commodity that could be revised and marketed in a variety of ways, including anything from generating maintenance schedules to tracking an entire building's inventory of partitions, equipment, or furniture. Architects and their clients are again realizing the benefits of comprehensive services.

Artificial Intelligence and Expert Systems

Automation, in its true sense, is computers taking over tasks and finishing them without the involvement of a human being. Many of the computer applications seen in architects' offices today are not truly automated, but are simply mechanized versions of previously manual techniques (12). In true automation, data bases are wholly integrated. Although many data bases in use today relate to each other by sharing data, such sharing is usually limited and, for the most part, not involved with the design process. Artificial intelligence (AI) is the field of computer science that deals with operating systems performing tasks normally requiring human intellectual activity. These include the ability to communicate in English (or other languages), to recognize objects by using the visual and tactile senses, and to solve problems. Moreover, as with human intelligence, AI involves the ability to reason and learn. The computer operating systems designed for AI involve the following (13):

- *Natural language,* communicating in written or spoken human languages.
- *Robotics,* electromechanical vision and ability to manipulate physical objects.
- *Automated programming,* programming that is self-generated from abstract or generalized task descriptions.
- *Knowledge-based systems,* systems that are able to interpret and react to unstructured situations such as in controlling robots or providing a variety of responses to an extensive range of possible events.
- *Expert systems,* a category of knowledge-based systems that are oriented to communicating with people, rather than equipment, and guiding them toward a problem solution.

It is within the realm of expert systems that architects will find the greatest benefit to and change in professional practice techniques. Expert systems solve problems that typically take hours, days, or more of human effort. They handle completely new problems and can accommodate

vagueness in response to inquiries. They reason through comparative choices based on their own accumulated knowledge, working through question-and-answer dialogues with their users. They also explain their decisions and conclusions, which makes them very comfortable for people to use.

For architects, the use of expert systems will integrate the aforementioned range of computer applications to such an extent that all aspects of professional practice, including design, will be enhanced. Several nations, most notably Japan, have set major goals in the research of AI in order to establish themselves as world leaders in information businesses (14). Since design of the built environment touches virtually every aspect of any nation's culture, architects and their practices can be expected to be significant participants in this paradigm.

BIBLIOGRAPHY

1. P. Driscoll, J. Mazzeki, and F. Wilson, *Journal of the American Institute of Architects,* 27 (July 1982).
2. J. G. Burch, Jr., F. R. Stratter, and G. Grudnitsky, *Information Systems: Theory and Practice,* 3rd ed., John Wiley & Sons, Inc., New York, 1983, p. 19.
3. A. Ralston and E. D. Reilly, Jr., eds., *Encyclopedia of Computer Science and Engineering,* 2nd ed., Van Nostrand Reinhold Co., Inc., New York, 1983, p. 715.
4. D. Haviland, *Managing Architectural Projects: The Process,* American Institute of Architects, Washington, D.C., 1981, p. 36.
5. *Ibid.,* p. 39.
6. H. Mileaf, *Techpointers,* Construction Industry Group, McGraw-Hill Information Systems Co., New York, Feb. 1985, p. 1.
7. C. Olson, *Building Design & Construction,* 93 (Aug. 1985).
8. F. Stitt, *Architectural Rules of Thumb,* Guidelines Publications, Grinda, Calif., 1974, p. 48.
9. S. Kostfed, *The Architect, Chapters in the History of the Profession,* Oxford University Press, New York, 1977, p. 74.
10. M. Schley, *Architectural Technology,* 50 (Summer 1985).
11. Ref. 3, p. 441.
12. H. Mileaf, *Techpointers,* Construction Industry Group, McGraw-Hill Information Systems Co., New York, Oct. 1984, p. 2.
13. D. LaCoe, *Robotics World,* 30 (Oct. 1984).
14. E. A. Feigenbaum and P. McCorduck, *The Fifth Generation,* Addison-Wesley Publishing Co., Inc., Reading, Mass., 1983, p. 20.

General References
Refs. 2, 3, 10, and 14 are good general references.

J. Patterson, *Information Methods for Design and Construction,* John Wiley & Sons, Inc., London, 1977. A relatively early account of principles and experiments in the use of computers in architectural planning and design.

W. Mitchell, *Computer-aided Architectural Design,* Petrocelli Caarter, New York, 1977.

J. Patterson, *Architects and The Micro Processor,* John Wiley & Sons, Inc., Chichester, UK, 1980. A sequel to the above.

Y. Masuda, *The Information Society as Post Industrial Society,* Institute for the Information Society, Tokyo, 1981. A highly readable and thoroughly stimulating account of Japan's master plan to be the world's foremost information society.

See also COMPUTER-AIDED DESIGN AND DRAFTING (CADD).

STEVEN C. GATSCHET, AIA
Mirick Pearson, Batcheler,
Architects
Philadelphia, Pennsylvania

CONCERT HALLS.   See MUSIC HALLS

CONCRETE—ARCHITECTURAL

The architectural concrete building is distinguished by the monolithic use of concrete for aesthetic finish as well as the frame, floors, and walls of the building. This continuous use of concrete in building elements that serve different functions allows the designer opportunity to conceive a building as a true whole and thus ultimately enhance an occupant's experience of its beauty. An architectural concrete facade is unique because it can be easily worked by the mold or formwork in depth at a small scale. This allows an interplay of light and shadow, and a resulting architectural texture that in other materials could only be achieved by intricate joinery (Fig. 1). There is structural continuity among column, beam, and floor as well as an architectural integration of function and finish that cannot be duplicated in other building types. However, this continuity also demands more complex analysis (than curtain-wall and steel frames) of reactions to structural and environmental loads imposed upon the building. This discussion focuses on the aesthetic qualities of concrete and the technical coordination required to achieve those aesthetics.

Although architectural concrete is produced on site, often under adverse weather conditions and by a workforce usually accustomed to placing concrete for other functions,

ie, roads, foundations, and structural frames, it is nonetheless required for the concrete to compete in aesthetic quality with materials finished in controlled environments or fabricated on a production line. The owner, designer, and contractor also recognize that the building is not built in highly specialized and incremental stages, but is assembled by a simultaneous process.

The concrete performs several functions at once (ie, weathertight envelope, structural frame, artistic expression). In constructing an architectural concrete building, these operations are not isolated, but are combined into one complex process, the installation of a finished material. This process is unique to the building type and provides great opportunity for artistic expression, cost economies, and/or failure.

Success is visible when the surface is consistent in its color and texture, the architectural volume is precisely aligned, and the natural cracking is controlled. To achieve this, the forms used to cast the concrete receive greater attention than the formwork used to cast structural concrete (ultimately concealed within the finishes of the building). The formwork is specially detailed to:

1. Withstand the hydraulic pressure of liquid concrete without leaking (design for full-liquid head in Fig. 2).
2. Be erected in the sequence envisioned by the design team (construction-oriented design in Fig. 3).

Figure 2. Design for full-liquid head. The formwork must be designed to withstand the complete hydraulic pressure generated by the concrete before it sets or else it will burst. A time-graduated placement is based on weather conditions, which are not in the complete control of the contractor.

Figure 1. Grand Coolee Dam, Bruer/Gatje, Papachristou and Smith. An example of the manipulation of depth of mold to create an interplay of light and shadow.

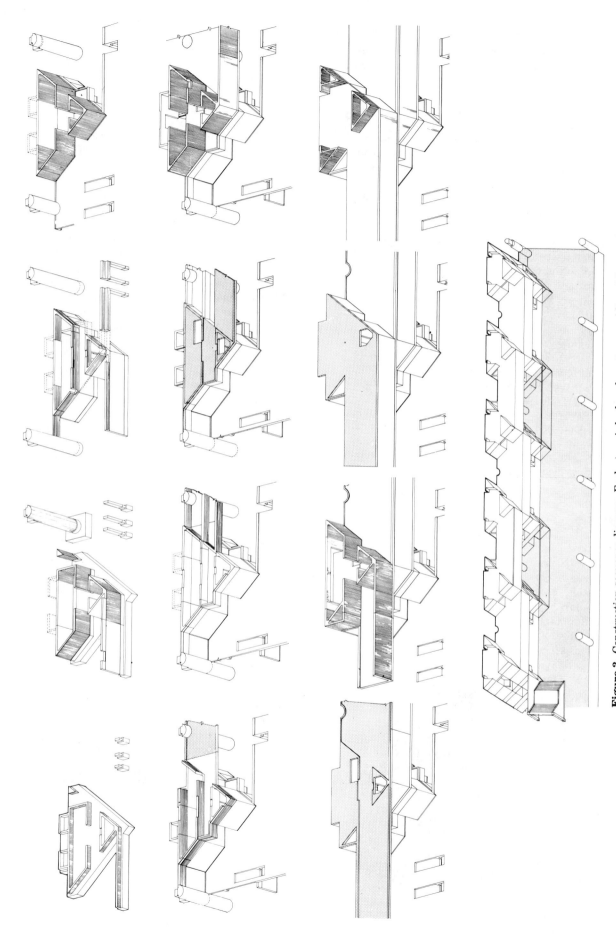

Figure 3. Construction-sequence diagram. Each stage is broken down to assemblies of formwork for that stage. The assembly in turn is detailed for placement volume, form ties, liner patterns, construction joints, and control joints.

715

3. Present a finish that is acceptable as cast or as modified after casting (bush-hammered, sandblasted, etc) (Fig. 4).

The formwork receives special input from the owner and architect because the finish is cast on site in the initial phase of the project; the means and methods of formwork construction dictate more than safe support of liquid concrete, ie, the formwork creates the finish; and the contracts of all other trades distinguish the concrete work that is exposed (architectural) from the concealed work (structural). The air conditioning, plumbing, and electrical work is more closely integrated into an architectural concrete building (than a steel frame) because there are fewer suspended ceilings (more concrete soffits) and fewer furred columns (more exposed concrete columns).

HISTORY

Concrete was used by Roman engineers in 200 B.C.; however, it was largely ignored during the following centuries and did not reemerge as a viable building material until the industrial revolution (Table 1). Advancements in reinforced concrete design made by the Europeans A. de Baudot, F. Hennebique, R. Maillart, and A. Perret showed that the material was capable of supporting structural loads and was an alternate to newly developed structural iron products. The standardization of concretes had enabled engineers to design with confidence. Dramatic examples of structural concrete technology are the interior vaults of the church of St. Jean de Montmartre, designed by A. de Baudot and built in 1894, and the long-span bridges in Switzerland, designed by R. Maillart and built in the early 1900s. Ernest Ransome and several structural engineers in the United States developed the technology of reinforced concrete for grain silos and for low-rise factories. Photographs of these buildings had a profound impact on the new age designers in Europe. At the turn of the century, the architects of the early modern movement broke from the traditional emphasis on applied ornamentation and presented straightforward, unadorned designs that reflected the machine-age aesthetic (modular and factory mass-produced), a concern for comprehensive planning, and a structural frame exposed in the final finish. This is best illustrated in the Cité Industrial presentation by T. Garnier in 1917. In this project, factories, housing, and public buildings were to be exposed reinforced concrete. Ransome, Garnier, and Perret pioneered the material for the industrial construction because the flat slab allowed more space from floor to ceiling (with flat plate design, dropped beams were not required); allowed greater daylight into the building (punched openings in bearing masonry eliminated); the concrete did not require additional treatment for fireproofing (as did steel structures); and, with some additional attention, a reasonable finish could be attained without adding another layer of construction (ie, terra cotta cladding or brick). In 1926, Le Corbusier's "Five Points of Architecture" advanced Garnier's artistic directions and Ransome's engineering advancements, and established reinforced concrete slabs and columns as a basic tenet of modern architecture.

At the Werkbund exhibition in Stuttgart, Germany, Le Corbusier, Mies Van der Rohe, Walter Gropius, Peter Behrens, and many other leading architects of the time designed and built a development of workers' housing that presented a new technology of reinforced concrete, combined with the machine-age aesthetic. Three factors restrained the growth of the building type: the worldwide depression during the 1930s, the rise of reactionary societies (unwilling to experiment) in Europe and Russia, and the problems encountered when reinforced concrete buildings were set in climates of heavy rainfall or recurring frost. However, the Villa Savoye in 1931 and the Swiss Pavilion in 1932, both designed by Le Corbusier, maintained the new tradition of concrete in architecture despite these restraints.

In 1939, R. Maillart designed "The Cement Hall," a thin shell arch that dramatically presented yet again the possibilities of concrete. During World War II, the demand for steel (armaments) surpassed the demand for concrete, with the result that steel technology, rapidly upgraded, was better prepared for the building boom after the war.

Le Corbusier had continued with only theoretical work during that time, but he returned to the built environment with the Unite d'Habitation, reemphasizing the principles first professed in the early 1900s by modern architects. This cast-in-place apartment building with rough, board-formed concrete surfaces became the most influential concrete building in its time. It was soon followed by his work in Chandigarh, which introduced this low energy

Figure 4. New York University Towers, I. M. Pei and Partners. An early use in the United States of architectural concrete for a high-rise residential complex.

technology to developing nations with spectacular results.

In the United States, I. M. Pei took the building type from its association with utilitarian factories and brought it to higher sophistication. The Kips Bay apartments and the Earth Sciences building at Massachusetts Institute of Technology (M.I.T.) (Fig. 5) exemplify architectural concrete design and construction as follows:

1. Design with construction orientation.
2. Architectural input into formwork design.
3. Concern for modular formwork.
4. Specification of cement color.
5. Construction of a mock-up.

Paul Rudolph, Louis Kahn, and Oscar Niemeyer continued using architectural concrete for their buildings around the world.

QUALITY CONTROLS AND REFERENCE STANDARDS

With the proliferation of the building type during the 1950s and 1960s came problems of inconsistent colors, textures, and tolerances. Owners, designers, and contractors unfamiliar with the special nature of the building type often suffered with architectural concrete that was neither durable nor visually acceptable. In response, the American Concrete Institute organized committees and published the *Guide to Cast-in-Place Architectural Concrete* (1) and several other standards addressing problems including placing concrete in hot and cold weather and curing concrete. The Portland Cement Association, the American Society for Testing and Materials (ASTM), the Concrete Reinforcing Steel Institute (CRSI), and the American Concrete Institute (ACI) all provide reference specifications for the industry.

Quoting or referencing the appropriate standards in contract documents is necessary, but does not ensure a quality finish because of the widely varying experience of contractors and a general misconception that whatever can be designed can be built. These concerns are acknowledged during the design phase and monitored through the construction phase by an individual versed in the building type. As the incremental stages of building (Fig. 6) become more specialized and fragmented (part of the industry-wide trend), it is all the more critical that one individual start at the initial design phase and continue by coordinating the interrelated trades with the final product, the architectural concrete building, foremost in mind.

This role of quality management has been described by James Shilstone as a concrete-process professional (2) and developed into a methodology of "construction oriented design" by Reginald Hough (3). An architectural concrete design must be first and foremost constructable. Architectural concrete requires more control over the means and methods of construction than other building types. At the same time, contract documents must clearly define the legal responsibilities of each participant in the building process. The designer must avoid the legal liabilities involved in trying to require particular means and methods

because this is the sole province of the contractor, but the designer must describe preliminary requirements that will develop an acceptable final product. This requires a sophisticated understanding of the roles of the building team members.

THE ROLE OF THE OWNER

As it is the owner who decides to build the building, it is he or she who chooses the material. The owner may employ the architect/engineer and contractor or construction manager to recommend materials based on needs, aesthetics, local availability, time factors, and cost, but it is the owner who ultimately decides upon architectural concrete and provides the leadership from the project's beginning to its end.

This choice is based on value engineering. An architectural concrete finish is often less expensive than the other finishes that must be applied over a structural frame. The cost to produce a visually acceptable finish, the architectural premium, must be separated from the cost to cast the structure. This architectural premium includes costs for special mix designs, mock-ups, upgraded form assemblies (ties and joinery), special form contact surfaces, reinforcing placement, precision and alignment, concrete placement, form removal, finishing, and/or sealing. From these items, a cost per finished square foot can be developed and then compared to other finishes such as sheet rock and paint, tile, glass, metal, or stone. The finish and structure of concrete can then be compared to other building systems (combinations of steel concrete and sheetrock, etc).

The owner assembles the building team and must make sure that each member of the team knows his or her role in the process. Employing an outside architectural concrete consultant to overview the activities of architect, engineer, and contractor, and independently report back to the owner does not assure the success of an architectural concrete building because this often only relieves the major players of their collective responsibility to produce a high quality product. The owner's initial program must establish requirements for each of the building team members.

During construction, the owner must be prepared to accept finished, yet structurally incomplete, sections prior to completion of the whole building. Since the finished concrete is also often the first trade on the job (as the structural frame), with roofing, glazing, and mechanical trades completing their work several months later, there is an obligation on the part of the owner to review the work during an interim stage of the building's construction. Upon completion of a section of architectural concrete work, the owner reviews the finish and has temporary protection installed over the completed concrete. The owner maintains this protection while the remaining trades (roof, glass, mechanicals, etc) complete their work. For other building types, the owner will generally wait until the entire project is complete before review and acceptance. For architectural concrete, this time frame is often too long because the finish (concrete) comes with the structural frame and an owner will not remove that structure once it is built upon. The concrete subcontractor, once

Table 1. Architectural Concrete Time Line

1. 55 B.C.
    Roman Amphitheater, Pompei, Italy
	14. 1889
	    Bridge (reinforced concrete arch), E
	    Ransome, San Francisco, California
		24. 1909
		    La Mouche Slaughterhouse, T.
		    Garnier, France

2. 27 B.C.
    Cement cures in water, Rome, Italy
	15. 1894
	    Church of St. Jean de Mont Martre
	    (exposed arches and vaults), A. de
	    Baudot, France
		25. 1909
		    Transit-mixed concrete

3. 1–199 A.D.
    Roman Colosseum, Basilica of
    Constantine, Pantheon Dome, Rome,
    Italy
	16. 1895
	    Factory at Tourcoing (concrete
	    structural frame), F. Hennebique,
	    Tourcoing, France
		26. 1912
		    Centenary Hall (ribbed dome), A.
		    Perret, Breslau, Germany

4. 1121
    Reading Abbey, Reading, UK
	17. 1901–1908
	    Arch bridges (continuity of two-way
	    slab and "mushroom" column), R.
	    Maillart, Switzerland
		27. 1916
		    Concrete-frame house, R. Van't Hoff,
		    Utrecht, The Netherlands

5. 1756
    Eddystone Lighthouse, J. Smeaton,
    Cornwall, UK
	18. 1902
	    Rue Franklin Apartments (concrete
	    frame), A. Perret, Paris, France
		28. 1917
		    Orly airport hangars (parabolic
		    vaults), E. Fressinet, Orly, France

6. 1796
    Roman cement patent, J. Parker,
    London, UK
	19. 1902
	    Ingalls building (reinforced-concrete
	    skyscraper), Ferro-Concrete Co.,
	    Cincinnati, Ohio
		29. 1918
		    Selma cargo ship (lightweight
		    concrete boat), R. J. Wig, United
		    States

7. 1824
    Portland cement patent, J. Aspdin,
    London, UK
	20. 1904
	    The Industrial City (reinforced
	    concrete, planned for use in all
	    building types), T. Garnier, Paris,
	    France
		30. 1919
		    Futurism, Sant'Elia, Italy

8. 1825–1843
    Thames Tunnel, Rotherlide, UK
	21. 1905
	    Rue de Ponthieu garage (exposed
	    concrete frame), A. Perret, France
		31. 1920
		    Five points of architecture, Le
		    Corbusier, 2nd International
		    Exposition

9. 1854
    Reinforced concrete patent, W.
    Wilkinson, London, UK
	22. 1907
	    Tilt-up wall construction, R. Aiken,
	    Zion City, Illinois
		32. 1922
		    Notre Dame du Raincy (vaults and
		    columns exposed), A. Perret, Raincy,
		    France

10. 1856. Reinforced concrete patent, F.
    Coignet, Paris, France
	23. 1908
	    Ingersol Terrace (tract houses cast-
	    in-place with modular forms), T.
	    Edison, Union, New Jersey
		33. 1928
		    Horticultural Hall (elliptical arches
		    exposed), Easton/Robertson,
		    Westminster, UK

11. 1867
    Reinforced concrete patent for wire
    mesh in plate slabs and arches, J.
    Monier, Paris, France
		34. 1931
		    Villa Savoye (concrete columns, slabs,
		    spiral stairs), Le Corbusier, Poissy,
		    France

12. 1871
    Portland cement, D. Saylor, United
    States
		35. 1932
		    Concrete pumped by compressed air

13. 1875
    Ward's Castle, R. Mook, Port Chester,
    New York		

this work is complete, cannot reasonably police the activity of the other subcontractors.

Lastly, the owner must prevent damage by graffiti and consider a program of cleaning. Concrete is a porous stone; the longer paint, rust, and grime remain on its surface, the more deeply it is absorbed. A number of sealers and coatings have been developed that prevent this absorption, but several result in a glossy finish. This sheen is incompatible with the desired stonelike quality, in some cases peels off when exposed to ultraviolet light, and in some cases will not allow the stone to breathe. An alternate treatment is applying a chemical that is absorbed within the first ¼ in. on the surface, prevents liquid penetration any further than that, and does not impart a sheen or discoloration to the surface. In this way, the stain remains on the surface and can be removed with relative ease. Selection of a graffiti and dirt-control system is often made after several experiments.

THE ROLE OF THE ARCHITECT

The architect conceptualizes the shape, color, and texture of the building in response to the owner's program require-

ments. The architect also addresses the constructability of the design by developing the following:

1. A shape that is compatible with the techniques used for concrete construction.
2. A layout of joints that allows for the natural tendency of the material to crack and allows the contractor to develop a productive cycle of work.
3. A pattern of tie holes that allows the location of form ties to support the concrete when it is initially placed.

Shapes. Shapes of architectural concrete buildings range from the elegant thin shells developed by Candela to the massive structures designed by Kenzo Tange. The designed shape should reflect the methodology of concrete construction. This is achieved by conceptualizing the structure as the result of a molding or forming process. Whereas the module of the curtain-wall facade is the grid of mullions, the module of the masonry is the brick, the module of a steel frame is the grid of beams, and the module of the concrete building is the size and shape of the formwork.

36. 1934
    Empire swimming pool (hinged arches with stiffening ribs), O. Williams, London, UK

37. 1935
    Hippodrome Raceway (cantilevered shell vaults), Torroja, Madrid, Spain

38. 1938
    Swiss Pavilion, Le Corbusier, Paris, France

39. 1938
    Air-entrained concrete sidewalks, N.Y. Depart. of Transportation, New York, New York

40. 1939–1943
    Ferrocement boats, P. L. Nervi

41. 1939
    Cement Hall (barrel vault), R. Maillart, Zurich, Switzerland

42. 1950
    Johnson's Wax Laboratory (cantilevered floors from hollow reinforced core), F. L. Wright, Racine, Wisconsin

43. 1950
    Exhibition Hall (ribbed dome, ferrocement), P. Nervi, Turin, Italy

44. 1951
    Cosmic Ray Pavilion (thin shell parabolas), F. Candela, University City, Mexico

45. 1952
    Unite d'Habitation (board-formed columns, spandrels, soffits), Le Corbusier, Marseilles, France

46. 1954
    Church of the Miraculous Virgin (double-curved vaults), F. Candela, Mexico City, Mexico

47. 1951–1960
    Secretariat, Courts of Justice, Parliament (rough-cast concrete, wood and steel forms), Le Corbusier, Chandigarh, India

48. 1957
    Cabero warehouse (folded-plate roof), F. Candela, Vallejo, Mexico

49. 1957
    Kips Bay Apartments (concrete warehouse), I. M. Pei, New York, New York

50. 1958
    Unesco Headquarters, Breuer/Nervi, Paris, France

51. 1959
    Monastere Sainte-Marie de la Tourette (board form and exposed aggregate), Le Corbusier, Lyons, France

52. 1960
    Kurashiki City Hall (New Brutalism), K. Tange, Kurashiki, Japan

53. 1960
    Hydraulic-pumped concrete in mobile trucks

54. 1960
    TWA Terminal (shell roof), E. Saarinen, New York, New York

55. 1962
    Air-traffic control towers, I. M. Pei/ Severud, Chicago, Illinois

56. 1963
    Yale Art and Architectural Building (bush-hammered/reeded texture), P. Rudolph, New Haven, Connecticut

57. 1963
    New Haven parking garage (continous-board form), P. Rudolph, New Haven, Connecticut

58. 1965
    Salk Institute (smooth-form finish), L. Kahn, La Jolla, California

59. 1967
    Marina City (concrete high rise), B. Goldberg, Chicago, Illinois

60. 1967
    Dallas City Hall, New York University Towers (board and fin-formed textures), I. M. Pei

61. 1962–1983
    National Assembly Building, L. Kahn, Dacca, Bangladesh

62. 1978
    National Gallery of Art, I. M. Pei, Washington, D.C.

63. 1985
    River City, B. Goldberg, Chicago, Illinois

64. 1986
    Javits Convention Center, I. M. Pei, New York, New York

The architect may conceptualize a series of forms to design the building much as he or she would use a combination of mullion patterns, bricks, or steel frames to design other types of buildings. The difference between these other materials and concrete is that the designer is "building" with materials (formwork) that are not ultimately part of the finished product; the form leaves only its impression (Fig. 7). In fact, an observer of the construction process might conclude that first a structure of formwork is constructed, then a second building is constructed in its place. This is a distinction that is carried throughout the building process by a construction-oriented design or a design oriented toward a methodology of construction. The characteristics of the formwork that have permanent effect on the architectural design are the form and form contact surface; the size, shape, and texture of the individual molding object; and the assembly, the individual forms combined to cast the concrete often in a repetitive manner, ie, cycles (the cycle is discussed in the section The Role of the Contractor).

Although reinforced concrete appears to be a material that can be shaped into an unlimited variety of forms, actual engineering design and building practice dictates a certain measure of standardization. In fact, some of the unpopularity of the architectural-concrete-building type derives from the misconception of the material's flexibility. The material's flexibility has already been dramatically exhibited; the present effort is now toward structures that can be repeated (with some modification) from job to job (eg, office and institutional buildings to apartments). The design profession and construction industry have standardized cements and reinforcing steel, and continue to simplify profiles, calculations, and reinforcing steel details much like, for example, the steel industry has done for connection details. Standardization of a job so that it can be constructed in series of cycles, although traditionally in the primary interest of the contractor, is best initiated by a modular architectural design that is intrinsic to the shape of the building.

The architect suggests a formwork assembly for typical conditions from which the contractor develops shop drawings. Once the architect approves these submittals, the contractor constructs a mock-up.

Designing the Pattern of Joints. The natural tendency of concrete to crack is considered by the location of shrinkage control joints and construction joints (Fig. 8). Concrete

Figure 5. Massachusetts Institute of Technology Earth Sciences building, I. M. Pei and Partners. The form establishes a pattern of joints that must be coordinated with columns, spandrels, fenestration, and ventilation of the building.

Figure 7. Installation of a gang form on successive wall lifts, illustrating the concept of designing with building materials not ultimately part of the finished product.

placement starts and ends at the construction joint. Because it is the plane between a cured and a new placement, the construction joint is a built-in plane of weakness at which the concrete will separate. The location of construction joints is checked by the structural engineer.

The placement is usually larger than the volume at which the concrete will crack and, as a result, the concrete will shrink and crack in a random manner (roughly 10 ft on center) if not controlled by a system of induced planes of weakness, ie, shrinkage-control joints. A rustication

form reduces the cross-sectional thickness of the wall and thus creates a plane of weakness at that location. In this way, the crack will most likely form in the shadow of the joint. The rustication form is also used to cover the butted edges of smooth form panels, prevent an overpour from a new placement onto a previous placement, and hide any misalignment of the panels.

The design indicates a pattern of joints that will incorporate the concrete's tendency to leak and shrink. The pattern of joints implies a size of panel or gang form (Fig.

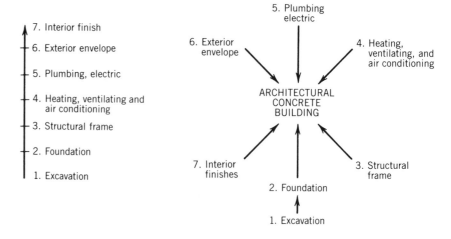

Figure 6. (a) Incremental stages and **(b)** simultaneous process of construction.

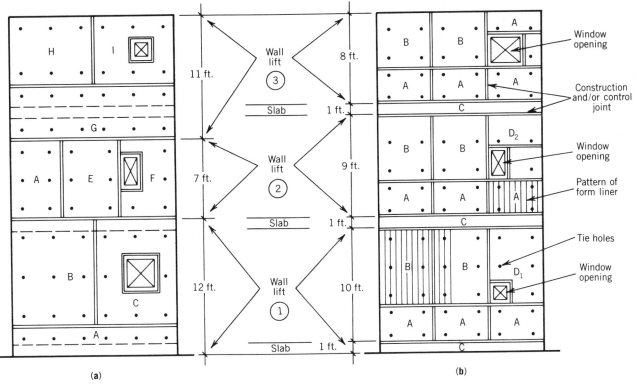

Figure 8. Designing a pattern of joints. **(a)** Not preferred. Note that there are eight different panel types. Successive wall lifts 2 and 3 are larger, and tie holes vary from wall lift to wall lift, making reuse impossible; **(b)** Preferred. Note that wall lifts 1–3 are smaller and window openings are larger so that formwork can be cut down or cut away, but reused for successive placements.

9). The greatest economy will be achieved by limiting the number of different panel types and developing a module of formwork that can be used over and over again throughout the job.

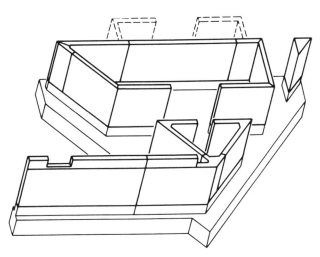

Figure 9. Wall lift. Three-dimensional view indicates how construction joints divide the length of wall into placements that foster the aesthetic characteristics required and prevent techniques that will diminish the final appearance. Joints limit the lengths of walls and thereby control concrete's natural tendency to crack and discourage diagonal lift lines associated with excessively long placements.

Texture. Texture can be achieved by changing the form contact surface or by altering the as-cast surface after it is cured. A variety of surface textures can be achieved by using different form contact surfaces (form liners). For a smooth and dense surface, fiber glass, steel, or high density overlay plywood are used. For a light grain, milled wood boards tightly fastened together and high grade plywood are applied. The wood absorbs water and leaves a sandy texture that is darker than the nonabsorptive liners. For a heavy porous and rough surface, rough-hewn boards are the desired materials. For a molded and patterned surface, modular panels with raised and depressed elements can be used.

Sand blasting can be either a light application, using a very fine sand spray which removes or steams the cement surface, or a heavy abrasive blasting which completely exposes the aggregate. Textures between these two extremes are also possible. In most architectural concrete jobs, the surface is at least lightly sandblasted to remove superficial cement paste that would otherwise weather away (due to acid rain), resulting in an uncontrolled and streaked pattern. The sand and stone are intentionally exposed to give a more granular appearance to the concrete. Bush-hammering fractures the surface by pounding (usually pneumatically) the concrete with a blunt hammer. Jack-hammering fractures the surface with a chisel.

Chemical surface retarders are applied to form contact surfaces to slow the set of cement paste on the finish surface of the concrete long enough so that the paste can be washed or brushed away to expose the matrix. By removing the cement paste from the surface of the concrete, the corresponding aesthetic problems of surface cracking (crazing), bug holes, and rain streaking are largely avoided. These techniques can vary with the skill of the mechanic and can be combined to present unique surfaces.

When the aggregate will be exposed by chemical or mechanical means, it is often preselected (gap-graded) so that the size of the aggregate stone is of a uniform diameter throughout.

Color. The selection of cement colors has been reduced in recent years. Mineral oxide pigments and color conditioning admixtures in liquid or granular form are more often used to give integral color. To produce the purest colors, the pigments and additives are generally used in a white cement mix. The precise color, its corresponding mix, reaction to form release agents, resistance to fading, etc, are all established during the mock-up stages of the job. For large jobs, repetition of the precise color from one placement of concrete to another is difficult to achieve because of variations in the mix, variations in the trucks used to transport the concrete, and the weather conditions. Different colors are commonly achieved by changing the type of sand and cement used in the design mix.

THE ROLE OF THE CONTRACTOR

Mock-up

Architectural concrete construction differs from structural concrete in its initial phases because it requires erection of a mock-up or test pour prior to the actual work in the field. In fact, this phase more closely resembles curtain-wall construction in that materials, assemblies, and installation techniques are tested and developed by the contractor to meet the architectural requirements and to suit the construction site. Through a process of trial and error, the test pours establish the formwork system, the detailing of construction and control joints, form ties, mix design, reinforcing steel installation, concrete placement and consolidation techniques, and the labor requirements for the work. The mock-up usually includes a window opening, the finish, and geometries that are typical to the architecture. Once approved, the mock-up serves as a standard of finish from which each job concrete placement is accepted or rejected.

Whereas the architect suggests a formwork design and erection sequence, it is the responsibility of the contractor to develop details suitable to the workforce that will cast the finishes required and provide the cost economies reflected in the bid. Critical to maintaining that cost economy is the development of a cycle.

Construction Cycling

In reinforced concrete construction, the basic cycle is as follows (Fig. 10):

1. Formwork assembly and carpentry, including mechanical coordination (embedments).
2. Placement of reinforcing steel.
3. Formwork close-up.

(a)   (b)   (c)

Figure 10. Casting process for a column with a duct cast into the concrete. **(a)** Reinforcing steel set around an inside form that will also act as an exhaust duct; **(b)** Formwork and bracing enclosing the mold; **(c)** Formwork and bracing removed (stripped), and the final casting exposed.

cracking are not critical items. Where the structural concrete is also ultimately exposed in the finished building (architectural concrete), the formwork must provide a higher grade of finish.

Formwork Shop Drawings. Formwork shop drawings respond to the results of the mock-up, the economies required by the construction cycling, and the final coordination with the other trades that have their work simultaneously cast in place (Fig. 11). The shop drawing explains the assembly in explicit detail so that the carpenters can construct the forms and install the form ties in the field (Fig. 12). The contractor's detailer takes the requirements from the architect and engineer and develops them so that the worker can install and remove the formwork from the cast concrete. With this in mind, the detailer determines the size and shape of the forms. Size of the form must respond to the type of machinery anticipated to move the formwork, the volume of concrete to be placed at one time, and the method for control of cracking. For example, the contractor may be able to mobilize a crane that can move formwork containing 100 yd^3 of concrete, but may not be able to supply that amount in a single work day.

Shape is determined by the techniques of casting the shape and removing (stripping) the formwork from the casting. For example, an irregular three-dimensional object may not allow removal without considerable damage to the finish concrete.

Formwork Assemblies. Several examples of formwork assemblies follow (Fig. 13).

Wall Assembly. The formwork is structurally designed to withstand the hydraulic pressure of freshly placed liquid

Figure 11. For an architectural concrete building, ceilings are often cast concrete and not suspended below the structure as in other building types. As a result, the conduit, normally concealed in the suspended ceiling, must be coordinated with the structural design and the cycle of construction.

4. Concrete placement.
5. Formwork removal (stripping).

This cycle is repeated until the building is complete. The cost of the cycle is impacted by the length of time to complete the cycle and the ability to reuse the formwork. Formwork made up from reusable panels provides the greatest economies. In structural concrete work, the formwork serves only to hold the liquid concrete; finish, alignment jointing, minor seepage of cement paste, and minor

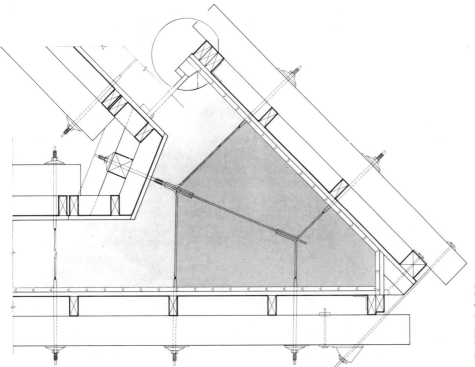

Figure 12. Acute corner, formwork detail. All of the materials that the workers must install for the casting process are detailed in the contractor's shop drawing. Note that the form ties provide an internal restraint to the radial pressure of liquid concrete.

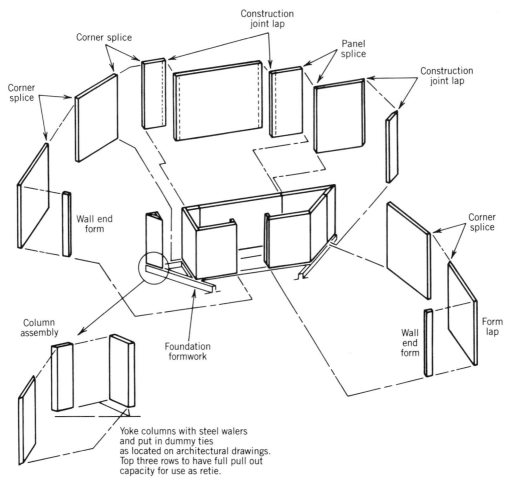

Figure 13. Formwork assembly. Exploded diagram explains how each panel forms a surface of the building and how the panels must be assembled together to form the concrete building. Typical formwork corners and splices between panels are identified on the drawing. Details at these locations reflect architectural concerns for alignment, form tightness, texture, and finish. They suggest but do not specify a means and method. The specific means and methods that will construct the final product are the sole responsibility of the contractor. Alternate details developed by the contractor are reviewed by the architect during the shop drawing and mock-up phases of the project.

concrete. This is done by through-wall ties that hold the two sides of the wall form together and provide the most efficient method of withstanding the outward pressure of the liquid concrete (Fig. 14). The ties are permanently embedded in the surface of the concrete. Care is taken so that the ends of the ties (tie holes on the finished concrete) form a pattern that is coordinated with the panel size and configuration. When the concrete functions as an exterior skin, the exposed tie hole should be sealed from liquid penetration and the tie protected from rusting. The liquid pressure of concrete is transferred from the ties to a system of beams (walers and strong backs).

These walers support the panel so that it will not move during placement and will precisely align the concrete with adjacent building elements such as curtain walls, door frames, and ceilings. Where this joint occurs, a reveal is usually specified. The reveal stops leakage from the new placement onto the one prior and visually forgives misalignment between successive placements.

The wall assembly must also consider the mobilization required to place the concrete. The concrete should be placed in horizontal layers; proper formwork assembly allows for this controlled placement of concrete. Special attention is devoted to the vibration and consolidation of concrete when textured form liners are used.

Plan at Corner. Corners are more visually prominent and require more precise alignment than walls. The corner is vulnerable to opening up from the hydraulic pressure (liquid and radial) of the freshly placed concrete. Installing the wall tie along the diagonal of the corner provides resistance directly opposite the pressure of liquid concrete; however, it would also result in the tie holes on the corner edge, an unacceptable condition. The plan detail at the corner suggests a method of resisting the hydraulic pressure and providing an architectural solution (Fig. 15).

The corner of a concrete structure may also abut door and window openings, and as such must match these elements in vertical and horizontal plumb or be detailed in

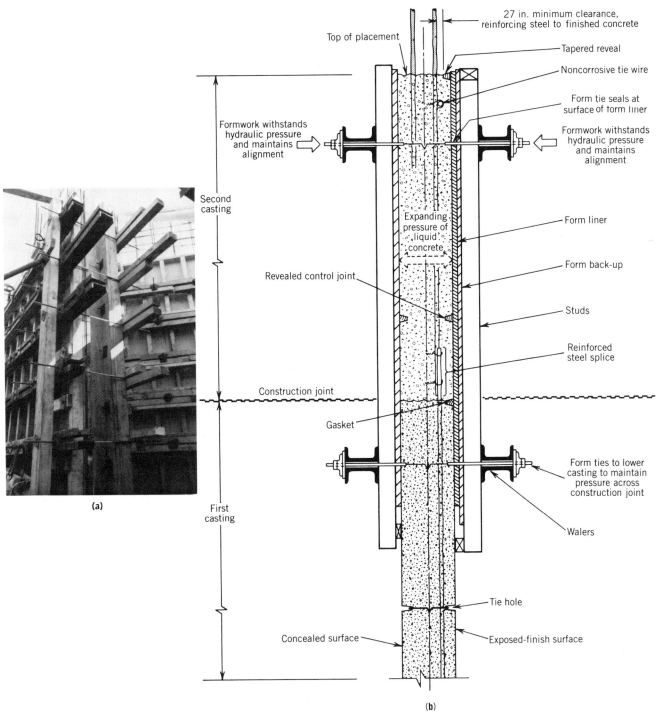

(a)

(b)

Figure 14. Wall assembly. **(a)** The end of an architectural concrete wall is specially braced to maintain alignment. Wall ends abut door, and window openings must be coordinated with the metal work so that an acceptable joint can be installed. The edge must be tightly sealed to prevent cement leaking through the panels. Note the tie rods, walers, and strong backs; **(b)** Note size and spacing of formwork. Bracing, reinforcing steel, and joints vary for architectural and engineering design.

a manner that allows for the different tolerances implicit in the different materials.

The Soffit and Beam Bottom. The architectural concrete soffit serves the same function as plaster, sheetrock, or suspended acoustical tile ceilings and therefore must equal the quality of finish. The concrete must be well consolidated and free of blemishes. This is achieved by close attention to the activity and techniques of construction. As shown in the beam section (Fig. 16), the bottom reinforcing steel is supported and wire tied in the structurally designed

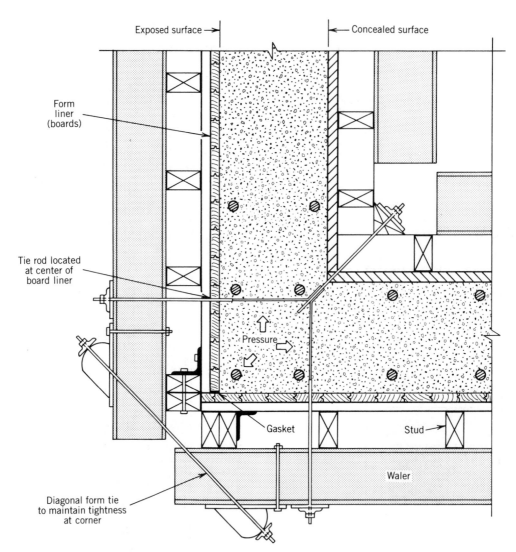

Figure 15. Plan at corner.

position by chairs. These chairs have round plastic tips that are colored to match the concrete and will generally provide a smooth soffit. Soffits and beam bottoms are cambered upward to absorb structural settlement and to avoid the visual discomfort of a sagging span. Since structural calculations of deflection are not consistently borne out in the field, an architectural camber is added to assure perception of flat or slightly arched span.

Along with formwork carpentry, installation of mechanical and electrical devices, and the tying of reinforcing steel in place, there is debris (sawdust, dirt, and wire) that is inadvertently deposited in the bottom of the form. If left in there when the concrete is placed, it will cast an undesirable imprint (ie, the coffee cup lid in Fig. 17). A small panel is designed in the formwork to be removed prior to placement of concrete and thereby allow a final clean-out of the form.

Curtain-wall Spandrels and Beam Fascias. The techniques employed to construct a spandrel illustrate the relationship between the process of construction and the finished product. Of particular importance is that concrete is placed in a continuous motion across the surface that will ultimately be exposed to view (Fig. 18). A discontinuous place-

ment may not be a structural problem, but may, under circumstances of high strength concrete and hot weather, cause discoloration or deposit lines diagonally across the exposed surface. These deposit lines become a line along which efflorescence collects and bleeds out onto the surface of the concrete. An architectural concrete placement plan avoids this pitfall. For example, concrete placed at an elapsed time of 45 min will be placed immediately adjacent to concrete placed at an elapsed time of 75 min. This 30-min lapse in continuity is concealed within the body of the total placement. With architectural concrete, timing and the finished product are closely related.

Beams are isolated from slabs to avoid the deposit lines that would otherwise result from the discontinuous placement of concrete across the exposed spandrel. Designing a construction joint between beam and slab will allow a continuous placement along the length of the beam and then a second placement of the slab over the beam.

Criteria for Workmanship

In addition to describing the concrete's texture and color and the appropriate formwork assemblies, contract documents specify the following:

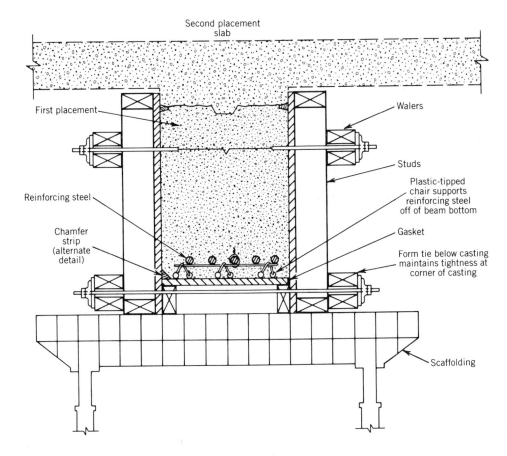

First placement

Second placement slab

Walers

Studs

Plastic-tipped chair supports reinforcing steel off of beam bottom

Reinforcing steel

Chamfer strip (alternate detail)

Gasket

Form tie below casting maintains tightness at corner of casting

Scaffolding

Figure 16. Beam section.

1. Minimum width of wall = 12 in.
2. Minimum exterior cover to any steel = 2 in.
3. Maximum deposit lift height = 18 in.
4. Maximum drop (free fall) = 3 ft.
5. Minimum time of a deposit to be covered by a subsequent deposit (in the same day's placement) = 15 min.
6. Minimum time from freshly mixed cement to final deposit = 90 min.
7. Limits of slump = 4 ± ½ in.
8. Maximum temperature = 90°F.
9. Use maximum recommended water-reducing admixture.
10. Use noncorrosive tie wire.
11. Use form ties that seal at the form contact surface.

With these criteria developed in the drawings and specifications, the contractor can produce work that meets the aesthetic requirements of the job.

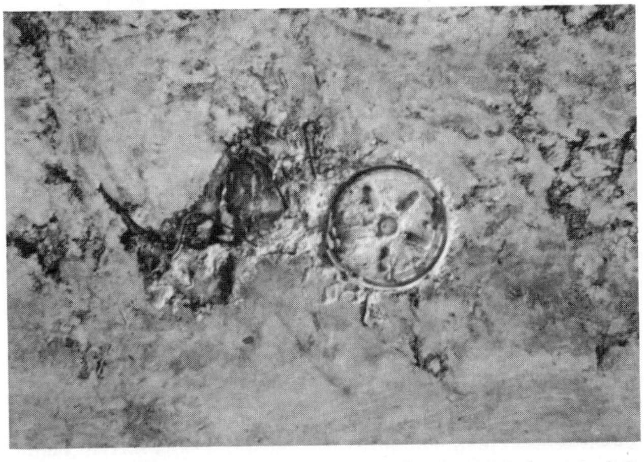

Architectural Concrete Inspection

Structural concrete requires inspection at the plant, site, and slab for strength, mix components, and placement and inspection of the reinforcing steel for compliance with approved shop drawings. When the structural work is ultimately exposed in the finished building, as with architectural concrete, additional inspections of the formwork are required. Especially when architectural concrete is not locally used and when the workforce is unaccustomed to its stricter requirements for finish, the intent of the contract documents must be represented by an individual on the site.

The architectural inspector reviews the formwork construction for compliance with the contract documents, the results of the on-site mock-up, and the approved materials and shop drawings. On a day-to-day basis, the inspector checks:

Figure 17. Debris. A coffee cup lid and other debris were left at the bottom of a form and then cast into the concrete. The result is totally unacceptable.

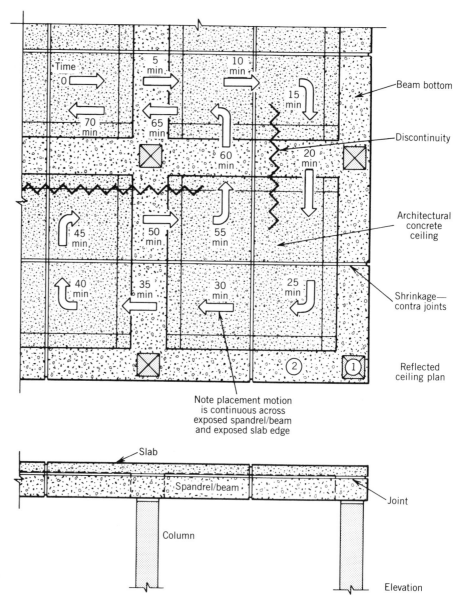

Figure 18. Curtain-wall spandrels and concrete ceilings.

1. The profile of the forms.
2. The bracing required to maintain the architectural alignment.
3. The tightness of the assembly to minimize leakage of cement paste.
4. Criteria for workmanship.
5. The quality of the form contact surface as it is repetitively used through several cycles.
6. The workers' coordination of structural and mechanical trades for items such as embedments, clearance of reinforcing steel from the finished surface.
7. Resolution of field conditions in cooperation with the design team.

THE ROLE OF THE ENGINEER AND STEEL DETAILER

The engineer calculates the quantity of steel reinforcement required to support the programmed loads within the envelope described by the architect and schematically indicates that steel on the contract drawings. The spacing of reinforcing steel considers the techniques employed to place the concrete in its final position in the form (Fig. 19). Efforts are made either to increase the thickness of walls or to cluster the reinforcement and thus allow proper consolidation of concrete. For example, overly dense concentrations of steel will prevent the proper consolidation of concrete on the form contact surface and create unsightly voids. For concrete exposed to the weather, special clearances between form contact surface and steel are specified. Steel detailing is also coordinated with the architectural location of expansion joints, control joints, construction joints, and cycle of construction. An architectural concrete specification will limit the size of concrete placement and thus, to a certain extent, determine the location of these joints. The contractor's steel detailer develops the exact lengths of the steel to be sent by workers in the field and notes them on the shop drawings. The shop drawings are then

(a)

(b)

Figure 19. Reinforcing steel design. **(a)** Reinforcing steel ("rebar") being installed in a wall; **(b)** Reinforcing steel spaced too closely together prevents the concrete from reaching its correct position in the form.

reviewed by the structural engineer and approved prior to the start of construction.

TROUBLESHOOTING

Because correction of cast blemishes in concrete is difficult, the prevention of mistakes takes on greater significance in architectural concrete work than in other trades (eg, masonry, sheetrock, or metal). This is because the methodology of repair for these other trades (ie, replacement of bricks, spackling, replacement of a metal panel) closely resembles the way in which the material was originally installed, whereas in concrete the repair procedure is quite different from the original installation. When a blemish

occurs in cast-in-place concrete, its repair rarely involves removal of the original casting. Repairs are on a spot basis and are developed by trial-and-error testing according to the specific characteristics of the problem. Terms used to describe defects that occur are

1. *Blistering.* Thin pieces of concrete (silver dollar size or larger) detach from the finished surface due to improper curing.
2. *Bug holes.* Individual small cavities caused by entrapped air or water not absorbed in the formation of concrete.
3. *Corrosion of metals in concrete.* Reinforcing steel aluminum conduit and tie wire too close to the finish concrete will rust through and stain the surface.
4. *Cracking.* Caused by shrinkage (loss of moisture), too infrequent isolation of concrete elements, or small delays in a concrete placement operation.
5. *Cold joints.* Caused when a continuous placement is interrupted to such a period of time sufficient for the concrete to have cured enough so that a structural joint is created where it was not designed.
6. *Crazing.* Shallow fine cracks uniformly distributed over the surface of the concrete caused by a higher water cement ratio or rapid drying of the surface.
7. *Discoloration.* (*1*) A change in color caused by a change from one truck to another with a slightly different color cement or differing water contents; or (*2*) a change in color due to the chemical content or absorptivity of the form contact surface.
8. *Dusting.* A powdered surface sometimes due to improper curing.
9. *Efflorescence.* A lime powder that bleeds out to the surface, often gathering in cracks.
10. *Form scabbing.* Cement paste pulled off the surface because the forms were stripped too early or a form release agent was improperly applied.
11. *Freeze–thaw deterioration.* A corrosion of the concrete exposed to frequent changes in weather due to inadequate air entrainment.
12. *Honeycombing.* Large voids in the concrete due to inadequate consolidation of the concrete.
13. *Lift lines.* Occur when there is a slight discontinuity in the placement, not enough to form a structural cold joint but enough to show.
14. *Leakage.* When the forms are not adequately tightened, cement paste will seep through the gap and cast undesirable fins or overpours onto the previous casting.
15. *Pop-outs.* Cone-shaped pieces of concrete that break away from the concrete. This is caused by impurities in the concrete rapidly expanding and breaking off from the concrete.
16. *Sand streaking.* When the cement paste on the surface is washed (by excess water) away, leaving the fine aggregate (sand) exposed in a streaking pattern.

17. *Spalling*. When concrete is hit and damaged so that parts break off.
18. *Scaling*. Superficial breaking away of the cement surface occurring in exterior concrete that lacked the correct air entrainment and was exposed due to deicing salts and frequent freeze–thaw cycles.

When the work is improperly detailed and the variety of trades that must be on the job at the same time are improperly coordinated, the final product is jeopardized. The finish will often suffer when the mix design does not account for the placement and consolidation technique. When the concrete is inadequately consolidated, unsightly voids will appear on the surface. If the formwork is not adequately tight or strong enough to withstand full-liquid head or does not lend itself to easy removal, the concrete finish will be less than desirable. Cast blemishes are many times impossible to correct.

A successful architectural concrete building is achieved when the process of construction is monitored for these aspects.

CONCLUSION

Concrete is chosen because it can be conveniently molded and textured by simple manipulation of formwork. An architectural concrete building by design efficiently combines structure and finish. The building type is particularly well suited to areas where steel factories and complex machinery are not readily available, but where a responsive labor force exists. The architectural concrete design incorporates these factors and allows the builder the freedom to achieve quality using the resources available. Concrete construction is a process where the final product and raw construction are done simultaneously. Up to and throughout this process, cooperation among the designer, engineer, carpenters, lathers, and masons is imperative. In today's fragmented construction industry, it is the nature of the links among these specialists that determines the project's ultimate success. These links are fostered by the architect's representative in the field. "This person must coordinate, maintain harmony, and, 'when push comes to shove', maintain control. At best, he is a master builder; at worst, a useless underfoot appendage—a nuisance to the contractor, and an unnecessary expense to his employer. Such men never have their name inscribed in cathedrals, and are known only to the men they work with from lathing apprentice to design architect"(4). Their roles are not defined by any institute code or guideline, but their influence makes all the difference.

BIBLIOGRAPHY

1. J. A. Dobrowolski, *Guide to Cast-in-Place Architectural Concrete Practice*, American Concrete Institute Committee 303, Detroit, Mich., 1974.
2. J. M. Shilstone, "Quality Management of Accelerated Construction," *Forming Economical Concrete Buildings, Proceedings of International Conference*, Portland Cement Association, Skokie, Ill., 1982.
3. R. D. Hough, "The Secret to Quality Architectural Concrete: Knowing Construction," *Archit. Rec.* (Mar. 1983).
4. J. C. Rowan, ed., "Concrete: Where Do We Go From There?" *Progress. Archit.* (Oct. 1966).

General References

R. Banham, *A Concrete Atlantis*, The M.I.T. Press, Cambridge, Mass., 1986.

M. Bill, *Robert Maillart: Bridges and Construction*, 3rd ed., Frederick A. Praeger Inc. Publishers, New York, 1969.

Color and Texture in Architectural Concrete, EP021-01A, Portland Cement Association, Skokie, Ill., 1980.

J. M. Shilstone, *Cast-in-Place Architectural Concrete, Monograph 03M350*, Construction Specifications Institute, Washington, D.C., Aug. 1974.

Kirk, Greene, and Moran in Shilstone, ed., *Concr. Constr.* (Nov. 1972).

Dabney, Johnson, Richardson, and Ford in Shilstone, ed., "Architectural Concrete: Design and Construction Practices," *Concr. Constr.* (Aug. 1982).

V. F. Pardon, *Le Corbusier*, Grosset and Dunlap Publishers, Italy, 1969.

R. E. Wilde, ed., *Concr. Int.* (Nov. 1985).

See also CONCRETE FORMING; CONCRETE—GENERAL PRINCIPLES.

ELIOT LOCITZER
HRH Construction Corp.
New York, New York

CONCRETE FORMING

Formwork, strong enough to withstand the pressure of liquid concrete, is used to contain the freshly placed concrete in the shape and location desired.

Formwork is the most significant and costly part of building a concrete structure. Good formwork built with quality materials will achieve the results expected by the architect. Proper planning and design will permit maximum reuse of form sections, thereby keeping forming costs down. Since formwork is usually considered a temporary structure, the contractor bears the responsibility for its stability and safety. The architect/engineer usually specifies the quality of formwork required, sequence of placement, stripping time, reshoring requirements, and all other pertinent information necessary to ensure proper results. The formwork specifications must be clear, concise, and tailored to the particular job. Architectural concrete formwork, in contrast to that of unexposed concrete, requires better quality of form contact surface; greater care in design, fabrication, and assembly to ensure tight joints and accurate profiles; stricter tolerances; and greater concern in the location of construction joints to allow good placing procedures, ensuring surfaces free from deposit seams, discoloration, and other placing defects. In addition to formwork drawings, the architect should require a mockup of exposed portions of the work. American Concrete Institute (ACI) Committee 347, (*Formwork for Concrete*) developed standards and guidelines based on safety, quality, and economy. This committee report, known as *Recommended Practice for Concrete Formwork,* was adopted as a standard of the ACI in July 1978 (1). This standard, although not written in specification language, will aid engineers and architects in the preparation of their specifications.

Using the specifications for a particular job, the concrete contractor develops a plan for the placing of concrete before bidding. Factors to be considered include site conditions, accessibility, weather, placing schedules, construction joints, and capacity of equipment to handle form sections and materials. Cost reduction can be accomplished by the proper selection of the forming system, maximum reuse of various form sections, and efficient field practices. In high-rise construction, where a floor is formed and cast every two or three days, the formwork must be designed to permit quick and easy removal to the next floor. The choice of whether to use prefabricated or job-built forms is usually predicated on the number of reuses for the various sections. It is not uncommon to use both on the same job. The selection of ties and other hardware is usually dictated by the form selection. Where the specifications restrict the location of form ties to rustication joints or limit the size of holes on the surface of the concrete, the selection of size and strength of form ties could be the determining factor for the design of the forms. The specified stripping time is an important factor in cost calculation. Cost increases proportionately with the time the form must be kept in place. Conversely, a faster rate of placement, which may require heavier forms to withstand the increased liquid concrete pressure, usually reduces forming costs. Proper selection of equipment to erect and strip forms, as well as to place concrete, is most important. Accessibility of the equipment must be planned. Municipal codes often restrict the use of some heavy equipment and force the selection of an alternate means of moving forms. The method of placement of concrete must also be considered. If the pumping of concrete proves to be more economical, then proper planning for site location of equipment must be a consideration.

Wall- and column-footing forming requirements are usually relatively simple. Low footing forms for walls can usually be braced to the side of excavation (Fig. 1). Deeper wall footings require more bracing and ties to withstand concrete pressure and are constructed the same as wall forms. Square or rectangular column footings can be formed by using external ties, internal ties, and simple forming (Fig. 2). If feasible, small sections of prefabricated wall forms are used horizontally to form footings. Round footings are usually formed with short lengths of fiber tubing.

Forming for vertical plumb walls can either be built in place (Fig. 3) or prefabricated. The basic parts of wall forms include sheathing to retain the concrete until it sets; studs to support the sheathing; wales to support the studs and align the forms; and wall ties to hold the forms at the desired spacing under the pressure of the fresh concrete. In job-built forms, the sheathing is usually boards or exterior-grade plywood. The four principal types of plywood used for formwork are

- Sanded, no overlaid, B–B concrete forming grade.
- Medium density overlaid (MDO).
- High density overlaid (HDO).
- Imported overlaid birch.

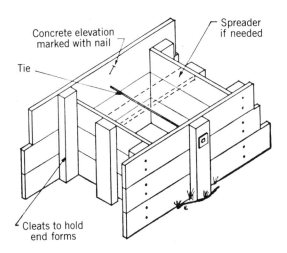

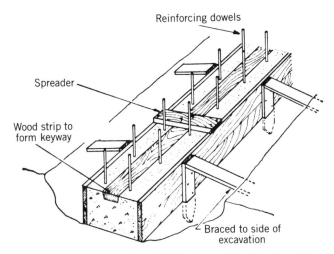

Figure 1. Low footing form (2). Courtesy of the American Concrete Institute.

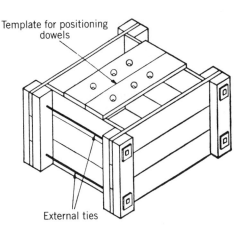

Figure 2. Two methods of forming column footings (2). Courtesy of the American Concrete Institute.

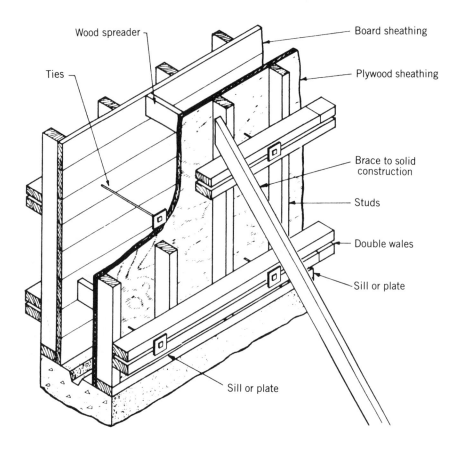

Figure 3. Typical wall form (2). Courtesy of the American Concrete Institute.

Overlaid plywood is exterior type, similar to other plywood, with the addition of resin-impregnated fiber faces on one or both sides. The B–B type is the least expensive; the overlaid types are more expensive. The better or more expensive grades offer a greater number of reuses, which reduces forming costs. In residential or industrial building forming, studs are usually 2 x 4s or 2 x 6s. The double wales are usually the same size. The choice of form lumber and selection of form ties is based on the size of the wall to be built and the lateral pressure on the form.

For structural concrete placed at controlled rates, ACI Committee 347 (1) has developed the formulas below for maximum lateral pressure on the form, prescribed conditions of temperature, rate of placement, vibration, weight of concrete, and slump. These are working formulas based on presently available experimental data; they are believed practical and are recommended for form design, but no claim is made for their theoretical precision. For walls with R not exceeding 7 ft/h,

$$p = 150 + \frac{9000\,R}{T}, \text{max}$$
$$= 2000 \text{ lb/ft}^2 \text{ or } 150\,h, \text{ whichever is less.} \tag{1}$$

For walls with $R = 7$–10 ft/h,

$$p = 150 + \frac{43{,}400}{T} + \frac{2800\,R}{T}, \text{max}$$
$$= 2000 \text{ lb/ft}^2 \text{ or } 150\,h, \text{ whichever is less.} \tag{2}$$

For walls with R greater than 10 ft/h,

$$p + 150\,h \tag{3}$$

where p = maximum lateral pressure, lb/ft^2; R = rate of replacement, ft/h; T = temperature of concrete in the forms, °F; and h = maximum height of fresh concrete in the form, ft. These formulas hold good for internally vibrated structural concrete of normal density, made with Type 1 cement and containing no pozzolans or admixtures, and with a slump of no more than 4 in. To adjust for the use of retarding admixtures or superplasticizers, a lower temperature than the temperature of concrete in the forms should be used. The admixture manufacturer's literature should be consulted for specific recommendations. Depth of vibration is limited to 4 ft below the top of concrete surface. Good placing procedures are assumed; for example, vibration is used for consolidation only, not for lateral movement of the concrete.

Equation 3 was added to the ACI recommendations in 1978 to provide guidance for form design pressure at rates faster than those originally covered. It should be remembered that Equations 1 and 2 were developed from data on actual measured form pressures. Until comparable data are available for faster placement rates, ACI Committee 347 does not feel justified in making more detailed recommendations, even though the discontinuity between Equations 2 and 3 is obvious.

Prefabricated modular forms are manufactured of wood,

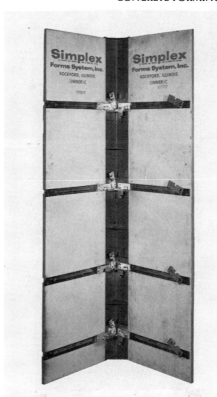

Figure 5. Unframed plywood panels backed by steel braces (2). Courtesy of the American Concrete Institute.

Where the form tie is a continuous single member (Fig. 7), break points can be provided a predetermined distance from the face of the wall to permit the tie to be broken back, leaving only a hole to be patched. The break point, or setback of tie metal from the face of the concrete, can vary from ¼ in. in residential work to 1½ in. or more for architectural concrete. Snap ties can be manufactured with a variety of different size cones in metal or plastic. The external wedge or tieholder holds the tie in place on the form and transmits the wet concrete pressure to the internal tie. For best results, forms should be stripped

Figure 4. Metal-framed plywood panels (2). Courtesy of the American Concrete Institute.

steel, aluminum, or fiber glass. The many proprietary systems can be classified as follows:

• Plywood on metal frame.
• All-aluminum.
• Unframed plywood with attached steel hardware.
• Unframed plywood with loose hardware.
• All-steel.

Some of these types are illustrated in Figures 4, 5, and 6. Prefabricated forms may be purchased outright, rented, or rented with an option to purchase. Usually, prefabricated forms permit a greater number of reuses.

The majority of job-built or prefabricated forms requires form ties. They resist the lateral pressure exerted by freshly placed concrete. Form ties should have a safety factor of 2. The number of form ties and their spacing will vary with the size and type of form used. The loading recommendations of the form and tie manufacturers should be followed when planning the form tie spacing. Many manufacturers offer technical service and layouts for individual job requirements.

A typical commercially available form tie consists of an internal tensile unit and an external holding device.

Figure 6. Unframed plywood panels with loose tying hardware (2). Courtesy of the American Concrete Institute.

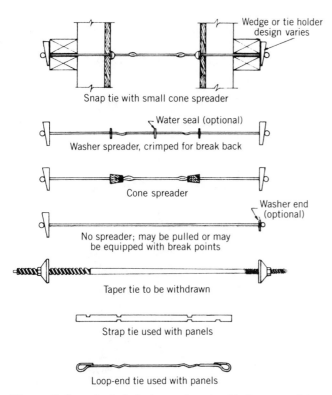

Figure 7. Some typical single-member ties (2). Courtesy of the American Concrete Institute.

and ties broken off as soon as possible after the concrete is placed in the forms. Another type of single continuous member is a taper tie (Fig. 7), which usually has two threaded ends that receive threaded nut washers or loose nuts and washers. This tie is removed from the wall when the form is stripped. Where the form tie is the internal disconnecting type (Fig. 8), the inner tensile unit is threaded. The coil type has two or four struts welded to coils at either end. The external member is a bolt with a threaded end to engage the coil tie. This type can be furnished with loose fitting cones for spreading the forms or with threaded cones, which screw onto the coil which is extended past the ends of the struts. A washer under the head of the bolt transmits the pressure exerted by the wet concrete on the form to the internal member. Another disconnect type has a solid, round rod threaded on both ends.

The external unit, larger in diameter, has a tapped hole in the tapered inner end for engaging the internal rod. A nut washer or loose nut and washer engage the external threaded end and hold the assembly to the form. Spreading can be accomplished by loose internal wood spreaders, which are removed as the concrete rises in the form. Galvanized wire snap ties should be avoided if they are being used to eliminate a future rust condition. After the snap tie is broken back, the base metal of the tie will be exposed and allow rusting to take place, thereby wasting the premium paid for galvanizing. Use of stainless steel wire snap ties is an expensive solution.

Ties can be manufactured with round metal or neoprene washers attached to the middle of the ties to minimize water leakage along the tie.

Before placing concrete in forms, it is necessary to apply a form release agent to minimize adhesions by the concrete and facilitate stripping. Care must be taken to select the proper release agent. Certain agents suitable for wood forms are not suitable for metal forms. Form manufacturers' instructions for applying agents must be followed. Form release agents must never be applied to reinforcing steel or any other surface where bonding of concrete is required.

Proper bracing of forms is necessary to prevent shifting of forms during the actual placing of concrete. During the placing of concrete, internal vibration is necessary to ensure proper consolidation. Care in vibration is necessary to keep the vibrator away from the surface of the form and from the wire ties. Whereas some forms can be designed for external vibration, continued use of external vibrators will eventually weaken and destroy the form. Revibration of previously placed layers of concrete will produce higher loads on the forms.

Whereas plumb walls are formed with the rows of ties parallel to the bottom of the wall, battered walls are formed in a different manner (Fig. 9). First, a determination must be made whether the batter is uniform or of a changing rate. Those walls with a changing rate are called warped walls and are the most costly to form. Comparing the rates of batter at each wall end will indicate if a uniform batter exists or if the wall is warped.

$$\text{rate of batter} = \frac{\text{bottom width} - \text{top width}}{\text{wall height}}$$

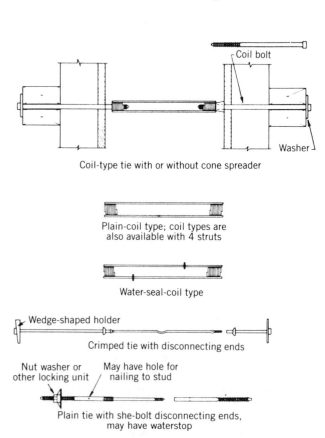

Figure 8. Some typical internal disconnecting ties (2). Courtesy of the American Concrete Institute.

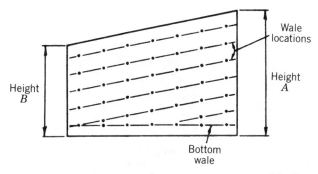

Figure 9. Variable-height battered wall (3). Courtesy of the Concrete Reinforcing Steel Institute.

Example:

$$\begin{aligned}
\text{wall height at end } A &= 20 \text{ ft}\\
\text{wall height at end } B &= 16 \text{ ft}\\
\text{bottom width at end } A &= 22 \text{ in.}\\
\text{bottom width at end } B &= 20 \text{ in.}\\
\text{top width} &= 12 \text{ in.}
\end{aligned}$$

$$\begin{aligned}
\frac{\text{rate of batter}}{(\text{at end } A)} &= \frac{22 \text{ in.} - 12 \text{ in.}}{20 \text{ ft}}\\
&= 0.5 \text{ in./ft}
\end{aligned}$$

$$\begin{aligned}
\frac{\text{rate of batter}}{(\text{at end } B)} &= \frac{20 \text{ in.} - 12 \text{ in.}}{16 \text{ ft}}\\
&= 0.5 \text{ in./ft}
\end{aligned}$$

Therefore, for this example, the rate of batter is uniform, and form ties positioned in wales that are parallel to the top of the wall will all be the same size. Note that the bottom wale is horizontal and each form tie could be a different size.

In vertical wall forming, where the architectural requirements call for a particular surface finish requiring the use of plastic form liners, care must be taken in the attachment of this material to the sheathing. Since there is expansion and contraction with temperature changes, buckling can occur unless relief is provided at joints. Plastic liners are available in numerous configurations in either a single-use type or a more durable multiuse type. In some cases, the architectural finish calls for a rough board or fluted finish. This can be accomplished with either wood or plastic liners. In all situations where rough or textured finishes are required, extra care must be taken to vibrate properly because it is extremely difficult or impossible to patch the surface to match the surrounding finish.

Rustication strips are available in wood, rubber, or plastic. Where ties are to be placed in the rustication, care must be taken in drilling the holes to avoid damaging the strips.

Where specifications call for the tie holes to be unfilled, care must be taken in breaking off the snap tie or removal of the cone from the coil tie. If there is concrete covering the cone on the surface of the wall, this concrete must be gently chipped away before removing the cone. The cone should also be tapped gently to break the bond with the concrete.

A gang form (Fig. 10) is an assembly of prefabricated panels joined together to make a much larger unit for convenience in erecting and stripping. Its size is limited by the contractor's ability to handle it easily and economically. Where the wall is small, with few reuses of form, gang forming is not economical. The gang form is usually braced with wales or strongbacks, either of wood or steel. Provisions for lifting must be incorporated into the form design. Economical applications for gang forms include a long plumb-retaining wall, Y-walls in a sewage treatment plant, and tanks. Form manufacturers offer technical assistance in selecting and designing the most economical system.

Several methods of forming curved walls are used, depending on the size of the radius. Where the radius is greater than 4 ft, plywood sheets attached to vertical studs can be used. On long radius curved walls, standard 2 x 8 ft prefabricated panels, with filler panels if necessary, are gang-formed. For medium radius curves, the use of horizontal sheathing boards with vertical studs is an acceptable alternative. The use of vertical sheathing requires special fabrication of the horizontal studs, usually out of 8 in. or wider lumber. Where the curved portion of the wall is a corner, with a small radius, the sheathing is usually two thin sheets of plywood supported by curved horizontal members or vertical members, as shown in Figures 11 and 12. Care must be taken in calculating the end dimension of the snap tie or bolt dimension of the coil-tie assembly because of the special sizes of form lumber used. A controlled rate of placement of the concrete is essential for thin tank walls where a fast rate of placement can cause an excessive buildup of liquid pressure.

The following tolerances suggested by ACI Committee 347 apply to finished walls of buildings. The forms should be constructed to give a finished wall within these limits, unless otherwise specified.

1. Variation from the plumb should not be more than ± 1 in. overall. High-rise structures (above 100 ft

Figure 10. Heavy-duty, metal-framed ganged panels (2). Courtesy of the American Concrete Institute.

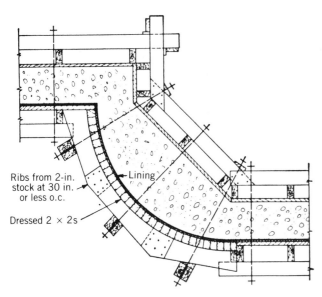

Figure 11. Small-radius corner form with vertical studs (2). Courtesy of the American Concrete Institute.

Figure 13. Rectangular column form with adjustable metal clamps (2). Courtesy of the American Concrete Institute.

high) or other special types of structures may require special tolerances as noted in ACI 347-78.

2. Variation from the plumb of conspicuous lines such as control joints should not be more than ± ¼ in. in any 20 ft, or more than ± ½ in. for the entire height.
3. Variation from the level or from specified grades for exposed horizontal grooves and conspicuous lines should be limited to ± ¼ in. in any bay or 20 ft of length, and ± ½ in. over the entire length.
4. Variation of the linear building lines from the established position in plan should not exceed ± 1 in.
5. Variation in distance between walls is limited to ± ¼ in. per 10 ft, but not more than ± ½ in. in any bay, and ± 1 in. in total variation.
6. Variation in the sizes and locations of wall openings should not be more than -¼ in. or + ½ in.

7. Variation in thickness is limited to -¼ in. or + ½ in.

Column forming requires special care and techniques because the rapid buildup of concrete pressure can cause difficulty in maintaining the design dimensions and shape. Square or rectangular column forming varies from loose board sheathing with backup yokes to heavy forming using steel wales (Fig. 13). Common practice is to use plywood, vertical lumber, and adjustable column clamps. Standard prefabricated panels, joined at the corners, make good column forms if the size is right (Fig. 14). Chamfer strips made from wood, sheet metal, or other material nailed to two opposite panels eliminate the sharp edges. If possi-

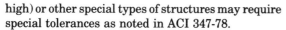
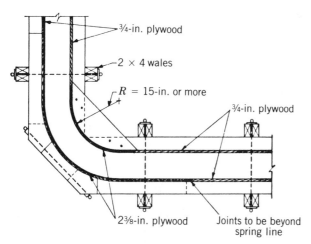

Figure 12. Small-radius corner form with curved horizontal members (2). Courtesy of the American Concrete Institute.

Figure 14. Square column form using prefabricated panels (2). Courtesy of the American Concrete Institute.

able in diameters from 6 to 48 in., and are economical and easy to use. Manufacturers offer a seamless type to minimize seams.

Reusable, round column forms are also manufactured of steel or fiber glass-reinforced plastic in the most common diameters (Fig. 16). Plastic forms are available in either one piece or two halves. Joining is accomplished with bolts or wedges. Column capitals are formed in a similar fashion, with two-piece forms easily joined together. The bracing of all column forms is necessary to maintain the proper position and keep the form plumb.

The majority of a structure's formwork cost is usually associated with the horizontal elements. No one forming system is applicable to all floor systems. Typical floor systems are shown in Figure 17. As in the case of wall forming, standardization and repeat use of formwork is desirable and most economical. Although there are typical methods of floor-forming systems, the components making up the systems vary with size of the bay.

Typical forming for flat slabs consists of plywood panels, carried by joists and stringers resting on shores. Stringers and shores can be either wood or steel. Construction of the formwork starts with the erection and bracing of shores, followed by the placing of stringers and joists. Deck panels placed over the joists complete the setup.

Where beam or girder forming is required, the forms can be assembled in boxes and either lifted into position or fabricated in place (Fig. 18). Form ties are not required unless the beams are too deep to permit side form bracing. In a steel frame structure, some method of hanging forms from the steel beam must be used. The common methods are shown in Figure 19. Spandrel beams, because of their critical location on the face of the building, require careful forming. Proper tying and bracing is necessary to maintain alignment.

Either wood forms or steel pans are used for forming concrete joists. The pans may rest on solid deck forms.

A system of forming slabs that combines deck form,

Figure 15. Fiber-tube column forms (2). Courtesy of the American Concrete Institute.

ble, the column form should be fabricated and lifted into place over the steel.

Lightweight fiber tubes are commonly used for forming round columns (Fig. 15). The fiber column forms are avail-

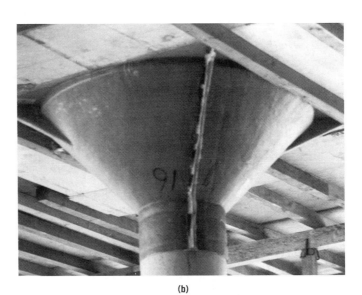

(a)   (b)

Figure 16. **(a)** One-piece round column form and **(b)** two-piece capital form of fiber glass-reinforced plastic (2). Courtesy of the American Concrete Institute.

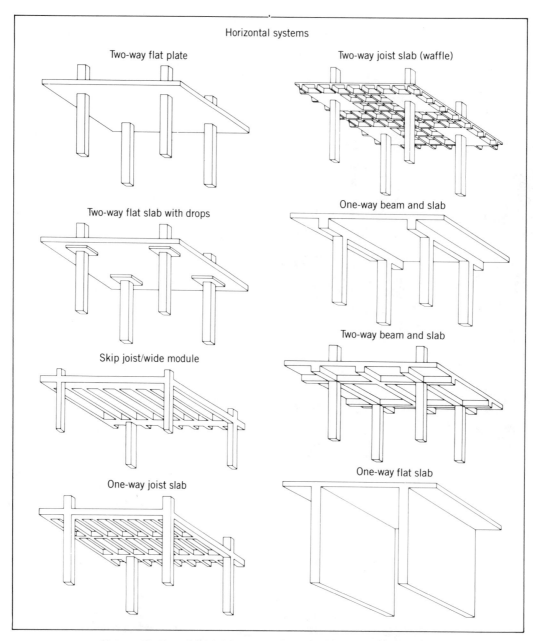

Figure 17. Typical floor systems (4). Courtesy of Ceco Industries, Inc.

beam form, supporting joists, and scaffolding is called a flying form. It is usually constructed in relatively large sections that require a crane to move. If conditions permit, the slab form can be supported on column-mounted hardware. Included in the hardware is a jack, which is used for raising and lowering the flying form. The hardware is mounted on the concrete columns with anchors and bolts. The flying form can combine wall and slab forms with bracing and shoring for use in bearing wall structures. The wall form is hinged to move inward so the form assembly can be lowered for movement to the next casting position.

The vertical shoring of slab-forming systems can be accomplished with wood, post shores, adjustable steel shores, or steel scaffold frames. A shoring plan is essential to ensure the safety of the construction crews and structural integrity. The reshoring procedure should be planned in advance and approved by the engineer.

After the formwork for beams or slabs is in place, bar supports, which are used to position reinforcing steel, must be put in place. Vertical steel in wall forms and column steel is also positioned with bar supports, usually wired to the reinforcing steel. Bar supports are available in a variety of configurations and sizes to meet the numerous field requirements. The use of the proper size item to maintain the designed cover or setback of reinforcing steel from the face of the concrete is essential. Those products are manufactured, under controlled conditions, in wire or plastic, or a combination of both. Where there are strict architectural requirements or the concrete surface is exposed

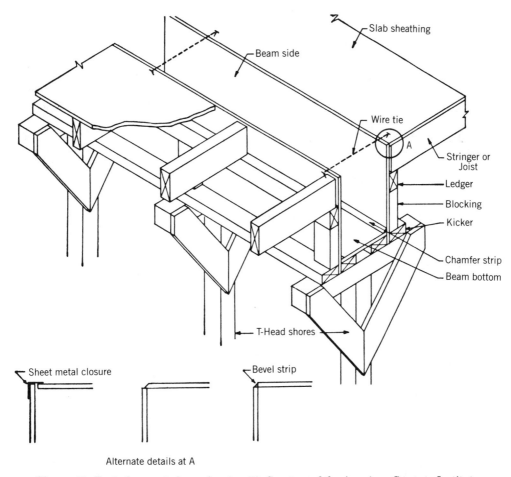

Figure 18. Typical concrete beam forming (2). Courtesy of the American Concrete Institute.

to the elements, the use of stainless steel, plastic-tipped or epoxy-coated wire chairs, or solid plastic chairs are recommended. The Concrete Reinforcing Steel Institute's *Manual of Standard Practice* gives suggested recommendations for use of bar supports under various conditions.

The forming of bridge substructures and superstructures is similar to other types of concrete construction. Because the substructure usually has heavier walls of mass concrete, the formwork must necessarily be heavier. Specifications normally call for the use of a form tie with a removable external member rather than a break-back type of tie to ensure the proper setback of tie metal. It is desirable to form pier columns without internal ties to obtain a better finish. Pier cap forms can be either supported from the column forms or from scaffold brackets anchored in the columns. Fiber glass or steel forms are often used in bridge work. Forming for the cast-in-place bridge deck or superstructure is usually hung from the steel or precast concrete beams (Fig. 20). Since the deck slab is usually even with or haunched to the top flange of the beam, different hanging devices are required. Properly designed formwork includes a live load factor, usually a minimum of 50 lb/ft^2, as well as the dead load of the concrete. The placing of the formwork is best done from the top flange of the beams. The hangers are set in the proper position on the top flange of the beam, with the

main supporting members called double wales placed next. The remaining forming is set in place after the wales are adjusted to the proper elevation. Particular care must be taken in forming the overhanging portion of the deck. Either prefabricated wood or adjustable steel brackets are used to carry the cantilever load back to the lower flange of the outside bridge beam. Stay-in-place corrugated metal forms are held in position by various methods to the top flange of the beam.

Stripping of deck forms is done from platforms suspended from equipment riding on top of the deck or from rails beneath the deck.

The forming of mass concrete structures such as gravity dams, turbine foundations, anchorage piers, and similar structures is frequently done with cantilever forms held in place with anchors (Fig. 21). The design load and size of the anchor depends on the height of the lift, which can vary from 4 to 8 ft, and the placement schedule, placing temperature, and anticipated concrete strength during the first five days after placement. Higher lifts require an additional tiedown to reduce the form deflection. Manufacturers offer technical assistance with the design of both forms and anchorages.

Underground tunnels are usually formed with a prefabricated steel form hinged at two or more places to permit stripping and moving. The size and weight of the form

For unfinished work, hanger ends
remain at concrete surface

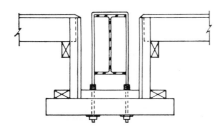

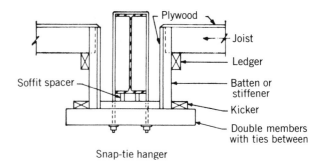

Coil-type hangers

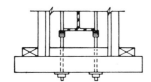

For exposed surfaces, where setback
is specified, recess to be grouted
when bolts are removed

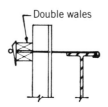

Fascia hanger

Figure 19. Typical steel beam forming (2). Courtesy of the American Concrete Institute.

depends on the diameter of the tunnel. A form that is designed to move forward within an adjacent form section that remains in place is called a telescoping form. Tunnel forms move along rails that are placed on the invert or bottom section of the tunnel. Positioning is accomplished by attachment to an anchorage unit embedded in the previously cast invert section (Fig. 22).

Vertical slip forming permits the continuous placement of concrete in walls of structures such as silos, water tanks, building cores, or external building walls (Fig. 23). The forms are moved by jacks riding on smooth steel rods.

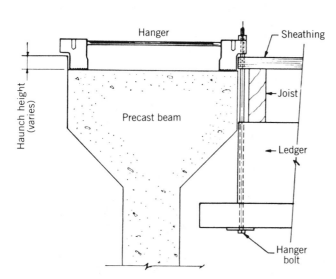

Figure 20. Forming method for deck slab supported on precast girder (2). Courtesy of the American Concrete Institute.

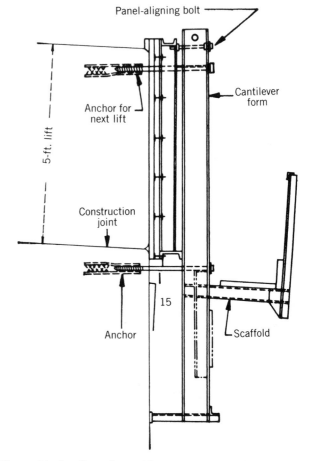

Figure 21. Cantilever form with one row of anchors (2). Courtesy of the American Concrete Institute.

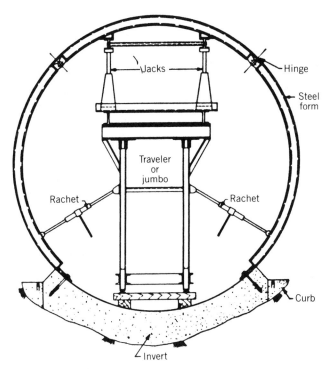

Figure 22. Telescoping tunnel form (2). Courtesy of the American Concrete Institute.

The rate of movement is controlled so that the forms leave the concrete after it is strong enough to retain its shape, while supporting its own weight.

Horizontal slipforms generally move on rails or on shaped beams. This system is used in the construction of tunnel inverts, drainage channels, canal linings, and similar structures. Whereas slip forming is usually more economical and faster than conventional forming, a crew trained in this technique is absolutely essential.

To achieve maximum economy in construction, the designer should strive for a simplified design, using standard dimensions and keeping the number of different structural component sizes to a minimum.

BIBLIOGRAPHY

1. Committee 347, "Recommended Practice for Concrete Formwork," American Concrete Institute, Detroit, Mich., July 1978.
2. M. K. Hurd, *Formwork for Concrete,* 4th ed, American Concrete Institute, Detroit, Mich., 1985.
3. *Concrete Formwork Digest II,* Concrete Reinforcing Steel Institute, Schaumburg, Ill., 1986.
4. *Concrete Buildings: New Formwork Perspectives,* Ceco Industries, Inc., Oak Brook, Ill., 1985.

General References

C. Backe, "Wall Forms: Selecting the Best Ganged System," *Concr. Constr.* **31**(1) (Jan. 1986).
"Choosing and Using Form Panel Boards," *Concr. Constr.* **30**(3) (Mar. 1985).
J. H. Ford, "Producing Architectural Concrete Using Plastic Form Liners and High Density Overlaid Plywoods," *Proceedings of The Second International Conference on Forming Economical Concrete Buildings,* Chicago, Ill., Nov. 28–30, 1984, American Concrete Institute, Detroit, Mich., 1986.

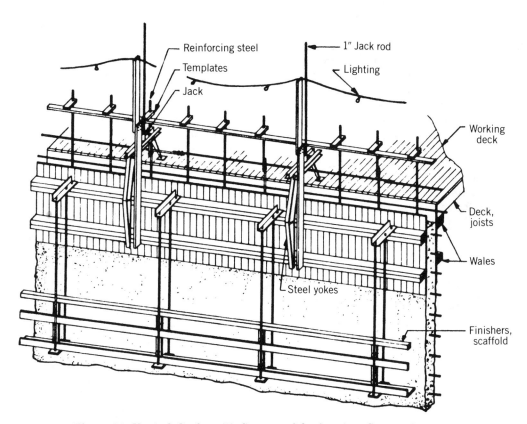

Figure 23. Vertical slip form (2). Courtesy of the American Concrete Institute.

R. Hough, "The Secret to Quality in Architectural Concrete: Knowing Construction," *Archit. Rec.* **171** (Mar. 1983).

See also CONCRETE—ARCHITECTURAL; CONCRETE—GENERAL PRINCIPLES; WOOD, STRUCTURAL PANEL COMPOSITES

ERNEST E. TROLIO
Concrete Industry Board, Inc.
New York, New York

CONCRETE—GENERAL PRINCIPLES

Concrete is an artificial conglomerate stone made principally of Portland cement and water combined with sand and stone aggregates. When freshly mixed, it is in a plastic state and can be placed in forms (usually made of wood, steel, or fiber glass). It then hardens into a solid mass, and after it gains sufficient strength, the forms are removed. Like natural stone, concrete is quite strong in compression, but relatively weak in tension. Therefore, steel reinforcing bars are generally located in the forms before the concrete is placed in order to accommodate any anticipated tensile stresses. Concrete is known as a formable or moldable structural material that can easily be used to make curvilinear members and surfaces. The basic ingredients are usually inexpensive and readily available, and the cost of a given construction is largely dependent on the complexity of the forms and amount of reinforcing steel needed.

HISTORY

The Greeks and the Romans used lime mortar to cement stone blocks together in early masonry construction. The mixing of lime and a type of volcanic sand called pozzuolana provided the Romans with a particularly durable mortar (1). This mortar mixed with stones could properly be called the first concrete, and the Pantheon provides remarkable evidence of its strength and durability. Concrete was not further adopted as a building material for many centuries, partly because of the lack of availability of suitable ingredients for making quality cement and the lack of technical knowledge about cements, but mostly because concrete was thought to be an unacceptable building material compared to stone or brick. It was not until the middle of the eighteenth century that concrete was again considered a viable building material. It then evolved as an extension of *pise* or rammed-earth construction. At that time, builders began mixing mortar with earth as a binding material (2). Francois Cointereaux, a French builder, promoted *pise* construction in France and the United Kingdom, convinced of the need for an economical building material that was virtually fireproof. Gradually, less earth and more cement and aggregates were used to make the material stronger.

The development of a greatly improved cement occurred in the United Kingdom in the early 1800s. It was stronger than the natural cements used previously and was also slower setting, which made construction easier. Although work on the improvement of cements was being done by many builders in France, the United Kingdom, and the United States, credit for this breakthrough is generally given to Joseph Aspdin, a mason in the UK. In 1824, he patented what he called Portland cement because in color it resembled a natural stone that was then quarried on the Isle of Portland. It is thought that Aspdin was responsible for the idea of using high temperatures to heat the cement ingredients to the point of vitrification, resulting in the fusing of materials into hard nodules that are now referred to as clinker (3).

During the 1850s, Francois Coignet, a French engineer, claimed to have invented monolithic construction in concrete, the molding or casting of building parts in one continuous mass. He also used iron bars in concrete, realizing that they could serve as tension elements. The invention of reinforced concrete is generally attributed to Francois Monier, a French gardener, who first worked with iron wire in concrete garden tubs and went on to build floor slabs of concrete with iron rods crossed at right angles in the plan (4). The first published scientific study of the behavior of reinforced concrete was by a U.S. mechanical engineer, William E. Ward, who built an iron and concrete residence in Port Chester, N.Y., in 1875. He conducted extensive experiments prior to construction and was the first to promote placing the iron near the bottom of the beam "for resisting the strain below the neutral axis"(5).

The development of the reinforced concrete skeletal frame occurred simultaneously at about the turn of the century in the United States and in Europe. Prior to that time, reinforced concrete buildings imitated those of stonework, using bearing walls and small window openings. The skeletal frame took advantage of the continuity between the beams and columns provided by reinforced concrete and made large openings possible. In the United States, first in California and later in New England, builder Ernest L. Ransome constructed buildings using square rods twisted to achieve a mechanical bond with the concrete in beams and floor slabs. He experimented with exposing the aggregates, introducing the possibility of textured or decorated surfaces which did not merely imitate masonry surfaces. His many large industrial and institutional buildings earned respect for concrete construction in the United States (6). The French contractor Francois Hennibique pioneered the construction of reinforced concrete frame buildings in Europe. The "Hennibique system" of monolithic construction, using bars near the top of the beams where they passed over columns and near the bottom edges of beams at midspan, was used in hundreds of buildings throughout Europe. He was the first to employ stirrups and bent-up bars to resist shear (Fig. 1) (7). Hennibique was an enlightened businessman who developed franchised branches of his firm throughout France and Belgium and took every opportunity to promote his system. Perhaps more than any other individual, he made reinforced concrete an acceptable building material appropriate for apartments, office buildings, and monumental architecture. Prior to his efforts, the material was thought suitable only for warehouses and factories. The stage was then set for the innovative designs in reinforced concrete produced in the twentieth century. The world

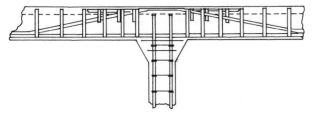

Figure 1. Connection between continuous girder and column in the Hennibique system.

of architecture was forever changed by the new forms and textures produced by such men as Antonio Gaudi, Auguste Perret, Eugene Freysinnet, Frank Lloyd Wright, Le Corbusier, Pier Luigi Nervi, Felix Candela, Eero Saarinen, and Louis Kahn.

BASIC CHARACTERISTICS

Concrete is a man-made material consisting of two basic types of ingredients: a paste, made of cement, air, and water, and aggregates, such as sand, gravel, and crushed rock. Freshly mixed and properly proportioned concrete has a hydraulic or plastic quality that enables it to be formed or molded into a desired shape. Due to hydration between the cement and water, the paste hardens, binding the aggregates together, making an artificial conglomerate stone. Hardened concrete develops sufficient compressive strength to serve as a major building material for roads, bridges, buildings, and sanitary and utility structures.

Almost all concrete used today contains embedded steel reinforcing bars at selected locations to carry tensile forces. These bars also help to control the stresses caused by thermal changes and cracking caused by shrinkage during the hardening process. Fortunately, steel and concrete have similar coefficients of thermal expansion, so the two materials remain bonded together during ambient temperature changes.

Concrete is considered to be of high quality if it is strong, durable, and economical and, if exposed, has an attractive surface finish. The quality of concrete is not only a function of the quality and proportions of the ingredients, but also depends on how the concrete is mixed, transported, placed in the forms, finished, and cured. It is important that the aggregates remain evenly dispersed throughout the mix so that the various particles of sand and gravel are completely surrounded by the cement paste. Careless handling can result in segregation of the paste and the aggregates, with a consequent loss in strength and durability. Excess or premature finishing of concrete can result in too much water being drawn to the surface, causing a weak, thin layer of material at that point. Finally, proper curing of the concrete is necessary as it hardens and gains strength. In many cases, this consists of maintaining an atmosphere of high humidity around the concrete for several days after placement in order to prevent the evaporation of moisture during the critical early stages of hydration. It is also necessary to prevent the freezing of concrete during this period.

Figure 2 shows a range of proportions by volume generally found to be suitable for concrete mixes with and without entrained air (8). (Entrained air is discussed below.) In general, given the same maximum aggregate size, a rich mix (high in cement content) will result in a stronger concrete than a lean mix, but will be less economical. A concrete that is too low in cement content will result in finishes of poor durability and appearance and a mix that is poor in workability. (Workability refers to the ease with which fresh concrete can be handled and placed.)

The single most influential factor in determining the strength of a concrete mixture is the ratio of water to cement. Other desirable qualities of hardened concrete, such as durability, abrasion resistance, and watertightness, also tend to vary with strength. Assuming that other factors are the same, a mix with a low water:cement ratio will be stronger. A minimum water:cement ratio of about 0.3 (by weight) is necessary to have enough water in the

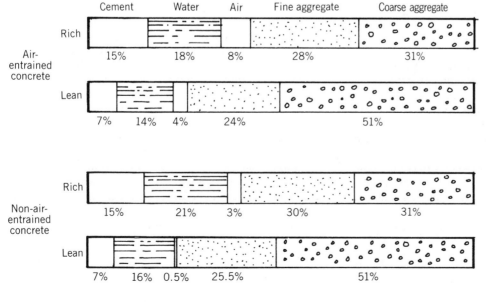

Figure 2. Proportions by volume of materials in concrete (8). Courtesy of the Portland Cement Association.

mix to ensure contact with all of the cement particles. From a practical standpoint, water:cement ratios are usually greater than this to achieve the necessary degree of workability. Depending on the strength and durability requirements, values in the 0.4–0.6 range are often used. The need for a low water:cement ratio, coupled with the need to avoid a high cement content (to ensure economy), indicates the desirability of using a mix of relatively stiff consistency with a large aggregate size.

THE INGREDIENTS OF CONCRETE

Air

Air is present in a concrete mix in the form of entrapped and entrained air voids. Air is entrapped during the mixing process and is undesirable. One of the goals of proper placement and consolidation of fresh concrete in the forms is the removal of such air voids. In contrast, entrained air results from the deliberate introduction of billions of tiny air bubbles (approximately 0.1 mm in diameter) into the mix. This is usually done when the cement is made (producing an air-entraining cement) or by the separate addition of a chemical when the concrete is mixed. Air entrainment improves concrete in two distinct ways. It greatly increases the resistance of hardened concrete to the detrimental effects of freezing and thawing. When water freezes and expands in the outer layer of a concrete surface, the small air spaces provide voids for this expansion and thereby relieve the pressure, which would otherwise tend to cause the breakup of this outer layer. The presence of these bubbles also tends to increase the workability of a concrete mix. One obvious advantage of a mix with entrained air is the ability to reduce the water content. In terms of negative effects, it has been observed that very high strengths with rich mixes are more difficult to obtain with air-entrained concrete. Two specifications of the American Society for Testing and Materials (ASTM) are available for establishing procedures for the field measurement of the air content in fresh concrete: ASTM C231 and ASTM C173.

Cement

Almost all of the cement used in concrete today is Portland cement or blends of Portland cement and pozzuolana. The raw ingredients of Portland cement include lime, silica, iron ore, and alumina. These are finely ground and mixed in proportions depending on the type of cement being produced. The mixture is then burned in a large kiln to form a clinker. The clinker is cooled and then pulverized into a very fine powder (similar in consistency to talcum powder). A small amount of gypsum is added to retard the setting time, and the mixture is then ready for shipping or packaging.

There are five basic types of Portland cement:

Type I: A general-purpose cement used when no special requirements are present.

Type II: A sulfate-resisting cement used for applications where it would be in contact with soils having a high sulfate content. It has a lower heat of hydration than Type I.

Type III: A high-early-strength cement that gains strength faster than Type I. It enables the forms to be removed sooner and reduces the length of time needed for protection from freezing during curing. (It does not take its initial set any faster, however.)

Type IV: A low heat of hydration cement for use in massive structures where the heat generated by normal cement would be excessive.

Type V: A very highly sulfate-resisting cement similar to Type II, but used for very severe sulfate situations.

The first three of these are produced in versions containing an air-entraining agent and are then labeled Types IA, IIA, and IIIA, respectively. ASTM specification C150 pertains to standards for Portland cement and C595 pertains to blended cements.

Water

Water used to make concrete should be reasonably clean, with only small concentrations of dissolved solids. Water suitable for human consumption is certainly satisfactory. In general, if the total of the dissolved solids remains below 2000 ppm (parts per million), the water is suitable for use in concrete. Certain salts, such as the carbonates of sodium and potassium, can have an effect on both the strength and the setting time of concrete, and if these exceed 1000 ppm, the water may be unsatisfactory. Water containing organic material such as algae must not be used because of its adverse effect on strength development (9). Seawater is not recommended because of its effect on the reinforcing steel in concrete.

Aggregates

The quality of the aggregates is very important to the production of quality concrete because, as shown in Figure 2, they make up a large fraction of the total volume. Aggregates are classified as fine or coarse, depending on their size. Fine aggregate is sand and consists of particles up to ¼ in. (6 mm) in width. All particles of fine aggregate must pass through a No. 4 sieve (16 openings/in.² or 6 mm in width of opening). There is some overlap in size, as coarse aggregate can have a certain fraction of small particles, but none so small as to pass through a No. 16 sieve (256 openings/in.² or 1.18 mm in width of opening). The maximum size of coarse aggregate varies. For most structural applications, a ¾–1½-in. maximum size is specified. It is more economical to use the largest practical aggregate size, but in order to achieve the necessary workability, it is recommended that the largest aggregate for a given application not exceed the least of:

1. Three-fourths of the clear distance between reinforcing bars.

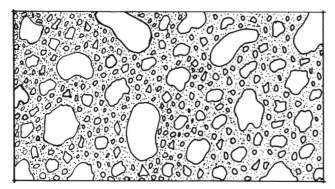

Figure 3. Sawn section of hardened concrete showing gradation of aggregate sizes.

2. One-fifth of the least dimension of linear elements such as walls, beams, and columns.
3. One-third the depth of slabs.

Aggregates for general-use concrete should be clean, hard, and well graded. Rocks with natural cleavage planes such as slate or shale must be avoided; certain flints are unacceptable because of their unstable nature when exposed to the weather or fire.

Figure 3 illustrates the need for maintaining a proper gradation of aggregate sizes to achieve a mix that is both strong and economical. The cost of concrete is often related to the amount of cement used, and having aggregates of many different sizes ensures that a smaller quantity of the cement and water paste is required. A concrete mix that has neither a deficiency nor an excess of a particular aggregate size is generally more workable and has less tendency to segregate. ASTM specifications C33 and C125 pertain to the grading of aggregates. The condition of the aggregates in terms of moisture content is important. Sand, in particular, can hold a great quantity of moisture, which could cause a detrimental increase in the water: cement ratio if left unchecked. On the other hand, very dry aggregate could actually absorb some of the mixing water and cause a decrease in workability. For these reasons, most concrete batching plants take close measurements of the water in the aggregates and adjust the quantity of mixing water accordingly. The reference condition that provides the basis for moisture adjustments in aggregates is called saturated-surface-dry (SSD), which means that the individual pieces have absorbed as much as they can internally, but have no surface moisture.

Admixtures

Admixtures are special-purpose ingredients that are added to the water or the cement before mixing or to the concrete during mixing. They are best used to meet the needs of selected construction conditions or those caused by certain materials deficiencies; it is not prudent to specify admixtures for universal or constant use. (Air entraining in cold climates is an exception.)

The more commonly used admixtures can be classified into four groups: air-entraining agents, workability agents, retarding agents, and accelerating agents. Air-entraining

agents (discussed previously) are commonly used to increase the freeze–thaw damage resistance of hardened concrete. They are also very beneficial in improving the workability of fresh concrete, especially harsh mixes that are deficient in fine sands.

Workability agents, apart from air-entraining ones, include water-reducing agents (and plasticizers), superplasticizers, and pozzuolana. Water-reducing chemicals act to prevent the formation of cement flocs, which tend to trap mixing water. This would indicate that less water could be used or that the workability of the mix could be enhanced. Many of these agents also have a retarding effect on the setting time of the mix. The superplasticizers are chemicals that tend to increase greatly the soupiness of a concrete mixture for a short time, meaning that very stiff mixes of high-strength concrete can be more easily placed and compacted. They are usually more expensive and used in larger quantities than other water reducers. Pozzuolana is a natural material such as diatomaceous earth and pumicites that possesses some slow-acting cementitious properties. Fly ash, a byproduct from the burning of coal, also acts like pozzuolana and is often readily available. It can be used to supplement a mix deficient in fines to aid in the development of strength and workability. Replacing some of the Portland cement with pozzuolana or fly ash as an economy measure may require an increase in curing time to achieve the required strength and durability.

Retarding agents lengthen the time period in which the concrete remains plastic and can be effectively used in hot-weather applications, when the ambient temperatures act to accelerate the rate of hydration. They are also used in the placement of large masses of concrete to prevent the occurrence of cold joints between placement layers.

Accelerating agents act to increase the rate of hydration, resulting in a reduction of the setting time and an increase in the rate of strength gain. This can be helpful in situations where rapid reuse of the concrete forms is desirable. This effect can also be beneficial in cold-weather concrete work, acting to reduce the time period in which the fresh concrete must be protected from freezing. The active ingredient is usually calcium chloride, which has been mistakenly referred to as an antifreeze agent. It is important to note that the addition of calcium chloride does not reduce the freezing point of fresh concrete. It merely increases the rate of hydration, which produces more heat.

There are other kinds of admixtures for special purposes, but the ones described above are the most widely used. All admixtures should be used with caution and their amounts carefully controlled. Improper or excess use can have detrimental effects on workability, shrinkage rate, strength gain, and final strength. When in doubt, tests are advisable to determine the effects of an admixture on a particular mix under the conditions of a particular job.

REINFORCING STEEL

Because of the inherent weakness in tension of plain concrete, reinforcing bars of steel are used extensively in concrete structures. Steel may also be used to supplement the strength of concrete in compression.

As the cement paste hardens, it bonds firmly to the steel bars, so the two materials act in a composite manner when subjected to the strains associated with tension, compression, and shear. Under normal building loads, the parts of beams and slabs that go into tension actually develop very minute, closely spaced cracks, and the total tensile load capacity is transferred to the steel bars. For this transfer to take place, proper bonding between the steel and concrete is essential. The bond is developed by three separate factors: the chemical adhesion between the cement and the steel; the surface roughness of the bar; and the deformations mechanically produced on the bars.

The various pieces of reinforcing to be used in a column or beam are welded together (or tied to each other with wire) to form a sort of three-dimensional "cage," which is placed in the form and secured firmly while the concrete is cast around it. Reinforcing for slabs consists of smaller bars evenly spaced near the top or bottom of the slab in a grid pattern. For slabs that rest on grade and for those carrying relatively light loads, the reinforcing can be in the form of a manufactured mat or coarse mesh of steel wires, called welded-wire fabric.

Reinforcing bar sizes are designated by a number representing the number of 1/8-in. increments contained in the nominal diameter of the bar. For example, a No. 9 bar has a nominal diameter of 1⅛ in. (The actual diameter varies somewhat because of the surface deformations.) Most bars used in building structures today are made of Grade 60 steel, which means the steel has a yield strength of at least 60,000 psi (400 Mpa). Some of the smaller bars, such as Nos. 3 and 4, are produced with Grade 40 steel. Reinforcing bars are manufactured to meet the requirements of ASTM A615.

The structural analysis and design of reinforced concrete buildings in the United States is governed by the provisions of *Building Code Requirements for Reinforced Concrete* (10), a document produced and maintained by the American Concrete Institute. This document contains requirements for the proper placement of reinforcing steel in concrete building elements, including specifications for spacing the bars to permit the plastic flow of the concrete around them. The same document spells out the required cover of concrete between the steel bars and the outside surface of the concrete for various situations to ensure adequate protection of the steel from damage by fire or corrosion from moisture.

TESTS FOR CONCRETE

There are a number of tests used to monitor the quality of the ingredients of concrete, the characteristics of the plastic mixture, and the strength of hardened concrete. Standard procedures are available for sampling and checking the aggregates for moisture content, the presence of foreign matter, and the adherence to grading specifications. Freshly mixed concrete is sampled to determine its air content and consistency. The most common test for consistency is called the "slump" test, in which the concrete is placed in a metal cone-shaped mold in three layers of equal volume. Each layer is "rodded" vertically with a standard ⅝-in. (15-mm) rod with a rounded end in order to consolidate the mix. The 12-in. (300-mm) tall cone is then lifted from the concrete, which slumps to a lesser height (Fig. 4). The distance it drops is referred to as the slump. A slump of less than 2 in. (50 mm) indicates a mix of stiff consistency and probably low workability. A slump of more than 5 in. (260 mm) indicates a mix that is too soupy and will flow very easily. Depending on the proportions of the ingredients, such a mix would probably result in concrete of reduced strength due to an excess of water and the resulting high water:cement ratio. ASTM specification C143 describes the slump test procedure in detail.

Before concrete is placed at the job site, test cylinders can be made for later testing in a compression machine. These are cured under highly controlled conditions in a laboratory to indicate the strength potential of the concrete as delivered and before it is subjected to handling and placing at the job. In many instances, field-cured cylinders are made to get an indication of the strength of the concrete in the actual structure. The standard cylinder is 6 in. (150 mm) in diameter and 12 in. (300 mm) in height. Before testing, the ends of each cylinder are capped by a thick layer of high-strength sulfur or plaster compound to make sure the ends are smooth and at right angles to the cylinder axis. A typical strength-gain curve for Type I Portland cement concrete is shown in Figure 5. The 28-day strength is generally accepted as the standard measure to compare various concretes even though some additional strength gain occurs after that time. Test measurements made before that time can serve to indicate whether or not a given concrete will reach its specified strength. The design strength at a specific age is called f'_c and is obtained by dividing the ultimate load capacity of the cylinder by its cross-sectional area. ASTM specifications C31, C192, C617, and C39 pertain to the making and testing of concrete cylinders.

There are other methods to estimate the strength of concrete after it has been fully cured at the job site. These may involve determining the surface hardness using instruments that strike the concrete surface in a measured fashion or fire a calibrated dart into it. These hardness determinations can be calibrated with the compressive strength. Nondestructive methods involving sound waves have also been developed.

The f'_c value as specified by the structural engineer

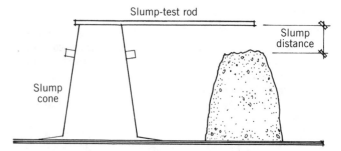

Figure 4. Slump-test apparatus.

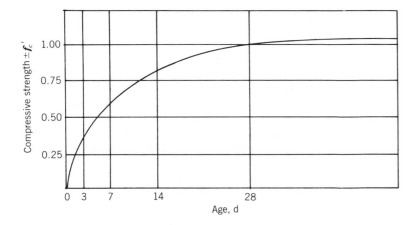

Figure 5. Typical strength-gain curve for concrete (Type I cement, moist cured at 70°F).

or the architect varies, depending on the strength requirements of the structure or its elements. For a slab-on-grade floor, the f'_c could be as low as 2500 psi (17 MPa); on the other hand, strengths as high as 10,000 psi (70 Mpa) might be called for in the lower-story columns of a high-rise building. For most structural elements, concrete strengths in the 3000–5000 psi (20–35 Mpa) range are specified.

MIXING, HANDLING, AND PLACING

Concrete may be mixed at the job site or a central plant and then trucked to the site or mixed in the truck while en route. Sometimes the mixing is partially done at the plant and completed in the truck. The quantity of concrete mixed at one time is called a batch; batching is the process of measuring the correct amount of each ingredient to be used. (Admixtures are usually premixed with the water.) Most batching is done by weight rather than volume. In general, the mixer is charged with the materials simultaneously, with a portion of the water being withheld until the end. The mixing time or the number of revolutions of the mixing drum is carefully controlled. Most truck mixers have drums that can turn at a slow speed after mixing has been completed. The ASTM specification pertaining to this type of mixing is C94, and this standard specifies that concrete shall be discharged from the mixer within 1½ h after water or cement has come into contact with the aggregates. Placing the concrete in the forms and consolidating it within this same time period is good practice.

Concrete is moved from the discharge location to its final place in the form by several means. Depending on the size of the job and the circumstances involved, fresh concrete may be transported by hand in wheelbarrows and rubber-tired buggies, by crane in buckets, by gravity in chutes, by motor-driven conveyer belts, or by hydraulic pumps. The last method is an easy way to get the concrete to inaccessible places in a hurry.

Regardless of the means, the main purpose is to move the concrete efficiently and without segregating the heavier coarse aggregates from the rest of the mix. Segregation results in concrete of nonuniform strength and workability characteristics. The portion with a high fraction of fines

will exhibit excess shrinkage cracking, and a high fraction of coarse aggregates in the mix will generate air voids and surface "honeycombing," that is, a surface that is weak and pock-marked by many air bubbles close together. Concrete should not be dropped or permitted to slide down a steep slope. It should be placed by the conveying device as close as is practical to its final location. It should not be placed at one end of a form and moved laterally by shovel or other means. If concrete must sustain a vertical drop of more than several feet, as in column and wall forms, an enclosing flexible chute should be used to minimize segregation. The top end of the chute should be large enough to avoid spillage, and the main body of the chute must be narrow enough to fit between the reinforcing bars within the formwork.

When conveyer systems, buggies, or other mechanisms are used to move concrete a considerable distance, provision must be made to ensure that a sufficient volume of concrete can be delivered to the appropriate place within the required time. If the in-place concrete stiffens and begins to set before the newly delivered concrete is placed against it, a cold joint results. This is a weakened interface in the slab or element where continuity and homogeneity were assumed in the design. (A construction joint is a planned cold joint between two different concrete pours or placements; these occur by design at selected locations where continuity is not important.)

CONSOLIDATION

After fresh concrete has been placed, it must be consolidated to remove air voids, making sure that the plastic mixture comes into complete contact with the reinforcing bars and fills all corners of the formwork. A mixture of high slump can be consolidated by hand merely by moving a round or flat rod up and down throughout the mixture. Most concrete used today, however, is stiff enough to require mechanical vibration to ensure proper consolidation. This is usually accomplished by using electric or air-actuated vibrators. The most popular type is the internal or immersion type of vibrator. It consists of a flexible shaft that vibrates with a high frequency, but low amplitude. The diameter of the shaft varies, depending on the size of the concrete member. The vibrator is lowered into the concrete and withdrawn at regular intervals, remaining in each location for about 5–10 s. Leaving the vibrator in one location for too long a time will cause segregation, as will using the vibrator to move the concrete horizontally in the form. External vibrators are also used, especially with thin or heavily reinforced sections where sufficient clearance for internal vibration is not present. These are usually attached to the outside of the formwork so that they affect a large area of the concrete. More time is required when external vibration is used.

FINISHING

Normally, the form is filled with concrete so that a slight excess occurs above the edges of the form. This is removed, or "struck off," by a straight edge or screed using a sawing or back-and-forth motion. For large slabs and pavements, the screed may be equipped with a mechanical vibration device so that surface vibration is accomplished during screeding. When finishing a floor slab or other wearing surface, the initial smoothing (called bullfloating) of the surface must take place right after the screeding, before any water bleeds to the surface. Because the aggregates have a density greater than that of water, they tend to settle slightly in the newly placed concrete, forcing a film of water to the surface. Screeding and bullfloating must take place before this bleeding occurs. A bullfloat is a flat rectangular piece of wood (or a light metal such as aluminum or magnesium) to which a long handle has been attached. It is drawn over the surface, removing any high spots and filling the voids. The coarse aggregates are forced to a position just below the surface, resulting in a smoother appearance. Overworking or excess floating can result in too much bleedwater coming to the surface, which will result in a weak layer of concrete at the wearing surface. A light sheen is normal.

Before any further finishing operations take place, the bleedwater must have evaporated and the concrete should have taken enough set to sustain foot pressure with only about ½ in. (6 mm) of indentation (11). Early finishing can ruin an otherwise potentially durable concrete surface.

Further finishing operations often consist of edging, jointing, more floating, or troweling with a steel trowel. Decorative patterns can also be made in the surface at this time.

Edging consists of using a special tool to round the edges and compact the concrete to avoid future chipping. Jointing consists of cutting grooves in the slab at selected intervals using hand tools or a special power saw. These regularly spaced grooves are called control joints and provide deliberately weakened places in the concrete to induce the inevitable shrinkage and temperature cracks to occur at these locations rather than in a random fashion.

Further floating by hand or using a machine with rotary blades can create a very smooth surface. The hardest and smoothest finish results from the successive use of steel trowels over a period of several hours, allowing the concrete to stiffen and harden considerably during the process. Concrete finishing of any type must be done with care and skill if the desired results are to be obtained.

CURING

Curing consists of keeping the finished concrete in a moist environment and controlling the temperature during the period of initial strength gain. This period can vary from a few days when Type III high-early-strength cement is used to several weeks for some massive structures using a mix that is lean in cement. Proper curing is essential to producing quality concrete; the curing time can affect the strength, hardness, durability, and watertightness of the final product.

One easy way of curing consists of keeping the concrete wet, not by adding water to newly placed concrete, but rather by preventing evaporation of moisture so that the hydration process is not affected. This can be accomplished by covering the concrete with wet burlap or some other absorptive material and keeping it wet. Plastic film or waterproof paper can also be used around the concrete to keep the air in contact with the concrete at a high humidity level. Chemical compounds that form an impervious membrane are used extensively on large flat areas such as paving. The compound eventually wears away after curing is complete.

During the curing period, the concrete temperature should be kept between 50 and 90°F (10 and 30°C). Higher temperatures lead not only to higher rates of evaporation, but also to more thermal expansion. When the temperature later drops (at nightfall), the new concrete will not have developed sufficient tensile strength for it to contract without cracking. Temperatures below 50°F (10°C) lead to a delayed rate of hydration, resulting in an increased curing period. Freezing temperatures can have very detrimental effects on the strength gain of concrete and, of course, prohibit the use of water as a curing medium. Saturated concrete is severely damaged when the water freezes. Heaters are often used with temporary enclosures of plastic or fabric to maintain proper temperatures during the curing period.

BIBLIOGRAPHY

1. J. O. Draffin, *Journal of the Western Society of Engineers* **48** (1), in *A Selection of Historic American Papers on Concrete*, American Concrete Institute, Detroit, Mich., Publication SP-52, 1976, p. 5.

2. P. Collins, *Concrete: The Vision of a New Architecture*, Faber and Faber, London, 1959, p. 21.

3. Ref. 1, p. 10.

4. Ref. 1, p. 29.

5. W. E. Ward, *Transactions of the American Society of Mechanical Engineers* **4**, 388 (1883).

6. Ref. 2, p. 62.

7. C. A. P. Turner, *Systems of Reinforced Concrete Construction*, Chapt. VIII, in *A Selection of Historic American Papers on Concrete*, American Concrete Institute, Detroit, Mich., Publication SP-52, 1976, p. 248.

8. *Design and Control of Concrete Mixtures*, 12th ed., Portland Cement Association, Skokie, Ill., 1979, p. 7.

9. *Ibid.*, p. 25.

10. *Building Code Requirements for Reinforced Concrete (ACI 318–83)*, American Concrete Institute, Detroit, Mich., 1983.

11. *Basic Concrete Construction Practices*, Portland Cement Association, Skokie, Ill., 1975, p. 239.

General References

Principles of Quality Concrete, Portland Cement Association, Skokie, Ill., 1975.

Significance of Tests and Properties of Concrete and Concrete-Making Materials, ASTM, Philadelphia, Pa., Publication STP 169B, 1978.

Commentary on Building Code Requirements for Reinforced Concrete (ACI 318–83), American Concrete Institute, Detroit, Mich., 1983.

Selected American Society for Testing and Materials (ASTM) Standards pertaining to Concrete.

ASTM C231-82: Test for Air Content of Freshly Mixed Concrete by the Pressure Method

ASTM C173-78: Test for Air Content of Freshly Mixed Concrete by the Volumetric Method

ASTM C150-85: Specification for Portland Cement

ASTM C595-86: Specification for Blended Hydraulic Cements

ASTM C33-86: Specification for Concrete Aggregates

ASTM C125-85: Definitions of Terms Relating to Concrete and Concrete Aggregates

ASTM A615-85: Specification for Deformed and Plain Billet-steel Bars for Concrete Reinforcement

ASTM C143-78: Test Method for Slump of Portland Cement Concrete

ASTM C31-85: Making and Curing Concrete Test Specimens in the Field

ASTM C192-81: Making and Curing Concrete Test Specimens in the Laboratory

ASTM C617-85: Practice for Capping Cylindrical Concrete Test Specimens

ASTM C39-86: Test for Compressive Strength of Cylindrical Concrete Specimens

ASTM C94-86: Specification for Ready-Mixed Concrete

See also CONCRETE—ARCHITECTURAL; CONCRETE FORMING; CONCRETE—LIGHTWEIGHT AGGREGATE; CONCRETE—POSTTENSIONING; CONCRETE—PRESTRESSED.

RONALD E. SHAEFFER
Florida A & M University
Tallahassee, Florida